2011
新疆生产建设兵团
统计年鉴

XINJIANG PRODUCTION & CONSTRUCTION GROUP
STATISTICAL YEARBOOK

新疆生产建设兵团统计局
国家统计局兵团调查总队 编
Compiled by Statistics Bureau of XPCG
and The Survey Office of XPCG of NBS

新疆生产建设兵团

XINJIANG PRODUCTION & CONSTRUCTION GROUP

统计年鉴

STATISTICAL YEARBOOK

2011

总第22期
No.22

中国统计出版社
China Statistics Press

（京）新登字041号

图书在版编目（CIP）数据

新疆生产建设兵团统计年鉴. 2011 : 汉英对照 / 新疆生产建设兵团统计局, 国家统计局兵团调查总队编.

--北京 : 中国统计出版社, 2011.8

ISBN 978-7-5037-6285-7

Ⅰ. ①新… Ⅱ. ①新… ②国… Ⅲ. ①生产建设兵团

—统计资料—新疆—2011—年鉴—汉、英 Ⅳ. ①E24-66

中国版本图书馆CIP数据核字(2011)第148421号

《新疆生产建设兵团统计年鉴2011》

作　　者　新疆生产建设兵团统计局　国家统计局兵团调查总队

责任编辑　佘竞雄　熊　威

责任校对　陈雪梅

装帧设计　新疆誉品空间设计工作室

出版发行　中国统计出版社

通信地址　北京市西城区月坛南街57号

邮　　编　100826

办公地址　北京市丰台区西三环南路甲6号

电　　话　(010)63376907

E-mail　yearbook@gj.stats.cn

印　　刷　新疆生产建设兵团印刷厂

经　　销　新华书店

开　　本　880×1230毫米　1/16

字　　数　1000千字

印　　张　39　彩页 1

版　　别　2011年8月第1版

版　　次　2011年8月第1次印刷

书　　号　ISBN 978-7-5037-6285-7/E·15

定　　价　238.00元　Price: 238.00 (RMB)

《新疆生产建设兵团统计年鉴2011》编辑委员会

《新疆生产建设兵团统计年鉴2011》编辑人员

NAME LIST OF EDITORIAL BOARD

NAME LIST OF EDITORIAL STAFF

兵团生产总值(亿元)及发展速度(%)

Toatal GDP and Growth Rate in XPCG(100 million yuan,%)

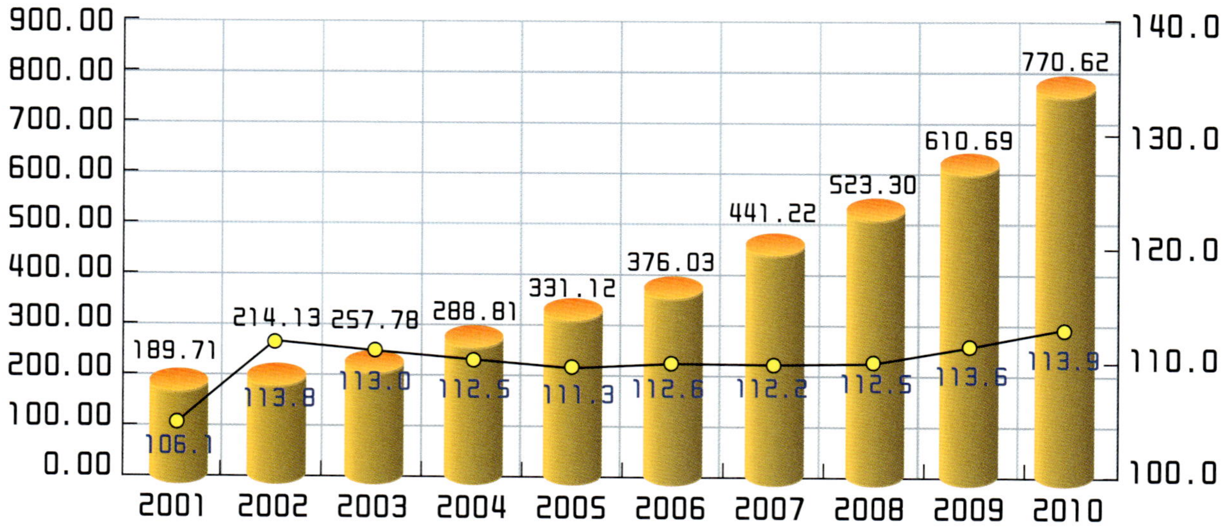

2010年兵团生产总值构成(%)

Composition of GDP in XPCG(%)

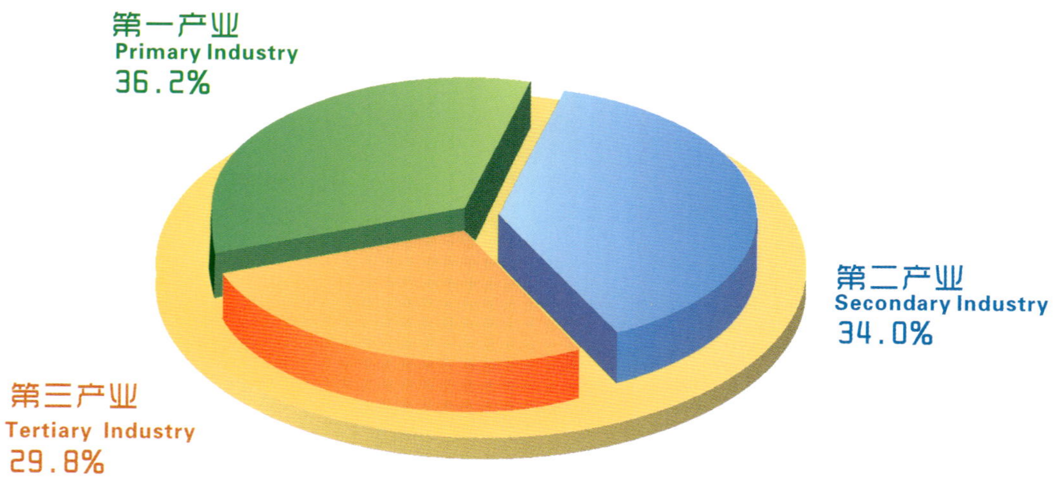

兵团人均生产总值(元)
Per Capita in XPCG(yuan)

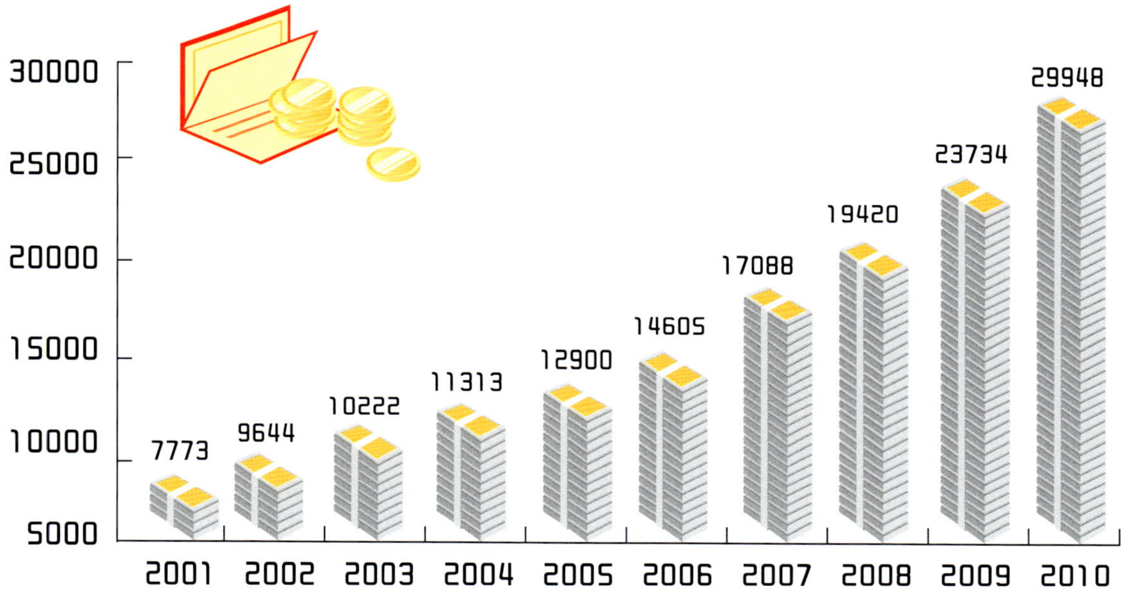

年末就业人员（万人）
Number of Employed Persons at the Year-end(10000 persons)

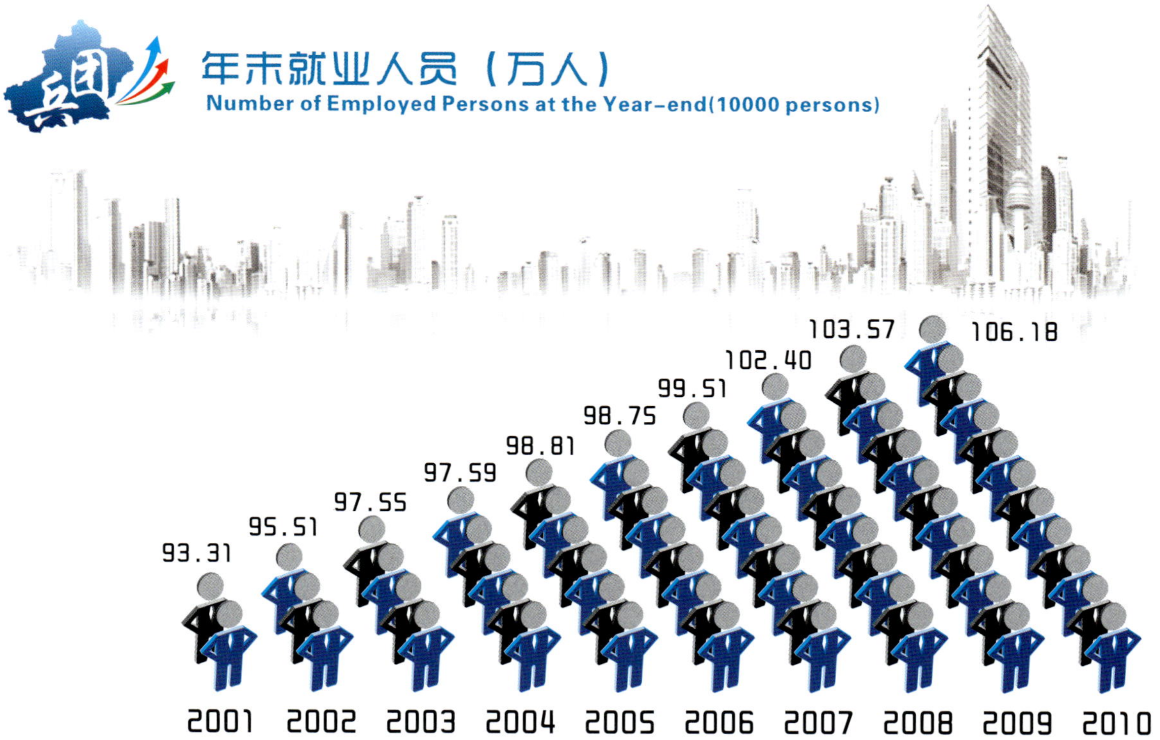

兵团农业总产值(亿元)及发展速度(%)

Gross Output Value of Farming, Forest, Animal Hasbandary and Fishery and Growth Rate(100 million yuan, %)

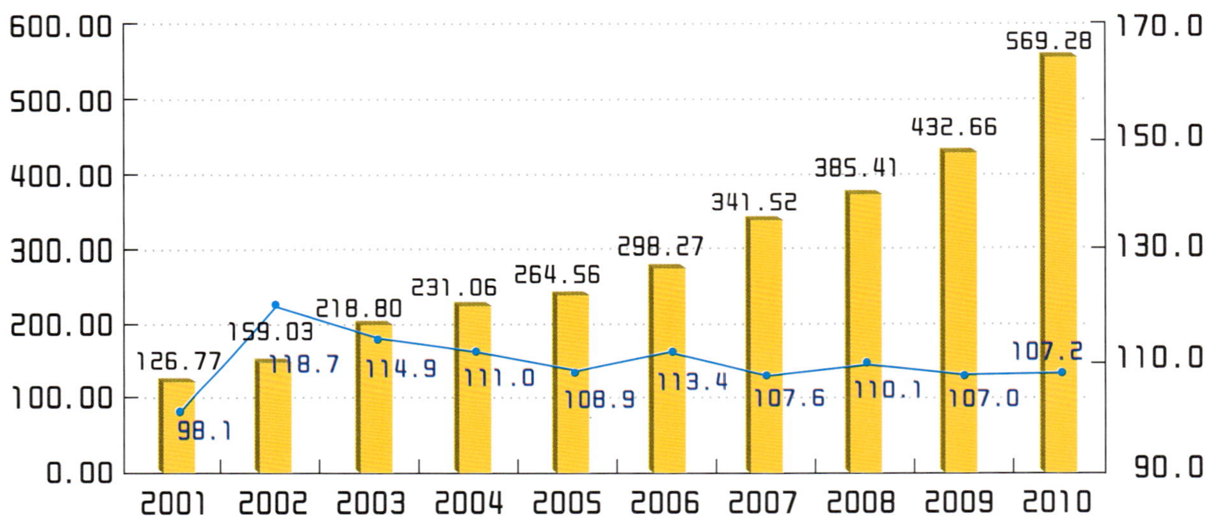

粮食、棉花产量（万吨）

Yield of Grain Corps and Cotton(10000 tons)

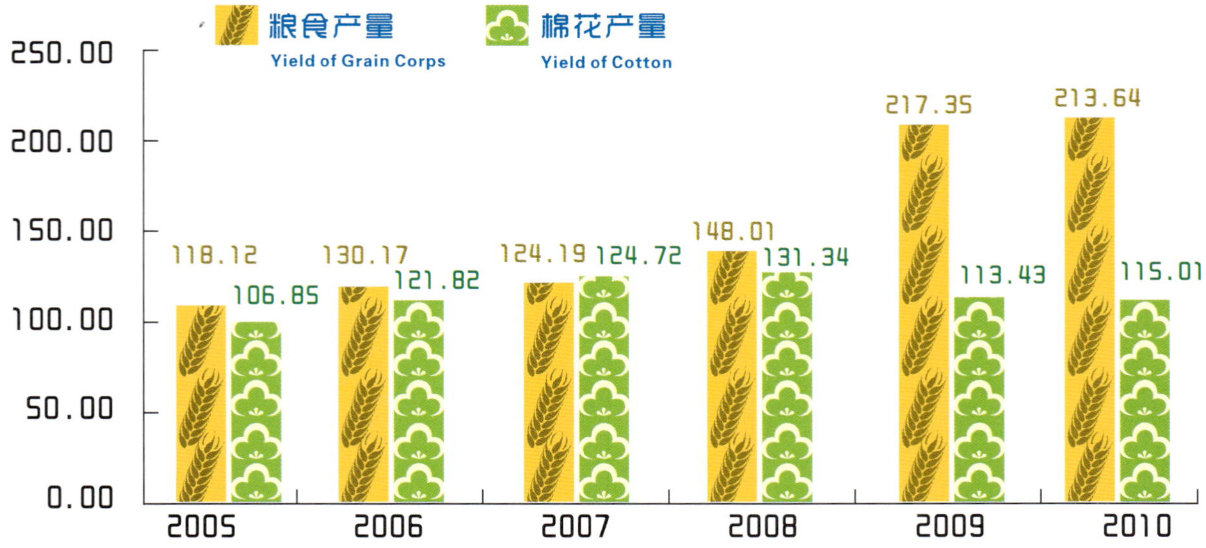

油料、甜菜产量（万吨）
Yield of Oil-bearing and Beetroots(10000 tons)

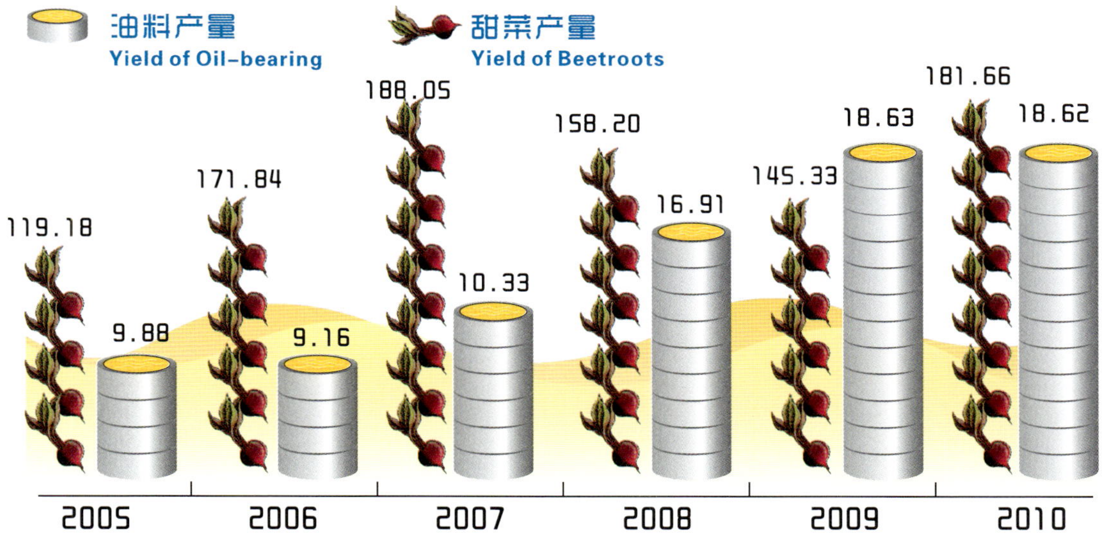

水果、肉类产量（万吨）
Output of Fruit and Meat(10000 tons)

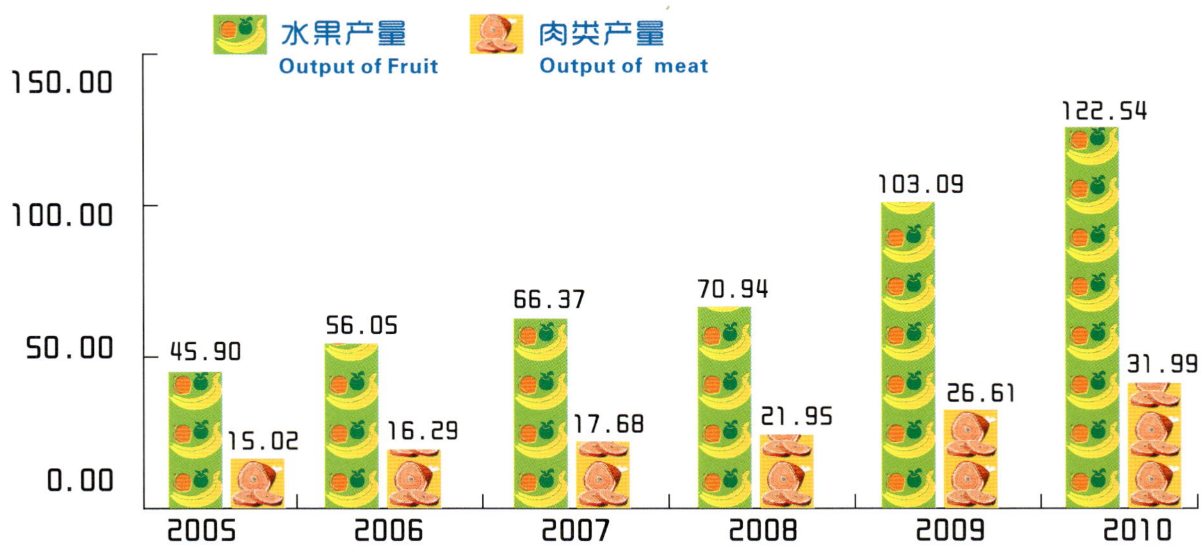

工业总产值(亿元)及发展速度(%)
Gross Output Value of Industry and Growth Rate(100 million yuan,%)

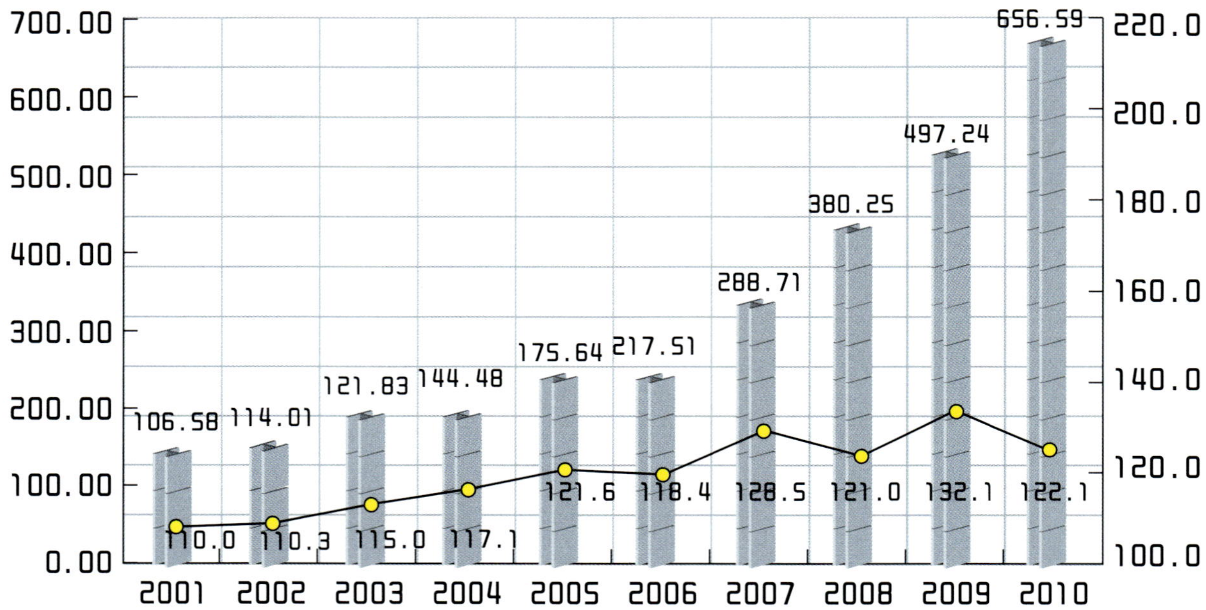

工业总产值构成(%)
Composition of Gross Output Value of Industry(%)

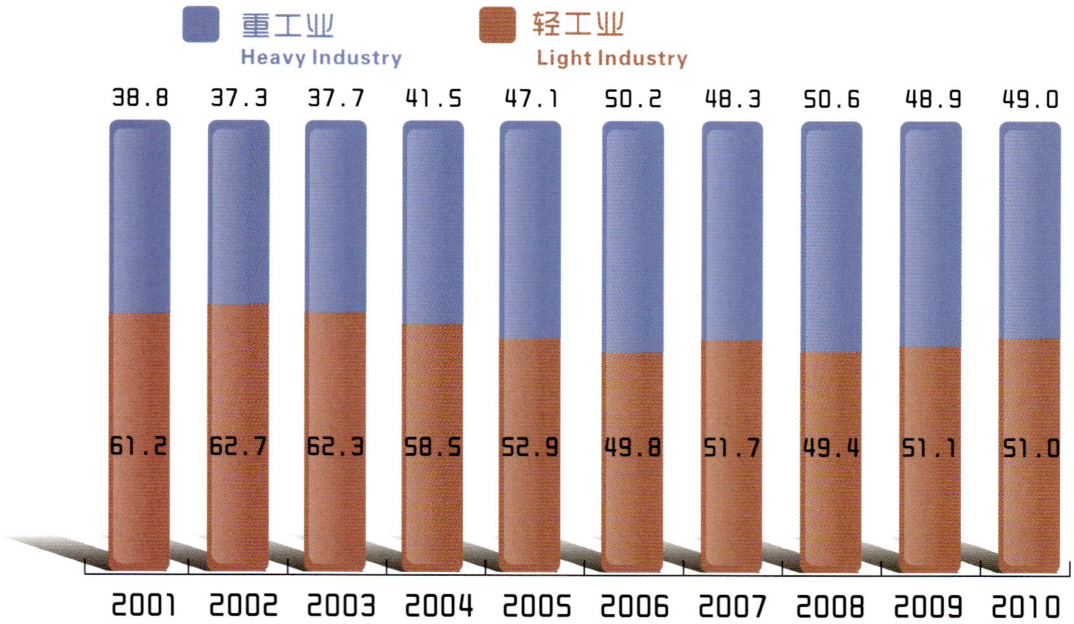

主要工业产品产量
Output of Main Industrial Products

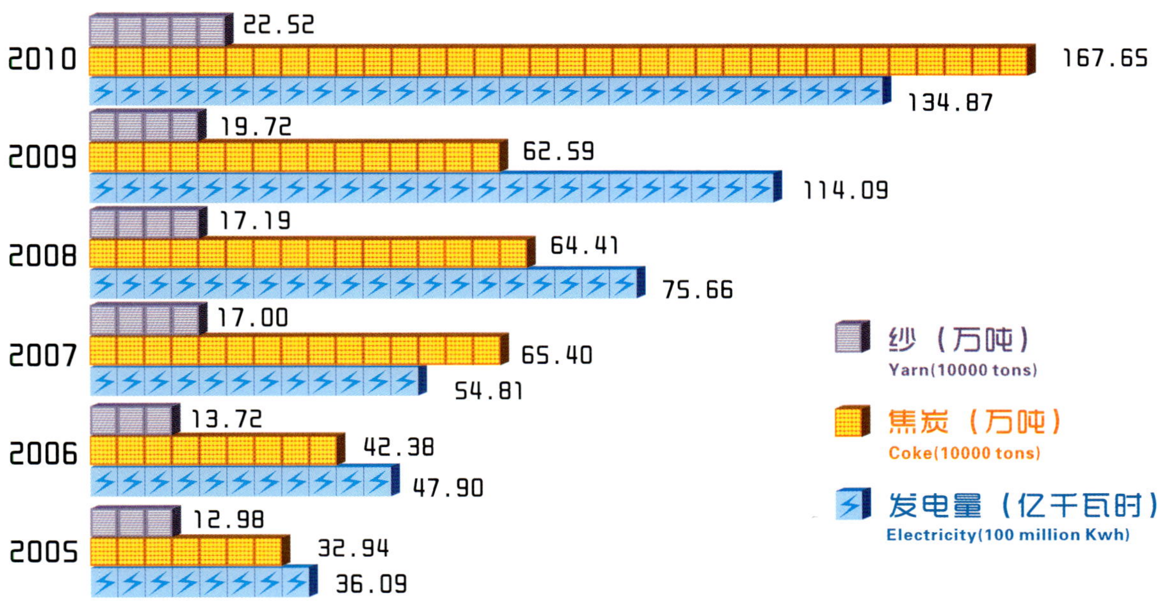

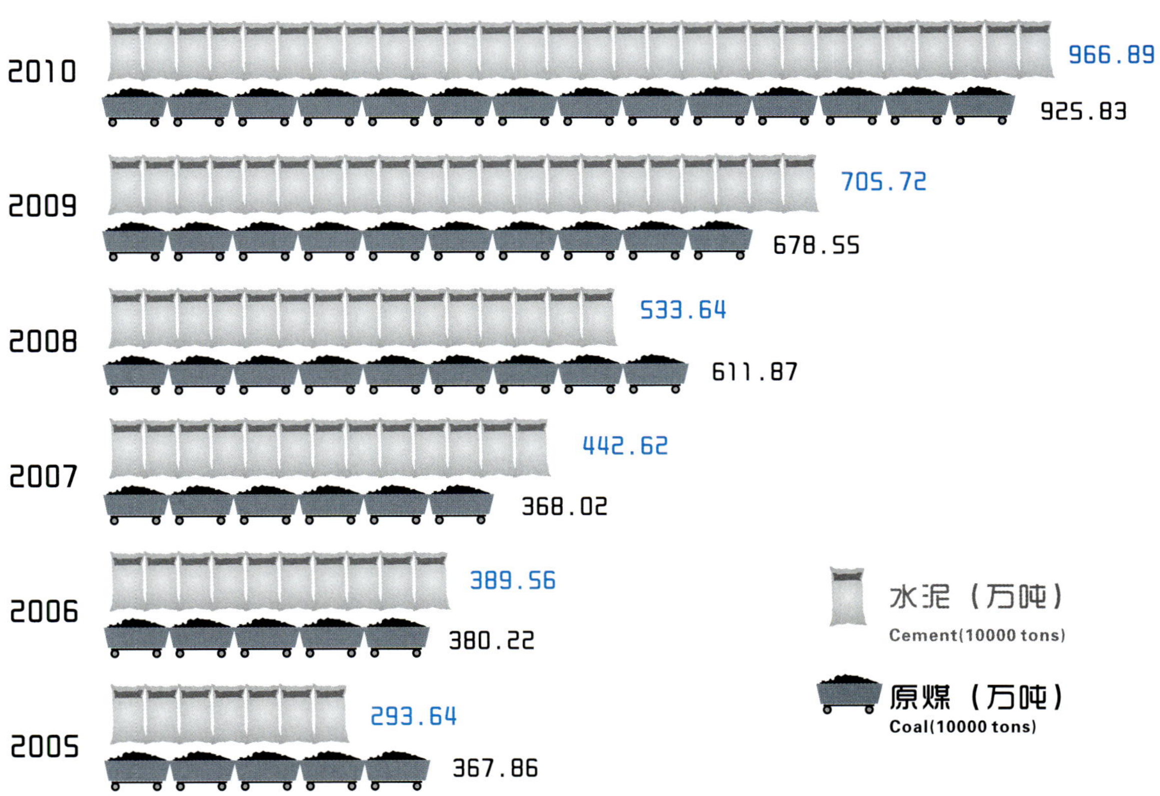

全社会固定资产投资(亿元)
Total Invesrment in Fixed Assets (100 million yuan)

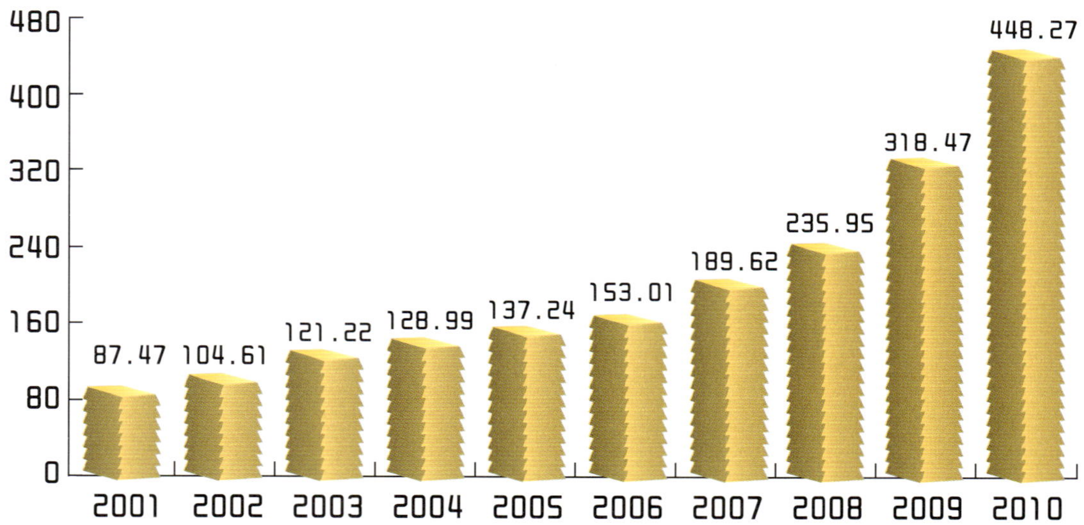

2010年按用途分全社会固定资产投资构成（%）
Composition of Investment in Fixed Assets by Use(%)

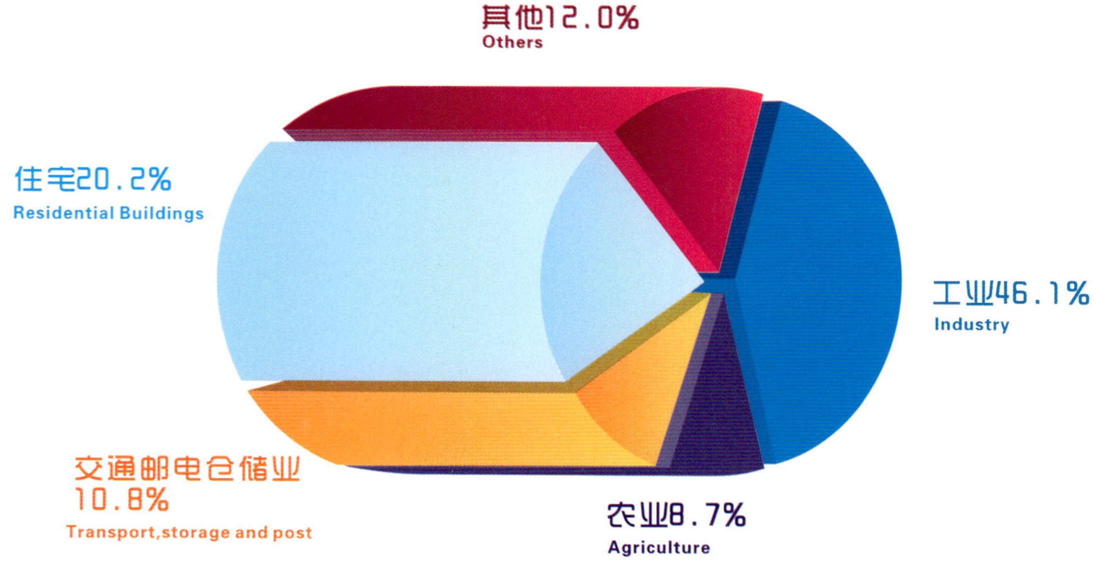

建筑业总产值(亿元)
Total Value of Construction(100 million yuan)

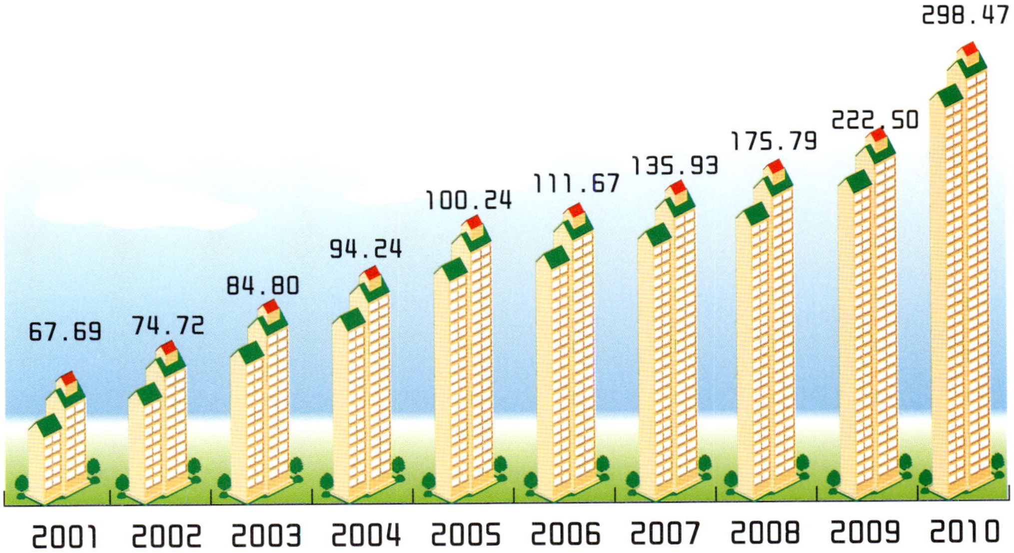

建筑企业生产情况
Production of Construction Enterprises

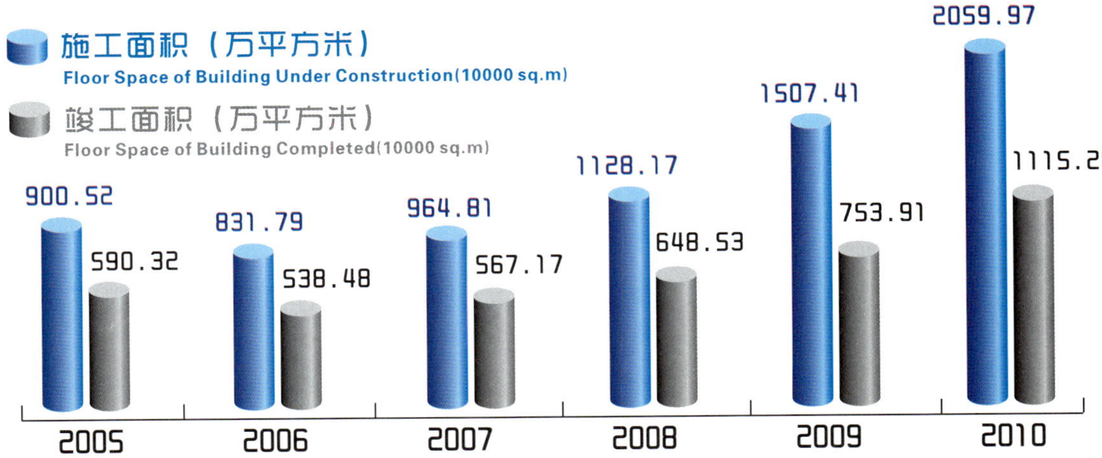

社会消费品零售总额(亿元)
Total Retail Sales of Consumer Goods(100 million yuan)

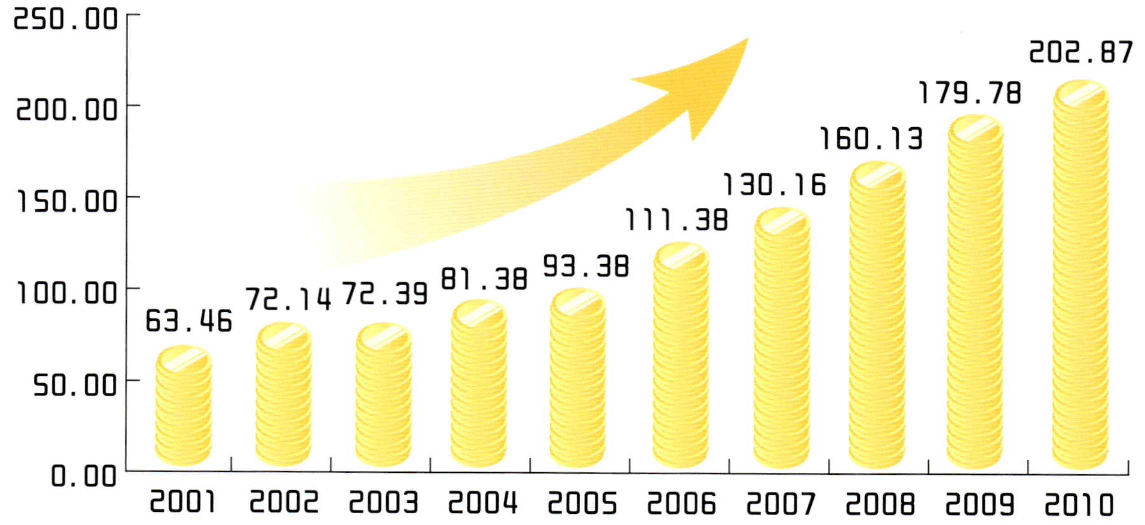

进出口情况
Imports and Exports

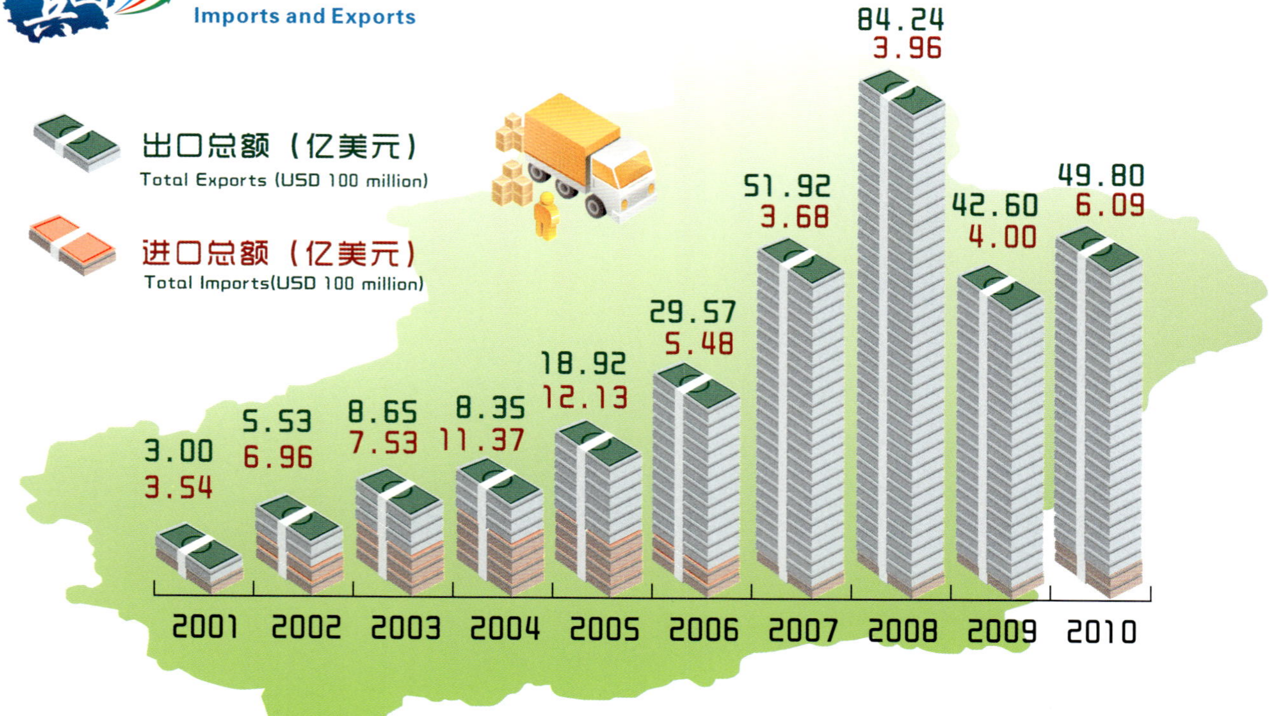

道路交通运输情况
Road Transporation

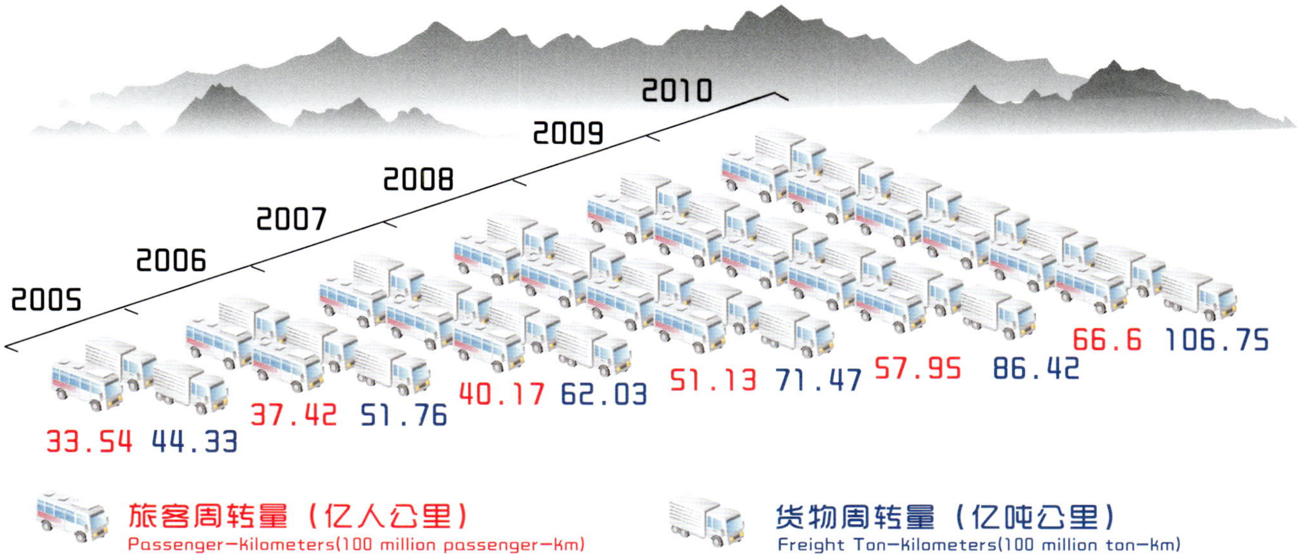

公路里程
Length of Highways

城镇居民、农牧工收入
Income in Urban and Farm

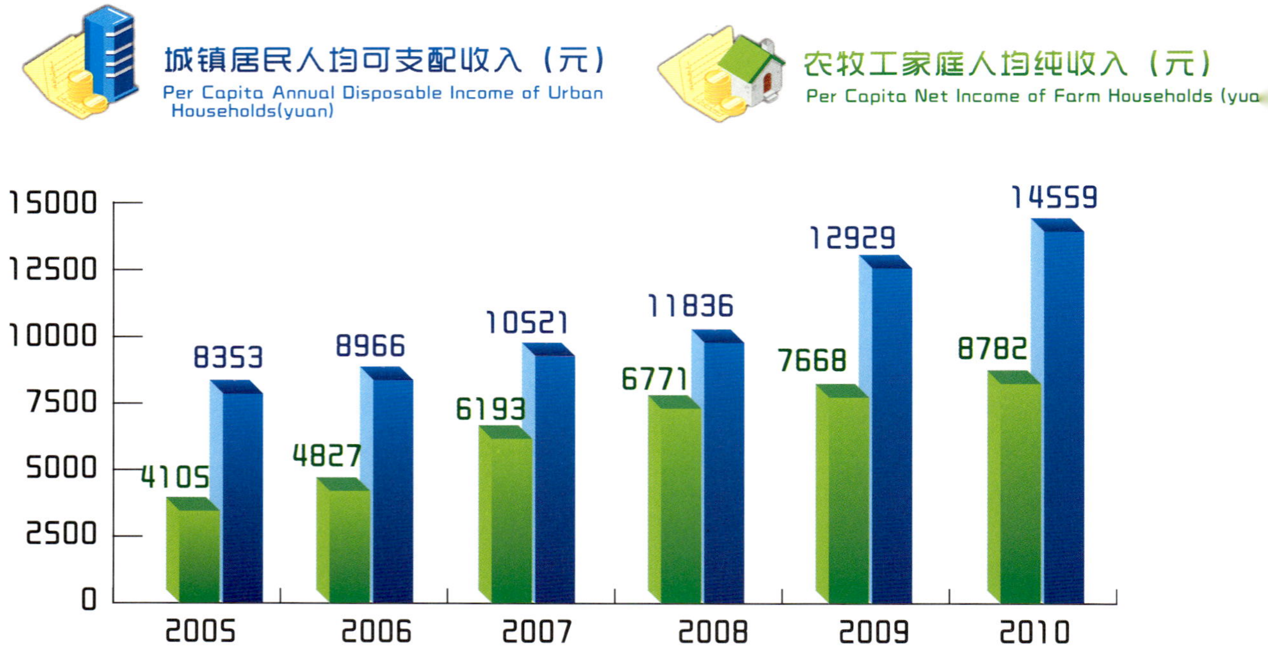

兵团在岗职工平均工资（元）
Average Annual Wage of Staff and Workers(yuan)

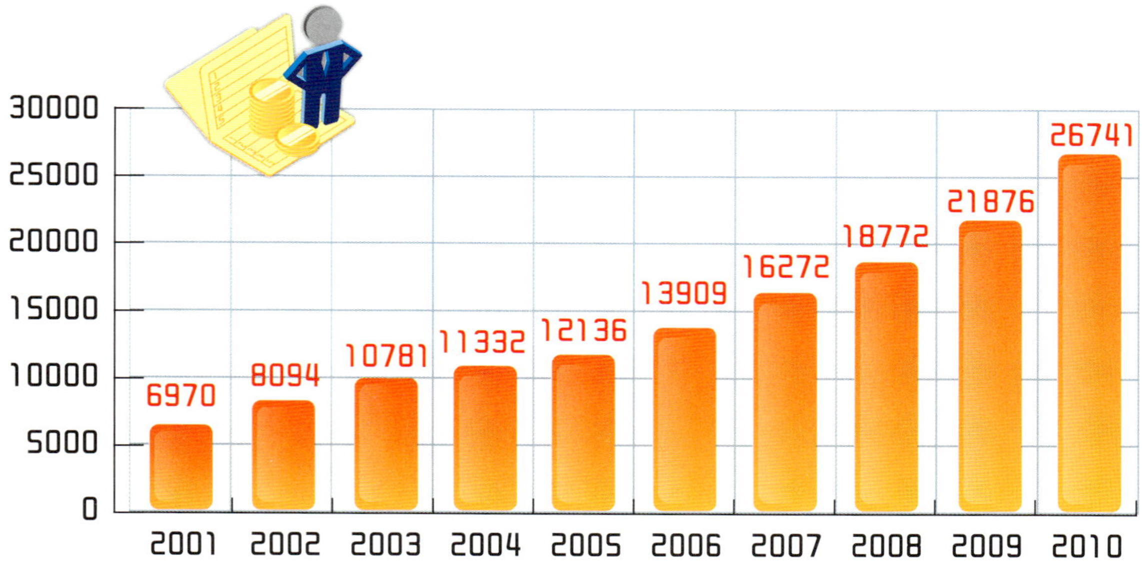

各级各类学校在校学生数（万人）
Number of Schools Enrollment by Level and Type of School(10000 persons)

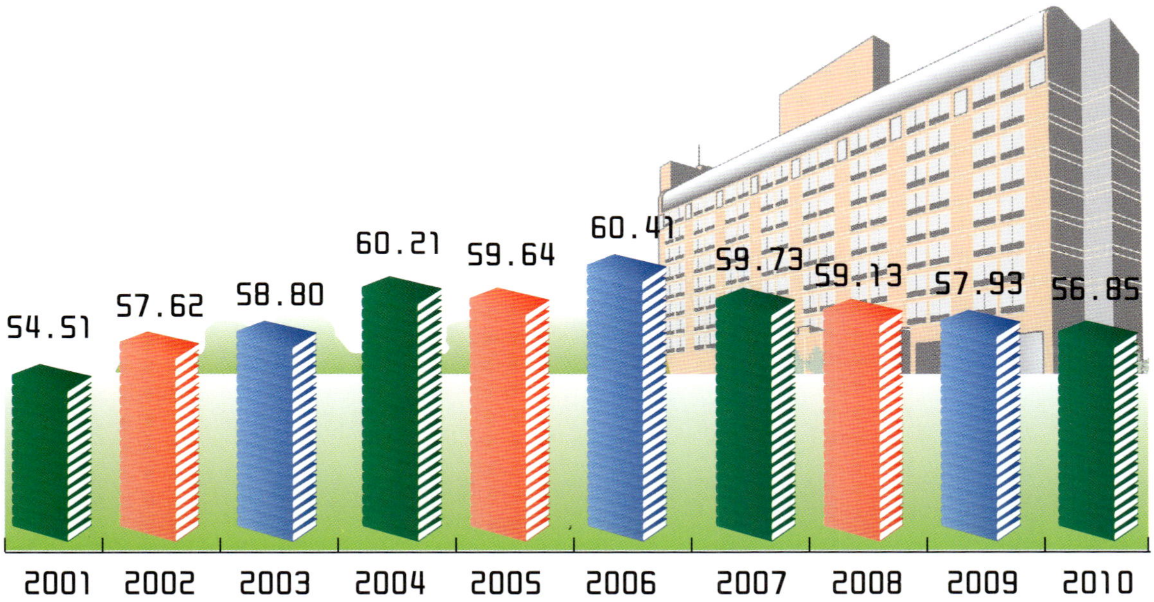

2010年兵团广播覆盖率（%）
Radio Broadcasting Coverage Rate in XPCG (%)

2010年兵团电视覆盖率（%）
TV Coverage Rate in XPCG (%)

2010年旅游业情况
Tourism

旅游人数：401.00万人
Number of Tourist (10000 persons)

旅游收入:16.90亿元
Income of Tourism (100 million yuan)

万人拥有卫生技术人员数(人)
Number of Medical Technical Personel Per 10000 Persons(person)

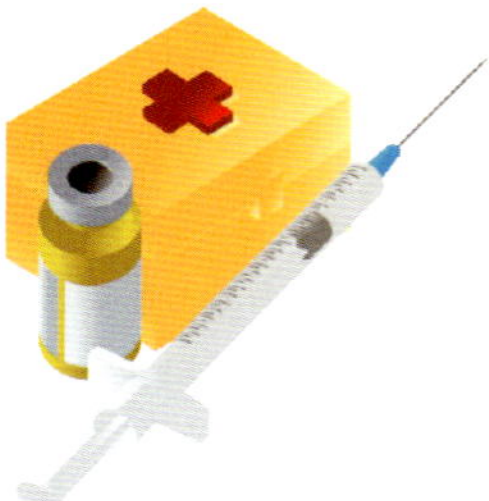

80人

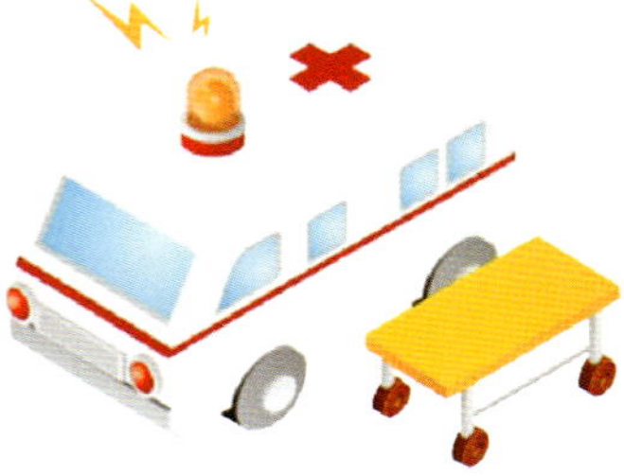

万名职工拥有科技人员(人)
Number of S&T Personel Per 10000 Staff and Workers(person)

1756人

编 者 说 明

一、《新疆生产建设兵团统计年鉴-2011》是一部全面反映新疆生产建设兵团国民经济和社会发展情况的综合性资料年刊，涵盖了兵团、各师和农牧团场2010年国民经济和社会发展各方面大量的统计数据、主要年份统计数据、沿天山北坡经济带自治区与兵团主要统计数据、新疆15个地州市主要统计数据及全国东、中、西部和东北三省主要统计数据；兵团、师、企业主要经济指标排序资料、与各省市主要指标排序及兵团检察院、法院情况、企业景气调查等资料。

二、全书内容分为特载和统计资料两部分，统计资料包括二十二篇：1.综合；2.国民经济核算；3.人口；4.就业人员和职工工资；5.固定资产投资；6.财务；7.价格指数；8.人民生活；9.农业；10.工业；11.建筑业；12.交通运输业；13.国内贸易；14.能源生产与消费；15.对外贸易、经济协作和旅游业；16.金融业；17.科学、教育、文化、卫生和城市；18.检察院、法院和司法局资料；19.企业景气调查；20.其他资料；21.农牧团场基本情况；22.各师、团主要经济指标排序。另附各省市区主要经济指标排序资料。各篇前设简要说明，对本篇章的主要内容、资料来源、统计范围、统计方法以及历史变动情况作简要概述。

三、《年鉴》中使用的度量衡单位均采用国际统一标准计量单位。

四、《年鉴》根据出版要求，标明的2011年为出版年份，正文为2010年度资料。

五、《年鉴》中符号含义的说明：

“…”或“－”表示数据不足本指标最小单位数；

“空格”表示无指标数据；

“#”表示其中的主要项；

六、本年鉴资料大部分来自年度统计报表，部分来自抽样调查和有关业务部门。为了便于读者使用，对某些指标在表下作了简要注释。凡以前发表过的统计数字与本年鉴有不一致的，以本年鉴为准。

七、在编辑过程中，得到了兵团机关有关部、委、办、局和自治区统计局、国家统计局的大力支持与协助，在此表示衷心感谢！限于编辑水平，对于《年鉴》存在的差错和缺点，敬请广大读者和各位统计同仁提出宝贵意见。

编　　者

二〇一一年八月

The Editors' Explanatory Notes

Ⅰ. Xinjiang Production & Construction Group Statistical Yearbook-2011 is a comprehensive data annual, which covers entirely national economy and social development of XPCG. The yearbook reflects various aspects of statistical data in 2010 at levels of XPCG and divisions; main statistical data in major years; main indicators between Xinjiang and XPCG on the economic belt of the northern slope of the Tianshan Mountains and main indicators on Xinjiang's 15 prefectures and cities, and data on the Eastern, Middle, Western and 3 Northeastern provinces to National total. Ranking data of main economic indicators on XPCG, divisions and enterprises and provinces; and data on XPCG Procurator's Office and the People's Court, and data on boom investigation of enterprises.

Ⅱ. The book contains two parts. Special Issue and data. Data includes twenty two parts, namely, 1. General Survey; 2. National Accounts; 3. Population; 4. Employment and Wages; 5. Investment in Fixed Assets; 6. Public Finance; 7. Price Indices; 8. People' s Livelihood 9. Agriculture; 10. Industry; 11. Construction; 12. Transportation; 13. Domestic Trade; 14. Energy production and consumption; 15.Foreign trade, Economic Cooperation and Tourism; 16. Financial intermediation; 17. Science, Education, Culture, Public Health and City; 18. Procurator's Offices, Courts and Judicial Affairs; 19. Enterprise Boom Survey; 20. Other Data; 21. Basic Conditions of Farms; 22. Ranking of Main Economic Indicators by Division and Farm. Ranking Data of Main Indicators by Province and City are attached in the appendix. In brief introduction at the beginning of each part, mainly coverage of this chapter, data sources, statistical coverage, statistical methods and historical changes are concerned.

Ⅲ. The units of measurement used in this book are internationally standard measurement units.

Ⅳ. According to publication request, the year marked in this book is 2011, but the year of data is 2010.

Ⅴ. Notations used in this book:

"..." or "-" indicates that the figure is not large enough to be measured with the smallest unit in the table;

"(Blank)" indicates that the data are not available;

"#" indicates the major items of the total.

Ⅵ. The major data sources of this yearbook are obtained from annual statistical reports, some from sample surveys and some from data provided by relative administrative departments. For the convenience of readers, brief notes concerning some indicators are placed at the lower part of relevant tables. In case of inconsistency of formerly issued some statistical data with this yearbook, this publication shall govern.

Ⅶ.In the course of compilation, the yearbook has received great support and assistance from many units of XPCG, Xinjiang Bureau of Statistics and National Bureau of Statistics. We would like to acknowledge them. Because of inadequate editing proficiency, readers and colleagues from statistical front are welcome to make precious opinions on mistakes and faults .

Editors
August 2011

目　　录
CONTENTS

特　载
Special Issue

一、综　合
Chapter 1 General Survey

二、国民经济核算

Chapter 2 National Accounts

三、人口

Chapter 3 Population

四、就业人员和职工工资

Chapter 4 Employment and Wages

五、固定资产投资

Chapter 5 Investment in Fixed Assets

六、财务
Chapter 6 Public Finance

七、价格指数

Chapter 7 Price Indices

八、人民生活

Chapter 8 People's Livelihood

九、农业
Chapter 9 Agriculture

十、工业
Chapter 10 Industry

十一、建筑业
Chapter 11 Construction

十二、交通运输业
Chapter 12 Communications and Transportation

十三、国内贸易

Chapter 13 Domestic Trade

十四、能源生产与消费

Chapter 14 Energy Production and Consumption

十五、对外贸易、经济技术协作和旅游业

Chapter 15 Foreign Trade, Economic and Technological Cooperation and Tourism

十六、金　融　业

Chapter 16 Financial Intermediation

十七、科技、教育、文化、卫生和城市

Chapter 17 Science, Education, Culture, Health and City

十八、检察院、法院和司法局资料

Chapter 18 Data on Procurator's Offices, Courts and Judicial Affairs

十九、企业景气调查

Chapter 19 Enterprise Climate Survey

二十、其他资料

Chapter 20 Other Data

二十一、团场基本情况

Chapter 21 Basic Conditions of Farms

二十二、各师、团主要经济指标排序

Chapter 22 Ranking of Main Economic Indicators by Division and Farm

附录各省(区)、直辖市主要经济指标排序

Appendix Ranking of Main Economic Indicators by Province

2011

BING TUAN

特　载

Special Issue

简要说明

一、本篇资料主要内容

本篇资料登载2010年新疆生产建设兵团国民经济和社会发展统计公报，反映兵团2010年经济和社会事业取得的成就。

二、本篇资料来源

本篇公报由兵团统计局国民经济综合统计处撰写，数据取自于兵团统计局、国家统计局兵团调查总队各专业统计年报和兵团有关部门统计年报。

Brief Introduction

1. Main Contents

This chapter carries the Statistical Communique on National Economy and Social Development of Xinjiang Production and Construction Group in 2010, reflecting achievements of economy and social undertakings of XPCG in 2010.

2. Sources of Data

This communique is written by the Comprehensive Office of Statistics Bureau of XPCG. Data in this communique are obtained from professional statistical annuals of the Statistics Bureau of XPCG, Survey Office of the National Bureau of Statistics of XPCG and statistical annuals of XPCG's relevant departments.

新疆生产建设兵团2010年
国民经济和社会发展统计公报

新疆生产建设兵团统计局　国家统计局兵团调查总队

2011年4月

2010年，兵团广大干部职工在兵团党委、兵团的正确领导下，以邓小平理论和“三个代表”重要思想为指导，深入贯彻落实科学发展观，全面落实兵团党委六届五次、六次全委（扩大）会议各项工作部署，紧紧抓住中央新疆工作座谈会支持新疆和兵团大建设、大开放、大发展的千载难逢机遇，求真务实，开拓进取，综合实力跨上新台阶，职工生活达到新水平，社会各项事业取得新进步。

一、综　　合

初步核算，全年兵团生产总值770.62亿元，比上年增长13.9%。其中，第一产业增加值278.81亿元，增长11.8%；第二产业增加值262.27亿元，增长21.2%；第三产业增加值229.54亿元，增长9.0 %。第一产业增加值占兵团生产总值比重为36%，第二产业增加值比重为34%，第三产业增加值比重为30%。

兵团控股的14家上市公司累计募集资金100.70亿元，其中发行上市募资38.32亿元，再融资62.31亿元。

国家级和兵团级农业产业化重点龙头企业68家，其中国家级11家。龙头企业带动农户40万户，销售收入过10亿元的企业有8家。

兵团国有及国有控股农工建交商企业实现利润40.26亿元，比上年增加27.69亿元。

初步统计，全年上缴各类税费90.74亿元。

全年以民生为主的“十件实事”完成投资70.73亿元。

全年居民消费价格比上年上涨4.3%（见表一），商品零售价格上涨4.6%，农业生产资料价格上涨3.1%，农产品生产价格上涨31.5%，工业品出厂价格上涨25.3%，原材料、燃料、动力购进价格上涨23.9%，固定资产投资价格上涨4.6%。

表一　居民消费价格增减变动情况

指　　　标	比上年增长%
居民消费价格总水平	4.3
#城　市	3.6
农　村	5.8
食　品	10.7
#粮　食	8.9
肉禽及其制品	13.0
蛋　类	12.3
水产品	7.4
烟　酒	2.0
衣　着	−0.8
家庭设备及用品	1.2
医疗保健及用品	2.0
交通和通讯工具	持平
娱乐教育文化用品及服务	1.2
居　住	2.7

年末从业人员106.18万人，比上年增长2.5%。年末在岗职工67.76万人，比上年增长0.8%。全年新增劳动力就业6.67万人。年末城镇登记失业率2.41%。建立零就业家庭24小时托底安置制度，帮助2334户零就业家庭至少一人实现就业。

全年四个季度企业家信心指数和企业景气指数均处于较景气区间。一至四季度企业家信心指数分别为144.2、139.0、137.0和144.6，分别比上年同期提高39.4点、24.5点、25.5点和17.3点；企业景气指数分别为124.9、125.5、138.5和135.6，分别比上年同期提高6.6点、3.6点、16.3点和15.0点。

二、农　　业

全年完成农业总产值569.28亿元，比上年增长7.2%。

农作物播种面积1119.20千公顷（1678.80万亩），增长1.0%。其中，粮食种植面积284.69千公顷（427.04万亩），下降9.3%；棉花种植面积497.98千公顷（746.97万亩），增长2.1%；油料种植面积67.78千公顷（101.67万亩），下降1.4%；甜菜种植面积25.52千公顷（38.28万亩），增长25.8%；蔬菜种植面积（含菜用瓜）79.68千公顷（119.52万亩），增长7.9%。

农作物精量半精量播种面积708.93千公顷（1063.39万亩），比上年下降6.7%，其中棉花精量播种面积364.53千公顷（546.80万亩），下降5.7%。测土配方施肥面积618.67千公顷（928.01万亩）。

有效灌溉面积1067.27千公顷（1600.90万亩）。高新节水灌溉面积682.16千公顷(1023.24万亩),其中当年新增29.23千公顷(43.58万亩)。

全年棉花产量115.01万吨,比上年增长1.4%;粮食产量213.64万吨,下降1.7%;油料产量18.62万吨,与上年持平;甜菜产量181.66万吨,增长25.0%。

年末牲畜存栏624.06万头(只),比上年增长6.5%。主要农、畜产品产量保持增长(见表二)。

全年水产品产量2.67万吨,比上年增长13.3%。

全年人工造林作业面积14.41千公顷(21.61万亩),下降16.9%,无林地和疏林地新封面积5.33千公顷(8.00万亩),增长3.9%。

全年农业机械总动力369.33万千瓦,比上年增长9.1%。

表二　主要农产品产量、畜牧业生产情况及其增长速度

指　　标	计量单位	绝对数	比上年增长%
粮　食	万吨	213.64	-1.7
棉　花	万吨	115.01	1.4
油　料	万吨	18.62	持平
甜　菜	万吨	181.66	25.0
蔬　菜	万吨	581.62	-2.9
#工业用番茄	万吨	441.31	-4.9
水　果	万吨	122.54	18.9
年末牲畜存栏头数	万头(只)	624.06	6.5
# 牛	万头	36.84	8.8
猪	万头	155.42	15.9
羊	万只	427.76	3.3
年内牲畜出栏头数	万头(只)	682.07	13.1
肉类总产量	万吨	31.99	20.2
羊毛产量	万吨	1.13	6.3
禽蛋产量	万吨	4.57	12.2
牛奶产量	万吨	44.31	15.3

年末拥有飞机29架,全年总飞行时间5482小时,起落4218架次,其中用于农林牧业飞行3320小时,起落3777架次;工业飞行1805小时,起落441架次。全年完成作业面积989.19千公顷(1483.78万亩)。

年末拥有水库125座,总库容32.78亿立方米。机电井15643眼,提水量22.67亿立方米。修建水闸114座,堤防建设长度2477.96千米。水利工程供水量125.59亿立方米。

三、工业与建筑业

全年全部工业增加值186.29亿元,比上年增长18.5%。规模以上工业增加值增长25.4%,其中,国有及国有控股企业增长14.4%,股份制企业增长27.5%,外商及港澳台商投资企业增长47.1%。按轻重工业分,轻工业增长24.9%,重工业增长28.2%。

全年规模以上工业中,煤炭开采和洗选业增加值比上年增长82.0%;农副食品加工业增长10.1%;食品制造业增长25.2%;饮料制造业增长52.3%;纺织业增长22.2%;化学原料及化学制品制造业增长6.1%;非金属矿物制品业增长45.0%;电力、热力的生产和供应业增长17.0%。

主要工业产品产量大部分保持增长(见表三)。

表三　全部工业主要产品产量及其增长速度

产品名称	计量单位	绝对数	比上年增长%
原　煤	万吨	925.83	36.4
发电量	亿千瓦时	134.87	18.2
食用植物油	万吨	30.73	-4.3
成品糖	万吨	17.24	24.2
乳制品	万吨	9.62	32.3
番茄酱	万吨	65.01	-4.2
饮料酒	万千升	14.97	75.7
软饮料	万吨	48.71	-0.2
纱	万吨	22.52	14.2
布	亿米	0.90	4.7
机制纸及纸板	万吨	12.70	-5.6
焦　炭	万吨	167.65	167.9
初级形态的塑料	万吨	73.33	10.9
塑料制品	万吨	31.44	21.4
水　泥	万吨	966.89	37.0

全年规模以上工业企业实现利润54.40亿元,比上年增长127.5%(见表四)。

表四　规模以上工业企业实现利润及增长速度

指　　标	绝对数(亿元)	比上年增长%
规模以上工业	54.40	127.8
# 国有控股企业	33.21	80.2
# 有限责任公司	32.02	140.3
股份有限公司	8.86	96.3
外商及港澳台商投资企业	2.51	48.5
# 私营企业	7.65	232.7

全年全社会建筑业增加值75.98亿元,比上年增长28.4%。建筑施工企业完成总产值298.47亿元,增长34.1%,其中国有及国有控股企业完成238.23亿元,增长27.7%。

全年全社会投标承包工程面积1959.71万平方米,增长44.0%。房屋建筑施工面积2059.97万平方米,增长36.7%,其中本年新开工面积1496.29万平方米,增长36.5%。房屋建筑竣工面积1115.28万平方米,增长47.9%。全部职工自有技术装备率5001元/人,自有动力装备率2.81千瓦/人。全员劳动生产率149112元/人,增长0.1%。

全年具有资质等级的总承包和专业承包建筑企业实现利润3.91亿元,增长26.9%,其中国有及国有控股企业实现利润3.13亿元,增长26.7%。

四、固定资产投资

全年全社会固定资产投资448.27亿元,比上年增长40.8%。其中,第一产业39.16亿元,增长7.8%;第二产业230.47亿元,增长55.6%;第三产业178.64亿元,增长33.3%(见表五)。南疆垦区投资88.05亿元,增长6.9%,北疆垦区投资360.22亿元,增长52.6%。

表五　全社会固定资产投资完成情况

指　　标	绝对数（亿元）	比上年增长%
全社会固定资产投资	448.27	40.8
# 房地产投资	33.53	37.9
按经济类型分		
# 国有经济	231.84	13.5
集体经济	0.52	18.5
私营个体	74.63	163.2
其　他	141.28	65.2
按用途分		
# 第一产业	39.16	7.8
第二产业	230.47	55.6
第三产业	178.64	33.3

房地产开发投资33.53亿元，比上年增长37.9%。商品房销售面积189.31万平方米，增长20.5%，其中住宅175.41万平方米，增长17.6 %。商品房待售面积47.48万平方米，增长34.2 %。商品房销售额50.31亿元，增长52.4%。

工业完成投资228.27亿元，比上年增长55.4%。其中制造业完成投资157.18亿元，增长71.3%；电力、燃气及水的生产和供应业完成投资62.95亿元，增长45.6%（见表六）。

交通运输业累计完成投资34.19亿元，比上年增长5.9%。新建改建公路2515公里，新建等级客运站33个。其中通营连公路建成1853公里，新增165个连队通公路。

农田水利及水利工程投资19.86亿元，比上年下降22.3%。

全年保障性住房建设完成投资59.50亿元，建设保障性住房9.73万户。

全年固定资产投资建设资金总额464.89亿元，本年资金来源450.80亿元。本年资金来源中，国家预算内资金57.23亿元，国内贷款80.70亿元，利用外资3.00亿元，自筹资金232.84亿元，其他资金77.02亿元。在自筹资金中，企事业单位自有资金182.33亿元，增长72.3%。

全年新增固定资产331.76亿元，比上年增长5.2%。主要新增生产能力或效益：原煤开采60万吨，水泥265万吨，棉纺锭40.06万锭，焦炭100万吨，电解铝20万吨，石墨及碳素制品30万吨，氮肥21.5万吨，发电装机容量17.02万千瓦，输电线路1354千米，医院1009个床位/4.31万平方米，各类学校28152个学生席位/14.62万平方米。

表六　分行业全社会固定资产投资及增长速度

指　　标	绝对数（万元）	比上年增长%
总计	4482739	40.8
农、林、牧、渔业	391574	7.8
采矿业	81513	−31.4
制造业	1571775	71.3
# 农副食品加工业	123679	105.3
食品制造业	102821	−4.8
饮料制造业	60254	436.8
纺织业	178100	33.2
石油加工、炼焦及核燃料加工业	67751	81.1
化学原料及化学制品制造业	432575	58.0
非金属矿物制品业	280798	100.8
有色金属冶炼及压延加工业	231279	692.8
电力、燃气及水的生产和供应业	629452	45.6
建筑业	21969	77.0
交通运输、仓储和邮政业	368571	6.6
信息传输、计算机服务和软件业	7246	41.1
批发和零售业	27854	50.0
住宿和餐饮业	19227	215.6
金融业	3537	183.6
房地产业	978130	57.7
租赁和商务服务业	1472	−46.8
科学研究、技术服务和地质勘查业	9689	−37.2
水利、环境和公共设施管理业	208267	−3.6
居民服务和其他服务业	5216	12.2
教育	95242	128.9
卫生、社会保障和社会福利业	25282	−13.0
文化、体育和娱乐业	21760	19.2
公共管理和社会组织	14963	−1.6

五、公路运输业

年末民用汽车保有量12.52万辆，比上年末增长17.1%，其中私人汽车10.38万辆，增长42.5%。民用轿车4.70万辆，增长30.4%，其中私人轿车3.93万辆，增长1.5倍。

全年民用汽车保有量中，载客汽车6.02万辆，增长27.9%；载货汽车3.19万辆，增长12.2%；农用运输车3.10万辆，增长5.1%。

全年道路运输旅客周转量66.60亿人公里、货物周转量106.75亿吨公里，分别比上年增长14.9%和23.5%（见表七）。

表七　道路运输业营运情况

指　　标	计量单位	绝对数	比上年增长%
货物周转量	亿吨公里	106.75	23.5
# 个体	亿吨公里	95.12	24.7
货运量	亿吨	1.19	21.4
# 个体	亿吨	1.08	21.8
旅客周转量	亿人公里	66.60	14.9
# 个体	亿人公里	38.05	19.6
客运量	亿人	1.10	11.8
# 个体	亿人	0.81	12.6
营运收入	亿元	53.15	24.8
# 个体纯收入	亿元	21.00	21.8

六、国内贸易

全年社会消费品零售总额202.87亿元，比上年增长19.4%。扣除物价因素实际增长14.1%。分行业看，批发和零售业零售额171.71亿元，增长19.1%；住宿和餐饮业零售额31.16亿元，增长21.0%。

批发零售业商品销售总额649.36亿元，增长8.8%，其中，限额以上批发和零售业商品销售总额476.96亿元，增长7.2%。限额以上批发和零售业商品销售类值中，棉麻类销售额比上年增长5.5%，石油及制品类增长17.0%，建筑及装潢材料类增长18.0%。

七、对外贸易、经济技术协作与旅游

全年货物进出口总额55.89亿美元，比上年增长19.3%。其中货物出口49.80亿美元，增长16.2%；货物进口6.09亿美元，增长52.5%(见表八)。

表八　货物进出口总额完成情况

指　　标	绝对数(万美元)	比上年增长%
进出口总额	558874	19.3
出口总额	498008	16.2
进口总额	60866	52.5
出口商品按类值分		
动物产品类	114	148.4
植物产品类	7239	192.4
食品饮料烟酒类	16922	-3.3
矿产品类	12942	1952.3
化工类	3592	-29.5
塑料制品类	19953	129.0
箱包类	9424	29.0
木制品类	2705	-49.2
纸浆类	739	-44.6
纺织原料及制品类	233045	4.9
鞋帽类	62950	9.4
矿物制品类	497	271.4
玻璃及陶制品	12040	55.3
珠宝类	33	
黑色金属类	6578	3.6
机电产品类	72784	25.8
汽车类	24969	74.7
医疗器械类	41	-71.9
杂项制品类	11400	0.2

注：数据为海关统计口径。

出口总额中兵团自产品出口额10亿美元，增长15.7%，占兵团出口总额20.1%。

新批外商投资企业10家，合同外资金额3590万美元，下降37.1%，实际使用外资3845万美元。

对外承包工程、劳务合作完成营业额3.08亿美元，增长28.1%。

全年招商引资项目483个，当年引进兵团以外项目到位资金199.26亿元，比上年增长39.3%。其中，第一产业3.75亿元，第二产业167.38亿元，第三产业28.13亿元。外省投资项目到位资金148.43亿元，外资项目到位资金5.59亿元，兵地融合项目到位资金41.90亿元，上市公司项目到位资金3.34亿元。城市、开发区、园区招商项目134个，到位资金137.35亿元。

年末有旅行社98家。旅游星级饭店50家。国家等级旅游景区26家，其中4A级景区5家。全国工农业旅游示范点12家。

全年接待旅游者401万人次，比上年增长21.0%。其中接待入境旅游游客13万人次，增长29.0%，出境旅游0.51万人次，增长50.0%。旅游总收入16.90亿元人民币，增长65.0%。

八、金融与保险业

驻疆各银行年末对兵团贷款余额875.46亿元，比年初增长25.1%。其中，中长期贷款443.26亿元，增长33.5%；短期贷款433.20亿元，增长17.8%。

兵团农业银行年末各项本外币存款余额746.56亿元，比年初增长2.0%。其中，个人存款342.22亿元，增长2.5%；单位存款402.50亿元，增长1.6%。各项贷款年末余额232.29亿元，增长2.4%。

年末有各级保险分支机构2051个。全年保险业务收入193.36亿元，与上年基本持平。各类保险赔款支出120.13亿元，下降10.8个百分点。

九、科学技术与教育

年末有各类学校554所，在校学生55.27万人，教职工4.36万人。其中，普通高等学校在校生4.68万人，比上年增长6.0%；招生1.34万人，增长5.6%；毕业生1.02万人，比上年增长5.9%(见表九)。小学适龄儿童入学率99.9%，初中适龄人口入学率96.1%。

表九　各类学校基本情况

计量单位：所、人

指　标	学校数	在校生数	新招生	教职工数	专任教师	毕业生数
合　计	554	552706	157203	43634	34786	151312
普通高等学校	4	46776	13370	4201	2741	10243
成人高等学校	2	10857	3909	948	612	3463
中等职业学校	23	35798	15110	2075	1305	13681
普通中学	251	190362	63429	17589	14541	62410
小　学	85	217600	33255	15568	13581	40186
幼儿园	189	51313	28130	3253	2006	21329

年末有科学研究与技术开发机构18个，各类专业技术人员11.85万人。

全年1项成果获国家科技进步二等奖；76项成果获兵团科技进步奖，其中一等奖3项，二等奖27项，三等奖46项。

十、文化、卫生和体育事业

年末有广播电视播出机构197座，其中兵、师电视台2座、广播电台1座、广播电视台13座。农牧团场广播电视播出机构176座，分场及工矿企业广播电视站5座。广播覆盖率96.0%，电视覆盖率98.2%，有线电视入户率60.0%。启动农村(团场)电影放映工作，全年放映22945场次，完成公益放映任务94.7%。以和平影院为龙头建立了兵团电影院线联盟。

年末有兵团文化中心1座，兵团军垦博物馆1座，国家三级图书馆1座，8个师建有文化中心(文化宫)。116个团场建有文化活动中心，1210个连队建有文化室，师团有文化广场102个。建有文化信息资源共享工程省级分中心1个、县级支中心81个，有不可移动的文物点500多处，兵团级爱国主义教育基地23个。三五九旅纪念馆等3个场馆入选全国第二期红色旅游景区名录。

年末有公开发行各级各类报纸18家，期刊16家，内部资料(刊型、报刊)25家。出版社1家，全年出版图书21种、7万余册。拥有网站66家，新华网、中新网、经济日报网、中广网均设有兵团频道。

年末有各类卫生机构1339个(含营利性卫生机构)，各类卫生人员24186人。其中，执业和执业助理医师8058人，注册护士7967人。每千人执业(助理)医师3.13人，每千人注册护士3.10人，每千人有医院床位6.91张。传染病报告发病率(甲乙类传染病) 338.07/10万，病死率0.2184%，婴儿死亡率6.47‰，孕产妇死亡率38/10万。

2010年，在第四届全国体育大会中，兵团代表团获男子三人篮球项目三等奖1枚，航空模型项目三等奖6枚，获全国体育道德风尚奖；在全国特奥运动会中，获6枚金牌、9枚银牌、8枚铜牌。

十一、人口、就业、人民生活与社会保障

初步预计，年末兵团总人口257.32万人。

兵团城镇居民人均可支配收入14559元，比上年增长12.6%，扣除价格因素，实际增长8.7%；团场农牧工家庭人均纯收入8782元，增长14.5%，扣除价格因素，实际增长8.2%。

在岗职工工资总额198.34亿元，增长25.9%。在岗职工平均工资26741元，比上年增加4865元，增长22.2%，扣除价格因素，实际增长17.2%。

年末参加基本养老保险人数129.42万人，其中参保职工81.47万人，退休人员52.64万人。参加失业保险62.66万人，参加职工基本医疗保险121.01万人，参加居民基本医疗保险97.36万人，参加工伤保险65.17万人，参加生育保险61.19万人。

全年有各类收养性单位111个。12.5万人得到居民最低生活保障。国家抚恤、补助各类优抚对象0.38万人。

全年受理劳动保障监察投诉案件1429件，结案1353件，结案率94.7%；接到行政复议案件43件，其中，立案受理42件，结案42件，结案率100%；处理劳动争议案件1247件，其中，调解611件，立案处理636件，结案率97.0%。

十二、资源、环境与安全生产

全年规模以上工业企业综合能源消费量797.88万吨标准煤，比上年增长17.4%。其中，煤炭消费量1157.01万吨，增长12.4%；汽油0.39万吨，增长15.1%；柴油2.00万吨，增长1.8%；天然气3920万立方米，增长37.1%；电120.89亿千瓦小时，增长36.2%；热力1217.56万百万千焦，增长35.5%。

全年工业废水排放总量4795.36万吨，工业废水中COD排放总量1.747万吨。工业废水排放达标率70.46%，工业重复用水率89.33%。工业废气中二氧化硫排放总量7.071万吨，工业烟尘排放总量2.199万吨，工业粉尘排放量1.389万吨，工业固体废物排放量4.61万吨，工业固体废物综合利用量421.56万吨，综合利用率60.49%。环境影响评价制度执行率95%以上，“三同时”执行率85%以上。

全年兵团工矿商贸企业共发生职工死亡事故24起，事故死亡27人，死亡人数与上年持平。亿元GDP生产安全事故死亡人数0.035人，下降12.4%。工矿商贸企业10万从业人员死亡人数4.69人，下降4.9%。煤矿百万吨死亡人数1.62人，下降35.2%。百万车公里事故死亡人数0.0155人，上升26.0%。

注：1. 生产总值、各产业增加值、总产值绝对数按现价计算，增长速度按可比价格计算。
2. 本公报数据为初步统计数，最终数据以《2011年兵团统计年鉴》为准。
3. 2010年末总人口数为初步预计数，最终数据以第六次全国人口普查暨兵团人口调查公报为准。
4. 南疆垦区为一、二、三、十四师，北疆垦区为四、五、六、七、八、九、十、建工师、十二、十三师及兵团直属单位。

Statistical Communiqué of Xinjiang Production & Construction Group on the 2010 National Economic and Social Development

Statistics Bureau of Xinjiang Production & Construction Group
The Survey Office of Xinjiang Production & Construction Group of National Bureau of Statistics

April 2011

In 2010, under the correct leadership of the CPC Committee of Xinjiang Production & Construction Group (Hereinafter shortened as XPCG) and XPCG, a great majority of cadres, staff and workers of XPCG, taking as the guidance of Deng Xiaoping Theory and the Important Thought of "Three Represents", implemented earnestly the scientific approach to the economic and social development, carried out arrangements set by the fifth and sixth full sessions (enlarged) of the sixth congress of the XPCG Committee of the CPC, firmly seized the golden opportunity of the grand construction, opening-up and development which the central work conference on Xinjiang's development supported, stayed realistic and pragmatic and blazed new trails in a pioneering spirit, the comprehensive strength reached a new high, life of workers and staff attained a new level and social undertakings achieved new progress.

Ⅰ. General Outlook

In 2010, the gross domestic product (GDP) of the year was 77.062 billion yuan, up by 13.9 percent over the previous year. Of this total, the value added of the primary industry was 27.881 billion yuan, up by 11.8 percent, that of the secondary industry was 26.227 billion yuan, up by 21.2 percent, and that of the tertiary industry was 22.954 billion yuan, up by 9.0 percent. The value added of the primary industry accounted for 36 percent of the GDP, that of the secondary industry made up 34 percent, and that of the tertiary industry represented 30 percent.

14 listed companies controlled by XPCG raised a cumulative capital of 10.07 billion yuan, of which 3.832 billion yuan came from the IPOs and 6.231 billion yuan was from refunding.

Number of the agricultural industrialized key leading enterprises was 68 at national and provincial levels, of which 11 were at national level. The leading enterprises promoted growth for 0.40 million farmers and number of enterprises with sales income of over 1 billion yuan was 8.

The total profit volume of XPCG's state-owned and state-holding enterprises of agriculture, industry, construction and commerce was 4.026 billion yuan, an increase of 2.769 billion yuan over the previous year.

According to preliminary statistics, 9.074 billion yuan of various taxes were turned over in 2010.

The investment completed in "ten good things" was 7.073 billion yuan.

The general level of consumer prices was up by 4.3 percent over the previous year (Table 1). The retail prices for commodities went up by 4.6 percent. The prices for means of agricultural production increased by 3.1 percent. The producer prices for farm products were up by 31.5 percent. The producer prices for manufactured goods were up by 25.3 percent. The purchasing prices for raw materials, fuels and power went up by 23.9 percent. The prices for investment in fixed assets were up by 4.6 percent.

Table 1: General level of Consumer Prices in 2010

Unit: %

Item	Increase over 2009(%)
General level of consumer prices	4.3
# Urban	3.6
Rural	5.8
Food	10.7
# Grain	8.9
Meat and Poultry	13.0
Eggs	12.3
Aquatic products	7.4
Tobaccos and alcohols	2.0
Clothing	-0.8
Household appliances and services	1.2
Medical, health and personal articles	2.0
Transportation and telecommunications	Even
Recreational, educational, cultural articles and services	1.2
Housing	2.7

At the end of 2010, the total of employed people in XPCG numbered 1.0618 million, up by 2.5 percent over

2009. Employed people on the job were 677. 6 thousand, up by 0. 8 percent over the previous year. The newly increased employed people numbered 66. 7 thousand. The urban unemployment rate through unemployment registration was 2. 41 percent at the end of 2010. The 24 hour minimum placement system for zero employment family was set up and 2, 334 households of zero employment families were assisted to realize at least one person was employed.

Entrepreneur confidence index and business climate index in the four quarters of the year were located at between better ranges. Entrepreneur confidence indices from the first quarter to the fourth quarter were 144. 2, 139. 0, 137. 0 and 144. 6, up by 39. 4, 24. 5, 25. 5, and 17. 3 points respectively over the corresponding period of the previous year. Business climate indices of four quarters were 124. 9, 125. 5, 138. 5 and 135. 6 respectively, up by 6. 6, 3. 6, 16. 3 and 15. 0 points respectively over the corresponding period of the previous year.

Ⅱ. Agriculture

In 2010, gross output value of agriculture was 56. 928 billion yuan, up by 7. 2% over the previous year.

The sown area of crops was 1,119. 20 thousand hectares (16. 788 million mu), up by 1. 0 percent over the previous year. Of this total, the sown area for grain was 284. 69 thousand hectares (4. 2704 million mu), down by 9. 3 percent. The sown area of cotton was 497. 98 thousand hectares (7. 4697 million mu), up by 2. 1 percent, that of oil-bearing crops was 67. 78 thousand hectares (1. 0167 million mu), down by 1. 4 percent, that of beetroot crop was 25. 52 thousand hectares (0. 3828 million mu), up by 25. 8 percent, and that of vegetables (including table gourds) was 79. 68 thousand hectares (1. 1952 million mu), up by 7. 9 percent.

The precision and semi-precision sown area of crops was 708. 93 thousand hectares (10. 6369 million mu), down by 6. 7 percent over the previous year. Of this total, the precision sown area of cotton was 364. 53 thousand hectares (5. 468 million mu), down by 5. 7percent. The area of soil analysis-based fertilization was 618. 67 thousand hectares (9. 2801 million mu).

The effectively irrigated area was 1, 067. 27 thousand hectares (16. 009 million mu). The area of high and new technology water-saving irrigation was 682. 16 thousand hectares (10. 2324 million mu), of which a newly increased area was 29. 23 thousand hectares (0. 4358 million mu).

The output of cotton in 2010 was 1. 1501 million tons, an increase of 1. 4 percent over the previous year, that of grain was 2. 1364 million tons, down by 1. 7 percent, that of edible oil was 186,200 tons, the same level as compared with that over the previous year, and that of beetroot was 1. 8166 million tons, up by 25. 0 percent.

Number of livestock at the end of 2010 was 6. 2406 million heads, up by 6. 5 percent over the previous year. Major farm products and livestock output kept growing (Table 2).

Table 2: Output of Major Farm Products ,livestock production in 2010

Item	Unit	Value	Increase over 2009(%)
Grain	10,000 tons	213. 64	-1. 7
Cotton	10,000 tons	115. 01	1. 4
Oil-bearing crops	10,000 tons	18. 62	Even
Beetroot	10,000 tons	181. 66	25. 0
Vegetables	10,000 tons	581. 62	-2. 9
# Industrial tomato	10,000 tons	441. 31	-4. 9
Fruits	10,000 tons	122. 54	18. 9
Number of livestock	10,000 heads	624. 06	6. 5
# Cattle	10,000 heads	36. 84	8. 8
Pig	10,000 heads	155. 42	15. 9
sheep	10,000 heads	427. 76	3. 3
Number of slaughtered livestock	10,000 heads	682. 07	13. 1
Total meat output	10,000 tons	31. 99	20. 2
Sheep wool output	10,000 tons	1. 13	6. 3
Poultry egg output	10,000 tons	4. 57	12. 2
Cow milk output	10,000 tons	44. 31	15. 3

The total output of aquatic products was 26. 7thousand tons, up by 13. 3 percent over the previous year.

The operation area of artificial afforestion was 14. 41 thousand hectares (216. 1 thousand mu), down by 16. 9 percent, and the newly sealed area without woods and with sparse woods was 5. 33 thousand hectares (80 thousand mu), up by 9. 1 percent.

The total power of agricultural machinery was 3. 6933 million kilowatts, up by 3. 9 percent over the previous year.

Possession of airplanes was 29 at the end of 2010. A total of flying time was 5,482 hours, with 4,218 sorties. The flying time for agriculture, forestry and animal husbandry was 3,320 hours, with 3. 777 sorties. The flying time for industry was 1,805 hours, with 441 sorties. The operation area completed was 989. 19 thousand hectares (14. 8378 million mu).

Number of reservoirs was 125, with a total capacity volume of 3. 278 billion cubic meters. Number of electric wells was 15,643, with a lifting capacity of 2. 267 billion cubic meters. 114 diversion gates were built and the total length of embankment construction was 2,477. 96 kilometers. The water supply volume of water conservancy projects was 12. 559 billion cubic meters.

Ⅲ. Industry and Construction

In 2010, the total value added of the industrial sector was 18. 629 billion yuan, up by 18. 5 percent over the previous year. The value added of industrial enterprises above the designated size was up by 25. 4 percent. Of this total, the value added of the state-owned and state-holding enterprises grew by 14. 4 percent, that of share-holding enterprises went by 27. 5 percent, and that of the enterprises by foreign investors and investors from Hong Kong, Macao and Taiwan rose by

47. 1 percent. Analyzed by light and heavy industries, the growth of the light industry was 24. 9 percent and that of the heavy industry was 28. 2 percent.

In 2010, of the industrial enterprises above the designated size, the growth of value added for the mining and washing of coal industry was 82. 0 percent over the previous year; for processing of food from agricultural products 10. 1 percent; for food manufacturing 25. 2 percent; for beverage manufacturing 52. 3 percent; for textile industry 22. 2 percent; for manufacture of raw chemical materials and chemical products 6. 1 percent; for manufacture of non-metallic mineral products 45. 0 percent; and for generation and supply of electric power and heat power 17. 0 percent.

Output of most major industrial products kept growing (Table 3).

Table 3: Output of Major Industrial Products in 2010

Item	Unit	Value	Increase over 2009(%)
Coal	10000 tons	925. 83	36. 4
Electricity	100 million kilowatt-hours	134. 87	18. 2
Edible Plant oil	10000 tons	30. 73	-4. 3
Machine-made sugar	10000 tons	17. 24	-24. 2
Dairy product	10000 tons	9. 62	32. 3
Tomato paste	10000 tons	65. 01	-4. 2
Beverage alcohol	10000 liters	14. 97	75. 7
Soft beverage	10000 tons	48. 71	-0. 2
Yarn	10000 tons	22. 52	14. 2
Cloth	10000 meters	0. 90	4. 7
Machine-made paper and paper board	10000 tons	12. 7	-5. 6
Coke	10000 tons	167. 65	167. 9
Preliminary plastics	10000 tons	73. 33	10. 9
Plastic product	10000 tons	31. 44	21. 4
Cement	10000 tons	966. 89	37. 0

The profits made by the industrial enterprises above the designated size in 2010 were 5. 440 billion yuan, up by 127. 5 percent over the previous year (Table 4).

Table 4: Profits and Growth of Industrial Enterprises above Designated Size and in 2010

Item	Value	Increase over 2009(%)
Industrial enterprises above designated size	54. 40	127. 8
# State-owned and state-holding enterprises	33. 21	80. 2
# Limited liability companies	31. 02	140. 3
Share-holding companies	8. 86	96. 3
Enterprises invested by foreigners or investors from Hong Kong, Macao, and Taiwan	2. 51	48. 5
# Private enterprises	7. 65	232. 7

In 2010, the value added of construction enterprises in XPCG was 7. 598 billion yuan, up by 28. 4 percent over the previous year. The total output value of construction enterprises was 29. 847 billion yuan, up by 34. 1 percent. Of this total, the total output value of state-owned and state-holding enterprises was 23. 823 billion yuan, up by 27. 7 percent.

The floor space of bidding contract buildings was 19. 5971 million square meters, up by 44. 0 percent. The floor space of buildings under construction was 20. 5997 million square meters, up by 36. 7 percent. Of this total, the floor space of new startup was 14. 9629 million square meters, up by 36. 5 percent, and that of buildings completed was 11. 1528 million square meters, up by 47. 9 percent. The level of technical equipment of overall staff and workers was 5,001 yuan per person and that of power equipment was 2. 81 kilowatts per person. Labor productivity was 149,112 yuan per person, up by 0. 1 percent.

The profits made by construction enterprises qualified for general contracts and specialized contracts reached 391 million yuan, up by 26. 9 percent, of which the profits made by the state-owned and state-holding enterprises were 313 million yuan, up by 26. 7 percent.

Ⅳ. Investment in Fixed Assets

The completed investment in fixed assets in 2010 was 44. 827 billion yuan, up by 40. 8 percent over the previous year. Of this total, the investment in the primary industry was 3. 916 billion yuan, up by 7. 8 percent; that in the secondary industry was 23. 047 billion yuan, up by 55. 6 percent and that in the tertiary industry was 17. 864 billion yuan, up by 33. 3 percent (Table 5). An analysis by regions showed that the investment in southern XPCG was 8. 805 billion yuan, up by 6. 9 percent, and that in northern XPCG was 36. 022 billion yuan, up by 52. 6 percent.

Table 5: Investment in Fixed Assets in 2010

Item	Value(100 million yuan)	Increase over 2009(%)
Investment in fixed assets	448. 27	40. 8
# Real estate investment	33. 53	37. 9
Classified by ownership		
# State-owned economy	231. 84	13. 5
Collective-owned economy	0. 52	18. 5
Private economy	74. 63	163. 2
Other	141. 28	65. 2
Classified by Use		
# The primary industry	39. 16	7. 8
The secondary industry	230. 47	55. 6
The tertiary industry	178. 64	33. 3

The investment in real estate was 3. 353 billion yuan, up by 37. 9 percent over the previous year. The floor space of sold commercial housing was 1. 8931 million square meters, up by 20. 5 percent. Of this total, the floor space of residential housing was 1. 7541 million square meters, up by 17. 6 percent. The floor space of empty commercial housing was 474,800 square meters, up by 34. 2 percent. The sales value of commercial housing was 5. 031 billion yuan, up by 52. 4

percent.

The completed investment in industry was 22. 827 billion yuan, up by 55. 4 percent over the previous year. Of this total, investment in manufacturing sector was 15. 718 billion yuan, up by 71. 3 percent and that of electric power, combustion gas and water production and supply sector was 6. 295 billion yuan, up by 45. 6 percent (Table 6).

The total investment in transport was 3. 419 billion yuan, up by 5. 9 percent over the previous year. Newly built and renovated highway was 2, 515 kilometers. 33 passenger stations were newly built. 1,853 kilometers of highway to villages and towns were completed and number of villages with the new access to highway covered by asphalt was 165.

The investment in water conservancy projects was 1. 986 billion yuan, down by 22. 3 percent over the previous year.

The investment in security residential housing construction was 5. 95 billion yuan and 97,300 security houses were constructed.

The total construction fund of investment in fixed assets was 46. 489 billion yuan and the fund source in 2010 was 45. 08 billion yuan. Of this total, the internal budgetary fund from the State was 5. 723 billion yuan, the domestic loan was 8. 07 billion yuan, the foreign capital utilization was 300 million yuan, the self-raised fund was 23. 284 billion yuan, and other fund was 7. 702 billion yuan. Of the self-raised fund, the fund from enterprises and institutions was 18. 233 billion yuan, up by 72. 3 percent.

The newly increased fixed assets were 33. 176 billion yuan, up by 5. 2 percent over the previous year. Main newly added production capacities and efficiency of fixed assets investment were: 600,000 tons of raw coal per annum, 2. 65 million tons of cement per annum, 400,600 spindles of cotton yarns, 1 million tons of coking, 200,000 tons of electrolytic aluminum, 300,000 tons of graphite and carbon products, 215,000 tons of nitrogen fertilizer, 170,200 kilowatts of installed generating electricity, 1, 354 kilometers of power transmission line, 1,009 beds and 43,100 square meters for hospitals, and 28,152 student seats and 146,200 square meters for various schools.

Table 6: Investment in Fixed Assets and Its Growth by Sector in 2010

Unit: 100 million yuan

Sector	Investment	Increase over 2009(%)
Total	4482739	40. 8
Agriculture, forestry, animal husbandry and fishing	391574	7. 8
Mining	81513	-31. 4
Manufacturing	1571775	71. 3
# Processing of food from agricultural products	123679	105. 3
Manufacture of foods	102821	-4. 8
Manfacture of beverage	60254	436. 8
Textile industry	178100	33. 2
Processing of Petroleum, Coking and Processing Nuclear fuel	67751	81. 1
Manufacture of raw chemical materials and chemical products	432575	58. 0
Manufacture of non-metallic mineral products	280798	100. 8
Smelting and Pressing of Non-Ferrous Metals	231279	692. 8
Production and Supply of Electricity, Gas and Water	629452	45. 6
Construction	21969	77. 0
Transport, Storage and Post	368571	6. 6
Information Transmission, Computer Services and Software	7246	41. 1
Wholesale and Retail Trade	27854	50. 0
Lodging and Catering Services	19227	215. 6
Banking	3537	183. 6
Real Estate	978130	57. 7
Leasing and Business Services	1472	-46. 8
Scientific Research, Technical Service and Geologic Prospecting	9689	-37. 2
Water Conservancy, Environment and Public Facilities Management	208267	-3. 6
Services to Households and Other Services	5216	12. 2
Education	95242	128. 9
Health, Social Security and Social Welfare	25282	-13. 0
Culture, Sports and Entertainment	21760	19. 2
Public Management and Social Organization	14963	-1. 6

Ⅴ. Road Transportation

By the end of 2010, the total number of motor vehicles for civilian use reached 125,200, up by 17. 1 percent over the previous year, of which private-owned vehicles numbered 103,800, up by 42. 5 percent. The total number of cars for civilian use stood at 47,000, up by 30. 4 percent, of which private-owned cars numbered 39,300, up by 1. 5 times.

Of the total vehicles for civilian use, number of passenger vehicles was 60,200, up by 27. 9 percent, that of load-carrying vehicles was 31,900, up by 12. 2 percent, and that of vehicles for agricultural use was 31,000, up by 5. 1 percent.

Highway passenger flow was 6. 66 billion person-kilometers and freight turnover was 10. 675 billion ton-kilometers, up by 14. 9 percent and 23. 5 percent over the previous year respectively (Table 7).

Table 7: Transportation Operation in 2010

Item	Unit	Value	Increase over 2009(%)
Freight turnover	100 million ton-kms	106.75	23.5
# Individual	100 million ton-kms	95.12	24.7
Freight traffic	100 million tons	1.19	21.4
# Individual	100 million tons	1.08	21.8
Passenger flow	100million person-kms	66.60	14.9
# Individual	100 million person-kms	38.05	19.6
Passenger traffic	100 million persons	1.10	11.8
# Individual	100 million persons	0.81	12.6
Operation income	100 million yuan	53.15	24.8
# Individual	100 million yuan	21.00	21.8

Ⅵ. Domestic Trade

In 2010, the total retail sales of consumer goods reached 20.287 billion yuan, a growth of 19.4 percent over the previous year, or a real growth of 14.1 percent after deducting price factors. Analyzed by different sectors, the sales of the wholesales and retail trade reached 17.171 billion yuan, up by 19.1 percent; that of the lodging and catering industry was 3.116 billion yuan, up by 21.0 percent.

The total sales of commodities of wholesale and retail sector were 64.936 billion yuan, up by 8.8 percent over the previous year. Of this total, the total sales of commodities of the wholesale and retail sector above the designated size was 47.696 billion yuan, up by 7.2 percent. Of the total sales of commodities above the designated size, the growth of cotton and flax sales was 5.5 percent over the previous year, that of coal and its products was 17.0 percent, and that of building and decoration materials was 18.0 percent.

Ⅶ. Foreign Trade, Economic and Technical Co-operation, and Tourism

The total value of imports and exports in 2010 reached 5.589 billion US dollars, up by 19.3 percent over the previous year. Of this total, the value of goods export was 4.98 billion US dollars, up by 16.2 percent, and the value of goods import was 609 million US dollars, up by 52.5 percent (Table 8).

Table 8: Import and Export by Major Categories in 2010

Unit: 100 million us dollars

Item	Value	Increase over 2009(%)
Total imports and exports	558874	19.3
Exports	498008	16.2
Imports	60866	52.5
Grouped by product category		
Animal products	114	148.4
Plant products	7239	192.4
Food, beverage, cigarette and alcohol	16922	-3.3
Minerals	12942	1952.3
Chemicals	3592	-29.5
Plastic products	19953	129.0
Cases and bags	9424	29.0
Wooden products	2705	-49.2
Paper pulp	739	-44.6
Textile material and textile articles	233045	4.9
Shoes and caps	62950	9.4
Mineral products	497	271.4
Glass and ceramics	12040	55.3
Jewelry	33	
Ferrous metals	6578	3.6
Mechanical and electronic products	72784	25.8
Automobile	24969	74.7
Medical equipment	41	-71.9
Miscellaneous products	11400	0.2

Note: Data were based on the Custom Statistics

Of the total exports, the value of goods exports produced by XPCG was 1 billion US dollars, up by 15.7 percent, representing 20.1 percent of it.

10 new foreign-funded ventures were approved, with a contract value of 35.90 million US dollars, down by 37.1 percent over the previous year and the actually utilized value of was 38.45 million US dollars.

The completed business revenue of foreign contract projects and labor cooperation was 308 million US dollars, up by 28.1 percent over the previous year.

483 projects were introduced and the actually utilized capital introduced outside of XPCG was 19.926 billion yuan, up by 39.3 percent over the previous year. Of this total, the actually utilized capital of the primary industry was 375 million yuan, that of the secondary industry was 16.738 billion yuan, and that of the tertiary industry was 2.813 billion yuan. The actually utilized capital of investment projects from other provinces was 14.843 billion yuan, that of foreign-funded projects was 559 million yuan and that of integrated projects between XPCG and Xinjiang was 4.19 billion yuan. The actually utilized capital of the projects from the listed companies was 334 million yuan. Number of projects introduced by cities, development districts and parks were 134, with an actually utilized capital of 13.735 billion yuan.

Travel agencies by the end of 2010 were 98. Number of star-rated hotels was 50. There were 26 tourist scenic spots at the national level, of which 5 for the 4A scenic spot. There were 12 national tourist demonstration spots of agriculture and industry.

In 2010, 4.01 million tourists were received, up by 21.0 percent over the previous year. Of this total, the number of inbound visitors was 130,000, up by 29.0 percent; and that of outbound Chinese visitors organized was 5,100, up by 50.0 percent. The total tourism income was 1.69 billion yuan, up by 65.0 percent.

Ⅷ. Banking and Insurance

By the end of 2010, balance of various loans to XPCG from various banks in Xinjiang was 87.546 billion yuan, up by 25.1 percent over the beginning of 2010. Of this total, the long-term loans were 44.326 billion yuan, up by 33.5 percent and the short-term loans were 43.32 billion yuan, up by 17.8 percent.

Various saving deposits in RMB and foreign currencies from XPCG Bank of Agriculture totaled 74.656 billion yuan, up by 2.0 percent over the beginning of 2010. Of this total, individual saving deposits were 34.222 billion yuan, up by 2.5 percent and that of units were 40.25 billion yuan, up by 1.6 percent. Balance of various loans by the end of 2010 was 23.229 billion yuan, up by 2.4 percent.

Number of insurance branches at various levels by the end of the year was 2,051. The premium of insurance business was 19.336 billion yuan, as same as that over the previous year. Indemnity of various insurances was 12.013 billion yuan, down by 10.8 percent.

Ⅸ. Science and Technology, and Education

Number of various schools by the end of the year was 554. Enrollment of various schools was 552,700 students, and teaching staff and workers were 43,600. Of this total, the general tertiary education enrollment was 46,800 students, up by 6.0 percent over the previous year. 13,400 students were enrolled, up by 5.6 percent. Number of graduates was 10,200, up by 5.9 percent over the previous year (Table 9). Enrollment rate of primary school-age children was 99.9 percent and that of junior secondary school-age people reached 96.1 percent.

Table 9: Basic statistics of Various Types of Schools

Unit: set, person

Item	School	Enrollment	New entrants	Teachers and staff	Full-time teachers	Graduates
Total	554	552706	157203	43634	34786	151312
Regular institutions	4	46776	13370	4201	2741	10243
Adult institutions	2	10857	3909	948	612	3463
Middle vocational	23	35798	15110	2075	1305	13681
Regular secondary	251	190362	63429	17589	14541	62410
Primary schools	85	217600	33255	15568	13581	40186
Kindergartens	189	51313	28130	3253	2006	21329

By the end of 2010, number of scientific research and technological development bodies was 18, with 118,500 various professionals and technicians.

In 2010, one result was awarded the second prize of the National Prize of Science and Technology Progress. 76 results were awarded the XPCG's Prize of Science and Technology Progress. Of this total, 3 items was awarded the first prize, 27 items were awarded the second prize and 46 items were awarded the third prize.

Ⅹ. Culture, Public Health and Sports

At the end of 2010, there were 197 radio broadcasting and TV stations, of which there were 2 TV stations, one radio broadcasting station and 13 radio broadcasting and TV stations of XPCG and divisions, 176 farm radio broadcasting and TV stations, and 5 radio broadcasting and TV stations of sub-farms and industrial mining enterprises. The radio broadcasting coverage rate was 96.0 percent, TV coverage was 98.2 percent, and cable TV household coverage was 60 percent. The film projection for countryside (farms) was launched, 2,945 numbers were shown, and 94.7 percent of the public welfare task was completed. The Alliance of XPCG Cinemas was established with the Peace Cinema as the flagship.

There were one cultural center, one army reclamation museum, one national third-level library, 8 cultural centers (cultural palaces) of divisions. There were 116 farm-based cultural activity centers, 1210 village-based cultural rooms, and 102 farm and division-based public cultural squares. One sub-center of shared cultural information resource project at the provincial level, 81 branch centers and over 500 fixed cultural sites were built. There were 23 patriotic educational bases at the XPCG level. The Memorial Hall of Brigade 359 and other halls were selected into the second phase list of national red tourist scenic spots.

By the end of 2010, there 18 various public newspapers, 16 journals and 25 internal materials (journal and newspaper) at various levels. It had one publishing house and 21 kinds of books with over 70,000 copies were published. It had 66 websites. Xinhua, China News, Economic Daily and China National Radio portals set up the XPCG channel.

By the end of 2010, there were 1,339 various health institutions (including profit-making institutions) and 24,186 various health workers. Of this total, there were 8,058 practicing doctors and assistant practicing doctors and 7,967 registered nurses. Number of practicing doctors and assistant practicing doctors per one thousand people was 3.13, that of registered nurses per one thousand was 3.10, and that of beds per one thousand people was 6.91. Reported annual incidence of A or B infectious diseases were 338.07 per 100 thousand, with the death rate standing at 0.2184 percent. Infant mortality rate was 6.47 per thousand and pregnant women death rate was 38 per 100 thousand.

In 2010, the delegation of XPCG Athletes was awarded one bronze medal of the 3-person basketball, 6 medals of model airplane and the sportsmanship prize at the Fourth National Games. 6 gold medals, 9 silver medals and 8 bronze medals were awarded at the Fifth National Special Olympics Games.

Ⅺ. Population, Employment and Social security

According to preliminary estimation, at the end of 2010, the total population of XPCG was 2,573,200.

The annual per capita disposable income of urban households in XPCG was 14,559 yuan, up by 12. 6 percent over the previous year, or a real increase of 8. 7 percent when price factors were deducted. The annual per capita net income of farm households was 8,782 yuan, up by 14. 5 percent, or a real increase of 8. 2 percent when price factors were deducted.

The total wages of workers on the job were 19. 834 billion yuan, up 25. 9 percent. The annual per capita wage of workers on the job was 26,741 yuan, an increase of 4,865 yuan over the previous year, up 22. 2 percent, or a real increase of 17. 2 percent when price factors were deducted.

At the end of 2010, a total of 1. 2942 million people participated in basic pension program. Of this total, 0. 8147 million were workers and staff and 0. 5264 million were retired persons. A total of 626,600 people participated in unemployment insurance program. A total of 1. 2101 million people participated in basic health insurance programs for staff and workers. A total of 973, 600 people participated in basic health insurance program for residents. A total of 0. 6517 million people participated in work accident insurance. A total of 0. 6119 million people participated in maternity insurance program.

There were 111 adoption institutions of various types. 125,000 people received the government minimum living allowance and 3,800 people were compensated and subsidized by the country.

1,429 cases of labor security supervision were received and 1,353 cases were settled, with a settlement rate of 94. 7 percent. 43 cases of administrative reconsideration were received, 42 cases were registered and 42 cases were settled, with a settlement rate of 100 percent. 1,247 cases of labor dispute were received, of which 611 cases were mediated and 636 cases were handled, with a settlement rate of 97. 0 percent.

Ⅻ. Resources, Environment and Work Safety

In 2010, the comprehensive energy consumption by industrial enterprises above designated size amounted to 7. 9788 million tons of standard coal equivalent, up 17. 4 percent over the previous year. Of this total, the consumption of coal was 11. 5701 million tons, up 12. 4 percent; gasoline 3,900 tons, up 15. 1 percent; diesel 20,000 tons, up 1. 8 percent; natural gas 39. 2 million cubic meters, up 37. 1 percent; electric power 12. 089 billion kilowatt hours, up 36. 2 percent; and heat power 12. 1756 million kilojoules, up 35. 5 percent.

The total emission of industrial sewage reached 47. 9536 million tons and that of COD in industrial sewage was 17,470 tons. The rate of industrial sewage discharge up to the standard was 70. 46 percent and that of the rate of industrial reused sewage was 89. 33 percent. Emission of sulfur dioxide in industrial waste gas was 70,710 tons, that of industrial smoke dust was 21,990 tons, and industrial dust was 13,890 tons. 46,100 tons of industrial solid wastes were discharged and the comprehensive utilization of industrial solid waste was 4. 2156 million tons, with the comprehensive utilization rate of 60. 49 percent. The implementation rate of the environment evaluation regulation was over 95 percent and that of the Three Simultaneous was more than 85 percent.

There were 24 death accidents in industrial, mining and trade enterprises, with 27 death tolls, as same as that over the previous year in terms of death toll. The death toll from work accidents every 100 million yuan worth of GDP was 0. 035 people, a decline of 12. 4 percent. Work accidents in industrial, mining and trade enterprises caused 4. 69 deaths out of every 100 thousand employees, down 4. 9 percent. The death toll for producing one million tons of coal in coal mines was 1. 62 persons, down 35. 2 percent. The road traffic death toll per 10 thousand vehicles-kilometers was 0. 0155 persons, an increase of 26. 0 percent.

Notes: 1. Gross domestic product, value added and total output value of different industries as quoted in this Communiqué are at current prices, whereas their growth rates are calculated at comparable prices.

2. All figures in this Communiqué are preliminary statistics. Data in the Statistic Book-2011 of XPCG shall be taken as final.

3. The total number of population at the end of 2010 is preliminary estimation. Data in the communiqué of the sixth national population census and population investigation in XPCG shall be taken as final.

4. Divisions in Southern Xinjiang include Division No. 1, Division No. 2, Division No. 3, and Division No. 14; Divisions in Northern Xinjiang include Division No. 4, Division No. 5 Division No. 6, Division No. 7, and Division No. 8, Division No. 9, Division No. 10 Division No. 12 Division No. 13, and the Construction and Industry Division.

2011

BING TUAN

第一篇

综　合

Chapter 1 General Survey

简要说明

一、本篇资料主要内容

本篇资料包括兵团各部门单位数，主要年份国民经济主要指标及发展速度和结构、效益情况，兵团各师主要指标资料，兵团主要指标占全国、全国农垦、新疆比重，兵团人口，自然资源以及全疆16个主要城 市平均气温、降水量、日照时数等内容。

二、本篇资料来源

主要年份国民经济主要指标、兵团各时期五年计划完成情况资料取自于历年兵团统计资料，兵团资料来自本书各篇。各部门机构数由兵团统计局、国家统计局兵团调查总队和兵团有关部门根据年报资料汇总整理。自然资源、水利工程及灌溉能力、包括土地、河流、水库等资料，来源于兵团国土资源局、兵团水利局年报资料。新疆16城市平均气温、降水量、日照时数由新疆维吾尔自治区统计局综合处提供。

Brief Introduction

1. Main Contents

This chapter contains number of units in various sectors of XPCG, main indicators, growth rate, structure and efficiency of national economy in major years, data on important indicators in the major years of XPCG, data on divisions of XPCG, percentage of XPCG's main indicators to the whole country, the farmland reclamation system and Xinjiang, XPXG's population, natural resource, and average temperature, precipitation and sunshine of 16 major cities in Xinjiang.

2. Sources of Data

Data on main indicators on national economy in major years, data on every period Five-Year Plan completed of XPCG are obtained from statistical data of XPCG over past years. Data of XPCG are from chapters of this book. Number of units in various sectors are compiled by the Statistics Bureau of XPCG and Survey Office of the National Bureau of Statistics of XPCG and XPCG's relevant departments according to data of statistical annuals. Natural resource, water conservancy, projects irrigation capacity and data including land, rivers and reservoirs are from statistical annuals of Land Resource Bureau and Water Conservancy Bureau of XPCG. Data on average temperature, precipitation and sunshine of 16 major cities in Xinjiang are provided by the Comprehensive Office of Statistics Bureau of Xinjiang.

1—1 各部门机构数

Grassroots Units in Various Sectors

计量单位:个 (unit)

部　　门	Sector	机构数 Grassroots Units		2010年比上年增长(%) Growth Rate in 2010 over 2009(%)
		2009	2010	
师机构	**Division Units**	**14**	**14**	
农业师	Agriculturial Division	13	13	
建筑工程师	Construction Engineer Division	1	1	
农牧团场	**Farm and Ranch**	**175**	**176**	
农　场	Farm	164	165	
牧　场	Ranch	11	11	
农村基层单位	**Rural Grassroots Units**			
乡政府	Township Enterprises	2	2	
村民委员会	Village Committees	29	29	
工业企业	**Industrial Enterprises**	**4 099**	**4 222**	**3.0**
国有企业	State-owned Industry	512	426	—16.8
# 法人企业	Corporative Enterprises	60	101	68.3
集体企业	Collective-owned Industry	9	7	—22.2
股份制企业	Share Holding Enterprises	673	848	26.0
其他企业	Other Enterprises	174	204	17.2
个　体	Individual	2 731	2 737	0.2
# 国有控股工业	State-controlled Shareholding Enterprises	713	618	—13.3
建筑业企业	**Construction Enterprises and Units**	**250**	**243**	**—2.8**
国有企业	State-owned Enterprises	115	112	—2.6
# 法人企业	Corporative Enterprises	12	16	33.3
集体企业	Collective-owned Enterprises	2	2	
股份制企业	Share-holding Enterprises	75	61	—18.7
私营企业	Private Enterprises	53	63	18.9
其他企业	Other Enterprises	5	5	
交通运输企业	**Transportation Enterprises**	**36**	**35**	**—2.8**
国有企业	State-owned Enterprises	5	12	140.0
# 法人企业	Corporative Enterprises	4	9	125.0
集体企业	Collective-owned Enterprises			
股份制企业	Share-holding Enterprises	31	23	—25.8

注:2007年起卫生机构数包含营利性机构。(下同)

1—1 续表　Continued

计量单位:个　　　　　　　　　　　　　　　　　　　　　　　　　　　　　　　(unit)

部　　门	Sector	机构数 Grassroots Units		2010 年比上年增长(%) Growth Rate in 2010 over 2009(%)
		2009	2010	
批发和零售、住宿和餐饮企业	**Wholesale and Retail Trade, Accommodation and Catering Services Industry Enterprises**	**1 347**	**1 499**	**11. 3**
国有企业	State-owned Enterprises	507	496	−2. 2
# 法人企业	Corporative Enterprises	161	166	3. 1
集体企业	Collective-owned Enterprises			
股份制企业	Share-holding Enterprises	12	14	16. 7
私营企业	Private Enterprises	438	493	12. 6
其他企业	Other Enterprises	390	462	18. 5
个　体	Individual		34	
卫生机构	**Health Institution**	**1 327**	**1 339**	**0. 9**
# 医　院	Hospitals	212	209	−1. 4
门诊部、所	Clinics	909	874	−3. 9
卫生防疫站	Sanitation and Antiepidemic Stations	92	105	14. 1
妇幼保健所、站	Maternity and Childcare Centers	1	1	
教育事业	**Education**			
普通高等学校	Regular Institutions of Higher Education	4	4	
成人高等学校	Adult Institutions of Higher Education	2	2	
中等专业学校	Specialized Secondary Schools	23	23	
技工学校	Technical school	10	10	
普通中学	Regular Secondary Schools	256	251	−2. 0
小　学	Primary Schools	105	85	−19. 0
艺术事业	**Art Institutions**			
艺术表演团体	Art Performance Troupes	9	9	
广播电视机构	**Broadcasting and Television Stations**			
兵团电视台	Cabled TV Stations of XPCG	1	1	
师(市)广播电视台	Cabled TV Stations of Divisions(City)	13	13	
团场广播电视播出机构	Cabled TV Stations of Farms	181	176	−2. 8
科研机构数	**Scientific and Research Institution**	**17**	**18**	
自然科学和技术领域	Field of Natural Sciences and Technology	13	14	
社会科学、人文科学领域	Field of Social Sciences and Humanities	1	1	
金融、保险业	**Banking and Insurance**			
银行系统合计	Sub-total of Banking System	10	10	
保险系统合计	Sub-total of Insurance System	2 079	2 051	−1. 3

Note: Number of health institutions included mercantil institutions since 2007. (the same as follow)

1—2 各师部门机构数

Number of Grassroots Units in Various Sectors by Division

计量单位：个 （2010 年） （unit）

单位	Unit	农牧团场 Farm and Ranch	#农场 Farm	#牧场 Ranch	农牧团场中农牧连队数 Brigade of Farm and Ranch	工业企业 Industry	建筑业企业 Const-ruction	交通运输企业 Transpo-rtation	批发和零售、住宿和餐饮企业 Wholesale and Retail Trade, Accommodation and Catering Services	房地产开发企业 Real Estate Trade
总　计	**Total**	**176**	**165**	**11**	**2 021**	**1 485**	**243**	**35**	**1 499**	**128**
一　师	Division 1	16	16		214	147	23	7	48	10
二　师	Division 2	18	18		181	108	14	1	85	4
三　师	Division 3	18	16	2	178	71	15	1	24	3
四　师	Division 4	21	19	2	208	100	19	1	58	2
五　师	Division 5	11	11		120	57	11	1	18	5
六　师	Division 6	19	18	1	229	116	16	9	35	17
七　师	Division 7	10	10		178	103	15	2	29	16
八　师	Division 8	18	17	1	322	478	76	7	803	44
九　师	Division 9	11	10	1	96	35	10	1	11	2
十　师	Division 10	11	11		100	56	11	1	16	1
建工师	Construction Division					24	13		8	2
十二师	Division 12	7	6	1	65	50	6	1	25	10
十三师	Division 13	11	9	2	87	103	9	1	7	5
十四师	Division 14	4	3	1	35	15	2	1	11	1
国资公司	State-owned Property Company					17	2		257	6
供销公司	Supply and Marketing Corporation General								46	
中基公司	Chalkis Company					3			3	
兵团直属	Directly under XPCG	1	1		8	2	1	1	15	

单位	Unit	普通高等学校 Regular Institutions of Higher Eductation	中等专业学校 Specialized Secondary Schools	技工学校 Technical Schools	普通中学 Regular Secondary Schools	小学 Primary Schools	医疗机构 Medical Insti-tutions	#医院 Hospital	科研机构 Scientific and Research Instit-ution
总　计	**Total**	**4**	**23**	**10**	**251**	**85**	**1 339**	**209**	**18**
一　师	Division 1	1	1	1	26	10	116	20	1
二　师	Division 2		1	1	25	4	117	20	1
三　师	Division 3		1		26	8	67	18	1
四　师	Division 4		1	1	25	3	56	21	1
五　师	Division 5		1	1	14	3	76	13	1
六　师	Division 6	1	1	1	28	18	152	21	1
七　师	Division 7		1	1	14	10	160	14	1
八　师	Division 8	1	2	1	34	22	382	30	2
九　师	Division 9		1		13		49	12	1
十　师	Division 10		1	1	12		33	12	1
建工师	Construction Division		1	1	5	1	18	2	1
十二师	Division 12		1		8		42	7	2
十三师	Division 13		1		13	2	41	13	1
十四师	Division 14				3	4	8	4	
国资公司	State-owned Property Company								
供销公司	Supply and Marketing Corporation General								
中基公司	Chalkis Company								
兵团直属	Directly under XPCG	1	9	1	5		22	2	3

1—3　主要年份国民经济主要指标

Main Indicators of National Economy in Major Years

指　　标	Item	1980	1985	1990	1995
年末总人口　（万人）	**Population at the Year-end　(10 000 persons)**	**220.08**	**222.24**	**214.35**	**228.79**
# 农牧团场人口	Population of Farms		170.96	162.30	171.37
年末就业人员　（万人）	**Employment at the Year-end　(10 000 persons)**	**93.00**	**103.43**	**106.3**	**106.55**
# 在岗职工人数	Staff and Workers	93.00	94.83	97.05	93.36
生产总值　（亿元）	**Gross Domestic Product　(100 million yuan)**	**10.19**	**20.13**	**45.69**	**121.60**
第一产业	Primary Industry	4.38	8.09	20.91	56.00
第二产业	Secondary Industry	4.10	7.93	14.69	31.87
工　业	Industry	3.24	5.80	11.51	23.89
建筑业	Construction	0.86	2.13	3.18	7.98
第三产业	Tertiary Industry	1.71	4.11	10.09	33.73
全社会固定资产投资　（亿元）	**Total Investment in Fixed Assets　(100 million yuan)**	**3.52**	**5.59**	**9.59**	**36.94**
# 国有单位	State-owned Units	3.52	4.97	8.85	30.72
# 第一产业	Primary Industry	1.76	1.10	2.37	5.94
第二产业	Secondary Industry	0.54	2.07	4.11	16.31
第三产业	Tertiary Industry	1.22	2.42	3.11	14.69
新增固定资产	Newly Increased Fixed Assets	2.07	3.79	8.36	28.98
物价总指数(上年=100)	**Price Indices(preceding year=100)**				
商品零售价格总指数	General Retail Price Index	104.2	108.1	104.1	116.7
居民消费价格总指数	General Consumer Price Index		107.8	105.0	119.7
农　业	**Agriculture**				
耕地总资源　（千公顷）	Cultivated Resource　(1 000 hectares)	905.40	918.80	937.80	948.49
总播面积　（千公顷）	Total Sown Area　(1 000 hectares)	740.28	727.51	780.80	813.00
农林牧渔业总产值　（亿元）	Gross Output Value of Farming, Forestry, Animal Husbandry and Fishery　(100 million yuan)	7.54	14.99	38.32	105.55
主要农产品产量　（万吨）	Output of Major Farm Products　(10000 tons)				
粮　食	Grain	92.26	103.65	156.63	145.26
棉　花	Cotton	3.48	8.27	19.48	38.19
油　料	Oil-bearing Crops	4.05	8.66	8.87	15.01
甜　菜	Beetroots	30.01	20.68	91.96	128.21
水　果	Fruits	2.55	3.13	8.42	15.79
肉　类	Meat	2.94	3.03	4.71	6.70
水产品	Aquatic Products	0.27	0.33	0.82	1.00
工　业	**Industry**				
工业总产值　（亿元）	Gross Industrial Output Value　(100 million yuan)	9.02	18.18	44.45	132.46
# 规模以上工业总产值	Gross Industrial Output Value above Designated Siaze				
主要工业产品产量	Output of Major Industrial Products				
布　（百万米）	Cloth　(1 million meter)	41.79	63.26	96.76	113.89
机制纸及纸板　（万吨）	Machine-Made Paper and Paperboards　(10 000 tons)	1.48	2.51	4.32	6.15
机制糖　（万吨）	Machine-Made Sugar　(10 000 tons)	3.87	5.15	5.78	10.89
原　煤　（万吨）	Crude Coal　(10 000 tons)	248.73	347.02	343.09	304.56
发电量　（亿千瓦时）	Electricity　(100 million kwh)	2.42	3.45	7.04	11.64
水　泥　（万吨）	Cement　(10 000 tons)	15.00	54.97	78.80	113.37
建筑业	**Construction**				
建筑业总产值　（亿元）	Gross Construction Output Value　(100 million yuan)	2.34	6.46	9.64	29.20
房屋施工面积　（万平方米）	Floor Space of Buildings Under Construction　(10 000 sq. m)	189.93	313.29	289.00	453.88
房屋竣工面积　（万平方米）	Floor Space of Buildings Completed　(10 000 sq. m)	153.08	205.11	193.00	267.81

1—3 续表 1 Continued

指 标	Item	2000	2005	2009	2010
年末总人口 (万人)	**Population at the Year-end (10 000 persons)**	**242.79**	**256.98**	**257.31**	**257.32**
# 农牧团场人口	Population of Farms	183.85	189.64	187.15	
年末就业人员 (万人)	**Employment at the Year-end (10 000 persons)**	**92.58**	**98.81**	**103.57**	**106.18**
# 在岗职工人数	Staff and Workers	70.23	66.54	67.20	67.76
生产总值 (亿元)	**Gross Domestic Product (100 million yuan)**	**176.41**	**331.12**	**610.69**	**770.62**
第一产业	Primary Industry	71.63	130.64	204.73	278.81
第二产业	Secondary Industry	48.53	83.35	206.57	262.27
工 业	Industry	32.16	56.50	148.70	186.29
建筑业	Construction	16.37	26.85	57.87	75.98
第三产业	Tertiary Industry	56.25	117.13	199.39	229.54
全社会固定资产投资 (亿元)	**Total Investment in Fixed Assets (100 million yuan)**	**73.61**	**137.24**	**318.47**	**448.27**
# 国有单位	State-owned Units	65.49	102.51	204.17	231.84
# 第一产业	Primary Industry	17.84	29.13	36.34	39.16
第二产业	Secondary Industry	18.35	39.53	148.13	230.47
第三产业	Tertiary Industry	37.42	68.58	134.00	178.64
新增固定资产	Newly Increased Fixed Assets	67.72	113.43	315.43	331.76
物价总指数(上年=100)	**Price Indices(preceding year=100)**				
商品零售价格总指数	General Retail Price Index	98.3	99.4	100.4	104.6
居民消费价格总指数	General Consumer Price Index	99.4	100.7	100.7	104.3
农 业	**Agriculture**				
耕地总资源 (千公顷)	Cultivated Resource (1 000 hectares)	1 064.57	1 052.08	1 044.87	1 241.82
总播面积 (千公顷)	Total Sown Area (1 000 hectares)	909.80	1 023.77	1 107.70	1 119.20
农林牧渔业总产值 (亿元)	Gross Output Value of Farming, Forestry, Animal Husbandry and Fishery (100 million yuan)	143.74	264.56	432.66	569.28
主要农产品产量 (万吨)	Output of Major Farm Products (10000 tons)				
粮 食	Grain	117.57	116.64	211.73	213.64
棉 花	Cotton	69.39	106.85	113.43	115.01
油 料	Oil-bearing Crops	14.97	9.88	18.63	18.62
甜 菜	Beetroots	106.07	119.18	145.33	181.66
水 果	Fruits	28.46	45.90	103.09	122.54
肉 类	Meat	12.52	15.02	26.61	31.99
水产品	Aquatic Products	1.29	2.00	2.36	2.67
工 业	**Industry**				
工业总产值 (亿元)	Gross Industrial Output Value (100 million yuan)	97.69	175.64	497.24	656.59
# 规模以上工业总产值	Gross Industrial Output Value above Designated Siaze		116.37	362.00	559.24
主要工业产品产量	Output of Major Industrial Products				
布 (百万米)	Cloth (1 million meter)	126.90	83.71	85.77	89.74
机制纸及纸板 (万吨)	Machine-Made Paper and Paperboards (10 000 tons)	4.99	6.33	13.45	12.70
机制糖 (万吨)	Machine-Made Sugar (10 000 tons)	10.64	15.32	13.88	17.24
原 煤 (万吨)	Crude Coal (10 000 tons)	335.92	367.86	678.55	925.83
发电量 (亿千瓦时)	Electricity (100 million kwh)	17.87	36.09	114.09	134.87
水 泥 (万吨)	Cement (10 000 tons)	169.00	293.64	705.72	966.89
建筑业	**Construction**				
建筑业总产值 (亿元)	Gross Construction Output Value (100 million yuan)	58.28	100.24	222.50	298.47
房屋施工面积 (万平方米)	Floor Space of Buildings Under Construction (10 000 sq. m)	703.50	900.52	1 507.41	2 059.97
房屋竣工面积 (万平方米)	Floor Space of Buildings Completed (10 000 sq. m)	500.96	590.32	753.91	1 115.28

1—3 续表 2　Continued

指　　标	Item	1980	1985	1990	1995
公路运输业	**Highways Transportation**				
客运量　（万人）	Passenger Traffic Volume　(10 000 persons)	57	388	1 246	2 400
货运量　（万吨）	Freight Traffic　(10 000 tons)	560	1 197	2 007	2 854
旅客周转量　（亿人公里）	Passenger-Kilometers　(100 million passenger-km)	0.73	3.18	9.53	14.85
货物周转量　（亿吨公里）	Freight Ton-Kilometers　(100 million ton-km)	6.65	10.32	18.66	27.24
国内商业	**Domestic Trade**				
社会消费品零售总额　（亿元）	Total Retail Sales of Consumer Goods　(100 million yuan)	7.87	10.67	19.70	35.71
商品销售总额	Total Sales Value	4.94	12.19	23.08	146.00
能　源　（规模以上工业企业）	**Energy (Industrial Enterprises above Designated Size)**				
综合能源消费量　（吨标准煤）	Comsuption of Comprehensive Energy (ton standard coal)				
对外经济贸易和旅游	**Foreign Trade and Tourism**				
进出口总额　（亿美元）	Total Exports and Imports　(USD 100 million)		0.02	0.20	1.82
进口总额	Total Imports		0.02	0.07	1.02
出口总额	Total Exports			0.13	0.80
旅游人数　（万人）	Tourists　(10 000 persons)			0.05	0.40
旅游外汇收入　（万美元）	Foreign Exchange Earnings from Tourism (USD 10 000)			41	50
金　融　（亿元）	**Finance　(100 million yuan)**				
金融机构各项贷款	Loans of Financial Institutions				
# 中长期贷款	Medium and Long-term Loans				
短期贷款	Short-term Loans				
兵团农行各项存款	Deposits of Agricultural Bank of XPCG				75.29
兵团农行各项贷款	Loans of Agricultural Bank of XPCG				59.47
保　险　（亿元）	**Insurance　(100 million yuan)**				
保险金额	Amount Insured			21	163
保险业务收入	Premium			0.39	1.95
已决赔款(给付)金额	Claim and Payment			0.25	0.81
职工生活	**Staff and Workers' Livelihood**				
城镇居民人均可支配收入　（元）	Per Capita Annual Disposable Income of Urban Households　(yuan)				
城镇居民家庭恩格尔系数(%)	Engle Coefficient of Urban Households　(%)				
农牧工人均纯收入　（元）	Per Capita Net Income of staff and Workers of Farm Households　(yuan)				
农牧工家庭恩格尔系数(%)	Engle Coefficient of Farm Households　(%)				
工　资	**Wages**				
在岗职工工资总额　（亿元）	Total Wages of Staff and Workers(100 million yuan)	7.61	10.07	17.95	39.59
在岗职工平均工资　（元）	Average Wage of Staff and Workers　(yuan)	821	1 053	1 877	4 183
教　育	Education				
专任教师数　（人）	Full-time Teachers　(person)				
普通高等学校	Institution of Higher Education	728	810	1 140	1 256
中等专业学校	Specialized Secondary Schools	83	536	892	776
普通中学	Regular Secondary Schools	18 056	17 808	14 293	9 814
小　学	Primary Schools	24 343	17 827	12 374	11 673
在校学生数　（人）	Student Enrollment　(person)				
普通高等学校	Institution of Higher Education	2 944	3 809	5 827	8 615
中等专业学校	Specialized Secondary Schools	1 024	20 070	15 346	21 267
普通中学	Regular Secondary Schools	242 592	307 214	200 822	107 491
小　学	Primary Schools	468 792	324 271	199 624	209 351
卫　生	**Health Care**				
医院床位数　（万张）	Hospital Beds　(10 000 units)	2.03	1.99	2.01	1.99
卫生技术人员数　（万人）	Medical Technical Personnel　(10 000 persons)	2.03	2.24	2.28	2.38
# 医　生	Doctors	0.46	0.79	0.98	1.01

注：本表价值量指标按当年价格计算。

1—3 续表 3 Continued

指 标	Item	2000	2005	2009	2010
公路运输业	**Highways Transportation**				
客运量 (万人)	Passenger Traffic Volume (10 000 persons)	5 206	7 458	9 860	11 019
货运量 (万吨)	Freight Traffic (10 000 tons)	4 637	6 552	9 766	11 853
旅客周转量 (亿人公里)	Passenger-Kilometers (100 million passenger-km)	23. 71	33. 54	57. 95	66. 60
货物周转量 (亿吨公里)	Freight Ton-Kilometers (100 million ton-km)	31. 28	44. 33	86. 42	106. 75
国内商业	**Domestic Trade**				
社会消费品零售总额 (亿元)	Total Retail Sales of Consumer Goods (100 million yuan)	54. 00	93. 38	179. 78	202. 87
商品销售总额 (亿元)	Total Sales Value (100 million yuan)	185. 43	369. 31	596. 92	649. 36
能 源 (规模以上工业企业)	**Energy (Industrial Enterprises above Designated Size)**				
综合能源消费量 (吨标准煤)	Comsuption of Comprehensive Energy (ton standard coal)		2 756 537	6 656 370	7 978 849
对外经济贸易和旅游	**Foreign Trade and Tourism**				
进出口总额 (亿美元)	Total Exports and Imports (USD 100 million)	7. 53	31. 05	46. 60	55. 89
进口总额	Total Imports	3. 03	12. 13	4. 00	6. 09
出口总额	Total Exports	4. 50	18. 92	42. 60	49. 80
旅游人数 (万人)	Tourists (10 000 persons)	133. 13	227. 54	340. 46	401. 00
旅游外汇收入 (万美元)	Foreign Exchange Earnings from Tourism (USD 10 000)	2 225	920	3 871	
金 融 (亿元)	**Finance (100 million yuan)**				
金融机构各项贷款	Loans of Financial Institutions			699. 81	875. 46
# 中长期贷款	Medium and Long-term Loans			322. 01	443. 26
短期贷款	Short-term Loans			367. 80	433. 20
兵团农行各项存款	Deposits of Agricultural Bank of XPCG	173. 54	358. 17	611. 58	746. 56
兵团农行各项贷款	Loans of Agricultural Bank of XPCG	117. 69	170. 90	184. 10	232. 29
保 险 (亿元)	**Insurance (100 million yuan)**				
保险金额	Amount Insured	533	22 152	50 747	45 773
保险业务收入	Premium	3. 83	105. 40	194. 61	193. 49
已决赔款(给付)金额	Claim and Payment	1. 88	44. 97	134. 62	120. 47
职工生活	**Staff and Workers' Livelihood**				
城镇居民人均可支配收入(元)	Per Capita Annual Disposable Income of Urban Households (yuan)		8 353	12 929	14 559
城镇居民家庭恩格尔系数(%)	Engle Coefficient of Urban Households (%)		37. 8	32. 4	29. 7
农牧工人均纯收入(元)	Per Capita Net Income of Staff and Workers of Farm Households(yuan)		4 105	7 668	8 782
农牧工家庭恩格尔系数(%)	Engle Coefficient of Farm Households (%)		33. 0	30. 9	26. 7
工 资	**Wages**				
在岗职工工资总额 (亿元)	Total Wages of Staff and Workers(100 million yuan)	51. 69	88. 73	157. 50	198. 34
在岗职工平均工资 (元)	Average Wage of Staff and Workers (yuan)	6 763	12 136	21 876	26 741
教 育	**Education**				
专任教师数 (人)	Full-time Teachers (person)				
普通高等学校	Institution of Higher Education	1 198	2 341	2 582	2 741
中等专业学校	Specialized Secondary Schools	914	1 100	1 297	1 305
普通中学	Regular Secondary Schools	9 347	13 679	14 305	14 541
小 学	Primary Schools	13 992	15 097	13 820	13 581
在校学生数 (人)	Student Enrollment (person)				
普通高等学校	Institution of Higher Education	11 735	30 663	44 149	46 776
中等专业学校	Specialized Secondary Schools	13 528	20 412	37 611	35 798
普通中学	Regular Secondary Schools	129 812	206 440	197 801	190 362
小 学	Primary Schools	288 707	269 811	227 854	217 600
卫 生	**Health Care**				
医院床位数 (万张)	Hospital Beds (10 000 units)	1. 73	1. 65	1. 76	1. 82
卫生技术人员数 (万人)	Medical Technical Personnel (10 000 persons)	2. 27	2. 06	2. 03	2. 06
# 医 生	Doctors	1. 03	0. 90	0. 81	0. 81

Note: Data in value terms in this table are calculated at current prices.

1—4　主要年份国民经济和社会发展主要比例和效益指标

Indicators on Proportions and Efficiency in National Economic and Social Development in Major Years

指　标	Item	1990	1995	2000	2005	2009	2010
人　口	**Population**						
出生率 (‰)	Birth Rate (‰)	11.48	9.98	9.40	6.38	5.61	5.74
死亡率 (‰)	Death Rate (‰)	4.35	4.45	5.30	4.65	4.39	5.11
自然增长率 (‰)	Natural Growth Rate (‰)	7.13	5.53	4.20	1.73	1.22	0.63
就　业	**Employment**						
就业者负担人口	Dependency Ratio	2.02	2.15	2.62	2.60	2.48	2.42
三次产业从业者比例（以第一产业为 100）	Employment Ratio by Type of Industry (Employment in primary industry=100)						
第一产业	Primary Industry	100.0	100.0	100.0	100.0	100.0	100.0
第二产业	Secondary Industry	58.3	62.7	48.8	39.8	40.6	43.1
第三产业	Tertiary Industry	35.5	49.3	62.4	64.4	73.5	75.2
城镇登记失业率 (%)	Registered Unemployment Rate in Urban Areas (%)			1.9	2.8	2.9	2.4
国民经济核算	**National Accounting**						
三次产业增加值比例（以第一产业为 100）	Ratio of Value-added by Type of Industry (Value-added in primary industry=100)						
第一产业	Primary Industry	100.0	100.0	100.0	100.0	100.0	100.0
第二产业	Secondary Industry	70.2	56.9	67.7	63.8	100.9	94.1
第三产业	Tertiary Industry	48.3	60.2	78.5	89.7	97.4	82.3
全社会劳动生产率(按增加值计算) (元/人)	Overall Labor Productivity(in terms of value-added per employee) (yuan/person)	4 330	11 401	18 670	33 719	59 301	73 483
第一产业	Primary Industry	3 843	11 063	15 882	26 760	42 449	57 484
第二产业	Secondary Industry	4 641	10 067	21 665	44 455	107 023	129 067
第三产业	Tertiary Industry	5 190	13 836	20 974	38 240	56 246	63 673
人均生产总值 (元)	Per Capita GDP (yuan)	2 134	5 390	7 276	12 900	23 734	29 964
固定资产投资	**Investment in Fixed Assets**						
全社会固定资产投资相当于生产总值比例 (%)	Proportion of Investment in Fixed Assets to GDP (%)	21.0	30.4	41.7	41.4	52.1	58.2
全社会房屋建筑面积竣工率 (%)	Rate of Total Floor Space of Buildings Completed in Constrcution (%)	83.7	70.8	87.5	77.7	49.9	54.5
固定资产交付使用率 (%)	Rate of Fixed Assets Completed and Put Into Use (%)	87.2	78.4	92.0	82.7	99.0	74.0
农　业	**Agriculture**						
人均耕地面积 (公顷)	Per Capita Cultivated Land (hectare)	0.44	0.42	0.44	0.41	0.48	0.48
农牧团场从业者人均耕地面积 (公顷)	Cultivated Land Per Agricultural Laborer (hectare)	1.22	1.27	1.57	1.53	1.83	1.80
每公顷耕地农业机械总动力 (千瓦)	Total Power of Agricultural Machinery per Hectare of Cultivated Land (kw)	1.28	1.48	1.69	2.41	2.72	2.97
每公顷耕地用电量 (千瓦小时)	Electric Power Consumption per Hectare of Cultivated Land (kwh)	235	777	1 013	1 522	2 039	2 259
每公顷耕地化肥施用量 (公斤)	Chemical Fertilizer Consumption per Hectare of Cultivated Land (kg)	179	255	273	361	888	956
每公顷耕地生产的农业产值 (元)	Agricultural Output Value per Hectare of Cultivated Land (yuan)	4 247	11 129	13 502	25 147	34 733	45 843
农牧团场从业者人均农产品产量(公斤)	Output of Farm Products per Agricultural Laborer (kg)						
粮　食	Grain	2 035	1 940	1 734	1 695	3 100	3 118

注：本表工业企业效益 2006 年以后统计口径为规模以上工业企业。

1—4 续表 Continued

指 标	Item	1990	1995	2000	2005	2009	2010
棉 花	Cotton	253	510	1 023	1 553	1 661	1 679
油 料	Oil-bearing Crops	115	200	221	144	273	272
甜 菜	Beetroots	1 195	1 712	1 564	1 732	2 128	2 651
肉 类	Meat	61	89	185	218	390	476
水产品	Aquatic Products	11	13	19	29	35	39
每公顷播种面积农产品产量 (公斤)	Output of Farm Crops per Hectare of Sown Area (kg)						
粮 食	Grain	4 259	4 873	5 367	6 146	6 895	7 504
棉 花	Cotton	1 146	1 435	1 690	1 939	2 325	2 310
油 料	Oil-bearing Crops	1 113	1 430	1 787	2 031	2 711	2 748
甜 菜	Beetroots	31 569	39 979	57 178	63 160	71 628	71 184
工业企业经济效益	**Economic Efficiency of Industry**						
总资产贡献率 (%)	Ratio of Total Assets to Industrial Output Value (%)			5.80	5.14	10.09	9.02
资产负债率 (%)	Assets-Liability Ratio (%)			75.22	69.11	63.88	64.02
成本费用利润率 (%)	Ratio of Profits to Industrial Cost (%)			3.64	2.20	7.28	10.86
流动资产周转次数 (次/年)	Number of Times of Annual Turnover Circulation Funds (times/year)		1.10	0.91	0.93	1.19	1.27
全员劳动生产率(按增加值计算) (元/人·年)	Overall Labor Productivity(in terms of value-added per employee) (yuan/person·year)			23 077	51 418	121 460	137 058
建筑业	**Construction**						
技术装备率 (元/人)	Value of Machinery per Laborer (yuan/person)	949	2 091	4 430	5 928	6 419	5 001
产值利税率(法人企业) (%)	Ratio of Per-tax Profits to Gross Output Value (corporative enterprise) (%)	−5.6	−2.4	2.5	3.9	5.1	4.9
全员劳动生产率(按总产值计算) (元/人)	Overall Labor Productivity (in terms of gross output value per employee) (yuan/person)	7 667	26 495	54 320	89 748	148 925	149 112
公路运输业	**Highways Transportation**						
客运量弹性系数	Elasticity of Passenger Traffic	0.99	1.04	1.11	0.95	0.93	0.85
货运量弹性系数	Elasticity of Freight Traffic	1.04	0.99	0.93	1.07	1.34	1.54
国内商业	**Domestic Trade**						
人均社会消费品零售额 (元)	Per Capita Retail Sales of Consumer Goods (yuan)	920	1 583	2 227	3 638	6 987	7 884
对外经济贸易	**Foreign Trade**						
进出口总额相当于生产总值比例 (%)	Proportion of Total Imports & Exports to GDP (%)	23.8	13.8	34.5	75.8	52.1	49.1
教 育	**Education**						
学龄儿童入学率 (%)	Rate of School-age Children Enrollment (%)	98.4	95.3	99.1	99.0	99.9	99.9
小学升学率 (%)	Rate of Graduates of Primary Schools Entering Junior Secondary Schools (%)	96.2	101.0	100.7	100.0	106.3	105.8
初中升学率 (%)	Rate of Graduates of Junior Secondary Schools Entering Senior Secondary Schools (%)	68.0	59.0	87.1	67.9	95.6	96.1
学校专任教师负担系数	Student-Full Time teachers Ratio						
高等学校	Colleges and Universities	8.4	11.6	11.7	14.8	17.2	17.1
中等学校	Secondary Schools	17.2	27.4	14.8	18.6	29.0	27.4
中学学校	Regular Secondary Schools	14.6	11.0	14.0	15.1	13.8	13.1
小学学校	Primary Schools	16.1	17.9	20.6	17.9	16.5	16.0
卫 生	**Health Care**						
每万人医院数 (个)	Numberof Hospitals per 10000 Persons (unit)	1.01	0.97	0.91	0.88	0.82	0.81
每万人医生数 (人)	Number of Doctors per 10000 Persons (unit)	45.91	44.06	42.51	35.11	31.34	31.32
每万人医院床位数 (张)	Number of Hospital Beds per 10000 Persons (unit)	93.73	86.78	71.00	64.81	68.25	70.70
医院病床使用率 (%)	Utilization Rate of Hospital Beds (%)	63.8	55.1	57.8	66.9	79.5	82.2

Note: Statistical scope of economic efficiency of industry in this table is above designated size since 2006.

1—5　主要年份国民经济主要指标比例关系

Percentage of Main National Economic Indicators in Major Years

计量单位：%　　　　(%)

指　　标	Item	1990	1995	2000	2005	2009	2010
年末就业人员	**Employment at the Year-end**						
第一产业	Plimary Industry	51.6	47.2	47.3	49.0	46.7	45.8
第二产业	Secondary Industry	30.1	29.6	23.1	19.5	19.0	19.8
第三产业	Tertiary Industry	18.3	23.2	29.6	31.5	34.3	34.4
生产总值	**Gross Domestic Product**						
第一产业	Plimary Industry	45.8	46.1	40.6	39.4	33.5	36.2
第二产业	Secondary Industry	32.1	26.2	27.5	25.2	33.8	34.0
第三产业	Tertiary Industry	22.1	27.7	31.9	35.4	32.7	29.8
全社会固定资产投资	**Total Investment in Fixed Assets**						
第一产业	Plimary Industry	24.7	16.1	24.3	21.2	11.4	8.7
第二产业	Secondary Industry	42.8	44.1	24.9	28.8	46.5	51.4
第三产业	Tertiary Industry	32.5	39.8	50.8	50.0	42.1	39.9
# 国有单位固定资产投资中	Of Investment in Fixed Assets of State-owned Units						
#能源工业	Energy Industry	6.9	7.8	9.8	11.4	13.0	6.2
运输仓储及邮政业	Transport, Storage and Postal Services Industry	5.4	2.5	7.1	12.1	10.1	7.7
固定资产投资资金来源结构	**Structure of Fund Sources**						
国家预算内	State Budgetary Appropriation	10.2	3.3	14.8	19.6	16.9	12.7
国内贷款	Domestic Loans	18.5	22.8	18.8	12.6	20.1	17.9
利用外资	Foreign Investment	12.7	3.6	0.1	1.4	1.0	0.7
自筹和其他	Fundraising and Others Investment	58.6	70.3	66.3	66.4	62.0	68.7
农林牧渔业总产值	**Gross Output Value of Farming, Forestry, Animal Husbandry and Fishery**						
农　业	Farming	86.0	87.7	87.2	81.1	77.5	79.1
林　业	Forestry	1.5	0.9	0.9	1.2	1.0	1.0
牧　业	Animal Husbandry	11.8	11.0	11.4	9.6	14.3	13.5
渔　业	Fishery	0.7	0.4	0.5	0.5	0.6	0.5
农林牧渔服务业	Services				7.6	6.6	5.9
工业总产值	**Gross Industrial Output Value**						
轻工业	Light Industry	77.9	82.5	67.8	52.9	51.1	51.0
重工业	Heavy Industry	22.1	17.5	32.2	47.1	48.9	49.0
社会消费品零售总额	**Total Retail Sales of Consumer Goods**						
批发和零售业	Wholesale and Retail Trade	51.5	48.8	57.7	78.2	80.2	84.6
住宿和餐饮业	Accommodation and Catering Trade	2.6	4.0	9.5	13.3	14.3	15.4
其他行业	Others	7.2	8.7	6.8	8.5	5.5	
制造业	Manufacturing	20.1	18.0	10.1			
农业生产者	Agriculture Workers	18.6	20.5	15.9			

注：本表价值量指标按当年价格计算。

Note: Data in value terms in this table are calculated at current prices.

1—6 按登记注册类型分国民经济主要指标比例关系

Percentage of Major National Economic Indicators by Types of Registration

计量单位:% (%)

指　　标	Item	1990	1995	2000	2005	2009	2010
年末就业人员	**Employment at the Year-end**						
国有企业	State-owned Enterprises	93.4	92.7	74.2	60.7	55.2	54.0
集体企业	Collective-owned Enterprises	3.3	1.3	0.7	0.1	…	…
股份制企业	Share Holding Enterprises				7.2	10.0	10.0
其他企业	Others			11.9	8.6	10.9	11.7
私营个体	Individuals	3.3	6.0	13.2	23.4	23.9	24.3
全社会固定资产投资	**Investment in Fixed Assets**						
国有企业	State-owned Enterprises	92.4	83.1	89.0	74.7	64.1	51.7
集体企业	Collective-owned Enterprises	0.1	7.3	0.1	0.1	0.1	0.1
股份制企业	Share Holding Enterprises				16.8	25.6	30.2
其他企业	Others		4.7	7.4	1.4	1.3	16.3
个　体	Individuals	7.5	4.9	3.5	7.0	8.9	1.7
工业总产值	**Gross Industrial Output Value**						
国有企业	State-owned Enterprises	96.9	92.4	72.4	32.0	16.3	12.6
集体企业	Collective-owned Enterprises	2.5	4.2	5.0	0.5	…	…
股份制企业	Share Holding Enterprises			14.7	58.1	72.3	74.9
其他企业	Others		2.5	3.9	3.5	5.1	6.6
个　体	Individuals	0.6	0.9	4.0	5.9	6.3	5.9
建筑业总产值	**Total Value of Construction**						
国有企业	State-owned Enterprises	92.7	95.6	97.2	42.2	29.6	32.1
集体企业	Collective-owned Enterprises	2.0	0.9	0.8	0.1	0.1	…
股份制企业	Share Holding Enterprises				52.8	63.8	60.2
私营企业	Private Enterprises			0.1	1.5	4.5	5.8
个　体	Individuals	5.3	3.5	1.9	0.2	2.0	1.9
公路货运量	**Freight Traffic of Highways**						
国有企业	State-owned Enterprises	75.2	58.2	22.7	8.7	5.5	6.7
集体企业	Collective-owned Enterprises	0.3	1.1	0.6			
股份制企业	Share Holding Enterprises			0.3	5.7	3.7	2.2
个　体	Individuals	24.5	40.7	76.4	85.6	90.8	91.1
社会消费品零售总额	**Total Retail Sales of Consumer Goods**						
国有企业	State-owned Enterprises	78.4	68.1	41.2	8.8	18.0	17.9
集体企业	Collective-owned Enterprises	4.2	2.2	0.5	1.7	…	…
股份制企业	Share Holding Enterprises		2.5	2.7	18.4	4.4	4.2
其他企业	Others	1.7	3.3	10.0	17.5	10.4	10.5
个　体	Individuals	15.7	23.9	45.6	53.6	67.2	67.4

注:本表价值量指标按当年价格计算。

Note: Data in value terms in this table are calculated at current prices.

1—7　主要时期国民经济主要指标平均增长速度

Average Growth Rates of Main National Economic Indicators in Major Periods

指　标	Item	"八五"时期年均增长速度(%) Average Annual Growth Rate in Seventh Five-Year Plan Period	"九五"时期年均增长速度(%) Average Annual Growth Rate in Eighth Five-Year Plan Period	"十五"时期年均增长速度(%) Average Annual Growth Rate in Ninth Five-Year Plan Period	"十一五"时期年均增长速度(%) Average Annual Growth Rate in Tenth Five-Year Plan Period	2010年比2009年增长(%) Increase Rate % in 2010 Against 2009
年末总人口	**Population at the Year-end**	**1.3**	**1.2**	**1.1**	**…**	**…**
年末在岗职工人数	**Staff and Workers**	**−0.8**	**−5.5**	**−1.1**	**0.4**	**0.8**
生产总值	**Gross Domestic Product**	**7.4**	**7.6**	**11.3**	**12.9**	**13.9**
第一产业	Primary Industry	6.6	7.3	9.7	9.3	11.8
第二产业	Secondary Industry	4.6	7.6	9.6	20.5	21.2
#工　业	Iudustry	4.1	6.1	10.5	21.9	18.5
建筑业	Coustruction	6.7	12.0	7.6	17.3	28.4
第三产业	Tertiary Industry	12.7	8.0	14.5	10.4	9.0
人均生产总值	Per Capiba GDP	6.3	6.0	10.0	12.9	13.9
全社会固定资产投资	**Total Investment in Fixed Assets**	**31.0**	**13.6**	**15.5**	**23.3**	**40.8**
第一产业	Primary Industry	22.1	35.6	16.0	7.5	7.8
第二产业	Secondary Industry	24.5	−9.7	16.6	40.5	55.6
第三产业	Tertiary Industry	43.1	20.5	14.8	16.2	33.3
在岗职工工资总额	**Total Wages of Staff and Workers on the Job**	**17.1**	**5.5**	**11.4**	**17.5**	**25.9**
在岗职工平均工资	**Average Wage of Staff and Workers on the job**	**17.4**	**10.1**	**12.4**	**17.1**	**22.2**
农　业	**Agriculture**					
农林牧渔业总产值	Gross Output Value of Farming, Forestry, Animal Husbandry and Fishery	6.6	9.4	10.2	9.0	7.2
主要农产品产量	Output of Major Farm Products					
粮　食	Grain	−1.5	−4.1	4.1	12.6	−1.7
棉　花	Cotton	14.4	12.7	7.3	1.5	1.4
油　料	Oil-bearing Crops	11.1	−0.1	−8.6	13.5	…
甜　菜	Beetroots	6.9	−3.7	4.3	8.8	25.0
水　果	Fruits	13.4	12.5	10.0	21.7	18.9
肉　类	Meat	7.3	13.3	12.8	16.3	20.2
水产品	Aquatic Products	4.0	5.2	9.2	5.9	13.3
工　业	**Industry**					
工业总产值	Gross Industrial Output Value	10.0	7.5	12.9	24.3	22.1
主要工业产品产量	Output of Major Industrial Products					
布	Cloth	3.3	2.2	−8.0	1.4	4.6
机制纸及纸板	Machine-Made Paper and Paperboards	7.3	−4.1	4.9	14.9	−5.6
机制糖	Machine-Made Sugar	13.5	−0.5	7.6	2.4	24.2
原　煤	Crude Coal	−2.4	2.0	1.8	20.3	36.4
发电量	Electricity	10.6	9.0	15.1	30.2	18.2
水　泥	Cement	7.5	8.3	11.7	26.9	37.0
建筑业	**Construction**					
建筑业总产值	Gross Construction Output Value	24.8	14.8	11.5	24.4	34.1
房屋施工面积	Floor Space of Buildings Under Construction	9.4	9.2	5.1	18.0	36.7
房屋竣工面积	Floor Space of Buildings Completed	6.8	13.3	3.3	13.6	47.9
公路运输业	**Highways Transportation**					
旅客周转量	Passenger-Kilometers	9.3	9.8	7.2	14.7	14.9
货物周转量	Freight Ton-Kilometers	7.9	2.8	7.2	19.2	23.5
社会消费品零售总额	**Total Retail Sales of Consumer Goods**	**12.6**	**8.6**	**11.6**	**16.8**	**19.4**
进出口总额	**Total Exports and Imports**	**58.6**	**30.2**	**32.8**	**12.2**	**19.3**

1－8　全国、全国农垦、新疆及新疆生产建设兵团国民经济主要指标指数

Indices of Main National Economic Indicators by the Whole Country, State Farmland Reclamation System, Xinjiang and XPCG

（2010 年，上年＝100）（2010, Preceding year＝100）

指　　标	Item	全　国 the Whole Country	全国农垦 State Farmland Reclamation System	新　疆 Xinjiang	新疆兵团 XPCG
年末总人口	**Population at the Year-end**	**100.4**	**100.9**	**101.1**	…
年末在岗职工人数	**Staff and Workers**		**97.7**	**102.5**	**100.8**
生产总值	**Gross Domestic Product**	**110.3**	**113.3**	**110.6**	**113.9**
第一产业	Primary Industry	104.3	111.4	104.5	111.8
第二产业	Secondary Industry	112.2	118.8	112.6	121.2
第三产业	Tertiary Industry	109.5	110.1	110.9	109.0
人均生产总值	Per Capita GDP		112.9	109.4	
全社会固定资产投资	**Total Investment in Fixed Assets**	**123.8**	**145.8**	**125.2**	**140.8**
农　业	**Agriculture**				
主要农产品产量	**Output of Major Farm Products**				
粮　食	Grain	102.9	106.5	101.6	98.3
棉　花	Cotton	93.5	101.9	98.2	101.4
油　料	Oil-bearing Crops	102.4	99.0	104.2	100.0
糖　料	Sugar	97.8	101.1	116.4	125.0
水　果	Fruits	104.9	105.1	105.1	118.9
肉　类	Meat	103.6	114.8	105.8	120.2
水产品	Aquatic Products	105.0	106.9	103.1	113.3
工　业	**Industry**				
主要工业产品产量	**Output of Major Industrial Products**				
原　煤	Crude Coal	109.0	177.1		136.4
发电量	Electricity	113.2	110.9		118.2
机制糖	Machine-Made Sugar	82.4	115.1		124.2
纱	Yarn	113.5	121.3		114.2
布	Cloth	106.2	99.2		104.6
机制纸及纸板	Machine-Made Paper and Paperboards		57.3		94.4
水　泥	Cement	114.4	122.8		137.0
公路运输	**Highways Transportation**				
旅客周转量	Passenger-Kilometers	116.1	—	125.1	123.5
货物周转量	Freight Ton-Kilometers	112.3	—	109.1	114.9
社会消费品零售总额	**Total Retail Sales of Consumer Goods**	**118.3**	**—**	**117.1**	**119.4**
进出口总额	**Total Exports and Imports**	**134.7**	**—**	**123.9**	**119.3**
进口总额	Total Exports	138.7	—		152.5
出口总额	Total Imports	131.3	116.2	119.8	116.2
职工生活	**Staff and Workers' Livelihood**				
城镇居民人均可支配收入	Per Capita Annual Disposable Income of Urban Households	111.3	—	111.3	112.6
农村居民人均纯收入	Per Capita Net Income of Rural Residents	114.9	—	119.6	114.5

注：1. 本表生产总值指标增长速度指标按可比价格计算。2. 全国指标来源于中国统计摘要。

Note: 1. Growth rate of GDP in this table is calculated at comparable prices.
　　2. Data on the whole country are provided though the China statistical abstract.

1—9　兵团主要指标占全国、全国农垦及新疆的比重

Proportion of Main Economic Indicators of XPCG to the Whole Country, State Farmland Reclamation System and Xinjiang

（2010 年）

指　　标	Item	全　国 the Whole Country	全国农垦 State Farmland Reclamation System	新　疆 Xinjiang	新疆兵团 XPCG
总人口　（万人）	**Total Population　(10000 persons)**	**133 972. 0**	**1 332. 30**	**2 181. 33**	**257. 32**
就业人员数　（万人）	**Employment　(10000 persons)**		**633. 21**	**894. 65**	**106. 18**
# 在岗职工人数	Staff and Workers		295. 50	245. 48	67. 76
生产总值　（亿元）	**Gross Domestic Product　(100 million yuan)**	**397 983. 3**	**3 381. 05**	**5 437. 47**	**770. 62**
第一产业	Primary Industry	40 497. 0	1 171. 10	1 078. 63	278. 81
第二产业	Secondary Industry	186 480. 9	1 342. 46	2 592. 15	262. 27
第三产业	Tertiary Industry	171 005. 4	867. 49	1 766. 69	229. 54
全社会固定资产投资　（亿元）	**Total Investment in Fixed Assets　(100 million yuan)**	**278 139. 8**	**1 811. 22**	**3 539. 69**	**448. 27**
农　业	**Agriculture**				
农林牧渔业增加值（亿元）	Value-added of Farming Forestry Annimal Husbandry and Fishery　(100 million yuan)	40 497. 0	1 171. 10	1 078. 61	278. 81
主要农产品产量　（万吨）	Output of Major Farm Products　(10000 tons)				
粮　食	Grain	54 647. 7	2 953. 29	1 170. 70	213. 64
棉　花	Cotton	596. 1	143. 93	247. 90	115. 01
油　料	Oil-bearing Crops	3 230. 1	80. 34	66. 62	18. 62
糖　料	Sugar	12 008. 5	766. 86	486. 97	181. 66
水　果	Fruits	21 401. 4	323. 40	596. 85	122. 54
肉　类	Meat	7 925. 8	256. 43	121. 74	31. 99
水产品	Aquatic Products	5 373	115. 17	10. 11	2. 67
工　业	**Industry**				
工业增加值　（亿元）	Value-added in Industry　(100 million yuan)	160 029. 6	1 081. 53	2 161. 39	186. 29
主要工业产品产量	Output of Major Industrial Products				
布　（百万米）	Cloth　(A million meter)	80 000. 0	648. 00	151. 48	89. 74
纱　（万吨）	Yarn　(10000 tons)	2 717. 0	51. 16	41. 58	22. 52
机制纸及纸板　（万吨）	Machine-Made Paper and Paperboards　(10000 tons)		61. 72	37. 10	12. 70
机制糖　（万吨）	Machine-Made Sugar　(10000 tons)	1 102. 9	205. 79	45. 10	17. 24
原　煤　（万吨）	Crude Coal　(10000 tons)	324 000. 0	2 901. 05	9 926. 73	925. 83
发电量　（亿千瓦时）	Electricity　(100 million kwh)	42 065. 4	156. 63	679. 32	134. 87
水　泥　（万吨）	Cement　(10000 tons)	188 000. 0	2 245. 07	2 401. 00	966. 89
建筑业	**Construction**				
建筑业增加值　（亿元）	Value-added in Construction　(100 million yuan)	26 451. 3	260. 93	430. 76	75. 98
房屋施工面积（万平方米）	Floor Space of Buildings Under Construction　(10000 sq. m)	700 572. 4	12 298. 00	6 620. 14	2 059. 97
房屋竣工面积（万平方米）	Floor Space of Buildings Completed　(10000 sq. m)	259 978. 7	—	2 891. 44	1 115. 28
公路运输	**Highways Transportation**				
旅客周转量　（亿人公里）	Passenger-Kilometers　(100 million passenger-km)	27 894. 0	—	670. 75	66. 60
货物周转量　（亿吨公里）	Freight Ton-Kilometers　(100 million ton-km)	141 838. 0	—	2 270. 78	106. 75
社会消费品零售总额　（亿元）	**Total Retail Sales of Consumer Goods　(100 million yuan)**	**156 998. 4**	**—**	**1 324. 48**	**202. 87**
进出口总额　（亿美元）	**Total Exports and Imports　(USD 100 million)**	**29 727. 6**	**—**	**171. 28**	**55. 89**
进口总额	Total Exports	13 948. 3	—	41. 58	6. 09
出口总额	Total Imports	15 779. 3	541. 58	129. 70	49. 80
生　活	**Wages**				
城镇居民人均可支配收入(元)	Per Capita Annual Disposable Income of Urban Households　(yuan)	19 109	—	13 644	14 559
农村居民人均纯收入(元)	Per Capita Net Income of Rural Residents　(yuan)	5 919	—	4 643	8 782

注：本表价值量指标按当年价格计算。

1—9 续表 Continued

（2010 年）

指　　标	Item	占全国比重（%） Ratio of XPCG to the Whole Country（%）	占全国农垦比重（%） Ratio of XPCG to State Farmland Reclamation System（%）	占新疆比重（%） Ratio of XPCG to Xinjiang（%）
总人口	**Total Population**	**0.2**	**19.3**	**11.8**
就业人员数	**Employment**		**16.8**	**11.9**
# 在岗职工人数	Staff and Workers		22.9	27.6
生产总值	**Gross Domestic Product**	**0.2**	**22.8**	**14.2**
第一产业	Primary Industry	0.7	23.8	25.8
第二产业	Secondary Industry	0.1	19.5	10.1
第三产业	Tertiary Industry	0.1	26.5	13.0
全社会固定资产投资	**Total Investment in Fixed Assets**	**0.2**	**24.7**	**12.7**
农　业	**Agriculture**			
农林牧渔业增加值	Value-added of Farming Forestry Annimal Husbandry and Fishery	0.7	23.8	25.8
主要农产品产量	Output of Major Farm Products			
粮　食	Grain	0.4	7.2	18.2
棉　花	Cotton	19.3	79.9	46.4
油　料	Oil-bearing Crops	0.6	23.2	27.9
糖　料	Sugar	1.5	23.7	37.3
水　果	Fruits	0.6	37.9	20.5
肉　类	Meat	0.4	12.5	26.3
水产品	Aquatic Products		2.3	26.4
工　业	**Industry**			
工业增加值	Value-added in Industry	0.1	17.2	8.6
主要工业产品产量	Output of Major Industrial Products			
布	Cloth	0.1	13.8	59.2
纱	Yarn	0.8	44.0	54.2
机制纸及纸板	Machine-Made Paper and Paperboards		20.6	34.2
机制糖	Machine-Made Sugar	1.6	8.4	38.2
原　煤	Crude Coal	0.3	31.9	9.3
发电量	Electricity	0.3	86.1	19.9
水　泥	Cement	0.5	43.1	40.3
建筑业	**Construction**			
建筑业增加值	Value-added in Construction	0.3	29.1	17.6
房屋施工面积	Floor Space of Buildings Under Construction	0.3	16.8	31.1
房屋竣工面积	Floor Space of Buildings Completed	0.4		38.6
公路运输	**Highways Transportation**			
旅客周转量	Passenger-Kilometers	0.2		9.9
货物周转量	Freight Ton-Kilometers	0.1		4.7
社会消费品零售总额	**Total Retail Sales of Consumer Goods**	**0.1**		**15.3**
进出口总额	**Total Exports and Imports**	**0.2**		**32.6**
进口总额	Total Exports	0.0		14.6
出口总额	Total Imports	0.3	9.2	38.4
生　活	**Wages**			
城镇居民人均可支配收入	Per Capita Annual Disposable Income of Urban Households	76.2		106.7
农村居民人均纯收入	Per Capita Net Income of Rural Residents	148.4		189.1

Note: Data in value terms in this table are calculated at current prices.

1—10 全国、全国农垦、新疆及新疆生产建设兵团人均国民经济主要指标

Per Capital Main National Indicators of the Whole Country, State Farmland Reclamation System, Xinjiang and XPCG

（2010 年）

指 标	Item	全 国 the Whole Country	全国农垦 State Farmland Reclamation System	新 疆 Xinjiang	新疆兵团 XPCG
生产总值 （元）	**Gross Domestic Product (yuan)**	**29 762**	**25 657**	**24 978**	**29 948**
全社会固定资产投资（元）	**Total Investment in Fixed Assets (yuan)**	**20 800**	**13 674**	**16 312**	**17 421**
农 业	**Agriculture**				
主要农产品产量 （公斤）	Output of Major Farm Products (mg)				
粮 食	Grain	409	2 230	540	830
棉 花	Cotton	5	109	114	447
油 料	Oil-bearing Crops	24	61	31	72
糖 料	Sugar	90	579	224	706
水 果	Fruits	160	244	275	476
肉 类	Meat	59	194	56	124
水产品	Aquatic Products	40	87	5	10
工 业	**Industry**				
主要工业产品产量	Output of Major Industrial Products				
布 （米）	Cloth (meter)	60	49	7	35
纱 （公斤）	Yarn (kg)	20	39	19	88
机制纸及纸板 （公斤）	Machine-Made Paper and Paperboards (kg)		47	17	49
机制糖 （公斤）	Machine-Made Sugar (kg)	8	155	21	67
原 煤 （公斤）	Crude Coal (kg)	2 423	2 190	4 575	3 598
发电量 （千瓦小时）	Electricity (kwh)	3 146	1 183	3 131	5 241
水 泥 （公斤）	Cement (kg)	1 406	1 695	1 106	3 758
社会消费品零售总额（元）	**Total Retail Sales of Consumer Goods (yuan)**	**11 741**	**—**	**6 104**	**7 884**
进出口总额 （美元）	**Total Exports and Imports (USD)**	**2 223**	**—**	**789**	**217**
进口总额	Total Exports	1 043	—	192	24
出口总额	Total Imports	1 180	409	598	194
职工生活	**Staff and Workers' Livelihood**				
城镇居民人均可支配收入 （元）	Per Capita Annual Disposable Income of Urban Households (yuan)	19 109	—	13 644	14 559
农村居民人均纯收入（元）	Per Capita Net Income of Rural Residents (yuan)	5 919	—	4 643	8 782
教 育 （人/万人）	**Education (person/10000 persons)**				
在校学生数	Student Enrollment				
普通高等学校	Institution of Higher Education	169	79	121	182
普通中学	Regular Secondary Schools	576	318	652	740
小 学	Primary Schools	743	380	892	846
卫 生	**Health Care**				
卫生技术人员数 （人/万人）	Medical Technical Personnel (person/10000 person)	44	45	56	80
# 医 生	Doctors	18	22	22	31
医院床位数 （张/万人）	Hospital Beds (unit/10000 persons)	33	43	50	71

注：本表价值量指标按当年价格计算。

1—10 续表 Continued

(2010 年)

指 标	Item	为全国的(%) Ratio of XPCG to the Whole Country (%)	为全国农垦的(%) Ratio of XPCG to State Farmland Reclamation System (%)	为新疆的(%) Ratio of XPCG to Xinjiang (%)
生产总值	**Gross Domestic Product**	**100.6**	**116.7**	**119.9**
全社会固定资产投资	**Total Investment in Fixed Assets**	**83.8**	**127.4**	**106.8**
农 业	**Agriculture**			
主要农产品产量	Output of Major Farm Products			
粮 食	Grain	203.1	37.2	153.8
棉 花	Cotton	9 932.3	411.3	392.1
油 料	Oil-bearing Crops	299.0	119.3	233.4
糖 料	Sugar	786.2	121.9	315.2
水 果	Fruits	297.6	195.0	173.2
肉 类	Meat	209.6	64.2	222.0
水产品	Aquatic Products	25.8	11.9	207.5
工 业	**Industry**			
主要工业产品产量	Output of Major Industrial Products			
布	Cloth	58.5	71.4	500.0
纱	Yarn	431.1	226.6	460.6
机制纸及纸板	Machine-Made Paper and Paperboards		105.9	290.3
机制糖	Machine-Made Sugar	817.1	43.1	319.0
原 煤	Crude Coal	148.5	164.3	78.6
发电量	Electricity	166.6	221.3	167.4
水 泥	Cement	267.3	221.7	339.7
社会消费品零售总额	**Total Retail Sales of Consumer Goods**	**67.1**		**129.2**
进出口总额	**Total Exports and Imports**	**9.8**		**27.5**
进口总额	Total Exports	2.3		12.4
出口总额	Total Imports	16.4	47.3	32.4
职工生活	**Staff and Workers' Livelihood**			
城镇居民人均可支配收入	Per Capita Annual Disposable Income of Urban Households	76.2		106.7
农村居民人均纯收入	Per Capita Net Income of Rural Residents	148.4		189.1
教 育	**Education**			
在校学生数	Student Enrollment			
普通高等学校	Institution of Higher Education	107.6	230.1	150.2
普通中学	Regular Secondary Schools	128.4	232.4	113.5
小 学	Primary Schools	113.8	222.3	94.8
卫 生	**Health Care**			
卫生技术人员数	Medical Technical Personnel	181.6	177.3	142.7
# 医 生	Doctors	174.0	142.5	141.0
医院床位数	Hospital Beds	214.2	162.9	141.4

Note: Data in value terms in this table are calculated at current prices.

1—11 国民经济主要指标分月变化情况

(2010年)

指标	Item	1月 1 Month	1—2月 1—2 Month
国民经济核算 (亿元)	**National Accounts (100 million yuan)**		
生产总值	Gross Domestic Product		
第一产业	Primary Industry		
第二产业	Secondary Industry		
# 工 业	Industry		
第三产业	Tertiary Industry		
生产总值增长速度(%)(比上年同期)	Gross Domestic Product Annual Growth Rate(%)(Ratio Last Year Same Period)		
第一产业	Primary Industry		
第二产业	Secondary Industry		
# 工 业	Industry		
第三产业	Tertiary Industry		
工 业	**Industry**		
规模以上工业增加值(亿元、现价)	Value-added of Industry above Designated Size(100 million yuan,Current Price)	8.08	14.75
# 轻工业	Light Industry	3.68	6.90
重工业	Heavy Industry	4.40	7.86
# 国有企业	State-owned Enterprises	0.55	0.95
股份制企业	Share-holding Corporations	7.00	12.84
# 大中型企业	Large and Medium Scale Enterprises	6.37	11.76
规模以上工业增加值增长速度(%)(比上年同期)	Value-added of Industry above Designated Size Annual Growth Rate(%)(Ratio Last Year Same Period)	64.2	30.8
# 轻工业	Light Industry	60.9	43.3
重工业	Heavy Industry	65.3	20.1
工业总产值(亿元、现价)	Gross Industrial Output Value(100 million yuan,Current Price)	30.97	59.52
# 轻工业	Light Industry	14.97	30.54
重工业	Heavy Industry	16.00	28.97
# 国有企业	State-owned Enterprises	5.60	11.66
股份制企业	Share-holding Corporations	22.79	42.84
# 国有控股企业	State-owned Holding Enterprises	25.81	48.93
# 大中型企业	Large and Medium Scale Enterprises	19.28	35.60
工业销售产值(亿元、现价)	Sales Value of Industry Products(100 million yuan,Current Price)	28.58	54.76
# 轻工业	Light Industry	14.01	27.77
重工业	Heavy Industry	14.57	26.99
# 国有企业	State-owned Enterprises	5.24	10.81
股份制企业	Share-holding Corporations	20.92	39.45
# 国有控股企业	State-owned Holding Enterprises	24.36	46.49
# 大中型企业	Large and Medium Size of Enterprises	19.12	35.76
工业产品销售率 (%)	Proportion of Indurtrial Product Sold (%)	92.3	92.0
# 轻工业	Light Industry	93.6	90.9
重工业	Heavy Industry	91.0	93.1
# 国有企业	State-owned Enterprises	93.6	92.7
股份制企业	Share-holding Corporations	91.8	92.1
# 国有控股企业	State-owned Holding Enterprises	94.4	95.0
# 大中型企业	Large and Medium Scale Enterprises	99.2	100.4
主要工业产品产量	Output of Major Industrial Products		
纱 (万吨)	Yarn 10 000 tons)	1.67	3.01
布 (亿米)	Cloth (100 million m)	0.04	0.07
机制糖 (万吨)	Maching-made Suagar (10 000 tons)	1.93	2.24
原煤 (万吨)	Crude Coal (10 000 tons)	50.03	91.47
发电量 (亿千瓦时)	Electrcity (100 million kwh)	10.46	18.97
水 泥 (万吨)	Cement (10 000 tons)	5.84	15.77
焦 炭 (吨)	Coke (ton)	4.71	9.27
番茄酱罐头 (吨)	Canned Ketchup (ton)	0.93	1.78

Main Indicators on National Economy by Month

1—3 月 1-3 Month	1—4 月 1-4 Month	1—5 月 1-5 Month	1—6 月 1-6 Month	1—7 月 1-7 Month	1—8 月 1-8 Month	1—9 月 1-9 Month	1—10 月 1-10 Month	1—11 月 1-11 Month	1—12 月 1-12 Month
83. 57			203. 92			426. 53			770. 62
8. 07			21. 23			105. 41			278. 81
32. 71			88. 40			173. 85			262. 27
30. 28			68. 18			119. 83			186. 29
42. 79			94. 29			147. 27			229. 54
12. 8			13. 1			13. 8			13. 9
12. 5			11. 1			8. 7			11. 8
24. 7			22. 0			25. 1			21. 2
23. 1			20. 6			23. 8			18. 5
5. 7			6. 5			6. 3			9. 0
21. 57	30. 11	38. 73	48. 16	59. 22	70. 51	81. 87	96. 32	110. 31	154. 10
10. 23	13. 88	17. 47	21. 38	25. 80	30. 78	36. 20	41. 49	47. 03	63. 34
11. 34	16. 22	21. 25	26. 78	33. 42	39. 73	45. 67	54. 82	63. 27	90. 76
1. 75	2. 04	2. 62	3. 27	4. 29	5. 01	6. 03	6. 99	7. 80	16. 80
17. 30	25. 23	32. 23	40. 21	50. 67	60. 04	68. 78	82. 64	94. 02	126. 80
16. 77	23. 32	29. 89	36. 72	43. 41	50. 66	58. 64	66. 45	74. 98	98. 64
21. 4	21. 9	21. 6	20. 6	23. 4	20. 1	18. 1	19. 0	20. 6	25. 4
35. 8	37. 0	35. 9	33. 8	35. 8	27. 0	20. 5	18. 0	17. 1	24. 9
10. 2	10. 7	12. 0	11. 8	15. 5	15. 8	15. 1	27. 8	25. 2	28. 2
101. 88	142. 04	182. 93	228. 33	269. 94	326. 11	392. 46	459. 97	533. 49	617. 79
54. 08	73. 80	93. 31	114. 53	133. 55	163. 28	197. 88	232. 37	269. 15	315. 35
47. 80	68. 24	89. 62	113. 80	136. 39	162. 82	194. 58	227. 60	264. 34	302. 44
21. 55	29. 41	36. 39	47. 96	55. 68	67. 00	86. 15	103. 24	118. 48	82. 27
73. 74	103. 42	134. 20	165. 15	196. 00	237. 80	282. 61	329. 91	385. 52	431. 66
81. 85	113. 69	145. 64	180. 46	212. 55	258. 05	306. 54	353. 44	403. 69	400. 24
59. 98	82. 41	105. 63	129. 52	153. 40	180. 52	207. 24	235. 24	264. 98	340. 32
95. 73	135. 72	176. 81	222. 56	263. 93	312. 53	365. 13	423. 25	496. 63	597. 40
49. 71	68. 81	88. 00	109. 65	128. 67	151. 68	174. 38	205. 75	241. 95	301. 50
46. 02	66. 91	88. 81	112. 92	135. 27	160. 86	190. 75	217. 50	254. 68	295. 90
18. 96	26. 89	33. 24	43. 78	51. 10	60. 49	73. 85	88. 01	102. 99	84. 33
70. 91	100. 33	131. 88	163. 80	194. 38	231. 17	268. 26	309. 38	364. 65	417. 42
78. 36	111. 15	142. 84	177. 75	209. 59	247. 97	285. 20	328. 36	377. 00	394. 24
61. 15	84. 61	108. 51	131. 36	154. 76	179. 87	202. 26	230. 06	260. 55	333. 51
94. 0	95. 6	96. 7	97. 5	97. 8	95. 8	93. 0	92. 0	93. 1	96. 7
91. 9	93. 2	94. 3	95. 7	96. 3	92. 9	88. 1	88. 5	89. 9	95. 6
96. 3	98. 1	99. 1	99. 2	99. 2	98. 8	98. 0	95. 6	96. 3	97. 8
88. 0	91. 4	91. 3	91. 3	91. 8	90. 3	85. 7	85. 2	86. 9	102. 5
96. 2	97. 0	98. 3	99. 2	99. 2	97. 2	94. 9	93. 8	94. 6	96. 7
95. 7	97. 8	98. 1	98. 5	98. 6	96. 1	93. 0	92. 9	93. 4	98. 5
101. 9	102. 7	102. 7	101. 4	100. 9	99. 6	97. 6	97. 8	98. 3	98. 0
4. 84	6. 71	8. 73	10. 68	12. 46	14. 55	16. 56	18. 32	20. 24	22. 52
0. 15	0. 24	0. 32	0. 40	0. 46	0. 53	0. 62	0. 71	0. 80	0. 90
2. 24	2. 24	4. 23	4. 23	4. 23	4. 23	4. 23	7. 53	12. 92	17. 24
162. 76	226. 72	304. 38	388. 47	455. 68	526. 52	613. 47	694. 08	786. 51	925. 83
23. 95	37. 64	47. 56	58. 82	70. 68	84. 32	96. 39	107. 66	119. 83	134. 87
52. 22	118. 17	217. 87	330. 78	447. 39	580. 00	735. 04	857. 62	935. 18	966. 89
14. 33	20. 73	26. 23	31. 17	35. 08	38. 86	43. 29	47. 88	66. 13	167. 65
2. 77	3. 65	4. 74	5. 93	7. 31	22. 53	55. 13	63. 39	65. 01	65. 01

1—11 续表

(2010 年)

指　　标	Item	1月 1 Month	1—2月 1-2 Month
塑料树脂及共聚物　(吨)	Plastics resin and　(ton)	5.84	10.17
规模以上工业企业财务指标	Financial Indicators of Industrial Enterprises above Designated Size		
产品销售收入　(亿元)	Sales Revenue　(10000 yuan)		40.90
税金总额　(亿元)	Total Tax　(10000 yuan)		1.81
利润总额　(亿元)	Total Profits　(10000 yuan)		1.62
# 亏损企业亏损额	Total Loss of Lost Enterprises		0.82
应收帐款净额　(亿元)	Net Accounts Receivable　(10000 yuan)		42.29
产成品　(亿元)	Semi-finished Products　(10000 yuan)		45.22
规模以上工业经济效益综合指数	Indices on Economic Benefit of Independent Accounting Industrial Enterprises above Designated Size		142.6
建筑业	**Construction**		
建筑业产值　(亿元)	Output Value of Contruction　(100 million yuan)		
建筑业产值增长速度(%)(比上年同期)	Output Value of Contruction Annual Growth Rate(%) (Ratio Last Year Same Period)		
竣工产值　(亿元)	Output Value Completed　(100 million yuan)		
房屋建筑施工面积　(万平方米)	Floor Space of Buildings under Construction　(10000 sq. m)		
# 新开工面积	Newly-opened Floor Space		
房屋建筑竣工面积　(万平方米)	Floor Space of Buildings Colmpleted　(10000 sq. m)		
道路运输业	**Highways Transportation**		
旅客周转量　(亿人公里)	Passenger-Kilometers　(100 million passenger-km)		
货物周转量　(亿吨公里)	Freight Ton-Kilometers　(100 million ton-km)		
国内商业	**Domestic Trade**		
社会消费品零售总额　(亿元)	Total Retail Sales of Consumer Goods　(100 million yuan)	10.68	22.03
社会消费品零售总额增长速度(%)(比上年同期)	Total Retail Sales of Consumer Goods Annual Growth Rate(%) (Ratio Last Year Same Period)	12.4	14.0
商品销售总额　(亿元)	Total Sales of Goods　(100 million yuan)	30.69	59.49
对外经济贸易	**Foreign Trade**		
进出口总额　(亿美元)	Total Exports and Imports　(USD 100 million)		6.80
# 出口总额	Total Exports		5.92
进出口总额增长速度(%)(比上年同期)	Total Exports and Imports Annual Growth Rate(%) (Ratio Last Year Same Period)		24.1
# 出口总额	Total Exports		18.7
全社会固定资产投资　(亿元)	**Total Investment in Fixed Assets　(100 million yuan)**		
第一产业	Primary Industry		
第二产业	Secondary Industry		
# 工　业	Industry		
第三产业	Tertiary Industry		
# 国　有	State-owned		
全社会固定资产投资增长速度(%)(比上年同期)	Total Investment in Fixed Assets Annual Growth Rate(%) (Ratio Last Year Same Period)		
第一产业	Primary Industry		
第二产业	Secondary Industry		
# 工　业	Industry		
第三产业	Tertiary Industry		
# 国　有	State-owned		
就业与收入	**Employment and Wages**		
在岗职工人数　(万人)	Staff and Workers on the Job　(10000 persons)		
# 团　场	Farm		
在岗职工工资总额　(亿元)	Total Wages of Staff and Workers on the Job　(100 million yuan)		
# 团　场	Farm		

Continued

1—3月 1-3 Month	1—4月 1-4 Month	1—5月 1-5 Month	1—6月 1-6 Month	1—7月 1-7 Month	1—8月 1-8 Month	1—9月 1-9 Month	1—10月 1-10 Month	1—11月 1-11 Month	1—12月 1-12 Month
14.91	20.95	26.73	31.75	37.67	42.91	48.11	54.41	62.85	73.33
67.04	101.03	137.23	167.60	198.81	242.32	285.56	318.04	368.05	
2.63	4.10	4.65	7.91	9.11	10.79	14.68	14.56	17.07	
3.08	6.75	8.68	11.24	12.78	15.81	18.69	24.25	30.86	
1.89	2.16	2.91	4.08	4.84	5.31	7.17	7.04	6.71	
43.42	43.52	44.13	46.94	49.20	52.57	51.19	47.54	50.06	
52.75	48.62	49.64	48.45	44.71	48.27	49.49	50.66	50.03	
133.5	162.4	164.0	161.2	161.0	162.2	165.0	174.0	182.8	
9.47		43.04	80.52		160.29	211.65			298.47
51.9		28.7	34.6		35.7	36.8			34.1
0.99		3.83	10.72		23.87	38.40			201.96
316.47		876.97	1 168.16		1 482.64	1 674.18			2 059.97
18.04		342.50	616.02		953.76	1 112.69			1 496.29
4.99		13.97	48.31		119.41	218.52			1 115.28
10.69			26.12			40.09			66.60
14.48			37.31			64.01			106.75
33.94	48.33	62.91	80.88	94.68	109.62	130.71	152.39	170.39	202.87
12.4	11.8	11.8	12.0	12.1	12.2	12.9	15.4	16.4	19.4
111.33	161.34	209.35	260.92	302.11	340.40	384.08	436.93	517.17	649.36
10.46	15.73	20.48	24.75	28.20	33.15	38.56	44.10		
8.95	13.50	17.88	21.68	24.73	29.21	34.19	39.32		
8.6	18.4	26.3	22.1	16.6	16.0	14.0	14.6		
	9.1	19.9	18.8	13.3	13.0	11.3	11.8		
16.77	38.70	75.64	130.81	184.35	243.21	306.40	354.40	405.94	448.27
0.78	3.41	8.59	12.84	16.77	21.16	24.45	28.59	32.18	39.16
14.58	26.60	48.13	78.40	103.40	131.90	164.22	183.14	212.08	230.47
14.53	26.47	48.00	77.72	102.37	130.82	163.14	182.05	210.48	228.27
1.41	8.69	18.92	39.57	64.18	90.15	117.73	142.67	161.68	178.64
8.42	19.13	39.86	70.29	101.29	132.45	163.65	190.41	213.94	231.84
92.4	61.4	48.8	52.1	42.4	44.9	43.6	43.4	41.0	40.8
−8.6	−14.3	20.0	6.5	6.0	6.7	1.2	2.7	5.4	7.8
187.3	172.3	128.3	133.7	101.3	95.7	86.0	74.0	62.6	55.6
186.5	172.0	128.1	133.7	101.1	95.6	86.0	73.9	62.5	55.4
−49.3	−15.1	−16.3	−2.1	3.0	11.9	16.7	25.1	27.4	33.3
33.0	12.1	23.3	22.3	22.1	27.1	20.2	18.5	14.9	13.5
65.13			70.15			82.93	80.08		67.76
41.13			41.85			52.47	49.06		41.19
31.11			65.39			108.49	123.54		198.34
15.17			30.66			50.50	57.34		96.89

1—12 各师主要国民经济指标

（2010 年）

指 标	Item	一 师 Devision 1	二 师 Devision 2	三 师 Devision 3	四 师 Devision 4
人口与劳动力 （万人）	**Population and Labor force (10 000 persons)**				
年末总人口	Year-end Population				
就业人员数	Employment	11. 52	7. 16	8. 30	9. 72
# 在岗职工人数	Staff and Workers	7. 57	4. 84	3. 78	7. 05
生产总值 （亿元）	**Gross Domestic Product (10 000 yuan)**	**104. 32**	**50. 01**	**38. 63**	**54. 60**
第一产业	Primary Industry	55. 74	21. 61	22. 05	19. 17
第二产业	Secondary Industry	28. 86	14. 95	6. 17	23. 46
工 业	Industry	22. 08	10. 74	3. 71	19. 71
建筑业	Construction	6. 78	4. 21	2. 46	3. 75
第三产业	Tertiary Industry	19. 72	13. 45	10. 41	11. 97
生产总值构成 （%）	**Composition of GDP (%)**				
第一产业	Primary Industry	53. 4	43. 2	57. 1	35. 1
第二产业	Secondary Industry	27. 7	29. 9	16. 0	43. 0
工 业	Industry	21. 2	21. 5	9. 6	36. 1
建筑业	Construction	6. 5	8. 4	6. 4	6. 9
第三产业	Tertiary Industry	18. 9	26. 9	26. 9	21. 9
全社会固定资产投资（亿元）	**Total Investment in Fixed Assets (100 million yuan)**	**45. 71**	**17. 31**	**22. 41**	**20. 78**
# 房地产开发	Real Estate Development	3. 51	1. 23	0. 16	0. 18
工 资	**Wages**				
职工工资总额 （亿元）	Total Wages of Staff and Workers (10 000 yuan)	24. 30	11. 87	9. 81	14. 73
职工平均货币工资 （元）	Average Wage of Staff and Workers (yuan)	30 581	23 880	25 490	20 844
农 业	**Agriculture**				
总播种面积 （千公顷）	Total Sown Area (1 000 hectares)	165. 33	65. 79	95. 38	118. 24
农林牧渔业总产值（亿元）	Gross Output Value of Farming, Forestry, Animal Husbandry and Fishery (100 million yuan)	113. 09	43. 80	47. 29	38. 94
农 业	Farming	99. 78	34. 13	39. 10	25. 32
林 业	Forestry	1. 24	0. 36	0. 51	0. 38
牧 业	Animal Husbandry	6. 29	6. 64	3. 52	10. 59
渔 业	Fishery	0. 46	0. 31	0. 12	0. 39
服务业	Services	5. 32	2. 36	4. 04	2. 26
主要农产品产量 （万吨）	Output of Major Farm Products (10 000 tons)				
粮 食	Grain	19. 35	6. 16	11. 75	48. 88
棉 花	Cotton	29. 37	6. 90	11. 57	1. 61
油 料	Oil-bearing Crops	0. 02	0. 08	0. 10	6. 23
甜 菜	Beetroots		39. 61		49. 74
水 果	Fruits	36. 12	21. 70	14. 61	9. 37
牲畜存栏头数（万头只）	Number of Livestock (10 000 heads)	54. 55	65. 27	55. 58	93. 10
肉 类	Meat	2. 09	3. 15	1. 58	4. 76
工 业	**Industry**				
工业总产值 （亿元）	Gross Industrial Output Value (10 000 yuan)	74. 28	35. 57	10. 50	44. 50
# 国有控股企业	State-owned and State-holding Entenrprises	54. 01	24. 28	8. 13	36. 58
# 轻工业	Light Industry	37. 50	24. 45	4. 49	26. 61
重工业	Heavy Industry	36. 78	11. 12	6. 01	17. 89
主要工业产品产量（万吨）	Output of Major Industrial Products (10 000 tons)				
纱	Yarn	1. 68	1. 83	0. 29	
布 （万米）	Cloth (10 000 meter)	0. 08		0. 02	
机制糖	Machine-made Sugar		6. 23		4. 50
原煤	Crude Coal	85. 01	224. 07		74. 11
发电量 （亿千瓦小时）	Electricity (10 000 million kwh)	11. 01	0. 40	1. 60	1. 84
水泥	Cement	451. 00	26. 47	11. 79	248. 21
建筑业施工产值 （亿元）	**Output Value of Construction (100 million yuan)**	**31. 80**	**15. 60**	**10. 28**	**12. 79**
道路运输业	**Highways Transportation**				
客运量 （万人）	Passenger Traffic Volume (10 000 persons)	955	862	336	1 036
货运量 （万吨）	Freight Traffic (10 000 tons)	2 093	917	263	926
旅客周转量 （亿人公里）	Passenger-Kilometers (100 million passenger-km)	6. 49	2. 74	1. 87	4. 54
货物周转量 （亿吨公里）	Freight Ton-Kilometers (100 million ton-km)	15. 83	4. 18	2. 51	7. 85
国内商业和对外经济贸易	**Domestic Trade And Foreign Trade**				
社会消费品零售总额（亿元）	Total Retail Sales of Consumer Goods (100 million yuan)	15. 86	17. 73	8. 43	8. 50
进出口总额 （万美元）	Total Exports and Imports (USD 10 000)	1 465	2 854	6 471	131 658

Main National Economic Indicators of XPCG's Division

五 师 Devision 5	六 师 Devision 6	七 师 Devision 7	八 师 Devision 8	九 师 Devision 9	十 师 Devision 10	建工师 Construction Devision	十二师 Devision 12	十三师 Devision 13	十四师 Devision 14
4. 57	11. 38	7. 69	27. 29	3. 22	2. 78	2. 56	2. 73	3. 42	1. 40
3. 87	6. 03	4. 61	16. 18	2. 24	2. 07	2. 38	1. 69	1. 93	1. 21
27. 60	**97. 50**	**64. 50**	**188. 50**	**13. 97**	**17. 02**	**23. 51**	**23. 20**	**21. 81**	**4. 79**
14. 54	33. 24	27. 99	55. 27	6. 55	6. 32	0. 02	4. 49	8. 13	2. 32
5. 61	34. 85	21. 11	72. 64	3. 05	6. 24	20. 93	12. 54	8. 92	1. 06
3. 98	24. 53	13. 63	60. 14	1. 89	4. 81	1. 07	11. 21	6. 86	0. 38
1. 63	10. 32	7. 48	12. 50	1. 16	1. 43	19. 86	1. 33	2. 06	0. 68
7. 45	29. 41	15. 40	60. 59	4. 37	4. 46	2. 56	6. 17	4. 76	1. 41
52. 7	34. 1	43. 4	29. 3	46. 9	37. 1	0. 1	19. 3	37. 3	48. 5
20. 3	35. 7	32. 7	38. 5	21. 8	36. 7	89. 0	54. 1	40. 9	22. 2
14. 4	25. 1	21. 1	31. 9	13. 5	28. 3	4. 5	48. 3	31. 4	7. 9
5. 9	10. 6	11. 6	6. 6	8. 3	8. 4	84. 5	5. 8	9. 5	14. 3
27. 0	30. 2	23. 9	32. 2	31. 3	26. 2	10. 9	26. 6	21. 8	29. 3
14. 71	**102. 23**	**36. 24**	**123. 46**	**7. 70**	**11. 81**	**4. 90**	**21. 03**	**11. 52**	**2. 62**
0. 99	4. 66	3. 08	9. 70	0. 47		0. 79	5. 05	1. 86	0. 04
9. 08	15. 88	10. 37	57. 26	3. 49	4. 75	16. 64	3. 84	5. 16	2. 20
23 164	24 868	22 930	32 560	15 627	20 540	26 709	22 625	27 064	17 764
59. 81	140. 63	109. 97	191. 27	77. 29	51. 11	0. 25	11. 03	18. 48	7. 14
28. 36	66. 88	55. 08	110. 10	13. 60	17. 50	0. 04	10. 22	16. 17	4. 93
25. 30	48. 64	42. 47	90. 50	9. 17	11. 70	0. 04	6. 95	11. 30	4. 06
0. 18	0. 50	0. 52	0. 90	0. 14	0. 39		0. 07	0. 14	0. 11
1. 73	12. 51	8. 82	13. 10	3. 76	3. 29		2. 75	2. 93	0. 65
0. 04	0. 21	0. 20	0. 46	…	0. 60		0. 19	0. 03	
1. 11	5. 02	3. 07	5. 14	0. 54	1. 51		0. 26	1. 78	0. 11
11. 08	47. 37	23. 73	13. 38	18. 33	4. 32	0. 03	2. 88	3. 53	0. 92
9. 26	10. 58	9. 65	32. 71		0. 80	0. 01	0. 06	2. 27	0. 20
0. 67	2. 51	2. 78	0. 20	1. 35	3. 87	0. 02	0. 26	0. 03	0. 01
2. 00	6. 66	25. 54	1. 07	47. 64	8. 28		0. 89		
3. 89	3. 68	2. 27	7. 28	0. 09	0. 31		6. 66	9. 52	5. 34
26. 43	93. 70	40. 13	57. 14	60. 11	19. 74		11. 15	31. 66	10. 84
0. 91	6. 00	2. 95	5. 19	1. 72	1. 30		0. 80	1. 11	0. 33
13. 91	71. 59	43. 07	227. 63	5. 98	10. 92	5. 18	10. 52	15. 45	1. 31
11. 36	14. 72	33. 49	146. 61	4. 37	6. 16	3. 44	7. 93	4. 90	0. 32
7. 24	28. 46	32. 03	89. 21	5. 23	3. 29	0. 04	7. 34	2. 98	0. 67
6. 67	43. 13	11. 04	138. 41	0. 75	7. 63	5. 14	3. 18	12. 47	0. 63
0. 88	1. 13	2. 99	13. 13				0. 50	0. 09	
0. 02	0. 01	0. 29	0. 46				0. 01		
		1. 71		4. 79					
	204. 21	48. 46	94. 51		102. 02		41. 81	45. 24	
4. 41		21. 22	92. 84	0. 35	1. 19			0. 02	
	33. 88		161. 43		4. 00	28. 25		1. 86	
6. 40	**40. 25**	**26. 78**	**42. 33**	**4. 34**	**7. 04**	**82. 18**	**5. 64**	**8. 83**	**2. 60**
292	2 121	1 296	892	366	371	234	645	517	120
139	1 905	1 023	1 888	183	191	123	1 450	657	5
1. 65	12. 76	9. 44	9. 81	1. 66	1. 33	0. 45	1. 15	1. 33	0. 22
2. 05	15. 20	11. 34	31. 15	2. 88	4. 14	0. 39	5. 01	2. 89	0. 18
6. 34	27. 90	15. 56	36. 26	5. 12	6. 05	0. 55	8. 65	4. 09	0. 35
13 228	31 460	5 956	63 030	7 727	19 054	274	7 060	10	25 375

1—13　人口和自然资源

Population and Natural Resources

指　　　标		Item		2010
人口		**Population**		
年末人口总数(万人)		Total Populatio(Year-end)	(10 000 persons)	257.32
人口密度(人/平方公里)		Population Density	(person/sq. km)	37.20
土地资源(千公顷)		**Land Resources**	**(1 000 hectares)**	
土地总面积		Total Areas of Land		6 917.25
农用地		Landfor Agriculture		4 202.40
耕地面积		Area of Cultivated Land		1 241.83
园地面积		Garden Area		150.89
林地面积		Woodland Area		895.08
牧草地面积		Pastureland Area		1 646.73
其他农用地		OtherLandfor Agriculture		267.87
建设用地		Land for Construction		258.13
居民点及工矿用地面积		Area for Residence and Factory		138.26
交通运输用地		Area for Transportation and Conveyance		10.97
水利设施用地		Area for Water Conservancy		108.90
未利用地		Land yet to be Unused		2 456.71
气　候		**Climate**		
年平均气温	(摄氏度)	Annual Average Temperature	(℃)	9.8
北　疆		North Xinjiang		7.4
南　疆		Sourth Xinjiang		12.9
东　疆		East Xinjiang		13.1
年平均降水量	(毫米)	Annual Average Precipitation	(mm)	217.6
北　疆		North Xinjiang		299.7
南　疆		Sourth Xinjiang		142.5
东　疆		East Xinjiang		36.0
年平均日照时数	(小时)	Average Sunshine Hours	(hour)	2 751.4
北　疆		North Xinjiang		2 703.3
南　疆		Sourth Xinjiang		2 689.9
东　疆		East Xinjiang		3 121.5
林木资源		**Forest Resources**		
森林资源面积	(万公顷)	Forest Resources Area	(10 000 hectares)	198.47
森林覆盖率	(%)	Forest-Coverage Rate	(%)	18.46
水利资源		**Water Resources**		
引用水	(亿立方米)	Amount of Water Supply	(100 million cu. m)	125.95
地表水资源(引用量)		Surface Water Volume		105.82
地下水资源		Ground Water Volume		20.13
水库:总座数	(座)	Reservoir:Number of Total	(unit)	125
库容量	(万立方米)	Reservoir Capacity	(10 000 cu. m)	327 839
大型水库:水库座数		Large-scale Reservoir :Number		11
库容量		Reservoir Capacity		182 671
中型水库:水库座数		Medium-scale Reservoir: Number		30
库容量		Reservoir Capacity		119 362
小型水库:水库座数		Small-scale Reservoir:Number		84
库容量		Reservoir Capacity		25 806

1—14 各师水库基本情况

Statistics on Reservoir by Division

单位	Unit	2009 水库座数(座) Number (unit)	2009 库容量(万立方米) Reservoir Capacity (10 000 cu. m)	2010 水库座数(座) Number (unit)	2010 库容量(万立方米) Reservoir Capacity (10 000 cu. m)
总计	**Total**	**125**	**327 838**	**125**	**327 839**
一师	Division 1	5	51 720	5	51 720
二师	Division 2	5	36 610	5	36 610
三师	Division 3	5	83 800	5	83 800
四师	Division 4	23	5 224	23	5 225
五师	Division 5	4	1 393	4	1 393
六师	Division 6	20	23 029	20	23 029
七师	Division 7	13	31 696	13	31 696
八师	Division 8	15	54 445	15	54 445
九师	Division 9	6	6 685	6	6 685
十师	Division 10	16	24 261	16	24 261
十二师	Division 12	5	4 330	5	4 330
十三师	Division 13	3	553	3	553
十四师	Division 14	3	1 592	3	1 592
兵团直属	Directly under XPCG	2	2 500	2	2 500

1—15 历年水利工程及灌溉能力

Water Conservancy Project and Irrigation Capacity

年份 Year	水库 Reservoir 座数(座) Number (unit)	水库 Reservoir 库容(万立方米) Reservoir Capacity (10 000 cu. m)	场外引水干渠 Trunk Canal 条数(条) Number (unit)	场外引水干渠 Trunk Canal 引水能力(立方米/秒) Water Supply Capacity (cu. m/second)	年实际引水量(亿立方米) Amount of Water Supply (100 million cu. m)	实际灌溉面积(千公顷) Actually Irrigated Area (1 000 hectares)
1978	68	218 974	214	2 447	69.18	725.00
1980	79	226 476	221	2 961	80.02	724.70
1985	91	265 968			89.47	725.30
1990	93	275 365			92.95	814.10
1991	93	276 067			89.93	834.00
1992	93	276 567			88.51	836.90
1993	93	276 567			87.53	840.00
1994	94	279 513			91.90	843.00
1995	101	280 935			96.60	847.40
1996	101	288 575			97.25	869.70
1997	104	291 926			113.39	880.30
1998	105	296 316			114.97	928.70
1999	105	296 316			116.51	962.00
2000	105	299 709			117.93	982.70
2001	108	303 553			120.30	1 072.30
2002	109	304 723			116.08	1 119.03
2003	113	314 692			123.63	1 151.64
2004	114	315 135			120.60	1 128.90
2005	114	316 250			123.89	1 164.48
2006	125	324 487			125.55	1 256.09
2007	125	327 346			123.84	1 222.30
2008	125	327 346			124.82	1 297.76
2009	125	327 838			116.43	1 326.50
2010	125	327 839			125.95	1 332.06

注:1.年实际引水量指:蓄水、引水、机电井、机电站及水轮泵、其他工程供水合计。
2.实际灌溉面积指:农田、园林、草场及其他面积合计。

Note:a) In the table amount of water supply refers to aggregate water-stored, water-supplyed, electromechanical well, electromechanical station, pump and other engineering water supply.
b) In the table actually irrigated area refers to aggregate farmland, orchard, grass field and other area.

1—16　主要城市平均气温

Monthly Average Temperature of Major Cities

计量单位:摄氏度　　(2010年)　　(℃)

城　市	City	一　月 Jan.	二　月 Feb.	三　月 Mar.	四　月 Apr.	五　月 May	六　月 June	七　月 July
乌鲁木齐市	Urumqi City	−10.6	−12.3	−4.4	8.7	16.2	22.5	24.0
克拉玛依市	Karamay City	−13.1	−14.5	−4.0	10.4	19.4	25.9	26.8
石河子市	Shi Hezi City	−12.7	−13.8	−5.5	10.0	18.8	24.4	25.6
阜康市	Fukang City	−13.6	−14.4	−5.5	9.9	18.3	24.5	25.7
米泉市	Miquan City	−11.5	−12.5	−4.3	10.3	18.5	24.9	26.4
伊宁市	Yining [Gulja] City	−4.4	−5.6	4.9	13.5	17.3	22.6	23.6
塔城市	Tacheng [Qoqek] City	−8.6	−12.1	−3.3	8.9	15.5	22.5	23.8
阿勒泰市	Altay City	−16.2	−18.1	−9.6	2.2	13.7	21.3	21.9
博乐市	Bole City	−13.3	−15.0	−4.5	9.2	17.9	23.2	24.1
库尔勒市	Korla City	−4.9	−0.7	7.2	14.0	19.3	26.8	27.9
阿克苏市	Aksu City	−4.8	−1.8	7.8	14.9	19.1	22.9	24.6
阿图什市	Artux City	−2.3	−0.7	10.0	16.9	20.2	23.0	26.3
喀什市	Kashgar [Kaxgar] City	−2.0	−0.4	10.4	16.7	19.5	22.5	25.8
和田市	Hotan City	−0.5	1.8	11.8	17.3	21.0	22.3	26.3
吐鲁番市	Turpan City	−4.4	1.8	9.1	18.2	25.1	32.3	33.3
哈密市	Hami [Kumul] City	−7.7	−3.3	2.9	11.9	19.7	26.8	28.3

城　市	City	八　月 Aug.	九　月 Sept.	十　月 Oct.	十一月 Nov.	十二月 Dec.	全年平均 Annual Average
乌鲁木齐市	Urumqi City	22.8	18.0	9.7	2.4	−8.2	7.4
克拉玛依市	Karamay City	25.7	20.3	11.0	2.2	−9.8	8.4
石河子市	Shi Hezi City	23.8	18.4	10.3	1.9	−10.3	7.6
阜康市	Fukang City	23.9	18.2	9.6	0.4	−10.8	7.2
米泉市	Miquan City	24.9	19.6	11.0	2.1	−8.9	8.4
伊宁市	Yining [Gulja] City	22.6	17.5	11.0	3.9	−2.9	10.3
塔城市	Tacheng [Qoqek] City	21.8	16.9	10.1	1.9	−8.6	7.4
阿勒泰市	Altay City	19.6	14.1	7.5	−2.1	−14.4	3.3
博乐市	Bole City	22.7	17.7	9.6	1.6	−9.6	7.0
库尔勒市	Korla City	27.9	20.2	12.5	3.6	−5.7	12.3
阿克苏市	Aksu City	25.5	18.6	12.6	4.3	−5.0	11.6
阿图什市	Artux City	27.4	19.6	14.2	6.7	−2.5	13.2
喀什市	Kashgar [Kaxgar] City	26.5	18.8	13.9	7.0	−2.1	13.1
和田市	Hotan City	27.4	20.2	14.6	7.6	−0.7	14.1
吐鲁番市	Turpan City	31.2	24.2	16.2	5.9	−5.4	15.6
哈密市	Hami [Kumul] City	25.1	18.5	10.5	2.0	−9.2	10.5

1—17 主要城市降水量

Monthly Precipitation of Major Cities

计量单位:毫米 （2010年） (milli meter)

城市	City	一月 Jan.	二月 Feb.	三月 Mar.	四月 Apr.	五月 May	六月 June	七月 July
乌鲁木齐市	Urumqi City	15.6	9.5	46.8	30.0	26.2	31.2	13.2
克拉玛依市	Karamay City	5.4	10.0	3.7	26.4	6.4	25.7	13.0
石河子市	Shi Hezi City	21.2	37.7	57.2	27.2	40.8	39.3	29.1
阜康市	Fukang City	19.3	6.3	26.5	14.4	15.2	25.7	10.7
米泉市	Miquan City	15.3	11.7	50.7	19.7	19.4	16.2	8.4
伊宁市	Yining [Gulja] City	27.8	64.5	86.1	39.1	22.3	29.2	35.2
塔城市	Tacheng [Qoqek] City	82.5	21.2	55.0	48.3	42.5	18.2	26.1
阿勒泰市	Altay City	75.0	26.6	53.3	8.1	25.6	6.0	10.6
博乐市	Bole City	11.8	3.6	33.2	14.7	22.8	46.2	12.4
库尔勒市	Korla City		1.5	0.7	10.1	7.7	1.5	7.1
阿克苏市	Aksu City		7.2	4.6		6.2	35.9	38.7
阿图什市	Artux City		15.9	8.2	0.5	12.7	47.9	56.5
喀什市	Kashgar [Kaxgar] City		18.7	11.4	0.3	35.0	29.1	32.2
和田市	Hotan City		11.3	15.8		23.5	31.5	2.8
吐鲁番市	Turpan City					0.4	2.5	1.1
哈密市	Hami [Kumul] City	2.5		1.0	6.1	7.6	20.4	6.5

城市	City	八月 Aug.	九月 Sept.	十月 Oct.	十一月 Nov.	十二月 Dec.	全年 Annual Total
乌鲁木齐市	Urumqi City	12.5	5.1	32.5	28.3	31.5	282.4
克拉玛依市	Karamay City	3.4	4.3	19.3	0.6	8.7	126.9
石河子市	Shi Hezi City	24.3	8.7	33.9	23.3	24.4	367.1
阜康市	Fukang City	5.2	8.6	31.4	25.1	19.8	208.2
米泉市	Miquan City	7.6	4.3	25.5	26.8	30.2	235.8
伊宁市	Yining [Gulja] City	10.6	13.2	85.8	25.6	26.0	465.4
塔城市	Tacheng [Qoqek] City	22.1	2.0	19.5	46.4	86.5	470.3
阿勒泰市	Altay City	19.2	3.6	26.3	41.3	42.9	338.5
博乐市	Bole City	7.0	8.5	24.2	15.1	2.9	202.4
库尔勒市	Korla City	2.4	2.2	6.3	2.8	2.5	44.8
阿克苏市	Aksu City	0.2	35.9	15.2	0.2		144.1
阿图什市	Artux City	0.3	62.5	15.4			219.9
喀什市	Kashgar [Kaxgar] City	0.8	49.1	15.0			191.6
和田市	Hotan City	0.3	13.3	13.4			111.9
吐鲁番市	Turpan City	0.1	0.4		1.1	1.4	7.0
哈密市	Hami [Kumul] City	4.4	8.3	1.2		6.9	64.9

1—18　主要城市日照时数

Monthly Sunshine Hours of Major Cities

计量单位:小时　　(2010年)　　(hour)

城　市	City	一　月 Jan.	二　月 Feb.	三　月 Mar.	四　月 Apr.	五　月 May	六　月 June	七　月 July
乌鲁木齐市	Urumqi City	107.8	99.2	219.8	286.9	309.1	315.3	301.7
克拉玛依市	Karamay City	77.2	121.0	181.9	274.2	332.3	317.3	301.9
石河子市	Shi Hezi City	81.8	66.8	177.9	239.1	296.6	288.7	301.7
阜康市	Fukang City	64.7	88.9	203.5	266.9	298.6	313.1	290.7
米泉市	Miquan City	49.3	62.2	186.8	258.5	285.2	301.4	286.6
伊宁市	Yining [Gulja] City	133.6	78.9	219.4	277.6	333.1	319.6	315.2
塔城市	Tacheng [Qoqek] City	103.9	143.5	200.3	275.7	334.3	342.3	325.0
阿勒泰市	Altay City	128.3	181.3	247.6	302.4	321.9	334.6	359.6
博乐市	Bole City	132.1	141.8	155.7	231.3	331.6	284.3	286.7
库尔勒市	Korla City	183.6	147.3	227.3	259.9	273.6	296.7	270.4
阿克苏市	Aksu City	184.2	173.7	203.4	250.8	270.8	243.6	268.4
阿图什市	Artux City	131.1	115.1	186.9	188.5	268.9	247.8	316.6
喀什市	Kashgar [Kaxgar] City	166.7	141.3	221.8	258.0	291.1	283.7	337.6
和田市	Hotan City	144.8	137.8	157.1	189.4	238.7	238.9	256.4
吐鲁番市	Turpan City	134.1	169.5	223.9	281.2	281.0	317.4	277.8
哈密市	Hami [Kumul] City	232.0	232.2	305.1	335.0	355.6	381.3	367.0

城　市	City	八　月 Aug.	九　月 Sept.	十　月 Oct.	十一月 Nov.	十二月 Dec.	全　年 Annual Total
乌鲁木齐市	Urumqi City	309.2	283.2	229.6	201.7	152.2	2 815.7
克拉玛依市	Karamay City	335.9	279.0	215.3	165.1	121.9	2 723.0
石河子市	Shi Hezi City	308.0	266.6	223.7	164.9	91.3	2 507.1
阜康市	Fukang City	295.2	283.2	229.4	151.1	119.3	2 604.6
米泉市	Miquan City	309.3	280.2	213.0	135.4	63.6	2 431.5
伊宁市	Yining [Gulja] City	304.3	278.7	226.4	202.9	167.4	2 857.1
塔城市	Tacheng [Qoqek] City	307.9	264.5	252.1	167.1	127.9	2 844.5
阿勒泰市	Altay City	321.5	287.7	252.8	154.1	143.7	3 035.5
博乐市	Bole City	296.3	234.8	167.1	112.6	136.6	2 510.9
库尔勒市	Korla City	280.3	265.7	218.6	222.8	167.4	2 813.6
阿克苏市	Aksu City	269.0	200.4	210.7	232.9	202.9	2 710.8
阿图什市	Artux City	267.0	191.4	229.8	212.2	183.8	2 539.1
喀什市	Kashgar [Kaxgar] City	286.5	211.2	243.0	235.4	209.7	2 886.0
和田市	Hotan City	253.7	181.3	251.4	251.5	198.9	2 499.9
吐鲁番市	Turpan City	302.4	268.4	227.8	125.8	40.8	2 650.1
哈密市	Hami [Kumul] City	344.1	304.3	285.2	244.3	206.7	3 592.8

2011

BING TUAN

第二篇

国民经济核算

Chapter 2 National Account

简要说明

一、本篇资料主要内容

本篇资料包括兵团生产总值及分产业情况等内容。

二、本篇资料来源

国民经济核算资料由兵团统计局国民经济核算处根据《兵团生产总值核算统计报表制度》收集、测算、整理提供。

Brief Introduction

1. Main contents

This chapter mainly contains data on gross domestic product and industries of XPCG.

2. Sources of Data

Relevant data on national accounts are collected, measure and calculate and compiled by <The Reporting Form System on GDP of XPCG> the National Accounts Section of the Statistics Bureau of XPCG.

2—1 生产总值

Gross Domestic Product

计量单位:万元 (10 000 yuan)

年 份 Year	单 位 Unit	收入总值 Gross National Income	生产总值 Gross Domestic Product	第一产业 Primary Industry	第二产业 Secondary Industry	工 业 Industry
	1950		2 351	579	1 018	
	1952		11 995	2 364	7 496	1 415
	1954		11 780	1 721	7 459	2 359
	1957		23 306	4 730	11 415	5 862
	1962		41 328	12 458	16 862	13 575
	1965		56 461	19 359	23 732	18 073
	1970		61 439	24 935	20 481	17 481
	1975		35 648	20 670	8 021	6 627
	1978		73 999	35 054	22 824	19 459
	1980	101 937	101 937	43 846	40 988	32 433
	1985	201 281	201 281	80 919	79 270	57 977
	1990	454 624	456 919	209 110	146 872	115 096
	1991	513 289	515 577	211 874	175 754	137 511
	1992	559 727	563 449	205 214	197 548	147 869
	1993	641 855	646 732	221 819	225 581	165 094
	1994	918 458	926 005	378 224	280 508	210 214
	1995	1 207 537	1 216 042	560 034	318 684	238 917
	1996	1 303 371	1 313 384	582 270	313 684	224 232
	1997		1 455 020	673 439	347 881	250 178
	1998		1 618 257	725 692	382 885	255 453
	1999		1 574 749	600 566	431 807	276 417
	2000		1 764 103	716 298	485 276	321 603
	2001		1 897 094	628 242	558 056	364 601
	2002		2 141 330	763 586	605 907	398 492
	2003		2 577 755	1 091 024	638 721	409 605
	2004		2 888 118	1 151 287	709 091	455 845
	2005	3 264 348	3 311 246	1 306 458	833 482	564 964
	2006	3 699 902	3 760 294	1 421 888	994 196	693 498
	2007	4 363 773	4 412 150	1 625 837	1 274 481	910 969
	2008	5 205 777	5 232 964	1 823 154	1 660 880	1 201 483
	2009	6 083 029	6 106 945	2 047 350	2 065 678	1 486 955
	2010	7 665 121	7 706 152	2 788 111	2 622 637	1 862 830
一 师	Division 1	1 029 547	1 043 212	557 369	288 659	220 861
二 师	Division 2	500 052	500 142	216 087	149 568	107 473
三 师	Division 3	386 342	386 345	220 536	61 681	37 093
四 师	Division 4	546 010	546 010	191 700	234 652	197 087
五 师	Division 5	257 926	276 030	145 464	56 082	39 771
六 师	Division 6	974 993	974 993	332 441	348 500	245 282
七 师	Division 7	636 030	645 039	279 955	211 055	136 288
八 师	Division 8	1 885 049	1 885 049	552 742	726 456	601 445
九 师	Division 9	139 530	139 690	65 504	30 491	18 871
十 师	Division 10	170 177	170 177	63 202	62 399	48 100
建 工 师	Construction Division	235 088	235 088	192	209 265	10 706
十 二 师	Division 12	232 005	232 005	44 871	125 424	112 097
十 三 师	Division 13	218 126	218 126	81 256	89 247	68 595
十 四 师	Division 14	47 938	47 938	23 222	10 655	3 813
国资公司	State-owned Property Company	91 264	91 264	1 651	41 509	40 289
供销公司	Supply and Marketing Corpor -ation General	5 714	5 714			
中基公司	Chalkis Company	−32 112	−32 112		−28 903	−28 903
兵团直属	Directly under XPCG	341 442	341 442	11 919	5 897	3 962

注:本表按当年价格计算。

2—1 续表 Continued

计量单位：万元 (10 000 yuan)

年份 Year	单位 Unit	建筑业 Construction	第三产业 Tertiary Industry	# 交通运输仓储和邮政业 Transport, Storage and Postal Services	# 批发和零售业 Wholesale and Retail Trade	人均生产总值（元） Per Capita GDP(yuan)
	1950	1 018	754	249	268	
	1952	6 081	2 135	645	667	439
	1954	5 100	2 600	741	738	723
	1957	5 553	7 161	1 948	1 883	764
	1962	3 287	12 008	2 761	3 290	478
	1965	5 659	13 370	3 516	3 770	465
	1970	3 000	16 023	4 679	4 839	330
	1975	1 394	6 957	2 052	2 358	177
	1978	3 365	16 121	4 508	5 666	374
	1980	8 555	17 103	5 165	5 832	464
	1985	21 293	41 092	9 501	14 343	900
	1990	31 776	100 937	17 594	27 614	2 134
	1991	38 243	127 949	21 828	39 810	2 391
	1992	49 679	160 687	28 215	47 854	2 590
	1993	60 487	199 332	30 070	65 951	2 953
	1994	70 294	267 273	32 801	78 609	4 189
	1995	79 767	337 324	37 523	97 204	5 390
	1996	89 452	417 430	46 209	120 406	5 672
	1997	97 703	433 700	49 502	111 275	6 156
	1998	127 432	509 680	60 794	131 220	6 755
	1999	155 390	542 376	65 213	135 516	6 523
	2000	163 673	562 529	66 867	145 006	7 276
	2001	193 455	710 796	91 208	180 913	7 773
	2002	207 415	771 837	93 276	176 029	8 644
	2003	229 116	848 010	101 599	176 541	10 222
	2004	253 246	1 027 740	101 724	185 673	11 313
	2005	268 518	1 171 306	115 084	196 842	12 900
	2006	300 698	1 344 210	134 448	235 352	14 605
	2007	363 512	1 511 832	157 708	277 496	17 088
	2008	459 397	1 748 930	174 244	331 738	20 291
	2009	578 723	1 993 917	195 454	375 456	23 734
	2010	759 807	2 295 404	229 614	394 095	29 948
一　师	Division 1	67 798	197 184	13 426	37 209	35 701
二　师	Division 2	42 095	134 487	12 410	27 396	25 938
三　师	Division 3	24 588	104 128	6 595	20 976	18 821
四　师	Division 4	37 565	119 658	18 823	30 272	24 756
五　师	Division 5	16 311	74 484	6 128	11 397	24 753
六　师	Division 6	103 218	294 052	39 577	75 566	31 462
七　师	Division 7	74 767	154 029	29 765	36 864	29 779
八　师	Division 8	125 011	605 851	74 599	51 302	32 263
九　师	Division 9	11 620	43 695	3 826	8 563	19 560
十　师	Division 10	14 299	44 576	7 807	7 793	22 698
建工师	Construction Division	198 559	25 631	505	1 054	49 206
十二师	Division 12	13 327	61 710	8 246	16 205	31 363
十三师	Division 13	20 652	47 623	5 471	8 094	27 313
十四师	Division 14	6 842	14 061	532	3 339	12 795
国资公司	State-owned Property Company	1 220	48 104	431	42 840	67 938
供销公司	Supply and Marketing Corpor -ation General		5 714	1 142	4 572	31 344
中基公司	Chalkis Company		−3 209		−3 441	−448 805
兵团直属	Directly under XPCG	1 935	323 626	331	14 094	88 522

Note: Data in value terms in this table are calculated at current prices.

2—2 生产总值构成

Composition of Gross Domestic Product

计量单位：% (生产总值=100，GDP=100) (%)

年 份 Year	单 位 Unit	第一产业 Primary Industry	第二产业 Secondary Industry	工 业 Industry	建筑业 Construction	第三产业 Tertiary Industry	# 交通运输仓储和邮政业 Transport, Storage and Postal Services	# 批发和零售业 Wholesale and Retail Trade
	1950	24.6	43.3		43.3	32.1	10.6	11.4
	1952	19.7	62.5	11.8	50.7	17.8	5.4	5.6
	1954	14.6	63.3	20.0	43.3	22.1	6.3	6.3
	1957	20.3	49.0	25.2	23.8	30.7	8.4	8.1
	1962	30.1	40.8	32.8	8.0	29.1	6.7	8.0
	1965	34.3	42.0	32.0	10.0	23.7	6.2	6.7
	1970	40.6	33.3	28.4	4.9	26.1	7.6	7.9
	1975	58.0	22.5	18.6	3.9	19.5	5.8	6.6
	1978	47.4	30.8	26.3	4.5	21.8	6.1	7.7
	1980	43.0	40.2	31.8	8.4	16.8	5.1	5.7
	1985	40.2	39.4	28.8	10.6	20.4	4.7	7.1
	1990	45.8	32.1	25.2	6.9	22.1	3.9	6.0
	1991	41.1	34.1	26.7	7.4	24.8	4.2	7.7
	1992	36.4	35.1	26.3	8.8	28.5	5.0	8.5
	1993	34.3	34.9	25.5	9.4	30.8	4.6	10.2
	1994	40.8	30.3	22.7	7.6	28.9	3.5	8.5
	1995	46.1	26.2	19.6	6.6	27.7	3.1	8.0
	1996	44.3	23.9	17.1	6.8	31.8	3.5	9.2
	1997	46.3	23.9	17.2	6.7	29.8	3.4	7.6
	1998	44.8	23.7	15.8	7.9	31.5	3.8	8.1
	1999	38.1	27.4	17.5	9.9	34.5	4.1	8.6
	2000	40.6	27.5	18.2	9.3	31.9	3.8	8.2
	2001	33.1	29.4	19.2	10.2	37.5	4.8	9.5
	2002	35.7	28.3	18.6	9.7	36.0	4.4	8.2
	2003	42.3	24.8	15.9	8.9	32.9	3.9	6.8
	2004	39.9	24.5	15.8	8.7	35.6	3.5	6.4
	2005	39.4	25.2	17.1	8.1	35.4	3.5	5.9
	2006	37.8	26.4	18.4	8.0	35.8	3.6	6.3
	2007	36.8	28.9	20.7	8.2	34.3	3.6	6.3
	2008	34.9	31.7	22.9	8.8	33.4	3.3	6.3
	2009	33.5	33.8	24.3	9.5	32.7	3.2	6.1
	2010	36.2	34.0	24.2	9.8	29.8	3.0	5.1
一 师	Division 1	53.4	27.7	21.2	6.5	18.9	1.3	3.6
二 师	Division 2	43.2	29.9	21.5	8.4	26.9	2.5	5.5
三 师	Division 3	57.1	16.0	9.6	6.4	26.9	1.7	5.4
四 师	Division 4	35.1	43.0	36.1	6.9	21.9	3.4	5.5
五 师	Division 5	52.7	20.3	14.4	5.9	27.0	2.2	4.1
六 师	Division 6	34.1	35.7	25.1	10.6	30.2	4.1	7.8
七 师	Division 7	43.4	32.7	21.1	11.6	23.9	4.6	5.7
八 师	Division 8	29.3	38.5	31.9	6.6	32.2	4.0	2.7
九 师	Division 9	46.9	21.8	13.5	8.3	31.3	2.7	6.1
十 师	Division 10	37.1	36.7	28.3	8.4	26.2	4.6	4.6
建工师	Construction Division	0.1	89.0	4.5	84.5	10.9	0.2	0.4
十二师	Division 12	19.3	54.1	48.3	5.8	26.6	3.6	7.0
十三师	Division 13	37.3	40.9	31.4	9.5	21.8	2.5	3.7
十四师	Division 14	48.5	22.2	7.9	14.3	29.3	1.1	7.0
国资公司	State-owned Property Company	1.8	45.5	44.2	1.3	52.7	0.5	46.9
供销公司	Supply and Marketing Corpor-ation General					100.0	20.0	80.0
中基公司	Chalkis Company							
兵团直属	Directly under XPCG	3.5	1.7	1.1	0.6	94.8	0.1	4.1

注：本表按当年价格计算。

Note: Data in value terms in this table are calculated at current prices.

2—3 生产总值

Gross Domestic Product

计量单位:万元 (10 000 yuan)

年份 Year	单位 Unit	收入总值 Gross National Income	生产总值 Gross Domestic Product	第一产业 Primary Industry	第二产业 Secondary Industry	工业 Industry
1950			4 696	1 461	2 158	
1952			22 761	6 237	14 127	2 274
1954			22 198	4 620	14 544	3 829
1957			44 008	12 661	21 899	9 417
1962			74 219	28 961	26 901	19 541
1965			114 099	52 144	42 467	29 719
1970			131 391	66 654	40 203	32 957
1975			76 948	50 342	15 472	12 554
1978		148 812	148 812	75 506	45 958	38 371
1980		185 848	185 848	79 728	77 801	64 566
1985		320 216	319 193	127 351	132 879	111 318
1990		465 754	468 049	213 569	153 543	121 767
1991		497 610	499 692	213 572	170 541	136 315
1992		523 779	523 779	209 986	179 336	141 457
1993		547 060	551 206	209 676	192 231	149 887
1994		601 063	605 561	246 711	194 218	153 297
1995		665 783	670 018	293 976	192 461	148 539
1996		676 694	681 353	288 342	184 847	138 603
1997			736 005	329 110	194 178	147 873
1998			810 571	367 233	209 632	151 970
1999			865 357	370 153	240 925	168 422
2000			964 777	417 586	277 391	199 923
(2000)			1 764 103	716 298	485 276	321 603
2001			1 871 389	680 008	522 488	348 355
2002			2 129 251	790 975	575 511	384 779
2003			2 405 517	953 114	613 211	403 054
2004			2 705 844	1 048 284	668 224	440 651
2005		2 982 125	3 012 939	1 137 769	766 482	530 464
(2005)		3 264 348	3 311 246	1 306 458	833 482	564 964
2006		3 640 854	3 687 941	1 415 562	967 167	672 943
2007		4 101 779	4 136 450	1 523 206	1 176 357	838 190
2008		4 627 811	4 652 765	1 661 328	1 395 790	1 020 578
2009		5 277 488	5 287 837	1 776 928	1 748 858	1 284 121
2010		5 999 375	6 025 403	1 986 104	2 119 104	1 522 183
一师	Division 1	775 738	785 948	388 779	230 252	175 860
二师	Division 2	395 840	395 917	163 553	120 878	87 506
三师	Division 3	297 811	297 814	159 876	48 952	29 688
四师	Division 4	438 191	438 191	149 426	193 302	163 438
五师	Division 5	185 913	201 519	96 902	46 198	33 419
六师	Division 6	751 904	751 904	236 012	276 475	195 608
七师	Division 7	518 070	518 070	208 295	174 123	115 547
八师	Division 8	1 479 873	1 479 873	377 508	612 110	514 169
九师	Division 9	102 572	102 704	44 371	21 563	12 459
十师	Division 10	133 018	133 018	46 610	49 121	37 919
建工师	Construction Division	185 969	185 969	111	162 352	7 088
十二师	Division 12	175 364	175 364	29 140	97 106	86 665
十三师	Division 13	168 682	168 682	60 080	69 641	53 478
十四师	Division 14	37 200	37 200	16 366	9 016	3 736
国资公司	State-owned Property Company	70 935	70 935	1 349	28 965	28 009
供销公司	Supply and Marketing Corpor -ation General	4 874	4 874			
中基公司	Chalkis Company	−27 879	−27 879		−25 176	−25 176
兵团直属	Directlt under XPCG	305 300	305 300	7 726	4 226	2 770

注:本表数据 2000 年(含 2000 年)以前按 1990 年可比价格计算,(2000)年以后按 2000 年可比价计算,2005 年及以后按 2005 年可比价计算。

2—3 续表 Continued

计量单位:万元 (10 000 yuan)

年 份 Year	单 位 Unit	建筑业 Construction	第三产业 Tertiary Industry	# 交通运输仓储和邮政业 Transport, Storage and Postal Services	# 批发和零售业 Wholesale and Retail Trade	人均生产总值(元) Per Capita GDP(yuan)
	1950	2 158	1 077	219	436	
	1952	11 853	2 397	354	843	833
	1954	10 715	3 034	730	1 194	1 363
	1957	12 482	9 448	1 573	3 622	1 443
	1962	7 360	18 357	2 668	5 739	858
	1965	12 748	19 488	3 460	6 581	939
	1970	7 246	24 534	4 694	8 764	706
	1975	2 918	11 134	2 097	4 340	382
	1978	7 587	27 348	4 384	10 631	752
	1980	13 235	28 319	5 421	10 377	846
	1985	21 561	58 963	9 969	22 154	1 427
	1990	31 776	100 937	17 569	27 615	2 186
	1991	34 226	115 579	18 625	36 291	2 318
	1992	37 879	134 457	20 840	41 005	2 408
	1993	42 344	149 299	21 865	49 370	2 517
	1994	40 921	164 632	22 890	46 701	2 739
	1995	43 922	183 581	24 761	50 371	2 970
	1996	46 244	208 164	28 515	57 162	2 942
	1997	46 305	212 717	29 179	51 756	3 114
	1998	57 662	233 706	32 995	58 320	3 384
	1999	72 503	254 279	34 918	60 594	3 585
	2000	77 468	269 800	36 284	66 162	3 979
	(2000)	163 673	562 529	66 867	145 006	7 276
	2001	174 133	668 893	83 023	168 012	7 667
	2002	190 732	762 765	87 238	173 330	8 595
	2003	210 157	839 192	95 204	176 456	9 539
	2004	227 573	989 336	99 526	180 846	10 599
	2005	236 018	1 108 688	110 760	193 192	11 738
	(2005)	268 518	1 171 306	115 084	196 842	12 900
	2006	294 224	1 305 212	128 209	229 587	14 324
	2007	338 167	1 436 887	142 698	259 848	16 020
	2008	375 212	1 595 647	156 787	283 473	18 042
	2009	464 737	1 762 051	170 237	323 712	20 550
	2010	596 921	1 920 195	198 324	329 153	23 416
一 师	Division 1	54 392	166 917	11 597	30 769	26 897
二 师	Division 2	33 372	111 486	10 719	23 051	20 533
三 师	Division 3	19 264	88 986	5 697	17 125	14 508
四 师	Division 4	29 864	95 463	16 258	23 408	19 868
五 师	Division 5	12 779	58 419	5 293	9 322	18 071
六 师	Division 6	80 867	239 417	34 186	62 934	24 263
七 师	Division 7	58 576	135 652	25 708	34 511	23 917
八 师	Division 8	97 941	490 255	64 432	41 141	25 328
九 师	Division 9	9 104	36 770	3 304	7 067	14 381
十 师	Division 10	11 202	37 287	6 743	6 319	17 742
建工师	Construction Division	155 264	23 506	436	896	38 925
十二师	Division 12	10 441	49 118	7 122	13 782	23 706
十三师	Division 13	16 163	38 961	4 725	6 688	21 121
十四师	Division 14	5 280	11 818	460	2 758	9 929
国资公司	State-owned Property Company	956	40 621	372	36 434	52 805
供销公司	Supply and Marketing Corpor -ation General		4 874	986	3 888	26 736
中基公司	Chalkis Company		−2 703		−2 927	−389 644
兵团直属	Directlt under XPCG	1 456	293 348	286	11 987	79 152

Note: Data prior to 2000 (including 2000) are calculated at comparable prices in 1990, data after 2000 are calculated at comparable prices in 2000, and data after 2005 are calculated at comparable pricesin 2005.

2—4 生产总值指数

Indices of Gross Domestic Product

计量单位:% （上年＝100,preceding year＝100） (%)

年份 Year	单位 Unit	收入总值 Gross National Income	生产总值 Gross Domestic Product	第一产业 Primary Industry	第二产业 Secondary Industry	工业 Industry
1951			141.1	156.3	96.2	
1952			343.6	273.2	680.8	
1954			143.2	109.9	156.5	139.8
1957			123.6	119.0	113.2	132.3
1962			90.3	106.9	81.5	77.0
1965			111.8	116.4	111.1	114.3
1970			119.7	121.5	131.0	126.2
1975			59.5	97.4	27.8	25.7
1978			174.0	144.6	213.6	250.2
1980			113.1	98.4	138.5	148.2
1985		112.8	112.7	107.5	113.2	118.1
1990		113.3	112.7	133.1	94.4	92.3
1991		106.9	106.8	100.0	111.1	111.9
1992		105.3	104.8	98.3	105.2	103.8
1993		105.1	105.2	99.9	107.2	106.0
1994		109.9	109.9	117.7	101.0	102.3
1995		110.8	110.6	119.2	99.1	96.9
1996		101.6	101.7	98.1	96.0	93.3
1997			108.0	114.1	105.0	106.7
1998			110.1	111.6	108.0	102.8
1999			106.8	100.8	114.9	110.8
2000			111.5	112.8	115.1	118.7
2001			106.1	94.9	107.7	108.3
2002			113.8	116.3	110.1	110.5
2003			113.0	108.4	113.3	115.2
2004			112.5	110.0	109.0	109.3
2005			111.3	108.5	114.7	120.4
2006		111.5	112.6	111.4	116.0	119.1
2007		112.7	112.2	107.6	121.6	124.6
2008		112.8	112.5	109.1	118.7	121.8
2009		114.0	113.6	107.0	125.3	125.8
2010		113.7	113.9	111.8	121.2	118.5
一师	Division 1	113.7	114.8	111.1	126.1	131.6
二师	Division 2	107.2	107.2	105.7	108.7	107.8
三师	Division 3	114.8	114.8	116.0	122.4	123.8
四师	Division 4	111.5	111.5	112.0	111.8	110.9
五师	Division 5	115.5	115.8	110.6	135.6	134.1
六师	Division 6	121.0	121.6	109.0	146.1	137.1
七师	Division 7	117.5	117.5	116.0	126.0	124.1
八师	Division 8	117.5	117.5	115.9	125.7	122.5
九师	Division 9	107.1	107.2	111.5	110.9	103.6
十师	Division 10	114.9	114.9	105.2	137.1	137.4
建工师	Construction Division	118.0	118.0	100.9	116.5	154.5
十二师	Division 12	117.3	117.3	105.1	121.6	121.3
十三师	Division 13	117.0	117.0	106.3	130.7	129.7
十四师	Division 14	117.1	117.1	121.7	131.1	146.8
国资公司	State-owned Property Company	111.8	111.8	169.3	83.8	82.6
供销公司	Supply and Marketing Corpor -ation General	107.8	107.8			
中基公司	Chalkis Company					
兵团直属	Directly under XPCG	100.2	100.2	89.4	114.2	74.8

注:本表数据2000年(含2000年)以前按1990年可比价格计算,2000年以后按2000年可比价计算,2005年及以后按2005年可比价计算。

2—4 续表 Continued

计量单位:% (%)

年 份 Year	单 位 Unit	建筑业 Construction	第三产业 Tertiary Industry	# 交通运输仓储和邮政业 Transport, Storage and Postal Service	# 批发和零售业 Wholesale and Retail Trade	人均生产总值 Per Capita GDP
	1951	96.2	210.5	212.3	211.0	
	1952	571.2	105.7	76.1	91.6	
	1954	163.5	151.1	294.4	165.8	186.2
	1957	102.2	167.8	150.4	186.2	102.3
	1962	96.5	82.9	91.9	95.2	83.1
	1965	104.4	102.1	97.5	95.7	96.7
	1970	158.7	101.0	106.9	102.3	111.4
	1975	43.6	50.7	52.0	55.9	65.4
	1978	122.7	232.4	212.3	221.5	158.3
	1980	105.0	104.4	106.9	102.0	111.0
	1985	93.2	124.4	113.5	137.8	113.5
	1990	103.5	109.6	105.4	117.7	113.1
	1991	107.7	114.5	106.0	131.4	106.0
	1992	110.7	116.3	111.9	113.0	103.9
	1993	111.8	111.0	104.9	120.4	104.5
	1994	96.6	110.3	104.7	94.6	108.8
	1995	107.3	111.5	108.2	107.9	108.4
	1996	105.3	113.4	115.2	113.5	99.1
	1997	100.1	102.2	102.3	90.5	105.8
	1998	124.5	109.9	113.1	112.7	108.7
	1999	125.7	108.8	105.8	103.9	105.9
	2000	106.8	106.1	103.9	109.2	111.0
	2001	106.4	118.9	124.2	115.9	105.4
	2002	109.5	114.0	105.1	103.2	112.1
	2003	110.2	117.9	109.1	121.5	111.0
	2004	108.3	117.9	104.5	102.5	111.1
	2005	103.7	112.1	111.3	106.8	110.8
	2006	109.6	111.4	111.4	116.6	112.2
	2007	114.8	110.1	111.3	113.2	111.8
	2008	111.0	111.0	109.9	109.1	112.6
	2009	123.9	110.4	108.5	111.2	113.9
	2010	128.4	109.0	116.5	101.7	113.9
一 师	Division 1	111.0	109.8	106.0	108.4	114.6
二 师	Division 2	111.3	107.7	107.6	102.6	109.3
三 师	Division 3	120.2	108.9	110.0	100.1	114.2
四 师	Division 4	116.7	110.1	115.4	108.3	112.4
五 师	Division 5	139.6	111.7	117.0	102.3	115.1
六 师	Division 6	173.5	112.8	122.8	102.3	120.0
七 师	Division 7	129.8	110.1	114.4	111.0	118.0
八 师	Division 8	145.4	109.6	122.3	88.4	117.8
九 师	Division 9	122.6	100.6	113.3	93.3	108.0
十 师	Division 10	136.3	104.8	106.0	105.5	116.1
建工师	Construction Division	115.2	129.4	97.5	135.3	113.2
十二师	Division 12	124.0	117.1	100.6	106.0	113.9
十三师	Division 13	133.9	113.3	117.0	102.9	115.7
十四师	Division 14	121.9	103.2	105.0	78.3	111.7
国资公司	State-owned Property Company	141.2	144.7	81.4	101.9	124.5
供销公司	Supply and Marketing Corpor -ation General		107.8	191.1	97.1	116.7
中基公司	Chalkis Company					
兵团直属	Directly under XPCG		100.3	102.1	134.4	106.4

Note: Data prior to 2000 (including 2000) are calculated at comparable prices in 1990, data after 2000 are calculated at comparable prices in 2000, and data after 2005 are calculated at comparable pricesin 2005.

2—5 三次产业对生产总值的贡献份额
Contribution Quotient of Three Industries to Gross Domestic Product

指　　标	Item	贡献份额(%) Contribution Quotient (%)		拉动百分点 Newly-added Percentage	
		2009	2010	2009	2010
生产总值	**Gross Domestic Product**	**100.00**	**100.00**	**13.64**	**13.94**
第一产业	**Primary Industry**	**18.20**	**28.36**	**2.48**	**3.95**
第二产业	**Secondary Industry**	**55.60**	**50.20**	**7.58**	**7.00**
工　业	Industry	41.50	32.28	5.66	4.50
建筑业	Construction	14.10	17.92	1.92	2.50
第三产业	**Tertiary Industry**	**26.20**	**21.44**	**3.58**	**2.99**
# 交通运输仓储和邮政业	Transport, Storage and Postal Services	2.11	3.81	0.29	0.53
批发和零售业	Wholesale and Retail Trade	5.12	0.74	0.70	0.10

2—6 总产出
Total Output

计量单位：万元　　(10 000 yuan)

指　　标	Item	按当年价计算 Calculated at Current Prices		按2005年可比价计算 Calculated at Comparable Prices in 2005	
		2009	2010	2009	2010
总产出	**Total Output**	**15 951 890**	**20 477 032**	**13 623 193**	**16 136 372**
第一产业	**Primary Industry**	**4 340 155**	**5 692 849**	**3 684 951**	**4 044 139**
# 农林牧渔服务业	Farming, Forestry, Animal Husbandry and Fishery Services	291 610	335 513	257 932	292 784
第二产业	**Secondary Industry**	**7 561 326**	**10 029 990**	**6 385 938**	**8 089 969**
工　业	Industry	5 348 695	7 043 279	4 620 171	5 745 336
建筑业	Construction	2 212 631	2 986 711	1 765 767	2 344 633
第三产业	**Tertiary Industry**	**4 050 409**	**4 754 193**	**3 552 304**	**4 002 264**
交通运输、仓储和邮政业	Transport, Storage and Postal Services	491 292	599 415	426 408	520 003
信息传输、计算机服务和软件业	Information Deliver, Computer Service and Software	78 474	86 540	74 754	82 054
批发和零售业	Wholesale and Retail Trade	825 765	1 078 153	716 945	886 547
住宿和餐饮业	Accommodation and Catering Services Industry	259 120	319 309	216 113	234 156
金融业	Finance	837 182	770 187	704 256	644 118
房地产业	Real Estate Trade	196 197	242 116	163 725	192 205
租赁和商务服务业	Leasing and Business Service	43 149	76 740	40 917	70 341
科学研究、技术服务和地质勘查业	Scientific Research, Technical Service and Geological Prospecting	86 883	93 503	80 987	91 733
水利、环境和公共设施管理业	Water Conservancy, Environment and Public Facilities Management	87 294	132 366	78 522	106 265
居民服务和其他服务业	Resident and Other Services	202 241	233 688	189 952	208 627
教　育	Education	260 535	348 163	235 721	209 177
卫生、社会保障和社会福利业	Health Care, Social Security and Welfare	241 927	252 038	220 251	214 845
文化、体育和娱乐业	Culture, Sports and Recreation	34 354	41 193	36 568	38 014
公共管理和社会组织	Public Management and Social Organization	405 996	480 782	367 185	423 179

2—7 各师按产业分总产出

Total Output by Branch of Industry and by Division

计量单位:万元 (2010 年) (10 000 yuan)

单位	Unit	合计 Total	第一产业 Primary Industry	# 农林牧渔服务业 Farming, Forestry, Animal Husbandry and Fishery Services	第二产业 Secondary Industry	工业 Industry
总计	**Total**	**20 477 032**	**5 692 849**	**335 513**	**10 029 990**	**7 043 279**
一师	Division 1	2 660 363	1 130 858	53 180	1 099 616	783 341
二师	Division 2	1 237 862	438 019	23 626	555 160	399 137
三师	Division 3	864 172	472 957	40 435	223 890	120 939
四师	Division 4	1 214 583	389 384	22 600	622 459	494 543
五师	Division 5	692 654	283 570	11 089	228 289	166 306
六师	Division 6	2 595 641	668 840	50 160	1 319 414	906 187
七师	Division 7	1 596 604	550 830	30 753	743 875	476 109
八师	Division 8	4 984 123	1 100 988	51 380	2 816 121	2 397 935
九师	Division 9	324 309	136 031	5 396	113 182	69 780
十师	Division 10	494 714	174 967	15 108	199 491	129 137
建工师	Construction Division	914 645	425		875 371	53 590
十二师	Division 12	809 155	102 182	2 644	419 882	363 457
十三师	Division 13	552 376	161 749	17 769	279 278	190 981
十四师	Division 14	111 293	49 262	1 139	40 120	14 130
国资公司	State-owned Property Company	381 296	8 946	7 556	286 163	274 165
供销公司	Supply and Marketing Corpor-ation General	22 662				
中基公司	Chalkis Company	163 306			162 243	162 243
兵团直属	Directly under XPCG	857 274	23 841	2 678	45 436	41 299

单位	Unit	建筑业 Construction	第三产业 Tertiary Industry	# 交通运输仓储和邮政业 Transport, Storage and Postal Services	# 批发和零售业 Wholesale and Retail Trade	按2005年可比价计算 Calculated at Comparable Prices in 2005
总计	**Total**	**2 986 711**	**4 754 193**	**599 415**	**1 078 153**	**16 136 372**
一师	Division 1	316 275	429 889	72 143	94 560	2 007 800
二师	Division 2	156 023	244 683	28 362	64 241	983 265
三师	Division 3	102 951	167 325	15 292	34 378	662 685
四师	Division 4	127 916	202 740	42 883	51 726	977 268
五师	Division 5	61 983	180 795	11 359	71 564	505 093
六师	Division 6	413 227	607 387	86 097	158 877	2 010 510
七师	Division 7	267 766	301 899	57 177	88 332	1 289 182
八师	Division 8	418 186	1 067 014	201 657	104 893	4 004 053
九师	Division 9	43 402	75 096	10 183	15 075	234 701
十师	Division 10	70 354	120 256	18 264	48 810	385 672
建工师	Construction Division	821 781	38 849	1 983	1 496	721 994
十二师	Division 12	56 425	287 091	17 036	189 255	627 864
十三师	Division 13	88 297	111 349	14 392	25 392	429 878
十四师	Division 14	25 990	21 911	1 115	6 031	86 893
国资公司	State-owned Property Company	11 998	86 187	4 089	61 048	282 633
供销公司	Supply and Marketing Corpor-ation General		22 662	2 016	20 646	19 916
中基公司	Chalkis Company		1 063		740	142 268
兵团直属	Directly under XPCG	4 137	787 997	15 367	41 089	764 697

2—8 按要素分列的分行业生产总值

Gross Domestic Product by Factor and Sector

计量单位:万元 (2010 年) (10 000 yuan)

指　标	Item	合计(按当年价计算) Total (Calculated at Current Prices)	劳动者报酬 Compensation of Laborers	生产税净额 Net Taxes on Production
收入总值	**Gross National Income**	**7 665 121**	**4 261 010**	**649 081**
生产总值	**Gross Domestic Product**	**7 706 152**	**4 302 041**	**649 081**
第一产业	**Primary Industry**	**2 788 111**	**2 092 920**	**−8 240**
# 农林牧渔服务业	Farming,Forestry,Animal Husbandry and Fishery Services	147 216	87 148	1 353
第二产业	**Secondary Industry**	**2 622 637**	**1 091 151**	**380 932**
工　业	Industry	1 862 830	583 298	284 218
建筑业	Construction	759 807	507 853	96 714
第三产业	**Tertiary Industry**	**2 295 404**	**1 117 970**	**276 389**
交通运输、仓储和邮政业	Transport,Storage and Postal Service	229 614	67 549	27 233
信息传输、计算机服务和软件业	Information Deliver,Computer Service and Software	48 541	11 871	3 470
批发和零售业	Wholesale and Retail Trade	394 095	143 674	43 224
住宿和餐饮业	Accommodation and Catering Services Industry	130 049	46 368	15 435
金融业	Finance	337 180	118 951	110 766
房地产业	Real Estate Trade	178 742	17 616	29 448
租赁和社会服务业	Leasing and Business Service	24 953	11 409	3 605
科学研究、技术服务和地质勘查业	Scientific Research,Technical Service and Geological Prospecting	45 316	28 712	4 589
水利、环境和公共设施管理业	Water Conservancy,Environment and Public Facilities Management	60 241	33 867	5 168
居民服务和其他服务业	Resident and Other Services	95 948	42 096	9 514
教　育	Education	253 231	183 463	12 925
卫生、社会保障和社会福利业	Health Care,Social Security and Welfare	159 076	107 494	8 943
文化、体育和娱乐业	Culture,Sports and Recreation	23 337	14 427	1 783
公共管理和社会组织	Public Management and Social Organization	315 081	290 473	286
国(地区)外净要素收入	**the Net Factor Income from Abroad(Region)**	**−41 031**	**−41 031**	

指　标	Item	固定资产折旧 Depreciation of Fixed Assets	营业盈余 Operating Surplus	按2005年可比价计算 Calculated at Comparable Prices in 2005
收入总值	**Gross National Income**	**994 806**	**1 760 224**	**5 999 375**
生产总值	**Gross Domestic Product**	**994 806**	**1 760 224**	**6 025 403**
第一产业	**Primary Industry**	**192 969**	**510 462**	**1 986 104**
# 农林牧渔服务业	Farming,Forestry,Animal Husbandry and Fishery Services	30 788	27 927	128 144
第二产业	**Secondary Industry**	**453 259**	**697 295**	**2 119 104**
工　业	Industry	384 927	610 387	1 522 183
建筑业	Construction	68 332	86 908	596 921
第三产业	**Tertiary Industry**	**348 578**	**552 467**	**1 920 195**
交通运输、仓储和邮政业	Transport,Storage and Postal Service	39 618	95 214	198 324
信息传输、计算机服务和软件业	Information Deliver,Computer Service and Software	10 588	22 612	46 077
批发和零售业	Wholesale and Retail Trade	45 380	161 817	329 153
住宿和餐饮业	Accommodation and Catering Services Industry	20 673	47 573	94 138
金融业	Finance	21 255	86 208	281 669
房地产业	Real Estate Trade	88 274	43 404	141 123
租赁和社会服务业	Leasing and Business Service	5 952	3 987	22 390
科学研究、技术服务和地质勘查业	Scientific Research,Technical Service and Geological Prospecting	5 911	6 104	42 182
水利、环境和公共设施管理业	Water Conservancy,Environment and PublicFacilities Management	11 816	9 390	48 299
居民服务和其他服务业	Resident and Other Services	12 418	31 920	81 374
教　育	Education	34 938	21 905	214 892
卫生、社会保障和社会福利业	Health Care,Social Security and Welfare	26 902	15 737	133 956
文化、体育和娱乐业	Culture,Sports and Recreation	3 778	3 349	21 725
公共管理和社会组织	Public Management and Social Organization	21 075	3 247	264 893
国(地区)外净要素收入	**the Net Factor Income from Abroad(Region)**			**−26 028**

2—9 各师按要素分生产总值

Gross Domestic Product by Factor and Division

计量单位:万元 （2010 年） （10000 yuan）

单 位	Unit	合计(按当年价计算) Total (Calculated at Current Prices)	劳动者报酬 Compensation of Laborers	生产税净额 Net Taxes on Production	固定资产折旧 Depreciation of Fixed Assets	营业盈余 Operating Surplus	按2005年可比价计算 Calculated at Comparable Prices in 2005
总 计	**Total**	**7 706 152**	**4 302 041**	**649 081**	**994 806**	**1 760 224**	**6 025 403**
一 师	Division 1	1 043 212	626 103	44 686	118 546	253 877	785 948
二 师	Division 2	500 142	333 281	30 365	62 356	74 140	395 917
三 师	Division 3	386 345	257 791	12 321	34 941	81 292	297 814
四 师	Division 4	546 010	304 492	53 821	49 092	138 605	438 191
五 师	Division 5	276 030	185 084	10 522	27 482	52 942	201 519
六 师	Division 6	974 993	519 698	62 342	112 098	280 855	751 904
七 师	Division 7	645 039	342 560	30 811	75 975	195 693	518 070
八 师	Division 8	1 885 049	904 416	192 001	349 070	439 562	1 479 873
九 师	Division 9	139 690	97 335	5 803	13 929	22 623	102 704
十 师	Division 10	170 177	88 566	8 907	24 298	48 406	133 018
建 工 师	Construction Division	235 088	173 823	28 588	18 522	14 155	185 969
十 二 师	Division 12	232 005	109 661	28 379	16 099	77 866	175 364
十 三 师	Division 13	218 126	114 545	17 444	26 736	59 401	168 682
十 四 师	Division 14	47 938	32 323	2 988	3 350	9 277	37 200
国资公司	State-owned Property Company	91 264	38 288	14 021	18 297	20 658	70 935
供销公司	Supply and Marketing Corpor-ation General	5 714	6 903	−4 960	2 232	1 539	4 874
中基公司	Chalkis Company	−32 112	7 089	2 062	8 878	−50 141	−27 879
兵团直属	Directly under XPCG	341 442	160 083	108 980	32 905	39 474	305 300

2—10 各师生产总值要素构成

Composition of Key Factor of Gross Domestic Product by Division

（2010 年，生产总值＝100）

单 位	Unit	劳动者报酬 Compensation of Laborers	生产税净额 Net Taxes on Production	固定资产折旧 Depreciation of Fixed Assets	营业盈余 Operating Surplus
总 计	**Total**	**55.8**	**8.4**	**12.9**	**22.9**
一 师	Division 1	60.0	4.3	11.4	24.3
二 师	Division 2	66.6	6.1	12.5	14.8
三 师	Division 3	66.7	3.2	9.1	21.0
四 师	Division 4	55.8	9.8	9.0	25.4
五 师	Division 5	67.0	3.8	10.0	19.2
六 师	Division 6	53.3	6.4	11.5	28.8
七 师	Division 7	53.1	4.8	11.8	30.3
八 师	Division 8	48.0	10.2	18.5	23.3
九 师	Division 9	69.7	4.1	10.0	16.2
十 师	Division 10	52.0	5.2	14.3	28.5
建 工 师	Construction Division	73.9	12.2	7.9	6.0
十 二 师	Division 12	47.3	12.2	6.9	33.6
十 三 师	Division 13	52.5	8.0	12.3	27.2
十 四 师	Division 14	67.4	6.2	7.0	19.4
国资公司	State-owned Property Company	42.0	15.4	20.0	22.6
供销公司	Supply and Marketing Corpor-ation General				
中基公司	Chalkis Company				
兵团直属	Directly under XPCG	46.9	31.9	9.6	11.6

注:本表按当年价格计算。

Note: Data in value terms in this table are calculated at current prices.

2—11 各师第一产业增加值

Value-added of Primary Industry by Division

计量单位:万元　　　　(2010 年)　　　　(10 000 yuan)

单　位	Unit	合计(按当年价计算) Total (Calculated at Current Prices)	劳动者报酬 Compensation of Laborers	生产税净额 Net Taxes on Production	固定资产折旧 Depreciation of Fixed Assets	营业盈余 Operating Surplus	按2005年可比价计算 Calculated at Comparable Prices in 2005
总　计	**Total**	**2 788 111**	**2 092 920**	**−8 240**	**192 969**	**510 462**	**1 986 104**
一　师	Division 1	557 369	409 873	−240	44 127	103 609	388 779
二　师	Division 2	216 087	183 742	103	21 120	11 122	163 553
三　师	Division 3	220 536	150 235	221	13 724	56 356	159 876
四　师	Division 4	191 700	149 928	44	10 440	31 288	149 426
五　师	Division 5	145 464	119 598	91	7 704	18 071	96 902
六　师	Division 6	332 441	233 601	−200	25 589	73 451	236 012
七　师	Division 7	279 955	171 325	37	16 532	92 061	208 295
八　师	Division 8	552 742	463 745	−8 814	26 009	71 802	377 508
九　师	Division 9	65 504	57 517	10	4 326	3 651	44 371
十　师	Division 10	63 202	41 328	35	7 478	14 361	46 610
建工师	Construction Division	192	139	−14	17	50	111
十二师	Division 12	44 871	27 505	34	1 959	15 373	29 140
十三师	Division 13	81 256	57 353		9 470	14 433	60 080
十四师	Division 14	23 222	16 762	253	1 157	5 050	16 366
国资公司	State-owned Property Company	1 651	1 011	200	1 346	−906	1 349
供销公司	Supply and Marketing Corporation General						
中基公司	Chalkis Company						
兵团直属	Directly under XPCG	11 919	9 258		1 971	690	7 726

2—12 各师农林牧渔业增加值

Value-added of Farming, Forestry, Animal Husbandry and Fishery by Division

计量单位:万元　　　　(2010 年)　　　　(10 000 yuan)

单　位	Unit	合　计 Total	农　业 Farming	林　业 Forestry	牧　业 Animal Husbandry	渔　业 Fishery	农林牧渔服务业 Farming, Forestry, Animal Husbandry and Fishery Services
总　计	**Total**	**2 788 111**	**2 261 353**	**23 960**	**343 041**	**12 541**	**147 216**
一　师	Division 1	557 369	502 266	5 917	27 666	2 382	19 138
二　师	Division 2	216 087	171 699	1 696	32 233	974	9 485
三　师	Division 3	220 536	185 321	1 660	15 337	515	17 703
四　师	Division 4	191 700	126 419	1 860	50 840	1 696	10 885
五　师	Division 5	145 464	132 026	714	6 910	200	5 614
六　师	Division 6	332 441	246 760	2 444	55 256	965	27 016
七　师	Division 7	279 955	218 162	2 359	43 306	965	15 163
八　师	Division 8	552 742	470 384	4 274	54 695	1 862	21 527
九　师	Division 9	65 504	43 023	646	18 994	9	2 832
十　师	Division 10	63 202	45 472	1 045	9 748	1 741	5 196
建工师	Construction Division	192	192				
十二师	Division 12	44 871	30 898	356	11 723	1 036	858
十三师	Division 13	81 256	59 095	501	12 572	85	9 003
十四师	Division 14	23 222	19 166	454	3 072		530
国资公司	State-owned Property Company	1 651			115		1 536
供销公司	Supply and Marketing Corporation General						
中基公司	Chalkis Company						
兵团直属	Directly under XPCG	11 919	10 470	34	574	111	730

注:本表按当年价格计算。

Note: Data in value terms in this table are calculated at current prices.

2—13 各师农林牧渔业增加值率

Rate of Value-added to Output Value of Farming, Forestry, Animal Husbandry and Fishery by Division

计量单位：% (2010 年) (%)

单 位	Unit	合 计 Total	农 业 Farming	林 业 Forestry	牧 业 Animal Husbandry	渔 业 Fishery	农林牧渔服务业 Farming, Forestry, Animal Husbandry and Fishery Services
总 计	**Total**	**48.98**	**50.21**	**44.00**	**44.64**	**41.27**	**43.85**
一 师	Division 1	49.29	50.34	47.75	43.99	51.29	35.99
二 师	Division 2	49.33	50.30	47.77	48.52	31.63	40.15
三 师	Division 3	46.63	47.40	32.26	43.55	43.79	43.78
四 师	Division 4	49.23	49.93	48.46	48.01	43.84	48.16
五 师	Division 5	51.30	52.19	39.47	39.99	47.62	50.63
六 师	Division 6	49.70	50.73	48.41	44.16	46.22	53.86
七 师	Division 7	50.82	51.37	45.67	49.09	47.68	49.31
八 师	Division 8	50.20	51.98	47.55	41.73	40.67	41.90
九 师	Division 9	48.15	46.94	46.68	50.54	47.37	52.48
十 师	Division 10	36.12	38.86	26.88	29.63	28.79	34.39
建 工 师	Construction Division	45.18	45.18				
十 二 师	Division 12	43.91	44.45	54.52	42.70	54.16	32.45
十 三 师	Division 13	50.24	52.28	35.18	42.95	33.86	50.67
十 四 师	Division 14	47.14	47.25	42.27	47.34		46.53
国资公司	State-owned Property Company	18.46			8.27		20.33
供销公司	Supply and Marketing Corporation General						
中基公司	Chalkis Company						
兵团直属	Directly under XPCG	49.99	53.67	35.05	44.84	39.93	27.26

注：本表按当年价格计算。

Note: Data in value terms in this table are calculated at current prices.

2—14 各师第二产业增加值

Value-added of Secondary Industry by Division

计量单位：万元 (2010 年) (10 000 yuan)

单 位	Unit	合计(按当年价计算) Total (Calculated at Current Prices)	劳动者报酬 Compensation of Laborers	生产税净额 Net Taxes on Production	固定资产折旧 Depreciation of Fixed Assets	营业盈余 Operating Surplus	按 2005 年可比价计算 Calculated at Comparable Prices in 2005
总 计	**Total**	**2 622 637**	**1 091 151**	**380 932**	**453 259**	**697 295**	**2 119 104**
一 师	Division 1	288 659	107 820	34 485	46 285	100 069	230 252
二 师	Division 2	149 568	70 530	19 940	21 245	37 853	120 878
三 师	Division 3	61 681	29 236	6 536	9 201	16 708	48 952
四 师	Division 4	234 652	89 094	46 878	23 647	75 033	193 302
五 师	Division 5	56 082	24 867	6 399	10 731	14 085	46 198
六 师	Division 6	348 500	146 870	43 874	42 882	114 874	276 475
七 师	Division 7	211 055	111 667	20 859	37 186	41 343	174 123
八 师	Division 8	726 456	208 428	126 546	193 542	197 940	612 110
九 师	Division 9	30 491	13 974	4 048	4 382	8 087	21 563
十 师	Division 10	62 399	24 587	6 230	10 481	21 101	49 121
建 工 师	Construction Division	209 265	154 078	26 578	16 687	11 922	162 352
十 二 师	Division 12	125 424	40 844	17 026	7 617	59 937	97 106
十 三 师	Division 13	89 247	34 792	13 466	9 832	31 157	69 641
十 四 师	Division 14	10 655	6 803	1 192	603	2 057	9 016
国资公司	State-owned Property Company	41 509	17 480	4 998	9 313	9 718	28 965
供销公司	Supply and Marketing Corporation General						
中基公司	Chalkis Company	−28 903	6 546	1 765	8 588	−45 802	−25 176
兵团直属	Directly under XPCG	5 897	3 535	112	1 037	1 213	4 226

2—15 各师工业增加值

Value-added in Industry by Division

计量单位:万元　　(2010年)　　(10 000 yuan)

单位	Unit	合计(按当年价计算) Total (Calculated at Current Prices)	劳动者报酬 Compensation of Laborers	生产税净额 Net Taxes on Production	固定资产折旧 Depreciation of Fixed Assets	营业盈余 Operating Surplus	按2005年可比价计算 Calculated at Comparable Prices in 2005
总计	**Total**	**1 862 830**	**583 298**	**284 218**	**384 927**	**610 387**	**1 522 183**
一师	Division 1	220 861	61 433	27 213	42 165	90 050	175 860
二师	Division 2	107 473	37 242	14 971	19 702	35 558	87 506
三师	Division 3	37 093	12 432	2 984	8 312	13 365	29 688
四师	Division 4	197 087	61 786	43 722	23 007	68 572	163 438
五师	Division 5	39 771	14 842	4 194	8 532	12 203	33 419
六师	Division 6	245 282	77 824	29 960	42 201	95 297	195 608
七师	Division 7	136 288	49 958	15 592	33 397	37 341	115 547
八师	Division 8	601 445	169 489	102 904	157 384	171 668	514 169
九师	Division 9	18 871	5 694	2 013	4 016	7 148	12 459
十师	Division 10	48 100	13 967	5 428	9 895	18 810	37 919
建工师	Construction Division	10 706	5 668	1 805	875	2 358	7 088
十二师	Division 12	112 097	25 241	15 205	6 891	64 760	86 665
十三师	Division 13	68 595	20 329	11 629	9 268	27 369	53 478
十四师	Division 14	3 813	1 141	373	566	1 733	3 736
国资公司	State-owned Property Company	40 289	17 286	4 366	9 241	9 396	28 009
供销公司	Supply and Marketing Corporation General						
中基公司	Chalkis Company	−28 903	6 546	1 765	8 588	−45 802	−25 176
兵团直属	Directly under XPCG	3 962	2 420	94	887	561	2 770

2—16 各师建筑业增加值

Value-added in Construction by Division

计量单位:万元　　(2010年)　　(10 000 yuan)

单位	Unit	合计(按当年价计算) Total (Calculated at Current Prices)	劳动者报酬 Compensation of Laborers	生产税净额 Net Taxes on Production	固定资产折旧 Depreciation of Fixed Assets	营业盈余 Operating Surplus	按2005年可比价计算 Calculated at Comparable Prices in 2005
总计	**Total**	**759 807**	**507 853**	**96 714**	**68 332**	**86 908**	**596 921**
一师	Division 1	67 798	46 387	7 272	4 120	10 019	54 392
二师	Division 2	42 095	33 288	4 969	1 543	2 295	33 372
三师	Division 3	24 588	16 804	3 552	889	3 343	19 264
四师	Division 4	37 565	27 308	3 156	640	6 461	29 864
五师	Division 5	16 311	10 025	2 205	2 199	1 882	12 779
六师	Division 6	103 218	69 046	13 914	681	19 577	80 867
七师	Division 7	74 767	61 709	5 267	3 789	4 002	58 576
八师	Division 8	125 011	38 939	23 642	36 158	26 272	97 941
九师	Division 9	11 620	8 280	2 035	366	939	9 104
十师	Division 10	14 299	10 620	802	586	2 291	11 202
建工师	Construction Division	198 559	148 410	24 773	15 812	9 564	155 264
十二师	Division 12	13 327	15 603	1 821	726	−4 823	10 441
十三师	Division 13	20 652	14 463	1 837	564	3 788	16 163
十四师	Division 14	6 842	5 662	819	37	324	5 280
国资公司	State-owned Property Company	1 220	194	632	72	322	956
供销公司	Supply and Marketing Corporation General						
中基公司	Chalkis Company						
兵团直属	Directly under XPCG	1 935	1 115	18	150	652	1 456

2—17 各师第三产业增加值

Value-added of Tertiary Industry by Division

计量单位:万元　　　　(2010 年)　　　　(10 000 yuan)

单位	Unit	合计(按当年价计算) Total (Calculated at Current Prices)	劳动者报酬 Compensation of Laborers	生产税净额 Net Taxes on Production	固定资产折旧 Depreciation of Fixed Assets	营业盈余 Operating Surplus	按2005年可比价计算 Calculated at Comparable Prices in 2005
总　计	**Total**	**2 295 404**	**1 117 970**	**276 389**	**348 578**	**552 467**	**1 920 195**
一　师	Division 1	197 184	108 410	10 441	28 134	50 199	166 917
二　师	Division 2	134 487	79 009	10 322	19 991	25 165	111 486
三　师	Division 3	104 128	78 320	5 564	12 016	8 228	88 986
四　师	Division 4	119 658	65 470	6 899	15 005	32 284	95 463
五　师	Division 5	74 484	40 619	4 032	9 047	20 786	58 419
六　师	Division 6	294 052	139 227	18 668	43 627	92 530	239 417
七　师	Division 7	154 029	59 568	9 915	22 257	62 289	135 652
八　师	Division 8	605 851	232 243	74 269	129 519	169 820	490 255
九　师	Division 9	43 695	25 844	1 745	5 221	10 885	36 770
十　师	Division 10	44 576	22 651	2 642	6 339	12 944	37 287
建工师	Construction Division	25 631	19 606	2 024	1 818	2 183	23 506
十二师	Division 12	61 710	41 312	11 319	6 523	2 556	49 118
十三师	Division 13	47 623	22 400	3 978	7 434	13 811	38 961
十四师	Division 14	14 061	8 758	1 543	1 590	2 170	11 818
国资公司	State-owned Property Company	48 104	19 797	8 823	7 638	11 846	40 621
供销公司	Supply and Marketing Corpor -ation General	5 714	6 903	−4 960	2 232	1 539	4 874
中基公司	Chalkis Company	−3 209	543	297	290	−4 339	−2 703
兵团直属	Directly under XPCG	323 626	147 290	108 868	29 897	37 571	293 348

2—18 各师交通运输、仓储和邮政业增加值

Value-added in Transport, Storage and Post Services by Division

计量单位:万元　　　　(2010 年)　　　　(10 000 yuan)

单位	Unit	合计(按当年价计算) Total (Calculated at Current Prices)	劳动者报酬 Compensation of Laborers	生产税净额 Net Taxes on Production	固定资产折旧 Depreciation of Fixed Assets	营业盈余 Operating Surplus	按2005年可比价计算 Calculated at Comparable Prices in 2005
总　计	**Total**	**229 614**	**67 549**	**27 233**	**39 618**	**95 214**	**198 324**
一　师	Division 1	13 426	3 180	2 360	2 587	5 299	11 597
二　师	Division 2	12 410	2 419	1 664	2 101	6 226	10 719
三　师	Division 3	6 595	4 905	622	468	600	5 697
四　师	Division 4	18 823	3 658	1 484	1 882	11 799	16 258
五　师	Division 5	6 128	576	852	911	3 789	5 293
六　师	Division 6	39 577	11 643	4 523	8 182	15 229	34 186
七　师	Division 7	29 765	1 644	2 365	3 691	22 065	25 708
八　师	Division 8	74 599	28 918	11 125	16 277	18 279	64 432
九　师	Division 9	3 826	615	534	367	2 310	3 304
十　师	Division 10	7 807	507	900	738	5 662	6 743
建工师	Construction Division	505	346	26	10	123	436
十二师	Division 12	8 246	6 545	1 151	829	−279	7 122
十三师	Division 13	5 471	815	647	571	3 438	4 725
十四师	Division 14	532	48	101	51	332	460
国资公司	State-owned Property Company	431	1 255	−1 239	655	−240	372
供销公司	Supply and Marketing Corpor -ation General	1 142	310	77	173	582	986
中基公司	Zhongji Company						
兵团直属	Directly under XPCG	331	165	41	125		286

2—19 各师批发和零售业增加值

Value-added in Wholesale and Retail Trade by Division

计量单位:万元 (2010年) (10 000 yuan)

单 位	Unit	合计(按当年价计算) Total (Calculated at Current Prices)	劳动者报酬 Compensation of Laborers	生产税净额 Net Taxes on Production	固定资产折旧 Depreciation of Fixed Assets	营业盈余 Operating Surplus	按2005年可比价计算 Calculated at Comparable Prices in 2005
总 计	**Total**	**394 095**	**143 674**	**43 224**	**45 380**	**161 817**	**329 153**
一 师	Division 1	37 209	4 513	3 377	2 046	27 273	30 769
二 师	Division 2	27 396	9 216	5 737	1 470	10 973	23 051
三 师	Division 3	20 976	11 150	3 123	1 889	4 814	17 125
四 师	Division 4	30 272	11 828	3 789	1 922	12 733	23 408
五 师	Division 5	11 397	2 902	335	601	7 559	9 322
六 师	Division 6	75 566	34 848	3 745	8 910	28 063	62 934
七 师	Division 7	36 864	5 135	3 501	5 407	22 821	34 511
八 师	Division 8	51 302	15 838	5 571	12 166	17 727	41 141
九 师	Division 9	8 563	1 572	394	418	6 179	7 067
十 师	Division 10	7 793	1 747	1 318	550	4 178	6 319
建工师	Construction Division	1 054	523	238	97	196	896
十二师	Division 12	16 205	14 876	3 547	646	−2 864	13 782
十三师	Division 13	8 094	2 897	956	509	3 732	6 688
十四师	Division 14	3 339	802	1 068	356	1 113	2 758
国资公司	State-owned Property Company	42 840	15 026	8 672	4 685	14 457	36 434
供销公司	Supply and Marketing Corpor -ation General	4 572	6 593	−5 037	2 059	957	3 888
中基公司	Chalkis Company	−3 441	442	228	269	−4 380	−2 927
兵团直属	Directly under XPCG	14 094	3 766	2 662	1 380	6 286	11 987

2—20 各师人均生产总值

Per Capita Gross Domestic Product by Division

计量单位:元 (yuan)

单 位	Unit	1980	1985	1990	1995	2000	2005	2009	2010
总 计	**Total**	**464**	**900**	**2 134**	**5 390**	**7 276**	**12 900**	**23 734**	**29 948**
一 师	Division 1	357	978	3 016	7 898	8 415	13 937	26 942	35 701
二 师	Division 2	566	971	2 454	5 667	7 145	12 063	21 246	25 938
三 师	Division 3	269	669	1 381	4 319	4 778	8 783	14 367	18 821
四 师	Division 4	421	750	1 833	4 880	6 873	10 630	20 172	24 756
五 师	Division 5	350	793	2 350	4 940	6 985	10 906	18 049	24 753
六 师	Division 6	376	957	1 732	4 691	6 272	11 516	24 080	31 462
七 师	Division 7	507	830	2 259	5 250	8 112	14 006	23 081	29 779
八 师	Division 8	577	932	2 319	5 219	8 011	12 246	24 449	32 263
九 师	Division 9	600	822	1 500	3 187	6 143	10 588	16 176	19 560
十 师	Division 10	427	735	1 663	3 307	4 745	10 679	18 562	22 698
建工师	Construction Division	467	1 004	1 684	4 283	8 295	23 443	41 472	49 206
十二师	Division 12	344	861	1 514	4 176	5 936	11 256	26 145	31 363
十三师	Division 13	155	459	1 030	2 797	5 806	10 387	21 470	27 313
十四师	Division 14		1 079	2 148	6 041	3 560	6 524	10 501	12 795
国资公司	State-owned Property Company						67 399	54 045	67 938
供销公司	Supply and Marketing Corpor -ation General							26 074	31 344
中基公司	Chalkis Company						205 952	277 863	−448 805
兵团直属	Directly under XPCG			2 165	10 798		44 247	80 655	88 522

注:本表按当年价格计算。

Note: Data in value terms in this table are calculated at current prices.

2011

BING TUAN

第三篇

人　口

Chapter 3 Population

简要说明

一、本篇资料主要内容

本篇资料反映兵团2010年及历年人口基本情况，包括兵团各师及兵团国资公司、供销公司、中基公司和兵直单位主要人口数据。如：总人口、人口出生率、死亡率、自然增长率、分民族人口数、分师按性别、职业分组的年末人口数；各师人口变动情况、各师分民族人口数，按县市、按师分列的农牧团场户数及人口数，以及各师计划生育情况。

二、本篇资料来源

本篇人口资料由兵团统计局社会科技贸易统计处根据《兵团劳动和人口统计报表制度》收集、汇总、整理提供。计划生育情况由兵团人口和计划生育委员会汇总、整理提供。

Brief Introduction

1. Main Contents

This chapter reflects the basic conditions of population of XPCG in 2009 and over past years, including main population of divisions, State-owned Property Corporation, Supply and Marketing Corporation General, Chalkis Corporation and units directly under XPCG population, such as birth rate, death rate, natural growth rate, population by nationalities, year-end population on sex, occupation by Division, population changes by division and population on nationality by division, households and population on farm by county and city and division, and family planning by division.

2. Sources of Data

Data on population are prepared by the Society Science Trade Statistical Section of the Statistics Bureau of XPCG according to <The Reporting Form System on Labor and Population of XPCG>. Data on Family Planning are provided by Family Planning Commission of XPCG.

3—1 年末人口数及构成

Population and Its Composition at the Year-end

年份 Year	年末人口数(人) Total Population atthe Year-end (person)			占总人口比重(%) Percentage to Total Population(%)		性别比(女=100) Sex Ratio (Female=100)
		男 Male	女 Female	男 Male	女 Female	
1952	273 279	206 666	66 613	75.6	24.4	310.2
1954	175 451	132 684	42 767	75.6	24.4	310.2
1957	311 470	231 874	79 596	74.4	25.6	291.3
1962	862 124	537 138	324 986	62.3	37.7	165.3
1965	1 293 151	741 413	551 738	57.3	42.7	134.4
1970	1 943 157	1 045 486	897 671	53.8	46.2	116.5
1975	1 771 097	921 502	849 595	52.0	48.0	108.5
1978	2 119 835	1 090 674	1 029 161	51.5	48.5	106.0
1980	2 200 755	1 127 050	1 073 705	51.2	48.8	105.0
1985	2 222 350	1 142 630	1 079 720	51.4	48.6	105.8
1990	2 143 528	1 110 475	1 033 053	51.8	48.2	107.5
1995	2 287 896	1 194 166	1 093 730	52.2	47.8	109.2
2000	2 427 920	1 272 719	1 155 201	52.4	47.6	110.2
2001	2 453 575	1 289 954	1 163 621	52.6	47.4	110.9
2002	2 501 189	1 311 750	1 189 439	52.4	47.6	110.3
2003	2 542 170	1 330 666	1 211 504	52.3	47.7	109.8
2004	2 563 837	1 341 213	1 222 624	52.3	47.7	109.7
2005	2 569 756	1 346 901	1 222 855	52.4	47.6	110.1
2006	2 579 435	1 352 541	1 226 894	52.4	47.6	110.2
2007	2 584 732	1 353 053	1 231 679	52.3	47.7	109.9
2008	2 573 077	1 344 445	1 228 632	52.3	47.7	109.4
2009	2 573 145	1 346 229	1 226 916	52.3	47.7	109.7
2010	2 573 203	1 351 079	1 222 124	52.5	47.5	110.6

3—2 各师按性别、职业分年末人口数

Population at the Year-end by Sex and Ocuppation and by Division

计量单位:人 (2010 年) (person)

单位	Unit	年末人口数 Total Population at the year-end	男 Male	女 Female	按农业非农业人口分 by Agriculture and Non-Agriculture: 农业人口 Agricultural Population	非农业人口 Non-Agricultural Population
总计	**Total**	**2 573 203**	**1 351 079**	**1 222 124**	**1 252 049**	**1 321 154**
一师	Division 1	292 305	156 974	135 331	146 992	145 313
二师	Division 2	191 003	102 327	88 676	92 386	98 617
三师	Division 3	206 072	112 373	93 699	152 516	53 556
四师	Division 4	220 366	112 915	107 451	125 797	94 569
五师	Division 5	111 406	57 810	53 596	60 277	51 129
六师	Division 6	310 716	163 758	146 958	161 403	149 313
七师	Division 7	217 186	113 049	104 137	78 013	139 173
八师	Division 8	581 248	296 436	284 812	244 758	336 490
九师	Division 9	70 817	36 574	34 243	33 204	37 613
十师	Division 10	74 809	39 402	35 407	26 097	48 712
建工师	Construction Division	49 926	29 661	20 265	88	49 838
十二师	Division 12	75 048	38 436	36 612	35 839	39 209
十三师	Division 13	80 290	43 065	37 225	52 212	28 078
十四师	Division 14	38 278	20 288	17 990	31 219	7 059
国资公司	State-owned Property Company	12 826	7 387	5 439		12 826
供销公司	Supply and Marketing Corporation General	1 672	928	744		1 672
中基公司	Chalkis Company	435	258	177		435
兵团直属	Directly under XPCG	38 800	19 438	19 362	11 248	27 552

3—3 人口出生率、死亡率、自然增长率

Birth Rate, Death Rate and Natural Growth Rate of Population

年份 Year	单位 Unit	出生数(人) Birth Population (person)	死亡数(人) Death Population (person)	出生率(‰) Birth Rate (‰)	死亡率(‰) Death Rate (‰)	自然增长率(‰) Natural Growth Rate(‰)
	1953	2 383	656	15.85	4.36	11.49
	1954	4 782	647	29.36	3.97	25.39
	1957	10 878	993	35.68	3.26	32.42
	1962	29 828	2 985	34.47	3.45	31.02
	1965	65 497	6 182	53.92	5.09	48.83
	1970	92 399	8 808	49.65	4.73	44.92
	1975	49 466	6 535	24.55	3.24	21.31
	1978	32 749	6 203	16.56	3.14	13.42
	1980	26 972	7 162	12.27	3.26	9.01
	1985	16 893	7 977	7.55	3.57	3.98
	1990	24 589	9 305	11.48	4.35	7.13
	1991	21 840	8 291	10.13	3.85	6.28
	1992	21 329	9 014	9.81	4.14	5.67
	1993	21 721	9 385	9.90	4.30	5.60
	1994	22 747	10 249	10.30	4.60	5.70
	1995	22 519	10 044	9.98	4.45	5.53
	1996	21 965	10 093	9.49	4.36	5.13
	1997	20 877	9 721	8.83	4.11	4.72
	1998	20 919	10 480	8.70	4.40	4.30
	1999	20 565	9 716	8.50	4.00	4.50
	2000	22 674	12 525	9.40	5.20	4.20
	2001	19 061	9 014	7.80	3.70	4.10
	2002	18 179	9 842	7.37	3.99	3.38
	2003	17 218	9 914	6.84	3.94	2.90
	2004	15 860	9 864	6.21	3.86	2.35
	2005	16 381	11 934	6.38	4.65	1.73
	2006	14 687	11 859	5.71	4.61	1.10
	2007	13 289	10 131	5.15	3.92	1.23
	2008	14 612	11 183	5.67	4.34	1.33
	2009	14 447	11 285	5.61	4.39	1.22
	2010	14 773	13 158	5.74	5.11	0.63
一　师	Division 1	1 555	992	5.32	3.39	1.93
二　师	Division 2	691	994	3.58	5.16	−1.57
三　师	Division 3	1 994	521	9.71	2.54	7.18
四　师	Division 4	1 374	1 027	6.23	4.66	1.57
五　师	Division 5	713	418	6.39	3.75	2.65
六　师	Division 6	2 019	1 770	6.52	5.71	0.80
七　师	Division 7	952	1 108	4.40	5.12	−0.72
八　师	Division 8	3 007	4 601	5.15	7.87	−2.73
九　师	Division 9	273	290	3.82	4.06	−0.24
十　师	Division 10	323	225	4.31	3.00	1.31
建工师	Construction Division	155	158	3.24	3.31	−0.06
十二师	Division 12	389	284	5.26	3.84	1.42
十三师	Division 13	582	403	7.29	5.05	2.24
十四师	Division 14	584	190	15.59	5.07	10.52
国资公司	State-owned Property Company	29	29	2.16	2.16	
供销公司	Supplyand Marketing Corporation General	4	5	2.40	2.99	−0.60
中基公司	Chalkis Company	4		5.59		5.59
兵团直属	Directly Under XPCG	125	143	3.23	3.69	−0.46

3－4 分民族人口数

Population by Nationality

计量单位:人 (person)

年 份 Year	单 位 Unit	年末人口数 Total Population at the year-end	汉 族 Han	维吾尔族 Uygur	哈萨克族 Kazak	回 族 Hui	蒙古族 Mongolian	其他民族 Others
1952		273 279						
1954		175 451	169 076	3 017	1 072	2 054	35	197
1957		311 470	295 759	6 132	4 525	4 429	125	500
1962		862 124	820 887	12 649	9 840	15 793	1 047	1 908
1965		1 293 151	1 229 105	19 652	16 884	22 011	2 407	3 092
1970		1 943 157	1 833 174	43 527	23 512	32 062	3 303	7 579
1975		1 771 097	1 624 096	67 479	20 545	33 828	3 011	22 138
1978		2 119 835	1 906 546	115 325	29 439	50 723	2 591	15 211
1980		2 200 755	1 985 191	124 422	31 199	52 645	4 485	2 813
1985		2 222 350	1 993 968	128 577	33 885	53 423	5 047	7 450
1990		2 143 528	1 897 473	138 856	35 921	55 521	5 812	9 945
1991		2 168 428	1 918 075	141 251	36 299	56 518	5 785	10 500
1992		2 181 926	1 927 650	143 365	36 858	56 953	5 901	11 199
1993		2 197 596	1 938 805	145 307	37 439	57 433	6 123	12 489
1994		2 223 957	1 963 330	146 008	37 863	57 569	6 284	12 903
1995		2 287 896	2 022 108	148 692	38 792	58 152	6 361	13 791
1996		2 343 308	2 076 765	148 510	38 710	58 897	6 150	14 276
1997		2 383 983	2 114 412	150 875	39 208	58 824	6 193	14 471
1998		2 407 148	2 132 512	153 918	40 141	59 266	6 130	15 181
1999		2 420 902	2 142 989	155 866	40 305	59 846	6 100	15 796
2000		2 427 920	2 143 676	157 511	40 713	62 175	5 941	17 904
2001		2 453 575	2 166 942	158 605	41 090	62 934	5 992	18 012
2002		2 501 189	2 204 494	164 962	42 702	64 705	6 172	18 154
2003		2 542 170	2 243 096	165 713	42 317	64 985	6 313	19 746
2004		2 563 837	2 256 983	174 198	42 359	65 645	6 425	18 227
2005		2 569 756	2 257 260	178 730	43 102	65 234	6 498	18 932
2006		2 579 435	2 264 260	181 859	43 169	65 458	6 465	18 224
2007		2 584 732	2 266 091	183 462	43 775	66 345	6 452	18 607
2008		2 573 077	2 247 742	188 953	44 437	66 673	6 473	18 799
2009		2 573 145	2 242 176	191 675	45 629	68 232	6 467	18 966
2010		2 573 203	2 234 309	197 525	45 663	69 073	6 583	20 050
一 师	Division1	292 305	266 051	20 690	390	2 132	155	2 887
二 师	Division2	191 003	183 965	3 527	6	1 228	562	1 715
三 师	Division3	206 072	95 636	108 464	10	713	55	1 194
四 师	Division4	220 366	177 584	10 565	21 406	6 917	2 326	1 568
五 师	Division5	111 406	98 134	4 158	3 142	4 128	1 005	839
六 师	Division6	310 716	284 205	1 377	6 572	15 356	692	2 514
七 师	Division7	217 186	210 165	174	684	4 636	488	1 039
八 师	Division8	581 248	550 665	6 269	3 321	14 680	696	5 617
九 师	Division9	70 817	66 846	93	2 492	874	223	289
十 师	Division10	74 809	72 717	107	434	1 102	80	369
建 工 师	Construction Division	49 926	48 510	472	26	489	66	363
十 二 师	Division12	75 048	54 182	3 140	2 929	14 165	91	541
十 三 师	Division13	80 290	63 419	10 472	3 743	1 913	70	673
十 四 师	Division14	38 278	12 063	26 120	2	71	1	21
国资公司	State-owned Property Company	12 826	12 332	333	11	108	12	30
供销公司	Supply and Marketing Corporation General	1 672	1 621	26		16	3	6
中基公司	Chalkis Company	435	416		1	13	1	4
兵团直属	Directly Under XPCG	38 800	35 798	1 538	494	532	57	381

3－5　各师计划生育情况

Family Planning by Division

（2010 年）

单　位	Unit	政策符合率(%) Match the Policy Rate (%) 汉族 Han	少数民族 Minority Nationalities	综合避孕率(%) Synthesize Cotrolled Birth Rate(%) 汉族 Han	少数民族 Minority Nationalities	独生子女领证率(%) Acceptance Rate of One-child Certificate(%) 汉族 Han	少数民族 Minority Nationalities
总　计	**Total**	**99.88**	**99.66**	**93.16**	**89.25**	**42.72**	**30.86**
一　师	Division 1	99.90	100.00	93.35	79.40	24.72	19.46
二　师	Division 2	100.00	100.00	93.45	93.40	32.45	50.96
三　师	Division 3	100.00	100.00	95.17	90.26	31.34	19.01
四　师	Division 4	100.00	100.00	94.16	88.48	37.51	32.70
五　师	Division 5	100.00	100.00	91.61	88.11	42.81	49.78
六　师	Division 6	99.76	98.18	92.00	92.63	45.72	40.33
七　师	Division 7	100.00	100.00	93.49	92.48	32.88	39.49
八　师	Division 8	99.73	98.16	92.81	89.53	60.42	51.14
九　师	Division 9	100.00	100.00	92.37	89.72	43.32	45.13
十　师	Division 10	100.00	100.00	93.05	89.51	38.10	45.07
建工师	Construction Division	100.00	100.00	94.95	91.33	77.87	84.39
十二师	Division 12	100.00	100.00	95.94	95.29	23.06	39.40
十三师	Division 13	100.00	100.00	95.89	92.18	34.08	40.14
十四师	Division 14	100.00	99.45	97.29	84.16	14.39	7.27
兵团直属	Directly under XPCG	100.00	100.00	84.61	91.67	47.91	35.07

单　位	Unit	已婚育龄妇女人数(人) Number of Women of Childbearing Age (person) 汉族 Han	少数民族 Minority Nationalities	采取节育措施人数(人) Number of Women Adopting Birth Control (person) 汉族 Han	少数民族 Minority Nationalities	独生子女领证人数(人) Acceptance Number of One-child Certificate (person) 汉族 Han	少数民族 Minority Nationalities
总　计	**Total**	**451 455**	**71 100**	**420 567**	**63 454**	**192 884**	**21 943**
一　师	Division 1	55 361	5 664	51 681	4 497	13 688	1 102
二　师	Division 2	36 881	1 880	34 466	1 756	11 967	958
三　师	Division 3	18 295	21 468	17 412	19 377	5 733	4 080
四　师	Division 4	34 111	8 983	32 119	7 948	12 794	2 937
五　师	Division 5	22 656	3 407	20 756	3 002	9 700	1 696
六　师	Division 6	53 999	5 430	49 679	5 030	24 689	2 190
七　师	Division 7	35 733	1 489	33 406	1 377	11 750	588
八　师	Division 8	122 742	7 898	113 922	7 071	74 156	4 039
九　师	Division 9	13 930	749	12 867	672	6 034	338
十　师	Division 10	17 095	639	15 907	572	6 514	288
建工师	Construction Division	7 144	173	6 783	158	5 563	146
十二师	Division 12	11 880	4 391	11 398	4 184	2 740	1 730
十三师	Division 13	13 391	3 413	12 841	3 146	4 563	1 370
十四师	Division 14	2 843	5 228	2 766	4 400	409	380
兵团直属	Directly under XPCG	5 394	288	4 564	264	2 584	101

2011

BING TUAN

第四篇

就业人员和职工工资

Chapter 4 Employment and Wages

简要说明

一、本篇资料主要内容

本篇资料反映兵团劳动经济方面的基本情况，包括各师及兵团国资公司、供销公司、中基公司、兵直单位主要劳动统计数据。如全社会就业人员数、在岗职工人数、在岗职工工资总额、平均工资等主要指标。

二、本篇统计范围

《兵团劳动和人口统计报表制度》调查范围为兵团范围内全部法人单位，包括国有单位、集体单位、其他各种经济类型单位。全社会就业人员统计范围为全兵团范围单位就业人员、个体劳动者及有劳动能力并从事各项劳动的人员。

三、本篇资料来源

本篇资料就业及工资情况由兵团统计局社会科技贸易统计处根据《兵团劳动和人口统计报表制度》汇总整理。兵团及各师社会救济情况由兵团民政局整理提供。

四、本篇调查方法

调查方法为全面调查。

Brief Introduction

1. Main Contents

Data in this chapter reflect the basic conditions of labor and Population of XPCG, including main labor statistical data of divisions, State-owned Property Corporation, Supply and Marketing Corporation General, Chalkis Corporation and units directly under XPCG, such as main indicators of number of employment, staff and workers on the job, total wages, average wage of staff and workers on the job.

2. Scope of Statistics

The Reporting Form System on Labor and Population of XPCG covers whole corporate units in XPCG, including State-owned units, collective-owned units and units of other ownership. Employment in the whole society covers number of employment, individual laborers and persons with labor capability and engaging in various labor.

3. Source of Data

Data in this chapter on employment and wages are prepared by the Society, Science and Trade Statistical Section of Statistics Bureau of XPCG according to The Reporting Form System on Labor. Social relief from XPCG and divisions are provided by the Bureau of Civil Affairs.

4. Methodology of Survey

It is a comprehensive survey.

4－1 按三次产业分全社会就业人员年末人数及构成

Number of Employed Persons and Composition of All Society at the Year-end by Type of Industry

年 份 Year	单 位 unit	年末就业人数(人) Total Number of Employed Persons at the Year-end (person)				构 成(%) Composition(%)		
			第一产业 Primary Industry	第二产业 Secondary Industry	第三产业 Tertiary Industry	第一产业 Primary Industry	第二产业 Secondary Industry	第三产业 Tertiary Industry
	1952	212 580	114 751	92 705	5 124	54.0	43.6	2.4
	1954	133 283	58 732	68 888	5 663	44.1	51.7	4.2
	1957	238 171	93 457	133 523	11 191	39.2	56.1	4.7
	1962	497 967	316 169	139 003	42 795	63.5	27.9	8.6
	1965	688 188	387 804	220 077	80 307	56.4	32.0	11.6
	1970	908 867	536 889	272 912	99 066	59.1	30.0	10.9
	1975	761 036	578 929	114 530	67 577	76.1	15.0	8.9
	1978	918 448	638 736	186 453	93 259	69.5	20.3	10.2
	1980	929 995	611 007	210 179	108 809	65.7	22.6	11.7
	1985	1 034 301	581 277	293 741	159 283	56.2	28.4	15.4
	1990	1 063 031	548 583	319 978	194 470	51.6	30.1	18.3
	1991	1 096 583	558 990	331 832	205 761	51.0	30.3	18.7
	1992	1 117 744	558 844	340 239	218 661	50.0	30.4	19.6
	1993	1 063 880	507 868	332 617	223 395	47.7	31.3	21.0
	1994	1 067 687	509 778	318 060	239 849	47.7	29.8	22.5
	1995	1 065 463	502 644	315 050	247 769	47.2	29.6	23.2
	1996	1 072 638	506 564	304 572	261 502	47.2	28.4	24.4
	1997	1 052 372	500 792	297 191	254 389	47.6	28.2	24.2
	1998	985 202	496 307	250 367	238 528	50.4	25.4	24.2
	1999	964 016	467 233	233 980	262 803	48.5	24.3	27.2
	2000	925 796	438 192	213 997	273 607	47.3	23.1	29.6
	2001	933 073	438 757	212 441	281 875	47.0	22.8	30.2
	2002	955 062	451 909	208 988	294 165	47.3	21.9	30.8
	2003	975 457	493 197	192 899	289 361	50.6	19.8	29.6
	2004	975 937	492 508	182 482	300 947	50.5	18.7	30.8
	2005	988 064	483 903	192 495	311 666	49.0	19.5	31.5
	2006	987 509	487 023	183 790	316 696	49.3	18.6	32.1
	2007	995 146	489 686	190 711	314 749	49.2	19.2	31.6
	2008	1 023 976	480 905	189 448	353 623	47.0	18.5	34.5
	2009	1 035 654	483 710	196 577	355 367	46.7	19.0	34.3
	2010	1 061 763	486 324	209 819	365 620	45.8	19.8	34.4
一 师	Division 1	115 170	66 728	16 151	32 291	58.0	14.0	28.0
二 师	Division 2	71 596	37 639	9 366	24 591	52.6	13.1	34.3
三 师	Division 3	82 962	55 529	9 009	18 424	66.9	10.9	22.2
四 师	Division 4	97 164	55 582	18 253	23 329	57.2	18.8	24.0
五 师	Division 5	45 711	26 020	5 976	13 715	56.9	13.1	30.0
六 师	Division 6	113 769	55 850	19 438	38 481	49.1	17.1	33.8
七 师	Division 7	76 853	35 410	12 869	28 574	46.1	16.7	37.2
八 师	Division 8	272 933	80 931	73 268	118 734	29.7	26.8	43.5
九 师	Division 9	32 245	19 378	2 449	10 418	60.1	7.6	32.3
十 师	Division 10	27 800	11 544	5 122	11 134	41.5	18.4	40.1
建 工 师	Construction Division	25 596	71	19 121	6 404	0.3	74.7	25.0
十 二 师	Division 12	27 320	11 532	6 082	9 706	42.2	22.3	35.5
十 三 师	Division 13	34 246	17 627	6 364	10 255	51.5	18.6	29.9
十 四 师	Division 14	13 958	9 483	1 066	3 409	67.9	7.6	24.4
国资公司	Stat-owned Property Company	7 445	334	2 923	4 188	4.5	39.3	56.3
供销公司	Supply and Mar keting Corporation General	1 129			1 129			100.0
中基公司	Chalkis Company	2 133	4	2 038	91	0.2	95.5	4.3
兵团直属	Direct Under XPCG	13 733	2 662	324	10 747	19.4	2.4	78.3

4—2 按从事职业分全社会就业人员年末人数

计量单位：人 （2010年）

指　标	Item	年末就业人数 Total Employed Persons at the Year-end
总　计	**Total**	**1 061 763**
第一产业	**Primary Industry**	**486 324**
农　业	Planting	410 744
林　业	Forestry	8 343
畜牧业	Animal Husbandry	32 872
渔　业	Fishery	923
农、林、牧、渔服务业	Farming,Forestry,Animal Husbandry and Fishery Services	33 442
第二产业	**Secondary Industry**	**209 819**
采矿业	Mining	12 410
制造业	Manufacturing	118 491
电力、煤气及水的生产和供应业	Production and Supply of Electricity,Gas and Water	15 001
建筑业	Construciton	63 917
第三产业	**Tertiary Industry**	**365 620**
交通运输、仓储和邮政业	**Transport,Storage,and Postal Service Industry**	**52 451**
# 道路运输业	Road Transport	44 914
# 公路旅客运输	Passenger Transport on Highways	24 461
道路货物运输	Freight Transport on Road	19 638
城市公共交通业	City Public Tramsport	3 821
航空运输业	Air Transport	201
装卸搬运和其他交通运输业	Pack,Unload Porterage and Other Transport	1 364
仓储业	Storage	936
邮政业	Postal Service	220
信息传输、计算机服务和软件业	**Postal Service,Computer Service and Software**	**2 159**
批发和零售业	**Wholesale and Retail Trade**	**93 702**
批发业	Wholesale Trade	13 776
零售业	Retail Trade	79 926
住宿和餐饮业	**Accommodation and Catering Services Industry**	**37 795**
住宿业	Accommodation Industry	5 797
餐饮业	Catering Services	31 998
金融业	**Finance**	**6 408**
银行业	Bank	1 661
证券业	Securities	33
保险业	Insurance	4 058
其他金融活动	Others	656
房地产业	**Real Estate Trade**	**4 695**
租赁和商务服务业	**Leasing and Business Service**	**8 903**
租赁业	Leasing	2 571
商务服务业	Business Service	6 332
科学研究、技术服务和地质勘查业	**Scientific Research,Technical Service and Geological Prospecting**	**6 866**
研究与实验发展	Research and Development	722
专业技术服务业	Professional Technique Service	5 017
科技交流和推广服务业	Technology Exchange and Expansion Service	910
地质勘查业	Geological Prospecting	217
水利、环境和公共设施管理业	**Water Conservancy,Environment and Public Facilities Management**	**8 648**
水利管理业	Water Conservancy Management	5 244
环境管理业	Environment Management	1 449
公共设施管理业	Public Facilities Management	1 955
居民服务和其他服务业	**Resident and Other Services**	**29 791**
居民服务业	Resident Services	18 177
其他服务业	Other Services	11 614
教　育	**Education**	**43 820**
卫生、社会保障和社会福利业	**Health Care,Social Security and Welfare**	**27 203**
卫　生	Health Care	25 682
社会保障业	Social Security	945
社会福利业	Social Welfare	576
文化、体育和娱乐业	**Culture,Sports and Entertainment**	**5 400**
新闻出版社	News Publishing House	408
广播、电视、电影和音像业	Broadcast,Television,Movie,Audio and Video	1 810
文化艺术业	Culture and Arts	811
体　育	Sports	103
娱乐业	Entertainment	2 268
公共管理和社会组织	**Public Management and Social Organization**	**37 779**

Number of Employed Persons of All Society by Occupation at the Year-end

(person)

单位就业人员 Employed Persons in Units	私营企业从业人员 Private Enterprises	个体劳动者 Induvidual Labors	乡村及其他人员 Rural Labors and Others	年末人数中:农牧团场人数 of Total:Population of Farms
682 509	**36 033**	**257 907**	**85 314**	**668 197**
361 722	**448**	**42 390**	**81 764**	**445 828**
312 353	10	23 572	74 809	377 048
7 158		547	638	7 963
13 491	248	14 449	4 684	30 129
572		331	20	650
28 148	190	3 491	1 613	30 038
153 391	**23 847**	**29 262**	**3 319**	**62 820**
10 008	36	1 432	934	4 667
75 675	22 721	18 875	1 220	37 992
14 855	85	56	5	2 018
52 853	1 005	8 899	1 160	18 143
167 396	**11 738**	**186 255**	**231**	**159 549**
4 693	**1 593**	**46 131**	**34**	**26 104**
2 096	1 589	41 208	21	25 085
1 276	1 082	22 092	11	9 074
615	507	18 506	10	15 602
64	4	3 753		98
201				
1 090		267	7	209
903		27	6	49
157		63		128
661	**347**	**1 151**		**375**
11 616	**3 783**	**78 303**		**44 443**
7 538	1 148	5 090		3 471
4 078	2 635	73 213		40 972
4 547	**889**	**32 255**	**104**	**18 106**
2 727	382	2 618	70	1 629
1 820	507	29 637	34	16 477
6 292	**43**	**59**	**14**	**20**
1 661				3
8		25		
4 028		30		
595	43	4	14	17
1 984	**1 310**	**1 401**		**760**
5 023	**807**	**3 073**		**738**
646	56	1 869		646
4 377	751	1 204		92
6 376	**474**	**16**		**285**
721		1		32
5 001	9	7		167
439	465	6		86
215		2		
8 227	**306**	**115**		**3 089**
5 181		63		1 828
1 341	107	1		239
1 705	199	51		1 022
8 449	**1 506**	**19 784**	**52**	**16 635**
6 221		11 931	25	10 599
2 228	1 506	7 853	27	6 036
43 076	**349**	**370**	**25**	**23 697**
25 571	**265**	**1 365**	**2**	**11 875**
24 110	246	1 324	2	11 626
945				137
516	19	41		112
3 102	**66**	**2 232**		**1 577**
401		7		
1 764		46		677
800		11		7
94		9		9
43	66	2 159		884
37 779				**11 845**

4—3 各师按从事职业分全社会就业人员年末人数

计量单位：人 （2010年）

指　　标	Item	总　计 Total	一　师 Division 1
总　　计	**Total**	**1 061 763**	**115 170**
第一产业	**Primary Industry**	**486 324**	**66 728**
农　业	Farming	410 744	58 305
林　业	Forestry	8 343	1 514
畜牧业	Animal Husbandry	32 872	1 995
渔　业	Fishery	923	94
农、林、牧、渔服务业	Farming,Forestry,Animal Husbandry and Fishery Services	33 442	4 820
第二产业	**Secondary Industry**	**209 819**	**16 151**
采矿业	Mining	12 410	635
制造业	Manufacturing	118 491	10 511
电力、煤气及水的生产和供应业	Production and Supply of Electricity,Gas and Water	15 001	1 219
建筑业	Construciton	63 917	3 786
第三产业	**Tertiary Industry**	**365 620**	**32 291**
交通运输、仓储和邮政业	**Transport,Storage,and Postal Service Industry**	**52 451**	**2 843**
# 道路运输业	Road Transport	44 914	2 588
# 公路旅客运输	Highway Traveller Conveyance	24 461	1 038
道路货物运输	Road Goods Conveyance	19 638	1 255
城市公共交通业	City Public Transport	3 821	63
航空运输业	Air Transport	201	
装卸搬运和其他交通运输业	Pack,Unload Porterage and Other Transport	1 364	
仓储业	Storage	936	
邮政业	Postal Service	220	76
信息传输、计算机服务和软件业	**Postal Service,Computer Service and Software**	**2 159**	**161**
批发和零售业	**Wholesale and Retail Trade**	**93 702**	**7 697**
批发业	Wholesale Trade	13 776	844
零售业	Retail Trade	79 926	6 853
住宿和餐饮业	**Accommodation and Catering Services Industry**	**37 795**	**2 945**
住宿业	Accommodation Industry	5 797	371
餐饮业	Catering Services	31 998	2 574
金融业	**Finance**	**6 408**	
银行业	Bank	1 661	
证券业	Securities	33	
保险业	Insurance	4 058	
其他金融活动	Others	656	
房地产业	**Real Estate Trade**	**4 695**	**622**
租赁和商务服务业	**Leasing and Business Service**	**8 903**	**268**
租赁业	Leasing	2 571	
商务服务业	Business Service	6 332	268
科学研究、技术服务和地质勘查业	**Scientific Research,Technical Service and Geological Prospecting**	**6 866**	**592**
研究与实验发展	Research and Development	722	
专业技术服务业	Professional Technique Service	5 017	446
科技交流和推广服务业	Technology Exchange and Expansion Service	910	26
地质勘查业	Geological Prospecting	217	120
水利、环境和公共设施管理业	**Water Conservancy,Environment and Public Facilities Management**	**8 648**	**847**
水利管理业	Water Conservancy Management	5 244	547
环境管理业	Environment Management	1 449	217
公共设施管理业	Public Facilities Management	1 955	83
居民服务和其他服务业	**Resident and Other Services**	**29 791**	**3 034**
居民服务业	Resident Services	18 177	1 998
其他服务业	Other Services	11 614	1 036
教　育	**Education**	**43 820**	**4 842**
卫生、社会保障和社会福利业	**Health Care,Social Security and Welfare**	**27 203**	**2 898**
卫　生	Health Care	25 682	2 737
社会保障业	Social Security	945	155
社会福利业	Social Welfare	576	6
文化、体育和娱乐业	**Culture,Sports and Entertainment**	**5 400**	**308**
新闻出版社	News Publishing House	408	36
广播、电视、电影和音像业	Broadcast,Television,Movie,Audio and Video	1 810	90
文化艺术业	Culture and Art	811	25
体　育	Sports	103	18
娱乐业	Entertainment	2 268	139
公共管理和社会组织	**Public Management and Social Organization**	**37 779**	**5 234**

Number of Employed Persons of All Society at the Year-end by Occupation and Division

(person)

二 师 Division 2	三 师 Division 3	四 师 Division 4	五 师 Division 5	六 师 Division 6	七 师 Division 7	八 师 Division 8	九 师 Division 9
71 596	**82 962**	**97 164**	**45 711**	**113 769**	**76 853**	**272 933**	**32 245**
37 639	**55 529**	**55 582**	**26 020**	**55 850**	**35 410**	**80 931**	**19 378**
31 588	49 070	45 870	21 348	46 095	30 843	67 189	15 094
1 357	1 170	423	1 207	363	538	464	203
1 553	2 232	6 311	901	4 035	2 167	6 492	3 009
63	62	183	34	58	106	191	
3 078	2 995	2 795	2 530	5 299	1 756	6 595	1 072
9 366	**9 009**	**18 253**	**5 976**	**19 438**	**12 869**	**73 268**	**2 449**
1 151	124	1 249	16	2 276	865	1 684	6
5 609	3 051	10 692	3 407	13 374	7 133	48 471	1 746
832	623	681	1 319	709	1 346	7 025	218
1 774	5 211	5 631	1 234	3 079	3 525	16 088	479
24 591	**18 424**	**23 329**	**13 715**	**38 481**	**28 574**	**118 734**	**10 418**
3 154	**1 595**	**3 403**	**1 079**	**6 321**	**6 799**	**19 961**	**883**
2 862	1 593	3 024	1 077	5 826	6 465	14 994	874
837	850	1 226	534	1 818	2 399	13 363	401
2 018	743	1 785	493	3 746	4 006	1 556	450
79				370		3 222	
73		76	2	35	79	1 073	9
115				78		493	
	2			12		114	
59	**15**	**30**	**6**	**172**	**40**	**1 450**	**143**
7 543	**3 768**	**5 102**	**3 359**	**8 995**	**7 375**	**33 703**	**2 928**
437	464	1 156	510	1 510	1 208	3 482	263
7 106	3 304	3 946	2 849	7 485	6 167	30 221	2 665
2 489	**2 051**	**3 027**	**1 672**	**4 562**	**3 204**	**11 849**	**1 290**
501	380	649	290	541	492	1 501	211
1 988	1 671	2 378	1 382	4 021	2 712	10 348	1 079
2			**10**	**848**	**4**	**3 552**	
				643		1 015	
						33	
				181		2 110	
2			10	24	4	394	
98	**38**	**18**	**162**	**780**		**1 961**	**28**
356	**52**	**110**	**254**	**354**	**51**	**4 927**	**31**
66	10	45	1	25	34	1 735	17
290	42	65	253	329	17	3 192	14
397	**151**	**427**	**274**	**257**	**479**	**1 160**	**98**
63			49		59	496	19
319	124	352	222	257	387	111	70
15	27	50	3		33	551	9
		25				2	
344	**332**	**909**	**75**	**811**	**1 101**	**2 992**	**377**
344	296	352	10	105	1 043	1 994	81
	36			149	21	548	296
		557	65	557	37	450	
1 852	**1 407**	**2 022**	**1 587**	**3 311**	**1 873**	**9 765**	**855**
1 253	705	1 461	1 156	1 543	1 267	5 408	712
599	702	561	431	1 768	606	4 357	143
2 907	**3 330**	**3 430**	**2 324**	**4 652**	**2 876**	**11 351**	**1 107**
2 324	**1 422**	**2 220**	**1 463**	**2 922**	**2 222**	**6 344**	**921**
2 184	1 374	2 159	1 411	2 730	2 150	6 024	854
86	44	49	30	148	3	182	50
54	4	12	22	44	69	138	17
307	**206**	**384**	**158**	**447**	**273**	**1 707**	**251**
12	27	16	15	24	32	57	17
106	32	195	93	204	127	402	31
	43	9		17		286	23
9						76	
180	104	164	50	202	114	886	180
2 759	**4 057**	**2 247**	**1 292**	**4 049**	**2 277**	**8 012**	**1 506**

4—3 续表

计量单位:人　　　　　　　　　　　　　　　　　　　　　　　　　　　　　　(2010 年)

指　　标	Item	十　师 Division 10	建工师 Construction Division
总　　计	**Total**	**27 800**	**25 596**
第一产业	**Primary Industry**	**11 544**	**71**
农　业	Farming	9 351	71
林　业	Forestry	358	
畜牧业	Animal Husbandry	751	
渔　业	Fishery	104	
农、林、牧、渔服务业	Farming, Forestry, Animal Husbandry and Fishery Services	980	
第二产业	**Secondary Industry**	**5 122**	**19 121**
采矿业	Mining	1 194	25
制造业	Manufacturing	1 813	932
电力、煤气及水的生产和供应业	Production and Supply of Electricity, Gas and Water	697	
建筑业	Construciton	1 418	18 164
第三产业	**Tertiary Industry**	**11 134**	**6 404**
交通运输、仓储和邮政业	**Transport, Storage, and Postal Service Industry**	**1 206**	**206**
# 道路运输业	Road Transport	1 172	137
# 公路旅客运输	Highway Traveller Conveyance	381	60
道路货物运输	Road Goods Conveyance	791	77
城市公共交通业	City Public Transport		69
航空运输业	Air Transport		
装卸搬运和其他交通运输业	Pack, Unload Porterage and Other Transport	10	
仓储业	Storage	16	
邮政业	Postal Service	8	
信息传输、计算机服务和软件业	**Postal Service, Computer Service and Software**	**30**	
批发和零售业	**Wholesale and Retail Trade**	**2 704**	**779**
批发业	Wholesale Trade	267	114
零售业	Retail Trade	2 437	665
住宿和餐饮业	**Accommodation and Catering Services Industry**	**1 212**	**230**
住宿业	Accommodation Industry	158	
餐饮业	Catering Services	1 054	230
金融业	**Finance**		6
银行业	Bank		
证券业	Securities		
保险业	Insurance		
其他金融活动	Others		6
房地产业	**Real Estate Trade**	**107**	**396**
租赁和商务服务业	**Leasing and Business Service**	**10**	**1 509**
租赁业	Leasing	4	353
商务服务业	Business Service	6	1 156
科学研究、技术服务和地质勘查业	**Scientific Research, Technical Service and Geological Prospecting**	**211**	**1 427**
研究与实验发展	Research and Development		
专业技术服务业	Professional Technique Service	161	1 427
科技交流和推广服务业	Technology Exchange and Expansion Service	50	
地质勘查业	Geological Prospecting		
水利、环境和公共设施管理业	**Water Conservancy, Environment and Public Facilities Management**	**399**	
水利管理业	Water Conservancy Management	63	
环境管理业	Environment Management	136	
公共设施管理业	Public Facilities Management	200	
居民服务和其他服务业	**Resident and Other Services**	**1 187**	**221**
居民服务业	Resident Services	748	88
其他服务业	Other Services	439	133
教　育	**Education**	**1 535**	**1 122**
卫生、社会保障和社会福利业	**Health Care, Social Security and Welfare**	**1 007**	**273**
卫　生	Health Care	940	196
社会保障业	Social Security	47	38
社会福利业	Social Welfare	20	39
文化、体育和娱乐业	**Culture, Sports and Entertainment**	**164**	**43**
新闻出版社	News Publishing House		15
广播、电视、电影和音像业	Broadcast, Television, Movie, Audio and Video	100	
文化艺术业	Culture and Art	3	
体　育	Sports		
娱乐业	Entertainment	61	28
公共管理和社会组织	**Public Management and Social Organization**	**1 362**	**192**

Continued

(person)

十二师 Division 12	十三师 Division 13	十四师 Division 14	国资公司 State-owned Property Company	供销公司 Supply and Marketing Corporation General	中基公司 Chalkis Company	兵团直属 Direct Under XPCG
27 320	**34 246**	**13 958**	**7 445**	**1 129**	**2 133**	**13 733**
11 532	**17 627**	**9 483**	**334**		**4**	**2 662**
9 316	15 132	8 810				2 662
76	616	54				
1 678	935	475	334		4	
15	13					
447	931	144				
6 082	**6 364**	**1 066**	**2 923**		**2 038**	**324**
750	2 342	29	64			
4 004	2 171	416	2 799		2 038	324
198	62	72				
1 130	1 789	549	60			
9 706	**10 255**	**3 409**	**4 188**	**1 129**	**91**	**10 747**
1 949	**2 023**	**464**	**226**	**220**		**119**
1 829	2 010	458		5		
765	394	395				
1 049	1 616	53				
18						
			201			
	7					
	6		13	215		
5		3				
	24	**7**				**22**
2 915	**1 771**	**731**	**2 833**	**868**	**70**	**561**
210	170	295	1 398	868	70	510
2 705	1 601	436	1 435			51
1 232	**816**	**370**	**459**			**387**
89	63	77	183			291
1 143	753	293	276			96
12	**25**	**7**	**13**			**1 929**
		3				
						1 767
12	25	4	13			162
136		**31**	**200**			**118**
228	**48**	**26**	**184**	**41**		**454**
228	47	4	2			
	1	22	182	41		454
	233	**37**				**1 123**
						36
	163	23				955
		14				132
	70					
46	**325**	**90**				
44	276	89				
2	43	1				
	6					
1 102	**1 151**	**153**	**250**		**21**	
664	840	117	217			
438	311	36	33		21	
976	**1 205**	**588**				**1 575**
383	**1 345**	**221**	**23**			**1 215**
356	1 282	194				1 091
19	11	27				56
8	52		23			68
131	**117**	**38**				**866**
		5				152
30	77	13				310
	4					401
101	36	20				3
596	**1 172**	**646**				**2 378**

4—4 按行业和登记注册类型分单位就业人员年末人数

计量单位:人 (2010年)

指 标	Item	单位就业人员年末人数 Number of Employed Persons in Units
总 计	**Total**	**682 509**
农、林、牧、渔业	**Farming, Forestry, Animal Husbandry and Fishery**	**413 001**
农 业	Farming	409 243
林 业	Forestry	26
畜牧业	Animal Husbandry	3 058
渔 业	Fishery	
农、林、牧、渔服务业	Services	674
采矿业	**Mining**	**6 916**
制造业	**Manufacturing**	**58 119**
电力、煤气及水的生产和供应业	**Production and Supply of Electricity, Gas and Water**	**11 126**
建筑业	**Construciton**	**47 259**
交通运输、仓储和邮政业	**Transport, Storage, and Postal Service Industry**	**2 726**
道路运输业	Road Transport	1 625
城市公共交通业	City Public Transport	67
航空运输业	Air Transport	201
装卸搬运和其他交通运输业	Pack, Unload Porterage and Other Transport	8
仓储业	Storage	324
邮政业	Postal Service	501
信息传输、计算机服务和软件业	**Postal Service, Computer Service and Software**	**895**
电信和其他信息传输服务业	Telecommunications and Other Information Deliver Service	799
计算机服务业	Computer Service	69
软件业	Software	27
批发和零售业	**Wholesale and Retail Trade**	**12 855**
批发业	Wholesale Trade	12 113
零售业	Retail Trade	742
住宿和餐饮业	**Accommodation and Catering Services Industry**	**3 026**
住宿业	Accommodation Industry	3 010
餐饮业	Catering Services	16
金融业	**Finance**	**6 324**
银行业	Bank	1 615
证券业	Securities	8
保险业	Insurance	4 331
其他金融活动	Others	370
房地产业	**Real Estate Trade**	**1 986**
#开发经营业	Development and Management	812
物业管理	Property Management	1 026
中介服务	Middle Service	49
租赁和商务服务业	**Leasing and Business Service**	**5 200**
租赁业	Leasing	
#商务服务业	Business Service	5 200
科学研究、技术服务和地质勘查业	**Scientific Research, Technical Service and Geological Prospecting**	**6 515**
研究与实验发展	Research and Development	963
专业技术服务业	Professional Technique Service	5 181
技术交流和推广服务业	Technology Exchange and Expansion Service	354
地质勘查业	Geological Prospecting	17
水利、环境和公共设施管理业	**Water Conservancy, Environment and Public Facilities Management**	**9 130**
水利管理业	Water Conservancy Management	7 384
环境管理业	Environment Management	1 138
公共设施管理业	Public Facilities Management	608
居民服务和其他服务业	**Resident and Other Services**	**1 776**
居民服务业	Resident Services	210
其他服务业	OtherS ervices	1 566
教 育	**Education**	**42 420**
#初等教育	Primary Education	6 402
中等教育	Secondary Education	29 032
高等教育	Higher Education	5 075
卫生、社会保障和社会福利业	**Health Care, Social Security and Welfare**	**24 590**
卫 生	Health Care	23 433
社会保障业	Social Security	788
社会福利业	Social Welfare	369
文化、体育和娱乐业	**Culture, Sports and Entertainment**	**2 049**
新闻出版社	News Publishing House	463
广播、电视、电影和音像业	Broadcast, Television, Movie, Audio and Video	790
文化艺术业	Culture and Arts	752
体 育	Sports	31
娱乐业	Entertainment	13
公共管理和社会组织	**Public Management and Social Organization**	**26 596**

Number of Employed Persons in Units at the Year-end by Types of Registration and Sector

(person)

国有单位 State-owned Units	集体单位 Collective-owned Units	有限责任公司 Limited Liability Corporations	股份有限责任公司 Share-holding Corporations Ltd	港澳台商投资 Units With Funds From Hong Kong, Macao & Twiwan	外商投资 Foreign Funded Units
573 136	**278**	**73 212**	**33 106**	**418**	**2 359**
412 099		**902**			
409 172		71			
26					
2 622		436			
279		395			
4 746		**2 170**			
11 091	**51**	**32 621**	**11 796**	**335**	**2 225**
5 360		**1 775**	**3 991**		
13 031		**21 348**	**12 880**		
1 768		**916**	**42**		
991		634			
		67			
		201			
		8			
276		6	42		
501					
608		**99**		**83**	**105**
600		11		83	105
8		61			
		27			
6 127		**6 474**	**254**		
5 891		5 968	254		
236		506			
2 152		**637**	**208**		**29**
2 152		621	208		29
		16			
2 609	**177**	**858**	**2 680**		
738	177		700		
			8		
1 828		531	1 972		
43		327			
930	**50**	**1 006**			
308	50	454			
477		549			
46		3			
3 115		**955**	**1 130**		
3 115		955	1 130		
4 693		**1 822**			
963					
3 376		1 805			
354					
		17			
9 019		**111**			
7 384					
1 057		81			
578		30			
448		**1 328**			
210					
238		1 328			
42 268		**116**	**36**		
6 402					
28 888		108	36		
5 075					
24 427		**74**	**89**		
23 344			89		
788					
295		74			
2 049					
463					
790					
752					
31					
13					
26 596					

4—5 单位就业人员和劳动报酬情况

计量单位:人、万元 (2010 年)

指 标	Item	单位数(个) Number of Units(unit)	单位就业人员年末人数 Number of Employed Persons in Units
总 计	**Total**	**2 225**	**682 509**
按企业、事业、机关分组	**Grouped by Enterprises, Institutions and Agencies**		
企 业	Enterprises	907	576 178
事 业	Institutions	1 057	82 117
机 关	Agencies	261	24 214
按国民经济行业分组	**Grouped by Sector**		
农、林、牧、渔业	**Farming, Forestry, Animal Husbandry and Fishery**	**180**	**413 001**
农 业	Farming	147	409 243
林 业	Forestry	1	26
畜牧业	Animal Husbandry	8	3 058
农、林、牧、渔服务业	Services	24	674
采矿业	**Mining**	**18**	**6 916**
制造业	**Manufacturing**	**208**	**58 119**
电力、煤气及水的生产和供应业	**Production and Supply of Electricity, Gas and Water**	**32**	**11 126**
建筑业	**Construciton**	**51**	**47 259**
交通运输、仓储和邮政业	**Transport, Storage, and Postal Service Industry**	**46**	**2 726**
道路运输业	Road Transport	34	1 625
城市公共交通业	City Public Transport	2	67
航空运输业	Air Transport	1	201
装卸搬运和其他交通运输业	Pack, Unload Porterage and Other Transport	1	8
仓储业	Storage	6	324
邮政业	Postal Service	2	501
信息传输、计算机服务和软件业	**Postal Service, Computer Service and Software**	**15**	**895**
电信和其他信息传输服务业	Telecommunications and Other Information Deliver Service	10	799
计算机服务业	Computer Service	4	69
软件业	Software	1	27
批发和零售业	**Wholesale and Retail Trade**	**158**	**12 855**
批发业	Wholesale Trade	136	12 113
零售业	Retail Trade	22	742
住宿和餐饮业	**Accommodation and Catering Services Industry**	**36**	**3 026**
住宿业	Accommodation Industry	35	3 010
餐饮业	Catering Services	1	16
金融业	**Finance**	**46**	**6 324**
银行业	Bank	13	1 615
证券业	Securities	1	8
保险业	Insurance	19	4 331
其他金融活动	Others	13	370
房地产业	**Real Estate Trade**	**64**	**1 986**
# 开发经营业	Development and Management	38	812
物业管理	Property Management	21	1 026
中介服务	Middle Service	2	49
租赁和商务服务业	**Leasing and Business Service**	**114**	**5 200**
# 商务服务业	Business Service	114	5 200
科学研究、技术服务和地质勘查业	**Scientific Research, Technical Service and Geological Prospecting**	**140**	**6 515**
研究与实验发展	Research and Development	16	963
专业技术服务业	Professional Technique Service	103	5 181
技术交流和推广服务业	Technology Exchange and Expansion Service	20	354
地质勘查业	Geological Prospecting	1	17
水利、环境和公共设施管理业	**Water Conservancy, Environment and Public Facilities Management**	**41**	**9 130**
水利管理业	Water Conservancy Management	26	7 384
环境管理业	Environment Management	7	1 138
公共设施管理业	Public Facilities Management	8	608
居民服务和其他服务业	**Resident and Other Services**	**24**	**1 776**
居民服务业	Resident Services	15	210
其他服务业	Other Services	9	1 566
教 育	**Education**	**327**	**42 420**
# 初等教育	Primary Education	63	6 402
中等教育	Secondary Education	212	29 032
高等教育	Higher Education	9	5 075
卫生、社会保障和社会福利业	**Health Care, Social Security and Welfare**	**268**	**24 590**
卫 生	Health Care	223	23 433
社会保障业	Social Security	17	788
社会福利业	Social Welfare	28	369
文化、体育和娱乐业	**Culture, Sports and Entertainment**	**54**	**2 049**
新闻出版社	News Publishing House	17	463
广播、电视、电影和音像业	Broadcast, Television, Movie, Audio and Video	17	790
文化艺术业	Culture and Arts	17	752
体 育	Sports	1	31
娱乐业	Entertainment	2	13
公共管理和社会组织	**Public Management and Social Organization**	**403**	**26 596**

Number of Employed Persons and Labor Remuneration

(person, 10 000 yuan)

# 女 性 Female	# 民族职工 Staff and Workers of MinorityNationalities	# 在岗职工 Fully Empolyed Staff and Workers	其他就业人员 Other Employed Persons
291 865	**56 272**	**677 570**	**4 939**
238 541	48 280	573 641	2 537
48 157	6 763	80 066	2 051
5 167	1 229	23 863	351
186 829	**40 221**	**411 922**	**1 079**
185 227	38 387	408 165	1 078
11	1	26	
1 335	1 778	3 058	
256	55	673	1
1 627	**260**	**6 911**	**5**
20 686	**4 075**	**57 621**	**498**
3 337	**1 137**	**11 091**	**35**
8 544	**885**	**47 204**	**55**
887	**93**	**2 581**	**145**
509	72	1 515	110
11		67	
20		201	
3		8	
104	5	289	35
240	16	501	
353	**84**	**894**	**1**
313	36	798	1
21	48	69	
19		27	
5 138	**523**	**12 383**	**472**
4 763	508	11 642	471
375	15	741	1
1 903	**167**	**2 967**	**59**
1 894	166	2 951	59
9	1	16	
3 591	**335**	**6 306**	**18**
743	96	1 598	17
3		8	
2 671	216	4 330	1
174	23	370	
876	**96**	**1 969**	**17**
370	27	796	16
413	61	1 026	
28	1	49	
1 571	**208**	**5 129**	**71**
1 571	208	5 129	71
1 958	**124**	**6 097**	**418**
354	33	958	5
1 462	79	4 804	377
136	12	318	36
6		17	
3 887	**335**	**8 880**	**250**
3 005	275	7 374	10
586	27	906	232
296	33	600	8
1 208	**47**	**1 766**	**10**
81	17	200	10
1 127	30	1 566	
26 491	**4 374**	**41 901**	**519**
4 313	1 020	6 346	56
18 375	2 988	28 799	233
2 463	253	4 991	84
15 840	**1 622**	**23 803**	**787**
15 187	1 593	22 721	712
461	20	739	49
192	9	343	26
859	**186**	**1 987**	**62**
224	27	439	24
359	34	785	5
265	122	719	33
6	3	31	
5		13	
6 280	**1 500**	**26 158**	**438**

4—5 续表 1

计量单位:人、万元　　　　(2010 年)

指　　标	Item	离开本单位仍保留劳动关系职工年末人数 Staff and Workers Who Have Left Their Working Units While Keeping Their Labour Contract Unchanged
总　　计	**Total**	**16 918**
按企业、事业、机关分组	**Grouped by Enterprises, Institutions and Agencies**	
企　业	Enterprises	15 976
事　业	Institutions	848
机　关	Agencies	94
按国民经济行业分组	**Grouped by Sector**	
农、林、牧、渔业	**Farming, Forestry, Animal Husbandry and Fishery**	**10 570**
农　业	Farming	10 566
林　业	Forestry	
畜牧业	Animal Husbandry	2
农、林、牧、渔服务业	Services	2
采矿业	**Mining**	**93**
制造业	**Manufacturing**	**1 064**
电力、煤气及水的生产和供应业	**Production and Supply of Electricity, Gas and Water**	**499**
建筑业	**Construciton**	**2 340**
交通运输、仓储和邮政业	**Transport, Storage, and Postal Service Industry**	**179**
道路运输业	Road Transport	101
城市公共交通业	City Public Transport	
航空运输业	Air Transport	9
装卸搬运和其他交通运输业	Pack, Unload Porterage and Other Transport	
仓储业	Storage	27
邮政业	Postal Service	42
信息传输、计算机服务和软件业	**Postal Service, Computer Service and Software**	**19**
电信和其他信息传输服务业	Telecommunications and Other Information Deliver Service	19
计算机服务业	Computer Service	
软件业	Software	
批发和零售业	**Wholesale and Retail Trade**	**456**
批发业	Wholesale Trade	381
零售业	Retail Trade	75
住宿和餐饮业	**Accommodation and Catering Services Industry**	**140**
住宿业	Accommodation Industry	140
餐饮业	Catering Services	
金融业	**Finance**	**42**
银行业	Bank	41
证券业	Securities	
保险业	Insurance	1
其他金融活动	Others	
房地产业	**Real Estate Trade**	**17**
# 开发经营业	Development and Management	1
物业管理	Property Management	16
中介服务	Middle Service	
租赁和商务服务业	**Leasing and Business Service**	**336**
# 商务服务业	Business Service	336
科学研究、技术服务和地质勘查业	**Scientific Research, Technical Service and Geological Prospecting**	**45**
研究与实验发展	Research and Development	27
专业技术服务业	Professional Technique Service	17
技术交流和推广服务业	Technology Exchange and Expansion Service	1
地质勘查业	Geological Prospecting	
水利、环境和公共设施管理业	**Water Conservancy, Environment and Public Facilities Management**	**344**
水利管理业	Water Conservancy Management	344
环境管理业	Environment Management	
公共设施管理业	Public Facilities Management	
居民服务和其他服务业	**Resident and Other Services**	**163**
居民服务业	Resident Services	163
其他服务业	Other Services	
教　育	**Education**	**135**
# 初等教育	Primary Education	11
中等教育	Secondary Education	101
高等教育	Higher Education	5
卫生、社会保障和社会福利业	**Health Care, Social Security and Welfare**	**313**
卫　生	Health Care	240
社会保障业	Social Security	4
社会福利业	Social Welfare	69
文化、体育和娱乐业	**Culture, Sports and Entertainment**	**32**
新闻出版社	News Publishing House	
广播、电视、电影和音像业	Broadcast, Television, Movie, Audio and Video	12
文化艺术业	Culture and Arts	20
体　育	Sports	
娱乐业	Entertainment	
公共管理和社会组织	**Public Management and Social Organization**	**131**

Continued

(person,10 000 yuan)

单位就业人员年平均人数 Average Annual Number of Persons Employed in Units	在岗职工平均人数 Average Annual Number of Staff and Workers	其他就业人员平均人数 Average Annual Number of Persons Employed in Others	离开本单位仍保留劳动关系职工平均人数 Staff and Workers Who Have Left Their Working Units While Keeping Their Labour Contract Unchanged	单位就业人员劳动报酬 Earnings of Employed Persons in Units	在岗职工工资总额 Wages of Fully Employed Staff and Workers	其他就业人员劳动报酬 Earnings of Other Employed Personsin Units
746 702	**741 702**	**5 000**	**17 277**	**1 990 638**	**1 983 365**	**7 273**
640 287	637 699	2 588	16 300	1 586 754	1 582 241	4 513
82 270	80 248	2 022	867	289 055	286 711	2 344
24 145	23 755	390	110	114 829	114 413	416
424 800	**423 810**	**990**	**11 104**	**970 113**	**968 907**	**1 206**
421 256	420 267	989	11 100	963 690	962 485	1 205
24	24			45	45	
2 999	2 999		2	4 543	4 543	
521	520	1	2	1 835	1 834	1
7 033	**7 029**	**4**	**105**	**22 854**	**22 847**	**7**
57 937	**57 193**	**744**	**1 142**	**154 436**	**152 881**	**1 555**
11 127	**11 102**	**25**	**526**	**33 184**	**33 133**	**51**
99 595	**99 540**	**55**	**1 909**	**273 979**	**273 934**	**45**
2 681	**2 544**	**137**	**225**	**7 913**	**7 744**	**169**
1 583	1 481	102	102	3 970	3 837	133
62	62			130	130	
204	204		8	841	841	
8	8			15	15	
329	294	35	72	954	918	36
495	495		43	2 003	2 003	
889	**888**	**1**	**41**	**4 304**	**4 302**	**2**
798	797	1	22	4 036	4 034	2
62	62		19	230	230	
29	29			38	38	
12 114	**11 739**	**375**	**476**	**40 535**	**39 847**	**688**
11 373	10 999	374	397	38 315	37 628	687
741	740	1	79	2 220	2 219	1
3 055	**2 995**	**60**	**143**	**5 888**	**5 788**	**100**
3 039	2 979	60	143	5 850	5 750	100
16	16			38	38	
6 146	**6 128**	**18**	**42**	**28 848**	**2 868**	**167**
1 602	1 585	17	41	11 011	1 084	166
8	8			122	122	
4 183	4 182	1	1	16 408	16 407	1
353	353			1 307	1 307	
1 938	**1 921**	**17**	**17**	**6 049**	**6 037**	**12**
809	793	16	1	3 302	3 292	10
992	992		16	2 006	2 006	
42	42			174	174	
5 273	**5 207**	**66**	**339**	**17 430**	**17 306**	**124**
5 273	5 207	66	339	17 430	17 306	124
6 821	**6 401**	**420**	**45**	**27 093**	**26 073**	**1 020**
940	935	5	27	3 547	3 540	7
5 515	5 136	379	17	22 328	21 379	949
349	313	36	1	1 175	1 111	64
17	17			43	43	
10 000	**9 760**	**240**	**349**	**28 980**	**28 728**	**251**
8 232	8 222	10	349	24 969	24 948	21
1 130	918	212		2 286	2 102	184
638	620	18		1 725	1 679	46
1 620	**1 610**	**10**	**162**	**2 517**	**2 484**	**33**
194	184	10	162	704	671	33
1 426	1 426			1 813	1 813	
42 683	**42 164**	**519**	**136**	**154 588**	**154 003**	**585**
6 426	6 367	59	10	22 213	22 171	42
29 219	28 979	240	102	105 224	104 922	302
5 123	5 042	81	5	21 458	21 356	102
24 430	**23 642**	**788**	**335**	**81 024**	**80 382**	**642**
23 296	22 606	690	262	77 552	77 012	540
769	698	71	4	2 278	2 199	79
365	338	27	69	1 194	1 171	23
2 032	**1 970**	**62**	**33**	**7 374**	**7 282**	**92**
469	445	24		1 734	1 707	27
765	760	5	14	2 657	2 648	9
754	721	33	19	2 829	2 773	56
31	31			128	128	
13	13			26	26	
26 528	**26 059**	**469**	**148**	**123 529**	**123 005**	**524**

4—5 续表 2

计量单位:人、万元 （2010 年）

指　　标	Item	离开本单位仍保留劳动关系职工生活费 Living Cost of Staff and Workers Who Have Left Their Working Units While Keeping Their Labour Contract Unchanged
总　计	**Total**	**8 017**
按企业、事业、机关分组	**Grouped by Enterprises, Institutions and Agencies**	
企　业	Enterprises	6 893
事　业	Institutions	811
机　关	Agencies	312
按国民经济行业分组	**Grouped by Sector**	
农、林、牧、渔业	**Farming, Forestry, Animal Husbandry and Fishery**	**3 586**
农　业	Farming	3 586
林　业	Forestry	
畜牧业	Animal Husbandry	
农、林、牧、渔服务业	Services	
采矿业	**Mining**	**71**
制造业	**Manufacturing**	**454**
电力、煤气及水的生产和供应业	**Production and Supply of Electricity, Gas and Water**	**1 130**
建筑业	**Construciton**	**417**
交通运输、仓储和邮政业	**Transport, Storage, and Postal Service Industry**	**264**
道路运输业	Road Transport	140
城市公共交通业	City Public Transport	
航空运输业	Air Transport	24
装卸搬运和其他交通运输业	Pack, Unload Porterage and Other Transport	
仓储业	Storage	35
邮政业	Postal Service	64
信息传输、计算机服务和软件业	**Postal Service, Computer Service and Software**	**49**
电信和其他信息传输服务业	Telecommunications and Other Information Deliver Service	49
计算机服务业	Computer Service	
软件业	Software	
批发和零售业	**Wholesale and Retail Trade**	**560**
批发业	Wholesale Trade	498
零售业	Retail Trade	62
住宿和餐饮业	**Accommodation and Catering Services Industry**	**57**
住宿业	Accommodation Industry	57
餐饮业	Catering Services	
金融业	**Finance**	**106**
银行业	Bank	104
证券业	Securities	
保险业	Insurance	2
其他金融活动	Others	
房地产业	**Real Estate Trade**	**10**
#开发经营业	Development and Management	
物业管理	Property Management	10
中介服务	Middle Service	
租赁和商务服务业	**Leasing and Business Service**	**192**
商务服务业	Business Service	192
科学研究、技术服务和地质勘查业	**Scientific Research, Technical Service and Geological Prospecting**	**38**
研究与实验发展	Research and Development	
专业技术服务业	Professional Technique Service	37
技术交流和推广服务业	Technology Exchange and Expansion Service	1
地质勘查业	Geological Prospecting	
水利、环境和公共设施管理业	**Water Conservancy, Environment and Public Facilities Management**	**30**
水利管理业	Water Conservancy Management	30
环境管理业	Environment Management	
公共设施管理业	Public Facilities Management	
居民服务和其他服务业	**Resident and Other Services**	**150**
居民服务业	Resident Services	150
其他服务业	Other Services	
教　育	**Education**	**86**
#初等教育	Primary Education	
中等教育	Secondary Education	84
高等教育	Higher Education	2
卫生、社会保障和社会福利业	**Health Care, Social Security and Welfare**	**412**
卫　生	Health Care	396
社会保障业	Social Security	2
社会福利业	Social Welfare	14
文化、体育和娱乐业	**Culture, Sports and Entertainment**	**30**
新闻出版社	News Publishing House	
广播、电视、电影和音像业	Broadcast, Television, Movie, Audio and Video	17
文化艺术业	Culture and Arts	13
体　育	Sports	
娱乐业	Entertainment	
公共管理和社会组织	**Public Management and Social Organization**	**375**

Continued

(person, 10 000 yuan)

单位就业人员平均工资(元) Average Money Wage of Employed Persons in Units (yuan)	在岗职工平均工资(元) Average Money Wage of Staff and Workers (yuan)	其他就业人员平均工资(元) Average Money Wage of Other Employed Persons (yuan)	离开本单位仍保留劳动关系的职工平均工资(元) Average Money Wage of Staff and Workers Who Have Left Their Working Units While Keeping Their Labour Contract Unchanged(yuan)	劳务派遣工平均劳动报酬 Number of Contract Workers at the Year-end
26 659	**26 741**	**14 546**	**4 640**	**19 343**
24 782	24 812	17 439	4 229	22 503
35 135	35 728	11 592	9 348	12 204
47 558	48 164	10 664	28 373	9 300
22 837	**22 862**	**12 183**	**3 229**	
22 877	22 902	12 182	3 230	
18 875	18 875			
15 148	15 148			
35 211	35 254	13 000		
32 496	**32 504**	**17 500**	**6 743**	
26 656	**26 731**	**20 897**	**3 977**	**17 387**
29 824	**29 844**	**20 560**	**21 479**	
27 509	**27 520**	**8 182**	**2 183**	**21 636**
29 514	**30 440**	**12 321**	**11 720**	
25 080	25 907	13 059	13 765	
20 887	20 887			
41 245	41 245		30 250	
19 125	19 125			
28 979	31 218	10 171	4 833	
40 465	40 465		14 953	
48 409	**48 444**	**18 000**	**11 854**	**30 342**
50 570	50 611	18 000	22 091	30 342
37 161	37 161			
13 000	13 000			
33 461	**33 944**	**18 344**	**11 769**	
33 690	34 211	18 361	12 554	
29 958	29 982	12 000	7 823	
19 272	**19 326**	**16 583**	**3 951**	
19 249	19 303	16 583	3 951	
23 625	23 625			
46 939	**46 804**	**93 000**	**25 262**	
68 739	68 425	98 059	25 293	
152 500	152 500			
39 225	39 232	7 000	24 000	
37 031	37 031			
31 214	**31 427**	**7 118**	**5 941**	
40 812	41 507	6 375	4 000	
20 217	20 217		6 063	
41 381	41 381			
33 055	**33 236**	**18 818**	**5 667**	**10 235**
33 055	33 236	18 818	5 667	10 235
39 720	**40 732**	**24 288**	**8 422**	**2 000**
37 736	37 862	14 200		
40 486	41 626	25 042	21 647	2 000
33 662	35 492	17 750	11 000	
25 235	25 235			
28 980	**29 435**	**10 483**	**857**	**11 995**
30 332	30 342	21 400	857	
20 228	22 895	8 679		11 995
27 042	27 082	25 667		11 995
15 535	**15 428**	**32 700**	**9 272**	
36 284	36 478	32 700	9 272	
12 712	12 712			
36 218	**36 525**	**11 266**	**6 346**	**14 063**
34 567	34 821	7 136		
36 012	36 206	12 592	8 216	9 600
41 886	42 356	12 642	3 600	
33 166	**34 000**	**8 147**	**12 296**	**6 167**
33 290	34 067	7 829	15 122	14 500
29 619	31 504	11 085	4 500	
32 726	34 657	8 556	2 014	2 000
36 289	**36 965**	**14 806**	**9 030**	**32 615**
36 974	38 369	11 125		
34 731	34 845	17 400	11 786	32 615
37 529	38 465	17 091	7 000	
41 161	41 161			
19 692	19 692			
46 565	**47 202**	**11 175**	**25 351**	**9 366**

4—6 各师单位就业人员年末人数

Number of Employed Persons at the Year-end by Division

计量单位：人 （2010年） (person)

单位 Unit		合计 Total	企业 Enterprises	事业 Institutions	机关 Agencies& Organizations	农、林、牧、渔业 Farming, Forestry, Animal Husbandry and Fishery	采矿业 Mining	制造业 Manufacturing	电力、煤气及水的生产和供应业 Production and Supply of Electricity, Gas and Water
总　计	**Total**	**682 509**	**576 178**	**82 117**	**24 214**	**413 001**	**6 916**	**58 119**	**11 126**
一　师	Division 1	76 089	64 223	8 164	3 702	47 711	689	6 244	1 407
二　师	Division 2	48 491	41 178	5 674	1 639	34 358	884	2 634	234
三　师	Division 3	38 106	29 998	5 391	2 717	24 720		485	423
四　师	Division 4	70 591	63 638	5 936	1 017	52 180	463	6 387	530
五　师	Division 5	38 768	34 141	4 021	606	29 435		2 068	807
六　师	Division 6	60 526	49 361	8 844	2 321	42 373	1 553	2 185	252
七　师	Division 7	46 131	38 444	6 186	1 501	32 070	374	1 813	925
八　师	Division 8	161 948	136 240	20 042	5 666	77 069	366	28 525	5 630
九　师	Division 9	23 091	19 839	2 630	622	18 178		952	128
十　师	Division 10	21 714	18 000	3 056	658	14 935	1 456	250	595
建工师	Construction Division	23 954	22 372	1 261	321	71		195	41
十二师	Division 12	17 163	15 616	1 547		12 586	740	1 797	82
十三师	Division 13	19 600	15 808	3 232	560	14 754	391	807	
十四师	Division 14	12 302	10 962	1 044	296	9 899		208	72
国资公司	State-owned Property Company	7 136	7 136					1 207	
供销公司	Supply and Marketing Corporation General	1 129	1 129						
中基公司	Chalkis Company	2 133	2 133					2 038	
兵团直属	Directlty under XPCG	13 637	5 960	5 089	2 588	2 662		324	

单位 Unit		建筑业 Construction	交通运输、仓储和邮政业 Transport, Storage and Postal Service	信息传输、计算机服务和软件业 Information Deliver, Computer Service and Software	批发和零售业 Wholesale and Retail Trade	住宿和餐饮业 Accommodation and Catering Services Industry	金融业 Finance	房地产业 Real Estate Trade	租赁和商务服务业 Leasing and Business Service
总　计	**Total**	**47 259**	**2 726**	**895**	**12 855**	**3 026**	**6 324**	**1 986**	**5 200**
一　师	Division 1	2 922	109	4	1 417	59		350	238
二　师	Division 2	1 325	112	3	578	274	2	96	695
三　师	Division 3	3 633	162		360	102		16	114
四　师	Division 4	2 518	107		618	600		9	57
五　师	Division 5	616	153	9	351	311	10	160	218
六　师	Division 6	547	164	45	223	29	848	139	741
七　师	Division 7	881	152		1 618	114		56	61
八　师	Division 8	13 270	853	770	563	865	3 514	204	2 057
九　师	Division 9	209	120	12	150	126		28	19
十　师	Division 10	402	73		153	87		3	18
建工师	Construction Division	20 213			80		6	221	170
十二师	Division 12	58	112	30	51	31		95	52
十三师	Division 13	134	33		66		11		45
十四师	Division 14	471	23		282		4	35	27
国资公司	State-owned Property Company	60	214		4 842	137		456	172
供销公司	Supply and Marketing Corporation General		220		868				41
中基公司	Chalkis Company				74				21
兵团直属	Directlty under XPCG		119	22	561	291	1 929	118	454

4—6 续表 Continued

计量单位:人 (2010 年) (person)

单 位	Unit	科学研究、技术服务和地质勘查业 Scientific Research, Technique Service and Geological Prospecting	水利、环境和公共设施管理业 Water Conservancy, Environment and Public Facilities Management	居民服务和其他服务业 Resident and Other Services	教 育 Education	卫生、社会保障和社会福利业 Health Care, Social Security and Welfare	文化、体育和娱乐业 Culture, Sports and Recreation	公共管理和社会组织 Public Management and Social Organization
总 计	**Total**	**6 515**	**9 130**	**1 776**	**42 420**	**24 590**	**2 049**	**26 596**
一 师	Division 1	504	3 189	32	4 693	2 577	149	3 795
二 师	Division 2	358	303		2 842	2 026	50	1 717
三 师	Division 3	159	481	39	3 294	1 267	66	2 785
四 师	Division 4	412	163	58	3 215	2 153	83	1 038
五 师	Division 5	274	75		2 177	1 364	48	692
六 师	Division 6	318	799	1	4 624	2 626	106	2 953
七 师	Division 7	469	1 291		2 750	1 894	113	1 550
八 师	Division 8	1 052	2 122	1 492	10 895	5 643	370	6 688
九 师	Division 9	88	381	20	1 078	860	65	677
十 师	Division 10	184	194	10	1 454	1 019	74	807
建工师	Construction Division	1 375			1 097	164		321
十二师	Division 12	16	30	22	970	274		217
十三师	Division 13	158		90	1 173	1 267	47	624
十四师	Division 14	25	89		583	218	12	354
国资公司	State-owned Property Company		13	12		23		
供销公司	Supply and Marketing Corporation General							
中基公司	Chalkis Company							
兵团直属	Directly under XPCG	1 123			1 575	1 215	866	2 378

4—7 各师少数民族单位就业人员年末人数

Number of Employed Persons of Minority Nationalties at the Year-end by Division

计量单位:人 (2010 年) (person)

单 位	Unit	合 计 Total	企 业 Enterprises	事 业 Institutions	机 关 Agencies& Organizations	农、林、牧、渔业 Farming, Forestry, Animal Husbandry and Fishery	采矿业 Mining	制造业 Manufacturing	电力、煤气及水的生产和供应业 Production and Supply of Electricity, Gas and Water
总 计	**Total**	**56 272**	**48 280**	**6 763**	**1 229**	**40 221**	**260**	**4 075**	**1 137**
一 师	Division 1	2 238	1 722	309	207	1 376	13	45	35
二 师	Division 2	1 683	1 440	190	53	1 025	19	294	
三 师	Division 3	9 332	7 432	1 605	295	6 831		175	3
四 师	Division 4	9 402	8 494	849	59	7 500	46	811	20
五 师	Division 5	3 723	3 287	384	52	2 907		186	79
六 师	Division 6	4 341	3 833	453	55	3 574	86	53	9
七 师	Division 7	1 159	920	208	31	761	2	29	29
八 师	Division 8	7 751	6 444	1 064	243	3 190	19	1 840	917
九 师	Division 9	649	546	84	19	522		13	
十 师	Division 10	523	433	71	19	370	27	19	12
建工师	Construction Division	338	312	23	3	1		7	3
十二师	Division 12	4 796	4 563	233		4 069	38	409	20
十三师	Division 13	3 188	2 669	457	62	2 629	10	20	
十四师	Division 14	6 178	5 628	505	45	5 444		64	10
国资公司	State-owned Property Company	175	175						
供销公司	Supply and Marketing Corporation General	36	36						
中基公司	Chalkis Company	85	85					81	
兵团直属	Directly under XPCG	675	261	328	86	22		29	

4—7 续表 Continued

计量单位:人 (2010 年) (person)

单位	Unit	建筑业 Construction	交通运输、仓储和邮政业 Transport, Storage and Postal Service	信息传输、计算机服务和软件业 Information Deliver, Computer Service and Software	批发和零售业 Wholesale and Retail Trade	住宿和餐饮业 Accommodation and Catering Services Industry	金融业 Finance	房地产业 Real Estate Trade	租赁和商务服务业 Leasing and Business Servic
总　计	**Total**	**885**	**93**	**84**	**523**	**167**	**335**	**96**	**208**
一　师	Division 1	61	7		37	6		12	7
二　师	Division 2	16	1		7	11		3	63
三　师	Division 3	340	21		54	8			
四　师	Division 4	34	2		18	62			
五　师	Division 5	45	16		8	25			27
六　师	Division 6	15	2	2	10	1	36	9	31
七　师	Division 7	14	5		34	4			3
八　师	Division 8	43	22	75	12	37	167	4	53
九　师	Division 9		3		3	5			
十　师	Division 10	3			1	1			
建工师	Construction Division	283			2			6	10
十二师	Division 12	9		6				17	
十三师	Division 13	16	1		8				
十四师	Division 14	6	9		90		1	10	6
国资公司	State-owned Property Company		1		130	1		29	3
供销公司	Supply and Marketing Corporation General		3		33				
中基公司	Chalkis Company				3				1
兵团直属	Directly under XPCG			1	73	6	131	6	4

单位	Unit	科学研究、技术服务和地质勘查业 Scientific Research, Technique Service and Geological Prospecting	水利、环境和公共设施管理业 Water Conservancy, Environment and Public Facilities Management	居民服务和其他服务业 Resident and Other Services	教育 Education	卫生、社会保障和社会福利业 Health Care, Social Security and Welfare	文化、体育和娱乐业 Culture, Sports and Recreation	公共管理和社会组织 Public Management and Social Organization
总　计	**Total**	**124**	**335**	**47**	**4 374**	**1 622**	**186**	**1 500**
一　师	Division 1	10	124		186	105	6	208
二　师	Division 2	7	2		91	82	3	59
三　师	Division 3	4	10	7	1 309	248	19	303
四　师	Division 4	12	3	8	552	272	3	59
五　师	Division 5	9	1		241	118	6	55
六　师	Division 6	4	8		301	134		66
七　师	Division 7	4	57		117	59	7	34
八　师	Division 8	37	102	30	526	210	23	444
九　师	Division 9	3	2	1	57	19	1	20
十　师	Division 10		9		23	30	5	23
建工师	Construction Division				14	9		3
十二师	Division 12	4		1	179	28		16
十三师	Division 13	2			257	179	2	64
十四师	Division 14	1	6		359	115		57
国资公司	State-owned Property Company		11					
供销公司	Supply and Marketing Corporation General							
中基公司	Chalkis Company							
兵团直属	Directly under XPCG	27			162	14	111	89

4—8 各师女性单位就业人员年末人数

Number of Female Employed Persons at the Year-end by Division

计量单位：人 (2010年) (person)

单位	Unit	合计 Total	企业 Enterprises	事业 Institutions	机关 Agencies & Organizations	农、林、牧、渔业 Farming, Forestry, Animal Husbandry and Fishery	采矿业 Mining	制造业 Manufacturing	电力、煤气及水的生产和供应业 Production and Supply of Electricity, Gas and Water
总计	**Total**	**291 865**	**238 541**	**48 157**	**5 167**	**186 829**	**1 627**	**20 686**	**3 337**
一师	Division 1	32 040	26 518	5 065	457	21 734	111	918	427
二师	Division 2	23 160	19 390	3 536	234	16 688	323	1 195	36
三师	Division 3	15 917	12 519	3 007	391	11 373		166	99
四师	Division 4	30 590	26 635	3 715	240	22 883	126	2 360	151
五师	Division 5	18 345	15 472	2 715	158	13 369		980	344
六师	Division 6	27 460	21 355	5 599	506	19 181	277	663	73
七师	Division 7	20 975	17 104	3 638	233	14 519	68	872	287
八师	Division 8	68 054	55 219	11 254	1 581	35 136	51	10 370	1 576
九师	Division 9	10 469	8 836	1 506	127	8 137		383	43
十师	Division 10	9 478	7 295	2 009	174	6 278	390	126	229
建工师	Construction Division	4 479	3 480	843	156	30		83	15
十二师	Division 12	7 749	6 835	914		5 492	181	1 019	37
十三师	Division 13	8 847	6 720	1 973	154	6 430	100	176	
十四师	Division 14	5 187	4 622	495	70	4 414		57	20
国资公司	State-owned Property Company	2 530	2 530					440	
供销公司	Supply and Marketing Corporation General	434	434						
中基公司	Chalkis Company	814	814					776	
兵团直属	Directly under XPCG	5 337	2 763	1 888	686	1 165		102	

单位	Unit	建筑业 Construction	交通运输、仓储和邮政业 Transport, Storage and Postal Service	信息传输、计算机服务和软件业 Information Deliver, Computer Service and Software	批发和零售业 Wholesale and Retail Trade	住宿和餐饮业 Accommodation and Catering Services Industry	金融业 Finance	房地产业 Real Estate Trade	租赁和商务服务业 Leasing and Business Service
总计	**Total**	**8 544**	**887**	**353**	**5 138**	**1 903**	**3 591**	**876**	**1 571**
一师	Division 1	976	52	4	587	39		159	71
二师	Division 2	406	44		264	156	2	43	235
三师	Division 3	530	58		200	58		6	37
四师	Division 4	334	30		305	361		4	16
五师	Division 5	218	59	2	116	180	4	60	136
六师	Division 6	186	76	10	82	22	363	66	268
七师	Division 7	361	42		692	81		16	25
八师	Division 8	2 375	314	315	228	556	2 323	96	432
九师	Division 9	92	31	4	53	92		16	8
十师	Division 10	98	34		82	64		2	9
建工师	Construction Division	2 797			31		3	104	99
十二师	Division 12	20	6	9		22		40	13
十三师	Division 13	84	10		28		6		20
十四师	Division 14	50	5		74		3	9	10
国资公司	State-owned Property Company	17	22		1 704	64		163	90
供销公司	Supply and Marketing Corporation General		72		350				12
中基公司	Chalkis Company				31				7
兵团直属	Directly under XPCG		32	9	311	208	887	92	83

4—8 续表 Continued

计量单位:人 (2010 年) (person)

单 位	Unit	科学研究、技术服务和地质勘查业 Scientific Research, Technique Service and Geological Prospecting	水利、环境和公共设施管理业 Water Conservancy, Environment and Public Facilities Management	居民服务和其他服务业 Resident and Other Services	教 育 Education	卫生、社会保障和社会福利业 Health Care, Social Security and Welfare	文化、体育和娱乐业 Culture, Sports and Recreation	公共管理和社会组织 Public Management and Social Organization
总 计	**Total**	**1 958**	**3 887**	**1 208**	**26 491**	**15 840**	**859**	**6 280**
一 师	Division 1	141	1 505	17	2 939	1 823	55	482
二 师	Division 2	102	118		1 931	1 335	18	264
三 师	Division 3	62	159	11	1 895	811	34	418
四 师	Division 4	157	73	19	1 980	1 490	47	254
五 师	Division 5	98	45		1 510	1 006	22	196
六 师	Division 6	111	432		2 882	1 816	84	868
七 师	Division 7	121	574		1 807	1 208	50	252
八 师	Division 8	341	749	1 065	6 452	3 570	175	1 930
九 师	Division 9	32	142	9	714	530	27	156
十 师	Division 10	44	78	4	1 020	744	30	246
建 工 师	Construction Division	318			706	137		156
十 二 师	Division 12	6	5	10	635	183		71
十 三 师	Division 13	37		63	803	888	18	184
十 四 师	Division 14	9	5		297	137	4	93
国资公司	State-owned Property Company		2	10		18		
供销公司	Supply and Marketing Corporation General							
中基公司	Chalkis Company							
兵团直属	Directly under XPCG	379			920	144	295	710

4—9 各师单位就业人员年平均人数

Average Annual Number of Employed Persons by Division

计量单位:人 (2010 年) (person)

单 位	Unit	合 计 Total	企 业 Enterprises	事 业 Institutions	机 关 Agencies & Organizations	农、林、牧、渔业 Farming, Forestry, Animal Husbandry and Fishery	采矿业 Mining	制造业 Manufacturing	电力、煤气及水的生产和供应业 Production and Supply of Electricity, Gas and Water
总 计	**Total**	**746 702**	**640 287**	**82 270**	**24 145**	**424 800**	**7 033**	**57 937**	**11 127**
一 师	Division 1	79 885	68 000	8 215	3 670	48 211	713	6 151	1 384
二 师	Division 2	49 753	42 451	5 679	1 623	34 785	904	2 708	226
三 师	Division 3	38 857	30 789	5 363	2 705	25 577		462	399
四 师	Division 4	70 773	63 819	5 949	1 005	52 164	542	6 196	530
五 师	Division 5	39 255	34 597	4 069	589	29 759		2 210	816
六 师	Division 6	64 107	53 014	8 790	2 303	44 535	1 545	1 942	257
七 师	Division 7	45 235	37 538	6 211	1 486	31 858	284	1 793	935
八 师	Division 8	176 000	150 363	20 020	5 617	84 276	348	28 284	5 688
九 师	Division 9	22 990	19 698	2 665	627	18 071		910	125
十 师	Division 10	24 097	20 418	3 030	649	15 587	1 496	250	583
建 工 师	Construction Division	62 387	60 549	1 365	473	71		269	41
十 二 师	Division 12	17 237	15 679	1 558		12 580	810	1 806	75
十 三 师	Division 13	19 383	15 607	3 226	550	14 610	391	787	
十 四 师	Division 14	12 478	11 187	1 002	289	10 074		248	68
国资公司	State-owned Property Company	6 993	6 993					1 188	
供销公司	Supply and Marketing Corporation General	1 131	1 131						
中基公司	Chalkis Company	2 448	2 448					2 359	
兵团直属	Directly under XPCG	13 693	6 006	5 128	2 559	2 642		374	

4—9 续表 Continued

计量单位：人 （2010 年） (person)

单 位	Unit	建筑业 Construction	交通运输、仓储和邮政业 Transport, Storage and Postal Service	信息传输、计算机服务和软件业 Information Deliver, Computer Service and Software	批发和零售业 Wholesale and Retail Trade	住宿和餐饮业 Accommodation and Catering Services Industry	金融业 Finance	房地产业 Real Estate Trade	租赁和商务服务业 Leasing and Business Service
总 计	**Total**	**99 595**	**2 681**	**889**	**12 114**	**3 055**	**6 146**	**1 938**	**5 273**
一 师	Division 1	5 571	100	4	1 422	60		339	209
二 师	Division 2	1 958	114	3	573	295	2	96	800
三 师	Division 3	3 608	156		363	102		16	123
四 师	Division 4	2 835	108		591	570		9	58
五 师	Division 5	606	134	9	391	303	10	156	210
六 师	Division 6	2 284	157	44	226	29	872	125	721
七 师	Division 7	875	149		1 022	140		56	64
八 师	Division 8	20 774	844	763	559	853	3 313	197	2 070
九 师	Division 9	209	115	13	158	127		28	19
十 师	Division 10	2 133	73		158	94		3	20
建 工 师	Construction Division	57 943			118		9	223	179
十 二 师	Division 12	58	114	32	52	30		91	49
十 三 师	Division 13	115	35		77		11		50
十 四 师	Division 14	566	23		201		4	31	23
国资公司	State-owned Property Company	60	217		4 707	137		453	168
供销公司	Supply and Marketing Corporation General		222		868				41
中基公司	Chalkis Company				69				20
兵团直属	Directly under XPCG		120	21	559	315	1 925	115	449

单 位	Unit	科学研究、技术服务和地质勘查业 Scientific Research, Technique Service and Geological Prospecting	水利、环境和公共设施管理业 Water Conservancy, Environment and Public Facilities Management	居民服务和其他服务业 Resident and Other Services	教 育 Education	卫生、社会保障和社会福利业 Health Care, Social Security and Welfare	文化、体育和娱乐业 Culture, Sports and Recreation	公共管理和社会组织 Public Management and Social Organization
总 计	**Total**	**6 821**	**10 000**	**1 620**	**42 683**	**24 430**	**2 032**	**26 528**
一 师	Division 1	489	3 952	31	4 752	2 594	143	3 760
二 师	Division 2	356	307		2 885	1 996	50	1 695
三 师	Division 3	159	481	39	3 280	1 253	66	2 773
四 师	Division 4	459	170	58	3 236	2 138	83	1 026
五 师	Division 5	263	79		2 202	1 386	48	673
六 师	Division 6	308	814	1	4 641	2 587	105	2 914
七 师	Division 7	468	1 302		2 762	1 880	113	1 534
八 师	Division 8	1 026	2 183	1 339	10 874	5 571	374	6 664
九 师	Division 9	88	365	14	1 123	875	67	683
十 师	Division 10	182	204	4	1 431	1 015	74	790
建 工 师	Construction Division	1 696			1 159	206		473
十 二 师	Division 12	16	30	22	970	273		229
十 三 师	Division 13	156		90	1 173	1 226	47	615
十 四 师	Division 14	19	95		550	221	11	344
国资公司	State-owned Property Company		18	22		23		
供销公司	Supply and Marketing Corporation General							
中基公司	Chalkis Company							
兵团直属	Directly under XPCG	1 136			1 645	1 186	851	2 355

4—10 各师单位就业人员劳动报酬

Labor Remuneration of Employed Persons by Division

计量单位:万元　　　　(2010 年)　　　　(10 000 yuan)

单　位	Unit	合　计 Total	企　业 Enterprises	事　业 Institutions	机　关 Agencies& Organizations	农、林、牧、渔业 Farming, Forestry, Animal Husbandry and Fishery	采矿业 Mining	制造业 Manufacturing	电力、煤气及水的生产和供应业 Production and Supply of Electricity, Gas and Water
总　计	**Total**	**1 990 638**	**1 586 754**	**289 055**	**114 829**	**970 113**	**22 854**	**154 436**	**33 184**
一　师	Division 1	243 796	193 799	33 607	16 389	128 894	2 709	20 375	4 660
二　师	Division 2	118 796	91 356	20 471	6 968	73 469	2 443	6 063	463
三　师	Division 3	98 597	70 614	15 868	12 115	56 629		1 033	909
四　师	Division 4	147 600	124 764	18 628	4 208	93 895	1 040	16 062	1 086
五　师	Division 5	90 888	75 281	12 595	3 012	64 216		4 019	1 878
六　师	Division 6	159 421	123 544	27 624	8 253	96 288	6 406	5 470	739
七　师	Division 7	103 744	78 945	17 946	6 853	63 609	1 134	4 056	3 070
八　师	Division 8	572 839	462 565	81 257	29 017	264 022	1 167	77 520	18 162
九　师	Division 9	35 605	26 583	5 851	3 171	22 257		2 527	310
十　师	Division 10	48 358	35 809	9 735	2 814	25 328	4 117	392	1 291
建 工 师	Construction Division	166 679	161 147	4 094	1 438	68		592	100
十 二 师	Division 12	38 787	32 750	6 037		25 513	2 586	3 419	212
十 三 师	Division 13	52 137	39 021	10 611	2 505	35 930	1 252	2 165	
十 四 师	Division 14	22 125	17 151	3 187	1 787	14 056		303	305
国资公司	State-owned Property Company	21 183	21 183					2 596	
供销公司	Supply and Marketing Corporation General	5 214	5 214						
中基公司	Chalkis Company	6 616	6 616					6 271	
兵团直属	Directly under XPCG	58 255	20 412	21 544	16 299	5 939		1 573	

单　位	Unit	建筑业 Construction	交通运输、仓储和邮政业 Transport, Storage and Postal Service	信息传输、计算机服务和软件业 Information Deliver, Computer Service and Software	批发和零售业 Wholesale and Retail Trade	住宿和餐饮业 Accommodation and Catering Services Industry	金融业 Finance	房地产业 Real Estate Trade	租赁和商务服务业 Leasing and Business Service
总　计	**Total**	**273 979**	**7 913**	**4 304**	**40 535**	**5 888**	**28 848**	**6 049**	**17 430**
一　师	Division 1	16 742	204	20	5 640	169		763	853
二　师	Division 2	4 351	311	9	1 569	494	11	201	1 912
三　师	Division 3	9 836	488		1 169	199		37	350
四　师	Division 4	7 978	295		2 011	1 049		27	180
五　师	Division 5	1 115	291	20	1 296	702	25	324	586
六　师	Division 6	5 070	476	152	543	90	4 635	399	2 737
七　师	Division 7	2 545	351		2 802	274		205	231
八　师	Division 8	64 589	3 093	3 913	2 029	1 600	13 970	1 178	6 770
九　师	Division 9	446	295	23	499	293		62	60
十　师	Division 10	3 882	123		351	165		11	77
建 工 师	Construction Division	154 813			328		47	447	385
十 二 师	Division 12	303	157	71	130	38		211	104
十 三 师	Division 13	337	127		372		73		260
十 四 师	Division 14	1 754	53		572		11	67	119
国资公司	State-owned Property Company	218	882		14 931	281		1 537	616
供销公司	Supply and Marketing Corporation General		509		4 419				286
中基公司	Chalkis Company				288				58
兵团直属	Directly under XPCG		258	96	1 586	534	10 077	580	1 846

4—10 续表 Continued

计量单位:万元 (2010 年) (10 000 yuan)

单位	Unit	科学研究、技术服务和地质勘查业 Scientific Research, Technique Service and Geological Prospecting	水利、环境和公共设施管理业 Water Conservancy, Environment and Public Facilities Management	居民服务和其他服务业 Resident and Other Services	教育 Education	卫生、社会保障和社会福利业 Health Care, Social Security and Welfare	文化、体育和娱乐业 Culture, Sports and Recreation	公共管理和社会组织 Public Management and Social Organization
总计	**Total**	**27 093**	**28 980**	**2 517**	**154 588**	**81 024**	**7 374**	**123 529**
一师	Division 1	2 837	13 216	99	19 350	10 118	415	16 729
二师	Division 2	1 851	957		10 726	6 510	172	7 283
三师	Division 3	421	1 351	291	10 346	3 037	133	12 368
四师	Division 4	1 871	349	128	10 586	6 488	284	4 271
五师	Division 5	1 572	157		6 974	4 209	202	3 302
六师	Division 6	1 199	1 392	3	15 542	7 954	425	9 901
七师	Division 7	1 296	3 069		8 296	5 298	428	7 081
八师	Division 8	4 191	7 179	1 673	45 362	22 817	1 315	32 291
九师	Division 9	190	520	31	2 737	1 826	143	3 385
十师	Division 10	749	422	12	4 653	3 332	273	3 180
建工师	Construction Division	4 366			3 550	544		1 438
十二师	Division 12	95	89	69	3 584	604		1 604
十三师	Division 13	667		139	4 626	3 226	171	2 794
十四师	Division 14	72	255		1 649	813	49	2 046
国资公司	State-owned Property Company		24	72		27		
供销公司	Supply and Marketing Corporation General							
中基公司	Chalkis Company							
兵团直属	Directly under XPCG	5 716			6 607	4 221	3 364	15 856

4—11 各师国有单位就业人员年末人数

Number of Employed Persons in State-owned Units at the Year-end by Division

计量单位:人 (2010 年) (person)

单位	Unit	合计 Total	企业 Enterprises	事业 Institutions	机关 Agencies & Organizations	农、林、牧、渔业 Farming, Forestry, Animal Husbandry and Fishery	采矿业 Mining	制造业 Manufacturing	电力、煤气及水的生产和供应业 Production and Supply of Electricity, Gas and Water
总计	**Total**	**573 136**	**466 805**	**82 117**	**24 214**	**412 099**	**4 746**	**11 091**	**5 360**
一师	Division 1	68 412	56 546	8 164	3 702	47 348	689	659	1 407
二师	Division 2	42 838	35 525	5 674	1 639	34 358	483		
三师	Division 3	34 425	26 317	5 391	2 717	24 720		485	423
四师	Division 4	61 263	54 310	5 936	1 017	52 180	463		530
五师	Division 5	36 238	31 611	4 021	606	29 362		89	807
六师	Division 6	54 733	43 568	8 844	2 321	42 373		84	156
七师	Division 7	45 635	37 948	6 186	1 501	32 070	374	1 667	925
八师	Division 8	114 303	88 595	20 042	5 666	76 674	366	5 168	831
九师	Division 9	22 004	18 752	2 630	622	18 178		10	128
十师	Division 10	20 781	17 067	3 056	658	14 935	1 240	131	71
建工师	Construction Division	8 822	7 240	1 261	321			5	
十二师	Division 12	17 076	15 529	1 547		12 586	740	1 760	82
十三师	Division 13	19 600	15 808	3 232	560	14 754	391	807	
十四师	Division 14	11 274	9 934	1 044	296	9 899			
国资公司	State-owned Property Company	2 013	2 013					84	
供销公司	Supply and Marketing Corporation General	1 110	1 110						
兵团直属	Directly under XPCG	12 609	4 932	5 089	2 588	2 662		142	

4—11 续表 Continued

计量单位:人 (2010 年) (person)

单位	Unit	建筑业 Construction	交通运输、仓储和邮政业 Transport, Storage and Postal Service	信息传输、计算机服务和软件业 Information Deliver, Computer Service and Software	批发和零售业 Wholesale and Retail Trade	住宿和餐饮业 Accommodation and Catering Services Industry	金融业 Finance	房地产业 Real Estate Trade	租赁和商务服务业 Leasing and Business Service
总计	**Total**	**13 031**	**1 768**	**608**	**6 127**	**2 152**	**2 609**	**930**	**3 115**
一师	Division 1	2 680	81	4	259	59		294	91
二师	Division 2	359	21	3	22	274	2	6	108
三师	Division 3		162		332	102		16	94
四师	Division 4		11		447	600			34
五师	Division 5	616	153		123	262		132	154
六师	Division 6		94	45	130	29	188	23	184
七师	Division 7	676	152		1 473	114		56	61
八师	Division 8	787	500	492	249	238	641	115	1 676
九师	Division 9	209	120	12	33	126			19
十师	Division 10	402	73		153	87		3	18
建工师	Construction Division	7 110						75	50
十二师	Division 12	58	112	30	51	31		45	52
十三师	Division 13	134	33		66		11		45
十四师	Division 14		23		37			29	5
国资公司	State-owned Property Company		13		1 781	20		63	29
供销公司	Supply and Marketing Corporation General		220		849				41
兵团直属	Directly under XPCG			22	122	210	1 767	73	454

单位	Unit	科学研究、技术服务和地质勘查业 Scientific Research, Technique Service and Geological Prospecting	水利、环境和公共设施管理业 Water Conservancy, Environment and Public Facilities Management	居民服务和其他服务业 Resident and Other Services	教育 Education	卫生、社会保障和社会福利业 Health Care, Social Security and Welfare	文化、体育和娱乐业 Culture, Sports and Recreation	公共管理和社会组织 Public Management and Social Organization
总计	**Total**	**4 693**	**9 019**	**448**	**42 268**	**24 427**	**2 049**	**26 596**
一师	Division 1	504	3 091	32	4 693	2 577	149	3 795
二师	Division 2	264	303		2 842	2 026	50	1 717
三师	Division 3	159	481	39	3 294	1 267	66	2 785
四师	Division 4	288	163	58	3 215	2 153	83	1 038
五师	Division 5	184	75		2 177	1 364	48	692
六师	Division 6	318	799	1	4 624	2 626	106	2 953
七师	Division 7	469	1 291		2 750	1 894	113	1 550
八师	Division 8	913	2 122	176	10 743	5 554	370	6 688
九师	Division 9	88	381	20	1 078	860	65	677
十师	Division 10	184	194	10	1 454	945	74	807
建工师	Construction Division				1 097	164		321
十二师	Division 12	16	30	22	970	274		217
十三师	Division 13	158		90	1 173	1 267	47	624
十四师	Division 14	25	89		583	218	12	354
国资公司	State-owned Property Company					23		
供销公司	Supply and Marketing Corporation General							
兵团直属	Directly under XPCG	1 123			1 575	1 215	866	2 378

4－12 各师国有单位就业人员年平均人数

Average Annual Number of Employed Persons in State-owned Units by Division

计量单位:人 (2010 年) (person)

单位	Unit	合计 Total	企业 Enterprises	事业 Institutions	机关 Agencies& Organizations	农、林、牧、渔业 Farming, Forestry, Animal Husbandry and Fishery	采矿业 Mining	制造业 Manufacturing	电力、煤气及水的生产和供应业 Production and Supply of Electricity, Gas and Water
总计	**Total**	**600 807**	**494 392**	**82 270**	**24 145**	**424 125**	**4 856**	**11 446**	**5 323**
一师	Division 1	71 843	59 958	8 215	3 670	47 931	713	720	1 384
二师	Division 2	43 388	36 086	5 679	1 623	34 785	488		
三师	Division 3	35 204	27 136	5 363	2 705	25 577		462	399
四师	Division 4	61 313	54 359	5 949	1 005	52 164	542		530
五师	Division 5	36 557	31 899	4 069	589	29 686		90	816
六师	Division 6	56 824	45 731	8 790	2 303	44 535		105	154
七师	Division 7	44 762	37 065	6 211	1 486	31 858	284	1 620	935
八师	Division 8	123 227	97 590	20 020	5 617	84 025	348	5 507	833
九师	Division 9	21 940	18 648	2 665	627	18 071		10	125
十师	Division 10	23 173	19 494	3 030	649	15 587	1 280	127	72
建工师	Construction Division	18 873	17 035	1 365	473			8	
十二师	Division 12	17 148	15 590	1 558		12 580	810	1 767	75
十三师	Division 13	19 383	15 607	3 226	550	14 610	391	787	
十四师	Division 14	11 404	10 113	1 002	289	10 074			
国资公司	State-owned Property Company	2 021	2 021					84	
供销公司	Supply and Marketing Corporation General	1 112	1 112						
兵团直属	Directly under XPCG	12 635	4 948	5 128	2 559	2 642		159	

单位	Unit	建筑业 Construction	交通运输、仓储和邮政业 Transport, Storage and Postal Service	信息传输、计算机服务和软件业 Information Deliver, Computer Service and Software	批发和零售业 Wholesale and Retail Trade	住宿和餐饮业 Accommodation and Catering Services Industry	金融业 Finance	房地产业 Real Estate Trade	租赁和商务服务业 Leasing and Business Service
总计	**Total**	**27 988**	**1 726**	**607**	**5 608**	**2 185**	**2 574**	**900**	**3 120**
一师	Division 1	4 716	72	4	256	60		286	89
二师	Division 2	468	21	3	21	295	2	7	107
三师	Division 3		156		337	102		16	104
四师	Division 4		11		431	570			35
五师	Division 5	606	134		124	254		128	152
六师	Division 6		92	44	137	29	170	19	169
七师	Division 7	670	149		927	140		56	64
八师	Division 8	2 114	496	490	253	239	620	108	1 687
九师	Division 9	209	115	13	36	127			19
十师	Division 10	2 133	73		158	94		3	20
建工师	Construction Division	16 899						75	53
十二师	Division 12	58	114	32	52	30		41	49
十三师	Division 13	115	35		77		11		50
十四师	Division 14		23		39			25	3
国资公司	State-owned Property Company		13		1 789	20		63	29
供销公司	Supply and Marketing Corporation General		222		849				41
兵团直属	Directly under XPCG			21	122	225	1 771	73	449

4—12 续表　Continued

计量单位：人　　　　（2010 年）　　　　(person)

单　位	Unit	科学研究、技术服务和地质勘查业 Scientific Research, Technique Service and Geological Prospecting	水利、环境和公共设施管理业 Water Conservancy, Environment and Public Facilities Management	居民服务和其他服务业 Resident and Other Services	教　育 Education	卫生、社会保障和社会福利业 Health Care, Social Security and Welfare	文化、体育和娱乐业 Culture, Sports and Recreation	公共管理和社会组织 Public Management and Social Organization
总　计	**Total**	**4 664**	**9 873**	**448**	**42 530**	**24 274**	**2 032**	**26 528**
一　师	Division 1	489	3 843	31	4 752	2 594	143	3 760
二　师	Division 2	258	307		2 885	1 996	50	1 695
三　师	Division 3	159	481	39	3 280	1 253	66	2 773
四　师	Division 4	319	170	58	3 236	2 138	83	1 026
五　师	Division 5	179	79		2 202	1 386	48	673
六　师	Division 6	308	814	1	4 641	2 587	105	2 914
七　师	Division 7	468	1 302		2 762	1 880	113	1 534
八　师	Division 8	887	2 183	189	10 721	5 489	374	6 664
九　师	Division 9	88	365	14	1 123	875	67	683
十　师	Division 10	182	204	4	1 431	941	74	790
建 工 师	Construction Division				1 159	206		473
十 二 师	Division 12	16	30	22	970	273		229
十 三 师	Division 13	156		90	1 173	1 226	47	615
十 四 师	Division 14	19	95		550	221	11	344
国资公司	State-owned Property Company					23		
供销公司	Supply and Marketing Corporation General							
兵团直属	Directly under XPCG	1 136			1 645	1 186	851	2 355

4—13　各师国有单位就业人员劳动报酬

Labor Remuneration of Employed Persons in State-owned Units by Division

计量单位：万元　　　　（2010 年）　　　　(10 000 yuan)

单　位	Unit	合　计 Total	企　业 Enterprises	事　业 Institutions	机　关 Agencies & Organizations	农、林、牧、渔业 Farming, Forestry, Animal Husbandry and Fishery	采矿业 Mining	制造业 Manufacturing	电力、煤气及水的生产和供应业 Production and Supply of Electricity, Gas and Water
总　计	**Total**	**1 567 940**	**1 164 056**	**289 055**	**114 829**	**968 495**	**14 342**	**25 449**	**15 136**
一　师	Division 1	216 547	166 551	33 607	16 389	128 274	2 709	1 484	4 661
二　师	Division 2	103 675	76 235	20 471	6 968	73 469	1 022		
三　师	Division 3	88 515	60 532	15 868	12 115	56 629		1 033	909
四　师	Division 4	121 739	98 903	18 628	4 208	93 896	1 040		1 086
五　师	Division 5	84 697	69 090	12 595	3 012	64 114		167	1 878
六　师	Division 6	135 458	99 581	27 624	8 253	96 288		191	383
七　师	Division 7	102 306	77 507	17 946	6 853	63 609	1 134	3 678	3 070
八　师	Division 8	414 873	304 599	81 257	29 017	263 193	1 167	12 627	2 484
九　师	Division 9	32 645	23 623	5 851	3 171	22 257		35	310
十　师	Division 10	46 190	33 641	9 735	2 814	25 328	3 432	190	143
建 工 师	Construction Division	44 351	38 819	4 094	1 438			21	
十 二 师	Division 12	38 636	32 598	6 037		25 513	2 586	3 340	212
十 三 师	Division 13	52 137	39 021	10 611	2 505	35 930	1 252	2 165	
十 四 师	Division 14	19 193	14 219	3 187	1 787	14 056			
国资公司	State-owned Property Company	7 068	7 068					164	
供销公司	Supply and Marketing Corporation General	5 128	5 128						
兵团直属	Directly under XPCG	54 784	16 941	21 544	16 299	5 939		354	

4—13 续表 Continued

计量单位:万元 （2010 年） （10 000 yuan）

单位	Unit	建筑业 Construction	交通运输、仓储和邮政业 Transport, Storage and Postal Service	信息传输、计算机服务和软件业 Information Deliver, Computer Service and Software	批发和零售业 Wholesale and Retail Trade	住宿和餐饮业 Accommodation and Catering Services Industry	金融业 Finance	房地产业 Real Estate Trade	租赁和商务服务业 Leasing and Business Service
总 计	**Total**	**68 472**	**5 078**	**2 901**	**20 155**	**4 408**	**14 449**	**2 500**	**10 930**
一 师	Division 1	14 593	154	20	958	169		579	366
二 师	Division 2	1 111	51	9	67	493	11	18	345
三 师	Division 3		488		988	199		37	285
四 师	Division 4		36		1 471	1 049			99
五 师	Division 5	1 115	291		495	594		262	280
六 师	Division 6		339	152	324	90	751	81	442
七 师	Division 7	1 695	351		2 592	274		204	231
八 师	Division 8	6 411	2 064	2 530	993	560	4 095	329	6 040
九 师	Division 9	446	295	23	93	293			60
十 师	Division 10	3 882	123		351	165		11	77
建 工 师	Construction Division	38 579						137	82
十 二 师	Division 12	303	157	71	130	38		137	104
十 三 师	Division 13	337	127		372		73		260
十 四 师	Division 14		52		152			43	5
国资公司	State-owned Property Company		41		6 471	58		186	122
供销公司	Supply and Marketing Corporation General		509		4 333				286
兵团直属	Directly under XPCG			96	365	426	9 519	476	1 846

单位	Unit	科学研究、技术服务和地质勘查业 Scientific Research, Technique Service and Geological Prospecting	水利、环境和公共设施管理业 Water Conservancy, Environment and Public Facilities Management	居民服务和其他服务业 Resident and Other Services	教育 Education	卫生、社会保障和社会福利业 Health Care, Social Security and Welfare	文化、体育和娱乐业 Culture, Sports and Recreation	公共管理和社会组织 Public Management and Social Organization
总 计	**Total**	**19 916**	**28 770**	**1 220**	**154 100**	**80 717**	**7 374**	**123 529**
一 师	Division 1	2 837	13 030	99	19 350	10 118	415	16 729
二 师	Division 2	1 432	957		10 726	6 510	172	7 283
三 师	Division 3	421	1 351	291	10 346	3 037	133	12 368
四 师	Division 4	957	349	128	10 586	6 488	284	4 271
五 师	Division 5	655	157		6 974	4 209	202	3 302
六 师	Division 6	1 199	1 392	3	15 542	7 954	425	9 901
七 师	Division 7	1 296	3 069		8 296	5 298	428	7 081
八 师	Division 8	3 630	7 179	448	44 874	22 644	1 315	32 291
九 师	Division 9	190	520	31	2 737	1 826	143	3 385
十 师	Division 10	749	422	12	4 653	3 198	273	3 180
建 工 师	Construction Division				3 550	544		1 438
十 二 师	Division 12	95	89	69	3 584	604		1 604
十 三 师	Division 13	667		139	4 626	3 226	171	2 794
十 四 师	Division 14	72	255		1 649	813	49	2 046
国资公司	State-owned Property Company					27		
供销公司	Supply and Marketing Corporation General							
兵团直属	Direct Under XPCG	5 716			6 607	4 221	3 364	15 856

4—14 各师国有单位女性就业人员年末人数

Number of Female Employed Persons in State-owned Units at the Year-end by Division

计量单位：人　　　　(2010 年)　　　　(person)

单位	Unit	合计 Total	企业 Enterprises	事业 Institutions	机关 Agencies & Organizations	农、林、牧、渔业 Farming, Forestry, Animal Husbandry and Fishery	采矿业 Mining	制造业 Manufacturing	电力、煤气及水的生产和供应业 Production and Supply of Electricity, Gas and Water
总　计	**Total**	**259 755**	**206 431**	**48 157**	**5 167**	**186 491**	**1 186**	**5 335**	**1 591**
一　师	Division 1	30 595	25 073	5 065	457	21 595	111	271	427
二　师	Division 2	20 972	17 202	3 536	234	16 688	218		
三　师	Division 3	15 371	11 973	3 007	391	11 373		166	99
四　师	Division 4	27 727	23 772	3 715	240	22 883	126		151
五　师	Division 5	17 215	14 342	2 715	158	13 338		58	344
六　师	Division 6	25 771	19 666	5 599	506	19 181		28	43
七　师	Division 7	20 843	16 972	3 638	233	14 519	68	826	287
八　师	Division 8	52 506	39 671	11 254	1 581	34 998	51	2 613	130
九　师	Division 9	10 033	8 400	1 506	127	8 137		4	43
十　师	Division 10	9 120	6 937	2 009	174	6 278	331	77	30
建工师	Construction Division	1 780	781	843	156			2	
十二师	Division 12	7 712	6 798	914		5 492	181	1 002	37
十三师	Division 13	8 847	6 720	1 973	154	6 430	100	176	
十四师	Division 14	4 995	4 430	495	70	4 414			
国资公司	State-owned Property Company	953	953					33	
供销公司	Supply and Marketing Corporation General	425	425						
兵团直属	Directly under XPCG	4 890	2 316	1 888	686	1 165		79	

单位	Unit	建筑业 Construction	交通运输、仓储和邮政业 Transport, Storage and Postal Service	信息传输、计算机服务和软件业 Information Deliver, Computer Service and Software	批发和零售业 Wholesale and Retail Trade	住宿和餐饮业 Accommodation and Catering Services Industry	金融业 Finance	房地产业 Real Estate Trade	租赁和商务服务业 Leasing and Business Service
总　计	**Total**	**2 810**	**625**	**208**	**2 796**	**1 389**	**1 266**	**395**	**827**
一　师	Division 1	922	36	4	98	39		119	49
二　师	Division 2	119	3		8	156	2	4	21
三　师	Division 3		58		193	58		6	28
四　师	Division 4		4		214	361			9
五　师	Division 5	218	59		45	155		52	108
六　师	Division 6		64	10	49	22	83	16	82
七　师	Division 7	296	42		671	81		16	25
八　师	Division 8	240	199	172	118	164	338	57	317
九　师	Division 9	92	31	4	12	92			8
十　师	Division 10	98	34		82	64		2	9
建工师	Construction Division	721						32	26
十二师	Division 12	20	6	9		22		20	13
十三师	Division 13	84	10		28		6		20
十四师	Division 14		5		20			7	4
国资公司	State-owned Property Company		2		862	8		17	13
供销公司	Supply and Marketing Corporation General		72		341				12
兵团直属	Directly under XPCG			9	55	167	837	47	83

4—14 续表 Continued

计量单位:人 (2010 年) (person)

单位	Unit	科学研究、技术服务和地质勘查业 Scientific Research, Technique Service and Geological Prospecting	水利、环境和公共设施管理业 Water Conservancy, Environment and Public Facilities Management	居民服务和其他服务业 Resident and Other Services	教育 Education	卫生、社会保障和社会福利业 Health Care, Social Security and Welfare	文化、体育和娱乐业 Culture, Sports and Recreation	公共管理和社会组织 Public Management and Social Organization
总计	**Total**	**1 490**	**3 847**	**214**	**26 412**	**15 734**	**859**	**6 280**
一师	Division 1	141	1 467	17	2 939	1 823	55	482
二师	Division 2	87	118		1 931	1 335	18	264
三师	Division 3	62	159	11	1 895	811	34	418
四师	Division 4	116	73	19	1 980	1 490	47	254
五师	Division 5	59	45		1 510	1 006	22	196
六师	Division 6	111	432		2 882	1 816	84	868
七师	Division 7	121	574		1 807	1 208	50	252
八师	Division 8	286	749	81	6 373	3 515	175	1 930
九师	Division 9	32	142	9	714	530	27	156
十师	Division 10	44	78	4	1 020	693	30	246
建工师	Construction Division				706	137		156
十二师	Division 12	6	5	10	635	183		71
十三师	Division 13	37		63	803	888	18	184
十四师	Division 14	9	5		297	137	4	93
国资公司	State-owned Property Company					18		
供销公司	Supply and Marketing Corporation General							
兵团直属	Directly under XPCG	379			920	144	295	710

4—15 各师国有单位少数民族就业人员年末人数

Number of Nationality Employed Persons in State-owned Units at the Year-end by Division

计量单位:人 (2010 年) (person)

单位	Unit	合计 Total				农、林、牧、渔业 Farming, Forestry, Animal Husbandry and Fishery	采矿业 Mining	制造业 Manufacturing	电力、煤气及水的生产和供应业 Production and Supply of Electricity, Gas and Water
			企业 Enterprises	事业 Institutions	机关 Agencies & Organizations				
总计	**Total**	**50 585**	**42 593**	**6 763**	**1 229**	**40 136**	**164**	**888**	**213**
一师	Division 1	2 143	1 627	309	207	1 334	13	34	35
二师	Division 2	1 298	1 055	190	53	1 025	14		
三师	Division 3	8 992	7 092	1 605	295	6 831		175	3
四师	Division 4	8 552	7 644	849	59	7 500	46		20
五师	Division 5	3 517	3 081	384	52	2 907		3	79
六师	Division 6	4 118	3 610	453	55	3 574			9
七师	Division 7	1 155	916	208	31	761	2	27	29
八师	Division 8	4 904	3 597	1 064	243	3 148	19	200	17
九师	Division 9	635	532	84	19	522			
十师	Division 10	502	412	71	19	370	22	16	1
建工师	Construction Division	95	69	23	3				
十二师	Division 12	4 773	4 540	233		4 069	38	397	20
十三师	Division 13	3 188	2 669	457	62	2 629	10	20	
十四师	Division 14	6 007	5 457	505	45	5 444			
国资公司	State-owned Property Company	99	99						
供销公司	Supply and Marketing Corporation General	36	36						
兵团直属	Directly under XPCG	571	157	328	86	22		16	

4—15 续表 Continued

计量单位:人　　　　(2010 年)　　　　(person)

单 位	Unit	建筑业 Construction	交通运输、仓储和邮政业 Transport, Storage and Postal Service	信息传输、计算机服务和软件业 Information Deliver, Computer Service and Software	批发和零售业 Wholesale and Retail Trade	住宿和餐饮业 Accommodation and Catering Services Industry	金融业 Finance	房地产业 Real Estate Trade	租赁和商务服务业 Leasing and Business Service
总　计	**Total**	**235**	**82**	**30**	**271**	**130**	**163**	**45**	**81**
一　师	Division 1	59	4		6	6		12	1
二　师	Division 2	5	1			11			1
三　师	Division 3		21		54	8			
四　师	Division 4		1		14	62			
五　师	Division 5	45	16		7	10			22
六　师	Division 6		2	2	5	1	11	1	
七　师	Division 7	12	5		34	4			3
八　师	Division 8	24	15	21	7	19	37	2	46
九　师	Division 9		3		2	5			
十　师	Division 10	3			1	1			
建工师	Construction Division	62						4	3
十二师	Division 12	9		6				6	
十三师	Division 13	16	1		8				
十四师	Division 14		9		5			10	1
国资公司	State-owned Property Company		1		94			4	
供销公司	Supply and Marketing Corporation General		3		33				
兵团直属	Directly under XPCG			1	1	3	115	6	4

单 位	Unit	科学研究、技术服务和地质勘查业 Scientific Research, Technique Service and Geological Prospecting	水利、环境和公共设施管理业 Water Conservancy, Environment and Public Facilities Management	居民服务和其他服务业 Resident and Other Services	教 育 Education	卫生、社会保障和社会福利业 Health Care, Social Security and Welfare	文化、体育和娱乐业 Culture, Sports and Recreation	公共管理和社会组织 Public Management and Social Organization
总　计	**Total**	**119**	**324**	**25**	**4 374**	**1 619**	**186**	**1 500**
一　师	Division 1	10	124		186	105	6	208
二　师	Division 2	4	2		91	82	3	59
三　师	Division 3	4	10	7	1 309	248	19	303
四　师	Division 4	12	3	8	552	272	3	59
五　师	Division 5	7	1		241	118	6	55
六　师	Division 6	4	8		301	134		66
七　师	Division 7	4	57		117	59	7	34
八　师	Division 8	37	102	8	526	209	23	444
九　师	Division 9	3	2	1	57	19	1	20
十　师	Division 10		9		23	28	5	23
建工师	Construction Division				14	9		3
十二师	Division 12	4		1	179	28		16
十三师	Division 13	2			257	179	2	64
十四师	Division 14	1	6		359	115		57
国资公司	State-owned Property Company							
供销公司	Supply and Marketing Corporation General							
兵团直属	Direct Under XPCG	27			162	14	111	89

4—16 各师非国有单位就业人员年末人数

Number of Employed Persons of Non-State-owned Units at the Year-end by Division

计量单位：人 (2010 年) (person)

单 位	Unit	合 计 Total	农、林、牧、渔业 Farming, Forestry, Animal Husbandry and Fishery	采矿业 Mining	制造业 Manufacturing	电力、煤气及水的生产和供应业 Production and Supply of Electricity, Gas and Water	建筑业 Construction	交通运输、仓储和邮政业 Transport, Storage and Postal Service	信息传输、计算机服务和软件业 Information Deliver, Computer Service and Software	批发和零售业 Wholesale and Retail Trade	住宿和餐饮业 Accommodation and Catering Services Industry
总 计	**Total**	**109 095**	**902**	**2 170**	**46 977**	**5 766**	**34 228**	**958**	**287**	**6 728**	**874**
一 师	Division 1	7 677	363		5 585		242	28		1 158	
二 师	Division 2	5 653		401	2 634	234	966	91		556	
三 师	Division 3	3 681					3 633			28	
四 师	Division 4	9 328			6 387		2 518	96		171	
五 师	Division 5	2 530	73		1 979				9	228	49
六 师	Division 6	5 793		1 553	2 101	96	547	70		93	
七 师	Division 7	496			146		205			145	
八 师	Division 8	47 417	395		23 306	4 799	12 483	353	278	314	627
九 师	Division 9	1 087			942					117	
十 师	Division 10	933		216	119	524					
建 工 师	Construction Division	15 132	71		190	41	13 103			80	
十 二 师	Division 12	37			37						
十 四 师	Division 14	1 028			208	72	471			245	
国资公司	State-owned Property Company	5 123			1 123		60	201		3 061	117
供销公司	Supply and Marketing Corporation General	19								19	
中基公司	Chalkis Company	2 133			2 038					74	
兵团直属	Directly under XPCG	1 028			182			119		439	81

单 位	Unit	金融业 Finance	房地产业 Real Estate Trade	租赁和商务服务业 Leasing and Business Service	科学研究、技术服务和地质勘查业 Scientific Research, Technique Service and Geological Prospecting	水利、环境和公共设施管理业 Water Conservancy, Environment and Public Facilities Management	居民服务和其他服务业 Resident and Other Services	教 育 Education	卫生、社会保障和社会福利业 Health Care, Social Security and Welfare
总 计	**Total**	**3 538**	**1 006**	**2 085**	**1 822**	**111**	**1 328**	**152**	**163**
一 师	Division 1		56	147		98			
二 师	Division 2		90	587	94				
三 师	Division 3			20					
四 师	Division 4		9	23	124				
五 师	Division 5	10	28	64	90				
六 师	Division 6	660	116	557					
七 师	Division 7								
八 师	Division 8	2 696	89	381	139		1 316	152	89
九 师	Division 9		28						
十 师	Division 10								74
建 工 师	Construction Division	6	146	120	1 375				
十 二 师	Division 12								
十 四 师	Division 14	4	6	22					
国资公司	State-owned Property Company		393	143		13	12		
供销公司	Supply and Marketing Corporation General								
中基公司	Chalkis Company			21					
兵团直属	Directly under XPCG	162	45						

4—17 全部职工年末人数构成及个体劳动者

Composition of All Staff and Workers and Individual Labors

年份 Year	单位 Unit	职工人数(人) Number of Staff and Workers (person)	#国有单位 State-owned Units	#集体单位 Collective-owned Units	构成(%)(职工人数=100) Composition(%) #国有单位 State-owned Units	#集体单位 Collective-owned Units	个体、私营劳动者(人) Self-employed Individuals (person)
1952		175 179	175 179		100		
1954		105 546	105 546		100		
1957		178 667	178 667		100		
1962		460 194	460 194		100		
1965		666 805	666 805		100		
1970		908 867	876 202	32 665	96.4	3.6	
1975		761 036	730 073	30 963	95.9	4.1	
1978		918 448	878 770	39 678	95.7	4.3	
1980		929 995	897 509	32 486	96.5	3.5	
1985		948 322	899 776	48 546	94.9	5.1	36 441
1990		970 507	935 170	35 337	96.4	3.6	34 688
1991		1 010 081	975 599	34 482	96.6	3.4	43 826
1992		1 019 011	985 260	33 751	96.7	3.3	49 164
1993		968 287	952 500	15 787	98.4	1.6	46 630
1994		946 458	931 186	15 272	98.4	1.6	50 157
1995		933 595	917 670	13 834	98.3	1.5	63 521
1996		926 722	905 277	15 352	97.7	1.7	65 350
1997		905 945	887 767	11 969	98.0	1.3	75 226
1998		797 348	778 136	8 865	97.6	1.1	86 118
1999		754 445	739 925	7 812	98.1	1.0	99 802
2000		702 257	683 518	5 962	97.3	0.8	121 965
2001		687 903	640 236	5 024	93.1	0.7	148 013
2002		691 027	629 468	3 916	91.1	0.6	168 816
2003		684 073	616 485	3 081	90.1	0.5	192 840
2004		669 986	604 264	2 878	90.2	0.4	215 344
2005		665 360	593 653	869	89.2	0.1	231 580
2006		662 285	586 691	567	88.6	0.1	238 058
2007		660 630	579 189	92	87.7	…	243 150
2008		673 220	584 917	225	86.9	…	262 118
2009		671 985	568 433	214	84.6	…	269 223
2010		677 570	568 885	278	84.0	…	293 940
一师	Division 1	75 691	68 054		89.9		25 250
二师	Division 2	48 447	42 817		88.4		18 472
三师	Division 3	37 775	34 094		90.3		12 345
四师	Division 4	70 486	61 162		86.8		25 145
五师	Division 5	38 698	36 184		93.5		6 943
六师	Division 6	60 278	54 534		90.5		40 438
七师	Division 7	46 117	45 621		98.9		27 512
八师	Division 8	161 801	114 213	228	70.6	…	103 396
九师	Division 9	22 353	21 398		95.7		6 479
十师	Division 10	20 667	19 745		95.5		6 086
建工师	Construction Division	23 848	8 804		36.9		1 642
十二师	Division 12	16 869	16 782	50	99.5		10 157
十三师	Division 13	19 277	19 277		100		8 014
十四师	Division 14	12 130	11 273		92.9		1 656
国资公司	State-owned Property Company	7 122	2 013		28.3		309
供销公司	Supply and Marketing Corporation General	931	912		98.0		
中基公司	Chalkis Company	2 086					
兵团直属	Directly Under XPCG	12 994	12 002		92.4		96

注:1998年及以后年份职工数据为在岗职工数据(下同)。

Note:Data Since 1998 refer to data of staff and workers on the job(the same as follows).

4—18 各师在岗职工年末人数

Number of Staff and Workers on the Job at the Year-end by Division

计量单位：人 （2010年） (person)

单 位	Unit	合 计 Total	企 业 Enterprises	事 业 Institutions	机 关 Agencies & Organizations	农、林、牧、渔业 Farming, Forestry, Animal Husbandry and Fishery	采矿业 Mining	制造业 Manufacturing	电力、煤气及水的生产和供应业 Production and Supply of Electricity, Gas and Water
总 计	**Total**	**677 570**	**573 641**	**80 066**	**23 863**	**411 922**	**6 911**	**57 621**	**11 091**
一 师	Division 1	75 691	64 139	7 938	3 614	47 711	689	6 202	1 407
二 师	Division 2	48 447	41 151	5 657	1 639	34 354	884	2 619	234
三 师	Division 3	37 775	29 882	5 247	2 646	24 699		462	411
四 师	Division 4	70 486	63 557	5 913	1 016	52 103	463	6 387	530
五 师	Division 5	38 698	34 109	3 984	605	29 424		2 066	807
六 师	Division 6	60 278	49 287	8 704	2 287	42 372	1 553	2 137	252
七 师	Division 7	46 117	38 444	6 172	1 501	32 070	374	1 813	925
八 师	Division 8	161 801	136 169	19 967	5 665	77 059	366	28 504	5 625
九 师	Division 9	22 353	19 619	2 149	585	18 177		848	111
十 师	Division 10	20 667	17 190	2 910	567	14 182	1 451	224	595
建 工 师	Construction Division	23 848	22 284	1 245	319	71		194	41
十 二 师	Division 12	16 869	15 358	1 511		12 585	740	1 635	82
十 三 师	Division 13	19 277	15 601	3 119	557	14 554	391	802	
十 四 师	Division 14	12 130	10 791	1 043	296	9 899		208	71
国资公司	State-owned Property Company	7 122	7 122					1 207	
供销公司	Supply and Marketing Corporation General	931	931						
中基公司	Chalkis Company	2 086	2 086					1 992	
兵团直属	Directly under XPCG	12 994	5 921	4 507	2 566	2 662		321	

单 位	Unit	建筑业 Construction	交通运输、仓储和邮政业 Transport, Storage and Postal Service	信息传输、计算机服务和软件业 Information Deliver, Computer Service and Software	批发和零售业 Wholesale and Retail Trade	住宿和餐饮业 Accommodation and Catering Services Industry	金融业 Finance	房地产业 Real Estate Trade	租赁和商务服务业 Leasing and Business Service
总 计	**Total**	**47 204**	**2 581**	**894**	**12 383**	**2 967**	**6 306**	**1 969**	**5 129**
一 师	Division 1	2 922	106	3	1 416	22		350	232
二 师	Division 2	1 325	112	3	576	274	2	96	692
三 师	Division 3	3 633	162		301	101		16	107
四 师	Division 4	2 518	107		618	600		9	57
五 师	Division 5	616	153	9	350	310	10	158	218
六 师	Division 6	547	164	45	222	29	831	139	740
七 师	Division 7	881	152		1 618	114		56	61
八 师	Division 8	13 264	853	770	561	864	3 513	204	2 055
九 师	Division 9	163	104	12	136	107		14	19
十 师	Division 10	402	73		147	87		2	18
建 工 师	Construction Division	20 213			73		6	221	170
十 二 师	Division 12	57	23	30	51	31		95	16
十 三 师	Division 13	134	31		66		11		37
十 四 师	Division 14	469	23		116		4	35	24
国资公司	State-owned Property Company	60	214		4 828	137		456	172
供销公司	Supply and Marketing Corporation General		185		705				41
中基公司	Chalkis Company				74				20
兵团直属	Directly under XPCG		119	22	525	291	1 929	118	450

4—18 续表 Continued

计量单位：人 （2010 年） (person)

单位	Unit	科学研究、技术服务和地质勘查业 Scientific Research, Technique Service and Geological Prospecting	水利、环境和公共设施管理业 Water Conservancy, Environment and Public Facilities Management	居民服务和其他服务业 Resident and Other Services	教育 Education	卫生、社会保障和社会福利业 Health Care, Social Security and Welfare	文化、体育和娱乐业 Culture, Sports and Recreation	公共管理和社会组织 Public Management and Social Organization
总计	**Total**	**6 097**	**8 880**	**1 766**	**41 901**	**23 803**	**1 987**	**26 158**
一师	Division 1	378	3 189	32	4 666	2 539	136	3 691
二师	Division 2	355	303		2 839	2 012	50	1 717
三师	Division 3	153	476	29	3 209	1 243	64	2 709
四师	Division 4	408	163	58	3 213	2 133	82	1 037
五师	Division 5	259	75		2 177	1 330	48	688
六师	Division 6	316	799	1	4 527	2 594	106	2 904
七师	Division 7	469	1 283		2 749	1 891	111	1 550
八师	Division 8	1 049	2 122	1 492	10 880	5 565	369	6 686
九师	Division 9	86	149	20	960	749	62	636
十师	Division 10	159	194	10	1 397	980	71	675
建工师	Construction Division	1 295			1 084	161		319
十二师	Division 12	16	25	22	970	274		217
十三师	Division 13	97		90	1 149	1 247	47	621
十四师	Division 14	25	89		583	218	12	354
国资公司	State-owned Property Company		13	12		23		
供销公司	Supply and Marketing Corporation General							
中基公司	Chalkis Company							
兵团直属	Directly under XPCG	1 032			1 498	844	829	2 354

4—19 各师在岗职工年平均人数

Average Annual Number of Staff and Workers on the Job by Division

计量单位：人 （2010 年） (person)

单位	Unit	合计 Total	企业 Enterprises	事业 Institutions	机关 Agencies & Organizations	农、林、牧、渔业 Farming, Forestry, Animal Husbandry and Fishery	采矿业 Mining	制造业 Manufacturing	电力、煤气及水的生产和供应业 Production and Supply of Electricity, Gas and Water
总计	**Total**	**741 702**	**637 699**	**80 248**	**23 755**	**423 810**	**7 029**	**57 193**	**11 102**
一师	Division 1	79 459	67 916	7 963	3 580	48 211	713	6 109	1 384
二师	Division 2	49 711	42 424	5 664	1 623	34 781	904	2 693	226
三师	Division 3	38 498	30 690	5 210	2 598	25 561		445	393
四师	Division 4	70 663	63 737	5 922	1 004	52 102	542	6 196	530
五师	Division 5	39 190	34 567	4 035	588	29 749		2 208	816
六师	Division 6	63 838	52 920	8 649	2 269	44 534	1 545	1 875	257
七师	Division 7	45 222	37 538	6 198	1 486	31 858	284	1 793	935
八师	Division 8	175 853	150 290	19 947	5 616	84 265	348	28 262	5 683
九师	Division 9	22 302	19 501	2 212	589	18 070		829	112
十师	Division 10	23 122	19 675	2 889	558	14 895	1 492	226	583
建工师	Construction Division	62 287	60 471	1 345	471	71		268	41
十二师	Division 12	16 958	15 434	1 524		12 579	810	1 656	75
十三师	Division 13	19 073	15 408	3 118	547	14 418	391	782	
十四师	Division 14	12 387	11 097	1 001	289	10 074		248	67
国资公司	State-owned Property Company	6 979	6 979					1 188	
供销公司	Supply and Marketing Corporation General	933	933						
中基公司	Chalkis Company	2 149	2 149					2 061	
兵团直属	Directly under XPCG	13 078	5 970	4 571	2 537	2 642		354	

4—19 续表 Continued

计量单位:人 (2010 年) (person)

单位	Unit	建筑业 Construction	交通运输、仓储和邮政业 Transport, Storage and Postal Service	信息传输、计算机服务和软件业 Information Deliver, Computer Service and Software	批发和零售业 Wholesale and Retail Trade	住宿和餐饮业 Accommodation and Catering Services Industry	金融业 Finance	房地产业 Real Estate Trade	租赁和商务服务业 Leasing and Business Service
总计	**Total**	**99 540**	**2 544**	**888**	**11 739**	**2 995**	**6 128**	**1 921**	**5 207**
一师	Division 1	5 571	98	3	1 421	22		339	203
二师	Division 2	1 958	114	3	571	295	2	96	797
三师	Division 3	3 608	156		304	101		16	116
四师	Division 4	2 835	108		591	570		9	58
五师	Division 5	606	134	9	390	302	10	154	210
六师	Division 6	2 284	157	44	225	29	855	125	720
七师	Division 7	875	149		1 022	140		56	64
八师	Division 8	20 768	844	763	557	852	3 312	197	2 068
九师	Division 9	163	105	13	140	108		14	19
十师	Division 10	2 133	73		152	94		2	20
建工师	Construction Division	57 943			111		9	223	179
十二师	Division 12	57	26	32	52	30		91	15
十三师	Division 13	115	33		77		11		45
十四师	Division 14	564	23		116		4	31	20
国资公司	State-owned Property Company	60	217		4 693	137		453	168
供销公司	Supply and Marketing Corporation General		187		705				41
中基公司	Chalkis Company				69				19
兵团直属	Directly under XPCG		120	21	543	315	1 925	115	445

单位	Unit	科学研究、技术服务和地质勘查业 Scientific Research, Technique Service and Geological Prospecting	水利、环境和公共设施管理业 Water Conservancy, Environment and Public Facilities Management	居民服务和其他服务业 Resident and Other Services	教育 Education	卫生、社会保障和社会福利业 Health Care, Social Security and Welfare	文化、体育和娱乐业 Culture, Sports and Recreation	公共管理和社会组织 Public Management and Social Organization
总计	**Total**	**6 401**	**9 760**	**1 610**	**42 164**	**23 642**	**1 970**	**26 059**
一师	Division 1	362	3 952	31	4 724	2 532	130	3 654
二师	Division 2	353	307		2 880	1 986	50	1 695
三师	Division 3	153	476	29	3 198	1 217	64	2 661
四师	Division 4	439	170	58	3 234	2 114	82	1 025
五师	Division 5	249	79		2 202	1 355	48	669
六师	Division 6	306	814	1	4 542	2 556	105	2 864
七师	Division 7	468	1 294		2 761	1 878	111	1 534
八师	Division 8	1 023	2 183	1 339	10 860	5 494	373	6 662
九师	Division 9	86	153	14	1 009	762	64	641
十师	Division 10	160	194	4	1 371	985	71	667
建工师	Construction Division	1 626			1 143	202		471
十二师	Division 12	16	25	22	970	273		229
十三师	Division 13	97		90	1 149	1 206	47	612
十四师	Division 14	19	95		550	221	11	344
国资公司	State-owned Property Company		18	22		23		
供销公司	Supply and Marketing Corporation General							
中基公司	Chalkis Company							
兵团直属	Directly under XPCG	1 044			1 571	838	814	2 331

4—20 各师国有单位在岗职工年末人数

Number of Staff and Workers on the Job in State-owned Units at the Year-end by Division

计量单位：人　　　　　　　　　　(2010 年)　　　　　　　　　　(person)

单位	Unit	合计 Total	企业 Enterprises	事业 Institutions	机关 Agencies& Organi-zations	农、林、牧、渔业 Farming,Fore-stry,Animal Husbandry and Fishery	采矿业 Mining	制造业 Manufac-turing	电力、煤气及水的生产和供应业 Production and Supply of Electricity, Gas and Water
总计	**Total**	**568 885**	**464 956**	**80 066**	**23 863**	**411 020**	**4 741**	**10 879**	**5 331**
一师	Division 1	68 054	56 502	7 938	3 614	47 348	689	657	1 407
二师	Division 2	42 817	35 521	5 657	1 639	34 354	483		
三师	Division 3	34 094	26 201	5 247	2 646	24 699		462	411
四师	Division 4	61 162	54 233	5 913	1 016	52 103	463		530
五师	Division 5	36 184	31 595	3 984	605	29 351		89	807
六师	Division 6	54 534	43 543	8 704	2 287	42 372		84	156
七师	Division 7	45 621	37 948	6 172	1 501	32 070	374	1 667	925
八师	Division 8	114 213	88 581	19 967	5 665	76 664	366	5 166	831
九师	Division 9	21 398	18 664	2 149	585	18 177		10	111
十师	Division 10	19 745	16 268	2 910	567	14 182	1 235	116	71
建工师	Construction Division	8 804	7 240	1 245	319			5	
十二师	Division 12	16 782	15 271	1 511		12 585	740	1 598	82
十三师	Division 13	19 277	15 601	3 119	557	14 554	391	802	
十四师	Division 14	11 273	9 934	1 043	296	9 899			
国资公司	State-owned Property Company	2 013	2 013					84	
供销公司	Supply and Marketing Corporation General	912	912						
兵团直属	Directly under XPCG	12 002	4 929	4 507	2 566	2 662		139	

单位	Unit	建筑业 Constr-uction	交通运输、仓储和邮政业 Transport, Storage and Postal Service	信息传输、计算机服务和软件业 Information Deliver, Computer Service and Software	批发和零售业 Wholesale and Retail Trade	住宿和餐饮业 Accommodat-ion and Catering Services Industry	金融业 Finance	房地产业 Real Estate Trade	租赁和商务服务业 Leasing and Business Service
总计	**Total**	**12 984**	**1 623**	**607**	**5 896**	**2 095**	**2 592**	**928**	**3 051**
一师	Division 1	2 680	78	3	258	22		294	85
二师	Division 2	359	21	3	22	274	2	6	108
三师	Division 3		162		273	101		16	87
四师	Division 4		11		447	600			34
五师	Division 5	616	153		122	262		131	154
六师	Division 6		94	45	129	29	171	23	184
七师	Division 7	676	152		1 473	114		56	61
八师	Division 8	787	500	492	249	238	641	115	1 674
九师	Division 9	163	104	12	33	107			19
十师	Division 10	402	73		147	87		2	18
建工师	Construction Division	7 110						75	50
十二师	Division 12	57	23	30	51	31		45	16
十三师	Division 13	134	31		66		11		37
十四师	Division 14		23		37			29	4
国资公司	State-owned Property Company		13		1 781	20		63	29
供销公司	Supply and Marketing Corporation General		185		686				41
兵团直属	Directly under XPCG			22	122	210	1 767	73	450

4—20 续表 Continued

计量单位：人 （2010 年） (person)

单位	Unit	科学研究、技术服务和地质勘查业 Scientific Research, Technique Service and Geological Prospecting	水利、环境和公共设施管理业 Water Conservancy, Environment and Public Facilities Management	居民服务和其他服务业 Resident and Other Services	教育 Education	卫生、社会保障和社会福利业 Health Care, Social Security and Welfare	文化、体育和娱乐业 Culture, Sports and Recreation	公共管理和社会组织 Public Management and Social Organization
总计	**Total**	**4 377**	**8 769**	**438**	**41 749**	**23 660**	**1 987**	**26 158**
一师	Division 1	378	3 091	32	4 666	2 539	136	3 691
二师	Division 2	264	303		2 839	2 012	50	1 717
三师	Division 3	153	476	29	3 209	1 243	64	2 709
四师	Division 4	288	163	58	3 213	2 133	82	1 037
五师	Division 5	181	75		2 177	1 330	48	688
六师	Division 6	316	799	1	4 527	2 594	106	2 904
七师	Division 7	469	1 283		2 749	1 891	111	1 550
八师	Division 8	913	2 122	176	10 728	5 496	369	6 686
九师	Division 9	86	149	20	960	749	62	636
十师	Division 10	159	194	10	1 397	906	71	675
建工师	Construction Division				1 084	161		319
十二师	Division 12	16	25	22	970	274		217
十三师	Division 13	97		90	1 149	1 247	47	621
十四师	Division 14	25	89		583	218	12	354
国资公司	State-owned Property Company					23		
供销公司	Supply and Marketing Corporation General							
兵团直属	Directly under XPCG	1 032			1 498	844	829	2 354

4—21 各师国有单位在岗职工年平均人数

Average Annual Number of Staff and Workers in State-owned Units by Division

计量单位：人 （2010 年） (person)

单位	Unit	合计 Total				农、林、牧、渔业 Farming, Forestry, Animal Husbandry and Fishery	采矿业 Mining	制造业 Manufacturing	电力、煤气及水的生产和供应业 Production and Supply of Electricity, Gas and Water
			企业 Enterprises	事业 Institutions	机关 Agencies & Organizations				
总计	**Total**	**596 659**	**492 656**	**80 248**	**23 755**	**423 135**	**4 852**	**11 242**	**5 304**
一师	Division 1	71 457	59 914	7 963	3 580	47 931	713	718	1 384
二师	Division 2	43 369	36 082	5 664	1 623	34 781	488		
三师	Division 3	34 845	27 037	5 210	2 598	25 561		445	393
四师	Division 4	61 223	54 297	5 922	1 004	52 102	542		530
五师	Division 5	36 509	31 886	4 035	588	29 676		90	816
六师	Division 6	56 623	45 705	8 649	2 269	44 534		105	154
七师	Division 7	44 749	37 065	6 198	1 486	31 858	284	1 620	935
八师	Division 8	123 139	97 576	19 947	5 616	84 014	348	5 506	833
九师	Division 9	21 365	18 564	2 212	589	18 070		10	112
十师	Division 10	22 213	18 766	2 889	558	14 895	1 276	118	72
建工师	Construction Division	18 851	17 035	1 345	471			8	
十二师	Division 12	16 869	15 345	1 524		12 579	810	1 617	75
十三师	Division 13	19 073	15 408	3 118	547	14 418	391	782	
十四师	Division 14	11 403	10 113	1 001	289	10 074			
国资公司	State-owned Property Company	2 021	2 021					84	
供销公司	Supply and Marketing Corporation General	914	914						
兵团直属	Directly under XPCG	12 036	4 928	4 571	2 537	2 642		139	

4—21 续表 Continued

计量单位:人 (2010 年) (person)

单 位	Unit	建筑业 Construction	交通运输、仓储和邮政业 Transport, Storage and Postal Service	信息传输、计算机服务和软件业 Information Deliver, Computer Service and Software	批发和零售业 Wholesale and Retail Trade	住宿和餐饮业 Accommodation and Catering Services Industry	金融业 Finance	房地产业 Real Estate Trade	租赁和商务服务业 Leasing and Business Service
总 计	**Total**	**27 941**	**1 589**	**606**	**5 377**	**2 127**	**2 557**	**898**	**3 061**
一 师	Division 1	4 716	70	3	255	22		286	83
二 师	Division 2	468	21	3	21	295	2	7	107
三 师	Division 3		156		278	101		16	97
四 师	Division 4		11		431	570			35
五 师	Division 5	606	134		123	254		127	152
六 师	Division 6		92	44	136	29	153	19	169
七 师	Division 7	670	149		927	140		56	64
八 师	Division 8	2 114	496	490	253	239	620	108	1 685
九 师	Division 9	163	105	13	36	108			19
十 师	Division 10	2 133	73		152	94		2	20
建 工 师	Construction Division	16 899						75	53
十 二 师	Division 12	57	26	32	52	30		41	15
十 三 师	Division 13	115	33		77		11		45
十 四 师	Division 14		23		39			25	2
国资公司	State-owned Property Company		13		1 789	20		63	29
供销公司	Supply and Marketing Corporation General		187		686				41
兵团直属	Directly under XPCG			21	122	225	1 771	73	445

单 位	Unit	科学研究、技术服务和地质勘查业 Scientific Research, Technique Service and Geological Prospecting	水利、环境和公共设施管理业 Water Conservancy, Environment and Public Facilities Management	居民服务和其他服务业 Resident and Other Services	教 育 Education	卫生、社会保障和社会福利业 Health Care, Social Security and Welfare	文化、体育和娱乐业 Culture, Sports and Recreation	公共管理和社会组织 Public Management and Social Organization
总 计	**Total**	**4 353**	**9 633**	**438**	**42 011**	**23 506**	**1 970**	**26 059**
一 师	Division 1	362	3 843	31	4 724	2 532	130	3 654
二 师	Division 2	258	307		2 880	1 986	50	1 695
三 师	Division 3	153	476	29	3 198	1 217	64	2 661
四 师	Division 4	319	170	58	3 234	2 114	82	1 025
五 师	Division 5	178	79		2 202	1 355	48	669
六 师	Division 6	306	814	1	4 542	2 556	105	2 864
七 师	Division 7	468	1 294		2 761	1 878	111	1 534
八 师	Division 8	887	2 183	189	10 707	5 432	373	6 662
九 师	Division 9	86	153	14	1 009	762	64	641
十 师	Division 10	160	194	4	1 371	911	71	667
建 工 师	Construction Division				1 143	202		471
十 二 师	Division 12	16	25	22	970	273		229
十 三 师	Division 13	97		90	1 149	1 206	47	612
十 四 师	Division 14	19	95		550	221	11	344
国资公司	State-owned Property Company					23		
供销公司	Supply and Marketing Corporation General							
兵团直属	Directly under XPCG	1 044			1 571	838	814	2 331

4—22 各师离开本单位仍保留劳动关系的职工年末人数

Number of Staff and Workers Leaving but still Maintaining Labor Relation at the Year-end by Division

计量单位：人　　　　(2010 年)　　　　(person)

单　位	Unit	合　计 Total	企　业 Enterprises	事　业 Institutions	机　关 Agencies& Organizations	农、林、牧、渔业 Farming, Forestry, Animal Husbandry and Fishery	采矿业 Mining	制造业 Manufacturing	电力、煤气及水的生产和供应业 Production and Supply of Electricity, Gas and Water
总　计	**Total**	**16 918**	**15 976**	**848**	**94**	**10 570**	**93**	**1 064**	**499**
一　师	Division 1	1 880	1 811	59	10	1 600	21	38	45
二　师	Division 2	418	411	7		327	3	7	
三　师	Division 3	152	152			2			
四　师	Division 4	1 714	1 332	347	35	1 072		179	34
五　师	Division 5	799	793	6		495		72	14
六　师	Division 6	3 628	3 622	5	1	3 326		213	
七　师	Division 7	3 511	3 373	138		2 207		239	
八　师	Division 8	2 493	2 234	227	32	1 133		266	390
九　师	Division 9	36	21	15		17			
十　师	Division 10	187	179	8		77	21		16
建工师	Construction Division	1 328	1 328						
十二师	Division 12	278	260	18		211	48		
十三师	Division 13	85	84	1		78			
十四师	Division 14	9	9			7			
国资公司	State-owned Property Company	236	236					44	
供销公司	Supply and Marketing Corporation General	87	87						
兵团直属	Directly under XPCG	77	44	17	16	18		6	

单　位	Unit	建筑业 Construction	交通运输、仓储和邮政业 Transport, Storage and Postal Service	信息传输、计算机服务和软件业 Information Deliver, Computer Service and Software	批发和零售业 Wholesale and Retail Trade	住宿和餐饮业 Accommodation and Catering Services Industry	金融业 Finance	房地产业 Real Estate Trade	租赁和商务服务业 Leasing and Business Service
总　计	**Total**	**2 340**	**179**	**19**	**456**	**140**	**42**	**17**	**336**
一　师	Division 1	47	12		20	30		12	
二　师	Division 2	1			70	2		1	
三　师	Division 3	146	4						
四　师	Division 4	5			10	27			53
五　师	Division 5		19		6	19			167
六　师	Division 6	11			18				32
七　师	Division 7	661			75	5			
八　师	Division 8	144	87	19	14	48	42		80
九　师	Division 9		3			3			
十　师	Division 10								
建工师	Construction Division	1 324							4
十二师	Division 12	1							
十三师	Division 13		4		2				
十四师	Division 14							2	
国资公司	State-owned Property Company		11		173	6		2	
供销公司	Supply and Marketing Corporation General		19		68				
兵团直属	Directly under XPCG		20						

4—22 续表 Continued

计量单位:人 (2010 年) (person)

单位	Unit	科学研究、技术服务和地质勘查业 Scientific Research, Technique Service and Geological Prospecting	水利、环境和公共设施管理业 Water Conservancy, Environment and Public Facilities Management	居民服务和其他服务业 Resident and Other Services	教育 Education	卫生、社会保障和社会福利业 Health Care, Social Security and Welfare	文化、体育和娱乐业 Culture, Sports and Recreation	公共管理和社会组织 Public Management and Social Organization
总　计	**Total**	**45**	**344**	**163**	**135**	**313**	**32**	**131**
一　师	Division 1		16		11	18		10
二　师	Division 2		3			4		
三　师	Division 3							
四　师	Division 4	5		163	64	46	20	36
五　师	Division 5	1			3	3		
六　师	Division 6				2	3		23
七　师	Division 7	1	308		2	12	1	
八　师	Division 8	34	17		38	135		46
九　师	Division 9	4				7	2	
十　师	Division 10				7	66		
建工师	Construction Division							
十二师	Division 12				3	15		
十三师	Division 13					1		
十四师	Division 14							
国资公司	State-owned Property Company							
供销公司	Supply and Marketing Corporation General							
兵团直属	Directly under XPCG				5	3	9	16

4—23 在岗职工人数变动情况

Increase and Decrease of Staff and Workers on the Job

计量单位:人 (2010 年) (person)

指标	Item	合计 Total	国有单位 State-owned Units	城镇集体单位 Urban Collective-owned Units	其他单位 Units of Other Types of Ownership
本年增加人数总计	**Added Staff and Workers This Year**	**99 035**	**45 693**	**20**	**53 322**
从农村招收	Recruited from Country-side	14 299	8 735		5 564
从城镇招收	Recruited fromCities and Towns	8 875	4 282		4 593
录用的退伍军人	Recruited Demobilized and Transferred Armymen	589	452		137
录用的大中专技工学校毕业生	Recruited Graduates	11 342	5 196	18	6 128
调　入	Transferredinto	8 243	5 419	2	2 822
# 由外省市、自治区调入	Transferred from Other Regions	225	113	2	110
其　他	Others	55 687	21 609		34 078
本年减少人数总计	**Decreased Staff and Workers**	**94 095**	**48 172**		**45 923**
离休、退休、退职	Retired and Resinged	11 930	10 970		960
开除、除名、辞退	Expelled, Expunged and Dismissed	2 516	1 004		1 512
终止、解除合同	Contract Closedor Terminated	12 438	4 853		7 585
离开本单位仍保留劳动关系的职工	Left and Keptthe Relation of Labor	846	682		164
死　亡	Death	1 212	1 143		69
调　出	Transferredout	9 385	7 765		1 620
# 调到外省市、自治区	Transferred to Other Regions	319	316		3
其　他	Others	55 768	21 755		34 013

4—24 各师在岗职工人数变动情况

Increase and Decrease of Staff and Workers on the Job by Division

计量单位：人　　　　（2010 年）　　　　(person)

单位	Unit	本年增加人数 Added Staff and Workers This Year	从农村招收 Recruited from Countryside	从城镇招收 Recruited from Cities and Towns	录用的退伍军人 Recruited Demobilized and Transfered Armymen	录用的大中专、技工学校毕业生 Recruited Graduates	调入 Transferred in	# 由外省市、自治区调入 Transferred from Other Regions	其他 Others
总　计	**Total**	**99 035**	**14 299**	**8 875**	**589**	**11 342**	**8 243**	**225**	**55 687**
一　师	Division 1	6 070	1 737	647	91	809	2 263	60	523
二　师	Division 2	3 784	1 266	241	16	903	907	3	451
三　师	Division 3	1 743	653	175		407	316		192
四　师	Division 4	4 115	1 545	1 332	73	555	541	1	69
五　师	Division 5	2 779	774	1 183	24	198	527		73
六　师	Division 6	4 975	1 211	618	60	720	847	1	1 519
七　师	Division 7	2 092	132	42	54	418	490	27	956
八　师	Division 8	58 098	4 852	3 333	173	5 207	958	111	43 575
九　师	Division 9	1 247		379	8	133	215	3	512
十　师	Division 10	1 640	442	48	15	151	202		782
建工师	Construction Division	7 932	30	117	13	723	450	16	6 599
十二师	Division 12	732	235	95	24	64	69	1	245
十三师	Division 13	937	158	263	11	360	70	2	75
十四师	Division 14	1 160	731	50	10	148	211		10
国资公司	State-owned Property Company	306	53	79	1	115	17		41
供销公司	Supply and Marketing Corporation General	6					5		1
中基公司	Chalkis Grorp	740	421	115		143	43		18
兵团直属	Directly under XPCG	679	59	158	16	288	112		46

单位	Unit	本年减少人数 Decreased Staff and Workers	离休、退休、退职 Retired and Resinged	开除、除名、辞退 Expelled, Expunged and Dismissed	终止解除合同 Contract Closed or Terminated	离开本单位仍保留劳动关系的职工 Left and Kept the Relation of Labor	死亡 Death	调出 Transferred out	# 调到外省市自治区 Transferred to Other Regions	其他 Others
总　计	**Total**	**94 095**	**11 930**	**2 516**	**12 438**	**846**	**1 212**	**9 385**	**319**	**55 768**
一　师	Division 1	6 662	1 418	190	2 126	237	82	2 384	11	225
二　师	Division 2	3 159	1 058	249	409	41	45	396	2	961
三　师	Division 3	1 534	594	350	193	4	61	197	27	135
四　师	Division 4	3 017	910	57	476	32	138	1 319	2	85
五　师	Division 5	1 924	709	18	347	13	145	652	3	40
六　师	Division 6	3 784	1 390	85	560	69	86	677		917
七　师	Division 7	3 936	1 102	52	1 052	77	125	1 458	239	70
八　师	Division 8	48 341	2 883	1 286	4 538	217	211	1 267	24	37 939
九　师	Division 9	996	599	1	28	3	36	248		81
十　师	Division 10	1 243	229	11	358	3	36	205	3	401
建工师	Construction Division	16 017	222	163	671	75	13	150	3	14 723
十二师	Division 12	708	329	6	222	2	72	65		12
十三师	Division 13	655	232	13	251		43	81		35
十四师	Division 14	303	44	1	109		105	44		
国资公司	State-owned Property Company	284	10	8	144	67	3	14	1	38
供销公司	Supply and Marketing Corporation General	34	15	9	6			2		2
中基公司	Chalkis Grorp	892	4		738			147		3
兵团直属	Directly under XPCG	606	182	17	210	6	11	79	4	101

4－25 各师国有单位在岗职工人数变动情况

Increase and Decrease of Staff and Workers on the Job in State-owned Units by Division

计量单位：人　　　　(2010 年)　　　　(person)

单　位	Unit	本年增加人数 Added Staff and Workers This Year	从农村招收 Recruited from Countryside	从城镇招收 Recruited from Cities and Towns	录用的退伍军人 Recruited Demobilized and Transfered Armymen	录用的大中专、技工学校毕业生 Recruited Graduates	调入 Transferred in	#由外省市、自治区调入 Transferred from Other Regions	其他 Others
总　计	**Total**	**45 693**	**8 735**	**4 282**	**452**	**5 196**	**5 419**	**113**	**21 609**
一　师	Division 1	3 803	1 059	187	86	648	1 361	60	462
二　师	Division 2	2 109	1 040	16	13	405	426	3	209
三　师	Division 3	1 337	411	175		384	305		62
四　师	Division 4	2 632	786	812	45	396	524	1	69
五　师	Division 5	1 908	736	741	24	170	175		62
六　师	Division 6	3 145	767	417	46	523	771	1	621
七　师	Division 7	2 081	132	42	54	415	482	27	956
八　师	Division 8	22 039	2 404	884	102	1 024	539	15	17 086
九　师	Division 9	1 080		377	8	119	199	3	377
十　师	Division 10	1 626	442	48	15	151	199		771
建 工 师	Construction Division	810		37	4	168	31		570
十 二 师	Division 12	732	235	95	24	64	69	1	245
十 三 师	Division 13	937	158	263	11	360	70	2	75
十 四 师	Division 14	907	562	34	10	140	151		10
国资公司	State-owned Property Company	78		43		35			
供销公司	Supply and Marketing Corporation General	6					5		1
兵团直属	Directly under XPCG	463	3	111	10	194	112		33

单　位	Unit	本年减少人数 Decreased Staff and Workers	离休、退休、退职 Retired and Resinged	开除、除名、辞退 Expelled, Expunged and Dismissed	终止解除合同 Contract Closed or Terminated	离开本单位仍保留劳动关系的职工 Left and Kept the Relation of Labor	死亡 Death	调出 Transferred out	#调到外省市自治区 Transferred to Other Regions	其他 Others
总　计	**Total**	**48 172**	**10 970**	**1 004**	**4 853**	**682**	**1 143**	**7 765**	**316**	**21 755**
一　师	Division 1	5 272	1 311	140	1 162	237	77	2 120	11	225
二　师	Division 2	2 055	1 015	226	146	39	37	341	2	251
三　师	Division 3	1 496	572	350	189	4	59	187	27	135
四　师	Division 4	2 727	818	51	361	32	132	1 267	2	66
五　师	Division 5	1 374	697	17	88	9	144	384	3	35
六　师	Division 6	3 064	1 350	24	272	68	82	646		622
七　师	Division 7	3 921	1 101	52	1 047	77	124	1 450	239	70
八　师	Division 8	22 601	2 368	80	621	143	179	618	24	18 592
九　师	Division 9	933	594	1	15	3	35	233		52
十　师	Division 10	1 032	221	9	161	3	34	204	3	400
建 工 师	Construction Division	1 559	125	4	121		10	51		1 248
十 二 师	Division 12	708	329	6	222	2	72	65		12
十 三 师	Division 13	655	232	13	251		43	81		35
十 四 师	Division 14	214	43	1	32		102	36		
国资公司	State-owned Property Company	85	6	4	7	65	2	1	1	
供销公司	Supply and Marketing Corporation General	34	15	9	6			2		2
兵团直属	Directly under XPCG	442	173	17	152		11	79	4	10

4－26 在岗职工工资总额及构成

Total Wages of Staff and Workers on the Job and Composition

年 份 Year	工资总额 (万元) Total Wages (10 000 yuan)	# 国有单位 State-owned Units	# 集体单位 Collective-owned Units	构成(%)(工资总额=100) Composition in Percentage # 国有单位 State-owned Units	# 集体单位 Collective-owned Units
1956	11 388	11 388		100.0	
1957	14 308	14 308		100.0	
1962	27 256	27 256		100.0	
1965	37 931	37 931		100.0	
1970	48 178	46 933	1 245	97.4	2.6
1975	43 450	42 173	1 277	97.1	2.9
1978	57 800	56 003	1 797	96.9	3.1
1980	76 082	74 178	1 904	97.5	2.5
1985	100 652	96 846	3 806	96.2	3.8
1990	179 535	175 000	4 535	97.5	2.5
1991	192 734	187 837	4 897	97.5	2.5
1992	205 133	199 473	5 660	97.2	2.8
1993	227 662	224 219	3 443	98.5	1.5
1994	301 018	295 942	5 076	98.3	1.7
1995	395 901	389 608	5 330	98.4	1.3
1996	445 281	436 160	6 569	98.0	1.5
1997	511 229	501 042	6 123	98.0	1.2
1998	480 237	469 085	4 755	97.7	1.0
1999	433 471	423 569	4 651	97.7	1.1
2000	516 897	500 038	4 390	96.7	0.8
2001	525 694	479 079	3 583	91.1	0.7
2002	594 249	524 738	3 026	88.3	0.5
2003	788 776	702 984	2 673	89.1	0.3
2004	830 326	728 785	3 439	87.8	0.4
2005	887 344	772 908	861	87.1	0.1
2006	998 870	866 335	677	86.7	0.1
2007	1 169 377	994 314	85	85.0	…
2008	1 386 606	1 158 836	844	83.6	0.1
2009	1 574 974	1 272 612	1 186	80.8	0.1
2010	1 983 365	1 562 590	1 500	78.8	0.1

注:1998 年及以后年份工资总额为在岗职工工资总额;
Note: Data on total wages since 1998 refer to wages of fully employed staff and workers.

4—27 各师在岗职工工资总额

Total Wages of Staff and Workers on the Job by Division

计量单位:万元　　　　(2010年)　　　　(10 000 yuan)

单　位	Unit	合　计 Total	企　业 Enterprises	事　业 Institutions	机　关 Agencies & Organizations	农、林、牧、渔业 Farming, Forestry, Animal Husbandry and Fishery	采矿业 Mining	制造业 Manufacturing	电力、煤气及水的生产和供应业 Production and Supply of Electricity, Gas and Water
总　计	**Total**	**1 983 365**	**1 582 241**	**286 711**	**114 413**	**968 907**	**22 847**	**152 881**	**33 133**
一　师	Division 1	242 991	193 641	33 081	16 269	128 894	2 709	20 283	4 660
二　师	Division 2	118 709	91 301	20 440	6 968	73 466	2 443	6 027	463
三　师	Division 3	98 132	70 473	15 630	12 029	56 588		1 016	892
四　师	Division 4	147 290	124 493	18 590	4 207	93 690	1 040	16 062	1 086
五　师	Division 5	90 782	75 224	12 547	3 011	64 193		4 016	1 878
六　师	Division 6	158 752	123 078	27 464	8 211	96 287	6 406	5 190	739
七　师	Division 7	103 695	78 945	17 898	6 853	63 609	1 134	4 056	3 070
八　师	Division 8	572 580	462 405	81 159	29 016	264 015	1 167	77 472	18 141
九　师	Division 9	34 851	26 290	5 441	3 120	22 254		2 374	299
十　师	Division 10	47 492	35 155	9 592	2 745	24 766	4 110	371	1 291
建工师	Construction Division	166 361	160 876	4 051	1 434	68		590	100
十二师	Division 12	38 367	32 397	5 970		25 512	2 586	3 186	212
十三师	Division 13	51 619	38 645	10 471	2 503	35 570	1 252	2 151	
十四师	Division 14	22 004	17 030	3 187	1 787	14 056		303	302
国资公司	State-owned Property Company	21 147	21 147					2 596	
供销公司	Supply and Marketing Corporation General	4 784	4 784						
中基公司	Chalkis Company	6 013	6 013					5 672	
兵团直属	Directly under XPCGP	57 796	20 345	21 192	16 260	5 939		1 516	

单　位	Unit	建筑业 Construction	交通运输、仓储和邮政业 Transport, Storage and Postal Service	信息传输、计算机服务和软件业 Information Deliver, Computer Service and Software	批发和零售业 Wholesale and Retail Trade	住宿和餐饮业 Accommodation and Catering Services Industry	金融业 Finance	房地产业 Real Estate Trade	租赁和商务服务业 Leasing and Business Service
总　计	**Total**	**273 934**	**7 744**	**4 302**	**39 847**	**5 788**	**28 682**	**6 037**	**17 306**
一　师	Division 1	16 742	199	18	5 636	112		763	847
二　师	Division 2	4 351	311	9	1 568	493	11	201	1 907
三　师	Division 3	9 836	488		1 105	197		37	340
四　师	Division 4	7 978	295		2 011	1 049		27	180
五　师	Division 5	1 115	291	20	1 289	702	25	323	586
六　师	Division 6	5 070	476	152	542	90	4 468	399	2 732
七　师	Division 7	2 545	351		2 802	274		205	231
八　师	Division 8	64 579	3 093	3 913	2 024	1 595	13 969	1 178	6 768
九　师	Division 9	418	283	23	450	258		53	60
十　师	Division 10	3 882	123		350	165		9	77
建工师	Construction Division	154 813			320		47	448	385
十二师	Division 12	302	43	71	130	38		211	38
十三师	Division 13	337	125		372		73		250
十四师	Division 14	1 748	53		463		11	67	116
国资公司	State-owned Property Company	218	882		14 895	281		1 537	616
供销公司	Supply and Marketing Corporation General		473		4 025				286
中基公司	Chalkis Company				288				54
兵团直属	Directly under XPCG		258	96	1 576	534	10 077	580	1 836

4—27 续表 Continued

计量单位:万元 (2010 年) (10 000 yuan)

单 位	Unit	科学研究、技术服务和地质勘查业 Scientific Research, Technique Service and Geological Prospecting	水利、环境和公共设施管理业 Water Conservancy, Environment and Public Facilities Management	居民服务和其他服务业 Resident and Other Services	教 育 Education	卫生、社会保障和社会福利业 Health Care, Social Security and Welfare	文化、体育和娱乐业 Culture, Sports and Recreation	公共管理和社会组织 Public Management and Social Organization
总 计	**Total**	**26 073**	**28 728**	**2 484**	**154 003**	**80 382**	**7 282**	**123 005**
一 师	Division 1	2 467	13 216	99	19 319	10 047	404	16 577
二 师	Division 2	1 843	957		10 715	6 489	172	7 283
三 师	Division 3	414	1 336	258	10 238	2 987	130	12 272
四 师	Division 4	1 806	349	128	10 584	6 452	284	4 270
五 师	Division 5	1 549	157		6 974	4 163	202	3 299
六 师	Division 6	1 199	1 392	3	15 428	7 923	425	9 833
七 师	Division 7	1 296	3 038		8 294	5 287	422	7 080
八 师	Division 8	4 184	7 179	1 672	45 341	22 687	1 313	32 289
九 师	Division 9	188	336	31	2 612	1 740	140	3 332
十 师	Division 10	676	406	12	4 621	3 267	270	3 095
建 工 师	Construction Division	4 105			3 510	541		1 434
十 二 师	Division 12	95	83	69	3 584	604		1 604
十 三 师	Division 13	590		139	4 604	3 193	171	2 792
十 四 师	Division 14	72	255		1 649	813	49	2 046
国资公司	State-owned Property Company		24	72		27		
供销公司	Supply and Marketing Corporation General							
中基公司	Chalkis Company							
兵团直属	Directly under XPCG	5 591			6 530	4 163	3 301	15 799

4—28 各师国有单位在岗职工工资总额

Total Wages of Staff and Workers on the Job in State-owned Units by Division

计量单位:万元 (2010 年) (10 000 yuan)

单 位	Unit	合 计 Total	企 业 Enterprises	事 业 Institutions	机 关 Agencies & Organizations	农、林、牧、渔业 Farming, Forestry, Animal Husbandry and Fishery	采矿业 Mining	制造业 Manufacturing	电力、煤气及水的生产和供应业 Production and Supply of Electricity, Gas and Water
总 计	**Total**	**1 562 590**	**1 161 466**	**286 711**	**114 413**	**967 288**	**14 335**	**25 114**	**15 110**
一 师	Division 1	215 832	166 482	33 081	16 269	128 274	2 709	1 483	4 661
二 师	Division 2	103 639	76 232	20 439	6 968	73 466	1 022		
三 师	Division 3	88 051	60 392	15 630	12 029	56 588		1 016	892
四 师	Division 4	121 494	98 697	18 590	4 207	93 690	1 040		1 086
五 师	Division 5	84 612	69 054	12 547	3 011	64 091		167	1 878
六 师	Division 6	135 074	99 400	27 463	8 211	96 287		191	383
七 师	Division 7	102 258	77 507	17 898	6 853	63 609	1 134	3 678	3 071
八 师	Division 8	414 762	304 587	81 159	29 016	263 186	1 167	12 624	2 485
九 师	Division 9	32 101	23 540	5 441	3 120	22 254		35	299
十 师	Division 10	45 333	32 996	9 592	2 745	24 766	3 425	178	143
建 工 师	Construction Division	44 304	38 819	4 051	1 434			21	
十 二 师	Division 12	38 215	32 245	5 970		25 512	2 586	3 108	212
十 三 师	Division 13	51 619	38 645	10 471	2 503	35 570	1 252	2 151	
十 四 师	Division 14	19 193	14 219	3 187	1 787	14 056			
国资公司	State-owned Property Company	7 068	7 068					164	
供销公司	Supply and Marketing Corporation General	4 698	4 698						
兵团直属	Directly under XPCG	54 337	16 885	21 192	16 260	5 939		298	

4—28 续表 Continued

计量单位:万元 (2010 年) (10 000 yuan)

单 位	Unit	建筑业 Construction	交通运输、仓储和邮政业 Transport, Storage and Postal Service	信息传输、计算机服务和软件业 Information Deliver, Computer Service and Software	批发和零售业 Wholesale and Retail Trade	住宿和餐饮业 Accommodation and Catering Services Industry	金融业 Finance	房地产业 Real Estate Trade	租赁和商务服务业 Leasing and Business Service
总 计	**Total**	**68 443**	**4 911**	**2 900**	**19 683**	**4 314**	**14 283**	**2 498**	**10 826**
一 师	Division 1	14 593	150	18	954	112		579	359
二 师	Division 2	1 111	51	9	67	493	11	18	345
三 师	Division 3		488		924	197		37	275
四 师	Division 4		36		1 471	1 049			99
五 师	Division 5	1 115	291		489	594		261	280
六 师	Division 6		339	152	322	90	585	81	442
七 师	Division 7	1 695	351		2 592	274		205	231
八 师	Division 8	6 411	2 064	2 531	993	560	4 095	329	6 038
九 师	Division 9	418	283	23	93	258			60
十 师	Division 10	3 882	123		350	165		9	77
建 工 师	Construction Division	38 579						137	83
十 二 师	Division 12	302	43	71	130	38		137	38
十 三 师	Division 13	337	125		372		73		250
十 四 师	Division 14		53		152			43	5
国资公司	State-owned Property Company		41		6 471	58		186	122
供销公司	Supply and Marketing Corporation General		473		3 939				286
兵团直属	Directly under XPCG			96	364	426	9 519	476	1 836

单 位	Unit	科学研究、技术服务和地质勘查业 Scientific Research, Technique Service and Geological Prospecting	水利、环境和公共设施管理业 Water Conservancy, Environment and Public Facilities Management	居民服务和其他服务业 Resident and Other Services	教育 Education	卫生、社会保障和社会福利业 Health Care, Social Security and Welfare	文化、体育和娱乐业 Culture, Sports and Recreation	公共管理和社会组织 Public Management and Social Organization
总 计	**Total**	**19 257**	**28 518**	**1 187**	**153 516**	**80 132**	**7 282**	**123 005**
一 师	Division 1	2 467	13 030	99	19 319	10 047	404	16 577
二 师	Division 2	1 432	957		10 715	6 489	172	7 283
三 师	Division 3	414	1 336	258	10 238	2 987	130	12 272
四 师	Division 4	957	349	128	10 584	6 452	284	4 270
五 师	Division 5	650	157		6 974	4 163	202	3 299
六 师	Division 6	1 199	1 392	3	15 428	7 923	425	9 833
七 师	Division 7	1 296	3 038		8 294	5 287	422	7 080
八 师	Division 8	3 630	7 179	448	44 854	22 569	1 313	32 289
九 师	Division 9	188	336	31	2 612	1 740	140	3 332
十 师	Division 10	676	406	12	4 621	3 134	270	3 095
建 工 师	Construction Division				3 510	541		1 434
十 二 师	Division 12	95	83	69	3 584	604		1 604
十 三 师	Division 13	590		139	4 604	3 193	171	2 792
十 四 师	Division 14	72	255		1 649	813	49	2 046
国资公司	State-owned Property Company					27		
供销公司	Supply and Marketing Corporation General							
兵团直属	Directly under XPCG	5 591			6 530	4 163	3 301	15 799

4—29 主要年份全部职工年平均工资及指数

Average Annual Wage of All Staff and Workers and Indices in Main Years

年 份 Year	平均工资(元) Average Annual Wage(yuan)			指数(上年=100) Indices(preceding year=100)		
	全部职工 All Staff and Workers	国有单位 State-owned Units	集体单位 Collective-owned Units	全部职工 All Staff and Workers	国有单位 State-owned Units	集体单位 Collective-owned Units
1956	852	852		100.0	100.0	
1957	827	827		97.1	97.1	
1962	580	580		100.7	100.7	
1965	608	608		103.4	103.4	
1970	534	540	381	104.9	104.4	104.4
1975	578	584	412	78.3	78.4	78.5
1978	638	643	453	111.5	110.9	110.8
1980	821	831	586	116.5	116.2	116.3
1985	1 053	1 067	789	111.3	111.1	115.2
1990	1 877	1 901	1 267	116.4	116.8	101.4
1995	4 183	4 187	3 770	133.1	133.3	114.9
2000	6 763	6 715	6 386	124.0	118.4	117.4
2005	12 136	11 925	9 373	107.1	107.0	92.0
2006	13 909	13 679	9 709	114.6	114.7	103.6
2007	16 272	15 987	9 517	117.0	116.9	98.0
2008	18 772	18 421	37 323	115.4	115.2	392.2
2009	21 876	21 393	56 218	116.5	116.1	150.6
2010	26 741	26 189	55 563	122.2	122.4	98.8

注:1998 年及以后年份为在岗职工平均工资。

Note: Data in this table are average annual wage of staff and workers on the job since 1998.

4—30 主要年份全国、新疆及兵团在岗职工平均工资及指数

Average Annual Wage and Indices of Staff and Workers on the Job by the Whole Country, Xinjiang and XPCG in Main Years

年 份 Year	平均工资(元) Average Annual Wage(yuan)			指数(上年=100) Indices(Preceding year=100)			兵团为全国的% XPCG as % of the Whole Country	兵团为新疆的% XPCG as % of Xinjiang
	全 国 the Whole Conutry	新 疆 Xinjiang	新疆兵团 XPCG	全 国 the Whole Conutry	新 疆 Xinjiang	新疆兵团 XPCG		
1978	615	717	638	106.6		111.5	103.7	89.0
1980	762	882	821	114.1	114.5	116.5	107.7	93.1
1985	1 148	1 277	1 053	117.9	115.7	111.3	91.7	82.5
1990	2 140	2 272	1 877	110.6	113.2	116.4	87.7	82.6
1995	5 500	5 348	4 183	121.2	125.8	133.1	76.1	78.2
2000	9 371	8 717	6 763	112.3	114.5	124.0	72.2	77.6
2005	18 364	15 558	12 136	114.6	107.4	107.1	66.1	78.0
2006	21 001	17 819	13 909	114.4	114.5	114.6	66.2	78.1
2007	24 932	21 434	16 272	118.7	120.3	117.0	65.3	75.9
2008	29 229	24 687	18 772	117.2	115.2	115.4	64.2	76.0
2009	32 736	27 753	21 876	112.0	112.4	116.5	66.8	78.8
2010	37 147	32 361	26 741	133.5	116.6	122.2	72.0	82.6

注:1998 年及以后年份为在岗职工平均工资。

Note: Data in this table are average annual wage of staff and workers on the job since 1998.

4—31 各师在岗职工平均工资

Average Annual Wage of Staff and Workers on the Job by Division

计量单位:元 （2010年） (yuan)

单位	Unit	合计 Total	企业 Enterprises	事业 Institutions	机关 Agencies & Organi-zations	农、林、牧、渔业 Farming, Forestry, Animal Husbandry and Fishery	采矿业 Mining	制造业 Manufac-turing	电力、煤气及水的生产和供应业 Production and Supply of Electricity, Gas and Water
总计	**Total**	**26 741**	**24 812**	**35 728**	**48 164**	**22 862**	**32 504**	**26 731**	**29 844**
一师	Division 1	30 581	28 512	41 544	45 445	26 735	37 999	33 202	33 675
二师	Division 2	23 880	21 521	36 087	42 930	21 122	27 027	22 379	20 487
三师	Division 3	25 490	22 963	30 000	46 301	22 138		22 820	22 687
四师	Division 4	20 844	19 532	31 391	41 905	17 982	19 188	25 924	20 496
五师	Division 5	23 164	21 762	31 095	51 202	21 578		18 190	23 015
六师	Division 6	24 868	23 257	31 753	36 187	21 621	41 464	27 681	28 747
七师	Division 7	22 930	21 031	28 876	46 117	19 966	39 940	22 621	32 840
八师	Division 8	32 560	30 768	40 687	51 667	31 332	33 540	27 412	31 921
九师	Division 9	15 627	13 481	24 597	52 971	12 315		28 641	26 679
十师	Division 10	20 540	17 868	33 202	49 188	16 627	27 543	16 429	22 142
建工师	Construction Division	26 709	26 604	30 117	30 444	9 577		22 026	24 390
十二师	Division 12	22 625	20 990	39 173		20 282	31 927	19 237	28 213
十三师	Division 13	27 064	25 081	33 583	45 757	24 671	32 008	27 503	
十四师	Division 14	17 764	15 346	31 836	61 841	13 953		12 226	45 119
国资公司	State-owned Property Company	30 301	30 301					21 851	
供销公司	Supply and Marketing Corporation General	51 275	51 275						
中基公司	Chalkis Company	27 981	27 981					27 518	
兵团直属	Directly under XPCG	44 194	34 078	46 361	64 091	22 480		42 839	

单位	Unit	建筑业 Constr-uction	交通运输、仓储和邮政业 Transport, Storage and Postal Service	信息传输、计算机服务和软件业 Information Deliver, Computer Service and Software	批发和零售业 Wholesale and Retail Trade	住宿和餐饮业 Accommod-ation and Catering Services Industry	金融业 Finance	房地产业 Real Estate Trade	租赁和商务服务业 Leasing and Business Service
总计	**Total**	**27 520**	**30 440**	**48 444**	**33 944**	**19 326**	**46 804**	**31 427**	**33 236**
一师	Division 1	30 053	20 347	60 333	39 664	50 682		22 504	41 704
二师	Division 2	22 223	27 281	29 000	27 454	16 725	54 500	20 938	23 925
三师	Division 3	27 261	31 276		36 362	19 505		23 250	29 293
四师	Division 4	28 141	27 324		34 034	18 402		30 000	30 966
五师	Division 5	18 399	21 739	22 667	33 056	23 245	24 800	20 948	27 895
六师	Division 6	22 197	30 287	34 432	24 089	31 069	52 260	31 928	37 940
七师	Division 7	29 085	23 564		27 415	19 557		36 554	36 125
八师	Division 8	31 095	36 647	51 286	36 341	18 722	42 176	59 817	32 726
九师	Division 9	25 644	26 952	17 846	32 164	23 907		38 000	31 316
十师	Division 10	18 200	16 808		23 053	17 585		46 500	38 250
建工师	Construction Division	26 718			28 847		52 556	20 067	21 503
十二师	Division 12	52 982	16 462	22 188	25 000	12 733		23 187	25 267
十三师	Division 13	29 296	37 909		48 338		66 182		55 622
十四师	Division 14	30 995	22 826		39 897		28 250	21 613	58 050
国资公司	State-owned Property Company	36 400	40 645		31 738	20 482		33 918	36 667
供销公司	Supply and Marketing Corporation General		25 299		57 091				69 756
中基公司	Chalkis Company				41 710				28 316
兵团直属	Directly under XPCG		21 533	45 619	29 022	16 952	52 350	50 417	41 249

4—31 续表 Continued

计量单位：元 (2010 年) (yuan)

单 位 Unit		科学研究、技术服务和地质勘查业 Scientific Research, Technique Service and Geological Prospecting	水利、环境和公共设施管理业 Water Conservancy, Environment and Public Facilities Management	居民服务和其他服务业 Resident and Other Services	教 育 Education	卫生、社会保障和社会福利业 Health Care, Social Security and Welfare	文化、体育和娱乐业 Culture, Sports and Recreation	公共管理和社会组织 Public Management and Social Organization
总 计	**Total**	**40 732**	**29 435**	**15 428**	**36 525**	**34 000**	**36 965**	**47 202**
一 师	Division 1	68 135	33 441	31 968	40 896	39 678	31 038	45 366
二 师	Division 2	52 218	31 182		37 206	32 673	34 300	42 965
三 师	Division 3	27 026	28 057	88 931	32 013	24 544	20 375	46 120
四 师	Division 4	41 128	20 524	22 034	32 727	30 522	34 610	41 656
五 师	Division 5	62 201	19 873		31 670	30 724	42 042	49 312
六 师	Division 6	39 167	17 106	32 000	33 968	30 996	40 457	34 333
七 师	Division 7	27 699	23 478		30 041	28 152	38 036	46 156
八 师	Division 8	40 897	32 885	12 490	41 751	41 295	35 206	48 468
九 师	Division 9	21 837	21 967	22 286	25 883	22 839	21 875	51 983
十 师	Division 10	42 219	20 948	31 000	33 705	33 168	37 972	46 408
建 工 师	Construction Division	25 244			30 709	26 767		30 444
十 二 师	Division 12	59 188	33 240	31 182	36 952	22 110		70 035
十 三 师	Division 13	60 845		15 456	40 068	26 479	36 468	45 618
十 四 师	Division 14	38 053	26 842		29 984	36 787	44 727	59 471
国资公司	State-owned Property Company		13 333	32 818		11 565		
供销公司	Supply and Marketing Corporation General							
中基公司	Chalkis Company							
兵团直属	Directly under XPCG	53 557			41 565	49 679	40 549	67 777

4—32 各师国有单位在岗职工平均工资

Average Annual Wage of Staff and Workers on the Job in State-owned Units by Division

计量单位：元 (2010 年) (yuan)

单 位 Unit		合 计 Total				农、林、牧、渔业 Farming, Forestry, Animal Husbandry and Fishery	采矿业 Mining	制造业 Manufacturing	电力、煤气及水的生产和供应业 Production and Supply of Electricity, Gas and Water
			企 业 Enterprises	事 业 Institutions	机 关 Agencies & Organizations				
总 计	**Total**	**26 189**	**23 576**	**35 728**	**48 164**	**22 860**	**29 545**	**22 338**	**28 484**
一 师	Division 1	30 205	27 787	41 544	45 445	26 762	37 999	20 650	33 675
二 师	Division 2	23 897	21 128	36 087	42 930	21 122	20 943		
三 师	Division 3	25 269	22 337	30 000	46 301	22 138		22 820	22 687
四 师	Division 4	19 845	18 177	31 391	41 905	17 982	19 188		20 496
五 师	Division 5	23 175	21 657	31 095	51 202	21 597		18 556	23 015
六 师	Division 6	23 855	21 748	31 753	36 187	21 621		18 229	24 857
七 师	Division 7	22 851	20 911	28 876	46 117	19 966	39 940	22 704	32 840
八 师	Division 8	33 682	31 215	40 687	51 667	31 326	33 540	22 928	29 826
九 师	Division 9	15 025	12 681	24 597	52 971	12 315		34 700	26 679
十 师	Division 10	20 408	17 583	33 202	49 188	16 627	26 839	15 110	19 917
建 工 师	Construction Division	23 502	22 788	30 117	30 444			26 000	
十 二 师	Division 12	22 654	21 013	39 173		20 282	31 927	19 218	28 213
十 三 师	Division 13	27 064	25 081	33 583	45 757	24 671	32 008	27 503	
十 四 师	Division 14	16 832	14 060	31 836	61 841	13 953			
国资公司	State-owned Property Company	34 971	34 971					19 500	
供销公司	Supply and Marketing Corporation General	51 404	51 404						
兵团直属	Directly under XPCG	45 145	34 263	46 361	64 091	22 480		21 403	

4—32 续表 Continued

计量单位:元　　　　　　　　　　（2010 年）　　　　　　　　　　(yuan)

单　位	Unit	建筑业 Construction	交通运输、仓储和邮政业 Transport, Storage and Postal Service	信息传输、计算机服务和软件业 Information Deliver, Computer Service and Software	批发和零售业 Wholesale and Retail Trade	住宿和餐饮业 Accommodation and Catering Services Industry	金融业 Finance	房地产业 Real Estate Trade	租赁和商务服务业 Leasing and Business Service
总　计	**Total**	**24 495**	**30 896**	**47 835**	**36 609**	**20 281**	**55 855**	**27 808**	**35 361**
一　师	Division 1	30 943	21 357	60 333	37 427	50 682		20 248	43 289
二　师	Division 2	23 733	24 143	29 000	31 857	16 725	54 500	25 143	32 206
三　师	Division 3		31 276		33 252	19 505		23 250	28 309
四　师	Division 4		32 818		34 132	18 402			28 229
五　师	Division 5	18 399	21 739		39 740	23 402		20 543	18 401
六　师	Division 6		36 837	34 432	23 706	31 069	38 216	42 737	26 178
七　师	Division 7	25 297	23 564		27 959	19 557		36 554	36 125
八　师	Division 8	30 326	41 613	51 643	39 229	23 423	66 050	30 444	35 836
九　师	Division 9	25 644	26 952	17 846	25 833	23 907			31 316
十　师	Division 10	18 200	16 808		23 053	17 585		46 500	38 250
建工师	Construction Division	22 829						18 200	15 566
十二师	Division 12	52 982	16 462	22 188	25 000	12 733		33 488	25 267
十三师	Division 13	29 296	37 909		48 338		66 182		55 622
十四师	Division 14		22 826		39 000			17 200	24 500
国资公司	State-owned Property Company		31 231		36 173	28 800		29 476	42 069
供销公司	Supply and Marketing Corporation General		25 299		57 423				69 756
兵团直属	Directly under XPCG			45 619	29 869	18 911	53 747	65 192	41 249

单　位	Unit	科学研究、技术服务和地质勘查业 Scientific Research, Technique Service and Geological Prospecting	水利、环境和公共设施管理业 Water Conservancy, Environment and Public Facilities Management	居民服务和其他服务业 Resident and Other Services	教　育 Education	卫生、社会保障和社会福利业 Health Care, Social Security and Welfare	文化、体育和娱乐业 Culture, Sports and Recreation	公共管理和社会组织 Public Management and Social Organization
总　计	**Total**	**44 236**	**29 605**	**27 096**	**36 542**	**34 089**	**36 965**	**47 202**
一　师	Division 1	68 135	33 906	31 968	40 896	39 678	31 038	45 366
二　师	Division 2	55 516	31 182		37 206	32 673	34 300	42 965
三　师	Division 3	27 026	28 057	88 931	32 013	24 544	20 375	46 120
四　师	Division 4	30 006	20 524	22 034	32 727	30 522	34 610	41 656
五　师	Division 5	36 528	19 873		31 670	30 724	42 042	49 312
六　师	Division 6	39 167	17 106	32 000	33 968	30 996	40 457	34 333
七　师	Division 7	27 699	23 478		30 041	28 152	38 036	46 156
八　师	Division 8	40 919	32 885	23 677	41 892	41 547	35 206	48 468
九　师	Division 9	21 837	21 967	22 286	25 883	22 839	21 875	51 983
十　师	Division 10	42 219	20 948	31 000	33 705	34 397	37 972	46 408
建工师	Construction Division				30 709	26 767		30 444
十二师	Division 12	59 188	33 240	31 182	36 952	22 110		70 035
十三师	Division 13	60 845		15 456	40 068	26 479	36 468	45 618
十四师	Division 14	38 053	26 842		29 984	36 787	44 727	59 471
国资公司	State-owned Property Company					11 565		
供销公司	Supply and Marketing Corporation General							
兵团直属	Directly under XPCG	53 557			41 565	49 679	40 549	67 777

4—33 各师按结构分团场职工年末人数

Number of Farm Staff and Workers at the Year-end by Composition and Division

计量单位:人 (2010 年) (person)

指 标	Item	合 计 Total	一 师 Division 1	二 师 Division 2	三 师 Division 3	四 师 Division 4	五 师 Division 5	六 师 Division 6	七 师 Division 7
总 计	**Total**	**438 474**	**43 856**	**37 382**	**27 979**	**56 035**	**31 222**	**46 863**	**35 098**
农业连队职工	Agriculture Brigade	330 907	33 858	28 927	19 909	44 972	23 526	35 993	25 043
连队干部	Brigade Staff	16 327	2 021	1 641	1 253	1 730	908	2 015	1 334
连队职工	Brigade Staff and Workers	314 580	31 837	27 286	18 656	43 242	22 618	33 978	23 709
# 承包职工	Contract Staff and Workers	285 737	29 455	25 455	16 385	39 927	21 077	32 921	21 143
# 承包土地职工	Contract for the Land Staff and Workers	267 359	28 307	23 676	15 423	36 656	19 515	30 996	20 260
# 承包土地超过 100 亩职工	Contract for theLand over 100 Acer	6 324	722				589	784	
# 机务职工	Agricultural Mechanization Staff and Workers	11 775	1 740	901	1 456	966	799	568	1 688
# 畜牧职工	Livestock Staff and Workers	10 328	548	729	672	2 261	706	471	690
团属轧花企业职工	Staff and Workers of Cotton Processing Enterprise Belong to Farm	11 196	999	727	1 054	147	1 452	1 080	1 047
团属工交建商服企业职工	Staff and Workers of Industry, Transportation, Construction and Domestic Enterprise Belong to Farm	34 695	2 555	2 292	1 871	3 899	2 578	3 181	3 560
团属事业单位职工	Staff and Workers of Institutions Belong to Farm	50 237	5 166	4 399	3 927	5 839	3 079	5 656	4 740
学校职工	Staff and Workers of School	23 727	2 399	1 658	2 607	2 619	1 492	2 976	2 130
医院职工	Staff and Workers of Hospital	11 420	1 235	893	673	1 325	663	1 489	1 194
其他事业单位职工	Other Staff and Workers of Institultions	15 090	1 532	1 848	647	1 895	924	1 191	1 416
团机关职工	Staff and Workers Belong to Farm	11 439	1 278	1 037	1 218	1 178	587	953	708

指 标	Item	八 师 Division	九 师 Division	十 师 Division 10	十二师 Division 12	十三师 Division 13	十四师 Division 14	兵团直属 Directly under XPCG
总 计	**Total**	**82 900**	**19 070**	**15 326**	**13 469**	**15 810**	**10 625**	**2 839**
农业连队职工	Agriculture Brigade	59 079	16 123	11 235	9 536	11 331	9 288	2 087
连队干部	Brigade Staff	2 853	623	611	394	637	244	63
连队职工	Brigade Staff and Workers	56 226	15 500	10 624	9 142	10 694	9 044	2 024
# 承包职工	Contract Staff and Workers	46 877	13 907	9 998	8 603	9 320	8 680	1 989
# 承包土地职工	Contract for the Land Staff and Workers	46 040	12 621	9 878	7 905	9 317	4 816	1 949
# 承包土地超过 100 亩职工	Contract for the Land over 100 Acer	3 772	171	230	48	5	3	
# 机务职工	Agricultural Mechanization Staff and Workers	2 936	174	216	56	255	2	18
# 畜牧职工	Livestock Staff and Workers	1 287	1 218	395	416	556	362	17
团属轧花企业职工	Staff and Workers of Cotton Processing Enterprise Belong to Farm	4 218		64		354	39	15
团属工交建商服企业职工	Staff and Workers of Industry, Transportation, Construction and Domestic Enterprise Belong to Farm	8 521	478	1 649	1 924	1 618	116	453
团属事业单位职工	Staff and Workers of Institutions Belong to Farm	9 006	1 827	1 822	1 606	1 993	935	242
学校职工	Staff and Workers of School	4 222	560	731	763	871	579	120
医院职工	Staff and Workers of Hospital	2 194	351	434	286	453	173	57
其他事业单位职工	Other Staff and Workers of Institutions	2 590	916	657	557	669	183	65
团机关职工	Staff and Workers Belong to Farm	2 076	642	556	403	514	247	42

4—34 工业法人企业单位就业人员和劳动报酬情况

计量单位：人，万元　　　　　　　　　　　　　　　　　　　　　　　　　　　　　（2010 年）

指　　标 Item	单位就业人员 Number of Persons Employed in Units	在岗职工 Fully Empolyed Staff and Workers	其他就业人员 Other Employed Persons	离开本单位仍保留劳动关系的职工人数 Staff and Workers Who Have Left Their Working Units While Keeping Their Labour Contract Unchanged
总　计 **Total**	**76 161**	**75 623**	**538**	**1 656**
采矿业 **Mining**	**6 916**	**6 911**	**5**	**93**
煤炭开采和洗选业 Coal Mining and Dressing	5 826	5 821	5	90
有色金属矿采选业 Nonferrous Metals Mining and Dressing	391	391		
非金属矿采选业 Nonmetal Metals Mining and Dressing	699	699		3
制造业 **Manufacturing**	**58 119**	**57 621**	**498**	**1 064**
农副产品加工业 Agriculture by-product Manufacturing	5 038	4 933	105	57
食品制造业 Food Production	4 621	4 421	200	6
饮料制造业 Beverage Production	4 458	4 458		112
纺织业 Textile Industry	10 317	10 285	32	401
纺织服装、鞋、帽制造业 Textile Garments，Shoe and Hat Manufacturing	33	33		
家具制造业 Furniture Manufacturing	24	24		
造纸及纸制品业 Papermaking and Paper Products	1 696	1 685	11	54
印刷业和记录媒介的复制 Printing and Record Medium Reproduction	432	412	20	6
石油加工、炼焦及核燃料加工 Petroleum Processing，Coking and Nuclear Material Processing	1 723	1 693	30	1
化学原料及化学制品制造业 Raw Chemical Materials and Chemical Products	11 298	11 280	18	1
医药制造业 Medical and Pharmaceutical Products	1 287	1 273	14	7
化学纤维制造业 Chemical Fiber	1 470	1 470		43
塑料制品业 Plastic Products	4 540	4 523	17	3
非金属矿物制品业 Nonmetal Mineral Products	8 796	8 756	40	133
黑色金属冶炼及压延加工业 Ferrous Metals Smelting and Rolling	389	389		
有色金属冶炼及压延加工业 Nonferrous Metals Smelting and Rolling	477	472	5	
金属制品业 Metal Products	599	597	2	10
通用设备制造业 General Equipment Manufacturing	84	84		201
专用设备制造业 Special Equipment Manufacturing	696	692	4	29
交通运输设备制造业 Transport Equipment Manufacturing	83	83		
电气机械及器材制造业 Electic Machine and Equipment Manufacturing	41	41		
废弃资源和废旧材料回收加工业 Abandon Resources and Discard Material Recovery processing	17	17		
电力、煤气及水的生产和供应业 **Production & Supply of Power，Gas & Water**	**11 126**	**11 091**	**35**	**499**
电力、热力的生产和供应业 Production and Supply of Power，Steam and Hot Water	10 500	10 466	34	471
燃气的生产和供应业 Production and Supply of Gas	222	221	1	26
水的生产和供应业 Production and Supply of Water	404	404		2

Employed Persons and Labor Remuneration in Industrial Corporative Enterprises

(person, 10 000 yuan)

单位就业人员平均人数 Average Number of Persons Employed in Units	在岗职工平均人数 Average Number of Fully Empolyed Staffand Workers	其他就业人员平均人数 Average Number of Other Employed Persons	离开本单位仍保留劳动关系的职工平均人数 Average of Staff and Workers Who Have Left Their Working Units While Keeping Their Labour Contract Unchanged	单位就业人员劳动报酬 Earnings of Employed Persons in Units	在岗职工工资总额 Wages of Fully Employed Staff and Workers	其他就业人员劳动报酬 Earnings of Other Employed Persons in Units	离开本单位仍保留劳动关系的职工生活费 Living Cost of Staff and Workers Who Have Left Their Working Units While Keeping Their Labour Contract Unchanged
76 097	**75 324**	**773**	**1 773**	**210 474**	**208 861**	**1 613**	**1 655**
7 033	**7 029**	**4**	**105**	**22 854**	**22 847**	**7**	**71**
5 938	5 934	4	102	19 896	19 889	7	69
391	391			1 252	1 252		
704	704		3	1 707	1 707		2
57 937	**57 193**	**744**	**1 142**	**154 436**	**152 881**	**1 555**	**454**
5 085	4 999	86	57	12 350	12 197	153	
4 912	4 473	439	6	12 799	11 995	804	5
4 121	4 121		119	13 518	13 518		117
10 757	10 725	32	433	21 639	21 580	59	42
33	33			71	71		
24	24			53	53		
1 589	1 578	11	63	3 593	3 583	10	45
436	405	31	6	755	686	69	
1 423	1 392	31	3	4 375	4 167	208	4
11 046	11 009	37	1	32 559	32 494	65	1
1 233	1 219	14	7	3 065	3 029	36	7
1 293	1 293		47	2 851	2 851		19
4 582	4 570	12	3	13 662	13 628	34	1
8 902	8 862	40	162	27 095	27 005	90	177
535	535			1 438	1 438		
417	412	5		1 122	1 108	14	
603	602	1	11	1 325	1 322	3	
105	105		195	191	191		36
703	698	5	29	1 649	1 639	10	
84	84			203	203		
38	38			82	82		
16	16			41	41		
11 127	**11 102**	**25**	**526**	**33 184**	**33 133**	**51**	**1 130**
10 538	10 514	24	498	31 323	31 273	50	1 072
193	192	1	26	675	674	1	56
396	396		2	1 186	1 186		1

4—35 各师工业法人企业在岗职工年末人数

计量单位：人　　　　　　　　　　　　　　　　　　　　　　　　（2010 年）

指　　标 Item	合　计 Total	一　师 Division 1	二　师 Division 2	三　师 Division 3	四　师 Division 4	五　师 Division 5	六　师 Division 6	七　师 Division 7
总　　计 Total	**75 623**	**8 298**	**3 737**	**873**	**7 380**	**2 873**	**3 942**	**3 112**
采矿业 Mining	**6 911**	**689**	**884**		**463**		**1 553**	**374**
煤炭开采和洗选业 Coal Mining and Dressing	5 821	689	401		463		1 553	374
有色金属矿采选业 Nonferrous Metals Mining and Dressing	391							
非金属矿采选业 Nonmetal Metals Mining and Dressing	699		483					
制造业 Manufacturing	**57 621**	**6 202**	**2 619**	**462**	**6 387**	**2 066**	**2 137**	**1 813**
农副产品加工业 Agriculture by-product Manufacturing	4 933	92	492		442	782		480
食品制造业 Food Production	4 421	7					27	107
饮料制造业 Beverage Production	4 458				2 700	55		
纺织业 Textile Industry	10 285	203	700			714		1 115
纺织服装、鞋、帽制造业 Textile Garments, Shoe and Hat Manufacturing	33							
家具制造业 Furniture Manufacturing	24							
造纸及纸制品业 Papermaking and Paper Products	1 685		147					
印刷业和记录媒介的复制 Printing and Record Medium Reproduction	412	67	27	4		34		9
石油加工及炼焦业 Petroleum Processing, Coking and Nuclear Material Processing	1 693						1 651	
化学原料及化学制品制造业 Raw Chemical Materials and Chemical Products	11 280	33		11	518	37	15	
医药制造业 Medical and Pharmaceutical Products	1 273	226	724	262				
化学纤维制造业 Chemical Fiber	1 470	1 468						
塑料制品业 Plastic Products	4 523	335	28	50		162	177	
非金属矿物制品业 Nonmetal Mineral Products	8 756	3 771	501	135	2 727		70	
黑色金属冶炼及压延加工业 Ferrous Metals Smelting and Rolling	389							
有色金属冶炼及压延加工业 Nonferrous Metals Smelting and Rolling	472							
金属制品业 Metal Products	597							63
通用设备制造业 General Equipment Manufacturing	84						84	
专用设备制造业 Special Equipment Manufacturing	692					282	40	39
交通运输设备制造业 Transport Equipment Manufacturing	83						73	
电气机械及器材制造业 Electic Machine and Equipment Manufacturing	41							
废弃资源和废旧材料回收加工业 Abandon Resources and Discard Material Recovery processing	17							
电力、煤气及水的生产和供应业 Production & Supply of Power, Gas & Water	**11 091**	**1 407**	**234**	**411**	**530**	**807**	**252**	**925**
电力、煤气及水有生产和供应业 Production and Supply of Power, Gas and Hot Water	10 466	1 350	234	411	530	807	252	925
燃气的生产和供应业 Production and Supply Electric Power and Hot Water	221							
水的生产和供应业 Production and Supply of Gas	404	57						

Number of Staff and Workers on the Job in Industry Corporative Enterprises at the Year-end by Division

(person)

八　师 Division 8	九　师 Division 9	十　师 Division 10	建工师 Construction Division	十二师 Division 12	十三师 Division 13	十四师 Division 14	国资公司 State-owned Property Company	中基公司 Chalkis Company	兵团直属 Directly under XPCG
34 495	**959**	**2 270**	**235**	**2 457**	**1 193**	**279**	**1 207**	**1 992**	**321**
366		**1 451**		**740**	**391**				
366		1 235		740					
					391				
		216							
28 504	**848**	**224**	**194**	**1 635**	**802**	**208**	**1 207**	**1 992**	**321**
336	848	174		37			1 068		182
2 000				498				1 782	
1 521				182					
6 569				901	78	5			
4							29		
24									
1 503		32				3			
44		18				70			139
					42				
10 613							53		
55						6			
							2		
3 709			26		36				
1 312			168			63	9		
85					291	13			
117					355				
230						48	46	210	
331									
10									
41									
				17					
5 625	**111**	**595**	**41**	**82**		**71**			
5 197	111	524		54		71			
221									
207		71	41	28					

4—36 各师工业法人企业在岗职工工资总额

计量单位：万元 （2010年）

指标 Item	合计 Total	一师 Division 1	二师 Division 2	三师 Division 3	四师 Division 4	五师 Division 5	六师 Division 6	七师 Division 7
总计 Total	**208 861**	**27 654**	**8 932**	**1 907**	**18 189**	**5 894**	**12 335**	**8 261**
采矿业 Mining	**22 847**	**2 709**	**2 443**		**1 040**		**6 406**	**1 134**
煤炭开采和洗选业 Coal Mining and Dressing	19 888	2 709	1 421		1 040		6 406	1 134
有色金属矿采选业 Nonferrous Metals Mining and Dressing	1 252							
非金属矿采选业 Nonmetal Metals Mining and Dressing	1 707		1 022					
制造业 Manufacturing	**152 881**	**20 285**	**6 026**	**1 015**	**16 063**	**4 016**	**5 190**	**4 056**
农副产品加工业 Agriculture by-product Manufacturing	12 196	248	1 267		1 254	1 516		1 090
食品制造业 Food Production	11 994	59					112	316
饮料制造业 Beverage Production	13 518				7 675	91		
纺织业 Textile Industry	21 581	569	1 503			1 376		2 526
纺织服装、鞋、帽制造业 Textile Garments, Shoe and Hat Manufacturing	72							
家具制造业 Furniture Manufacturing	53							
造纸及纸制品业 Papermaking and Paper Products	3 583		389					
印刷业和记录媒介的复制 Printing and Record Medium Reproduction	686	74	47	8		76		17
石油加工及炼焦业 Petroleum Processing, Coking and Nuclear Material Processing	4 167						4 039	
化学原料及化学制品制造业 Raw Chemical Materials and Chemical Products	32 494	95		48	936	111	51	
医药制造业 Medical and Pharmaceutical Products	3 030	612	1 778	561				
化学纤维制造业 Chemical Fiber	2 851	2 847						
塑料制品业 Plastic Products	13 628	934	54	78		347	334	
非金属矿物制品业 Nonmetal Mineral Products	27 005	14 847	988	320	6 198		108	
黑色金属冶炼及压延加工业 Ferrous Metals Smelting and Rolling	1 437							
有色金属冶炼及压延加工业 Nonferrous Metals Smelting and Rolling	1 108							
金属制品业 Metal Products	1 322							45
普通机械制造业 Ordinary Machinery	191						191	
专用设备制造业 Special Purposes Equipment	1 639					499	164	62
交通运输设备制造业 Transport Equipment	203						191	
电气机械及器材制造业 Electic Machine and Equipment Manufacturing	82							
废弃资源和废旧材料回收加工业 Abandon Resources and Discard Material Recovery processing	41							
电力、煤气及水的生产和供应业 Production & Supply of Power, Gas & Water	**33 133**	**4 660**	**463**	**892**	**1 086**	**1 878**	**739**	**3 071**
电力、燃力的生产和供应业 Production and Supply of Power, Steam and Hot Water	31 273	4 526	463	892	1 086	1 878	739	3 071
燃气的生产和供应业 Production and Supply of Gas	674							
水的生产和供应业 Production and Supply of Water	1 186	134						

Total Wages of Stsff and Workers on the Job in Industry Corporative Enterprise by Division

(10 000 yuan)

八 师 Division 8	九 师 Division 9	十 师 Division 10	建工师 Construction Division	十二师 Division 12	十三师 Division 13	十四师 Division 14	国资公司 State-owned Property Company	中基公司 Chalkis Company	兵团直属 Directly under XPCG
96 780	**2 673**	**5 771**	**690**	**5 984**	**3 403**	**605**	**2 596**	**5 671**	**1 516**
1 167		**4 110**		**2 586**	**1 252**				
1 167		3 425		2 586					
					1 252				
		685							
77 472	**2 374**	**371**	**590**	**3 186**	**2 151**	**303**	**2 596**	**5 671**	**1 516**
693	2 374	305		78			2 152		1 219
5 831				685				4 991	
5 163				589					
13 629				1 793	164	21			
8							64		
53									
3 117		38				39			
60		28				79			297
					128				
30 977							276		
40						39			
							4		
11 705			92		84				
3 971			498			55	20		
525					893	19			
226					882				
466						51	80	680	
914									
12									
82									
				41					
18 141	**299**	**1 290**	**100**	**212**		**302**			
16 712	299	1 147		158		302			
674									
755		143	100	54					

4—37 各师私营企业就业人员及个体劳动者人数

Private Enterprises Employed Persons and Individual Labors by Division

计量单位：人 （2010 年） （person）

单位 Unit	年末人数 Population (Year end)	第一产业 Primary Industry	# 农业 Farming	第二产业 Secondary Industry	# 工业 Industry	第三产业 Tertiary Industry	# 交通运输、仓储和邮政业 Transport, Storage and Postal Service	# 批发和零售业 Wholesale and Retail Trade	# 住宿和餐饮业 Accommodation and Catering Services Industry
总计 Total	**293 940**	**42 838**	**23 582**	**53 109**	**43 205**	**197 993**	**47 724**	**82 086**	**33 144**
一师 Division 1	25 250	5 752	4 587	3 701	2 983	15 797	2 556	7 347	2 841
二师 Division 2	18 472	2 470	632	2 484	2 172	13 518	2 885	7 143	2 087
三师 Division 3	12 345	2 031	1 458	1 940	1 553	8 374	1 507	3 550	1 913
四师 Division 4	25 145	8 122	3 619	5 837	3 524	11 186	3 250	4 115	1 947
五师 Division 5	6 943	107		495	488	6 341	881	2 957	1 338
六师 Division 6	40 438	5 128	1 354	12 307	10 158	23 003	6 056	8 554	4 418
七师 Division 7	27 512	5 777	3 837	3 873	2 251	17 862	6 520	6 760	2 993
八师 Division 8	103 396	10 207	6 581	17 601	16 302	75 588	17 740	30 908	10 546
九师 Division 9	6 479	161	43	667	571	5 651	763	2 651	1 130
十师 Division 10	6 086			624	535	5 462	1 119	2 465	1 083
建工师 Construction Division	1 642			285	285	1 357	206	696	230
十二师 Division 12	10 157	1 902	720	1 396	1 107	6 859	1 832	2 707	1 190
十三师 Division 13	8 014	1 181	751	1 586	1 041	5 247	1 976	1 624	816
十四师 Division 14	1 656			313	235	1 343	433	446	370
国资公司 State-owned Property Company	309					309		163	146
兵团直属 Directly Under XPCG	96					96			96

4—38 各师社会救济情况

Social Relief by Division

（2010 年）

单位 Unit	城镇居民最低生活保障人数（人） Bottommost Living Security of Urban Households (person)	城镇居民最低生活保障家庭数（户） Number of Bottommost Living Security of Urban Households (household)	城镇临时救济人次数（人次） Temporarily Relief of Urban Households (person-time)	农村定期救济人数（人） Periodic Relief of Rural Households (person)	农村定期救济户数（户） Number of Periodic Relief of Rural Households (household)	农村临时救济人次数（人次） Temporarily Relief of Rural Households (person-time)
总计 Total	**119 480**	**71 986**	**32 719**	**1 879**	**1 800**	**110**
一师 Division 1	9 018	4 460		316	297	
二师 Division 2	7 044	3 816	6 855	176	160	
三师 Division 3	15 713	9 920	2 220	310	300	
四师 Division 4	12 274	6 204		195	193	
五师 Division 5	6 805	5 272	1 760			
六师 Division 6	9 653	7 853	2 595	66	66	
七师 Division 7	12 607	7 401	5 497	215	190	
八师 Division 8	16 642	12 166		53	53	
九师 Division 9	3 402	1 861	3 061	59	59	
十师 Division 10	5 856	3 624	3 184	63	58	75
建工师 Construction Division	1 884	1 221	944			
十二师 Division 12	3 796	2 073	2 440	46	46	
十三师 Division 13	7 178	3 447	1 776	90	88	
十四师 Division 14	5 036	1 548	590	290	290	
兵团直属 Directly under XPCG	2 572	1 120	1 797			35

2011 BING TUAN

第五篇

固定资产投资

Chapter 5 Investment in Fixed Assets

简要说明

一、本篇资料主要内容

本篇资料反映一定时期兵团全社会固定资产投资规模、速度和结构，固定资产投资资金来源和固定资产投资效果等情况。主要指标有固定资产投资按经济类型、产业分组；主要年份房屋建筑施工面积、竣工面积；固定资产投资及新增固定资产按行业分组。

二、本篇资料统计范围

固定资产投资统计范围为城乡建设投资、房地产开发投资、其他固定资产投资、城镇集体固定资产投资、农村集体固定资产投资、私人、私营固定资产投资。

三、本篇资料来源

本篇资料由兵团统计局工业交通投资统计处根据《兵团固定资产投资统计报表制度》搜集、汇总、整理、提供。

四、本篇调查方法

调查方法为全面调查。统计数据资料起点为50万元以上的固定资产投资项目。

Brief Introduction

1. Main Contents

Data in this chapter reflect the size, growth, structure, source of fund and results of the investment in fixed assets of the whole society of XPCG during a given period of time. Main indicators cover investment in fixed assets grouped by economic status, industry; floor space of buildings under construction and completed in major years, newly increased investment in fixed assets by sector.

2. Scope of Statistics

Statistics on investment in fixed assets cover investment in capital construction projects in urban and rural areas, real estate development, other investment in fixed assets, urban collective-owned investment in fixed assets, rural collective-owned investment in fixed assets and private investment in fixed assets.

3. Sources of Data

Data in this chapter are collected and prepared according to Statistical Reporting From System of Investment in Fixed Assets of XPCG and provided by Industry Communications Assets Statistical Section of Statistics Bureau of XPCG.

4. Methodology of Survey

Survey method of investment in fixed assets statistics is complete statistical. The starting point of statistical data in this chapter is projects of investment in fixed assets with over 500000 yuan.

5—1 按用途分全社会固定资产投资

Total Investment in Fixed Assets by Use

计量单位:万元 (10 000 yuan)

年份 单位 Year Unit	投资总额(万元) Total (10 000 yuan)	第一产业 Primary Industry	第二产业 Secondary Industry	第三产业 Tertiary Industry	构成(%) Composition(%) 第一产业 Primary Industry	第二产业 Secondary Industry	第三产业 Tertiary Industry
1950	2 434	1 850		584	76.0		24.0
1952	11 311	3 996	4 495	2 820	35.3	39.8	24.9
1954	4 924	1 753	1 880	1 291	35.6	38.2	26.2
1957	12 227	7 129	574	4 524	58.3	4.7	37.0
1962	10 636	5 908	2 187	2 541	55.5	20.6	23.9
1965	12 471	5 567	3 451	3 453	44.6	27.7	27.7
1970	13 907	4 177	6 509	3 221	30.0	46.8	23.2
1975	6 258	3 882	570	1 806	62.0	9.1	28.9
1978	14 575	7 787	3 463	3 325	53.4	23.8	22.8
1980	35 225	17 613	5 424	12 188	50.0	15.4	34.6
1985	55 895	11 008	20 707	24 180	19.7	37.0	43.3
1990	95 876	23 696	41 055	31 125	24.7	42.8	32.5
1991	130 459	39 248	43 599	47 612	30.1	33.4	36.5
1992	177 138	55 727	41 025	80 386	31.4	23.2	45.4
1993	214 062	37 211	71 449	105 402	17.4	33.4	49.2
1994	266 079	32 554	96 563	136 962	12.2	36.3	51.5
1995	369 435	59 381	163 096	146 958	16.1	44.1	39.8
1996	431 918	101 575	139 720	190 623	23.5	32.4	44.1
1997	462 669	159 089	94 446	209 134	34.4	20.4	45.2
1998	524 012	203 079	87 551	233 382	38.8	16.7	44.5
1999	595 072	169 556	100 606	324 910	28.5	16.9	54.6
2000	736 077	178 403	183 486	374 188	24.3	24.9	50.8
2001	874 698	242 417	157 184	475 097	27.7	18.0	54.3
2002	1 046 123	254 546	264 479	527 098	24.3	25.3	50.4
2003	1 212 157	316 902	314 953	580 302	26.1	26.0	47.9
2004	1 289 870	318 885	357 342	613 643	24.7	27.7	47.6
2005	1 372 367	291 324	395 231	685 812	21.2	28.8	50.0
2006	1 530 067	352 619	485 149	692 299	23.1	31.7	45.2
2007	1 896 156	370 202	815 803	710 151	19.5	43.0	37.5
2008	2 359 518	341 029	1 052 493	965 996	14.5	44.6	40.9
2009	3 184 664	363 353	1 481 274	1 340 037	11.4	46.5	42.1
2010	4 482 739	391 574	2 304 709	1 786 456	8.7	51.4	39.9
一师 Division 1	457 128	59 603	189 189	208 336	13.0	41.4	45.6
二师 Division 2	173 051	9 946	38 318	124 787	5.8	22.1	72.1
三师 Division 3	224 109	35 316	53 502	135 291	15.7	23.9	60.4
四师 Division 4	207 801	32 127	88 775	86 899	15.5	42.7	41.8
五师 Division 5	147 081	24 475	26 497	96 109	16.6	18.0	65.4
六师 Division 6	1 022 272	51 646	708 580	262 046	5.1	69.3	25.6
七师 Division 7	362 386	20 902	198 962	142 522	5.8	54.9	39.3
八师 Division 8	1 234 618	72 120	830 326	332 172	5.8	67.3	26.9
九师 Division 9	76 984	17 786	13 777	45 421	23.1	17.9	59.0
十师 Division 10	118 109	14 441	16 619	87 049	12.2	14.1	73.7
建工师 Construction Division	48 998		22 851	26 147		46.6	53.4
十二师 Division 12	210 284	18 679	73 468	118 137	8.9	34.9	56.2
十三师 Division 13	115 210	27 115	25 978	62 117	23.5	22.6	53.9
十四师 Division 14	26 246	3 256	6 786	16 204	12.4	25.9	61.7
国资公司 State-owned Property Company	30 604	3 037	9 374	18 193	9.9	30.6	59.5
供销公司 Supply and Marketing Corporation General	1 066			1 066			100.0
中基公司 Chalkis Company	656		554	102		84.5	15.5
兵团直属 Directly under XPCG	26 136	1 125	1 153	23 858	4.3	4.4	91.3

5—2 按登记注册类型分全社会固定资产投资

Total Investment in Fixed Assets by Registration Status

计量单位:万元 (10 000 yuan)

年份 Year	单位 unit	合计 Total	国有 State-owned	集体 Collective	私营个体 Private Individual	其他 Other
1950		2 434	2 434			
1952		11 311	11 311			
1954		4 924	4 924			
1957		12 227	12 227			
1962		10 636	10 636			
1965		12 471	12 471			
1970		13 907	13 907			
1975		6 258	6 258			
1978		14 575	14 575			
1980		35 225	35 225			
1985		55 895	49 707	1 045	5 143	
1990		95 876	88 549	103	7 224	
1991		130 459	122 554	109	7 796	
1992		177 138	164 515	3 154	9 469	
1993		214 062	194 029	6 509	13 524	
1994		266 079	233 550	16 606	15 923	
1995		369 435	307 170	26 884	18 055	17 326
1996		431 918	383 573	8 855	20 000	19 490
1997		462 669	427 089	3 212	25 319	7 049
1998		524 012	476 926	1 634	39 375	6 077
1999		595 072	547 936	1 144	27 414	18 578
2000		736 077	654 858	815	25 620	54 784
2001		874 698	732 942	750	30 810	110 196
2002		1 046 123	823 534	165	61 997	160 427
2003		1 212 157	946 698	555	67 102	197 802
2004		1 289 870	886 215	1 249	90 751	311 655
2005		1 372 367	1 025 106	640	96 195	250 426
2006		1 530 067	1 082 649	338	119 611	327 469
2007		1 896 156	1 461 604	2 764	139 507	292 281
2008		2 359 518	1 573 090	1 295	210 846	574 287
2009		3 184 664	2 041 739	4 381	283 537	855 007
2010		4 482 739	2 318 366	5 190	746 337	1 412 846
一 师	Division 1	457 128	245 302	4 780	36 005	171 041
二 师	Division 2	173 051	130 185		7 472	35 394
三 师	Division 3	224 109	189 667		26 363	8 079
四 师	Division 4	207 801	106 727		30 136	70 938
五 师	Division 5	147 081	121 136		4 801	21 144
六 师	Division 6	1 022 272	279 103		366 731	376 438
七 师	Division 7	362 386	158 032	410	39 069	164 875
八 师	Division 8	1 234 618	674 033		170 493	390 092
九 师	Division 9	76 984	64 403		7 490	5 091
十 师	Division 10	118 109	88 043		23 413	6 653
建工师	Construction Division	48 998	23 738			25 260
十二师	Division 12	210 284	92 185		28 291	89 808
十三师	Division 13	115 210	84 691		4 831	25 688
十四师	Division 14	26 246	20 953		721	4 572
国资公司	State-owned Property Company	30 604	13 700			16 904
供销公司	Supply and Marketing Corporation General	1 066	1 066			
中基公司	Chalkis Company	656				656
兵团直属	Directlyunder XPCG	26 136	25 402		521	213

5—3 主要年份全社会固定资产投资

Total Investment in Fixed Assets in Major Years

指 标	Item	1995	2000	2005	2009	2010
投资总额(万元)	**Total Investment (10000 yuan)**	**369 435**	**736 077**	**1 372 367**	**3 184 664**	**4 482 739**
按构成分	Grouped by Purpose of Funds					
建筑工程	Construction	220 505	478 559	807 589	1 867 088	2 562 841
安装工程	Installation		45 119	73 180	213 567	240 155
设备工器具购置	Purchase of Equipment and Instrucments	131 925	167 744	393 636	837 907	1 406 475
其他费用	Others	17 005	44 655	97 962	266 102	273 268
按用途分	Grouped by Use					
第一产业	Primary Industry	59 381	178 403	291 324	363 353	391 574
第二产业	Secondary Industry	163 096	183 486	395 231	1 481 274	2 304 709
第三产业	Tertiary Industry	146 958	374 188	685 812	1 340 037	1 786 456
投资总额构成(%)	**Composition of Total Investment(%)**					
按构成分	Grouped by Purpose of Funds					
建筑工程	Construction	59.7	65.0	58.9	58.6	57.2
安装工程	Installation		6.1	5.3	6.7	5.3
设备工器具购置	Purchase of Equipment and Instrucments	35.7	22.8	28.7	26.3	31.4
其他费用	Others	4.6	6.1	7.1	8.4	6.1
按用途分	Grouped by Use					
第一产业	Primary Industry	16.1	24.2	21.2	11.4	8.7
第二产业	Secondary Industry	44.1	24.9	28.8	46.5	51.4
第三产业	Tertiary Industry	39.8	50.9	50.0	42.1	39.9
固定资产投资资金来源(万元)	**Grouped by Source of Funds(10000 yuan)**	**374 823**	**735 029**	**1 363 818**	**3 276 535**	**4 508 010**
国家预算内资金	State Budgetary Appropriation	12 390	108 567	267 787	555 594	572 337
国内贷款	Domestic Loans	85 354	138 289	171 798	657 486	807 025
债 券	Bonds					
利用外资	Foreign Investment	13 659	716	19 198	31 602	30 037
自筹资金	Fund Raising	185 885	294 522	682 183	1 544 026	2 328 397
其他资金	Others	77 535	192 935	222 852	487 827	770 214
固定资产投资资金来源构成	**Composition of Source of Funds(%)**					
国家预算内资金	State Budgetary Appropriation	3.3	14.8	19.6	16.9	12.7
国内贷款	Domestic Loans	22.8	18.8	12.6	20.1	17.9
债 券	Bonds					
利用外资	Foreign Investment	3.6	0.1	1.4	1.0	0.7
自筹资金	Fund Raising	49.6	40.1	50.0	47.1	51.6
其他资金	Others	20.7	26.2	16.4	14.9	17.1
房屋建筑面积(万平方米)	**Floor Space of Buildings (10000 sq. m)**					
施工面积	Floor Space under Construction	346	568	685	1 199	1 630
# 住 宅	Residential Buildings	172	378	389	661	1 019
竣工面积	Floor Space Completed	245	497	532	598	888
# 住 宅	Residential Buildings	145	367	349	378	632

5—4 全社会固定资产投资及构成

Total Investment in Fixed Assets and its Composition

(2010年)

指 标	Item	合 计 Total	按登记注册类型分 Grouped by Registration Status 国 有 State-owned	集 体 Collective	私营个体 Private Individual	其 他 Other	# 房地产开发 Real Estate Development
投资总额 (万元)	**Total Investment (10 000 yuan)**	**4 482 739**	**2 318 366**	**5 190**	**746 337**	**1 412 846**	**335 344**
按建设性质分	Grouped by Type of Construction						
# 新 建	New Construction	1 783 429	589 043	2 600	331 417	860 369	335 344
扩 建	Expansion	859 879	397 104	2 590	199 520	260 665	
改 建	Reconstruction	774 494	699 315		23 258	51 921	
按构成分	Grouped by Purpose of Funds						
建筑工程	Construction	2 562 841	1 609 216	1 610	331 102	620 913	289 361
安装工程	Installation	240 155	97 827	780	55 206	86 342	8 672
设备工器具购置	Purchase of Equipment and Instrucments	1 406 475	479 934	2 800	300 459	623 282	5 599
其他费用	Others	273 268	131 389		59 570	82 309	31 712
按用途分	Grouped by Use						
第一产业	Primary Industry	391 574	293 007		71 693	26 874	
第二产业	Secondary Industry	2 304 709	663 057	5 190	504 365	1 132 097	
第三产业	Tertiary Industry	1 786 456	1 362 302		170 279	253 875	335 344
投资总额构成 (%)	**Composition of Total Investment (%)**						
按建设性质分	Grouped by Type of Construction						
# 新 建	New Construction	39. 8	25. 4	50. 1	44. 4	60. 9	100. 0
扩 建	Expansion	19. 2	17. 1	49. 9	26. 7	18. 4	
改 建	Reconstruction	17. 3	30. 2		3. 1	3. 7	
按构成分	Grouped by Purpose of Funds						
建筑工程	Construction	57. 2	69. 4	31. 0	44. 4	44. 0	86. 3
安装工程	Installation	5. 3	4. 2	15. 0	7. 4	6. 1	2. 6
设备工器具购置	Purchase of Equipment and Instrucments	31. 4	20. 7	54. 0	40. 2	44. 1	1. 7
其他费用	Others	6. 1	5. 7		8. 0	5. 8	9. 4
按用途分	Grouped by Use						
第一产业	Primary Industry	8. 7	12. 6		9. 6	1. 9	
第二产业	Secondary Industry	51. 4	28. 6	100. 0	67. 6	80. 1	
第三产业	Tertiary Industry	39. 9	58. 8		22. 8	18. 0	100. 0
固定资产投资资金来源 (万元)	**Grouped by Source of Funds (10 000 yuan)**	**4 508 010**	**2 234 362**	**5 190**	**749 661**	**1 518 797**	**382 384**
国家预算内资金	State Budgetary Appropriation	572 337	560 193	130	6 537	5 477	
国内贷款	Domestic Loans	807 025	518 907		18 962	269 156	58 443
债 券	Bonds						
利用外资	Foreign Investment	30 037	2 849			27 188	
自筹资金	und Raising	2 328 397	761 654	2 510	536 613	1 027 620	74 171
其他资金	Others	770 214	390 759	2 550	187 549	189 356	249 770
固定资产投资资金来源构成 (%)	**Composition of Source of Funds (%)**	**100. 0**	**100. 0**	**100. 0**	**100. 0**	**100. 0**	**100. 0**
国家预算内资金	State Budgetary Appropriation	12. 7	25. 1	2. 5	0. 9	0. 3	
国内贷款	Domestic Loans	17. 9	23. 2		2. 5	17. 7	15. 3
债 券	Bonds						
利用外资	Foreign Investment	0. 7	0. 1			1. 8	
自筹资金	Fund Raising	51. 6	34. 1	48. 4	71. 6	67. 7	19. 4
其他资金	Others	17. 1	17. 5	49. 1	25. 0	12. 5	65. 3

注：按登记注册类型分中"新建"不含房地产开发投资。

Note: The new construction grouped by registration status excluding investment in real estate development.

5—5　按行业分全社会固定资产投资

Total Investment in Fixed Assets by Sector

计量单位：万元　　　　(2010 年)　　　　(10 000 yuan)

指　标	Item	合　计 Total	按登记注册类型分 Grouped by Registration Status 国　有 State-owned	集　体 Collective	私营个体 Private Individual	其　他 Other
总　计	**Total**	**4 482 739**	**2 318 366**	**5 190**	**746 337**	**1 412 846**
第一产业	**Primary Industry**	**391 574**	**293 007**		**71 693**	**26 874**
农、林、牧、渔业	Farming, Forestry, Animal Husbandary and Fishery	391 574	293 007		71 693	26 874
第二产业	**Secondary Industry**	**2 304 709**	**663 057**	**5 190**	**504 365**	**1 132 097**
采矿业	Mining	81 513	58 788	2 180	600	19 945
制造业	Manufacturing	1 571 775	370 193	3 010	498 925	699 647
电力、煤气及水的生产和供应业	Production and Supply of Power, Gas and Water	629 452	232 132		4 840	392 480
建筑业	Construction	21 969	1 944			20 025
第三产业	**Tertiary Industry**	**1 786 456**	**1 362 302**		**170 279**	**253 875**
交通运输、仓储及邮政电信业	Transport, Storage and Postal Service Indusery	368 571	344 395		7 430	16 746
信息传输、计算机服务和软件业	Information Deliver, Computer Service and Software	7 246	7 246			
批发和零售业	Wholesale and Retail Trade	27 854	20 421		2 502	4 931
住宿和餐饮业	Aocommodation and Catering Services Industry	19 227	5 792		1 840	11 595
金融业	Finance and Insurance	3 537	3 537			
房地产业	Real Estate Industry	978 130	611 634		153 611	212 885
租赁和商务服务业	Leasing and Business Service	1 472	672			800
科学研究、技术服务和地质勘查业	Scientific Reasearch, Technical Service and Geological Prospecting	9 689	9 689			
水利、环境和公共设施管理业	Water Conservancy, Enviromment and public Facilities Management	208 267	200 933		1 400	5 934
居民服务和其他服务业	Resident and Other Services	5 216	1 116		3 200	900
教　育	Education	95 242	94 946		296	
卫生、社会保障和社会福利业	Health care, Social Security and Welfare	25 282	25 282			
文化、体育和娱乐业	Calture, Spotrs and Recreation	21 760	21 676			84
公共管理和社会组织	Public Management and Social Organization	14 963	14 963			

5—6　按建设性质分全社会固定资产投资

Total Investment in Fixed Assets by Type of Construction

计量单位：万元　　　　(2010 年)　　　　(10 000 yuan)

单　位	Unit	投资总额 Total	# 新　建 New Construction	# 扩　建 Expansion	# 改　建 Reconst-ruction	# 单纯生活设施 Pure Life-Facilities	# 单　纯购　置 Purely Purchase
总　计	**Total**	**4 482 739**	**2 118 773**	**859 879**	**774 494**	**628 377**	**100 601**
农、林、牧、渔业	Farming, Forestry, Animal Husbandry and Fishery	391 574	42 626	108 888	179 728		60 332
采矿业	Mining	81 513	8 849	44 030	28 634		
制造业	Manufacturing	1 571 775	1 087 140	431 891	45 604	1 380	5 760
电力、煤气及水的生产和供应业	Production & Supply of Power, Gas & Water	629 452	492 256	82 186	53 935		1 075
建筑业	Construction	21 969				176	21 793
交通运输、仓储和邮政业	Transport, Storage and Postal Service	368 571	34 528	86 571	245 055		2 417
信息传输、计算机服务和软件业	Information Deliver, Computer Service and Software	7 246		200	7 046		
批发和零售业	Wholesale and Retail Trade	27 854	10 016	14 504	2 573		761
住宿和餐饮业	Accommodation and Catering Services Industry	19 227	16 155	1 422	1 650		
金融业	Finance	3 537	28	600			2 909
房地产业	Real Estate Trade	978 130	349 859	287	1 880	626 104	
租赁和商务服务业	Leasing and Business Service	1 472			800		672
科学研究、技术服务和地质勘查业	Scientific Research, Technique Service and Geological Prospecting	9 689	2 629	1 606	5 387		67
水利、环境和公共设施管理业	Water Conservancy, Environment and Public Facilities Management	208 267	49 499	17 758	140 232	206	177
居民服务和其他服务业	Resident and Other Services	5 216	505	1 220	3 491		
教　育	Education	95 242	8 200	36 579	49 549	511	183
卫生、社会保障和社会福利业	Health Care, Social Security and Welfare	25 282	2 457	17 771	1 579		3 475
文化、体育和娱乐业	Culture, Sports and Recreation	21 760	9 151	8 683	3 746		180
公共管理和社会组织	Public Management and Social Organization	14 963	4 875	5 683	3 605		800

5—7 各师按用途分第一产业全社会固定资产投资

Total Investment in Fixed Assets of Primary Industry by Use and Division

计量单位：万元　　　　（2010年）　　　　（10 000 yuan）

单位	Unit	合计 Total	国有 State-owned	集体经济 Collective	私营个体 Private Individual	其他 Other
总计	**Total**	**391 574**	**293 007**		**71 693**	**26 874**
一师	Division 1	59 603	45 305		7 298	7 000
二师	Division 2	9 946	7 696		2 250	
三师	Division 3	35 316	35 316			
四师	Division 4	32 127	20 066		11 481	580
五师	Division 5	24 475	21 319		3 156	
六师	Division 6	51 646	36 459		3 760	11 427
七师	Division 7	20 902	15 408		5 494	
八师	Division 8	72 120	45 159		23 961	3 000
九师	Division 9	17 786	11 754		6 032	
十师	Division 10	14 441	6 159		6 665	1 617
建工师	Construction Division					
十二师	Division 12	18 679	17 935		744	
十三师	Division 13	27 115	27 115			
十四师	Division 14	3 256	2 925		331	
国资公司	State-owned Property Company	3 037				3 037
供销公司	Supply and Marketing Corporation General					
中基公司	Chalkis Company					
兵团直属	Directly under XPCG	1 125	391		521	213

5—8 各师按用途分第二产业全社会固定资产投资

Total Investment in Fixed Assets of Secondry Industry and by Use and Division

计量单位：万元　　　　（2010年）　　　　（10 000 yuan）

单位	Unit	合计 Total	国有 State-owned	集体 Collective	私营个体 Private Individual	其他 Other
总计	**Total**	**2 304 709**	**663 057**	**5 190**	**504 365**	**1 132 097**
一师	Division 1	189 189	49 016	4 780	15 597	119 796
二师	Division 2	38 318	12 177		5 222	20 919
三师	Division 3	53 502	29 025		18 648	5 829
四师	Division 4	88 775	12 565		13 885	62 325
五师	Division 5	26 497	11 520		545	14 432
六师	Division 6	708 580	39 568		344 293	324 719
七师	Division 7	198 962	31 468	410	6 759	160 325
八师	Division 8	830 326	422 892		91 028	316 406
九师	Division 9	13 777	11 938		1 458	381
十师	Division 10	16 619	12 913		820	2 886
建工师	Construction Division	22 851	3 471			19 380
十二师	Division 12	73 468	8 274		5 720	59 474
十三师	Division 13	25 978	14 040			11 938
十四师	Division 14	6 786	3 037		390	3 359
国资公司	State-owned Property Company	9 374				9 374
供销公司	Supply and Marketing Corporation General					
中基公司	Chalkis Company	554				554
兵团直属	Directly under XPCG	1 153	1 153			

5—9 各师按用途分第三产业全社会固定资产投资

Total Investment in Fixed Assets of Tertiary by Use and Prefectrue

计量单位:万元 (2010 年) (10 000 yuan)

单 位	Unit	合 计 Total	国 有 State-owned	集体经济 Collective	私营个体 Private Individual	其 他 Other
总 计	**Total**	**1 786 456**	**1 362 302**		**170 279**	**253 875**
一 师	Division 1	208 336	150 981		13 110	44 245
二 师	Division 2	124 787	110 312			14 475
三 师	Division 3	135 291	125 326		7 715	2 250
四 师	Division 4	86 899	74 096		4 770	8 033
五 师	Division 5	96 109	88 297		1 100	6 712
六 师	Division 6	262 046	203 076		18 678	40 292
七 师	Division 7	142 522	111 156		26 816	4 550
八 师	Division 8	332 172	205 982		55 504	70 686
九 师	Division 9	45 421	40 711			4 710
十 师	Division 10	87 049	68 971		15 928	2 150
建 工 师	Construction Division	26 147	20 267			5 880
十 二 师	Division 12	118 137	65 976		21 827	30 334
十 三 师	Division 13	62 117	43 536		4 831	13 750
十 四 师	Division 14	16 204	14 991			1 213
国资公司	State-owned Property Company	18 193	13 700			4 493
供销公司	Supply and Marketing Corporation General	1 066	1 066			
中基公司	Chalkis Company	102				102
兵团直属	Directly under XPCG	23 858	23 858			

5—10 各师按构成分全社会固定资产投资

Total Investment in Fixed Assets by Composition and by Division

计量单位:万元 (2010 年) (10 000 yuan)

单 位	Unit	合 计 Total	建筑工程 Construction Works	安装工程 Works of Installation	设备工具器具购置 Purchase of Equip-ment and Devices	其他费用 Other Expenses
总 计	**Total**	**4 482 739**	**2 562 841**	**240 155**	**1 406 475**	**273 268**
一 师	Division 1	457 128	273 784	24 312	133 422	25 610
二 师	Division 2	173 051	130 057	8 413	27 424	7 157
三 师	Division 3	224 109	145 612	12 576	43 472	22 449
四 师	Division 4	207 801	136 568	8 007	50 556	12 670
五 师	Division 5	147 081	108 333	1 594	26 496	10 658
六 师	Division 6	1 022 272	529 976	70 740	370 585	50 971
七 师	Division 7	362 386	199 191	22 956	126 188	14 051
八 师	Division 8	1 234 618	516 352	74 029	533 862	110 375
九 师	Division 9	76 984	58 179	1 395	15 779	1 631
十 师	Division 10	118 109	97 582	6 090	13 298	1 139
建 工 师	Construction Division	48 998	23 721	1 994	21 404	1 879
十 二 师	Division 12	210 284	174 386	3 858	22 074	9 966
十 三 师	Division 13	115 210	108 247	250	5 382	1 331
十 四 师	Division 14	26 246	18 836	1 333	5 906	171
国资公司	State-owned Property Company	30 604	22 556	2 204	4 152	1 692
供销公司	Supply and Marketing Corporation General	1 066	966			100
中基公司	Chalkis Company	656	150	50	456	
兵团直属	Directly under XPCG	26 136	18 345	354	6 019	1 418

5—11 各师按建设性质分全社会固定资产投资

Total Investment in Fixed Assets by Type of Construction and by Division

计量单位:万元　　(2010年)　　(10 000 yuan)

单　位	Unit	投资总额 Total	# 新　建 New Construction	# 扩　建 Expansion	# 改　建 Reconstruction	# 单纯生活设施 Pure Life Facilities	# 单纯购置 Purely Purchase
总　计	**Total**	**4 482 739**	**2 118 773**	**859 879**	**774 494**	**628 377**	**100 601**
一　师	Division 1	457 128	232 814	68 943	81 990	59 710	13 451
二　师	Division 2	173 051	46 235	26 175	47 793	48 861	3 987
三　师	Division 3	224 109	47 865	51 804	60 361	60 736	2 948
四　师	Division 4	207 801	56 514	65 279	24 698	54 165	7 145
五　师	Division 5	147 081	26 785	27 283	48 285	41 564	3 164
六　师	Division 6	1 022 272	569 509	230 163	153 410	66 776	2 414
七　师	Division 7	362 386	162 916	70 442	70 270	52 864	5 894
八　师	Division 8	1 234 618	777 239	184 420	148 860	105 325	18 774
九　师	Division 9	76 984	6 306	38 195	13 729	14 254	4 500
十　师	Division 10	118 109	15 420	23 838	32 788	37 669	8 394
建工师	Construction Division	48 998	7 885	766	4 542	14 925	20 880
十二师	Division 12	210 284	91 132	41 582	40 094	36 037	1 439
十三师	Division 13	115 210	52 393	2 948	39 964	19 905	
十四师	Division 14	26 246	6 135	8 850	1 443	7 202	2 616
国资公司	State-owned Property Company	30 604	18 193	7 395	5 016		
供销公司	Supply and Marketing Corporation General	1 066		1 066			
中基公司	Chalkis Company	656			554		102
兵团直属	Directly under XPCG	26 136	1 432	10 730	697	8 384	4 893

5—12 按行业分全社会固定资产投资资金来源

Funds Source of Total Investment in Fixed Assets by Sector

计量单位:万元　　(2010年)　　(10 000 yuan)

指　标	Item	资金来源合计 Total of Capital Sources	国家预算内资金 State Budgetary Appropriation	国内贷款 Domestic Loans	利用外资 Foreign Investment	自筹资金 Fund Raising	其他资金 Others
总　计	Total	**4 508 010**	**572 337**	**807 025**	**30 037**	**2 328 397**	**770 214**
农、林、牧、渔业	Farming, Forestry, Animal Husbandary and Fishery	393 064	118 308	19 129		166 138	89 489
采矿业	Mining	75 745	1 278	31 630		41 637	1 200
制造业	Manufacturing	1 599 541	5 218	475 794	25 666	1 052 570	40 293
电力、煤气及水的生产和供应业	Production and Supply of Power, Gas and Water	665 044	25 831	165 613		461 014	12 586
建筑业	Construction	22 169	180	811		21 178	
交通运输、仓储及邮政电信业	Transport, Storage and Postal Service Indusery	325 611	103 737	28 025		179 278	14 571
信息传输、计算机服务和软件业	Information Deliver, Computer Service and Software	9 017	1 008			8 009	
批发和零售业	Wholesale and Retail Trade	28 004	1 348			12 822	13 834
住宿和餐饮业	Aocommodation and Catering Services Industry	16 823			3 251	11 432	2 140
金融业	Finance and Insurance	3 509				3 509	
房地产业	Real Estate Industry	1 004 340	144 129	63 488		209 916	586 807
租赁和商务服务业	Leasing and Business Service	1 472				1 472	
科学研究、技术服务和地质勘查业	Scientific Reasearch, Technical Service and Geological Prospecting	9 456	6 991			2 329	136
水利、环境和公共设施管理业	Water Conservancy, Environment and public Facilities Management	187 458	64 397	16 463		102 869	3 729
居民服务和其他服务业	Resident and Other Services	5 216	392			3 904	920
教　育	Education	99 004	68 648	6 000		21 312	3 044
卫生、社会保障和社会福利业	Health Care, Social Security and Welfare	24 437	10 984		1 120	11 553	780
文化、体育和娱乐业	Calture, Spotrs and Recreation	23 055	9 279	72		13 549	155
公共管理和社会组织	Public Management and Social Organization	15 045	10 609			3 906	530

5—13 各师全社会固定资产资金来源

Funds Source Total Investment in Fixed Assets by Divisi

计量单位:万元 (2010 年) (10 000 yuan)

单位	Unit	资金来源合计 Total of Capital Sources	国家预算内资金 State Budgetary Appropriation	国内贷款 Domestic Loans	利用外资 Foreign Investment	自筹资金 Fund Raising	其他资金 Others
总计	**Total**	**4 508 010**	**572 337**	**807 025**	**30 037**	**2 328 397**	**770 214**
一师	Division 1	466 362	56 986	58 831	1 729	301 960	46 856
二师	Division 2	144 407	50 664	7 536		37 858	48 349
三师	Division 3	224 761	92 766	13 449	1 120	102 789	14 637
四师	Division 4	216 171	49 016	16 763		103 458	46 934
五师	Division 5	135 458	30 316	6 779		51 063	47 300
六师	Division 6	996 249	55 695	40 136		796 295	104 123
七师	Division 7	375 539	40 613	104 857	22 365	150 162	57 542
八师	Division 8	1 246 213	72 581	466 315	4 823	522 345	180 149
九师	Division 9	76 984	21 920	1 300		27 560	26 204
十师	Division 10	117 209	27 294	5 764		28 863	55 288
建工师	Construction Division	55 058	1 843	2 311		25 144	25 760
十二师	Division 12	254 375	24 390	51 222		103 736	75 027
十三师	Division 13	109 278	24 902	1 000		49 214	34 162
十四师	Division 14	26 246	16 735			6 832	2 679
国资公司	State-owned Property Company	32 128		23 969		8 159	
供销公司	Supply and Marketing Corporation General	1 045	445	420		180	
中基公司	Chalkis Company	656				656	
兵团直属	Directly under XPCG	29 871	6 171	6 373		12 123	5 204

5—14 按行业分全社会新增固定资产

Total Newly Increased Fixed Assets by Sector

计量单位:万元 (2010 年) (10 000 yuan)

指标	Item	新增固定资产 Newly Increased Fixed Assets	国有 State-owned	集体 Collective	私营个体 Private and Individuals	其他 Other
总计	**Total**	**3 317 601**	**1 900 523**	**5 190**	**509 563**	**902 325**
农、林、牧、渔业	Farming, Forestry, Animal Husbandary and Fishery	383 319	294 887		72 811	15 621
采矿业	Mining	59 828	45 785	2 180	600	11 263
制造业	Manufacturing	1 018 778	91 833	3 010	312 667	611 268
电力、煤气及水的生产和供应业	Production and Supply of Power, Gas and Water	232 991	185 062		1 840	46 089
建筑业	Construction	21 793	1 768			20 025
交通运输、仓储及邮政电信业	Transport, Storage and Postal Service Indusery	401 625	393 839		5 870	1 916
信息传输、计算机服务和软件业	Information Deliver, Computer Service and Software	3 463	3 463			
批发和零售业	Wholesale and Retail Trade	26 994	20 346		2 002	4 646
住宿和餐饮业	Aocommodation and Catering Services Industry	10 632	9 532		1 100	
金融业	Finance and Insurance	3 006	3 006			
房地产业	Real Estate Industry	812 157	515 803		107 777	188 577
租赁和商务服务业	Leasing and Business Service	672	672			
科学研究、技术服务和地质勘查业	Scientific Reasearch, Technical Service and Geological Prospecting	11 967	11 967			
水利、环境和公共设施管理业	Water Conservancy, Envirommnent and public Facilities Management	169 850	167 047		1 400	1 403
居民服务和其他服务业	Resident and Other Services	5 746	1 646		3 200	900
教育	Education	95 780	95 484		296	
卫生、社会保障和社会福利业	Health care, Social Security and Welfare	25 757	25 757			
文化、体育和娱乐业	Calture, Spotrs and Recreation	17 031	16 414			617
公共管理和社会组织	Public Management and Social Organization	16 212	16 212			

5—15 各师按行业分全社会新增固定资产

Total Newly Increased Fixed Assets by Sector and Division

（2010 年）

单　位	Unit	新增固定资产（万元）Newly Increased Fixed Assets (10 000 yuan)	第一产业 Primary Industry	第二产业 Secondary Industry	第三产业 Tertiary Indusry
总　计	**Total**	**3 317 601**	**383 319**	**1 333 390**	**1 600 892**
一　师	Division 1	395 838	53 079	105 589	237 170
二　师	Division 2	191 485	9 368	62 807	119 310
三　师	Division 3	243 373	33 139	82 056	128 178
四　师	Division 4	199 185	29 642	85 452	84 091
五　师	Division 5	111 145	25 057	12 084	74 004
六　师	Division 6	625 218	44 207	342 095	238 916
七　师	Division 7	195 624	23 927	66 879	104 818
八　师	Division 8	695 191	73 461	355 181	266 549
九　师	Division 9	81 917	23 637	15 782	42 498
十　师	Division 10	119 829	15 868	16 610	87 351
建工师	Construction Division	35 739		23 446	12 293
十二师	Division 12	242 659	19 005	122 231	101 423
十三师	Division 13	102 133	18 263	17 587	66 283
十四师	Division 14	30 143	9 717	7 748	12 678
国资公司	State-owned Property Company	24 443	4 037	15 272	5 134
供销公司	Supply and Marketing Corporation General	3 100			3 100
中基公司	Chalkis Company	656		554	102
兵团直属	Directly under XPCG	19 923	912	2 017	16 994

5—16 各师按登记注册类型分全社会新增固定资产

Total Newly Increased Fixed Assets by Registration Status and Division

（2010 年）

单　位	Unit	新增固定资产（万元）Newly Increased Fixed Assets (10 000 yuan)	国　有 State-owned	集　体 Collective	私营个体 Private Individual Economy	其　他 Others
总　计	**Total**	**3 317 601**	**1 900 523**	**5 190**	**509 563**	**902 325**
一　师	Division 1	395 838	273 647	4 780	26 345	91 066
二　师	Division 2	191 485	153 000		6 782	31 703
三　师	Division 3	243 373	232 131		4 148	7 094
四　师	Division 4	199 185	103 599		25 216	70 370
五　师	Division 5	111 145	98 892		4 801	7 452
六　师	Division 6	625 218	244 857		247 044	133 317
七　师	Division 7	195 624	117 277	410	35 912	42 025
八　师	Division 8	695 191	267 274		102 937	324 980
九　师	Division 9	81 917	69 116		7 190	5 611
十　师	Division 10	119 829	91 116		22 673	6 040
建工师	Construction Division	35 739	10 258			25 481
十二师	Division 12	242 659	107 115		16 953	118 591
十三师	Division 13	102 133	79 148		8 320	14 665
十四师	Division 14	30 143	25 457		721	3 965
国资公司	State-owned Property Company	24 443	5 134			19 309
供销公司	Supply and Marketing Corporation General	3 100	3 100			
中基公司	Chalkis Company	656				656
兵团直属	Directly under XPCG	19 923	19 402		521	

5—17 房地产开发投资

Investment in Real Estate Development

指　　标	Item	2009	2010
房地产开发投资　　(万元)	**Investment for Real-estate Development　(10 000 yuan)**	**243 223**	**335 344**
按构成分	Grouped by Field of Investment		
建筑工程	Construction Works	185 372	289 361
安装工程	Works of Installation	17 866	8 672
设备工器具购置	Purchase of Equipment and Devices	3 805	5 599
其他费用	Other Expenses	36 180	31 712
按工程用途分	Grouped by Purpose of Works		
住　宅	Flat	190 795	290 062
办公楼	Office Building	467	2 725
商业营业用房	Houses for Business Use	44 617	32 688
其　他	Others	7 344	9 869
新增固定资产　　(万元)	**Newly Increased Fixed Assets　(10 000 yuan)**	**150 381**	**268 554**
本年购置土地面积　　(万平方米)	**Land Area Purchased for the Current Year　(10 000 sq. m)**	**70. 11**	**45. 37**
商品房屋施工面积　　(万平方米)	**Floor Space of Construction for Commercial Houses　(10 000 sq. m)**	**291. 93**	**450. 74**
住　宅	Flat	248. 45	374. 18
办公楼	Office Building	0. 79	3. 67
商业营业用房	Houses for Business Use	40. 39	58. 90
其　他	Others	2. 30	13. 99
商品房屋竣工面积　　(万平方米)	**Completed Area of Commercial Houses　(10 000 sq. m)**	**106. 51**	**199. 13**
住　宅	Flat	95. 65	181. 53
办公楼	Office Building	0. 50	0. 79
商业营业用房	Houses for Business Use	9. 03	15. 22
其　他	Others	1. 33	1. 59
商品房屋销售建筑面积 (万平方米)	**Floor Space of Sales and Construction for Commercial Houses　(10 000 sq. m)**	**157. 05**	**189. 31**
住　宅	Flat	149. 21	175. 41
办公楼	Office Building	0. 30	0. 24
商业营业用房	Houses for Business Use	7. 49	13. 53
其　他	Others	0. 05	0. 13
竣工房屋造价　　(元/平方米)	**Price of Completed Houses　(yuan/sq. m)**	**1 265**	**1 111**
商品房屋销售额　　(万元)	**Sales Sum of Commercial Houses　(10 000 yuan)**	**330 128**	**503 080**
#住　宅	Flat	301 206	440 437

5—18 各师房地产开发投资

（2010 年）

指　　标	Item	合计 Total	一师 Division 1	二师 Division 2	三师 Division 3
房地产开发投资 （万元）	**Investment for Real-estate Development (10 000 yuan)**	**335 344**	**35 108**	**12 251**	**1 550**
按构成分	Grouped by Field of Investment				
建筑工程	Construction Works	289 361	27 337	10 486	1 494
安装工程	Works of Installation	8 672	1 792	116	40
设备工器具购置	Purchase of Equipment and Devices	5 599	3 606	299	
其他费用	Other Expenses	31 712	2 373	1 350	16
按工程用途分	Grouped by Purpose of Works				
住　宅	Flat	290 062	21 092	11 305	860
办公楼	Office Building	2 725			
商业营业用房	Houses for Business Use	32 688	13 584	946	690
其　他	Others	9 869	432		
新增固定资产 （万元）	**Newly Increased Fixed Assets (10 000 yuan)**	**268 554**	**36 404**	**11 040**	**1 850**
本年购置土地面积 （万平方米）	**Land Area Purchased for the Current Year (10 000 sq. m)**	**45. 37**	**6. 93**		**0. 10**
商品房屋施工面积 （万平方米）	**Floor Space of Construction for Commercial Houses (10 000 sq. m)**	**450. 74**	**32. 48**	**8. 48**	**1. 90**
住　宅	Flat	374. 18	24. 01	7. 95	1. 26
办公楼	Office Building	3. 67			
商业营业用房	Houses for Business Use	58. 90	8. 47	0. 53	0. 64
其　他	Others	13. 99			
商品房屋竣工面积 （万平方米）	**Completed Area of Commercial Houses (10 000 sq. m)**	**199. 13**	**26. 53**	**6. 05**	**1. 28**
住　宅	Flat	181. 53	21. 96	5. 52	0. 64
办公楼	Office Building	0. 79			
商业营业用房	Houses for Business Use	15. 22	4. 57	0. 53	0. 64
其　他	Others	1. 59			
商品房屋销售建筑面积 （万平方米）	**Floor Space of Sales and Construction for Commercial Houses (10 000 sq. m)**	**189. 31**	**27. 72**	**4. 29**	**2. 29**
住　宅	Flat	175. 41	21. 27	4. 29	1. 69
办公楼	Office Building	0. 24	0. 08		
商业营业用房	Houses for Business Use	13. 53	6. 31		0. 60
其　他	Others	0. 13	0. 06		
竣工房屋造价 （元/平方米）	**Price of Completed Houses (yuan/sq. m)**	**1 111**	**1 071**	**1 601**	**1 155**
商品房屋销售额 （万元）	**Sales Sum of Commercial Houses (10 000 yuan)**	**503 080**	**63 202**	**8 344**	**3 566**
# 住　宅	Flat	440 437	37 213	8 344	2 359

Investment in Real Estate Development by Division

四 师 Division 4	五 师 Division 5	六 师 Division 6	七 师 Division 7	八 师 Division 8	九 师 Division 9	十 师 Division 10	建工师 Construction Division	十二师 Division 12	十三师 Division 13	十四师 Division 14	国资公司 State-owned Property Company
1 839	**9 885**	**46 563**	**30 836**	**97 019**	**4 710**		**7 885**	**50 491**	**18 581**	**433**	**18 193**
1 450	7 806	40 017	25 600	89 157	4 331		5 717	42 002	17 514	433	16 017
		759		661			737	2 353	38		2 176
		1 559	120					15			
389	2 079	4 228	5 116	7 201	379		1 431	6 121	1 029		
339	9 134	45 227	29 458	87 474	4 710		6 429	42 193	15 712	433	15 696
		175		479			296	1 270	145		360
1 500	684	380	869	7 942			1 160	1 772	2 644		517
	67	781	509	1 124				5 256	80		1 620
1 839	**11 526**	**37 314**	**29 619**	**78 993**	**5 230**		**4 382**	**23 005**	**21 785**	**433**	**5 134**
	0.71	**4.32**	**12.52**	**16.70**	**0.12**			**0.43**	**3.54**		
0.96	**18.68**	**57.00**	**22.06**	**127.47**	**3.60**		**15.32**	**87.92**	**32.46**	**1.65**	**40.76**
0.34	16.08	56.24	21.22	105.74	3.60		13.64	76.41	29.61	1.65	16.43
				1.36			0.32	0.79	0.17		1.03
0.62	2.60	0.37	0.61	16.24			0.90	2.55	2.45		22.92
		0.39	0.23	4.13			0.46	8.17	0.23		0.38
0.96	**9.00**	**29.54**	**17.49**	**72.23**	**3.60**		**2.21**	**10.81**	**15.49**	**0.30**	**3.64**
0.34	8.80	29.54	17.08	64.63	3.60		2.21	8.70	14.57	0.30	3.64
								0.79			
0.62	0.20		0.39	7.32				0.27	0.68		
			0.02	0.28				1.05	0.24		
0.96	**5.28**	**31.66**	**17.18**	**52.55**	**3.60**	**0.13**	**4.88**	**22.29**	**14.07**	**0.30**	**2.11**
0.34	5.07	31.48	16.93	48.29	3.60	0.04	4.62	21.61	13.77	0.30	2.11
				0.16							
0.62	0.21	0.18	0.25	4.03		0.09	0.26	0.68	0.30		
				0.07							
1 518	**1 156**	**1 060**	**1 104**	**1 001**	**1 132**		**1 980**	**1 427**	**1 177**	**843**	**1 237**
3 374	**11 272**	**70 434**	**37 386**	**153 351**	**8 350**	**230**	**13 450**	**93 046**	**32 067**	**450**	**4 558**
374	10 596	70 027	36 399	133 450	8 350	74	12 247	85 288	30 708	450	4 558

5—19 全社会固定资产投资新增生产能力(或效益)

Newly Increased Production Capacity or Efficiency of Total Investment in Fixed Assets

(2010年)

能力(或效益)名称		Item		合 计 Total
大中型拖拉机	(千瓦)	Large and Medium Tractors	(kw)	135 230
	(台)		(set)	2 420
手扶拖拉机	(千瓦)	Mini-Tractors	(kw)	8 964
	(台)		(set)	1 224
联合收割机	(千瓦)	Combine	(kw)	30 068
	(台)		(set)	230
机引农具	(部)	Towing Farm Machinery	(unit)	4 107
植保机械	(部)	Crop Protection machinery	(unit)	95
造　林	(千公顷)	Afforested Area	(1 000 hectares)	12.72
果树定植	(千公顷)	Fruit Tree Planting	(1 000 hectares)	22.16
畜禽生产用房	(万平方米)	Buildings for Animaland Poulty Production	(10 000 sq. m)	39.92
草原建设	(千公顷)	Steppe Development	(1 000 hectares)	3.01
畜牧机械	(部)	Livestock Machine	(unit)	36
水泥晒场	(万平方米)	Field for Cement Insolate	(10 000 sq. m)	15.8
有效灌溉面积	(千公顷)	Effective Irrigated Area	(1 000 hectares)	52.41
# 喷灌面积		Spray Irrigated Area		29.29
新建公路	(公里)	Length of New Highways	(km)	120
改建公路	(公里)	Length of Reconstructed Highways	(km)	2 573
新挖灌渠	(公里)	Newly Dug Irrigation Canal	(km)	118
新挖排渠	(公里)	Newly dug Drainage Canal	(km)	243
渠道防渗	(公里)	Canal Antiseepage	(km)	1 016
水库	(万立方米/座)	Reservoin	(10 000cu. m/unit)	
汽　车	(辆)	Motor Vehicles	(unit)	1 015
住　房	(万平方米)	Housing	(10 000 sq. m)	631.71
仓　库	(万平方米/座)	Storehouses	(10 000 sq. m/unit)	6.19/40
中、高等学校学生席位	(座位:个)	University or College and Secondary School Number of Student Seat	(unit)	10 764
小学学校学生席位	(座位:个)	Primary Number of Student Seat	(unit)	17 388
医　院	(床位:个)	Hospital	(Beds:unit)	1 009
	(万平方米)		(10 000 sq. m)	4.31
发电机组容量	(万千瓦)	Capacity of Generation Setes	(10 000 tons)	17.02
输电线路	(公里)	Transmission Line	(km)	1 354
# 11万伏及以上的		110 000 V and Above it		134
变电设备	(万千伏安/台)	Power Equipment	(10 000 kilovotampere/set)	22.88/291
煤炭开采	(万吨/年)	Coal Mining	(10 000 tons/year)	60
洗煤	(万吨/年)	Coal Dressing	(10 000 tons/year)	60
焦炭	(万吨/年)	Coke	(10 000 tons/year)	100
铁矿选矿处理量	(万吨/年)	Prdding Mining and Dressing	(10 000 tons/year)	10
水泥	(万吨/年)	Cement	(10 000 tons/year)	265
棉纺绽	(锭)	Cotton Hasp	(ingot)	400 560
啤酒	(万吨/年)	Beer	(10 000 tons/year)	9
其他酒	(万吨/年)	Other Wine	(10 000 tons/year)	3.3
石墨及炭素制品	(万吨/年)	Graphite and Carbon Products	(10 000 tons/year)	30
润滑油(综合能力)	(万吨/年)	Lubricating Oil(Synthetic Ability)	(10 000 tons/year)	0.2
平板玻璃	(万重量箱/年)	Plate Glass	(10 000 weight case)	60
氮肥	(万吨/年)	Nitrogen Fertilizer	(10 000 tons/year)	21.5
钾肥	(万吨/年)	Potash Fertilizer	(10 000 tons/year)	1
电解铝	(万吨/年)	Electrolyzed Aluminum	(10 000 tons/year)	20
镍冶炼	(吨/年)	Nickle Rolling	(ton/year)	19 510

5—20 各师房地产开发投资新增固定资产

Investment in Real Estate Development in Newly Increased Fixed Assets by Division

计量单位:万元 (2010 年) (10 000 yuan)

单位	Unit	新增固定资产 Newly Increased Fixed Assets	国有 State-owned	集体 Collective	私营个体 Private and individuals	其他 Other
总计	**Total**	**268 554**	**21 822**		**77 160**	**169 572**
一师	Division 1	36 404				36 404
二师	Division 2	11 040				11 040
三师	Division 3	1 850			1 850	
四师	Division 4	1 839			1 500	339
五师	Division 5	11 526	11 526			
六师	Division 6	37 314			13 781	23 533
七师	Division 7	29 619			24 839	4 780
八师	Division 8	78 993			21 870	57 123
九师	Division 9	5 230				5 230
十师	Division 10					
建工师	Construction Division	4 382				4 382
十二师	Division 12	23 005	5 162		5 000	12 843
十三师	Division 13	21 785			8 320	13 465
十四师	Division 14	433				433
国资公司	State-owned Property Company	5 134	5 134			
供销公司	Supply and Marketing Corporation General					
中基公司	Chalkis Company					
兵团直属	Directly under XPCG					

5—21 按行业分全社会施工和竣工房屋建筑面积及竣工房屋价值

Floor Space of Buildings Under Construction and Completed and Value of Buildings Completed by Sector

(2010 年)

指标	Item	施工房屋面积合计(平方米) Floor Space Under Construction (sq. m)	#本年新开工 Started in this Year	竣工房屋面积(平方米) Floor Space Completed (sq. m)	竣工房屋价值(万元) Value of Buildings Completed (10 000 yuan)	竣工房屋造价(元/平方米) Price of Buildings Completed (yuan/sq. m)
总计	**Total**	**16 304 196**	**10 844 413**	**8 880 158**	**973 843**	**1 097**
农、林、牧、渔业	Farming Forestry Animal Husbandry and Fishery	481 313	375 294	291 262	19 714	677
采矿业	Mining	4 024	2 500	2 500	430	1 720
制造业	Manufacturing	2 944 740	1 013 467	1 034 459	101 415	980
电力、煤气及水的生产和供应业	Production & Supply of Power Gas & Water	339 901	168 334	98 813	9 574	969
建筑业	Construction					
交通运输、仓储和邮政业	Transport Storage and Postal Service	165 291	139 515	99 454	12 340	1 241
信息传输、计算机服务和软件业	Information Deliver Computer Service and Software					
批发和零售业	Wholesale and Retail Trade	177 894	154 248	147 175	19 200	1 305
住宿和餐饮业	Accommodation and Catering ServicesIndustry	108 010	93 088	35 383	6 188	1 749
金融业	Finance	4 734	4 214	520	69	1 327
房地产业	Real Estate Trade	11 206 525	8 194 813	6 574 132	722 184	1 099
租赁和商务服务业	Leasing and Business Service					
科学研究、技术服务和地质勘查业	Scientific Research Technique Service and Geological Prospecting	32 756	30 051	31 943	6 176	1 933
水利、环境和公共设施管理业	Water Conservancy Environment and Public Facilities Management	30 654	26 369	24 699	3 014	1 220
居民服务和其他服务业	Resident and Other Services	2 245	1 960	2 245	377	1 679
教育	Education	413 633	374 357	292 095	38 278	1 311
卫生、社会保障和社会福利业	Health Care Social Security and Welfare	143 660	91 514	88 638	14 398	1 624
文化、体育和娱乐业	Culture Sports and Recreation	148 939	113 387	85 133	11 338	1 332
公共管理和社会组织	Public Management and Social Organization	99 877	61 302	71 707	9 148	1 276

5—22 各师全社会施工、竣工房屋建筑面积及竣工房屋价值

Floor Space of Buildings Under Construction and Completed and Value of Buildings Completed by Division

(2010 年)

单 位	Unit	施工房屋面积（平方米） Floor Space Under Construction (sq. m)	竣工房屋面积（平方米） Floor Space Completed (sq. m)	竣工房屋价值（万元） Value of Buildings Completed (10 000 yuan)	竣工房屋造价（元/平方米） Price of Buildings Completed (yuan/sq. m)
总 计	**Total**	**16 304 196**	**8 880 158**	**973 843**	**1 097**
一 师	Division 1	1 264 689	1 028 466	109 931	1 069
二 师	Division 2	824 604	522 201	75 397	1 444
三 师	Division 3	1 241 448	865 119	81 895	947
四 师	Division 4	878 900	842 179	82 629	981
五 师	Division 5	748 120	344 110	43 114	1 253
六 师	Division 6	2 225 138	1 160 103	109 883	947
七 师	Division 7	981 952	459 924	54 907	1 194
八 师	Division 8	4 253 712	1 889 384	196 095	1 038
九 师	Division 9	303 682	204 818	21 135	1 032
十 师	Division 10	465 687	442 823	59 941	1 354
建工师	Construction Division	311 102	62 674	9 183	1 465
十二师	Division 12	1 316 385	510 411	69 441	1 361
十三师	Division 13	662 979	327 081	34 995	1 070
十四师	Division 14	244 256	112 535	8 975	798
国资公司	State-owned Property Company	418 624	47 397	5 884	1 241
供销公司	Supply and Marketing Corporation General				
中基公司	Chalkis Company				
兵团直属	Directly under XPCG	162 918	60 933	10 438	1 713

5—23 各师全社会住宅建设投资及竣工面积

Total Investment in Housing Construction and Floor Space of Housing Buildings Completed by Division

(2010 年)

单 位	Unit	住宅投资（万元） Housing Construction Investment (10 000 yuan)	# 经济适用房 Economic Houses	# 国有 State -owned	# 个体 Private -owned	竣工面积（平方米） Completed Floor Space (sq. m)	# 经济适用房 Economic Houses	# 国有 State -owned	# 个体 Private -owned
总 计	**Total**	**904 656**	**113 191**	**594 443**	**128 565**	**6 317 138**	**1 164 756**	**4 229 895**	**743 386**
一 师	Division 1	78 589	14 832	48 826	80	716 570	165 503	420 945	800
二 师	Division 2	55 805		45 135		400 494		345 216	
三 师	Division 3	58 768	200	57 878	890	644 980		638 299	6 681
四 师	Division 4	54 484	43 995	52 297	1 810	592 965	494 616	571 102	18 091
五 师	Division 5	50 592	332	48 088		284 613	11 610	284 613	
六 师	Division 6	111 499	28 664	63 609	14 827	660 862	205 303	365 500	98 814
七 师	Division 7	82 322	2 347	52 334	25 797	381 268	19 560	210 507	145 258
八 师	Division 8	192 293	6 333	92 307	47 932	1 386 644	100 026	620 254	221 372
九 师	Division 9	18 744		14 034		135 713		99 685	
十 师	Division 10	35 400	2 825	20 317	13 833	281 902	19 800	174 323	96 749
建工师	Construction Division	21 354		15 534		62 674		22 259	
十二师	Division 12	77 574	13 663	37 213	19 238	345 793	148 338	203 216	104 570
十三师	Division 13	35 617		19 905	4 158	289 671		143 987	51 051
十四师	Division 14	7 635		7 202		78 174		75 174	
国资公司	State-owned Property Company	15 696		11 480		36 415		36 415	
供销公司	Supply and Marketing Corporation General								
中基公司	Chalkis Company								
兵团直属	Directly under XPCG	8 284		8 284		18 400		18 400	

5－24 按用途分国有单位固定资产投资及构成

Investment in Fixed Assets of State-owned Units and its Composition by Use

年份 Year	单位 Unit	投资总额（万元） Total (10 000yuan)	第一产业 Primary Industry	第二产业 Secondary Industry	第三产业 Tertiary Industry	构成(%) Composition(%) 第一产业 Primary Industry	第二产业 Secondary Industry	第三产业 Tertiary Industry
	1950	2 434	1 850		584	76.0		24.0
	1952	11 311	3 996	4 495	2 820	35.3	39.8	24.9
	1954	4 924	1 753	1 880	1 291	35.6	38.2	26.2
	1957	12 227	7 129	574	4 524	58.3	4.7	37.0
	1962	10 636	5 908	2 187	2 541	55.5	20.6	23.9
	1965	12 471	5 567	3 451	3 453	44.6	27.7	27.7
	1970	13 907	4 177	6 509	3 221	30.0	46.8	23.2
	1975	6 258	3 882	570	1 806	62.0	9.1	28.9
	1978	14 575	7 787	3 463	3 325	53.4	23.8	22.8
	1980	35 225	17 613	5 424	12 188	50.0	15.4	34.6
	1985	49 707	8 268	20 236	21 203	16.6	40.7	42.7
	1990	88 549	22 061	40 952	25 536	24.9	46.2	28.9
	1991	122 554	37 522	43 526	41 506	30.6	35.5	33.9
	1992	164 515	53 182	41 001	70 332	32.3	24.9	42.8
	1993	194 029	33 910	65 657	94 462	17.5	33.8	48.7
	1994	233 550	27 513	84 524	121 513	11.8	36.2	52.0
	1995	307 170	40 081	125 398	141 691	13.1	40.8	46.1
	1996	383 573	93 072	127 607	162 894	24.2	33.3	42.5
	1997	427 089	149 472	86 913	190 704	35.0	20.3	44.7
	1998	476 926	185 765	78 433	212 728	39.0	16.4	44.6
	1999	547 936	149 426	87 225	311 285	27.3	15.9	56.8
	2000	654 858	151 904	150 739	352 215	23.2	23.0	53.8
	2001	732 942	193 836	124 480	414 626	26.4	17.0	56.6
	2002	823 534	216 017	158 589	448 928	26.2	19.3	54.5
	2003	946 698	275 194	180 012	491 492	29.1	19.0	51.9
	2004	886 215	286 248	131 962	468 005	32.3	14.9	52.8
	2005	1 025 106	230 603	206 062	588 441	22.5	20.1	57.4
	2006	1 082 649	300 356	208 762	573 531	27.7	19.3	53.0
	2007	1 461 604	300 603	579 909	581 092	20.6	39.7	39.7
	2008	1 573 090	273 011	570 208	729 871	17.4	36.2	46.4
	2009	2 041 739	275 959	745 922	1 019 858	13.5	36.5	50.0
	2010	2 318 366	293 007	663 057	1 362 302	12.6	28.6	58.8
一　师	Division 1	245 302	45 305	49 016	150 981	18.5	20.0	61.5
二　师	Division 2	130 185	7 696	12 177	110 312	5.9	9.4	84.7
三　师	Division 3	189 667	35 316	29 025	125 326	18.6	15.3	66.1
四　师	Division 4	106 727	20 066	12 565	74 096	18.8	11.8	69.4
五　师	Division 5	121 136	21 319	11 520	88 297	17.6	9.5	72.9
六　师	Division 6	279 103	36 459	39 568	203 076	13.1	14.2	72.7
七　师	Division 7	158 032	15 408	31 468	111 156	9.8	19.9	70.3
八　师	Division 8	674 033	45 159	422 892	205 982	6.7	62.7	30.6
九　师	Division 9	64 403	11 754	11 938	40 711	18.3	18.5	63.2
十　师	Division 10	88 043	6 159	12 913	68 971	7.0	14.7	78.3
建工师	Construction Division	23 738		3 471	20 267		14.6	85.4
十二师	Division 12	92 185	17 935	8 274	65 976	19.4	9.0	71.6
十三师	Division 13	84 691	27 115	14 040	43 536	32.0	16.6	51.4
十四师	Division 14	20 953	2 925	3 037	14 991	14.0	14.5	71.5
国资公司	State-owned Property Company	13 700			13 700			100.0
供销公司	Supply and Marketing Corporation General	1 066			1 066			100.0
中基公司	Chalkis Company							
兵团直属	Directly under XPCG	25 402	391	1 153	23 858	1.6	4.5	93.9

5—25 各师按行业分国有单位固定资产投资

Investment in Fixed Assets of State-owned Units by Sector and Division

计量单位：万元　　　　(2010 年)　　　　(10 000 yuan)

单位	Unit	投资总额 Total	农、林、牧、渔业 Farming Forestry Animal Husbandary	采矿业 Mining	制造业 Manufac-turing	电力、煤气及水的生产和供应业 Production and Supply of Power Gas and Water	建筑业 Constru-ction	交通运输、仓储及邮政电信业 Transport, Storage and Postal Service Industry	信息传输、计算机服务和软件业 Information Deliver, Computer Service and Software	批发零售业 Wholesale and Retail Trade	住宿和餐饮业 Accommo-dation and Catering Services Industry
总　计	**Total**	**2 318 366**	**293 007**	**58 788**	**370 193**	**232 132**	**1 944**	**344 395**	**7 246**	**20 421**	**5 792**
一　师	Division 1	245 302	45 305	254	32 193	16 569		69 711	1 900	753	
二　师	Division 2	130 185	7 696	2 444	4 876	4 676	181	12 703		57	
三　师	Division 3	189 667	35 316		8 537	20 225	263	19 436	1 082	1 433	
四　师	Division 4	106 727	20 066	8 730	1 863	1 972		2 560			
五　师	Division 5	121 136	21 319	889	1 275	9 356		21 768		450	1 503
六　师	Division 6	279 103	36 459	13 482	18 100	7 986		66 149	103	328	1 840
七　师	Division 7	158 032	15 408	9 484		21 984		42 871		750	
八　师	Division 8	674 033	45 159	17 369	279 958	125 565		49 750	3 464	2 067	1 027
九　师	Division 9	64 403	11 754		1 043	10 895		11 214		3 037	278
十　师	Division 10	88 043	6 159	4 283	4 950	3 680		7 861		10 452	
建工师	Construction Division	23 738			1 205	766	1 500	1 700			
十二师	Division 12	92 185	17 935		2 395	5 879		14 630		450	1 144
十三师	Division 13	84 691	27 115	1 853	10 073	2 114		18 928		160	
十四师	Division 14	20 953	2 925		2 572	465		4 048		484	
国资公司	State-owned Property Company	13 700									
供销公司	Supply and Marketing Corporation General	1 066						1 066			
中基公司	Chalkis Company										
兵团直属	Directly under XPCG	25 402	391		1 153				697		

单位	Unit	金融业 Finance	房地产业 Real Estate Trade	租赁和商务服务业 Leasing and Business Service	科学研究、技术服务和地质勘查业 Scientific Research Technical Service and Geological Prospecting	水利、环境和公共设施管理业 Water Con-servancy, Enviro nment and Public Facilities Management	居民服务和其他服务业 Resident and Other Services	教育 Education	卫生、社会保障和社会福利业 Health Care, Social Security and Welfare	文化体育和娱乐业 Culture, Sports and Recreation	公共管理和社会组织 Public Man-agerment and Social Organ-ization
总　计	**Total**	**3 537**	**611 634**	**672**	**9 689**	**200 933**	**1 116**	**94 946**	**25 282**	**21 676**	**14 963**
一　师	Division 1		49 600	672	1 461	17 551	820	6 057	545	1 771	140
二　师	Division 2		49 496		4 535	31 014		6 973	2 522	716	2 296
三　师	Division 3		60 389		822	20 126		7 810	2 170	4 785	7 273
四　师	Division 4		52 317		430	6 832		9 641		2 316	
五　师	Division 5	600	49 125		344	4 546		8 364	451	709	437
六　师	Division 6		65 843		143	51 031	238	10 948	719	5 341	393
七　师	Division 7		52 334		282	4 544	53	5 311	4 635	376	
八　师	Division 8		92 813		1 129	34 133	5	15 274	4 233	1 666	421
九　师	Division 9		14 034			2 210		7 452	1 496	990	
十　师	Division 10		21 931		67	18 265		4 283	2 238	2 161	1 713
建工师	Construction Division		16 930			1 637					
十二师	Division 12		37 731			8 033		1 563	2 348	26	51
十三师	Division 13		19 905		420	643		2 313	860	307	
十四师	Division 14		7 202			368		687	251	512	1 439
国资公司	State-owned Property Company		13 700								
供销公司	Supply and Marketing Corporation General										
中基公司	Chalkis Company										
兵团直属	Directly under XPCG	2 937	8 284		56			8 270	2 814		800

5—26 各师按构成分国有单位固定资产投资

Investment in Fixed Assets of State-owned Units by Composition and by Division

计量单位：万元 (2010 年) (10 000 yuan)

单 位	Unit	投资总额 Total	建筑工程 Construction Works	安装工程 Works of Installation	设备工具器具购置 Purchase of Equip-ment and Devices	其他费用 Other Expenses
总 计	**Total**	**2 318 366**	**1 609 216**	**97 827**	**479 934**	**131 389**
一 师	Division 1	245 302	185 724	9 877	38 231	11 470
二 师	Division 2	130 185	106 873	5 889	13 331	4 092
三 师	Division 3	189 667	134 163	8 962	28 860	17 682
四 师	Division 4	106 727	93 781	750	7 660	4 536
五 师	Division 5	121 136	97 161	1 474	15 624	6 877
六 师	Division 6	279 103	226 782	5 705	27 014	19 602
七 师	Division 7	158 032	134 443	3 051	12 428	8 110
八 师	Division 8	674 033	269 505	52 261	302 183	50 084
九 师	Division 9	64 403	51 754	1 249	10 398	1 002
十 师	Division 10	88 043	76 376	4 617	5 911	1 139
建 工 师	Construction Division	23 738	19 018	1 277	2 024	1 419
十 二 师	Division 12	92 185	80 961	1 026	6 813	3 385
十 三 师	Division 13	84 691	82 122	192	2 075	302
十 四 师	Division 14	20 953	17 755	1 143	1 884	171
国资公司	State-owned Property Company	13 700	13 700			
供销公司	Supply and Marketing Corporation General	1 066	966			100
中基公司	Chalkis Company					
兵团直属	Directly under XPCG	25 402	18 132	354	5 498	1 418

5—27 各师按建设性质分国有单位固定资产投资

Investment in Fixed Assets of State-owned Units by Type of Construction and by Division

计量单位：万元 (2010 年) (10 000 yuan)

单 位	Unit	合 计 Total	# 新 建 New Construction	# 扩 建 Expansion	# 改 建 Reconstruction	# 单纯生活设施 Pure Life Facilities	# 单纯购置 Purely Purchase
总 计	**Total**	**2 318 366**	**623 716**	**397 104**	**699 315**	**575 157**	**22 459**
一 师	Division 1	245 302	52 388	59 581	77 710	49 313	6 090
二 师	Division 2	130 185	29 069	9 028	40 724	48 861	2 503
三 师	Division 3	189 667	31 751	34 324	59 543	60 706	2 948
四 师	Division 4	106 727	430	31 943	21 437	52 317	600
五 师	Division 5	121 136	19 946	16 466	43 160	41 564	
六 师	Division 6	279 103	18 230	58 050	138 556	64 113	154
七 师	Division 7	158 032		34 463	70 270	52 334	965
八 师	Division 8	674 033	400 969	51 044	129 207	92 813	
九 师	Division 9	64 403	1 096	35 324	13 729	14 254	
十 师	Division 10	88 043	13 140	20 241	30 099	21 931	2 632
建 工 师	Construction Division	23 738	3 724	766	4 542	13 206	1 500
十 二 师	Division 12	92 185	11 464	22 938	28 834	28 254	695
十 三 师	Division 13	84 691	22 474	2 948	39 364	19 905	
十 四 师	Division 14	20 953	4 116	8 192	1 443	7 202	
国资公司	State-owned Property Company	13 700	13 700				
供销公司	Supply and Marketing Corporation General	1 066		1 066			
中基公司	Chalkis Company						
兵团直属	Directly under XPCG	25 402	1 219	10 730	697	8 384	4 372

5—28 各师国有单位固定资产投资资金来源

Funds Source of Investment in State-owned Units Fixed Assets by Division

计量单位：万元　　　　(2010年)　　　　(10 000 yuan)

指　标	Item	资金来源合计 Total of Capital Sources	国家预算内资金 State Budgetary Appropriation	国内贷款 Domestic Loans	利用外资 Foreign Investment	自筹资金 Fund Raising	其他资金 Others
总　计	**Total**	**2 234 362**	**560 193**	**518 907**	**2 849**	**761 654**	**390 759**
一　师	Division 1	250 121	54 883	31 811	1 729	149 243	12 455
二　师	Division 2	102 427	49 846	3 026		24 174	25 381
三　师	Division 3	190 934	92 766	13 249	1 120	70 607	13 192
四　师	Division 4	106 967	47 704	10 226		16 118	32 919
五　师	Division 5	108 537	28 599	4 279		33 377	42 282
六　师	Division 6	255 461	55 501	27 349		128 641	43 970
七　师	Division 7	151 544	39 372	14 857		61 816	35 499
八　师	Division 8	648 175	71 539	380 373		130 532	65 731
九　师	Division 9	64 403	20 860	1 300		26 534	15 709
十　师	Division 10	87 143	26 725	5 064		26 951	28 403
建工师	Construction Division	26 621	1 843	1 311		5 764	17 703
十二师	Division 12	92 614	22 550	5 642		35 309	29 113
十三师	Division 13	84 280	24 902			36 444	22 934
十四师	Division 14	20 953	16 607			3 841	505
国资公司	State-owned Property Company	14 000		14 000			
供销公司	Supply and Marketing Corporation General	1 045	445	420		180	
中基公司	Chalkis Company						
兵团直属	Directly under XPCG	29 137	6 051	6 000		12 123	4 963

5—29 各师国有单位施工、竣工房屋建筑面积及价值

Floor Space of Buildings Under Construction and Completed and Value of Buildings Completed in State-owned Units by Division

(2010年)

单　位	Unit	施工房屋面积合计（平方米） Floor Space Under Construction (sqm)	#本年新开工 Started in this Year	竣工房屋面积（平方米） Floor Space Completed (sq. m)	竣工房屋价值（万元） Value of Buildings Completed (10 000 yuan)	竣工房屋造价（元/平方米） Price of Buildings Completed (yuan/sq. m)
总　计	**Total**	**8 657 706**	**6 384 232**	**5 447 484**	**619 591**	**1 137**
一　师	Division 1	620 941	539 503	561 033	61 041	1 088
二　师	Division 2	724 689	340 542	442 566	61 894	1 399
三　师	Division 3	1 110 456	933 530	823 994	77 358	939
四　师	Division 4	679 359	586 968	669 638	65 551	979
五　师	Division 5	652 440	504 291	340 780	42 844	1 257
六　师	Division 6	684 922	637 432	433 308	50 860	1 174
七　师	Division 7	452 830	420 621	232 390	30 793	1 325
八　师	Division 8	1 756 393	966 992	791 214	87 976	1 112
九　师	Division 9	241 135	134 650	159 431	16 181	1 015
十　师	Division 10	346 824	304 006	332 360	44 427	1 337
建工师	Construction Division	188 509	163 477	22 259	3 082	1 385
十二师	Division 12	343 342	280 537	262 774	37 867	1 441
十三师	Division 13	336 554	243 251	170 404	16 303	957
十四师	Division 14	225 806	173 559	107 985	8 472	785
国资公司	State-owned Property Company	134 115	66 690	36 415	4 504	1 237
供销公司	Supply and Marketing Corporation General					
中基公司	Chalkis Company					
兵团直属	Directly under XPCG	159 391	88 183	60 933	10 438	1 713

5—30 农业及水利投资完成情况

Completion of Investment in Agriculture and Water Conservancy

计量单位:万元 (2010 年) (10 000 yuan)

指 标	Item	投资总额 Total Investment	# 国有单位 State-owned	资金来源合计 Total of Capital Sources	国家预算内资金 State Budgetary Appropriation
农业及水利投资总额	**Total Investment in Agriculture and Water Conservancy**	**497 713**	**399 066**	**479 049**	**173 781**
开垦荒地	Reclaimed Wildland Area	3 250	3 250	3 250	3 250
改造中低产田	Reform Farm Land With Low output	45 904	45 904	45 580	39 635
农田水利及水利工程	Farm Land Irrigation Engineering	198 574	197 060	179 910	99 452
# 新挖灌渠	Newly Dug Irrigation Canal	1 569	1 569	1 569	484
新挖排渠	Newly Dug Drainage Canal	4 790	4 790	4 790	2 267
渠道防渗	Anti-seepage Canal	44 355	44 355	45 797	28 557
喷、微灌	Spay-Irrigated and Micro-Irrigation	35 045	34 535	34 945	15 109
农业机械购置	Purchase for Agricalture Machinery	55 615	4 100	55 615	7 053
造 林	Afforestation	21 226	19 495	21 316	5 659
畜牧业	Animal Husbandry	43 325	20 125	42 738	4 562
其 它	Others	129 819	109 132	130 640	14 170

指 标	Item	国内贷款 Domestic Loans	利用外资 Foreign Investment	自筹资金 Fund Raising	其 他 Others
农业及水利投资总额	**Total Investment in Agriculture and Water Conservancy**	**22 129**		**193 115**	**90 024**
开垦荒地	Reclaimed Wildland Area				
改造中低产田	Reform Farm Land With Low Output			5 915	30
农田水利及水利工程	Farm Land Irrigation Engineering	4 395		70 785	5 278
# 新挖灌渠	Newly Dug Irrigation Canal			1 085	
新挖排渠	Newly Dug Drainage Canal	36		2 487	
渠道防渗	Anti-seepage Canal	1 291		15 524	425
喷、微灌	Spay-Irrigated and Micro-Irrigation			17 862	1 974
农业机械购置	Purchase for Agriculture Machinery	160		3 530	44 872
造 林	Afforestation			12 267	3 390
畜牧业	Animal Husbandry	10 203		12 963	15 010
其 它	Others	7 371		87 655	21 444

5—31 各师农业及水利投资完成情况

Completion of Investment in Agriculture and Water Conservancy by Division

计量单位:万元 (2010 年) (10 000 yuan)

单 位	Unit	投资总额 Total Investment in Agriculture	开垦荒地 Reclaimed Wildland Area	改造中低产田 Reform Farm Land with Low Output	农田水利及水利工程 Farmland Irrigation Engineering	# 新挖灌渠 Newly Dug Irrigation Canal	# 新挖排渠 Newly Dug Drainage Canal
总 计	**Total**	**497 713**	**3 250**	**45 904**	**198 574**	**1 569**	**4 790**
一 师	Division 1	72 625			38 588		2 060
二 师	Division 2	40 051		624	34 281	482	
三 师	Division 3	48 655		7 098	22 260		858
四 师	Division 4	37 097	3 250	2 945	9 347	622	95
五 师	Division 5	28 549		759	11 003		
六 师	Division 6	63 638		1 500	23 568		250
七 师	Division 7	22 529		2 077	8 193		253
八 师	Division 8	88 189		15 990	22 045		30
九 师	Division 9	19 510		1 307	6 538		
十 师	Division 10	19 021		730	7 707		
建 工 师	Construction ivision						
十 二 师	Division 12	22 998		1 155	10 150	465	424
十 三 师	Division 13	27 105		11 529	2 737		
十 四 师	Division 14	3 584		190	2 157		820
国资公司	State-owned Property Company	3 037					
供销公司	Supply and Marketing Corporation General						
中基公司	Chalkis Company						
兵团直属	Directly under XPCG	1 125					

单 位	Unit	# 渠道防渗 Anti-seepage Canal	# 喷、微灌 Spay-Irrigated and Micro-Irrigation	农业机械购置 Purchase of Agricultural Machines	造 林 Afforestation	畜牧业 Animal Husbandry	其 他 Others
总 计	**Total**	**44 355**	**35 045**	**55 615**	**21 226**	**43 325**	**129 819**
一 师	Division 1	15 677	6 060	8 876	3 876	1 634	19 651
二 师	Division 2	3 275	2 056	1 340	825	638	2 343
三 师	Division 3	2 495	4 385	1 381	1 614	1 758	14 544
四 师	Division 4	1 923	3 363	6 395	1 687	6 257	7 216
五 师	Division 5	2 440	4 489	2 956	798	336	12 697
六 师	Division 6	3 898	5 876	2 260	4 868	10 050	21 392
七 师	Division 7	5 481	225	4 284	1 345	1 398	5 232
八 师	Division 8	4 359	1 282	16 106	4 511	11 689	17 848
九 师	Division 9	485	3 359	4 500		1 125	6 040
十 师	Division 10	1 933	1 004	5 668	300	520	4 096
建 工 师	Construction ivision						
十 二 师	Division 12	490	1 178	997	976	3 937	5 783
十 三 师	Division 13	1 537	1 200		248	733	11 858
十 四 师	Division 14	362	568	331	176		730
国资公司	State-owned Property Company					3 037	
供销公司	Supply and Marketing Corporation General						
中基公司	Chalkis Company						
兵团直属	Directly under XPCG			521	2	213	389

2011

BING TUAN

第六篇

财　务

Chapter 6 Public Finance

简要说明

一、本篇资料反映2010年兵团国有及国有控股企业资产、主营业务收入、营业税金及附加、企业管理费用支出、营业外收入和支出和利润总额，盈利1000万以上国有企业情况。中华联合财产保险股份公司在本篇中简称为中华保险。

二、本篇资料由兵团财务局提供。

Brief Introduction

1. Main Contents

Data in this chapter reflect the conditions of assets of State-owned and State-holding enterprises, main business income, payable business tax and surcharges, management expenses, extra business revenue and expenditure and profit total amount, enterprises with a profit of over 10 million yuan. The brief name of China United Property Insurance Company is called China Insurance in this chapter.

2. Sources of Data

Data in this chapter are provided by the Financial Bureau of XPCG.

6—1 历年国有及国有控股企业年末固定资产(1951—2010年)

Year-end Fixed Assets of State-owned and State-controlled Shareholding Enterprises over the Years(1951—2010)

计量单位:万元 (10 000 yuan)

年 份 Year	年末固定资产 Year-end Fixed Assets		年 份 Year	年末固定资产 Year-end Fixed Assets	
	原 值 Original Value	净 值 Net Value		原 值 Original Value	净 值 Net Value
1951	1 824	1 824	1981	146 718	87 631
1952	3 369	3 369	1982	165 703	99 891
1953	6 071	5 485	1983	176 135	104 141
1954	8 642	7 474	1984	205 176	121 190
1955	11 419	9 502	1985	210 326	127 114
1956	15 079	12 211	1986	251 174	153 479
1957	20 382	16 424	1987	278 465	174 624
1958	31 933	27 088	1988	285 797	187 176
1959	47 685	41 084	1989	325 862	216 598
1960	51 991	45 774	1990	377 860	253 976
1961	71 098	58 895	1991	440 031	309 211
1962	91 905	76 867	1992	518 094	362 604
1963	85 201	70 223	1993	666 525	480 289
1964	99 055	77 824	1994	848 349	619 784
1965	100 492	76 945	1995	1 198 480	851 377
1966	68 500	53 156	1996	1 538 539	1 112 888
1967	78 300	56 853	1997	1 834 230	1 340 750
1968	90 200	57 889	1998	2 224 568	1 626 352
1969	96 000	59 097	1999	2 397 769	1 709 282
1970	99 232	62 059	2000	2 385 124	1 676 272
1971	102 400	64 125	2001	2 549 525	1 792 884
1972	105 156	65 728	2002	2 846 283	2 002 413
1973	112 295	66 882	2003	3 063 855	2 153 063
1974	141 404	92 385	2004	3 448 049	2 421 280
1975	85 222	46 554	2005	4 100 982	2 667 261
1976	91 392	48 836	2006	4 501 324	2 931 719
1977	94 494	52 677	2007	5 060 407	3 277 708
1978	106 621	58 708	2008	5 853 140	3 639 694
1979	119 817	66 230	2009	6 869 041	4 283 575
1980	132 295	77 133	2010	8 058 931	4 993 187

6－2　按行业分国有及国有控股企业年末固定资产原值(1980－2010年)

Original Value of Year-end Fixed Assets of State-owned and State-controlled Shareholding Enterprises by Sector(1980－2010)

计量单位:万元　　(10 000 yuan)

年　份 Year	合　计 Total	农　业 Agriculture	工　业 Industry	建筑业 Construction and Installation	交通运输业 Transportation	商品流通企业 Commodity Circulation
1980	132 295	84 355	35 543	3 351	6 987	2 059
1981	146 718	91 426	39 282	5 818	7 649	2 544
1982	165 703	103 228	44 193	6 582	8 315	3 385
1983	176 135	108 071	46 949	7 080	9 159	4 876
1984	205 176	115 252	57 704	13 223	10 624	8 374
1985	210 326	122 079	60 283	8 348	10 885	8 731
1986	251 174	127 623	82 389	14 674	12 792	13 697
1987	278 465	133 923	100 429	15 777	14 722	13 614
1988	285 797	127 461	107 266	17 612	15 209	18 250
1989	325 862	137 945	130 526	20 063	17 161	20 168
1990	377 860	154 493	154 150	23 986	19 698	25 533
1991	440 031	176 441	182 156	27 516	25 703	28 216
1992	518 094	213 634	206 884	33 516	30 088	33 973
1993	666 525	284 488	262 878	41 217	35 134	42 808
1994	848 349	360 295	334 765	52 313	38 910	62 066
1995	1 198 480	524 775	451 348	68 747	52 447	101 163
1996	1 538 539	673 053	551 027	92 772	62 989	158 695
1997	1 834 230	852 675	604 035	103 467	68 231	205 822
1998	2 224 568	1 027 912	799 619	109 702	65 638	221 697
1999	2 397 769	1 125 450	827 609	111 734	69 311	263 665
2000	2 385 124	1 198 322	762 842	113 774	57 539	252 647
2001	2 549 525	1 383 590	733 891	122 718	46 540	262 786
2002	2 846 283	1 520 347	861 152	132 288	48 293	284 203
2003	3 063 855	1 645 733	866 215	135 397	27 884	388 626
2004	3 448 049	1 810 322	1 000 895	137 553	29 162	470 117
2005	4 100 982	2 119 150	1 255 836	147 698	21 600	556 698
2006	4 501 324	2 350 620	1 334 933	159 442	20 873	635 456
2007	5 060 407	2 626 552	1 612 408	189 607	27 174	604 666
2008	5 853 140	2 967 283	1 886 592	301 655	25 794	671 816
2009	6 869 041	3 242 464	2 640 312	317 285	24 850	644 130
2010	8 058 931	3 515 157	3 649 944	351 421	29 671	512 738

6—3 各师国有及国有控股企业年末固定资产原值

Original Value of Year-end Fixed Assets of State-owned and State-controlled Shareholding Enterprises by Division

计量单位:万元 (2010 年) (10 000 yuan)

单位 Unit		合计 Total	农业 Agriculture	工业 Industry	建筑业 Construction and Installation	交通运输业 Transportation
总计	**Total**	**8 058 931**	**3 515 157**	**3 649 944**	**351 421**	**29 671**
一师	Division 1	1 202 015	540 430	621 996	24 530	
二师	Division 2	452 113	321 551	74 598	15 865	952
三师	Division 3	338 162	217 547	42 352	63 042	4 420
四师	Division 4	555 986	221 778	299 747	6 079	1 073
五师	Division 5	258 817	182 354	57 141	3 365	1 677
六师	Division 6	687 072	461 763	175 516	158	1 876
七师	Division 7	748 944	300 906	306 576	68 424	3 167
八师	Division 8	2 482 170	596 533	1 799 311	7 542	
九师	Division 9	182 483	111 603	60 167	3 594	2 070
十师	Division 10	242 476	198 347	41 047		721
建工师	Construction Division	135 553	91 014	39 991	310	
十二师	Division 12	211 390	190 409	16 605	765	291
十三师	Division 13	51 389	32 515	11 807	1 678	86
十四师	Division 14	161 224	1 357	5 970	152 474	
国资公司	State-owned Property Company	264 688		91 927	3 595	13 338
兵团直属	Directly under XPCG	84 449	47 050	5 193		

单位 Unit		商品流通业 Commodity Circulation	商业 Commerce	外贸 Foreign Trade	物资 Materials	供销 Supply and Marketing
总计	**Total**	**512 738**	**372 092**	**8 367**	**8 232**	**124 047**
一师	Division 1	15 059	607			14 452
二师	Division 2	39 147	31 842	190	1 683	5 432
三师	Division 3	10 801	10 483	318		
四师	Division 4	27 309	17 618	2 387		7 304
五师	Division 5	14 280	13 265		122	893
六师	Division 6	47 759	38 093		5 196	4 470
七师	Division 7	69 871	7 475	469	1 045	60 882
八师	Division 8	78 784	52 984			25 800
九师	Division 9	5 049	4 471	43		535
十师	Division 10	2 361	34	199		2 128
建工师	Construction Division	4 238	4 076	162		
十二师	Division 12	3 320	1 771			1 549
十三师	Division 13	5 303	202	4 599		502
十四师	Division 14	1 423	1 255		66	101
国资公司	State-owned Property Company	155 828	155 709		120	
兵团直属	Directly under XPCG	32 206	32 206			

6—4 各师国有及国有控股企业年末固定资产净额

Net Value of Year-end Fixed Assets of State-owned and State-controlled Shareholding Enterprises by Division

计量单位:万元　　(2010 年)　　(10 000 yuan)

单　位	Unit	合　计 Total	农　业 Agriculture	工　业 Industry	建筑业 Construction and Installation	交通运输业 Transportation
总　计	**Total**	**4 979 681**	**1 717 287**	**2 681 801**	**208 257**	**18 476**
一　师	Division 1	696 057	211 800	457 064	17 134	
二　师	Division 2	300 095	205 154	58 600	8 529	711
三　师	Division 3	172 621	103 630	30 680	28 486	3 378
四　师	Division 4	266 033	49 988	194 717	3 384	736
五　师	Division 5	142 211	98 929	29 524	1 616	1 241
六　师	Division 6	402 277	214 936	146 556	124	1 365
七　师	Division 7	500 505	177 947	227 585	49 494	1 867
八　师	Division 8	1 748 101	337 223	1 350 410	3 323	
九　师	Division 9	85 710	48 071	30 878	1 953	1 530
十　师	Division 10	118 800	91 927	25 011		355
建工师	Construction Division	85 174	52 811	28 246	221	
十二师	Division 12	104 185	85 975	15 444	541	186
十三师	Division 13	25 023	11 041	9 615	1 337	80
十四师	Division 14	96 369	1 165	4 515	89 684	
国资公司	State-owned Property Company	183 728		70 463	2 431	7 025
兵团直属	Directly under XPCG	52 791	26 690	2 493		

单　位	Unit	商品流通业 Commodity Circulation	商　业 Commerce	外　贸 Foreign Trade	物　资 Materials	供　销 Supply and Marketing
总　计	**Total**	**353 860**	**266 282**	**4 968**	**5 090**	**77 520**
一　师	Division 1	10 058	527			9 531
二　师	Division 2	27 100	23 164	127	909	2 901
三　师	Division 3	6 448	6 369	78		
四　师	Division 4	17 208	10 425	1 799		4 984
五　师	Division 5	10 902	10 671		55	176
六　师	Division 6	39 295	33 413		3 233	2 648
七　师	Division 7	43 612	4 934	171	775	37 733
八　师	Division 8	57 145	40 665			16 480
九　师	Division 9	3 278	2 949	19		310
十　师	Division 10	1 507	30	168		1 309
建工师	Construction Division	3 897	3 741	155		
十二师	Division 12	2 037	995			1 042
十三师	Division 13	2 950	131	2 451		368
十四师	Division 14	1 006	935		33	37
国资公司	State-owned Property Company	103 809	103 725		85	
兵团直属	Directly under XPCG	23 608	23 608			

6—5 各师国有及国有控股企业年末流动资产

Year-end Current Assets of State-owned and State-controlled Shareholding Enterprises by Division

计量单位:万元 (2010 年) (10 000 yuan)

单 位 Unit		合 计 Total	农 业 Agriculture	工 业 Industry	建筑业 Construction and Installation	交通运输业 Transportation
总 计	**Total**	**11 274 435**	**3 465 580**	**2 729 022**	**843 336**	**14 104**
一 师	Division 1	1 665 474	631 832	645 723	56 847	
二 师	Division 2	447 118	268 514	34 078	43 783	614
三 师	Division 3	644 641	295 270	81 900	45 060	2 251
四 师	Division 4	600 799	261 395	215 454	11 608	1 870
五 师	Division 5	429 429	261 114	29 704	8 978	2 045
六 师	Division 6	751 279	380 211	186 689	6 026	496
七 师	Division 7	503 144	239 155	146 327	39 641	917
八 师	Division 8	2 363 280	568 608	1 084 304	67 791	
九 师	Division 9	183 776	105 914	42 233	16 921	1 274
十 师	Division 10	122 418	107 184	10 638		112
建工师	Construction Division	386 124	95 619	61 120	57 447	
十二师	Division 12	247 360	180 343	27 328	15 142	305
十三师	Division 13	78 925	29 832	18 345	2 415	17
十四师	Division 14	429 895	4 722	559	422 707	
国资公司	State-owned Property Company	1 016 521		135 922	48 970	4 202
兵团直属	Directly under XPCG	1 404 252	35 869	8 697		

单 位 Unit		商品流通业 Commodity Circulation	商 业 Commerec	外 贸 Foreign Trade	物 资 Materials	供 销 Suply and Marketing
总 计	**Total**	**4 222 393**	**2 834 271**	**30 048**	**64 436**	**1 293 638**
一 师	Division 1	331 072	3 892			327 180
二 师	Division 2	100 129	11 961	120	33 768	54 280
三 师	Division 3	220 161	217 940	2 222		
四 师	Division 4	110 471	26 951	1 770		81 750
五 师	Division 5	127 587	18 804		1 238	107 545
六 师	Division 6	177 858	64 606		10 827	102 425
七 师	Division 7	77 103	9 312	2 161	2 634	62 996
八 师	Division 8	642 578	125 292			517 286
九 师	Division 9	17 434	8 443	378		8 614
十 师	Division 10	4 484	829	370		3 285
建工师	Construction Division	171 939	165 394	6 545		
十二师	Division 12	24 242	8 840			15 403
十三师	Division 13	28 315	133	16 482		11 700
十四师	Division 14	1 906	231		501	1 174
国资公司	State-owned Property Company	827 427	811 958		15 468	
兵团直属	Directly under XPCG	1 359 686	1 359 686			

6—6 各师国有及国有控股企业年末总资产

Year-end Total Assets of State-owned and State-controlled Shareholding Enterprises by Division

计量单位:万元　　　　(2010 年)　　　　(10 000 yuan)

单　位 Unit		合　计 Total	农　业 Agriculture	工　业 Industry	建筑业 Construction and Installation	交通运输业 Transportation
总　计	**Total**	**20 596 641**	**6 715 603**	**7 195 548**	**1 206 431**	**45 388**
一　师	Division 1	2 877 958	1 001 199	1 422 626	91 313	
二　师	Division 2	883 550	576 299	107 297	56 857	6 274
三　师	Division 3	1 047 884	540 108	174 385	87 638	8 105
四　师	Division 4	1 132 683	446 144	504 563	15 367	2 674
五　师	Division 5	674 068	448 561	65 536	14 252	5 220
六　师	Division 6	1 645 767	756 544	612 365	7 613	1 888
七　师	Division 7	1 176 066	518 403	425 322	96 136	3 804
八　师	Division 8	5 181 872	1 150 537	3 228 961	83 049	
九　师	Division 9	323 889	196 495	81 451	19 868	3 438
十　师	Division 10	300 486	243 028	46 218		502
建工师	Construction Division	661 328	250 267	128 471	59 706	
十二师	Division 12	499 423	361 659	93 356	16 851	599
十三师	Division 13	209 161	134 154	36 120	4 509	105
十四师	Division 14	608 160	8 095	3 953	599 216	
国资公司	State-owned Property Company	1 410 363		253 282	54 054	12 780
兵团直属	Directly under XPCG	1 963 984	84 109	11 642		

单　位 Unit		商品流通业 Commodity Circulation	商　业 Commerce	外　贸 Foreign Trade	物　资 Materials	供　销 Supply and Marketing
总　计	**Total**	**5 433 671**	**3 909 686**	**42 104**	**74 422**	**1 407 459**
一　师	Division 1	362 820	4 423			358 397
二　师	Division 2	136 822	41 413	1 241	36 631	57 538
三　师	Division 3	237 646	235 346	2 300		
四　师	Division 4	163 936	67 039	5 404		91 492
五　师	Division 5	140 499	31 168		1 356	107 975
六　师	Division 6	267 358	146 385		14 875	106 097
七　师	Division 7	132 401	22 700	2 332	3 539	103 831
八　师	Division 8	719 325	182 972			536 353
九　师	Division 9	22 636	12 580	397		9 658
十　师	Division 10	10 738	5 445	538		4 755
建工师	Construction Division	222 884	213 369	9 515		
十二师	Division 12	26 958	10 418			16 540
十三师	Division 13	34 274	285	20 377		13 611
十四师	Division 14	−3 105	−4 873		557	1 211
国资公司	State-owned Property Company	1 090 246	1 072 783		17 464	
兵团直属	Directly under XPCG	1 868 233	1 868 233			

6－7 国有及国有控股企业主营业务收入(1979－2010年)

Main Business Income of State-owned and State-controlled Shareholding Enterprises(1979－2010)

计量单位:万元 (10 000 yuan)

年 份 Year	合 计 Total	农 业 Agriculture	工 业 Industry	建筑业 Construction and Installation	交通运输业 Transportation	商品流通业 Commodity Circulation
1979	171 816	90 388	29 475	5 962	6 744	39 247
1980	200 547	109 296	34 204	4 128	7 059	45 860
1981	218 198	121 538	35 709	6 169	6 414	48 341
1982	257 817	140 783	38 153	8 009	7 410	63 462
1983	305 120	166 004	46 752	14 016	8 185	70 163
1984	355 300	160 637	55 127	27 729	9 476	102 331
1985	306 995	123 211	57 700	19 331	9 107	97 646
1986	396 858	142 933	73 392	34 386	10 640	135 507
1987	557 759	247 556	90 064	44 956	13 087	162 096
1988	722 603	315 754	117 925	53 683	14 566	220 675
1989	792 980	359 030	127 402	56 751	16 786	233 191
1990	991 592	498 526	142 788	58 576	18 841	272 861
1991	1 398 548	666 837	168 097	68 467	26 961	468 186
1992	1 622 073	688 691	196 919	90 296	28 933	617 234
1993	2 167 075	920 930	286 103	137 341	30 560	792 141
1994	2 083 751	966 299	313 336	148 476	32 565	623 145
1995	2 978 017	1 354 316	363 080	172 991	31 875	1 055 755
1996	3 486 683	1 388 985	392 145	186 225	30 258	1 489 040
1997	3 611 481	1 565 781	389 380	202 006	34 438	1 419 876
1998	3 744 763	1 587 475	432 385	268 733	32 047	1 424 123
1999	3 458 441	1 351 546	443 893	284 729	25 869	1 352 404
2000	3 791 107	1 514 993	484 737	350 986	21 388	1 419 003
2001	3 337 440	1 223 521	434 814	376 807	16 241	1 286 057
2002	3 758 252	1 422 510	475 300	446 961	16 111	1 397 370
2003	4 441 033	1 671 487	524 604	490 699	14 691	1 739 552
2004	5 198 307	1 619 767	649 885	522 813	10 739	2 395 103
2005	6 718 567	2 005 357	722 023	493 342	10 914	3 486 931
2006	7 390 183	2 254 430	777 327	565 145	12 521	3 780 760
2007	9 069 015	2 609 118	1 171 507	775 284	12 228	4 500 878
2008	9 616 740	2 711 233	1 245 247	930 883	14 867	4 714 510
2009	10 625 814	2 664 132	1 726 262	1 176 041	13 927	5 045 452
2010	10 456 802	3 188 776	2 403 822	1 512 417	19 472	3 332 315

6—8　国有及国有控股企业应缴税金(1979—2010年)

Payable Taxes of State-owned and State-controlled Shareholding Enterprises(1979—2010)

计量单位:万元　　(10 000 yuan)

年　份 Year	合　计 Total	农　业 Agriculture	工　业 Industry	建筑业 Construction and Installation	交通运输业 Transportation	商品流通企业 Commodity Circulation
1979	4 971	1 966	2 724		186	95
1980	5 405	1 848	3 153	96	199	109
1981	5 444	1 793	3 341		182	128
1982	6 154	2 400	3 401		211	142
1983	7 608	3 183	3 860	118	241	206
1984	8 120	2 796	4 536	158	282	348
1985	8 756	2 874	4 990	105	294	493
1986	10 954	2 636	6 429	122	333	1 434
1987	13 971	4 489	7 151	197	419	1 715
1988	19 467	6 589	9 115	828	497	2 438
1989	26 780	8 453	13 869	1 137	561	2 760
1990	35 089	10 541	18 865	1 484	781	3 418
1991	42 036	11 996	21 571	2 012	1 113	5 344
1992	50 865	14 280	25 774	2 737	1 174	6 900
1993	54 347	16 670	20 975	3 762	1 268	11 672
1994	54 164	22 478	26 725	4 345	1 254	−638
1995	80 977	24 338	30 293	6 278	1 209	18 859
1996	93 801	25 818	29 645	6 071	1 402	30 865
1997	93 719	29 887	33 812	6 132	1 319	22 569
1998	103 827	28 847	36 745	7 576	1 085	29 574
1999	117 382	27 849	40 663	8 501	1 164	39 205
2000	90 695	25 730	39 957	11 076	1 010	12 922
2001	86 890	25 959	33 757	10 966	728	15 480
2002	101 002	27 462	36 193	14 011	606	22 730
2003	104 083	22 220	36 387	15 485	540	29 451
2004	148 227	19 212	46 475	16 378	740	65 422
2005	241 672	14 961	64 583	16 962	879	144 287
2006	215 054	19 168	70 391	20 861	686	103 948
2007	281 330	17 200	97 847	29 511	570	136 202
2008	336 312	21 784	123 859	34 106	982	155 581
2009	431 143	31 418	147 954	51 092	1 353	199 326
2010	349 777	32 158	218 946	66 463	1 634	30 576

6—9　各师国有及国有控股企业主营业务收入净额

Majin Business Net Income of State-owned and State-controlled Shareholding Enterprises by Division

计量单位:万元　　　　(2010 年)　　　　(10 000 yuan)

单　位	Unit	合　计 Total	农　业 Agriculture	工　业 Industry	建筑业 Construction and Installation	交通运输业 Transportation
总　计	**Total**	**1 211 214**	**293 281**	**626 416**	**89 340**	**2 169**
一　师	Division 1	205 375	98 319	93 294	9 855	
二　师	Division 2	47 365	26 320	9 476	3 889	34
三　师	Division 3	32 892	17 102	3 506	2 684	1 110
四　师	Division 4	111 054	17 776	72 679	3 086	533
五　师	Division 5	32 273	20 300	3 429	1 642	409
六　师	Division 6	36 196	−323	29 186	37	−4
七　师	Division 7	45 618	6 500	27 097	5 612	275
八　师	Division 8	421 043	77 179	315 484	5 079	
九　师	Division 9	14 384	3 366	6 680	1 205	420
十　师	Division 10	3 865	2 555	622		11
建工师	Construction Division	29 089	10 172	9 751	3 990	
十二师	Division 12	24 577	16 595	4 232	1 547	
十三师	Division 13	2 174	−3 925	3 365	610	24
十四师	Division 14	50 199	8	1 239	47 910	
国资公司	State-owned Property Company	108 258		43 321	2 194	−643
兵团直属	Directly under XPCG	46 852	1 337	3 054		

单　位	Unit	商品流通业 Commodity Circulation	商　业 Commerce	外　贸 Foreign Trade	物　资 Materials	供　销 Supply and Marketing
总　计	**Total**	**200 008**	**149 366**	**2 398**	**2 097**	**46 147**
一　师	Division 1	3 907	210			3 697
二　师	Division 2	7 646	3 305	18	1 144	3 179
三　师	Division 3	8 490	8 490			
四　师	Division 4	16 980	7 505	835		8 640
五　师	Division 5	6 494	4 585		256	1 653
六　师	Division 6	7 299	2 002			5 297
七　师	Division 7	6 133	1 073		567	4 493
八　师	Division 8	23 300	7 614			15 686
九　师	Division 9	2 713	1 421	53		1 239
十　师	Division 10	677		89		588
建工师	Construction Division	5 176	4 833	343		
十二师	Division 12	2 203	1 650			553
十三师	Division 13	2 099	11	1 060		1 028
十四师	Division 14	1 043	949			94
国资公司	State-owned Property Company	63 386	63 256		130	
兵团直属	Directly under XPCG	42 461	42 461			

6—10　各师国有及国有控股企业营业税金及附加

Business Tax and Extra Charges of State-owned and State-controlled Shareholding Enterprises by Division

计量单位:万元　　　　(2010 年)　　　　(10 000 yuan)

单　位	Unit	合　计 Total	农　业 Agriculture	工　业 Industry	建筑业 Construction and Installation	交通运输业 Transportation
总　计	**Total**	**103 778**	**9 254**	**36 327**	**50 941**	**516**
一　师	Division 1	7 708	7	3 531	4 136	
二　师	Division 2	5 688	89	866	4 454	7
三　师	Division 3	2 817	64	22	2 431	186
四　师	Division 4	19 270	876	16 053	1 865	24
五　师	Division 5	2 520	921	87	1 369	75
六　师	Division 6	1 946	373	890	41	24
七　师	Division 7	4 508	816	793	2 724	23
八　师	Division 8	18 624	1 529	12 424	4 256	
九　师	Division 9	1 459	3	184	1 025	140
十　师	Division 10	1 192	1 068	108		3
建工师	Construction Division	5 827	2 796	646	1 769	
十二师	Division 12	2 079	694	203	1 075	2
十三师	Division 13	872		51	795	1
十四师	Division 14	24 024		84	23 882	
国资公司	State-owned Property Company	4 242		365	1 119	32
兵团直属	Directly under XPCG	1 002	18	21		

单　位	Unit	商品流通业 Commodity Circulation	商　业 Commerce	外　贸 Foreign Trade	物　资 Materials	供　销 Supply and Marketing
总　计	**Total**	**6 740**	**5 828**	**57**	**593**	**262**
一　师	Division 1	34	4			30
二　师	Division 2	273	242	1	18	12
三　师	Division 3	114	114			
四　师	Division 4	451	306	41		104
五　师	Division 5	69	68		1	
六　师	Division 6	619	113		505	1
七　师	Division 7	152	72		40	40
八　师	Division 8	415	379			36
九　师	Division 9	108	92	1		15
十　师	Division 10	14		1		13
建工师	Construction Division	616	616			
十二师	Division 12	105	100			6
十三师	Division 13	24	5	14		5
十四师	Division 14	58	58			
国资公司	State-owned Property Company	2 725	2 695		29	
兵团直属	Directly under XPCG	963	963			

6—11 各师国有及国有控股企业应缴税金

Payable Taxes of State-owned and State-controlled Shareholding Enterprises by Division

计量单位:万元 (2010 年) (10 000 yuan)

指标	Item	合计 Total	一师 Division 1	二师 Division 2	三师 Division 3	四师 Division 4	五师 Division 5	六师 Division 6	七师 Division 7	八师 Division 8
本年应缴税金总计	**Total Payable Taxesin This Year**	**349 777**	**46 875**	**20 106**	**9 855**	**58 357**	**11 251**	**16 374**	**13 232**	**84 328**
增值税	Value Added Tax	126 645	23 177	11 419	3 799	23 619	6 920	6 325	4 860	36 373
消费税	Consumption Tax	17 242	535	6		14 257	24			
营业税	Business Tax	61 578	4 073	3 657	2 533	2 600	2 282	1 124	4 493	10 504
资源税	Resource Tax	3 258	634	529		387		384	144	644
城市维护建设税	Urban Maintenanceand Development Tax	11 682	1 659	438	148	1 070	119	120	733	4 375
教育费附加	Additional Education fee	6 546	824	249	92	1 251	81	156	379	1 833
关税	Tariff	11 584						1 920		191
# 本年已交进口关税	Import Tariff	9 665								191
本年已交出口关税	Export Tariff	1 920						1 920		
企业所得税	Enterprise Income Tax	72 343	11 136	1 371	1 954	13 588	799	3 903	1 153	17 743
其他各税	Other	38 899	4 837	2 437	1 330	1 584	1 026	2 444	1 469	12 663

指标	Item	九师 Division 9	十师 Division 10	建工师 Construction Division	十二师 Division 12	十三师 Division 13	十四师 Division 14	国资公司 State-owned Property Company	兵团直属 Directly under XPCG
本年应缴税金总计	**Total Payable Taxesin This Year**	**6 141**	**2 785**	**30 584**	**11 866**	**8 465**	**2 771**	**16 856**	**9 933**
增值税	Value Added Tax	2 410	1 070	1 912	2 661	3 922	1 112	1 249	−4 183
消费税	Consumption Tax		352		229		178	1 649	12
营业税	Business Tax	1 101	502	20 136	4 314	1 482	616	1 679	484
资源税	Resource Tax			1	107	259		170	
城市维护建设税	Urban Maintenanceand Development Tax	153	39	1 387	369	173	80	586	233
教育费附加	Additional Education fee	103	27	701	198	143	45	340	124
关税	Tariff		306		4		271	1 777	7 115
# 本年已交进口关税	Import Tariff		306		4		271	1 777	7 115
本年已交出口关税	Export Tariff								
企业所得税	Enterprise Income Tax	1 155	129	2 699	2 677	2 021	172	6 378	5 464
其他各税	Other	1 219	360	3 749	1 307	465	297	3 028	683

6—12　各师国有及国有控股企业管理费用支出

计量单位:万元　　(2010 年)

指　标	Item	合计 Total	一师 Division 1	二师 Division 2	三师 Division 3	四师 Division 4	五师 Division 5	六师 Division 6
管理费用支出总计	**Total Expenditures on Administration Expenses**	**586 820**	**120 550**	**35 250**	**26 756**	**58 390**	**15 599**	**33 815**
职工薪酬	Wages	280 119	38 701	19 582	12 391	32 605	6 343	19 937
离退休人员医疗费补助	Medical Treatment Fee Subsidy for Retirees	14 802	2 072	1 004	714	453	263	163
业务招待费	Business Reception Fee	24 506	2 935	1 336	1 591	2 194	591	1 913
印花税	Stamp Taxes	2 448	579	19	185	94	51	150
土地使用税	Land Use Taxes	3 219	515	222	109	144	55	173
房产税	House Property Taxes	5 532	335	294	104	201	66	426
车船使用税	Car and Ship Use Taxes	91	16	1	3	4	1	3
坏账损失	Bad Loan Loss	2 788	1 506	−8	−1	36	3	324
# 提取的坏帐准备	Bad Loan Preparation Withdrawn	2 179	1 538	−45	−1	15	3	−41
技术开发费	Technique Development Fee	2 113	783	62	2	97	2	1
技术转让费	Techigue Transfer Fee	70	30				10	
土地使用费	Land Use Fee	554	96	40	27	60		
排污费	Pollution Discharge Fee	1 598	169	56	20	57	19	24
绿化费	Greening Fee	3 021	321	198	128	150	46	262
折旧费	Depreciation	73 428	16 701	6 008	4 480	5 961	3 232	5 346
修理费	Repairing	7 835	914	386	672	673	617	389
物料消耗	Material Depletion	7 395	898	692	422	738	295	499
低值易耗品摊销	Low Value Easy Consumables Apportion	1 325	84	84	101	140	21	100
住房公积金	Housing Provident Fund	6 906	874	277	556	343	328	242
递延资产摊销	Deferred Assets Apportion	25 357	3 234	2 791	4 458	2 760	812	956
无形资产摊销	Intangible Assets Apportion	4 357	871	236	49	298	1	938
差旅费	Public Errand Fee	12 643	1 328	884	813	1 104	353	658
办公费	Administrative Expenses	12 653	1 106	1 034	655	1 098	371	572
存货盘亏、毁废(减盘盈)	Inventory, Defacement (InventoryOverage Reduction)	−4 755	70	46	17	64		−1 804
其　他	Others	128 243	57 930	4 130	2 625	9 117	2 119	7 635
减:家庭农场实际上交管理费	Reduce: Real Turnover Managerial Expenses of Family-Run Farms	29 428	11 518	4 125	3 365			5 091
管理费用支出净额	**Net Amount of Managerial Fee**	**586 820**	**120 550**	**35 250**	**26 756**	**58 390**	**15 599**	**33 815**

Expenditures on Administration Expenses of State-owned and State-controlled Shareholding Enterpriese by Division

(10 000 yuan)

七 师 Division 7	八 师 Division 8	九 师 Division 9	十 师 Division 10	建工师 Construction Division	十二师 Division 12	十三师 Division 13	十四师 Division 14	国资公司 State-owned Property Company	兵团直属 Directly under XPCG
28 578	**105 399**	**19 127**	**15 849**	**44 210**	**22 340**	**9 697**	**3 501**	**38 836**	**8 924**
11 871	49 071	6 570	8 565	22 347	15 314	10 925	2 011	17 133	6 755
3 680	4 002	1 083	775	155	233	173		19	14
1 543	2 604	1 043	780	3 127	1 204	423	228	2 038	954
85	571	37	17	170	78	36	8	235	134
240	1 068	70	19	190	73	6	5	293	37
276	2 510	134	36	119	194	8	4	533	291
5	32	5	2	7	1	4	1	5	1
−78	691		188	77	25	15	2	8	
−98	677		11	77	31	2	2	7	
5	535	48		60				293	225
	30								
34	159	38	14			70		16	
25	955	59	3		7	194		1	8
361	924	42	122	11	155	287	13	1	
2 775	11 981	2 124	3 059	2 239	1 336	2 027	145	3 852	2 160
274	2 102	389	43	336	156	79	34	646	125
912	1 727	186	83	200	276	346	105	1	17
55	315	34	3	42	73	123	1	117	32
194	981	504	238	1 593	68	65	67	521	56
184	7 807	1	266	14	1 507	243	6	57	263
42	913	38	3	103	223	85	56	425	76
649	2 002	466	367	1 960	267	251	138	1 059	344
529	2 022	458	912	1 723	498	460	155	837	222
1	−122	12	42		31	73		−3 244	60
4 918	12 519	5 785	562	9 736	3 709	−6 107	666	13 988	−1 089
			250		3 089	87	143		1 760
28 578	**105 399**	**19 127**	**15 849**	**44 210**	**22 340**	**9 697**	**3 501**	**38 836**	**8 924**

6—13　各师营业外收入及营业外支出

计量单位：万元　　　　　　　　　　　　　　　　　　　　　　　　　　　　　　　（2010 年）

指　标	Item	合　计 Total	一　师 Division 1	二　师 Division 2	三　师 Division 3	四　师 Division 4	五　师 Division 5	六　师 Division 6
营业外收入	**Extra-Business Revenue**	**545 090**	**92 991**	**36 807**	**55 773**	**54 313**	**18 184**	**65 791**
处理固定资产净收益	Net Gains of Fixed Assets Disposal	11 580	854	468	635	752	7	1 418
固定资产盘盈	Inventory Losses of Fixed Assets	42						9
教育费附加返还款	Repyament of Enucation Surtax	4						
罚款收入	Penalty Income	2 306	275	115	253	100	43	139
物资现金溢余收入	Surplus Income of Materials and Cash	70		2	8	1		12
其他社会性收入	Other Social Income	390 762	45 234	30 455	42 042	51 606	16 840	53 724
其　他	Others	140 326	46 628	5 766	12 834	1 855	1 294	10 490
营业外支出	**Extra-Business Expenditures**	**478 957**	**77 601**	**31 959**	**50 515**	**49 340**	**21 716**	**62 244**
处理固定资产净损失	Net Losses of Fixed Assets Disposal	8 142	1 788	302	430	198	154	237
固定资产盘亏	Inventory Losses of Fixed Assets	65			15			47
非常损失	Abnormal Losses	635	381	5		61		30
赔偿金、违约金	Solatium and Penalty	3 711	415	219	163	84	109	396
公益性捐赠支出	Public Welfare Donation Expenditure	974	232	90	13	128	105	86
中小学校经费	Fund for Primary and Secondary Schools	117 578	245	14 345	19 820	1 529	8 823	22 796
技工学校经费	Fund for Technical Schools	17		17				
安置老残干部	Settlement Allowance of Veteran and Disabled Cadres	707		332				
专职政法人员经费	Fund for Full-Time Political-Legal Functionaries	1 221		97	141	72		137
边防民兵值勤经费	Fund on Duty for Frontier Defence Militia	7 862	10	412	1 145	682	840	819
防汛抢险支出	Expenditure For Flood and Emergency Control	1 015	19	197	347	173	1	58
政府行政经费	Governmental Administration Fund	4 007		228	663		744	40
其他社会性支出	Other Social Expenditure	307 198	69 995	15 402	25 863	45 907	10 848	34 837
其　他	Others	25 826	4 518	314	1 915	508	94 2 759	

Extra-Business Revenue and Extra-Business Expenditures by Division

(10 000 yuan)

七 师 Division 7	八 师 Division 8	九 师 Division 9	十 师 Division 10	建工师 Construction Division	十二师 Division 12	十三师 Division 13	十四师 Division 14	国资公司 State-owned Property Company	兵团直属 Directly under XPCG
41 173	**56 013**	**26 563**	**34 468**	**4 587**	**10 139**	**21 532**	**7 318**	**16 353**	**3 084**
2 018	1 247	217	331	504	991	98	26	1 895	118
	28					5			
3									
75	769	18	95	19	66	58	8	256	15
1	20		25		3				
29 859	46 492	14 434	28 921	2 208	6 865	15 663	4 379	271	1 771
9 217	7 458	11 893	5 096	1 857	2 214	5 707	2 905	13 930	1 181
31 372	**63 698**	**18 884**	**30 421**	**974**	**8 697**	**22 428**	**4 802**	**1 102**	**3 204**
2 022	739	586	105	352	169	517		511	33
					2				
	58				29	55		16	
141	590	6	20	93	1 199	46	2	190	38
33	121	4	83	9	4	28		22	16
14 646	16 175	5 147	6 915		32	4 822	2 282		
	373	2							
53	434	57			37	29	165		
694	1 110	900	476		181	335	258		
17	91	4	100			9			
	2 333								
12 284	36 570	9 660	21 919	1	6 817	13 035	2 043		2 017
1 482	5 104	2 517	803	518	228	3 551	51	363	1 100

6－14　各师国有及国有控股企业利润总额

Profit Amount of State-owned and State-controlled Shareholding Enterprises by Division

计量单位：万元　　(2010 年)　　(10 000 yuan)

单　位　Unit	合　计 Total	农　业 Agriculture	工　业 Industry	建筑业 Construction and Installation	交通运输业 Transportation
总　计　Total	**402 648**	**56 862**	**268 688**	**15 313**	**－27**
一　师　Division 1	91 458	25 219	54 699	5 258	
二　师　Division 2	11 266	6 022	2 351	1 161	80
三　师　Division 3	14 691	12 589	883	－1 948	68
四　师　Division 4	47 319	2 108	40 799	898	50
五　师　Division 5	9 566	6 655	513	840	107
六　师　Division 6	3 943	－9 039	10 816	－16	－160
七　师　Division 7	4 576	－2 183	5 278	1 522	50
八　师　Division 8	155 422	16 207	128 169	1 228	
九　师　Division 9	－1 314	－4 653	3 989	－133	44
十　师　Division 10	－738	－982	100		－67
建工师　Construction Division	3 151	－38	388	3 588	
十二师　Division 12	9 596	3 261	2 407	1 532	
十三师　Division 13	10 485	3 819	4 518	748	－11
十四师　Division 14	－1 105	－3 156	1 479	251	3
国资公司　State-owned Property Company	20 622		10 573	385	－192
兵团直属　Directly under XPCG	23 707	1 032	1 726		

单　位　Unit	商品流通业 Commodity Circulation	商　业 Commerce	外　贸 Foreign Trade	物　资 Materials	供　销 Supply and Marketing
总　计　Total	**61 811**	**44 164**	**321**	**1 473**	**15 853**
一　师　Division 1	6 282	－64			6 346
二　师　Division 2	1 653	586	4	579	485
三　师　Division 3	3 100	3 091	9		
四　师　Division 4	3 464	1 377	311		1 777
五　师　Division 5	1 451	1 184		17	250
六　师　Division 6	2 342	1 077		860	405
七　师　Division 7	－92	－63	－42	52	－39
八　师　Division 8	9 818	4 222			5 597
九　师　Division 9	－561	－400	－1		－161
十　师　Division 10	212	1	20		191
建工师　Construction Division	－787	－762		－27	1
十二师　Division 12	2 395	2 392	4		
十三师　Division 13	1 411	696			715
十四师　Division 14	318	15	16		286
国资公司　State-owned Property Company	9 855	9 864		－9	
兵团直属　Directly under XPCG	20 950	20 950			

6—15 盈利1000万元以上国有及国有控股企业主要经济指标

Main Economic Indicators of State-owned and State-controlled Shareholding Enterprises with Profits above Ten Millions Yuan

计量单位:万元　　(2010年)　　(10 000 yuan)

单 位	Unit	职工平均人数(人) Average Number of Staff and Workers(person)	盈利总额 Total Profits	营业收入 Business Income	营业税金及附加 Business Tax and Extra Charges	财务费用 Financial Expenses
总　计	**Total**					
农　业	**Agriculture**					
一师一团	Farm 1 Division 1	4 362	2 633	64 768		−520
一师二团	Farm 2 Division 1	3 418	3 019	48 324		−134
一师三团	Farm 3 Division 1	4 179	2 850	68 478		20
一师五团	Farm 5 Division 1	3 458	1 300	35 457		204
一师七团	Farm 7 Division 1	3 011	1 339	50 194		−247
一师八团	Farm 8 Division 1	2 554	1 653	40 653		−59
一师十团	Farm 10 Division 1	4 211	2 061	44 709	…	−180
一师十二团	Farm 12 Division 1	2 185	1 343	23 449		323
一师十三团	Farm 13 Division 1	3 467	1 849	43 442		185
一师十四团	Farm 14 Division 1	3 915	1 534	26 938		437
一师十六团	Farm 16 Division 1	3 974	1 683	42 841		−439
一师塔水处	Ta Water Conservancy Office of Division 1	2 739	1 057	32 589	4	−101
一师沙水处	Sha Water Conservancy Office of Division 1	352	1 131	16 964		−67
二师二十九团	Farm 29 Division 2	5 883	2 459	68 794	19	897
二师三十团	Farm 30 Division 2	3 135	1 604	33 597	…	378
二师三十三团	Farm 33 Division 2	3 316	1 365	29 218	36	325
二师三十四团	Farm 34 Division 2	2 575	1 219	23 723		97
二师三十六团	Farm 36 Division 2	2 141	1 504	16 697	28	−57
三师四十二团	Farm 42 Division 3	1 210	1 233	15 837	1	−26
三师四十四团	Farm 44 Division 3	2 889	1 459	26 137	8	312
三师四十五团	Farm 45 Division 3	6 438	2 349	20 803	…	256
三师四十九团	Farm 49 Division 3	3 439	1 632	29 399		106
三师五十团	Farm 50 Division 3	1 998	1 196	23 816		360
三师五十一团	Farm 51 Division 3	1 751	1 100	23 883		256
三师五十三团	Farm 53 Division 3	1 322	1 106	25 430		337
三师伽师总场	Jiashi Farm Division 3	3 419	1 320	16 173	1	250
五师八十三团	Farm 83 Division 5	6 276	1 859	61 477	426	382
五师八十六团	Farm 86 Division 5	4 292	1 952	52 499	45	193
五师九十团	Farm 90 Division 5	3 698	1 899	40 365	1	52
六师一〇五团	Farm 105 Division 6	2 630	1 895	30 411		814
六师军户场	Junhu Farm Division 6	3 078	1 065	16 113		493
七师一二五团	Farm 125 Division 7	5 839	1 175	72 039	338	1 085
八师一二一团	Farm 121 Division 8	9 201	2 088	72 010		2 548
八师一四一团	Farm 141 Division 8	3 005	1 280	48 226	97	474
八师一四二团	Farm 142 Division 8	4 440	1 688	71 534	23	1 066
八师一四四团	Farm 144 Division 8	3 306	1 267	63 105	…	1 348
八师石河子总场	Shihezi Farm Division 8	8 386	2 454	127 550	1 128	2 150
八师一四七团	Farm 147 Division 8	3 583	2 639	53 911		852
八师一五二团	Farm 152 Division 8	2 347	3 036	33 771	215	67
八师一五〇团	Farm 150 Division 8	4 670	1 686	65 452	17	872
十师一八四团场	Farm 184 Division 10	1 576	1 350	20 348	159	−189
十师一八八团场	Farm 188 Division 10	2 569	1 009	15 764	38	−118
十二师一〇四团	Farm 104 Division 12	3 650	1 211	42 134	2 223	320
十三师红星一场	Red Star No. 1 Farm Division 13	1 732	1 378	20 139	60	82
十三师红山农场	Hongshan Farm Division 13	2 680	1 879	22 344	191	906
兵团直属二二二团	Directly Under XPCG Farm 222	2 761	1 049	18 935	18	664
工业	**Industry**					
阿拉尔统众国有资产经营有限责任公司	Alaer Tongzhong State-owned Property Management Company	19	1 515			5 343
新疆青松建材化工(集团)股份有限公司	XJ Qingsong Building Materialand Chemical Industry Co.,Ltd	4 813	37 601	192 467	1 648	4 901

6—15 续表 1　Continued

计量单位:万元　　　　(2010 年)　　　　(10 000 yuan)

单　位	Unit	资产总额 Total Assets	固定资产原值 Original Value of Fixed Assets	固定资产净值 Net Value of Fixed Assets	流动资产 Ciuculating Assets	负债总额 Total Liabilities
总　计	**Total**					
农　业	**Agriculture**					
一师一团	Farm 1 Division 1	84 942	39 930	12 951	51 150	75 660
一师二团	Farm 2 Division 1	77 094	34 831	8 964	56 930	78 902
一师三团	Farm 3 Division 1	93 790	53 478	22 696	60 741	88 457
一师五团	Farm 5 Division 1	62 234	40 308	14 200	40 339	59 888
一师七团	Farm 7 Division 1	74 657	36 455	16 073	49 832	67 050
一师八团	Farm 8 Division 1	46 494	28 763	10 190	31 225	40 893
一师十团	Farm 10 Division 1	94 624	47 371	16 372	68 566	88 569
一师十二团	Farm 12 Division 1	53 697	32 538	9 995	33 260	60 678
一师十三团	Farm 13 Division 1	67 244	29 765	8 867	43 146	64 749
一师十四团	Farm 14 Division 1	47 151	34 217	12 448	28 810	44 119
一师十六团	Farm 16 Division 1	75 901	40 670	16 433	52 640	62 821
一师塔水处	Ta Water Conservancy Office of Division 1	72 310	24 738	15 805	40 464	62 980
一师沙水处	Sha Water Conservancy Office of Division 1	19 693	6 587	3 540	15 069	15 835
二师二十九团	Farm 29 Division 2	105 135	70 189	45 005	48 976	75 229
二师三十团	Farm 30 Division 2	51 621	21 056	12 415	36 112	42 757
二师三十三团	Farm 33 Division 2	61 600	39 030	24 562	28 035	46 064
二师三十四团	Farm 34 Division 2	42 713	38 902	23 171	18 423	34 276
二师三十六团	Farm 36 Division 2	47 714	24 967	14 790	15 430	38 309
三师四十二团	Farm 42 Division 3	31 525	8 125	4 781	22 829	20 277
三师四十四团	Farm 44 Division 3	80 259	24 982	14 070	43 476	75 995
三师四十五团	Farm 45 Division 3	92 007	39 452	10 000	63 008	76 006
三师四十九团	Farm 49 Division 3	53 488	23 543	13 280	27 155	54 041
三师五十团	Farm 50 Division 3	42 061	17 033	7 439	24 728	52 810
三师五十一团	Farm 51 Division 3	31 886	20 082	6 967	18 958	44 731
三师五十三团	Farm 53 Division 3	49 099	30 570	16 885	18 846	42 746
三师伽师总场	Jiashi Farm Division 3	62 501	18 711	11 363	30 741	56 103
五师八十三团	Farm 83 Division 5	116 447	39 093	16 063	84 990	103 846
五师八十六团	Farm 86 Division 5	82 331	30 118	17 356	53 848	68 698
五师九十团	Farm 90 Division 5	48 228	27 441	15 612	24 286	39 436
六师一〇五团	Farm 105 Division 6	48 879	32 714	18 371	25 806	39 676
六师军户场	Junhu Farm Division 6	41 492	19 115	8 835	21 593	36 365
七师一二五团	Farm 125 Division 7	117 042	68 456	40 488	58 864	104 103
八师一二一团	Farm 121 Division 8	146 299	60 142	30 150	82 321	145 715
八师一四一团	Farm 141 Division 8	51 676	33 609	20 315	20 057	43 177
八师一四二团	Farm 142 Division 8	94 519	50 915	26 923	43 752	102 982
八师一四四团	Farm 144 Division 8	59 442	33 139	17 192	28 017	64 062
八师石河子总场	Shihezi Farm Division 8	116 466	54 902	26 587	69 840	98 338
八师一四七团	Farm 147 Division 8	44 666	30 453	14 437	23 223	46 744
八师一五二团	Farm 152 Division 8	36 609	15 647	8 317	24 391	25 356
八师一五〇团	Farm 150 Division 8	91 328	35 228	20 914	34 347	69 432
十师一八四团场	Farm 184 Division 10	63 298	39 897	24 822	31 166	48 116
十师一八八团场	Farm 188 Division 10	29 887	18 957	5 852	14 286	26 908
十二师一〇四团	Farm 104 Division 12	101 283	36 189	22 654	46 265	95 815
十三师红星一场	Red Star No. 1 Farm Division 13	70 107	29 053	12 055	45 423	55 605
十三师红山农场	Hongshan Farm Division 13	82 875	41 758	21 181	36 355	78 163
兵团直属二二二团	Directly Under XPCG Farm 222	72 941	41 568	24 674	27 971	41 986
工业	**Industry**					
阿拉尔统众国有资产经营有限责任公司	Alaer Tongzhong State-owned Property Management Company	304 672	538	472	141 049	293 211
新疆青松建材化工(集团)股份有限公司	XJ Qingsong Building Materialand Chemical Industry Co. ,Ltd	500 147	276 869	212 387	214 336	236 833

6—15 续表 2 Continued

计量单位:万元 (2010 年) (10 000 yuan)

单 位	Unit	流动负债 Liquid Liabilities	长期负债 Long-tem Liabilities	所有者权益 Creditors' Equity	实收资本 Paid-up Capital
总 计	**Total**				
农 业	**Agriculture**				
一师一团	Farm 1 Division 1	74 465	1 195	9 282	4 749
一师二团	Farm 2 Division 1	78 427	475	−1 808	2 678
一师三团	Farm 3 Division 1	86 087	2 370	5 333	6 233
一师五团	Farm 5 Division 1	56 657	3 232	2 346	6 889
一师七团	Farm 7 Division 1	65 567	1 483	7 607	3 798
一师八团	Farm 8 Division 1	40 478	415	5 601	5 107
一师十团	Farm 10 Division 1	85 963	2 606	6 055	9 973
一师十二团	Farm 12 Division 1	57 156	3 522	−6 981	3 984
一师十三团	Farm 13 Division 1	60 431	4 318	2 495	7 292
一师十四团	Farm 14 Division 1	43 606	514	3 032	3 617
一师十六团	Farm 16 Division 1	62 041	780	13 080	4 580
一师塔水处	Ta Water Conservancy Office of Division 1	60 943	2 037	9 330	1 859
一师沙水处	Sha Water Conservancy Office of Division 1	14 833	1 002	3 858	578
二师二十九团	Farm 29 Division 2	66 459	8 770	29 906	10 561
二师三十团	Farm 30 Division 2	41 277	1 480	8 864	3 774
二师三十三团	Farm 33 Division 2	45 583	481	15 536	8 137
二师三十四团	Farm 34 Division 2	33 909	367	8 437	6 757
二师三十六团	Farm 36 Division 2	30 298	8 011	9 405	4 114
三师四十二团	Farm 42 Division 3	18 686	1 592	11 248	5 271
三师四十四团	Farm 44 Division 3	72 970	3 025	4 264	8 562
三师四十五团	Farm 45 Division 3	73 460	2 546	16 001	11 123
三师四十九团	Farm 49 Division 3	53 677	365	−554	3 293
三师五十团	Farm 50 Division 3	50 130	2 679	−10 749	3 635
三师五十一团	Farm 51 Division 3	37 775	6 956	−12 845	5 083
三师五十三团	Farm 53 Division 3	39 951	2 796	6 353	4 739
三师伽师总场	Jiashi Farm Division 3	52 587	3 516	6 398	5 537
五师八十三团	Farm 83 Division 5	101 193	2 653	12 601	6 922
五师八十六团	Farm 86 Division 5	67 738	961	13 633	5 081
五师九十团	Farm 90 Division 5	33 539	5 897	8 792	7 702
六师一〇五团	Farm 105 Division 6	37 078	2 598	9 202	5 922
六师军户场	Junhu Farm Division 6	32 050	4 315	5 127	1 642
七师一二五团	Farm 125 Division 7	82 639	21 464	12 939	10 425
八师一二一团	Farm 121 Division 8	133 805	11 910	585	8 740
八师一四一团	Farm 141 Division 8	39 883	3 294	8 499	2 105
八师一四二团	Farm 142 Division 8	91 295	11 686	−8 463	3 418
八师一四四团	Farm 144 Division 8	64 062		−4 620	3 531
八师石河子总场	Shihezi Farm Division 8	69 916	28 422	18 128	6 133
八师一四七团	Farm 147 Division 8	43 187	3 557	−2 078	1 646
八师一五二团	Farm 152 Division 8	24 448	907	11 253	4 122
八师一五〇团	Farm 150 Division 8	68 723	710	21 896	4 917
十师一八四团场	Farm 184 Division 10	42 279	5 836	15 182	13 486
十师一八八团场	Farm 188 Division 10	21 483	5 425	2 979	9 475
十二师一〇四团	Farm 104 Division 12	73 720	22 095	5 468	6 433
十三师红星一场	Red Star No. 1 Farm Division 13	42 641	12 964	14 502	6 807
十三师红山农场	Hongshan Farm Division 13	55 325	22 838	4 712	9 078
兵团直属二二二团	Directly Under XPCG Farm 222	26 185	15 801	30 955	10 440
工业	**Industry**				
阿拉尔统众国有资产经营有限责任公司	Alaer Tongzhong State-owned Property Management Company	163 941	129 270	11 461	5 000
新疆青松建材化工(集团)股份有限公司	XJ Qingsong Building Materialand Chemical Industry Co. ,Ltd	124 788	112 045	263 314	47 870

6—15 续表 3　Continued

计量单位:万元　　　　(2010 年)　　　　(10 000 yuan)

单　　位	Unit	职工平均人数(人) Average Number of Staff and Workers-(person)	盈利总额 Total Profits	营业收入 Business Income	营业税金及附加 Business Tax and Extra Charges	财务费用 Financial Expenses
新疆塔里木农业综合开发股份有限公司	XJ Tarimu Agicultural Comprehensive Development Stock Co. ,Ltd	5 579	6 236	175 544	1 033	6 092
一师电力公司	Division 1 Electricity Company	1 246	1 506	56 245	394	4 255
阿克苏塔河矿业有限责任公司	Akesu Tahe Mining Co. ,Ltd	686	5 181	19 334	413	3 203
库车科兴煤炭实业有限责任公司	Kuche Kexing Coal Industry Minerals	337	4 930	15 494	335	3 106
新疆塔里木河种业股份有限公司	XJ Tarimu River Seed Stock Co. ,Ltd	1 141	2 705	34 795	45	—16
库尔勒金川矿业有限公司	Kuerle Jinchuan Mining Co. ,Ltd	203	1 843	11 539	502	156
新疆伊力特集团有限公司	XJ Yilite Group Co. ,Ltd	1 864	19 310	108 484	15 335	3 103
四师电力公司	Division 4 Electricity Company	511	1 621	19 065	41	834
新疆绿华糖业有限责任公司	XJ Luhua Suger Co. ,Ltd	443	3 022	21 151	86	75
伊犁南岗建材(集团)有限责任公司	Yili Nangang Building Materials Co. ,Ltd	2 881	17 610	94 740	529	3 697
新疆伊力特实业股份有限公司	XJ Yilite Industry Co. ,Ltd	1 657	19 585	105 200	15 300	700
六师国有资产经营有限责任公司	Division 6 State-owned Property Management Company	3 840	12 947	247 844	1 051	9 812
七师电力公司	Division 7 Electricity Company	935	1 480	70 140	360	9 103
七师奎屯锦业纺织有限责任公司	Division 7 Kuitun Jingye Spinning Co. ,Ltd	1 111	2 710	43 408	244	1 315
新疆天业(集团)有限公司	XJ Tianye(Group) Stock Co. ,Ltd.	12 781	121 765	740 133	8 605	51 585
新疆天富电力(集团)有限责任公司	XJ Tianfu Thermoelectricity Stock Co. ,Ltd	7 615	11 634	194 572	3 765	17 505
新疆绿翔糖业有限责任公司	XJ Luxiang Suger Ltd. ,Co.	555	4 340	32 733	155	298
新疆昌平矿业有限责任公司	XJ Changping Mining Co. ,Ltd	767	1 983	10 429	322	816
十三师国有资产经营有限公司	Division 13 State-owned Property Management Company	225	4 212	9 444	203	289
和田昆仑山枣业有限责任公司	Hetian Kunlunshan Jujubes Industry Co. ,Ltd.	70	1 067	13 945	32	322
新疆天康控股(集团)有限公司	XJ Tiankang Share-Controled(Group) Co. ,Ltd	2 020	10 476	271 801	267	5 212
新疆科神农业装备科技开发有限公司	Keshen Agriculture Equipment Technology Development Co. ,Ltd	218	1 068	3 785	19	—18
建筑安装	**Construction and Installation**					
新疆塔里木建筑安装工程集团有限公司	Talimu Construction and Installation Co. ,Ltd	1 250	2 496	62 808	2 609	1 139
新疆阿拉尔水利水电工程总公司	Alaer Water Conservancy and Water Electricity Engineering Company	2 594	2 749	50 197	1 527	147
阿拉尔市新苑房地产开发有限责任公司	Alaer Xinyuan Real Estate Co. ,Ltd	6	1 638	8 296	434	—51
小海子水利建筑安装工程有限公司	Division 3 Xiaohaizi Water Conservancy and Water Electricity Engineering Co. ,Ltd	1 745	2 258	35 885	1 000	—115
新疆北方建设集团有限公司	The North Construction Group of XJ	1 250	1 247	66 040	1 993	244
石河子天筑建设(集团)有限责任公司	Division 8 ShiHezi Taian Construction and Installation Company	1 506	1 228	124 389	4 256	769
新疆兵团第四建筑安装工程公司	The 4 th Construction and Installation Co. ,Ltd of XPCG	849	1 612	74 352	2 147	220
新疆兵团建设工程(集团)有限责任公司	XPCG Construction and Installation Co. ,Ltd	9 358	2 079	737 636	22 072	8 029
新疆北新路桥建设股份有限公司	Beixin Road and Bridge Building Share-holding Co. ,Ltd. of XPCG Construction Group	1 432	7 318	248 034	5 253	2 608
商　业	**Domestic Trade**					
三师农资公司	Division 3 Agricultural Production Materials Supplying Company	138	1 140	72 510	…	583
三师棉麻公司	Division 3 Cotton and Flax Company	424	1 462	156 475	5	1 086
新疆西部牧业股份有限公司	XJ West Animal Husb and ry(Group) Industry Co. ,Ltd.	364	3 160	30 829	7	465
新疆泉牲牧业有限责任公司	XJ Quanshen Animal Husb and ry(Group) Industry Co. ,Ltd.	46	1 043	5 120		20
新疆天恒基投资有限公司	XPCG Tianhenji Invest Co. ,Ltd.	95	3 355	42 600	1 802	554
兵团石油有限公司	XPCG Petroleum Co. ,Ltd.	1 681	6 203	384 997	320	892
兵团烟草有限责任公司	XPCG Tobacco Co. ,Ltd.	176	1 364	38 623	1 932	—21
新疆康地种业科技股份有限公司	XJ Kangdi Seed Industry Technological Stock Co. ,Ltd.	187	3 248	17 998	14	77
兵团供销合作总公司	XPCG Supplying and Marketing Co. ,Ltd.	1 082	1 517	450 730	198	5 931
兵团投资公司	XPCG Invest Co. ,Ltd.	27	6 772	2 383	140	593
新疆银隆国际贸易股份有限公司	XJ Yinlong International Trade Co. ,Ltd.	526	14 848	287 794	308	3 516
供　销	**Supply and Marketing**					
一师供销(集团)有限公司	Division 1 Supply and Marketing Company	202	2 108	101 162	31	—324
一师棉麻公司	Division 1 Cotton and Flax Company	94	4 141	357 152	2	389
四师供销社	Division 4 Supply and Marketing Company	221	1 777	112 867	104	1 598
新疆西部银力棉业(集团)有限责任公司	XJ Western Yinli Cotton(Group) Industry Co. ,Ltd.	182	5 788	389 004	36	1 846
新疆石河子市银力实业股份有限公司	Shihezi Yinli Industry Investment Co. ,Ltd.	18	1 145	109 589	6	—544
新疆西部银力机械采棉有限公司	XJ Western Yinli Cotton Harvwsted by Machine Co. ,Ltd.	70	1 010	2 760		—1

6—15 续表 4 Continued

计量单位:万元　　(2010 年)　　(10 000 yuan)

单　位	Unit	资产总额 Total Assets	固定资产原值 Original Value of Fixed Assets	固定资产净值 Net Value of Fixed Assets	流动资产 Ciuculating Assets	负债总额 Total Liabilities
新疆塔里木农业综合开发股份有限公司	XJ Tarimu Agicultural Comprehensive Development Stock Co.,Ltd	348 330	122 413	83 629	213 295	280 774
一师电力公司	Division 1 Electricity Company	193 368	173 637	130 831	42 549	162 791
阿克苏塔河矿业有限责任公司	Akesu Tahe Mining Co.,Ltd	32 339	25 232	13 357	10 922	28 745
库车科兴煤炭实业有限责任公司	Kuche Kexing Coal Industry Minerals	18 381	11 501	2 464	6 822	9 276
新疆塔里木河种业股份有限公司	XJ Tarimu River Seed Stock Co.,Ltd	33 535	13 069	9 140	22 611	19 902
库尔勒金川矿业有限公司	Kuerle Jinchuan Mining Co.,Ltd	29 254	15 935	13 265	10 448	20 970
新疆伊力特集团有限公司	XJ Yilite Group Co.,Ltd	200 941	57 022	28 015	126 746	93 374
四师电力公司	Division 4 Electricity Company	53 925	42 307	28 902	15 966	34 303
新疆绿华糖业有限责任公司	XJ Luhua Suger Co.,Ltd	26 890	11 133	7 996	18 771	18 327
伊犁南岗建材(集团)有限责任公司	Yili Nangang Building Materials Co.,Ltd	210 902	181 199	123 893	51 692	143 938
新疆伊力特实业股份有限公司	XJ Yilite Industry Co.,Ltd	148 837	50 000	25 200	80 232	43 887
六师国有资产经营有限责任公司	Division 6 State-owned Property Management Company	761 168	185 526	151 303	325 978	591 681
七师电力公司	Division 7 Electricity Company	267 903	212 647	166 560	87 851	209 853
七师奎屯锦业纺织有限责任公司	Division 7 Kuitun Jingye Spinning Co.,Ltd	42 840	30 851	22 241	20 110	34 942
新疆天业(集团)有限公司	XJ Tianye(Group) Stock Co.,Ltd.	2 302 201	1 215 775	967 038	750 600	1 628 427
新疆天富电力(集团)有限责任公司	XJ Tianfu Thermoelectricity Stock Co.,Ltd	964 669	556 151	376 475	392 097	748 575
新疆绿翔糖业有限责任公司	XJ Luxiang Suger Ltd.,Co.	42 040	32 502	14 817	22 480	17 782
新疆昌平矿业有限责任公司	XJ Changping Mining Co.,Ltd	45 613	11 378	7 956	25 028	32 017
十三师国有资产经营有限公司	Division 13 State-owned Property Management Company	87 378	14 780	13 775	23 558	63 754
和田昆仑山枣业有限责任公司	Hetian Kunlunshan Jujubes Industry Co.,Ltd.	27 109	6 176	5 579	16 403	17 451
新疆天康控股(集团)有限公司	XJ Tiankang Share-Controled(Group) Co.,Ltd	231 145	81 176	62 380	124 279	121 377
新疆科神农业装备科技开发有限公司	Keshen Agriculture Equipment Technology Development Co.,Ltd	3 250	760	581	2 667	848
建筑安装	**Construction and Installation**					
新疆塔里木建筑安装工程集团有限公司	Talimu Construction and Installation Co.,Ltd	40 502	8 197	7 337	20 692	30 081
新疆阿拉尔水利水电工程总公司	Alaer Water Conservancy and Water Electricity Engineering Company	60 674	26 600	17 536	36 719	47 702
阿拉尔市新苑房地产开发有限责任公司	Alaer Xinyuan Real Estate Co.,Ltd	8 336	8	4	5 767	6 621
小海子水利建筑安装工程有限公司	Division 3 Xiaohaizi Water Conservancy and Water Electricity Engineering Co.,Ltd	29 169	4 438	2 115	25 942	24 756
新疆北方建设集团有限公司	The North Construction Group of XJ	57 094	30 765	22 282	29 186	33 333
石河子天筑建设(集团)有限责任公司	Division 8 ShiHezi Taian Construction and Installation Company	83 049	7 542	3 323	67 791	81 009
新疆兵团第四建筑安装工程公司	The 4 th Construction and Installation Co.,Ltd of XPCG	35 121	8 129	6 501	26 010	42 419
新疆兵团建设工程(集团)有限责任公司	XPCG Construction and Installation Co.,Ltd	541 937	148 168	87 128	377 309	514 236
新疆北新路桥建设股份有限公司	Beixin Road and Bridge Building Share-holding Co.,Ltd. of XPCG Construction Group	290 004	77 909	43 046	197 989	211 291
商　业	**Domestic Trade**					
三师农资公司	Division 3 Agricultural Production Materials Supplying Company	47 729	1 750	1 065	44 675	39 874
三师棉麻公司	Division 3 Cotton and Flax Company	207 970	11 188	8 053	195 663	200 325
新疆西部牧业股份有限公司	XJ West Animal Husb and ry(Group)Industry Co.,Ltd.	73 198	19 540	14 137	47 360	20 108
新疆泉牲牧业有限责任公司	XJ Quanshen Animal Husb and ry(Group)Industry Co.,Ltd.	5 155	1 386	895	4 260	1 548
新疆天恒基投资有限公司	XPCG Tianhenji Invest Co.,Ltd.	247 993	3 619	3 433	196 741	204 040
兵团石油有限公司	XPCG Petroleum Co.,Ltd.	62 982	35 148	20 741	26 879	29 391
兵团烟草有限责任公司	XPCG Tobacco Co.,Ltd.	12 835	2 744	1 367	7 831	4 589
新疆康地种业科技股份有限公司	XJ Kangdi Seed Industry Technological Stock Co.,Ltd.	22 733	4 750	2 394	16 545	8 544
兵团供销合作总公司	XPCG Supplying and Marketing Co.,Ltd.	457 812	59 538	38 148	382 698	389 393
兵团投资公司	XPCG Invest Co.,Ltd.	1 510 544	1 852	1 200	1 034 364	1 118 412
新疆银隆国际贸易股份有限公司	XJ Yinlong International Trade Co.,Ltd.	188 377	21 035	17 346	167 102	167 353
供　销	**Supply and Marketing**					
一师供销(集团)有限公司	Division 1 Supply and Marketing Company	107 395	7 269	4 675	81 443	96 872
一师棉麻公司	Division 1 Cotton and Flax Company	255 797	7 760	5 353	250 026	252 373
四师供销社	Division 4 Supply and Marketing Company	91 492	7 304	4 984	81 750	83 631
新疆西部银力棉业(集团)有限责任公司	XJ Western Yinli Cotton(Group)Industry Co.,Ltd.	522 010	27 033	16 711	503 873	498 479
新疆石河子市银力实业股份有限公司	Shihezi Yinli Industry Investment Co.,Ltd.	248 319	2 699	1 706	246 527	240 302
新疆西部银力机械采棉有限公司	XJ Western Yinli Cotton Harvwsted by Machine Co.,Ltd.	9 868	8 506	5 672	4 196	3 828

6—15 续表 5　Continued

计量单位:万元　　(2010 年)　　(10 000 yuan)

单　位	Unit	流动负债 Liquid Liabilities	长期负债 Long-tem Liabilities	所有者权益 Creditors' Equity	实收资本 Paid-up Capital
新疆塔里木农业综合开发股份有限公司	XJ Tarimu Agicultural Comprehensive Development Stock Co. ,Ltd	211 340	69 433	67 556	32 100
一师电力公司	Division 1 Electricity Company	42 514	120 277	30 577	29 063
阿克苏塔河矿业有限责任公司	Akesu Tahe Mining Co. ,Ltd	27 400	1 345	3 595	1 185
库车科兴煤炭实业有限责任公司	Kuche Kexing Coal Industry Minerals	9 276		9 105	5 230
新疆塔里木河种业股份有限公司	XJ Tarimu River Seed Stock Co. ,Ltd	18 910	992	13 633	6 500
库尔勒金川矿业有限公司	Kuerle Jinchuan Mining Co. ,Ltd	15 597	5 373	8 284	6 700
新疆伊力特集团有限公司	XJ Yilite Group Co. ,Ltd	84 374	9 000	107 566	18 300
四师电力公司	Division 4 Electricity Company	15 097	19 206	19 622	17 446
新疆绿华糖业有限责任公司	XJ Luhua Suger Co. ,Ltd	18 327		8 562	6 103
伊犁南岗建材(集团)有限责任公司	Yili Nangang Building Materials Co. ,Ltd	71 638	72 299	66 964	17 384
新疆伊力特实业股份有限公司	XJ Yilite Industry Co. ,Ltd	34 887	9 000	104 950	44 100
六师国有资产经营有限责任公司	Division 6 State-owned Property Management Company	390 940	200 741	169 487	65 333
七师电力公司	Division 7 Electricity Company	68 579	141 275	58 050	23 491
七师奎屯锦业纺织有限责任公司	Division 7 Kuitun Jingye Spinning Co. ,Ltd	22 159	12 783	7 898	7 601
新疆天业(集团)有限公司	XJ Tianye(Group) Stock Co. ,Ltd.	702 959	925 468	673 774	125 000
新疆天富电力(集团)有限责任公司	XJ Tianfu Thermoelectricity Stock Co. ,Ltd	433 949	314 626	216 095	98 000
新疆绿翔糖业有限责任公司	XJ Luxiang Suger Ltd. ,Co.	17 782		24 258	20 110
新疆昌平矿业有限责任公司	XJ Changping Mining Co. ,Ltd	31 171	846	13 596	12 563
十三师国有资产经营有限公司	Division 13 State-owned Property Management Company	48 828	14 925	23 624	14 248
和田昆仑山枣业有限责任公司	Hetian Kunlunshan Jujubes Industry Co. ,Ltd.	17 442	9	9 658	4 641
新疆天康控股(集团)有限公司	XJ Tiankang Share-Controled(Group) Co. ,Ltd	81 848	39 529	109 768	11 657
新疆科神农业装备科技开发有限公司	Keshen Agriculture Equipment Technology Development Co. ,Ltd	848		2 403	894
建筑安装	**Construction and Installation**				
新疆塔里木建筑安装工程集团有限公司	Talimu Construction and Installation Co. ,Ltd	27 801	2 281	10 421	7 801
新疆阿拉尔水利水电工程总公司	Alaer Water Conservancy and Water Electricity Engineering Company	41 246	6 456	12 973	3 758
阿拉尔市新苑房地产开发有限责任公司	Alaer Xinyuan Real Estate Co. ,Ltd	6 621		1 715	800
小海子水利建筑安装工程有限公司	Division 3 Xiaohaizi Water Conservancy and Water Electricity Engineering Co. ,Ltd	22 120	2 636	4 413	3 132
新疆北方建设集团有限公司	The North Construction Group of XJ	32 808	525	23 761	23 385
石河子天筑建设(集团)有限责任公司	Division 8 ShiHezi Taian Construction and Installation Company	80 914	95	2 041	7 488
新疆兵团第四建筑安装工程公司	The 4 th Construction and Installation Co. ,Ltd of XPCG	42 419		−7 298	2 262
新疆兵团建设工程(集团)有限责任公司	XPCG Construction and Installation Co. ,Ltd	337 485	176 751	27 701	53 658
新疆北新路桥建设股份有限公司	Beixin Road and Bridge Building Share-holding Co. ,Ltd. of XPCG Construction Group	126 575	84 716	78 713	18 945
商　业	**Domestic Trade**				
三师农资公司	Division 3 Agricultural Production Materials Supplying Company	39 423	451	7 855	6 499
三师棉麻公司	Division 3 Cotton and Flax Company	200 325		7 645	1 539
新疆西部牧业股份有限公司	XJ West Animal Husb and ry(Group) Industry Co. ,Ltd.	9 750	10 358	53 090	11 700
新疆泉牲牧业有限责任公司	XJ Quanshen Animal Husb and ry(Group) Industry Co. ,Ltd.	1 548		3 607	1 688
新疆天恒基投资有限公司	XPCG Tianhenji Invest Co. ,Ltd.	182 360	21 680	43 953	17 008
兵团石油有限公司	XPCG Petroleum Co. ,Ltd.	29 391		33 592	22 324
兵团烟草有限责任公司	XPCG Tobacco Co. ,Ltd.	4 589		8 246	1 860
新疆康地种业科技股份有限公司	XJ Kangdi Seed Industry Technological Stock Co. ,Ltd.	8 544		14 189	7 500
兵团供销合作总公司	XPCG Supplying and Marketing Co. ,Ltd.	371 775	17 618	68 418	62 557
兵团投资公司	XPCG Invest Co. ,Ltd.	175 549	942 863	392 131	256 015
新疆银隆国际贸易股份有限公司	XJ Yinlong International Trade Co. ,Ltd.	166 954	399	21 023	6 370
供　销	**Supply and Marketing**				
一师供销(集团)有限公司	Division 1 Supply and Marketing Company	96 872		10 524	9 607
一师棉麻公司	Division 1 Cotton and Flax Company	245 817	6 556	3 425	2 219
四师供销社	Division 4 Supply and Marketing Company	83 631		7 861	7 218
新疆西部银力棉业(集团)有限责任公司	XJ Western Yinli Cotton(Group) Industry Co. ,Ltd.	498 374	105	23 531	12 339
新疆石河子市银力实业股份有限公司	Shihezi Yinli Industry Investment Co. ,Ltd.	240 302		8 017	7 000
新疆西部银力机械采棉有限公司	XJ Western Yinli Cotton Harvwsted by Machine Co. ,Ltd.	3 828		6 040	4 539

2011 BING TUAN

第七篇

价格指数

Chapter 7 Price Indices

简要说明

一、本篇资料主要内容

本篇资料反映生产、流通、消费与投资、建设施工环节的价格变动趋势和变动幅度，主要包括1978年以来各种价格指数、居民消费价格指数、商品零售价格指数、农业生产资料价格指数、工业品出厂价格指数、原材料、燃料、动力购进价格指数、建筑安装工程价格指数、固定资产投资价格指数等。

二、本篇资料来源

本篇资料由国家统计局新疆调查总队、国家统计局兵团调查总队住户调查处、农业调查处整理提供。

Brief Introduction

1. Main Contents

Data in this chapter reflect production, circulation, consumption and investment, price fluctuation trend and change range of construction cycle, mainly including general price indices, residential consumer price indices, commodity retail sale price indices, price indices of means of farming production, purchase price indices of farming produce, ex-factory price in dices of industrial products, purchase price indices of raw materials, fuel, and power price in dices of building and installation works and price indices of investment in fixed assets.

2. Sources of Data

Data in this chapter are provided and compiled by the Survey Office of Xinjiang and by Household Survey Section and Agriculture Survey Section of the Survey Office of XPCG of National Bureau of Statistics of China.

7—1 各种物价总指数(1978—2010 年)

General Price Indices(1978—2010)

年 份 Year	居民消费价格指数 Consumers Price Index	城市居民消费价格指数 Urban Areas	农村居民消费价格指数 Rural Areas	商品零售价格指数 Retail Price Index for Commodities
上年＝100 Preceding year＝100				
1978	101.2	101.4	100.3	101.4
1980	102.8	104.1	102.0	104.2
1985	107.8	109.5	106.4	108.1
1990	105.0	104.5	105.9	104.1
1995	119.7	118.4	122.5	116.7
1996	110.5	110.4	110.6	108.8
1997	103.7	103.5	103.9	101.8
1998	100.2	99.9	100.8	99.7
1999	97.4	97.7	96.8	96.2
2000	99.4	100.1	97.6	98.3
2001	104.0	104.0	103.8	102.5
2002	99.4	98.9	100.9	97.9
2003	100.4	100.5	100.2	99.2
2004	102.7	102.1	104.5	100.7
2005	100.7	100.6	101.2	99.4
2006	101.3	101.0	102.0	101.8
2007	105.5	104.6	107.2	105.1
2008	108.1	107.3	109.5	108.5
2009	100.7	100.2	102.0	100.4
2010	104.3	103.6	105.8	104.6
1978 年＝100				
1978	100.0	100.0	100.0	100.0
1980	105.1	106.6	103.8	107.8
1985	120.9	125.6	117.9	124.2
1990	194.3	206.0	184.0	197.6
1995	392.7	422.7	364.2	381.0
1996	433.9	466.7	402.9	414.6
1997	450.0	483.0	418.6	422.0
1998	450.9	482.5	421.9	420.8
1999	439.2	471.4	408.4	404.8
2000	436.5	471.9	398.6	397.9
2001	454.0	490.8	413.8	407.8
2002	451.3	485.4	417.5	399.3
2003	453.1	487.8	418.3	396.1
2004	465.3	498.1	437.1	398.9
2005	468.6	501.1	442.3	396.5
2006	474.7	506.1	451.1	403.6
2007	500.8	529.4	483.6	424.2
2008	541.4	568.0	529.5	460.3
2009	545.2	569.1	540.1	462.1
2010	568.6	589.6	571.4	483.4

7—2 居民消费价格分类指数

Consumer Price Indices by Category

（上年=100） （2010年） (preceding year=100)

指　　标	Item	全　区 Province	城　市 Urban Areas	农　村 Rural Areas
居民消费价格指数	**Consumers'Price Index**	**104.3**	**103.6**	**105.8**
食　品	**Food**	**110.7**	**109.5**	**113.1**
粮　食	Grain	108.9	108.5	109.4
大　米	Rice	129.6	129.6	129.6
面　粉	Flour	95.7	96.4	94.9
粮食制品	Grain Products	100.9	100.8	101.7
其　　它	Others	116.6	116.8	116.6
淀　粉	Starches and Tubers	105.7	104.5	107.6
干豆类及豆制品	Bean and Its Products	109.6	109.7	109.4
油　脂	Oil or Fat	107.6	104.3	112.9
肉禽及其制品	Meat,Poultry and Their Products	113.0	111.9	115.0
蛋	Eggs	112.3	110.7	115.1
水产品	Aquatic Products	107.4	108.0	106.4
菜	Vegetables	120.0	117.5	124.9
鲜　菜	Fresh Vegetables	120.0	117.3	125.6
干菜及菜制品	Dried Vegetables and Vegetable Products	108.1	108.5	107.3
薯　类	Tubers	130.9	133.0	124.6
调味品	Flavoring	105.4	107.1	102.7
糖	Sugar	108.1	106.7	109.8
食　糖	Sugar	118.5	114.6	122.8
糖　果	Candy	102.2	101.7	103.5
巧克力制品	Chocolate Goods	105.5	108.3	101.5
糖类小食品	Sugar Foodstuff	103.8	103.6	104.0
茶及饮料	Tea and Beverages	101.7	101.4	102.2
干鲜瓜果	Dried and Fresh Melons and Fruits	114.1	112.1	118.3
鲜瓜果	Fresh Fruits	112.7	109.8	118.1
干(坚)果品	Dried(nut) Fruits and Melon and Fruits Products	117.6	117.0	119.2
糕点饼干	Cake,Cookie,Bread	101.9	102.4	100.9
液体乳及乳制品	Milk and Its Products	108.7	107.7	111.4
在外用膳食品	Catering Trade	105.8	105.4	107.3
主　食	Staple Food	103.4	103.0	104.7
炒　菜	Fried Dishes	105.9	105.5	107.2
地方小吃	Local Snack	110.6	109.9	113.0
其他食品	Other Food and Food Processing	101.8	102.4	100.5
烟酒及用品	**Tobacco,Liquor and Articles**	**102.0**	**102.6**	**100.8**
烟　草	Tobacco	98.7	98.9	98.2
酒	Liquor	105.3	106.4	103.3
吸烟饮酒用品	Articles	103.8	104.5	101.5
衣　着	**Clothing**	**99.2**	**98.2**	**101.8**
服　装	Garments	99.3	98.2	102.0
衣着材料	Clothing Material	102.7	103.2	102.2
棉　布	Cotton Cloth	103.8	104.8	102.8

7—2 续表 Continued

(上年=100) (2010 年) (preceding year=100)

指标	Item	全区 Province	城市 Urban Areas	农村 Rural Areas
棉花化纤混纺布	Blend Cloth	102.3	103.2	101.6
化纤布	Chemical Fiber Cloth	101.1	101.2	101.0
毛线	Wool	103.7	103.9	103.6
鞋袜帽	Footwear and Hats	98.4	97.2	101.4
鞋	Shoes	98.0	96.5	101.9
袜子	Socks and Stockings	100.3	100.5	99.9
帽子	Hats	99.9	100.0	99.8
衣着加工服务	Clothing Processing	102.4	105.1	99.4
家庭设备及用品及维修服务	**Household Facilities and Articles**	**101.2**	**100.9**	**101.9**
耐用消费品	Durable Consumer Goods	100.0	99.6	100.6
家具	Furniture	101.3	101.0	101.9
家庭设备	Household Facilities	99.1	98.7	99.8
室内装饰品	Interior Decorations	100.3	100.5	99.8
床上用品	Bed Articles	101.1	101.7	99.8
家庭日用杂品	Daily Use Household Articles	100.5	100.5	100.7
家庭服务及加工维修服务	Household Service	110.2	107.4	116.9
医疗保健和个人用品	**Medicine and Personal Articles**	**102.0**	**102.0**	**101.9**
医疗保健	Medicine and Health Care	101.7	101.8	101.3
医疗器具及用品	Medical Appliances and Articles	103.2	103.1	103.3
中药材及中成药	Traditional Chinese Medicine	107.2	107.7	106.2
西药	Western Medicine	100.4	100.7	99.8
保健器具及用品	Health Appliances and Articles	100.4	100.4	100.6
医疗保健服务	Medical and Health Service	100.1	100.1	100.2
个人用品及服务	Personal Articles and Services	102.5	102.3	103.0
交通和通讯	**Transportation and Communication**	**100.0**	**99.7**	**100.5**
交通	Transportation	101.7	101.1	102.9
通讯	Communication	98.4	98.5	98.0
娱乐教育文化用品及服务	**Recreation, Education, Culture Articles and Services**	**101.2**	**101.4**	**100.7**
文娱用耐用消费品	Durable Consumer Goods for Recreational Use	97.5	96.4	100.1
教育	Education	101.9	102.3	101.0
文化娱乐	Cultural and Recreational	100.9	100.8	101.0
文化娱乐用品	Culture and Recreation Articles	100.4	99.7	102.0
书报杂志	Newspapers and Magazines	101.0	101.2	100.6
文娱费	Recreation	101.3	101.6	100.3
旅游及外出	Touristry and Outside	105.2	107.5	100.2
居住	**Residence**	**102.7**	**101.7**	**104.7**
建房及装修材料	Building and Finishing Materials	103.5	101.3	108.1
租房	Tenancy	103.3	102.3	105.1
自有住房	Housing	101.6	101.8	101.5
水、电、燃料	Water, Electricity and Fuels	102.5	101.9	103.7
服务项目价格指数	**Services**	**101.5**	**101.6**	**101.3**

7—3　各市县居民消费价格分类指数

（上年=100）　　（2010 年）

指　　标	Item	乌鲁木齐市 Urumqi City	喀什市 Kashgar [Kaxgar] City	伊宁市 Yining [Gulja] City	和田市 Hotan City	克拉玛依市 Karamay City	哈密市 Hami [Kumul] City
居民消费价格总指数	**Consumers'Price Index**	**102.7**	**104.8**	**106.2**	**104.4**	**104.5**	**105.0**
食　品	**Food**	**108.5**	**111.7**	**112.0**	**110.4**	**111.3**	**113.3**
粮　食	Grain	108.8	106.4	107.4	105.1	123.6	106.9
大　米	Rice	131.3	123.6	127.5	123.8	167.5	121.7
面　粉	Flour	95.1	94.6	94.4	94.7	100.2	95.1
粮食制品	Grain Products	100.3	101.4	98.5	102.7	102.0	100.8
其　它	Others	116.7	119.6	116.0	105.7	114.5	114.5
淀　粉	Starches and Tubers	99.8	109.7	112.3	117.6	99.0	96.6
干豆类及豆制品	Bean and Its Products	108.2	120.5	129.0	117.1	109.9	115.7
油　脂	Oil or Fat	101.6	110.0	106.6	107.2	106.1	100.4
肉禽及其制品	Meat,Poultry and Their Products	109.9	116.5	114.8	112.1	109.1	111.7
蛋	Eggs	110.4	115.2	116.0	104.2	111.1	105.8
水产品	Aquatic Products	111.2	112.7	97.6	109.0	104.1	111.8
菜	Vegetables	110.8	119.3	130.4	126.8	126.2	133.2
鲜　菜	Fresh Vegetables	110.1	119.9	132.1	128.1	126.7	132.3
干菜及菜制品	Dried Vegetables and Vegetable Products	105.8	100.3	113.9	109.1	113.1	124.5
薯　类	Tubers	132.2	113.7	126.4	115.4	133.9	162.3
调味品	Tlavoring	106.3	102.3	102.7	103.7	103.8	107.2
糖	Sugar	101.7	113.0	113.8	107.2	104.0	114.5
食　糖	Sugar	102.3	124.2	121.7	118.1	107.0	133.2
糖　果	Candy	100.3	100.0	111.8	100.0	104.7	103.7
巧克力制品	Chocolate Goods	105.5	136.2	122.5	112.3	100.0	120.1
糖制小食品	Sugar Foodstuff	103.5	109.2	100.0	104.0	104.2	101.3
茶及饮料	Tea and Beverages	99.5	101.9	105.6	100.2	100.3	103.4
干鲜瓜果	Dried and Fresh Melons and Fruits	111.7	113.8	109.7	121.0	104.9	122.8
鲜瓜果	Fresh Fruits	107.4	114.7	106.9	122.3	105.3	126.6
干(坚)果	Dried(nut)Fruits and Melon and Fruits Products	123.6	109.5	117.4	115.7	101.1	114.9
糕点饼干	Cake,Cookie,Bread	103.6	101.2	102.9	101.0	100.2	100.7
液体乳及乳制品	Milk and Its Products	108.5	104.1	103.9	98.5	104.9	103.7
在外用膳食品	Catering Trade	106.0	107.3	101.9	105.5	102.9	103.2
主　食	Staple Food	103.4	101.6	100.6	103.5	100.2	102.5
炒　菜	Fried Dishes	105.4	103.1	103.4	108.4	100.5	103.9
地方小吃	Local Snack	114.3	125.7	100.9	100.0	108.1	103.2
其他食品	Other Food and Food Processing	101.2	100.4	100.3	101.1	107.5	98.7
烟酒及用品	**Tobacco,Liquor and Articles**	**101.6**	**100.6**	**105.2**	**102.9**	**101.8**	**98.9**
烟　草	Tobacco	98.4	99.1	97.0	98.3	101.2	96.6
酒	Liquor	104.8	102.2	112.6	107.7	102.5	101.4
吸烟饮酒用品	Articles	105.6	101.1	102.7	100.0	100.4	97.3
衣　着	**Clothing**	**94.7**	**99.4**	**105.0**	**100.1**	**101.6**	**95.1**
服　装	Garments	95.8	99.1	105.1	100.1	101.1	89.5
衣着材料	Clothing Material	100.5	102.1	109.2	101.4	104.5	106.3
棉　布	Cotton Cloth	101.1	103.3	103.1	102.7	109.9	108.1

Consumer Price Indices by Category in Cities and Counties

(preceding year=100)

昌吉市 Changji City	库尔勒市 Korla City	阿克苏市 Aksu City	焉耆回族自治县 Yanqi Hui Autonomous County	塔城市 Tacheng [Qoqek] City	阿勒泰市 Altay City	乌苏市 Usu City	博乐市 Bole [Bortala] City	吐鲁番市 Turpan City	库车县 Kuqa County	阿图什市 Artux City	莎车县 Shache [Yarkant] County	奎屯市 Kuytun City	石河子市 Shihezi City
103.6	**104.5**	**106.1**	**104.7**	**105.2**	**104.6**	**105.5**	**105.7**	**104.6**	**105.2**	**104.3**	**107.3**	**103.3**	**103.7**
108.7	**111.1**	**110.4**	**111.5**	**113.1**	**112.0**	**112.6**	**111.5**	**110.9**	**111.7**	**111.2**	**114.9**	**108.0**	**107.0**
102.4	105.4	109.6	107.6	106.4	106.2	109.3	113.8	106.2	110.6	106.0	110.9	100.2	105.4
113.3	112.4	123.7	118.7	122.7	118.9	124.8	130.8	120.3	142.9	124.4	129.8	105.0	111.9
97.0	100.7	98.4	96.1	94.8	96.0	91.5	105.2	94.6	83.3	94.0	93.5	98.0	98.5
99.2	100.2	102.0	101.6	100.0	100.9	107.5	100.8	106.6	106.3	100.2	102.7	98.0	101.3
115.2	128.6	132.2	122.8	110.7	113.1	147.5	105.4	108.4	116.9	109.4	125.8	101.7	114.3
129.4	101.6	109.4	110.7	100.0	100.0	97.1	115.5	133.3	101.1	100.0	110.6	100.0	100.6
112.2	108.2	103.7	116.1	109.9	118.3	114.0	104.9	109.8	125.4	101.4	111.3	123.0	116.6
104.9	107.9	102.6	109.8	121.3	117.9	102.4	106.8	103.8	123.3	116.2	109.3	113.7	111.1
114.4	116.2	112.6	112.0	112.2	115.4	113.2	112.3	112.7	107.3	115.3	119.9	105.5	104.6
104.9	114.4	115.2	108.1	109.5	108.9	110.0	104.2	116.2	107.7	113.4	132.4	108.8	105.0
107.5	106.5	105.9	105.3	101.8	101.4	105.0	104.8	106.2	104.7	114.5	111.1	104.9	108.1
108.6	123.0	111.4	122.7	126.2	123.3	127.9	125.2	126.4	126.5	123.8	108.8	122.6	113.7
109.3	125.0	110.3	120.6	128.3	124.9	128.5	133.8	126.3	132.1	124.7	109.2	123.0	115.7
100.2	98.5	119.8	118.4	100.0	111.9	114.9	102.8	102.2	104.7	104.0	106.7	100.7	105.3
96.9	142.1	118.8	147.7	98.2	125.7	144.1	93.4	134.2	100.0	122.9	103.7	133.6	96.3
106.9	100.5	113.4	100.8	105.8	113.8	102.1	104.3	100.4	103.8	101.4	100.0	100.0	103.0
105.8	104.2	106.6	111.6	110.9	105.5	108.5	112.8	106.8	109.2	104.7	110.6	104.7	110.4
114.9	111.5	125.8	131.5	121.5	118.7	131.3	121.1	118.2	121.2	113.1	126.5	112.7	117.9
102.6	103.3	98.9	98.1	100.0	100.0	100.5	113.0	100.7	103.4	100.0	107.0	100.0	108.4
100.0	100.5	100.0	108.0	103.4	101.5	100.0	106.4	100.0	102.2	100.0	97.5	103.4	99.3
100.3	100.7	105.9	103.5	120.6	100.0	102.1	100.0	100.0	100.7	100.0	102.7	100.0	114.3
105.1	101.3	109.8	100.2	98.3	100.9	99.9	100.7	104.0	99.5	106.3	106.0	100.0	101.6
104.4	119.4	105.7	119.5	118.0	122.1	119.7	116.3	116.3	120.2	107.2	120.3	113.2	105.7
104.0	119.1	98.8	120.0	122.4	128.2	122.5	115.1	110.0	130.6	107.0	117.0	119.5	100.4
105.5	121.1	121.9	118.7	102.1	100.0	112.1	118.7	122.0	104.0	108.7	130.7	100.0	124.6
100.0	101.9	103.7	102.8	100.0	100.0	100.9	100.0	102.7	100.4	100.0	101.4	105.7	101.7
118.7	102.5	107.3	103.4	125.3	108.6	107.7	104.5	101.6	101.3	100.6	111.3	101.0	113.7
105.9	101.5	113.1	107.4	104.6	102.0	108.3	103.7	101.1	109.3	103.0	113.2	100.3	103.9
102.8	103.5	107.4	103.7	106.6	103.8	100.0	101.9	101.1	107.0	100.0	107.5	101.9	104.2
110.6	100.4	116.9	109.0	100.0	101.1	107.9	101.2	100.0	106.7	103.2	118.2	100.0	104.1
105.2	100.0	113.3	109.6	116.5	100.0	114.2	111.8	103.1	117.6	110.0	115.0	101.9	102.7
100.4	100.0	113.3	100.3	103.2	100.0	100.0	100.0	100.0	100.0	100.0	100.0	101.4	101.0
105.4	**101.5**	**106.4**	**101.2**	**100.1**	**100.3**	**100.4**	**103.5**	**98.4**	**100.6**	**100.3**	**100.6**	**104.1**	**101.3**
100.8	100.0	99.2	97.8	100.0	99.6	95.6	101.1	93.0	97.7	97.9	98.8	103.9	99.7
110.1	103.4	111.5	105.8	100.5	101.3	105.0	105.4	104.9	105.5	103.2	102.7	104.5	102.5
99.8	100.8	114.4	100.0	97.8	100.0	100.0	111.9	100.0	100.0	100.0	101.5	100.6	105.6
99.4	**99.1**	**106.1**	**99.8**	**99.1**	**100.7**	**101.7**	**101.5**	**100.9**	**100.9**	**100.3**	**103.8**	**100.6**	**101.9**
99.0	98.2	103.6	98.8	98.6	102.5	100.3	102.2	99.7	100.8	100.4	104.9	100.7	100.4
101.5	100.2	104.8	101.9	108.6	100.4	100.0	102.2	102.9	100.5	100.6	106.7	101.8	103.4
108.9	101.2	107.2	103.4	113.3	100.0	100.0	103.3	113.3	100.0	100.0	106.3	100.0	106.4

7—3 续表

（上年=100）　　　　（2010 年）

指　　标	Item	乌鲁木齐市 Urumqi City	喀什市 Kashgar [Kaxgar] City	伊宁市 Yining [Gulja] City	和田市 Hotan City	克拉玛依市 Karamay City	哈密市 Hami [Kumul] City
棉花化纤混纺布	Blend Cloth	101.5	104.2	103.3	101.0	107.8	103.9
化纤布	Chemical Fiber Cloth	100.0	101.4	101.4	101.5	100.0	111.4
毛　线	Wool	100.8	100.0	124.6	100.0	101.8	100.0
鞋袜帽	Footwear and Hats	90.9	98.6	104.1	100.0	100.6	100.8
鞋	Shoes	90.0	100.0	104.4	100.1	101.0	101.1
袜　子	Socks and Stockings	100.0	92.5	102.7	100.0	97.3	100.0
帽　子	Hats	97.1	101.0	100.9	100.0	100.4	100.0
衣着加工服务费	Clothing Processing	100.7	106.4	103.5	100.0	113.6	108.7
家庭设备及用品及维修服务	**Household Facilities and Articles**	**100.7**	**99.2**	**101.3**	**101.8**	**100.8**	**98.3**
耐用消费品	Durable Consumer Goods	99.3	96.9	100.0	99.9	99.8	96.8
家　具	Furniture	101.4	95.8	101.3	100.0	99.7	99.2
家庭设备	Household Facilities	97.9	97.7	99.4	99.8	99.9	95.8
室内装饰品	Interior Decorations	101.0	98.7	103.0	101.4	99.6	100.0
床上用品	Bed Articles	106.1	99.4	100.0	96.6	100.0	91.2
家庭日用杂品	Daily Use Household Articles	99.6	101.8	99.9	108.4	100.0	101.5
家庭服务及加工维修服务	Household Service	113.9	102.3	111.8	100.0	110.2	103.2
医疗保健和个人用品	**Medicine and Personal Articles**	**101.4**	**102.9**	**100.9**	**101.2**	**100.7**	**105.6**
医疗保健	Medicine and Health care	101.8	101.1	100.2	101.1	99.8	106.7
医疗器具及用品	Medical Appliances and Articles	97.7	117.2	111.1	100.0	104.9	112.9
中药材及中成药	Traditional Chinese Medicine	105.5	104.8	96.5	104.0	96.3	119.7
西　药	Western Medicine	100.8	98.9	102.4	100.6	101.4	100.7
保健器具及用品	Health Appliances and Articles	100.0	100.3	99.9	99.8	99.2	102.7
医疗保健服务	Medical and Health Service	100.0	100.5	98.7	100.0	100.0	100.0
个人用品及服务	Personal Articles and Services	100.4	105.8	102.0	101.4	101.8	103.8
交通和通讯	**Transportation and Communication**	**99.3**	**100.3**	**100.5**	**100.9**	**101.0**	**99.3**
交　通	Transportation	100.8	102.3	101.3	102.7	102.7	101.1
通　讯	Communication	97.8	97.9	99.9	99.7	99.1	97.2
娱乐教育文化用品及服务	**Recreation, Education, Culture Articles and Services**	**101.9**	**99.6**	**103.4**	**100.6**	**101.1**	**102.2**
文娱用耐用消费品	Durable Consumer Goods for Recreational Use	92.1	92.0	99.5	99.5	99.4	96.3
教　育	Education	102.2	100.0	101.6	100.0	102.7	102.3
文化娱乐	Cultural and Recreational Articles	99.9	104.3	99.5	101.1	102.1	100.9
文化娱乐用品	Culture and Recreation	98.9	100.5	98.8	99.7	100.0	98.7
书报杂志	Newspapers and Magazines	100.3	110.7	99.8	102.5	104.8	100.0
文娱费	Recreation	100.8	103.0	100.0	102.3	103.0	106.4
旅　游	Touristry and Outside	108.5	106.8	114.4	114.4	100.6	115.2
居　住	**Residence**	**99.9**	**104.1**	**105.1**	**102.5**	**101.3**	**103.3**
建房及装修材料	Building and Finishing Materials	99.2	101.6	101.3	101.0	102.9	102.1
租　房	Tenancy	102.6	100.0	100.0	100.0	100.0	104.8
自有住房	Housing	100.3	105.7	102.0	100.7	103.1	100.6
水、电、燃料	Water, Electricity and Fuels	100.0	105.9	107.3	104.8	100.0	104.8
服务项目价格指数	**Services**	**101.7**	**102.0**	**102.5**	**100.7**	**102.2**	**102.7**

Continued

(preceding year=100)

昌吉市 Changji City	库尔勒市 Korla City	阿克苏市 Aksu City	焉耆回族自治县 Yanqi Hui Autonomous County	塔城市 Tacheng [Qoqek] City	阿勒泰市 Altay City	乌苏市 Usu City	博乐市 Bole [Bortala] City	吐鲁番市 Turpan City	库车县 Kuqa County	阿图什市 Artux City	莎车县 Shache [Yarkant] County	奎屯市 Kuytun City	石河子市 Shihezi City
105.3	100.0	102.7	103.3	101.3	101.6	100.0	101.6	100.0	100.0	102.2	102.6	105.8	101.0
98.6	100.0	100.0	100.0	106.9	100.0	100.0	102.8	100.0	100.0	100.0	106.2	100.6	108.0
100.0	100.0	111.6	102.0	100.8	100.0	100.0	100.0	100.7	102.2	100.0	111.6	100.0	99.0
99.8	100.6	110.8	100.9	100.0	100.0	105.4	100.1	103.2	102.2	100.0	99.6	100.0	105.3
100.1	100.5	108.7	101.5	100.0	100.0	109.1	100.2	103.9	102.6	100.0	99.5	98.4	107.3
97.9	101.9	119.6	97.7	100.0	100.0	100.0	100.0	100.0	100.0	100.0	100.0	102.1	100.1
99.4	100.0	106.6	97.7	100.0	100.0	100.0	100.0	100.0	100.0	100.0	99.5	104.8	99.9
100.4	100.0	119.0	101.1	101.2	84.5	100.0	100.3	100.0	100.0	100.0	106.7	100.0	100.3
101.0	**100.6**	**102.7**	**102.3**	**102.7**	**99.8**	**100.9**	**100.4**	**101.1**	**105.1**	**99.9**	**104.2**	**100.2**	**100.9**
100.8	100.2	100.4	104.3	98.5	99.2	100.0	100.3	99.9	101.1	100.0	102.8	98.3	97.5
100.2	101.2	102.6	110.9	100.0	100.5	100.0	100.0	100.0	100.3	100.0	104.1	98.2	97.0
100.9	99.8	98.7	100.5	97.8	98.2	100.0	100.5	99.9	101.8	100.0	102.0	98.3	97.7
97.1	101.2	99.7	100.0	100.0	100.0	100.0	100.4	100.2	100.0	100.0	100.0	99.8	107.5
101.9	103.0	101.7	100.0	100.0	100.0	100.0	100.0	102.6	100.0	100.0	100.9	98.4	100.1
101.4	100.3	106.5	97.6	99.9	100.0	100.3	100.8	103.3	98.5	99.3	102.4	104.1	102.1
103.9	100.8	109.4	110.6	147.5	101.2	108.7	100.0	101.6	140.8	100.0	120.3	102.0	107.7
101.8	**101.1**	**102.7**	**101.1**	**102.8**	**104.9**	**98.0**	**104.3**	**101.7**	**101.0**	**100.9**	**101.0**	**100.7**	**104.7**
101.5	100.7	101.2	100.1	103.1	106.8	94.3	103.9	101.0	100.4	101.8	100.3	100.3	104.4
100.0	101.9	110.6	97.1	100.9	100.0	100.0	100.2	124.9	106.4	100.0	100.0	100.0	115.0
108.5	102.3	101.7	102.6	110.5	123.9	91.6	119.2	101.8	97.1	105.6	102.2	101.4	116.0
98.5	99.9	101.0	99.7	105.1	101.0	91.4	98.6	100.2	101.5	99.7	99.3	99.9	101.7
102.8	100.0	100.6	100.2	102.3	100.1	100.0	103.5	99.9	98.9	105.5	100.2	99.4	101.6
100.3	100.0	101.2	98.0	100.0	100.0	100.0	100.0	100.0	102.0	101.6	100.2	100.0	100.0
102.3	101.7	105.0	102.6	102.2	101.5	102.9	104.9	102.7	101.9	99.5	102.0	101.3	105.2
99.4	**101.5**	**101.2**	**99.6**	**100.6**	**99.6**	**100.9**	**101.7**	**100.5**	**99.3**	**98.3**	**102.2**	**98.6**	**101.2**
101.2	102.9	103.1	101.1	101.0	102.1	101.9	104.3	102.9	101.8	101.9	106.2	100.3	102.9
97.8	99.5	98.6	98.5	100.0	96.7	100.0	99.3	99.1	95.4	94.4	97.8	96.9	99.2
100.9	**102.5**	**101.6**	**102.3**	**99.9**	**100.0**	**101.0**	**102.1**	**101.0**	**101.6**	**100.2**	**100.4**	**100.0**	**99.3**
99.0	99.3	96.8	103.2	98.7	99.4	100.3	99.2	99.2	99.2	100.0	101.6	98.2	92.6
102.4	105.0	103.8	102.6	100.4	100.0	100.0	106.8	100.6	101.1	100.0	100.0	100.6	101.1
100.5	101.2	102.0	100.5	99.9	100.8	104.4	101.5	103.6	101.4	101.2	100.1	100.8	100.4
100.7	101.1	99.4	100.0	99.9	100.0	109.1	103.3	100.0	100.1	103.2	100.2	101.9	99.9
100.6	102.1	100.0	100.0	99.4	102.3	100.0	100.0	102.6	102.9	100.0	100.0	100.0	101.6
100.0	100.0	106.9	101.7	100.0	100.0	100.0	100.0	110.5	101.6	100.0	100.0	100.0	100.0
99.4	101.8	99.1	100.0	100.0	100.0	100.0	93.6	104.8	106.4	100.0	100.0	100.3	102.2
101.9	**101.6**	**106.4**	**101.7**	**103.7**	**100.8**	**106.8**	**104.1**	**102.7**	**104.5**	**101.2**	**108.2**	**103.6**	**103.7**
104.2	101.4	104.5	102.7	105.6	101.4	104.1	106.2	104.8	108.5	98.6	117.6	103.0	104.3
107.8	100.0	111.1	105.0	100.2	100.0	104.2	106.6	100.0	100.0	100.0	116.4	100.0	107.1
100.4	105.1	100.0	102.3	100.0	100.7	116.1	100.0	100.3	100.7	100.3	102.0	100.6	100.2
100.6	100.7	108.9	100.8	103.9	100.7	106.5	104.1	102.9	104.0	103.6	102.7	105.2	104.0
101.4	**102.2**	**103.3**	**101.3**	**102.0**	**99.5**	**102.4**	**102.5**	**101.1**	**103.2**	**100.2**	**101.2**	**100.3**	**101.5**

7—4 商品零售价格分类指数

Retail Price Indices by Category of Commodities

（上年=100）　　（2010年）　　（preceding year=100）

指　　标	Item	全　区 Province	城　市 Urban Areas	农　村 Rural Areas
商品零售价格总指数	**General Retail Price Index**	**104.6**	**103.9**	**106.4**
食品类	**Food**	**110.6**	**109.4**	**113.4**
粮　食	Grain	109.7	109.3	110.3
油　脂	Oil or Fat	107.8	104.1	113.7
肉禽及其制品	Meat,Poultry and Their Products	111.6	110.7	113.6
猪　肉	Pork	104.3	103.5	106.1
牛　肉	Beef	111.0	109.4	114.1
羊　肉	Lamb	118.0	116.3	122.1
鸡	Chicken	113.9	113.7	114.1
鲜　蛋	Fresh Egg	112.5	111.2	115.1
水产品	Aquatic Products	108.1	109.2	105.3
鲜　果	Fresh Fruits	111.3	108.2	117.8
糕　点	Cake	102.5	103.1	100.9
饮料、烟酒	**Beverage,Tobacco and Wine**	**101.7**	**101.8**	**101.2**
茶及饮料	Tea and Drinks	101.9	101.6	102.3
#饮　料	Beverage	101.0	101.4	100.2
烟　草	Tobacco	98.6	98.7	98.3
酒	Liquor	104.9	105.5	103.4
服装鞋帽	**Garments,Shoes and Hats**	**98.0**	**96.4**	**101.6**
服　装	Garments	98.2	96.8	101.7
鞋袜帽	Shoes,Stocks and Hats	97.3	95.4	101.6
#鞋	Shoes	96.6	94.3	102.1
纺织品类	**Textiles**	**103.5**	**104.0**	**101.4**
棉　布	Cotton Cloth	104.2	103.9	104.6
棉花化纤混纺布	Blend Cloth	102.4	102.6	101.7
化纤布	Chemical Fiber Cloth	100.7	100.3	101.8
毛　线	Woolen Fabric	103.4	102.9	104.4
家用电器及音响器材	**Electric Household Appliance and Sound Apparatus**	**97.8**	**97.0**	**99.7**
家庭设备	Household Facilities	98.6	98.3	99.2
文娱用耐用消费品	Durable Consuming Goods for Entertainment	96.8	95.1	100.1
音响器材类	Sound Apparatus	99.5	99.2	100.1

7—4 续表 Continued

（上年=100） （2010 年） （preceding year=100）

指 标	Item	全 区 Province	城 市 Urban Areas	农 村 Rural Areas
文化办公用品	**Cultural and Office Goods**	**99.2**	**98.3**	**101.1**
日用品	**Articse for Daily Use**	**100.7**	**100.7**	**100.6**
日用百货	Merchandise for Daily Use	100.7	100.9	100.1
日用杂品	Sundries for Daily Use	100.6	100.4	101.1
洗涤用品	Washing and Cleaning Goods	101.6	101.8	100.8
其他日用品	Other Daily-use Goods	99.1	98.5	100.4
体育娱乐用品	**Sports and Entertainment Goods**	**97.5**	**96.5**	**100.1**
体育用品	Sports Goods	99.8	99.6	100.2
娱乐用品	Recreational Goods	95.6	94.1	100.0
交通、通信用品	**Traffic and Telecommunication Goods**	**96.8**	**95.8**	**98.6**
交通运输机械	Traffic and Transport Machinery	99.3	98.6	100.8
通讯器材类	Telecommunication Apparatus	93.7	92.2	96.3
家 具	**Furniture**	**101.3**	**101.2**	**101.4**
化妆品类	**Cosmetics**	**99.5**	**99.6**	**99.3**
金银珠宝类	**Gold and Silver Jewels**	**110.7**	**108.0**	**118.1**
中西药品及医疗保健用品类	**Chinese and Western Medicine, Medical-care and Healthy Goods**	**102.6**	**102.3**	**103.4**
医疗器具及用品	Medical-care Apparatus and Goods	102.0	100.1	105.3
中药材及中成药	Chinese Herbs and Patent Medicine	107.5	107.0	108.3
西 药	Western Medicine	100.6	100.8	100.0
保健品及器具	Health Goods and Devices	100.4	100.2	101.4
书报杂志及电子出版物类	**Books, Magazines and Electronic Publications**	**103.0**	**103.9**	**100.6**
教材及参考书	Texts and Reference Books	106.9	109.6	101.1
书报杂志	Newspapers and Magazines	100.9	101.0	100.6
电子音像制品	Electronic Audio and Video Products	101.2	101.6	100.0
燃料类	**Fuels**	**107.7**	**107.1**	**109.2**
煤炭及制品类	Coal and Its Products	102.0	99.9	104.1
石油及制品类	Oil and its Products	110.3	109.2	114.3
建筑材料及五金电料类	**Building Materials and Hardwares**	**103.0**	**101.4**	**105.9**
建筑装璜材料	Building Decoration Materials	104.2	102.3	108.1
五金电料类	Hardwares and Electrical Apparatus	99.6	99.0	100.6

7—5　各市县商品零售价格分类指数

（上年＝100）　　　　　　　　　　　　　　　　　　　　　　　　　　　　（2010年）

指　　标	Item	乌鲁木齐市 Urumqi City	喀什市 Kashgar [Kaxgar] City	伊宁市 Yining [Gulja] City	和田市 Hotan City	克拉玛依市 Karamay City	哈密市 Hami [Kumul] City
商品零售价格总指数	**General Retail Price Index**	**103.4**	**105.1**	**106.5**	**105.2**	**104.2**	**105.1**
食品类	**Food**	**108.6**	**112.0**	**111.8**	**111.3**	**111.5**	**114.0**
粮　食	Grain	109.4	106.0	107.4	107.0	123.6	106.6
油　脂	Oil or Fat	102.1	110.8	106.7	107.2	106.1	101.1
肉禽及其制品	Meat, Poultry and Their Products	109.7	116.3	114.8	112.5	108.7	112.8
猪　肉	Pork	102.2	113.7	103.2	119.7	105.5	108.5
牛　肉	Beef	106.8	113.8	113.6	113.9	109.2	109.6
羊　肉	Lamb	114.2	117.1	128.9	110.5	118.8	122.5
鸡	Chicken	115.0	118.1	104.5	111.3	103.9	104.2
鲜　蛋	Fresh Egg	111.4	115.6	117.5	104.5	115.0	105.6
水产品	Aquatic Products	111.1	110.9	97.9	109.0	104.1	112.2
鲜　果	Fresh Fruits	107.4	114.7	106.9	122.3	105.3	126.6
糕　点	Cake	104.0	101.1	102.8	101.0	100.2	100.8
饮料、烟酒	**Beverage, Tobacco and Wine**	**101.2**	**100.3**	**105.1**	**103.1**	**101.3**	**99.9**
茶及饮料	Tea and Drinks	99.5	102.1	105.0	99.6	100.2	103.2
#饮　料	Beverage	99.5	101.3	104.8	100.7	99.2	99.2
烟　草	Tobacco	98.4	99.1	97.1	98.3	101.2	96.9
酒	Liquor	105.0	102.1	110.5	107.7	102.5	101.4
服装鞋帽	**Garments, Shoes and Hats**	**94.4**	**99.2**	**104.7**	**100.0**	**100.9**	**94.2**
服　装	Garments	96.0	99.3	105.1	100.1	101.1	89.3
鞋袜帽	Shoes, Stocks and Hats	90.9	99.1	104.1	100.0	100.6	100.8
#鞋	Shoes	89.9	100.0	104.4	100.0	101.0	101.0
纺织品类	**Textiles**	**104.6**	**101.1**	**104.9**	**99.3**	**101.4**	**99.1**
棉　布	Cotton Cloth	101.1	103.3	103.1	102.7	109.9	108.1
棉花化纤混纺布	Blend Cloth	101.5	104.2	103.3	101.0	107.8	103.9
化纤布	Chemical Fiber Cloth	100.0	101.4	101.4	101.5	100.0	111.4
毛　线	Woolen Fabric	100.8	100.0	124.6	100.0	101.8	100.0
家用电器及音响器材	**Electric Household Appliance and Sound Apparatus**	**96.2**	**95.4**	**99.4**	**99.7**	**99.7**	**96.2**
家庭设备	Household Facilities	97.9	98.1	99.4	99.8	99.9	95.7
文娱用耐用消费品	Durable Consuming Goods for Entertainment	93.6	91.9	99.5	99.3	99.3	96.0
音响器材类	Sound Apparatus	99.8	95.6	97.9	100.0	100.0	100.0

Retail Price Indices by Category of Commoditles in Cities and Counties

(preceding year=100)

昌吉市 Changji City	库尔勒市 Korla City	阿克苏市 Aksu City	焉耆回族自治县 Yanqi Hui Autonomous County	塔城市 Tacheng [Qoqek] City	阿勒泰市 Altay City	乌苏市 Usu City	博乐市 Bole [Bortala] City	吐鲁番市 Turpan City	库车县 Kuqa County	阿图什市 Artux City	莎车县 Shache [Yarkant] County	奎屯市 Kuytun City	石河子市 Shihezi City
104.0	**104.5**	**106.2**	**104.7**	**105.7**	**106.1**	**104.9**	**105.7**	**105.5**	**103.7**	**105.1**	**107.9**	**103.8**	**103.9**
108.3	**110.7**	**110.6**	**111.2**	**112.4**	**113.4**	**111.3**	**111.0**	**111.4**	**110.0**	**111.6**	**113.9**	**109.1**	**107.0**
102.5	105.6	109.0	107.8	106.4	106.8	108.6	112.5	106.2	109.8	106.8	112.5	100.3	105.5
105.1	110.9	102.6	109.6	121.3	122.1	102.1	106.9	103.8	116.0	118.0	109.4	117.0	109.2
113.0	111.9	112.6	110.6	112.2	116.5	111.7	111.3	112.5	108.3	115.2	118.4	106.4	104.9
102.9	108.9	103.8	97.6	105.4	109.5	107.8	110.1	101.8	99.3	101.2	113.5	97.9	102.5
109.0	119.8	118.6	114.4	110.0	111.6	112.6	107.4	114.6	108.4	114.2	121.4	113.5	107.9
123.9	123.0	124.2	123.7	124.3	125.5	126.9	120.7	118.9	113.4	122.6	122.2	125.0	115.2
116.5	113.5	109.3	110.3	108.4	123.4	110.4	117.8	110.8	117.3	110.4	117.0	107.7	102.7
104.6	115.0	115.2	108.6	111.0	109.8	109.8	105.3	117.1	111.1	113.7	134.5	109.8	104.6
107.7	105.8	105.2	105.4	101.8	101.7	104.5	105.4	106.2	104.0	115.2	110.8	102.2	108.5
104.0	119.1	98.8	120.0	122.4	128.2	122.5	115.1	110.0	130.6	107.0	117.0	119.5	100.4
100.0	102.2	103.7	102.6	100.0	100.0	100.9	100.0	102.7	100.8	100.0	101.8	107.0	101.2
104.0	**101.0**	**105.6**	**101.2**	**99.7**	**100.2**	**100.3**	**102.4**	**100.0**	**101.3**	**102.4**	**101.8**	**103.3**	**101.9**
104.1	101.2	108.1	100.2	98.3	101.0	99.9	100.5	104.0	99.7	106.5	104.6	100.0	104.6
106.2	102.0	106.0	100.3	100.0	99.2	99.8	100.8	103.0	99.5	98.7	99.2	100.0	108.0
101.0	100.0	99.3	97.7	100.0	98.9	95.8	102.6	92.9	98.2	98.0	99.1	104.7	99.7
108.3	102.0	111.5	106.0	100.5	101.2	104.8	103.7	104.9	105.6	102.5	103.2	103.5	102.2
99.3	**99.1**	**105.9**	**99.0**	**99.0**	**101.4**	**102.4**	**101.3**	**100.8**	**101.3**	**100.1**	**104.0**	**101.4**	**102.7**
99.0	98.2	102.8	98.5	98.6	102.3	100.4	101.6	99.7	101.3	100.1	105.0	101.4	101.8
99.8	100.5	111.2	100.1	100.0	100.0	105.5	101.0	103.2	101.4	100.0	99.8	99.4	104.7
100.1	100.4	108.7	101.3	100.0	100.0	108.4	101.6	103.9	102.6	100.0	99.6	98.3	107.2
103.0	**101.7**	**104.3**	**101.2**	**102.5**	**100.2**	**100.0**	**101.1**	**102.8**	**100.3**	**100.3**	**104.8**	**100.2**	**101.3**
108.9	101.2	107.2	103.4	113.3	100.0	100.0	103.3	113.3	100.0	100.0	106.3	100.0	106.4
105.3	100.0	102.7	103.3	101.3	101.6	100.0	101.6	100.0	100.0	102.2	102.6	105.8	101.0
98.6	100.0	100.0	100.0	106.9	100.0	100.0	102.8	100.0	100.0	100.0	106.2	100.6	108.0
100.0	100.0	111.6	102.0	100.8	100.0	100.0	100.0	100.7	102.2	100.0	111.6	100.0	99.0
101.0	**99.5**	**97.2**	**101.4**	**98.8**	**98.5**	**100.0**	**99.8**	**99.6**	**101.3**	**100.0**	**102.1**	**98.3**	**95.6**
101.2	99.8	98.7	100.5	97.8	98.0	100.0	100.4	99.9	102.3	100.0	102.1	98.4	98.0
100.9	99.0	95.3	103.0	99.7	98.9	100.0	99.2	99.1	99.6	100.0	102.1	97.8	91.9
93.8	100.0	99.9	100.0	100.0	100.0	100.0	100.0	100.0	100.0	100.0	101.3	100.0	100.0

7—5 续表

（上年=100） （2010年）

指标	Item	乌鲁木齐市 Urumqi City	喀什市 Kashgar [Kaxgar] City	伊宁市 Yining [Gulja] City	和田市 Hotan City	克拉玛依市 Karamay City	哈密市 Hami [Kumul] City
文化办公用品	**Cultural and Office Goods**	**97.1**	**100.7**	**99.3**	**99.8**	**100.0**	**97.4**
日用品	**Articles for Daily Use**	**100.7**	**99.5**	**100.9**	**102.4**	**100.3**	**101.6**
日用百货	Daily Merchandise	101.2	95.6	101.2	99.7	100.4	102.0
日用杂品	Sundries for Daily Use	100.0	100.5	100.0	109.3	100.0	101.2
洗涤用品	Washing and Cleaning Goods	101.9	102.0	101.2	100.3	100.4	101.9
其他日用品	Other Daily Goods	97.4	98.7	101.0	100.0	100.3	100.4
体育娱乐用品	**Sports and Creational Goods**	**94.0**	**99.4**	**98.5**	**100.0**	**100.3**	**98.6**
体育用品	Sports Goods	99.6	99.0	99.2	100.1	100.5	97.6
娱乐用品	Recreational Goods	89.3	99.9	97.9	100.0	100.0	99.8
交通、通信用品	**Traffic and Telecommunication Goods**	**94.8**	**94.5**	**100.3**	**99.1**	**99.0**	**95.2**
交通运输机械	Traffic and Transport Machinery	98.3	97.1	101.4	99.2	99.9	97.3
通讯器材类	Telecommunication Apparatus	90.2	90.5	99.4	99.0	97.9	92.1
家　具	**Furniture**	**101.9**	**95.5**	**101.3**	**100.0**	**99.7**	**99.1**
化妆品类	**Cosmetic Products**	**99.3**	**101.0**	**102.4**	**101.9**	**99.9**	**101.9**
金银珠宝类	**Gold and Silver Jewels**	**107.6**	**112.0**	**112.9**	**115.3**	**105.7**	**106.5**
中西药品及医疗保健用品类	**Chinese and Western Medicine, Medical-car e and Healthy Goods**	**102.6**	**101.6**	**100.1**	**101.4**	**100.1**	**108.7**
医疗器具及用品	Medical-care Apparatus and Goods	97.7	117.2	111.1	100.0	104.9	112.9
中药材及中成药	Chinese Herbs and Patent Medicine	109.0	104.8	96.5	104.0	96.3	119.7
西　药	Western Medicine	100.8	99.4	102.4	100.8	101.4	100.7
保健器具及用品	Health Apparatus and Goods	100.0	100.2	99.9	99.9	99.2	103.1
书报杂志及电子出版物类	**Books, Magazines and Electronic Publications**	**104.9**	**103.9**	**101.1**	**100.8**	**101.4**	**102.3**
教材及参考书	Texts and Reference Books	115.9	100.5	102.7	100.0	101.0	107.3
书报杂志	Newspapers and Magazines	100.3	111.1	99.8	102.3	104.8	100.0
电子音像制品	Electronic Audio and Video Products	103.2	97.6	100.0	100.0	97.5	94.0
燃料类	**Fuels**	**106.8**	**118.2**	**115.2**	**110.4**	**106.6**	**105.3**
煤炭及制品类	Coal and its Products	100.0	106.5	94.3	105.8	100.7	96.2
石油及制品类	Oil and its Products	107.3	123.7	118.5	111.4	110.0	110.6
建筑器材及五金电料类	**Building Apparatus and Hardware**	**100.0**	**102.6**	**101.3**	**100.9**	**102.9**	**102.8**
建筑装璜材料	Building Decoration Materials	100.8	103.1	102.8	101.3	104.3	102.5
五金电料类	Hardware and Electrical Apparatus	97.3	100.4	96.1	100.0	100.4	103.6

Continued

(preceding year=100)

昌吉市 Changji City	库尔勒市 Korla City	阿克苏市 Aksu City	焉耆回族自治县 Yanqi Hui Autonomous County	塔城市 Tacheng [Qoqek] City	阿勒泰市 Altay City	乌苏市 Usu City	博乐市 Bole [Bortala] City	吐鲁番市 Turpan City	库车县 Kuqa County	阿图什市 Artux City	莎车县 Shache [Yarkant] County	奎屯市 Kuytun City	石河子市 Shihezi City
96.9	**101.1**	**100.0**	**99.1**	**93.5**	**100.0**	**107.3**	**103.2**	**100.0**	**98.1**	**103.2**	**99.9**	**100.0**	**94.6**
100.3	**100.4**	**103.8**	**101.2**	**100.4**	**99.8**	**102.0**	**101.3**	**100.7**	**100.6**	**100.5**	**100.9**	**101.0**	**102.2**
99.4	100.7	104.2	98.1	100.3	99.4	104.3	99.4	100.3	101.0	99.8	101.0	100.2	102.5
98.4	100.0	104.8	97.2	100.0	100.0	100.0	104.1	100.0	100.0	100.0	105.2	103.3	101.5
102.2	100.4	104.6	106.0	102.1	99.7	101.8	102.4	101.8	100.0	101.2	99.6	100.0	103.9
98.7	100.0	102.5	100.0	100.0	100.0	100.4	100.0	100.0	101.4	100.3	100.8	101.0	98.4
97.8	**100.0**	**104.4**	**100.5**	**99.8**	**100.0**	**100.0**	**100.0**	**100.0**	**100.0**	**100.2**	**100.3**	**100.4**	**99.1**
99.5	100.0	100.0	101.3	100.0	100.0	100.0	100.0	100.0	100.0	100.3	100.5	100.1	102.9
96.1	100.0	106.3	99.5	99.6	100.0	100.0	100.0	100.0	100.0	100.0	100.0	100.7	94.9
95.7	**99.5**	**97.7**	**96.4**	**99.5**	**96.2**	**100.0**	**99.2**	**98.1**	**92.3**	**93.2**	**102.7**	**96.2**	**96.6**
96.2	99.9	100.0	100.0	99.5	99.9	100.0	100.0	100.5	95.8	100.3	106.6	100.0	98.5
95.2	98.6	94.6	94.9	99.6	93.0	100.0	98.2	96.7	88.6	87.0	100.0	93.5	93.9
99.9	**101.6**	**102.6**	**110.8**	**100.0**	**100.6**	**100.0**	**100.0**	**100.0**	**100.3**	**100.0**	**104.2**	**98.2**	**96.4**
98.5	**100.3**	**100.8**	**102.1**	**100.0**	**102.4**	**100.0**	**100.4**	**100.0**	**97.0**	**99.4**	**100.3**	**100.4**	**103.0**
108.6	**107.4**	**113.0**	**112.2**	**109.3**	**114.6**	**118.1**	**118.2**	**114.0**	**136.9**	**113.9**	**125.6**	**101.7**	**111.6**
103.2	**100.9**	**101.6**	**100.4**	**107.3**	**107.4**	**91.4**	**105.7**	**102.8**	**100.1**	**102.3**	**100.2**	**100.0**	**106.7**
100.0	101.9	110.6	97.1	100.9	100.0	100.0	100.2	124.9	106.4	100.0	100.0	100.0	115.0
109.1	102.6	101.7	102.7	110.5	120.2	91.6	116.1	101.6	96.8	106.2	102.5	101.3	116.0
99.9	99.8	101.0	99.3	105.1	100.6	89.1	100.0	100.2	101.8	99.6	99.2	99.9	101.7
103.1	100.0	100.6	100.2	102.3	100.1	100.0	105.1	99.9	99.2	106.0	100.2	97.8	101.4
100.5	**103.6**	**100.3**	**102.1**	**99.7**	**100.9**	**100.0**	**99.8**	**101.0**	**105.1**	**100.0**	**100.0**	**100.3**	**101.4**
100.6	108.0	100.9	103.6	100.0	100.0	100.0	99.5	100.0	112.4	100.0	100.0	101.1	101.3
100.7	103.2	100.0	100.0	99.4	102.2	100.0	100.0	102.6	102.9	100.0	100.0	100.0	101.5
100.0	100.0	100.0	100.0	99.5	100.0	100.0	100.0	100.0	100.0	100.0	100.0	100.0	101.2
105.8	**107.2**	**123.3**	**105.5**	**110.4**	**108.3**	**106.8**	**109.7**	**112.1**	**102.2**	**111.9**	**110.6**	**115.1**	**110.2**
94.7	99.6	114.9	100.9	98.5	102.8	94.1	96.0	116.2	98.9	96.1	108.6	100.0	99.0
108.7	110.1	126.1	108.5	115.0	112.2	118.3	116.4	108.2	106.9	116.0	111.6	124.3	113.8
104.4	**102.6**	**105.3**	**102.6**	**104.5**	**101.1**	**104.0**	**103.9**	**103.5**	**106.0**	**99.3**	**112.5**	**102.2**	**102.5**
106.0	103.0	105.3	103.1	105.8	100.9	107.1	105.3	105.2	112.7	98.8	115.5	102.3	102.8
99.3	101.8	105.1	101.1	89.8	101.8	100.0	101.1	100.0	99.2	100.0	102.8	101.6	102.0

7—6 农业生产资料价格指数

Price Indices of Agricultural Means of Production by Category

(上年=100) (preceding year=100)

指 标	Item	2000	2005	2009	2010
农业生产资料价格指数	**General Index**	**97.9**	**105.3**	**99.5**	**103.1**
农用手工工具	Farm-oriented Handwork Implemen	99.1	104.9	100.5	101.0
饲料类	Forage	93.5	101.3	110.4	114.0
产品畜	Animal for Products	94.4	89.4	108.4	127.1
半机械化农具	Semi-mechanized Farm Tools	97.8	100.9	100.7	101.7
机械化农具	Mechanized Farm Machinery	97.7	102.5	102.3	100.1
化学肥料	Chemical Fertilizer	92.8	110.2	93.2	95.3
农药及农药械	Pesticide and Its Appliances	98.5	102.8	105.4	101.7
农用机油	Oil for Farm Machinery	110.3	111.0	101.1	110.1
其他农业生产资料	Others General Index	98.4	105.5	96.1	100.7
农业生产服务	The Agriculture Produces Service			102.0	102.0

7—7 各市县农业生产资料价格指数

Price Indices of Agricultural Means of Production by Category in Cities and Counties

(上年=100) (2010年) (preceding year=100)

指 标	Item	全 区 Province	塔城市 Kashgar [Kaxgar] City	阿勒泰市 Altay City	乌苏市 Usu City	博乐市 Bole [Bortala] City	吐鲁番市 Turpan City	库车县 Kuqa County	阿图什市 Artux City	莎车县 Shache [Yarkant] County	焉耆回族自治县 Yanqi Hui Autonomous County
农业生产资料价格指数	**General Index**	**103.1**	**98.0**	**101.4**	**101.5**	**103.4**	**100.8**	**101.8**	**104.4**	**104.3**	**104.8**
农用手工工具	Farm-oriented Handwork Implemen	101.0	100.0	100.0	100.0	108.0	100.0	100.0	100.0	100.0	99.2
饲料类	Forage	114.0	109.3	106.3	112.0	118.0	92.9	136.7	111.5	113.0	117.1
产品畜	Animal for Products	127.1	127.2	103.8	101.4	113.3	110.2	88.5	119.3	152.7	108.2
半机械化农具	Semi-mechanized Farm Tools	101.7	99.4	100.0	100.0	100.0	100.0	100.0	100.0	102.9	100.0
机械化农具	Mechanized Farm Machinery	100.1	89.6	100.5	100.0	100.0	100.0	100.0	105.1	104.7	100.0
化学肥料	Chemical Fertilizer	95.3	95.9	98.3	94.5	100.5	100.5	91.1	99.5	86.5	103.9
农药及农药械	Pesticide and Its Appliances	101.7	94.9	103.2	102.3	100.4	100.0	100.0	100.0	102.6	105.7
农用机油	Oil for Farm Machinery	110.1	92.3	109.7	115.7	105.4	108.7	116.1	118.0	115.3	114.4
其他农业生产资料	Others General Index	100.7	94.7	100.2	98.0	98.8	99.8	90.8	101.5	104.7	100.1
农业生产服务	The Agriculture Produces Service	102.0	106.2	100.0	101.9	100.2	100.0	101.9	104.2	104.5	102.7

7—8 兵团农产品生产价格分类指数

EX-Factory Price Indices of Farm Products by Category of XPCCG

(上年=100) (preceding year=100)

指　　标	Item	2009	2010
农产品生产价格总指数	**General Farm Products Price Index**	**106.6**	**125.3**
种植业产品	Farm Products	106.1	128.2
谷物及其他作物	Cereal and Others	110.9	132.8
谷　物(原粮)	Cereal(Original Cereal)	107.7	110.3
小　麦	Tubers	103.5	102.3
稻　谷	Rice	106.7	126.9
玉　米	Corn	109.3	115.2
棉花(籽棉)	Cotton(seed)	110.5	137.6
细绒棉	Long-staple Cotton	110.5	137.6
甜　菜	Beetroots	100.7	113.2
蔬菜园艺作物	Vegetable and Horticulture Crop	96.8	114.5
蔬　菜	Vegetable	96.8	114.5
水果、坚果、饮料和香料	Fruit Nut Beverage and Spice Crop	95.8	118.5
水果、坚果	Fruit and Nut	95.8	118.5
园林水果	Horticulture Fruit	95.6	118.6
苹　果	Apple	95.4	122.0
香　梨	Snow Flake Peras	94.0	110.8
葡　萄	Grapes	100.3	122.8
瓜果类	Melon	99.1	116.4
西　瓜	Melon	99.7	121.4
甜　瓜	Muskmelon	98.8	113.3
牧业(畜产品)	Output Value of Animal Husbandry	100.9	108.6
牲畜饲养	Livestock Feeding	103.4	111.9
活牛(毛重)	Cattle and Buffaloes	104.5	103.3
活羊(毛重)	Sheep and Goats	102.3	113.7
牛　奶	Milk	105.6	114.7
绵羊毛	Sheep Wool	99.5	112.0
猪的饲养	Pork Feeding	95.7	103.1
活猪(毛重)	Pig	95.7	103.1
家禽的饲养	Poultry Feeding	105.1	108.6
鸡	Chicken	104.9	109.8
禽　蛋	Poultry Eggs	105.4	107.4
鸡　蛋	Egg	105.4	107.4
渔　业	Fishery	104.7	106.3
淡水鱼类	Classified by Kind	104.7	106.3
鲤　鱼	Carp	104.7	106.3

7—9 兵团各师农产品生产价格分类指数

Ex-Factory Price Indices of Farm Products by Category of XPCG by Division

（上年＝100）　　（2010 年）　　(preceding year＝100)

单位	Unit	农产品生产价格总指数 Ceneral Farm Products Price	种植业产品 Farm Products	谷物及其他作物 Cereal and Others	谷物 Cereal	棉花（籽棉） Cotton (seed)	甜菜 Beetroots	蔬菜园艺作物 Vegetable and Horticulture	蔬菜 Vegatable
兵团	**XPCG**	**125.3**	**128.2**	**132.8**	**110.3**	**137.6**	**113.2**	**114.5**	**114.5**
一师	Division 1	137.6	139.1	148.4	115.2	150.3		122.5	122.5
二师	Division 2	116.9	118.4	127.7	101.1	132.5	104.0	105.8	105.8
三师	Division 3	122.5	126.4	133.6	106.6	140.0		110.6	110.6
四师	Division 4	110.5	112.2	107.1	106.9	130.1	106.6	114.1	114.1
五师	Division 5	131.7	133.4	135.8	110.7	139.2	117.1	107.2	107.2
六师	Division 6	124.6	130.2	133.1	105.2	145.2		115.1	115.1
七师	Division 7	113.6	114.0	130.6	105.0	136.6	125.0	106.4	106.4
八师	Division 8	127.1	132.2	128.6	104.9	137.9		107.8	107.8
九师	Division 9	116.6	117.3	114.9	109.2		122.6	137.7	137.7
十师	Division 10	113.3	116.4	123.1	110.1	146.5	116.5	109.0	109.0
十二师	Division 12	125.9	133.2	116.5	108.3	142.0	103.3	116.0	116.0
十三师	Division 13	119.0	123.4	135.6	103.5	140.2		115.8	115.8
十四师	Division 14	93.3	91.9			129.0			

单位	Unit	水果、坚果、饮料和香料 Fruit Nut Beverage and Spice Crop	水果、坚果 Fruit and Nut	园林水果 Hurticulture Fruit	瓜果类 Melon	牧业（畜产品） Output Value of Animal	牲畜饲养 Livestock Feeding	活牛（毛重） Cattle and Buffaloes
兵团	**XPCG**	**118.5**	**118.5**	**118.6**	**116.4**	**108.6**	**111.9**	**103.3**
一师	Division 1	117.8	117.8	117.8		114.3	119.7	103.8
二师	Division 2	107.8	107.8	103.0	107.8	109.8	117.1	106.0
三师	Division 3	108.3	111.5	111.4		112.0	112.2	115.4
四师	Division 4	117.0	117.0	117.0	112.6	108.3	106.5	106.5
五师	Division 5	114.5	114.5	114.2		107.1	112.0	108.4
六师	Division 6	144.2	144.2	144.3	143.7	103.4	106.0	106.9
七师	Division 7	123.4	123.4	110.9	172.9	111.6	114.0	109.1
八师	Division 8	110.2	110.2	111.2	124.5	112.3	113.6	108.7
九师	Division 9	126.1	126.1	119.9	131.3	115.2	116.4	114.2
十师	Division 10	90.3	90.3	129.4	82.4	105.4	108.4	111.0
十二师	Division 12	117.6	117.6	127.7	117.3	109.7	113.2	106.1
十三师	Division 13	104.7	104.7		104.7	102.3	104.9	99.7
十四师	Division 14					106.4		

单位	Unit	活羊（毛重） Sheep and Goats	牛奶 Milk	绵羊毛 Sheep Wool	猪的饲养 Pork Feeding	家禽的饲养 Poultry Feeding	禽蛋 Poultry Eggs	渔业 Fishery	淡水鱼类 Classified by Kind
兵团	**XPCG**	**113.7**	**114.7**	**112.0**	**103.1**	**108.6**	**107.4**	**106.3**	**106.3**
一师	Division 1	117.8	131.4	101.8	101.4	103.9	103.1	108.7	108.7
二师	Division 2	119.8	110.9	160.9	102.8	109.1	112.5	107.1	107.1
三师	Division 3	110.9	102.8	102.6	109.5	105.2		104.5	104.5
四师	Division 4	112.2	111.5	103.6	103.2	109.6	108.1	109.0	109.0
五师	Division 5	109.1	112.2	118.6	100.9	105.0	104.3	104.0	104.0
六师	Division 6	106.5	113.5		100.0	107.7	107.2	104.9	104.9
七师	Division 7	115.4	116.2	102.5	107.6	108.8	111.0	109.6	109.6
八师	Division 8	114.3	114.6	105.7	105.3	106.2	108.0	118.0	118.0
九师	Division 9	115.9	116.2	128.7	105.9	108.7	107.5	100.8	100.8
十师	Division 10	112.0	106.0	104.0	102.0	101.7	101.2	103.7	103.7
十二师	Division 12	109.1	117.5	119.5	102.9	112.3	120.4	103.8	103.8
十三师	Division 13	106.8	108.2	92.9	95.2	104.5	105.2	108.6	108.6
十四师	Division 14								

7—10 工业品出厂价格分类指数

Ex-Factory Price Indices of Industrial Products by Category

（上年=100） (preceding year=100)

指 标	Item	1995	2000	2005	2009	2010
全部工业品	**Total Industrial Products**	**117.2**	**129.4**	**116.6**	**85.5**	**125.3**
轻工业	Light Industry	125.1	97.3	99.6	97.5	108.9
以农产品为原料	Using Farm Produces as Raw Materials	126.9	97.1	98.4	96.6	111.2
以非农产品为原料	Using Non-farm Produces as Raw Materials	113.2	103.5	101.9	99.9	104.6
重工业	Heavy Industry	110.0	141.8	122.5	83.3	128.7
采 掘	Mining and Quarrying	113.7	164.2	136.2	72.9	153.1
原 料	Raw Materials	108.2	114.3	114.2	93.4	114.0
加 工	Manufacturing	112.8	98.6	104.1	86.5	105.6
生产资料	Means of Production	112.2	138.0	118.4	84.5	127.1
采 掘	Mining and Quarrying	113.7	164.0	136.0	73.1	151.9
原 料	Raw Materials	111.2	113.7	114.3	93.4	115.1
加 工	Manufacturing	114.0	97.7	100.4	91.5	107.3
生活资料	Consumer Goods	124.6	96.6	101.3	98.5	104.1
食 品	Food	130.0	93.0	101.7	98.0	104.4
衣 着	Clothing	121.7	100.3	96.4	102.4	101.5
一般日用品	Articles for Daily Use	122.6	98.1	101.1	98.1	101.4
耐用消费品	Durable Consumer Goods	101.5	99.7	99.2	108	102.3
按工业行业分	**Grouped by Setors**					
冶金工业	Metallurgical Industry	100.8	103.9	101.9	78.6	114.4
电力工业	Power Industry	120.2	104.8	100.9	102.4	100.7
煤炭及炼焦工业	Coal and coking Industry	113.2	98.2	109.4	107.6	104.0
石油工业	Petroleum Industry	101.1	162.2	130.5	80.3	141.6
化学工业	Chemical Industry	133.3	102.6	106.1	89.5	112.1
机械工业	Machine Buiding Industry	105.5	97.4	112.4	99.9	97.4
建筑材料工业	Buiding Materials Industry	101.5	98.4	99.4	105.1	101.1
森林工业	Timber Industry	88.1	99.7	99.9	103.8	101.7
食品工业	Food Industry	130.0	92.2	101.1	98.0	104.9
纺织工业	Textile Industry	119.9	101.8	92.1	95.5	122.8
缝纫工业	Tailoring Industry		101.7	96.3	102.5	101.5
皮革工业	Leather Industry	123.6	95.7	100.0	99.4	101.1
造纸工业	Paper Industry	149.2	98.4	102.6	92.3	127.8
文教艺术用品工业	Cultural,Educational and Handicraft Articles	108.5	98.2	99.7	100.1	101.1
其他工业	Other Industry	157.1	98.8	104.0	101.2	107.7

7—11 兵团工业品出厂价格分类指数
Ex-Factory Price Indices of Industrial Products by Category of XPCG

（上年=100） (preceding year=100)

指　　标	Item	2009	2010
全部工业品	**Total Industrial Products**	**99.0**	**108.2**
轻工业	Light Industry	98.4	109.7
以农产品为原料	Using Farm Produces as Raw Materials	98.1	112.4
以非农产品为原料	Using Non-farm Produces as Raw Materials	99.9	100.8
重工业	Heavy Industry	101.9	104.9
采　掘	Mining and Quarrying	104.0	108.4
原　料	Raw Materials	101.6	104.8
加　工	Manufacturing	96.6	98.4
生产资料	Means of Production	97.7	109.5
采　掘	Mining and Quarrying	103.8	106.2
原　料	Raw Materials	101.6	104.9
加　工	Manufacturing	96.5	112.5
生活资料	Consumer Goods	103.2	104.5
食　品	Food	103.1	104.5
衣　着	Clothing	100.3	106.2
一般日用品	Articles for Daily Use	108.4	100.8
按工业行业分	**Grouped by Sector**		
煤炭开采和洗选业	Coal Mining and Dresing	104.7	100.1
有色金属矿采选业	Nonferrous Metals Mining and Dressing	87.0	132.3
非金属矿采选业	Nonmetal Mineral Mining and Dressing	115.1	102.6
农副食品加工业	Farm and Sideline Food Processing	102.3	116.0
食品制造业	Food Manufacturing	106.2	93.2
饮料制造业	Beverage Manufacturing	101.0	103.7
纺织业	Textile Industry	94.8	124.1
造纸及纸制品业	Paper Making and Paper Products	93.5	98.5
印刷业及记录媒介的复制	Printing Industry and Recording Media	100.2	100.0
文教体育用品制造业	Cultural,Educational and SportsProdrcts Manufacturing		100.0
石油加工、炼焦及核燃料加工业	Petroleum Processing,Coking and Nuclear Material Processing	100.7	106.2
化学原料及化学制品制造业	Chemical Materials and Chemical Products Manufacturing	102.9	105.2
医药制造业	Pharmaceuticals Manufacturing	100.0	105.4
塑料制品业	Plastic Products Manufacturing	88.0	99.7
非金属矿物制品业	Nonmetal Mineral Products Manufacturing	103.7	101.0
黑色金属冶炼及压延加工业	Ferrous Metals Smelting and Rolling	100.3	99.3
金属制品业	Matal Product Manufacturing	81.6	110.1
通用设备制造业	General Equipment Manufacturing	102.6	95.1
专用设备制造业	General Equipment Manufacturing	100.0	100.1
电力、热力的生产和供应业	Electricity and Heat Production and Supply	103.8	102.0
燃气的生产和供应业	Gas Production and Supply	100.0	100.0
水的生产和供应业	Water Production and Supply	109.5	99.5

7—12 原材料、燃料及动力购进价格分类指数

Purchasing Price Indices of Raw Materials, Fuels and Power Purchased by Category

（上年＝100） (preceding year＝100)

指　　标	Iterm	1995	2000	2005	2009	2010
全部原材料价格指数	**Total of Raw Material**	**116.9**	**115.2**	**110.7**	**90.6**	**123.9**
燃料、动力类	Fuels and Power	117.0	137.9	132.0	82.0	137.6
黑色金属材料类	Materials of Ferrous Metals	96.1	100.5	113.8	82.6	105.0
# 钢　材	Rolled Steel	96.1	104.8	112.9	85.3	102.5
其　他	Other	96.5	95.5	114.9	77.3	112.3
有色金属材料和电线类	Materials of Non-Ferrous Metal and wires	125.1	112.2	108.5	78.5	139.6
化工原料类	Chemical Raw Materials	125.4	104.4	113.0	100.0	106.8
木材及纸浆类	Wood and Paper Pulp	100.9	100.5	102.0	98.9	104.0
建筑材料及非金属矿类	Building Materials and Non-metal Ore	95.5	100.4	103.9	105.8	103.0
其他工业原材料及半成品类	Other Industrial Raw Materials and Semi-finished Category	103.2	111.4	105.5	97.7	101.1
农副产品类	Agricultural and Side-line Produces	152.0	97.2	91.9	99.3	118.7
纺织原料类	Textile Raw Materials	125.1	95.2	93.0	96.1	144.2

7—13 固定资产投资价格指数

Price Indices of Investment in Fixed Assets

（上年＝100） (preceding year＝100)

指　　标	Item	1995	2000	2005	2009	2010
固定资产投资	**Investment in Fixed Assets**	**106.2**	**103.6**	**102.8**	**98.0**	**104.6**
建筑安装工程	**Construction and Installation**	**105.1**	**105.5**	**102.7**	**98.1**	**105.9**
直接工程费	Expenses of Direct Project	105.2	105.5	102.7		
# 人工费	Manpower Expenses	120.1	108.2	103.8	109.1	110.6
材料费	Material Expenses	102.3	104.9	102.3	92.8	104.8
# 钢　材	Rolled Steel	96.3	108.3	101.7	86.0	104.4
木　材	Timber	106.8	102.2	102.5	101.6	104.8
水　泥	Cement	109.7	100.6	100.1	100.5	104.7
地方材料	Local Materials	103.4	102.8	102.0	97.7	104.6
化工材料	Chemical Materials		107.4	109.1	95.1	104.9
电　料	Electrical Wire		99.2	104.0	95.5	105.1
其他材料	Other Materials	92.8	102.9	99.9	99.6	101.7
机械使用费	Expenses of Machine Use		104.4	102.3	101.9	103.3
间接费用	Indirect Expense	104.8	105.3			
设备工器具	**Purchase of Equipment, Tools and Instruments**	**112.7**	**97.4**	**104.8**	**95.0**	**100.4**
其他费用	**Others**	**125.0**	**103.2**	**100.0**	**103.5**	**105.2**

7—14 建筑安装工程价格指数

Price Indices of Construction and Installation Engineering

（上年=100） (preceding year=100)

指　　标	Item	1995	2000	2005	2009	2010
建筑安装工程价格总指数	**General Drice Index**	**105.1**	**105.5**	**102.7**	**98.1**	**105.9**
直接费用价格指数	Price Indices of Direct Expenses	105.2	105.5	102.7		
# 人工费	Labour Cost	120.1	108.2	103.8	109.1	110.6
材料费	Materials	102.3	104.9	102.3	92.8	104.8
机械费用费	Machinery Use Expenses		104.4	102.3	101.9	103.3
间接费用价格指数	Price Indices of Indirect Expenses	104.8	105.3			

7—15 房屋销售价格指数

Sale Price Indices of Houses

（上年=100） （2010年） (preceding year=100)

指　　标	Item	一季度 First Quarter	二季度 Second Quarter	三季度 Third Quarter	四季度 Fourth Quarter
房屋销售价格指数	**Sale Price Indices of Houses**	**106.8**	**107.5**	**107.4**	**108.3**
新建房	New Constraction Houses	107.0	108.2	108.2	108.6
住　宅	Residential Buildings	106.9	107.9	108.0	108.5
经济适用房	Economical Houses	99.5	100.0	100.0	100.0
普通住宅	General Residential Buildings	107.5	108.4	108.5	108.8
多层住宅	Multilayer Buildings	106.5	108.5	109.9	110.8
高层住宅	High-layer Buildings	108.5	108.8	108.1	107.9
高档住宅	Upscale Residential Buildings	98.9	105.2	106.5	118.0
非住宅	Non-Residential Buildings	108.5	113.8	111.7	110.4
办公楼	Office Buildings	111.1	127.4	124.3	122.0
商业用房	Houses for Business Use	110.1	113.8	111.6	110.3

2011 BING TUAN

第八篇

人民生活

Chapter 8 People's Livelihood

简要说明

一、本篇资料主要内容

本篇资料反映兵团人民生活现状及发展变化情况，分为城镇居民生活和农牧团场农牧工家庭生活两部分。

二、本篇资料来源

城镇居民生活状况数据来源于国家统计局兵团调查总队住户调查处城镇住户抽样调查，调查内容主要包括家庭人口及其构成、家庭现金收支、主要商品购买数量及支出金额、劳动就业状况、居住状况和耐用消费品拥有量等。

农牧团场农牧工家庭生活状况数据来源于国家统计局兵团调查总队住户调查处农牧团场农牧工住户抽样调查，调查内容包括农牧团场农牧工家庭基本情况、家庭现金收支、劳动力就业状况、居住状况、主要消费品消费量、耐用消费品拥有量等。

三、本篇调查方法

统计调查方法为抽样调查。

Brief Introduction

1. Main Contents

Data in this chapter show the conditions and development of people's livelihood in XPCG, consisting of two parts on the life of urban and farm households respectively.

2. Sources of Data

Data on the livelihood of the urban residents in this chapter come from the data collected through sample survey on the urban households by the Household Survey Section of the Society and Economy Investigation Brigade of XPCG. The main content of the survey includes household population and its composition, cash income and expenditure of the household, quantity and expenditure on major commodities purchased, labor employment, the housing condition and the possession of durable consumer goods.

Data on the livelihood of the farm residents come from data collected through the sample survey on farm households by the Household Survey Section of Survey Office of the National Bureau of Statistics of XPCG. The main content of the survey includes the basic condition of the farm households, cash income and expenditure of the household, labor employment, the housing condition, consumption of major consumer goods and the quantity of durable consumer goods owned.

3. Methodology of Survey

Survey method is sampled one.

8—1 城镇居民家庭生活基本情况

Basic Living Conditions of Urban Households

（抽样调查 Sampled Survey）

指 标	Item	2009	2010
调查户数(户)	**Number of Households Surveyed(household)**	**580**	**580**
平均每户家庭人口(人)	**Average Household Size (person)**	**2.78**	**2.78**
平均每户就业人口(人)	**Average Number of Employed Persons per Household(person)**	**1.45**	**1.54**
平均每人居住建筑面积(平方米)	**Per Capita Residence Floor Space of Building(sq. m)**	**29.94**	**29.53**
平均每人全部年收入(元)	**Per Capita Annual Income(yuan)**	**14 469.93**	**16 266.06**
# 可支配收入	Disposable Income	12 929.37	14 559.10
工资性收入	Income of Wages and Salaries	11 379.44	12 987.31
经营净收入	Net Income from Management	407.64	575.35
财产性收入	Property Income	246.66	127.36
转移性收入	Transfer Income	2 436.19	2 576.04
平均每人消费性支出(元)	**Per Capita Annual Living Expenditures for Consumption(yuan)**	**9 697.61**	**11 792.53**
食 品	Food	3 140.50	3 504.60
衣 着	Clothing	1 178.88	1 342.85
居 住	Residence	976.52	1 511.48
家庭设备用品及服务	Household Facilities, Articles and Service	599.06	985.33
医疗保健	Medicine and Medical Service	854.98	875.00
交通通讯	Transport, Post and Communication Services	1 204.67	1 726.43
教育文化娱乐服务	Education, Cultural and Recreation Services	1 340.34	1 454.34
其他商品和服务	Other Goods and Services	402.66	392.50
平均每人消费性支出构成	**Composition of Per Capita Annual Living**	**100.00**	**100.00**
(人均消费支出=100)	**(Per Capita Annual Living Expenditures for Consumption=100)**		
食 品	Food	32.38	29.72
衣 着	Clothing	12.16	11.39
居 住	Residence	10.07	12.82
家庭设备用品及服务	Household Facilities, Articles and Service	6.18	8.35
医疗保健	Medicine and Medical Service	8.82	7.42
交通通讯	Transport, Post and Communication Services	12.42	14.64
教育文化娱乐服务	Education, Cultural and Recreation Services	13.82	12.33
其他商品和服务	Other Goods and Services	4.15	3.33

8—2 城镇居民家庭年人均购买主要商品数量

Per Capita Major Commodities Purchased by Urban Households Annually

(抽样调查 Sampled Survey)

指　　标	Item	2009	2010
大米(千克)	Rice(kg)	29.78	31.42
面粉(千克)	Flour(kg)	19.90	18.03
食用植物油(千克)	Edible Vegetable Oil(kg)	10.42	9.88
猪肉(千克)	Pork(kg)	14.49	13.87
牛肉(千克)	Beef(kg)	2.35	2.64
羊肉(千克)	Mutton(kg)	2.45	2.30
鸡(千克)	Chicken(kg)	7.57	7.26
鸭(千克)	Duck(kg)	1.07	0.95
鲜蛋(千克)	Fresh Eggs(kg)	8.91	9.02
鱼(千克)	Fish(kg)	6.60	6.21
虾(千克)	Shrimp(kg)	0.66	0.65
鲜菜(千克)	Fresh Vegetables(kg)	109.66	108.07
白酒(千克)	Liquor(kg)	1.56	1.55
果酒(千克)	Fruit Wine(kg)	0.30	0.25
啤酒(千克)	Beer(kg)	3.17	3.12
碳酸饮料(千克)	Aerated beverages(kg)	2.07	1.94
鲜果(千克)	Fresh Fruits(kg)	37.43	32.74
鲜瓜(千克)	Fresh Melons(kg)	30.12	23.43
糕点(千克)	Cake(kg)	5.46	4.97
鲜乳品(千克)	Milk(kg)	17.88	16.11
奶粉(千克)	Milk Powder(kg)	0.33	0.26
酸奶(千克)	Yogurt(kg)	3.79	3.32
服装(件)	Clothing(piece)	7.02	6.53
鞋(双)	Shoes(pair)	2.40	2.38
水(吨)	Water(ton)	29.82	30.32
电(千瓦时)	Electricity(kwh)	239.69	247.70
煤炭(千克)	Coal(kg)	42.67	50.24
罐装液化石油气(千克)	Bottle Packs Liquefied Petrolum Gas(kg)	18.45	13.86
管道天然气(立方米)	Pipe Natural Gas(stere)	11.72	23.32

8—3 城镇居民家庭平均每百户年底耐用消费品拥有量

Possession of Durable Consumer Goods Owned Per-100 Urban Households at Year-end in Urban Households

（抽样调查 Sampled Survey）

指标	Item	2009	2010
摩托车(辆)	Motorcycle(unit)	33.07	33.39
助力车(辆)	Helping Hand Car(unit)	19.01	16.85
家用汽车(辆)	Automobile(unit)	6.03	8.41
洗衣机(台)	Washing Machine(set)	88.25	89.90
电冰箱(台)	Refrigerator(set)	75.74	78.36
彩色电视机(台)	Color Television Set(set)	107.56	108.36
家用电脑(台)	Computer(set)	51.44	55.00
组合音响(套)	Hi-Fi Stereo Component System(set)	23.06	23.31
摄像机(架)	Pickup Camera(set)	5.17	5.19
照相机(架)	Camera(set)	32.15	34.28
钢琴(架)	Piano(set)	2.11	2.48
其他中高档乐器(件)	Other Medium and High Grade Musical Instrument(piece)	5.39	7.03
微波炉(台)	Oven(set)	30.46	31.03
空调器(台)	Air Conditioner(set)	12.33	12.28
淋浴热水器(台)	Shower(set	64.79	65.69
消毒碗柜(台)	Disinfection Cupboard(set)	3.80	3.73
洗碗机(台)	Dishwasher(set)	0.80	0.41
健身器材(套)	Healthy Equipment(set)	3.00	2.94
固定电话(部)	Telephone(set)	78.86	78.95
移动电话(部)	Mobile Telephone(set)	152.17	161.21

8—4 各师(市)城镇居民家庭年人均收支情况

Per Capita Annual Income and Expendture of Urban Households by Division and City

计量单位:元　　（2010 年）　　(yuan)

单位	Unit	家庭总收入 Households Gross Income	可支配收入 Disposable Income	家庭总支出 Households Gross Expenditure	消费性支出 Expenditure for Consumption
兵团	**XPCG**	**16 266.06**	**14 559.10**	**17 310.65**	**11 792.53**
一师	Division 1	16 194.43	14 925.84	18 995.17	11 181.88
二师	Division 2	17 365.62	14 996.79	17 457.05	13 808.74
三师	Division 3	16 030.93	13 740.24	18 222.22	12 748.50
四师	Division 4	16 298.99	14 509.99	20 114.70	13 223.88
五师	Division 5	16 262.12	14 018.90	13 948.69	9 659.72
六师	Division 6	14 851.24	13 979.23	13 957.49	11 408.51
七师	Division 7	16 996.95	14 987.09	15 033.38	11 097.38
八师	Division 8	16 768.41	15 043.30	14 683.66	10 885.12
九师	Division 9	15 734.99	13 923.78	16 946.27	9 938.85
十师	Division 10	16 045.76	13 651.01	16 245.29	11 067.96
建工师	Contrction Division	18 991.24	15 969.14	23 505.93	13 470.84
十二师	Division 12	15 868.27	14 075.64	17 168.75	11 354.60
十三师	Division 13	17 266.10	14 936.78	18 857.95	10 989.85
十四师	Division 14	17 896.95	14 548.64	15 513.12	9 438.19
石河子市	Shihezi City	16 768.41	15 043.30	14 683.66	10 885.12
五家渠市	Alaer City	14 851.24	13 979.23	13 957.49	11 408.51
阿拉尔市	Tumushuke City	15 258.09	14 721.79	18 507.38	11 520.22
图木舒克市	Wujiaqu City	15 645.34	13 419.28	18 393.49	12 770.03

注:一师数据包含阿拉尔市,三师数据包含图木舒克市,六师数据包含五家渠市,八师数据包含石河子市。

Note:Data of Division 1 included Alaer City,data of division 3 included Tumushuke City,data of Division 6 included Wujiaqu City,data of Division 8 included Shihezi City.

8—5 农牧团场农牧工家庭基本情况

Basic Conditions of Farm Households

(抽样调查 Sampled Survey)

指　　标	Item	2009	2010
调查户数(户)	**Number of Households Surveyed (household)**	**720**	**720**
调查户常住人口(人)	**Number of Residents Residents Surveyed (person)**	**2 359**	**2 286**
调查户劳动力总人数(人)	**Number of Laborers per Household (person)**	**1 469**	**1 514**
平均每户常住人口(人)	Average Number of Permanent Residents per Household(person)	3.40	3.27
平均每户整半劳动力(含本人)(人)	Average Number of Laborers per Household(Including oneself)(person)	2.10	2.16
户均经营耕地面积(亩)	Per Household Area of Cultivated Land Managed(mu)	64.92	63.50
平均每人经营耕地面积(亩)	Per capita Area of Cultivated Land Managed(mu)	19.09	19.42
总收入	**Total Revenue(yuan)**	**30 427.48**	**39 502.82**
工资性收入	Wages Income	945.89	928.92
家庭经营收入	Household Business Income	28 713.24	37 561.77
财产性收入	Property Income	154.15	250.78
转移性收入	Transfer Income	614.20	761.35
总支出(元)	**Total Expenditure(yuan)**	**29 231.13**	**39 765.50**
# 家庭经营费用支出	Expenditure for Household Business	20 776.76	27 718.51
购置生产性固定资产支出	Purchasing Productive Fixed Assets	559.00	726.07
生活消费支出	Expenditure for Consumption	5 154.98	7 175.62
转移性和财产性支出	Expenditure for Transfer and Property	1 017.26	1 439.51
人均年纯收入(元)	**Per capita Aet Income(yuan)**	**7 668.71**	**8 782.55**
工资收入	Wages Income	945.89	928.92
家庭经营收入	Household Business Income	5 966.97	6 874.16
财产性收入	Property Income	154.15	250.78
转移性收入	Transfer Income	601.70	728.69
现金收入(元)	**Cash Income(yuan)**	**30 431.96**	**39 362.96**
工资收入	Wages Income	943.50	925.78
家庭经营收入	Household Business Income	28 828.07	37 622.14
财产性收入	Property Income	49.64	59.82
转移性收入	Transfer Income	610.75	755.22
现金支出(元)	**Cash Expenditure(yuan)**	**29 128.19**	**39 719.03**
# 家庭经营费用支出	Expenditure for Household Business	20 730.91	27 705.65
购置生产性固定资产支出	Purchasing Productive Fixed Assets	559.00	726.07
生活消费支出	Expenditure for Consumption	5 115.04	7 143.36
转移性和财产性支出	Expenditure for Transfer and Property	1 016.89	1 438.48
住房面积(平方米/人)	**Per capita Floor Space of Residence(sq. m/person)**	**23.94**	**25.78**
# 楼房面积	Storied Building	1.77	3.25
砖瓦平房面积	Tile Bungalow	13.01	16.04
其　他	Others	9.16	6.49
住房结构(平方米/人)	**Structure of Residence(sq. m/person)**		
# 钢筋混泥土结构面积	Steel reinforced concrete	4.96	6.31
砖木结构面积	Brick and wood	12.56	14.61
其　他	Others	6.42	4.86

注:团场住户资料为抽样调查数据,统计范围为抽中团场连队住户家庭情况。
Note: Data on farm households are sampled survey and the statstical scope refers to conditions of farm worker households surveyed.

8—6 农牧团场农牧工住户人均总收入、纯收入及构成

Per Capita Annual Gross and Net Income and It's Composition of Farm Households

计量单位:元 (抽样调查 Sampled Survey) (yuan)

指 标	Item	2009	2010	构成(%) Composition 2009	构成(%) Composition 2010
全年总收入	**Annual Gross Income**	**30 427.48**	**39 502.82**	**100.0**	**100.0**
工资性收入	Wages Income	945.89	928.92	3.1	2.4
家庭经营收入	Household business income	28 713.24	37 561.77	94.4	95.1
财产性收入	Property Income	154.15	250.78	0.5	0.6
转移性收入	Transfer Income	614.20	761.35	2.0	1.9
全年总支出	**Annual Gross Expenditure**	**29 231.13**	**39 765.50**	**100.0**	**100.0**
# 家庭经营费用支出	Expenditure for Household Business	20 776.76	27 718.51	71.1	69.7
生活消费支出	Expenditure for Consumption	5 154.98	7 175.62	17.6	18.0
全年纯收入	**Annual Net Income**	**7 668.71**	**8 782.55**	**100.0**	**100.0**
工资性收入	Wages Income	945.89	928.92	12.3	10.6
家庭经营收入	Household Business Income	5 966.97	6 874.16	77.8	78.3
财产性纯收入	Property Income	154.15	250.78	2.0	2.8
转移性纯收入	Transfer Income	601.70	728.69	7.9	8.3
全年可支配收入	**Annual Disposable Income**	**6 663.95**	**7 375.70**	**100.0**	**100.0**

8—7 农牧团场农牧工住户人均生活消费支出及构成

Per Capita Annual Living Expenditure and It's Composition of Farm Households

计量单位:元 (抽样调查 Sampled Survey) (yuan)

指 标	Item	2009	2010	构成(%) Composition 2009	构成(%) Composition 2010
生活消费支出	**Expenditure of Services**	**5 154.98**	**7 175.62**	**100.0**	**100.0**
# 服务性支出	Expenditure for Consumption	1 860.00	2 204.28	36.1	30.7
食 品	Food	1 594.45	1 916.74	30.9	26.7
# 主 食	Staple Food	417.28	472.99	26.2	6.6
副 食	Non-Staple Food	510.69	642.98	32.0	9.0
衣 着	Clothing	360.66	488.98	7.0	6.8
居 住	Residence	775.54	1 484.30	15.0	20.7
家庭设备、用品及服务	Household Facilities, Articles and Services	254.35	401.77	4.9	5.6
交通和通讯	Transportation and Communications	790.37	1 232.81	15.3	17.2
文教娱乐用品及服务	Cultural, Education and Recreation Services	849.33	969.86	16.5	13.5
医疗保健	Medicines and Medical Services	401.75	484.32	7.8	6.8
其他商品和服务	Other Commodities and Services	128.53	196.84	2.5	2.7

8—8 农牧团场农牧工住户人均现金收入

Per Capita Income in Cash of Farm Household

计量单位:元　　(抽样调查 Sampled Survey)　　(yuan)

指　标	Item	2009	2010
期内现金收入	**Annual Total Income In Cash**	**30 431.96**	**39 362.96**
工资性收入	Wages Income	943.50	925.78
在非企业组织中劳动得到收入	From Non-enterprise Organization	165.34	212.66
在本乡地域内劳动得到收入	From Local	755.10	701.70
# 在企业中劳动得到收入	Form Local Enterprise	406.88	363.11
# 在国家投资基建项目得到收入	From Item of State Capital Constructuon Investment	0.13	0.32
# 提供其他劳务收入	From Others	348.09	338.27
外出从业得到收入	Out of Migrant Workers	23.06	11.42
家庭经营现金收入	Income of Household Business cash	28 828.07	37 622.14
第一产业	Primary Industry	28 743.02	37 531.41
农　业	Agriculture	27 999.84	36 769.73
# 出售农产品收入	Income From Farm Product Sales	27 543.78	36 250.39
林　业	Forestry	24.82	3.40
# 出售林业产品收入	Income from Forestry product Sales	19.04	2.43
牧　业	Animal Husbandry	718.36	758.28
# 出售牧业产品收入	Income from Livestock product Sales	718.23	757.65
第二产业	Secondary Industry	1.93	5.45
第三产业	Tertiary Industry	83.12	85.28
# 第三产业服务性现金收入	Tertiary Industry Service Cash Income	83.07	85.28
交通、运输、邮电业	Transport, Postal and Telecommunications Services	22.77	26.04
批零贸易业、餐饮业	Wholesale, Retail Sale and Catering Services	41.53	47.57
社会服务业	Social Services	0.33	3.68
文教卫生业	Cultural, Education, and Health Services	2.81	2.63
其他行业	Others	15.64	5.36
财产性收入	Property Income	49.64	59.82
转移性收入	Transfer Income	610.75	755.22
非收入现金所得	**Non-income Gain**	**4 866.83**	**8 182.92**
非借贷性现金所得	Non-Loan Gain	294.35	290.66
# 保险赔款	Insurance Reparations	9.38	7.65
出售财物	Property Sales	120.56	100.09
借贷性现金所得	Loan cash Gain	4 572.48	7 838.26
银行、信用社贷款	Loan of Banks and Credit cooperatives	1 919.04	2 822.91
借入款	Borrowed Money	736.58	924.91
收回借出款	Loaned Money Recovery	105.44	143.51
取回存款	Deposit Withdrawal	1 757.46	3 887.49
收回其他投资款	Other Investment Money Recovery	3.84	14.87
其　他	Others	50.12	44.57

8－9 农牧团场农牧工住户家庭平均每百户耐用消费品拥有量

Possession of Durable Consumer Goods Owned by Per-100 Farm Households

（抽样调查 Sampled Survey）

指　　标	Item	2009	2010
洗衣机(台)	Washing Machine (set)	82	89
电冰箱(台)	Refrigerator (set)	41	54
空调机(台)	Air Conditioner (unit)	2	1
热水器(台)	Water-heater(set)	22	29
抽油烟机(台)	Smoke Absorber(unit)	18	25
摩托车(辆)	Motorcycle	85	82
电话机(部)	Telephone(unit)	80	71
移动电话(部)	Mobile Telephone(unit)	120	92
黑白电视机(台)	Black and White TV (set)	1	
彩色电视机(台)	Color TV (set)	103	99
# 接入有线电视网的	Connect into the Cable TV	92	89
影碟机	Video-disc (set)	35	28
照相机(架)	Camera (set)	7	8
家用计算机(台)	Household-use Computer(set)	10	15
# 接入互联网的	Connect into the Internet	7	11

8－10 农牧团场农牧工住户居民人均食品消费量

Per Capita Consumption of Food of Farm Households

（抽样调查 Sampled Survey）

指　　标	Item	2009	2010
粮食消费量(公斤)	Grain(kg)	145.18	156.82
蔬菜及菜制品消费(公斤)	Fresh Vegetable and Manofacture of Vegetable(kg)	61.56	65.99
油脂类消费量(公斤)	Edible Oil(kg)	11.20	11.38
豆制品消费量(公斤	Bean Ware(kg)	1.69	3.26
瓜果类消费量(公斤)	Melon fruits(kg)	34.10	29.35
猪牛羊肉消费量(公斤)	Pork, and Mutton(kg)	12.69	13.22
家禽、其他肉禽及制品消费量(公斤)	Poultry and Manufacture of Poultry(kg)	5.71	7.26
蛋、奶类及其制品消费量(公斤)	Eggs, Milk and Related Products(kg)	9.82	10.90
水产品消费量(公斤)	Apuatic Products(kg)	3.44	3.99
食糖消费量(公斤)	Sugar(kg)	0.89	0.91
酒类消费量(元)	Liquor(yuan)	8.30	9.96

8—11 农牧团场农牧工住户人均出售产品情况

Per Capita Products Sales of Farm Households

(抽样调查 Sampled Survey)

指　　标	Item	2009 数量(公斤) Quantity (kg)	2009 金额(元) sum (yuan)	2010 数量(公斤) Quantity (kg)	2010 金额(元) sum (yuan)
谷　物	Cereal	1 486. 32	2 663. 81	1 458. 85	2 503. 99
豆　类	Pulse	102. 37	368. 81	81. 01	329. 98
棉　花	Cotton	3 532. 34	20 161. 98	3 142. 08	27 050. 18
油　料	Oil Bearing Crops	148. 36	580. 24	154. 01	710. 88
甜　菜	Beetroots	875. 33	249. 96	1 390. 26	505. 74
蔬　菜	Vegetables	308. 04	317. 09	230. 97	304. 76
瓜　类	Melons	209. 28	192. 87	351. 32	283. 61
园林水果	Fruit	328. 57	673. 46	333. 98	958. 92
专用农产品	Special Farming Procucts		1 974. 58		3 264. 16
# 酱用西红柿	Tomato for Catsup	2 440. 48	766. 10	2 902. 47	2 440. 48
打　瓜	Seed Melons	99. 13	965. 11	121. 87	1 404. 14
肉猪及猪肉总重量	Pigand Pork	26. 06	367. 59	27. 93	456. 35
菜羊及羊肉总重量	Sheep, Goats and Mutton	7. 65	184. 65	4. 94	159. 72
肉牛及牛肉总重量	Cattle, Buffaloesand Beef	1. 43	34. 36	1. 67	47. 68
家禽总重量	Poultry	0. 38	5. 16	0. 18	2. 75
蛋　类	Poultry Eggs	0. 04	0. 34	0. 01	0. 20
奶　类	Milk	2. 05	4. 17		
仔、幼、育肥畜禽和小动物	Infant, Young and Fatlerned Livestock and small Snimals		115. 54		80. 20
其他牧业产品	Other Animal Procucts		0. 22		1. 15

8—12 各师农牧团场农牧工住户人均纯收入

Per Capita Net Income of Farm Households by Division

计量单位:元　　(2010 年)　　(yuan)

单　位	Unit	全年纯收入 Annual Net Income	工资性收入 Wages-Income	家庭经营收入 Hoesehold Business Income	财产性收入 Property Income	转移性收入 Transfer Income	全年可支配收入 Annual Disposable Income
兵　团	**XPCG**	**8 782. 55**	**928. 92**	**6 874. 16**	**250. 78**	**728. 69**	**7 375. 70**
一　师	Division 1	10 875. 15	314. 58	10 062. 42	202. 69	295. 46	9 446. 49
二　师	Division 2	10 101. 90	835. 52	8 611. 63	157. 69	497. 06	8 688. 54
三　师	Division 3	8 219. 16	122. 64	8 032. 04	64. 48		8 079. 40
四　师	Division 4	7 555. 62	1 025. 94	5 474. 44	525. 32	529. 92	5 755. 54
五　师	Division 5	9 327. 91	1 018. 91	8 058. 62	34. 58	215. 80	7 540. 98
六　师	Division 6	9 026. 45	1 317. 61	6 105. 54	344. 07	1 259. 23	6 380. 26
七　师	Division 7	9 569. 44	488. 63	8 857. 42	1. 13	222. 26	8 462. 84
八　师	Division 8	10 211. 40	1 652. 61	7 165. 04	360. 51	1 033. 24	8 652. 72
九　师	Division 9	6 870. 34	585. 86	4 432. 08	26. 75	1 825. 65	5 923. 48
十　师	Division 10	7 777. 38	1 567. 56	5 379. 81	234. 13	595. 88	5 735. 92
十 二 师	Division 12	8 053. 47	1 852. 01	4 799. 07	15. 36	1 387. 03	6 174. 03
十 三 师	Division 13	8 680. 90	1 071. 70	6 397. 56	932. 94	278. 70	7 985. 72
十 四 师	Division 14	5 154. 68	106. 86	3 237. 85	138. 61	1 671. 36	5 154. 68

2011

BING TUAN

第九篇

农　业

Chapter 9 Agriculture

简要说明

一、本篇资料主要内容

本篇资料反映兵团农业生产和农牧团经济基本情况。主要内容包括农场劳动力、耕地资源、农业机械拥有量、农林牧渔业总产值、主要农产品产量、农牧团场基本情况和乡镇企业基本情况等统计资料。

二、本篇统计范围

包括全社会除农业科研机构进行的农业生产以外的所有农业生产内容。如各种专业性农、林、牧、渔场的农业生产活动；兵团各级机关、团体、学校进行的农业生产活动；集体所有制农场农业生产活动；工矿企业经营的农、林、牧、渔业生产活动；以及农牧团场各种经济组织、农户经营的农林牧渔业生产活动和农工家庭兼营的商品性工业生产活动等。

1.农业:指对各种农作物的种植活动。包括谷物、豆类、薯类、棉花、油料、糖料、麻类、烟叶、蔬菜、园艺作物、水果、坚果、饮料和香料作物、中草药及其他作物的种植。

2.林业:包括林木的栽培(不包括茶园、桑园和果园的栽培、管理和收获等活动),木材和竹材的采运,林产品的采集。

3.牧业：包括牲畜饲养和放牧、家禽饲养。

4.渔业：包括水生动物的养殖和捕捞。

5.农、林、牧、渔服务业:指对农、林、牧、渔业生产活动进行的各种支持性服务。但不包括各种科学技术和专业性技术服务活动。

三、本篇资料来源

本篇资料由国家统计局兵团调查总队农业调查处根据《兵团农林牧渔业统计报表制度》收集、汇总、整理、提供。

四、本篇调查方法

统计调查方法为全面统计。

Brief Introduction

1. Main Contents

Data in this chapter reflect the basic conditions of agricultural production and farm economy of XPCG. Contents mainly include farm labor force, resources of cultivated land, farming machinery possession, total output value of farming, forestry, animal husbandry and fishery, output of major farming products, farms and township enterprises.

2. Scope of Statistics

The statistical scope includes all agricultural production contents except for agricultural production of agricultural scientific research institutions, such as production activities of farms specializing in farming, forestry, animal husbandry and fishery; production activities of administrative agencies, institutions and schools, production activities of collective farms run by townships and villages; production activities of farming, forestry, animal husbandry and fishery run by industrial and mining enterprises; and production activities of farming, forestry, animal husbandry, and fishery undertaken by rural economic units of various types and by households, and commercial industrial activities Undertaken by rural households as sideline production.

2.1. Agriculture: refers to cultivation of farm crops, including cereals, beans, tuber crops, cotton, oil-bearing crops, sugar crops, hemp, tobacco leaves, vegetables, gardening plants, fruits, nuts, crops for beverages and spices, medicinal herbs and other farm crops.

2.2. Forestry: includes the planting of trees (excluding the operations of planting, management and harvesting on tea plantations, mulberry fields and orchards), cutting and transport of timber and bamboo and collection of forest products.

2.3. Animal husbandry: includes the raising and grazing of domestic animals and poultry.

2.4. Fishery: includes cultivation and catching of aquatic animals.

2.5. Services in support of agriculture, forestry, animal husbandry and fishery: include supporting services to production activities in agriculture, forestry, animal husbandry and fishery but do not include activities of science and technology and professional services.

3. Sources of Data

Data in this chapter are collected and prepared by the Agriculture Survey Section of Survey Office of XPCG of National Bureau of Statistics China according to the Comprehensive Statistical Reporting Form System on Farming , Forestry, Animal Husbandry and Fishery of XPCG.

4. Methodology of Survey

Survey method is comprehensive statistics.

9－1 各师国有农林牧渔场基本情况

Basic Statistics of State-owned Farms by Division

（2010 年）

指 标 Item	合 计 Total	一 师 Division 1	二 师 Division 2	三 师 Division 3	四 师 Division 4	五 师 Division 5	六 师 Division 6	七 师 Division 7
团场总数(个) Total Regiment Farms(unit)	**176**	**16**	**18**	**18**	**21**	**11**	**19**	**10**
农 场 Number of Farms	165	16	18	16	19	11	18	10
林 场 Number of Forest Farms								
牧 场 Number of Ranch	11			2	2		1	
渔 场 Number of Fishing Ground								
团场劳动力合计(人) Total Labour on Farms(person)	**825 386**	**74 691**	**71 547**	**69 420**	**94 744**	**35 303**	**102 236**	**64 675**
# 劳动力年龄内的 Inside of Labor Force Age	811 142	74 663	67 639	69 148	93 348	35 303	101 167	64 675
场内实有就业人员 Persons Actually Engaged on Farms	688 546	71 202	52 791	68 913	80 448	35 205	88 664	59 639
# 劳动力年龄内的 Inside of Labor Force Age	682 535	71 174	52 444	68 615	79 970	35 205	88 520	59 639
# 男 Male	374 614	39 329	29 204	36 624	44 088	18 700	47 345	31 331
女 Female	313 932	31 873	23 587	32 289	36 360	16 505	41 319	28 308
农业就业人员 Persons Engaged in Agriculture	460 806	52 259	36 309	55 194	55 502	25 320	55 670	31 282
# 种植业就业人员 Persons Engaged in Farming	384 129	42 780	30 629	49 410	45 537	20 924	46 033	26 874
牧业就业人员 Persons Engaged in Stock-Raising	30 798	1 537	1 503	2 064	6 318	828	3 936	2 093
工业就业人员 Persons Engaged in Industry	46 939	2 847	3 328	2 309	4 663	1 887	8 015	5 001
建筑业就业人员 Persons Engaged in Construction	19 865	1 954	785	1 734	3 110	688	2 224	2 027
交通运输业、仓储及邮电通迅业就业人员 Persons Engaged in Transportation, Storage and Postal Service and Telecommunications	27 264	1 003	2 174	570	2 876	643	5 172	6 203
信息传输、计算机服务和软件业就业人员 Persons Engaged in Information Deliver, Computer Service and Software	351	114	54	12	25	2	49	40
批发和零售业就业人员 Persons Engaged in Wholesale and Retail Trade	42 936	4 198	3 078	2 176	3 967	1 783	6 332	6 285
住宿和餐饮业就业人员 Persons Engaged in Accommodation and Catering Services Industry	18 706	1 458	1 351	1 231	2 003	773	2 387	2 563
其他就业人员 Employed Persons in Other Trades	71 679	7 369	5 712	5 687	8 302	4 109	8 815	6 238

9—1续表　Continued

（2010年）

指　标 Item	八　师 Division 8	九　师 Division 9	十　师 Division 10	十二师 Division 12	十三师 Division 13	十四师 Division 14	兵团直属 Divectly Under XPCG
团场总数(个) Total Reginent Farms(unit)	**18**	**11**	**11**	**7**	**11**	**4**	**1**
农　场 Number of Farms	17	10	10	7	9	3	1
林　场 Number of Forest Farms							
牧　场 Number of Ranch	1	1	1		2	1	
渔　场 Number of Fishing Ground							
团场劳动力合计(人) Total Labour on Farms(person)	**186 663**	**26 373**	**20 654**	**25 746**	**34 243**	**15 937**	**3 154**
# 劳动力年龄内的 Inside of Labor Force Age	179 163	26 352	20 651	25 733	34 243	15 903	3 154
场内实有就业人员 Persons Actually Engaged on Farms	115 976	25 081	19 101	25 671	30 675	12 026	3 154
# 劳动力年龄内的 Inside of Labor Force Age	115 976	22 366	19 101	23 670	30 675	12 026	3 154
# 男 Male	62 919	14 131	10 513	14 655	17 644	6 490	1 641
女 Female	53 057	10 950	8 588	11 016	13 031	5 536	1 513
农业就业人员 Persons Engaged in Agriculture	77 318	19 360	11 523	11 878	17 627	9 457	2 107
# 种植业就业人员 Persons Engaged in Farming	62 242	15 094	9 351	9 590	15 132	8 584	1 949
牧业就业人员 Persons Engaged in Stock-Raising	5 483	3 009	751	1 822	935	487	32
工业就业人员 Persons Engaged in Industry	10 423	766	1 421	2 519	3 377	132	251
建筑业就业人员 Persons Engaged in Construction	3 078	250	754	1 361	1 655	78	167
交通运输业、仓储及邮电通迅业就业人员 Persons Engaged in Transportation,Storage and Postal Service and Telecommunications	2 365	651	798	2 270	2 010	441	88
信息传输、计算机服务和软件业就业人员 Persons Engaged in Information Deliver,Computer Service and Software	24	3			24	4	
批发和零售业就业人员 Persons Engaged in Wholesale and Retail Trade	7 369	1 094	1 125	3 274	1 705	420	130
住宿和餐饮业就业人员 Persons Engaged in Accommodation and Catering Services Industry	3 284	570	518	1 377	816	277	98
其他就业人员 Employed Persons in Other Trades	12 115	2 387	2 962	2 992	3 461	1 217	313

9—2 农、林、牧、渔业总产值

Gross Output Value of Farming, Forestry, Animal Husbandry and Fishery

年份 单位 Year Unit	农林牧渔业总产值（万元） Total (10 000 yuan)	农业 Farming	林业 Forestry	牧业 Animal Husbandry	渔业 Fishery	农林牧渔服务业 Services	构成% Composition% # 农业 Farming	# 牧业 Animal Husbandry
1950	1 105	1 105					100.0	
1952	4 494	3 854		640			85.8	14.2
1954	3 153	2 521		632			80.0	20.0
1957	8 233	6 668		1 565			81.0	19.0
1962	21 809	15 224	224	3 488	126		69.8	16.0
1965	34 818	26 714	533	5 121	122		76.7	14.7
1970	44 521	34 112	583	5 623	160		76.6	12.6
1975	37 313	28 131	384	6 325	119		75.4	17.0
1978	62 305	46 629	498	9 664	131		74.8	15.5
1980	75 351	59 751	900	8 386	179		79.3	11.1
1985	149 853	113 893	6 116	19 981	599		76.0	13.3
1990	383 188	320 256	5 776	45 352	2 645		83.6	11.8
1991	412 351	355 452	5 741	48 245	2 913		86.2	11.7
1992	418 635	357 515	6 324	51 911	2 885		85.4	12.4
1993	472 704	399 803	6 127	63 111	3 663		84.6	13.4
1994	726 673	623 309	6 459	92 039	4 866		85.8	12.7
1995	1 055 545	925 635	7 260	116 540	6 110		87.7	11.0
1996	1 111 518	971 700	7 829	125 932	6 057		87.4	11.3
1997	1 311 916	1 165 546	8 988	130 511	6 871		88.8	9.9
1998	1 400 265	1 240 444	9 962	143 172	6 687		88.6	10.2
1999	1 205 981	1 050 362	11 238	137 693	6 688		87.1	11.4
2000	1 414 310	1 253 291	12 949	141 028	7 042		88.6	10.0
2001	1 267 685	1 081 188	16 944	161 583	7 970		85.3	12.7
2002	1 590 270	1 367 883	29 778	182 708	9 901		86.0	11.5
2003	2 187 989	1 775 231	43 331	207 217	10 305	151 905	81.1	9.5
2004	2 315 994	1 831 921	33 233	245 737	11 861	193 242	79.1	10.6
2005	2 645 643	2 142 398	32 343	255 228	14 136	201 538	81.0	9.6
2006	2 982 673	2 431 520	30 798	272 286	15 493	232 576	81.5	9.1
2007	3 415 178	2 748 722	33 475	367 703	18 238	247 040	80.5	10.8
2008	3 854 118	2 981 537	35 718	525 293	22 626	288 944	77.4	13.6
2009	4 326 567	3 353 245	43 031	618 642	24 232	287 417	77.5	14.3
2010	5 692 849	4 504 030	54 456	768 463	30 387	335 513	79.1	13.5
一师 Division 1	1 130 858	997 758	12 391	62 885	4 644	53 180	88.2	5.6
二师 Division 2	438 019	341 330	3 550	66 434	3 079	23 626	77.9	15.2
三师 Division 3	472 957	390 984	5 146	35 216	1 176	40 435	82.7	7.4
四师 Division 4	389 384	253 186	3 838	105 891	3 869	22 600	65.0	27.2
五师 Division 5	283 570	252 974	1 809	17 278	420	11 089	89.2	6.1
六师 Division 6	668 840	486 417	5 049	125 126	2 088	50 160	72.7	18.7
七师 Division 7	550 830	424 677	5 165	88 211	2 024	30 753	77.1	16.0
八师 Division 8	1 100 988	904 983	8 988	131 059	4 578	51 380	82.2	11.9
九师 Division 9	136 031	91 650	1 384	37 582	19	5 396	67.4	27.6
十师 Division 10	174 967	117 028	3 888	32 895	6 048	15 108	66.9	18.8
建工师 Construction Division	425	425					100.0	
十二师 Division 12	102 182	69 519	653	27 453	1 913	2 644	68.0	26.9
十三师 Division 13	161 749	113 031	1 424	29 274	251	17 769	69.9	18.1
十四师 Division 14	49 262	40 560	1 074	6 489		1 139	82.3	13.2
国资公司 State-owned Property Company	8 946			1 390		7 556		15.5
兵团直属 Directly Under XPCG	23 841	19 508	97	1 280	278	2 678	81.8	5.4

注：本表按当年价格计算。1998 年至 2006 年农业总产值按兵团第二次全国农业普查结果进行校验修订，下同。

Note: Data in this table are calculated at current prices. Data of farming , forestry , animal husbandry and fishery from 1998 to 2006 are calculated at result of XPCG Second China Agriculture Census, (the same as follow).

9—3 农、林、牧、渔业总产值及指数

Gross Output Value of Farming, Forestry, Animal Husbandry and Fishery and Related Indices

年份 单位 Year Unit	绝对数(万元) Gross Output Value of Farming, Forestry, Animal Husbandry and Fishery(10 000 yuan)					
	农林牧渔业总产值 Total	农业 Farming	林业 Forestry	牧业 Animal Husbandry	渔业 Fishery	农林牧渔服务业 Services
1950	2 788	2 788				
1952	11 856	9 721		2 135		
1954	8 465	6 358		2 107		
1957	22 037	16 822		5 215		
1962	47 359	35 740	1 232	9 678	709	
1965	90 593	70 870	2 793	15 965	965	
1970	112 053	88 401	3 228	19 476	948	
1975	87 107	65 013	1 764	19 745	585	
1978	126 393	96 902	2 232	26 648	611	
1980	147 898	118 924	3 317	25 057	600	
1985	241 561	190 289	10 038	40 036	1 198	
1990	388 892	332 603	6 274	46 989	3 026	
1991	416 132	361 196	6 531	45 515	2 890	
1992	426 479	369 854	7 002	46 924	2 699	
1993	424 020	367 118	6 415	47 531	2 956	
1994	474 733	414 320	6 059	51 053	3 301	
1995	548 982	483 787	6 180	55 150	3 865	
1996	549 215	480 021	6 126	58 998	4 070	
1997	637 627	563 999	6 783	62 322	4 523	
1998	735 421	655 331	7 141	68 516	4 433	
1999	769 507	682 722	7 534	74 292	4 959	
2000	850 899	761 350	8 050	76 146	5 353	
2001	835 151	740 405	9 346	79 682	5 718	
2002	991 718	882 968	15 149	86 875	6 726	
2003	1 139 699	910 682	20 053	97 892	7 020	104 052
2004	1 265 396	1 006 406	16 407	109 597	7 587	125 399
2005	1 378 114	1 107 445	15 233	119 731	8 520	127 185
2006	2 952 458	2 413 419	30 804	267 998	15 482	224 755
2007	3 214 280	2 616 086	33 279	303 085	17 719	244 111
2008	3 759 743	2 987 512	31 735	436 073	20 309	284 114
2009	4 125 448	3 161 755	42 183	613 245	23 129	285 136
2010	4 638 925	3 513 010	59 095	707 674	28 591	330 555
一　师 Division 1	884 910	762 695	11 400	55 085	4 273	51 457
二　师 Division 2	377 943	288 212	3 228	60 516	2 875	23 112
三　师 Division 3	385 879	309 445	4 215	31 434	1 126	39 659
四　师 Division 4	352 874	225 676	3 784	97 812	3 549	22 053
五　师 Division 5	218 758	189 579	1 827	16 133	404	10 815
六　师 Division 6	550 807	373 707	4 613	121 035	1 990	49 462
七　师 Division 7	488 962	372 491	4 943	79 021	1 847	30 660
八　师 Division 8	864 751	684 556	8 970	116 704	3 880	50 641
九　师 Division 9	117 397	78 113	1 349	32 626	19	5 290
十　师 Division 10	156 410	100 531	3 634	31 224	5 834	15 187
建工师 Construction Division	371	371				
十二师 Division 12	89 255	59 520	483	24 808	1 844	2 600
十三师 Division 13	139 133	91 620	1 359	28 616	231	17 307
十四师 Division 14	52 448	44 135	1 082	6 100		1 131
国资公司 State-owned Property Company	8 848			1 418		7 430
兵团直属 Directly Under XPCG	18 959	14 988	89	976	265	2 641

注：本表 2005 年(含 2005 年)以前数据按 1990 年可比价格计算，2006 年以后数据按价格缩减指数计算。分师数据相加不等于合计。
Note: Data in this table are calculated at 1990 comparable prices before 2005(including 2005), and data after 2006 are calculated at price indices cut. Data of divisions added not same as total.

9—3 续表 Continued

年份 Year	单位 Unit	指数(%)(上年=100) Indices of Gross Output Value of Farming, Forestry, Animal Husbandry and Fishery(%)(preceding year=100))					
		农林牧渔业总产值 Total	农业 Farming	林业 Forestry	牧业 Animal Husbandry	渔业 Fishery	农林牧渔服务业 Services
1950		100. 0	100. 0				
1952		276. 3	236. 6		1 173. 1		
1954		103. 2	106. 1		95. 2		
1957		129. 9	125. 2		148. 0		
1962		103. 9	101. 4	96. 0	112. 5	87. 7	
1965		115. 1	114. 4	101. 3	127. 2	115. 0	
1970		113. 7	113. 0	144. 8	113. 6	82. 0	
1975		99. 5	107. 7	70. 5	85. 0	106. 4	
1978		140. 4	141. 9	104. 9	141. 7	265. 7	
1980		112. 0	114. 2	106. 6	101. 9	86. 1	
1985		106. 0	102. 2	184. 6	110. 6	116. 5	
1990		124. 1	131. 0	94. 5	98. 5	113. 7	
1991		104. 5	105. 7	104. 1	96. 9	95. 5	
1992		102. 5	102. 4	107. 2	103. 1	93. 4	
1993		99. 4	99. 3	91. 6	101. 3	109. 5	
1994		112. 0	112. 9	94. 5	107. 4	111. 7	
1995		115. 6	116. 8	102. 0	108. 0	117. 1	
1996		100. 0	99. 2	99. 1	107. 0	105. 3	
1997		116. 1	117. 5	110. 7	105. 8	111. 1	
1998		115. 3	116. 2	105. 3	109. 9	98. 0	
1999		104. 6	104. 2	105. 5	108. 4	111. 9	
2000		110. 6	111. 5	106. 8	102. 5	107. 9	
2001		98. 1	97. 2	116. 1	104. 6	106. 8	
2002		118. 7	119. 3	162. 1	109. 0	117. 6	
2003		114. 9	103. 1	132. 4	112. 7	104. 4	111. 1
2004		111. 0	110. 5	81. 8	112. 0	108. 1	120. 5
2005		109. 1	109. 6	92. 8	114. 0	112. 3	101. 4
2006		113. 4	114. 2	96. 5	112. 3	114. 0	110. 6
2007		107. 6	107. 5	108. 7	111. 8	110. 3	103. 8
2008		110. 1	108. 7	94. 8	118. 6	111. 4	115. 0
2009		107. 0	106. 0	118. 1	116. 7	102. 2	98. 7
2010		107. 2	104. 8	137. 3	114. 4	118. 0	115. 0
一 师	Division 1	108. 2	108. 4	122. 2	114. 3	108. 7	96. 7
二 师	Division 2	101. 3	97. 6	110. 2	120. 6	102. 9	104. 2
三 师	Division 3	112. 6	111. 2	85. 2	102. 8	100. 9	142. 4
四 师	Division 4	109. 8	107. 1	159. 6	117. 2	110. 7	102. 7
五 师	Division 5	108. 5	107. 4	101. 6	125. 3	109. 5	106. 5
六 师	Division 6	106. 4	101. 2	168. 2	119. 4	95. 8	117. 9
七 师	Division 7	113. 7	114. 2	97. 7	116. 4	103. 8	104. 2
八 师	Division 8	110. 8	110. 4	131. 8	108. 5	117. 6	119. 0
九 师	Division 9	109. 6	103. 9	121. 2	124. 0	100. 0	117. 7
十 师	Division 10	103. 4	101. 3	114. 5	89. 3	151. 7	151. 9
建工师	Construction Division	112. 4	112. 4				
十二师	Division 12	102. 0	97. 2	70. 4	113. 2	131. 5	117. 8
十三师	Division 13	103. 6	98. 5	124. 7	108. 5	155. 0	126. 8
十四师	Division 14	140. 8	148. 7	120. 4	109. 2	100. 0	104. 3
国资公司	State-owned Property Company	163. 0			284. 7		150. 7
兵团直属	Directly Under XPCG	101. 3	99. 3	102. 3	110. 5	107. 7	117. 4

9—4　各师按行业分列的农业总产值

计量单位:万元　　　　(2010 年)

指　　标	Item	合　计 Total	一　师 Division 1	二　师 Division 2	三　师 Division 3	四　师 Division 4
农林牧渔业总产值总计	**Total Gross Output Value of Farming, Forestry, Animal Husbandry and Fishery**	**5 692 849**	**1 130 858**	**438 019**	**472 957**	**389 384**
农业产值合计	**Output Value of Farming**	**4 504 030**	**997 758**	**341 330**	**390 984**	**253 186**
谷物及其他作物	Cereal and Others	3 331 773	689 927	190 187	280 343	204 065
谷　物	Cereal	410 219	38 682	12 241	23 159	94 315
薯　类	Tubers	24 798	2 350	18	215	8 042
油料作物	Oil-bearing Crops	86 464	146	309	549	23 801
豆　类	Soybeans	11 011			52	6 675
棉　花	Cotton(lint)	2 548 981	638 197	152 572	251 350	36 778
#棉　籽	Cotton Seed	319 090	74 543	18 035	27 018	5 538
麻类(熟麻皮)	Fiber Crops	1 422	968			436
甜　菜	Beetroots	66 473		13 267		16 996
烟　叶	Tobacco	41				18
其他作物	Others	182 364	9 584	11 780	5 018	17 004
蔬菜园艺作物	Vegetable and Horticultural Crops	492 340	29 695	78 223	9 413	22 062
#工业用番茄	Tomato for Industry	179 774		21 827	432	3 901
工业用辣椒	Hot Pepper for Industry	88 224	22 333	48 758	35	4 255
水果、饮料和香料作物	Fruit, Beverage and Spice Crop	665 015	277 848	72 920	100 011	26 999
#水　果	Fruit	587 608	266 227	71 174	69 354	24 156
瓜　类	Melon	42 159	805	1 077	8 668	2 586
药　材(种植)	Medical Materials(Planting)	14 902	288		1 217	60
林业产值合计	**Output Value of Forestry**	**54 456**	**12 391**	**3 550**	**5 146**	**3 838**
林木的培育和种植	Nurturing and Planting of Wood	40 414	3 974	3 111	2 506	2 994
林产品	Wood Products	10 847	7 748		2 596	
木材采运	Timber Conveyance	3 195	669	439	44	844
牧业产值合计	**Output Value of Animal Husbandry**	**768 463**	**62 885**	**66 434**	**35 216**	**105 891**
牲畜饲养	Livestock Feeding	429 633	43 130	28 544	22 413	66 283
牛	Cattle and Buffaloes	82 425	8 769	4 559	3 066	18 435
羊	Sheep and Goats	193 692	15 568	18 822	16 191	30 612
其他牲畜饲养	Others	5 152	136	109	382	2 664
奶产品	Milk Products	129 292	17 353	3 667	1 996	10 678
毛绒产品	Hair and Cashere Products	16 010	1 277	632	512	3 874
其他牲畜产品	Other Livestock Products	3 062	27	755	266	20
猪的饲养	Pork Feeding	260 758	15 825	29 780	10 671	26 664
家禽的饲养	Poultry Feeding	64 027	3 114	3 271	1 852	9 044
#禽　蛋	Poultry Eggs	32 809	1 672	1 119	1 016	5 340
其他动物及产品	Other Animal and Products	14 044	816	4 839	280	3 899
狩猎及捕捉动物	Hunting and Catching Animal	1				1
渔业产值合计	**Output Value of Fishery**	**30 387**	**4 644**	**3 079**	**1 176**	**3 869**
农林牧渔服务业产值合计	**Output Value of Farming, Forestry, Animal Husbandry and Fishery Services**	**335 513**	**53 180**	**23 626**	**40 435**	**22 600**

注:本表按当年价格计算。

Gross Output Value of Agriculture by Sector and Division

(10000 yuan)

五 师 Division 5	六 师 Division 6	七 师 Division 7	八 师 Division 8	九 师 Division 9	十 师 Division 10	建工师 Contrction Division	十二师 Division 12	十三师 Division 13	十四师 Division 14	国资公司 State-owned Property Company	兵团直属 Directly Under XPCG
283 570	**668 840**	**550 830**	**1 100 988**	**136 031**	**174 967**	**425**	**102 182**	**161 749**	**49 262**	**8 946**	**23 841**
252 974	**486 417**	**424 677**	**904 983**	**91 650**	**117 028**	**425**	**69 519**	**113 031**	**40 560**		**19 508**
228 925	371 184	297 266	784 646	81 669	92 511	336	27 742	64 425	7 910		10 637
23 604	89 596	42 942	26 522	33 522	8 211	49	3 770	7 661	1 833		4 112
894	3 865		486	237	200		6 730	696	115		950
3 502	12 732	12 665	739	5 807	22 558	137	1 351	233	66		1 869
	4	174	2 640	1	1 456		4		5		
199 330	238 456	217 336	736 524		17 425	150	1 666	54 193	4 199		805
21 075	32 084	29 064	100 467		1 999	16	404	8 152	575		120
					18						
631	2 490	10 327	334	18 920	3 147		289				72
	23										
964	24 018	13 822	17 401	23 182	39 496		13 932	1 642	1 692		2 829
7 596	91 269	109 648	91 991	8 829	15 608		15 161	10 778	247		1 820
5 274	50 744	51 057	38 540	5 127	117		2 631				124
88	4 099	1 102	1 181		6 004		96				273
16 453	21 831	11 132	27 772	568	7 912	89	26 056	37 828	31 112		6 484
14 627	11 975	9 652	24 658	258	1 337		24 935	31 949	30 922		6 384
443	9 856	1 420	3 114	310	6 575	89	1 047	5 879	190		100
	2 133	6 631	574	584	997		560		1 291		567
1 809	**5 049**	**5 165**	**8 988**	**1 384**	**3 888**		**653**	**1 424**	**1 074**		**97**
1 583	4 882	5 160	8 492	1 259	3 853		653	1 180	670		97
				1	32			188	282		
226	167	5	496	124	3			56	122		
17 278	**125 126**	**88 211**	**131 059**	**37 582**	**32 895**		**27 453**	**29 274**	**6 489**	**1 390**	**1 280**
7 967	64 345	52 002	53 332	32 171	17 026		17 324	19 625	4 442		1 029
1 872	15 661	7 788	5 240	3 683	4 821		3 489	4 274	460		308
4 855	37 193	12 252	5 184	24 389	9 853		4 138	10 650	3 627		358
	523	131	70	200			30	761	146		
399	7 388	30 409	42 089	2 169	2 006		9 451	1 356	31		300
841	3 580	1 422	749	1 730	346		216	659	109		63
								1 925	69		
5 873	50 325	24 273	64 877	3 170	12 900		6 442	7 730	936	1 192	100
3 363	10 057	10 020	12 336	1 836	2 636		3 665	1 518	1 016	198	101
2 212	3 970	4 763	7 098	887	1 484		1 811	648	723	28	38
75	399	1 916	514	405	333		22	401	95		50
420	**2 088**	**2 024**	**4 578**	**19**	**6 048**		**1 913**	**251**			**278**
11 089	**50 160**	**30 753**	**51 380**	**5 396**	**15 108**		**2 644**	**17 769**	**1 139**	**7 556**	**2 678**

Note: Data in this table are calculated at current prices.

9－5　各师农林牧渔业生产中间消耗

计量单位:万元*　　　　(2010年)

指　标	Item	合计 Total	一师 Division 1	二师 Division 2	三师 Division 3	四师 Division 4
农林牧渔业生产中间消耗总计	**Total Indermediate Production Consumption**	**2 904 738**	**573 489**	**221 932**	**252 421**	**197 684**
农　业	Farming	**2 242 677**	**495 492**	**169 631**	**205 663**	**126 767**
中间物质消耗	Intermediate Material Consumption	1 380 120	304 058	125 586	115 961	83 369
用种量	Quantity of Seed	129 217	18 101	16 092	6 254	13 124
#谷　物	Cereal	32 715	2 361	1 046	1 959	6 846
棉　籽	Cotton Seed	35 689	12 327	1 184	3 015	725
役畜用饲料、饲草	Animal Feed and Grass	9 116	1 267	62	3 163	179
#饲料用粮	Grain for Animal Feed	1 755		8	1 127	31
农作物秸秆	Farm Crop Strain	1 750	421	4	268	24
肥　料	Fertilizers	492 730	142 519	45 984	47 026	31 025
#化学肥料	Chemical Fertilizers	339 858	87 557	29 657	30 695	25 062
燃　料	Fuel	153 600	21 011	8 469	15 524	10 835
#柴　油	Diesel	120 672	15 146	7 231	10 849	9 386
农　药	Pesticide	53 920	9 097	4 595	3 532	4 912
农用塑料簿膜	Farm Plastic Film	74 106	14 645	5 773	5 681	2 752
用电量	Electricity Consumed	85 493	7 491	5 019	6 974	2 486
小农具购置费	Purchases of Small Farm Implements	18 056	7 768	412	1 655	724
办公用品购置	Purchases of Office Equipment	10 347	2 844	489	1 442	744
其他物质消耗	Other Material Consumption	353 535	79 315	38 691	24 710	16 588
生产服务支出	Expenditures of Production Service	862 557	191 434	44 045	89 702	43 398
#修理费	Fix Fee	38 348	8 086	3 712	3 130	3 426
种植业保险费支出	Premium Expenditure of Farming	33 955	4 526	3 267	3 010	2 864
外雇排灌费	Hired Irrigation and Drainage Fee	149 892	32 121	10 171	19 741	5 163
外雇机耕费	Hired Mechanical Cultivation Fee	142 798	30 563	9 585	15 449	10 035
林　业	**Forestry**	**30 496**	**6 474**	**1 854**	**3 486**	**1 978**
#中间物质消耗	Indermediate Material Consumption	21 593	4 471	1 325	2 455	1 353
牧　业	**Animal Husbandry**	**425 422**	**35 219**	**34 201**	**19 879**	**55 051**
中间物质消耗	Indermediate Material Consumption	383 942	31 461	31 383	18 309	47 888
用种量	Quantity of Seed	7 410	103	30	17	453
饲料、饲草	Animal Feed and Grass	335 986	27 646	25 233	17 354	42 488
#饲料用粮	Grain for Animal Feed	117 493	6 029	9 850	3 398	20 032
饲料作物	Animal Feed Crop	22 971	3 632	555	1 980	1 530
农作物秸秆	Farm Crop Straw	27 907	3 731	1 189	1 646	3 189
饲　草	Forage	47 044	2 997	2 011	2 522	5 991
燃　料	Fuel	7 819	512	752	223	919
用电量	Electricity Consumed	3 564	222	442	84	461
畜牧用药品	Medicine for Animal Husbandry	9 704	1 019	1 337	272	1 132
其他物质消耗	Other Material Consumption	19 459	1 959	3 589	359	2 435
生产服务支出	Expenditures of Production Service	41 480	3 758	2 818	1 570	7 163
#牧业保险费支出	Premium Expenditure of Animal Husbandry	4 187	336	827	124	200
配种费	Stockimg Fee	3 099	356	225	115	814
防疫费	Prevention Fee	5 804	630	379	359	1 048
渔　业	**Fishery**	**17 846**	**2 262**	**2 105**	**661**	**2 173**
#中间物质消耗	Intermediate Material Consumption	15 023	1 876	1 919	577	1 915
农林牧渔服务业合计	**Farming, Forestry, Animal Husbandry and Fishery Services**	**188 297**	**34 042**	**14 141**	**22 732**	**11 715**

Intermediate Production Consumption of Farming, Forestry, Animal, Husbandry and Fishery by Division

(10 000 yuan)

五 师 Division 5	六 师 Division 6	七 师 Division 7	八 师 Division 8	九 师 Division 9	十 师 Division 10	建工师 Contrction Division	十二师 Division 12	十三师 Division 13	十四师 Division 14	国资公司 State-owned Property Company	兵团直属 Directly Under XPCG
138 106	**336 399**	**270 875**	**548 246**	**70 527**	**111 765**	**233**	**57 311**	**80 493**	**26 040**	**7 295**	**11 922**
120 948	**239 657**	**206 515**	**434 599**	**48 627**	**71 556**	**233**	**38 621**	**53 936**	**21 394**		**9 038**
92 729	146 955	106 652	248 113	33 179	45 346	141	26 156	30 453	16 251		5 171
5 688	15 910	11 639	18 155	6 746	9 504	51	2 329	2 274	1 628		1 722
2 047	6 371	2 816	2 435	3 830	702	5	295	647	236		1 119
1 513	2 316	2 770	10 837		303	1	13	615	34		36
	41		28		25		926	1 170	2 255		
	14						16	146	413		
	10		22				16	182	803		
26 743	38 026	34 643	71 948	10 831	12 624	39	11 490	11 191	7 582		1 059
20 523	26 275	25 891	57 097	8 428	11 712	39	3 579	8 289	4 106		948
8 806	18 665	13 233	32 842	5 190	10 749	5	2 633	2 469	1 793		1 376
7 373	14 682	11 631	25 064	4 372	9 712	2	873	2 225	1 144		982
3 325	6 246	3 448	11 743	548	4 643	9	263	948	529		82
4 614	9 831	7 681	16 154	2 101	2 784	13	359	1 165	250		303
6 909	16 568	5 547	24 845	1 930	1 008	24	1 920	3 885	507		380
112	1 066	1 272	2 459	577	1 318		138	460			95
673	400	2 128	913	221	188		75	195	30		5
35 859	40 202	27 061	69 026	5 035	2 503		6 023	6 696	1 677		149
28 219	92 702	99 863	186 486	15 448	26 210	92	12 465	23 483	5 143		3 867
2 472	4 061	5 560	3 068	816	2 494		387	486	150		500
1 992	3 649	2 870	7 574	2 037	1 288			526	50		302
2 914	20 604	15 076	26 677	1 849	5 373		3 018	4 646	1 439		1 100
1 791	20 559	12 810	29 023	2 201	4 605	26	1 497	3 654	450		550
1 095	**2 605**	**2 806**	**4 714**	**738**	**2 843**		**297**	**923**	**620**		**63**
940	2 228	2 078	3 268	420	1 371		293	806	547		38
10 368	**69 870**	**44 905**	**76 364**	**18 588**	**23 147**		**15 730**	**16 702**	**3 417**	**1 275**	**706**
9 853	66 590	39 167	69 213	16 384	18 696		14 558	15 717	3 140	1 173	410
185	2 922	97	652	143	466		2 056	254	32		
8 838	57 801	36 453	63 588	14 669	15 074		9 440	13 011	2 966	1 031	394
4 359	25 534	9 967	24 202	3 168	3 448		2 624	2 594	1 117	1 031	140
293	2 887	5 652	4 076	894	473		138	778	48		35
838	4 971	2 709	3 112	1 130	1 295		906	2 826	235		130
833	5 866	4 398	7 981	6 092	4 453		1 279	2 180	441		
270	706	711	1 323	510	866		370	572	45	38	2
128	290	600	831	109	116		118	109	16	24	14
221	1 351	967	1 531	361	805		335	237	61	75	
211	3 520	339	1 288	592	1 369		2 239	1 534	20	5	
515	3 280	5 738	7 151	2 204	4 451		1 172	985	277	102	296
60	21	904	1 467	189	57			2			
87	264	329	260	120	328		90	70	29		12
149	630	785	748	268	433		213	103	42	5	12
220	**1 123**	**1 059**	**2 716**	**10**	**4 307**		**877**	**166**			**167**
170	976	744	2 519	8	3 175		854	139			151
5 475	**23 144**	**15 590**	**29 853**	**2 564**	**9 912**		**1 786**	**8 766**	**609**	**6 020**	**1 948**

9—6　各师农业生产条件

（2010年）

指　标	Item	合　计 Total	一　师 Division 1	二　师 Division 2	三　师 Division 3	四　师 Division 4
耕地总资源　（千公顷）	**Cultivated Resource　(1 000 hectares)**					
年初耕地总资源	Cultivated Recource in Beginning of the Year	1 245.65	177.07	78.05	98.45	114.83
年内增加的耕地总资源	Increased Cultivated Recource in the Current Year	1.38				0.02
# 园地改耕地	Newly Reclaimed Wildland Area					
年内减少的耕地总资源	Decreased Cultivated Resource in the Current Year	5.21	1.54	0.30	0.12	0.64
# 国家基建占地	Land Covered by Country's Capital Construction	0.63	0.09		0.04	0.02
其他基建占地	Land Covered by Other Capital Construction					
退耕还林还草占地	Land Converted to Forestry and Grass Land	0.07		0.02		0.01
耕地改园地	Land Converted to Garden Area	3.47	1.44			0.59
年末实有耕地总资源	Cultivated Resoure at the Year-end	1 241.83	175.53	77.75	98.33	114.21
# 水　田	Paddy Fields	7.76	0.05			7.29
旱　地	Dry Fields	54.77				30.86
水浇地	Irrigated Land	1 179.30	175.49	77.75	98.32	76.06
农业主要能源及物资消耗	**Main Engery and Material Consumption in Farm**					
乡村办水电站数　（个）	Hydro-Power Station Run by Village　(Unit)	31		5		5
装机容量　（万千瓦）	Installed Capacity　(10 000 kwh)	5.53		1.03		0.26
发电量　（万千瓦小时）	Electricity Generation　(10 000 kwh)	18 871		995		1 094
农村用电量　（万千瓦小时）	Electricity Consumed in Rural Areas　(10 000 kwh)	280 471	29 913	16 228	17 221	13 950
农用化肥施用量	Consumption of Farm Chemical Fertilizers					
按实物量计算　（吨）	Compution Based on Material Objects　(ton)	1 187 312	299 350	98 637	100 828	87 391
氮　肥	Nitrogenous Fertilizers	543 819	101 323	50 263	56 569	36 742
磷　肥	Phosphate Fertilizers	242 348	69 467	17 170	30 767	20 877
钾　肥	Potash Fertilizers	86 874	18 309	10 076	5 945	6 646
复合肥	Compound Fertilizers	314 271	110 251	21 128	7 547	23 126
按折纯法计算　（吨）	Compution Based on Purity Deduction　(ton)	545 451	135 786	45 887	46 505	40 926
氮　肥	Nitrogenous Fertilizers	252 379	46 811	22 889	25 726	16 917
磷　肥	Phosphate Fertilizers	98 380	24 838	7 311	14 195	8 925
钾　肥	Potash Fertilizers	39 793	8 533	4 823	2 868	3 106
复合肥	Compound Fertilizers	154 899	55 604	10 864	3 716	11 978
农用塑料薄膜使用量　（吨）	Consumption of Farm Plastic Film　(ton)	53 361	11 113	4 375	4 212	2 109
# 地膜使用量	Consumption of Ground Plastic Film	50 080	10 223	4 151	4 161	1 864
地膜覆盖面积　（公顷）	Areas Covered by Ground Plastic Pellicle　(hectare)	10 596 127	1 924 097	758 217	837 521	458 971
农用柴油使用量　（吨）	Consumption of Diesel　(ton)	170 518	22 188	11 586	15 327	13 442
农药使用量(实物量)　（公斤）	Consumption of Pesticide (Material Objects)　(kg)	8 733 897	1 020 973	675 404	539 060	778 281
农田水利建设情况	**Farmland Irrigation Development**					
有效灌溉面积　（千公顷）	Irrigated Area　(1 000 hectares)	1 072.68	152.45	71.14	93.02	78.99
# 高新节水灌溉面积	Pelaxe and New Water-Saving Irrigated Area	682.16	97.84	46.23	56.25	22.60
旱涝保收面积　（千公顷）	Area with Stable Yields Despite Drought or Flood　(1 000 hectares)	897.99	146.17	67.69	63.85	64.20
机电排灌面积　（千公顷）	Electrical Irrigation and Drainage Area　(1 000 hectares)	528.82	105.63	40.00	52.29	18.10
机电井　（眼）	Machine Well　(unit)	16 738	1 318	857	3 716	582

注：本表耕地总资源数据来源于兵团国土资源局。年初耕地总资源根据第二次全国土地调查数据进行校验修订。

Agriculture Production Conditions by Division

五 师 Division 5	六 师 Division 6	七 师 Division 7	八 师 Division 8	九 师 Division 9	十 师 Division 10	建工师 Contrc tion Division	十二师 Division 12	十三师 Division 13	十四师 Division 14	兵团直属 Divectly Under XPCG
61.36	182.96	114.48	237.84	67.93	58.76	0.28	14.11	25.57	8.07	5.89
	0.97	0.05	0.05					0.23		0.06
0.09	0.84	0.11	1.34	0.16				0.04	0.01	0.02
0.03	0.03	0.06	0.35					0.01		
	0.04									
0.05	0.61		0.75					0.03		
61.27	183.09	114.42	236.55	67.77	58.76	0.28	14.11	25.76	8.06	5.93
	0.30		0.10						0.02	
	1.54			22.37						
61.27	181.26	114.42	236.45	45.40	58.76	0.28	14.11	25.76	8.04	5.93
16		1		1				3		
3.46		0.30		0.23				0.25		
15 722		554		239				267		
21 354	56 445	16 483	77 777	6 215	3 875	84	4 823	13 204	1 721	1 179
71 621	95 865	87 866	206 304	29 767	47 086	138	13 234	29 954	13 221	6 050
30 914	41 357	46 387	112 869	15 322	23 084	93	5 441	14 187	5 820	3 448
7 868	24 161	17 189	24 746	7 079	9 786	30	2 922	6 281	3 461	544
5 462	4 915	5 433	17 264	1 616	4 382	5	1 438	4 711	370	302
27 377	25 432	18 857	51 425	5 750	9 834	10	3 433	4 775	3 570	1 756
33 121	44 745	41 618	94 379	13 622	20 406	68	5 977	14 019	5 981	2 411
14 382	19 523	22 101	53 143	7 206	10 452	52	2 345	6 692	2 761	1 379
3 287	10 317	6 981	10 571	2 960	3 678	14	1 337	2 474	1 280	212
2 462	2 179	2 574	7 862	711	1 650	1	620	2 119	167	118
12 990	12 726	9 962	22 803	2 745	4 626	1	1 675	2 734	1 773	702
3 334	5 961	5 067	12 431	1 454	1 817	10	243	850	152	233
3 138	5 870	4 301	11 967	1 270	1 771	10	158	812	151	233
606 974	1 307 441	1 182 951	2 390 753	304 035	506 726	2 784	45 263	178 218	45 531	46 645
9 824	20 137	16 951	34 273	5 850	13 363		1 399	2 982	1 708	1 488
616 904	1 169 005	617 006	1 738 561	116 518	820 580	4 000	98 554	424 240	91 811	23 000
57.13	175.09	106.51	186.03	45.42	58.70	0.25	16.02	21.96	4.08	5.89
44.79	83.24	81.74	166.40	26.30	32.84	0.17	3.69	15.62	1.21	3.24
57.13	143.09	106.18	167.98	31.16	4.77	0.25	16.02	19.53	4.08	5.89
41.13	92.12	20.61	107.82	20.23	2.74	0.25	3.48	17.70	0.83	5.89
1 257	2 373	594	2 787	781	208	10	252	1 805	73	125

Note: Data of Cultivated resource in this table come from the Land and Resources Bureau of XPCG.

9—7　各师农业机械年末拥有量

(2010 年)

指　　标		Item		合　计 Total	一　师 Division 1	二　师 Division 2	三　师 Division 3	四　师 Division 4
农业机械总动力	**(千瓦)**	**Total Power of Agricultural Machinery**	**(kw)**	**3 693 346**	**561 352**	**257 768**	**234 670**	**267 202**
柴油机动力		Diesel Engine Power		2 761 372	433 507	200 948	170 828	205 495
汽油机动力		Gasoline Engine Power		49 719	2 584	2 176	4 872	3 900
电动机动力		Electric Motor Power		882 255	125 261	54 644	58 970	57 807
其它机械动力		Other POwer						
主要机械与设备	**(千瓦)**	**Farming Machinery**	**(kw)**	**3 556 939**	**556 329**	**251 682**	**229 013**	**259 314**
大中型拖拉机	(台)	Large and Medium Agricultural Tractors	(unit)	36 819	3 858	2 981	1 993	3 316
	(千瓦)		(kw)	1 660 162	246 605	133 287	109 587	136 806
小型拖拉机	(台)	Mini-Tractors	(unit)	37 343	6 634	2 473	2 161	1 336
	(千瓦)		(kw)	466 041	79 225	32 314	27 005	15 235
大中型机引农具	(部)	Large and Medium Tractor Towing Farm Machinery	(unit)	70 872	6 715	5 054	4 242	5 202
小型机引农具	(部)	Small Tractor Towing Farm Machinery	(unit)	33 523	3 565	2 917	919	1 474
农用排灌柴油机	(台)	Farming Irrigated Machinery	(unit)	3 176	379	163	573	180
	(千瓦)		(kw)	64 186	10 138	3 575	10 477	4 457
农用排灌电动机	(台)	Diesel Engines	(unit)	20 610	2 655	1 757	2 434	681
	(千瓦)		(kw)	768 985	119 748	48 646	53 904	47 768
农用水泵	(台)	Farm Pump	(unit)	19 286	2 253	1 320	3 361	923
节水灌溉机械	(套)	Water-saving Irrigated Machinery	(set)	14 131	1 937	1 383	1 122	704
联合收割机	(台)	Combine Harvesters	(set)	1 670	191	73	24	388
	(千瓦)		(kw)	200 650	30 124	8 704	3 321	36 986
自走式收割机	(台)	Self-Propelled Combine Harvesters	(set)	79	10	2		52
	(千瓦)		(kw)	3 736	480	141		2 600
机动脱粒机	(台)	Mechanical Sheller	(set)	1 249	15	14	9	218
	(千瓦)		(kw)	6 663	651	304	88	1 479
渔业机械	(台)	Fishery Machinery	(set)	116	17	17	8	
	(千瓦)		(kw)	1 638	376	345	171	
农用运输车	(辆)	Farm Heavy-Dt	(set)	20 606	5 349	579	1 910	224
	(千瓦)		(kw)	344 324	65 543	11 464	24 460	9 522

Year-end Possession of Farming Machinery by Division

五 师 Division 5	六 师 Division 6	七 师 Division 7	八 师 Division 8	九 师 Division 9	十 师 Division 10	建工师 Contrc tion Division	十二师 Division 12	十三师 Division 13	十四师 Division 14	兵团直属 Divectly Under XPCG
261 181	**556 236**	**293 648**	**675 052**	**135 382**	**192 807**	**413**	**68 809**	**130 958**	**39 155**	**18 713**
155 521	428 656	234 991	493 186	94 398	169 603	40	48 317	78 655	35 649	11 578
650	3 952	1 464	6 287	5 678	3 800		10 460		380	3 516
105 010	123 628	57 193	175 579	35 306	19 404	373	10 032	52 303	3 126	3 619
237 344	**549 883**	**273 709**	**633 344**	**128 483**	**183 980**	**413**	**69 618**	**131 097**	**38 505**	**14 225**
3 043	4 845	3 016	6 978	1 047	3 367		346	546	1 298	185
96 724	212 619	144 751	353 141	43 744	104 662		18 387	27 070	25 564	7 215
2 770	8 760	1 718	5 522	1 777	1 333	3	721	1 862	153	120
32 973	112 006	22 528	66 709	23 743	17 335	40	9 170	24 054	2 024	1 680
2 286	10 705	7 273	16 718	1 793	3 367		434	4 990	1 719	374
2 522	7 751	1 497	5 081	1 696	3 833		734	1 166	246	122
12	183	34	204	6	1 391		8	26	17	
300	3 836	3 000	2 396	220	24 217		32	723	815	
1 245	2 732	1 393	3 957	881	352		243	2 058	97	125
72 164	121 052	50 354	140 649	35 083	13 302		8 878	52 206	2 856	2 375
143	2 363	619	3 720	839	820	10	217	2 306	267	125
1 137	899	780	3 067	406	1 811		30	551	264	40
69	296	139	280	97	86		11	11	2	3
13 031	32 652	20 608	31 268	11 701	9 445		1 019	1 090	101	600
	4		10		1					
	80		229		206					
34	382	22	172	269	28		34	47	3	2
366	848	30	949	25	923		460	463	53	24
	4		11		59					
	76		196		474					
563	3 210	2 252	2 580	433	404		1 110	1 404	403	185
13 423	66 712	32 435	31 128	13 809	10 668		30 246	25 491	7 092	2 331

9—8 主要农业机械化作业项目水平

Level of Major Agricultural Mechanization

计量单位:千公顷　　(1 000 hectares)

指　标	Item	2009	2010
当年实际机耕面积(按耕地面积计算)	**Machine-Cultivated Area in the Current Year (Computed Based on Cultivated Area)**	**1 066.57**	**1 076.61**
当年机械播种面积(按播种面积计算)	**Machine-Sown Area in the Current Year (Computed Based on Sown Area)**	**1 061.86**	**1 113.43**
地膜覆盖栽培面积	**Cultivated Area with Plastic Film**	**599.62**	**620.96**
# 机械覆膜面积	Area of Plastic Film Layed with Machine	599.04	620.88
化学除草面积	**Area of Chemical Weeding**	**827.66**	**908.96**
# 机械化除面积	Area of Mechanized Weeding	827.53	908.48
中耕作业面积	**Cultivation Area**	**587.67**	**651.14**
# 机械中耕面积	Area of Mechanical Cultivation	587.67	651.14
机械施肥作业面积	**Area of Mechanical Fertilization**	**773.05**	**820.01**
# 液氨施肥面积	Area of Liquid Ammonia Application	65.91	42.99
化肥深施面积	Area of Deep Fertilizer Application	661.18	743.02
病虫害防治面积	**Area of Pest Control**	851.70	908.48
# 机力防治面积	Area of Mechanic Control	851.70	908.48
机电灌溉面积	**Machine-Irrigated Area**	**672.69**	**683.52**
# 喷灌面积	Spay-Irrigated Area	76.18	60.73
当年机械收割面积	**Machine-Harvested Area**	**582.55**	**691.33**
# 机收小麦面积	Wheat Area Harvested by Machine	185.65	156.18
机收水稻面积	Rice Area Harvested by Machine	21.49	18.19
机收玉米面积	Corn Area Havested by Machine	52.79	81.91
机收棉花面积	Cotton Area Havested by Machine	116.04	172.00
机收油料面积	Oil-Bearing Crops Area Harvested by Machine	67.22	67.29
机收甜菜面积	Beetroots Area Harvested by Machine	7.79	13.50
机收饲料面积	Animal Feed Area Harvested by Machine	55.62	40.59
机械秸秆还田面积	**Area of Straw Turning to Fields by Machine**	**674.87**	**709.24**
# 切粉碎还田	Area of Straw Shredding to Fields	620.54	659.75
机械植树面积	**Machine-Planting Trees Area**	12.62	10.49
收获牧草数量(吨)	**Quantity of Haveast Animal Grass(ton)**	**1 801 846**	**1 810 328**
# 机械收割牧草	Machine-Havested Forage	1 801 846	1 810 328
机械收割农作物茎杆(吨)	**Crop Stalk Harvested by Machine(ton)**	**950 037**	**926 278**
# 青黄储数量	Silage Quantity	724 440	736 552
机械剪毛羊只数(万只)	**Sheep Shearing with Machine(10 000 heads)**	**38.86**	**38.69**
飞机作业面积	**Area of Airplane Operation**	**242.74**	**233.58**
# 飞机播种水稻	Rice Area Sown by Airplane	1.22	1.53
飞机化除面积	**Area of Weed Control by Airplane**	**22.21**	**19.80**
飞机防治病虫害面积	**Area of Pest Control by Airplane**	**135.59**	**120.53**
飞机施肥面积	**Area of Fertilization by Airplane**	**5.19**	**5.76**
附:农机管理标准化农场(个)	Attached:Farm of Agricultural Machinery Management Standardization(Unit)	121	119
农机管理标准化连队(个)	Brigade of Agricultural Machinery Management Standardization(Unit)	1 360	1 376
农机管理标准化机组(个)	Groups of Agricultural Machinery Management Standardization(Unit)	16 122	13 355

9—9 农作物播种面积、产量

Sown Areas and Yield of Farm Crops

(2010 年)

指 标	Item	正复播播种面积(千公顷) Total Sown Area (1 000 hectares)	正复播总产量(吨) Total Yield of Major Farm Crops (ton)	每公顷产量(公斤) Yield of Major Farm Crops Per Hectare (kg)	复播面积(千公顷) Multiple Sown Area (1 000 hectares)
农作物总播种面积	**Total Sown Area**	**1 119. 20**			**37. 56**
粮食作物合计	**Sown Area of Grain Crops**	**284. 69**	**2 136 355**	**7 504**	**13. 02**
谷 物	Cereal	269. 59	2 064 212	7 657	8. 99
水 稻	Rice	18. 19	181 557	9 981	0. 22
小 麦	Wheat	156. 18	963 275	6 168	
# 冬小麦	Winter Wheat	99. 05	619 915	6 259	
春小麦	Spring Wheat	57. 13	343 360	6 010	
玉 米	Corn	85. 61	857 216	10 013	8. 56
高 梁	Sorghum	2. 80	27 009	9 646	
大 麦	Barley	6. 60	34 767	5 268	
其他谷物	Other Cereal	0. 21	388	1 848	0. 21
豆 类	Pulse	9. 06	28 850	3 184	4. 03
# 大豆(黄豆、黑豆等)	Soja	8. 04	25 912	3 223	4. 02
绿 豆	Green Bean	0. 03	99	3 300	0. 01
薯 类	Tubers	6. 04	43 293	7 168	
油料作物	**Oil Bearing Crops**	**67. 78**	**186 233**	**2 748**	**9. 63**
花 生	Peanuts	0. 49	1 704	3 478	
油菜籽	Rapeseeds	21. 95	56 753	2 586	
芝 麻	Sesame	0. 04	71	1 775	
胡 麻	Flax	0. 01	19	1 900	
向日葵籽	Sunflower	41. 01	119 212	2 907	9. 63
其他油料	Other	4. 28	8 474	1 980	
棉 花	**Cotton**	**497. 98**	**1 150 137**	**2 310**	**0. 27**
# 长绒棉	Long Staple Cotton	19. 78	36 251	1 833	
麻 类	**Hemp Crops**	**0. 40**	**6 569**	**16 423**	
# 亚 麻	Flax	0. 22	1 496	6 800	
甜 菜	**Beetroots**	**25. 52**	**1 816 603**	**71 184**	
烟 叶	**Tobacco**	**0. 01**	**45**	**4 500**	
药 材	**Medicial Materials**	**4. 96**			
# 枸 杞	Chinese Wolf Berry	2. 34	3 449	1 474	
蔬菜(含菜用瓜)	**Vegetables**	**79. 68**	**5 816 228**	**72 995**	**1. 58**
瓜果类	**Melons**	**10. 78**	**427 993**	**39 703**	**0. 09**
# 西 瓜	Muskmelon	3. 85	202 539	52 608	0. 09
# 甜 瓜	Strawbery	6. 89	225 025	32 660	
其他作物	**Other Farm Crops**	**147. 40**			**12. 97**
打瓜籽	Melon Seed	49. 73	87 500	1 760	0. 25
啤酒花	Hops	3. 07	8 673	2 825	
苜蓿(包括当年新播)	Lucerne	39. 97	281 917	7 092	1. 28
其他饲料	Other Animal Feed	17. 38			6. 57
# 青贮玉米	Silage Corn	16. 48	1 021 090	61 959	6. 40
绿 肥(包括翻掉播种面积)	Green Manure	4. 35			4. 13
其它作物(包括安息茴香)	Others	32. 90			0. 74

9—10　农作物总播种面积

计量单位：千公顷

年份 Year	单位 Unit	农作物总播种面积 Total Sown Area	粮食作物播种面积 Sown Area of Grain Crops	谷物 Cereal	#水稻 Rice	#小麦 Wheat	#冬麦 Winter Wheat	#玉米 Corn	#大麦 Barley	豆类 Pulse	薯类 Tubers
1950		55.68	41.83	41.33	6.56	18.96		6.61		0.50	
1952		108.14	80.71	80.08	13.21	45.15	13.73	14.54	0.67	0.63	
1954		59.11	44.71	43.44	4.82	28.09	15.50	6.69	1.11	1.27	
1957		147.58	92.36	88.57	6.59	42.03	21.65	25.33	2.67	3.79	
1962		430.59	284.53	279.69	8.05	129.30	72.66	90.99	3.94	4.84	
1965		514.75	321.58	314.29	19.50	197.82	113.23	79.08	3.10	7.29	
1970		656.59	432.07	424.54	36.80	247.11	130.65	116.69	4.61	7.53	
1975		675.75	446.98	438.22	32.09	253.49	168.77	105.34	0.10	4.49	4.27
1978		740.19	469.23	445.24	35.93	277.15	148.01	100.89	8.70	16.38	7.61
1980		740.28	441.08	420.82	33.43	288.21	160.29	80.41	7.36	14.81	5.45
1985		727.51	362.03	354.81	29.17	278.09	144.02	42.65	2.26	5.55	1.67
1990		780.80	369.07	359.80	32.00	244.13	132.67	54.40	23.93	8.00	1.27
1991		807.80	338.90	331.40	29.40	237.80	92.87	44.50	16.80	6.40	1.10
1992		810.20	339.90	332.30	29.40	241.00	122.70	43.90	12.30	6.60	1.00
1993		786.93	332.92	313.86	26.04	226.52	133.06	36.86	16.15	18.02	1.04
1994		787.31	263.18	239.72	22.20	146.38	85.37	31.85	32.77	22.48	0.98
1995		813.00	299.02	287.41	27.91	190.09	97.66	49.34	15.80	10.65	0.96
1996		831.40	324.05	314.32	29.47	205.15	110.71	52.73	21.90	8.29	1.44
1997		864.19	321.03	306.63	33.23	207.60	102.16	37.76	24.70	12.88	1.52
1998		892.03	268.81	254.71	25.69	180.02	92.57	37.10	9.19	11.69	2.41
1999		914.72	245.53	234.50	27.91	157.68	68.15	38.09	5.66	9.28	1.75
2000		909.80	221.03	207.38	26.33	142.67	63.68	28.82	9.18	11.69	1.96
2001		919.71	209.22	190.84	20.22	123.71	50.91	35.34	10.47	16.58	1.80
2002		931.80	207.69	193.08	19.01	118.53	52.78	41.96	10.90	12.57	2.04
2003		932.40	162.33	143.58	15.30	76.38	38.23	37.77	11.87	16.10	2.65
2004		983.65	179.11	157.84	14.89	84.15	24.66	50.56	6.52	17.92	3.35
2005		1 023.77	192.06	173.17	13.61	103.54	44.80	46.88	7.23	16.62	2.27
2006		1 032.81	191.47	178.40	23.24	97.95	49.07	44.59	11.46	10.48	2.59
2007		1 040.94	173.18	159.51	25.45	73.01	34.33	43.02	15.26	7.46	6.21
2008		1 068.90	235.40	215.30	23.93	119.68	41.58	59.60	10.53	10.66	9.44
2009		1 107.70	313.99	292.46	21.77	197.06	82.74	63.35	7.26	14.62	6.91
2010		1 119.20	284.69	269.59	18.19	156.18	99.05	85.61	6.60	9.06	6.04
一　师	Division 1	165.33	22.10	21.68	8.66	4.62	3.68	8.30			0.42
二　师	Division 2	65.79	9.64	9.64	0.45	6.53		2.66			
三　师	Division 3	95.38	20.75	20.67	0.33	8.06	7.32	12.21		0.05	0.03
四　师	Division 4	118.24	63.96	55.82	8.27	29.91	12.30	13.16	1.78	6.20	1.94
五　师	Division 5	59.81	16.88	16.55		11.72	5.42	4.83			0.33
六　师	Division 6	140.63	54.62	53.52	0.22	35.12	26.09	17.51	0.67	0.01	1.09
七　师	Division 7	109.97	26.61	26.43		15.00	14.83	11.36		0.18	
八　师	Division 8	191.27	20.85	19.05	0.17	12.96	12.02	5.85		1.64	0.16
九　师	Division 9	77.29	26.82	26.72		17.85	10.23	5.56	3.31		0.10
十　师	Division 10	51.11	6.06	5.03		2.79		2.24		0.97	0.06
建工师	Construction Division	0.25	0.07	0.07		0.07	0.07				
十二师	Division 12	11.03	4.11	2.68		2.03	1.94	0.65			1.43
十三师	Division 13	18.48	5.14	4.99		3.56		0.59	0.84		0.15
十四师	Division 14	7.14	3.19	3.15		2.59	1.82	0.56		0.01	0.03
兵团直属	Directly Under XPCG	7.48	3.89	3.59	0.09	3.37	3.33	0.13			0.30

注：2001年至2006年种植业数据按兵团第二次全国农业普查结果进行校验修订，下同。

Total Sown Areas of Farm Crops

(1 000 hectares)

油 料 Oil-bearing Crops	# 油菜籽 Rapes-eeds	# 向日葵籽 Helian-thus	棉 花 Cotton	# 长绒棉 Long-staple Cotton	甜 菜 Beetroots	烟 叶 Tobacco	药 材 Medicinal Materials	蔬 菜 Vegeta-bles	瓜果类 Melons	# 甜 瓜 Musk-melon	打瓜籽 Melon Seed	苜 蓿 Lucerne	绿 肥 Green Manure
7. 64	3. 14		2. 46									0. 17	
9. 54	3. 93		13. 98									0. 11	
4. 35	2. 15	0. 49	4. 62									1. 47	
4. 54	2. 44	1. 10	27. 57		0. 19							12. 93	0. 93
23. 00	17. 18	1. 60	19. 86	3. 40	8. 47	4. 59		23. 84				41. 93	0. 15
32. 27	26. 71	3. 18	43. 56	6. 77	10. 02	1. 27		15. 53				67. 54	4. 82
32. 06	22. 00		45. 59	3. 95	11. 92	0. 51		17. 99				85. 11	
41. 11	27. 59	5. 37	36. 58		8. 55	0. 54	1. 84	22. 26				53. 33	11. 27
57. 41	35. 14	9. 83	41. 67	13. 49	13. 00	0. 93	1. 86	23. 68	15. 15			93. 31	12. 00
69. 89	36. 31	21. 17	65. 09	20. 86	18. 11	0. 12	2. 47	19. 94	14. 34			86. 60	10. 47
89. 01	43. 74	40. 51	110. 03	18. 78	8. 25	0. 01	0. 39	13. 88	17. 59	5. 53	67. 09	35. 69	17. 05
79. 73	44. 20	30. 20	170. 00	36. 53	29. 13	0. 07	0. 60	13. 67	9. 00	2. 67	6. 73	35. 73	57. 47
81. 50	49. 70	28. 40	212. 20	39. 70	30. 70	0. 10	0. 20	12. 20	9. 20	2. 70	15. 70	35. 10	62. 10
62. 40	36. 20	22. 70	229. 60	4. 40	31. 20	0. 10	0. 20	13. 00	10. 10	3. 20	32. 30	32. 20	50. 20
70. 10	37. 94	25. 23	215. 92	12. 90	22. 83	0. 15	2. 72	13. 57	10. 05	5. 43	32. 07	29. 97	44. 73
104. 51	59. 80	40. 67	270. 35	2. 88	31. 20	0. 25	3. 59	13. 18	9. 33	4. 92	10. 79	30. 33	33. 39
104. 91	50. 17	51. 99	266. 03	4. 21	32. 07	0. 11	1. 88	16. 14	8. 33	3. 85	8. 89	26. 13	35. 29
58. 69	30. 73	26. 28	284. 24	5. 17	41. 46	0. 20	1. 15	16. 40	8. 18	3. 79	12. 17	25. 02	46. 76
55. 96	26. 07	28. 50	315. 44	14. 47	41. 54	0. 48	1. 14	14. 93	10. 17	5. 46	11. 21	24. 37	52. 17
71. 96	32. 90	35. 66	362. 56	5. 02	50. 99	0. 20	1. 03	18. 09	11. 49	6. 99	10. 45	25. 80	54. 35
101. 63	40. 01	54. 65	381. 38	8. 14	37. 88	0. 09	1. 38	23. 25	15. 40	7. 92	16. 89	26. 84	48. 12
83. 81	32. 05	47. 92	410. 72	31. 08	18. 55	0. 03	1. 73	32. 81	13. 39	8. 10	25. 79	28. 39	45. 55
55. 94	22. 00	29. 96	470. 94	37. 88	25. 91	0. 03	3. 40	32. 84	13. 48	7. 45	14. 97	38. 09	34. 01
58. 58	22. 00	32. 46	463. 30	23. 60	21. 78	0. 07	7. 06	47. 02	13. 44	6. 96	14. 65	46. 24	23. 32
71. 61	31. 60	34. 62	494. 06	35. 58	17. 04	0. 07	5. 89	46. 11	11. 59	5. 58	27. 91	41. 65	17. 78
58. 64	25. 77	30. 29	533. 59	35. 20	17. 18	0. 01	4. 33	56. 61	11. 08	6. 05	22. 61	57. 80	10. 43
48. 63	21. 10	24. 37	551. 08	39. 06	18. 87	0. 02	3. 42	48. 28	11. 21	6. 46	37. 96	61. 30	10. 31
38. 25	19. 82	14. 06	588. 11	52. 48	26. 34		1. 30	40. 49	10. 40	6. 99	46. 10	47. 35	13. 01
39. 93	15. 58	19. 33	613. 06	54. 75	27. 55		1. 78	47. 00	9. 59	6. 85	43. 45	46. 18	11. 30
72. 00	20. 21	49. 46	563. 16	13. 06	24. 44		3. 26	56. 28	8. 39	4. 70	26. 99	41. 67	8. 59
68. 72	21. 18	43. 91	487. 86	13. 88	20. 29		4. 11	73. 84	11. 56	7. 34	47. 49	40. 47	5. 11
67. 78	21. 95	41. 01	497. 98	19. 78	25. 52	0. 01	4. 96	79. 68	10. 78	6. 89	49. 73	39. 97	4. 35
0. 10	0. 07	0. 03	118. 49	19. 40				6. 87	0. 23	0. 05	4. 49	0. 69	0. 18
0. 37		0. 37	27. 07		4. 92		0. 01	14. 66	0. 39	0. 27	5. 45	0. 32	2. 12
0. 35		0. 02	51. 07	0. 38			0. 57	1. 98	2. 67	1. 50	0. 09	3. 54	0. 27
22. 99	17. 77	5. 20	10. 15		6. 01		0. 01	5. 07	0. 61	0. 15	3. 50	1. 69	0. 85
3. 01		3. 01	34. 41		0. 50		0. 33	2. 08	0. 10	0. 02	0. 37	0. 77	0. 33
7. 58		6. 02	52. 17		0. 87	0. 01	0. 04	15. 22	1. 46	1. 18	4. 62	0. 62	
8. 89		7. 78	43. 72		3. 07		1. 66	14. 72	0. 40	0. 06	1. 97	3. 55	0. 60
0. 72		0. 69	143. 73		0. 29		0. 03	12. 40	0. 69	0. 07	1. 69	1. 74	
7. 58	4. 10	1. 84			8. 47		0. 02	1. 40	0. 08	0. 02	8. 69	24. 00	
13. 23		13. 23	6. 33		1. 22		1. 00	2. 02	1. 91	1. 90	16. 00	1. 74	
0. 10		0. 02	0. 04						0. 04				
0. 96		0. 96	0. 38		0. 14		0. 19	2. 12	0. 24	0. 13	0. 29	0. 34	
0. 15	0. 01	0. 14	9. 33					0. 85	1. 85	1. 50	0. 33	0. 61	
0. 05			0. 89				0. 59	0. 09	0. 08	0. 04	1. 89	0. 35	
1. 70		1. 70	0. 20		0. 03		0. 51	0. 20	0. 03		0. 35	0. 01	

Note: Data of farming from 2001 to 2006 are calculated at result of XPCG Second China Agriculture Census. (the same as follow)

9—11　农作物总产量

计量单位:万吨、吨

年　份 Year	单　位 Unit	粮食作物合计 Total Grain Crops	谷　物 Cereal	#水　稻 Rice	#小　麦 Wheat	#冬　麦 Winter Wheat	#玉　米 Corn	#大　麦 Barley	豆　类 Pulse	薯　类 Tubers
1950		3.29	3.27	0.92	1.29		0.53		0.02	
1952		9.96	9.94	2.77	4.48	1.37	1.77	0.11	0.02	
1954		7.18	7.08	1.16	3.80	2.53	1.31	0.16	0.10	
1957		12.24	12.03	0.98	5.25	2.77	4.36	0.23	0.21	
1962		30.92	30.74	1.10	9.48	5.97	15.48	0.14	0.18	
1965		56.11	55.67	3.75	27.08	19.60	23.29	0.25	0.44	
1970		77.63	77.13	7.34	33.11	19.70	34.32	0.56	0.50	
1975		65.39	64.95	7.28	30.84	20.32	23.26	0.09	0.44	
1978		87.60	86.09	12.12	44.48	27.32	24.81	1.01	1.51	0.91
1980		93.09	91.91	11.17	55.79	33.30	21.11	0.85	1.18	0.83
1985		104.10	103.49	12.15	76.01	42.06	14.16	0.29	0.61	0.45
1990		157.18	155.91	21.89	90.38	52.07	33.44	6.86	1.27	0.55
1991		135.12	134.38	19.70	81.57	47.45	27.60	3.63	0.74	0.48
1992		146.07	145.03	17.65	93.74	50.04	27.43	3.35	1.04	0.42
1993		141.80	138.35	15.06	88.37	53.16	24.96	5.45	3.45	0.47
1994		111.22	106.36	14.37	55.57	33.76	20.82	11.45	4.85	0.49
1995		145.77	143.51	19.53	80.37	45.85	36.00	5.58	2.26	0.51
1996		161.57	160.06	19.78	87.93	50.02	41.91	6.83	1.51	0.73
1997		159.72	156.72	22.56	94.34	48.64	29.34	7.73	3.00	0.75
1998		139.49	136.70	14.43	86.06	44.13	29.24	3.41	2.78	1.59
1999		134.44	132.29	16.86	78.15	36.32	29.99	1.86	2.15	0.96
2000		118.71	115.71	19.28	70.13	33.06	21.74	3.24	3.00	1.14
2001		113.31	107.90	13.70	63.93	27.55	25.24	4.26	4.43	0.98
2002		120.88	116.31	14.52	64.82	30.65	30.07	4.84	3.28	1.29
2003		94.53	87.94	11.36	41.80	21.69	27.72	5.62	4.82	1.77
2004		105.25	97.86	10.21	45.84	13.63	37.33	3.24	5.42	1.97
2005		118.12	111.64	11.34	60.79	27.31	34.60	3.36	5.01	1.47
2006		130.17	125.12	21.43	61.53	31.84	34.25	6.92	3.17	1.88
2007		124.19	117.93	22.61	45.50	22.18	36.75	10.49	2.54	3.72
2008		148.01	139.18	22.86	57.90	23.20	53.76	3.13	3.15	5.68
2009		217.35	207.31	20.13	119.62	52.30	60.27	4.34	4.41	5.63
2010		213.64	206.42	18.16	96.33	61.99	85.72	3.48	2.89	4.33
一　师	Division 1	193 524	190 666	87 017	29 307	24 942	73 261			2 858
二　师	Division 2	61 645	61 625	2 944	41 120		17 561			20
三　师	Division 3	117 489	117 019	2 500	44 547	40 742	69 812		140	330
四　师	Division 4	488 762	454 979	85 984	204 618	92 113	126 834	11 992	18 616	15 167
五　师	Division 5	110 786	108 776		63 133	35 625	45 643			2 010
六　师	Division 6	473 732	465 112	1 708	238 963	172 957	220 609	3 832	9	8 611
七　师	Division 7	237 273	236 853		94 238	93 316	142 539		420	
八　师	Division 8	133 764	125 838	944	69 475	65 539	54 894		6 816	1 110
九　师	Division 9	183 315	182 719		102 233	63 555	66 713	13 773	5	591
十　师	Division 10	43 179	39 937		17 609		22 328		2 821	421
建工师	Construction Division	273	273		273	273				
十二师	Division 12	28 758	19 603		12 020	11 453	7 583		5	9 150
十三师	Division 13	35 322	34 397		25 041		4 186	5 170		925
十四师	Division 14	9 176	8 958		4 999	3 900	3 955		18	200
兵团直属	Directly Under XPCG	19 357	17 457	460	15 699	15 500	1 298			1 900

Total Yield of Farm Crops

(10 000 tons, ton)

油　料			棉　花		甜　菜	烟　叶	蔬　菜	瓜果类		打瓜籽	苜　蓿
Oil-bearing Crops	# 油菜籽 Rapeseeds	# 向日葵籽 Helianthus	Cotton	# 长绒棉 Long-staple Cotton	Beetroots	Tobacco	Vegetables	Melons	# 甜　瓜 Muskmelon	Melon Seed	Lucerne
0. 19	0. 06		0. 04								
0. 49	0. 24		0. 33								
0. 21	0. 09	0. 03	0. 19								
0. 21	0. 09	0. 08	1. 09		0. 34						
0. 63	0. 49	0. 06	0. 60	0. 10	7. 16	0. 51	29. 73				
1. 18	0. 90	0. 20	2. 81	0. 21	15. 13	0. 18	33. 33				
1. 06	0. 68		2. 28	0. 12	18. 09	0. 05	23. 28				
1. 51	0. 92	0. 27	1. 03		9. 87	0. 06	8. 49				
2. 29	1. 17	0. 62	1. 95	0. 55	12. 55	0. 14	22. 60	15. 87			16. 90
4. 05	1. 92	1. 54	3. 48	0. 94	30. 01	0. 04	30. 95	20. 66			14. 67
8. 66	3. 33	4. 89	8. 27	1. 32	20. 68	0. 01	28. 98	44. 12	12. 80	4. 87	9. 16
8. 87	3. 63	4. 47	19. 48	3. 42	91. 96	0. 03	43. 68	32. 44	6. 34	0. 81	14. 80
9. 94	5. 22	4. 30	23. 37	4. 18	90. 36	0. 02	37. 35	33. 28	6. 89	1. 65	12. 55
8. 38	4. 49	3. 50	23. 63	0. 52	109. 86	0. 02	37. 80	31. 34	7. 34	3. 40	15. 45
8. 53	3. 85	3. 89	24. 58	1. 46	80. 27	0. 04	38. 61	25. 37	8. 58	2. 71	10. 07
12. 75	5. 45	6. 89	33. 29	0. 37	107. 57	0. 06	38. 94	24. 67	7. 79	1. 26	11. 44
15. 01	4. 40	10. 29	38. 19	0. 56	128. 21	0. 03	49. 53	25. 40	8. 17	1. 12	10. 21
7. 47	2. 76	4. 54	36. 90	0. 62	151. 86	0. 05	53. 60	22. 53	7. 61	1. 61	10. 89
8. 37	2. 64	5. 56	47. 34	1. 90	167. 32	0. 10	53. 31	29. 43	11. 09	1. 51	10. 82
12. 43	4. 40	7. 78	59. 70	0. 70	227. 71	0. 03	63. 53	27. 91	11. 34	1. 38	11. 40
17. 82	5. 56	11. 68	61. 23	1. 14	160. 45	0. 01	93. 02	37. 10	13. 66	1. 85	12. 06
14. 97	4. 16	10. 35	69. 39	3. 72	106. 07		140. 36	35. 54	11. 69	3. 05	12. 75
12. 04	4. 51	7. 02	64. 45	6. 01	150. 35	0. 01	128. 38	41. 79	15. 87	1. 84	20. 82
13. 41	5. 05	7. 72	82. 17	3. 73	132. 80	0. 04	223. 54	47. 55	16. 19	1. 83	27. 36
18. 00	8. 24	9. 12	85. 46	5. 56	105. 82	0. 04	265. 03	39. 35	13. 70	3. 66	38. 78
14. 05	5. 73	7. 97	93. 40	6. 40	107. 25		339. 99	39. 00	16. 63	3. 42	41. 56
9. 88	3. 15	6. 24	106. 85	6. 84	119. 18	0. 01	284. 39	39. 29	18. 46	5. 72	41. 20
9. 16	4. 79	3. 76	121. 82	10. 71	171. 84		270. 13	42. 40	24. 74	6. 75	31. 39
10. 33	3. 97	5. 71	124. 72	11. 51	188. 05		291. 03	35. 17	20. 67	7. 07	32. 09
16. 91	2. 44	14. 03	131. 34	2. 71	158. 20		373. 83	32. 13	13. 58	4. 95	21. 55
18. 63	5. 24	12. 63	113. 43	2. 67	145. 33		598. 78	43. 77	22. 16	9. 55	27. 86
18. 62	5. 68	11. 92	115. 01	3. 63	181. 66	…	581. 62	42. 80	22. 50	8. 75	28. 19
229	131	91	293 651	35 731			152 317	9 104	1 250	5 168	11 279
800		800	69 024		396 149		906 810	10 329	5 360	5 010	6 199
1 027		77	115 706	520			77 525	88 233	48 743	168	54 356
62 293	50 006	12 171	16 126		497 402	24	252 211	30 893	5 995	6 370	18 724
6 664		6 664	92 550		20 000		180 861	5 926	430	857	3 207
25 101		22 722	105 834		66 610	21	1 274 547	54 137	34 877	11 681	3 725
27 772		23 342	96 534		255 380		1 396 141	25 888	2 023	4 480	43 602
2 008		1 945	327 050		10 703		1 149 641	47 327	2 595	3 038	42 990
13 496	6 566	4 834			476 444		149 462	3 903	835	14 712	64 612
38 650		38 650	8 011		82 760		75 135	85 982	85 542	32 831	14 958
151		52	53					2 970			
2 642		2 642	581		8 895		137 517	7 668	1 888	546	219
343	50	293	22 679				52 225	52 264	34 500	512	2 864
128			1 985				2 736	2 115	987	1 544	14 742
4 929		4 929	353		2 260		9 100	1 254		583	440

9—12　农作物公顷产量

计量单位：公斤/公顷

年　份 Year	单　位 Unit	粮食作物合计 Total Grain Crops	谷　物 Cereal	#水　稻 Rice	#小　麦 Wheat	#冬　麦 Winter Wheat	#玉　米 Corn	#大　麦 Barley	豆　类 Pulse	薯　类 Tubers
	1950	787	791	1 403	683		803		450	
	1952	1 234	1 241	2 093	990	998	1 215	1 725	285	
	1954	1 606	1 630	2 408	1 350	1 635	1 965	1 439	818	
	1957	1 325	1 358	1 493	1 245	1 283	1 725	875	548	
	1962	1 087	1 099	1 373	735	825	1 703	689	375	
	1965	1 745	1 771	1 920	1 373	1 733	2 948	814	608	
	1970	1 797	1 817	1 995	1 343	1 508	2 940	1 223	660	
	1975	1 463	1 482	2 273	1 215	1 208	2 205	885	983	
	1978	1 867	1 913	3 373	1 605	1 845	2 459	1 161	922	1 200
	1980	2 110	2 164	3 341	1 936	2 077	2 625	1 148	800	1 518
	1985	2 875	2 904	4 165	2 733	2 920	3 320	1 283	1 099	2 676
	1990	4 259	4 318	6 841	3 702	3 925	6 147	2 867	1 588	4 381
	1991	3 987	4 040	6 701	3 430	5 109	6 202	2 161	1 156	4 359
	1992	4 297	4 352	6 003	3 890	4 078	6 248	2 722	1 576	4 167
	1993	4 259	4 393	5 783	3 901	3 995	6 772	3 375	1 913	4 536
	1994	4 226	4 417	6 473	3 796	3 954	6 537	3 493	2 159	4 956
	1995	4 875	4 976	6 997	4 228	4 695	7 296	3 532	2 120	5 271
	1996	4 986	5 069	6 712	4 286	4 518	7 948	3 117	1 822	5 069
	1997	4 975	5 087	6 789	4 544	4 761	7 770	3 131	2 329	4 961
	1998	5 189	5 305	5 617	4 781	4 767	7 881	3 706	2 379	6 581
	1999	5 475	5 600	6 041	4 956	5 329	7 873	3 284	2 324	5 509
	2000	5 371	5 525	7 321	4 916	5 192	7 544	3 530	2 573	5 806
	2001	5 416	5 654	6 775	5 168	5 412	7 141	4 069	2 672	5 456
	2002	5 820	6 024	7 637	5 469	5 807	7 166	4 444	2 614	6 343
	2003	5 824	6 125	7 425	5 473	5 673	7 340	4 736	2 992	6 694
	2004	5 877	6 200	6 860	5 447	5 528	7 383	4 977	3 023	5 893
	2005	6 150	6 447	8 333	5 871	6 097	7 381	4 646	3 012	6 485
	2006	6 798	7 013	9 222	6 282	6 488	7 680	6 038	3 027	7 259
	2007	7 171	7 393	8 884	6 233	6 461	8 542	6 873	3 407	5 997
	2008	6 288	6 465	9 551	4 838	5 580	9 021	2 971	2 953	6 019
	2009	6 922	7 088	9 247	6 070	6 321	9 514	5 981	3 020	8 146
	2010	7 504	7 657	9 981	6 168	6 259	10 013	5 268	3 184	7 168
一　师	Division 1	8 757	8 795	10 048	6 344	6 778	8 827			6 805
二　师	Division 2	6 395	6 393	6 542	6 297		6 602			
三　师	Division 3	5 662	5 661	7 576	5 527	5 566	5 718		2 800	11 000
四　师	Division 4	7 642	8 151	10 397	6 841	7 489	9 638	6 737	3 003	7 818
五　师	Division 5	6 563	6 573		5 387	6 573	9 450			6 091
六　师	Division 6	8 673	8 690	7 764	6 804	6 629	12 599	5 719	900	7 900
七　师	Division 7	8 917	8 962		6 283	6 292	12 547		2 333	
八　师	Division 8	6 416	6 606	5 553	5 361	5 452	9 384		4 156	6 938
九　师	Division 9	6 835	6 838		5 727	6 213	11 999	4 161		5 910
十　师	Division 10	7 125	7 940		6 311		9 968		2 908	7 017
建工师	Construction Division	3 900	3 900		3 900	3 900				
十二师	Division 12	6 997	7 315		5 921	5 904	11 666			6 399
十三师	Division 13	6 872	6 893		7 034		7 095	6 155		6 167
十四师	Division 14	2 876	2 844		1 930	2 143	7 062		1 800	6 667
兵团直属	Directly Under XPCG	4 976	4 863	5 111	4 658	4 655	9 985			6 333

Yield of Farm Crops Per Hectare

(kg/hectare)

油 料 Oil-bearing Crops	# 油菜籽 Rapeseeds	# 向日葵籽 Helianthus	棉 花 Cotton	# 长绒棉 Long-staple Cotton	甜 菜 Beetroots	烟 叶 Tobacco	蔬 菜 Vegetables	瓜果类 Melons	# 甜 瓜 Musk-melon	打瓜籽 Melon Seed	苜 蓿 Lucerne
249	188		163		1 000						
514	615		236								
483	435	675	411								
463	353	705	395		17 895						
274	285	405	302	295	8 453	1 104	12 549				
366	338	623	645	316	15 100	1 443	21 470				
331	308		500	313	15 176	907	12 936				
367	330	495	282		11 544	1 185	3 810				
399	332	631	468	408	9 654	753	9 544	10 478			1 811
579	527	725	535	448	16 571	142	15 519	14 404			1 693
973	761	1 207	752	703	25 067	259	20 879	25 078	23 160	726	2 567
1 113	820	1 482	1 146	936	31 569	437	31 959	36 040	23 786	1 205	4 142
1 220	1 051	1 513	1 101	1 052	29 433	965	30 611	36 173	25 500	1 049	3 576
1 343	1 240	1 544	1 029	1 173	35 212	1 035	29 076	31 027	22 924	1 054	4 798
1 217	1 015	1 544	1 138	1 128	35 160	144	28 453	25 245	15 799	844	3 361
1 220	912	1 694	1 231	1 283	34 478	171	29 545	26 444	15 842	1 172	3 773
1 430	877	1 979	1 435	1 330	39 979	160	30 688	30 492	21 221	1 260	3 907
1 273	898	1 728	1 298	1 199	36 628	435	32 683	27 543	20 079	1 323	4 353
1 496	1 013	1 951	1 501	1 313	40 279	877	35 707	28 938	20 311	1 347	4 440
1 727	1 337	2 182	1 647	1 394	44 658	291	35 119	24 291	16 223	1 321	4 419
1 753	1 390	2 137	1 606	1 400	42 357	72	40 009	24 091	17 247	1 095	4 493
1 787	1 298	2 160	1 690	1 197	57 178		42 780	26 542	14 432	1 183	4 491
2 152	2 050	2 342	1 369	1 588	58 027	4 800	39 091	31 004	21 302	1 228	5 466
2 289	2 296	2 378	1 773	1 579	60 972	5 114	47 542	35 381	23 260	1 251	5 918
2 514	2 607	2 635	1 730	1 561	62 098	6 143	57 477	33 951	24 556	1 312	9 312
2 397	2 224	2 630	1 750	1 819	62 425		60 058	35 198	27 488	1 511	7 191
2 031	1 493	2 559	1 939	1 752	63 160	6 050	58 903	35 046	28 576	1 507	6 721
2 395	2 415	2 677	2 071	2 041	65 241		66 715	40 772	35 391	1 465	6 630
2 587	2 550	2 953	2 034	2 102	68 258		61 922	36 673	30 176	1 627	6 948
2 349	1 206	2 836	2 332	2 079	64 732		66 423	38 297	28 883	1 833	5 171
2 711	2 476	2 875	2 325	1 926	71 628		81 092	37 866	30 189	2 010	6 884
2 748	2 586	2 907	2 310	1 833	71 184	4 500	72 995	39 703	32 660	1 760	7 092
2 290	1 871	3 033	2 478	1 842			22 171	39 583	25 000	1 151	16 346
2 162		2 162	2 550		80 518		61 856	26 485	19 852	919	19 372
2 934		3 850	2 266	1 368			39 154	33 046	32 495	1 867	15 355
2 710	2 814	2 341	1 589		82 762		49 746	50 644	39 967	1 820	11 079
2 214		2 214	2 690		40 000		86 952	59 260	21 500	2 316	4 165
3 311		3 774	2 029		76 563	2 100	83 742	37 080	29 557	2 528	6 008
3 124		3 000	2 208		83 186		94 847	64 720	33 717	2 274	12 282
2 789		2 819	2 275		36 907		92 713	68 590	37 071	1 798	24 707
1 780	1 601	2 627			56 251		106 759	48 788	41 750	1 693	2 692
2 921		2 921	1 266		67 836		37 196	45 017	45 022	2 052	8 597
1 510		2 600	1 325					74 250			
2 752		2 752	1 529		63 536		64 867	31 950	14 523	1 883	644
2 287	5 000	2 093	2 431				61 441	28 251	23 000	1 552	4 695
2 560			2 230				30 400	26 438	24 675	817	42 120
2 899		2 899	1 765		75 333		45 500	41 800		1 666	44 000

9—13　农作物种植面积构成

Composition of Farm Crops Area

计量单位:%　　　　　　　　　　　　　　　　　　　　　　　　　　　　(%)

指　标	Item	1990	1995	2000	2005	2009	2010
农作物总播种面积	**Total Sown Areas of Farm Crops**	**100.0**	**100.0**	**100.0**	**100.0**	**100.0**	**100.0**
粮食作物	Grain Crops	47.3	36.8	24.3	18.8	28.3	25.4
谷　物	Cereal	97.5	96.1	93.8	90.2	93.1	94.7
稻　谷	Rice	8.9	9.7	12.7	7.9	7.4	6.8
小　麦	Wheat	67.9	66.1	68.8	59.8	67.4	57.9
玉　米	Corn	15.1	17.2	13.9	27.1	21.7	31.8
大　麦	Barley	6.7	5.5	4.4	4.2	2.5	2.5
其它谷物	Other Cereal	1.5	1.5	0.2	1.1	1.0	1.0
豆　类	Pulse	2.2	3.6	5.3	8.7	4.7	3.2
薯　类	Tubers	0.3	0.3	0.9	1.2	2.2	2.1
油料作物	Oil-bearing Crops	10.2	12.9	9.2	4.8	6.2	6.1
# 花　生	Peanuts	0.2	0.1	0.1	0.2	0.2	0.7
油菜籽	Rapeseeds	55.4	47.8	38.2	43.4	30.8	32.4
芝　麻	Sesame					0.4	0.1
胡麻籽	Linseed	1.3	0.7	0.2	3.4	0.4	…
向日葵	Sunflower	37.9	49.6	57.2	50.1	63.9	60.5
棉　花	Cotton	21.8	32.7	45.1	53.8	44.0	44.5
# 长绒棉	Long-staple Cotton	21.5	1.6	7.5	7.1	2.8	4.0
麻　类	Hemp Crops	0.1	…	…	0.3	…	…
# 亚　麻	Flax		100.0	95.8	100.0	100.0	100.0
甜　菜	Beetsroots	3.7	4.0	2.1	1.8	1.9	2.3
烟　叶	Tobacco	…	…	…			…
药　材	Medicinal Materials	0.1	0.2	0.2	0.3	0.4	0.4
蔬　菜	Vegetables	1.8	2.0	3.6	4.7	6.7	7.1
瓜果类	melons	1.1	1.0	1.5	1.1	1.0	1.0
其他农作物	Other Farm Crops	13.9	10.4	14.0	14.4	11.5	13.2
# 苜　蓿	Lucerne	4.6	3.2	3.1	41.5	31.8	27.1

注:2005年数据按兵团第二次农业普查结果进行校验修订。
Note:2005 are calculated at result of XPCG Second China Agriculture Census.

9—14 各师农作物复播面积

Multiple Cropping Areas of Farm Crops by Division

计量单位:千公顷 (2010 年) (1 000 hectares)

指 标	Item	合 计 Total	一 师 Division 1	二 师 Division 2	三 师 Division 3	四 师 Division 4	五 师 Division 5	六 师 Division 6	七 师 Division 7
农作物复播面积	**Total Multiple Cropping Area**	**37.56**	**4.92**	**2.63**	**6.79**	**9.50**	**1.81**	**0.43**	**9.10**
粮食作物	Grain Crops	13.02	1.98	0.51	5.76	4.01			0.15
谷 物	Cereal	8.99	1.98	0.51	5.71	0.18			
水 稻	Rice	0.22	0.22						
玉 米	Corn	8.56	1.76	0.51	5.64	0.04			
其他谷物	Other Cerea	0.21			0.07	0.14			
豆 类	Pulse	4.03			0.05	3.83			0.15
# 大豆(黄豆、黑豆等)	Soja	4.02			0.05	3.82			0.15
油料作物	Oil-bearing Crops	9.63				3.77	1.48	0.12	4.10
# 向日葵籽	Sunflower	9.63				3.77	1.48	0.12	4.10
棉 花	Cotton	0.27							
蔬菜(含菜用瓜)	Vegetables	1.58	0.22		0.07	0.04		0.31	0.35
瓜果类	Melons	0.09	0.01		0.07	0.01			
其他作物	Other Farm Crops	12.97	2.71	2.12	0.89	1.67	0.33		4.50
打瓜籽	Melon Seed	0.25				0.23			
苜蓿(包括当年新播)	Lucerne	1.28			0.02	0.24			0.69
其他饲料	Other Animal Feed	6.57	1.88		0.60	0.35			3.34
# 青贮玉米	Silage Corn	6.40	1.88		0.53	0.35			3.34
绿 肥(包括翻掉播种面积)	Green Manure	4.13	0.09	2.12	0.27	0.85	0.33		0.47
其它作物(包括安息茴香)	Others	0.74	0.74						

指 标	Item	八 师 Division 8	九 师 Division 9	十 师 Division 10	建工师 Construction Division	十二师 Division 12	十三师 Division 13	十四师 Division 14	兵团直属 Division 7
农作物复播面积	**Total Multiple Cropping Area**	**0.77**				**0.78**	**0.23**	**0.54**	**0.06**
粮食作物	Grain Crops						0.07	0.54	
谷 物	Cereal						0.07	0.54	
水 稻	Rice								
玉 米	Corn						0.07	0.54	
其他谷物	Other Cereal								
豆 类	Pulse								
# 大豆(黄豆、黑豆等)	Soja								
油料作物	Oil-bearing Crops	0.02				0.02	0.06		0.06
# 向日葵籽	Helianthus	0.02				0.02	0.06		0.06
棉 花	Cotton					0.27			
蔬菜(含菜用瓜)	Vegetables	0.12				0.47			
瓜果类	Melons								
其他作物	Other Farm Crops	0.63				0.02	0.10		
打瓜籽	Melon Seed					0.02			
苜蓿(包括当年新播)	Lucerne	0.33							
其他饲料	Other Animal Feed	0.30					0.10		
# 青贮玉米	Silage Corn	0.30							
绿 肥(包括翻掉播种面积)	Green Manure								
其它作物(包括安息茴香)	Others								

9—15　各师蔬菜播种面积

Sown Areas of Vegetable by Division

计量单位:公顷　　　　(2010 年)　　　　(hectare)

指　标	Item	合计 Total	一师 Division 1	二师 Division 2	三师 Division 3	四师 Division 4	五师 Division 5	六师 Division 6	七师 Division 7
总　计	**Total**	**79 678**	**6 866**	**14 660**	**1 980**	**5 069**	**2 076**	**15 223**	**14 720**
叶菜类	Genus	4 278	456	280	750	448	74	447	730
# 大白菜	Greens	2 308	312	127	556	219	35	182	374
瓜菜类	Genus	1 399	62	60	99	211	29	154	147
# 黄　瓜	Cucumber	636	36	39	60	123	17	65	127
块根、块茎类	Root tuber	2 198	103	70	253	412	29	625	197
# 萝　卜	Radish	797	54	26	96	83	14	151	116
胡萝卜	Carrot	1 162	36	37	120	287	12	426	80
茄果菜类	Fruit	68 945	6 037	14 112	614	3 635	1 887	13 602	13 448
# 番　茄	Tomato	47 652	63	5 776	319	1 716	1 792	12 453	12 836
# 工业用番茄	Tomato for Industry	45 482		5 710	105	1 328	1 744	12 248	12 534
辣　椒	Pepper	20 055	5 913	8 276	125	1 525	61	1 045	421
# 工业用辣椒	Hot Pepper for Industry	17 852	5 851	8 207	13	1 149	8	736	203
葱蒜类	Garlic	1 089	45	44	79	167	11	299	39
# 大　葱	Shallot	686	25	32	56	90	8	188	37
菜用豆类	Mean	928	96	69	129	161	36	59	131
# 四季豆	Legumina	412	39	31	64	93	13	32	43
豇　豆	Cownea	372	50	37	63	36	23	24	32
水生菜类	Aquatic Vegetable	4	2						
其它蔬菜	Other Vegetable	837	65	25	56	35	10	37	28

指　标	Item	八师 Division 8	九师 Division 9	十师 Division 10	十二师 Division 12	十三师 Division 13	十四师 Division 14	兵团直属 Directly Under XPCG
总　计	**Total**	**12 400**	**1 399**	**2 022**	**2 122**	**846**	**90**	**205**
叶菜类	Genus	461	32	148	258	157	37	
# 大白菜	Greens	294	9	80	42	56	22	
瓜菜类	Genus	133	22	227	69	62	6	118
# 黄　瓜	Cucumber	82	10	20	10	45	2	
块根、块茎类	Root tuber	152	27	85	134	89	22	
# 萝　卜	Radish	95	8	53	62	30	9	
胡萝卜	Carrot	41	7	22	30	57	7	
茄果菜类	Fruit	11 458	1 287	1 534	928	303	13	87
# 番　茄	Tomato	10 297	1 236	129	861	129	4	41
# 工业用番茄	Tomato for Industry	9 826	1 191	52	703			41
辣　椒	Pepper	1 051	39	1 396	56	98	3	46
# 工业用辣椒	Hot Pepper for Industry	243		1 365	31			46
葱蒜类	Garlic	45	13	9	225	110	3	
# 大　葱	Shallot	35	6	6	194	8	1	
菜用豆类	Mean	86	5	7	45	95	9	
# 四季豆	Legumina	43		4	9	36	5	
豇　豆	Cownea	38		3	6	56	4	
水生菜类	Aquatic Vegetable	2						
其它蔬菜	Other Vegetable	63	13	12	463	30		

9—16 各师蔬菜产量

Yield of Vegetable by Division

计量单位:吨 (2010 年) (ton)

指 标	Item	合 计 Total	一 师 Division 1	二 师 Division 2	三 师 Division 3	四 师 Division 4	五 师 Division 5	六 师 Division 6	七 师 Division 7
总 计	**Total**	**5 816 228**	**152 317**	**906 810**	**77 525**	**252 211**	**180 861**	**1 274 547**	**1 396 141**
叶菜类	Genus	240 140	18 492	10 951	26 387	19 707	4 420	28 427	55 178
# 大白菜	Greens	145 004	14 079	5 791	19 429	11 343	2 564	15 881	28 880
瓜菜类	Genus	73 976	2 462	2 399	3 075	10 293	2 399	10 386	12 022
# 黄 瓜	Cucumber	40 213	987	1 817	2 302	6 389	1 200	4 799	10 388
块根、块茎类	Root tuber	113 141	3 285	3 174	10 091	18 307	2 030	31 524	14 546
# 萝 卜	Radish	45 330	1 670	1 163	3 809	4 824	889	7 733	9 118
胡萝卜	Carrot	56 752	1 117	1 878	4 927	11 219	634	21 755	5 249
茄果菜类	Fruit	5 263 429	124 587	886 421	29 514	191 795	169 153	1 183 273	1 299 786
# 番 茄	Tomato	4 605 983	2 242	611 400	21 246	135 027	166 132	1 141 955	1 264 513
# 工业用番茄	Tomato for Industry	4 413 084	12	607 303	12 250	112 989	162 807	1 110 951	1 228 136
辣 椒	Pepper	603 098	120 684	273 073	3 989	47 693	1 804	35 850	22 913
# 工业用辣椒	Hot Pepper for Industry	509 159	118 973	271 443	320	34 265	350	21 029	7 765
葱蒜类	Garlic	61 104	965	945	2 196	5 433	439	16 832	4 351
# 大 葱	Shallot	37 579	591	701	1 510	3 243	335	8 861	4 189
菜用豆类	Mean	33 713	2 162	1 840	4 177	4 826	2 011	1 975	7 051
# 四季豆	Legumina	14 049	890	1 049	1 863	2 313	549	1 053	2 495
豇 豆	Cownea	14 368	1 046	791	2 289	1 275	1 462	862	1 898
水生菜类	Aquatic Vegetable	202	70			6			
其它蔬菜	Other Vegetable	25 636	271	1 007	1 880	1 379	255	1 868	1 876
食用菌(干鲜混合)	Edible Mushroom(Dry,Fvesh,Mix)	4 887	23	73	205	465	154	262	1 331

指 标	Item	八 师 Division 8	九 师 Division 9	十 师 Division 10	十二师 Division 12	十三师 Division 13	十四师 Division 14	兵团直属 Directly Under XPCG
总 计	**Total**	**1 149 641**	**149 462**	**75 135**	**137 517**	**52 225**	**2 736**	**9 100**
叶菜类	Genus	42 865	1 415	6 602	15 675	8 930	1 091	
# 大白菜	Greens	31 420	508	5 816	4 310	4 170	813	
瓜菜类	Genus	8 314	1 583	6 402	4 912	5 141	99	4 489
# 黄 瓜	Cucumber	4 121	996	879	2 085	4 204	46	
块根、块茎类	Root tuber	8 792	1 087	5 569	9 018	4 954	764	
# 萝 卜	Radish	5 463	428	3 864	4 150	1 929	290	
胡萝卜	Carrot	1 911	399	1 453	3 039	2 951	220	
茄果菜类	Fruit	1 078 065	143 381	55 612	77 931	18 816	484	4 611
# 番 茄	Tomato	1 025 245	139 555	8 770	76 204	10 469	130	3 095
# 工业用番茄	Tomato for Industry	978 906	133 961	3 910	58 764			3 095
辣 椒	Pepper	40 734	3 258	46 488	1 181	3 831	84	1 516
# 工业用辣椒	Hot Pepper for Industry	6 801		46 097	600			1 516
葱蒜类	Garlic	3 397	509	216	17 953	7 827	41	
# 大 葱	Shallot	2 341	206	150	14 921	520	11	
菜用豆类	Mean	3 466	283	219	529	4 917	257	
# 四季豆	Legumina	1 783	15	40	121	1 726	152	
豇 豆	Cownea	1 166	9	179	126	3 160	105	
水生菜类	Aquatic Vegetable	126						
其它蔬菜	Other Vegetable	4 445	819	505	10 001	1 330		
食用菌(干鲜混合)	Edible Mushroom(Dry,Fresh,Mix)	171	385	10	1 498	310		

9—17　造林面积、水果及水产品生产情况

Forestation Area, Fruits and Aquatic Production

年　份 Year	当年人工造林面积 Afforestation Area in the Current Year	年末实有果园面积(公顷) Orchard Area at the Year-end (hectare)	# 结果面积 Orchard Area In the Current Year	水果总产量(吨) Total Output of Fruits (ton)	养殖面积(公顷) Culture Area (hectare)	水产品产量(吨) Aquatic Products(ton)
1950	71					
1952	674					
1954	466					
1957	1 063					
1962	1 863	4 514	505	805	2 227	1 869
1965	3 457	6 403	1 715	4 374	5 729	2 974
1970	1 151	7 099	3 608	10 727	9 300	2 775
1975	1 173	9 823	4 918	14 506	18 200	1 813
1978	2 516	12 111	6 120	25 717	18 943	2 956
1980	4 103	12 871	6 591	26 607	20 514	2 715
1985	28 391	12 107	6 811	31 318	30 248	3 269
1990	7 085	22 637	9 256	84 213	29 611	8 184
1995	7 369	29 538	14 796	157 912	30 795	10 003
2000	13 399	36 948	20 697	284 584	28 368	12 894
2001	18 916	40 037	18 567	249 823	22 491	13 612
2002	48 928	51 612	23 943	303 376	24 787	16 295
2003	83 670	54 353	25 437	320 979	25 846	16 608
2004	37 982	58 662		390 294	31 841	17 640
2005	21 831	71 005	33 692	459 012	31 908	20 026
2006	9 428	81 060	36 711	560 500	32 183	20 838
2007	16 247	93 881	45 046	663 672	33 238	22 443
2008	14 274	101 357	54 269	709 367	33 718	22 396
2009	17 349	129 216	65 249	1 030 865	32 481	23 569
2010	14 409	176 445	90 664	1 225 376	32 853	26 701

9—18　牲畜年末头数及主要畜产品产量

Year-end Number of Livestock and Output of Major Livestock Products

年　份 Year	大小牲畜年末头数(万头、万只) Year-end Number of Livestock(head)	大牲畜 Large Animals	猪 Pigs	羊 Sheep and Goats	肉类产量(吨) Output of Meat (ton)	羊毛产量(吨) Wool (ton)	牛奶产量(吨) Cow Milk (ton)	禽蛋产量(吨) Poultry Eggs (ton)
1950	18.15	4.45	1.21	12.48		21		
1952	49.11	4.69	1.77	42.65		98		
1954	52.99	5.44	2.18	45.38	3 178	438	455	
1957	74.25	7.55	6.88	59.83	5 502	1 159	1 945	
1962	144.61	17.97	13.95	112.68	9 727	2 057	7 624	709
1965	210.05	28.43	20.74	160.88	19 459	3 434	10 799	1 393
1970	234.46	28.32	28.13	178.02	12 851	5 240	12 974	1 599
1975	245.15	30.85	27.24	187.06	15 611	5 823	12 223	1 765
1978	269.12	29.22	51.92	187.98	20 704	5 705	16 307	2 291
1980	267.09	27.10	47.32	192.67	29 406	5 692	14 106	2 442
1985	289.79	25.29	30.60	233.90	30 289	6 987	24 908	13 054
1990	331.10	25.75	32.40	272.94	47 102	8 545	43 455	15 365
1995	327.84	22.55	42.46	262.83	67 000	7 587	62 300	20 837
2000	403.97	23.90	51.35	328.72	106 875	8 528	75 908	24 568
2001	402.37	22.78	51.53	328.06	113 101	8 204	77 852	25 095
2002	425.56	24.38	52.60	348.58	120 627	8 511	84 028	26 746
2003	446.56	26.23	51.32	369.01	127 828	9 036	95 231	29 529
2004	481.61	30.65	52.81	398.15	138 426	9 892	122 662	31 239
2005	502.66	32.13	57.20	413.33	150 238	10 181	164 817	28 121
2006	510.40	32.06	63.38	414.96	162 900	10 419	193 608	28 207
2007	533.63	31.78	75.88	425.97	176 803	11 216	247 299	31 099
2008	536.20	34.49	106.87	394.84	219 482	11 326	328 228	34 771
2009	586.19	37.95	134.09	414.15	266 130	10 639	384 414	40 760
2010	624.06	40.88	155.42	427.76	319 923	11 314	443 099	45 731

注：1998年至2006年牧业数据按兵团第二次全国农业普查结果进行校验修订。

Note: Data of animal hunbandry from 1998 to 2006 are calculated at result of XPCG Second China Agriclture Census.

9—19 各师林业生产情况

Forestry Production by Division

计量单位:公顷 (2010 年) (hectare)

单 位 Unit	当年荒山荒地造林面积 Afforestation Area in of Waste Mountain and Wasteland in the Current Year	# 人工造林面积 Afforestation Area	当年造林面积按造林方式分 Woodland Restored from Cultivated Land 用材林 Timber Forest	经济林 Economic Forest	防护林 Wind break	薪炭林 Firewood Forest	特种用途林 Forest for Special Purpose	年末实有封山育林面积 Area of Planting Trees
总 计 Total	**19 742**	**14 409**	**23**	**1 371**	**18 348**			**280 851**
一 师 Division 1	1 907	1 907	15	892	1 000			23 011
二 师 Division 2	3 393	727			3 393			22 396
三 师 Division 3	1 480	1 480			1 480			
四 师 Division 4	632	632			632			
五 师 Division 5	438	438			438			
六 师 Division 6	3 541	1 541			3 541			27 713
七 师 Division 7	923	923			923			73 746
八 师 Division 8	4 750	4 750	8		4 742			
九 师 Division 9	1 533	866		13	1 520			132 651
十 师 Division 10	366	366		12	354			
十二师 Division 12	144	144		42	102			
十三师 Division 13	122	122			122			1 334
十四师 Division 14	513	513		412	101			
兵团直属 Directly Under XPCG								

单 位 Unit	当年零星(四旁)植树(万株) Fragmentary Planting (10 000 stubs)	年末实有育苗面积 Actual Sapling Breeding Area	当年苗木产量(万株) Output of Breeding and Trees(10 000 stubs)	幼林抚育作业面积 Tending Area of Young Growth	成林抚育面 积 Tending Area of Forest	核桃产量(吨) Walnut Output (ton)	木材采伐量(立方米) Timber Felling Output in (cu. m)
总 计 Total	**261.84**	**1 373**	**7 681.63**	**231 537**	**152 510**	**2 920**	**58 941**
一 师 Division 1	57.14	118	577.99	9 188	29 407	2 566	13 367
二 师 Division 2	18.78	47	1 826.50	21 592	15 381		8 876
三 师 Division 3		80	1 039.70	3 079	6 362	176	294
四 师 Division 4	4.23	172	601.09	19 006	3 209		17 700
五 师 Division 5	5.00	15	118.60	14 487	7 272		3 751
六 师 Division 6	55.75	114	474.70	31 742	20 358		2 185
七 师 Division 7	100.80	126	363.50	37 706	25 406		85
八 师 Division 8		394	1 510.90	12 428	17 766		6 602
九 师 Division 9	12.39	39	520.40	14 158	4 872		2 420
十 师 Division 10		110	489.35	53 751	15 308		70
十二师 Division 12		114	85.00	66	400		
十三师 Division 13	7.35	42	63.90	4 245	3 564	75	896
十四师 Division 14				9 215	2 531	103	2 695
兵团直属 Directly Under XPCG	0.40	2	10.00	874	674		

9—20　各师水果生产情况

Fruit Production by Division

（2010 年）

指　　标	Item	合　计 Total	一　师 Division 1	二　师 Division 2	三　师 Division 3	四　师 Division 4	五　师 Division 5	六　师 Division 6
年末实有面积(公顷)	**Actual Area at the Year-end(hectare)**	**176 445**	**52 145**	**33 132**	**30 478**	**10 755**	**4 186**	**5 969**
苹　果	Apples	14 962	5 894	695	2 279	4 184	194	24
# 红富士苹果	Hongfushi Apples	10 819	5 336	385	1 927	2 124	173	11
黄元帅苹果	Huangyuangshuai Apples	1 483	516	187	273	328	10	
梨	Pears	17 278	5 845	9 959	1 382	43		
# 香　梨	Snow Flake Pears	14 817	5 138	9 231	436			
砀山梨	Duck Pears	1 878	655	370	829			
葡　萄	Grapes	34 018	191	1 358	391	4 032	3 907	5 913
# 无核葡萄	Seedless Grapes	7 949	8	107	4	229	405	757
红提葡萄	Hongti Grapes	10 103	123	317	152	1 575	3 501	989
酿酒葡萄	Grapes of Make Wining	12 441		403		1 652		3 820
桃	Peachs	2 431	91	117	116	971	45	2
# 蟠　桃	Pan Peachs	904	3	56		399	29	2
杏	Apricots	4 945	1 210	1 599	638	1 171	13	
红　枣	Jujubes	101 967	38 859	19 208	25 535	245	27	27
石　榴	Pomegranate	56			56			
其　他	Other	788	55	196	81	109		3
产　量(吨)	**Output(ton)**	**1 225 376**	**361 246**	**217 023**	**146 134**	**93 681**	**38 883**	**36 791**
苹　果	Apples	200 450	92 852	9 392	31 902	39 210	1 292	137
# 红富士苹果	Hongfushi Apples	113 424	60 112	1 883	21 209	14 096	765	38
黄元帅苹果	huanyuanshuai Apples	56 125	31 019	6 542	9 480	4 199	300	
梨	Pears	353 340	127 938	177 197	46 513	1 105		
# 香　梨	Snow Flake Pears	283 118	109 320	157 638	16 149	1		
砀山梨	Dangshan Pears	56 748	17 457	12 909	26 165			
葡　萄	Grapes	369 239	3 366	9 571	10 195	31 467	37 282	36 575
# 无核葡萄	Seedless Grapes	125 771	270	219	190	1 340	1 081	3 970
红提葡萄	Hongti Grapes	118 634	2 207	2 112	6 876	16 202	36 151	10 236
酿酒葡萄	Grapes of Make Wining	94 410	85	2 128		12 737		22 079
桃	Peachs	32 768	1 268	2 124	1 308	15 790	255	5
# 蟠　桃	Pan Peachs	13 494	40	1 320		6 683	145	1
杏	Apricots	19 560	2 775	2 767	7 592	5 112		
红　枣	Jujubes	245 981	132 469	15 877	47 239	259	54	18
石　榴	Pomegranate	83			83			
其　他	Other	3 955	578	95	1 302	738		56

9—20 续表　Continued

（2010 年）

指　　标	Item	七　师 Division 7	八　师 Division 8	九　师 Division 9	十　师 Division 10	十二师 Division 12	十三师 Division 13	十四师 Division 14	兵团直属 Directly Under XPCG
年末实有面积（公顷）	**Actual Area at the Year-end(hectare)**	**1 468**	**8 993**	**256**	**181**	**4 097**	**10 556**	**12 925**	**1 304**
苹　果	Apples	751	291	159	168	28	1	294	
# 红富士苹果	Hongfushi Apples	514	42		91	28		188	
黄元帅苹果	Huangyuangshuai Apples	83	7		22			57	
梨	Pears	2				12	1	34	
# 香　梨	Snow Flake Pears					12			
砀山梨	Dangshan Pears							24	
葡　萄	Grapes	658	7 551	23	3	3 517	5 044	126	1 304
# 无核葡萄	Seedless Grapes	24	1 066	7		694	4 584	64	
红提葡萄	Hongti Grapes	250	1 249		2	1 855	90		
酿酒葡萄	Grapes of Make Wining		4 613			592	67		1 294
桃	Peachs	30	590	1	10	439		19	
# 蟠　桃	Pam Peachs	21	36	1	10	347			
杏	Apricots	1		57		26	19	211	
红　枣	Jujubes	19	424			73	5 309	12 241	
石　榴	Pomegranate								
其　他	Other	7	137	16		2	182		
产　量(吨)	**Output(ton)**	**22 723**	**72 814**	**947**	**3 116**	**66 592**	**95 230**	**53 396**	**16 800**
苹　果	Apples	12 895	2 085	672	2 961	92	23	6 937	
# 红富士苹果	Hongfushi Apples	8 431	455		2 225	92		4 118	
黄元帅苹果	huanyuanshuai Apples	1 540	93	26	734			2 192	
梨	Pears	66		8		10	35	468	
# 香　梨	Snow Flake Pears					10			
砀山梨	Dangshan Pears							217	
葡　萄	Grapes	8 978	63 081	211	38	61 647	86 460	3 568	16 800
# 无核葡萄	Seedless Grapes	699	13 541	13		19 471	83 120	1 857	
红提葡萄	Hongti Grapes	3 928	10 814		21	27 994	2 092	1	
酿酒葡萄	Grapes of Make Wining	24	31 857			7 843	1 000		16 657
桃	Peachs	681	6 540		117	4 653		27	
# 蟠　桃	Pam Peachs	421	811		117	3 956			
杏	Apricots	9	3			50	972	280	
红　枣	Jujubes	39	110			70	7 730	42 116	
石　榴	Pomegranate								
其　他	Other	55	995	56		70	10		

9—21　畜牧业生产情况

Animal Husbandry Production

计量单位:万头(只)　　(2010年)　　(10 000 heads)

指　标	Item	合计 Total	牛 Cattle and Buffaloes	#奶牛 Cows	马 Horses	驴 Donkeys	骡 Mules	骆驼 Camels
年初数	**Number at the Beginning of the Year**	**586.19**	**33.85**	**17.25**	**2.30**	**1.34**	**0.01**	**0.45**
年内增加	**Increase in the Year**	**782.37**	**29.95**	**10.56**	**1.23**	**0.57**		**0.15**
繁殖成活数	Number of Breeding Survival	519.38	14.56	7.08	0.68	0.27		0.09
买入数	Buy in	261.69	15.36	3.45	0.55	0.30		0.06
其　他	Other	1.30	0.03	0.03				
年内减少	**Decrease in the Year**	**744.50**	**26.96**	**7.90**	**1.13**	**0.68**	**0.01**	**0.19**
成、幼畜死亡数	Death of Adult and Infant Animals	9.06	0.35	0.25	0.02			
卖出数	Sold out	621.12	21.77	6.53	0.93	0.52	0.01	0.17
#仔　畜	Infant Animals	52.34	1.92	1.34	0.01	0.05		
自宰自食数	Slaughtered and Eaten by Peasants Themselves	113.29	4.68	0.97	0.18	0.16		0.02
其　他	Other	1.03	0.16	0.15				
年末实有数	**Number at the Year-end**	**624.06**	**36.84**	**19.91**	**2.40**	**1.23**		**0.41**
#实际参加农事劳役的	Draught Animal	0.96	0.56	0.02	0.18	0.22		
#能繁殖的母畜	Reproducable Female Animals	319.32	19.41	11.22	0.81	0.59		0.13
年内仔畜死亡	**Death of Infant Animals in the Year**	**6.47**	**0.21**	**0.12**				

指　标	Item	猪 Pigs	羊 Goats	山羊 Milk Goats	绵羊 Sheep	#细毛羊及改良羊 Fine Wool Sheep and Improved Sheep	家禽 Poultry	兔 Rabbits
年初数	**Number at the Beginning of the Year**	**134.09**	**414.15**	**37.64**	**376.51**	**135.83**		
年内增加	**Increasein the Year**	**298.33**	**452.14**	**57.80**	**394.34**	**106.91**		
繁殖成活数	Number of Breeding Survival	242.10	261.68	25.49	236.19	69.59		
买入数	Buy in	55.18	190.24	32.31	157.93	37.32		
其　他	Other	1.05	0.22		0.22			
年内减少	**Decreasein the Year**	**277.00**	**438.53**	**55.23**	**383.30**	**114.01**		
成、幼畜死亡数	Death of Adult and Infant Animals	4.55	4.14	0.70	3.44	0.84		
卖出数	Sold out	238.65	359.07	40.45	318.62	100.92	881.06	63.60
#仔　畜	Infant Animals	38.83	11.53	1.69	9.84	3.74		
自宰自食数	Slaughtered and Eaten by Peasants Themselves	33.44	74.81	14.07	60.74	11.95	209.78	37.40
其　他	Other	0.36	0.51	0.01	0.50	0.30		
年末实有数	**Number at the Year-end**	**155.42**	**427.76**	**40.21**	**387.55**	**128.73**	**573.13**	**28.32**
#实际参加农事劳役的	Draught Animal							
#能繁殖的母畜	Reproducable Female Animals	19.99	278.39	24.82	253.57	69.10		
年内仔畜死亡	**Death of Infant Animals in the Year**	**2.11**	**4.15**	**0.50**	**3.65**	**0.82**		

9—22 各师畜牧业生产情况

Animal Husbandry Production by Division

计量单位:万头(只) (2010年) (10 000 heads)

指 标	Item	合 计 Total	一 师 Division 1	二 师 Division 2	三 师 Division 3	四 师 Division 4	五 师 Division 5	六 师 Division 6	七 师 Division 7
年初数	**Number at the Beginning of the Year**	**586.19**	**54.41**	**63.03**	**50.89**	**91.54**	**23.91**	**91.24**	**35.87**
年内增加	**Increase in the Year**	**782.37**	**51.25**	**67.35**	**51.66**	**113.10**	**22.67**	**141.92**	**57.25**
繁殖成活数	Number of Breeding Survival	519.38	40.71	53.76	40.33	65.12	16.13	76.92	30.93
买入数	Buy in	261.69	10.15	13.59	11.33	47.97	6.54	65.00	26.32
其 他	Other	1.30	0.39			0.01			
年内减少	**Decrease in the Year**	**744.50**	**51.11**	**65.11**	**46.97**	**111.54**	**20.15**	**139.46**	**52.99**
成、幼畜死亡数	Death of Adult and Infant Animals	9.06	1.11	0.58	0.14	0.53	0.44	1.11	1.21
卖出数	Sold out	621.12	36.94	59.11	21.89	105.22	17.92	121.39	30.31
# 仔 畜	Infant Animals	52.34	3.55	4.64	0.93	2.67	0.66	3.40	2.00
自宰自食数	Slaughtered and Eaten by Peasants Themselves	113.29	12.89	5.42	24.94	5.48	1.79	16.96	21.47
其 他	Other	1.03	0.17			0.31			
年末实有数	**Number at the Year-end**	**624.06**	**54.55**	**65.27**	**55.58**	**93.10**	**26.43**	**93.70**	**40.13**
# 实际参加农事劳役的	Draught Animal	0.96	0.04	0.08	0.57	0.02		0.05	
# 能繁殖的母畜	Reproducable Female Animals	319.32	29.26	27.30	34.08	48.76	14.36	43.58	17.60
年内仔畜死亡	**Death of Infant Animals in the Year**	**6.47**	**0.51**	**0.69**	**0.20**	**0.44**	**0.35**	**0.22**	**1.01**

指 标	Item	八 师 Division 8	九 师 Division 9	十 师 Division 10	十二师 Division 12	十三师 Division 13	十四师 Division 14	国资公司 State-owned property company	兵团直属 Directly Under XPCG
年初数	**Number at the Beginning of the Year**	**51.19**	**50.37**	**18.30**	**9.52**	**30.48**	**10.86**	**3.87**	**0.71**
年内增加	**Increase in the Year**	**95.64**	**70.25**	**33.78**	**15.21**	**34.02**	**10.93**	**16.65**	**0.69**
繁殖成活数	Number of Breeding Survival	80.06	42.74	20.64	7.91	19.06	8.58	16.04	0.45
买入数	Buy in	15.51	27.51	13.14	7.08	14.96	2.35		0.24
其 他	Other	0.07			0.22			0.61	
年内减少	**Decrease in the Year**	**89.69**	**60.51**	**32.34**	**13.58**	**32.84**	**10.95**	**16.61**	**0.65**
成、幼畜死亡数	Death of Adult and Infant Animals	1.27	0.20	0.28	0.15	0.18		1.85	0.01
卖出数	Sold out	82.68	56.82	29.60	12.61	22.67	8.76	14.76	0.44
# 仔 畜	Infant Animals	17.88	0.29	0.31	1.36	1.86	0.02	12.76	0.01
自宰自食数	Slaughtered and Eaten by Peasants Themselves	5.33	3.49	2.46	0.68	9.99	2.19		0.20
其 他	Other	0.41			0.14				
年末实有数	**Number at the Year-end**	**57.14**	**60.11**	**19.74**	**11.15**	**31.66**	**10.84**	**3.91**	**0.75**
# 实际参加农事劳役的	Draught Animal			0.01			0.19		
# 能繁殖的母畜	Reproducable Female Animals	14.12	43.78	13.30	4.42	19.06	8.14	0.98	0.58
年内仔畜死亡	**Death of Infant Animals in the Year**	**1.35**	**1.36**	**0.13**	**0.08**	**0.12**			**0.01**

9—23　各师牲畜年底头数

Number of Livestock by Division

计量单位:万头(只)　　　　(2010 年)　　　　(10 000 heads)

指　标	Unit	合计 Total	牛 Cattle and Buffaloes	#奶牛 Cows	马 Horses	驴 Donkeys	骡 Mules	骆驼 Camels
总　计	**Total**	**624.06**	**36.84**	**19.91**	**2.40**	**1.23**		**0.41**
一　师	Division 1	54.55	4.85	2.41	0.03	0.05		0.01
二　师	Division 2	65.27	1.70	0.67	0.02	0.09		
三　师	Division 3	55.58	2.07	0.70	0.16	0.43		0.01
四　师	Division 4	93.10	7.95	4.30	1.25	0.05		
五　师	Division 5	26.43	1.05	0.14	0.04	0.01		0.01
六　师	Division 6	93.70	4.22	1.54	0.27	0.14		0.16
七　师	Division 7	40.13	3.55	2.59	0.05			0.01
八　师	Division 8	57.14	5.58	5.05	0.11	0.01		
九　师	Division 9	60.11	1.74	0.48	0.16			
十　师	Division 10	19.74	1.41	0.80		0.04		
十二师	Division 12	11.15	1.35	1.05	0.08			0.01
十三师	Division 13	31.66	1.09	0.10	0.20	0.13		0.13
十四师	Division 14	10.84	0.16		0.03	0.28		0.07
国资公司	State-owned Property Company	3.91						
兵团直属	Direct Lyunder XPCG	0.75	0.12	0.08				

指　标	Item	猪 Pigs	羊 Goats	山羊 Milk Goats	绵羊 Sheep	#细毛羊及改良羊 Fine Wool Sheep and Improved Sheep	家禽 Poultry	兔 Rabbits
总　计	**Total**	**155.42**	**427.76**	**40.21**	**387.55**	**128.73**	**573.13**	**28.32**
一　师	Division 1	12.42	37.19	3.68	33.51	0.87	20.22	2.98
二　师	Division 2	21.96	41.50	2.02	39.48	9.60	32.58	1.86
三　师	Division 3	7.22	45.69	7.61	38.08		19.58	3.72
四　师	Division 4	15.78	68.07	2.04	66.03	40.36	125.82	4.33
五　师	Division 5	4.79	20.53	0.60	19.93	10.41	36.82	0.89
六　师	Division 6	27.38	61.53	10.95	50.58	30.16	97.69	1.59
七　师	Division 7	7.83	28.69	2.98	25.71	12.26	51.80	7.57
八　师	Division 8	40.35	11.09	1.01	10.08	7.52	90.41	1.97
九　师	Division 9	1.88	56.33	2.53	53.80	11.67	10.58	0.69
十　师	Division 10	3.58	14.71	0.60	14.11	2.53	21.40	
十二师	Division 12	3.54	6.17	0.40	5.77	0.24	34.08	0.40
十三师	Division 13	4.15	25.96	5.12	20.84		15.81	0.80
十四师	Division 14	0.50	9.80	0.57	9.23	2.71	8.99	1.32
国资公司	State-owned Property Company	3.91					6.25	
兵团直属	Direct Lyunder XPCG	0.13	0.50	0.10	0.40	0.40	1.10	0.20

9—24 各师大牲畜生产情况

Large Animals Production by Division

计量单位:万头(只) (2010 年) (10 000 heads)

指标	Item	合计 Total	一师 Division 1	二师 Division 2	三师 Division 3	四师 Division 4	五师 Division 5	六师 Division 6	七师 Division 7
年初数	**Number at the Beginning of the Year**	**37.95**	**4.61**	**2.13**	**2.68**	**8.22**	**0.95**	**4.45**	**3.22**
年内增加	**Increase in the Year**	**31.90**	**2.99**	**1.19**	**1.76**	**8.54**	**0.95**	**4.73**	**2.74**
繁殖成活数	Number of Breeding Survival	15.60	2.38	0.77	1.30	3.31	0.42	1.45	1.47
买入数	Buy in	16.27	0.61	0.42	0.46	5.22	0.53	3.28	1.27
其他	Other	0.03				0.01			
年内减少	**Decrease in the Year**	**28.97**	**2.66**	**1.51**	**1.77**	**7.51**	**0.79**	**4.39**	**2.35**
成、幼畜死亡数	Death of Adult and Infant Animals	0.37	0.01	0.03		0.03		0.06	0.02
卖出数	Sold out	23.40	2.05	1.27	0.88	7.15	0.67	3.47	1.36
# 仔畜	Infant Animals	1.98	0.30	0.13	0.09	0.27	0.05	0.07	0.18
自宰自食数	Slaughtered and Eaten by Peasants Themselves	5.04	0.59	0.21	0.89	0.33	0.12	0.86	0.97
其他	Other	0.16	0.01						
年末实有数	**Number at the Year-end**	**40.88**	**4.94**	**1.81**	**2.67**	**9.25**	**1.11**	**4.79**	**3.61**
# 实际参加农事劳役的	Draught Animal	0.96	0.04	0.08	0.57	0.02		0.05	
# 能繁殖的母畜	Reproducable Female Animals	20.94	2.55	1.03	1.77	4.46	0.68	1.90	1.88
年内仔畜死亡	**Death of Infant Animals in the Year**	**0.21**	**0.01**	**0.02**		**0.01**	**0.01**		**0.02**

指标	Item	八师 Division 8	九师 Division 9	十师 Division 10	十二师 Division 12	十三师 Division 13	十四师 Division 14	兵团直属 Directly Under XPCG
年初数	**Number at the Beginning of the Year**	**5.22**	**1.45**	**1.26**	**1.23**	**1.84**	**0.57**	**0.12**
年内增加	**Increase in the Year**	**2.84**	**1.63**	**1.78**	**1.04**	**1.27**	**0.36**	**0.08**
繁殖成活数	Number of Breeding Survival	1.96	0.72	0.50	0.43	0.69	0.13	0.07
买入数	Buy in	0.86	0.91	1.28	0.61	0.58	0.23	0.01
其他	Other	0.02						
年内减少	**Decrease in the Year**	**2.36**	**1.18**	**1.59**	**0.83**	**1.56**	**0.39**	**0.08**
成、幼畜死亡数	Death of Adult and Infant Animals	0.20			0.02			
卖出数	Sold out	1.86	1.04	1.53	0.72	1.03	0.31	0.06
# 仔畜	Infant Animals	0.62		0.04	0.09	0.12	0.01	0.01
自宰自食数	Slaughtered and Eaten by Peasants Themselves	0.15	0.14	0.06	0.09	0.53	0.08	0.02
其他	Other	0.15						
年末实有数	**Number at the Year-end**	**5.70**	**1.90**	**1.45**	**1.44**	**1.55**	**0.54**	**0.12**
# 实际参加农事劳役的	Draught Animal			0.01			0.19	
# 能繁殖的母畜	Reproducable Female Animals	3.07	0.99	0.80	0.77	0.76	0.18	0.10
年内仔畜死亡	**Death of Infant Animals in the Year**	**0.12**		**0.01**	**0.01**			

9—25　各师牛生产情况

Cattle and Buffaloes Production by Division

计量单位:万头(只)　　　　(2010 年)　　　　(10 000 heads)

指　　标	Item	合　计 Total	一　师 Division 1	二　师 Division 2	三　师 Division 3	四　师 Division 4	五　师 Division 5	六　师 Division 6	七　师 Division 7
年初数	**Number at the Beginning of the Year**	**33.85**	**4.48**	**1.98**	**2.08**	**6.98**	**0.89**	**3.88**	**3.16**
年内增加	**Increase in the Year**	**29.95**	**2.86**	**1.15**	**1.50**	**7.73**	**0.95**	**4.54**	**2.70**
繁殖成活数	Number of Breeding Survival	14.56	2.33	0.74	1.10	2.97	0.42	1.33	1.44
买入数	Buy in	15.36	0.53	0.41	0.40	4.75	0.53	3.21	1.26
其　他	Other	0.03				0.01			
年内减少	**Decrease in the Year**	**26.96**	**2.49**	**1.43**	**1.51**	**6.76**	**0.79**	**4.20**	**2.31**
成、幼畜死亡数	Death of Adult and Infant Animals	0.35	0.01	0.03		0.03		0.04	0.02
卖出数	Sold out	21.77	1.92	1.19	0.67	6.49	0.67	3.35	1.34
# 仔　畜	Infant Animals	1.92	0.29	0.11	0.08	0.26	0.05	0.07	0.18
自宰自食数	Slaughtered and Eaten by Peasants Themselves	4.68	0.55	0.21	0.84	0.24	0.12	0.81	0.95
其　他	Other	0.16	0.01						
年末实有数	**Number at the Year-end**	**36.84**	**4.85**	**1.70**	**2.07**	**7.95**	**1.05**	**4.22**	**3.55**
# 实际参加农事劳役的	Draught Animal	0.56		0.07	0.39			0.01	
# 能繁殖的母畜	Reproducable Female Animals	19.41	2.51	0.98	1.46	3.98	0.65	1.71	1.86
年内仔畜死亡	**Death of Infant Animals in the Year**	**0.21**	**0.01**	**0.02**		**0.01**	**0.01**		**0.02**

指　　标	Item	八　师 Division 8	九　师 Division 9	十　师 Division 10	十二师 Division 12	十三师 Division 13	十四师 Division 14	兵团直属 Directly Under XPCG
年初数	**Number at the Beginning of the Year**	**5.10**	**1.29**	**1.26**	**1.15**	**1.31**	**0.17**	**0.12**
年内增加	**Increase in the Year**	**2.82**	**1.58**	**1.74**	**1.02**	**1.06**	**0.22**	**0.08**
繁殖成活数	Number of Breeding Survival	1.94	0.68	0.50	0.42	0.57	0.05	0.07
买入数	Buy in	0.86	0.90	1.24	0.60	0.49	0.17	0.01
其　他	Other	0.02						
年内减少	**Decrease in the Year**	**2.34**	**1.13**	**1.59**	**0.82**	**1.28**	**0.23**	**0.08**
成、幼畜死亡数	Death of Adult and Infant Animals	0.20			0.02			
卖出数	Sold out	1.84	1.00	1.53	0.71	0.85	0.15	0.06
# 仔　畜	Infant Animals	0.62		0.04	0.09	0.12		0.01
自宰自食数	Slaughtered and Eaten by Peasants Themselves	0.15	0.13	0.06	0.09	0.43	0.08	0.02
其　他	Other	0.15						
年末实有数	**Number at the Year-end**	**5.58**	**1.74**	**1.41**	**1.35**	**1.09**	**0.16**	**0.12**
# 实际参加农事劳役的	Draught Animal			0.01			0.08	
# 能繁殖的母畜	Reproducable Female Animals	3.04	0.95	0.77	0.76	0.59	0.05	0.10
年内仔畜死亡	**Death of Infant Animals in the Year**	**0.12**		**0.01**	**0.01**			

9－26 各师奶牛生产情况

Cows Production by Division

计量单位:万头(只) (2010年) (10 000 heads)

指标	Item	合计 Total	一师 Division 1	二师 Division 2	三师 Division 3	四师 Division 4	五师 Division 5	六师 Division 6	七师 Division 7
年初数	**Number at the Beginning of the Year**	**17.25**	**2.11**	**0.63**	**0.66**	**3.41**	**0.06**	**1.41**	**2.40**
年内增加	**Increase in the Year**	**10.56**	**1.16**	**0.45**	**0.24**	**2.79**	**0.16**	**0.37**	**1.62**
繁殖成活数	Number of Breeding Survival	7.08	1.10	0.33	0.21	1.44	0.05	0.24	0.99
买入数	Buy in	3.45	0.06	0.12	0.03	1.34	0.11	0.13	0.63
其　他	Other	0.03				0.01			
年内减少	**Decrease in the Year**	**7.90**	**0.86**	**0.41**	**0.20**	**1.90**	**0.08**	**0.24**	**1.43**
成、幼畜死亡数	Death of Adult and Infant Animals	0.25	0.01	0.01		0.02			
卖出数	Sold out	6.53	0.78	0.40	0.11	1.82	0.08	0.24	0.84
# 仔　畜	Infant Animals	1.34	0.22	0.08	0.04	0.02	0.04	0.03	0.18
自宰自食数	Slaughtered and Eaten by Peasants Themselves	0.97	0.07		0.09	0.06			0.59
其　他	Other	0.15							
年末实有数	**Number at the Year-end**	**19.91**	**2.41**	**0.67**	**0.70**	**4.30**	**0.14**	**1.54**	**2.59**
# 实际参加农事劳役的	Draught Animal	0.02			0.02				
# 能繁殖的母畜	Reproducable Female Animals	11.22	1.49	0.40	0.41	2.30	0.09	0.61	1.81
年内仔畜死亡	**Death of Infant Animals in the Year**	**0.12**							

指标	Item	八师 Division 8	九师 Division 9	十师 Division 10	十二师 Division 12	十三师 Division 13	十四师 Division 14	兵团直属 Directly Under XPCG
年初数	**Number at the Beginning of the Year**	**4.49**	**0.47**	**0.58**	**0.86**	**0.09**		**0.08**
年内增加	**Increase in the Year**	**2.44**	**0.17**	**0.52**	**0.45**	**0.13**		**0.06**
繁殖成活数	Number of Breeding Survival	1.83	0.16	0.29	0.27	0.11		0.06
买入数	Buy in	0.59	0.01	0.23	0.18	0.02		
其　他	Other	0.02						
年内减少	**Decrease in the Year**	**1.88**	**0.16**	**0.30**	**0.26**	**0.12**		**0.06**
成、幼畜死亡数	Death of Adult and Infant Animals	0.20			0.01			
卖出数	Sold out	1.45	0.14	0.30	0.25	0.06		0.06
# 仔　畜	Infant Animals	0.55		0.02	0.09	0.06		0.01
自宰自食数	Slaughtered and Eaten by Peasants Themselves	0.08	0.02			0.06		
其　他	Other	0.15						
年末实有数	**Number at the Year-end**	**5.05**	**0.48**	**0.80**	**1.05**	**0.10**		**0.08**
# 实际参加农事劳役的	Draught Animal							
# 能繁殖的母畜	Reproducable Female Animals	2.79	0.25	0.41	0.50	0.08		0.08
年内仔畜死亡	**Death of Infant Animals in the Year**	**0.12**						

9—27　各师马生产情况

Horse Production by Division

计量单位:万头(只)　　　　(2010年)　　　　(10 000 heads)

指　标	Item	合计 Total	一师 Division 1	二师 Division 2	三师 Division 3	四师 Division 4	五师 Division 5	六师 Division 6	七师 Division 7
年初数	**Number at the Beginning of the Year**	**2.30**	**0.02**	**0.02**	**0.15**	**1.19**	**0.04**	**0.26**	**0.04**
年内增加	**Increase in the Year**	**1.23**	**0.04**	**0.02**	**0.11**	**0.77**		**0.09**	**0.02**
繁殖成活数	Number of Breeding Survival	0.68	0.02	0.01	0.10	0.34		0.07	0.02
买入数	Buy in	0.55	0.02	0.01	0.01	0.43		0.02	
其　他	Other								
年内减少	**Decrease in the Year**	**1.13**	**0.03**	**0.02**	**0.10**	**0.71**		**0.08**	**0.01**
成、幼畜死亡数	Death of Adult and Infant Animals	0.02						0.02	
卖出数	Sold out	0.93	0.02	0.02	0.09	0.62		0.03	
# 仔　畜	Infant Animals	0.01				0.01			
自宰自食数	Slaughtered and Eaten by Peasants Themselves	0.18	0.01		0.01	0.09		0.03	0.01
其　他	Other								
年末实有数	**Number at the Year-end**	**2.40**	**0.03**	**0.02**	**0.16**	**1.25**	**0.04**	**0.27**	**0.05**
# 实际参加农事劳役的	Draught Animal	0.18			0.14	0.02		0.01	
# 能繁殖的母畜	Reproducable Female Animals	0.81	0.01	0.01	0.06	0.47	0.02	0.08	0.02
年内仔畜死亡	**Death of Infant Animals in the Year**								

指　标	Item	八师 Division 8	九师 Division 9	十师 Division 10	十二师 Division 12	十三师 Division 13	十四师 Division 14	兵团直属 Directly Under XPCG
年初数	**Number at the Beginning of the Year**	**0.11**	**0.16**		**0.07**	**0.21**	**0.03**	
年内增加	**Increase in the Year**	**0.02**	**0.05**		**0.02**	**0.08**	**0.01**	
繁殖成活数	Number of Breeding Survival	0.02	0.04		0.01	0.05		
买入数	Buy in		0.01		0.01	0.03	0.01	
其　他	Other							
年内减少	**Decrease in the Year**	**0.02**	**0.05**		**0.01**	**0.09**	**0.01**	
成、幼畜死亡数	Death of Adult and Infant Animals							
卖出数	Sold out	0.02	0.04		0.01	0.07	0.01	
# 仔　畜	Infant Animals							
自宰自食数	Slaughtered and Eaten by Peasants Themselves		0.01			0.02		
其　他	Other							
年末实有数	**Number at the Year-end**	**0.11**	**0.16**		**0.08**	**0.20**	**0.03**	
# 实际参加农事劳役的	Draught Animal						0.01	
# 能繁殖的母畜	Reproducable Female Animals	0.03	0.04		0.01	0.06		
年内仔畜死亡	**Death of Infant Animals in the Year**							

9—28 各师猪生产情况

Pig Production by Division

计量单位:万头(只) (2010年) (10 000 heads)

指 标	Item	合计 Total	一师 Division 1	二师 Division 2	三师 Division 3	四师 Division 4	五师 Division 5	六师 Division 6	七师 Division 7
年初数	**Number at the Beginning of the Year**	**134.09**	**11.76**	**20.47**	**6.99**	**12.54**	**2.98**	**24.50**	**6.34**
年内增加	**Increase in the Year**	**298.33**	**17.82**	**31.94**	**9.85**	**32.92**	**8.76**	**48.48**	**21.93**
繁殖成活数	Number of Breeding Survival	242.10	14.43	28.93	8.49	22.34	6.00	40.92	14.62
买入数	Buy in	55.18	3.00	3.01	1.36	10.58	2.76	7.56	7.31
其 他	Other	1.05	0.39						
年内减少	**Decrease in the Year**	**277.00**	**17.16**	**30.45**	**9.62**	**29.68**	**6.95**	**45.60**	**20.44**
成、幼畜死亡数	Death of Adult and Infant Animals	4.55	0.69	0.23	0.03	0.08	0.34	0.22	0.27
卖出数	Sold out	238.65	11.35	27.53	4.51	27.96	5.87	41.78	13.68
# 仔 畜	Infant Animals	38.83	1.70	3.00	0.20	1.08	0.37	2.14	1.43
自宰自食数	Slaughtered and Eaten by Peasants Themselves	33.44	5.02	2.69	5.08	1.64	0.74	3.60	6.49
其 他	Other	0.36	0.10						
年末实有数	**Number at the Year-end**	**155.42**	**12.42**	**21.96**	**7.22**	**15.78**	**4.79**	**27.38**	**7.83**
# 能繁殖的母畜	Reproducable Female Animals	19.99	1.18	2.69	1.03	2.07	0.75	3.76	1.18
年内仔畜死亡	**Death of Infant Animals in the Year**	**2.11**	**0.20**	**0.26**	**0.05**	**0.09**	**0.23**	**0.03**	**0.21**

指 标	Item	八师 Division 8	九师 Division 9	十师 Division 10	十二师 Division 12	十三师 Division 13	十四师 Division 14	国资公司 Stat-owned Pronerty Company	兵团直属 Directly Under XPCG
年初数	**Number at the Beginning of the Year**	**32.82**	**1.35**	**3.14**	**2.96**	**3.76**	**0.48**	**3.87**	**0.13**
年内增加	**Increase in the Year**	**81.29**	**3.57**	**10.61**	**6.59**	**7.05**	**0.77**	**16.65**	**0.10**
繁殖成活数	Number of Breeding Survival	70.85	2.74	9.01	2.97	3.99	0.74	16.04	0.03
买入数	Buy in	10.39	0.83	1.60	3.62	3.06	0.03		0.07
其 他	Other	0.05						0.61	
年内减少	**Decrease in the Year**	**73.76**	**3.04**	**10.17**	**6.01**	**6.66**	**0.75**	**16.61**	**0.10**
成、幼畜死亡数	Death of Adult and Infant Animals	0.83		0.01				1.85	
卖出数	Sold out	69.12	2.45	9.19	5.88	3.83	0.67	14.76	0.07
# 仔 畜	Infant Animals	14.63	0.15	0.27	0.91	0.18	0.01	12.76	
自宰自食数	Slaughtered and Eaten by Peasants Themselves	3.55	0.59	0.97	0.13	2.83	0.08		0.03
其 他	Other	0.26							
年末实有数	**Number at the Year-end**	**40.35**	**1.88**	**3.58**	**3.54**	**4.15**	**0.50**	**3.91**	**0.13**
# 能繁殖的母畜	Reproducable Female Animals	4.67	0.21	0.61	0.28	0.52	0.03	0.98	0.03
年内仔畜死亡	**Death of Infant Animals in the Year**	**0.81**	**0.18**	**0.04**	**0.01**				

9—29　各师羊生产情况

Sheep and Goats Production by Division

计量单位:万头(只)　　　　(2010年)　　　　(10 000 heads)

指　　标	Item	合　计 Total	一　师 Division 1	二　师 Division 2	三　师 Division 3	四　师 Division 4	五　师 Division 5	六　师 Division 6	七　师 Division 7
年初数	**Number at the Beginning of the Year**	**414.15**	**38.04**	**40.43**	**41.22**	**70.78**	**19.98**	**62.29**	**26.31**
年内增加	**Increase in the Year**	**452.14**	**30.44**	**34.22**	**40.05**	**71.64**	**12.96**	**88.71**	**32.58**
繁殖成活数	Number of Breeding Survival	261.68	23.90	24.06	30.54	39.47	9.71	34.55	14.84
买入数	Buy in	190.24	6.54	10.16	9.51	32.17	3.25	54.16	17.74
其　他	Other	0.22							
年内减少	**Decrease in the Year**	**438.53**	**31.29**	**33.15**	**35.58**	**74.35**	**12.41**	**89.47**	**30.20**
成、幼畜死亡数	Death of Adult and Infant Animals	4.14	0.41	0.32	0.11	0.42	0.10	0.83	0.92
卖出数	Sold out	359.07	23.54	30.31	16.50	70.11	11.38	76.14	15.27
# 仔　畜	Infant Animals	11.53	1.55	1.51	0.64	1.32	0.24	1.19	0.39
自宰自食数	Slaughtered and Eaten by Peasants Themselves	74.81	7.28	2.52	18.97	3.51	0.93	12.50	14.01
其　他	Other	0.51	0.06			0.31			
年末实有数	**Number at the Year-end**	**427.76**	**37.19**	**41.50**	**45.69**	**68.07**	**20.53**	**61.53**	**28.69**
# 能繁殖的母畜	Reproducable Female Animals	278.39	25.53	23.58	31.28	42.23	12.93	37.92	14.54
年内仔畜死亡	**Death of Infant Animals in the Year**	**4.15**	**0.30**	**0.41**	**0.15**	**0.34**	**0.11**	**0.19**	**0.78**

指　　标	Item	八　师 Division 8	九　师 Division 9	十　师 Division 10	十二师 Division 12	十三师 Division 13	十四师 Division 14	兵团直属 Directly Under XPCG
年初数	**Number at the Beginning of the Year**	**13.15**	**47.57**	**13.90**	**5.33**	**24.88**	**9.81**	**0.46**
年内增加	**Increase in the Year**	**11.51**	**65.05**	**21.39**	**7.58**	**25.70**	**9.80**	**0.51**
繁殖成活数	Number of Breeding Survival	7.25	39.28	11.13	4.51	14.38	7.71	0.35
买入数	Buy in	4.26	25.77	10.26	2.85	11.32	2.09	0.16
其　他	Other				0.22			
年内减少	**Decrease in the Year**	**13.57**	**56.29**	**20.58**	**6.74**	**24.62**	**9.81**	**0.47**
成、幼畜死亡数	Death of Adult and Infant Animals	0.24	0.20	0.27	0.13	0.18		0.01
卖出数	Sold out	11.70	53.33	18.88	6.01	17.81	7.78	0.31
# 仔　畜	Infant Animals	2.63	0.14		0.36	1.56		
自宰自食数	Slaughtered and Eaten by Peasants Themselves	1.63	2.76	1.43	0.46	6.63	2.03	0.15
其　他	Other				0.14			
年末实有数	**Number at the Year-end**	**11.09**	**56.33**	**14.71**	**6.17**	**25.96**	**9.80**	**0.50**
# 能繁殖的母畜	Reproducable Female Animals	6.38	42.58	11.89	3.37	17.78	7.93	0.45
年内仔畜死亡	**Death of Infant Animals in the Year**	**0.42**	**1.18**	**0.08**	**0.06**	**0.12**		**0.01**

9—30 各师绵羊生产情况

Sheep Production by Division

计量单位:万头(只)　　　　(2010年)　　　　(10 000 heads)

指　　标	Item	合　计 Total	一　师 Division 1	二　师 Division 2	三　师 Division 3	四　师 Division 4	五　师 Division 5	六　师 Division 6	七　师 Division 7
年初数	**Number at the Beginning of the Year**	**376.51**	**33.54**	**38.80**	**36.24**	**69.24**	**19.50**	**50.31**	**23.50**
年内增加	**Increase in the Year**	**394.34**	**26.76**	**32.44**	**32.78**	**69.97**	**12.25**	**63.96**	**25.47**
繁殖成活数	Number of Breeding Survival	236.19	20.58	23.17	25.61	38.65	9.51	27.89	12.24
买入数	Buy in	157.93	6.18	9.27	7.17	31.32	2.74	36.07	13.23
其　他	Other	0.22							
年内减少	**Decrease in the Year**	**383.30**	**26.79**	**31.76**	**30.94**	**73.18**	**11.82**	**63.69**	**23.26**
成、幼畜死亡数	Death of Adult and Infant Animals	3.44	0.27	0.26	0.08	0.42	0.10	0.57	0.81
卖出数	Sold out	318.62	20.07	29.48	15.54	69.09	11.01	53.66	12.34
# 仔　畜	Infant Animals	9.84	1.42	1.33	0.41	1.30	0.24	0.75	0.32
自宰自食数	Slaughtered and Eaten by Peasants Themselves	60.74	6.39	2.02	15.32	3.36	0.71	9.46	10.11
其　他	Other	0.50	0.06			0.31			
年末实有数	**Number at the Year-end**	**387.55**	**33.51**	**39.48**	**38.08**	**66.03**	**19.93**	**50.58**	**25.71**
# 能繁殖的母畜	Reproducable Female Animals	253.57	22.74	22.71	26.65	41.24	12.63	31.66	12.36
年内仔畜死亡	**Death of Infant Animals in the Year**	**3.65**	**0.24**	**0.36**	**0.11**	**0.34**	**0.11**	**0.13**	**0.71**

指　　标	Item	八　师 Division 8	九　师 Division 9	十　师 Division 10	十二师 Division 12	十三师 Division 13	十四师 Division 14	兵团直属 Directly Under XPCG
年初数	**Number at the Beginning of the Year**	**12.15**	**45.26**	**13.68**	**4.85**	**19.85**	**9.23**	**0.36**
年内增加	**Increase in the Year**	**10.51**	**62.32**	**20.37**	**7.22**	**20.38**	**9.44**	**0.47**
繁殖成活数	Number of Breeding Survival	6.67	37.37	10.95	4.20	11.60	7.40	0.35
买入数	Buy in	3.84	24.95	9.42	2.80	8.78	2.04	0.12
其　他	Other				0.22			
年内减少	**Decrease in the Year**	**12.58**	**53.78**	**19.94**	**6.30**	**19.39**	**9.44**	**0.43**
成、幼畜死亡数	Death of Adult and Infant Animals	0.23	0.19	0.27	0.11	0.12		0.01
卖出数	Sold out	10.93	51.03	18.28	5.62	13.82	7.48	0.27
# 仔　畜	Infant Animals	2.57	0.14		0.32	1.04		
自宰自食数	Slaughtered and Eatenby Peasants Themselves	1.42	2.56	1.39	0.44	5.45	1.96	0.15
其　他	Other				0.13			
年末实有数	**Number at the Year-end**	**10.08**	**53.80**	**14.11**	**5.77**	**20.84**	**9.23**	**0.40**
# 能繁殖的母畜	Reproducable Female Animals	5.83	40.71	11.74	3.05	14.32	7.56	0.37
年内仔畜死亡	**Death of Infant Animals in the Year**	**0.37**	**1.06**	**0.08**	**0.05**	**0.08**		**0.01**

9—31　各师肉类生产情况

Meat Production by Division

（2010 年）

指标	Item	合计 Total	一师 Division 1	二师 Division 2	三师 Division 3	四师 Division 4	五师 Division 5	六师 Division 6	七师 Division 7
总产肉量(吨)	**Output of Meat(ton)**	**319 923**	**20 899**	**31 547**	**15 760**	**47 581**	**9 113**	**59 965**	**29 477**
牛	Beef	37 231	2 758	2 124	2 047	10 094	1 170	6 548	3 251
马	Horse	1 474	29	26	94	1 004		85	15
驴	Donkey	528	128	35	92	24		48	10
骡	Mule	12							
骆驼	Camel	334	24		16			99	31
肉猪	Pork	171 065	11 199	20 411	7 245	19 551	4 827	30 943	14 857
羊	Goats and sheep	81 694	5 525	6 566	5 548	13 941	2 279	17 203	6 201
山羊	Goat	9 419	735	188	756	447	149	3 880	1 944
绵羊	Sheep	72 275	4 790	6 378	4 792	13 494	2 130	13 323	4 257
家禽	Poultry	24 389	986	1 179	627	2 693	784	4 907	4 328
兔	Rabbit	1 981	241	109	91	274	53	132	784
其他肉产量	Others	1 215	9	1 097					
平均产肉量(公斤/头、只)	**Average Yield of Meat (kg/head)**								
牛	Beef	152	127	165	143	156	158	160	154
马	Horse	134	97	130	94	143		142	150
驴	Donkey	84	107	88	66	60		96	100
骡	Mule	120							
骆驼	Camel	176	240		160			165	155
肉猪	Pork	73	76	75	77	69	77	72	79
绵羊	Sheep	20	19	21	16	19	19	21	19
家禽	Poultry	2	2	2	2	2	2	2	2
兔	RabbitX	2	2	2	2	2	2	2	2

指标	Item	八师 Division 8	九师 Division 9	十师 Division 10	十二师 Division 12	十三师 Division 13	十四师 Division 14	国资公司 State-owned Property Company	兵团直属 Directly Under XPCG
总产肉量(吨)	**Output of Meat(ton)**	**51 943**	**17 206**	**13 019**	**8 006**	**11 096**	**3 251**	**697**	**363**
牛	Beef	2 191	1 996	1 855	1 076	1 624	373		124
马	Horse	31	62		16	100	12		
驴	Donkey				7	85	99		
骡	Mule						12		
骆驼	Camel					114	50		
肉猪	Pork	42 511	2 413	7 003	4 169	4 590	611	658	77
羊	Goats and sheep	2 246	11 985	3 296	1 130	3 797	1 867		110
山羊	Goat	138	439	99	4	578	57		5
绵羊	Sheep	2 108	11 546	3 197	1 126	3 219	1 810		105
家禽	Poultry	4 813	679	865	1 591	663	199	39	36
兔	Rabbit	151	56		9	37	28		16
其他肉产量	Others		15		8	86			
平均产肉量(公斤/头、只)	**Average Yield of Meat (kg/head)**								
牛	Beef	160	177	120	152	140	162		177
马	Horse	155	124		160	111	120		
驴	Donkey					71	90		
骡	Mule						120		
骆驼	Camel					163	250		
肉猪	Pork	73	83	71	82	71	83	33	77
绵羊	Sheep	22	22	16	20	18	19		25
家禽	Poultry	2	2	2	2	2	2	3	2
兔	Rabbit	2	2		2	2	2		2

9—32 各师畜产品产量

Output of Livestock Products by Division

(2010 年)

指标	Item	合计 Total	一师 Division 1	二师 Division 2	三师 Division 3	四师 Division 4	五师 Division 5	六师 Division 6	七师 Division 7
羊毛 (吨)	Wool (ton)	11 314	941	665	601	2 648	483	1 827	1 120
绵羊毛 (吨)	Sheep Wool (ton)	11 087	924	664	583	2 631	481	1 749	1 070
# 细羊毛	Fine Wool	5 067	297	132	113	1 510	217	1 192	653
半细羊毛	Semi-Fine Wool	3 282	444	532	320	531		557	265
山羊毛 (吨)	Goat Wool (ton)	227	17	1	18	17	2	78	50
山羊绒 (公斤)	Cashmere (kg)	57 379	2 926	2 143	1 721	3 097	280	26 712	1 667
牛奶 (吨)	Cow Milk (ton)	443 099	61 352	12 986	5 399	48 215	1 588	23 488	103 314
羊奶 (吨)	Sheep Milk (ton)	1 519			965			85	
牛皮 (张)	Oxhide (sheet)	37 292	2 982	1 957	7 600	2 471	856	8 100	4 560
绵羊皮 (张)	Sheep Skin (sheet)	457 119	30 446	15 012	71 267	22 317	7 460	97 400	85 462
山羊皮 (张)	Goat Skin (sheet)	137 072	16 934	7 370	32 950	10 353	2 100	30 100	16 625
驼毛 (吨)	Camel Hair (ton)	18						14	
蜂群数 (箱)	Bee Cluster (box)	47 789	320	753	210	23 777		3 245	11 164
蜂蜜产量 (吨)	Honey (ton)	2 865	87	52	14	1 863		177	145
禽蛋产量 (吨)	Poultry Eggs (ton)	45 731	2 078	1 570	1 252	8 754	3 404	5 270	6 316
年末养鹿 (头)	Deer (head)	28 331	1 035	23 805	447	899		275	742
年内产鹿茸(公斤)	Pilose Antler (kg)	30 639	1 768	23 793	833	1 928		20	586

指标	Item	八师 Division 8	九师 Division 9	十师 Division 10	十二师 Division 12	十三师 Division 13	十四师 Division 14	国资公司 State-owned Property Company	兵团直属 Directly Under XPCG
羊毛 (吨)	Wool (ton)	524	1 229	388	100	619	139		30
绵羊毛 (吨)	Sheep Wool (ton)	523	1 229	388	98	578	139		30
# 细羊毛	Fine Wool	425	252	94	85	65	32		
半细羊毛	Semi-Fine Wool	63	347	108	13	72			30
山羊毛 (吨)	Goat Wool (ton)	1			2	41			
山羊绒 (公斤)	Cashmere (kg)	1 150	4 433	210	1 174	11 516	150		200
牛奶 (吨)	Cow Milk (ton)	134 860	7 121	8 018	31 265	4 625	88		780
羊奶 (吨)	Sheep Milk (ton)					461	8		
牛皮 (张)	Oxhide (sheet)	830	1 300	511	834	4 291	800		200
绵羊皮 (张)	Sheep Skin (sheet)	7 621	26 349	13 600	4 985	55 700	18 000		1 500
山羊皮 (张)	Goat Skin (sheet)	2 512	2 262	983	183	12 400	2 300		
驼毛 (吨)	Camel Hair (ton)					2	2		
蜂群数 (箱)	Bee Cluster (box)	5 253	150	1 940		502	475		
蜂蜜产量 (吨)	Honey (ton)	190	2	231		84	20		
禽蛋产量 (吨)	Poultry Eggs (ton)	9 871	1 078	1 894	2 357	860	926	56	45
年末养鹿 (头)	Deer (head)	377	693						58
年内产鹿茸(公斤)	Pilose Antler (kg)	695	886		50				80

9—33 各师渔业生产情况

Fishery Production by Division

（2010 年）

单 位	Unit	淡水鱼产量（吨）Aquatic Products(ton)	#捕捞产量 Catching Output	淡水鱼产量按品种分(吨) Classified by Kind(ton) 草 鱼 Grass carp	鲤 鱼 Carp	鲢 鱼 Silver Carp	其 他 Others
总 计	**Total**	**26 701**	**313**	**6 727**	**9 603**	**6 422**	**4 030**
一 师	Division 1	3 372		2 091	392	564	325
二 师	Division 2	2 713	67	1 044	1 040	380	249
三 师	Division 3	1 156		515	182	118	341
四 师	Division 4	3 904	70	1 118	1 838	871	77
五 师	Division 5	418	3	37	85	274	22
六 师	Division 6	2 133		192	765	771	405
七 师	Division 7	1 868		308	812	542	206
八 师	Division 8	5 239		543	1 996	1 459	1 241
九 师	Division 9	14			6	8	
十 师	Division 10	3 915	173	843	824	1 130	1 118
十二师	Division 12	1 471		5	1 365	100	1
十三师	Division 13	193		19	150		24
十四师	Division 14						
兵团直属	Diretly Under XPCG	305		12	68	204	21

单 位	Unit	养殖产量(吨) Cultureed Output (ton)	#池塘养殖 Puddle and Pond	水库养殖 Reservoirs	其他养殖 Other	养殖面积(公顷) Culture Area (hectare)	#池塘养殖 Puddle and Pond	水库养殖 Reservoirs	其他养殖 Other
总 计	**Total**	**26 388**	**15 160**	**6 882**	**4 346**	**32 853**	**2 094**	**23 956**	**6 803**
一 师	Division 1	3 372	1 666	1 483	223	8 529	203	8 300	26
二 师	Division 2	2 646	2 646			216	216		
三 师	Division 3	1 156	616	511	29	4 643	116	4 517	10
四 师	Division 4	3 834	3 083	172	579	705	283	286	136
五 师	Division 5	415	130	33	252	252	38	14	200
六 师	Division 6	2 133	822	1 311		2 595	133	2 462	
七 师	Division 7	1 868	666	575	627	2 375	82	2 187	106
八 师	Division 8	5 239	3 772	1 425	42	3 074	848	2 216	10
九 师	Division 9	14		14		160		160	
十 师	Division 10	3 742		1 148	2 594	9 667	13	3 339	6 315
十二师	Division 12	1 471	1 470	1		139	130	9	
十三师	Division 13	193	172	21		54	17	37	
十四师	Division 14								
兵团直属	Directly Under XPCG	305	117	188		444	15	429	

9—34 按不同类型分国有农林牧渔场基本情况

Basic Conditions of State-owned Farms by Different Types

（2010 年）

指标 Item	团场合计 Total	# 中心团场 Center Farm	# 小城镇团场 Small Town Farms	# 植棉团场 Cotton-planting Farm	# 边境团场 Border Farms	# 贫困团场 Needy Farms	# 南疆困难和边境团场 Needy and Border Farms of South XJ
团场总数(个) Total Reginent Farms(unit)	**176**	**33**	**38**	**101**	**58**	**61**	**77**
农场 Number of Farms	165	33	38	100	52	51	71
林场 Number of Forest Farms							
牧场 Number of Ranch	11			1	6	10	6
渔场 Number of Fishing Ground							
团场劳动力合计(人) Total Labour on Farms(person)	**825 386**	**256 905**	**315 907**	**688 279**	**190 508**	**172 920**	**267 199**
# 劳动力年龄内的 Inside of Labor Force Age	811 142	248 858	313 729	675 117	189 746	171 652	266 149
场内实有就业人员 Persons Actually Engaged on Farms	688 546	205 210	255 437	562 996	173 496	151 302	248 310
# 劳动力年龄内的 Inside of Labor Force Age	682 535	204 909	255 128	562 049	170 377	146 353	244 909
# 男 Male	374 614	112 167	139 251	303 946	95 552	83 831	135 272
女 Female	313 932	93 043	116 186	259 050	77 944	67 471	113 038
农业就业人员 Persons Engaged in Agriculture	460 806	137 525	162 055	377 637	121 691	104 799	182 001
# 种植业就业人员 Persons Engaged in Farming	384 129	114 551	136 604	318 358	100 799	85 501	154 846
牧业就业人员 Persons Engaged in Stock-Raising	30 798	7 889	8 301	19 365	11 110	11 177	13 354
工业就业人员 Persons Engaged in Industry	46 939	13 133	20 093	37 318	9 712	8 755	12 037
建筑业就业人员 Persons Engaged in Construction	19 865	5 928	8 537	15 757	4 778	3 876	6 534
交通运输业、仓储及邮电通迅业就业人员 Persons Engaged in Transportation, Storage and Postal Service and Telecommunications	27 264	7 035	11 875	22 207	5 652	6 227	6 271
信息传输、计算机服务和软件业就业人员 Persons Engaged in Information Deliver, Computer Service and software	351	112	165	310	55	24	71
批发和零售业就业人员 Persons Engaged in Wholesale and Retail Trade	42 936	13 079	17 729	36 172	8 698	7 380	11 001
住宿和餐饮业就业人员 Persons Engaged in Accomodation and catering Services Industry	18 706	5 048	8 232	15 464	3 974	3 766	5 379
其他就业人员 Employed Persons in Other Trades	71 679	23 350	26 751	58 131	18 936	16 475	25 016

注：本篇资料只包括纳入团场序列的 176 个团场资料，贫困团场数据不含且末支队。

Note: Data in this table only include 176 farms and data of needy farms in this chapter is not including Qiemo Detachment. (the same as follow)

9—35　按不同类型分团场农业总产值

Gross Output Value of Agriculture for Farms by Different Types

计量单位:万元　　　　(2010 年)　　　　(10 000 yuan)

指　标	Item	团场合计 Total	# 中心团场 Center Farm	# 小城镇团场 Small Town Farms	# 植棉团场 Cotton-planting Farm	# 边境团场 Border Farms	# 贫困团场 Needy Farms	# 南疆困难和边境团场 Needy and Border Farms of South XJ
农林牧渔业总产值总计	**Total Gross Output Value of Farming, Forestry, Animal Husbandry and Fishery**	**5 249 479**	**1 497 690**	**1 939 856**	**4 585 806**	**1 042 193**	**865 653**	**1 524 221**
农业产值合计	**Output Value of Farming**	**4 134 253**	**1 180 667**	**1 520 869**	**3 703 974**	**752 433**	**608 785**	**1 152 796**
谷物及其他作物	Cereal and Others	3 050 618	870 063	1 137 025	2 718 604	613 627	454 645	882 126
谷　物	Cereal	389 948	110 774	134 929	249 337	189 951	122 505	213 762
薯　类	Tubers	23 823	6 529	3 536	4 169	15 348	8 950	15 463
油料作物	Oil-bearing Crops	83 051	15 336	26 246	31 894	55 427	36 565	55 978
豆　类	Soybeans	10 286	3 636	1 837	4 840	5 663	2 125	5 720
棉花(皮棉)	Cotton(lint)	2 302 943	665 435	899 796	2 302 776	224 326	168 931	462 753
# 棉　籽	Cotton Seed	288 852	81 364	110 109	288 829	26 215	22 285	51 593
麻类(熟麻皮)	Fiber Crops	1 422		18	974	281	191	281
甜　菜	Beetroots	66 148	19 292	20 353	32 096	36 195	34 147	36 195
烟　叶	Tobacco	41			23		18	
其他作物	Others	172 956	49 061	50 310	92 495	86 436	81 213	91 974
蔬菜园艺作物	Vegetable and Horticultural Crops	475 971	128 010	208 710	410 345	66 245	62 911	74 802
# 工业用番茄	Tomato for Industry	175 470	53 539	78 746	159 986	16 262	24 959	16 682
工业用辣椒	Hot Pepper for Industry	85 198	29 489	25 564	65 292	12 301	9 645	12 336
水果、饮料和香料作物	Fruit, Beverage and Spice Crop	593 329	178 977	168 058	562 139	68 602	88 522	189 401
# 水　果	Fruit	518 661	150 458	147 061	500 750	51 620	66 576	142 727
瓜　类	Melon	40 617	12 977	11 600	27 933	15 342	17 347	23 053
药　材(种植)	Medical Materials(Planting)	14 335	3 617	7 076	12 886	3 959	2 707	6 467
林业产值合计	**Output Value of Forestry**	**52 081**	**15 313**	**16 817**	**44 974**	**15 818**	**11 740**	**21 896**
林木的培育和种植	Nurturing and Planting of Wood	39 106	11 654	12 219	32 768	12 678	10 248	15 767
林产品	Wood Procucts	9 953	2 916	3 347	9 866	1 818	640	4 657
木材采运	Timber Conveyance	3 022	743	1 251	2 340	1 322	852	1 472
牧业产值合计	**Output Value of Animal Husbandry**	**735 252**	**204 773**	**283 734**	**555 700**	**207 241**	**187 413**	**242 351**
牲畜饲养	Livestock Feeding	413 034	103 293	140 225	295 703	141 301	131 737	162 773
牛	Cattle and Buffaloes	79 724	18 321	22 010	54 026	29 243	24 160	31 999
羊	Sheep and Goats	187 877	53 601	62 420	120 939	78 652	79 494	94 272
其他牲畜饲养	Others	5 130	1 069	600	2 088	2 961	1 994	3 365
奶产品	Milk Products	121 548	25 487	49 557	105 467	22 454	18 302	24 320
毛绒产品	Hair and Cashere Products	15 693	4 218	5 247	10 153	7 900	6 431	8 450
其他牲畜产品	Other Livestock Products	3 062	597	391	3 030	91	1 356	367
猪的饲养	Pork Feeding	249 380	80 165	117 084	201 137	48 133	35 365	58 737
家禽的饲养	Poultry Feeding	59 145	15 804	21 998	49 068	14 021	16 912	16 733
# 禽　蛋	Poultry Eggs	29 060	8 711	10 016	24 002	8 073	8 035	9 764
其他动物及产品	Other Animal and Products	13 692	5 511	4 427	9 791	3 785	3 399	4 107
狩猎及捕捉动物	Hunting and Catching Animal	1			1	1		1
渔业产值合计	**Output Value of Fishery**	**23 048**	**10 684**	**7 986**	**15 758**	**8 508**	**9 935**	**9 060**
农林牧渔服务业产值合计	**Output Value of Farming, Forestry, Animal Husbandry and Fishery Services**	**304 845**	**86 253**	**110 450**	**265 400**	**58 193**	**47 780**	**98 118**

注:本表按当年价格计算。

Note: Data in this table are calculated at current prices.

9—36 按不同类型分团场农作物播种面积

Total Sown Areas of Farm Crops for Farms by Different Types

计量单位:千公顷 (2010 年) (1 000 hectares)

指标	Item	团场正复播播种面积 Total Sown Area	# 中心团场 Center Farm	# 小城镇团场 Small Town Farms	# 植棉团场 Cotton-planting Farm	# 边境团场 Border Farms	# 贫困团场 Needy Farms	# 南疆困难和边境团场 Needy and Border Farms of South XJ
农作物总播种面积	**Total Sown Areas of Farm crops**	**1 039.15**	**289.87**	**369.95**	**792.98**	**317.37**	**245.73**	**413.18**
粮食作物合计	Sown Area of Grain Crops	272.53	73.20	84.39	164.01	127.47	86.8	150.48
谷物	Cereal	257.98	69.29	81.71	158.75	118.72	82.96	141.64
水稻	Rice	15.08	4.09	2.20	13.13	6.67	1.48	7.00
小麦	Wheat	150.10	40.48	44.01	81.06	77.98	55.79	88.08
玉米	Corn	83.18	23.18	33.01	64.25	27.21	21.29	39.63
谷子	Millet							
高粱	Sorghum	2.80		1.79	0.24	0.27	0.18	0.27
大麦	Barley	6.60	1.54	0.70		6.59	4.15	6.59
其他谷物	Other Cereal	0.22			0.07		0.07	0.07
豆类	Pulse	8.54	2.62	1.80	4.19	5.1	1.63	5.16
# 大豆(黄豆、黑豆等)	Soja	7.53	2.00	1.45	4.15	4.11	0.66	4.17
绿豆	Green Bean	0.04			0.04	0.01		0.01
红小豆	Red Small Bean							
薯类	Vepetables	6.01	1.29	0.88	1.07	3.65	2.21	3.68
油料作物	Oil Bearing Crops	66.67	11.68	17.11	22.83	45.5	28.74	45.88
# 花生	Peanuts	0.48		0.09	0.48	0.02	0.01	0.40
油菜籽	Rapeseeds	21.96	0.66	0.82	0.07	21.47	6.09	21.47
芝麻	Sesame	0.04	0.03	0.02	0.04			
胡麻	Flax	0.01		0.01	0.01			
向日葵籽	Sunflower	39.98	9.49	15.84	19.95	20.87	19.77	20.87
棉花	Cotton	441.48	130.24	183.57	441.24	46.4	33.47	93.63
# 长绒棉	Long Staple Cotton	14.63	0.77	2.96	14.63		1.15	0.38
麻类	Hemp Crops	0.40		0.01	0.18	0.20	0.04	0.20
# 亚麻	Flax	0.22			0.01	0.19	0.03	0.19
甜菜	Beetroots	25.37	7.65	7.74	11.36	14.63	14.07	14.63
烟叶	Tobacco	0.01			0.01			
药材	Medicinal Materials	4.87	0.56	2.73	4.17	1.54	0.23	2.69
蔬菜	Vegetables	75.82	22.93	29.75	65.57	11.53	12.24	13.39
瓜果类(含菜用瓜)	Melons	10.29	2.93	2.52	6.34	4.47	5.23	6.83
其他作物	Other Farm Crops	141.71	40.68	42.13	77.27	65.63	64.91	85.45
# 苜蓿(包括当年新播)	Lucerne	39.52	8.09	12.26	12.75	28.55	29.17	32.04

9—37　按不同类型分团场农作物总产量

Yield of Farm Crops for Farms by Different Types

计量单位：吨　　　　（2010 年）　　　　(ton)

指　标	Item	团场合计 Total	# 中心团场 Total output	# 小城镇团场 Small Town Farms	# 植棉团场 Cotton-planting Farm	# 边境团场 Border Farms	# 贫困团场 Needy Farms	# 南疆困难和边境团场 Needy and Border Farms of South XJ
粮食作物	**Grain Crops**	**2 054 595**	**585 424**	**718 815**	**1 258 070**	**976 357**	**622 557**	**1 097 047**
谷　物	Cereal	1 984 594	566 425	706 536	1 238 200	933 961	603 654	1 054 293
水　稻	Rice	153 323	40 074	21 934	136 649	72 248	13 329	74 748
小　麦	Wheat	932 338	289 375	283 934	481 460	530 407	357 996	576 860
玉　米	Corn	836 769	227 869	381 078	618 249	293 470	211 355	364 685
高　粱	Sorghum	27 009		15 641	1 682	3 081	1 867	3 081
大　麦	Barley	34 767	9 107	3 949		34 755	18 943	34 755
其他谷物	Other Cereal	388			160		164	164
豆　类	Pulse	26 781	8 792	4 691	12 778	14 582	4 779	14 740
# 大　豆（黄豆、黑豆等）	Soja	23 843	6 907	3 755	12 679	11 707	1 940	11 847
绿　豆	Green Bean	99			99	54		54
红小豆	Red Small Bean							
薯　类	Vepetables	43 220	10 207	7 588	7 092	27 814	14 124	28 014
油料作物	**Oil Bearing Crops**	**183 184**	**30 945**	**50 097**	**67 409**	**118 694**	**72 888**	**119 772**
# 花　生	Peanuts	1 704		510	1 704	123	40	1 201
油菜籽	Rapeseeds	56 753	869	1 192	131	55 527	12 877	55 527
芝　麻	Sesame	71	44	27	71			
胡　麻	Flax	19		19	19			
向日葵籽	Sunflower	116 262	27 812	47 794	59 595	58 738	56 055	58 738
棉　花	**Cotton**	**1 035 912**	**302 947**	**409 550**	**1 035 485**	**103 746**	**74 694**	**213 636**
# 长绒棉	Long Staple Cotton	29 407	1 470	4 708	29 407		2 480	520
麻　类	**Hemp Crops**	**6 569**		**33**	**5 080**	**1 352**	**210**	**1 352**
# 亚　麻	Flax	1 496			40	1 319	177	1 319
甜　菜	**Beetroots**	**1 809 821**	**546 565**	**549 839**	**904 317**	**970 096**	**910 789**	**970 096**
烟　叶	**Tobacco**	**45**			**21**		**24**	
药　材	**Medicinal Materials**							
蔬　菜	**Vegetables**	**5 647 486**	**1 802 132**	**2 344 357**	**4 973 982**	**736 468**	**885 690**	**808 865**
瓜果类（含菜用瓜）	**Melons**	**414 848**	**140 716**	**102 899**	**275 642**	**172 248**	**181 614**	**254 488**
其他作物	**Other Farm Crops**							
# 苜蓿（包括当年新播）	Lucerne	277 791	62 886	103 772	182 388	123 769	136 247	176 862

9－38　按不同类型分团场蔬菜及特种作物生产情况

Vegetable and Special kind Crop Production for Farms by Different Types

计量单位：吨　　(2010 年)　　(ton)

指　　标	Item	团场合计 Total	# 中心团场 Total	# 小城镇团场 Small Town Farms	# 植棉团场 Cotton-planting Farm	# 边境团场 Border Farms	# 贫困团场 Needy Farms	# 南疆困难和边境团场 Needy and Border Farms of South XJ
蔬菜合计	**Total**	**5 647 486**	**1 802 132**	**2 344 357**	**4 973 982**	**736 468**	**885 690**	**808 865**
叶菜类	Genus	214 622	57 351	58 610	182 809	37 611	37 048	60 444
# 大白菜	Greens	123 296	34 053	33 263	109 466	22 886	19 431	39 412
瓜菜类	Genus	70 493	11 889	20 819	56 414	20 670	16 555	23 601
# 黄瓜	Melon	37 898	7 117	10 106	32 430	10 987	9 876	13 092
块根、块茎类	Root tuber	109 667	24 205	34 045	79 088	31 000	21 643	40 982
# 萝卜	Radish	43 009	13 384	15 935	31 322	11 844	9 670	15 817
# 胡萝卜	Carrot	55 606	9 379	11 331	38 185	16 774	8 107	21 174
茄果菜类	Fruit	5 130 694	1 657 808	2 190 587	4 578 864	616 649	788 613	645 191
# 番茄	Tomato	4 497 126	1 435 199	1 977 018	4 057 001	493 582	706 220	514 331
# 工业用番茄	Tomato for Industry	4 311 077	1 396 575	1 895 923	3 889 164	439 288	660 641	451 288
辣椒	Pepper	581 687	211 142	196 543	473 267	114 387	67 941	118 265
# 工业用辣椒	Hot Pepper for Industry	493 200	182 185	143 070	400 202	88 324	54 296	88 644
葱蒜类	Garlic	60 152	28 803	22 847	30 844	19 813	7 027	21 940
菜用豆类	Shallot	32 878	9 486	7 192	29 679	7 284	7 784	11 246
# 四季豆	Mean	13 607	3 553	3 430	12 127	2 744	2 949	4 513
# 豇　豆	Legumina	13 977	4 491	3 144	12 914	3 059	4 173	5 227
水生菜类	Cownea	202		126	202	6		6
其他蔬菜	Aquatic Vegetable	24 529	10 643	8 507	13 693	2 568	6 425	4 383
食用菌(干鲜混合)	Edibte Mushroom (Dry, Fresh, Mix)	4 249	1 947	1 624	2 389	867	595	1 072
花卉种植面积(公顷)	**Edibte Mushroom (Dry, Fresh, Mix)**	**173**	**64**	**91**	**163**	**4**	**13**	**14**
鲜切花(万枝)	**Fresh Flower(10 000 sets)**	**119**	**16**	**90**	**113**	**16**	**6**	**16**
盆栽观赏植物(包括盆景)(盆)	**Potted Plant(set)**	**1 102 507**	**820 500**	**282 007**	**952 507**	**32 000**	**110 000**	**60 000**
药　材	**Medical Materials**	**8 861**	**190**	**3 793**	**7 580**	**1 607**	**487**	**3 095**
# 枸　杞	Chinese Wolf Berry	3 449	190	2 573	3 259	146	146	626

9—39　按不同类型分团场水果生产情况

Fruit Production for Farms by Different Types

（2010 年）

指　标	Item	团场合计 Total	# 中心团场 Center Farm	# 小城镇团场 Small Town Farms	# 植棉团场 Cotton-planting Farm	# 边境团场 Border Farms	# 贫困团场 Needy Farms	# 南疆困难和边境团场 Needy and Border Farms of South XJ
年末实有面积(公顷)	**Actural Area at the Year-end(hectare)**	**161 861**	**48 431**	**44 394**	**149 157**	**20 780**	**25 902**	**60 838**
苹　果	Apples	14 600	3 274	6 258	12 685	6 847	5 126	9 128
# 红富士苹果	Hongfushi Apples	10 602	2 553	4 732	9 728	4 819	3 659	6 791
黄元帅苹果	Huangyuanshuai Apples	1 425	333	680	1 073	695	468	945
国光苹果	Guoguang Apples	91	35	19	74	8	44	42
梨	Pears	15 235	9 083	6 530	14 784	92	654	1 481
# 雪花梨	Snow Flake Pears	3	3		3	3		3
鸭　梨	Duck Pears	36	25		36	2		4
香　梨	Fragrant Pear	13 143	8 262	6 074	12 947	15	303	449
砀山梨	Dangshan Pear	1 530	683	434	1 529	26	186	862
葡　萄	Grapes	33 149	8 071	13 617	30 428	6 602	5 494	7 007
# 无核葡萄	Seedless Grapes	7 901	2 811	3 897	7 295	1 226	3 019	1 244
红提葡萄	Hongti Grapes	9 669	3 388	4 208	9 402	3 357	1 227	3 510
酿酒葡萄	Grapes of Make Wining	12 332	1 316	4 154	10 792	1 492	773	1 492
桃	Peachs	2 407	955	128	1 634	1 025	159	1 161
# 蟠　桃	Pan peachs	899	76	56	559	438	66	438
杏	Apricots	4 914	694	1 040	2 432	2 060	2 381	2 562
红　枣	Jujubes	90 765	26 015	16 767	86 441	4 032	11 861	39 245
石　榴	Pomegranate	50	22	2	50			50
其　他	Other	741	317	52	703	122	227	204
产　量(吨)	**Output(ton)**	**1 147 817**	**358 880**	**409 999**	**1 068 412**	**172 794**	**186 861**	**348 802**
苹　果	Apples	191 089	35 685	79 674	171 096	72 201	65 149	102 391
# 红富士苹果	Hongfushi Apples	105 865	23 974	40 334	101 498	30 037	36 298	50 328
黄元帅苹果	Huangyuanshuai Apples	54 819	6 914	34 082	45 662	33 324	12 853	42 148
国光苹果	Guoguang Apples	2 923	1 111	407	2 257	79	1 425	988
梨	Pears	323 327	167 120	118 317	317 341	3 535	9 269	49 992
# 雪花梨	Snow Flake Pears	102	85		88	87	1	87
鸭　梨	Duck Pears	605	335		581	93	6	156
香　梨	Fragrant Pear	258 771	135 095	99 100	255 441	880	5 187	16 984
砀山梨	Dangshan Pear	51 647	27 291	18 775	51 636	1 497	1 927	27 652
葡　萄	Grapes	365 743	85 949	164 637	332 448	64 572	73 889	74 983
# 无核葡萄	Seedless Grapes	125 324	39 218	76 905	116 064	13 308	55 490	13 705
红提葡萄	Hongti Grapes	117 624	35 499	47 229	115 395	38 246	8 230	45 123
酿酒葡萄	Grapes of make wining	93 262	5 719	26 406	73 219	9 897	4 210	9 897
桃	Peachs	32 522	10 936	1 546	20 221	16 131	1 890	17 466
# 蟠　桃	Pan Peachs	13 418	880	804	7 220	6 925	850	6 925
杏	Apricots	19 432	3 642	2 130	12 413	4 850	8 023	12 000
红　枣	Jujubes	211 811	53 274	42 931	211 244	10 727	28 449	89 807
石　榴	Pomegranate	83	60		83			83
其　他	Other	3 810	2 214	764	3 566	778	192	2 080

9—40 按不同类型分团场牲畜年底头数

Number of Livestock for Farms by Different Types

计量单位:万头(只) (2010 年) (10 000 heads)

指 标	Item	合 计 Total	牛 Cattle and Buffaloes	#奶 牛 Cows	马 Horses	驴 Donkeys	骡 Mules	骆 驼 Camels
团场总计	**Total**	**597.81**	**34.96**	**18.54**	**2.38**	**1.23**		**0.41**
#中心团场	Center Farms	184.66	7.79	4.26	0.48	0.58		0.16
#小城镇团场	Small Town Farms	198.35	10.87	6.52	0.20	0.56		0.14
#植棉团场	Cotton-Planting Farms	395.19	23.80	13.47	0.81	1.08		0.29
#边境团场	Border Farms	235.78	12.70	5.83	1.32	0.41		0.27
#贫困团场	Needy Farms	224.07	11.12	4.77	1.18	0.59		0.31
#南疆困难团场和边境团场	Needy and Border Farms of South XJ	289.29	14.69	6.52	1.50	0.95		0.27

指 标	Item	猪 Pigs	羊 Goats	山 羊 Milk Goats	绵 羊 Sheep	#细毛羊及改良羊 Fine Wool Sheep and Improved Sheep	家 禽 Poultry	兔 Rabbits
团场总计	**Total**	**143.44**	**415.39**	**38.27**	**377.12**	**126.79**	**534.48**	**27.18**
#中心团场	Center Farms	48.98	126.67	10.73	115.94	38.25	153.20	10.22
#小城镇团场	Small Town Farms	70.50	116.08	9.91	106.17	52.50	168.91	11.67
#植棉团场	Cotton-Planting Farms	119.94	249.27	27.55	221.72	68.65	449.57	22.88
#边境团场	Border Farms	24.63	196.45	11.82	184.63	75.66	178.00	6.65
#贫困团场	Needy Farms	17.38	193.49	15.40	178.09	47.76	152.07	5.21
#南疆困难团场和边境团场	Needy and Border Farms of South XJ	31.62	240.26	19.74	220.52	78.37	202.94	10.46

9—41　按不同类型分团场肉类生产情况

Meat Production for Farms by Different Types

计量单位：吨　　（2010 年）　　(ton)

指　　标	Item	团场合计 Total	# 中心团场 Center Farm	# 小城镇团场 Small Town Farms	# 植棉团场 Cotton-planting Farm	# 边境团场 Border Farms	# 贫困团场 Needy Farms	# 南疆困难和边境团场 Needy and Border Farms of South XJ
肉类总产量	**Output of Meat**	**308 732**	**89 217**	**124 731**	**230 295**	**88 424**	**77 881**	**104 331**
牛	Beef	36 596	8 013	9 983	23 571	14 314	11 867	16 132
马	Horse	1 474	204	81	457	918	464	1 012
驴	Donkey	520	140	207	457	213	280	364
骡	Mule	12		12	12	12	12	12
骆　驼	Camel	334	144	65	210	243	288	243
肉　猪	Pork	163 735	51 881	75 968	132 091	32 439	22 951	39 726
羊	Goat	79 754	21 418	27 057	50 995	35 698	35 247	41 396
# 绵　羊	Sheep	70 674	20 424	23 216	43 229	33 802	31 649	38 746
家　禽	Poultry	23 168	5 705	9 850	19 658	4 187	6 435	4 941
兔	Rabbit	1 924	895	980	1 652	376	227	481
其他肉产量	Others	1 215	817	528	1 192	24	110	24

9—42　按不同类型分团场畜产品产量

Output of Livestock Products for Farms by Different Types

（2010 年）

指　　标	Item	团场合计 Total	# 中心团场 Center Farm	# 小城镇团场 Small Town Farms	# 植棉团场 Cotton-planting Farm	# 边境团场 Border Farms	# 贫困团场 Needy Farms	# 南疆困难和边境团场 Needy and Border Farms of South XJ
绵羊毛　（吨）	Sheep Wool　(ton)	10 933	3 254	3 692	7 167	5 181	4 450	5 767
# 细羊毛	Fine Wool	5 026	1 221	2 019	3 338	2 450	1 376	2 595
半细羊毛	Semi-Fine Wool	3 203	1 468	940	2 266	1 276	1 463	1 508
山羊毛　（吨）	Goat Wool　(ton)	218	62	112	177	47	35	65
山羊绒　（公斤）	Cashmere　(kg)	55 379	12 759	15 285	34 103	25 644	31 757	27 384
奶类产量　（吨）	Milk　(ton)	419 467	90 451	168 362	354 305	84 445	68 484	90 259
# 牛　奶	Cow Milk	417 948	89 983	168 362	353 627	83 612	67 580	88 846
羊　奶	Sheep Milk	1 519	468		678	833	904	1 413
牛　皮　（张）	Oxhide　(sheet)	35 732	8 131	10 662	28 941	8 237	8 373	15 537
绵羊皮　（张）	Sheep Skin　(sheet)	578 843	140 435	222 425	476 243	148 502	151 973	254 602
山羊皮　（张）	Goat Skin　(sheet)	448 433	115 286	187 322	359 971	128 391	125 867	200 991
驼　毛　（吨）	Camel Hair　(ton)	18	12	2	12	18	18	18
蜂群数　（箱）	Bee Cluster　(box)	47 789	7 996	9 527	23 941	16 645	11 533	17 030
蜂蜜产量　（吨）	Honey　(ton)	2 865	572	475	1 222	1 680	1 278	1 701
禽蛋产量　（吨）	Poultry Eggs　(ton)	40 595	12 721	13 397	33 882	11 929	11 195	14 045
年末养鹿　（头）	Deer　(head)	27 717	17 017	9 916	24 408	1 498	1 636	1 945
年内产鹿茸　（公斤）	Pilose Antler　(kg)	29 382	18 462	10 828	26 283	2 311	2 295	3 144

9—43 乡镇企业分行业主要经济指标

Main Economic Indicators of Village Enterprises by Sector

计量单位:万元 (2010年) (10 000 yuan)

指 标	Item	企业个数（个） Enterprise (unit)	就业人员年末数（人） Employees(Year-end) (person)	增加值 Value-added	总产值 Total Output Value
总 计	**Total**	**1 608**	**51 878**	**337 930**	**1 137 011**
农 业	Farming	208	4 048	13 189	33 099
工 业	Industry	1 062	40 713	289 022	998 049
采矿业	Mining and Dressing	60	3 432	20 054	61 652
制造业	Manufacturing	964	36 003	262 384	924 283
电力、燃气及水的生产和供应业	Production and Supply of Electricity, Gas and Water	38	1 278	6 584	12 114
建筑业	Construction	37	2 275	15 220	45 399
# 资质等级企业	Qualification Grade	7	530	8 202	24 022
交通运输仓储业	Transportation and Storage	35	1 870	9 624	22 688
批发零售业	Wholesale and Retail Trade	64	962	6 231	27 121
住宿及餐饮业	Accommodation and Catering Services	142	1 243	2 993	6 687
# 餐饮业	Catering Services	56	528	1 371	2 883
居民服务、其他服务业和娱乐业	Resident, Other Services and Recreation	57	691	622	990
其 他	Others	3	76	1 029	2 978

指 标	Item	营业收入 Business Income	利润总额 Total Profits	上交税金 Payable Taxes	劳动者报酬 Earnings
总 计	**Total**	**1 119 811**	**102 088**	**29 843**	**91 015**
农 业	Farming	28 754	1 581	334	4 786
工 业	Industry	970 209	89 516	26 611	68 686
采矿业	Mining and Dressing	59 231	6 824	2 188	5 657
制造业	Manufacturing	896 712	81 813	24 142	60 906
电力、燃气及水的生产和供应业	Production and Supply of Electricity, Gas and Water	14 266	879	281	2 123
建筑业	Construction	44 668	3 567	1 057	7 267
# 资质等级企业	Qualification Grade	27 862	1 600	422	3 719
交通运输仓储业	Transportation and Storage	27 817	2 218	614	5 765
批发零售业	Wholesale and Retail Trade	36 223	3 547	797	1 719
住宿及餐饮业	Accommodation and Catering Services	7 575	1 333	247	1 694
# 餐饮业	Catering Services	2 895	377	97	714
居民服务、其他服务业和娱乐业	Resident, Other Services and Recreation	1 997	231	137	760
其 他	Others	2 568	95	46	338

9—44　各师乡镇企业主要经济指标

Main Economic Indicators of Village Enterprises by Division

计量单位:万元　　　　(2010年)　　　　(10 000 yuan)

单　位	Unit	企业个数(个) Enterprise (unit)	就业人员年末数(人) Employees(Year-end) (person)	增加值 Added Value	总产值 Gross Output Value
总　计	**Total**	**1 608**	**51 878**	**337 930**	**1 137 011**
一　师	Division 1	82	3 235	15 952	59 194
二　师	Division 2	103	3 810	51 978	187 646
三　师	Division 3	80	2 650	25 380	46 178
四　师	Division 4	154	4 396	57 725	174 202
五　师	Division 5	44	1 573	14 188	42 721
六　师	Division 6	230	8 130	42 192	168 617
七　师	Division 7	264	6 221	19 508	69 836
八　师	Division 8	141	6 697	26 653	133 191
九　师	Division 9	153	3 325	4 487	11 754
十　师	Division 10	61	1 969	25 861	78 961
十二师	Division 12	195	3 486	16 695	41 100
十三师	Division 13	94	5 917	35 682	117 026
十四师	Division 14	7	469	1 629	6 585

单　位	Unit	营业收入 Business Income	利润总额 Total Profits	上交税金 Payable Taxes	劳动者报酬 Earnings
总　计	**Total**	**1 119 811**	**102 088**	**29 843**	**91 015**
一　师	Division 1	58 350	3 986	1 899	6 188
二　师	Division 2	160 267	15 766	2 181	6 515
三　师	Division 3	64 840	1 380	560	6 230
四　师	Division 4	170 999	29 281	4 374	13 480
五　师	Division 5	44 101	3 752	720	2 398
六　师	Division 6	149 043	10 442	3 331	6 528
七　师	Division 7	67 981	4 474	2 317	11 744
八　师	Division 8	147 331	4 951	4 304	15 191
九　师	Division 9	16 856	3 278	582	4 596
十　师	Division 10	81 563	9 311	1 585	4 369
十二师	Division 12	40 440	1 850	620	4 405
十三师	Division 13	111 674	12 872	7 021	8 796
十四师	Division 14	6 366	745	349	575

2011 BING TUAN

第十篇

工　业

Chapter 10 Industry

简要说明

一、本篇资料主要内容

本篇资料反映兵团全部工业经济主要发展情况。包括：全部工业企业按师和主要指标分组的企业单位数、工业总产值和工业总产值指数及构成。规模以上工业企业按师和主要指标分组的主要经济指标和经济效益指标，包括企业单位数、工业总产值、工业销售产值、工业增加值、财务指标、效益指标和主要工业产品生产能力等。大中型工业企业主要指标。主要工业产品产量。

二、本篇统计范围

工业统计调查范围为隶属于兵团管理和在兵团辖区范围内的全部工业企业和个体工业。包括：工业法人企业、工业产业活动单位及个体工业。规模以上工业企业统计范围：2006年及以前为全部国有及年主营业务收入在500万元以上的非国有 工业法人企业。2007年起调整为年主营业务收入在500万元以上的全部工业法人企业。

三、本篇资料来源

本篇资料由兵团统计局工业交通投资统计处根据《兵团工业统计报表制度》收集、汇总、整理、提供。

四、本篇调查方法

统计调查方法为全面调查。

Brief Introduction

1. Main Contents

Data in this chapter reflect industrial economic development of XPCG, including the number of all industrial enterprises by division and by main indicators, gross industrial output value, indices of gross industrial output value and composition. Main economic indicators and efficiency indicators of industrial enterprises above designated size by division and main indicators, including number of enterprises, gross industrial output value, industrial sales value, industrial value-added, main economic indicators, efficiency indicators and production capacity of main products. Main indicators of large and medium scale enterprises. Output of main industrial products.

2. Scope of Statistics

Industrial statistics cover all industrial enterprises and individual enterprises within XPCG, including corporate industrial enterprises, units of industrial activities and individual enterprises.

The statistics of industrial enterprises above designated size cover all State-owned and non State-owned industrial corporation enterprises with annual main income of over 5 million yuan in 2006 and before 2006, From 2007 on, it was adjusted as all industrial corporation enterprises with annual main income of over 5 million yuan.

3. Sources of Data

The industrial enterprises statistics in this chapter are collected according to the Comprehensive Statistical reporting on Industrial of XPCG, which are provided by Industry Communications and Assets Statistical Section of Statistics Bureau of XPCG.

4. Methodology of Survey

Survey method is comprehensive statistics.

10—1 工业企业单位数

Number of Industrial Enterprises

计量单位：个 (unit)

年份 单位	Year Unit	工业单位数 Number of Industrial Enterprises	国有企业 State-owned	集体企业 Collective-owned	股份制企业 Share Holding	其他企业 Others	个体 Individuals	轻工业 Light Industry	重工业 Heavy Industry	# 法人企业 Corporative Enterprise	# 大中型企业 Large Scale and Medium Scale
	1952	42	42					17	25	29	
	1954	87	87					52	35	40	
	1957	115	115					84	31	32	
	1962	319	319					170	149	108	
	1965	268	268					170	118	108	
	1970	352	352					190	162	119	
	1975	351	351					186	165	5	
	1978	507	498	9				229	278	75	
	1980	647	626	21				296	351	102	6
	1985	2 220	1 060	104			1 056	1 350	870	168	16
	1990	2 182	1 224	153			805	1 426	756	291	22
	1991	3 045	1 216	160			1 669	1 622	1 423	303	22
	1992	3 086	1 190	193			1 703	1 970	1 116	343	37
	1993	3 313	1 249	174			1 890	2 104	1 209	327	37
	1994	3 307	1 235	202		14	1 856	2 286	1 021	344	43
	1995	2 859	1 278	232		24	1 325	1 862	997	388	48
	1996	2 872	1 265	264		46	1 297	1 899	973	407	47
	1997	2 837	1 197	197		36	1 407	1 893	944	344	49
	1998	3 411	1 061	149		39	2 162	2 306	1 105	305	43
	1999	3 453	1 030	127	13	24	2 259	2 317	1 136	291	51
	2000	4 053	952	113	25	49	2 914	2 595	1 458	270	50
	2001	4 691	895	97	86	58	3 555	3 088	1 603	273	47
	2002	4 796	877	68	71	61	3 719	3 176	1 620	240	42
	2003	4 390	710	62	92	26	3 500	3 256	1 134	220	37
	2004	3 006	565	55	296	164	1 926	1 866	1 140	480	35
	2005	3 064	607	47	294	149	1 967	1 849	1 215	447	39
	2006	3 005	561	21	297	140	1 986	1 745	1 260	450	45
	2007	2 909	484	12	340	120	1 953	1 665	1 244	433	63
	2008	4 035	535	11	623	187	2 679	2 024	2 011	722	64
	2009	4 099	512	9	673	174	2 731	2 364	1 735	691	68
	2010	4 222	426	7	848	204	2 737	2 319	1 903	1 103	80
一　师	Division 1	251	42		100	5	104	146	105	109	6
二　师	Division 2	218	34		56	18	110	141	77	60	6
三　师	Division 3	157	55		15	1	86	80	77	28	1
四　师	Division 4	458	24		60	16	358	295	163	82	7
五　师	Division 5	223	35		21	1	166	119	104	26	3
六　师	Division 6	700	17		94	5	584	424	276	91	9
七　师	Division 7	288	60	2	32	9	185	194	94	49	6
八　师	Division 8	996	60	4	279	135	518	392	604	450	29
九　师	Division 9	178	25		10		143	113	65	10	1
十　师	Division 10	174	27	1	22	6	118	86	88	34	2
建工师	Construction Division	41	10		11	3	17	16	25	14	
十二师	Division 12	237	12		36	2	187	152	85	40	3
十三师	Division 13	198	16		86	1	95	76	122	77	3
十四师	Division 14	81	3		11	1	66	74	7	12	
国资公司	State-owned Property Company	17	4		13			13	4	16	2
中基公司	Chalkis Company	3	1		2			2	1	3	2
兵团直属	Directly under XPCG	2	1			1		2		2	

注：1. 1980 年以前大中型企业无资料记载。2. 从 1999 年开始将股份制企业由其他企业中分列出来。
Note: a) Data on Large-scale and Medium-scale enterprises are not recorded before 1980.
b) Since 1999 share holding enterprises have been Listed separately from other enterprises.

10—2　工业总产值及构成

Gross Output Value of Industry and Its Composition

年　份 Year	工业总产值 Gross Industrial Output Value	按登记注册类型分 Grouped by Status of Registration 国有企业 State-owned	集体企业 Collective-owned	股份制企业 Share Holding	其他企业 Others	个　体 Individuals	按轻重工业分 Grouped by Light &Heavy Industry 轻工业 Light-Industry	重工业 Heavy Industry
绝对数(万元) Value(10 000yuan)								
1952	3 221	3 221					1 894	1 327
1954	5 703	5 703					3 895	1 808
1957	14 638	14 638					11 183	3 455
1962	37 186	37 186					24 877	12 309
1965	53 113	53 113					38 154	14 959
1970	64 289	64 289					43 152	21 137
1975	16 547	16 547					9 399	7 148
1978	54 511	54 190	321				36 413	18 098
1980	90 241	89 273	968				62 627	27 614
1985	181 801	175 319	4 355			2 127	127 109	54 692
1990	444 490	430 738	11 285			2 467	346 263	98 227
1995	1 324 568	1 223 435	55 531		32 808	12 794	1 092 950	231 618
(1995)	709 290	626 295	46 612		25 937	10 446	504 498	204 792
1996	816 230	708 635	62 569		35 425	9 601	560 863	255 367
1997	902 717	736 889	68 689		85 481	11 658	621 152	281 565
1998	882 052	728 583	46 083		88 114	19 272	581 068	300 984
1999	909 347	706 322	53 359	85 625	36 216	27 825	602 190	307 157
2000	976 926	707 326	48 681	143 456	38 000	39 463	661 985	314 941
2001	1 065 752	645 515	32 633	275 324	31 382	80 898	652 365	413 387
2002	1 140 143	656 184	33 986	327 585	32 766	89 622	715 376	424 767
(2002)	1 023 562	539 603	33 986	327 585	32 766	89 622	607 543	416 019
2003	1 218 342	513 379	27 425	498 566	78 700	100 272	758 540	459 802
2004	1 444 790	496 279	8 725	768 169	85 089	86 528	845 478	599 312
2005	1 756 428	562 559	8 537	1 019 391	61 861	104 080	929 263	827 165
2006	2 175 070	642 417	3 337	1 199 136	197 694	132 486	1 084 057	1 091 013
2007	2 887 118	700 813	3 388	1 713 611	256 348	212 958	1 492 025	1 395 093
2008	3 802 504	809 698	5 021	2 525 149	207 314	255 322	1 879 540	1 922 964
2009	4 972 441	811 616	1 433	3 592 201	252 071	315 120	2 541 882	2 430 559
2010	6 565 904	822 694	1 705	4 919 366	434 125	388 014	3 350 177	3 215 727
构成(%) Composition(%)								
1952		100.0					58.8	41.2
1954		100.0					68.3	31.7
1957		100.0					76.4	23.6
1962		100.0					66.9	33.1
1965		100.0					71.8	28.2
1970		100.0					67.1	32.9
1975		100.0					56.8	43.2
1978		99.4	0.6				66.8	33.2
1980		98.9	1.1				69.4	30.6
1985		96.4	2.4			1.2	69.9	30.1
1990		96.9	2.5			0.6	77.9	22.1
1995		92.4	4.2		2.5	0.9	82.5	17.5
(1995)		88.3	6.6		3.6	1.5	71.1	28.9
1996		86.8	7.7		4.3	1.2	68.7	31.3
1997		81.6	7.6		9.5	1.3	68.8	31.2
1998		82.6	5.2		10.0	2.2	65.9	34.1
1999		77.7	5.9	9.4	4.0	3.0	66.2	33.8
2000		72.4	5.0	14.7	3.9	4.0	67.8	32.2
2001		60.6	3.1	25.8	2.9	7.6	61.2	38.8
2002		57.5	3.0	28.7	2.9	7.9	62.7	37.3
(2002)		52.7	3.3	32.0	3.2	8.8	59.4	40.6
2003		42.1	2.3	40.9	6.5	8.2	62.3	37.7
2004		34.3	0.6	53.2	5.9	6.0	58.5	41.5
2005		32.0	0.5	58.0	3.5	6.0	52.9	47.1
2006		29.5	0.2	55.1	9.1	6.1	49.8	50.2
2007		24.3	0.1	59.3	8.9	7.4	51.7	48.3
2008		21.3	0.1	66.4	5.5	6.7	49.4	50.6
2009		16.3	…	72.3	5.1	6.3	51.1	48.9
2010		12.6	…	74.9	6.6	5.9	51.0	49.0

注：1.本表绝对数按当年价计算。2.(1995)年以后棉花加工按加工费计算总产值。3.本表2003年以后数据按照新口径统计，剔除了纤维原料初加工业；(2002)年前为老口径。(下表同)

Note: a) Data in value terms in this table are calculated at current prices. b) Gross output Value of cotton processing are calculated at processing expenses after 1995. c) Data in 2003 are calculated at new caliber, removing the initial processing on the fiber raw materials. Data prior to 2002 are at old caliber(the same as follows).

10—3 工业总产值及指数

Gross Output Value of Industry and Its Indices

年份 Year	工业总产值 Gross Industrial Output Value	国有企业 State-owned	集体企业 Collective-owned	股份制企业 Share Holding	其他企业 Others	个体 Individuals
绝对数(万元) **Value(10 000yuan)**						
1952	5 176	5 176				
1954	9 257	9 257				
1957	23 516	23 516				
1962	53 529	53 529				
1965	87 337	87 337				
1970	121 201	121 201				
1975	31 346	31 346				
1978	107 490	106 964	526			
1980	150 486	148 827	1 659			
1985	307 673	296 220	7 676			3 777
1990	474 344	458 596	13 011			2 737
1995	763 589	696 893	33 547		24 415	8 734
(1995)	476 580	419 996	31 603		17 284	7 697
1996	528 720	459 819	37 667		23 172	8 062
1997	580 119	466 933	39 853		63 627	9 706
1998	595 015	478 847	30 348		71 844	13 976
1999	648 562	508 993	39 611	53 353	25 501	21 104
2000	682 724	490 948	35 783	95 834	30 075	30 084
2001	751 101	457 104	23 368	185 860	22 605	62 164
2002	828 380	463 369	26 993	243 229	23 230	71 559
(2002)	765 015	400 004	26 993	243 229	23 230	71 559
2003	879 565	361 880	19 300	375 203	45 197	77 985
2004	1 030 142	320 823	7 062	562 416	66 060	73 781
2005	1 253 271	364 282	6 928	722 647	79 044	80 370
2006	2 080 206	614 459	3 192	1 146 950	189 090	126 515
2007	2 795 428	678 556	3 280	1 659 190	248 207	206 195
2008	3 494 627	744 140	4 615	2 320 695	190 528	234 649
2009	5 022 973	819 898	1 448	3 628 851	254 441	318 335
2010	6 071 109	760 697	1 577	4 548 651	401 410	358 774
环比指数(%) **Indices(Preceding=100)**						
1952	100. 0	100. 0				
1954	135. 3	135. 3				
1957	135. 3	135. 3				
1962	86. 3	86. 3				
1965	126. 4	126. 4				
1970	130. 5	130. 5				
1975	24. 7	24. 7				
1978	247. 2	246. 0				
1980	119. 0	119. 1	108. 7			
1985	121. 7	119. 3	172. 9			
1990	110. 9	112. 9	77. 8			55. 7
1995	113. 2	111. 1	120. 0		195. 6	128. 5
(1995)						
1996	110. 9	109. 5	119. 2		134. 1	104. 7
1997	109. 7	101. 5	105. 8		274. 6	120. 4
1998	102. 6	102. 6	76. 1		112. 9	144. 0
1999	109. 0	106. 3	130. 5	132. 6	101. 2	151. 0
2000	105. 3	96. 5	90. 3	179. 6	117. 9	147. 4
2001	110. 0	93. 1	65. 3	193. 9	75. 2	206. 6
2002	110. 3	101. 4	115. 5	130. 9	102. 8	115. 1
2003	115. 0	90. 5	71. 5	154. 3	194. 6	109. 0
2004	117. 1	88. 6	36. 6	149. 9	146. 2	94. 6
2005	121. 6	113. 6	98. 1	128. 5	119. 7	120. 6
2006	118. 4	109. 2	37. 4	118. 2	170. 2	121. 6
2007	128. 5	105. 6	98. 3	138. 4	125. 6	155. 6
2008	121. 0	106. 2	136. 2	135. 4	74. 3	110. 2
2009	132. 1	101. 3	28. 8	143. 7	122. 8	124. 7
2010	122. 1	93. 7	110. 0	126. 6	159. 2	113. 9

注:(1)本表 2005 年以前绝对数为可比价数据,环比指数按可比价计算。(2)2006 年绝对数为价格指数缩减数据,环比指数按价格指数缩减法计算。

Note: a) Data in this table before 2005 are value data and indices are calulated at comparable prices. b) Data of Value in 2006 and indices are calculated at price indices cut.

10—4　工业企业数及工业总产值

Number of Industrial Enterprises and Output Value

计量单位:万元　　(2010 年)　　(10 000 yuan)

指　标	Item	企业数（个） Number of Enterprises (unit)	工业总产值当年价格 At Current Prices
总　计	**Total**	**1 485**	**6 177 890**
# 国有控股企业	State-controlled Shareholding Enterprises	618	4 002 400
按登记注册类型分	**Grouped by Statusof Registration**		
内资企业	Domestic Enterprises	1 462	5 892 104
国有企业	State-owned Enterprises	426	822 694
集体企业	Collective-owned Enterprises	7	1 705
股份合作企业	Share Cooperative Enterprises	11	48 559
有限责任公司	Limited Liability Corporations	414	3 457 164
国有独资公司	State-owned Corporations with Private-Funds	12	45 277
其他有限责任公司	Other Limited Liability Corporations	402	3 411 887
股份有限公司	Share-holding Corporations Ltd.	22	602 777
私营企业	Private Enterprises	574	950 752
私营独资企业	Private-funded Enterprises	145	85 697
私营合伙企业	Private Partnership Enterprises	17	5 630
私营有限责任公司	Private Limited Liabilit yCorporations	394	798 172
私营股份有限公司	Private Share-holding Corporations Ltd.	18	61 253
其他企业	Other Enterprises	8	8 452
港、澳、台商投资企业	Enterprises with Funds from Hong Kong, Macao and Taiwan	7	75 834
合资经营企业(港或澳、台)	Joint-Venture Enterprises(with funds from Hong Kong, Macaoand Taiwan)	4	51 315
港、澳、台商独资经营企业	Enterprises with Funds from Hong Kong, Macaoand Taiwan	2	24 134
港、澳、台商投资股份有限公司	Share—holding Corporations Ltd. from Hong Kong, Macao and Taiwan	1	385
外商投资企业	Foreign Funded Enterprises	16	209 952
中外合资经营企业	Joint-Venture Enterprises	9	122 404
中外合作经营企业	Cooperative Enterprises	1	34 464
外商投资	Foreign-Funded Enterprises	5	49 940
外商投资股份有限公司	Foreign-Funded Enterprises Share-holding Corporations Ltd.	1	3 144
按轻重工业分	**Grouped by Light & Heavy Industry**		
轻工业	Light Industry	653	3 148 996
重工业	Heavy Industry	832	3 028 894
按企业规模分	**Grouped by Size of Enterprises**		
大型企业	Large-Scale Enterprises	6	1 103 831
中型企业	Medium-Scale Enterprises	74	2 299 400
小型企业	Small-Scale Enterprises	1 405	2 774 659
按工业行业分	**Grouped by Sector**		
采矿业	**Mining**	**81**	**269 968**
煤炭开采和洗选业	Coal Mining and Dressing	24	179 001
烟煤和无烟煤的开采洗选	Soft Coal and Hard Coal Mining and Dressing	24	179 001
黑色金属矿采选业	Ferrous Metals Mining and Dressing	9	12 889
铁矿采选	Prdding Mining and Dressing	9	12 889
有色金属矿采选业	Nonferrous Metals Mining and Dressing	4	21 030
常用有色金属矿采选	Common Nonferrous Metals Mining and Dressing	3	21 030
镍钴矿采选	Nickle and Cobalt Minerals Mining and Dressing	3	21 030
稀有稀土金属矿采选	Rare Thulium Metals Mining and Dressing	1	
钨钼矿采选	Tungsten and Molybdenum Minerals Mining and Dressing	1	
非金属矿采选业	Nonmetal Mineral Mining and Dressing	44	57 047
土砂石开采	Gravel and Sand Mining	36	30 392
石灰石、石膏开采	Lime and Gypsum Mining	8	22 062
建筑装饰用石开采	Construction and Decorative Stone Mining	3	2 013
耐火土石开采	Refractory Stone Mining	1	228
粘土及其他土砂石开采	Clay and Other Gravel Mining	24	6 089
化学矿采选	Chemical Mineral Mining and Dressing	1	1 200
采　盐	Salt Mining	2	2 516
石棉及其他非金属矿采选	Asbestos and Other Nonmetal Minerals Mining and Dressing	5	22 940
石棉、云母矿采选	Asbestos and Mica Minerals Mining and Dressing	1	12 803
其他非金属矿采选	Other Nonmetal Minerals Mining and Dressing	4	10 137

注:本表按当年价格计算,不含连队办工业(村办)及个体工业。(下表同)
Note: This table is not including county-run and individual industry(the same as follows).

10－4 续表 1 Continued

计量单位:万元 (2010 年) (10 000 yuan)

指　　标	Item	企业数（个）Number of Enterprises (unit)	工业总产值 当年价格 At Current Prices
制造业	**Manufacturing**	**1 297**	**5 477 670**
农副食品加工业	Farm and Sideline Food Processing	242	1 053 214
谷物磨制	Cereal Grain Grinding	46	80 568
饲料加工	Forage Processing	27	310 627
植物油加工	Plant Oil Processing	87	370 013
食用植物油加工	Edible Plant Oil Processing	87	370 013
制　糖	Sugar Making	4	86 580
屠宰及肉类加工	Slaughtering and Meat Processing	24	92 421
畜禽屠宰	Livestock and Fowl Slaughtering	19	87 985
肉制品及副产品加工	Meat Product and Sideline Product Processing	5	4 436
水产品加工	Aquatic Production Processing	1	988
水产品冷冻加工	Aquatic Production Refrigeration Processing	1	988
蔬菜、水果和坚果加工	Vegetable Fruit and Nuts Processing	26	40 181
其他农副食品加工	Other Farm and Sideline Food Processing	27	71 836
淀粉及淀粉制品的制造	Starch and Starch Products Manufacturing	5	17 417
豆制品制造	Bean Ware Manufacturing	1	219
蛋品加工	Egg Ware Processing	2	3 950
其他未列明的农副食品加工	Other Unlisted Farm and Sideline Food Processing	19	50 250
食品制造业	Food Manufacturing	93	659 219
焙烤食品制造	Bakery Products Manufacturing	5	4 610
糕点、面包制造	Pastry and dread Manufacturing	2	23
饼干及其他焙烤食品制造	Cookie and Other Bakery Products Manufacturing	3	4 587
糖果、巧克力及蜜饯制造	Candy,Chocolate and Sweetmeat Manufacturing	1	12
糖果、巧克力制造	Candy and Chocolate Manufacturing	1	12
方便食品制造	Convenient Food Manufacturing	5	30 101
米、面制品制造	Rice and Flour Manufacturing	3	2 953
方便面及其他方便食品制造	Cohvenient Noodles and Other Convenient Food Manufacturing	2	27 148
液体乳及乳制品制造	Liquid Milk and Dairy Products Manufacturing	20	114 693
罐头制造	Canned Fod Manufacturing	45	426 855
蔬菜、水果罐头制造	Canned Vegetable and Fruit Manufacturing	45	426 855
调味品、发酵制品制造	Condiment and Fermented Products Manufacturing	9	43 894
味精制造	Gourmet Powder Manufacturing	2	20 482
酱油、食醋及类似制品的制造	Soy Sauce,Edible Vinegar and Similar Products Manufacturing	4	13 648
其他调味品、发酵制品制造	Other Gourmet Powder and Fermented Products Manufacturing	3	9 764
其他食品制造	Other Food Manufacturing	8	39 055
食品及饲料添加剂制造	Food and Forage Additive Manufacturing	4	30 032
其他未列明的食品制造	Other Non-list Food Manufacturing	4	9 023
饮料制造业	Beverage Manufacturing	52	306 422
酒精制造	Alcohol Manufacturing	1	440
酒的制造	Liquor Brewing	35	237 686
白酒制造	White Liquor Brewing	17	141 118
啤酒制造	Beer Brewing	5	51 033
葡萄酒制造	Grape Wine Brewing	13	45 535
软饮料制造	Soft Beverage Manufacturing	16	68 296
瓶(罐)装饮用水制造	Bottled (Canned) Drinkable Water Manufacturing	8	1 456
果菜汁及果菜汁饮料制造	Fruit and Vegetable Juice Fruit and Vegetable Juice Beverage Manufacturing	6	22 158
茶饮料及其他软饮料制造业	Tea Beverage and Other Soft Beverage Manufacturing	2	44 683
纺织业	Textile Industry	85	677 438
棉、化纤纺织及印染精加工	Cotton Chemical Fibre and Dying Fine Processing	66	637 182
棉、化纤纺织加工	Cotton and Chemical Textile Processing	66	637 182
毛纺织和染整精加工	Woolen Textile Dying and Finishing Fine Processing	7	11 360
毛条加工	Woolen Hair Textile	2	1 530
毛纺织	Woolen Textile	5	9 830
麻纺织	Homp Crops Textile	1	7 598

10—4 续表 2 Continued

计量单位:万元 (2010 年) (10 000 yuan)

指 标	Item	企业数(个) Number of Enterprises (unit)	工业总产值 当年价格 At Current Prices
纺织制成品制造	Textile Products Manufacturing	9	8 072
棉及化纤制品制造	Cotton and Chemical Fibre Products Manufacturing	3	7 146
绳、索、缆的制造	Rope and Cordage Manufacturing	3	193
纺织带和帘子布制造	Textile Belt and Cord Fabric Manufacturing	2	724
其他纺织制成品制造	Other Textile Products Manufacturing	1	10
针织品、编织品及其制品制造	Knitted Fabrics and Products Manufacturing	2	13 226
棉、化纤针织品及编织品制造	Cotton and Chemical Fabrics and Products Manufacturing	1	13 179
毛针织品及编织品制造	Woolen Knitted Products Manufacturing	1	47
纺织服装、鞋、帽制造业	Textile Clothing Shoes and Hats Manufacturing	10	1 274
纺织服装制造	Textile Clothing Manufacturing	10	1 274
皮革、毛皮、羽毛(绒)及其制品业	Leather,Furriery,Fecather and Its Manufacturing	2	885
皮革鞣制加工	Leather Tan Processing	1	430
羽毛(绒)加工及制品制造	Feather and Ite Processing and Manufacturing	1	455
羽毛(绒)制品加工	Feather and Its Processing and Manufacturing	1	455
木材加工及木、竹、藤、棕、草制造	Timber Processing,Wood,Bamboo,Rattan,Palm Fibre and Straw Products	17	8 907
锯材、木片加工	Sawed Wood and Chip Processing	5	1 817
锯材加工	Sawed Wood Processing	2	456
木片加工	Chip Processing	3	1 361
人造板制造	Artificial Board Manufacturing	9	2 695
胶合板制造	Veneer Manufacturing	6	2 195
刨花板制造	Board Manufacturing	1	313
其他人造板、材制造	Other Artificial Board Maufacturing	2	186
木制品制造	Wooden Products Manufacturing	3	4 395
木容器制造	Wooden Container Aanufacturing	1	3 972
软木制品及其他木制品制造	Soft Woodem and Other Wooden Products Manufacturing	2	423
家具制造业	Furniture Manufacturing	11	12 310
木质家具制造	Wooden Furniture Manufacturing	11	12 310
造纸及纸制品业	Paper Making and Paper Products	38	78 912
纸浆制造	Paper pulp Manufacturing	1	2 436
造 纸	Paper Making	9	26 345
机制纸及纸板制造	Machine-Made Paper and Paper Board Manufacturing	9	26 345
纸制品制造	Paper Products Manufacturing	28	50 131
纸和纸板容器的制造	Paper and Paper Board Receptacle Manufacturing	17	35 758
其他纸制品制造	Other Paper Products Manufacturing	11	14 373
印刷业和记录媒介的复制	Printing Industry and Recording Media	34	9 264
印 刷	Printing	33	9 248
书、报、刊印刷	Book Newspaper and Magazine Printing	24	4 882
本册印制	Book Form Printing	5	187
包装装潢及其他印刷	Packing Decorates	4	4 178
装订及其他印刷服务活动	Bookbinding and Other Printing Service Activities	1	16
文教体育用品制造业	Cultural educational and Sports Products Manufacturing	1	158
文化用品制造	Cultural Products Manufacturing	1	158
墨水、墨汁制造	Ink and Lipuid ink manufacturing	1	158
石油加工、炼焦及核燃料加工业	Petroleum Processing,Coking and Nuclear Material Processing	11	114 145
炼 焦	Coking	11	114 145
化学原料及化学制品制造业	Chemical Materials and Chemical Products Manufacturing	109	1 035 313
基础化学原料制造	Basic Chemical Materials Manufacturing	6	122 597
无机碱制造	Inorganic Alkali Manufacturing	1	96 621
无机盐制造	Inorganic Salts Manufacturing	3	25 771
其他基础化学原料制造	Other Basic Chemical Materials Manufacturing	2	205
肥料制造	Fertilizer Manufacturing	62	63 561
钾肥制造	Potassium Fertilizer Manufacturing	2	1 842
复混肥料制造	Compound Fertilizer Manufacturing	19	25 162
有机肥料及微生物肥料制造	Organic Fertilizer and Microbial Fertilizer Manufacturing	24	18 509
其他肥料制造	Other Fertilizer Manufacturing	17	18 048

10—4 续表 3 Continued

计量单位:万元 (2010 年) (10 000 yuan)

指标	Item	企业数(个) Number of Enterprises (unit)	工业总产值 当年价格 At Current Prices
农药制造	Pesticide Manufacturing	3	2 292
化学农药制造	Chemical Pesticide Manufactaring	2	2 059
生物化学农药及微生物农药制造	Biological Chemical and Microbe Pesticide	1	233
涂料、油墨、颜料及类似产品	Paint Printing Ink Dyestuff and Similar Products Manufacturing	12	4 068
涂料制造	Paint Manufacturing	10	2 729
油墨及类似产品制造	Printing Ink and Similar Products Manufacturing	1	1 029
密封用填料及类似品制造	Hermetic Material and Similar Products Manufacturing	1	310
合成材料制造	Synthesize Material Manufacturing	4	826 508
初级形态的塑料及合成树脂制造	Primary Plastics and Synthesize Resin Manufacturing	4	826 508
专用化学产品制造	Special Chemical Products Manufacturing	14	8 500
化学试剂和助剂制造	Chemical Reagent and Assistant Manufacturing	4	1 191
专项化学用品制造	Special Chemical Products Manufacturing	4	2 386
炸药及火工产品制造	Explosive and Pyrotechnics Manufacturing	2	990
动物胶制造	Animal Gum Manufacturing	1	3 562
其他专用化学产品制造	Other Special Chemical Products Manufacturing	3	371
日用化学产品制造	Daily Chemical Products Manufacturing	8	7 787
肥皂及合成洗涤剂制造	Soap and Synthetic Detergent Manufacturing	1	26
香料、香精制造	Perfume and Essence Manufacturing	3	7 393
其他日用化学产品制造	Other Daily Chemical Products Manufacturing	4	368
医药制造业	Pharmaceuticals Manufacturing	9	50 919
化学药品制剂制造	Chemical Pharmaceutical Manufacturing	2	21 120
中药饮片加工	Chinese Patent Drugs Troche Processing	2	432
中成药制造	Chinese Patent Drugs Manufacturing	4	28 147
卫生材料及医药用品制造	Chinese Patent Drugs Manufacturing	1	1 219
化学纤维制造业	Chemical Fibre Manufacturing	4	225 309
纤维素纤维原料及纤维制造	Cellulose Material and Fibre Manufacturing	4	225 309
化纤浆粕制造	Chemical Fibre Pulp Manufacturing	3	122 860
人造纤维(纤维素纤维)制造	Artificial Cellulose Material and Fibre Manufacturing	1	102 449
橡胶制品业	Rubber Products Manufacturing	3	1 330
橡胶板、管、带的制造	Rubber Board,Pipe and Structural Section Manufacturing	2	689
橡胶零件制造	Rubber Part Manufacturing	1	642
塑料制品业	Plastic Products Manufacturing	192	296 024
塑料薄膜制造	Plastic Film Manufacturing	35	76 733
塑料板、管、型材的制造	Plastic Board Pipe and Structural Section Manufacturing	105	168 032
塑料丝、绳及编织品的制造	Plastic Silk Rope and Knitted Products Manufacturing	16	17 981
泡沫塑料制造	Foam Plastics Manufacturing	14	6 474
塑料包装箱及容器制造	Plastic Packing Cases and Container Manufacturing	9	8 598
塑料零件制造	Plastic patr Manufactwring	2	519
日用塑料制造	Daily Use Plastics Manufacturing	3	6 373
日用塑料杂品制造	Daily Use Plastics Products Manufacturing	3	6 373
其他塑料制品制造	Other Plastic Products Manufacturing	8	11 313
非金属矿物制品业	Nonmetal Mineral Products Manufacturing	169	533 662
水泥、石灰和石膏的制造	Cement Lime and Gypsum Manufacturing	21	349 630
水泥制造	Cement Manufacturing	21	349 630
水泥及石膏制品制造	Cement and Gypsum Products Manufacturing	40	99 801
水泥制品制造	Cement Product Manufacturing	20	80 554
砼结构构件制造	Concrete Structural Component Manufacturing	13	12 840
轻质建筑材料制造	Light Building Material Manufacturing	4	1 444
其他水泥制品制造	Other Cement and Gypsum Products Manufacturing	3	4 963
砖瓦、石材及其他建筑材料制造	Brick Tile Stone and Other Building Material Manufacturing	92	49 307
粘土砖瓦及建筑砌块制造	Clay Brick Tile and Building Brick Manufacturing	70	38 615
建筑陶瓷制品制造	Building Ceramics Product Manufacturing	4	857
建筑用石加工	Stone for Building Processing	3	342
防水建筑材料制造	Waterproof Building Material Manufacturing	3	3 534
隔热和隔音材料制造	Heat and Sound Insulation Material Manufacturing	4	2 531
其他建筑材料制造	Other Building Material Manufacturing	8	3 429

10－4 续表 4　Continued

计量单位:万元　　　　(2010 年)　　　　(10 000 yuan)

指　　标	Item	企业数(个) Number of Enterprises (unit)	工业总产值 当年价格 At Current Prices
玻璃及玻璃制品制造	Glass and Glass Producs Manufacturing	11	28 610
平板玻璃制造	Board Glass Products Manufacturing	2	1 820
技术玻璃制品制造	Technical Glass Products Manufacturing	1	50
日用玻璃制品及玻璃包装容器	Daily Use Glass Products and Glass Packing Container Manufacturing	4	16 135
玻璃保温容器制造	Glass Packing Container Manufacturing	1	972
玻璃纤维增强塑料制品制造	Glass Fibre and Enhanced Glass Producs Manufacturing	2	4 917
其他玻璃制品制造	Other Glass Producs Manufacturing	1	4 716
耐火材料制品制造	Fire-Resistant Material Producs Manufacturing	3	5 036
耐火陶瓷制品及其他耐火材料制造	Fire-Resistant Material Producs and Others Manufacturing	3	5 036
石墨及其他非金属矿物制品制造	Craphite and Other Nonmetal Mineral Products Manuracturing	2	1 277
石墨及碳素制品制造	Craphite and Carbon Element Products Manuracturing	1	610
其他非金属矿物制品制造	Other Nonmetal Mineral Products Manuracturing	1	667
黑色金属冶炼及压延加工业	Ferrous Metals Smelting and Rolling	12	63 909
炼　铁	Prddling	4	22 808
钢压延加工	Steel Rolling	7	37 981
铁合金冶炼	Prdding Alloy Smelting	1	3 120
有色金属冶炼及压延加工业	Nonferrous Metals Smelting and Rolling	5	197 464
常用有色金属冶炼	Common Nonferrous Metals Smelting	3	190 671
铝冶炼	Aluminum Smelting	1	178 409
镁冶炼	Magnesium Smelting	2	12 263
稀有稀土金属冶炼	Rare Metals and Rare Soil Smelting	1	
其他稀有金属冶炼	Other Rare Metals Smelting	1	
有色金属压延加工	Nonferrous Metals Rolling	1	6 793
常用有色金属压延加工	Common Nonferrous Metals Rolling	1	6 793
金属制品业	Metal Product Manufacturing	57	68 132
结构性金属制品制造	Structural Metal Product Manufacturing	38	27 700
金属结构制造	Metal Structural Manufacturing	17	18 032
金属门窗制造	Metal Door and Window Manufacturing	21	9 668
金属工具制造	Metal Tools Manufacturing	5	1 296
农用及园林用金属工具制造	Agriculture and Horticultural Use Metal Tools Manufacturing	5	1 296
集装箱及金属包装容器制造	Container and Metal Packing Vessel Manufacturing	4	30 215
金属压力容器制造	Metal Pressure Container Manufacturing	1	572
金属包装容器制造	Metal Packing Vessel Manufacturing	3	29 644
金属丝绳及其制品的制造	Metal Rope and Product Manufacturing	3	1 221
建筑、安全用金属制品制造	Construction and Safety Use Metal Product Manufacturing	2	331
其他建筑、安全用金属制品制造	Other Construction and Safety Use Metal Product Manufacturing	2	331
其他金属制品制造	Other Metal Product Manufacturing	5	7 368
其他未列明的金属制品制造	Other Non-list Metal Product Manufacturing	5	7 368
通用设备制造业	General Equipment Manufacturing	28	17 469
泵、阀门、压缩机及类似机械	Pump Valve Compressor and Similar Machine Manufacturing	2	1 625
泵及真空设备制造	Pump and Vacuum Equipments Manufacturing	2	1 625
轴承、齿轮、传动和驱动部件	Bearing, Gear, Transmission and Driving Component Manufacturing	1	100
齿轮及真空设备制造	Gear, Transmission and Driving Component Manufacturing	1	100
风机、衡器、包装设备等通用设备	Fans, Weighing Apparatus and Packing Equipment Manufacturing	7	7 607
风机、风扇制造	Fans Manufacturing	2	735
其他通用设备制造	Other General Equipment Manufacturing	5	6 872
通用零部件制造及机械修理	General Spare Parts Manufacturing and Machine Repairing	11	2 935
金属密封件制造	Metal Airproof Parts Manufacturing	1	13
紧固件、弹簧制造	Tight Firmware and Spring	1	1 735
机械零部件加工及设备修理	Machine Spare Parts Manufacturing and Equipment Repairing	8	1 187
其他通用零部件制造	Other General Spare Parts Manufacturing	1	
金属铸、锻加工	Metal Casting and Forging	7	5 203
钢铁铸件制造	Steel Cast Manufacturing	7	5 203
专用设备制造业	Special Equipment Manufacturing	70	38 830

10—4 续表 5 Continued

计量单位:万元 (2010 年) (10 000 yuan)

指 标	Item	企业数（个） Number of Enterprises (unit)	工业总产值当年价格 At Current Prices
食品、饮料、烟草及饲料生产专用设备制造	Food Beverage Tobacco and Forage Special Equipment Manufacturing	2	831
农副食品加工专用设备制造	Farm and Sideline Food Processing Special Equipment Manufacturing	2	831
纺织、服装和皮革工业专用设备制造	Textile Clothing and Leather Industry Special Equipment Manufacturing	2	95
纺织专用设备制造	Textile Special Equipment Manufacturing	2	95
农、林、牧、渔专用机械制造	Special Machine Manufacturing for Farming Forestry Livestock and Fishing	64	37 526
机械化农业及园艺机具制造	Mechanized Agriculture and Horticultural Implement Manufacturing	37	26 550
农林牧渔机械配件制造	Machinery Component Manufacturing for Farming Forestry Livestock and Fishing	8	866
其他农林牧渔业机械制造	Other Machine Manufacturing for Farming Forestry Livestock and Fishing	19	10 111
环保、社会公共安全及其他专用设备制造	Environmental Protection,Society Pubic Safety and Other Special Equipment Manufacturing	2	377
其他专用设备制造	Other Special Equipment Manufacturing	2	377
交通运输设备制造业	Transportation Equipment Manufacturing	18	7 725
汽车制造	Automobile Manufacturing	17	7 629
汽车整车制造	Entire Automobile Manufactaring	1	5 025
汽车车身	Automobile Carriage and Trailer Manufacturing	1	72
汽车零部件及配件制造	Automobile Parts and Fitting Manufacturing	1	381
汽车修理	Automobile Repairing	14	2 151
交通器材及其他交通运输设备制造	Transportation Equipment and Others Manufacturing	1	96
交通管理用金属标及及设施制造	Transportation Metal Sign and Equipment Manufacturing	1	96
电气机械及器材制造业	Electric Machine and Equipment Manufacturing	19	10 769
输配电及控制设备制造	Electricity Transmission and Distribution and Control Equipment Manufacturing	12	2 728
电容器及其配套设备制造	Capacitor and Its Kit Equipments Manufacturing	1	
配电开关控制设备制造	Electricity Switch Control Equipments Manufacturing	6	1 544
电力电子元器件制造	Electric Power Electronics Parts Manufacturing	1	200
其他输配电及控制设备制造	Other Electricity Transmission and Distribution and Control Equipment Manufacturing	4	985
电线、电缆、光缆及电工器材制造	Wire,Cable,Optical Fibre and Electric Equipment Manufacturing	2	1 883
电线电缆制造	Wire, Cable Manufacturing	1	1 268
其他电工器材制造	Other Electric Equipment Manufacturing	1	616
非电力家用器具制造	Non-Electricity Household Equipment Manufacturing	1	146
燃气、太阳能及类似能源的器具制造	Gas, Solar Energy and Similar Energy Tool Manufacturing	1	146
照明器具制造	Illuminate EquipmentManufacturing	3	5 791
照明灯具制造	Illuminate Lamp Manufacturing	3	5 791
其他电气机械及器材制造	Other Electric Machine and Equipment Manufacturing	1	219
其他未列明的电气机械制造	Other Non-list Electric Machine and Equipment Manufacturing	1	219
仪器仪表及文化、办公用机械制造业	Apparatus,Appearance,culture and Handle official Bussiness Machine Manufacturing	1	985
通用仪器仪表制造	Geheral Apparatas and Appearance Manufacturing	1	985
供应用仪表及其他通用仪器制造	Appearance used for Provide and General Apparatus Manufacturing	1	985
工艺品及其他制造业	Handicraft Product and Other Manufacturing	1	342
工艺美术品制造	Handicraft Manufacturing	1	342
地毯、挂毯制造	Carpet and Arras Manufacturing	1	342
废弃资源和废旧材料回收加工业	Abandon Resources and Discard Material Recovery Processing	4	7 342
非金属废料和碎屑的加工处理	Nonmetal Waste Handle and Broken Bits Processing	1	6 933
非金属废料和碎屑的加工处理	Nonmetal Waste Handle and Broken Bits Processing	3	410
电力、燃气及水的生产和供应业	**Electric Power Gas and Water Production and Supply**	**107**	**430 252**
电力、热力的生产和供应业	Electricity and Heat Production and Supply	83	413 456
电力生产	Electricity Production	31	289 723
火力发电	Coal-Fired Generation	8	244 076
水力发电	Hydropower Generation	22	37 850
其他能源发电	Other Energy Generation	1	7 798
电力供应	Electricity Supply	13	102 556
热力生产和供应	Heat Production and Supply	39	21 176
燃气生产和供应业	Gass Production and Supply	4	5 071
水的生产和供应业	Water Production and Supply	20	11 725
自来水的生产和供应	Tap Water Production and Supply	20	11 725

10—5 工业总产值行业构成

Composition of Gross Output Value of Industry by Sector

（2010年）

指 标	Item	构 成（%）Composition（%）
总 计	**Total**	**100.0**
# 国有控股企业	State-controlled Shareholding Enterprises	64.8
按登记注册类型分	**Grouped by Statusof Registration**	
内资企业	Domestic Enterprises	95.4
国有企业	State-owned Enterprises	13.3
集体企业	Collective-owned Enterprises	…
股份合作企业	Share Cooperative Enterprises	0.8
有限责任公司	Limited Liability Corporations	56.0
国有独资公司	State-owned Corporations with Private-Funds	0.7
其他有限责任公司	Other Limited Liability Corporations	55.2
股份有限公司	Share-holding Corporations Ltd.	9.8
私营企业	Private Enterprises	15.4
私营独资企业	Private-funded Enterprises	1.4
私营合伙企业	Private Partnership Enterprises	0.1
私营有限责任公司	Private Limited Liabilit yCorporations	12.9
私营股份有限公司	Private Share-holding Corporations Ltd.	1.0
其他企业	Other Enterprises	0.1
港、澳、台商投资企业	Enterprises with Funds from Hong Kong, Macao and Taiwan	1.2
合资经营企业（港或澳、台）	Joint-Venture Enterprises(with funds from Hong Kong, Macaoand Taiwan)	0.8
港、澳、台商独资经营企业	Enterprises with Funds from Hong Kong, Macaoand Taiwan	0.4
港、澳、台商投资股份有限公司	Share—holding Corporations Ltd. from Hong Kong, Macao and Taiwan	…
外商投资企业	Foreign Funded Enterprises	3.4
中外合资经营企业	Joint-Venture Enterprises	2.0
中外合作经营企业	Cooperative Enterprises	0.6
外商投资	Foreign-Funded Enterprises	0.8
外商投资股份有限公司	Foreign-Funded Enterprises Share-holding Corporations Ltd.	0.1
按轻重工业分	**Grouped by Light & Heavy Industry**	
轻工业	Light Industry	51.0
重工业	Heavy Industry	49.0
按企业规模分	**Grouped by Size of Enterprises**	
大型企业	Large-Scale Enterprises	17.9
中型企业	Medium-Scale Enterprises	37.2
小型企业	Small-Scale Enterprises	44.9
按工业行业分	**Grouped by Sector**	
采矿业	**Mining**	**4.4**
煤炭开采和洗选业	Coal Mining and Dressing	2.9
烟煤和无烟煤的开采洗选	Soft Coal and Hard Coal Mining and Dressing	2.9
黑色金属矿采选业	Ferrous Metals Mining and Dressing	0.2
铁矿采选	Prdding Mining and Dressing	0.2
有色金属矿采选业	Nonferrous Metals Mining and Dressing	0.3
常用有色金属矿采选	Common Nonferrous Metals Mining and Dressing	0.3
镍钴矿采选	Nickle and Cobalt Minerals Mining and Dressing	0.3
稀有稀土金属矿采选	Rare Thulium Metals Mining and Dressing	
钨钼矿采选	Tungsten and Molybdenum Minerals Mining and Dressing	
非金属矿采选业	Nonmetal Mineral Mining and Dressing	0.9
土砂石开采	Gravel and Sand Mining	0.5
石灰石、石膏开采	Lime and Gypsum Mining	0.4
建筑装饰用石开采	Construction and Decorative Stone Mining	…
耐火土石开采	Refractory Stone Mining	…
粘土及其他土砂石开采	Clay and Other Gravel Mining	0.1
化学矿采选	Chemical Mineral Mining and Dressing	…
采 盐	Salt Mining	…
石棉及其他非金属矿采选	Asbestos and Other Nonmetal Minerals Mining and Dressing	0.4
石棉、云母矿采选	Asbestos and Mica Minerals Mining and Dressing	0.2
其他非金属矿采选	Other Nonmetal Minerals Mining and Dressing	0.2

注：本表按当年价格计算，不含连队办工业（村办）及个体工业。（下表同）
Note: This table is not including county-run and individual industry(the same as follows).

10—5 续表 1 Continued

(2010 年)

指 标	Item	构 成(%) Composition(%)
制造业	**Manufacturing**	**88.6**
农副食品加工业	Farm and Sideline Food Processing	17.0
谷物磨制	Cereal Grain Grinding	1.3
饲料加工	Forage Processing	5.0
植物油加工	Plant Oil Processing	6.0
食用植物油加工	Edible Plant Oil Processing	6.0
制 糖	Sugar Making	1.4
屠宰及肉类加工	Slaughtering and Meat Processing	1.5
畜禽屠宰	Livestock and Fowl Slaughtering	1.4
肉制品及副产品加工	Meat Product and Sideline Product Processing	0.1
水产品加工	Aquatic Production Processing	…
水产品冷冻加工	Aquatic Production Refrigeration Processing	…
蔬菜、水果和坚果加工	Vegetable Fruit and Nuts Processing	0.7
其他农副食品加工	Other Farm and Sideline Food Processing	1.2
淀粉及淀粉制品的制造	Starch and Starch Products Manufacturing	0.3
豆制品制造	Bean Ware Manufacturing	…
蛋品加工	Egg Ware Processing	0.1
其他未列明的农副食品加工	Other Unlisted Farm and Sideline Food Processing	0.8
食品制造业	Food Manufacturing	10.7
焙烤食品制造	Bakery Products Manufacturing	0.1
糕点、面包制造	Pastry and dread Manufacturing	…
饼干及其他焙烤食品制造	Cookie and Other Bakery Products Manufacturing	0.1
糖果、巧克力及蜜饯制造	Candy,Chocolate and Sweetmeat Manufacturing	…
糖果、巧克力制造	Candy and Chocolate Manufacturing	…
方便食品制造	Convenient Food Manufacturing	0.5
米、面制品制造	Rice and Flour Manufacturing	…
方便面及其他方便食品制造	Cohvenient Noodles and Other Convenient Food Manufacturing	0.4
液体乳及乳制品制造	Liquid Milk and Dairy Products Manufacturing	1.9
罐头制造	Canned Food Manufacturing	6.9
蔬菜、水果罐头制造	Canned Vegetable and Fruit Manufacturing	6.9
调味品、发酵制品制造	Condiment and Fermented Products Manufacturing	0.7
味精制造	Gourmet Powder Manufacturing	0.3
酱油、食醋及类似制品的制造	Soy Sauce,Edible Vinegar and Similar Products Manufacturing	0.2
其他调味品、发酵制品制造	Other Gourmet Powder and Fermented Products Manufacturing	0.2
其他食品制造	Other Food Manufacturing	0.6
食品及饲料添加剂制造	Food and Forage Additive Manufacturing	0.5
其他未列明的食品制造	Other Non-list Food Manufacturing	0.1
饮料制造业	Beverage Manufacturing	5.0
酒精制造	Alcohol Manufacturing	…
酒的制造	Liquor Brewing	3.8
白酒制造	White Liquor Brewing	2.3
啤酒制造	Beer Brewing	0.8
葡萄酒制造	Grape Wine Brewing	0.7
软饮料制造	Soft Beverage Manufacturing	1.1
瓶(罐)装饮用水制造	Bottled (Canned) Drinkable Water Manufacturing	…
果菜汁及果菜汁饮料制造	Fruit and Vegetable Juice Fruit and Vegetable Juice Beverage Manufacturing	0.4
茶饮料及其他软饮料制造业	Tea Beverage and Other Soft Beverage Manufacturing	0.7
纺织业	Textile Industry	11.0
棉、化纤纺织及印染精加工	Cotton Chemical Fibre and Dying Fine Processing	10.3
棉、化纤纺织加工	Cotton and Chemical Textile Processing	10.3
毛纺织和染整精加工	Woolen Textile Dying and Finishing Fine Processing	0.2
毛条加工	Woolen Hair Textile	…
毛纺织	Woolen Textile	0.2
麻纺织	Homp Crops Textile	0.1

10—5 续表 2 Continued

(2010 年)

指 标	Item	构 成（%） Composition（%）
纺织制成品制造	Textile Products Manufacturing	0.1
棉及化纤制品制造	Cotton and Chemical Fibre Products Manufacturing	0.1
绳、索、缆的制造	Rope and Cordage Manufacturing	…
纺织带和帘子布制造	Textile Belt and Cord Fabric Manufacturing	…
其他纺织制成品制造	Other Textile Products Manufacturing	…
针织品、编织品及其制品制造	Knitted Fabrics and Products Manufacturing	0.2
棉、化纤针织品及编织品制造	Cotton and Chemical Fabrics and Products Manufacturing	0.2
毛针织品及编织品制造	Woolen Knitted Products Manufacturing	…
纺织服装、鞋、帽制造业	Textile Clothing Shoes and Hats Manufacturing	…
纺织服装制造	Textile Clothing Manufacturing	…
皮革、毛皮、羽毛(绒)及其制品业	Leather, Furriery, Fecather and Its Manufacturing	…
皮革鞣制加工	Leather Tan Processing	…
羽毛(绒)加工及制品制造	Feather and Its Processing and Manufacturing	…
羽毛(绒)制品加工	Feather and Its Processing and Manufacturing	…
木材加工及木、竹、藤、棕、草制造	Timber Processing, Wood, Bamboo, Rattan, Palm Fibre and Straw Products	0.1
锯材、木片加工	Sawed Wood and Chip Processing	…
锯材加工	Sawed Wood Processing	…
木片加工	Chip Processing	…
人造板制造	Artificial Board Manufacturing	…
胶合板制造	Veneer Manufacturing	…
刨花板制造	Board Manufacturing	…
其他人造板、材制造	Other Artificial Board Maufacturing	…
木制品制造	Wooden Products Manufacturing	0.1
木容器制造	Wooden Container Aanufacturing	0.1
软木制品及其他木制品制造	Soft Woodem and Other Wooden Products Manufacturing	…
家具制造业	Furniture Manufacturing	0.2
木质家具制造	Wooden Furniture Manufacturing	0.2
造纸及纸制品业	Paper Making and Paper Products	1.3
纸浆制造	Paper pulp Manufacturing	…
造 纸	Paper Making	0.4
机制纸及纸板制造	Machine-Made Paper and Paper Board Manufacturing	0.4
纸制品制造	Paper Products Manufacturing	0.8
纸和纸板容器的制造	Paper and Paper Board Receptacle Manufacturing	0.6
其他纸制品制造	Other Paper Products Manufacturing	0.2
印刷业和记录媒介的复制	Printing Industry and Recording Media	0.1
印 刷	Printing	0.1
书、报、刊印刷	Book Newspaper and Magazine Printing	0.1
本册印制	Book Form Printing	…
包装装潢及其他印刷	Packing Decorates	0.1
装订及其他印刷服务活动	Bookbinding and Other Printing Service Activities	…
文教体育用品制造业	Cultural educational and Sports Products Manufacturing	…
文化用品制造	Cultural Products Manufacturing	…
墨水、墨汁制造	Ink and Lipuid ink manufacturing	…
石油加工、炼焦及核燃料加工业	Petroleum Processing, Coking and Nuclear Material Processing	1.8
炼 焦	Coking	1.8
化学原料及化学制品制造业	Chemical Materials and Chemical Products Manufacturing	16.8
基础化学原料制造	Basic Chemical Materials Manufacturing	2.0
无机碱制造	Inorganic Alkali Manufacturing	1.6
无机盐制造	Inorganic Salts Manufacturing	0.4
其他基础化学原料制造	Other Basic Chemical Materials Manufacturing	…
肥料制造	Fertilizer Manufacturing	1.0
钾肥制造	Potassium Fertilizer Manufacturing	…
复混肥料制造	Compound Fertilizer Manufacturing	0.4
有机肥料及微生物肥料制造	Organic Fertilizer and Microbial Fertilizer Manufacturing	0.3
其他肥料制造	Other Fertilizer Manufacturing	0.3

10—5 续表 3 Continued

(2010 年)

指　　标	Item	构成(%) Composition(%)
农药制造	Pesticide Manufacturing	…
化学农药制造	Chemical Pesticide Manufactaring	…
生物化学农药及微生物农药制造	Biological Chemical and Microbe Pesticide	…
涂料、油墨、颜料及类似产品	Paint Printing Ink Dyestuff and Similar Products Manufacturing	0.1
涂料制造	Paint Manufacturing	…
油墨及类似产品制造	Printing Ink and Similar Products Manufacturing	…
密封用填料及类似品制造	Hermetic Material and Similar Products Manufacturing	…
合成材料制造	Synthesize Material Manufacturing	13.4
初级形态的塑料及合成树脂制造	Primary Plastics and Synthesize Resin Manufacturing	13.4
专用化学产品制造	Special Chemical Products Manufacturing	0.1
化学试剂和助剂制造	Chemical Reagent and Assistant Manufacturing	…
专项化学用品制造	Special Chemical Products Manufacturing	…
炸药及火工产品制造	Explosive and Pyrotechnics Manufacturing	…
动物胶制造	Animal Gum Manufacturing	0.1
其他专用化学产品制造	Other Special Chemical Products Manufacturing	…
日用化学产品制造	Daily Chemical Products Manufacturing	0.1
肥皂及合成洗涤剂制造	Soap and Synthetic Detergent Manufacturing	…
香料、香精制造	Perfume and Essence Manufacturing	0.1
其他日用化学产品制造	Other Daily Chemical Products Manufacturing	…
医药制造业	Pharmaceuticals Manufacturing	0.8
化学药品制剂制造	Chemical Pharmaceutical Manufacturing	0.3
中药饮片加工	Chinese Patent Drugs Troche Processing	…
中成药制造	Chinese Patent Drugs Manufacturing	0.5
卫生材料及医药用品制造	Chinese Patent Drugs Manufacturing	…
化学纤维制造业	Chemical Fibre Manufacturing	3.6
纤维素纤维原料及纤维制造	Cellulose Material and Fibre Manufacturing	3.6
化纤浆粕制造	Chemical Fibre Pulp Manufacturing	2.0
人造纤维(纤维素纤维)制造	Artificial Cellulose Material and Fibre Manufacturing	1.7
橡胶制品业	Rubber Products Manufacturing	…
橡胶板、管、带的制造	Rubber Board, Pipe and Structural Section Manufacturing	…
橡胶零件制造	Rubber Part Manufacturing	…
塑料制品业	Plastic Products Manufacturing	4.8
塑料薄膜制造	Plastic Film Manufacturing	1.2
塑料板、管、型材的制造	Plastic Board Pipe and Structural Section Manufacturing	2.7
塑料丝、绳及编织品的制造	Plastic Silk Rope and Knitted Products Manufacturing	0.3
泡沫塑料制造	Foam Plastics Manufacturing	0.1
塑料包装箱及容器制造	Plastic Packing Cases and Container Manufacturing	0.1
塑料零件制造	Plastic patr Manufactwring	…
日用塑料制造	Daily Use Plastics Manufacturing	0.1
日用塑料杂品制造	Daily Use Plastics Products Manufacturing	0.1
其他塑料制品制造	Other Plastic Products Manufacturing	0.2
非金属矿物制品业	Nonmetal Mineral Products Manufacturing	8.6
水泥、石灰和石膏的制造	Cement Lime and Gypsum Manufacturing	5.7
水泥制造	Cement Manufacturing	5.7
水泥及石膏制品制造	Cement and Gypsum Products Manufacturing	1.6
水泥制品制造	Cement Product Manufacturing	1.3
砼结构构件制造	Concrete Structural Component Manufacturing	0.2
轻质建筑材料制造	Light Building Material Manufacturing	…
其他水泥制品制造	Other Cement and Gypsum Products Manufacturing	0.1
砖瓦、石材及其他建筑材料制造	Brick Tile Stone and Other Building Material Manufacturing	0.8
粘土砖瓦及建筑砌块制造	Clay Brick Tile and Building Brick Manufacturing	0.6
建筑陶瓷制品制造	Building Ceramics Product Manufacturing	…
建筑用石加工	Stone for Building Processing	…
防水建筑材料制造	Waterproof Building Material Manufacturing	0.1
隔热和隔音材料制造	Heat and Sound Insulation Material Manufacturing	…
其他建筑材料制造	Other Building Material Manufacturing	0.1

10－5 续表 4　Continued

（2010 年）

指　　标	Item	构　成（%） Composition（%）
玻璃及玻璃制品制造	Glass and Glass Producs Manufacturing	0.5
平板玻璃制造	Board Glass Products Manufacturing	…
技术玻璃制品制造	Technical Glass Products Manufacturing	…
日用玻璃制品及玻璃包装容器	Daily Use Glass Products and Glass Packing Container Manufacturing	0.3
玻璃保温容器制造	Glass Packing Container Manufacturing	…
玻璃纤维增强塑料制品制造	Glass Fibre and Enhanced Glass Producs Manufacturing	0.1
其他玻璃制品制造	Other Glass Producs Manufacturing	0.1
耐火材料制品制造	Fire-Resistant Material Producs Manufacturing	0.1
耐火陶瓷制品及其他耐火材料制造	Fire-Resistant Material Producs and Others Manufacturing	0.1
石墨及其他非金属矿物制品制造	Craphite and Other Nonmetal Mineral Products Manuracturing	…
石墨及碳素制品制造	Craphite and Carbon Element Products Manuracturing	…
其他非金属矿物制品制造	Other Nonmetal Mineral Products Manuracturing	…
黑色金属冶炼及压延加工业	Ferrous Metals Smelting and Rolling	1.0
炼　铁	Prddling	0.4
钢压延加工	Steel Rolling	0.6
铁合金冶炼	Prdding Alloy Smelting	0.1
有色金属冶炼及压延加工业	Nonferrous Metals Smelting and Rolling	3.2
常用有色金属冶炼	Common Nonferrous Metals Smelting	3.1
铝冶炼	Aluminum Smelting	2.9
镁冶炼	Magnesium Smelting	0.2
稀有稀土金属冶炼	Rare Metals and Rare Soil Smelting	0.0
其他稀有金属冶炼	Other Rare Metals Smelting	0.0
有色金属压延加工	Nonferrous Metals Rolling	0.1
常用有色金属压延加工	Common Nonferrous Metals Rolling	0.1
金属制品业	Metal Product Manufacturing	1.1
结构性金属制品制造	Structural Metal Product Manufacturing	0.4
金属结构制造	Metal Structural Manufacturing	0.3
金属门窗制造	Metal Door and Window Manufacturing	0.2
金属工具制造	Metal Tools Manufacturing	…
农用及园林用金属工具制造	Agriculture and Horticultural Use Metal Tools Manufacturing	…
集装箱及金属包装容器制造	Container and Metal Packing Vessel Manufacturing	0.5
金属压力容器制造	Metal Pressure Container Manufacturing	…
金属包装容器制造	Metal Packing Vessel Manufacturing	0.5
金属丝绳及其制品的制造	Metal Rope and Product Manufacturing	…
建筑、安全用金属制品制造	Construction and Safety Use Metal Product Manufacturing	…
其他建筑、安全用金属制品制造	Other Construction and Safety Use Metal Product Manufacturing	…
其他金属制品制造	Other Metal Product Manufacturing	0.1
其他未列明的金属制品制造	Other Non-list Metal Product Manufacturing	0.1
通用设备制造业	General Equipment Manufacturing	0.3
泵、阀门、压缩机及类似机械	Pump Valve Compressor and Similar Machine Manufacturing	…
泵及真空设备制造	Pump and Vacuum Equipments Manufacturing	…
轴承、齿轮、传动和驱动部件	Bearing, Gear, Transmission and Driving Component Manufacturing	…
齿轮及真空设备制造	Gear, Transmission and Driving Component Manufacturing	…
风机、衡器、包装设备等通用设备	Fans, Weighing Apparatus and Packing Equipment Manufacturing	0.1
风机、风扇制造	Fans Manufacturing	…
其他通用设备制造	Other General Equipment Manufacturing	0.1
通用零部件制造及机械修理	General Spare Parts Manufacturing and Machine Repairing	…
金属密封件制造	Metal Airproof Parts Manufacturing	…
紧固件、弹簧制造	Tight Firmware and Spring	…
机械零部件加工及设备修理	Machine Spare Parts Manufacturing and Equipment Repairing	…
其他通用零部件制造	Other General Spare Parts Manufacturing	0.0
金属铸、锻加工	Metal Casting and Forging	0.1
钢铁铸件制造	Steel Cast Manufacturing	0.1
专用设备制造业	Special Equipment Manufacturing	0.6

10－5 续表 5 Continued

（2010 年）

指　　标	Item	构　成（%）Composition（%）
食品、饮料、烟草及饲料生产专用设备制造	Food Beverage Tobacco and Forage Special Equipment Manufacturing	…
农副食品加工专用设备制造	Farm and Sideline Food Processing Special Equipment Manufacturing	…
纺织、服装和皮革工业专用设备制造	Textile Clothing and Leather Industry Special Equipment Manufacturing	…
纺织专用设备制造	Textile Special Equipment Manufacturing	…
农、林、牧、渔专用机械制造	Special Machine Manufacturing for Farming Forestry Livestock and Fishing	0.6
机械化农业及园艺机具制造	Mechanized Agriculture and Horticultural Implement Manufacturing	0.4
农林牧渔机械配件制造	Machinery Component Manufacturing for Farming Forestry Livestock and Fishing	…
其他农林牧渔业机械制造	Other Machine Manufacturing for Farming Forestry Livestock and Fishing	0.2
环保、社会公共安全及其他专用设备制造	Environmental Protection, Society Pubic Safety and Other Special Equipment Manufacturing	…
其他专用设备制造	Other Special Equipment Manufacturing	…
交通运输设备制造业	Transportation Equipment Manufacturing	0.1
汽车制造	Automobile Manufacturing	0.1
汽车整车制造	Entire Automobile Manufactaring	0.1
汽车车身	Automobile Carriage and Trailer Manufacturing	…
汽车零部件及配件制造	Automobile Parts and Fitting Manufacturing	…
汽车修理	Automobile Repairing	…
交通器材及其他交通运输设备制造	Transportation Equipment and Others Manufacturing	…
交通管理用金属标及及设施制造	Transportation Metal Sign and Equipment Manufacturing	…
电气机械及器材制造业	Electric Machine and Equipment Manufacturing	0.2
输配电及控制设备制造	Electricity Transmission and Distribution and Control Equipment Manufacturing	…
电容器及其配套设备制造	Capacitor and Its Kit Equipments Manufacturing	0.0
配电开关控制设备制造	Electricity Switch Control Equipments Manufacturing	…
电力电子元器件制造	Electric Power Electronics Parts Manufacturing	…
其他输配电及控制设备制造	Other Electricity Transmission and Distribution and Control Equipment Manufacturing	…
电线、电缆、光缆及电工器材制造	Wire, Cable, Optical Fibre and Electric Equipment Manufacturing	…
电线电缆制造	Wire, Cable Manufacturing	…
其他电工器材制造	Other Electric Equipment Manufacturing	…
非电力家用器具制造	Non-Electricity Household Equipment Manufacturing	…
燃气、太阳能及类似能源的器具制造	Gas, Solar Energy and Similar Energy Tool Manufacturing	…
照明器具制造	Illuminate EquipmentManufacturing	0.1
照明灯具制造	Illuminate Lamp Manufacturing	0.1
其他电气机械及器材制造	Other Electric Machine and Equipment Manufacturing	…
其他未列明的电气机械制造	Other Non-list Electric Machine and Equipment Manufacturing	…
仪器仪表及文化、办公用机械制造业	Apparatus, Appearance, culture and Handle official Bussiness Machine Manufacturing	…
通用仪器仪表制造	Geheral Apparatas and Appearance Manufacturing	…
供应用仪表及其他通用仪器制造	Appearance used for Provide and General Apparatus Manufacturing	…
工艺品及其他制造业	Handicraft Product and Other Manufacturing	…
工艺美术品制造	Handicraft Manufacturing	…
地毯、挂毯制造	Carpet and Arras Manufacturing	…
废弃资源和废旧材料回收加工业	Abandon Resources and Discard Material Recovery Processing	0.1
非金属废料和碎屑的加工处理	Nonmetal Waste Handle and Broken Bits Processing	0.1
非金属废料和碎屑的加工处理	Nonmetal Waste Handle and Broken Bits Processing	…
电力、燃气及水的生产和供应业	**Electric Power Gas and Water Production and Supply**	**7.0**
电力、热力的生产和供应业	Electricity and Heat Production and Supply	6.7
电力生产	Electricity Production	4.7
火力发电	Coal-Fired Generation	4.0
水力发电	Hydropower Generation	0.6
其他能源发电	Other Energy Generation	0.1
电力供应	Electricity Supply	1.7
热力生产和供应	Heat Production and Supply	0.3
燃气生产和供应业	Gass Production and Supply	0.1
水的生产和供应业	Water Production and Supply	0.2
自来水的生产和供应	Tap Water Production and Supply	0.2

10—6 各师工业总产值

计量单位:万元 (2010 年)

指标	Item	合计 Total	一师 Division 1	二师 Division 2	三师 Division 3
总 计	**Total**	**6 177 890**	**742 761**	**355 699**	**105 004**
# 国有控股企业	State-controlled Shareholding Enterprises	4 002 400	540 097	242 765	81 251
按登记注册类型分	**Grouped by Status of Registration**				
内资企业	Domestic Enterprises	5 892 104	727 372	355 204	105 004
国有企业	State-owned Enterprises	822 694	106 825	46 794	81 251
集体企业	Collective-owned Joing Enterprises	1 705			
股份合作企业	Share Cooperative Enterprises	48 559	8 608		
有限责任公司	Limited Liability Corporations	3 457 164	441 875	209 313	90
国有独资公司	State-owned Corporations with Private-Funds	45 277	18 531		
其他有限责任公司	Other Limited Liability Corporations	3 411 887	423 344	209 313	90
股份有限公司	Share-holding Corporations Ltd.	602 777	73 104	43 987	
私营企业	Private Enterprises	950 752	96 961	55 110	23 662
私营独资企业	Private-funded Enterprises	85 697	557	27 400	1 502
私营合伙企业	Private Partnership Enterprises	5 630			
私营有限责任公司	Private Limited Liability Corporations	798 172	96 405	27 710	22 160
私营股份有限公司	Private Share-holding Corporations Ltd.	61 253			
其他企业	Other Enterprises	8 452			
港、澳、台商投资企业	Enterprises with Funds from Hong Kong Macao and Taiwan	75 834	15 389		
合资经营企业(港或澳、台)	Joint-Venture Enterprises(with funds from Hong Kong Macao and Taiwan)	51 315			
港、澳、台商独资经营企业	Enterprises with Funds from Hong Kong,Macao and Taiwan	24 134	15 389		
港澳台商投资股份有限公司	Share—holding Corporations Ltd. from Hong Kong,Macao and Taiwan	385			
外商投资企业	Foreign-Funded Enterprises	209 952		495	
中外合资经营企业	Joint-Venture Enterprises	122 404		495	
中外合作经营企业	Cooperative Enterorises	34 464			
外资企业	Foreign-Funded Enterprises	49 940			
外商投资股份有限公司	Foreign-Funded Enterprises Share-holding Corporations Ltd.	3 144			
按轻重工业分	**Grouped by Light & Heavy Industry**				
轻工业	Light Industry	3 148 996	374 996	244 549	44 902
重工业	Heavy Industry	3 028 894	367 765	111 150	60 102
按企业规模分	**Grouped by Size of Enterprises**				
大型企业	Large-Scale Enterprises	1 103 831	73 104		
中型企业	Medium-Scale Enterprises	2 299 400	291 474	128 162	7 615
小型企业	Small-Scale Enterprises	2 774 659	378 183	227 537	97 389
按工业行业分	**Grouped by Sector**				
采矿业	**Mining**	**269 968**	**22 507**	**45 216**	**145**
煤炭开采和洗选业	Coal Mining and Dressing	179 001	22 315	29 121	
黑色金属矿采选业	Ferrous Metals Mining and Dressing	12 889			
有色金属矿采选业	Nonferrous Metals Miningand Dressing	21 030			
非金属矿采选业	Nonmetal Mineral Miningand Dressing	57 047	192	16 096	145

注:本表按当年价格计算,不含连队办工业(村办)及个体工业。(下表同)

Total Output Value of Industry by Division

(10 000 yuan)

四 师 Division 4	五 师 Division 5	六 师 Division 6	七 师 Division 7	八 师 Division 8	九 师 Division 9	十 师 Division 10	建工师 Construction Division	十二师 Division 12	十三师 Division 13	十四师 Division 14
444 980	**139 099**	**715 931**	**430 729**	**2 276 280**	**59 846**	**109 186**	**51 769**	**105 202**	**154 481**	**13 054**
365 811	113 609	147 240	334 940	1 466 148	43 700	61 554	34 402	79 328	48 955	3 196
436 923	139 099	707 187	379 590	2 109 233	59 846	109 186	51 319	105 202	154 481	13 054
47 577	53 609	77 761	164 226	135 875	20 349	26 298	19 225	18 022	3 442	
				1 369		336				
4 993	221		23 742			10 996				
199 238	84 967	491 743	130 938	1 224 405	36 109	56 724	15 195	80 881	151 027	11 163
373				309		3 817	516	3 035	18 696	
198 865	84 967	491 743	130 938	1 224 096	36 109	52 907	14 679	77 845	132 331	11 163
114 343			29 921	243 560		2 488		904		
68 307	302	137 322	30 762	499 645	3 388	12 344	16 899	4 159		1 891
6 505		8 128	85	27 868		12 344	1 308			
1 604			705	1 430						1 891
32 787	302	129 194	29 972	436 505	3 388		15 591	4 159		
27 411				33 842						
2 466		360		4 378				1 236	12	
		8 745	51 139	561						
			51 139	176						
		8 745								
				385						
8 057				166 486			450			
8 057				113 402			450			
				49 940						
				3 144						
266 127	72 399	284 642	320 343	892 137	52 345	32 901	419	73 377	29 824	6 722
178 853	66 700	431 289	110 386	1 384 143	7 501	76 285	51 350	31 825	124 657	6 332
108 043				922 684						
141 567	43 016	373 480	161 345	724 232	25 724	19 526		36 302	20 557	
195 370	96 083	342 451	269 384	629 364	34 122	89 660	51 769	68 900	133 924	13 054
4 048	**420**	**66 434**	**8 508**	**32 954**		**19 128**	**794**	**10 576**	**58 609**	
4 048		65 184	8 508	11 433		12 578		9 376	15 809	
	420								12 469	
									21 030	
		1 250		21 521		6 550	794	1 200	9 300	

Note: This table is not including county-run and individual industry(the same as follows).

10－6 续表1　Continued

计量单位:万元　　　　(2010年)　　　　(10 000 yuan)

指　　标	Item	国资公司 Stateowned Property Company	中基公司 Chalkis Company	兵团直属 Directly under XPCG
总　　计	**Total**	**277 594**	**160 101**	**36 175**
# 国有控股企业	State-controlled Shareholding Enterprises	277 594	160 101	1 711
按登记注册类型分	**Grouped by Status of Registration**			
内资企业	Domestic Enterprises	277 594	160 101	1 711
国有企业	State-owned Enterprises	1 324	18 405	1 711
集体企业	Collective-owned Joing Enterprises			
股份合作企业	Share Cooperative Enterprises			
有限责任公司	Limited Liability Corporations	181 799	141 696	
国有独资公司	State-owned Corporations with Private-Funds			
其他有限责任公司	Other Limited Liability Corporations	181 799	141 696	
股份有限公司	Share-holding Corporations Ltd.	94 470		
私营企业	Private Enterprises			
私营独资企业	Private-funded Enterprises			
私营合伙企业	Private Partnership Enterprises			
私营有限责任公司	Private Limited Liability Corporations			
私营股份有限公司	Private Share-holding Corporations Ltd.			
其他企业	Other Enterprises			
港、澳、台商投资企业	Enterprises with Funds from Hong Kong Macao and Taiwan			
合资经营企业(港或澳、台)	Joint-Venture Enterprises(with funds from Hong Kong Macao and Taiwan)			
港、澳、台商独资经营企业	Enterprises with Funds from Hong Kong,Macao and Taiwan			
港澳台商投资股份有限公司	Share—holding Corporations Ltd. from Hong Kong,Macao and Taiwan			
外商投资企业	Foreign-Funded Enterprises			34 464
中外合资经营企业	Joint-Venture Enterprises			
中外合作经营企业	Cooperative Enterorises			34 464
外资企业	Foreign-Funded Enterprises			
外商投资股份有限公司	Foreign-Funded Enterprises Share-holding Corporations Ltd.			
按轻重工业分	**Grouped by Light & Heavy Industry**			
轻工业	Light Industry	275 444	141 696	36 175
重工业	Heavy Industry	2 150	18 405	
按企业规模分	**Grouped by Size of Enterprises**			
大型企业	Large-Scale Enterprises			
中型企业	Medium-Scale Enterprises	184 704	141 696	
小型企业	Small-Scale Enterprises	92 889	18 405	36 175
按工业行业分	**Grouped by Sector**			
采矿业	**Mining**	**630**		
煤炭开采和洗选业	Coal Mining and Dressing	630		
黑色金属矿采选业	Ferrous Metals Mining and Dressing			
有色金属矿采选业	Nonferrous Metals Miningand Dressing			
非金属矿采选业	Nonmetal Mineral Miningand Dressing			

10—6 续表 2 Continued

计量单位:万元 (2010 年) (10 000 yuan)

指　　标	Item	合　计 Total	一　师 Division 1	二　师 Division 2	三　师 Division 3
制造业	**Manufacturing**	**5 477 670**	**659 019**	**297 821**	**77 336**
农副食品加工业	Farm and Sideline Food Processing	1 053 214	114 316	73 942	21 659
食品制造业	Food Manufacturing	659 219	19 658	79 340	
饮料制造业	Beverage Manufacturing	306 422	3 183	11 430	1 082
纺织业	Textile Industry	677 438	39 620	38 470	9 765
纺织服装、鞋、帽制造业	Textile Clothing Shoes and Hats Manufacturing	1 274			
皮革、毛皮、羽毛(绒)及其制品业	Leather,Furriery,Fecather and Its Manufacturing	885		455	
木材加工及木、竹、藤、棕、草制品业	Timber Processing Wood Bamboo Rattan Palm Fibreand Straw Products	8 907	180	1 765	
家具制造业	Furniture Manufacturing	12 310		328	
造纸及纸制品业	Paper Makingand Paper Products	78 912	2 094	11 600	
印刷业和记录媒介的复制	Printing Industry and Recording Media	9 264	587	271	
文教体育用品制造业	Cultural educational and Sports Products Manufacturing	158			
石油加工、炼焦及核燃料加工业	Petroleum Processing Coking and Nuclear Material Processing	114 145			
化学原料及化学制品制造业	Chemical Materials and Chemical Products Manufacturing	1 035 313	14 741	6 236	1 794
医药制造业	Pharmaceuticals Manufacturing	50 919	10 488	27 185	11 595
化学纤维制造业	Chemical Fibre Manufacturing	225 309	182 816		
橡胶制品业	Rubber Products Manufacturing	1 330			
塑料制品业	Plastic Products Manufacturing	296 024	59 603	13 860	21 463
非金属矿物制品业	Nonmetal Mineral Products Manufacturing	533 662	198 569	27 347	8 927
黑色金属冶炼及压延加工业	Ferrous Metals Smelting and Rolling	63 909	5 016		
有色金属冶炼及压延加工业	Nonferrous Metals Smelting and Rolling	197 464			
金属制品业	Metal Product Manufacturing	68 132	75		358
通用设备制造业	General Equipment Manufacturing	17 469		1 821	
专用设备制造业	Special Equipment Manufacturing	38 830	6 873	3 509	225
交通运输设备制造业	Transportation Equipment Manufacturing	7 725	1 054		469
电气机械及器材制造业	Electric Machine and Equipment Manufacturing	10 769			
仪器仪表及文化、办公用机械制造	Apparatus Appearance Culture and Handle Official Bussiness Machine Manufacturing	985			
工艺品及其他制造业	Handicraft Product and Other Manufacturing	342			
废弃资源和废弃旧材料回收加工业	Abandon Resources and Discard Material Recovery Processing	7 342	147	263	
电力、燃气及水的生产和供应业	**Electric Power Gasand Water Production and Supply**	**430 252**	**61 235**	**12 661**	**27 523**
电力、热力的生产和供应业	Electricity and Heat Production and Supply	413 456	59 001	12 661	26 721
燃气生产和供应业	Gas Production and Supply	5 071			
水的生产和供应业	Water Production and Supply	11 725	2 234		802

10—6 续表 3

计量单位:万元 (2010 年)

指 标	Item	四 师 Division 4	五 师 Division 5	六 师 Division 6	七 师 Division 7
制造业	**Manufacturing**	**421 003**	**114 691**	**634 198**	**346 152**
农副食品加工业	Farm and Sideline Food Processing	85 227	45 046	62 505	86 026
食品制造业	Food Manufacturing	18 490	86	89 240	107 044
饮料制造业	Beverage Manufacturing	143 778	853	14 504	6 725
纺织业	Textile Industry	11 032	19 401	89 672	113 225
纺织服装、鞋、帽制造业	Textile Clothing Shoes and Hats Manufacturing				
皮革、毛皮、羽毛(绒)及其制品业	Leather, Furriery, Fecather and Its Manufacturing				
木材加工及木、竹、藤、棕、草制品业	Timber Processing Wood Bamboo Rattan Palm Fibreand Straw Products	313		675	227
家具制造业	Furniture Manufacturing			263	
造纸及纸制品业	Paper Makingand Paper Products	2 929		8 052	
印刷业和记录媒介的复制	Printing Industry and Recording Media		322	385	129
文教体育用品制造业	Cultural educational and Sports Products Manufacturing				
石油加工、炼焦及核燃料加工业	Petroleum Processing Coking and Nuclear Material Processing	11 002		99 150	
化学原料及化学制品制造业	Chemical Materials and Chemical Products Manufacturing	23 396	17 282	9 384	4 211
医药制造业	Pharmaceuticals Manufacturing				
化学纤维制造业	Chemical Fibre Manufacturing				
橡胶制品业	Rubber Products Manufacturing	675			
塑料制品业	Plastic Products Manufacturing	8 326	24 924	33 323	10 369
非金属矿物制品业	Nonmetal Mineral Products Manufacturing	110 604	1 890	12 002	7 223
黑色金属冶炼及压延加工业	Ferrous Metals Smelting and Rolling		3 120	10 500	
有色金属冶炼及压延加工业	Nonferrous Metals Smelting and Rolling			178 409	
金属制品业	Metal Product Manufacturing	3 308		6 047	8 698
通用设备制造业	General Equipment Manufacturing	100		3 167	
专用设备制造业	Special Equipment Manufacturing	1 325	1 768	2 742	2 075
交通运输设备制造业	Transportation Equipment Manufacturing	148		5 406	
电气机械及器材制造业	Electric Machine and Equipment Manufacturing	350		8 772	200
仪器仪表及文化、办公用机械制造	Apparatus Appearance Culture and Handle Official Bussiness Machine Manufacturing				
工艺品及其他制造业	Handicraft Product and Other Manufacturing				
废弃资源和废弃旧材料回收加工业	Abandon Resources and Discard Material Recovery Processing				
电力、燃气及水的生产和供应业	**Electric Power Gasand Water Production and Supply**	**19 930**	**23 988**	**15 299**	**76 069**
电力、热力的生产和供应业	Electricity and Heat Production and Supply	19 910	23 988	9 876	75 428
燃气生产和供应业	Gas Production and Supply			2 780	
水的生产和供应业	Water Production and Supply	20		2 644	641

Continued

(10 000 yuan)

八　师 Division 8	九　师 Division 9	十　师 Division 10	建工师 Construction Division	十二师 Division 12	十三师 Division 13	十四师 Division 14	国资公司 State-owned Property Company	中基公司 Chalkis Company	兵团直属 Directly under XPCG
2 076 055	**55 253**	**77 335**	**50 556**	**89 371**	**95 782**	**9 858**	**276 964**	**160 101**	**36 175**
143 324	48 091	22 623		29 953	11 775	2 016	272 249		34 464
177 146	3 193	3 670		16 801	20		2 836	141 696	
112 445	337	2 006		6 289	3 460	330			
339 371	47	1 008		13 179	2 647				
915							359		
430									
5 132				196	419				
8 846		2 874							
45 393		211		481	7 873	280			
1 665		99				4 095			1 711
				158					
123					3 870				
942 547	472	3 852	1 540	641	7 282	751	1 185		
1 364	287								
42 492									
14			642						
81 888	2 156	18 701	2 197	3 773	14 316	1 125			
98 652	670	18 605	34 892	6 035	7 924	244	79		
13 828			8 813		22 634				
6 793					12 263				
26 459		2 433	1 075			1 017	256	18 405	
7 253			1 399	3 729					
17 540		1 254		220	1 300				
649									
1 446									
				985					
342									
				6 933					
167 271	**4 593**	**12 723**	**419**	**5 254**	**90**	**3 196**			
161 720	4 203	12 313		4 350	90	3 196			
2 291									
3 261	390	411	419	904					

10－7 各师工业总产值指数

Indices of Gross Output Value of Industry by Division

计量单位:%　　（2010 年,上年=100）（2010,preceding year=100）　　（%）

单位 Unit	工业总产值 Gross Industrial Output Value	国有企业 State-owned	集体企业 Collective-owned	股份制企业 Share Holding	其他企业 Others	个体 Individuals	轻工业 Light Industry	重工业 Heavy Industry
总计 Total	**122.1**	**93.7**	**110.0**	**126.6**	**159.2**	**113.9**	**123.0**	**126.2**
一师 Division 1	137.8	93.9		148.4	184.5	138.5	139.4	133.1
二师 Division 2	121.8	48.8		146.2	10 068.3	90.2	125.8	128.6
三师 Division 3	121.9	120.9		116.8		123.5	116.5	120.5
四师 Division 4	123.6	109.6		127.9	143.1	91.0	119.1	140.9
五师 Division 5	118.6	143.1		116.5	5.1	84.5	115.8	127.1
六师 Division 6	149.6	226.6		167.8	56.9	107.5	122.4	217.9
七师 Division 7	125.4	87.9		121.3	8 917.1	133.3	137.0	112.0
八师 Division 8	114.5	89.4	95.2	114.9	122.5	222.8	128.6	108.2
九师 Division 9	114.6	108.9		122.7		92.6	147.0	70.4
十师 Division 10	143.1	43.2		311.6		219.6	137.0	125.2
建工师 Construction Division	129.2	191.8		110.5	83.3	106.0	282.8	135.4
十二师 Division12	114.6	92.4		178.6		62.5	134.2	218.0
十三师 Division13	130.7	21.3		129.5	2.6	477.5	67.5	140.9
十四师 Division14	188.1			309.9	56.9	182.2	210.2	152.7
国资公司 State-owned Property Company	108.9	59.7		109.3			107.7	68.1
中基公司 Chalkis Company	138.2	218		131.9			89.7	152.9
兵团直属 Directly under XPCG	95.3	104.4			97.6		96.6	

注:本表按价格指数缩减法计算。
Note: Data in this table are calculated at price index.

10—8 规模以上工业企业数、总产值、销售产值及产销率

Numbers, Gross Output Value, Sale Value and Production-sale Ratio of Industrial Enterprises above Designated Size

计量单位:万元 (2010 年) (10 000 yuan)

指标	Item	企业单位数(个) Number of Enterprises (unit)	# 亏损企业 Losses	工业总产值(当年价格) Gross Industrial Output Value (At Current Prices)
总计	**Total**	**570**	**66**	**5 592 355**
# 国有控股企业	State-controlled Shareholding Enterprises	218	34	3 595 039
按登记注册类型分	**Grouped by Status of Registration**			
内资企业	Domestic Enterprises	553	61	5 308 804
国有企业	State-owned Enterprises	60	10	469 594
有限责任公司	Limited Liability Corporations	268	25	3 336 003
国有独资公司	State-owned Corporations with Private-Funds	7		43 935
其他有限责任公司	Other Limited Liability Corporations	261	25	3 292 068
股份有限公司	Share-holding Corporations Ltd.	21	5	602 284
私营企业	Private Enterprises	188	20	846 833
私营独资企业	Private-funded Enterprises	18	2	50 167
私营合作企业	Private Cooperative Enterprises	2		2 391
私营有限责任公司	Private Limited Liability Corporations	157	15	734 733
私营股份有限公司	Private Share-holding Corporations Ltd.	11	3	59 542
其他企业	Other Enterprises	16	1	54 090
港、澳、台商投资企业	Enterprises with Funds from Hong Kong, Macao and Taiwan	4	2	75 272
合资经营企业(港或澳、台)	Joint-Venture Enterprises(with funds from Hong Kong, Macao and Taiwan)	2	1	51 139
港、澳、台商独资经营企业	Enterprises with Funds from Hong Kong, Macao and Taiwan	2	1	24 133
外商投资企业	Foreign Funded Enterprises	13	3	208 279
中外合资经营企业	Joint-Venture Enterprises	6	1	120 731
中外合作经营企业	Cooperative Enterprises	1		34 464
外资企业	Foreign-Funded Enterprises	5	2	49 940
外商投资股份有限公司	Foreign-Funded Enterprises	1		3 144
按轻重工业分	**Grouped by Light & Heavy Industry**			
轻工业	Light Industry	300	44	2 875 843
重工业	Heavy Industry	270	22	2 716 512
按企业规模分	**Grouped by Size of Enterprises**			
大型企业	Large-Scale Enterprises	6	1	1 103 831
中型企业	Medium-Scale Enterprises	74	11	2 299 399
小型企业	Small-Scale Enterprises	490	54	2 189 125
按工业行业分	**Grouped by Sector**			
采矿业	**Mining**	**32**	**1**	**198 140**
煤炭开采和洗选业	Coal Mining and Dressing	14	1	140 905
黑色金属矿采选业	Ferrous Metals Mining and Dressing	6		10 141
有色金属矿采选业	Nonferrous Metals Mining and Dressing	3		21 030
非金属矿采选业	Nonmetal Mineral Mining and Dressing	9		26 064
制造业	**Manufacturing**	**507**	**59**	**4 993 026**
农副食品加工业	Farm and Sideline Food Processing	112	16	876 071
谷物磨制	Cereal Grain Grinding	14	2	45 146
饲料加工	Forage Processing	13	2	292 844
植物油加工	Plant Oil Processing	38	7	261 523
制　糖	Sugar Making	4		86 580
食品制造业	Food Manufacturing	70	14	653 052
液体乳及乳制品制造	Liquid Milk and Dairy Products Manufacturing	13	1	113 291
罐头制造	Canned Food Manufacturing	41	11	425 191

10—8 续表 1　Continued

计量单位:万元　　(2010 年)　　(10 000 yuan)

指　　标	Item	工业销售产值(当年价格) Sale Value of Industry (At Current Prices)	# 出口交货值 Export Commodities	产销率(%) Ratio of Production & Marketing (%)
总　计	**Total**	**5 408 062**	**282 068**	**96.7**
# 国有控股企业	State-controlled Shareholding Enterprises	3 540 618	263 292	98.5
按登记注册类型分	**Grouped by Status of Registration**			
内资企业	Domestic Enterprises	5 154 811	271 807	97.1
国有企业	State-owned Enterprises	481 165	11 259	102.5
有限责任公司	Limited Liability Corporations	3 218 433	226 920	96.5
国有独资公司	State-owned Corporations with Private-Funds	40 115		91.3
其他有限责任公司	Other Limited Liability Corporations	3 178 318	226 920	96.5
股份有限公司	Share-holding Corporations Ltd.	595 949	25 113	98.9
私营企业	Private Enterprises	807 611	8 515	95.4
私营独资企业	Private-funded Enterprises	45 726		91.1
私营合作企业	Private Cooperative Enterprises	1 918		80.2
私营有限责任公司	Private Limited Liability Corporations	701 480	8 515	95.5
私营股份有限公司	Private Share-holding Corporations Ltd.	58 487		98.2
其他企业	Other Enterprises	51 653		95.5
港、澳、台商投资企业	Enterprises with Funds from Hong Kong,Macao and Taiwan	39 494	2 805	52.5
合资经营企业(港或澳、台)	Joint-Venture Enterprises(with funds from Hong Kong,Macao and Taiwan)	10 666	2 805	20.9
港、澳、台商独资经营企业	Enterprises with Funds from Hong Kong,Macao and Taiwan	28 828		119.5
外商投资企业	Foreign Funded Enterprises	213 757	7 456	102.6
中外合资经营企业	Joint-Venture Enterprises	124 184	6 099	102.9
中外合作经营企业	Cooperative Enterprises	34 613		100.4
外资企业	Foreign-Funded Enterprises	51 854	1 358	103.8
外商投资股份有限公司	Foreign-Funded Enterprises	3 106		98.8
按轻重工业分	**Grouped by Light & Heavy Industry**			
轻工业	Light Industry	2 750 129	212 031	95.6
重工业	Heavy Industry	2 657 933	70 037	97.8
按企业规模分	**Grouped by Size of Enterprises**			
大型企业	Large-Scale Enterprises	1 093 884	3 622	99.1
中型企业	Medium-Scale Enterprises	2 239 603	215 835	97.4
小型企业	Small-Scale Enterprises	2 074 575	62 611	94.8
按工业行业分	**Grouped by Sector**			
采矿业	**Mining**	**187 685**		**94.7**
煤炭开采和洗选业	Coal Mining and Dressing	131 468		93.3
黑色金属矿采选业	Ferrous Metals Mining and Dressing	11 883		117.2
有色金属矿采选业	Nonferrous Metals Mining and Dressing	20 815		99.0
非金属矿采选业	Nonmetal Mineral Mining and Dressing	23 518		90.2
制造业	**Manufacturing**	**4 823 012**	**282 068**	**96.6**
农副食品加工业	Farm and Sideline Food Processing	828 438	855	94.6
谷物磨制	Cereal Grain Grinding	44 445		98.4
饲料加工	Forage Processing	294 913		100.7
植物油加工	Plant Oil Processing	214 837		82.1
制　糖	Sugar Making	89 890	855	103.8
食品制造业	Food Manufacturing	575 840	197 958	88.2
液体乳及乳制品制造	Liquid Milk and Dairy Products Manufacturing	112 423		99.2
罐头制造	Canned Food Manufacturing	346 849	183 719	81.6

10—8 续表 2 Continued

计量单位:万元 (2010 年) (10 000 yuan)

指 标	Item	企业单位数(个) Number of Enterprises (unit)	# 亏损企业 Losses	工业总产值(当年价格) Gross Industrial Output Value (At Current Prices)
蔬菜、水果罐头制造	Vegetable and Fruit Canned Food Manufacturing	41	11	425 191
饮料制造业	Beverage Manufacturing	30	4	298 854
酒的制造	Liquor Brewing	24	4	231 535
软饮料制造	Soft Beverage Manufacturing	6		67 319
纺织业	Textile Industry	41	4	640 934
棉、化纤纺织及印染精加工	Cotton,Chemical Fibre and Dying Fine Processing	34	2	602 863
木材加工及木、竹、藤、棕、草制品业	Timber Processing Wood Bamboo Rattan PalmFibre and Straw Products	2	1	5 249
家具制造业	Furniture Manufacturing	2	1	7 741
造纸及纸制品业	Paper Making and Paper Products	15	4	65 279
造 纸	Paper Making	6	2	26 087
印刷业和记录媒介的复制	Printing Industry and Recording Media	3		6 377
石油加工、炼焦及核燃料加工业	Oil Processing,Coking Plant and Nuclear Elding Processing	9	1	113 552
炼 焦	Coking Plant	9	1	113 552
化学原料及化学制品制造业	Chemical Materials and Chemical Products Manufacturing	35	5	1 003 257
基础化学原料制造	Basic Chemical Materials Manufacturing	3	2	122 264
合成材料制造	Complex Materials Manufacturing	3		826 508
医药制造业	Pharmaceuticals Manufacturing	5		44 422
化学纤维制造业	Chemical Fibre Manufacturing	3		224 659
纤维素纤维原料及纤维制造	Cellulose Material and Fibre Manufacturing	3		224 659
化纤浆粕制造	Chemical Fibre Pulp Manufacturing	2		122 210
人造纤维(纤维素纤维)制造	Artificial Cellulose Material and Fibre Manufacturing	1		102 449
橡胶制品业	Rubber Products Manufacturing	1		642
塑料制品业	Plastic Products Manufacturing	73	4	212 020
塑料薄膜制造	Plastic Film Manufacturing	14		39 248
塑料板、管、型材的制造	Plastic Board,Pipe and Structural Section Manufacturing	44	2	135 782
非金属矿物制品业	Nonmetal Mineral Products Manufacturing	54		470 099
水泥、石灰和石膏的制造	Cement,Lime and Gypsum Manufacturing	18		346 429
水泥制造	Cemen Manufacturing	18		346 429
黑色金属冶炼及压延加工业	Ferrous Metals Smelting and Rolling	8	2	60 265
有色金属冶炼及压延加工业	Nonferrous Metals Smelting and Rolling	4		197 464
常用有色金属冶炼	Common Nonferrous Metals Smelting	3		190 671
金属制品业	Metal Product Manufacturing	10		53 561
通用设备制造业	General Equipment Manufacturing	11	1	14 717
专用设备制造业	Special Equipment Manufacturing	15	1	25 904
交通运输设备制造业	Transportation Equipment Manufacturing	1	1	5 025
电气机械及器材制造业	ElectricMachine and Equipment Manufacturing	2		6 949
废弃资源和废旧材料回收加工业	Abandon Resources and Discard Material Recovery Processing	1		6 933
电力、煤气及水的生产和供应业	**Electricity,Gasand Water Productionand Supply**	**31**	**6**	**401 189**
电力、热力的生产和供应业	Electricity and Heat Production and Supply	26	5	390 952
电力生产	Electricity Production	13	3	283 334
火力发电	Coal-Fired Generation	8	2	244 076
热力生产和供应	Heat Production and Supply	6		11 639
燃气生产和供应业	Gass Production and Supply	2		4 499
水的生产和供应业	Water Production and Supply	3	1	5 739

10－8 续表 3 Continued

计量单位:万元　　(2010 年)　　(10 000 yuan)

指　　标	Item	工业销售产值(当年价格) Sale Value of Industry (At Current Prices)	# 出口交货值 Export Commodities	产销率(%) Ratio of Production & Marketing (%)
蔬菜、水果罐头制造	Vegetable and Fruit Canned Food Manufacturing	346 849	183 719	81.6
饮料制造业	Beverage Manufacturing	292 703		97.9
酒的制造	Liquor Brewing	233 598		100.9
软饮料制造	Soft Beverage Manufacturing	59 106		87.8
纺织业	Textile Industry	676 243	7 018	105.5
棉、化纤纺织及印染精加工	Cotton,Chemical Fibre and Dying Fine Processing	640 349	3 622	106.2
木材加工及木、竹、藤、棕、草制品业	Timber Processing Wood Bamboo Rattan PalmFibre and Straw Products	5 099		97.1
家具制造业	Furniture Manufacturing	7 741	5 603	100.0
造纸及纸制品业	Paper Making and Paper Products	60 941		93.4
造　纸	Paper Making	23 482		90.0
印刷业和记录媒介的复制	Printing Industry and Recording Media	6 269		98.3
石油加工、炼焦及核燃料加工业	Oil Processing,Coking Plant and Nuclear Elding Processing	114 469	5 697	100.8
炼　焦	Coking Plant	114 469	5 697	100.8
化学原料及化学制品制造业	Chemical Materials and Chemical Products Manufacturing	1 003 662	63 258	100.0
基础化学原料制造	Basic Chemical Materials Manufacturing	123 967	3 622	101.4
合成材料制造	Complex Materials Manufacturing	826 765	59 636	100.0
医药制造业	Pharmaceuticals Manufacturing	35 086	598	79.0
化学纤维制造业	Chemical Fibre Manufacturing	214 065		95.3
纤维素纤维原料及纤维制造	Cellulose Material and Fibre Manufacturing	214 065		95.3
化纤浆粕制造	Chemical Fibre Pulp Manufacturing	106 257		86.9
人造纤维(纤维素纤维)制造	Artificial Cellulose Material and Fibre Manufacturing	107 808		105.2
橡胶制品业	Rubber Products Manufacturing	642		100.0
塑料制品业	Plastic Products Manufacturing	214 019	176	100.9
塑料薄膜制造	Plastic Film Manufacturing	38 174		97.3
塑料板、管、型材的制造	Plastic Board,Pipe and Structural Section Manufacturing	141 613	176	104.3
非金属矿物制品业	Nonmetal Mineral Products Manufacturing	462 641		98.4
水泥、石灰和石膏的制造	Cement,Lime and Gypsum Manufacturing	343 036		99.0
水泥制造	Cemen Manufacturing	343 036		99.0
黑色金属冶炼及压延加工业	Ferrous Metals Smelting and Rolling	58 420		96.9
有色金属冶炼及压延加工业	Nonferrous Metals Smelting and Rolling	154 342		78.2
常用有色金属冶炼	Common Nonferrous Metals Smelting	148 929		78.1
金属制品业	Metal Product Manufacturing	51 131	906	95.5
通用设备制造业	General Equipment Manufacturing	13 841		94.0
专用设备制造业	Special Equipment Manufacturing	30 028		115.9
交通运输设备制造业	Transportation Equipment Manufacturing	5 025		100.0
电气机械及器材制造业	ElectricMachine and Equipment Manufacturing	5 436		78.2
废弃资源和废旧材料回收加工业	Abandon Resources and Discard Material Recovery Processing	6 933		100.0
电力、煤气及水的生产和供应业	**Electricity,Gasand Water Productionand Supply**	**397 365**		**99.0**
电力、热力的生产和供应业	Electricity and Heat Production and Supply	387 127		99.0
电力生产	Electricity Production	278 943		99.0
火力发电	Coal-Fired Generation	239 685		98.5
热力生产和供应	Heat Production and Supply	11 546		98.2
燃气生产和供应业	Gass Production and Supply	4 499		100.0
水的生产和供应业	Water Production and Supply	5 739		100.0

10—9 各师规模以上工业企业单位数

Number of Industrial Enterprises above Designated Size by Division

计量单位:个 (2010年) (unit)

指标	Item	合计 Total	一师 Division 1	二师 Division 2	三师 Division 3
总计	**Total**	**570**	**87**	**43**	**13**
# 国有控股企业	State-controlled Shareholding Enterprises	218	23	18	6
按登记注册类型分	**Grouped by Status of Registration**				
内资企业	Domestic Enterprises	553	86	43	13
国有企业	State-owned Enterprises	60	5	1	6
有限责任公司	Limited Liability Corporations	268	38	23	
国有独资公司	State-owned Corporations with Private-Funds	7	1		
其他有限责任公司	Other Limited Liability Corporations	261	37	23	
股份有限公司	Share-holding Corporations Ltd.	21	1	6	
私营企业	Private Enterprises	188	40	13	7
私营独资企业	Private-funded Enterprises	18		7	
私营合作企业	Private Cooperative Enterprises	2			
私营有限责任公司	Private Limited Liability Corporations	157	40	6	7
私营股份有限公司	Private Share-holding Corporations Ltd.	11			
其他企业	Other Enterprises	4			
港、澳、台商投资企业	Enterprises with Funds from Hong Kong, Macao and Taiwan	4	1		
合资经营企业(港或澳、台)	Joint-Venture Enterprises(with funds from Hong Kong, Macao and Taiwan)	2			
港、澳、台商独资经营企业	Enterprises with Funds from Hong Kong, Macao and Taiwan	2	1		
外商投资企业	Foreign Funded Enterprises	13			
中外合资经营企业	Joint-Venture Enterprises	6			
中外合作经营企业	Cooperative Enterprises	1			
外资企业	Foreign-Funded Enterprises	5			
外商投资股份有限公司	Foreign-Funded Enterprises	1			
按轻重工业分	**Grouped by Light & Heavy Industry**				
轻工业	Light Industry	300	41	29	2
重工业	Heavy Industry	270	46	14	11
按企业规模分	**Grouped by Size of Enterprises**				
大型企业	Large-Scale Enterprises	6	1		
中型企业	Medium-Scale Enterprises	74	5	6	1
小型企业	Small-Scale Enterprises	490	81	37	12
按工业行业分	**Grouped by Sector**				
采矿业	**Mining**	**32**	**2**	**2**	
煤炭开采和洗选业	Coal Mining and Dressing	14	2	1	
黑色金属矿采选业	Ferrous Metals Mining and Dressing	6			
有色金属矿采选业	Nonferrous Metals Mining and Dressing	3			
非金属矿采选业	Nonmetal Mineral Mining and Dressing	9		1	
制造业	**Manufacturing**	**507**	**81**	**40**	**11**
农副食品加工业	Farm and Sideline Food Processing	112	23	7	
谷物磨制	Cereal Grain Grinding	14	2		
饲料加工	Forage Processing	13		1	
植物油加工	Plant Oil Processing	38	13		
制糖	Sugar Making	4		1	
食品制造业	Food Manufacturing	70	3	13	
液体乳及乳制品制造	Liquid Milk and Dairy Products Manufacturing	13	2		
罐头制造	Canned Food Manufacturing	41		11	

10—9 续表 1

计量单位:个　　　　　　　　　　　　　　　　　　　　　　(2010 年)

指　　标	Item	四　师 Division 4	五　师 Division 5	六　师 Division 6	七　师 Division 7
总　计	**Total**	**58**	**15**	**58**	**26**
# 国有控股企业	State-controlled Shareholding Enterprises	33	12	12	14
按登记注册类型分	**Grouped by Status of Registration**				
内资企业	Domestic Enterprises	57	15	57	24
国有企业	State-owned Enterprises	10	4	4	6
有限责任公司	Limited Liability Corporations	20	11	31	7
国有独资公司	State-owned Corporations with Private-Funds				
其他有限责任公司	Other Limited Liability Corporations	20	11	31	7
股份有限公司	Share-holding Corporations Ltd.	2			2
私营企业	Private Enterprises	22		22	6
私营独资企业	Private-funded Enterprises	3			
私营合作企业	Private Cooperative Enterprises	1			
私营有限责任公司	Private Limited Liability Corporations	14		22	6
私营股份有限公司	Private Share-holding Corporations Ltd.	4			
其他企业	Other Enterprises	1			
港、澳、台商投资企业	Enterprises with Funds from Hong Kong, Macao and Taiwan			1	2
合资经营企业(港或澳、台)	Joint-Venture Enterprises(with funds from Hong Kong, Macao and Taiwan)				2
港、澳、台商独资经营企业	Enterprises with Funds from Hong Kong, Macao and Taiwan			1	
外商投资企业	Foreign Funded Enterprises	1			
中外合资经营企业	Joint-Venture Enterprises	1			
中外合作经营企业	Cooperative Enterprises				
外资企业	Foreign-Funded Enterprises				
外商投资股份有限公司	Foreign-Funded Enterprises				
按轻重工业分	**Grouped by Light & Heavy Industry**				
轻工业	Light Industry	40	9	28	16
重工业	Heavy Industry	18	6	30	10
按企业规模分	**Grouped by Size of Enterprises**				
大型企业	Large-Scale Enterprises	1			
中型企业	Medium-Scale Enterprises	6	3	9	6
小型企业	Small-Scale Enterprises	51	12	49	20
按工业行业分	**Grouped by Sector**				
采矿业	**Mining**	**2**		**2**	**1**
煤炭开采和洗选业	Coal Mining and Dressing	2		2	1
黑色金属矿采选业	Ferrous Metals Mining and Dressing				
有色金属矿采选业	Nonferrous Metals Mining and Dressing				
非金属矿采选业	Nonmetal Mineral Mining and Dressing				
制造业	**Manufacturing**	**55**	**13**	**54**	**22**
农副食品加工业	Farm and Sideline Food Processing	21	6	7	3
谷物磨制	Cereal Grain Grinding	8			
饲料加工	Forage Processing	1			1
植物油加工	Plant Oil Processing	1	5	2	1
制　糖	Sugar Making	1			1
食品制造业	Food Manufacturing	5		9	6
液体乳及乳制品制造	Liquid Milk and Dairy Products Manufacturing	3			1
罐头制造	Canned Food Manufacturing			5	5

Continued

(unit)

八 师 Division 8	九 师 Division 9	十 师 Division 10	建工师 Construction Division	十二师 Division 12	十三师 Division 13	十四师 Division 14	国资公司 Stateowned Property Company	中基公司 Chalkis Company	兵团直属 Directly under XPCG
137	**8**	**25**	**10**	**26**	**43**	**6**	**10**	**3**	**2**
44	4	9	2	11	15	1	10	3	1
127	8	25	9	26	43	6	10	3	1
13	2	2		3	2			1	1
41	3	18	2	17	41	5	9	2	
		1		1	4				
41	3	17	2	16	37	5	9	2	
7		1		1			1		
63	3	1	7	3		1			
5		1	2						
						1			
51	3		5	3					
7									
1				2					
10			1						1
4			1						
									1
5									
1									
83	6	8		14	9	2	9	2	2
54	2	17	10	12	34	4	1	1	
4									
25	1	2		3	3		2	2	
108	7	23	10	23	40	6	8	1	2
1		**2**		**2**	**18**				
1		1		1	3				
					6				
					3				
		1		1	6				
129	**7**	**19**	**10**	**21**	**25**	**5**	**10**	**3**	**2**
19	3	6		4	3	1	8		1
2	1	1							
3							6		1
10		2		1	1	1	1		
	1								
25	3	1		2			1	2	
6				1					
14	3						1	2	

10－9 续表 2

计量单位:个　　　　(2010 年)

指　标	Item	合 计 Total	一 师 Division1	二 师 Division2	三 师 Division3
蔬菜、水果罐头制造	Vegetable and Fruit Canned Food Manufacturing	41		11	
饮料制造业	Beverage Manufacturing	30	2	2	
酒的制造	Liquor Brewing	24	1	2	
软饮料制造	Soft Beverage Manufacturing	6	1		
纺织业	Textile Industry	41	6	2	1
棉、化纤纺织及印染精加工	Cotton,Chemical Fibre and Dying Fine Processing	34	6	2	1
木材加工及木、竹、藤、棕、草制品业	Timber Processing Wood Bamboo Rattan PalmFibre and Straw Products	2		1	
家具制造业	Furniture Manufacturing	2			
造纸及纸制品业	Paper Making and Paper Products	15	2	3	
造　纸	Paper Making	6		1	
印刷业和记录媒介的复制	Printing Industry and Recording Media	3	1		
石油加工、炼焦及核燃料加工业	Oil Processing,Coking Plant and Nuclear Elding Processing	9			
炼　焦	Coking Plant	9			
化学原料及化学制品制造业	Chemical Materials and Chemical Products Manufacturing	35	8	2	
基础化学原料制造	Basic Chemical Materials Manufacturing	3			
合成材料制造	Complex Materials Manufacturing	3			
医药制造业	Pharmaceuticals Manufacturing	5	1	2	1
化学纤维制造业	Chemical Fibre Manufacturing	3	2		
纤维素纤维原料及纤维制造	Cellulose Material and Fibre Manufacturing	3	2		
化纤浆粕制造	Chemical Fibre Pulp Manufacturing	2	1		
人造纤维(纤维素纤维)制造	Artificial Cellulose Material and Fibre Manufacturing	1	1		
橡胶制品业	Rubber Products Manufacturing	1			
塑料制品业	Plastic Products Manufacturing	73	20	2	8
塑料薄膜制造	Plastic Film Manufacturing	14	5	1	1
塑料板、管、型材的制造	Plastic Board,Pipe and Structural Section Manufacturing	44	13	1	7
非金属矿物制品业	Nonmetal Mineral Products Manufacturing	54	9	4	1
水泥、石灰和石膏的制造	Cement,Lime and Gypsum Manufacturing	18	5	3	1
水泥制造	Cemen Manufacturing	18	5	3	1
黑色金属冶炼及压延加工业	Ferrous Metals Smelting and Rolling	8	1		
有色金属冶炼及压延加工业	Nonferrous Metals Smelting and Rolling	4			
常用有色金属冶炼	Common Nonferrous Metals Smelting	3			
金属制品业	Metal Product Manufacturing	10			
通用设备制造业	General Equipment Manufacturing	11		1	
专用设备制造业	Special Equipment Manufacturing	15	3	1	
交通运输设备制造业	Transportation Equipment Manufacturing	1			
电气机械及器材制造业	ElectricMachine and Equipment Manufacturing	2			
废弃资源和废旧材料回收加工业	Abandon Resources and Discard Material Recovery Processing	1			
电力、煤气及水的生产和供应业	**Electricity,Gasand Water Productionand Supply**	**31**	**4**	**1**	**2**
电力、热力的生产和供应业	Electricity and Heat Production and Supply	26	3	1	2
电力生产	Electricity Production	13	1		1
火力发电	Coal-Fired Generation	8	1		1
热力生产和供应	Heat Production and Supply	6	1		
燃气生产和供应业	Gass Production and Supply	2			
水的生产和供应业	Water Production and Supply	3	1		

Continued

(unit)

四 师 Division 4	五 师 Division 5	六 师 Division 6	七 师 Division 7	八 师 Division 8	九 师 Division 9	十 师 Division 10	建工师 Construction Division	十二师 Division 12	十三师 Division 13	十四师 Division 14
		5	5	14	3					
8	1	2	2	9		1		2	1	
7	1	2	2	5		1		2	1	
1				4						
3	1	6	4	16				1	1	
	1	5	4	14					1	
				1						
				2						
1				6					3	
1				3					1	
										1
1		7							1	
1		7							1	
4	2	4	1	7		2	1	1	1	1
1				1					1	
				3						
				1						
				1						
				1						
				1						
							1			
3	2	7	3	10	1	5	2	3	6	1
1	1			3				1	1	
	1	5	2	5	1	4	1		3	1
7		2	1	14		4	3	4	5	
4				4			1			
4				4			1			
		1		2			2		2	
		1		1					2	
		1							2	
1		1	2	4						1
		3		3			1	3		
1	1	1		8						
		1								
		2								
								1		
1	**2**	**2**	**3**	**7**	**1**	**4**		**3**		**1**
1	2	1	3	5	1	4		2		1
1	1		3	4		2				
			2	3		1				
		1				2		2		
		1		1						
				1				1		

10—9 续表 3　Continued

计量单位：个　　（2010 年）　　(unit)

指　标	Item	国资公司 Stateowned Property Company	中基公司 Chalkis Company	兵团直属 Directly under XPCG
蔬菜、水果罐头制造	Vegetable and Fruit Canned Food Manufacturing	1	2	
饮料制造业	Beverage Manufacturing			
酒的制造	Liquor Brewing			
软饮料制造	Soft Beverage Manufacturing			
纺织业	Textile Industry			
棉、化纤纺织及印染精加工	Cotton, Chemical Fibre and Dying Fine Processing			
木材加工及木、竹、藤、棕、草制品业	Timber Processing Wood Bamboo Rattan PalmFibre and Straw Products			
家具制造业	Furniture Manufacturing			
造纸及纸制品业	Paper Making and Paper Products			
造　纸	Paper Making			
印刷业和记录媒介的复制	Printing Industry and Recording Media			1
石油加工、炼焦及核燃料加工业	Oil Processing, Coking Plant and Nuclear Elding Processing			
炼　焦	Coking Plant			
化学原料及化学制品制造业	Chemical Materials and Chemical Products Manufacturing	1		
基础化学原料制造	Basic Chemical Materials Manufacturing			
合成材料制造	Complex Materials Manufacturing			
医药制造业	Pharmaceuticals Manufacturing			
化学纤维制造业	Chemical Fibre Manufacturing			
纤维素纤维原料及纤维制造	Cellulose Material and Fibre Manufacturing			
化纤浆粕制造	Chemical Fibre Pulp Manufacturing			
人造纤维(纤维素纤维)制造	Artificial Cellulose Material and Fibre Manufacturing			
橡胶制品业	Rubber Products Manufacturing			
塑料制品业	Plastic Products Manufacturing			
塑料薄膜制造	Plastic Film Manufacturing			
塑料板、管、型材的制造	Plastic Board, Pipe and Structural Section Manufacturing			
非金属矿物制品业	Nonmetal Mineral Products Manufacturing			
水泥、石灰和石膏的制造	Cement, Lime and Gypsum Manufacturing			
水泥制造	Cemen Manufacturing			
黑色金属冶炼及压延加工业	Ferrous Metals Smelting and Rolling			
有色金属冶炼及压延加工业	Nonferrous Metals Smelting and Rolling			
常用有色金属冶炼	Common Nonferrous Metals Smelting			
金属制品业	Metal Product Manufacturing		1	
通用设备制造业	General Equipment Manufacturing			
专用设备制造业	Special Equipment Manufacturing			
交通运输设备制造业	Transportation Equipment Manufacturing			
电气机械及器材制造业	ElectricMachine and Equipment Manufacturing			
废弃资源和废旧材料回收加工业	Abandon Resources and Discard Material Recovery Processing			
电力、煤气及水的生产和供应业	**Electricity, Gasand Water Productionand Supply**			
电力、热力的生产和供应业	Electricity and Heat Production and Supply			
电力生产	Electricity Production			
火力发电	Coal-Fired Generation			
热力生产和供应	Heat Production and Supply			
燃气生产和供应业	Gass Production and Supply			
水的生产和供应业	Water Production and Supply			

10—10 各师规模以上工业企业总产值

Gross Output Value of Industrial Enterprise above Designated Size by Division

计量单位:万元 （2010 年） (10 000yuan)

指　　标	Item	合　计 Total	一　师 Division 1	二　师 Division 2	三　师 Division 3
总　　计	**Total**	**5 592 355**	**686 654**	**299 833**	**64 642**
# 国有控股企业	State-controlled Shareholding Enterprises	3 595 039	491 670	192 520	44 384
按登记注册类型分	**Grouped by Status of Registration**				
内资企业	Domestic Enterprises	5 308 804	671 265	299 833	64 642
国有企业	State-owned Enterprises	469 594	57 712	12 803	44 384
有限责任公司	Limited Liability Corporations	3 336 003	440 070	194 425	
国有独资公司	State-owned Corporations with Private-Funds	43 935	18 531		
其他有限责任公司	Other Limited Liability Corporations	3 292 068	421 539	194 425	
股份有限公司	Share-holding Corporations Ltd.	602 284	73 104	43 987	
私营企业	Private Enterprises	846 833	91 773	48 618	20 258
私营独资企业	Private-funded Enterprises	50 167		24 522	
私营合作企业	Private Cooperative Enterprises	2 391			
私营有限责任公司	Private Limited Liability Corporations	734 733	91 773	24 096	20 258
私营股份有限公司	Private Share-holding Corporations Ltd.	59 542			
其他企业	Other Enterprises	54 090	8 608		
港、澳、台商投资企业	Enterprises with Funds from Hong Kong, Macao and Taiwan	75 272	15 389		
合资经营企业(港或澳、台)	Joint-Venture Enterprises(with funds from Hong Kong, Macao and Taiwan)	51 139			
港、澳、台商独资经营企业	Enterprises with Funds from Hong Kong, Macao and Taiwan	24 133	15 389		
外商投资企业	Foreign Funded Enterprises	208 279			
中外合资经营企业	Joint-Venture Enterprises	120 731			
中外合作经营企业	Cooperative Enterprises	34 464			
外资企业	Foreign-Funded Enterprises	49 940			
外商投资股份有限公司	Foreign-Funded Enterprises	3 144			
按轻重工业分	**Grouped by Light & Heavy Industry**				
轻工业	Light Industry	2 875 843	350 787	214 216	19 210
重工业	Heavy Industry	2 716 512	335 867	85 617	45 432
按企业规模分	**Grouped by Size of Enterprises**				
大型企业	Large-Scale Enterprises	1 103 831	73 104		
中型企业	Medium-Scale Enterprises	2 299 399	291 474	128 162	7 615
小型企业	Small-Scale Enterprises	2 189 125	322 076	171 671	57 027
按工业行业分	**Grouped by Sector**				
采矿业	**Mining**	**198 140**	**22 315**	**41 924**	
煤炭开采和洗选业	Coal Mining and Dressing	140 905	22 315	29 121	
黑色金属矿采选业	Ferrous Metals Mining and Dressing	10 141			
有色金属矿采选业	Nonferrous Metals Mining and Dressing	21 030			
非金属矿采选业	Nonmetal Mineral Mining and Dressing	26 064		12 803	
制造业	**Manufacturing**	**4 993 026**	**603 329**	**245 936**	**41 253**
农副食品加工业	Farm and Sideline Food Processing	876 071	90 713	55 858	
谷物磨制	Cereal Grain Grinding	45 146	9 401		
饲料加工	Forage Processing	292 844		5 032	
植物油加工	Plant Oil Processing	261 523	56 437		
制　糖	Sugar Making	86 580		30 013	
食品制造业	Food Manufacturing	653 052	19 658	78 196	
液体乳及乳制品制造	Liquid Milk and Dairy Products Manufacturing	113 291	8 892		
罐头制造	Canned Food Manufacturing	425 191		68 500	

10—10 续表 1

计量单位：万元　　　　　　　　　　　　　　　　　　　　　　　　　　　　　　(2010 年)

指　　标	Item	四　师 Division 4	五　师 Division 5	六　师 Division 6	七　师 Division 7
总　　计	**Total**	**423 658**	**101 742**	**644 116**	**320 077**
# 国有控股企业	State-controlled Shareholding Enterprises	357 941	78 383	146 727	227 007
按登记注册类型分	**Grouped by Status of Registration**				
内资企业	Domestic Enterprises	415 601	101 742	635 371	268 938
国有企业	State-owned Enterprises	43 073	20 200	41 386	93 850
有限责任公司	Limited Liability Corporations	198 865	81 542	479 969	92 719
国有独资公司	State-owned Corporations with Private-Funds				
其他有限责任公司	Other Limited Liability Corporations	198 865	81 542	479 969	92 719
股份有限公司	Share-holding Corporations Ltd.	114 343			29 921
私营企业	Private Enterprises	54 854		114 016	28 706
私营独资企业	Private-funded Enterprises	3 298			
私营合作企业	Private Cooperative Enterprises	500			
私营有限责任公司	Private Limited Liability Corporations	24 795		114 016	28 706
私营股份有限公司	Private Share-holding Corporations Ltd.	26 261			
其他企业	Other Enterprises	4 466			23 742
港、澳、台商投资企业	Enterprises with Funds from Hong Kong, Macao and Taiwan			8 745	51 139
合资经营企业(港或澳、台)	Joint-Venture Enterprises(with funds from Hong Kong, Macao and Taiwan)				51 139
港、澳、台商独资经营企业	Enterprises with Funds from Hong Kong, Macao and Taiwan			8 745	
外商投资企业	Foreign Funded Enterprises	8 057			
中外合资经营企业	Joint-Venture Enterprises	8 057			
中外合作经营企业	Cooperative Enterprises				
外资企业	Foreign-Funded Enterprises				
外商投资股份有限公司	Foreign-Funded Enterprises				
按轻重工业分	**Grouped by Light & Heavy Industry**				
轻工业	Light Industry	254 156	64 199	265 724	233 905
重工业	Heavy Industry	169 502	37 543	378 392	86 172
按企业规模分	**Grouped by Size of Enterprises**				
大型企业	Large-Scale Enterprises	108 043			
中型企业	Medium-Scale Enterprises	141 568	43 016	373 480	161 345
小型企业	Small-Scale Enterprises	174 047	58 726	270 636	158 732
按工业行业分	**Grouped by Sector**				
采矿业	**Mining**	**4 048**		**41 069**	**2 306**
煤炭开采和洗选业	Coal Mining and Dressing	4 048		41 069	2 306
黑色金属矿采选业	Ferrous Metals Mining and Dressing				
有色金属矿采选业	Nonferrous Metals Mining and Dressing				
非金属矿采选业	Nonmetal Mineral Mining and Dressing				
制造业	**Manufacturing**	**400 766**	**81 678**	**596 438**	**247 789**
农副食品加工业	Farm and Sideline Food Processing	79 761	39 463	59 564	22 472
谷物磨制	Cereal Grain Grinding	18 465			
饲料加工	Forage Processing	10 788			2 045
植物油加工	Plant Oil Processing	7 766	27 511	33 235	11 217
制　糖	Sugar Making	21 633			9 210
食品制造业	Food Manufacturing	17 972		86 918	107 044
液体乳及乳制品制造	Liquid Milk and Dairy Products Manufacturing	8 854			8 862
罐头制造	Canned Food Manufacturing			51 465	98 183

Continued

(10 000 yuan)

八　师 Division 8	九　师 Division 9	十　师 Division 10	建工师 Construction Division	十二师 Division 12	十三师 Division 13	十四师 Division 14	国资公司 Stateowned Property Company	中基公司 Chalkis Company	兵团直属 Directly under XPCG
2 159 199	**55 716**	**87 358**	**30 949**	**99 282**	**134 676**	**11 907**	**276 270**	**160 101**	**36 175**
1 398 752	43 667	44 198	13 600	75 235	39 845	3 028	276 270	160 101	1 711
1 993 892	55 716	87 357	30 499	99 282	134 676	11 907	276 270	160 101	1 711
91 426	16 267	10 082		16 123	2 172			18 405	1 711
1 199 700	36 109	55 372	13 600	77 617	132 504	10 016	181 799	141 696	
		3 817		2 892	18 696				
1 199 700	36 109	51 556	13 600	74 725	113 808	10 016	181 799	141 696	
243 067		2 488		904			94 470		
454 657	3 340	8 419	16 899	3 403		1 891			
12 620		8 419	1 308						
						1 891			
408 756	3 340		15 591	3 403					
33 281									
5 042		10 996		1 236					
165 308			450						34 464
112 224			450						
									34 464
49 940									
3 144									
840 778	50 363	24 785		71 887	26 890	5 986	275 085	141 696	36 175
1 318 421	5 353	62 573	30 949	27 395	107 786	5 921	1 185	18 405	
922 684									
724 232	25 724	19 526		36 302	20 556		184 704	141 696	
512 283	29 992	67 832	30 949	62 980	114 120	11 907	91 566	18 405	36 175
6 744		**19 128**		**10 576**	**50 031**				
6 744		12 578		9 376	13 349				
					10 141				
					21 030				
		6 550		1 200	5 511				
1 986 192	**52 187**	**56 440**	**30 949**	**83 999**	**84 646**	**8 879**	**276 270**	**160 101**	**36 175**
113 012	47 171	20 384		29 529	9 542	1 891	272 249		34 464
6 179	8 709	2 391							
25 912							214 603		34 464
71 899		5 644		2 362	6 472	1 891	37 089		
	25 724								
176 455	3 193	2 394		16 691			2 836	141 696	
72 937				13 746					
59 319	3 193						2 836	141 696	

10—10 续表 2

计量单位:万元　　　　　　　　　　　　　　　　　　　　　　　　　　　　　　(2010 年)

指　　标	Item	合　计 Total	一　师 Division1	二　师 Division2	三　师 Division3
蔬菜、水果罐头制造	Vegetable and Fruit Canned Food Manufacturing	425 191		68 500	
饮料制造业	Beverage Manufacturing	298 854	3 183	10 160	
酒的制造	Liquor Brewing	231 535	2 023	10 160	
软饮料制造	Soft Beverage Manufacturing	67 319	1 160		
纺织业	Textile Industry	640 934	39 256	38 470	7 615
棉、化纤纺织及印染精加工	Cotton,Chemical Fibre and Dying Fine Processing	602 863	39 256	38 470	7 615
木材加工及木、竹、藤、棕、草制品业	Timber Processing Wood Bamboo Rattan PalmFibre and Straw Products	5 249		1 277	
家具制造业	Furniture Manufacturing	7 741			
造纸及纸制品业	Paper Making and Paper Products	65 279	2 094	10 413	
造　纸	Paper Making	26 087		5 999	
印刷业和记录媒介的复制	Printing Industry and Recording Media	6 377	571		
石油加工、炼焦及核燃料加工业	Oil Processing,Coking Plant and Nuclear Elding Processing	113 552			
炼　焦	Coking Plant	113 552			
化学原料及化学制品制造业	Chemical Materials and Chemical Products Manufacturing	1 003 257	12 344	1 463	
基础化学原料制造	Basic Chemical Materials Manufacturing	122 264			
合成材料制造	Complex Materials Manufacturing	826 508			
医药制造业	Pharmaceuticals Manufacturing	44 422	10 488	21 120	11 595
化学纤维制造业	Chemical Fibre Manufacturing	224 659	182 816		
纤维素纤维原料及纤维制造	Cellulose Material and Fibre Manufacturing	224 659	182 816		
化纤浆粕制造	Chemical Fibre Pulp Manufacturing	122 210	80 367		
人造纤维(纤维素纤维)制造	Artificial Cellulose Material and Fibre Manufacturing	102 449	102 449		
橡胶制品业	Rubber Products Manufacturing	642			
塑料制品业	Plastic Products Manufacturing	212 020	39 944	2 127	18 031
塑料薄膜制造	Plastic Film Manufacturing	39 248	16 235	1 476	3 460
塑料板、管、型材的制造	Plastic Board,Pipe and Structural Section Manufacturing	135 782	19 529	651	14 571
非金属矿物制品业	Nonmetal Mineral Products Manufacturing	470 099	193 406	22 363	4 012
水泥、石灰和石膏的制造	Cement,Lime and Gypsum Manufacturing	346 429	172 027	20 557	4 012
水泥制造	Cemen Manufacturing	346 429	172 027	20 557	4 012
黑色金属冶炼及压延加工业	Ferrous Metals Smelting and Rolling	60 265	4 666		
有色金属冶炼及压延加工业	Nonferrous Metals Smelting and Rolling	197 464			
常用有色金属冶炼	Common Nonferrous Metals Smelting	190 671			
金属制品业	Metal Product Manufacturing	53 561			
通用设备制造业	General Equipment Manufacturing	14 717		980	
专用设备制造业	Special Equipment Manufacturing	25 904	4 191	3 509	
交通运输设备制造业	Transportation Equipment Manufacturing	5 025			
电气机械及器材制造业	ElectricMachine and Equipment Manufacturing	6 949			
废弃资源和废旧材料回收加工业	Abandon Resources and Discard Material Recovery Processing	6 933			
电力、煤气及水的生产和供应业	**Electricity,Gasand Water Productionand Supply**	**401 189**	**61 010**	**11 974**	**23 389**
电力、热力的生产和供应业	Electricity and Heat Production and Supply	390 952	59 001	11 974	23 389
电力生产	Electricity Production	283 334	15 367		5 120
火力发电	Coal-Fired Generation	244 076	15 367		5 120
热力生产和供应	Heat Production and Supply	11 639	2 300		
燃气生产和供应业	Gass Production and Supply	4 499			
水的生产和供应业	Water Production and Supply	5 739	2 009		

Continued

(10 000 yuan)

四 师 Division 4	五 师 Division 5	六 师 Division 6	七 师 Division 7	八 师 Division 8	九 师 Division 9	十 师 Division 10	建工师 Construction Division	十二师 Division 12	十三师 Division 13	十四师 Division 14
		51 465	98 183	59 319	3 193					
140 418	853	14 504	6 725	111 377		2 006		6 168	3 460	
139 918	853	14 504	6 725	45 718		2 006		6 168	3 460	
500				65 659						
11 032	18 423	89 351	91 339	329 622				13 179	2 647	
	18 423	82 569	91 339	322 543					2 647	
				3 972						
				7 741						
822				44 077					7 873	
822				18 351					915	
										4 095
11 002		99 150							3 400	
11 002		99 150							3 400	
22 202	11 891	7 043	529	934 103		2 670	1 423	641	7 014	751
18 629				96 621					7 014	
				826 508						
				1 219						
				41 842						
				41 842						
				41 842						
							642			
6 855	9 426	23 729	8 347	67 337	1 824	17 725	1 135	3 571	10 844	1 125
1 660	4 975			7 966				805	2 672	
	4 452	15 053	2 022	57 429	1 824	15 228	685		3 214	1 125
107 639		9 672	4 993	90 360		11 261	17 538	3 886	4 969	
103 312				33 607			12 914			
103 312				33 607			12 914			
		10 500		13 653			8 813		22 634	
		178 409		6 793					12 263	
		178 409							12 263	
1 738		2 259	6 340	23 801						1 017
		2 346		6 590			1 399	3 403		
1 325	1 621	1 020		14 238						
		5 025								
		6 949								
								6 933		
18 844	**20 064**	**6 609**	**69 983**	**166 263**	**3 529**	**11 789**		**4 707**		**3 028**
18 844	20 064	3 829	69 983	161 720	3 529	11 789		3 803		3 028
18 844	7 798		69 983	156 140		10 082				
			67 463	152 992		3 134				
		3 829				1 707		3 803		
		2 780		1 719						
				2 825				904		

10—10 续表 3　Continued

计量单位：万元　　　　（2010 年）　　　　(10 000 yuan)

指　　标	Item	国资公司 Stateowned Property Company	中基公司 Chalkis Company	兵团直属 Directly under XPCG
蔬菜、水果罐头制造	Vegetable and Fruit Canned Food Manufacturing	2 836	141 696	
饮料制造业	Beverage Manufacturing			
酒的制造	Liquor Brewing			
软饮料制造	Soft Beverage Manufacturing			
纺织业	Textile Industry			
棉、化纤纺织及印染精加工	Cotton, Chemical Fibre and Dying Fine Processing			
木材加工及木、竹、藤、棕、草制品业	Timber Processing Wood Bamboo Rattan PalmFibre and Straw Products			
家具制造业	Furniture Manufacturing			
造纸及纸制品业	Paper Making and Paper Products			
造　纸	Paper Making			
印刷业和记录媒介的复制	Printing Industry and Recording Media			1 711
石油加工、炼焦及核燃料加工业	Oil Processing, Coking Plant and Nuclear Elding Processing			
炼　焦	Coking Plant			
化学原料及化学制品制造业	Chemical Materials and Chemical Products Manufacturing	1 185		
基础化学原料制造	Basic Chemical Materials Manufacturing			
合成材料制造	Complex Materials Manufacturing			
医药制造业	Pharmaceuticals Manufacturing			
化学纤维制造业	Chemical Fibre Manufacturing			
纤维素纤维原料及纤维制造	Cellulose Material and Fibre Manufacturing			
化纤浆粕制造	Chemical Fibre Pulp Manufacturing			
人造纤维(纤维素纤维)制造	Artificial Cellulose Material and Fibre Manufacturing			
橡胶制品业	Rubber Products Manufacturing			
塑料制品业	Plastic Products Manufacturing			
塑料薄膜制造	Plastic Film Manufacturing			
塑料板、管、型材的制造	Plastic Board, Pipe and Structural Section Manufacturing			
非金属矿物制品业	Nonmetal Mineral Products Manufacturing			
水泥、石灰和石膏的制造	Cement, Lime and Gypsum Manufacturing			
水泥制造	Cemen Manufacturing			
黑色金属冶炼及压延加工业	Ferrous Metals Smelting and Rolling			
有色金属冶炼及压延加工业	Nonferrous Metals Smelting and Rolling			
常用有色金属冶炼	Common Nonferrous Metals Smelting			
金属制品业	Metal Product Manufacturing		18 405	
通用设备制造业	General Equipment Manufacturing			
专用设备制造业	Special Equipment Manufacturing			
交通运输设备制造业	Transportation Equipment Manufacturing			
电气机械及器材制造业	ElectricMachine and Equipment Manufacturing			
废弃资源和废旧材料回收加工业	Abandon Resources and Discard Material Recovery Processing			
电力、煤气及水的生产和供应业	**Electricity, Gasand Water Productionand Supply**			
电力、热力的生产和供应业	Electricity and Heat Production and Supply			
电力生产	Electricity Production			
火力发电	Coal-Fired Generation			
热力生产和供应	Heat Production and Supply			
燃气生产和供应业	Gass Production and Supply			
水的生产和供应业	Water Production and Supply			

10—11 各师规模以上工业企业销售产值

Sale Value of Industrial Enterprises above Designated Size by Division

计量单位:万元 (2010 年) (10 000 yuan)

指 标	Item	合 计 Total	一 师 Division 1	二 师 Division 2	三 师 Division 3
总 计	**Total**	**5 408 062**	**658 439**	**272 613**	**62 599**
# 国有控股企业	State-controlled Shareholding Enterprises	3 540 618	471 089	172 693	41 174
按登记注册类型分	**Grouped by Status of Registration**				
内资企业	Domestic Enterprises	5 154 811	637 488	272 614	62 599
国有企业	State-owned Enterprises	481 165	57 537	9 480	41 174
有限责任公司	Limited Liability Corporations	3 218 433	416 225	179 844	
国有独资公司	State-owned Corporations with Private-Funds	40 115	15 594		
其他有限责任公司	Other Limited Liability Corporations	3 178 318	400 631	179 844	
股份有限公司	Share-holding Corporations Ltd.	595 949	72 282	41 529	
私营企业	Private Enterprises	807 611	84 736	41 762	21 426
私营独资企业	Private-funded Enterprises	45 726		21 231	
私营合作企业	Private Cooperative Enterprises	1 918			
私营有限责任公司	Private Limited Liability Corporations	701 480	84 736	20 531	21 426
私营股份有限公司	Private Share-holding Corporations Ltd.	58 487			
其他企业	Other Enterprises	51 653	6 708		
港、澳、台商投资企业	Enterprises with Funds from Hong Kong, Macao and Taiwan	39 494	20 951		
合资经营企业(港或澳、台)	Joint-Venture Enterprises(with funds from Hong Kong, Macao and Taiwan)	10 666			
港、澳、台商独资经营企业	Enterprises with Funds from Hong Kong, Macao and Taiwan	28 828	20 951		
外商投资企业	Foreign Funded Enterprises	213 757			
中外合资经营企业	Joint-Venture Enterprises	124 184			
中外合作经营企业	Cooperative Enterprises	34 613			
外资企业	Foreign-Funded Enterprises	51 854			
外商投资股份有限公司	Foreign-Funded Enterprises	3 106			
按轻重工业分	**Grouped by Light & Heavy Industry**				
轻工业	Light Industry	2 750 129	331 379	194 483	15 484
重工业	Heavy Industry	2 657 933	327 060	78 130	47 115
按企业规模分	**Grouped by Size of Enterprises**				
大型企业	Large-Scale Enterprises	1 093 884	72 281		
中型企业	Medium-Scale Enterprises	2 239 603	280 110	115 092	8 263
小型企业	Small-Scale Enterprises	2 074 575	306 048	157 521	54 336
按工业行业分	**Grouped by Sector**				
采矿业	**Mining**	**187 685**	**19 379**	**34 331**	
煤炭开采和洗选业	Coal Mining and Dressing	131 468	19 379	24 851	
黑色金属矿采选业	Ferrous Metals Mining and Dressing	11 883			
有色金属矿采选业	Nonferrous Metals Mining and Dressing	20 815			
非金属矿采选业	Nonmetal Mineral Mining and Dressing	23 518		9 480	
制造业	**Manufacturing**	**4 823 012**	**578 050**	**226 310**	**39 210**
农副食品加工业	Farm and Sideline Food Processing	828 438	81 144	52 105	
谷物磨制	Cereal Grain Grinding	44 445	9 170		
饲料加工	Forage Processing	294 913		2 683	
植物油加工	Plant Oil Processing	214 837	47 336		
制 糖	Sugar Making	89 890		27 708	
食品制造业	Food Manufacturing	575 840	18 979	68 582	
液体乳及乳制品制造	Liquid Milk and Dairy Products Manufacturing	112 423	9 214		
罐头制造	Canned Food Manufacturing	346 849		58 886	

10—11 续表 1

计量单位:万元　　　　(2010 年)

指　　标	Item	四　师 Division 4	五　师 Division 5	六　师 Division 6	七　师 Division 7
总　　计	**Total**	**421 470**	**100 204**	**574 839**	**298 155**
# 国有控股企业	State-controlled Shareholding Enterprises	359 295	78 633	137 738	236 144
按登记注册类型分	**Grouped by Status of Registration**				
内资企业	Domestic Enterprises	413 169	100 204	566 962	287 489
国有企业	State-owned Enterprises	41 393	19 782	41 376	116 099
有限责任公司	Limited Liability Corporations	201 537	80 422	419 847	93 746
国有独资公司	State-owned Corporations with Private-Funds				
其他有限责任公司	Other Limited Liability Corporations	201 537	80 422	419 847	93 746
股份有限公司	Share-holding Corporations Ltd.	114 818			16 765
私营企业	Private Enterprises	51 068		105 739	38 506
私营独资企业	Private-funded Enterprises	3 295			
私营合作企业	Private Cooperative Enterprises	500			
私营有限责任公司	Private Limited Liability Corporations	22 334		105 739	38 506
私营股份有限公司	Private Share-holding Corporations Ltd.	24 939			
其他企业	Other Enterprises	4 353			22 374
港、澳、台商投资企业	Enterprises with Funds from Hong Kong, Macao and Taiwan			7 877	10 665
合资经营企业(港或澳、台)	Joint-Venture Enterprises(with funds from Hong Kong, Macao and Taiwan)				10 665
港、澳、台商独资经营企业	Enterprises with Funds from Hong Kong, Macao and Taiwan			7 877	
外商投资企业	Foreign Funded Enterprises	8 301			
中外合资经营企业	Joint-Venture Enterprises	8 301			
中外合作经营企业	Cooperative Enterprises				
外资企业	Foreign-Funded Enterprises				
外商投资股份有限公司	Foreign-Funded Enterprises				
按轻重工业分	**Grouped by Light & Heavy Industry**				
轻工业	Light Industry	253 373	63 402	238 021	208 357
重工业	Heavy Industry	168 097	36 802	336 818	89 798
按企业规模分	**Grouped by Size of Enterprises**				
大型企业	Large-Scale Enterprises	108 518			
中型企业	Medium-Scale Enterprises	141 042	48 811	320 233	159 022
小型企业	Small-Scale Enterprises	171 910	51 393	254 606	139 133
按工业行业分	**Grouped by Sector**				
采矿业	**Mining**	**3 993**		**41 069**	**2 306**
煤炭开采和洗选业	Coal Mining and Dressing	3 993		41 069	2 306
黑色金属矿采选业	Ferrous Metals Mining and Dressing				
有色金属矿采选业	Nonferrous Metals Mining and Dressing				
非金属矿采选业	Nonmetal Mineral Mining and Dressing				
制造业	**Manufacturing**	**398 633**	**80 140**	**527 161**	**223 816**
农副食品加工业	Farm and Sideline Food Processing	80 201	31 955	53 572	21 335
谷物磨制	Cereal Grain Grinding	18 082			
饲料加工	Forage Processing	11 668			2 045
植物油加工	Plant Oil Processing	7 766	21 750	28 790	9 553
制　糖	Sugar Making	21 663			9 738
食品制造业	Food Manufacturing	17 321		68 414	56 005
液体乳及乳制品制造	Liquid Milk and Dairy Products Manufacturing	8 379			10 984
罐头制造	Canned Food Manufacturing			39 066	45 021

Continued

(10 000 yuan)

八 师 Division 8	九 师 Division 9	十 师 Division 10	建工师 Construction Division	十二师 Division 12	十三师 Division 13	十四师 Division 14	国资公司 Stateowned Property Company	中基公司 Chalkis Company	兵团直属 Directly under XPCG
2 146 196	**59 947**	**81 102**	**33 685**	**94 113**	**129 828**	**10 865**	**265 171**	**162 512**	**36 324**
1 398 662	47 825	41 669	13 897	70 016	39 363	3 028	265 171	162 512	1 711
1 975 833	59 947	81 102	33 204	94 113	129 828	10 865	265 171	162 512	1 711
92 728	17 044	10 082		13 381	2 655			16 724	1 711
1 197 920	39 563	49 245	13 897	75 095	127 173	9 447	168 685	145 788	
		3 282		2 777	18 462				
1 197 920	39 563	45 963	13 897	72 318	108 711	9 447	168 685	145 788	
251 208		1 956		904			96 487		
429 058	3 340	7 644	19 307	3 608		1 418			
12 248		7 644	1 308						
						1 418			
383 262	3 340		17 998	3 608					
33 548									
4 918		12 175		1 125					
170 363			481						34 613
115 402			481						
									34 613
51 854									
3 106									
827 622	53 935	19 920		67 183	25 467	5 406	263 985	145 788	36 324
1 318 574	6 012	61 182	33 685	26 930	104 361	5 459	1 186	16 724	
913 085									
733 401	30 781	17 498		31 749	20 091		187 722	145 788	
499 710	29 166	63 604	33 685	62 364	109 737	10 865	77 449	16 724	36 324
6 798		**17 981**		**10 109**	**51 720**				
6 798		10 550		8 909	13 614				
					11 883				
					20 815				
		7 431		1 200	5 407				
1 979 575	**55 760**	**51 332**	**33 685**	**79 389**	**78 108**	**7 837**	**265 171**	**162 512**	**36 324**
103 503	52 419	15 781		29 323	9 316	1 418	261 754		34 613
6 064	8 782	2 348							
25 544							218 361		34 613
62 874		4 661		2 362	6 404	1 418	21 924		
	30 781								
180 673	1 516	2 122		14 210			2 231	145 788	
72 496				11 350					
54 342	1 516						2 231	145 788	

10—11 续表 2

计量单位:万元 （2010 年）

指 标	Item	合 计 Total	一 师 Division1	二 师 Division2	三 师 Division3
蔬菜、水果罐头制造	Vegetable and Fruit Canned Food Manufacturing	346 849		58 886	
饮料制造业	Beverage Manufacturing	292 703	2 814	10 009	
酒的制造	Liquor Brewing	233 598	1 944	10 009	
软饮料制造	Soft Beverage Manufacturing	59 106	870		
纺织业	Textile Industry	676 243	42 885	36 987	8 263
棉、化纤纺织及印染精加工	Cotton, Chemical Fibre and Dying Fine Processing	640 349	42 885	36 987	8 263
木材加工及木、竹、藤、棕、草制品业	Timber Processing Wood Bamboo Rattan PalmFibre and Straw Products	5 099		1 258	
家具制造业	Furniture Manufacturing	7 741			
造纸及纸制品业	Paper Making and Paper Products	60 941	1 885	7 384	
造 纸	Paper Making	23 482		3 516	
印刷业和记录媒介的复制	Printing Industry and Recording Media	6 269	571		
石油加工、炼焦及核燃料加工业	Oil Processing, Coking Plant and Nuclear Elding Processing	114 469			
炼 焦	Coking Plant	114 469			
化学原料及化学制品制造业	Chemical Materials and Chemical Products Manufacturing	1 003 662	11 648	1 722	
基础化学原料制造	Basic Chemical Materials Manufacturing	123 967			
合成材料制造	Complex Materials Manufacturing	826 765			
医药制造业	Pharmaceuticals Manufacturing	35 086	7 092	19 417	7 222
化学纤维制造业	Chemical Fibre Manufacturing	214 065	174 001		
纤维素纤维原料及纤维制造	Cellulose Material and Fibre Manufacturing	214 065	174 001		
化纤浆粕制造	Chemical Fibre Pulp Manufacturing	106 257	66 193		
人造纤维(纤维素纤维)制造	Artificial Cellulose Material and Fibre Manufacturing	107 808	107 808		
橡胶制品业	Rubber Products Manufacturing	642			
塑料制品业	Plastic Products Manufacturing	214 019	39 250	2 937	19 816
塑料薄膜制造	Plastic Film Manufacturing	38 174	15 416	1 584	4 582
塑料板、管、型材的制造	Plastic Board, Pipe and Structural Section Manufacturing	141 613	19 851	1 353	15 234
非金属矿物制品业	Nonmetal Mineral Products Manufacturing	462 641	189 410	21 771	3 909
水泥、石灰和石膏的制造	Cement, Lime and Gypsum Manufacturing	343 036	168 476	19 964	3 909
水泥制造	Cemen Manufacturing	343 036	168 476	19 964	3 909
黑色金属冶炼及压延加工业	Ferrous Metals Smelting and Rolling	58 420	4 304		
有色金属冶炼及压延加工业	Nonferrous Metals Smelting and Rolling	154 342			
常用有色金属冶炼	Common Nonferrous Metals Smelting	148 929			
金属制品业	Metal Product Manufacturing	51 131			
通用设备制造业	General Equipment Manufacturing	13 841		689	
专用设备制造业	Special Equipment Manufacturing	30 028	4 069	3 451	
交通运输设备制造业	Transportation Equipment Manufacturing	5 025			
电气机械及器材制造业	ElectricMachine and Equipment Manufacturing	5 436			
废弃资源和废旧材料回收加工业	Abandon Resources and Discard Material Recovery Processing	6 933			
电力、煤气及水的生产和供应业	**Electricity, Gasand Water Productionand Supply**	**397 365**	**61 010**	**11 974**	**23 389**
电力、热力的生产和供应业	Electricity and Heat Production and Supply	387 127	59 001	11 974	23 389
电力生产	Electricity Production	278 943	15 367		5 120
火力发电	Coal-Fired Generation	239 685	15 367		5 120
热力生产和供应	Heat Production and Supply	11 546	2 300		
燃气生产和供应业	Gass Production and Supply	4 499			
水的生产和供应业	Water Production and Supply	5 739	2 009		

Continued

(10 000 yuan)

四 师 Division 4	五 师 Division 5	六 师 Division 6	七 师 Division 7	八 师 Division 8	九 师 Division 9	十 师 Division 10	建工师 Construction Division	十二师 Division 12	十三师 Division 13	十四师 Division 14
		39 066	45 021	54 342	1 516					
140 143	667	14 324	5 431	108 196		2 017		6 053	3 050	
139 643	667	14 324	5 431	50 460		2 017		6 053	3 050	
500				57 736						
10 840	25 320	88 078	119 458	330 716				11 490	2 207	
	25 320	82 415	119 458	322 814					2 207	
				3 842						
				7 741						
737				42 966					7 970	
737				18 314					915	
										3 988
9 763		101 948							2 758	
9 763		101 948							2 758	
21 831	12 420	6 591	530	935 864		2 533	1 423	623	6 795	494
18 453				98 719					6 795	
				826 765						
				1 356						
				40 064						
				40 064						
				40 064						
							642			
5 912	8 388	21 337	9 712	71 028	1 824	17 533	1 166	3 542	10 650	924
1 548	4 405			7 145				822	2 672	
	3 982	13 095	3 584	62 064	1 824	15 553	685		3 464	924
109 355		9 328	4 993	86 355		11 346	17 526	3 608	5 041	
105 048				32 427			13 212			
105 048				32 427			13 212			
		10 500		13 341			11 393		18 882	
		137 489		5 413					11 440	
		137 489							11 440	
1 444		2 259	6 352	23 339						1 013
		1 811		6 198			1 535	3 608		
1 087	1 390	1 049		18 983						
		5 025								
		5 436								
								6 933		
18 844	**20 064**	**6 609**	**72 033**	**159 822**	**4 188**	**11 789**		**4 615**		**3 028**
18 844	20 064	3 829	72 033	155 278	4 188	11 789		3 710		3 028
18 844	7 798		72 033	149 699		10 082				
			69 513	146 551		3 134				
		3 829				1 707		3 710		
		2 780		1 719						
				2 825				904		

10—11 续表 3　Continued

计量单位:万元　　(2010 年)　　(10 000 yuan)

指　标	Item	国资公司 Stateowned Property Company	中基公司 Chalkis Company	兵团直属 Directly under XPCG
蔬菜、水果罐头制造	Vegetable and Fruit Canned Food Manufacturing	2 231	145 788	
饮料制造业	Beverage Manufacturing			
酒的制造	Liquor Brewing			
软饮料制造	Soft Beverage Manufacturing			
纺织业	Textile Industry			
棉、化纤纺织及印染精加工	Cotton,Chemical Fibre and Dying Fine Processing			
木材加工及木、竹、藤、棕、草制品业	Timber Processing Wood Bamboo Rattan PalmFibre and Straw Products			
家具制造业	Furniture Manufacturing			
造纸及纸制品业	Paper Making and Paper Products			
造　纸	Paper Making			
印刷业和记录媒介的复制	Printing Industry and Recording Media			1 711
石油加工、炼焦及核燃料加工业	Oil Processing,Coking Plant and Nuclear Elding Processing			
炼　焦	Coking Plant			
化学原料及化学制品制造业	Chemical Materials and Chemical Products Manufacturing	1 186		
基础化学原料制造	Basic Chemical Materials Manufacturing			
合成材料制造	Complex Materials Manufacturing			
医药制造业	Pharmaceuticals Manufacturing			
化学纤维制造业	Chemical Fibre Manufacturing			
纤维素纤维原料及纤维制造	Cellulose Material and Fibre Manufacturing			
化纤浆粕制造	Chemical Fibre Pulp Manufacturing			
人造纤维(纤维素纤维)制造	Artificial Cellulose Material and Fibre Manufacturing			
橡胶制品业	Rubber Products Manufacturing			
塑料制品业	Plastic Products Manufacturing			
塑料薄膜制造	Plastic Film Manufacturing			
塑料板、管、型材的制造	Plastic Board,Pipe and Structural Section Manufacturing			
非金属矿物制品业	Nonmetal Mineral Products Manufacturing			
水泥、石灰和石膏的制造	Cement,Lime and Gypsum Manufacturing			
水泥制造	Cemen Manufacturing			
黑色金属冶炼及压延加工业	Ferrous Metals Smelting and Rolling			
有色金属冶炼及压延加工业	Nonferrous Metals Smelting and Rolling			
常用有色金属冶炼	Common Nonferrous Metals Smelting			
金属制品业	Metal Product Manufacturing		16 724	
通用设备制造业	General Equipment Manufacturing			
专用设备制造业	Special Equipment Manufacturing			
交通运输设备制造业	Transportation Equipment Manufacturing			
电气机械及器材制造业	ElectricMachine and Equipment Manufacturing			
废弃资源和废旧材料回收加工业	Abandon Resources and Discard Material Recovery Processing			
电力、煤气及水的生产和供应业	**Electricity,Gasand Water Productionand Supply**			
电力、热力的生产和供应业	Electricity and Heat Production and Supply			
电力生产	Electricity Production			
火力发电	Coal-Fired Generation			
热力生产和供应	Heat Production and Supply			
燃气生产和供应业	Gass Production and Supply			
水的生产和供应业	Water Production and Supply			

10—12 各师规模以上工业企业主要经济指标

Main Economic Indicators of Industrial Enterprises above Designated Size by Division

计量单位：万元 (2010 年) (10 000 yuan)

单 位	Unit	工业总产值（当年价格）Gross Industrial Output Value (at current prices)	工业增加值（当年价格）Added Value of Industry (atcurrent prices)	资产合计 Total Assets	固定资产合计 Fixed Assets	流动资产合计 Circulation Assets	负债合计 Total Liabilities	#流动负债合计 Liquid Liabilities	所有者权益合计 Creditors Equity	#国家资本 National Capital
总 计	**Total**	**5 592 355**	**1 541 040**	**10 420 284**	**4 654 642**	**4 368 690**	**6 670 888**	**4 497 871**	**3 722 236**	**656 916**
一 师	Division 1	686 654	207 408	1 375 486	600 408	471 220	765 658	461 052	606 952	71 092
二 师	Division 2	299 833	95 274	451 845	201 676	213 954	316 971	273 744	134 874	52 065
三 师	Division 3	64 642	19 277	152 204	99 894	51 537	120 619	46 701	31 485	22 555
四 师	Division 4	423 658	189 298	685 873	276 881	302 135	379 343	252 687	306 532	62 275
五 师	Division 5	101 742	26 927	292 022	140 488	139 426	221 171	161 590	70 741	20 172
六 师	Division 6	644 116	176 721	1 125 134	397 497	527 708	757 775	553 783	363 808	131 644
七 师	Division 7	320 077	100 621	656 750	339 200	263 129	487 881	302 689	168 868	66 062
八 师	Division 8	2 159 199	565 601	4 102 937	2 138 074	1 557 499	2 535 073	1 555 074	1 549 172	121 371
九 师	Division 9	55 716	15 562	77 176	28 341	43 838	43 160	39 242	34 015	33 200
十 师	Division 10	87 358	38 940	153 990	86 155	59 897	87 959	54 313	65 591	22 847
建 工 师	Construction Division	30 949	8 006	29 425	11 830	15 142	21 592	21 146	6 802	158
十 二 师	Division 12	99 282	27 491	211 586	63 131	98 288	150 142	108 555	61 394	24 759
十 三 师	Division 13	134 676	51 953	185 297	75 088	79 825	119 220	88 578	66 056	17 586
十 四 师	Division 14	11 907	3 111	21 718	10 922	10 075	14 821	11 744	6 897	2 066
国资公司	State-owned Property Compan	276 270	40 011	274 082	50 095	150 154	143 770	123 185	130 023	8 000
中基公司	Chalkis Company	160 101	−29 124	610 556	131 497	376 716	499 086	437 375	111 469	
兵团直属	Directly under XPCG	36 175	3 962	14 204	3 464	8 149	6 648	6 414	7 556	1 064

单 位	Unit	主营业务收入 Main Business Income	主营业务成本 Main Business Cost	主营业务税金及附加 Main Business Tax and Affixture	营业费用 Operation Expenses	管理费用 Administrative Expenses	营业利润 Business Profits	利润总额 Total Profits	利税总额 Total Profits and Taxes	就业人员年平均人数（人）Average Annual Exployees (Person)
总 计	**Total**	**5 532 077**	**4 413 207**	**49 078**	**214 465**	**213 252**	**498 138**	**544 021**	**782 473**	**112 437**
一 师	Division 1	652 181	514 578	4 943	21 525	28 087	85 515	96 042	132 610	12 219
二 师	Division 2	253 782	180 018	1 943	21 714	16 524	31 564	27 344	40 043	6 546
三 师	Division 3	53 718	46 607	145	410	2 198	5 450	5 473	6 945	1 561
四 师	Division 4	404 869	256 984	18 821	17 724	19 460	79 995	84 012	124 103	10 129
五 师	Division 5	136 561	122 888	360	1 731	3 976	7 445	6 700	9 721	3 056
六 师	Division 6	565 349	455 896	1 789	24 618	18 572	44 892	47 652	68 449	10 203
七 师	Division 7	308 864	248 012	1 444	13 522	10 324	20 578	15 125	25 891	6 631
八 师	Division 8	2 213 675	1 767 854	14 815	73 313	68 435	218 576	253 045	341 772	42 753
九 师	Division 9	61 925	53 276	204	1 397	3 564	5 223	6 018	8 752	1 123
十 师	Division 10	82 947	61 284	1 067	2 826	5 554	13 422	13 704	17 647	3 059
建 工 师	Construction Division	30 934	27 837	164	917	1 831	1 783	1 825	3 173	997
十 二 师	Division 12	102 004	79 221	906	4 195	7 470	8 601	9 144	12 416	3 905
十 三 师	Division 13	132 355	101 323	1 845	6 028	5 908	19 100	19 217	27 576	4 776
十 四 师	Division 14	10 900	7 412	23	156	451	1 302	1 301	1 602	266
国资公司	State-owned Property Company	275 122	233 406	265	13 844	13 990	10 415	12 952	15 688	2 432
中基公司	Chalkis Company	211 456	225 750	345	9 044	5 154				2 359
兵团直属	Directly under XPCG	35 436	30 861	1	1 501	1 755	1 331	1 316	1 333	422

10—13　规模以上工业企业主要经济指标

计量单位：万元　　　　　　　　　　　　　　　　　　　　　　　　　　　　　　　　（2010 年）

指　　标	Item	工业增加值（当年价） Added Value of Industry (At current Prices)	资产合计 Total Assets	流动资产合计 Circulating Assets
总　　计	**Total**	**1 541 040**	**10 420 284**	**4 368 690**
# 国有控股企业	State-controlled Shareholding Enterprises	1 050 108	8 054 982	3 170 651
按登记注册类型分	**Grouped by Status of Registration**			
内资企业	Domestic Enterprises	1 465 448	10 037 681	4 236 613
国有企业	State-owned Enterprises	168 001	1 190 203	415 959
有限责任公司	Limited Liability Corporations	867 628	5 996 550	2 576 952
国有独资公司	State-owned Corporations with Private-Funds	26 601	126 639	25 355
其他有限责任公司	Other Limited Liability Corporations	841 027	5 869 911	2 551 598
股份有限公司	Share-holding Corporations Ltd.	232 995	1 818 375	778 149
私营企业	Private Enterprises	181 981	976 597	434 963
私营独资企业	Private-funded Enterprises	14 072	39 294	21 616
私营合作企业	Private Cooperative Enterprises	511	6 703	4 086
私营有限责任公司	Private Limited Liability Corporations	156 607	838 189	353 786
私营股份有限公司	Private Share-holding Corporations Ltd.	10 791	92 410	55 475
其他企业	Other Enterprises	14 843	55 957	30 590
港、澳、台商投资企业	Enterprises with Funds from Hong Kong, Macao and Taiwan	22 069	122 968	75 779
合资经营企业（港或澳、台）	Joint-Venture Enterprises(with funds from Hong Kong, Macao and Taiwan)	14 830	70 481	41 496
港、澳、台商独资经营企业	Enterprises with Funds from Hong Kong, Macao and Taiwan	7 239	52 487	34 284
外商投资企业	Foreign Funded Enterprises	53 523	259 636	56 297
中外合资经营企业	Joint-Venture Enterprises	40 415	180 672	27 010
中外合作经营企业	Cooperative Enterprises	3 096	11 403	6 834
外资企业	Foreign-Funded Enterprises	8 681	64 349	21 111
外商投资股份有限公司	Foreign-Funded Enterprises	1 331	3 211	1 344
按轻重工业分	**Grouped by Light & Heavy Industry**			
轻工业	Light Industry	633 378	4 225 427	2 193 275
重工业	Heavy Industry	907 662	6 194 857	2 175 415
按企业规模分	**Grouped by Size of Enterprises**			
大型企业	Large-Scale Enterprises	387 433	2 920 705	1 012 859
中型企业	Medium-Scale Enterprises	598 998	4 335 857	1 872 876
小型企业	Small-Scale Enterprises	554 609	3 163 722	1 482 955

Main Economic Indicators of Industrial Enterprises above Designated Size

(10 000 yuan)

# 应收账款净额 Net Amunt of Accounts Receivable	# 产成品 Finished Product	固定资产合计 Fixed Assets	累计折旧 Accumulated Depreciation	负债合计 Total Liabilities	# 流动负债合计 Liquid Liabilities	# 长期负债合计 Long-term Lialbilties	所有者权益合计 Creditors Equity	主营业务收入 Main Business Income
621 657	**693 535**	**4 654 642**	**1 291 584**	**6 670 888**	**4 497 871**	**2 084 969**	**3 722 236**	**5 532 077**
462 587	473 872	3 636 622	1 083 048	5 171 171	3 276 178	1 844 690	2 876 978	3 619 112
594 433	672 048	4 413 305	1 223 921	6 449 664	4 311 507	2 055 418	3 560 859	5 243 752
85 880	54 903	605 365	292 508	813 123	478 055	331 381	374 817	511 062
390 826	456 430	2 891 562	590 382	4 064 452	2 824 727	1 205 140	1 924 423	3 052 669
3 178	3 386	38 728	14 746	51 437	37 685	13 752	75 182	40 042
387 648	453 044	2 852 834	575 636	4 013 015	2 787 043	1 191 388	1 849 241	3 012 628
45 433	59 679	419 830	254 436	956 744	571 356	367 720	861 631	822 731
67 503	95 889	474 756	75 918	586 133	409 525	151 178	373 293	807 011
5 901	8 348	14 604	2 273	19 763	17 626	433	19 221	44 643
2	686	2 602	355	4 071	4 071		2 632	2 097
53 073	73 706	427 128	67 297	499 298	345 629	148 303	326 491	704 683
8 527	13 149	30 422	5 993	63 002	42 198	2 442	24 949	55 589
4 790	5 148	21 793	10 678	29 212	27 844		26 695	50 279
12 486	16 853	45 092	9 115	84 980	68 869	16 111	37 987	63 168
14 483	14 039	27 176	2 779	50 221	50 221		20 259	34 867
−1 997	2 814	17 916	6 336	34 759	18 649	16 111	17 728	28 300
14 738	4 634	196 245	58 547	136 245	117 495	13 440	123 391	225 157
10 486	2 616	151 394	47 060	99 366	93 012	1 045	81 306	136 461
410	438	2 010	5 323	5 913	5 913		5 490	33 686
3 186	1 561	41 298	5 079	30 035	17 640	12 395	34 314	51 903
656	18	1 542	1 085	930	930		2 282	3 106
326 386	492 890	1 624 823	494 128	2 699 785	2 205 863	427 397	1 505 442	2 843 448
295 271	200 645	3 029 819	797 456	3 971 103	2 292 008	1 657 572	2 216 794	2 688 629
100 243	16 344	1 366 917	255 668	1 764 240	895 304	858 324	1 156 465	1 094 298
270 674	341 739	1 835 292	684 329	2 787 602	1 995 426	763 013	1 536 569	2 360 084
250 740	335 452	1 452 433	351 587	2 119 046	1 607 141	463 632	1 029 202	2 077 695

10—13 续表 1

计量单位:万元　　　　(2010 年)

指　　标	Item	主营业务成　本 Main Business Cost	主营业务税金及附加 Main Business Tax and Affixture	其他业务利　润 Profits of Other Business	营　业费　用 Operation Expenses
总　　计	**Total**	**4 413 207**	**49 078**	**26 196**	**214 465**
# 国有控股企业	State-controlled Shareholding Enterprises	2 863 980	39 801	16 995	135 993
按登记注册类型分	**Grouped by Status of Registration**				
内资企业	Domestic Enterprises	4 183 668	49 029	25 805	193 562
国有企业	State-owned Enterprises	433 007	3 786	2 125	13 900
有限责任公司	Limited Liability Corporations	2 426 471	22 723	13 619	109 116
国有独资公司	State-owned Corporations with Private-Funds	21 766	874	382	2 108
其他有限责任公司	Other Limited Liability Corporations	2 404 705	21 849	13 237	107 008
股份有限公司	Share-holding Corporations Ltd.	616 182	19 172	7 387	44 991
私营企业	Private Enterprises	670 903	2 894	2 584	23 361
私营独资企业	Private-funded Enterprises	31 640	162	2 200	3 767
私营合作企业	Private Cooperative Enterprises	1 495	1		8
私营有限责任公司	Private Limited Liability Corporations	593 393	2 429	2 194	17 764
私营股份有限公司	Private Share-holding Corporations Ltd.	44 374	302	−1 811	1 823
其他企业	Other Enterprises	37 105	454	89	2 194
港、澳、台商投资企业	Enterprises with Funds from Hong Kong, Macao and Taiwan	51 382		180	3 029
合资经营企业(港或澳、台)	Joint-Venture Enterprises(with funds from Hong Kong, Macao and Taiwan)	28 388		25	1 577
港、澳、台商独资经营企业	Enterprises with Funds from Hong Kong, Macao and Taiwan	22 994		155	1 453
外商投资企业	Foreign Funded Enterprises	178 157	49	212	17 874
中外合资经营企业	Joint-Venture Enterprises	100 972	47	163	14 610
中外合作经营企业	Cooperative Enterprises	29 556		29	1 467
外资企业	Foreign-Funded Enterprises	45 223		18	1 635
外商投资股份有限公司	Foreign-Funded Enterprises	2 406	2	2	161
按轻重工业分	**Grouped by Light & Heavy Industry**				
轻工业	Light Industry	2 334 015	31 897	14 549	142 324
重工业	Heavy Industry	2 079 192	17 181	11 647	72 141
按企业规模分	**Grouped by Size of Enterprises**				
大型企业	Large-Scale Enterprises	771 282	23 038	4 173	32 472
中型企业	Medium-Scale Enterprises	1 972 617	12 567	7 958	103 671
小型企业	Small-Scale Enterprises	1 669 308	13 473	14 065	78 322

Continued

(10 000 yuan)

管理费用 Administ-rative Expenses	财务费用 Financial Expenses	#利息支出 Intrest Exjpend-iture	营业利润 Business Profits	利润总额 Total Profits	亏损企业亏损总额 Total Loss	利税总额 Total Profits and Taxes	本年应交增值税 Value Added Taxes Payable	全部就业人员年平均人数(人) Average Number of Employees (person)
213 252	**167 396**	**157 863**	**498 138**	**544 021**	**95 618**	**782 473**	**189 374**	**112 437**
156 524	139 589	132 482	302 425	332 126	85 328	516 042	144 115	73 576
205 247	162 903	153 618	472 350	518 883	94 296	747 705	179 793	108 558
32 736	13 064	13 031	22 382	26 477	4 417	48 658	18 395	18 218
98 982	112 030	104 262	294 465	320 172	75 461	463 578	120 683	54 192
2 443	1 544	95	12 706	12 709		18 010	4 427	1 656
96 539	110 486	104 167	281 759	307 463	75 461	445 568	116 256	52 536
46 641	21 332	21 395	81 167	88 606	6 846	134 531	26 752	15 096
25 276	15 096	13 549	67 191	76 450	7 556	92 741	13 397	20 140
1 616	1 010	1 007	8 604	8 586	78	9 317	570	898
91	205	205	297	297		306	8	65
20 806	12 285	10 804	55 041	63 913	5 255	78 686	12 344	17 554
2 763	1 597	1 534	3 250	3 655	2 222	4 433	476	1 623
1 613	1 381	1 381	7 146	7 178	16	8 197	566	912
1 676	601	614	6 264	4 015	659	4 404	389	1 105
1 104	515	439	3 310	1 056	35	1 056		797
572	87	175	2 954	2 959	624	3 348	389	308
6 330	3 892	3 631	19 523	21 123	663	30 363	9 191	2 774
2 555	3 507	3 274	15 626	16 670	147	23 110	6 392	1 440
1 380	134	116	1 147	1 132		1 136	4	285
2 108	252	243	2 498	3 050	516	5 594	2 544	780
287	−1	−1	253	270		524	252	269
100 664	68 665	61 810	158 857	187 689	83 997	291 186	71 599	57 830
112 588	98 731	96 053	339 281	356 332	11 621	491 287	117 775	54 607
36 239	51 566	49 627	184 716	201 629	4 164	274 464	49 798	20 743
94 961	70 126	65 105	106 196	126 977	73 165	231 076	91 532	51 587
82 052	45 704	43 131	207 226	215 415	18 289	276 933	48 044	40 107

10—13 续表 2

计量单位:万元　　(2010 年)

指　　标	Item	工业增加值(当年价) Added Value of Industry (At current Prices)	资产合计 Total Assets	流动资产合计 Circulating Assets
按工业行业分	**Grouped by Sector**			
采矿业	**Mining**	**128 076**	**570 617**	**130 638**
煤炭开采和洗选业	Coal Mining and Dressing	99 761	480 666	95 678
黑色金属矿采选业	Ferrous Metals Mining and Dressing	3 386	11 720	7 259
有色金属矿采选业	Nonferrous Metals Mining and Dressing	14 785	54 491	13 503
非金属矿采选业	Nonmetal Mineral Mining and Dressing	10 145	23 740	14 199
制造业	**Manufacturing**	**1 217 560**	**8 047 300**	**3 776 758**
农副食品加工业	Farm and Sideline Food Processing	164 235	953 004	600 637
食品制造业	Food Manufacturing	77 794	1 400 676	756 730
饮料制造业	Beverage Manufacturing	121 437	376 931	197 187
纺织业	Textile Industry	172 972	994 061	431 006
木材加工及木、竹、藤、棕、草制品业	Timber Processing Wood Bamboo Rattan PalmFibre and Straw Products	557	5 527	5 120
家具制造业	Furniture Manufacturing	383	1 852	1 274
造纸及纸制品业	Paper Making and Paper Products	18 033	79 573	37 678
印刷业和记录媒介的复制	Printing Industry and Recording Media	1 858	7 965	3 595
石油加工、炼焦及核燃料加工业	Oil Processing, Coking Plant and Nuclear Elding Processing	31 756	261 081	80 960
化学原料及化学制品制造业	Chemical Materials and Chemical Products Manufacturing	257 929	1 868 295	679 467
医药制造业	Pharmaceuticals Manufacturing	12 951	60 153	39 403
化学纤维制造业	Chemical Fibre Manufacturing	43 218	258 418	97 529
塑料制品业	Plastic Products Manufacturing	195	301	256
非金属矿物制品业	Nonmetal Mineral Products Manufacturing	53 497	245 917	159 404
黑色金属冶炼及压延加工业	Ferrous Metals Smelting and Rolling	177 170	1 004 981	318 338
有色金属冶炼及压延加工业	Nonferrous Metals Smelting and Rolling	9 099	66 547	46 032
金属制品业	Metal Product Manufacturing	45 378	272 107	191 041
通用设备制造业	General Equipment Manufacturing	10 769	76 529	59 164
专用设备制造业	Special Equipment Manufacturing	4 058	15 642	11 252
交通运输设备制造业	Transportation Equipment Manufacturing	6 506	53 956	40 934
电气机械及器材制造业	ElectricMachine and Equipment Manufacturing	647	3 830	2 822
废弃资源和废旧材料回收加工业	Abandon Resources and Discard Material Recovery Processing	2 155	8 013	5 388
仪器仪表及文化、办公用机械制造	Apparatus, Appearance, Culture and Handle Official Bussiness Machine Manufacturing	4 963	31 944	11 542
电力、煤气及水的生产和供应业	**Electricity, Gasand Water Productionand Supply**	**195 404**	**1 802 367**	**461 294**
电力、热力的生产和供应业	Electricity and Heat Production and Supply	188 809	1 737 996	452 187
燃气生产和供应业	Gass Production and Supply	3 462	30 267	3 823
水的生产和供应业	Water Production and Supply	3 133	34 105	5 284

Continued

(10 000 yuan)

# 应收账款净额 Net Amunt of Accounts Receivable	# 产成品 Finished Product	固定资产合计 Fixed Assets	累计折旧 Accumulated Depreciation	负债合计 Total Liabilities	# 流动负债合计 Liquid Liabilities	# 长期负债合计 Long-term Lialbilties	所有者权益合计 Creditors Equity	主营业务收入 Main Business Income
12 311	**14 888**	**262 001**	**58 681**	**341 242**	**224 599**	**111 904**	**229 214**	**181 713**
7 184	9 404	219 103	46 259	286 676	186 396	96 706	193 850	129 267
1 818	777	3 815	1 307	8 004	7 391	608	3 716	11 934
851	1 474	31 433	5 120	29 726	16 297	12 425	24 745	21 140
2 458	3 233	7 651	5 995	16 836	14 516	2 166	6 904	19 371
563 013	**677 233**	**3 367 641**	**858 025**	**5 115 667**	**3 813 996**	**1 225 191**	**2 905 794**	**4 845 612**
28 466	150 939	251 194	90 486	596 640	554 385	39 882	351 680	874 589
208 821	196 485	472 904	163 266	995 011	861 793	112 417	399 840	646 799
22 994	23 100	122 746	55 187	171 060	147 776	3 006	205 871	287 593
35 720	60 211	519 983	129 321	621 063	419 970	194 267	368 580	660 157
2 834	153	384	61	4 658	4 658		859	5 102
173	191	577	565	624	424	200	1 048	7 725
5 315	6 504	36 174	15 690	44 752	37 366	3 089	34 718	60 234
190	1 422	3 553	2 415	3 273	3 028	234	4 692	6 362
5 082	13 025	78 863	20 348	212 119	116 202	94 832	47 963	110 054
94 687	43 316	1 091 300	129 308	1 239 300	738 778	499 265	628 317	958 351
7 265	14 922	16 340	7 842	45 776	42 641	3 135	14 377	31 213
11 535	31 672	147 620	12 033	170 802	98 026	60 836	82 625	215 103
228		42	9	199	199		102	673
29 758	46 442	71 667	42 385	120 625	117 063	1 123	124 174	208 916
49 007	18 265	424 508	159 440	476 525	297 409	174 212	527 015	435 113
4 431	6 856	18 024	5 411	49 118	46 674	2 445	16 428	60 818
2 087	42 649	66 066	9 016	225 719	215 819	9 900	46 358	154 722
35 845	5 820	16 731	6 918	49 592	47 178	2 311	26 634	49 545
3 788	4 283	3 763	3 154	10 507	9 185	1 321	5 127	14 655
13 176	8 771	12 127	2 518	45 187	39 057	5 968	8 719	39 018
208	11	995	184	4 868	3 864	1 000	−1 039	6 654
1 413	2 198	2 625	1 986	4 416	4 416		3 597	5 285
−7		9 456	484	23 835	8 087	15 749	8 109	6 933
46 333	**1 414**	**1 025 000**	**374 878**	**1 213 979**	**459 276**	**747 874**	**587 228**	**504 752**
45 205	1 186	984 970	355 798	1 178 370	437 498	734 044	558 466	491 224
218	229	20 550	8 530	23 853	15 953	7 900	6 413	7 619
910		19 479	10 550	11 755	5 825	5 930	22 349	5 909

10—13 续表 3

计量单位:万元 （2010 年）

指　　标	Item	主营业务成　本 Main Business Cost	主营业务税金及附加 Main Business Tax and Affixture	其他业务利　润 Profits of Other Business	营　业费　用 Operation Expenses
按工业行业分	**Grouped by Sector**				
采矿业	**Mining**	**101 636**	**4 608**	**853**	**4 336**
煤炭开采和洗选业	Coal Mining and Dressing	69 020	3 496	514	2 140
黑色金属矿采选业	Ferrous Metals Mining and Dressing	9 526	326		256
有色金属矿采选业	Nonferrous Metals Mining and Dressing	9 993	279	124	615
非金属矿采选业	Nonmetal Mineral Mining and Dressing	13 097	508	215	1 325
制造业	**Manufacturing**	**3 915 974**	**41 938**	**23 846**	**201 620**
农副食品加工业	Farm and Sideline Food Processing	737 953	2 277	8 167	33 607
食品制造业	Food Manufacturing	571 073	1 168	2 283	44 881
饮料制造业	Beverage Manufacturing	166 772	23 919	2 259	30 704
纺织业	Textile Industry	552 030	2 639	—253	18 270
木材加工及木、竹、藤、棕、草制品业	Timber Processing Wood Bamboo Rattan PalmFibre and Straw Products	4 479	13		392
家具制造业	Furniture Manufacturing	7 373	20		142
造纸及纸制品业	Paper Making and Paper Products	51 109	369	75	1 794
印刷业和记录媒介的复制	Printing Industry and Recording Media	3 952	8		93
石油加工、炼焦及核燃料加工业	Oil Processing,Coking Plant and Nuclear Elding Processing	88 805	224	684	2 387
化学原料及化学制品制造业	Chemical Materials and Chemical Products Manufacturing	740 575	5 749	2 050	22 420
医药制造业	Pharmaceuticals Manufacturing	21 169	431	135	3 721
化学纤维制造业	Chemical Fibre Manufacturing	183 910	564	1 734	6 772
塑料制品业	Plastic Products Manufacturing	599	2	15	12
非金属矿物制品业	Nonmetal Mineral Products Manufacturing	172 574	985	2 701	6 799
黑色金属冶炼及压延加工业	Ferrous Metals Smelting and Rolling	323 466	2 609	1 513	16 086
有色金属冶炼及压延加工业	Nonferrous Metals Smelting and Rolling	56 586	114	504	1 623
金属制品业	Metal Product Manufacturing	132 569	566	1 316	10 035
通用设备制造业	General Equipment Manufacturing	43 643	100	589	603
专用设备制造业	Special Equipment Manufacturing	11 625	48	76	567
交通运输设备制造业	Transportation Equipment Manufacturing	33 011	52		602
电气机械及器材制造业	ElectricMachine and Equipment Manufacturing	6 328	4		31
废弃资源和废旧材料回收加工业	Abandon Resources and Discard Material Recovery Processing	4 191	68		76
仪器仪表及文化、办公用机械制造	Apparatus,Appearance,Culture and Handle Official Bussiness Machine Manufacturing	2 180	11		6
电力、煤气及水的生产和供应业	**Electricity,Gasand Water Productionand Supply**	**395 597**	**2 532**	**1 497**	**8 509**
电力、热力的生产和供应业	Electricity and Heat Production and Supply	386 775	2 426	1 481	6 026
燃气生产和供应业	Gass Production and Supply	4 271	79		2 219
水的生产和供应业	Water Production and Supply	4 550	27	15	264

Continued

(10 000 yuan)

管理费用 Administrative Expenses	财务费用 Financial Expenses	# 利息支出 Intrest Exjpenditure	营业利润 Business Profits	利润总额 Total Profits	亏损企业亏损总额 Total Loss	利税总额 Total Profits and Taxes	本年应交增值税 Value Added Taxes Payable	全部就业人员年平均人数(人) Average Number of Employees (person)
22 274	**7 471**	**5 300**	**45 376**	**44 459**	**765**	**67 317**	**18 250**	**8 994**
18 153	6 586	4 473	33 849	32 488	765	50 070	14 086	7 079
458	218	171	989	983		1 861	553	340
1 302	414	403	8 329	8 450		11 569	2 841	379
2 360	253	253	2 209	2 539		3 816	770	1 196
164 029	**125 018**	**117 634**	**408 194**	**452 007**	**90 248**	**638 523**	**144 578**	**92 190**
37 117	13 373	12 577	62 790	66 005	9 233	80 177	11 896	11 975
20 331	27 820	23 109	−28 124	−29 006	63 707	−18 537	9 301	10 607
9 972	4 253	4 252	42 407	48 302	5 216	86 439	14 219	5 462
19 294	14 233	12 625	51 554	70 168	4 407	97 089	24 283	22 092
126	3	2	133	133	21	251	105	117
112	32	17	45	64	6	116	31	75
2 970	253	687	3 333	5 259	1 237	7 626	1 998	2 280
600	42	42	579	627		703	68	269
4 739	3 821	3 846	9 908	10 423	125	15 210	4 563	2 385
15 267	37 687	37 227	134 096	135 658	4 450	167 891	26 484	10 931
3 531	700	697	3 086	3 120		5 599	2 048	1 227
3 176	6 940	6 776	15 868	15 868		23 350	6 918	1 975
34	4	4	42	42		60	16	38
8 619	2 184	2 159	22 239	20 096	354	23 854	2 772	5 254
29 971	11 220	11 246	67 655	82 262		114 769	29 899	11 494
1 594	812	717	−28	84	1 127	1 610	1 411	991
751	200	216	9 690	9 823		17 478	7 089	1 779
1 378	595	565	4 199	4 087		4 775	588	1 227
1 363	93	93	926	949	50	1 324	326	609
2 231	195	226	3 085	3 379	14	3 804	373	1 120
338	256	256	−301	−300	300	−275	21	73
202	74	70	821	819		958	70	176
316	228	228	4 192	4 146		4 255	98	34
26 950	**34 907**	**34 929**	**44 568**	**47 555**	**4 605**	**76 633**	**26 546**	**11 253**
25 722	34 533	34 540	44 180	47 172	4 414	75 615	26 017	10 801
686	164	164	385	381		695	235	168
542	210	225	3	2	191	322	293	284

10—14 规模以上工业企业主要经济效益指标

（2010 年）

指 标	Item	工业经济效益综合指数 Comprehensive Index of industry Economic Results	总资产贡献率（%） Ratio of Total Assets to Industrial Output Value （%）
总 计	**Total**	**195.73**	**9.02**
# 国有控股企业	State-controlled Shareholding Enterprises	191.70	8.05
按登记注册类型分	**Grouped by Status of Registration**		
内资企业	Domestic Enterprises	194.43	8.98
国有企业	State-owned Enterprises	139.56	5.18
有限责任公司	Limited Liability Corporations	211.76	9.47
国有独资公司	State-owned Corporations with Private-Funds	403.02	14.30
其他有限责任公司	Other Limited Liability Corporations	209.49	9.37
股份有限公司	Share-holding Corporations Ltd.	205.44	8.57
私营企业	Private Enterprises	184.90	10.88
私营独资企业	Private-funded Enterprises	340.60	26.27
私营合作企业	Private Cooperative Enterprises	174.15	7.61
私营有限责任公司	Private Limited Liability Corporations	181.44	10.68
私营股份有限公司	Private Share-holding Corporations Ltd.	166.80	6.46
其他企业	Other Enterprises	252.69	17.12
港、澳、台商投资企业	Enterprises with Funds from Hong Kong, Macao and Taiwan	213.16	4.08
合资经营企业（港或澳、台）	Joint-Venture Enterprises(with funds from Hong Kong, Macao and Taiwan)	1 229.58	2.12
港、澳、台商独资经营企业	Enterprises with Funds from Hong Kong, Macao and Taiwan	249.65	6.71
外商投资企业	Foreign Funded Enterprises	258.78	13.09
中外合资经营企业	Joint-Venture Enterprises	339.04	14.60
中外合作经营企业	Cooperative Enterprises	187.86	10.97
外资企业	Foreign-Funded Enterprises	169.60	9.07
外商投资股份有限公司	Foreign-Funded Enterprises	152.45	16.28
按轻重工业分	**Grouped by Light & Heavy Industry**		
轻工业	Light Industry	163.79	8.35
重工业	Heavy Industry	229.98	9.48
按企业规模分	**Grouped by Size of Enterprises**		
大型企业	Large-Scale Enterprises	272.04	11.10
中型企业	Medium-Scale Enterprises	158.34	6.83
小型企业	Small-Scale Enterprises	205.30	10.12

Main Indicators on Economic Benefit of Industrial Enterprises above Designated Size

资本保值增值率(%) Ratio of Capital Hold and Rise (%)	资产负债率(%) Assets Liability Ratio (%)	流动资产周转次数(次/年) Number of Times of Annual Turnover Circulating Assets (times/year)	全员劳动生产率(元/人·年) Over Labor Productivity (yuan/person-year)	工业成本费用利润率(%) Ratio of Profits to Industrial Cost (%)	工业销售率(%) Ratio of Industrial Products Sold (%)	工业增加值率(%) Ratio of Value Added to GrossIndustrial Output Value (%)
138. 13	**64. 02**	**1. 27**	**137 058**	**10. 86**	**96. 70**	**27. 56**
125. 91	64. 20	1. 14	142 724	10. 08	98. 49	29. 21
138. 62	64. 25	1. 24	134 992	10. 93	97. 10	27. 60
136. 46	68. 32	1. 23	92 217	5. 37	102. 46	35. 78
139. 62	67. 78	1. 18	160 103	11. 66	96. 48	26. 01
530. 54	40. 62	1. 58	160 631	45. 62	91. 30	60. 54
135. 56	68. 37	1. 18	160 086	11. 31	96. 54	25. 55
117. 46	52. 62	1. 06	154 342	12. 15	98. 95	38. 69
204. 81	60. 02	1. 86	90 358	10. 41	95. 37	21. 49
514. 09	50. 29	2. 07	156 700	22. 57	91. 15	28. 05
167. 67	60. 73	0. 51	78 687	16. 48	80. 22	21. 39
191. 10	59. 57	1. 99	89 215	9. 92	95. 47	21. 31
408. 14	68. 18	1. 00	66 488	7. 23	98. 23	18. 12
138. 13	52. 20	1. 64	162 752	16. 97	95. 50	27. 44
248. 74	69. 11	0. 83	199 718	7. 08	52. 47	29. 32
8 103. 68	71. 25	0. 84	186 071	3. 34	20. 86	29. 00
118. 01	66. 22	0. 83	235 032	11. 79	119. 45	30. 00
111. 47	52. 48	4. 00	192 945	10. 24	102. 63	25. 70
113. 59	55. 00	5. 05	280 660	13. 70	102. 86	33. 48
118. 28	51. 86	4. 93	108 629	3. 48	100. 43	8. 98
106. 10	46. 68	2. 46	111 293	6. 20	103. 83	17. 38
107. 00	28. 95	2. 31	49 488	9. 48	98. 80	42. 34
138. 37	63. 89	1. 30	109 524	7. 09	95. 63	22. 02
137. 97	64. 10	1. 24	166 217	15. 08	97. 84	33. 41
125. 99	60. 40	1. 08	186 778	22. 62	99. 10	35. 10
131. 16	64. 29	1. 26	116 114	5. 67	97. 40	26. 05
170. 04	66. 98	1. 40	138 282	11. 49	94. 77	25. 33

10—14 续表 1

（2010 年）

指　　　标	Item	工业经济效益综合指数 Comprehensive Index of industry Economic Results	总资产贡献率（%） Ratio of Total Assets to Industrial Output Value（%）
按工业行业分	**Grouped by Sector**		
采矿业	**Mining**	**296.33**	**12.73**
煤炭开采和洗选业	Coal Mining and Dressing	299.00	11.35
黑色金属矿采选业	Ferrous Metals Mining and Dressing	187.65	17.34
有色金属矿采选业	Nonferrous Metals Mining and Dressing	592.55	21.97
非金属矿采选业	Nonmetal Mineral Mining and Dressing	187.02	17.14
制造业	**Manufacturing**	**191.73**	**9.40**
农副食品加工业	Farm and Sideline Food Processing	188.70	9.73
食品制造业	Food Manufacturing	73.16	0.33
饮料制造业	Beverage Manufacturing	320.60	24.06
纺织业	Textile Industry	174.89	11.04
木材加工及木、竹、藤、棕、草制品业	Timber Processing Wood Bamboo Rattan PalmFibre and Straw Products	238.06	4.57
家具制造业	Furniture Manufacturing	177.38	7.14
造纸及纸制品业	Paper Making and Paper Products	159.19	10.45
印刷业和记录媒介的复制	Printing Industry and Recording Media	178.56	9.36
石油加工、炼焦及核燃料加工业	Oil Processing, Coking Plant and Nuclear Elding Processing	182.95	7.30
化学原料及化学制品制造业	Chemical Materials and Chemical Products Manufacturing	281.22	10.98
医药制造业	Pharmaceuticals Manufacturing	164.37	10.47
化学纤维制造业	Chemical Fibre Manufacturing	250.53	11.66
塑料制品业	Plastic Products Manufacturing	162.85	21.06
非金属矿物制品业	Nonmetal Mineral Products Manufacturing	174.37	10.58
黑色金属冶炼及压延加工业	Ferrous Metals Smelting and Rolling	256.13	12.54
有色金属冶炼及压延加工业	Nonferrous Metals Smelting and Rolling	111.29	3.50
金属制品业	Metal Product Manufacturing	264.70	6.50
通用设备制造业	General Equipment Manufacturing	149.40	6.98
专用设备制造业	Special Equipment Manufacturing	135.86	9.05
交通运输设备制造业	Transportation Equipment Manufacturing	136.04	7.47
电气机械及器材制造业	ElectricMachine and Equipment Manufacturing	83.94	−0.48
废弃资源和废旧材料回收加工业	Abandon Resources and Discard Material Recovery Processing	229.42	12.83
仪器仪表及文化、办公用机械制造	Apparatus, Appearance, Culture and Handle Official Bussiness Machine Manufacturing	1 529.42	14.03
电力、煤气及水的生产和供应业	**Electricity, Gasand Water Productionand Supply**	**205.00**	**6.19**
电力、热力的生产和供应业	Electricity and Heat Production and Supply	206.45	6.34
燃气生产和供应业	Gass Production and Supply	283.92	2.84
水的生产和供应业	Water Production and Supply	115.81	1.60

Continued

资本保值增值率(%) Ratio of Capital Hold and Rise (%)	资产负债率(%) Assets Liability Ratio (%)	流动资产周转次数(次/年) Number of Times of Annual Turnover Circulating Assets (times/year)	全员劳动生产率(元/人·年) Over Labor Productivity (yuan/person-year)	工业成本费用利润率(%) Ratio of Profits to Industrial Cost (%)	工业销售率(%) Ratio of Industrial Products Sold (%)	工业增加值率(%) Ratio of Value Added to GrossIndustrial Output Value (%)
180.80	**59.80**	**1.39**	**142 402**	**32.76**	**94.72**	**64.64**
199.88	59.64	1.35	140 925	33.88	93.30	70.80
133.61	68.30	1.64	99 586	9.40	117.18	33.39
124.36	54.55	1.57	390 107	68.56	98.98	70.30
97.01	70.92	1.36	84 823	14.90	90.23	38.92
140.57	**63.57**	**1.28**	**132 071**	**10.26**	**96.59**	**24.39**
140.20	62.61	1.46	137 148	8.03	94.56	18.75
116.37	71.04	0.85	73 342	−4.37	88.18	11.91
135.40	45.38	1.46	222 331	22.82	97.94	40.63
167.21	62.48	1.53	78 296	11.62	105.51	26.99
1 221.76	84.28	1.00	47 598	2.66	97.14	10.61
373.29	33.71	6.06	51 112	0.84	100.00	4.95
125.30	56.24	1.60	79 093	9.37	93.35	27.62
222.73	41.09	1.77	69 085	13.38	98.31	29.14
123.63	81.25	1.36	133 150	10.45	100.81	27.97
130.41	66.33	1.41	235 961	16.63	100.04	25.71
110.36	76.10	0.79	105 552	10.72	78.98	29.15
160.91	66.10	2.21	218 824	7.90	95.28	19.24
138.13	66.12	2.63	51 434	6.43	100.00	30.46
124.49	49.05	1.31	101 822	10.57	100.94	25.23
160.86	47.42	1.37	154 141	21.61	98.41	37.69
109.21	73.81	1.32	91 821	0.14	96.94	15.10
363.36	82.95	0.81	255 073	6.84	78.16	22.98
135.28	64.80	0.84	87 766	8.84	95.46	20.11
126.57	67.17	1.30	66 630	6.95	94.04	27.57
161.35	83.75	0.95	58 085	9.38	115.92	25.11
140.58	127.12	2.36	88 577	−4.31	100.00	12.87
239.45	55.11	0.98	122 443	18.03	78.22	31.01
138.13	74.61	0.60	1 459 724	151.85	100.00	71.59
117.56	**67.35**	**1.09**	**173 646**	**10.21**	**99.05**	**48.71**
116.87	67.80	1.09	174 807	10.41	99.02	48.29
709.27	78.81	1.99	206 057	5.19	100.00	76.95
107.70	34.47	1.12	110 306	0.03	100.00	54.59

10—15 规模以上国有及国有控股工业企业数、总产值、销售产值及产销率
Number, Gross Output Value, Sale Value and Production-Sale Ratio of State-owned and State-Controlled Shareholding Industrial Enterprises above Designated Size

计量单位:万元 (2010 年) (10 000 yuan)

指 标	Item	企业单位数（个） Number of Enterprises (unit)	#亏损企业 Losses	工业总产值（当年价格） Gross Industrial Output Value (At Current Prices)
总 计	**Total**	**218**	**34**	**3 595 039**
按轻重工业分	**Grouped by Light & Heavy Industry**			
轻工业	Light Industry	112	22	1 514 293
重工业	Heavy Industry	106	12	2 080 746
按企业规模分	**Grouped by Size of Enterprises**			
大型企业	Large-Scale Enterprises	5	1	980 193
中型企业	Medium-Scale Enterprises	54	9	1 724 901
小型企业	Small-Scale Enterprises	159	24	889 945
按工业行业分	**Grouped by Sector**			
采矿业	**Mining**	**24**	**1**	**173 098**
煤炭开采和洗选业	Coal Mining and Dressing	14	1	140 905
黑色金属矿采选业	Ferrous Metals Mining and Dressing	4		6 623
有色金属矿采选业	Nonferrous Metals Mining and Dressing	1		2 906
非金属矿采选业	Nonmetal Mineral Mining and Dressing	5		22 665
制造业	**Manufacturing**	**167**	**27**	**3 026 957**
农副食品加工业	Farm and Sideline Food Processing	43	9	509 867
谷物磨制	Cereal Grain Grinding	7	2	21 694
饲料加工	Forage Processing	8	2	229 416
植物油加工	Plant Oil Processing	10	3	94 575
制 糖	Sugar Making	4		86 580
食品制造业	Food Manufacturing	29	8	376 734
液体乳及乳制品制造	Liquid Milk and Dairy Products Manufacturing	7		57 479
罐头制造	Canned Food Manufacturing	17	7	296 247
蔬菜、水果罐头制造	Vegetable and Fruit Canned Food Manufacturing	17	7	296 247
饮料制造业	Beverage Manufacturing	14	3	174 841
酒的制造	Liquor Brewing	13	3	172 315
软饮料制造	Soft Beverage Manufacturing	1		2 526
纺织业	Textile Industry	9		186 963
棉、化纤纺织及印染精加工	Cotton Chemical Fibre and Dying Fine Processing	8		173 784
木材加工及木、竹、藤、棕、草制品业	Timber Processing, Wood, Bamboo, Rattan, Palm Fibre and Straw Products	1		1 277
家具制造业	Furniture Manufacturing	1		630
造纸及纸制品业	Paper Making and Paper Products	2	1	21 005
造纸	Paper Making	2	1	21 005
印刷业和记录媒介的复制	Printing Industry and Recording Media	1		1 711
石油加工、炼焦及核燃料加工业	Oil Processing, Coking Plant and Nuclear Elding Processing	2		53 519
炼 焦	Coking Plant	2		53 519
化学原料及化学制品制造业	Chemical Materials and Chemical Products Manufacturing	14	2	972 018
基础化学原料制造	Basic Chemical Materials Manufacturing	3	2	122 264
合成材料制造	Complex Materials Manufacturing	3		826 508
医药制造业	Pharmaceuticals Manufacturing	4		43 203
化学纤维制造业	Chemical Fiber Manufacturing	2		182 816
纤维素纤维原料及纤维制造	Cellulose Material and Fibre Manufacturing	2		182 816
化纤浆粕制造	Chemical Fibre Pulp Manufacturing	1		80 367
人造纤维(纤维素纤维)制造	Artificial Cellulose Material and Fibre Manufacturing	1		102 449
塑料制品业	Plastic Products Manufacturing	14	2	88 874
塑料薄膜制造	Plastic Film Manufacturing	4		17 134
塑料板、管、型材的制造	Plastic Board Pipe and Structural Section Manufacturing	9	2	68 441
非金属矿物制品业	Nonmetal Mineral Products Manufacturing	21		366 717
水泥、石灰和石膏的制造	Cement Lime and Gypsum Manufacturing	14		322 401
水泥制造	Cemen Manufacturing	14		322 401
金属制品业	Metal Product Manufacturing	4		28 344
通用设备制造业	General Equipment Manufacturing	1	1	598
专用设备制造业	Special Equipment Manufacturing	4	1	10 907
废弃资源和废旧材料回收加工业	Abandon Resources and Discard Material Recovery Processing	1		6 933
电力、煤气及水的生产和供应业	**Electric Power Gas and Water Production and Supply**	**27**	**6**	**394 984**
电力、热力的生产和供应业	Electricity and Heat Production and Supply	24	5	389 245
电力生产	Electricity Production	13	3	283 334
火力发电	Coal-Fired Generation	8	2	244 076
热力生产和供应	Heat Production and Supply	4		9 932
水的生产和供应业	Water Production and Supply	3	1	5 739

10—15 续表1 Continued

计量单位:万元 (2010年) (10 000 yuan)

指标	Item	工业销售产值(当年价格) Sale Value of Industry (At Current Prices)	#出口交货值 Export Commodities	产销率(%) Ratio of Production & Marketing (%)
总 计	**Total**	**3 540 618**	**263 292**	**98.49**
按轻重工业分	**Grouped by Light & Heavy Industry**			
轻工业	Light Industry	1 464 821	194 337	96.73
重工业	Heavy Industry	2 075 797	68 955	99.77
按企业规模分	**Grouped by Size of Enterprises**			
大型企业	Large-Scale Enterprises	976 525	3 622	99.63
中型企业	Medium-Scale Enterprises	1 729 692	214 427	100.28
小型企业	Small-Scale Enterprises	834 401	45 243	93.76
按工业行业分	**Grouped by Sector**			
采矿业	**Mining**	**160 777**		**92.91**
煤炭开采和洗选业	Coal Mining and Dressing	131 468		93.30
黑色金属矿采选业	Ferrous Metals Mining and Dressing	6 519		98.43
有色金属矿采选业	Nonferrous Metals Mining and Dressing	2 671		91.91
非金属矿采选业	Nonmetal Mineral Mining and Dressing	20 119		88.80
制造业	**Manufacturing**	2 988 682	263 292	98.73
农副食品加工业	Farm and Sideline Food Processing	493 510	855	94.73
谷物磨制	Cereal Grain Grinding	21 662		98.65
饲料加工	Forage Processing	233 913		101.96
植物油加工	Plant Oil Processing	69 521		73.51
制 糖	Sugar Making	89 890	855	103.82
食品制造业	Food Manufacturing	342 724	187 274	93.78
液体乳及乳制品制造	Liquid Milk and Dairy Products Manufacturing	55 611		96.75
罐头制造	Canned Food Manufacturing	266 345	179 134	93.41
蔬菜、水果罐头制造	Vegetable and Fruit Canned Food Manufacturing	266 345	179 134	93.41
饮料制造业	Beverage Manufacturing	176 613		100.93
酒的制造	Liquor Brewing	174 232		101.04
软饮料制造	Soft Beverage Manufacturing	2 380		94.22
纺织业	Textile Industry	206 584	5 610	110.49
棉、化纤纺织及印染精加工	Cotton Chemical Fibre and Dying Fine Processing	195 095	2 264	112.26
木材加工及木、竹、藤、棕、草制品业	Timber Processing, Wood, Bamboo, Rattan, Palm Fibre and Straw Products	1 258		98.48
家具制造业	Furniture Manufacturing	630		100.00
造纸及纸制品业	Paper Making and Paper Products	19 070		90.67
造纸	Paper Making	19 070		90.79
印刷业和记录媒介的复制	Printing Industry and Recording Media	1 711		100.00
石油加工、炼焦及核燃料加工业	Oil Processing,Coking Plant and Nuclear Elding Processing	57 818	5 697	108.03
炼 焦	Coking Plant	57 818	5 697	108.03
化学原料及化学制品制造业	Chemical Materials and Chemical Products Manufacturing	972 747	63 258	100.08
基础化学原料制造	Basic Chemical Materials Manufacturing	123 967	3 622	101.39
合成材料制造	Complex Materials Manufacturing	826 765	59 636	100.03
医药制造业	Pharmaceuticals Manufacturing	33 731	598	78.07
化学纤维制造业	Chemical Fiber Manufacturing	174 001		95.18
纤维素纤维原料及纤维制造	Cellulose Material and Fibre Manufacturing	174 001		95.18
化纤浆粕制造	Chemical Fibre Pulp Manufacturing	66 193		82.36
人造纤维(纤维素纤维)制造	Artificial Cellulose Material and Fibre Manufacturing	107 808		105.23
塑料制品业	Plastic Products Manufacturing	94 986		106.88
塑料薄膜制造	Plastic Film Manufacturing	18 119		104.35
塑料板、管、型材的制造	Plastic Board Pipe and Structural Section Manufacturing	73 764		108.46
非金属矿物制品业	Nonmetal Mineral Products Manufacturing	364 208		99.32
水泥、石灰和石膏的制造	Cement Lime and Gypsum Manufacturing	320 374		99.37
水泥制造	Cemen Manufacturing	320 374		99.37
金属制品业	Metal Product Manufacturing	26 056		91.93
通用设备制造业	General Equipment Manufacturing	588		98.31
专用设备制造业	Special Equipment Manufacturing	15 515		142.25
废弃资源和废旧材料回收加工业	Abandon Resources and Discard Material Recovery Processing	6 933		100.00
电力、煤气及水的生产和供应业	**Electric Power Gas and Water Production and Supply**	**391 159**		**99.03**
电力、热力的生产和供应业	Electricity and Heat Production and Supply	385 420		99.02
电力生产	Electricity Production	278 943		96.30
火力发电	Coal-Fired Generation	239 685		95.60
热力生产和供应	Heat Production and Supply	9 839		99.07
水的生产和供应业	Water Production and Supply	5 739		100.00

10—16　规模以上国有及国有控股工业企业主要经济指标

计量单位:万元　　　　(2010年)

指　　标	Item	工业增加值（当年价） Added Value of Industry (At current Prices)	资产合计 Total Assets	流动资产合计 Circulating Assets	#应收账款净额 Net Amunt of Accounts Receivable
总　计	**Total**	**1 050 108**	**8 054 982**	**3 170 651**	**462 587**
按轻重工业分	**Grouped by Light & Heavy Industry**				
轻工业	Light Industry	307 753	2 590 609	1 430 993	236 166
重工业	Heavy Industry	742 355	5 464 373	1 739 658	226 421
按企业规模分	**Grouped by Size of Enterprises**				
大型企业	Large-Scale Enterprises	357 885	2 647 087	946 508	96 514
中型企业	Medium-Scale Enterprises	459 021	3 601 594	1 466 981	237 505
小型企业	Small-Scale Enterprises	233 202	1 806 301	757 162	128 568
按工业行业分	**Grouped by Sector**				
采矿业	**Mining**	**111 244**	**524 945**	**111 103**	**10 639**
煤炭开采和洗选业	Coal Mining and Dressing	99 761	480 666	95 678	7 184
黑色金属矿采选业	Ferrous Metals Mining and Dressing	2 022	4 548	1 595	605
有色金属矿采选业	Nonferrous Metals Mining and Dressing	1 236	20 220	2 162	422
非金属矿采选业	Nonmetal Mineral Mining and Dressing	8 225	19 511	11 668	2 428
制造业	**Manufacturing**	**747 594**	**5 763 602**	**2 603 547**	**405 950**
农副食品加工业	Farm and Sideline Food Processing	101 959	599 005	372 921	12 674
食品制造业	Food Manufacturing	5 478	1 069 255	603 554	171 961
饮料制造业	Beverage Manufacturing	86 638	283 699	150 865	11 223
纺织业	Textile Industry	54 167	263 339	145 094	18 356
木材加工及木、竹、藤、棕、草制品业	Timber Processing, Wood, Bamboo, Rattan, Palm Fibre and Straw Products	390	1 630	1 253	43
家具制造业	Furniture Manufacturing	192	956	631	139
造纸及纸制品业	Paper Making and Paper Products	6 837	34 986	16 904	1 274
印刷业和记录媒介的复制	Printing Industry and Recording Media	866	2 801	1 315	309
石油加工、炼焦及核燃料加工业	Oil Processing, Coking Plant and Nuclear Elding Processing	16 173	243 143	73 012	3 172
化学原料及化学制品制造业	Chemical Materials and Chemical Products Manufacturing	250 169	1 824 605	653 554	87 049
医药制造业	Pharmaceuticals Manufacturing	12 544	57 199	37 219	7 265
化学纤维制造业	Chemical Fiber Manufacturing	31 752	236 820	91 078	10 933
塑料制品业	Plastic Products Manufacturing	17 257	152 099	111 063	15 292
非金属矿物制品业	Nonmetal Mineral Products Manufacturing	150 453	856 487	250 865	27 482
金属制品业	Metal Product Manufacturing	4 490	59 973	46 241	29 744
通用设备制造业	General Equipment Manufacturing	299	4 061	3 701	122
专用设备制造业	Special Equipment Manufacturing	2 968	41 600	32 737	8 919
废弃资源和废旧材料回收加工业	Abandon Resources and Discard Material Recovery Processing	4 963	31 944	11 542	−7
电力、煤气及水的生产和供应业	**Electric Power Gas and Water Production and Supply**	**191 271**	**1 766 434**	**456 002**	**45 998**
电力、热力的生产和供应业	Electricity and Heat Production and Supply	188 138	1 732 330	450 718	45 088
水的生产和供应业	Water Production and Supply	3 133	34 105	5 284	910

Main Economic Indicators of State-owned and State-controlled Shareholding Industrial Enterprises above Designated Size

(10 000 yuan)

# 产成品 Finished Product	固定资产合计 Fixed Assets	累计折旧 Accumulated Depreciation	负债合计 Total Liabilities	流动负债合计 Liquid Liabilities	# 长期负债合计 Long-term Lialbilties	所有者权益合计 Creditors Equity	主营业务收入 Main Business Income
473 872	**3 636 622**	**1 083 048**	**5 171 171**	**3 276 178**	**1 844 690**	**2 876 978**	**3 619 112**
350 414	851 524	354 632	1 717 987	1 462 942	218 726	868 350	1 516 520
123 458	2 785 098	728 416	3 453 184	1 813 236	1 625 964	2 008 628	2 102 592
12 049	1 168 736	235 077	1 600 112	852 830	736 669	1 046 975	976 939
267 825	1 546 944	632 696	2 300 365	1 582 678	691 849	1 296 143	1 813 053
193 998	920 942	215 275	1 270 694	840 670	416 172	533 860	829 120
12 990	**237 757**	**52 767**	**317 886**	**205 001**	**109 302**	**206 899**	**154 535**
9 404	219 103	46 259	286 676	186 396	96 706	193 850	129 267
598	2 577	834	2 987	2 377	608	1 561	6 623
256	9 752	100	15 585	3 597	11 988	4 615	2 671
2 733	6 325	5 575	12 638	12 632		6 873	15 974
459 696	**2 397 570**	**665 754**	**3 666 033**	**2 630 177**	**995 964**	**2 092 057**	**2 969 595**
111 082	146 516	67 852	369 751	344 104	25 468	227 843	519 166
149 727	324 550	131 776	792 708	682 164	109 138	276 546	389 612
13 868	81 298	34 459	127 583	107 249	1 042	156 117	162 896
26 284	102 427	74 133	176 980	160 758	12 719	83 679	201 147
22	369	51	800	800		830	1 260
177	326	476				777	614
1 645	17 440	11 777	17 364	17 141	223	17 622	18 707
	1 454	1 588	735	501	234	2 066	1 750
8 845	70 765	17 888	202 644	107 813	94 832	40 499	54 116
40 152	1 076 032	124 680	1 210 974	710 927	499 180	613 631	926 554
14 684	15 571	7 733	44 077	40 942	3 135	13 122	30 452
30 600	140 236	11 561	169 721	96 945	60 836	67 099	175 370
36 118	34 373	31 194	67 189	66 171	1 005	84 910	90 077
12 422	354 924	142 744	383 632	214 636	166 445	471 918	340 634
3 369	13 438	4 487	38 286	38 183		21 384	25 633
2 490	306	1 617	3 117	3 117		944	586
8 210	8 089	1 255	36 637	30 640	5 958	4 963	24 088
	9 456	484	23 835	8 087	15 749	8 109	6 933
1 186	**1 001 295**	**364 526**	**1 187 252**	**440 999**	**739 424**	**578 023**	**494 982**
1 186	981 815	353 977	1 175 497	435 174	733 494	555 673	489 073
	19 479	10 550	11 755	5 825	5 930	22 349	5 909

10—16 续表 1

计量单位:万元 (2010 年)

指　标	Item	主营业务成本 Main Business Cost	主营业务税金及附加 Main Business Tax and Affixture	其他业务利润 Profits of Other Business	营业费用 Operation Expenses
总　计	**Total**	**2 863 980**	**39 801**	**16 995**	**135 993**
按轻重工业分	**Grouped by Light & Heavy Industry**				
轻工业	Light Industry	1 263 141	24 992	8 782	87 542
重工业	Heavy Industry	1 600 839	14 809	8 213	48 451
按企业规模分	**Grouped by Size of Enterprises**				
大型企业	Large-Scale Enterprises	675 775	22 511	3 844	28 188
中型企业	Medium-Scale Enterprises	1 519 836	10 848	8 012	75 347
小型企业	Small-Scale Enterprises	668 369	6 442	5 139	32 458
按工业行业分	**Grouped by Sector**				
采矿业	**Mining**	**86 587**	**4 140**	**729**	**3 658**
煤炭开采和洗选业	Coal Mining and Dressing	69 020	3 496	514	2 140
黑色金属矿采选业	Ferrous Metals Mining and Dressing	4 997	187		229
有色金属矿采选业	Nonferrous Metals Mining and Dressing	1 814	83		
非金属矿采选业	Nonmetal Mineral Mining and Dressing	10 756	374	215	1 289
制造业	**Manufacturing**	**2 387 967**	**33 213**	**14 773**	**126 394**
农副食品加工业	Farm and Sideline Food Processing	444 619	1 160	5 193	22 286
食品制造业	Food Manufacturing	363 135	669	613	29 257
饮料制造业	Beverage Manufacturing	78 353	21 226	1 289	16 950
纺织业	Textile Industry	171 857	787	−284	7 500
木材加工及木、竹、藤、棕、草制品业	Timber Processing, Wood, Bamboo, Rattan, Palm Fibre and Straw Products	718	8		316
家具制造业	Furniture Manufacturing	488	5		25
造纸及纸制品业	Paper Making and Paper Products	16 821	128		609
印刷业和记录媒介的复制	Printing Industry and Recording Media	1 305	1		35
石油加工、炼焦及核燃料加工业	Oil Processing, Coking Plant and Nuclear Elding Processing	42 971	204	99	1 055
化学原料及化学制品制造业	Chemical Materials and Chemical Products Manufacturing	715 334	5 646	1 994	21 650
医药制造业	Pharmaceuticals Manufacturing	20 485	363	135	3 664
化学纤维制造业	Chemical Fiber Manufacturing	153 645	558	1 734	6 772
塑料制品业	Plastic Products Manufacturing	81 557	41	2 465	3 312
非金属矿物制品业	Nonmetal Mineral Products Manufacturing	249 630	2 339	1 262	12 407
金属制品业	Metal Product Manufacturing	23 530	38	273	87
通用设备制造业	General Equipment Manufacturing	499	2		68
专用设备制造业	Special Equipment Manufacturing	20 840	26		398
废弃资源和废旧材料回收加工业	Abandon Resources and Discard Material Recovery Processing	2 180	11		6
电力、煤气及水的生产和供应业	**Electric Power Gas and Water Production and Supply**	**389 427**	**2 448**	**1 493**	**5 942**
电力、热力的生产和供应业	Electricity and Heat Production and Supply	384 877	2 421	1 478	5 678
水的生产和供应业	Water Production and Supply	4 550	27	15	264

Continued

(10 000 yuan)

管理费用 Administrative Expenses	财务费用 Financial Expenses	# 利息支出 Interest Expenditure	营业利润 Operation Business Profits	利润总额（亏损为负） Total Profits as Negative	亏损企业亏损总额 Total Loss	利税总额 Total Profits and Taxes	本年应交增值税 Value Added Taxes Payable	全部就业人员年平均人数（人） Average Number of Employees (person)
156 524	**139 589**	**132 482**	**302 425**	**332 126**	**85 328**	**516 042**	**144 115**	**73 576**
60 907	45 698	41 092	23 660	33 558	75 547	103 061	44 511	29 656
95 617	93 891	91 390	278 765	298 568	9 781	412 981	99 604	43 920
32 414	45 556	44 979	177 507	183 740	4 164	251 069	44 818	15 669
85 591	66 121	61 297	57 966	72 932	70 060	156 843	73 063	40 919
38 519	27 912	26 206	66 952	75 454	11 104	108 130	26 234	16 988
20 648	**6 794**	**4 655**	**36 679**	**35 637**	**765**	**55 165**	**15 389**	**8 317**
18 153	6 586	4 473	33 849	32 488	765	50 070	14 086	7 079
206	69	43	735	735		1 080	158	231
169	−2	−2	604	604		1 061	374	46
2 119	142	142	1 491	1 810		2 954	770	961
109 803	**98 071**	**93 081**	**221 486**	**249 358**	**79 959**	**385 040**	**102 469**	**54 275**
25 593	7 564	7 161	24 838	28 437	6 492	38 448	8 851	6 921
12 793	23 460	19 081	−50 677	−50 333	62 986	−45 475	4 189	6 147
6 173	2 638	2 635	28 788	32 578	5 196	65 332	11 528	4 149
6 972	4 449	4 340	9 141	10 213		20 491	9 490	7 735
62	2	2	155	155		224	61	72
26	−1	−1	71	71		90	14	25
1 772	−243	197	−780	75	683	1 195	993	1 079
375	−2		185	184		198	12	137
4 285	4 086	4 111	1 555	2 072		5 213	2 936	2 034
13 948	37 202	36 622	130 330	131 880	4 387	163 758	26 231	10 320
3 339	642	639	3 054	3 089		5 500	2 048	1 164
2 813	6 940	6 776	6 768	6 768		14 066	6 740	1 654
3 445	1 049	1 075	3 575	3 841	150	5 259	1 377	2 455
25 264	9 541	9 668	57 776	73 352		103 122	27 431	8 913
866	312	309	1 227	1 230		1 488	220	657
268	40	40	−50	−50	50	−30	18	120
1 494	165	201	1 340	1 651	14	1 908	231	659
316	228	228	4 192	4 146		4 255	98	34
26 073	**34 724**	**34 746**	**44 260**	**47 132**	**4 605**	**75 837**	**26 257**	**10 984**
25 531	34 514	34 521	44 258	47 130	4 414	75 515	25 964	10 700
542	210	225	3	2	191	322	293	284

10—17　规模以上国有及国有控股工业企业主要经济效益指标

（2010 年）

指　标	Item	工业经济效益综合指数 Comprehensive Index of industry Economic Results	总资产贡献率（%） Ratio of Total Assets to Industrial Output Value（%）
总　计	**Total**	**191.70**	**8.05**
按轻重工业分	**Grouped by Light & Heavy Industry**		
轻工业	Light Industry	130.60	5.56
重工业	Heavy Industry	235.17	9.23
按企业规模分	**Grouped by Size of Enterprises**		
大型企业	Large-Scale Enterprises	300.30	11.18
中型企业	Medium-Scale Enterprises	147.21	6.06
小型企业	Small-Scale Enterprises	187.59	7.44
按工业行业分	**Grouped by Sector**		
采矿业	**Mining**	**280.65**	**11.40**
煤炭开采和洗选业	Coal Mining and Dressing	299.00	11.35
黑色金属矿采选业	Ferrous Metals Mining and Dressing	230.97	24.68
有色金属矿采选业	Nonferrous Metals Mining and Dressing	336.82	5.24
非金属矿采选业	Nonmetal Mineral Mining and Dressing	180.38	15.87
制造业	**Manufacturing**	**185.69**	**8.30**
农副食品加工业	Farm and Sideline Food Processing	179.86	7.61
食品制造业	Food Manufacturing	−4.27	−2.47
饮料制造业	Beverage Manufacturing	340.68	23.96
纺织业	Textile Industry	132.96	9.43
木材加工及木、竹、藤、棕、草制品业	Timber Processing, Wood, Bamboo, Rattan, Palm Fibre and Straw Products	161.69	13.84
家具制造业	Furniture Manufacturing	153.52	9.36
造纸及纸制品业	Paper Making and Paper Products	91.94	3.98
印刷业和记录媒介的复制	Printing Industry and Recording Media	137.82	7.06
石油加工、炼焦及核燃料加工业	Oil Processing, Coking Plant and Nuclear Elding Processing	111.91	3.83
化学原料及化学制品制造业	Chemical Materials and Chemical Products Manufacturing	285.42	10.98
医药制造业	Pharmaceuticals Manufacturing	165.77	10.73
化学纤维制造业	Chemical Fiber Manufacturing	205.62	8.80
塑料制品业	Plastic Products Manufacturing	111.26	4.16
非金属矿物制品业	Nonmetal Mineral Products Manufacturing	276.45	13.17
金属制品业	Metal Product Manufacturing	109.59	3.00
通用设备制造业	General Equipment Manufacturing	28.30	0.24
专用设备制造业	Special Equipment Manufacturing	111.70	5.07
废弃资源和废旧材料回收加工业	Abandon Resources and Discard Material Recovery Processing	1 527.79	14.03
电力、煤气及水的生产和供应业	**Electric Power Gas and Water Production and Supply**	**204.00**	**6.26**
电力、热力的生产和供应业	Electricity and Heat Production and Supply	207.26	6.35
水的生产和供应业	Water Production and Supply	115.81	1.60

Main Indicators on Enconomic Bendfit of State-owned and State-controlled Shareholding Industrial Enterprises above Designated Size

资本保值增值率(%) Ratio of Capital Hold and Rise (%)	资产负债率(%) Assets Liability Ratio (%)	流动资产周转次数(次/年) Number of Times of Annual Turnover Circulating Assets (times/year)	全员劳动生产率(元/人、年) Over Labor Productivity (yuan/person. year)	工业成本费用利润率(%) Ratio of Profits to Industrial Cost (%)	工业销售率(%) Ratio of Industrial Products Sold (%)	工业增加值率(%) Ratio of Value Added to Gross industrial Output Value(%)
125. 91	**64. 20**	**1. 14**	**142 724**	**10. 08**	**98. 49**	**29. 21**
112. 13	66. 32	1. 06	103 774	2. 30	96. 73	20. 32
132. 97	63. 19	1. 21	169 024	16. 24	99. 76	35. 68
125. 62	60. 45	1. 03	228 403	23. 50	99. 63	36. 51
116. 53	63. 87	1. 24	112 178	4. 17	100. 28	26. 61
157. 39	70. 35	1. 10	137 275	9. 83	93. 76	26. 20
194. 11	**60. 56**	**1. 39**	**133 754**	**30. 28**	**92. 88**	**64. 27**
199. 88	59. 64	1. 35	140 925	33. 88	93. 30	70. 80
125. 91	65. 68	4. 15	87 528	13. 36	98. 43	30. 53
131. 56	77. 08	1. 24	268 644	30. 52	91. 91	42. 53
112. 65	64. 77	1. 37	85 590	12. 65	88. 77	36. 29
124. 44	**63. 61**	**1. 14**	**137 742**	**9. 16**	**98. 74**	**24. 70**
124. 16	61. 73	1. 39	147 318	5. 69	96. 79	20. 00
96. 00	74. 14	0. 65	8 912	−11. 74	90. 97	1. 45
134. 58	44. 97	1. 08	208 816	31. 29	101. 01	49. 55
106. 54	67. 21	1. 39	70 029	5. 35	110. 49	28. 97
125. 91	49. 08	1. 01	54 109	14. 09	98. 48	30. 51
125. 91		0. 97	76 774	13. 13	100. 00	30. 47
86. 10	49. 63	1. 11	63 361	0. 39	90. 79	32. 55
103. 93	26. 24	1. 33	63 205	10. 74	100. 00	50. 62
110. 19	83. 34	0. 74	79 515	3. 95	108. 03	30. 22
128. 98	66. 37	1. 42	242 412	16. 73	100. 08	25. 74
100. 73	77. 06	0. 82	107 768	10. 98	78. 07	29. 04
130. 68	71. 67	1. 93	191 972	3. 98	95. 18	17. 37
100. 09	44. 17	0. 81	70 295	4. 30	106. 88	19. 42
153. 58	44. 79	1. 36	168 802	24. 71	99. 32	41. 03
113. 12	63. 84	0. 55	68 336	4. 96	91. 93	15. 84
94. 92	76. 75	0. 16	24 899	−5. 76	98. 31	49. 95
132. 09	88. 07	0. 74	45 036	7. 21	142. 25	27. 21
125. 91	74. 61	0. 60	1 459 722	151. 85	100. 00	71. 59
116. 57	**67. 21**	**1. 09**	**171 284**	**10. 33**	**99. 03**	**47. 63**
116. 96	67. 86	1. 09	175 830	10. 46	99. 02	48. 33
107. 70	34. 47	1. 12	110 306	0. 03	100. 00	54. 59

10－18　各师规模以上工业企业主要经济效益指标

Main Indicators on Economic Benefit of Industrial Enterprises above Designated Size by Division

（2010 年）

单　　位 Unit	工业经济效　益综合指数 Comprehensive Index of industry Economic Results	总资产贡献率（%） Ratio of Total Assets to Industrial Output Value (%)	资本保值增值率（%） Ratio of Capital Hold and Rise (%)	资　产负债率（%） Assets Liability Ratio (%)	流动资产周转次数（次/年） Number of Times of Annual Turnover Circulating Assets (rimes-/year)	全员劳动生产率（元/人、年） Over Labor Productivity (yuan/person-year)	工业成本费　用利润率（%） Ratio of Profits to Industrial Cost (%)	工　业销售率（%） Ratio of Industrial Products Sold (%)	工　业增加值率（%） Ratio of Value Added to Gross Industrial Output Value (%)
总　计 Total	**195.73**	**9.02**	**138.13**	**64.02**	**1.27**	**137 058**	**10.86**	**96.70**	**27.56**
一　师 Division 1	245.12	11.08	164.34	55.66	1.38	169 742	16.40	95.89	30.21
二　师 Division 2	213.33	10.36	202.31	70.15	1.19	145 546	12.13	90.92	31.78
三　师 Division 3	195.86	5.34	303.66	79.25	1.04	123 492	10.85	96.84	29.82
四　师 Division 4	310.01	19.08	135.05	55.31	1.34	186 887	27.91	99.48	44.68
五　师 Division 5	137.74	5.04	193.21	75.74	0.98	88 112	5.00	98.49	26.47
六　师 Division 6	205.00	7.16	143.31	67.35	1.07	173 205	9.30	89.24	27.44
七　师 Division 7	178.44	6.36	171.75	74.29	1.17	151 743	5.25	93.15	31.44
八　师 Division 8	203.21	9.98	128.85	61.79	1.42	132 295	12.79	99.40	26.19
九　师 Division 9	197.22	11.45	99.13	55.92	1.41	138 577	10.32	107.59	27.93
十　师 Division 10	232.72	12.15	166.14	57.12	1.38	127 298	19.37	92.84	44.58
建工师 Construction Division	146.94	11.35	88.98	73.38	2.04	80 302	5.92	108.84	25.87
十二师 Division 12	145.83	7.15	158.68	70.96	1.04	70 400	9.76	94.79	27.69
十三师 Division 13	216.28	15.67	134.59	64.34	1.66	108 779	16.69	96.40	38.58
十四师 Division 14	202.77	9.66	178.85	68.24	1.08	116 972	15.22	91.25	26.13
国资公司 State-owned Property Company	193.02	7.10	150.55	52.46	1.83	164 519	4.88	95.98	14.48
中基公司 Chalkis Company	－137.85	－6.95	67.95	81.74	0.56	－123 460	－22.22	101.51	－18.19
兵团直属 Directly under XPCG	171.26	10.20	111.89	46.81	4.35	93 883	3.84	100.41	10.95

10—19 各师规模以上国有及国有控股工业企业主要经济指标

Main Economic Indicators of State-owned and State-Controlled Shareholding Industrial Enterprises above Designated Division

计量单位:万元 (2010 年) (10 000 yuan)

单位	Unit	工业总产值(当年价格) Gross Industrial Output Value (atcurrent)	工业增加值(当年价) Added Value of Industry (At current Prices)	资产合计 Total Assets	固定资产合计 Fixed Assets	流动资产合计 Circulating Assets	负债合计 Total Liabilities	#流动负债合计 Liquid Liabilities	所有者权益合计 Creditors Equity	#国家资本 National Capital
总计	**Total**	**3 595 039**	**1 050 108**	**8 054 982**	**3 636 622**	**3 170 651**	**5 171 171**	**3 276 178**	**2 876 978**	**642 163**
一师	Division 1	491 670	154 636	1 123 313	506 564	325 660	588 101	295 385	534 275	70 005
二师	Division 2	192 520	63 182	326 079	128 060	171 746	236 471	196 134	89 608	49 995
三师	Division 3	44 384	12 801	131 770	90 458	41 312	110 525	36 608	21 245	22 555
四师	Division 4	357 941	168 193	627 634	245 518	277 527	351 897	228 090	275 736	61 375
五师	Division 5	78 383	24 425	274 689	134 968	128 279	212 527	152 946	62 162	20 172
六师	Division 6	146 727	58 998	569 074	210 683	197 272	369 499	199 330	199 435	129 848
七师	Division 7	227 007	74 015	550 524	300 294	199 442	408 840	225 959	141 684	65 472
八师	Division 8	1 398 752	403 310	3 132 163	1 645 502	1 128 211	1 972 357	1 196 800	1 154 360	119 621
九师	Division 9	43 667	13 475	70 590	26 832	39 570	39 843	36 320	30 747	33 200
十师	Division 10	44 198	22 778	99 718	69 708	28 015	57 834	26 660	41 884	20 730
建工师	Construction Division	13 600	4 025	6 097	3 588	2 336	2 782	2 774	3 315	158
十二师	Division 12	75 235	20 172	188 838	56 682	82 072	133 022	93 601	55 816	24 759
十三师	Division 13	39 845	16 945	59 482	28 775	19 396	38 679	22 374	20 782	13 588
十四师	Division 14	3 028	1 402	7 575	5 946	1 629	5 204	2 138	2 371	1 622
国资公司	State-owned Property Company	276 270	40 011	274 082	50 095	150 154	143 770	123 185	130 023	8 000
中基公司	Chalkis Company	160 101	−29 124	610 556	131 497	376 716	499 086	437 375	111 469	
兵团直属	Direcly under XPCG	1 711	866	2 801	1 454	1 315	735	501	2 066	1 064

单位	Unit	主营业务收入 Main Business Income	主营业务成本 Main Business Cost	主营业务税金及附加 Main Business Tax and Affixture	营业费用 Operation Expenses	管理费用 Administrative Expenses	营业利润 Business Profits	利润总额 Total Profits	利税总额 Total Profits and Taxes	就业人员年平均人数(人) Average Annual Exployees (Person)
总计	**Total**	**3 619 112**	**2 863 980**	**39 801**	**135 993**	**156 524**	**302 425**	**332 126**	**516 042**	**73 576**
一师	Division 1	454 978	361 027	3 745	13 645	21 417	55 275	65 743	98 664	8 558
二师	Division 2	157 377	112 441	1 645	13 867	12 807	13 706	10 091	21 570	4 685
三师	Division 3	33 777	29 204	25	107	1 685	2 792	2 801	3 826	890
四师	Division 4	342 873	214 435	18 412	16 367	17 569	64 886	69 951	109 103	9 182
五师	Division 5	114 990	103 581	338	1 444	3 502	5 656	5 623	8 620	2 822
六师	Division 6	132 220	94 182	638	7 010	10 683	12 522	13 371	20 712	4 305
七师	Division 7	225 859	180 391	1 176	11 371	7 468	11 965	11 597	21 746	4 902
八师	Division 8	1 452 927	1 141 250	10 710	40 747	46 370	157 741	170 816	233 220	25 029
九师	Division 9	49 985	43 176	183	1 159	3 229	3 928	4 732	7 235	941
十师	Division 10	40 178	29 190	648	1 794	3 632	5 828	6 020	8 768	2 359
建工师	Construction Division	11 300	9 019	76	697	578	1 660	1 666	2 271	170
十二师	Division 12	71 715	55 070	702	3 033	5 750	6 290	6 789	9 378	3 027
十三师	Division 13	39 578	28 389	874	1 781	2 143	6 190	6 200	9 608	1 721
十四师	Division 14	3 028	2 164	19	50	175	439	439	685	57
国资公司	State-owned Property Company	275 122	233 406	265	13 844	13 990	10 415	12 952	15 688	2 432
中基公司	Chalkis Company	211 456	225 750	345	9 044	5 154	−57 052	−56 846	−55 249	2 359
兵团直属	Direcly under XPCG	1 750	1 305	1	35	375	185	184	198	137

10—20 各师规模以上国有及国有控股工业企业主要经济效益指标

Main Indicators on Economic Benefit of State-owned and State-controlled Shareholding Industrial Enterprises above Designated Size by Division

(2010 年)

单 位 Unit		工业经济效益综合指数 Comprehensive Index of industry Economic Results	总资产贡献率(%) Ratio of Total Assets to Industrial Output Value(%)	资本保值增值率(%) Ratio of Capital Hold and Rise (%)	资产负债率(%) Assets Liability Ratio (%)	流动资产周转次数(次/年) Number of Times of Annual Turnover Circulating Assets (times/year)	全员劳动生产率(元/人·年) Over Labor Productivity (yuan/person-year)	工业成本费用利润率(%) Ratio of Profits to Industrial Cost (%)	工业销售率(%) Ratio of Industrial Products Sold (%)	工业增加值率(%) Ratio of Value Added to Gross Industrial Output Value(%)
总 计	**Total**	**191.70**	**8.05**	**125.91**	**64.20**	**1.14**	**142 724**	**10.08**	**98.49**	**29.21**
一 师	Division 1	247.08	10.32	158.78	52.35	1.40	180 692	15.86	95.81	31.45
二 师	Division 2	171.44	7.85	142.74	72.52	0.92	134 859	7.03	89.70	32.82
三 师	Division 3	187.19	3.73	259.91	83.88	0.82	143 828	8.72	92.77	28.84
四 师	Division 4	304.63	18.39	138.74	56.07	1.24	183 177	27.48	100.38	46.99
五 师	Division 5	132.17	4.87	169.77	77.37	0.90	86 552	4.96	100.32	31.16
六 师	Division 6	178.02	5.10	104.68	64.93	0.67	137 046	11.03	93.87	40.21
七 师	Division 7	176.67	6.57	145.97	74.26	1.13	150 990	5.42	104.03	32.60
八 师	Division 8	218.15	9.26	117.36	62.97	1.29	161 137	13.29	99.99	28.83
九 师	Division 9	196.15	10.37	104.70	56.44	1.26	143 194	9.93	109.52	30.86
十 师	Division 10	195.26	9.23	121.59	58.00	1.43	96 558	17.17	94.28	51.54
建工师	Construction Division	362.87	37.75	129.34	45.63	4.84	236 791	16.12	102.19	29.60
十二师	Division 12	139.83	6.06	144.26	70.44	0.87	66 639	10.29	93.06	26.81
十三师	Division 13	230.38	16.35	186.18	65.03	2.04	98 458	18.90	98.79	42.53
十四师	Division14	289.97	11.70	103.67	68.70	1.86	245 966	16.94	100.00	46.30
国资公司	State-owned Property Company	193.02	7.10	150.55	52.46	1.83	164 519	4.88	95.98	14.48
中基公司	Chalkis Company	−137.85	−6.95	67.95	81.74	0.56	−123 460	−22.22	101.51	−18.19
兵团直属	Directly under XPCG	137.80	7.06	103.93	26.24	1.33	63 205	10.74	100.00	50.62

10—21 个体工业主要指标

Main Indicators of Individual Industry

计量单位:万元 (2010 年) (10 000 yuan)

指 标	Item	户数(户) Household (household)	工业总产值 Gross Industrial (当年价格) (At Current Prices)	就业人员年平均人数(人) Average Annual Employee(person)
总 计	**Total**	**2 737**	**388 014**	**17 399**
按轻重工业分	**Grouped by Light & Heavy Industry**			
轻工业	LightIndutry	1 666	201 181	9 306
重工业	HeavyIndustry	1 071	186 833	8 093
按师分	**Grouped by Division of XPCG**			
一 师	Division 1	104	10 096	600
二 师	Division 2	110	12 964	816
三 师	Division 3	86	11 251	853
四 师	Division 4	358	26 709	1 902
五 师	Division 5	166	6 807	586
六 师	Division 6	584	167 909	4 992
七 师	Division 7	185	32 017	1 612
八 师	Division 8	518	37 859	1 892
九 师	Division 9	143	6 545	431
十 师	Division 10	118	14 489	456
建工师	Construction Division	17	361	66
十二师	Division 12	187	33 008	2 170
十三师	Division 13	95	27 216	893
十四师	Division 14	66	783	130

10—22 大中型工业企业主要指标

Main Indicators of Large-scale and Medium-scale Industrial Enterprises

计量单位:万元 (10 000 yuan)

指　　标	Item	2009	2010
企业单位数(个)	Number of Enterprises(unit)	68	80
# 亏损企业(个)	Loss(unit)	21	12
工业总产值(按当年价格计算)	Gross Industrial Output Value(atCurrantPrices)	2 554 044	3 403 231
工业销售产值(按当年价格计算生产法)	Sales Value of Industry Products(at Current Prices Produce Approach)	2 437 488	3 333 487
# 出口交货值	Delivery Value of Industry Export	122 352	219 457
流动资产小计	Circulating Assets	2 169 673	2 885 735
# 应收账款净额	Net Accounts Receivable	310 795	370 917
存　货	Stock	584 327	759 837
# 产成品	Finished Product	262 711	358 083
固定资产小计	Fixed Assets	2 662 366	3 202 209
固定资产原价	Original Fixed Assets	2 908 734	3 623 073
累计折旧	Accumulated Depreciation	755 252	939 997
资产总计	Total Assets	5 661 741	7 256 562
流动负债合计	Liquid Liabilities	1 988 989	2 890 730
长期负债合计	Long-term Liabilities8	1 579 143	1 621 337
负债合计	Total Liabilities	3 571 942	4 551 842
所有者权益合计	CreditorsEquity	2 089 447	2 693 034
主营业务收入	Main Business Income	2 503 001	3 454 382
主营业务成本	Main Business Cost	2 064 423	2 743 899
主营业务税金及附加	Main Business Tax and Affixture	24 470	35 605
其他业务利润	Profits of Other Business	11 005	12 131
营业费用	Operation Expenses	94 068	136 143
管理费用	Adiministrative Expenses	103 165	131 200
财务费用	Financial Expenses	94 617	121 692
# 利息支出	Intrest Exjpenditure	93 200	114 732
营业利润	Business Profits	146 167	290 912
补贴收入	Subsidy Income9	18 736	14 921
利润总额(亏损为负)	Total Profits(Negative as Loss)	176 115	328 606
# 应交所得税	Income Tax Payable	27 608	40 372
利税总额	Total Profits and Tax	291 370	505 540
本年应付工资总额	Total Wages Payable	155 950	245 131
本年应付福利费总额	Total Welfare Payable	5 359	6 847
本年应交增值税	Value Added Taxes Payable	103 860	141 330
本年进项税额	Receipt Tax	399 559	364 688
本年销项税额	Sale Tax	474 653	468 173
全部职工(就业人员)年平均人数(人)	Average Number of Staff and Workers(person)	61 394	72 330

10－23　大中型工业企业名录一览表

List of Industrial Enterprises by Type of Large-scale and Medium-scale Enterprises

（2010 年）

单　　位	Unit	规　模　Scale	行业类型	Sector　Type
新疆青松建材化工(集团)股份有限公司	XJ Qingsong Building Material and Chemical Industry Co.,Ltd.	大型 LargeScale	水泥制造	Cement Manufacturing
库车县科兴煤炭实业有限责任公司	Kuchen Kexin Coal Industry Co.,Ltd.	中型 Medium Scale	烟煤和无烟煤的开采洗选	Soft Coal and Hard Coal Mining and Dressing
新疆海龙化纤有限公司	XJ Hailong Chemcial Fibre Co.,Ltd.	中型 Medium Scale	人造纤维(纤维素纤维)制造	Artifical Textile Processing
一师电力公司	Division 1 Electricity Company	中型 Medium Scale	电力供应	Electricity Supply
新疆青松水泥有限责任公司	XJ Qingsong Cement Co.,Ltd.	中型 Medium Scale	水泥制造	Cement Manufacturing
阿拉尔新农棉浆有限责任公司	Alaer Xingnong Textile Co.,Ltd.	中型 Medium Scale	化纤浆粕制造	Textile Processing
二师三十六团石棉矿	Asbestos Minerals of Farm 36 Division 2	中型 Medium Scale	石棉、云母矿采选	Asbestos and Mica Minerals Mining and Dressing
二师华世丹药业股份有限公司	Division 2 Huashidan Drug Stock Co.,Ltd.	中型 Medium Scale	化学药品制剂制造	Chemical Drug Preparation Manufacturing
二师金川矿业有限公司	Division 2 Jinchuan Union Minerals Co.,Ltd.	中型 Medium Scale	烟煤和无烟煤的开采洗选	Soft Coal and Hard Coal Mining and Dressing
二师二十九团鸿盛纺织有限公司	Hingshen Textile Co.,Ltd. of Farm 29 Division 2	中型 Medium Scale	棉、化纤纺织加工	Cotton and Chemical Textile Processing
二师银纺棉业有限责任公司	Division 2 Yinfang Cotton Industry Co.,Ltd.	中型 Medium Scale	棉、化纤纺织加工	Cotton and Chemical Textile Processing
二师绿原糖业有限公司	Division 2 Luyuan Sugar Industry Co.,Ltd.	中型 Medium Scale	制糖	Sugar Making
图木舒克市前海棉纺织有限责任公司	Tumushuke Qianhai Textile Co.,Ltd.	中型 Medium Scale	棉、化纤纺织加工	Cotton and Chemical Textile Processing
四师电力公司	Division 4 Electricity Company	中型 Medium Scale	水力发电	Hydropower Generation
四师七十一团双新煤业集团公司	Shuangxin Coal Industry Co.,Ltd. of Farm 71 Division 4	中型 Medium Scale	炼焦	Coking
四师伊力特实业股份有限公司	Division 4 Yilite Industry Co.,Ltd.	大型 Large Scale	白酒制造	White Liquor Brewing
四师博乐南岗建材有限责任公司	Division 4 Bortala Nangang Building Materials Co.,Ltd.	中型 Medium Scale	水泥制造	Cement Manufacturing
四师伊犁南岗建材有限责任公司	Division 4 Yili Nangang Building Materials Co.,Ltd.	中型 Medium Scale	水泥制造	Cement Manufacturing
四师伊力特绿华糖业有限责任公司	Division 4 Yilite LuHua SugarIndustry Co.,Ltd.	中型 Medium Scale	制糖	Sugar Making
四师伊犁南岗化工有限责任公司	Division 4 Yili Nangang Chemical Industry Co.,Ltd.	中型 Medium Scale	无机盐制造	Inorganic Salt Manufacturing
五师电力公司	Division 5 Electricity Company	中型 Medium Scale	电力供应	Electricity Supply
新疆新赛精纺有限公司	Division 5 Bosai Textile Co.,Ltd.	中型 Medium Scale	棉、化纤纺织加工	Cottonand Chemical Textile Processing
五师新疆博乐新赛油脂有限公司	Division 5 Bole Xinsai Oil Co.,Ltd.	中型 Medium Scale	食用植物油加工	Edible Plant Oil Processing
六师大黄山煤矿	Division 6 Dahuangshan Coal Minerals	中型 Medium Scale	烟煤和无烟煤的开采洗选	Soft Coal and Hard Coal Mining and Dressing
五家渠中基制品有限责任公司	Wujiaqu Zhongji Product Stock Co.,Ltd.	中型 Medium Scale	蔬菜、水果和坚果加工	Canned Vegetable and Fruit Manufacturing
新疆光大山河化工科技有限公司	XJ Guangda Shanhe Chemical Engineering Technology	中型 Medium Scale	棉及化纤制品制造	Cotton and Chemical Textile Manufacturing
六师铝业有限责任公司	Division 6 Alumium Industry Co.,Ltd.	中型 Medium Scale	铝冶炼	Alumium Smelting
五家渠华孚有限公司	Wujiaqu Huafu Co.,Ltd.	中型 Medium Scale	棉、化纤纺织加工	Cotton and Chemical Textile Processing
新疆大黄山鸿基焦化有限责任公司	Dahuangshan Hongji Coking Co.,Ltd.	中型 Medium Scale	炼焦	Coking
新疆新光油脂有限公司	XJ Xinguang Oil Co.,Ltd.	中型 MediumScale	食用植物油加工	Edible Plant Oil Processing
新疆天达生物工程有限公司	XJ Tianda Biological Engineering Co.,Ltd.	中型 Medium Scale	味精制造	Gourmet Powder Manufacturing
呼图壁县万维纺织有限公司	Hutubi Wanwei Textile Co.,Ltd.	中型 Medium Scale	棉、化纤纺织加工	Cotton and Chemical Textile Processing
七师电力公司	Division 7 Electricity Industry Company	中型 Medium Scale	电力供应	Electricity Supply
七师柳沟红番茄制品有限公司	Division 7 Liugouhong Tomato Products Co.,Ltd.	中型 Medium Scale	蔬菜、水果罐头制造	Canned Vegetable and FruitManufacturing
七师伊犁特糖业有限公司	Division 7 Yilite Sugar Industry Co.,Ltd.	中型 MediumScale	制糖	Sugar Making
七师一三零团昌恒纺织有限责任公司	Changheng Textile Co.,Ltd. of Farm 130 Division 7	中型 Medium Scale	棉、化纤纺织加工	Cotton and Chemical Textile Processing
七师奎屯锦业纺织有限责任公司	Division 7 Huitun Jinye Textile Co.,Ltd.	中型 Medium Scale	棉、化纤纺织加工	Cotton and Chemical Textile Processing
七师奎屯天北矿业投资有限公司	Division 8 Huitun Tianbei Union Minerals Co.,Ltd.	中型 Medium Scale	烟煤和无烟煤的开采洗选	Soft Coal and Hard Coal Mining and Dressing
八师天业股份有限公司(母公司)	XJ Tianye Co.,Ltd.	大型 Large Scale	无机碱制造	Inorganic Alkali Manufacturing
八师石河子八棉纺织有限公司	Division 8 Eight-one Cotton Textile Co.,Ltd.	中型 Medium Scale	棉、化纤纺织加工	Cotton and Chemical Textile Processing

10—23 续表 Continued

(2010 年)

单 位	Unit	规 模 Scale	行业类型	Sector Type
八师白杨水泥制品有限责任公司	Division 8 Baiyang Cement Product Co. ,Ltd.	中型 Medium Scale	水泥制品制造	Cement Manufacturing
八师石河子南山水泥厂	Division 8 Shihezi South Mountain Cement Factory	中型 Medium Scale	水泥制造	Cement Manufacturing
八师石河子中发化工有限责任公司	Division 8 Shihezi Zhongfa Chemical Industry Co. ,Ltd.	中型 Medium Scale	初级形态的塑料及合成树脂制造	Early Class of Plastics and Synthesize Resin Manufacturing
八师如意毛纺织有限公司	Division 8 Ruyi Woolen Textile Co. ,Ltd.	中型 Medium Scale	毛纺织	Woolen Textile
八师石河子开发区天业化工有限责任公司	Shihezi Development Zones Tianye ChemicalIndustry Co. ,Ltd.	中型 Medium Scale	初级形态的塑料及合成树脂制造	Early Class of Plastics and Synthesize Resin Manufacturing
八师华兴玻璃有限公司	Division 8 Hnaxin Glass Co. ,Ltd.	中型 Medium Scale	日用玻璃制品及玻璃包装容器制造	Daily Use Glass Products and Glass Packing Container Manufacturing
八师爱立泽纺织有限公司	Division 8 Ailize Textile Co. ,Ltd.	中型 Medium Scale	棉、化纤纺织加工	Cotton and Chemical Textile Processing
八师石河子郑氏化纤有限公司	Division 8 Shihezi Zhengshi Chemcial Fibre Co. ,Ltd.	中型 Medium Scale	化纤浆粕制造	Textile Processing
八师唐成棉业有限公司	Division 8 Tangcheng Cotton Industry Co. ,Ltd.	中型 Medium Scale	棉、化纤纺织加工	Cotton and Chemical Textile Processing
八师石河子市义展纺织有限公司	Division 8 Shihezi Yizhan Textile Co. ,Ltd.	中型 Medium Scale	棉、化纤纺织加工	Cotton and Chemical Textile Processing
八师石河子天富南热电有限公司	Division 8 Shihezi XJ Tianfu South Thermoelectricity Co. ,Ltd	中型 Medium Scale	火力发电	Hydropower Generation
八师天富热电股份有限公司(母公司)	Division 8 Tianfu Thermoelectricity Co. ,Ltd	大型 Large Scale	火力发电	Hydropower Generation
八师天宏纸业股份有限公司(母公司)	Division 8 Tianhong Paper Industry Stock Co. ,Ltd.	中型 Medium Scale	机制纸及纸板制造	Machine-Made Paper and Paper Board Manufacturing
八师石河子市长运生化有限责任公司	Division 8 Shihezi Changyun Chemical Industry Co. ,Ltd.	中型 MediumScale	食品及饲料添加剂制造	Food and Forage Additive Manufacturing
八师石河子银河纺织有限责任公司	Division 8 Shihezi Yinhe Textile Co. ,Ltd.	中型 Medium Scale	棉、化纤纺织加工	Cotton and Chemical Textile Processing
八师康师傅(新疆)顶益方便面食品有限公司	Division 8 Kang Teacher Conveninent Noodles Food Co. ,Ltd.	中型 Medium Scale	方便面及其他方便食品制造	Convenient Food Manufacturing
八师石河子顶津食品有限公司	Division 8 Shihezi Dingjing Food Co. ,Ltd.	中型 Medium Scale	茶饮料及其他软饮料制造	Tea Beverage and Other Soft Beverage Manufacturing
八师天盛实业有限公司	Division 8 Tianshen Industry Co. ,Ltd.	大型 Large Scale	棉、化纤纺织加工	Cotton and Chemical Textile Processing
八师天业节水灌溉股份有限公司	Division 8 Tianye Water-Saving Irrigated Co. ,Ltd.	中型 Medium Scale	塑料板、管、型材的制造	Plastic Board,Pipe and Structural Section Manufacturing
八师天富煤业有限公司	Division 8 Tianfu CoalIndustry Co. ,Ltd.	中型 Medium Scale	烟煤和无烟煤的开采洗选	Soft Coal and Hard Coal Mining and Dressing
八师天宏新八棉产业有限公司	Division 8 Tianhong Eight Cotton Textile Co. ,Ltd.	中型 Medium Scale	棉、化纤纺织加工	Cotton and Chemical Textile Processing
八师石河子开发区天业热电有限责任公司	Division 8 Shihezi Development Zones Tianye Thermoelectricity Co. ,Ltd	中型 Medium Scale	火力发电	Hydropower Generation
八师石河子开发区青松天业水泥有限公司	Division 8 Shihezi Development Zones Qinsong Tianye CementCo. ,Ltd.	中型 Medium Scale	水泥制造	Cement Manufacturing
八师华芳石河子纺织有限公司	Division8 Huafang Shihezi Textile Stock Co. ,Ltd.	中型 Medium Scale	棉、化纤纺织加工	Cotton and Chemical Textile Processing
八师燕京啤酒有限公司	Division 8 Yanjing Beer Co. ,Ltd.	中型 Medium Scale	啤酒制造	Beer Manufacturing
八师石河子天富农电有限责任公司	Division 8 Tianfu Agriculture Thermoelectricity Co. ,Ltd	中型 Medium Scale	电力供应	Electricity Supply
八师天业天辰化工有限公司	Division 8 Tianye Tianchen Chemical Industry Co. ,Ltd.	大型 Large Scale	初级形态的塑料及合成树脂制造	Early Class of Plastics and Synthesize Resin Manufacturing
新疆绿翔糖业有限责任公司	XJ Luxiang Sugar Industry Co. ,Ltd.	中型 Medium Scale	制糖	Sugar Making
十师电力工业有限公司	Division 10 Electricity Company	中型 Medium Scale	水力发电	Hydropower Generation
新疆屯南煤业有限责任公司	XJ Tunnan CoalIndustry Co. ,Ltd.	中型 Medium Scale	烟煤和无烟煤的开采洗选	Soft Coal and Hard Coal Mining and Dressing
十二师天润乳业生物制品有限公司	Division 12 Milk Industry Biology Product Stock Co. ,Ltd.	中型 Medium Scale	液体乳及乳制品制造	Liquid Milk and Dairy Products Manufacturing
十二师芳婷针纺织有限公司	Division 12 Fangtin Knit Textile Co. ,Ltd.	中型 Medium Scale	棉、化纤针织品及编织品制造	Cotton and Chemical Fabrics and Products Manufacturing
十二师昌平矿业有限责任公司	Division 12 Changpin Minerals Industr yCo. ,Ltd.	中型 Medium Scale	烟煤和无烟煤的开采洗选	Soft Coal and Hard Coal Mining and Dressing
十三师红山煤业总厂	Division 13 Hongshan Coal Minerals	中型 Medium Scale	烟煤和无烟煤的开采洗选	Soft Coal and Hard Coal Mining and Dressing
哈密红山化工有限责任公司	Hami Hongshan Chemical Industry Co. ,Ltd.	中型 Medium Scale	无机盐制造	Inorganic Salt Manufacturing
新疆红星科健镁合金有限公司	XJ Hongxin Kejian Magnesium Alloys Co. ,Ltd.	中型 Medium Scale	镁冶炼	Magnesium Smelting
河南宏展实业有限责任公司	Henan Hongzhan Industry Co. ,Ltd.	中型 Medium Scale	饲料加工	Forage Processing
新疆天康畜牧生物技术股份有限公司	XJ Tiankang Livestock Biology Stock Co. ,Ltd.	中型 Medium Scale	饲料加工	Forage Processing
新疆中基番茄制品有限责任公司	XJ Chalkis Tomato Products Co. ,Ltd.	中型 Medium Scale	蔬菜、水果罐头制造	Canned Vegetable and fruit Manufacturing
天津中辰番茄制品有限责任公司	Tianjin Zhongchen Tomato Products Ltd. Co.	中 型 Medium Scale	蔬菜、水果罐头制造	Canned Vegetable and fruit Manufacturing

10—24　主要年份工业主要产品产量

Output of Major Industrial Products in Major Years

年　份 Year	原　煤 （吨） Coal （ton）	石　棉 （吨） Asbestos （ton）	大　米 （吨） Rice （ton）	小麦粉 （吨） Wheat Flour （ton）	食用植物油 （吨） Edible Vegetable Oil（ton）	机制糖 （吨） Mechine-made Sugar （ton）	乳制品 （吨） Dairy Products （ton）	罐　头 （吨） Canned Food （ton）
1952	114 988		624	2 249	73			
1954	172 498		5 440	19 695	834			
1957	437 310		7 689	55 020	4 115			
1962	1 400 893	45	6 104	71 637	2 878	3 754	180	
1965	2 109 957	118	11 310	128 506	7 298	21 095	79	
1970	3 358 500	5 396	25 520	277 448	7 263	19 391	186	
1975	1 221 653	7 293	21 704	76 124	2 010	410	88	
1978	2 231 556	6 742	48 660	188 020	6 438	18 965	119	
1980	2 487 251	11 524	45 898	260 252	13 930	38 734	247	
1985	3 470 200	17 223	101 219	300 037	36 659	51 455	1 442	2 802
1990	3 430 868	29 503	101 488	308 284	46 922	57 764	6 566	22 519
1995	3 045 604	23 122	83 893	298 271	94 443	108 931	3 606	33 674
1996	3 241 383	44 959	110 434	355 400	119 549	144 392	2 904	38 457
1997	3 267 857	45 749	90 861	210 600	106 814	172 767	3 094	35 337
1998	3 361 853	43 629	123 035	218 500	118 221	202 187	1 979	58 732
1999	3 578 650	45 408	74 023	235 600	175 129	192 253	1 812	64 121
2000	3 359 203	48 297	89 859	200 000	188 294	106 382	1 828	118 115
2001	3 369 597	39 441	96 004	219 700	160 783	133 361	3 264	81 253
2002	3 712 242	36 717	68 027	291 000	157 100	135 424	4 422	209 296
2003	3 827 877	54 001	78 615	257 800	170 243	141 312	22 394	246 229
2004	4 022 989	72 901	83 856	220 754	195 112	132 153	18 000	349 193
2005	3 678 606	65 127	62 556	228 301	183 453	153 181	28 270	244 885
2006	3 802 198	67 066	70 995	221 239	193 055	163 530	36 806	368 127
2007	3 680 162	67 607	92 225	224 882	206 789	215 862	54 555	462 234
2008	6 118 672	52 578	83 365	173 797	231 440	183 140	63 441	413 255
2009	6 785 468	70 021	88 010	200 273	321 172	138 751	72 774	694 945
2010	9 258 299	73 010	78 849	224 662	307 264	172 356	96 244	675 695

年　份 Year	味　精 （吨） Monosodium Glutamate （ton）	饮料酒 （吨） Beverage Wine （ton）	#白　酒 White Spirit	饲　料 （吨） Forage （ton）	纱 （吨） Yarn （ton）	布 （万米） Cloth （10 000 m）	呢　绒 （万米） Woolen Goods （10 000 m）	服　装 （万件） Garments （10 000 pieces）
1952					458	330		
1954								
1957								
1962		1 639	1 082		4 704	2 935		136
1965		1 103	1 103		9 180	4 644	63	127
1970		1 729	1 729		14 365	7 235	110	
1975		1 369	1 186		8 737	104	99	
1978		2 965	2 682		8 164	4 237	93	35
1980	62	6 048	5 130		9 434	4 179	117	36
1985	328	23 564	11 570	32 485	15 473	6 326	250	42
1990	1 229	28 022	19 201	95 021	38 481	9 676	322	97
1995	3 138	35 496	24 243	177 178	77 636	11 389	307	450
1996	3 790	30 736	25 243	173 703	79 820	11 740	331	413
1997	4 806	43 287	37 381	188 759	94 173	12 129	274	365
1998	5 219	46 472	42 322	175 732	79 773	10 667	259	230
1999	5 059	50 514	46 420	204 982	110 702	11 348	195	342
2000	3 901	56 041	45 870	230 703	121 422	12 690	127	337
2001	2 781	53 683	43 805	281 683	108 206	12 080	103	347
2002	2 132	53 304	43 308	273 454	106 380	8 913	141	396
2003	2 615	51 352	27 139	285 113	113 048	8 237	99	441
2004	2 300	41 709	27 905	322 014	111 769	9 073	101	367
2005	1 702	40 618	26 176	359 075	129 765	8 371	134	393
2006	2 417	43 613	28 426	404 414	137 192	7 865	164	363
2007	25	85 647	35 040	475 142	169 995	7 346	184	230
2008	1 900	102 124	30 625	567 810	171 880	6 896	207	199
2009	15 913	85 185	36 164	1 019 585	197 163	8 577	214	359
2010	20 910	149 712	42 969	1 083 029	225 210	8 974	172	384

注：从 2003 年起，饮料酒与白酒执行新的计量单位：千升。

Note: Since 2003 beverage wine and white spirit are carried out new calculationUnit: 1000 Liter.

10－24 续表 1 Continued

年份 Year	皮鞋（双） Leather Shoes (pair)	人造板（立方米） Artificial Board (cu. m)	机制纸及纸板（吨） Machine-made Paper and Paper-boards (ton)	发电量（万千瓦时） Electricity (10 000kwh)	#水电 Hydro-power	焦炭（吨） Coke (ton)	硫酸（吨） Sulfuric Acid (ton)	烧碱（吨） Caustic Soda (ton)
1952	3 100			152		8 808		
1954	3 100			134				
1957	22 900			374				
1962	274 931		2 500	5 289	1 458	96 534	1 722	147
1965	194 129		6 739	8 804	4 018	78 200	4 382	563
1970	286 900		8 387	19 712	14 081	140 236	7 151	901
1975	79 900		880	10 785	8 024	16 714	7 889	454
1978	115 876		7 250	25 425	16 283	135 991	2 516	1 352
1980	208 583		14 797	24 244	14 743	65 895	6 907	1 121
1985	347 800	4 162	25 122	34 516	22 456	85 400	9 328	1 972
1990	415 029	11 024	43 248	70 384	38 189	105 775	13 945	7 479
1995	163 300	16 812	61 507	116 385	48 757	158 828	24 911	10 087
1996	123 300	6 917	53 683	129 717	50 944	121 062	32 917	12 206
1997	66 200	6 566	55 816	144 314	55 641	132 423	27 904	16 442
1998	45 700	4 222	56 661	156 839	56 181	81 089	29 104	16 045
1999	54 900	5 035	49 005	169 883	59 323	100 247	33 817	18 750
2000	40 000	1 424	49 893	178 745	58 050	130 414	34 852	20 257
2001	71 700	1 358	45 796	179 445	62 055	150 505	37 293	26 064
2002	20 600	610	56 600	191 905	63 060	174 121	34 705	33 965
2003	26 000	5 525	65 929	211 594	64 887	212 500	40 285	47 503
2004	9 700	10 339	66 854	256 317	65 148	265 016	47 855	56 192
2005	1 300	368	63 310	360 926	68 229	329 425	69 419	158 231
2006	6 800	4 760	86 993	478 980	71 501	423 818	65 988	215 416
2007	4 900	65 083	53 813	548 057	92 387	654 022	66 026	231 955
2008		8 740	60 380	756 605	93 887	644 057	80 288	302 270
2009	800	19 196	134 531	1 140 950	94 034	625 903	112 739	451 851
2010	1 100	15 839	127 026	1 348 687	102 408	1 676 530	90 539	505 264

年份 Year	农用化肥（吨） Farm Chemical Ferrilizer (ton)	酒精（吨） Alcohol (ton)	塑料制品（吨） Plastic Products (ton)	水泥（吨） Cement (ton)	砖（万块） Brick (10 000 piece)	钢（吨） Steel (ton)	钢材（吨） Steel Products (ton)	改装汽车（辆） Modified Truck (unit)
1952					2 994	705	618	
1954					7 538			
1957					14 911			
1962	1 643	243		4 421	5 676	1 974	2 199	
1965	4 099	2 154		87 530	27 714	2 647	2 009	
1970	12 842	1 729		104 963	18 741	10 298	5 152	107
1975	3 026	1 503		2 800	3 854	13 090	5 466	192
1978	16 593	1 287		76 620	29 134	10 425	9 009	263
1980	1 249	3 188		150 015	58 489	10 465	7 701	425
1985	6 036	3 364	3 126	549 700	117 797	18 620	13 547	1 007
1990	7 449	4 442	9 216	787 995	117 247	25 034	20 880	749
1995	2 708	16 814	28 281	1 133 672	143 609	21 121	16 577	225
1996	5 340	18 608	37 541	1 283 000	139 001	19 585	16 562	164
1997	17 946	18 385	43 172	1 362 000	156 385	9 541	7 493	50
1998	19 254	21 550	51 595	1 552 400	158 205	14 890	15 404	137
1999	20 695	24 433	47 614	1 586 100	179 070	12 849	11 127	125
2000	12 295	10 355	67 712	1 690 000	188 493			121
2001	25 838	11 744	108 657	1 944 600	181 088			
2002	19 187	11 224	84 742	2 282 300	161 291			
2003	13 585	15 070	116 694	2 535 600	148 229			1
2004	9 612	12 957	148 549	2 710 637	148 661			
2005	16 313	11 064	148 197	2 936 374	146 527			
2006	13 485	7 917	175 474	3 895 625	163 241			
2007	7 707	7 587	230 318	4 426 243	149 723			
2008	31 068	8 592	233 440	5 336 441	139 128			
2009	17 416	7 000	259 075	7 057 155	179 967	26 255	52 858	152
2010	11 528	5 193	314 388	9 668 886	205 101	17 219	69 901	136

10—25　工业主要产品产量
Output of Major Industrial Products

指　　标		Item		2010
原煤	（吨）	Coal	（ton）	9 258 299
小麦粉	（吨）	Wheate Flour	（ton）	224 662
大米	（吨）	Rice	（ton）	78 849
配混合饲料	（吨）	Forage	（ton）	1 083 029
食用植物油	（吨）	Edible Vegetable Oil	（ton）	307 264
机制糖	（吨）	Sugar	（ton）	172 356
鲜冷藏冻肉	（吨）	Fresh Refuigerates Meet	（ton）	40 110
方便面	（吨）	Convenient Noodles	（ton）	23 874
乳制品	（吨）	Dairy Products	（ton）	96 244
# 液体乳		Liquid Milk	（ton）	64 952
罐头	（吨）	Canned Food	（ton）	675 695
# 番茄酱罐头		Canned Ketchup		650 109
味精	（吨）	Monosodium Glutamate	（ton）	20 910
酱油	（吨）	Soy	（ton）	3 083
发酵酒精（折 96 度，商品量）	（千升）	YmolyticAlcohol	（1000 liter）	5 193
饮料酒	（千升）	AlcoholBeverage	（1000 liter）	149 712
# 白酒（折 65 度，商品量）		WhiteSpirit		42 969
啤酒		Beer		98 286
葡萄酒		Wine		6 495
软饮料	（吨）	Soft Drink	（ton）	487 162
# 碳酸饮料		Carbonated Beverag		21 523
果汁及果汁饮料		Fruit Juice and Berverage		283 947
瓶（罐）装饮用水		Drinking Water Bottled		46 150
纱	（吨）	Yarn	（ton）	225 210
布	（万米）	Cloth	（10000 m）	8 974
# 棉布		Cotton Cloth		8 964
呢绒	（万米）	Woolen Goods	（10000 m）	172
服装	（万件）	Garments	（10 000 pieces）	383.97
# 梭织服装		Loom Clothing		376.24
人造板	（立方米）	Artificial Board	（cu. meter）	15 839
家具	（件）	Funiture	（unit）	282 242
纸浆	（吨）	Paper Pulp	（ton）	31 298
机制纸及纸板	（吨）	Machine-made Paper and Paper Boards	（ton）	127 026
# 新闻纸		News Paper		13 839
纸制品	（吨）	Paper Products	（ton）	66 779
焦炭	（吨）	Coke	（ton）	1 676 530
# 机械化焦炉生产的焦炭	（吨）	Coke Turnedout by Mechanized Coke Oven	（ton）	661 282
硫酸（折 100%）	（吨）	Sulfuric Acid	（ton）	90 539
盐酸（含量 31%以上）	（吨）	Hydrochloric Acid（with Content of 31%）	（ton）	125 364
氢氧化钠（烧碱）（折 100%）	（吨）	Caustic Soda	（ton）	505 264

10—25 续表 Continued

指 标		Item		2010
电石	(吨)	Calcium Carhide	(ton)	1 092 745
合成氨(无水氨)	(吨)	Synthetic Ammonia	(ton)	3 430
农用氮、磷、钾化学肥料总计(折纯)	(吨)	Chemical Fertilizer	(ton)	11 528
化学农药	(吨)	Chemical Pesticides	(ton)	380
涂料	(吨)	Paint	(ton)	6 894
塑料树脂及共聚物	(吨)	Plastics resin and	(ton)	733 286
# 聚氯乙烯树脂		Corvic		731 593
化学原料药	(吨)	Chemical Medicine	(ton)	35
中成药	(吨)	Traditional Chinese Medicine	(ton)	2 445
化学纤维用浆粕	(吨)	Chemical Fibre Pulp	(ton)	103 167
# 化学纤维		Chemical Fibre		64 517
塑料制品	(吨)	Plastic Produces	(ton)	314 388
# 塑料薄膜		Plastic Pellicle		76 427
塑料管及其附件		Plastic PipeandIts Enclosure		182 508
水泥熟料	(万吨)	Cement Chamotte	(10000 tons)	647.05
# 预分解窑熟料		Predecomposing Kiln Chamotle		497.77
水泥	(万吨)	Cement	(10000 tons)	966.89
商品混凝土	(立方米)	Merchandise concrete	(cu. meter)	2 629 638
水泥排水管	(吨)	Cement Sewage Duct	(ton)	2 235
水泥电杆	(根)	Cement Electric Pole Piece	(unit)	112 050
砖(折标准砖)	(万块)	Brick(standardBrick)	(10000 pieces)	205 101
瓦	(万片)	Tile	(10000 pieces)	240
平板玻璃	(重量箱)	Plate Glass	(weight cases)	281 888
日用玻璃制品	(吨)	Household Glass Products	(ton)	87 137
耐火材料制品	(吨)	Fire-Resistant Material Producs	(ton)	73 553
生铁	(吨)	PigIron	(ton)	86 687
粗钢	(吨)	CrudeSteel	(ton)	17 219
钢材	(吨)	RolledSteel	(ton)	69 901
铁合金	(吨)	IronAlloys	(ton)	4 100
电解铝	(吨)	Electrolyzed Aluminum	(ton)	120 000
镁	(吨)	Magnesium	(ton)	3 462
泵	(台)	Pump	(unit)	3 346
弹簧	(吨)	Spring	(ton)	3 470
改装汽车	(辆)	Modified Truck	(unit)	136
发电量	(万千瓦时)	Electricity	(10000 kwh)	1 348 687
# 火电		Thermalpower		1 230 549
水电		Hydropower		102 408
供热量	(万百万千焦)	Volume of Heat Supply	(10 billion kj)	4 052
自来水生产量	(万吨)	Tap Water Production	(10000 tons)	7 998

10－26　各师工业主要产品产量

（2010 年）

指　标	Item	合　计 Total	一　师 Division 1	二　师 Division 2	三　师 Division 3	四　师 Division 4	五　师 Division 5
原　煤（吨）	Coal (ton)	9 258 299	850 062	2 240 690		741 130	
小麦粉（吨）	Wheate Flour (ton)	224 662	2 022	2 733	28 330	32 123	6 700
大　米（吨）	Rice (ton)	78 849	26 804	1 286		50 702	
配混合饲料（吨）	Forage (ton)	1 083 029	36 009	34 916	3 478	57 635	9 645
食用植物油（吨）	Edible Vegetable Oil (ton)	307 264	45 510	29 369	10 919	8 110	35 585
机制糖（吨）	Mechine Make Sugar (ton)	172 356		62 305		45 048	
乳制品（吨）	Dairy Products (ton)	96 244	8 642			4 137	161
#液体乳	Liquid Milk	64 952	7 361			456	161
罐　头（吨）	Canned Food (ton)	675 695		99 559			
#番茄酱罐头	Canned Ketchup	650 109		75 673			
饮料酒（千升）	Alcohol Beverage (1 000 liter)	149 712	591	6 501	573	31 809	253
白酒（折 65 度，商品量）	White Spirit	42 969	591	6 001	5	22 683	253
啤　酒	Beer	98 286				8 199	
葡萄酒	Wine	6 495		500	66	927	
软饮料（吨）	Soft Drink (ton)	487 162	34 113	1 800	8 497	8 938	4 173
纱（吨）	Yarn (ton)	225 210	16 825	18 313	2 870		8 753
布（万米）	Cloth (10 000 m)	8 974	839		211		155
呢绒（万米）	Woolen Piece Goods (10 000 m)	172					
服　装（万件）	Garments (10 000 piece)	384					3
家　具（件）	Funiture (unit)	282 242	4 510	8 337	9 920	8 921	
机制纸及纸板（吨）	Machine-made Paper and Paper Boards (ton)	127 026		30 809		5 154	
焦　炭（吨）	Coke (ton)	1 676 530				64 947	
#机械化焦炉生产的焦炭	Coke Turned out by Mechanized Coke Oven	661 282				64 947	
硫　酸（折 100%）（吨）	Sulfuric Acid (ton)	90 539	54 578				
盐　酸（含量 31%以上）（吨）	Hydrochloric Acid(with Content of 31%) (ton)	125 364	8 698				
氢氧化钠(烧碱)(折 100%)（吨）	Caustic Soda (ton)	505 264					
电　石（吨）	Calcium Carhide (ton)	1 092 745				77 846	
塑料树脂及共聚物（吨）	Plastics resin and (ton)	733 286		400			1 293
#聚氯乙烯树脂	Corvic	731 593					
塑料制品（吨）	Plastic Produces (ton)	314 388	45 780	13 842	15 850	9 788	22 842
#塑料薄膜	Plastic Pellicle	76 427	26 589	2 355	2 799	1 733	7 146
塑料制管子及其附件	Plastic Stick and Pipe Section	182 508	13 259	10 386	12 629	966	4 156
水泥熟料（吨）	Cement Familiar Material (ton)	6 470 484	3 487 632	173 037	86 426	2 184 507	
#预分解窑熟料	Beforehand Resolve Kiln Familiar Material	4 977 678	2 695 844			1 983 429	
水　泥（吨）	Cement (ton)	9 668 886	4 510 010	264 656	117 860	2 482 076	
砖（折标准砖）（万块）	Brick (standard Brick) (10 000 piece)	205 101	19 816	7 730	20 453	16 919	5 045
发电量（万千瓦时）	Electricity (10 000 kwh)	1 348 687	110 080	3 958	16 000	18 435	44 126
火　电	Coal-Fired Generation	1 230 549	94 389	2 938	16 000	9 468	11 391
水　电	Hydropower Generation	102 408	15 691	1 020		8 967	17 005
供热量（万百万千焦）	Volume of Heat Supply (10 billion KJ)	4 052	564	72	99	41	182
自来水生产量（万吨）	Top Water Production (10 000 ton)	7 998	2 150		739	10	870

Output of Major Industrial Products by Division

六师 Division 6	七师 Division 7	八师 Division 8	九师 Division 9	十师 Division 10	建工师 Construction Division	十二师 Division 12	十三师 Division 13	十四师 Division 14	国资公司 State-owned Property Company	中基公司 Chalkis Company	兵团直属 Directly under XPCG
2 042 141	484 627	945 114		1 020 188		418 067	452 355		63 925		
72 495	4 718	23 523	37 974	9 121		395	2 483	2 045			
						57					
17 609	38 795	130 723	21 014	2 934			1 444		609 657		119 170
42 097	43 137	59 391	505	3 627		367	6 086	997	21 564		
	17 130		47 873								
47	3 587	52 430		109		27 131					
47		29 945				26 982					
98 703	134 873	113 239	7 014	800		900	1 700		5 102	213 805	
98 703	134 873	113 239	7 014	800		900			5 102	213 805	
2 284	5 534	93 690	1 782	900		5 103	692				
2 284	5 534	3 401	322	900		303	692				
		90 087									
		202				4 800					
1 467		425 662	1 148	1 240		124					
11 289	29 942	131 318				5 041	859				
138	2 888	4 602				141					
		172									
2		3	1			367		1	7		
8 483	14 100		197 204	2 490		23 037		5 240			
53 565		36 035		580		883					
1 476 335						1 100	134 148				
596 335											
		35 961									
		116 666									
		505 264									
		1 014 899									
21 125		710 468									
21 125		710 468									
55 334	11 369	110 501	2 523	11 983	210	3 366	9 534	1 466			
18 663	1 936	9 419		2 487		2 370	930				
35 716	4 301	89 497	1 522	5 507		1 137	3 216	216			
298 405		221 600		18 877							
298 405											
338 834		1 614 310		40 000	282 500		18 640				
39 050	4 852	31 539	5 290	6 932	6 511	15 167	25 797				
	212 166	928 385	3 451	11 860			226				
	202 412	882 283	3 022	8 646							
	9 754	46 102	429	3 214			226				
259	301	2 221	104	101		100		8			
210	2 233	636	637	28	485						

10－27　规模以上工业企业主要工业产品生产能力

Production Capacity of Major Industrial Products above Designated Size

主要产品名称		Item		2010
原煤(按核定能力填报)	(万吨)	Coal	(10 000 tons)	868.00
发电设备容量总计	(万千瓦)	Generate Electricity Equipment Capacity	(10 000 kw)	235.93
石　棉	(吨)	Asbestos	(ton)	70 500
小麦粉	(万吨)	Wheate Flour	(10 000 tons)	15.25
精制食用植物油	(万吨)	Refined Edible Vegetable Oil	(10 000 tons)	27.55
成品糖	(日处理糖料量吨)	Machine-madeSugar	(daily disposal)	15 000
成品糖	(年产糖量吨)	Machile-madeSugar	(annual outpput)	247 500
配混合饲料	(万吨)	Forage	(10 000 tons)	175
方便面	(万吨)	Convenient Noodles	(10 000 tons)	22.18
乳制品	(万吨)	Dairy Products	(10 000 tons)	23.77
# 液体乳		Liqui Milk		20.38
罐头	(万吨)	Canned Food	(10 000 tons)	144.00
# 番茄酱罐头		Monosodium Glutamate		129.00
发酵酒精(折96度,商品量)	(千升)	Zymolytic Alcohol	(1 000 L)	4 000
白　酒	(千升)	White Spirit	(1 000 L)	35 750
葡萄酒	(千升)	Wine	(1 000 L)	103 000
碳酸饮料	(万吨)	Carbonicacid beverage	(10 000 tons)	2.80
果汁及果汁饮料	(万吨)	Fruit Juice and Berverage	(10 000 tons)	1.23
瓶(罐)装饮用水	(万吨)	Drinking Water Bottled	(10 000 tons)	39.56
棉纺锭(环锭纺)	(万锭)	Cotton Hasp	(10 000 ingot)	233
气流纺锭(转杯纺)	(万头)	AirCurrent Hasp	(10 000 head)	5
棉布织机	(台)	Cotton Cloth Machine	(set)	2 546
毛纺锭	(锭)	Wool Hasp	(ingot)	15 000
毛织机	(台)	Wool Weavw Machine	(set)	94.00
纸　浆	(万吨)	Paper Pulp	(10 000 tons)	3.49
机制纸及纸板	(万吨)	Machine-made Paper and Paper Boards	(10 000 tons)	2.86
焦　炭	(万吨)	Coke	(10 000 tons)	390.70
# 机械化焦炉生产的焦炭		Coke Turned out by Mechanized Coke Oven		390.70
硫酸(折100%)	(万吨)	Sulfuric Acid	(10 000 tons)	5.00
盐酸(含量31%以上)	(万吨)	Hydrochloric Acid (with Content of 31%)	(10 000 tons)	35.00
烧　碱(折100%)	(万吨)	CausticSoda	(10 000 tons)	60.00
碳化钙(电石)(折300升/千克)	万吨	CarbonizationCalcium	(10 000 tons)	114.00
初级形态的塑料	(万吨)	PlasticofElementaryConfiguration	(10 000 tons)	71.00
# 聚氯乙烯树脂		Corvic		71.00
水泥熟料	(万吨)	Familiar Cement	(10 000 tons)	889.50
# 窑外分解窑熟料(预分解窑料)		Beforeh and Resolve Kiln Familiar Material		705.00
水　泥	(万吨)	Cement	(10 000 tons)	1291.50

2011

BING TUAN

第十一篇

建筑业

Chapter 11 Construction

简要说明

一、本篇资料主要内容

本篇资料反映兵团建筑业概况和发展情况。主要包括建筑业企业规模、生产经营和效益情况，主要指标企业个数、从业人员数、建筑业总产值、房屋建筑面积、机械设备、资产负债、企业总收入、利润税金、劳动生产率、技术装备率等。

二、本篇统计范围

建筑业统计范围为全部法人、产业活动单位和个体。

三、本篇资料来源

本篇资料由兵团统计局工业交通投资统计处根据《兵团建筑业统计报表制度》收集、汇总、整理、提供。

四、本篇调查方法

统计调查方法为全面调查。

Brief Introduction

1. Main Contents

Data in this chapter show the general situation and development of construction in XPCG, including scale, production and management, efficiency of construction enterprises, main indicators including number of enterprises, employed persons, gross output value of construction, floor space of buildings, machinery and equipment, assets and liabilities, total revenue of enterprises, profits and taxes, labor productivity, per capita machinery, etc.

2. Scope of Statistics

The statistical scope of construction in this chapter is corporate enterprises, units of industrial activities and individuals.

3. Sources of Data

The data in this chapter are collected, prepared and provided by Industry Communications and Assets Statistical Section of Statistics Bureau of XPCG according to the Comprehensive Statistical Reporting Form System on Construction of XPCG.

4. Methodology of Survey

Survey method is comprehensive statistics.

11—1 建筑业单位基本情况

Basic Conditions of Construction Units

年份 单位 Year Unit	企业个数(个) Number of Construction Enterprises (unit)				职工年平均人数(万人) Average Annual Number of Employees(10 000 persons)			
	合计 Total	国有企业 State-owned Enterprises	集体企业 Collective-owned Enterprises	其他 Others	合计 Total	国有企业 State-owned Enterprises	集体企业 Collective-owned Enterprises	其他 Others
1951	57	57			0.83	0.83		
1952	172	172			2.55	2.55		
1954	207	207			3.59	3.59		
1957	142	142			4.62	4.62		
1962	185	185			7.84	7.84		
1965	201	201			12.49	12.49		
1970	171	171			10.24	10.24		
1975	170	170			3.25	3.25		
1978	106	106			3.22	3.22		
1980	264	264			7.28	7.28		
1985	317	317			11.69	11.69		
1990	238	233	5		11.28	11.05	0.23	
1991	238	232	6		12.05	11.93	0.12	
1992	237	231	6		12.39	12.26	0.13	
1993	252	244	8		11.89	11.76	0.13	
1994	257	250	7		10.26	10.15	0.11	
1995	269	261	7	1	10.48	10.38	0.10	…
1996	274	264	9	1	10.59	10.09	0.50	…
1997	278	266	11	1	10.89	10.78	0.11	…
1998	268	258	9	1	10.75	10.59	0.16	…
1999	258	250	6	2	11.27	11.16	0.10	0.01
2000	253	246	5	2	10.53	10.41	0.11	0.01
2001	253	242	3	8	11.94	10.53	0.09	1.32
2002	236	200	3	33	11.47	7.90	0.03	3.54
2003	250	179	7	64	10.83	5.87	0.05	4.91
2004	282	173	6	103	10.62	4.82	0.02	5.78
2005	303	162	2	139	10.98	4.99	0.02	5.97
2006	296	141	2	153	10.96	5.14	0.02	5.80
2007	275	143	1	131	12.49	6.12	0.02	6.35
2008	258	134	2	122	13.47	6.12	0.01	7.34
2009	250	115	2	133	14.94	4.93	0.01	10.00
2010	243	112	2	129	20.02	6.78	0.01	13.23
一师 Division 1	23	13		10	1.70	0.69		1.01
二师 Division 2	14	11		3	0.83	0.31		0.52
三师 Division 3	15	11		4	0.62	0.15		0.47
四师 Division 4	19	12		7	0.77	0.16		0.61
五师 Division 5	11	6		5	0.33	0.06		0.27
六师 Division 6	16	5		11	1.94	0.18		1.76
七师 Division 7	15	10		5	1.61	1.15		0.46
八师 Division 8	76	5	2	69	4.98	0.75	0.01	4.22
七师 Division 9	10	8		2	0.30	0.11		0.19
十师 Division 10	11	10		1	0.43	0.22		0.21
建工师 Construction Division	13	6		7	5.26	2.25		3.01
十二师 Division 12	6	5		1	0.41	0.23		0.18
十三师 Division 13	9	8		1	0.64	0.44		0.20
十四师 Division 14	2			2	0.09			0.09
国资公司 State-owned Property Company	2	1		1	0.09	0.06		0.03
兵团直属 Directly under XPCG	1	1			0.02	0.02		

注:企业个数不含个体。
Note: Number of construction enterprises not includs individuals.

11—2 按经济类型分建筑业总产值

Total Output Value of Construction by Economic Sectors

计量单位:万元 (10 000 yuan)

年份 Year	单位 Unit	合计 Total	国有企业 State-owned Enterprises	集体企业 Collective-owned Enterprises	其他 Others
	1950	2 061	2 061		
	1952	13 267	13 267		
	1954	10 740	10 740		
	1957	19 821	19 821		
	1962	9 978	9 978		
	1965	21 437	21 437		
	1970	11 676	11 676		
	1975	3 899	3 899		
	1978	9 631	9 631		
	1980	23 431	23 431		
	1985	64 608	64 524		84
	1990	96 386	88 298	1 298	6 790
	1991	123 241	115 070	1 486	6 685
	1992	168 792	152 357	2 046	14 389
	1993	227 419	214 695	2 655	10 069
	1994	254 158	238 234	3 624	12 300
	1995	291 989	274 991	2 663	14 335
	1996	317 436	302 006	2 644	12 786
	1997	355 600	337 188	2 501	15 911
	1998	448 314	421 830	4 129	22 355
	1999	527 145	510 193	3 980	12 972
	2000	582 768	567 042	4 685	11 041
	2001	676 917	584 312	3 701	88 904
	2002	747 247	508 803	1 778	236 666
	2003	848 001	450 195	3 599	394 207
	2004	942 376	387 958	2 200	552 218
	2005	1 002 400	423 107	819	578 474
	2006	1 116 687	497 224	982	618 481
	2007	1 359 304	697 029	197	662 078
	2008	1 757 883	821 465	980	935 438
	2009	2 225 015	659 113	980	1 564 922
	2010	2 984 683	957 905	980	2 025 798
一 师	Division 1	318 028	127 687		190 341
二 师	Division 2	156 023	63 124		92 899
三 师	Division 3	102 766	11 060		91 706
四 师	Division 4	127 916	21 871		106 045
五 师	Division 5	64 053	8 708		55 345
六 师	Division 6	402 489	43 856		358 633
七 师	Division 7	267 766	188 790		78 976
八 师	Division 8	423 289	70 457	980	351 852
九 师	Division 9	43 402	14 014		29 388
十 师	Division 10	70 354	51 484		18 870
建工师	Construction Division	821 781	263 447		558 334
十二师	Division 12	56 425	35 011		21 414
十三师	Division 13	88 297	43 192		45 105
十四师	Division 14	25 990			25 990
国资公司	State-owned Property Company	11 998	11 098		900
兵团直属	Directly under XPCG	4 106	4 106		

注:其他含个体。

Note: Others is including individuals.

11—3 建筑企业总产值、全员劳动生产率

Total Value of Construction and Labour Productivity of Construction Enterprises

年份 Year	单位 Unit	建筑业总产值（万元） Total value of construction (10 000 yuan)	# 国有法人企业 State-owned Corporative Enterprises	# 国有产业活动单位 State-owned Number of Basic Units	# 集体企业 Collective-owned Enterprises	全员劳动生产率（元/人） Labour Productivity (Yuan/Person)	# 国有法人企业 State-owned Corporative Enterprises	# 国有产业活动单位 State-owned Number of Basic Units	# 集体企业 Collective-owned Enter-Prises
1950		2 061	174	1 887					
1952		13 267	2 302	10 965					
1954		10 740	6 154	4 586					
1957		19 821	5 844	13 977					
1962		9 978	3 235	6 743					
1965		21 437	13 142	8 295					
1970		11 676	8 119	3 557					
1975		3 899	3 022	877					
1978		9 631	2 746	6 885		2 991	1 760	4 148	
1980		23 431	5 589	15 574		2 907	1 583	4 758	
1985		64 608	43 956	13 691		4 931	5 460	5 651	
1990		96 386	54 589	30 596	1 298	7 667	8 271	7 409	5 643
1991		123 241	65 665	45 745	1 486	9 369	9 314	10 124	12 383
1992		168 792	86 289	60 839	2 046	12 040	12 052	12 955	15 738
1993		227 419	128 616	86 079	2 655	18 280	19 636	16 522	20 423
1994		254 158	151 954	86 280	3 624	23 573	26 565	19 476	32 945
1995		291 989	177 922	97 069	2 663	26 495	33 194	19 336	26 630
1996		317 436	187 131	114 875	2 644	28 776	33 062	25 931	5 288
1997		355 600	205 954	131 234	2 501	31 204	35 146	26 674	22 736
1998		448 314	255 230	166 600	4 129	39 665	43 480	35 297	25 806
1999		527 145	286 422	223 771	3 980	45 629	52 845	38 984	39 800
2000		582 768	328 140	238 902	4 685	54 320	60 542	47 876	42 591
2001		676 917	310 954	273 358	3 701	55 826	59 684	51 374	41 122
2002		747 247	303 757	205 046	1 778	63 906	65 944	62 299	59 267
2003		848 001	252 620	197 575	3 599	76 510	80 603	72 105	70 431
2004		942 376	161 164	207 781	1 852	88 251	81 586	78 349	72 062
2005		1 002 400	206 623	216 484	819	89 748	93 920	77 316	40 935
2006		1 116 687	289 223	208 001	982	96 530	109 554	83 200	49 100
2007		1 359 304	479 840	217 189	197	106 696	124 848	95 447	
2008		1 757 883	554 869	266 596	980	130 504	130 383	142 565	70 000
2009		2 225 015	353 224	305 889	980	148 925	124 515	145 953	69 979
2010		2 984 683	577 052	380 853	980	149 112	134 555	153 101	70 000
一师	Division 1	318 028	41 370	86 317		187 108	168 788	195 067	
二师	Division 2	156 023	53 323	9 801		188 434	249 057	103 605	
三师	Division 3	102 766		11 060		166 504		72 430	
四师	Division 4	127 916		21 871		165 245		135 006	
五师	Division 5	64 053		8 708		196 421		159 487	
六师	Division 6	402 489		43 856		207 897		249 749	
七师	Division 7	267 766	136 122	52 668		165 738	179 108	134 597	
八师	Division 8	423 289	70 457		980	84 943	94 459		70 000
九师	Division 9	43 402	1 235	12 779		143 005	209 322	119 654	
十师	Division 10	70 354		51 484		165 150		231 805	
建工师	Construction Division	821 781	263 447			156 078	116 678		
十二师	Division 12	56 425		35 011		137 824		152 156	
十三师	Division 13	88 297		43 192		137 835		98 477	
十四师	Division 14	25 990				304 333			
国资公司	State-owned Property Company	11 998	11 098			133 757	185 896		
兵团直属	Directly under XPCG	4 106		4 106		245 868		245 868	

注：1. 全员劳动生产率按总产值计算

Note: Labour productivity are calculated by construction output value.

11—4 各师按构成分建筑业总产值

Total Output Value of Construction by Composition and Division

计量单位:万元　　　　（2010年）　　　　(10 000 yuan)

单　位	Unit	总产值 Output Value of Construction	建筑工程 Construction Engineering	安装工程 Installation Engineering	其　他 Others
总　计	**Total**	**2 984 683**	**2 833 746**	**137 815**	**13 122**
一　师	Division 1	318 028	306 752	9 375	1 901
二　师	Division 2	156 023	151 848	1 719	2 456
三　师	Division 3	102 766	101 037	1 449	280
四　师	Division 4	127 916	121 903	5 950	63
五　师	Division 5	64 053	63 269	784	
六　师	Division 6	402 489	341 342	60 810	337
七　师	Division 7	267 766	257 863	9 882	21
八　师	Division 8	423 289	389 101	30 087	4 101
九　师	Division 9	43 402	42 976	337	89
十　师	Division 10	70 354	66 586	1 984	1 784
建 工 师	Construction Division	821 781	808 063	12 893	825
十 二 师	Division 12	56 425	56 004	187	234
十 三 师	Division 13	88 297	85 950	1 337	1 010
十 四 师	Division 14	25 990	25 769	200	21
国资公司	State-owned Property Company	11 998	11 998		
兵团直属	Directly under XPCG	4 106	3 285	821	

11—5 建筑业单位生产情况

Production of Construction Units

（2010年）

指　标 Item	合　计 Total	国有法人企业 State-owned Corporative Enterprises	国有产业活动单位 State-owned Number of Basic Units	集体企业 Collective-owned Enterprises	有限责任公司 Limited Liability Corporations	股份有限公司 Stock Ltd. co.	其　他 Others
建筑业总产值(万元) Construction Output Value(10 000 yuan)	2 984 683	577 052	380 853	980	1 245 737	295 482	484 579
# 建筑工程产值 Construction	2 833 746	564 617	351 065	980	1 213 235	293 604	410 245
安装工程产值 Installation	137 815	11 610	23 054		31 904	1 857	69 390
其他产值 Others	13 122	825	6 735		598	21	4 943
竣工产值 Completion Output Value	2 019 554	365 933	338 326	980	859 144	50 967	404 204
房屋建筑施工面积(万平方米) Floor Space of Building Under Construction(10 000 sq. m)	2 059.97	332.22	279.80		1 139.09	9.19	299.67
# 本年新开工面积 Newly-opened Areas	1 496.29	160.00	264.66		796.78	6.21	268.64
房屋建筑竣工面积(万平方米) Floor Space of Building Completed (10 000 sq. m)	1 115.28	145.91	206.43		544.24	9.00	209.70
# 住宅面积 Floor Space of Residence	708.56	104.49	158.65		340.48	6.89	98.05
自有施工机械设备净值(万元) Net Value of Working Machinery and Equipment(10 000 yuan)	100 094	14 071	13 829		35 590	30 631	5 973
自有施工机械设备总台数(台) Self-owned Total Number of Working Machinery and Equipment(set)	16 894	2 322	2 408		8 824	1 446	1 894
自有施工机械设备总功率(千瓦) Self-owned Total Power of Working Machinery and Equipment (kw)	562 911	72 894	57 507		289 897	118 240	24 373
职工年平均人数(人) Average Annual Nnmber of staff and workers(peron)	200 164	42 886	24 876	140	94 918	8 784	28 560

注:本表含个体。

Note:This table is including individuals.

11—6 按登记注册类型、行业和资质等级分建筑业总产值

Total Value of Construction Grouped by Types of Registration, Sector and Qualification Grade

计量单位:万元 (2010年) (10 000 yuan)

指 标 Item	建筑业总产值 Total Value of Construction	# 在外省完成的产值 Output Value Realized in Other Provinces	# 装修装饰产值 Output Value of Decoration	按构成分建筑业总产值 Total Output Value of Construction Sectors		
				建筑工程 Construction Works	安装工程 Installation Works	其 他 Others
总 计 Total	**2 984 683**	**165 274**	**23 519**	**2 833 746**	**137 815**	**13 122**
按登记注册类型分组 Grouped by Types of Reyistration						
# 国有企业 State-owned Enterprises	957 905	25 114	7 670	915 682	34 664	7 559
集体企业 Collective Enterprises	980			980		
有限责任公司 Limited Liability Company	1 245 737	21 212	10 048	1 213 235	31 904	598
股份有限公司 Stock Ltd. co.	295 482	118 948	242	293 604	1 857	21
私营企业 Private Enterprises	172 660		1 935	163 712	5 256	3 692
按国民经济行业分 Grouped by Sector						
房屋和土木工程建筑业 Civil Engineering and Building Sector	2 909 493	165 274	22 315	2 797 883	99 400	12 210
建筑安装业 Installation of Wire, Tube and Equipments	63 130		280	25 674	37 163	293
建筑装饰业 Repair and Decoration	1 668		668	677	658	333
其他建筑业 Others	10 392		256	9 512	594	286
按资质等级分组 Grouped by Enterprise Qualification Grade						
施工总承包 Contruction Contract	2 345 978	165 274	14 405	2 313 865	26 979	5 135
一 级 First Class	1 165 622	146 646	9 328	1 151 905	12 893	825
二 级 Second Class	778 494	18 628	2 532	766 147	12 347	
三 级 Third Class	401 862		2 545	395 813	1 739	4 310
专业承包 Professional Contract	92 109		291	59 277	32 832	
一 级 First Glass						
二 级 Second Glass	40 582			38 217	2 365	
三 级 Third Glass	51 527		291	21 060	30 467	
资质等级外企业 Outside Qualification Grade	546 596		8 823	460 604	78 004	7 987

注:本表含个体。
Note: This table is including individuals.

11—7 建筑业施工单位房屋施工面积

Floor Space of Buildings under Construction of Construction Units

计量单位:万平方米 (10 000 sq. m)

年份 单位	Year Unit	房屋施工面积合计 Total Floor Space of Buildings under Construction	# 国有法人企业 State-owned Corporative Enterprises	# 国有产业活动单位 State-owned Number of Basic Units	# 集体企业 Collective-owned Enterprises	# 本年新开工面积 New-opened Area in this yesr
	1950	6.99	1.70	5.29		6.99
	1952	21.52	9.10	12.42		19.37
	1954	28.50	24.74	3.76		25.65
	1957	75.11	68.58	6.53		59.39
	1962	71.56	18.21	53.35		59.98
	1965	140.22	63.73	76.49		111.63
	1970	164.55	56.88	107.67		129.60
	1975	77.97	52.33	25.64		54.58
	1978	123.16	37.87	85.29		100.86
	1980	189.93	43.90	146.03		151.94
	1985	313.29	217.39	95.90		170.94
	1990	289.00	147.00	137.00	5.00	164.70
	1991	352.75	172.19	174.92	5.64	201.07
	1992	403.52	197.33	198.08	8.11	230.01
	1993	440.05	236.46	194.52	9.07	288.22
	1994	446.05	266.95	171.47	7.63	245.04
	1995	453.88	276.63	174.01	3.24	300.31
	1996	467.07	280.78	182.80	3.49	280.50
	1997	445.23	271.53	169.22	4.48	289.69
	1998	534.58	311.69	216.70	6.19	372.70
	1999	698.38	326.75	364.95	6.69	522.73
	2000	703.50	389.19	308.47	5.83	546.10
	2001	776.99	356.71	340.02	5.42	584.30
	2002	671.64	247.45	189.67	2.59	477.00
	2003	774.00	216.99	215.80	5.77	590.16
	2004	873.66	152.17	208.57	3.73	648.75
	2005	900.52	142.36	253.32		617.92
	2006	831.79	161.74	166.39	0.10	576.73
	2007	964.81	223.95	157.98	0.10	697.12
	2008	1 128.17	318.98	156.79		791.88
	2009	1 507.41	265.92	182.06		1 096.40
	2010	2 059.97	332.22	279.80		1 496.29
一 师	Division 1	285.36	38.89	55.73		237.52
二 师	Division 2	141.18	56.17	4.81		63.09
三 师	Division 3	77.83		4.36		74.58
四 师	Division 4	94.30		17.09		71.71
五 师	Division 5	58.20		6.27		54.22
六 师	Division 6	198.54		25.79		188.27
七 师	Division 7	79.99	21.66	30.08		64.70
八 师	Division 8	495.36	49.07			329.63
九 师	Division 9	56.36		11.63		37.65
十 师	Division 10	59.12		43.59		46.74
建 工 师	Construction Division	310.30	149.62			159.54
十 二 师	Division 12	78.23		43.08		72.32
十 三 师	Division 13	79.59		35.16		64.53
十 四 师	Division 14	25.20				24.57
国资公司	State-owned Property Company	18.20	16.81			5.66
兵团直属	Directly under XPCG	2.21		2.21		1.56

注:本表含个体。

Note: This table is including individuals.

11—8 建筑业施工单位房屋竣工面积

Floor Space of Buildings Completed of Construction Units

计量单位:万平方米 (10 000 sq. m)

年份 单位 Year Unit		房屋竣工面积合计 Total Floor Space of Buildings under Construction	#国有法人企业 State-owned Corporative Enterprises	#国有产业活动单位 State-owned Number of Basic Units	#集体企业 Collective-owned Enterprises	#住宅竣工面积 Completed Floor Space of Residence
	1950	6.43	0.54	5.89		2.65
	1952	19.80	9.10	10.70		8.87
	1954	26.22	15.02	11.20		15.84
	1957	69.10	20.37	48.73		32.72
	1962	68.64	11.82	56.82		32.68
	1965	132.06	47.25	84.81		79.22
	1970	152.55	31.87	120.68		95.61
	1975	72.14	38.98	33.16		42.67
	1978	108.71	18.21	90.50		56.78
	1980	153.08	17.79	135.29		88.77
	1985	205.11	129.96	75.15		96.68
	1990	193.00	79.00	110.00	4.00	82.00
	1991	237.12	98.10	135.96	3.06	96.08
	1992	250.98	95.15	150.67	5.16	117.39
	1993	234.87	93.82	136.36	4.69	97.64
	1994	279.30	134.90	138.55	5.85	143.34
	1995	267.81	130.47	134.94	2.40	134.60
	1996	293.98	135.96	155.99	2.04	153.83
	1997	276.60	131.89	141.84	2.82	156.59
	1998	345.94	169.05	173.11	3.78	207.90
	1999	531.45	194.64	331.31	5.50	431.33
	2000	500.96	233.35	263.33	4.27	341.49
	2001	558.63	211.81	301.83	4.73	398.40
	2002	461.86	157.06	177.62	1.68	309.54
	2003	512.97	114.58	193.67	3.36	300.94
	2004	567.18	68.00	189.81	3.73	343.72
	2005	590.32	72.50	220.59		391.71
	2006	538.48	99.00	128.80		277.66
	2007	567.17	112.63	131.15		348.93
	2008	648.53	135.94	108.63		438.91
	2009	753.91	91.14	142.13		523.49
	2010	1 115.28	145.91	206.43		708.56
一 师	Division 1	163.03	13.92	45.38		109.27
二 师	Division 2	61.46	13.38	4.79		51.86
三 师	Division 3	49.76		4.36		35.94
四 师	Division 4	58.67		16.37		32.48
五 师	Division 5	35.64		6.25		23.55
六 师	Division 6	147.24		24.21		73.56
七 师	Division 7	51.89	7.67	23.59		45.16
八 师	Division 8	268.28	43.75			124.86
九 师	Division 9	20.90		5.12		16.04
十 师	Division 10	43.93		31.27		32.87
建工师	Construction Division	110.14	59.83			92.64
十二师	Division 12	45.86		21.30		20.21
十三师	Division 13	41.94		21.58		36.43
十四师	Division 14	6.97				4.12
国资公司	State-owned Property Company	7.36	7.36			7.36
兵团直属	Directly under XPCG	2.21		2.21		2.21

注:本表含个体。

Note: This table is including individuals.

11—9 建筑业施工单位技术装备

Machinery and Equipment of Construction Units

年份 单位 Year Unit		自有施工机械设备 Self-owned Working Machinery and Equipment			动力装备率(千瓦/人) Power of Machinery per Laborer(kw/person)		技术装备率(元/人) Value of Machines per Laborer(yuan/person)	
		台数(台) Total Numbers (set)	总功率(万千瓦) Total Power (10 000 kw)	净值(万元) NetValue (10 000 yuan)	全部职工 Total Workers and Staff	# 国有法人企业 State-owned Corporative Enterprises	全部职工 Total Workers and Staff	# 国有法人企业 State-owned Corporative Enterprises
	1952	9	0.02	13	0.02		9	
	1954	26	0.06	35	0.02		9	
	1957	43	0.10	58	0.02		13	
	1962	246	0.57	495	0.07		63	
	1965	782	1.81	1 006	0.17		81	
	1970	1 944	4.50	2 363	0.44		231	
	1975	332	0.76	337	0.23		103	
	1978	471	1.09	606	0.34		188	
	1980	1 158	2.68	1 490	0.37		205	
	1985	8 600	20.09	6 463	3.20	3.10	553	879
	1990	13 662	31.58	10 701	2.80	3.80	949	1 250
	1991	14 929	36.15	13 044	3.00	4.00	1 082	1 500
	1992	15 400	37.56	17 536	3.00	4.10	1 400	1 938
	1993	16 301	37.43	18 562	3.10	4.20	1 561	1 957
	1994	15 785	36.74	19 269	3.50	4.60	1 813	3 257
	1995	17 953	39.27	21 916	3.75	4.40	2 091	4 089
	1996	19 397	39.01	29 264	3.68	4.65	2 763	4 463
	1997	18 362	39.56	36 287	3.63	4.52	3 332	5 012
	1998	20 158	41.46	39 695	3.87	4.86	3 692	4 378
	1999	20 141	41.13	44 820	3.65	5.42	3 977	5 608
	2000	20 530	41.21	46 680	3.91		4 430	6 201
	2001	23 302	42.23	55 199	3.54	4.15	4 623	6 158
	2002	22 733	39.87	62 798	3.48	3.89	5 475	6 641
	2003	23 946	44.83	71 820	4.14	5.12	6 631	8 307
	2004	19 110	41.74	46 710	3.93	4.60	4 398	7 009
	2005	20 021	43.86	65 116	3.99	4.75	5 928	6 775
	2006	21 821	48.00	77 172	4.38	18.18	7 042	29 232
	2007	22 792	54.92	101 929	4.40	5.91	8 161	11 537
	2008	20 508	61.56	85 499	4.57	3.23	6 349	4 113
	2009	20 141	57.83	95 899	3.87	2.24	6 419	3 416
	2010	16 894	56.29	100 094	2.81	3.10	5 001	5 295
一 师	Division 1	1 744	4.56	14 868	2.69	2.55	8 747	9 002
二 师	Division 2	1 352	4.05	2 814	4.89	4.48	3 398	1 762
三 师	Division 3	1 128	3.13	5 080	5.07	5.14	8 231	8 097
四 师	Division 4	959	1.95	2 620	2.52	5.15	3 384	8 454
五 师	Division 5	490	0.69	3 590	2.11	2.89	11 009	9 368
六 师	Division 6	898	1.48	2 126	0.77	1.78	1 098	1 574
七 师	Division 7	1 262	1.95	5 445	1.21	1.37	3 370	2 851
八 师	Division 8	3 448	11.47	10 617	2.30	2.30	2 131	2 131
九 师	Division 9	467	1.39	1 991	4.57	6.11	6 560	9 299
十 师	Division 10	426	1.45	1 808	3.40	0.25	4 243	470
建工师	Construction Division	3 870	22.36	47 321	4.25	4.25	8 988	8 988
十二师	Division 12	291	0.61	289	1.49	1.49	706	31
十三师	Division 13	342	0.53	1 205	0.82	1.08	1 882	268
十四师	Division 14	170	0.32	41	3.76	4.59	484	590
国资公司	State-owned Property Company							
兵团直属	Directlyunder XPCG	47	0.35	279	20.96		16 677	

注:1.本表含个体。2.2003年以前为非自有机械设备。
Note:a)This table is including individuals. b)Data in this table is not self-owned machinery and equipment before 2003.

11—10 资质建筑法人企业主要财务指标

Major Financial Indicators of Qualification Construction Corporative Enterprises

计量单位:万元 (2010年) (10 000 yuan)

指 标 Item	合 计 Total	按登记注册类型分 Grouped by Types of Registration			
		国有企业 State-owned Enterprises	股份合作企业 Share Cooperative Enterprises	有限责任公司 Limited Liability Corporations	股份有限公司 Stock Co.，Ltd.
资本金合计 **Total Principal Value**	**219 150**	**55 894**	**2 653**	**119 248**	**21 943**
流动资产小计 Circulating Assets	1 171 680	199 883	7 024	664 735	206 327
# 存 货 Stock	233 709	36 850	1 645	124 780	58 650
固定资产小计 Fixed Assets	221 676	62 713	6 443	99 999	44 958
固定资产原价 Original Value of Fixed Assets	305 595	88 151	4 028	120 788	81 134
# 生产经营用 Used for Production and Management	240 641	54 589	2 134	94 915	80 994
累计折旧 Accumulated Depreciation	118 626	30 119	1 149	46 441	36 195
# 本年折旧 Depreciationin the Current Year	26 304	6 489	372	7 757	10 846
# 在建工程 Under Construction	16 812	4 623	3 564	8 033	19
资产合计 **Total Assets**	**1 540 402**	**272 065**	**13 809**	**843 919**	**301 115**
流动负债小计 Liquid Liabilities	1 021 807	204 811	11 156	584 498	133 850
长期负债小计 Long-term Liabilities	199 853	6 531		108 606	84 716
负债合计 **Total Liabilities**	**1 221 660**	**211 342**	**11 156**	**693 104**	**218 566**
所有者权益合计 **Creditors' Equity**	**318 742**	**60 723**	**2 653**	**150 815**	**82 549**
工程结算收入 Revenue of Project Settlement Accounts	2 039 327	543 846	9 825	1 076 655	269 411
工程结算成本 Cost of Project Settlement Accounts	1 866 650	513 335	6 794	979 132	239 933
工程结算税金及附加 Taxes and Extra Charges on Project Settlement Accounts	61 519	15 925	24	35 164	6 049
工程结算利润 Profits of Project Settlement Accounts	109 600	14 288	2 972	61 252	23 429
其他业务利润 Other Business Profit	11 674	3 970	28	4 779	1 943
管理费用 Management Expenses	75 367	11 439	1 104	42 895	15 888
利润总额 Total Profits	39 082	8 218	1 816	18 474	7 886

11—10 续表 Continued

计量单位:万元 (2010 年) (10 000 yuan)

指标 Item	私营企业 Private Enterprises	按国民经济行业分 Grouped by Sector 房屋和土木工程建筑业 Civil Engineering and Building Sector	建筑安装业 Construction and Installation	建筑装饰业 Repair and Decoration
资本金合计 Total Principal Value	**19 412**	**214 955**	**4 033**	**162**
流动资产小计 Circulating Assets	93 711	1 141 402	29 503	775
# 存　货 Stock	11 784	217 131	16 039	539
固定资产小计 Fixed Assets	7 563	215 827	5 574	275
固定资产原价 Original Value of Fixed Assets	11 494	298 680	6 547	368
# 生产经营用 Used for Produce and Management	8 009	234 846	5 722	73
累计折旧 Accumulated Depreciation	4 722	117 099	1 433	94
# 本年折旧 Depreciationin the Current Year	840	25 910	383	11
# 在建工程 Under Construction	573	16 352	460	
资产合计 Total Assets	**109 494**	**1 503 301**	**36 041**	**1 060**
流动负债小计 Liquid Liabilities	87 492	992 263	28 881	663
长期负债小计 Long-term Liabilities		199 847	6	
负债合计 Total Liabilities	**87 492**	**1 192 110**	**28 887**	**663**
所有者权益合计 Creditors' Equity	**22 002**	**311 191**	**7 154**	**397**
工程结算收入 Revenue of Project Settlement Accounts	139 590	2 004 740	33 479	1 108
工程结算成本 Cost of Project Settlement Accounts	127 456	1 834 946	30 806	898
工程结算税金及附加 Taxes and Extra Charges on Project Settlement Accounts	4 357	60 786	723	10
工程结算利润 Profits of Project Settlement Accounts	7 659	107 449	1 951	200
其他业务利润 Other Business Profit	954	11 218	455	1
管理费用 Management Expenses	4 041	74 424	814	129
利润总额 Total Profits	2 688	37 920	1 098	64

11—11 各师资质建筑法人企业主要财务指标

Major Financial Indicators of Qualification Construction Corporative Enterprises by Division

计量单位:万元 (2010 年) (10 000 yuan)

指标 Item	合计 Total	一师 Division 1	二师 Division 2	三师 Division 3	四师 Division 4	五师 Division 5	六师 Division 6	七师 Division 7	八师 Division 8
资本金合计 Total Principal Value	**219 150**	**20 142**	**13 051**	**7 156**	**2 558**	**528**	**12 806**	**27 878**	**40 496**
流动资产小计 Circulating Assets	1 171 680	91 035	43 782	45 722	11 343	8 978	81 462	47 837	212 874
# 存货 Stock	233 709	7 294	3 248	9 667	2 385	1 419	4 978	1 428	95 578
固定资产小计 Fixed Assets	221 676	32 256	8 529	5 353	3 277	4 819	2 555	25 986	19 893
固定资产原价 Original Value of Fixed Assets	305 595	38 868	15 865	7 450	5 932	3 365	4 808	35 560	33 900
# 生产经营用 Used for Produce and Management	240 641	28 873	12 962	5 611	5 932	3 365	2 517	9 814	31 208
累计折旧 Accumulated Depreciation	118 626	11 756	7 335	3 286	2 656	1 749	2 860	9 593	14 937
# 本年折旧 Depreciationin the Current Year	26 304	2 603	876	556	183	237	374	3 116	2 115
# 在建工程 Under Construction	16 812	5 145		844		3 204	3	19	924
资产合计 Total Assets	**1 540 402**	**129 069**	**56 857**	**53 078**	**14 995**	**14 253**	**91 062**	**80 051**	**242 468**
流动负债小计 Liquid Liabilities	1 021 807	88 772	43 207	41 070	10 990	11 922	75 584	50 364	191 024
长期负债小计 Long-term Liabilities	199 853	6 910		2 636		535		525	95
负债合计 Total Liabilities	**1 221 660**	**95 682**	**43 207**	**43 706**	**10 990**	**12 457**	**75 584**	**50 889**	**191 119**
所有者权益合计 Creditors' Equity	**318 742**	**33 387**	**13 650**	**9 372**	**4 005**	**1 796**	**15 478**	**29 162**	**51 349**
工程结算收入 Revenue of Project Settlement Accounts	2 039 327	154 786	121 868	94 639	51 954	32 263	124 839	146 447	366 843
工程结算成本 Cost of Project Settlement Accounts	1 866 650	138 548	113 525	85 778	47 682	29 563	114 788	137 713	341 794
工程结算税金及附加 Taxes and Extra Charges on Project Settlement Accounts	61 519	4 570	4 401	3 176	1 829	1 320	3 705	3 210	10 543
工程结算利润 Profits of Project Settlement Accounts	109 600	11 496	3 652	5 685	1 693	1 377	6 345	5 464	14 508
其他业务利润 Other Business Profit	11 674	2 966	476	381	426	261	119	990	2 112
管理费用 Management Expenses	75 367	5 339	2 951	3 433	1 227	672	3 312	3 685	11 086
利润总额 Total Profits	39 082	6 995	1 161	3 229	850	840	2 478	2 364	5 285

11—11 续表 Continued

计量单位:万元 (2010年) (10 000 yuan)

指标 Item	九师 Division 9	十师 Division 10	建工师 Construction Division	十二师 Division 12	十三师 Division 13	十四师 Division 14	国资公司 State-owned Property Company
资本金合计 Total Principal Value	**2 386**	**749**	**84 935**	**2 042**	**500**	**1 315**	**2 608**
流动资产小计 Circulating Assets	16 185	7 150	571 002	10 113	16 138	2 328	5 731
# 存货 Stock	8 247	107	92 026	3 788	2 324		1 220
固定资产小计 Fixed Assets	2 904	546	110 346	100	541	1 556	3 015
固定资产原价 Original Value of Fixed Assets	3 456	188	151 112	147	765	1 387	2 792
# 生产经营用 Used for Produce and Management	3 456	177	135 575	18	679	454	
累计折旧 Accumulated Depreciation	1 546	35	62 169	46	223	197	238
# 本年折旧 Depreciationin the Current Year	252	2	15 814	19	60	27	70
# 在建工程 Under Construction	993	392	4 520			366	402
资产合计 Total Assets	**19 088**	**7 903**	**790 575**	**11 130**	**16 851**	**4 275**	**8 747**
流动负债小计 Liquid Liabilities	230	7 140	468 179	8 643	15 944	2 644	6 094
长期负债小计 Long-term Liabilities	16 458	14	172 128	6			546
负债合计 Total Liabilities	**16 688**	**7 154**	**640 307**	**8 649**	**15 944**	**2 644**	**6 640**
所有者权益合计 Creditors' Equity	**2 400**	**749**	**150 268**	**2 481**	**907**	**1 631**	**2 107**
工程结算收入 Revenue of Project Settlement Accounts	28 691	18 728	797 696	19 987	38 870	23 110	18 606
工程结算成本 Cost of Project Settlement Accounts	25 897	17 861	719 551	18 665	36 256	21 753	17 276
工程结算税金及附加 Taxes and Extra Charges on Project Settlement Accounts	981	280	24 456	593	1 075	764	616
工程结算利润 Profits of Project Settlement Accounts	1 813	587	53 688	729	1 539	593	431
其他业务利润 Other Business Profit	192	4	3 521	75	138	1	12
管理费用 Management Expenses	1 422	435	40 117	323	944	349	72
利润总额 Total Profits	568	201	13 457	339	748	247	320

第十二篇 交通运输业

Chapter 12 Communications and Transportation

简要说明

一、本篇资料主要内容

本篇资料反映兵团系统内公路里程、道路运输企业生产及历年发展基本状况。包括兵团现有公路里程、道路运输业基本情况及按经济类型分列的民用车辆年末保有量、客（货）运量、周转量和法人企业财务状况等。

二、本篇统计范围

统计范围为兵团管辖道路及所属道路运输法人企业、产业活动单位和个体运输户。

三、本篇资料来源

公路里程由兵团交通局整理提供，道路运输业生产及财务状况由兵团统计局工业交通投资统计处根据《兵团交通运输业统计报表制度》收集、汇总、整理、提供。

四、本篇调查方法

统计调查方法为全面调查。

Brief Introduction

1. Main Contents

Data in this chapter show comprehensively length of highways, the basic conditions of road and transportation development, including the basic situations of road transportation in XPCG, year-end possession of civil vehicle, freight traffic and passenger traffic, and financial conditions of enterprises with independent accounting system.

2. Scope of Statistics

The statistical scope covers road of XPCG road and transportation enterprises with independent accounting system industrial active units and individual transportation units.

3. Sources of Data

Data on length of highways are provided by the Transportation Bureau of XPCG. Data on production of road and transportation enterprise and individual transportation are collected, prepared and provided by Industry Communications and Assets Statistical Section of Statistics Bureau of XPCG according to the Comprehensive Statistical Reporting Form System on Communications and Transportation of XPCG.

4. Methodology of Survey

Survey method is comprehensive statistics.

12—1 按登记注册类型分道路运输业单位数

Number of Road Transportation Units by Types of Registration

计量单位:个 (unit)

年份 Year	单位 Unit	合计 Total	法人企业 Corporative Enterprises	国有企业 State-owned Enterprises	集体企业 Collective-owned Enterprises	股份制企业 Share Holding System Enterprises	产业活动单位 Number of Basic Units
	1980	207	15	14	1		192
	1981	208	15	14	1		193
	1982	209	15	14	1		194
	1983	210	20	19	1		190
	1984	218	21	20	1		197
	1985	236	19	18	1		217
	1986	239	17	16	1		222
	1987	258	24	20	4		234
	1988	260	25	21	4		235
	1989	270	24	20	4		246
	1990	269	23	20	3		246
	1991	264	23	19	4		241
	1992	286	25	21	4		261
	1993	278	24	21	3		251
	1994	250	30	25	5		220
	1995	227	30	24	6		197
	1996	190	32	28	4		158
	1997	171	29	23	6		142
	1998	116	25	22	1	2	91
	1999	90	24	20	1	3	66
	2000	90	25	21	1	3	65
	2001	50	22	17	1	4	28
	2002	44	19	14		5	25
	2003	36	21	15		6	15
	2004	37	28	12		16	9
	2005	38	29	12		17	9
	2006	36	29	12		17	7
	2007	33	28	13		15	5
	2008	30	26	10		16	4
	2009	36	33	4		29	3
	2010	35	32	9		23	3
一师	Division 1	7	6	1		5	1
二师	Division 2	1	1			1	
三师	Division 3	1	1	1			
四师	Division 4	1	1	1			
五师	Division 5	1	1			1	
六师	Division 6	9	8			8	1
七师	Division 7	2	1	1			1
八师	Division 8	7	7	1		6	
九师	Division 9	1	1	1			
十师	Division 10	1	1	1			
建工师	Construction Division						
十二师	Division 12	1	1	1			
十三师	Division 13	1	1	1			
十四师	Division 14	1	1			1	
国资公司	State-owned Property Company						
供销公司	Supply and Marketing Corporation General						
中基公司	Chalkis Company						
兵团直属	Directly under XPCG	1	1			1	

12—2 道路运输业基本情况

Basic Statistics for Road Transportation

年份 Year	单位 Unit	民用汽车年末保有量（辆） Year-end Number of Civil Motor Vehicles (unit)	运量 Traffic: 客运量（万人） Passenger Traffic (10 000 persons)	运量 Traffic: 货运量（万吨） Freight Traffic (10 000 tons)	周转量 Kilometers: 旅客周转量（万人公里） Passenger-Kilometers (10 000 passenger-km)	周转量 Kilometers: 货物周转量（万吨公里） Freight Ton-Kilometers (10 000 ton-km)
	1950	1 277	13	15	16 512	2 866
	1952	1 761	11	143	17 272	14 946
	1954	2 194	9	176	12 557	19 058
	1957	2 530	17	260	9 672	27 890
	1962	3 277	54	269	9 065	30 433
	1965	3 964	44	677	22 057	64 620
	1970	5 824	28	563	10 765	68 000
	1975	1 760		142		29 910
	1978	4 882	40	394	6 250	50 085
	1980	6 941	57	560	7 304	66 461
	1985	12 913	388	1 197	31 821	103 233
	1990	17 135	1 246	2 007	95 259	186 613
	1991	18 729	1 349	2 053	112 043	210 988
	1992	20 442	1 484	2 395	112 794	226 582
	1993	22 492	1 866	2 551	123 806	233 909
	1994	24 004	2 085	2 594	138 724	263 911
	1995	25 818	2 400	2 854	148 470	272 375
	1996	26 506	2 549	3 000	163 677	276 232
	1997	28 410	2 843	3 406	168 478	288 030
	1998	29 375	3 822	3 817	198 387	308 591
	1999	30 345	4 213	4 475	204 099	309 891
	2000	31 925	5 206	4 637	237 061	312 763
	2001	35 010	5 936	4 717	272 149	319 858
	2002	37 186	6 303	7 229	281 738	332 954
	2003	38 896	6 623	6 128	285 844	384 837
	2004	36 442	7 082	5 494	293 678	416 363
	2005	62 689	7 458	6 552	335 394	443 260
	2006	66 306	7 882	7 158	374 164	517 592
	2007	72 106	8 197	8 329	401 687	620 291
	2008	98 780	9 139	8 765	511 314	714 652
	2009	106 906	9 860	9 766	579 487	864 163
	2010	125 197	11 019	11 853	665 999	1 067 475
一师	Division 1	16 877	955	2 093	64 856	158 322
二师	Division 2	5 395	862	917	27 395	41 827
三师	Division 3	4 907	336	263	18 674	25 128
四师	Division 4	5 276	1 036	926	45 400	78 466
五师	Division 5	4 560	292	139	16 504	20 490
六师	Division 6	12 567	2 121	1 905	127 554	152 007
七师	Division 7	8 952	1 296	1 023	94 357	113 410
八师	Division 8	45 422	892	1 888	98 136	311 536
九师	Division 9	2 494	366	183	16 560	28 773
十师	Division 10	2 844	371	191	13 295	41 393
建工师	Construction Division	922	234	123	4 548	3 933
十二师	Division 12	2 746	645	1 450	11 514	50 044
十三师	Division 13	4 679	517	657	13 348	28 898
十四师	Division 14	1 277	120	5	2 225	1 740
国资公司	State-owned Property Compan	378	36	8	498	119
供销公司	Supply and Marketing Corporation General	165	26	10	240	114
中基公司	Chalkis Company	73	8	1	252	11
兵团直属	Directly under XPCG	5 663	906	71	110 643	11 264

注：从 2005 年起，民用汽车保有量包括农用运输车（下同）。

Note: Year-end number of civil motor vehicles is includes trucks for agriculture use from 2005(the same as follows).

12—3 全部车辆年末保有量

Year-end Number of All Motor Vehicles

计量单位:辆 (2010 年) (unit)

指标	Item	合计 Total	国有法人企业 State-owned Corporative Enterprises	股份制法人企业 Share Holding System Corporative Enterprises	产业活动单位 Number of Basic Units	其他单位 Other Unit	私人 Private	个体 Individuals
总计	**Total**	**445 020**	**338**	**962**	**205**	**90 215**	**353 300**	**111 243**
民用汽车	**Civil Motor Vehicles**	**125 197**	**308**	**962**	**203**	**19 885**	**103 839**	**47 152**
载客汽车	Buses and Cars	60 187	162	275	52	10 992	48 706	12 071
# 大型	Large Scale	2 290	98	214	50	429	1 499	1 242
中型	Medium Scale	2 066	25	45		499	1 497	1 151
小型	Small Scale	50 041	39	16	2	9 172	40 812	7 255
微型	Miniature Scale	5 790				892	4 898	2 423
# 轿车	Car	46 969	39	12		7 634	39 284	6 154
载货汽车	Trucks	31 863	146	687	85	3 384	27 561	26 892
# 重型	Large Scale	9 536	118	550	80	964	7 824	8 136
中型	Medium Scale	8 631	26	15	1	248	8 341	8 164
轻型	Small Scale	11 923	1	121	4	1 951	9 846	9 397
微型	Miniature Scale	1 773	1	1		221	1 550	1 195
# 普通载货	Ordinary Trucks	24 996	136	665		2 736	21 459	21 093
农用运输车	Tucks for Agriculture Use	31 000				4 015	26 985	7 905
三轮	Three-wheeled	14 528				911	13 617	3 675
四轮	Four-wheeled	16 472				3 104	13 368	4 230
其他汽车	Others	2 147			66	1 494	587	284
摩托车	**Motorcycles**	**245 853**				**55 114**	**190 739**	**38 257**
普通	Ordinary	218 712				54 187	164 525	33 913
轻便	Easy and Convenient	27 141				927	26 214	4 344
拖拉机	**Tractor**	**69 229**				**13 077**	**56 152**	**22 689**
大中型	Large Scale	31 992				7 196	24 796	9 626
小型方向盘式	Small Scale	37 237				5 881	31 356	13 063
挂车	**Trailer Trucks**	**3 254**	**30**			**1 764**	**1 460**	**2 639**
其他类型车	**Others**	**1 487**			**2**	**375**	**1 110**	**506**

12—4 各师按登记注册类型分民用汽车年末保有量

Year-end Number of Civil Motor Vehicles by Types of Registration and Division

计量单位:辆 (2010 年) (unit)

指标	Item	合计 Total	国有法人企业 State-owned Corporative Enterprises	股份制法人企业 Share Holding System Corporative Enterprises	产业活动单位 Number of Basic Units	其他单位 Other Unit	私人 Private	个体 Individuals
总计	**Total**	**125 197**	**308**	**962**	**203**	**19 885**	**103 839**	**47 152**
一师	Division 1	16 877			110	1 271	15 496	2 389
二师	Division 2	5 395		5		733	4 657	1573
三师	Division 3	4 907				711	4 196	1 114
四师	Division 4	5 276	11			769	4 496	3 024
五师	Division 5	4 560				562	3 998	2 095
六师	Division 6	12 567			81	1 005	11 481	11 263
七师	Division 7	8 952	99		12	740	8 101	4 791
八师	Division 8	45 422	30	649		7 327	37 416	13 421
九师	Division 9	2 494	58			352	2 084	883
十师	Division 10	2 844	10			382	2 452	2139
建工师	Construction Division	922				550	372	153
十二师	Division 12	2 746	100			411	2 235	1916
十三师	Division 13	4 679				227	4 452	2 160
十四师	Division 14	1 277		3		213	1 061	165
国资公司	State-owned Property Company	378				372	6	
供销公司	Supply and Marketing Corporation General	165				165		
中基公司	Chalkis Company	73				67	6	
兵团直属	Directly under XPCG	5 663		305		4 028	1 330	66

12—5 各师全部车辆年末保有量

Year-end Number of All Motor Vehicles by Division

计量单位：辆 （2010 年） （unit）

指 标	Item	合 计 Total	一 师 Division 1	二 师 Division 2	三 师 Division 3	四 师 Division 4	五 师 Division 5	六 师 Division 6	七 师 Division 7	八 师 Division 8
总 计	**Total**	**445 020**	**58 284**	**33 427**	**28 582**	**32 865**	**19 621**	**51 232**	**42 157**	**113 755**
民用汽车	**Civil Motor Vehicles**	**125 197**	**16 877**	**5 395**	**4 907**	**5 276**	**4 560**	**12 567**	**8 952**	**45 422**
载客汽车	Buses and Cars	60 187	6 490	2 511	1 769	2 886	1 633	4 220	3 075	25 738
# 大 型	Large Scale	2 290	265	76	124	104	49	338	145	1 013
中 型	Medium Scale	2 066	169	159	141	138	94	195	169	633
小 型	Small Scale	50 041	5 499	1 628	1 151	2 589	998	2 614	2 561	23 514
微 型	Miniature Scale	5 790	557	648	353	55	492	1 073	200	578
# 轿 车	Car	46 969	4 381	1 593	1 199	2 151	940	2 618	2 020	23 514
载货汽车	Trucks	31 863	1 834	993	625	1 805	859	3 368	2 262	15 098
# 重 型	Large Scale	9 536	1 151	182	162	392	117	563	338	4 999
中 型	Medium Scale	8 631	302	355	281	691	219	1 749	1 123	2 491
轻 型	Small Scale	11 923	256	246	131	669	359	685	578	7 522
微 型	Miniature Scale	1 773	125	210	51	53	164	371	223	86
# 普通载货	Ordinary Trucks	24 996	806	606	440	1 118	686	1 668	2 032	14 990
农用运输车	Tucks for Agriculture Use	31 000	8 022	1 844	2 380	557	1 991	4 790	3 508	3 873
三 轮	Three-wheeled	14 528	4 299	994	1 235	159	865	2 497	1 513	863
四 轮	Four-wheeled	16 472	3 723	850	1 145	398	1 126	2 293	1 995	3 010
其他汽车	Others	2 147	531	47	133	28	77	189	107	713
摩托车	**Motorcycles**	**245 853**	**32 305**	**23 012**	**19 648**	**24 193**	**9 404**	**25 665**	**28 170**	**54 006**
普 通	Ordinary	218 712	27 638	20 318	15 919	23 250	8 305	22 375	22 083	53 246
轻 便	Easy and Convenient	27 141	4 667	2 694	3 729	943	1 099	3 290	6 087	760
拖拉机	**Tractor**	**69 229**	**8 417**	**4 763**	**3 873**	**3 353**	**5 588**	**12 280**	**4 708**	**12 506**
大中型	Large Scale	31 992	3 147	2 723	2 157	1 522	2 694	3 612	2 501	6 978
小型方向盘式	Small Scale	37 237	5 270	2 040	1 716	1 831	2 894	8 668	2 207	5 528
挂 车	**Trailer Trucks**	**3 254**	**420**		**14**	**3**	**3**	**629**	**213**	**1 776**
其他类型车	**Others**	**1 487**	**265**	**257**	**140**	**40**	**66**	**91**	**114**	**45**

指 标	Item	九 师 Division 9	十 师 Division 10	建工师 Constr-uction Division	十二师 Division 12	十三师 Division 13	十四师 Division 14	国资公司 State-owned Property Company	供销公司 Supply and Marketing Corporation General	中基公司 Chalkis Company	兵团直属 Directly under XPCG
总 计	**Total**	**12 050**	**15 942**	**940**	**6 764**	**15 596**	**6 308**	**414**	**179**	**203**	**6 701**
民用汽车	**Civil Motor Vehicles**	**2 494**	**2 844**	**922**	**2 746**	**4 679**	**1 277**	**378**	**165**	**73**	**5 663**
载客汽车	Buses and Cars	1 181	1 525	541	1 099	1 274	677	264	156	63	5 085
# 大 型	Large Scale	30	24	25	34	11	14	9	2	1	26
中 型	Medium Scale	68	32	42	35	75	11	9	26	3	67
小 型	Small Scale	992	916	402	463	858	505	187	128	46	4 990
微 型	Miniature Scale	91	553	72	567	330	147	59		13	2
# 轿 车	Car	794	894	465	530	861	470	166	126	49	4 198
载货汽车	Trucks	760	712	308	1 243	1 306	185	110	9	10	376
# 重 型	Large Scale	141	223	135	458	473	16				186
中 型	Medium Scale	308	264	89	436	253	27	9			34
轻 型	Small Scale	291	169	60	199	381	138	94	8	3	134
微 型	Miniature Scale	20	56	24	150	199	4	7	1	7	22
# 普通载货	Ordinary Trucks	723	426	178	203	516	170	39	9	10	376
农用运输车	Tucks for Agriculture Use	466	490		395	2 093	405				186
三 轮	Three-wheeled	103	136		158	1 325	246				135
四 轮	Four-wheeled	363	354		237	768	159				51
其他汽车	Others	87	117	73	9	6	10	4			16
摩托车	**Motorcycles**	**6 646**	**7 804**	**8**	**2 315**	**8 513**	**3 286**	**31**	**1**	**130**	**716**
普 通	Ordinary	6 284	7 431	6	1 210	7 086	2 724		1	128	708
轻 便	Easy and Convenient	362	373	2	1 105	1 427	562	31		2	8
拖拉机	**Tractor**	**2 827**	**5 189**	**3**	**1 689**	**2 256**	**1 455**	**2**			**320**
大中型	Large Scale	1 050	3 414		267	440	1 302				185
小型方向盘式	Small Scale	1 777	1 775	3	1 422	1 816	153	2			135
挂 车	**Trailer Trucks**	**59**	**87**	**7**		**43**					
其他类型车	**Others**	**24**	**18**		**14**	**105**	**290**	**3**	**13**		**2**

12—6 各师按用途分民用汽车年末保有量

Year-end Number of Civil Motor Vehicles by Purpose and Division

计量单位：辆　　　　（2010 年）　　　　(unit)

单 位	Unit	合 计 Total	载客汽车 Buses and Cars	# 轿 车 Car	载货汽车 Trucks	# 普通载货 Ordinary Trucks	农用运输车 Tucks for Agriculture Use	其他汽车 Others Motor Vehicles
总 计	**Total**	**125 197**	**60 187**	**46 969**	**31 863**	**24 996**	**31 000**	**2 147**
一 师	Division 1	16 877	6 490	4 381	1 834	806	8 022	531
二 师	Division 2	5 395	2 511	1 593	993	606	1 844	47
三 师	Division 3	4 907	1 769	1 199	625	440	2 380	133
四 师	Division 4	5 276	2 886	2 151	1 805	1 118	557	28
五 师	Division 5	4 560	1 633	940	859	686	1 991	77
六 师	Division 6	12 567	4 220	2 618	3 368	1 668	4 790	189
七 师	Division 7	8 952	3 075	2 020	2 262	2 032	3 508	107
八 师	Division 8	45 422	25 738	23 514	15 098	14 990	3 873	713
九 师	Division 9	2 494	1 181	794	760	723	466	87
十 师	Division 10	2 844	1 525	894	712	426	490	117
建 工 师	Construction Division	922	541	465	308	178		73
十 二 师	Division 12	2 746	1 099	530	1 243	203	395	9
十 三 师	Division 13	4 679	1 274	861	1 306	516	2 093	6
十 四 师	Division 14	1 277	677	470	185	170	405	10
国资公司	State-owned Property Company	378	264	166	110	39		4
供销公司	Supply and Marketing Corporation General	165	156	126	9	9		
中基公司	Chalkis Company	73	63	49	10	10		
兵团直属	Directly under XPCG	5 663	5 085	4 198	376	376	186	16

12—7 各师按营运性质分民用汽车年末保有量

Year-end Number of Civil Motor Vehicles by Operation Kind and Division

计量单位：辆　　　　（2010 年）　　　　(unit)

单 位	Unit	合 计 Total	营运 Operation	非营运 Not Operation	# 特种 Special	# 进口 Import	# 新注册 Newly registered	报废汽车 Discard Motor Vehicles	载客汽车客位（人） Passenger Vehicles Capacity (People)	# 私人 Private	载货汽车吨位（吨） Trucks Capacity (Ton)	# 私人 Private
总 计	**Total**	**125 197**	**41 063**	**84 134**	**1 653**	**1 944**	**14 021**	**831**	**400 784**	**306 256**	**312 343**	**260 323**
一 师	Division 1	16 877	2 377	14 500	260	48	968	194	41 473	34 282	29 539	29 349
二 师	Division 2	5 395	1 583	3 812	53	30	174	6	16 556	11 747	7 345	7 203
三 师	Division 3	4 907	1 114	3 793	233	96	212	19	13 941	9 930	5 455	5 252
四 师	Division 4	5 276	3 024	2 252	173	13	611	52	19 153	14 695	14 518	14 203
五 师	Division 5	4 560	1 066	3 494	82	13	772	25	10 174	7 171	4 949	4 587
六 师	Division 6	12 567	6 805	5 762	193	7	467	30	33 183	26 132	22 813	21 859
七 师	Division 7	8 952	4 890	4 062	96	18	952	171	22 732	15 594	17 107	16 550
八 师	Division 8	45 422	13 421	32 001	156	1 405	8 004	136	169 685	151 671	166 146	129 333
九 师	Division 9	2 494	939	1 555	78	5	379	27	7 285	4 602	5 814	5 511
十 师	Division 10	2 844	1 259	1 585	112	3	715	36	8 870	6 864	7 556	7 366
建 工 师	Construction Division	922	153	769	72	136	39	17	4 488	2 043	2 477	1 114
十 二 师	Division 12	2 746	1 981	765	11	8	64	36	6 675	5 097	12 756	7 687
十 三 师	Division 13	4 679	1 913	2 766	10	2	223	4	8 993	7 284	9 413	9 413
十 四 师	Division 14	1 277	167	1 110	50	9	216	2	3 700	2 627	781	616
国资公司	State-owned Property Company	378		378				2	1 679	30	271	
供销公司	Supply and Marketing Corporation General	165		165		1	8	1	938		21	
中基公司	Chalkis Company	73		73			4	2	322	24	14	
兵团直属	Directly under XPCG	5 663	371	5 292	74	150	213	71	30 937	6 463	5 368	280

12—8 各师道路运输客运量

Passenger Traffic of Road Transportation by Division

计量单位:万人　　　　(2010 年)　　　　(10 000 persons)

单　位	Unit	合　计 Total	国　有 法人企业 State-owned Corporative Enterprises	股份制 法人企业 Share Holding System Corporative Enterprises	产　业 活动单位 Number of Basic Units	其他单位 Other Unit	个　体 Individuals
总　计	**Total**	**11 019**	**244**	**1 329**	**49**	**1 283**	**8 114**
一　师	Division 1	955	1			42	912
二　师	Division 2	862				41	821
三　师	Division 3	336					336
四　师	Division 4	1 036				58	978
五　师	Division 5	292		65			227
六　师	Division 6	2 121		766		1	1 354
七　师	Division 7	1 296	185		49	68	994
八　师	Division 8	892		488			404
九　师	Division 9	366	48			13	305
十　师	Division 10	371	10				361
建工师	Construction Division	234				49	185
十二师	Division 12	645					645
十三师	Division 13	517				45	472
十四师	Division 14	120		10			110
国资公司	State-owned Property Company	36				36	
供销公司	Supply and Marketing Corporation General	26				26	
中基公司	Chalkis Company	8				8	
兵团直属	Directly under XPCG	906				896	10

12—9 各师道路运输货运量

Freight Traffic of Road Transportation by Division

计量单位:万吨　　　　(2010 年)　　　　(10 000 tons)

单　位	Unit	合　计 Total	国　有 法人企业 State-owned Corporative Enterprises	股份制 法人企业 Share Holding System Corporative Enterprises	产　业 活动单位 Number of Basic Units	其他单位 Other Unit	个　体 Individuals
总　计	**Total**	**11 853**	**27**	**256**	**667**	**100**	**10 803**
一　师	Division 1	2 093			534	6	1 553
二　师	Division 2	917				2	915
三　师	Division 3	263					263
四　师	Division 4	926				4	922
五　师	Division 5	139					139
六　师	Division 6	1 905			133		1 772
七　师	Division 7	1 023				1	1 022
八　师	Division 8	1 888	17	243			1 628
九　师	Division 9	183	3			2	178
十　师	Division 10	191					191
建工师	Construction Division	123				42	81
十二师	Division 12	1 450	4				1 446
十三师	Division 13	657	3				654
十四师	Division 14	5					5
国资公司	State-owned Property Company	8				8	
供销公司	Supply and Marketing Corporation General	10				10	
中基公司	Chalkis Company	1				1	
兵团直属	Directly under XPCG	71		13		24	34

12—10 按登记注册类型分旅客周转量

Passenger-kilometers by Types of Registration

计量单位：万人公里 (10 000 passenger-km)

年 份 单 位	Year Unit	合 计 Total	国有法人企业 State-owned Corporative Enterprises	股份制法人企业 Share Holding System Corporative Enterprises	产业活动单位 Number of Basic Units	集体企业 Collective-owned Enterprises	其他单位 Other Unit	个 体 Individuals
	1980	7 304	7 183		121			
	1981	9 642	9 373		269			
	1982	11 062	10 650		412			
	1983	14 413	13 616		650		53	93
	1984	16 676	14 992		1 312		136	236
	1985	31 821	24 079		2 683		1 844	3 214
	1986	49 549	29 765		8 561		4 092	7 131
	1987	66 691	38 639		12 833		5 549	9 670
	1988	84 915	49 395		17 630		7 170	10 720
	1989	96 379	58 761		18 880		7 570	11 168
	1990	95 259	54 542		21 615		8 111	10 991
	1991	112 043	63 953		29 976		6 079	12 035
	1992	112 794	66 852		25 655		6 913	13 374
	1993	123 806	61 055		29 744		6 727	26 280
	1994	138 724	55 495		23 778		9 106	50 345
	1995	148 470	50 857		21 731	770	10 300	64 812
	1996	163 677	55 330		15 137	420	12 816	79 974
	1997	168 478	59 630		12 056	119	10 931	85 742
	1998	198 387	62 109		12 407		22 808	101 064
	1999	204 099	53 385		10 477	860	21 432	117 944
	2000	237 061	55 483		8 784	7 616	25 242	139 936
	2001	272 149	35 150	39 584	7 904		33 520	155 992
	2002	281 738	38 801	47 660	4 446		17 267	173 564
	2003	285 844	55 575	54 278	3 847		6 733	165 411
	2004	293 678	60 841	48 726	4 942		5 827	173 342
	2005	335 394	63 827	53 085	5 088		11 187	202 207
	2006	374 164	57 772	62 446	4 750		4 865	244 330
	2007	401 687	57 155	83 538	4 850		5 637	250 507
	2008	511 314	54 091	86 915	4 404		80 658	285 247
	2009	579 487	52 663	105 740	1 350		101 525	318 209
	2010	665 999	54 296	103 467	1 552		126 224	380 460
一 师	Division 1	64 856	1 036				2 458	61 362
二 师	Division 2	27 395					2 022	25 373
三 师	Division 3	18 674						18 674
四 师	Division 4	45 400					2 367	43 033
五 师	Division 5	16 504		2 335				14 169
六 师	Division 6	127 554		35 444			90	92 020
七 师	Division 7	94 357	42 332		1 552		3 267	47 206
八 师	Division 8	98 136		65 647				32 489
九 师	Division 9	16 560	7 300				1 173	8 087
十 师	Division 10	13 295	3 628					9 667
建 工 师	Construction Division	4 548					2 460	2 088
十 二 师	Division 12	11 514						11 514
十 三 师	Division 13	13 348					1 299	12 049
十 四 师	Division 14	2 225		41				2 184
国资公司	State-owned Property Company	498					498	
供销公司	Supply and Marketing Corporation General	240					240	
中基公司	Chalkis Company	252					252	
兵团直属	Directly under XPCG	110 643					110 098	545

12—11 按登记注册类型分货物周转量

Freight Ton-kilometers by Types of Registration

计量单位:万吨公里 (10 000 ton-km)

年份 单位	Year Unit	合计 Total	国有法人企业 State-owned Corporative Enterprises	股份制法人企业 Share Holding System Corporative Enterprises	产业活动单位 Number of Basic Units	集体企业 Collective-owned Enterprises	其他单位 Other Unit	个体 Individuals
	1980	66 461	31 248		34 522			691
	1981	64 372	27 357		35 674			1 341
	1982	70 733	31 339		36 357			3 038
	1983	79 511	38 134		34 605			6 772
	1984	96 752	38 591		48 376			9 785
	1985	102 923	32 775		44 940	128		25 080
	1986	104 746	33 952		46 276	113		24 405
	1987	135 573	41 624		57 606	787	11 552	24 003
	1988	162 176	48 735		62 624	968	20 352	29 496
	1989	177 825	52 168		71 247	1 026	20 408	32 976
	1990	186 613	60 412		79 530	948	17 303	28 420
	1991	210 988	72 649		87 676	1 332	18 194	31 137
	1992	226 582	73 031		95 551	1 372	21 879	34 749
	1993	233 909	75 099		95 167	128	28 201	35 314
	1994	263 911	75 549		87 755	1 429	42 117	57 061
	1995	272 375	69 199		75 972	1 843	43 755	81 606
	1996	276 232	64 612		66 347	2 357	49 548	93 367
	1997	288 030	60 514		66 850	2 990	29 961	127 714
	1998	308 591	54 259		47 795	2 056	30 473	174 008
	1999	309 891	51 568		33 351	8 069	25 234	191 671
	2000	312 763	38 040		20 664	2 933	21 638	229 489
	2001	319 858	20 711	6 026	26 205	343	13 282	253 292
	2002	332 954	4 078	11 812	14 116		15 837	287 112
	2003	384 837	44 410	19 865	6 370		4 648	309 544
	2004	416 363	37 474	29 150	8 067		5 073	336 598
	2005	443 260	39 937	33 880	7 777		1 327	360 339
	2006	517 592	7 893	38 720	12 745		1 502	456 732
	2007	620 291	16 380	54 078	14 226		840	534 768
	2008	714 652	15 350	46 067	15 110		427	637 698
	2009	864 163	2 350	76 236	22 088		535	762 954
	2010	1 067 475	17 105	47 591	49 858		1 702	951 219
一 师	Division 1	158 322			14 858		246	143 218
二 师	Division 2	41 827					107	41 720
三 师	Division 3	25 128						25 128
四 师	Division 4	78 466					144	78 322
五 师	Division 5	20 490						20 490
六 师	Division 6	152 007			35 000			117 007
七 师	Division 7	113 410					5	113 405
八 师	Division 8	311 536	1 197	37 758				272 581
九 师	Division 9	28 773	692				78	28 003
十 师	Division 10	41 393						41 393
建工师	Construction Division	3 933					786	3 147
十二师	Division 12	50 044	12 600					37 444
十三师	Division 13	28 898	2 616					26 282
十四师	Division 14	1 740						1 740
国资公司	State-owned Property Company	119					119	
供销公司	Supply and Marketing Corporation General	114					114	
中基公司	Chalkis Company	11					11	
兵团直属	Directly under XPCG	11 264		9 833			92	1 339

12—12 各师公路里程

Total Length of Highways by Division

计量单位:公里 （2010 年） (km)

单位	Unit	按行政等级分 by Administrative level 合计 Total	省道 Provinces	县道 Country	乡道 Townships	专用道 Special	村道 Village
总计	**Total**	**32 058**	**3 957**	**5 476**	**11 225**	**3 750**	**7 650**
一师	Division 1	2 866	566	230	1 038	159	873
二师	Division 2	3 090	237	609	488	770	986
三师	Division 3	2 410	380	436	736	364	494
四师	Division 4	2 719	187	243	1 449	363	477
五师	Division 5	2 077	236	237	877	157	570
六师	Division 6	4 593	902	902	2 170		619
七师	Division 7	2 581	259	843	677	19	783
八师	Division 8	3 251	621	340	919	110	1 261
九师	Division 9	1 491	118	333	274	398	368
十师	Division 10	2 829	451	193	497	1 108	580
建工师	Construction Division	25			25		
十二师	Division 12	646		318	318		10
十三师	Division 13	2 257		515	1 528	208	6
十四师	Division 14	1 223		277	229	94	623

单位	Unit	按技术等级分 by Technique level 合计 Total	一级 Level	二级 Level 2	三级 Level 3	四级 Level 4	等外 BelowLevel4
总计	**Total**	**32 058**	**15**	**1 314**	**5 400**	**8 403**	**16 926**
一师	Division 1	2 866		335	550	649	1 332
二师	Division 2	3 090		222	531	634	1 703
三师	Division 3	2 410	4	111	681	842	772
四师	Division 4	2 719	7	39	540	993	1 140
五师	Division 5	2 077		153	215	477	1 232
六师	Division 6	4 593		275	435	1 071	2 812
七师	Division 7	2 581		17	539	642	1 383
八师	Division 8	3 251	2	56	697	930	1 566
九师	Division 9	1 491		48	170	494	779
十师	Division 10	2 829	2	14	336	930	1 547
建工师	Construction Division	25				4	21
十二师	Division 12	646		30	200	157	259
十三师	Division 13	2 257		14	377	347	1 519
十四师	Division 14	1 223			129	233	861

12—13 道路运输法人企业财务状况

Financial Indicators of Road Transportation Corporative Enterprises

计量单位:万元 (2010年) (10 000 yuan)

指　标	Item	合　计 Total	国有企业 State-owned Enterprises	股份制企业 Share Holding System Enterprises
企业单位数(个)	Number of Enterprises(unit)	32	9	23
# 亏损企业	Loss	3	1	2
年初存货	Stock at the Beginning of the Year	1 851	483	1 368
资产总计	Total Assets	85 904	29 743	56 161
流动资产合计	Working Capitals	34 218	9 716	24 502
# 存　货	Stock at the Year-end	1 926	621	1 305
固定资产原价	Original Fixed Assets	43 074	16 842	26 232
累计折旧	Accumulation Depreciation	15 983	6 065	9 918
# 本年折旧	Current Year Depreciation	4 725	1 776	2 949
负债合计	Total Liabilities	576 074	23 633	552 441
所有者权益合计	Creditors Equity	28 297	6 110	22 187
# 实收资本	Paid-up Capital	19 890	6 348	13 542
# 国家资本	National Capital	6 689	5 718	971
个人资本	Individual Capital	10 022	510	9 512
主营业务收入	Revenue from Principal Business	49 951	17 908	32 043
主营业务成本	Cost of Principal Business	39 953	14 034	25 919
主营业务税金及附加	Taxes and Other Charges on Principal Business	1 326	401	925
主营业务利润	Profits from Principal Business	7 990	2 994	4 996
其他业务利润	Profits from Other Business	723	438	285
经营费用	Business Expenses	682	479	203
管理费用	Administrative Expenses	5 572	2 862	2 710
# 税金	Taxes	327	270	57
财产保险费	Property Insurance Expenses	204	26	178
差旅费	Travel Allowance	115	69	46
财务费用	Financial Expenses	128	20	108
# 利息净支出	Intrest Expenditure	112	19	93
营业利润	Operating Profits	3 013	550	2 463
利润总额	Total Profits	3 587	756	2 831
应交所得税	Income Tax Payable	249	101	148
劳动、失业保险费	Unemployment Insurance Expenses	42	19	23
养老保险和医疗保险费	Old-pension and Medical Insurance Expenses	878	388	490
住房公积金及住房补贴	Housing Fund and Housing Allowance	233	105	128
本年应付工资总额	Total Accrued wages of Current Year	5 467	2 351	3 116
本年应付福利费总额	Total Accrued welfarism of Current Year	255	122	133
全部从业人员年平均人数(人)	Average Annual Number of Persons Employed (person)	1 887	734	1 153

2011

BING TUAN

第十三篇

国内贸易

Chapter 13 Domestic Trade

简要说明

一、本篇资料主要内容

本篇资料反映兵团国内贸易基本情况、批发和零售市场的发展和批发和零售业商品流转情况、住宿和餐饮业经营情况以及主要财务状况。主要内容包括：批发和零售业、住宿和餐饮业基本情况、商品流转和经营情况及财务状况；社会消费品零售总额；限额以上连锁批发和零售业及餐饮业经营情况；亿元以上商品交易市场概况及交易情况等。

二、本篇统计范围

（一）批发和零售业商品流转情况统计范围为批发和零售业的法人企业、产业活动单位和个体经营户。

（二）住宿和餐饮业基本情况统计范围为住宿和餐饮业的法人企业、产业活动单位和个体经营户。

（三）社会消费品零售总额统计范围为批发和零售业、住宿和餐饮业以及其他行业有零售业务的法人企业、产业活动单位和个体经营户对城乡居民和社会集团的消费品零售额总和。

（四）限额以上连锁店（公司）基本情况统计范围为限额以上批发和零售、餐饮业的连锁集团、法人企业和产业活动单位。

（五）限额以上批发和零售、住宿和餐饮业企业及个体经营户统计限额标准：批发业，年主营业务收入2000万元及以上；零售业，年主营业务收入500万元及以上；住宿和餐饮业，年主营业务收入200万元及以上。

三、本篇资料来源

本篇资料由兵团统计局社会科技贸易统计处根据《兵团批发和零售业、住宿和餐饮业统计报表制度》整理提供。

四、本篇调查方法

调查方法为全面调查。

Brief Introduction

1. Main Contents

Data in this chapter reflect the development of XPCG's domestic market, development of wholesale and retail trade, and circulation of commodities through wholesale and retail trades, and the operation of hotels and catering services. Main contents include the basic conditions of the wholesale and retail trades, hotels and catering services; circulation of commodities (in operation and financial terms); total retail sales of consumer goods; development of chain stores of wholesale and retail trades and catering services above designated size; basic statistics on commodity exchange markets of transaction value over 100 million yuan.

2. Scope of Statistics

(1) The statistics of circulation of commodities through wholesale and retail trades cover corporation enterprises, economic active establishments and self-employed individuals of wholesale and retail trades.

(2) The statistics of hotels and catering services cover corporation enterprises, economic active establishments and self-employed individuals of hotels and catering services.

(3) The statistics of total retail sales of consumer goods cover corporation enterprises, economic active establishments and self-employed individuals of wholesale and retail trades, hotels and catering services, and other sectors with retail business

(4) The statistics of chain stores cover chain groups, corporation enterprises, economic active establishments of wholesale and retail trades and catering services above designated size.

(5) Criteria for wholesale and retail sale trades, hotels and catering services above designated size are as follows: wholesale trade, main business income over 20 million yuan; retail trade, main business income over 5 million yuan; hotels and catering services, main business income over 2 million yuan.

3. Sources of Data

Data in this chapter are compiled and provided by the Society, Science and Trade Statistics Section of the Statistics Bureau of XPCG in accordance with the Statistical Reporting Form System on Wholesale and retail Trades, hotels and Catering Services.

4. Methods of Survey

It is comprehensive statistics.

13—1 国内贸易基本情况

Basic Conditions of Domestic Trade

指 标	Item	1978	1985	1990	1995	2000	2005	2009	2010
法人企业 (个)	**Number of Corporation Unit (unit)**	**52**	**87**	**132**	**277**	**178**	**718**	**965**	**967**
批发和零售业	Wholesale and Retail Trades	47	79	118	244	170	634	882	869
住宿和餐饮业	Accommodation and Catering Trade	5	8	14	33	8	84	83	98
产业活动单位 (个)	**Number of Economic Active Unit (unit)**	**74**	**111**	**160**	**790**	**300**	**1 099**	**543**	**532**
批发和零售业	Wholesale and Retail Trades	63	97	143	727	256	944	520	488
住宿和餐饮业	Accommodation and Catering Trade	11	14	17	63	44	155	23	44
年末从业人员 (人)	**Number of Employed Persons at the Year-end (person)**	**1 507**	**6 348**	**10 855**	**11 820**	**20 663**	**25 949**	**23 461**	**23 114**
批发和零售业	Wholesale and Retail Trades	1 109	5 766	9 856	10 683	18 795	20 160	17 802	16 731
住宿和餐饮业	Accommodation and Catering Trade	398	582	999	1 137	1 868	5 789	5 659	6 383
批发和零售业	**Wholesale and Retail Trades**								
商品购进总额 (亿元)	Total Purchases Value (100 million yuan)	4. 25	11. 50	23. 85	146. 37	189. 94	358. 25	526. 29	652. 88
商品销售总额 (亿元)	Total Sales Value (100 million yuan)	4. 80	12. 19	23. 08	146. 00	185. 43	369. 31	596. 92	649. 36
年末库存总额 (亿元)	Stock at the Year-end (100 million yuan)	1. 68	3. 10	9. 31	36. 20	64. 69	93. 48	107. 70	150. 50
社会消费品零售总额 (亿元)	**Total Retail Sales of Consumer Goods (100 million yuan)**	**5. 71**	**10. 67**	**19. 70**	**35. 71**	**54. 00**	**93. 38**	**179. 78**	**202. 87**
按销售单位所在地分	Grouped by Location of Establishments								
城 镇	Urban								178. 20
# 城 区	Urban Areas								114. 57
乡 村	Rural								24. 67
按行业分	Goruped by Sector								
批发和零售业	Wholesale and Retail Trade	2. 76	5. 44	10. 15	17. 42	31. 18	73. 03	144. 22	171. 71
住宿和餐饮业	Accommodation and Catering Trade	0. 10	0. 34	0. 50	1. 42	5. 12	12. 42	25. 76	31. 16
其他行业	Others	2. 85	4. 89	9. 05	16. 87	17. 70	7. 93	9. 80	

注：年末从业人员为法人企业、非同业限额以上产业活动单位及限额以上个体。

Note: Number of eplioyedpersons at the year-end includs corporation unit, economic active unit above designated in different Sector and individual units.

13—2 批发和零售业基本情况

Basic Conditions of Wholesale and Retail Trades

计量单位：万元　　(2010 年)　　(10 000 yuan)

指 标	Item	法人企业（个） Number of Corporation Enterprises (unit)	商品购进总额 Total Purchases Value	商品销售总额 Total Sales Value	年末库存总额 Stock at the Year-end
总 计	**Total**	**869**	**6 528 847**	**6 493 650**	**1 504 993**
按规模分	**Grouped by Size of Enterprises**				
限额以上	Above Designated Size	135	5 047 740	4 766 562	1 157 100
限额以下	Below Designated Size	734	1 481 107	1 727 088	347 893
按师分	**Grouped by Division**				
一 师	Division 1	12	770 886	707 555	182 888
二 师	Division 2	8	341 593	334 534	69 270
三 师	Division 3	6	345 416	310 813	101 981
四 师	Division 4	10	313 012	355 154	60 421
五 师	Division 5	9	320 328	367 259	63 221
六 师	Division 6	21	592 208	559 594	114 434
七 师	Division 7	11	361 774	338 914	104 505
八 师	Division 8	700	1 184 499	1 220 126	411 081
九 师	Division 9	5	73 853	76 876	19 507
十 师	Division 10	6	100 635	97 784	19 159
建 工 师	Construction Division	4	33 152	34 254	750
十 二 师	Division 12	11	89 051	88 970	6 182
十 三 师	Division 13	2	111 070	100 006	38 182
十 四 师	Division 14	10	46 465	54 039	3 693
国资公司	State-owned Property Company	36	933 842	1 034 421	74 099
供销公司	Supply and Marketing Corporation General	6	581 072	513 263	144 906
中基公司	Chalkis Company	3	443	1 653	489
兵团直属	Direct under XPCG	9	329 547	298 436	90 229

13—3 限额以上批发和零售业基本情况

(2010 年)

指标	Item	法人企业(个) Number of Corporation Enterprises(unit)	非批发零售业产业活动单位及个体户(个) Industries Activty Units and Individual Unibs are not Belong to Wholesale and Retail (unit)
总计	**Total**	**135**	**50**
批发业	**Wholesale Trade**	**96**	**29**
按批发行业分组	**Group by Wholesale Trade Sector**		
农畜产品批发	Wholesale of Farm Produce and Livestock Products	43	9
谷物、豆及薯类批发	Wholesale of Cereal, Pulse and Tubers	1	2
种子、饲料批发	Wholesale of Seed and Animal Forage	10	6
棉、麻批发	Wholesale of Cotton and Hemp Crops	29	
其他农畜产品批发	Other Wholesale of Farm Produce and Livestock Products	3	1
食品、饮料及烟草制品批发	Wholesale of Food, Beverages and Tobaccos	7	1
米、面制品及食用油批发	Wholesale of Rice, Flour and Edible Oil	1	
果品、蔬菜批发	Wholesale of Fruit and Vegetable	2	1
饮料及茶叶批发	Wholesale of Beverage and Tea	1	
烟草制品批发	Wholesale of Tobaccos	1	
其他食品批发	Other Wholesale	2	
纺织、服装及日用品批发	Wholesale of Textiles, Garments and Daily Consumer Articles	4	
纺织品、针织品及原料批发	Wholesale of Textiles, Garments and Daily Consumer Articles	2	
服装批发	Wholesale of Garments	1	
其他日用品批发	Wholesale of Other Daily Consumer Articles	1	
医药及医疗器材批发	Wholesale of Medicines and Mdedical Appliances	4	
西药批发	Wholesale of Western Medicines	4	
矿产品、建材及化工产品批发	Wholesale of Mineral Products, Building Materials and Chemical Products	29	18
煤炭及制品批发	Wholesale of Coal and Related Products	1	
石油及制品批发	Wholesale of Petroleum and Related Products	2	
金属及金属矿批发	Wholesale of Metal and Materials	4	
建材批发	Wholesale of Building Materials Products	8	
化肥批发	Wholesale of Chemical Fertilizer	13	18
其他化工产品批发	Wholesale of Other Chemical Products	1	
机械设备、五金交电及电子产品批发	Wholesale of Machinery, Hardware and Electronic Equipment	5	1
农业机械批发	Wholesale of Agricultural Machinery	4	
汽车、摩托车及零配件批发	Wholesale of Motor Vehicles, Motorcycle and Accessories	1	
其他机械设备及电子产品批发	Other Wholesale of Machinery and Electronic Equipment		1
贸易经纪与代理	Trade Broker and Agency	2	
其他批发	Other Wholesale	2	
其他未列明的批发	Other Not Listed Wholesale	2	
按登记注册类型分组	**Grouped by Status of Registration**		
内资企业	Domestic Enterprises	96	29
国有企业	State-owned Enterprises	33	26
有限责任公司	Limited Liability Corporations	36	1
国有独资公司	State-owned Corporations with Private-Funds	4	
其他有限责任公司	Other Limited Liability Corporations	32	1
股份有限公司	State-controlled Corporations Ltd.	5	
私营企业	Private Enterprises	22	1
私营有限责任公司	Private Limited Liability Corporations	20	
私营股份有限公司	Private Share-holding Corporations Ltd.	2	1
其他企业	Other Enterprises		1

Basic Conditions of Enterprises above Designated Size in Wholesale and Retail Trades

年末从业人员（人）Number of Engaged Persons at the Year-end (person)	商品购进总额（万元）Total Purchases Value (10 000 yuan)	商品销售总额（万元）Total Sales Value (10 000 yuan)	批发 Wholesale Value	零售 Retail Value	年末库存总额（万元）Stock at the Year-end (10 000 yuan)
13 434	**5 047 740**	**4 766 562**	**4 228 478**	**538 084**	**1 157 100**
9 667	**4 543 142**	**4 238 163**	**4 206 705**	**31 458**	**1 134 547**
4 441	2 923 241	2 548 062	2 548 062		903 802
109	16 291	15 987	15 987		7 831
1 811	80 326	103 091	103 091		18 242
2 394	2 803 763	2 404 149	2 404 149		873 095
127	22 862	24 835	24 835		4 633
557	96 027	109 444	108 273	1 171	16 525
24	15 971	16 817	16 817		7 078
128	27 512	33 680	33 680		334
29	3 266	3 617	3 617		433
128	32 462	38 895	37 724	1 171	2 552
248	16 817	16 435	16 435		6 128
113	13 475	16 124	16 124		2 076
14	8 008	8 854	8 854		839
5	3 183	2 912	2 912		365
94	2 284	4 358	4 358		872
451	43 156	45 853	44 102	1 751	8 182
451	43 156	45 853	44 102	1 751	8 182
3 791	1 370 013	1 413 030	1 384 494	28 536	196 561
25	3 565	3 044	3 044		523
1 821	425 388	464 140	439 725	24 415	18 587
58	22 357	24 393	24 393		832
125	135 174	134 456	134 456		6 171
1 759	762 613	766 058	761 937	4 121	170 448
3	20 916	20 939	20 939		
188	63 990	69 055	69 055		4 043
122	23 318	23 290	23 290		3 628
50	2 374	3 212	3 212		415
16	38 298	42 553	42 553		
15	9 294	9 829	9 829		312
111	23 945	26 767	26 767		3 047
111	23 945	26 767	26 767		3 047
9 667	4 543 142	4 238 163	4 206 705	31 458	1 134 547
5 920	3 196 554	2 872 209	2 841 943	30 265	895 627
2 002	799 032	809 327	808 156	1 171	152 411
295	112 945	121 401	120 230	1 171	5 673
1 707	686 087	687 926	687 926		146 739
1 425	261 512	276 639	276 639		55 577
317	278 794	273 034	273 012	22	28 647
288	223 053	213 336	213 314	22	28 256
29	55 741	59 699	59 699		391
3	7 250	6 955	6 955		2 285

13—3 续表

（2010 年）

指　　标	Item	法人企业（个）Number of Corporation Enterprises(unit)	非批发零售业产业活动单位及个体户(个) Industries Activty Units and Individual Unibs are not Belong to Wholesale and Retail (unit)
按控股情况分组	**Grouped by Share-holding Controlled**		
国有控股	Share-holding Controlled of State-owned	64	
集体控股	Share-holding Controlled of Collective-owned	1	
私人控股	Share-holding Controlled of Private	23	
其他	Other	8	
按经营形式分组	**Grouped by Operate Form**		
独立门店	Store of Independent	48	22
连锁总店	Total Store of Catena	3	
其他	Other	45	7
零售业	**Retail Trade**	**39**	**21**
按零售行业分组	**Group by Retail Trade Sector**		
综合零售	Integrated Retail	5	11
食品、饮料及烟草制品专门零售	Retail of Food, Beverage and Tobaccos	1	1
纺织、服装及日用品专门零售	Retail of Textiles, Garments and Daily Consumer Articles	2	2
文化、体育用品及器材专门零售	Retail of Culture, Sports Appliances and Equipments	1	
医药及医疗器材专门零售	Retail of Medicines and Mdedical Appliances	7	1
汽车、摩托车、燃料及零配件专门零售	Retail of Motor Vehicles, Motorcycles Fuel and Parts	17	3
家用电器及电子产品专门零售	Special Retail of Household Electric Appliances and Electronic Products	5	1
五金、家具及室内装修材料专门零售	Special Retail of Hardware, Furniture and Decoration Materials		1
无店铺及其他零售	Non-shop and Other Retails	1	1
按登记注册类型分组	**Grouped by Status of Registration**		
内资企业	Domestic Enterprises	39	9
国有企业	State-owned Enterprises	14	9
有限责任公司	Limited Liability Corporations	10	
国有独资公司	State-owned Corporations with Private-Funds	3	
其他有限责任公司	Other Limited Liability Corporations	7	
私营企业	Private Enterprises	15	
私营有限责任公司	Private Limited Liability Corporations	15	
个体工商户	Individual		12
按控股情况分组	**Grouped by Share-holding Controlled**		
国有控股	Share-holding Controlled of State-owned	20	
私人控股	Share-holding Controlled of Collective-owned	18	
其他	Other	1	
按经营形式分组	**Grouped by Operate Form**		
独立门店	Store of Independent	20	15
连锁总店	Total Store of Catena	8	
连锁门店	Store of Catena	10	
其他	Other	1	6
按零售业态分组	**Group by Retail Trade Form**		
有店铺零售	Store Retail Trade Form	39	21
便利店	Convenience Store		2
超市	Supermarket	1	7
大型超市	Large Supermarket	2	
百货店	General Store	2	3
专业店	Profession Store	33	2
专卖店	Monopoly Store	1	3
家居建材商店	Building Material Store		1
购物中心	Shopping Center		2
厂家直销中心	Factory Sales in Directly Center		1

Continued

年末从业人员（人） Number of Engaged Persons at the Year-end (person)	商品购进总额（万元） Total Purchases Value (10 000 yuan)	商品销售总额（万元） Total Sales Value (10 000 yuan)	批　发 Wholesale Value	零　售 Retail Value	年末库存总额（万元） Stock at the Year-end (10 000 yuan)
8 037	3 840 304	3 583 813	3 554 602	29 211	971 288
19	63 135	65 123	65 123		6 747
347	241 067	231 682	231 660	22	29 273
616	187 229	157 112	157 112		85 450
6 613	2 406 838	2 358 260	2 328 719	29 541	470 679
180	24 450	23 481	21 563	1 918	3 044
2 874	2 111 855	1 856 424	1 856 424		660 825
3 767	**504 598**	**528 399**	**21 773**	**506 626**	**22 553**
1 218	73 633	74 699	1 093	73 607	6 608
46	2 613	2 722		2 722	535
94	1 243	2 470		2 470	320
88	6 361	6 656		6 656	747
363	11 147	11 850	386	11 464	1 566
1 852	396 957	417 300	16 847	400 453	11 588
81	9 163	9 121	1 528	7 593	968
10	554	510		510	68
15	2 926	3 071	1 919	1 152	152
3 310	462 973	486 252	21 559	464 692	20 418
1 962	377 815	398 695	10 526	388 169	13 675
769	36 566	39 256	8 436	30 820	2 818
324	8 890	10 340	1 809	8 531	737
445	27 675	28 916	6 627	22 288	2 081
579	48 592	48 301	2 596	45 704	3 925
579	48 592	48 301	2 596	45 704	3 925
457	41 626	42 148	214	41 934	2 134
2 236	379 525	401 674	11 289	390 384	13 944
710	57 787	58 487	2 596	55 891	4 668
130	14 253	14 253	6 607	7 645	
1 736	146 134	154 499	11 237	143 262	8 090
364	10 327	10 558	386	10 172	1 695
1 377	306 269	322 778	8 964	313 814	9 615
290	41 869	40 564	1 186	39 378	3 152
3 767	504 599	528 399	21 773	506 625	22 552
25	770	783		783	166
378	39 685	38 815	214	38 601	1 956
316	20 698	21 444		21 444	2 048
518	9 663	10 836	94	10 742	1 937
2 330	424 442	445 930	20 473	425 457	15 082
106	4 040	4 087	207	3 880	488
10	554	510		510	68
78	1 160	2 391		2 391	139
6	3 587	3 605	785	2 820	668

13－4　各师限额以上批发和零售业基本情况

Basic Conditions of Enterprises above Designated Size in Wholesale and Retail Trades by Division

（2010 年）

单　位	Unit	法人企业（个） Number of Corporation Enterprises (unit)	非批发零售业产业活动单位及个体户(个) Number of economic active unit is not belong to wholesale andretail trades and individual units.(unit)	年末从业人员（人） Number of Engaged Persons at the Year-end (person)	商品购进总额（万元） Total Purchases Value (10 000 yuan)
总　计	**Total**	**135**	**50**	**13 434**	**5 047 740**
一　师	Division 1	8	9	1 688	598 026
二　师	Division 2	5	3	692	203 484
三　师	Division 3	5		272	299 425
四　师	Division 4	8	10	1 128	237 515
五　师	Division 5	7	5	669	257 019
六　师	Division 6	4	4	254	200 783
七　师	Division 7	3	5	697	213 273
八　师	Division 8	42	5	1 577	1 010 304
九　师	Division 9	3		143	20 256
十　师	Division 10	1	3	148	30 015
建工师	Construction Division	4		69	29 096
十二师	Division 12	1	2	69	8 107
十三师	Division 13	2	4	143	70 684
十四师	Division 14	6		130	42 065
国资公司	State-owned Property Company	25		4 087	927 864
供销公司	Supply and Marketing Corporation General	6		1 213	580 916
兵团直属	Directly under XPCG	5		455	318 908

单　位	Unit	商品销售总额（万元） Total Sales Value (10 000 yuan)	批　发 Wholesale Value	零　售 Retail Value	年末库存总额（万元） Stock at the Year-end (10 000 yuan)
总　计	**Total**	**4 766 562**	**4 228 478**	**538 084**	**1 157 100**
一　师	Division 1	562 363	553 876	8 487	133 816
二　师	Division 2	207 851	170 919	36 931	32 107
三　师	Division 3	229 928	227 678	2 250	90 025
四　师	Division 4	260 542	251 896	8 646	50 431
五　师	Division 5	288 932	287 135	1 797	44 577
六　师	Division 6	191 839	191 129	711	36 380
七　师	Division 7	168 765	168 765		72 085
八　师	Division 8	824 652	751 713	72 937	349 490
九　师	Division 9	19 615	19 615		4 499
十　师	Division 10	29 071	22 130	6 941	4 140
建工师	Construction Division	29 772	27 881	1 891	433
十二师	Division 12	10 292	9 509	783	1 974
十三师	Division 13	67 609	67 609		28 770
十四师	Division 14	48 335	48 335		2 957
国资公司	State-owned Property Company	1 026 105	629 395	396 710	71 435
供销公司	Supply and Marketing Corporation General	513 215	513 215		144 696
兵团直属	Directly under XPCG	287 677	287 678		89 285

13—5 批发和零售业商品销售类值

Enterprises in Wholesale and Retail Trades by Category of Commodities

计量单位:万元 (2010 年) (10 000 yuan)

指 标	Item	商品销售总额 Total Sales Value	限额以上 Wholesale Value	限额以下 Retail Value
总 计	**Total**	**6 493 650**	**4 766 562**	**1 727 088**
粮油、食品、饮料、烟酒类	Grain, oil, Food, Beverage, Tobacco and Liquor	714 668	159 695	554 973
# 粮油、食品类	Grain, oil and Food	394 269	104 578	289 691
服装鞋帽、针、纺织品类	Clothing, Shoes, Hats and Textiles	183 042	26 266	156 775
化妆品类	Cosmetics	37 483	5 766	31 717
金银珠宝类	Gold, Silver and Jewelry	6 774	602	6 173
日用品类	Articles for Daily Use	121 211	8 329	112 882
五金、电料类	Hardware and Electrical Materials	41 390	4 495	36 894
体育、娱乐用品类	Sports and Recreation Articles	8 067	929	7 138
书报杂志类	Newspapers and Magazines	13 718	6 938	6 780
电子出版物及音像制品类	E—journal and Video Products	7 656	645	7 011
家用电器和音像器材类	Houshold Appliances and Video Equipments	56 937	13 247	43 690
中西药品类	Traditional Chinese and Western Medicine	93 337	56 433	36 904
文化办公用品类	Cultural and Official Goods	32 515	4 446	28 069
家具类	Furniture	27 244	49	27 195
通讯器材类	Communication Appliances	16 595	940	15 655
煤炭及制品类	Coal and Related Product	24 470	4 672	19 799
木材及制品类	Wood and Wooden Product	3 418		3 418
石油及制品类	Petroleum and Related Product	965 301	923 171	42 130
化工材料及制品类	Raw Chemical Materials and Related Products	716 851	612 031	104 820
金属材料类	Metal Materials	163 727	137 671	26 057
建筑及装璜材料类	Building and Decoration Materials	111 039	46 223	64 815
机电产品及设备类	Mechanical and Electrical Products	134 806	80 178	54 628
汽车类	Automobile	44 058	25 393	18 665
种子饲料类	Seed and feedstuff	193 792	101 220	92 572
棉麻类	Cotton and Hemp	2 500 381	2 494 182	6 199
其他类	Others	275 174	53 042	222 131

13—6 限额以上批发和零售业商品销售、库存数量

Number of Commodities Sales and Inventory of Enterprises above Designated Size in Wholesale and Retail Trade

计量单位:吨 (2010 年) (ton)

指 标	Item	购进量 Total Purchases Quantities	销售量 Total Sale Quantities	年末库存数 量 Year-end Inventory
粮 食	Grain	31 987	21 717	30 784
棉 花	Cotton	1 389 753	1 328 155	367 096
化学肥料	Chemical Fertilizers	1 364 736	1 323 854	169 995
化学农药	Chemical Pesticide	27 679	17 541	3 692
农用薄膜	Farming Pellicle	15 500	13 331	3 577
煤 炭	Coal	346 055	305 314	104 119
汽 油	Gasoline	286 810	287 994	14 015
柴 油	Diesel Oil	419 509	422 669	17 139
钢 材	Steel Products	170 844	199 453	7 438
水 泥	Cement	17 589	18 084	

13—7 限额以上批发和零售业商品销售类值

Enterprises above Designated Size in Wholesale and Retail Trades by Category of Commodities

计量单位:万元　　(2010 年)　　(10 000 yuan)

指　　标	Item	商品销售总额 Total Sales Value	批　发 Wholesale Value	零　售 Retail Value
总　　计	**Total**	**4 766 562**	**4 228 478**	**538 084**
粮油、食品、饮料、烟酒类	Grain,oil,Food,Beverage,Tobacco and Liquor	159 695	123 568	36 128
# 粮油、食品类	Grain ,Oil and Food	104 578	80 827	23 751
粮油类	Grain and oil	28 992	20 610	8 382
肉禽蛋类	Meat,Poultry and Eggs	7 733	3 101	4 633
水产品类	Aquatic Products	1 222	14	1 207
蔬菜类	Vegetables	23 829	20 746	3 084
干鲜果类	Dried and Fresh Melons and Fruits	35 194	32 819	2 376
饮料类	Beverages	8 143	3 987	4 156
烟酒类	Tobacco and Liquor	46 975	38 755	8 220
服装鞋帽、针、纺织品类	Clothing,Shoes,Hats and Textiles	26 266	16 290	9 977
# 服装类	Clothing	4 886	130	4 756
鞋帽类	Shoes and Hats	3 121	49	3 072
针、纺织品类	Knitwear and Textiles	18 260	16 111	2 149
化妆品类	Cosmetics	5 766	4 400	1 366
金银珠宝类	Gold,Silver and Jewelry	602	16	586
日用品类	Articles for Daily Use	8 329	169	8 160
# 洗涤用品类	Washing Articles	5 901	102	5 800
儿童玩具类	Children Toys	1 124	4	1 120
五金、电料类	Hardware and Electrical Materials	4 495	3 116	1 380
体育、娱乐用品类	Sports and Recreation Articles	929	7	922
书报杂志类	Newspapers and Magazines	6 938	5	6 933
电子出版物及音像制品类	E-journal and Video Products	645	61	584
家用电器和音像器材类	Houshold Appliances and Video Equipments	13 247	1 765	11 482
中西药品类	Traditional Chinese and Western Medicine	56 433	44 972	11 461
# 西药类	Western Medicines	49 195	39 564	9 631
中草药及中成药类	Chinese Herb Medicine and Traditional Chinese Medicine	6 649	5 358	1 290
文化办公用品类	Cultural and Official Goods	4 446	55	4 391
家具类	Furniture	49	1	48
通讯器材类	Communication Appliances	940	7	933
煤炭及制品类	Coal and Related Products	4 672	4 672	
石油及制品类	Petroleum and Related Products	923 171	499 710	423 461
化工材料及制品类	Raw Chemical Materials and Related Products	612 031	612 031	
# 化肥类	Chemical Fertilizer	471 652	471 652	
金属材料类	Metal Materials	137 671	137 671	
建筑及装璜材料类	Building and Decoration Materials	46 223	46 223	
机电产品及设备类	Mechanical and Electrical Products	80 178	80 178	
# 农机类	Agricultural Machinery	16 808	16 808	
汽车类	Automobile	25 393	11 043	14 351
种子饲料类	Seed and Feedstuff	101 220	101 220	
棉麻类	Cotton and Hemp	2 494 182	2 491 957	2 225
其他类	Others	53 042	49 343	3 699

13－8 限额以下批发和零售业商品销售类值

Enterprises below Designated Size in Wholesale and Retail Trade by Category of Commodities

计量单位:万元 (2010 年) (10 000 yuan)

指　　标	Item	商品销售总额 Total Sales Value	批　发 Wholesale Value	零　售 Retail Value
总　　计	**Total**	**1 727 088**	**548 071**	**1 179 017**
食品、饮食、烟酒类	Food,Beverage,Tobacco and Liquor	554 973	106 292	448 681
# 粮油、食品类	Grain,oil andFood	289 691	67 861	221 829
服装、鞋帽、针、纺织品类	Clothing,Shoes,Hats and Textiles	156 775	7 844	148 931
化妆品类	Cosmetics	31 717	1 387	30 330
金银珠宝类	Gold,Silver and Jewelry	6 173		6 173
日用品类	Articles for Daily Use	112 882	4 494	108 388
五金、电料类	Hardware and Electrical Materials	36 894	2 499	34 395
体育、娱乐用品类	Sports and Recreation Articles	7 138	711	6 427
书报、杂志类	Newspapers and Magazines	6 780	57	6 723
电子出版物及音像制品类	E-journal and Video Products	7 011	2 228	4 783
家用电器和音像器材类	Houshold Appliances and Video Equipments	43 690	1 953	41 737
中西药品类	Traditional Chinese and Western Medicine	36 904	1 031	35 873
文化、办公用品类	Cultural and Official Goods	28 069	4 951	23 118
家具类	Furniture	27 195	4 650	22 545
通讯器材类	Communication Appliances	15 655	4 336	11 319
煤炭及制品类	Coal and Related Products	19 799	3 939	15 860
木材及制品类	Wood and Wooden Products	3 418	845	2 573
石油及制品类	Petroleum and Related Products	42 130	20 960	21 170
化工材料及制品类	Raw Chemical Materials and Related Products	104 820	104 820	
金属材料类	Metal Materials	26 057	26 057	
建筑及装璜材料类	Building and Decoration Materials	64 815	33 768	31 048
机电产品及设备类	Mechanical and Electrical Products	54 628	43 657	10 971
汽车类	Automobiles	18 665	8 484	10 181
种子饲料类	Seed and feedstuff	92 572	92 572	
棉麻类	Cotton and Hemp	6 199	6 199	
其他类	Others	222 131	64 336	157 795
按师分	**Group by Division**			
一　　师	Division 1	145 193	25 398	119 795
二　　师	Division 2	126 684	14 329	112 354
三　　师	Division 3	80 885	15 702	65 183
四　　师	Division 4	94 612	37 930	56 682
五　　师	Division 5	78 327	27 515	50 812
六　　师	Division 6	367 755	144 781	222 974
七　　师	Division 7	170 150	40 883	129 267
八　　师	Division 8	395 475	181 988	213 487
九　　师	Division 9	57 261	15 441	41 820
十　　师	Division 10	68 713	24 270	44 444
建 工 师	Construction Division	4 482	1 752	2 730
十 二 师	Division 12	78 678	235	78 443
十 三 师	Division 13	32 398	3 976	28 422
十 四 师	Division 14	5 704	3 405	2 299
国资公司	State-owned Property Company	8 316	6 168	2 148
供销公司	Supply and Marketing Corporation General	48	48	
中基公司	Chalkis Company	1 653	1 653	
兵团直属	Direct under XPCG	10 756	2 598	8 158

13—9 限额以上住宿和餐饮业经营情况

Basic Conditions of Enterprises above Designated Size in Accommodation and Catering Services Industry

(2010 年)

单 位	Unit	法人企业(个) Number of Corporation Enterprises (unit)	非住宿和餐饮业产业活动单位及个体户(个) Industries Activty Units and Individual Units are not Belong to Accommodation and Catering Services Industry (unit)	年末从业人员(人) Number of Engaged Persons at the Year-end (person)	营业额(万元) Business Revenue (10 000 yuan)
总 计	**Total**	**31**	**36**	**4 933**	**47 116**
住宿业	**Hotels**	**29**	**12**	**3 887**	**36 707**
按住宿行业分组	**Group by Hotels Sector**				
旅游饭店	Travel Hotel	26	8	3 527	33 234
一般旅馆	General Hotel	3	4	360	3 474
按登记注册类型分	**Grouped by Types of Registration**				
内资企业	Domestic Enterprises	28	11	3 828	36 182
国有企业	State-owned Enterprises	20	8	2 544	23 052
有限责任公司	Limited Liability Corporations	5	2	696	7 938
其他有限责任公司	Other Limited Liability Corporations	5	2	696	7 938
股份有限公司	Share-holding Corporations Ltd	1		208	2 100
私营企业	Private Enterprises	2	1	380	3 094
私营有限责任公司	Private Co. ltd	2	1	380	3 094
港、澳、台商投资企业	Enterprises with Funds from HongKong Macao and TaiWan	1		29	212
合资经营企业(港或澳、台资)	Joint-venture Enterprises	1		29	212
个体工商户	Individual		1	30	314
按控股情况分组	**Grouped by Share-holding Controlled**				
国有控股	Share-holding Controlled of State-owned	24		2 742	24 263
私人控股	Share-holding Controlled of Private	4		390	3 716
其他	Other	1		29	212
按经营形式分组	**Grouped by Operate Form**				
独立门店	Store of Independent	29	10	3 756	34 923
其他	Other		2	131	1 784
按星级分组	**Group by Hotels Star**				
四星	4 Stars	5		942	8 497
三星	3 Stars	19		1 967	17 732
二星	2 Stars	2		90	630
其他	Other	3		162	1 332
餐饮业	**Catering Services**	**2**	**24**	**1 046**	**10 409**
按餐饮行业小类分组	**Grouped by Catering Trade**				
正餐服务	Restaurant	1	19	885	7 563
快餐服务	Snack Counter	1		51	1 131
其他餐饮服务	Other		5	110	1 715
按登记注册类型分组	**Grouped by Types of Registration**				
内资企业	Domestic Enterprises	2	3	142	2 133
国有企业	State-owned Enterprises		3	42	755
有限责任公司	Limited Liability Corporations	1		51	1 131
其他有限责任公司	Other Limited Liability Corporations	1		51	1 131
私营企业	Private Enterprises	1		49	248
私营有限责任公司	Private Co. ltd	1		49	248
个体工商户	Individual		21	904	8 275
按控股情况分组	**Grouped by Share-holding Controlled**				
私人控股	Share-holding Controlled of Private	1		49	248
其他	Other	1		51	1 131
按经营形式分组	**Grouped by Operate Form**				
独立门店	Store of Independent	2	24	1 046	10 408

13—9 续表 1 Continued

(2010 年)

单 位	Unit	客房收入 Rooms Income	餐费收入 Catering Services Income	商品销售收入 Total Sales Income	其他收入 Others	客房间数（间） Rooms (unit)	床位数（个） Beds (unit)	餐位数（位） Dinner Seat (unit)
总 计	**Total**	**20 804**	**22 328**	**1 408**	**2 576**	**6 594**	**12 792**	**24 080**
住宿业	**Hotels**	**20 279**	**13 724**	**163**	**2 542**	**6 306**	**12 247**	**14 497**
按住宿行业分组	**Group by Hotels Sector**							
旅游饭店	Travel Hotel	18 679	12 334	101	2 121	5 839	11 314	12 477
一般旅馆	General Hotel	1 600	1 389	62	421	467	933	2 020
按登记注册类型分	**Grouped by Types of Registration**							
内资企业	Domestic Enterprises	19 925	13 583	163	2 512	6 086	11 871	14 237
国有企业	State-owned Enterprises	12 899	7 849	149	2 155	3 814	7 281	8 741
有限责任公司	Limited Liability Corporations	3 311	4 367	13	246	947	1 816	3 304
其他有限责任公司	Other Limited Liability Corporations	3 311	4 367	13	246	947	1 816	3 304
股份有限公司	Share-holding Corporations Ltd	1 258	840	1		280	526	1 110
私营企业	Private Enterprises	2 457	527		110	1 045	2 248	1 082
私营有限责任公司	Private Co. ltd	2 457	527		110	1 045	2 248	1 082
港、澳、台商投资企业	Enterprises with Funds from HongKong Macao and TaiWan	200			12	72	128	
合资经营企业(港或澳、台资)	Joint-venture Enterprises	200			12	72	128	
个体工商户	Individual	153	141		19	148	248	260
按控股情况分组	**Grouped by Share-holding Controlled**							
国有控股	Share-holding Controlled of State-owned	12 760	9 354	14	2 134	3 659	6 945	9 023
私人控股	Share-holding Controlled of Private	2 118	1 549		50	453	832	1 652
其他	Other	200			12	72	128	
按经营形式分组	**Grouped by Operate Form**							
独立门店	Store of Independent	19 125	13 312	53	2 434	6 034	11 837	13 347
其他	Other	1 154	412	111	108	272	410	1 150
按星级分组	**Group by Hotels Star**							
四星	4 Stars	4 764	3 483		250	924	1 691	2 872
三星	3 Stars	9 015	7 220	14	1 483	2 914	5 576	7 303
二星	2 Stars	342	200		88	145	260	500
其他	Other	958			375	201	378	
餐饮业	**Catering Services**	**525**	**8 604**	**1 245**	**34**	**288**	**545**	**9 583**
按餐饮行业小类分组	**Grouped by Catering Trade**							
正餐服务	Restaurant	526	6 545	459	34	288	545	7 893
快餐服务	Snack Counter		404	726				900
其他餐饮服务	Other		1 655	60				790
按登记注册类型分组	**Grouped by Types of Registration**							
内资企业	Domestic Enterprises	100	1 216	818		64	128	2 042
国有企业	State-owned Enterprises	100	590	66		64	128	842
有限责任公司	Limited Liability Corporations		404	726				900
其他有限责任公司	Other Limited Liability Corporations		404	726				900
私营企业	Private Enterprises		222	26				300
私营有限责任公司	Private Co. ltd		222	26				300
个体工商户	Individual	426	7 388	427	34	224	417	7 541
按控股情况分组	**Grouped by Share-holding Controlled**							
私人控股	Share-holding Controlled of Private		222	26				300
其他	Other		404	726				900
按经营形式分组	**Grouped by Operate Form**							
独立门店	Store of Independent	526	8 604	1 245	34	288	545	9 583

13—10 各师住宿和餐饮业基本情况

Basic Conditions of Enterprises in Accommodation and Catering Services Industry by Division

计量单位：万元　　　　(2010 年)　　　　(10 000 yuan)

单　位	Unit	法人企业（个）Number of Corporation Enterprises (unit)	营业额 Business Revenue	客房收入 Rooms Income	餐费收入 Catering Services Income	商品销售额 Total Sales Income	其他收入 Others
总　计	**Total**	**98**	**367 301**	**50 962**	**297 593**	**13 990**	**4 756**
一　师	Division 1	3	33 992	3 643	27 554	2 777	19
二　师	Division 2	2	32 583	4 092	26 716	1 248	524
三　师	Division 3	2	20 673	3 622	16 909		142
四　师	Division 4	5	25 700	5 414	19 626	66	594
五　师	Division 5	4	13 193	2 315	10 744		135
六　师	Division 6	6	61 972	5 238	51 529	3 811	1 394
七　师	Division 7	1	27 639	1 306	23 506	2 820	7
八　师	Division 8	53	94 033	16 827	74 804	1 420	982
九　师	Division 9	2	10 501	988	9 368	45	100
十　师	Division 10	3	10 089	998	8 838	253	
建工师	Construction Division		894		894		
十二师	Division 12	4	8 883	1 554	7 028	277	23
十三师	Division 13		13 117	658	11 386	1 058	16
十四师	Division 14	1	1 312	140	1 172		
国资公司	State-owned Property Company	3	2 388	560	1 691		137
供销公司	Supply and Marketing Corporation General	4	664		664		
兵团直属	Direct under XPCG	5	9 670	3 609	5 163	215	683

13—11 按行业分社会消费品零售总额

Total Retail Sales of Consumer Goods by Sector

计量单位：万元　　　　(10 000 yuan)

年　份 Year	社会消费品零售总额 Total Retail Sales of Consumer Goods	批发和零售业 Wholesale and Retail Trade	住宿和餐饮业 Accommodation and Catering Trade	其他行业 Others		
					制造业 Manufacturing	农业生产者 Agricultural Producers
1950	2 446	1 400		1 046	426	372
1952	5 883	3 738	92	2 053	1 073	588
1954	4 113	2 201	78	1 834	687	975
1957	8 696	5 679	166	2 851	1 226	975
1962	28 383	15 821	1 443	11 119	4 697	3 853
1965	30 601	17 309	1 125	12 167	2 378	8 168
1970	40 069	18 940	621	20 508	4 436	9 643
1975	42 846	20 844	693	21 309	1 279	12 018
1978	57 076	27 604	1 040	28 432	4 640	16 654
1980	78 701	33 315	1 709	43 677	6 763	32 425
1985	106 667	54 362	3 387	48 918	13 993	25 167
1990	197 041	101 462	5 046	90 533	39 582	36 665
1995	357 082	174 160	14 176	168 746	64 310	73 105
2000	540 004	311 797	51 238	176 969	54 540	85 715
2005	933 828	730 375	124 180	79 273		
2006	1 113 810	888 232	145 256	80 322		
2007	1 301 564	1 039 298	170 338	91 928		
2008	1 601 327	1 298 088	203 666	99 573		
2009	1 797 787	1 442 178	257 596	98 013		
2010	2 028 683	1 717 101	311 582			

13—12 主要年份按销售单位所在地分社会消费品零售总额

Total Retail Sales of Consumer Goods Grouped by Location of Sales Units in Major Years

计量单位：万元 (10 000 yuan)

年 份 Year	社会消费品零售总额 Total Retail Sales of Consumer Goods	市 City	县 County	县以下 Under County Level
1950	2 446	797	133	1 516
1952	5 883	2 030	378	3 475
1954	4 113	1 501	247	2 365
1957	8 696	5 679	566	2 451
1962	28 383	10 821	2 097	15 465
1965	30 601	11 309	2 278	17 014
1970	40 069	12 940	2 336	24 793
1975	42 846	13 925	2 526	26 395
1978	57 076	18 588	3 098	35 390
1980	78 701	18 406	6 083	54 212
1985	106 667	26 757	10 126	69 784
1990	197 041	58 951	15 868	122 222
1995	357 082	118 745	19 064	219 273
2000	540 004	246 592	34 561	258 851
2005	933 828	523 264	26 790	383 774
2006	1 113 810	651 042	27 228	435 540
2007	1 301 564	779 761	32 557	489 246
2008	1 601 327	959 678	36 475	605 174
2009	1 797 787	1 046 321	42 926	708 540

注：2002 年"社会消费品零售总额"按 2003 年新口径调整，下同。

Note: Total Retail Sales of Consumer Goods Data in 2002 are calulated on 2003 new caliber(the same as follows).

13—13 按销售单位所在地分社会消费品零售总额

Total Retail Sales of Consumer Goods Grouped by Location of Sales Units

计量单位：万元 (2010 年) (10 000 yuan)

单 位	Unit	社会消费品零售总额 Total Retail Sales of Consumer Goods	城 镇 Urban	#城 区 Urban Areas	乡 村 Rural
总 计	**Total**	**2 028 683**	**1 782 012**	**1 145 699**	**246 671**
一 师	Division 1	158 613	134 821	44 491	23 792
二 师	Division 2	177 251	154 872	116 047	22 379
三 师	Division 3	84 343	83 419	26 230	924
四 师	Division 4	85 020	81 759	31 308	3 261
五 师	Division 5	63 353	55 836	36 396	7 517
六 师	Division 6	279 024	198 845	130 101	80 179
七 师	Division 7	155 593	148 057	271	7 536
八 师	Division 8	362 649	301 535	288 552	61 114
九 师	Division 9	51 233	47 595	46 410	3 638
十 师	Division 10	60 475	55 535	1 002	4 941
建工师	Construction Division	5 515	5 515	5 515	
十二师	Division 12	86 530	86 530	86 530	
十三师	Division 13	40 866	31 186	13 540	9 680
十四师	Division 14	3 471	3 279	90	192
国资公司	State-owned Property Company	400 550	379 133	305 374	21 418
供销公司	Supply and Marketing Corporation General	664	664	408	
兵团直属	Direct under XPCG	13 534	13 433	13 433	101

13—14 各师按行业分社会消费品零售总额

Total Retail Sales of Consumer Goods by Sector and Division

计量单位:万元 (2010 年) (10 000 yuan)

单 位	Unit	社会消费品零售总额 Total Retail Sales of Consumer Goods	批发和零售业 Wholesale and Retail Trade	住宿和餐饮业 Accommodation and Catering Trade
总 计	**Total**	**2 028 683**	**1 717 101**	**311 582**
一 师	Division 1	158 613	128 282	30 332
二 师	Division 2	177 251	149 286	27 965
三 师	Division 3	84 343	67 433	16 909
四 师	Division 4	85 020	65 328	19 692
五 师	Division 5	63 353	52 609	10 744
六 师	Division 6	279 024	223 684	55 340
七 师	Division 7	155 593	129 267	26 326
八 师	Division 8	362 649	286 425	76 224
九 师	Division 9	51 233	41 820	9 413
十 师	Division 10	60 475	51 384	9 091
建工师	Construction Division	5 515	4 621	894
十二师	Division 12	86 530	79 226	7 304
十三师	Division 13	40 866	28 422	12 444
十四师	Division 14	3 471	2 299	1 172
国资公司	State-owned Property Company	400 550	398 859	1 691
供销公司	Supply and Marketing Corporation General	664		664
兵团直属	DirectunderXPCG	13 534	8 158	5 376

13—15 限额以上连锁店(公司)基本情况

Basic Conditions of Chain Stores(Companies) above Designated Size

(2010 年)

指 标	Item	连锁门店数(个) Branches of Chain Stores(unit)	直营店 Under Direct Management	加盟店 Through License Arrangement	年末零售营业面积(平方米) Total Retail Sales from Perational Area (sq·m)	年末从业人员(人) Number of Employed Persons at the Year-end (person)	商品购进总额 Total Purchases (10 000 yuan)	销售总额(营业总收入)(万元) Total Sales (Business Revenue) (10 000 yuan)	# 商品零售额 Retail Sales
总 计	**Total**	**487**	**317**	**170**	**19 449**	**834**	**30 833**	**29 117**	**29 026**
# 国有控股	State-owned and State-controlled shareholding	384	276	108	10 665	433	22 464	21 149	21 129
批发和零售业	**Wholesale and Retail Trades**	**487**	**317**	**170**	**19 449**	**834**	**30 833**	**29 117**	**29 026**
# 便利店	Neighbourhood Markdt	82	16	66	3 175	96	1 503	1 256	1 256
超 市	Supermarket	234	234		2 500	234	17 548	16 442	16 442
专业店	Professional Store	171	67	104	13 774	504	11 782	11 419	11 328
分单位	**Grouped by Unit**								
二 师	Division 2	62	20	42	4 300	63	1 178	1 177	1 157
四 师	Division 4	20	20		800	37	777	831	760
五 师	Division 5	234	234		2 500	234	17 548	16 442	16 442
八 师	Division 8	83	21	62	7 984	364	7 591	7 138	7 138
十 师	Division 10	82	16	66	3 175	96	1 503	1 256	1 256
国资公司	State-owned Property Company	6	6		690	40	2 236	2 273	2 273

13—16 限额以上批发和零售业法人企业主要财务指标

Main Financial Indicators of Enterprises above Designated Size in Wholesale and Retail Trade

计量单位:万元 (2010 年)

指 标	Item	年初存货 Inventories at the Beginning of the Year	流动资产合计 Working Capitals	#应收帐款 Account Receivable	#存货 Inventories
总 计	**Total**	**650 194**	**2 828 244**	**196 701**	**1 035 113**
批发业	**Wholesale Trade**	**634 340**	**2 774 215**	**192 276**	**1 018 330**
按批发行业分组	**Group by Wholesale Trade Sector**				
农畜产品批发	Wholesale of Farm Produce and Livestock Products	435 184	2 197 483	125 354	801 341
食品、饮料及烟草制品批发	Wholesale of Food, Beverages and Tobaccos	14 132	54 332	1 657	15 996
纺织、服装及日用品批发	Wholesale of Textiles, Garments and Daily Consumer Articles	1 423	6 677	717	2 014
医药及医疗器材批发	Wholesale of Medicines and Mdedical Appliances	5 826	22 659	7 845	7 867
矿产品、建材及化工产品批发	Wholesale of Mineral Products, Building Materials and Chemical Products	173 332	465 032	52 309	182 397
机械设备、五金交电及电子产品批发	Wholesale of Machinery, Hardware and Electronic Equipment	2 100	13 582	2 554	5 380
贸易经纪与代理	Trade Agent and Agency	298	2 249	900	283
其他批发	Other Wholesale	2 045	12 200	939	3 052
按登记注册类型分组	**Grouped by Status of Registration**				
内资企业	Domestic Enterprises	634 340	2 774 215	192 276	1 018 330
国有企业	State-owned Enterprises	410 396	1 976 240	122 887	746 694
有限责任公司	Limited Liability Corporations	150 454	495 865	55 176	182 117
股份有限公司	State-controlled Corporations Ltd.	58 420	238 465	8 820	60 453
私营企业	Private Enterprises	15 070	63 645	5 393	29 066
按控股情况分组	**Grouped by Share-holding Controlled**				
国有控股	Share-holding Controlled of State-owned	553 581	2 537 620	160 647	890 882
集体控股	Share-holding Controlled of Collective-owned	6 320	24 736	17 989	6 747
私人控股	Share-holding Controlled of Private	16 189	87 263	9 151	29 753
其他	Other	58 250	124 596	4 488	90 948
按经营形式分组	**Grouped by Operate Form**				
独立门店	Store of Independent	286 197	1 239 699	131 239	396 629
连锁总店	Total Store of Catena	2 684	9 537	3 035	3 008
其他	Other	345 459	1 524 979	58 001	618 693
零售业	**Retail Trade**	**15 854**	**54 029**	**4 425**	**16 783**
按零售行业分组	**Group by Retail Trade Sector**				
综合零售	Integrated Retail	2 470	9 044	591	3 133
食品、饮料及烟草制品专门零售	Retail of Food, Beverage and Tobaccos	490	1 131		
纺织、服装及日用品专门零售	Wholesale of Textiles, Garments and Daily Consumer Articles	184	204	5	181
文化、体育用品及器材专门零售	Retail of Culture, Sports Appliances and Equipments	443	3 651	200	625
医药及医疗器材专门零售	Retail of Medicines and Mdedical Appliances	1 456	4 110	1 165	1 724
汽车、摩托车、燃料及零配件专门零售	Retail of Motor Vehicles, Motorcycles Fuel and Parts	10 158	32 633	2 069	10 316
家用电器及电子产品专门零售	Special Retail of Household Electric Appliances and Electronic Products	636	2 997	278	764
无店铺及其他零售	Non-shop and Other Retails	17	260	118	42
按登记注册类型分组	**Grouped by Status of Registration**				
内资企业	Domestic Enterprises	15 854	54 029	4 425	16 783
国有企业	State-owned Enterprises	10 379	26 759	635	10 594
有限责任公司	Limited Liability Corporations	2 804	14 268	3 045	2 724
私营企业	Private Enterprises	2 671	13 003	745	3 466
按控股情况分组	**Grouped by Share-holding Controlled**				
国有控股	Share-holding Controlled of State-owned	12 199	31 439	1 620	12 290
私人控股	Share-holding Controlled of Collective-owned	3 639	15 211	1 527	4 469
其他	Other	16	7 379	1 278	24
按经营形式分组	**Grouped by Operate Form**				
独立门店	Store of Independent	5 255	28 898	3 728	6 220
连锁总店	Total Store of Catena	1 537	3 538	266	1 241
连锁门店	Store of Catena	8 477	20 440	432	8 484
其他	Other	585	1 153		838
按零售业态分组	**Group by Retail Trade Form**				
有店铺零售	Store Retail Trade Form	15 854	54 029	4 425	16 783
超市	Supermarket	89	315	4	150
大型超市	Large Supermarket	1 490	7 165	587	1 819
百货店	General Store	891	1 563		1 165
专业店	Profession Store	13 058	44 447	3 684	13 345
专卖店	Monopoly Store	327	539	151	306

13—16 续表 1

计量单位:万元 (2010 年)

指 标	Item	流动资产年平均余额 Working Capitals Average Surplus Amount of Year	长期投资合计 Long-term Investment	固定资产合计 Total Value of Fixed Assets	固定资产原价 Original Value of Fixed Assets
总 计	**Total**	**1 830 135**	**103 316**	**306 202**	**430 718**
批发业	**Wholesale Trade**	**1 795 064**	**103 311**	**275 052**	**382 649**
按批发行业分组	**Group by Wholesale Trade Sector**				
农畜产品批发	Wholesale of Farm Produce and Livestock Products	1 399 527	58 619	204 763	284 234
食品、饮料及烟草制品批发	Wholesale of Food, Beverages and Tobaccos	44 819	775	16 362	20 051
纺织、服装及日用品批发	Wholesale of Textiles, Garments and Daily Consumer Articles	7 111		964	1 159
医药及医疗器材批发	Wholesale of Medicines and Mdedical Appliances	21 035	3 440	2 764	4 173
矿产品、建材及化工产品批发	Wholesale of Mineral Products, Building Materials and Chemical Products	302 484	35 861	47 748	69 540
机械设备、五金交电及电子产品批发	Wholesale of Machinery, Hardware and Electronic Equipment	7 989		1 245	1 820
贸易经纪与代理	Trade Agent and Agency	2 040		6	7
其他批发	Other Wholesale	10 061	4 616	1 199	1 665
按登记注册类型分组	**Grouped by Status of Registration**				
内资企业	Domestic Enterprises	1 795 064	103 311	275 052	382 649
国有企业	State-owned Enterprises	1 110 918	48 488	194 855	279 036
有限责任公司	Limited Liability Corporations	395 941	35 151	49 014	63 299
股份有限公司	State-controlled Corporations Ltd.	237 337	19 544	28 698	36 250
私营企业	Private Enterprises	50 867	128	2 484	4 064
按控股情况分组	**Grouped by Share-holding Controlled**				
国有控股	Share-holding Controlled of State-owned	1 589 368	97 921	258 906	359 170
集体控股	Share-holding Controlled of Collective-owned	33 940		605	605
私人控股	Share-holding Controlled of Private	49 641	5 390	2 657	4 312
其他	Other	122 115		12 884	18 562
按经营形式分组	**Grouped by Operate Form**				
独立门店	Store of Independent	767 666	45 619	142 946	208 029
连锁总店	Total Store of Catena	2 795	826	1 871	2 922
其他	Other	1 024 603	56 867	130 235	171 698
零售业	**Retail Trade**	**35 071**	**5**	**31 150**	**48 069**
按零售行业分组	**Group by Retail Trade Sector**				
综合零售	Integrated Retail	7 586		6 035	8 792
食品、饮料及烟草制品专门零售	Retail of Food, Beverage and Tobaccos	1 159		458	458
纺织、服装及日用品专门零售	Wholesale of Textiles, Garments and Daily Consumer Articles	206		1	1
文化、体育用品及器材专门零售	Retail of Culture, Sports Appliances and Equipments	3 480		1 249	1 966
医药及医疗器材专门零售	Retail of Medicines and Mdedical Appliances	3 323	5	292	680
汽车、摩托车、燃料及零配件专门零售	Retail of Motor Vehicles, Motorcycles Fuel and Parts	16 222		22 855	35 642
家用电器及电子产品专门零售	Special Retail of Household Electric Appliances and Electronic Products	2 859		127	225
无店铺及其他零售	Non-shop and Other Retails	237		133	306
按登记注册类型分组	**Grouped by Status of Registration**				
内资企业	Domestic Enterprises	35 071	5	31 150	48 069
国有企业	State-owned Enterprises	13 512		20 599	32 753
有限责任公司	Limited Liability Corporations	11 730	5	9 785	13 755
私营企业	Private Enterprises	9 829		766	1 561
按控股情况分组	**Grouped by Share-holding Controlled**				
国有控股	Share-holding Controlled of State-owned	18 052		26 919	41 715
私人控股	Share-holding Controlled of Collective-owned	11 321	5	1 068	2 054
其他	Other	5 699		3 162	4 300
按经营形式分组	**Grouped by Operate Form**				
独立门店	Store of Independent	21 538	5	9 777	14 245
连锁总店	Total Store of Catena	3 622		597	906
连锁门店	Store of Catena	8 888		15 833	25 784
其他	Other	1 023		4 943	7 134
按零售业态分组	**Group by Retail Trade Form**				
有店铺零售	Store Retail Trade Form	35 071	5	31 150	48 069
超市	Supermarket	223		2	3
大型超市	Large Supermarket	5 959		390	799
百货店	General Store	1 404		5 644	7 990
专业店	Profession Store	26 811	5	25 076	39 156
专卖店	Monopoly Store	675		39	121

Continued

(10 000 yuan)

累计折旧 Accumulation Depreciation	# 本年折旧 Current Year Depreciation	资产总计 Total Assets	流动负债合计 Working Liability	# 应付帐款 Account Payable	长期负债合计 Lang-term Liabilities	负债合计 Total Liabilities	所有者权益合计 Total Owners' Equities	实收资本 Paicl-up Capitals
155 713	**20 561**	**3 358 317**	**2 705 067**	**170 296**	**60 047**	**2 793 384**	**564 933**	**351 508**
137 092	**17 930**	**3 259 930**	**2 674 004**	**160 842**	**59 830**	**2 760 264**	**499 666**	**340 494**
104 222	11 838	2 525 601	2 114 817	53 447	53 499	2 192 360	333 241	210 060
3 689	360	78 185	44 549	7 240	2 549	47 312	30 873	17 525
194	84	7 759	4 614	153		4 614	3 145	1 587
1 408	711	34 654	26 872	11 605	698	27 570	7 084	6 491
26 175	4 781	576 060	459 895	82 991	2 985	464 015	112 045	95 453
629	81	14 996	12 030	2 904	100	13 165	1 831	1 595
1	1	2 289	1 645	208		1 645	644	520
773	76	20 386	9 583	2 294		9 583	10 803	7 262
137 092	17 930	3 259 930	2 674 004	160 842	59 830	2 760 265	499 666	340 494
109 340	13 499	2 256 885	1 944 552	81 814	22 774	1 991 381	265 504	177 463
15 705	2 697	613 779	446 691	59 578	26 794	475 859	137 920	94 180
10 466	1 424	322 870	229 324	10 213	10 262	239 587	83 284	64 360
1 580	310	66 396	53 438	9 237		53 438	12 958	4 491
129 555	16 911	2 978 392	2 452 447	149 122	59 830	2 536 598	441 794	308 672
204	25	45 937	43 988	23		43 988	1 949	1 300
1 654	310	96 061	75 058	10 082		75 058	21 003	12 478
5 678	684	139 541	102 512	1 614		104 621	34 920	18 043
72 299	12 741	1 480 347	1 182 439	65 328	26 572	1 220 691	259 656	161 168
1 050	131	12 341	8 329	613		8 864	3 477	2 220
63 743	5 059	1 767 243	1 483 237	94 901	33 258	1 530 710	236 533	177 106
18 621	**2 631**	**98 387**	**31 063**	**9 454**	**217**	**33 120**	**65 267**	**11 014**
2 757	377	15 923	11 870	5 025		12 421	3 502	834
150	20	3 284	836	57		836	2 448	1 239
		205	235	86		235	−31	80
717	64	4 929	1 033	501		2 321	2 608	164
389	58	4 524	3 235	1 970		3 235	1 289	1 597
14 338	2 074	65 976	11 040	1 762	217	11 257	54 719	6 592
98	21	3 124	2 612	54		2 612	512	299
173	17	422	202			202	220	210
18 621	2 631	98 387	31 063	9 455	217	33 120	65 267	11 015
13 706	1 886	57 872	8 629	898		9 918	47 954	5 305
4 120	606	26 025	12 342	4 886		12 893	13 132	3 878
796	139	14 490	10 092	3 670	217	10 309	4 181	1 832
16 497	2 194	70 819	16 771	3 098		18 611	52 208	8 038
986	212	17 026	12 501	5 157	217	12 718	4 308	1 977
1 138	226	10 542	1 791	1 199		1 791	8 751	1 000
5 071	701	40 314	16 739	7 053	217	18 244	22 070	2 839
459	63	5 939	2 637	936		2 637	3 302	2 731
10 900	1 672	45 847	6 329	326		6 329	39 518	5 141
2 191	195	6 286	5 359	1 140		5 910	376	304
18 621	2 631	98 387	31 063	9 454	217	33 120	65 267	11 014
1	1	317	257	204		257	60	100
410	143	8 185	5 934	3 681		5 934	2 251	350
2 346	234	7 421	5 679	1 140		6 230	1 191	384
15 782	2 224	81 886	18 694	4 222	217	20 199	61 687	9 381
82	30	577	500	208		500	77	800

13—16 续表 2

计量单位:万元　　　　（2010 年）

指　　标	Item	国家资本 State-owned Capitals	集体资本 Collective-owned Capitals	法人资本 Corporative Capitals	个人资本 Individual Capitals
总　计	**Total**	**238 951**	**35 460**	**47 894**	**29 203**
批发业	**Wholesale Trade**	**233 043**	**35 460**	**44 242**	**27 749**
按批发行业分组	**Group by Wholesale Trade Sector**				
农畜产品批发	Wholesale of Farm Produce and Livestock Products	131 775	35 430	16 581	26 275
食品、饮料及烟草制品批发	Wholesale of Food, Beverages and Tobaccos	17 524		1	
纺织、服装及日用品批发	Wholesale of Textiles, Garments and Daily Consumer Articles	1 283		151	153
医药及医疗器材批发	Wholesale of Medicines and Mdedical Appliances	6 105			386
矿产品、建材及化工产品批发	Wholesale of Mineral Products, Building Materials and Chemical Products	67 401	30	27 088	934
机械设备、五金交电及电子产品批发	Wholesale of Machinery, Hardware and Electronic Equipment	1 193		402	
贸易经纪与代理	Trade Agent and Agency	500		18	2
其他批发	Other Wholesale	7 262			
按登记注册类型分组	**Grouped by Status of Registration**				
内资企业	Domestic Enterprises	233 043	35 460	44 242	27 749
国有企业	State-owned Enterprises	113 348	34 104	29 035	976
有限责任公司	Limited Liability Corporations	80 855	1 080	3 665	8 580
股份有限公司	State-controlled Corporations Ltd.	38 839	276	9 585	15 660
私营企业	Private Enterprises			1 957	2 533
按控股情况分组	**Grouped by Share-holding Controlled**				
国有控股	Share-holding Controlled of State-owned	215 387	34 410	41 550	17 326
集体控股	Share-holding Controlled of Collective-owned		1 050	250	
私人控股	Share-holding Controlled of Private			2 207	10 271
其他	Other	17 656		235	153
按经营形式分组	**Grouped by Operate Form**				
独立门店	Store of Independent	120 550	731	30 097	9 790
连锁总店	Total Store of Catena	2 190			30
其他	Other	110 303	34 729	14 144	17 929
零售业	**Retail Trade**	**5 908**		**3 652**	**1 454**
按零售行业分组	**Group by Retail Trade Sector**				
综合零售	Integrated Retail	181		203	450
食品、饮料及烟草制品专门零售	Retail of Food, Beverage and Tobaccos	1 239			
纺织、服装及日用品专门零售	Wholesale of Textiles, Garments and Daily Consumer Articles				80
文化、体育用品及器材专门零售	Retail of Culture, Sports Appliances and Equipments	164			
医药及医疗器材专门零售	Retail of Medicines and Mdedical Appliances	878		480	240
汽车、摩托车、燃料及零配件专门零售	Retail of Motor Vehicles, Motorcycles Fuel and Parts	3 237		2 904	451
家用电器及电子产品专门零售	Special Retail of Household Electric Appliances and Electronic Products			65	234
无店铺及其他零售	Non-shop and Other Retails	210			
按登记注册类型分组	**Grouped by Status of Registration**				
内资企业	Domestic Enterprises	5 908		3 652	1 454
国有企业	State-owned Enterprises	2 401		2 904	
有限责任公司	Limited Liability Corporations	3 508		203	168
私营企业	Private Enterprises			545	1 287
按控股情况分组	**Grouped by Share-holding Controlled**				
国有控股	Share-holding Controlled of State-owned	4 908		3 107	22
私人控股	Share-holding Controlled of Collective-owned			545	1 432
其他	Other	1 000			
按经营形式分组	**Grouped by Operate Form**				
独立门店	Store of Independent	1 532		65	1 242
连锁总店	Total Store of Catena	2 039		480	212
连锁门店	Store of Catena	2 237		2 904	
其他	Other	101		203	
按零售业态分组	**Group by Retail Trade Form**				
有店铺零售	Store Retail Trade Form	5 908		3 652	1 454
超市	Supermarket				100
大型超市	Large Supermarket				350
百货店	General Store	181		203	
专业店	Profession Store	4 927		3 449	1 004
专卖店	Monopoly Store	800			

Continued

(10 000 yuan)

主营业务收入 Revenue from Principal Business	主营业务成本 Cost of Principal Business	主营业务税金及附加 Taxes and Other Changes on Principal Business	主营业务利润 Profits from Principal Business	其他业务收入 Revenue from Other Business	其他业务利润 Profits from Other Business	营业费用 Business Expenses	管理费用 Administrative Expenses	# 税金 Taxes
4 196 637	**3 939 488**	**3 833**	**228 542**	**18 254**	**8 165**	**111 669**	**53 420**	**2 811**
3 788 252	**3 556 422**	**3 393**	**204 426**	**15 790**	**6 868**	**93 846**	**52 193**	**2 088**
2 361 358	2 221 387	613	130 254	9 949	4 939	41 364	31 507	1 297
100 641	87 401	1 989	11 200	212	75	3 193	3 586	26
14 344	11 853	34	2 457			570	653	1
39 345	36 162	32	3 151	64	62	1 706	1 955	46
1 211 740	1 143 765	657	53 222	4 222	1 126	43 847	12 975	639
26 976	24 516	48	2 413	537	48	1 433	594	62
9 445	8 678	10	757			433	104	1
24 402	22 661	11	972	806	619	1 300	819	18
3 788 252	3 556 422	3 393	204 426	15 790	6 868	93 846	52 193	2 088
2 497 224	2 358 732	686	108 621	11 640	4 998	55 708	27 471	1 481
785 490	729 778	2 345	48 397	1 500	968	24 620	15 077	340
299 995	272 744	313	37 081	1 673	1 480	11 060	7 939	161
205 543	195 168	49	10 326	977	−579	2 458	1 705	106
3 361 477	3 163 552	3 186	171 520	14 754	7 392	83 159	46 590	1 941
65 123	61 708	4	2 620			792	591	31
207 412	195 878	43	11 491	977	−579	2 652	2 310	107
154 240	135 285	160	18 795	59	55	7 244	2 702	9
2 024 797	1 891 385	2 737	111 058	13 155	4 545	43 998	29 147	1 085
23 586	20 712	13	776	152	25	1 845	724	39
1 739 868	1 644 326	643	92 593	2 483	2 298	48 003	22 322	964
408 385	**383 066**	**440**	**24 116**	**2 464**	**1 297**	**17 823**	**1 228**	**723**
26 265	21 810	153	4 303	1 112	980	2 971	1 011	86
1 943	1 681	2	260	133	57	272	105	3
75	48		27			13	19	
5 999	4 680	1	1 318	45	40	577	368	145
10 044	8 545	22	1 478	72	62	660	528	13
354 875	337 550	255	16 306	1 093	151	13 221	−1 085	451
7 275	6 925	6	344	8	7	97	218	23
1 910	1 828	1	81			11	64	2
408 385	383 066	440	24 116	2 464	1 297	17 823	1 228	723
330 839	316 207	198	13 670	1 050	102	12 746	−1 117	588
35 701	28 179	141	7 381	457	342	2 930	1 676	88
41 846	38 680	100	3 065	957	854	2 147	669	46
345 038	327 605	261	16 409	1 201	176	14 154	−108	654
50 707	46 349	132	4 227	1 263	1 121	2 854	1 179	62
12 640	9 112	48	3 480			815	157	7
122 571	110 261	238	12 067	1 534	1 121	6 408	1 389	218
9 074	7 826	14	1 234	205	119	832	450	15
275 843	264 578	166	10 341	725	57	10 498	−854	437
898	400	22	475			85	243	53
408 385	383 066	440	24 116	2 464	1 297	17 823	1 228	723
835	704	1	131			104	31	10
18 376	15 842	104	2 430	1 112	980	1 901	444	18
7 054	5 264	48	1 742			966	537	58
381 078	360 451	284	19 579	1 334	300	14 765	66	635
1 043	805	3	234	18	17	87	151	1

13—16 续表 3

计量单位:万元　　　　(2010 年)

指　标	Item	# 差旅费 Travel Allowance	# 工会经费 Trade Unions Funds	财务费用 Financial Expenses	# 利息支出 Intrest Expenditure
总　计	**Total**	**2 063**	**558**	**31 808**	**25 631**
批发业	**Wholesale Trade**	**1 867**	**450**	**31 454**	**25 491**
按批发行业分组	**Group by Wholesale Trade Sector**				
农畜产品批发	Wholesale of Farm Produce and Livestock Products	909	277	22 299	18 153
食品、饮料及烟草制品批发	Wholesale of Food, Beverages and Tobaccos	105	31	972	651
纺织、服装及日用品批发	Wholesale of Textiles, Garments and Daily Consumer Articles	48	6	23	23
医药及医疗器材批发	Wholesale of Medicines and Mdedical Appliances	41	11	184	162
矿产品、建材及化工产品批发	Wholesale of Mineral Products, Building Materials and Chemical Products	676	112	7 382	6 084
机械设备、五金交电及电子产品批发	Wholesale of Machinery, Hardware and Electronic Equipment	25	4	303	159
贸易经纪与代理	Trade Agent and Agency	1		60	40
其他批发	Other Wholesale	62	9	231	218
按登记注册类型分组	**Grouped by Status of Registration**				
内资企业	Domestic Enterprises	1 867	450	31 454	25 491
国有企业	State-owned Enterprises	850	268	18 648	17 612
有限责任公司	Limited Liability Corporations	851	123	8 040	4 831
股份有限公司	State-controlled Corporations Ltd.	65	51	3 128	1 952
私营企业	Private Enterprises	100	8	1 638	1 096
按控股情况分组	**Grouped by Share-holding Controlled**				
国有控股	Share-holding Controlled of State-owned	1 504	420	24 903	21 775
集体控股	Share-holding Controlled of Collective-owned	23	1	1 746	1 746
私人控股	Share-holding Controlled of Private	149	24	2 155	1 613
其他	Other	191	5	2 650	357
按经营形式分组	**Grouped by Operate Form**				
独立门店	Store of Independent	1 156	277	12 415	11 189
连锁总店	Total Store of Catena	15	5	70	69
其他	Other	695	168	18 969	14 233
零售业	**Retail Trade**	**196**	**108**	**354**	**140**
按零售行业分组	**Group by Retail Trade Sector**				
综合零售	Integrated Retail	36	10	29	14
食品、饮料及烟草制品专门零售	Retail of Food, Beverage and Tobaccos	1	5	6	
纺织、服装及日用品专门零售	Wholesale of Textiles, Garments and Daily Consumer Articles	1	1	11	10
文化、体育用品及器材专门零售	Retail of Culture, Sports Appliances and Equipments	10		−28	−28
医药及医疗器材专门零售	Retail of Medicines and Mdedical Appliances	28	5	137	52
汽车、摩托车、燃料及零配件专门零售	Retail of Motor Vehicles, Motorcycles Fuel and Parts	109	85	214	109
家用电器及电子产品专门零售	Special Retail of Household Electric Appliances and Electronic Products	11	2	−19	−19
无店铺及其他零售	Non-shop and Other Retails			4	3
按登记注册类型分组	**Grouped by Status of Registration**				
内资企业	Domestic Enterprises	196	108	354	140
国有企业	State-owned Enterprises	111	81	172	66
有限责任公司	Limited Liability Corporations	38	14	88	54
私营企业	Private Enterprises	47	14	95	21
按控股情况分组	**Grouped by Share-holding Controlled**				
国有控股	Share-holding Controlled of State-owned	143	92	233	112
私人控股	Share-holding Controlled of Collective-owned	50	17	123	30
其他	Other	3		−2	−2
按经营形式分组	**Grouped by Operate Form**				
独立门店	Store of Independent	79	24	36	−14
连锁总店	Total Store of Catena	22	11	131	62
连锁门店	Store of Catena	83	70	167	72
其他	Other	12	4	20	20
按零售业态分组	**Group by Retail Trade Form**				
有店铺零售	Store Retail Trade Form	196	108	354	140
超市	Supermarket	20			
大型超市	Large Supermarket	4	5	10	−5
百货店	General Store	12	5	19	19
专业店	Profession Store	149	99	297	103
专卖店	Monopoly Store	11		29	24

Continued

(10 000 yuan)

营业利润 Operating Profits	投资收益 Total Profits	补贴收入 Revenue from Allowance	营业外收入 Revenue Outside Business	利润总额 Total Profits	应交所得税 Income Tax Payable	劳动、失业保险费 Unemployment Insurance	养老保险和医疗保险费 Old-Pension and Medical Insurance	住房公积金和住房补贴 Housing Fund and Housing Allowance	本年应付工资总额 Total Accrued wages of Current Year
55 527	**1 303**	**9 361**	**25 669**	**71 232**	**15 007**	**1 368**	**4 641**	**1 730**	**41 450**
48 474	**1 258**	**9 361**	**25 216**	**64 103**	**13 377**	**640**	**3 598**	**1 414**	**32 202**
39 739	502	2 359	6 363	42 832	8 818	268	2 077	582	13 286
3 514		129	546	4 164	595	206	290	122	2 547
1 211			1	1 196	71	1	31	14	320
−631	49		175	279	113	5	124	17	1 069
4 330	707	6 203	17 853	14 361	3 476	138	903	639	13 884
52		281		340	90	18	61	18	545
160			15	179	36		11		78
99		389	263	752	177	4	101	23	473
48 474	1 258	9 361	25 216	64 103	13 377	640	3 598	1 414	32 202
23 742	381	6 309	18 571	31 331	7 504	367	1 795	992	20 937
8 134	450	2 748	6 091	15 954	2 782	242	1 059	350	7 926
12 652		74	521	12 195	3 054	29	699	67	2 687
3 946	428	230	32	4 623	38	3	44	6	653
37 835	830	8 893	24 816	52 044	12 338	633	3 459	1 379	30 078
55				372	93	3	40	11	285
3 769	428	365	177	4 566	134	4	62	7	767
6 815		104	222	7 121	812	1	37	18	1 072
32 060	507	2 413	12 183	33 378	6 561	542	2 132	996	21 601
277		181	710	498	173	2	63	27	354
16 136	751	6 768	12 322	30 227	6 644	96	1 402	391	10 247
7 053	**45**		**453**	**7 129**	**1 630**	**728**	**1 043**	**316**	**9 248**
1 273			64	1 279	302	89	208	26	1 655
65			13	−53		38	16	23	242
−16				−16					16
440				356	145	3	118	38	359
214			50	257	60	4	81	6	547
5 020	45		306	5 235	1 110	590	604	217	6 296
55			1	50	10	2	14	6	106
2			19	21	3		3		26
7 053	45		453	7 129	1 630	728	1 043	316	9 248
2 886			306	2 977	599	588	661	238	6 020
3 160	45		114	3 120	770	130	258	71	2 148
1 008			33	1 032	262	10	125	7	1 081
3 350			394	3 373	711	712	807	292	7 462
1 193			60	1 205	281	15	178	7	1 381
2 510	45			2 551	639		58	17	406
4 971	45		56	4 923	1 379	78	417	111	3 586
72			63	−3	13	40	85	27	693
1 884			300	2 066	198	525	454	160	4 783
127			35	143	41	84	88	19	186
7 053	**45**		**453**	**7 129**	**1 630**	**728**	**1 043**	**316**	**9 248**
−4				−4	3		10		50
1 056			29	1 046	238	5	102		637
221			35	237	62	84	97	26	968
5 795	45		369	5 850	1 328	638	817	288	7 481
−15			21				18	3	112

13—16 续表 4

计量单位：万元 （2010 年）

指　标	Item	本年应付福利费总额 Total Accrued welfarism of Current Year	本年应交增值税 Current Year VAT Payable	全部从业人员年平均人数（人） Average Annual Number of Employed Persons (person)	资产减值损　失 Loss of Property Reduces
总　计	**Total**	**3 683**	**25 214**	**11 839**	**279**
批发业	**Wholesale Trade**	**2 713**	**21 675**	**8 835**	**279**
按批发行业分组	**Group by Wholesale Trade Sector**				
农畜产品批发	Wholesale of Farm Produce and Livestock Products	963	6 452	4 131	114
食品、饮料及烟草制品批发	Wholesale of Food, Beverages and Tobaccos	161	1 330	525	61
纺织、服装及日用品批发	Wholesale of Textiles, Garments and Daily Consumer Articles	27	443	113	
医药及医疗器材批发	Wholesale of Medicines and Mdedical Appliances	51	315	446	24
矿产品、建材及化工产品批发	Wholesale of Mineral Products, Building Materials and Chemical Products	1 404	9 923	3 327	2
机械设备、五金交电及电子产品批发	Wholesale of Machinery, Hardware and Electronic Equipment	61	314	167	79
贸易经纪与代理	Trade Agent and Agency	2	95	15	
其他批发	Other Wholesale	45	2 803	111	
按登记注册类型分组	**Grouped by Status of Registration**				
内资企业	Domestic Enterprises	2 713	21 675	8 835	279
国有企业	State-owned Enterprises	1 922	10 226	5 126	119
有限责任公司	Limited Liability Corporations	521	7 443	1 994	226
股份有限公司	State-controlled Corporations Ltd.	221	3 587	1 420	−65
私营企业	Private Enterprises	49	419	295	
按控股情况分组	**Grouped by Share-holding Controlled**				
国有控股	Share-holding Controlled of State-owned	2 588	20 211	7 873	138
集体控股	Share-holding Controlled of Collective-owned	6	43	19	
私人控股	Share-holding Controlled of Private	52	606	341	26
其他	Other	67	814	602	115
按经营形式分组	**Grouped by Operate Form**				
独立门店	Store of Independent	1 648	11 798	6 075	143
连锁总店	Total Store of Catena	55	32	181	2
其他	Other	1 010	9 845	2 579	135
零售业	**Retail Trade**	**970**	**3 539**	**3 004**	
按零售行业分组	**Group by Retail Trade Sector**				
综合零售	Integrated Retail	68	404	682	
食品、饮料及烟草制品专门零售	Retail of Food, Beverage and Tobaccos	5	22	40	
纺织、服装及日用品专门零售	Wholesale of Textiles, Garments and Daily Consumer Articles		1	16	
文化、体育用品及器材专门零售	Retail of Culture, Sports Appliances and Equipments	45	8	90	
医药及医疗器材专门零售	Retail of Medicines and Mdedical Appliances	8	227	348	
汽车、摩托车、燃料及零配件专门零售	Retail of Motor Vehicles, Motorcycles Fuel and Parts	842	2 804	1 765	
家用电器及电子产品专门零售	Special Retail of Household Electric Appliances and Electronic Products	1	56	53	
无店铺及其他零售	Non-shop and Other Retails	1	18	10	
按登记注册类型分组	**Grouped by Status of Registration**				
内资企业	Domestic Enterprises	970	3 539	3 004	
国有企业	State-owned Enterprises	814	2 317	1 734	
有限责任公司	Limited Liability Corporations	122	1 051	692	
私营企业	Private Enterprises	34	171	578	
按控股情况分组	**Grouped by Share-holding Controlled**				
国有控股	Share-holding Controlled of State-owned	850	2 726	2 214	
私人控股	Share-holding Controlled of Collective-owned	64	338	709	
其他	Other	57	475	81	
按经营形式分组	**Grouped by Operate Form**				
独立门店	Store of Independent	287	1 601	1 211	
连锁总店	Total Store of Catena	13	101	352	
连锁门店	Store of Catena	650	1 836	1 371	
其他	Other	21	2	70	
按零售业态分组	**Group by Retail Trade Form**				
有店铺零售	Store Retail Trade Form	970	3 539	3 004	
超市	Supermarket	7	7	42	
大型超市	Large Supermarket	35	176	316	
百货店	General Store	26	222	324	
专业店	Profession Store	898	3 135	2 259	
专卖店	Monopoly Store	4		63	

13—17 分师限额以上批发和零售业法人企业主要财务指标

Main Financial Indicators of Enterprises above Designated Size in Wholesale and Retail Trade by Division

计量单位:万元 (2010 年) (10 000 yuan)

单位	Unit	年初存货 Inventories at the Beginning of the Year	流动资产合计 Working Capitals	#应收帐款 Account Receivable	#存货 Inventories	流动资产年平均余额 Working Capitals Average Surplus Amount of Year	长期投资合计 Long-term Investment
总计	**Total**	**650 194**	**2 828 244**	**196 701**	**1 035 113**	**1 830 135**	**103 316**
一师	Division 1	80 349	363 021	26 088	129 778	289 913	18 240
二师	Division 2	28 963	95 737	5 665	33 562	85 521	3 160
三师	Division 3	32 050	249 050	25 550	55 620	78 110	3 642
四师	Division 4	45 065	103 879	8 138	45 806	93 849	4 351
五师	Division 5	33 605	161 741	4 966	44 807	50 221	1 180
六师	Division 6	21 814	100 683	47 459	31 908	90 557	993
七师	Division 7	35 723	93 094	1 135	48 317	83 852	2 052
八师	Division 8	123 889	759 402	33 442	304 681	391 607	16 972
九师	Division 9	3 848	12 874	3 185	4 557	12 812	50
十师	Division 10	225	3 285	158	429	2 589	100
建工师	Construction Division	621	7 248	2 525	433	4 640	220
十二师	Division 12	1 205	23 649	8	1 808	13 435	30
十三师	Division 13	14 060	19 040	735	14 407	20 574	120
十四师	Division 14	4 642	35 388	3 233	5 616	18 161	1 417
国资公司	State-owned Property Company	77 263	179 731	7 419	71 106	124 335	28 502
供销公司	Supply and Marketing Corporation General	89 478	395 324	24 595	152 993	244 859	7 318
兵团直属	Directly under XPCG	57 394	225 101	2 401	89 285	225 101	14 968

单位	Unit	固定资产合计 Total Value of Fixed Assets	固定资产原价 Original Value of Fixed Assets	累计折旧 Accumulation Depreciation	#本年折旧 Current Year Depreciation	资产总计 Total Assets	流动负债合计 Working Liability
总计	**Total**	**306 202**	**430 718**	**155 713**	**20 561**	**3 358 317**	**2 705 067**
一师	Division 1	21 300	28 801	9 226	1 445	426 225	367 225
二师	Division 2	10 576	16 740	6 164	1 335	111 348	103 215
三师	Division 3	20 395	20 304	4 171	2 281	273 108	245 781
四师	Division 4	7 192	10 509	3 317	888	116 304	100 369
五师	Division 5	14 233	19 047	4 867	872	178 272	142 243
六师	Division 6	2 019	3 132	1 289	179	103 931	75 216
七师	Division 7	43 560	69 636	26 077	3 521	140 472	96 361
八师	Division 8	63 805	100 621	36 815	1 901	848 864	733 327
九师	Division 9	921	1 406	485	156	14 536	11 815
十师	Division 10	1 309	2 128	818	68	4 755	2 770
建工师	Construction Division	1 523	2 071	548	88	9 011	6 476
十二师	Division 12	545	708	162	11	24 613	24 736
十三师	Division 13	1 210	1 774	563	142	20 767	17 234
十四师	Division 14	6 533	7 239	800	98	48 841	36 055
国资公司	State-owned Property Company	55 586	89 480	37 327	5 351	308 923	109 895
供销公司	Supply and Marketing Corporation General	38 307	36 311	19 458	2 225	468 020	402 417
兵团直属	Directly under XPCG	17 186	20 813	3 627		260 327	229 934

13－17 续表 1 Continued

计量单位:万元 (2010 年) (10 000 yuan)

单 位	Unit	# 应付帐款 Account Payable	长期负债合计 Lang-term Liabilities	负债合计 Total Liabilities	所有者权益合计 Total Owners' Equities	实收资本 Paicl-up Capitals	国家资本 State-owned Capitals
总 计	**Total**	**170 296**	**60 047**	**2 793 384**	**564 933**	**351 508**	**238 951**
一 师	Division 1	19 865	992	374 773	51 452	39 514	34 033
二 师	Division 2	33 599	820	104 586	6 762	7 177	6 321
三 师	Division 3	5 520	451	246 232	26 877	8 839	8 736
四 师	Division 4	18 053		100 369	15 935	12 535	12 233
五 师	Division 5	3 613	2 540	146 047	32 225	26 846	26 846
六 师	Division 6	2 085		75 416	28 514	5 374	5 090
七 师	Division 7	3 286	21 013	121 263	19 209	6 217	3 673
八 师	Division 8	29 778	881	737 456	111 408	67 466	20 924
九 师	Division 9	5 428	67	11 882	2 654	2 899	2 899
十 师	Division 10	121		3 076	1 680	910	910
建工师	Construction Division	623		6 876	2 135	2 300	2 300
十二师	Division 12	136	949	25 685	－1 072	476	476
十三师	Division 13	2 447		17 382	3 384	1 559	1 559
十四师	Division 14	4 617	9	36 064	12 778	6 464	5 173
国资公司	State-owned Property Company	9 796	29 900	139 795	169 128	93 933	43 948
供销公司	Supply and Marketing Corporation General	28 708	2 425	416 334	51 687	55 929	54 629
兵团直属	Directly under XPCG	2 623		230 149	30 178	13 072	9 202

单 位	Unit	集体资本 Collective-owned Capitals	法人资本 Corporative Capitals	个人资本 Individual Capitals	主营业务收入 Revenue from Principal Business	主营业务成本 Cost of Principal Business	主营业务税金及附加 Taxes and Other Changes on Principal Business
总 计	**Total**	**35 460**	**47 894**	**29 203**	**4 196 637**	**3 939 488**	**3 833**
一 师	Division 1	276	4 819	385	518 476	496 663	97
二 师	Division 2		501	356	165 284	160 196	64
三 师	Division 3	30	50	22	229 928	217 618	129
四 师	Division 4		100	202	173 837	159 869	173
五 师	Division 5				265 854	239 624	3
六 师	Division 6			284	166 782	161 650	2
七 师	Division 7		2 544		93 858	86 165	74
八 师	Division 8	33 679	1 695	11 168	724 338	689 158	248
九 师	Division 9				19 615	17 962	6
十 师	Division 10				6 857	6 258	13
建工师	Construction Division				29 772	28 855	11
十二师	Division 12				9 509	8 790	
十三师	Division 13				52 499	49 921	14
十四师	Division 14		1 191	100	44 839	40 320	33
国资公司	State-owned Property Company	425	34 949	14 611	895 945	830 822	2 534
供销公司	Supply and Marketing Corporation General	1 050	250		511 566	484 449	132
兵团直属	Directly under XPCG		1 795	2 075	287 680	261 169	299

13－17 续表 2 Continued

计量单位:万元 (2010 年) (10 000 yuan)

单 位	Unit	主营业务利润 Profits from Principal Business	其他业务收入 Revenue from Other Business	其他业务利润 Profits from Other Business	营业费用 Business Expenses	管理费用 Administrative Expenses	# 税 金 Taxes
总 计	**Total**	**228 542**	**18 254**	**8 165**	**111 669**	**53 420**	**2 811**
一 师	Division 1	21 715	1 169	1 095	5 439	5 624	270
二 师	Division 2	5 024	366	363	4 400	2 269	153
三 师	Division 3	12 181			2 882	4 518	134
四 师	Division 4	13 795	29	5	4 801	5 285	77
五 师	Division 5	6 158	51	11	3 801	2 262	48
六 师	Division 6	5 130	390	353	855	1 210	81
七 师	Division 7	7 619	4 977	862	1 871	2 630	168
八 师	Division 8	34 932	2 731	977	14 350	7 340	506
九 师	Division 9	854	54	53	904	838	8
十 师	Division 10	586	115	25	357	298	21
建 工 师	Construction Division	905	633	381	278	698	61
十 二 师	Division 12	418	2 388	1 276	301	290	23
十 三 师	Division 13	2 564	136	130	1 697	752	17
十 四 师	Division 14	4 486	13		1 519	1 105	5
国资公司	State-owned Property Company	60 471	3 554	995	38 052	6 117	801
供销公司	Supply and Marketing Corporation General	15 349	1 649	1 639	16 602	7 694	439
兵团直属	Directly under XPCG	36 355			13 558	4 492	

单 位	Unit	# 差旅费 Travel Allowance	# 工会经费 Trade Unions Funds	财务费用 Financial Expenses	# 利息支出 Intrest Expenditure	营业利润 Operating Profits	投资收益 Total Profits
总 计	**Total**	**2 063**	**558**	**31 808**	**25 631**	**55 527**	**1 303**
一 师	Division 1	145	69	192	138	11 555	
二 师	Division 2	80	15	224	197	－1 506	49
三 师	Division 3	210	56	1 687	1 464	3 094	
四 师	Division 4	162	29	1 611	1 611	2 104	279
五 师	Division 5	208	9	742	742	2 119	
六 师	Division 6	36	14	2 311	2 300	1 334	228
七 师	Division 7	29	15	2 913	2 905	1 067	
八 师	Division 8	273	59	4 908	4 254	8 884	347
九 师	Division 9	83	8	212	212	－254	
十 师	Division 10	6	4	－13	－14	－31	
建 工 师	Construction Division	44	5	146	141	165	
十 二 师	Division 12	6	4	119	119	1 311	
十 三 师	Division 13	24	7	110	87	143	
十 四 师	Division 14	97	3	986	922	876	1
国资公司	State-owned Property Company	408	144	3 175	1 701	17 345	400
供销公司	Supply and Marketing Corporation General	252	117	8 976	8 855	－7 319	
兵团直属	Directly under XPCG			3 510		14 641	

13—17 续表 3 Continued

计量单位:万元 (2010 年) (10 000 yuan)

单位	Unit	补贴收入 Revenue from Allowance	营业外收入 Revenue Outside Business	利润总额 Total Profits	应交所得税 Income Tax Payable	劳动、失业保险费 Unemployment Insurance	养老保险和医疗保险费 Old-Pension and Medical Insurance
总计	**Total**	**9 361**	**25 669**	**71 232**	**15 007**	**1 368**	**4 641**
一师	Division 1		8 356	11 670	1 480	105	798
二师	Division 2	1 811	2 018	1 195	359	94	379
三师	Division 3			3 094	878	20	263
四师	Division 4	70	621	2 658	648	3	230
五师	Division 5	7	718	2 346	330	2	129
六师	Division 6	160	224	1 541	367	5	86
七师	Division 7	881	1 196	522	206	45	210
八师	Division 8	1 069	1 383	10 971	2 340	105	603
九师	Division 9	184	123	71	15	62	19
十师	Division 10	181	223	191	14	2	45
建工师	Construction Division	20	88	273	43	2	40
十二师	Division 12		5	233	78	1	41
十三师	Division 13		968	1 119	281	1	43
十四师	Division 14	50	887	1 806	47	9	35
国资公司	State-owned Property Company	463	1 070	18 152	3 846	862	930
供销公司	Supply and Marketing Corporation General	4 269	7 303	781	1 064	52	792
兵团直属	Directly under XPCG	196	487	14 607	3 012		

单位	Unit	住房公积金和住房补贴 Housing Fund and Housing Allowance	本年应付工资总额 Total Accrued Wages of Current Year	本年应付福利费总额 Total Accrued Welfarism of Current Year	本年应交增值税 Current Year VAT Payabele	全部从业人员平均人数(人) Average Annual Number of Employed Persons(person)	资产减值损失 Loss of Property Reduces
总计	**Total**	**1 730**	**41 450**	**3 683**	**25 214**	**11 839**	**279**
一师	Division 1	133	3 814	44	1 239	1 509	
二师	Division 2	73	1 217	134	2 666	497	24
三师	Division 3	92	1 992	62	322	286	
四师	Division 4	77	3 134	184	2 012	832	
五师	Division 5	68	876	115	9	465	
六师	Division 6	56	857	51	47	143	
七师	Division 7	69	1 429	67	313	596	117
八师	Division 8	143	3 647	221	1 489	1 324	63
九师	Division 9	63	392	62	32	144	
十师	Division 10	20	206	33	26	133	2
建工师	Construction Division	19	328	25	131	75	
十二师	Division 12	5	186			51	
十三师	Division 13	32	345	43	618	73	
十四师	Division 14	28	484	36	270	131	
国资公司	State-owned Property Company	651	15 988	1 853	11 765	4 059	−65
供销公司	Supply and Marketing Corporation General	201	5 165	557	2 206	1 055	
兵团直属	Directly under XPCG		1 392	195	2 069	466	140

13－18 限额以上住宿和餐饮业法人企业主要财务指标

Main Financial Indicators of Enterprises above Designated Size in Accommodation and Catering Services Industry

计量单位:万元 （2010 年） （10 000 yuan）

指 标	Item	年初存货 Inventories at the Beginning of the Year	流动资产合计 Working Capitals	#应收帐款 Account Receivable	#存货 Inventories
总 计	**Total**	**1 585**	**18 142**	**1 315**	**1 613**
住宿业	**Hotels**	**1 549**	**17 597**	**1 259**	**1 526**
按住宿行业分组	**Group by Hotels Sector**				
旅游饭店	Travel Hotel	1 444	17 103	1 254	1 410
一般旅馆	General Hotel	105	494	5	116
按登记注册类型分	**Grouped by Types of Registration**				
内资企业	Domestic Enterprises	1 543	17 385	1 259	1 517
国有企业	State-owned Enterprises	1 095	11 124	711	1 106
有限责任公司	Limited Liability Corporations	241	3 345	380	202
股份有限公司	Share-holding Corporations Ltd	68	2 312	126	57
私营企业	Private Enterprises	139	604	42	152
港、澳、台商投资企业	Enterprises with Funds from HongKong Macao and TaiWan	7	212		9
按控股情况分组	**Grouped by Share-holding Controlled**				
国有控股	Share-holding Controlled of State-owned	1 305	16 364	1 173	1 262
私人控股	Share-holding Controlled of Private	237	1 021	86	255
其他	Other	7	212		9
按经营形式分组	**Grouped by Operate Form**				
独立门店	Store of Independent	1 549	17 597	1 259	1 526
按星级分组	**Group by Hotels Star**				
四星	4 Stars	300	3 094	120	338
三星	3 Stars	1 136	12 422	844	1 131
二星	2 Stars	92	1 509	290	29
其他	Other	21	572	5	29
餐饮业	**Catering Services**	**36**	**545**	**56**	**87**
按餐饮行业分组	**Grouped by Catering Trade**				
正餐服务	Restaurant		40		3
快餐服务	Snack Counter	36	505	56	84
按登记注册类型分组	**Grouped by Types of Registration**				
内资企业	Domestic Enterprises	36	545	56	87
有限责任公司	Limited Liability Corporations	36	505	56	84
私营企业	Private Enterprises		40		3
按控股情况分组	**Grouped by Share-holding Controlled**				
私人控股	Share-holding Controlled of Private		40		3
其他	Other	36	505	56	84
按经营形式分组	**Grouped by Operate Form**				
独立门店	Store of Independent	36	545	56	87

13－18 续表 1

计量单位:万元　　　　(2010 年)

指　标	Item	流动资产年平均余额 Working Capitals Average Surplus Amount of Year	长期投资合计 Long-term Investment	固定资产合计 Total Value of Fixed Assets	固定资产原价 Original Value of Fixed Assets
总　计	**Total**	**15 116**	**656**	**45 135**	**76 829**
住宿业	**Hotels**	**14 602**	**630**	**45 068**	**76 694**
按住宿行业分组	**Group by Hotels Sector**				
旅游饭店	Travel Hotel	14 327	630	44 086	75 131
一般旅馆	General Hotel	275		982	1 563
按登记注册类型分	**Grouped by Types of Registration**				
内资企业	Domestic Enterprises	14 376	630	44 636	75 972
国有企业	State-owned Enterprises	8 832	103	37 311	60 633
有限责任公司	Limited Liability Corporations	2 838	360	4 562	7 504
股份有限公司	Share-holding Corporations Ltd	2 251	168	2 693	7 685
私营企业	Private Enterprises	455		70	151
港、澳、台商投资企业	Enterprises with Funds from HongKong Macao and TaiWan	226		432	722
按控股情况分组	**Grouped by Share-holding Controlled**				
国有控股	Share-holding Controlled of State-owned	13 495	630	44 083	75 165
私人控股	Share-holding Controlled of Private	880		553	807
其他	Other	226		432	722
按经营形式分组	**Grouped by Operate Form**				
独立门店	Store of Independent	14 602	630	45 068	76 694
按星级分组	**Group by Hotels Star**				
四星	4 Stars	2 864	5	6 011	10 926
三星	3 Stars	10 966	270	36 751	62 177
二星	2 Stars	284	355	896	1 356
其他	Other	488		1 409	2 235
餐饮业	**Catering Services**	**514**	**26**	**67**	**135**
按餐饮行业分组	**Grouped by Catering Trade**				
正餐服务	Restaurant	73		17	47
快餐服务	Snack Counter	441	26	50	88
按登记注册类型分组	**Grouped by Types of Registration**				
内资企业	Domestic Enterprises	514	26	67	135
有限责任公司	Limited Liability Corporations	441	26	50	88
私营企业	Private Enterprises	73		17	47
按控股情况分组	**Grouped by Share-holding Controlled**				
私人控股	Share-holding Controlled of Private	73		17	47
其他	Other	441	26	50	88
按经营形式分组	**Grouped by Operate Form**				
独立门店	Store of Independent	514	26	67	135

Continued

(10 000 yuan)

累计折旧 Accumulation Depreciation	# 本年折旧 Current Year Depreciation	资产总计 Total Assets	流动负债合计 Working Liability	# 应付帐款 Account Payable	长期负债合计 Lang-term Liabilities	负债合计 Total Liabilities	所有者权益合计 Total Owners' Equities
32 210	**2 277**	**73 974**	**29 748**	**5 286**	**4 417**	**34 205**	**39 769**
32 142	**2 255**	**73 336**	**29 348**	**5 162**	**4 417**	**33 805**	**39 531**
31 561	2 219	71 581	28 623	5 128	4 417	33 076	38 504
581	36	1 756	725	34		729	1 027
31 837	2 235	72 686	29 125	5 157	4 397	33 563	39 123
23 822	1 738	52 396	19 167	3 828	1 956	21 157	31 238
2 942	141	11 019	3 777	897	208	3 985	7 034
4 992	333	8 597	5 497	247	2 233	7 730	867
81	23	674	685	185		690	−16
305	19	651	222	5	20	242	409
31 583	2 200	71 089	27 412	4 481	4 397	31 844	39 245
254	35	1 597	1 713	677		1 719	−122
305	19	651	222	5	20	242	409
32 142	2 255	73 336	29 347	5 163	4 417	33 804	39 532
4 915	609	9 253	4 158	1 399		4 164	5 089
25 927	1 497	56 557	22 899	3 720	4 397	27 326	29 231
460	100	5 258	1 429	16		1 429	3 828
840	49	2 269	861	28	20	885	1 383
68	**22**	**638**	**400**	**124**		**400**	**238**
31	7	57	11			11	45
37	16	581	389	124		389	192
68	22	638	400	124		400	238
37	16	581	389	124		389	192
31	7	57	11			11	45
31	7	57	11			11	45
37	16	581	389	124		389	192
68	22	638	400	124		400	238

13－18 续表 2

计量单位:万元 (2010 年)

指　　标	Item	实收资本 Paicl-up Capitals	国家资本 State-owned Capitals	法人资本 Corporative Capitals
总　计	**Total**	**41 051**	**37 436**	**2 247**
住宿业	**Hotels**	**40 621**	**37 436**	**1 892**
按住宿行业分组	**Group by Hotels Sector**			
旅游饭店	Travel Hotel	39 644	36 659	1 892
一般旅馆	General Hotel	976	776	
按登记注册类型分	**Grouped by Types of Registration**			
内资企业	Domestic Enterprises	40 216	37 436	1 588
国有企业	State-owned Enterprises	31 123	30 035	1 088
有限责任公司	Limited Liability Corporations	5 261	4 268	500
股份有限公司	Share-holding Corporations Ltd	3 132	3 132	
私营企业	Private Enterprises	700		
港、澳、台商投资企业	Enterprises with Funds from HongKong Macao and TaiWan	405		304
按控股情况分组	**Grouped by Share-holding Controlled**			
国有控股	Share-holding Controlled of State-owned	38 571	37 436	1 088
私人控股	Share-holding Controlled of Private	1 644		500
其他	Other	405		304
按经营形式分组	**Grouped by Operate Form**			
独立门店	Store of Independent	40 621	37 436	1 892
按星级分组	**Group by Hotels Star**			
四星	4 Stars	5 726	3 694	1 088
三星	3 Stars	33 346	32 598	500
二星	2 Stars	368	368	
其他	Other	1 181	776	304
餐饮业	**Catering Services**	**430**		**355**
按餐饮行业分组	**Grouped by Catering Trade**			
正餐服务	Restaurant	30		
快餐服务	Snack Counter	400		355
按登记注册类型分组	**Grouped by Types of Registration**			
内资企业	Domestic Enterprises	430		355
有限责任公司	Limited Liability Corporations	400		355
私营企业	Private Enterprises	30		
按控股情况分组	**Grouped by Share-holding Controlled**			
私人控股	Share-holding Controlled of Private	30		
其他	Other	400		355
按经营形式分组	**Grouped by Operate Form**			
独立门店	Store of Independent	430		355

Continued

(10 000 yuan)

个人资本 Individual Capitals	港澳台资本 Capitals from HongKong Macao and TaiWan Capitals	主营业务收入 Revenue from Principal Business	主营业务成本 Cost of Principal Business	主营业务税金及附加 Taxes and Other Changes on Principal Business	主营业务利润 Profits from Principal Business	其他业务收入 Revenue from Other Business	其他业务利润 Profits from Other Business	营业费用 Business Expenses
1 267	**101**	**28 111**	**11 499**	**1 573**	**13 192**	**968**	**455**	**9 881**
1 192	**101**	**26 733**	**10 706**	**1 518**	**12 662**	**968**	**455**	**9 475**
992	101	25 572	10 581	1 376	11 768	696	183	8 690
200		1 161	126	142	894	273	273	786
1 192		26 521	10 703	1 507	12 464	968	455	9 339
		17 793	6 644	1 058	9 176	784	339	6 997
492		4 929	1 815	237	2 878	180	112	1 358
		2 100	1 801	114	184			51
700		1 700	444	98	226	5	4	933
	101	212	3	11	198			136
48		23 140	9 540	1 344	11 342	950	438	8 081
1 144		3 382	1 163	163	1 122	18	17	1 258
	101	212	3	11	198			136
1 192	101	26 733	10 706	1 518	12 662	968	455	9 475
944		8 651	3 107	446	4 165	33	−111	3 164
248		16 460	7 406	923	7 219	547	197	5 199
		562	191	24	347	116	96	191
	101	1 060	3	125	931	273	273	922
75		**1 378**	**793**	**55**	**530**			**406**
30		248	128	16	104			
45		1 131	664	40	427			406
75		1 378	793	55	530			406
45		1 131	664	40	427			406
30		248	128	16	104			
30		248	128	16	104			
45		1 131	664	40	427			406
75		1 378	793	55	530			406

13－18 续表 3

计量单位:万元 (2010 年)

指　　标	Item	管理费用 Administrative Expenses	# 税金 Taxes	# 差旅费 Travel Allowance	# 工会经费 Trade Unions Funds
总　计	**Total**	**7 362**	**666**	**130**	**38**
住宿业	**Hotels**	**7 144**	**666**	**125**	**38**
按住宿行业分组	**Group by Hotels Sector**				
旅游饭店	Travel Hotel	6 772	619	119	34
一般旅馆	General Hotel	372	47	6	4
按登记注册类型分	**Grouped by Types of Registration**				
内资企业	Domestic Enterprises	7 089	662	123	38
国有企业	State-owned Enterprises	4 670	521	85	34
有限责任公司	Limited Liability Corporations	1 600	137	17	4
股份有限公司	Share-holding Corporations Ltd	397	1	18	
私营企业	Private Enterprises	423	3	3	
港、澳、台商投资企业	Enterprises with Funds from HongKong Macao and TaiWan	55	4	2	
按控股情况分组	**Grouped by Share-holding Controlled**				
国有控股	Share-holding Controlled of State-owned	5 954	602	114	37
私人控股	Share-holding Controlled of Private	1 136	60	8	
其他	Other	55	4	2	
按经营形式分组	**Grouped by Operate Form**				
独立门店	Store of Independent	7 144	666	125	38
按星级分组	**Group by Hotels Star**				
四星	4 Stars	1 849	172	27	8
三星	3 Stars	4 578	392	83	22
二星	2 Stars	383	54	8	4
其他	Other	334	48	8	4
餐饮业	**Catering Services**	**218**		**5**	
按餐饮行业分组	**Grouped by Catering Trade**				
正餐服务	Restaurant	107			
快餐服务	Snack Counter	111		5	
按登记注册类型分组	**Grouped by Types of Registration**				
内资企业	Domestic Enterprises	218		5	
有限责任公司	Limited Liability Corporations	111		5	
私营企业	Private Enterprises	107			
按控股情况分组	**Grouped by Share-holding Controlled**				
私人控股	Share-holding Controlled of Private	107			
其他	Other	111		5	
按经营形式分组	**Grouped by Operate Form**				
独立门店	Store of Independent	218		5	

Continued

(10 000 yuan)

财务费用 Financial Expenses	# 利息支出 Intrest Expenditure	营业利润 Operating Profits	补贴收入 Revenue from Allowance	营业外收入 Revenue Outside Business	利润总额 Total Profits	应交所得税 Income Tax Payable	劳动、失业保险费 Unemployment Insurance	养老保险和医疗保险费 Old-Pension and Medical Insurance
232	**194**	**−1 592**	**185**	**151**	**−1 291**	**205**	**135**	**918**
231	**194**	**−1 497**	**185**	**151**	**−1 196**	**203**	**133**	**876**
231	195	−1 506	185	110	−1 344	184	108	855
	−1	9		41	148	19	25	21
226	189	−1 500	185	151	−1 197	202	133	871
154	128	−1 292	185	128	−978	179	97	710
67	66	254		17	265	16	29	69
−4	−4	−260			−260		7	90
9		−202		5	−225	8		2
5	5	2			2	1		5
217	190	−1 170	185	129	−859	194	133	867
9		−330		21	−338	8	1	4
5	5	2			2	1		5
231	194	−1 497	185	151	−1 196	203	133	876
26	8	−52		43	−32	108	7	192
200	181	−1 546	185	67	−1 433	81	100	646
1		158			158	2	1	14
5	4	−56		41	110	12	25	24
1		**−95**			**−95**	**2**	**2**	**42**
		−4			−4	2		1
1		−91			−91		2	41
1		−95			−95	2	2	42
1		−91			−91		2	41
		−4			−4	2		1
		−4			−4	2		1
1		−91			−91		2	41
1		−95			−95	2	2	42

13—18 续表 4

计量单位:万元 (2010 年)

指 标	Item	住房公积金和住房补贴 Housing Fund and Housing Allowance	本年应付工资总额 Total Accrued wages of Current Year	本年应付福利费总额 Total Accrued welfarism of Current Year	全部从业人员年平均人数(人) Average Annual Number of Employed Persons (person)
总　计	**Total**	**229**	**6 516**	**653**	**3 241**
住宿业	**Hotels**	**212**	**6 339**	**640**	**3 141**
按住宿行业分组	**Group by Hotels Sector**				
旅游饭店	Travel Hotel	193	5 992	617	2 963
一般旅馆	General Hotel	19	347	23	178
按登记注册类型分	**Grouped by Types of Registration**				
内资企业	Domestic Enterprises	213	6 275	640	3 109
国有企业	State-owned Enterprises	200	4 484	400	2 168
有限责任公司	Limited Liability Corporations	13	984	114	527
股份有限公司	Share-holding Corporations Ltd		451	79	208
私营企业	Private Enterprises		356	47	206
港、澳、台商投资企业	Enterprises with Funds from HongKong Macao and TaiWan		64		32
按控股情况分组	**Grouped by Share-holding Controlled**				
国有控股	Share-holding Controlled of State-owned	212	5 612	535	2 710
私人控股	Share-holding Controlled of Private		663	105	399
其他	Other		64		32
按经营形式分组	**Grouped by Operate Form**				
独立门店	Store of Independent	212	6 339	640	3 141
按星级分组	**Group by Hotels Star**				
四星	4 Stars	45	1 805	188	935
三星	3 Stars	148	3 993	420	1 960
二星	2 Stars	1	198	9	78
其他	Other	19	343	23	168
餐饮业	**Catering Services**	**17**	**177**	**13**	**100**
按餐饮行业分组	**Grouped by Catering Trade**				
正餐服务	Restaurant		83		49
快餐服务	Snack Counter	17	94	13	51
按登记注册类型分组	**Grouped by Types of Registration**				
内资企业	Domestic Enterprises	17	177	13	100
有限责任公司	Limited Liability Corporations	17	94	13	51
私营企业	Private Enterprises		83		49
按控股情况分组	**Grouped by Share-holding Controlled**				
私人控股	Share-holding Controlled of Private		83		49
其他	Other	17	94	13	51
按经营形式分组	**Grouped by Operate Form**				
独立门店	Store of Independent	17	177	13	100

13－19 各师限额以上住宿和餐饮业法人企业主要财务指标

Main Financial Indicators of Enterprises above Designated Size in Accommodation and Catering Services Industry by Division

计量单位：万元 （2010 年） （10 000 yuan）

单 位	Unit	年初存货 Inventories at the Beginning of the Year	流动资产合计 Working Capitals	# 应收帐款 Account Receivable	# 存货 Inventories	流动资产年平均余额 Working Capitals Average Surplus Amount of Year	长期投资合计 Long-term Investment
总 计	**Total**	**1 585**	**18 142**	**1 315**	**1 613**	**15 116**	**656**
一 师	Division 1	115	314		107	119	
二 师	Division 2	91	587	7	100	404	5
三 师	Division 3	45	613	4	42	614	
四 师	Division 4	136	3 061	53	183	2 757	18
五 师	Division 5	183	2 991	524	126	1 766	355
六 师	Division 6	47	830	113	97	721	26
七 师	Division 7	184	301	102	106	335	
八 师	Division 8	448	5 490	317	442	5 246	168
九 师	Division 9	29	422		58	441	
十 师	Division 10	16	170	32	22	128	30
国资公司	State-owned Property Company	13	474	26	27	1 289	5
兵团直属	Directly under XPCG	278	2 891	137	304	1 296	50

单 位	Unit	固定资产合计 Total Value of Fixed Assets	固定资产原价 Original Value of Fixed Assets	累计折旧 Accumulation Depreciation	# 本年折旧 Current Year Depreciation	资产总计 Total Assets	流动负债合计 Working Liability
总 计	**Total**	**45 135**	**76 829**	**32 210**	**2 277**	**73 974**	**29 748**
一 师	Division 1	1 171	1 837	666	44	1 584	385
二 师	Division 2	737	1 845	1 108	134	1 608	972
三 师	Division 3	2 916	4 737	1 821	200	3 615	929
四 师	Division 4	10 120	18 149	8 029	695	14 009	3 287
五 师	Division 5	3 607	5 922	2 316	185	10 480	4 181
六 师	Division 6	793	1 150	357	53	1 675	635
七 师	Division 7	1 729	3 061	1 332	86	2 103	1 208
八 师	Division 8	9 811	19 811	10 014	628	19 243	12 753
九 师	Division 9	2 716	3 238	1 021	104	3 138	615
十 师	Division 10	331	427	96	13	549	291
国资公司	State-owned Property Company	1 011	1 659	648	51	1 692	1 018
兵团直属	Directly under XPCG	10 190	14 992	4 802	85	14 280	3 474

13－19 续表 1 Continued

计量单位:万元 （2010 年） (10 000 yuan)

单 位	Unit	# 应付帐款 Account Payable	长期负债合计 Lang-term Liabilities	负债合计 Total Liabilities	所有者权益合计 Total Owners' Equities	实收资本 Paicl-up Capitals	国家资本 State-owned Capitals
总 计	**Total**	**5 286**	**4 417**	**34 205**	**39 769**	**41 051**	**37 436**
一 师	Division 1	12	821	1 205	379	901	201
二 师	Division 2	293		972	636	924	924
三 师	Division 3	96		929	2 685	2 101	2 101
四 师	Division 4	499	1 132	4 418	9 591	15 626	14 538
五 师	Division 5	2 312		4 181	6 299	4 920	4 920
六 师	Division 6	124		635	1 040	448	48
七 师	Division 7		4	1 212	890	1 797	1 797
八 师	Division 8	1 371	2 253	15 018	4 225	7 616	6 737
九 师	Division 9			638	2 500	2 022	2 022
十 师	Division 10	1		291	258	386	386
国资公司	State-owned Property Company	148	208	1 226	465	500	452
兵团直属	Directly under XPCG	432		3 480	10 800	3 811	3 311

单 位	Unit	法人资本 Corporative Capitals	个人资本 Individual Capitals	港澳台资本 Capitals from HongKong Macao and TaiWan Capitals	主营业务收入 Revenue from Principal Business	主营业务成本 Cost of Principal Business
总 计	**Total**	**2 247**	**1 267**	**101**	**28 111**	**11 499**
一 师	Division 1	500	200		849	342
二 师	Division 2				2 232	1 251
三 师	Division 3				1 407	383
四 师	Division 4	1 088			4 801	873
五 师	Division 5				2 517	2 196
六 师	Division 6	355	45		1 337	684
七 师	Division 7				608	262
八 师	Division 8	304	474	101	7 850	3 655
九 师	Division 9				987	160
十 师	Division 10				470	397
国资公司	State-owned Property Company		48		1 125	307
兵团直属	Directly under XPCG		500		3 928	990

13—19 续表 2 Continued

计量单位:万元 (2010 年) (10 000 yuan)

单 位	Unit	主营业务税金及附加 Taxes and Other Changes on Principal Business	主营业务利润 Profits from Principal Business	其他业务收入 Revenue from Other Business	其他业务利润 Profits from Other Business	营业费用 Business Expenses	管理费用 Administrative Expenses
总 计	**Total**	**1 573**	**13 192**	**968**	**455**	**9 881**	**7 362**
一 师	Division 1	58	450	31	31	180	276
二 师	Division 2	191	790	287	145	520	424
三 师	Division 3	88	937			524	191
四 师	Division 4	267	3 661	279	234	2 706	1 279
五 师	Division 5	131	383	95	24	85	624
六 师	Division 6	50	603	88	72	512	241
七 师	Division 7	34	312			322	201
八 师	Division 8	409	3 787	68	56	1 565	2 706
九 师	Division 9	55	762	12	10	592	328
十 师	Division 10	24	49	9	8		57
国资公司	State-owned Property Company	58	760	95	32	476	155
兵团直属	Directly under XPCG	210	698	5	-158	2 400	880

单 位	Uni	#税 金 Taxes	#差旅费 Travel Allowance	#工会经费 Trade Unions Funds	财务费用 Financial Expenses	#利息支出 Intrest Expenditure	营业利润 Operating Profits
总 计	**Total**	**666**	**130**	**38**	**232**	**194**	**-1 592**
一 师	Division 1	25	5	3	1		25
二 师	Division 2	69	6	1	13	12	-22
三 师	Division 3	59	15		10		211
四 师	Division 4	128	27	12	-22	-25	-67
五 师	Division 5	51	10	11	4	4	-53
六 师	Division 6	6	7	2	2		-78
七 师	Division 7	19		1	4	4	-215
八 师	Division 8	139	38		168	165	-645
九 师	Division 9	58	4	5	-1	-1	-147
十 师	Division 10	3	1	1			
国资公司	State-owned Property Company	10	4	2	41	39	121
兵团直属	Directly under XPCG	99	12		13	-4	-723

13—19 续表 3　Continued

计量单位:万元　　(2010 年)　　(10 000 yuan)

单　位	Unit	补贴收入 Revenue from Allowance	营业外收入 Revenue Outside Business	利润总额 Total Profits	应交所得税 Income Tax Payable	劳动、失业保险费 Unemployment Insurance
总　计	**Total**	**185**	**151**	**−1 291**	**205**	**135**
一　师	Division 1	30	14	40	8	
二　师	Division 2		7	−35	11	4
三　师	Division 3		27	239	52	2
四　师	Division 4		4	−69	72	3
五　师	Division 5	33	20	−79		3
六　师	Division 6			−77	2	2
七　师	Division 7		19	−196	1	3
八　师	Division 8	123	5	−525	58	35
九　师	Division 9		42	22		26
十　师	Division 10					1
国资公司	State-owned Property Company			117	1	2
兵团直属	Directly under XPCG		13	−726		55

单　位	Unit	养老保险和医疗保险费 Old-Pension and Medical Insurance	住房公积金和住房补贴 Housing Fund and Housing Allowance	本年应付工资总额 Total Accrued Wages of Current Year	本年应付福利费总额 Total Accrued Welfarism of Current Year	全部从业人员平均人数(人) Average Annual Number of Employed Persons(person)
总　计	**Total**	**918**	**229**	**6 516**	**653**	**3 241**
一　师	Division 1	15	5	198	19	119
二　师	Division 2	89	10	596	46	295
三　师	Division 3	29	6	197	4	102
四　师	Division 4	255	57	1 105	56	561
五　师	Division 5	116	21	716	59	287
六　师	Division 6	50	18	185	17	80
七　师	Division 7	21	8	250	5	131
八　师	Division 8	228	28	1 828	298	891
九　师	Division 9	18	43	295	23	127
十　师	Division 10	22	23	137	22	67
国资公司	State-owned Property Company	24	2	188	11	98
兵团直属	Directly under XPCG	51	8	822	93	483

13－20　亿元以上商品交易市场基本情况

Basic Statistics on Commodity Exchange Markets of Transaction Value over 100 Million Yuan

(2010 年)

指　标	Item	市场数(个) Number of Market (unit)	摊位总数(个) Number of Booths (unit)	年末出租摊位数(个) Number of Rented Booths at the Yearend (unit)	年末营业面积(平方米) Operating Area (sq. m)	成交额(万元) Turnover (10 000 yuan)
总　计	**Total**	**10**	**4 371**	**3 824**	**234 862**	**289 964**
按市场类别分组	**Group by Type of Markets**					
综合市场	Integrated Markets	4	2 098	1 987	133 463	168 027
工业消费品综合市场	Industrial Products Integrated Markets	1	731	731	55 860	66 490
农产品综合市场	Farm Produce Comprehensive Markets	1	480	480	60 000	70 970
其他综合市场	Other Comprehensive Markets	2	887	776	17 603	30 567
专业市场	Special Markets	6	2 273	1 837	101 399	121 937
生产资料市场	Productions Markets	1	72	72	8 757	19 921
农用生产资料市场	Agricultural Productions Markets	1	72	72	8 757	19 921
农产品市场	Agricultural Products Markets	2	510	510	37 401	27 743
肉食禽蛋市场	Meat, Poultry and Eggs Markets	1	120	120	30 001	10 816
其他农产品市场	Other Agricultural Products Markets	1	390	390	7 400	16 927
食品、饮料及烟酒市场	Food, Beverages, Tobacco and Liquor Markets	2	1 101	780	49 950	54 438
食品饮料市场	Food and Beverages Markets	1	825	548	32 946	24 849
其他食品饮料及烟酒市场	Other Food, Beverages, Tobacco and Liquor Markets	1	276	232	17 004	29 589
纺织、服装、鞋帽市场	Textile, Garments, Footwear and Hat Wear Markets	1	590	475	5 291	19 835
服装市场	Garments Markets	1	590	475	5 291	19 835
按营业状态分组	**Group by Business Appearance**					
常年营业	Throughout the Year	10	4 371	3 824	234 862	289 964
按经营方式分组	**Group by Management Way**					
以批发为主	Wholesale	4	948	904	115 762	131 296
以零售为主	Retail	6	3 423	2 920	119 100	158 668
按经营环境分组	**Group by Operate Environment Way**					
露天式	Open-air Type	1	120	120	30 001	10 816
封闭式	Closed Type	6	3 085	2 663	126 857	160 009
其他	Other	3	1 166	1 041	78 004	119 139

13—21 亿元以上商品交易市场商品销售类值

Commodity Exchange Markets by Category of Commodities of Transaction Value over 100 Million Yuan

(2010 年)

指　标	Item	年末出租摊位数（个） Number of Rented Booths at the Yearend (unit)	成交额（万元） Turnover (10 000yuan)
总　计	**Total**	**3 824**	**289 964**
食品、饮料、烟酒类	Food,Beverages,Tobacco and Liquor	1 526	171 229
粮油、食品类	Grain and Oil,Food	1 399	146 167
# 粮油类	GrainandOil	77	16 027
肉禽蛋类	Meat,Poultry and Eggs	278	31 710
水产品类	Aquatic Products	142	19 453
蔬菜类	Vegetables	598	53 929
干鲜果品类	Dried and Fresh Melons and Fruits	262	24 601
饮料类	Beverages	45	10 699
烟酒类	Tobacco and Liquor	82	14 363
服装、鞋帽、针纺织品类	Clothing,Shoes,Hats and Textiles	1 383	41 938
服装类	Clothing	1 152	32 623
鞋帽类	Footwear and Hats	181	7 729
针纺织品类	Knitwear and Textiles	50	1 586
化妆品类	Cosmetics	56	3 246
金银珠宝类	Gold,Silver and Jeweller	37	2 052
日用品类	Articles for DailyUse	268	11 917
# 洗涤用品类	Washing Articles	118	8 998
儿童玩具类	Children Toys	15	628
五金、电料类	Hardware & Electrical Materials	50	2 773
体育、娱乐用品类	Sports & Recreational Articles	10	1 034
书报杂志类	Newspapers and Magazines	11	432
电子出版物及音像制品类	E-ournal and Video Products	13	2 515
家用电器和音像器材类	Household Appliances and Vide Equipments	66	11 963
中西药品类	Traditional Chinese and Western Medicine	27	4 654
# 西药类	Western Medicine	15	3 186
中草药及中成药类	Traditional Chinese	3	635
文化办公用品类	Cultural and official Goods	24	3 592
家具类	Furniture	10	456
通讯器材类	Communication Appliances	95	2 113
木材及制品类	Wood and Wooden Products	2	21
建筑及装潢材料类	Building and Decoration Materials	8	546
机电产品及设备类	Mechanical & Electrical Products	8	717
# 农机类	Agricultural Machinery	4	472
汽车类	Automobile	1	1 131
种子饲料类	Seed and Feedstuff	93	23 478
其他类	Others	136	4 157

2011

BING TUAN

第十四篇

能源生产与消费

Chapter 14 Energy Production and Consumption

简要说明

一、本篇资料主要内容

本篇资料反映兵团规模以上工业法人企业分行业主要能源品种的消费、库存量及能源、加工转换量，分行业能源消费量；兵团道路运输企业主要能源品种的消费量。

二、本篇统计范围

统计范围为兵团规模以上工业法人企业，兵团道路交通运输法人企业。

三、本篇资料来源

本篇资料由兵团统计局工业交通投资统计处根据《兵团能源、主要物资消费统计报表制度》整理提供。

四、本篇调查方法

统计调查方法为全面调查。

Brief Introduction

1. Main Contents

Data in this chapter show energy consumption and inventory of industrial enterprises and output of energy processing conversion of industrial enterprises by category of energy above designated size, consumption by industrial branch; consumption of main energy varieties of road transportation enterprises.

2. Scope of Statistics

The statistical scope covers industrial corporate enterprises above designated size, road communication and transportation corporate enterprises of XPCG.

3. Sources of Data

The data in this chapter are prepared and provided by Industry Communications and Assets Statistical Section of Statistics Bureau of XPCG according to the Comprehensive Statistical Reporting Form System on Energy and Main Supplies Consumption.

4. Methodology of Survey

Survey method is comprehensive statistics.

14—1 规模以上工业企业能源消费与库存量

Energy Consumption and Inventory of Industrial Enterprises above Designated Size

（2010 年）

指标	Item	年初库存量 Inventory at the Beginning of the year	本年消费量 Consumption in the Year	工业生产消费 Industry Consumption	非工业生产消费 Non-industry Consumption	# 车辆用油 Vehicle Oil	年末库存量 Inventory at the Year-end
能源合计（吨标准煤）	**Total Energy Production (tons of SCE)**	**2 298**	**11 990 861**	**11 942 977**	**47 885**		
原　煤　（吨）	Coal (ton)	1 333 454	11 570 092	11 547 836	22 256	12	1 418 202
洗精煤　（吨）	Dressing Coal (ton)	95 893	552 418	552 418			66 480
其他洗煤　（吨）	Other Dressing Coal (ton)		6 437	6 418	19		
煤制品　（吨）	Coal Ware (ton)	12 000	16 897	16 897			
焦　炭　（吨）	Coke (ton)	135 538	887 855	887 855			269 327
其他焦化产品　（吨）	Other Coking Product (ton)	280	6 119	6 119			
焦炉煤气　（万立方米）	Coke Oven Coal Gas (10000 cu. m)		793	793			
天然气　（万立方米）	Natural Gas (10 000 cu. m)		3 920	3 796	124	7	
原　油　（吨）	Crude Oil (ton)		8	8			
汽　油　（吨）	Gasoline (ton)	75	3 905	2 084	1 814	2 696	50
柴　油　（吨）	Diesel Oil (ton)	782	20 037	11 967	8 057	13 365	1 347
燃料油　（吨）	Fuel Oil (ton)	116	161	154	7		119
液化石油气　（吨）	Liquefied Petroleum Gas (ton)		118	118			
润滑油脂　（吨）	Lubrication (ton)		7	7			
石油焦　（吨）	Petroleum Coke (ton)		320	320			
石油沥青　（吨）	Petroleum Asphalt (ton)		425	425			
其他石油制品　（吨）	Other Petroleum Products (ton)	3	1 238	1 238			167
热　力　（百万千焦）	Heat (million KJ)		12 175 602	11 900 392	275 210		
电　力　（万千瓦时）	Electricity (10 000 kwh)		1 208 854	1 202 759	5 329	31	
煤矸石用于燃料　（吨）	Coal Gangue Used for Fuel (ton)		26 639	26 639			
余热余压　（百万千焦）	Remaining Hot and Pressure (million KJ)		1 033 368	1 033 368			
其他燃料　（吨标准煤）	Other Fuel (tons of SCE)		8 069	8 069			

注：由于规模以上工业统计口径变化，本表 2009 年数据与《2010 年兵团统计年鉴》相同指标数据不可比。
Note：Due to changes of statistical caliber, same item in 2007 in this tabel are not same as statistical yearbook-2008 of XPCG.（the same as follow）

14—2 规模以上工业加工转换企业按能源品种分能源加工转换量

Output of Energy Processing Conversion of Industrial Processing Conversion Enterprises above Designated Size by Category of Energy

（2010 年）

指标	Item	工业生产消费 Industry Consumption	加工转换投入合计 Total Processing Conversion Devoted	火电投入 Thermal Power Consumption	供热投入 Heating Consumption	原煤入洗 Coal Dressing	炼焦投入 Coking Consumption	能源转换产出量 Energy Output Conversion	回收利用 Recycling
能源合计（吨标准煤）	**Total Energy Production (tons of SCE)**	**9 748 222**	**7 594 094**	**4 536 328**	**1 654 245**	**310 354**	**1 093 167**	**3 932 321**	**34 104**
原　煤　（吨）	Coal (ton)	10 494 659	9 450 804	6 140 546	2 270 783	365 766	673 709		
洗精煤　（吨）	Dressing Coal (ton)	552 418	533 231				533 231	309 616	
煤制品　（吨）	Coal Ware (ton)	13 094	13 094				13 094		
焦　炭　（吨）	Coke (ton)	537 906						791 454	
其他焦化产品　（吨）	Other Coking Product (ton)							50 769	
焦炉煤气　（万立方米）	Coke Oven Coal Gas (10000 cu. m)	793	793	793				793	
天然气　（万立方米）	Natural Gas (10 000 cu. m)	1 330							
汽　油　（吨）	Gasoline (ton)	291	41	41					
柴　油　（吨）	Diesel Oil (ton)	5 896	960	946	14				
燃料油　（吨）	Fuel Oil (ton)	154							
其他石油制品　（吨）	Other Petroleum Products (ton)	6							
热　力　（百万千焦）	Heat (million KJ)	3 421 460						37 975 814	
电　力　（万千瓦时）	Electricity (10 000 kwh)	586 150						1 235 997	
煤矸石用于燃料　（吨）	Coal Gangue Used for Fuel (ton)	12 549	12 549	12 549				29 437	
余热余压　（百万千焦）	Remaining Hot and Pressure (million KJ)	1 033 368	150 543	150 543					1 000 123

14—3 规模以上工业企业按行业分产值能耗

Output Value Energy Consumption of Industrial Enterprises above Designated Size by Industrial Branch

指 标	Item	企业单位数（个）Number of Enterprises (unit)	2009 综合能源消费量（吨标准煤）Comsuption of Comprehensive Energy(ton standard coal)	2009 产值能耗（吨标准煤/万元）Energy Comsuption of Output Value (ton standard coal)
总　计	**Total**	**569**	**6 795 004**	**1.6450**
按工业行业大类分列	**Grouped by Sector**			
采矿业	**Mining**	**31**	**30 391**	**0.2460**
煤炭开采和洗选业	Coal Mining and Dressing	14	21 258	0.2454
石油和天然气开采业	Petroleum and Natural Gas Extraction			
黑色金属矿采选业	Ferrous Metals Mining and Dressing	6	1 210	0.1749
有色金属矿采选业	Nonferrous Metals Mining and Dressing	3	2 332	0.1947
非金属矿采选业	Nonmetal Minerals Mining and Dressing	8	5 591	0.3097
其他采矿业	Other Minerals Mining and Dressing			
制造业	**Manufacturing**	**508**	**4 892 366**	**1.3288**
农副食品加工业	Food Processing	113	233 696	0.3166
食品制造业	Food Manufacturing	68	310 546	0.6632
饮料制造业	Beverage Production	31	48 899	0.2334
烟草制品业	Tobacco Processing			
纺织业	Textile Industry	42	169 496	0.4103
纺织服装、鞋、帽制造业	Textile Clothing Shoes and Hats Manufacturing			
皮革、毛皮、羽毛(绒)及其制品业	Leather Furs Downand Related Products			
木材加工及木、竹、藤、棕、草制品业	Timber Processing Bamboo Cane Palm Fiber and Straw Products	2	599	0.1758
家具制造业	Furniture Manufacturing	2	121	0.0200
造纸及纸制品业	Paper making and Paper Products	16	33 703	0.5845
印刷业和记录媒介的复制	Printing Industry and Recording Media	3	160	0.0753
文教体育用品制造业	Cultural Educational and Sports Goods			
石油加工、炼焦及核燃料加工业	Petroleum, Processing Coking and Nucler Fuel	9	168 515	2.8984
化学原料及化学制品制造业	Raw Chemical Materials and Chemical Products	35	2 643 054	2.8692
医药制造业	Medical and Pharmaceutical Products	5	18 010	0.4553
化学纤维制造业	Chemical Fiber	3	82 876	0.6117
橡胶制品业	Rubber Products	1	44	0.0908
塑料制品业	Plastic Products	71	20 091	0.1149
非金属矿物制品业	Nonmetal Mineral Products	55	1 010 043	3.0930
黑色金属冶炼及压延加工业	Ferrous Metals Smelting and Rolling	7	86 369	2.3109
有色金属冶炼及压延加工业	Non-Ferrous Metals Smelting and Rolling	4	54 346	8.1297
金属制品业	Metal Products	11	2 857	0.1067
通用设备制造业	Ordinary Machinery	10	1 301	0.1159
专用设备制造业	Special Purpose Equipment	16	3 201	0.0882
交通运输设备制造业	Transport Equipment	1	1 734	0.4801
电气机械及器材制造业	Electric Equipment and Machinery	2	2 705	0.5091
通信设备、计算机及其他电子设备制造业	Correspondence Equipments, Computer and other Electronics Equipments			
仪器仪表及文化、办公用机械制造业	Apparatus, Appearance, Culture and Handle official Bussiness Machine Manufacturing			
工艺品及其他制造业	Arts and Crafts Products and Other Manufacturing			
废弃资源和废旧材料回收加工业	Worn-out Resource and Material Reclaim and Processing	1		
电力、燃气及水的生产和供应业	**Electricity Gasand Water Production and Supply**	**30**	**1 872 247**	**5.7544**
电力、热力的生产和供应业	Electricity and Heat Production and Supply	25	1 868 215	5.8793
燃气生产和供应业	Gas Production and Supply	2	753	0.2963
水的生产和供应业	Water Production and Supply	3	3 279	0.6486
按轻重工业分	**Grouped by Light & Heavy Industry**			
轻工业	Light Industry	303	924 242	0.4373
重工业	Heavy Industry	266	5 870 762	2.9107

14—3 续表 Continued

指 标	Item	2010 综合能源消费量（吨标准煤） Comsuption of Comprehensive Energy (ton standard coal)	2010 产值能耗（吨标准煤/万元） Energy Comsuption of Output Value (ton standard coal)
总 计	**Total**	**7 978 849**	**1.4350**
按工业行业大类分列	**Grouped by Sector**		
采矿业	**Mining**	**48 095**	**0.2438**
煤炭开采和洗选业	Coal Mining and Dressing	37 140	0.2636
石油和天然气开采业	Petroleum and Natural Gas Extraction		
黑色金属矿采选业	Ferrous Metals Mining and Dressing	1 333	0.1314
有色金属矿采选业	Nonferrous Metals Mining and Dressing	3 677	0.1749
非金属矿采选业	Nonmetal Minerals Mining and Dressing	5 945	0.2358
其他采矿业	Other Minerals Mining and Dressing		
制造业	**Manufacturing**	**5 679 576**	**1.1438**
农副食品加工业	Food Processing	267 080	0.2887
食品制造业	Food Manufacturing	307 093	0.5302
饮料制造业	Beverage Production	64 710	0.2145
烟草制品业	Tobacco Processing		
纺织业	Textile Industry	222 253	0.3458
纺织服装、鞋、帽制造业	Textile Clothing Shoes and Hats Manufacturing		
皮革、毛皮、羽毛(绒)及其制品业	Leather Furs Downand Related Products		
木材加工及木、竹、藤、棕、草制品业	Timber Processing Bamboo Cane Palm Fiber and Straw Products	296	0.2150
家具制造业	Furniture Manufacturing	169	0.0220
造纸及纸制品业	Paper making and Paper Products	38 694	0.5837
印刷业和记录媒介的复制	Printing Industry and Recording Media	283	0.0444
文教体育用品制造业	Cultural Educational and Sports Goods		
石油加工、炼焦及核燃料加工业	Petroleum, Processing Coking and Nucler Fuel	267 000	2.3526
化学原料及化学制品制造业	Raw Chemical Materials and Chemical Products	2 754 820	2.7618
医药制造业	Medical and Pharmaceutical Products	18 472	0.4158
化学纤维制造业	Chemical Fiber	89 430	0.3981
橡胶制品业	Rubber Products	53	0.0830
塑料制品业	Plastic Products	23 551	0.1126
非金属矿物制品业	Nonmetal Mineral Products	1 212 731	2.5507
黑色金属冶炼及压延加工业	Ferrous Metals Smelting and Rolling	93 593	1.6833
有色金属冶炼及压延加工业	Non-Ferrous Metals Smelting and Rolling	299 123	1.5148
金属制品业	Metal Products	3 341	0.0587
通用设备制造业	Ordinary Machinery	1 791	0.1345
专用设备制造业	Special Purpose Equipment	2 548	0.0933
交通运输设备制造业	Transport Equipment	1 761	0.3506
电气机械及器材制造业	Electric Equipment and Machinery	3 674	0.5287
通信设备、计算机及其他电子设备制造业	Correspondence Equipments, Computer and other Electronics Equipments		
仪器仪表及文化、办公用机械制造业	Apparatus, Appearance, Culture and Handle official Bussiness Machine Manufacturing		
工艺品及其他制造业	Arts and Crafts Products and Other Manufacturing		
废弃资源和废旧材料回收加工业	Worn-out Resource and Material Reclaim and Processing	7 110	0.9741
电力、燃气及水的生产和供应业	**Electricity Gasand Water Production and Supply**	**2 251 178**	**5.6653**
电力、热力的生产和供应业	Electricity and Heat Production and Supply	2 246 465	5.8028
燃气生产和供应业	Gas Production and Supply	1 064	0.2366
水的生产和供应业	Water Production and Supply	3 649	0.6365
按轻重工业分	**Grouped by Light & Heavy Industry**		
轻工业	Light Industry	1 040 575	0.3639
重工业	Heavy Industry	6 938 274	2.5687

14—4 规模以上工业企业按行业分主要能源消费

(2010年)

指 标	Item	原 煤 (吨) Coal (ton)	焦 炭 (吨) Coke (ton)	天然气 (万立方米) Natural Gas (10 000 cu. m)	汽 油 (吨) Gasoline (ton)
总 计	**Total**	**11 570 092**	**887 855**	**3 920**	**3 905**
按工业行业大类分列	**Grouped by Sector**				
采矿业	**Mining**	**134 443**		**1**	**355**
煤炭开采和洗选业	Coal Mining and Dressing	127 674		1	298
石油和天然气开采业	Petroleum and Natural Gas Extraction				
黑色金属矿采选业	Ferrous Metals Mining and Dressing	899			3
有色金属矿采选业	Nonferrous Metals Mining and Dressing	1 118			22
非金属矿采选业	Nonmetal Minerals Mining and Dressing	4 752			32
其他采矿业	Other Minerals Mining and Dressing				
制造业	**Manufacturing**	**5 882 351**	**887 855**	**3 919**	**2 909**
农副食品加工业	Food Processing	358 852	9 736	171	610
食品制造业	Food Manufacturing	380 984		731	404
饮料制造业	Beverage Production	48 956		89	185
烟草制品业	Tobacco Processing				
纺织业	Textile Industry	79 847			205
纺织服装、鞋、帽制造业	Textile Clothing Shoes and Hats Manufacturing				
皮革、毛皮、羽毛(绒)及其制品业	Leather Furs Downand Related Products				
木材加工及木、竹、藤、棕、草制品业	Timber Processing Bamboo Cane Palm Fiber and Straw Products	344			5
家具制造业	Furniture Manufacturing				19
造纸及纸制品业	Paper making and Paper Products	17 184		1	25
印刷业和记录媒介的复制	Printing Industry and Recording Media	173			29
文教体育用品制造业	Cultural Educational and Sports Goods				
石油加工、炼焦及核燃料加工业	Petroleum, Processing Coking and Nucler Fuel	838 785			49
化学原料及化学制品制造业	Raw Chemical Materials and Chemical Products	2 370 926	821 663	2 614	187
医药制造业	Medical and Pharmaceutical Products	24 103			86
化学纤维制造业	Chemical Fiber	18 962			18
橡胶制品业	Rubber Products	8			
塑料制品业	Plastic Products	9 447		5	167
非金属矿物制品业	Nonmetal Mineral Products	1 517 536	61	267	736
黑色金属冶炼及压延加工业	Ferrous Metals Smelting and Rolling	30 412	56 330	33	32
有色金属冶炼及压延加工业	Non-Ferrous Metals Smelting and Rolling	173 066			24
金属制品业	Metal Products	577		8	16
通用设备制造业	Ordinary Machinery	734	65		42
专用设备制造业	Special Purpose Equipment	1 813			45
交通运输设备制造业	Transport Equipment	2 392			17
电气机械及器材制造业	Electric Equipment and Machinery	150			4
通信设备、计算机及其他电子设备制造业	Correspondence Equipments, Computer and other Electronics Equipments				
仪器仪表及文化、办公用机械制造业	Apparatus, Appearance, Culture and Handle official Bussiness Machine Manufacturing				
工艺品及其他制造业	Arts and Crafts Products and Other Manufacturing				
废弃资源和废旧材料回收加工业	Worn-out Resource and Material Reclaim and Processing	7 100			4
电力、燃气及水的生产和供应业	**Electricity Gas and Water Production and Supply**	**5 553 298**			**641**
电力、热力的生产和供应业	Electricity and Heat Production and Supply	5 552 770			626
燃气生产和供应业	Gas Production and Supply				1
水的生产和供应业	Water Production and Supply	528			14
按轻重工业分	**Grouped by Light & Heavy Industry**				
轻工业	Light Industry	960 717	9 736	991	1 614
重工业	Heavy Industry	10 609 375	878 119	2 929	2 291

Main Energy Consumption of Industrial Enterprises above Designated Size by Industrial Branch

柴 油 （吨） Diesel Oil (ton)	燃料油 （吨） Fuel Oil (ton)	液 化 石油气 （吨） Liquefied Petroleum Gas (ton)	其 他 石油制品 （吨） Other Petroleum Products (ton)	热 力 （百万千焦） Heat (million kj)	电 力 （万千瓦时） Electricity (10 000 kwh)	煤矸石 用于燃料 （吨） Coal Gangue Used for Fuel (ton)	其他燃料 （吨标准煤） Other Fuel (tons of SCE)
20 037	**161**	**118**	**1 238**	**12 175 602**	**1 208 854**	**8 069**	**26 639**
1 984			**45**		**15 477**		
710			39		11 401		
65					483		
61					2 245		
1 148			6		1 348		
15 374	**7**	**118**	**1 193**	**11 971 715**	**1 089 010**	**8 069**	**26 639**
872	7	1	1 078	1 079 859	22 139		
799			28	1 984 600	26 012		
143				1 146 388	7 141		
199			1	1 952 231	84 075		
8					25		
				3 345	23		
80				547 958	6 013		
18				1 261	84		
126					8 718		12 549
3 914				3 056 071	606 725		
40				6 254	761		
128			51	1 764 753	12 655		
30					20		
186				81 166	11 405		
7 717		112	35	235 607	108 531	8 069	14 090
767				54 544	5 240		
229					181 627		
29				22 101	1 686		
31				18 779	430		
54		5		16 798	1 102		
					37		
4					2 902		
					1 659		
2 679	**154**			**203 887**	**104 367**		
2 671	154			175 578	101 642		
				20 800	289		
8				7 509	2 436		
2 321	7	1	1 158	8 495 088	167 464		
17 716	154	117	80	3 680 514	1 041 390	8 069	26 639

14—5 规模以上工业企业按行业分水消费

Water Consumption of Industrial Enterprises above Designated Size by Industrial Branch

计量单位:万立方米　　(2010 年)　　(10 000 cu. m)

指　标	Item	工业取水总量合计 Water Used by Industry	地表水 Surface Water	地下水 Ground Water	自来水 Tap Water	重复用水 Recycling Water
总　计	**Total**	**16 702.88**	**4 622.51**	**9 728.82**	**1 708.33**	**45 378.56**
按工业行业大类分列	**Grouped by Sector**					
采矿业	**Mining**	**607.35**	**30.79**	**540.09**	**11.56**	**45.43**
煤炭开采和洗选业	Coal Mining and Dressing	82.79	30.79	40.44	11.56	19.23
石油和天然气开采业	Petroleum and Natural Gas Extraction					
黑色金属矿采选业	Ferrous Metals Mining and Dressing	75.18		75.18		1.20
有色金属矿采选业	Nonferrous Metals Mining and Dressing	55.06		55.06		25.00
非金属矿采选业	Nonmetal Minerals Mining and Dressing	394.32		369.41		
其他采矿业	Other Minerals Mining and Dressing					
制造业	**Manufacturing**	**8 328.13**	**796.85**	**5 965.17**	**947.81**	**39 436.14**
农副食品加工业	Food Processing	1 090.24	156.08	842.56	91.56	311.53
食品制造业	Food Manufacturing	1 580.64	29.14	1 392.40	159.10	1 484.00
饮料制造业	Beverage Production	493.21		455.39	37.82	55.30
烟草制品业	Tobacco Processing					
纺织业	Textile Industry	565.22	0.40	478.53	86.29	560.54
纺织服装、鞋、帽制造业	Textile Clothing Shoes and Hats Manufacturing					
皮革、毛皮、羽毛(绒)及其制品业	Leather Furs Downand Related Products					
木材加工及木、竹、藤、棕、草制品业	Timber Processing Bamboo Cane Palm Fiber and Straw Products	0.22	0.05		0.16	
家具制造业	Furniture Manufacturing	0.54			0.54	
造纸及纸制品业	Paper making and Paper Products	578.59	6.21	558.90	13.49	2.03
印刷业和记录媒介的复制	Printing Industry and Recording Media	1.31			1.31	
文教体育用品制造业	Cultural Educational and Sports Goods					
石油加工、炼焦及核燃料加工业	Petroleum,Processing Coking and Nucler Fuel	138.92	10.52	128.40		0.72
化学原料及化学制品制造业	Raw Chemical Materials and Chemical Products	1 735.25	23.61	1 697.39	14.26	36 389.21
医药制造业	Medical and Pharmaceutical Products	62.04	1.51	4.53	56.00	
化学纤维制造业	Chemical Fiber	1 265.55	405.36		287.67	572.53
橡胶制品业	Rubber Products	0.04				
塑料制品业	Plastic Products	119.71	0.44	89.51	29.60	9.38
非金属矿物制品业	Nonmetal Mineral Products	581.24	163.53	232.10	147.08	45.70
黑色金属冶炼及压延加工业	Ferrous Metals Smelting and Rolling	16.14		5.00	4.50	5.20
有色金属冶炼及压延加工业	Non-Ferrous Metals Smelting and Rolling	78.00		77.55	0.45	
金属制品业	Metal Products	3.56		0.30	2.89	
通用设备制造业	Ordinary Machinery	6.45		0.02	6.42	
专用设备制造业	Special Purpose Equipment	5.05		2.59	2.46	
交通运输设备制造业	Transport Equipment	2.17			2.17	
电气机械及器材制造业	Electric Equipment and Machinery	0.31			0.31	
通信设备、计算机及其他电子设备制造业	Correspondence Equipments,Computer and other Electronics Equipments					
仪器仪表及文化、办公用机械制造业	Apparatus,Appearance,culture and Handle official Bussiness Machine Manufacturing					
工艺品及其他制造业	Arts and Crafts Products and Other Manufacturing					
废弃资源和废旧材料回收加工业	Worn-out Resource and Material Reclaim and Processing	3.73			3.73	
电力、燃气及水的生产和供应业	**Electricity Gas and Water Production and Supply**	**7 767.40**	**3 794.87**	**3 223.56**	**748.96**	**5 896.99**
电力、热力的生产和供应业	Electricity and Heat Production and Supply	3 180.02	1 824.87	1 093.56	261.58	5 896.99
燃气生产和供应业	Gas Production and Supply	1.87			1.87	
水的生产和供应业	Water Production and Supply	4 585.51	1 970.00	2 130.00	485.51	
按轻重工业分	**Grouped by Light & Heavy Industry**					
轻工业	Light Industry	10 302.30	2 592.20	5 910.20	1 227.33	2 986.62
重工业	Heavy Industry	6 400.58	2 030.31	3 818.62	481.00	42 391.94

14—6 各师规模以上工业企业主要能源消费

Main Energy Consumption of Industrial Entrprises above Designated Size by Division

（2010 年）

指 标	Item	合 计 Total	一 师 Division 1	二 师 Division 2	三 师 Division 3	四 师 Division 4	五 师 Division 5	六 师 Division 6	七 师 Division 7	八 师 Division 8
能源合计（吨标准煤）	**Total Energy Production (tons of SCE)**	**11 990 861**	**1 241 686**	**193 749**	**76 986**	**778 404**	**176 373**	**1 480 234**	**1 015 082**	**6 149 763**
原 煤 （吨）	Coal (ton)	11 570 092	1 467 443	210 163	99 722	823 305	222 443	865 889	1 344 908	5 599 757
焦 炭 （吨）	Coke (ton)	887 855	61	1 628		63 118		65	1 044	763 314
天然气（万立方米）	Crude Oil (10 000 cu. m)	3 920		186		89		6		2 614
汽 油 （吨）	Gasolin (ton)	3 905	725	477	142	450	125	230	109	383
柴 油 （吨）	Diesel Oil (ton)	20 037	6 770	1 553	353	1 263	301	188	310	4 695
燃料油 （吨）	Fuel Oil (ton)	161						7		154
液化石油气（吨）	Liquefied Petroleum Gas (ton)	118	5	112						
其他石油制品（吨）	Other Petroleum Products (ton)	1 238	145	45			985			
热 力（百万千焦）	Heat (million KJ)	12 175 602	1 879 608	473 545		641 687	156 847	1 430		8 300 205
电 力（万千瓦时）	Electricity (10 000 kwh)	1 208 854	91 995	15 078	4 094	68 629	6 991	209 395	42 952	735 817
其他燃料（吨标准煤）	Other Fuel (tons of SCE)	8 069								
煤矸石用于燃料（吨）	Coal Gangue Used for Fuel (ton)	26 639		14 090				12 549		

指 标	Item	九 师 Division 9	十 师 Division 10	建工师 Construction Division	十二师 Division 12	十三师 Division 13	十四师 Division 14	国资公司 State-owned Property Company	中基公司 Chalkis Company	兵团直属 Directly under XPCG
能源合计（吨标准煤）	**Total Energy Production (tons of SCE)**	**97 173**	**115 526**	**23 114**	**77 204**	**480 053**	**970**	**17 817**	**64 684**	**2 043**
原 煤 （吨）	Coal (ton)	95 546	148 811	6 493	93 373	500 637	962	15 470	73 131	2 039
焦 炭 （吨）	Coke (ton)	2 295				56 330				
天然气（万立方米）	Crude Oil (10 000 cu. m)			300	1			170	554	
汽 油 （吨）	Gasolin (ton)	41	462	54	224	103	38	148	124	70
柴 油 （吨）	Diesel Oil (ton)	131	1 639	245	696	1 535	40	76	229	13
燃料油 （吨）	Fuel Oil (ton)									
液化石油气（吨）	Liquefied Petroleum Gas (ton)				1					
其他石油制品（吨）	Other Petroleum Products (ton)				35				28	
热 力（百万千焦）	Heat (million KJ)	675 845	1 631	293	1 269	2 345		16 770	22 866	1 261
电 力（万千瓦时）	Electricity (10 000 kwh)	2 766	4 968	4 858	6 026	8 298	136	2 931	3 577	343
其他燃料（吨标准煤）	Other Fuel (tons of SCE)			8 069						
煤矸石用于燃料（吨）	Coal Gangue Used for Fuel (ton)									

14—7 各师规模以上工业企业水消费

Water Consumption of Industrial Enterprises above Designated Size by Division

计量单位:万立方米　　(2010 年)　　(10 000 cu. m)

单 位	Unit	工业取水总量合计 Water used by Industry	地表水 Surface Water	地下水 Ground Water	自来水 Tap water	重复用水 Recycling water
总 计	**Total**	**16 702.88**	**4 622.51**	**9 728.82**	**1 708.33**	**45 378.56**
一 师	Division 1	4 917.39	3 712.55	114.72	487.59	1 335.94
二 师	Division 2	336.38	14.03	263.30	59.05	121.00
三 师	Division 3	182.75	9.00	44.88	128.87	4.54
四 师	Division 4	675.39	183.46	422.59	63.61	160.88
五 师	Division 5	289.72	230.81	41.64	17.27	185.66
六 师	Division 6	1 483.66	10.03	1 459.42	14.22	414.26
七 师	Division 7	658.53	395.29	245.50	17.75	117.76
八 师	Division 8	6 004.00		5 739.04	264.95	42 320.59
九 师	Division 9	196.23	55.13	141.10		49.98
十 师	Division 10	394.96		382.76	12.20	43.93
建 工 师	Construction Division	12.98			2.93	
十 二 师	Division 12	776.25	12.21	244.00	520.02	
十 三 师	Division 13	281.49		256.58		44.24
十 四 师	Division 14	4.97			4.97	0.10
国资公司	State-owned Property Company	57.25		30.08	27.18	22.08
中基公司	Chalkis Company	426.99		343.21	83.78	557.60
兵团直属	Directly under XPCG	3.94			3.94	

14—8 各师规模以上工业企业总产值能耗

Output Value Energy Consumption of Industrial Enterprises above Designated Size by Division

单 位	Unit	企业单位数(个) Number of Enterprises (unit)	2009		2010	
			综合能源消费量(吨标准煤) Comsuption of Comprehensive Energy(ton standard coal)	产值能耗(吨标准煤/万元) Energy Comsuption of Output Value (ton standard coal /10 000yuan)	综合能源消费量(吨标准煤) Comsuption of Comprehensive Energy(ton standard coal)	产值能耗(吨标准煤/万元) Energy Comsuption of Output Value (ton standard coal /10 000yuan)
总 计	**Total**	**569**	**6 795 004**	**1.6450**	**7 978 849**	**1.4350**
一 师	Division 1	87	746 290	1.6120	918 354	1.3379
二 师	Division 2	43	136 399	0.6218	166 016	0.5542
三 师	Division 3	13	22 158	0.4401	57 157	0.8842
四 师	Division 4	58	569 045	1.8333	673 540	1.5898
五 师	Division 5	15	77 044	0.9690	98 717	0.9706
六 师	Division 6	58	211 874	0.7202	555 519	0.8625
七 师	Division 7	26	559 532	2.7153	663 511	2.2124
八 师	Division 8	137	3 989 049	2.2787	4 272 061	1.9893
九 师	Division 9	8	38 064	1.0077	57 593	1.0337
十 师	Division 10	25	76 327	1.1970	81 617	0.9346
建 工 师	Construction Division	10	18 617	0.7086	22 125	0.7149
十 二 师	Division 12	26	29 894	0.4146	43 938	0.4410
十 三 师	Division 13	43	211 409	2.1557	283 920	2.1082
十 四 师	Division 14	5	850	0.1358	860	0.0722
国资公司	State-owned Property Company	10	20 172	0.0772	17 817	0.0645
中基公司	Chalkis Company	3	85 702	0.5447	64 061	0.4001
兵团直属	Directly under XPCG	2	2 578	0.0747	2 043	0.0565

14—9 规模以上工业企业主要能源按工业行业分年末库存量

Year-end Main Energy Inventory of Industrial Enterprises above Designated Size by Industrial Branch

(2010 年)

计量单位:吨 (ton)

指标	Item	原煤 Coal	焦炭 Coke	汽油 Gasoline	柴油 Diesel Oil	燃料油 Fuel Oil	其他石油制品 Other Petroleum Products
总计	**Total**	**1 418 202**	**269 327**	**50**	**1 347**	**119**	**167**
按工业行业大类分列	**Grouped by Sector**						
采矿业	**Mining**	**3 552**		**14**	**55**		**1**
煤炭开采和洗选业	Coal Mining and Dressing	2 785		12	25		
石油和天然气开采业	Petroleum and Natural Gas Extraction						
黑色金属矿采选业	Ferrous Metals Mining and Dressing	52					
有色金属矿采选业	Nonferrous Metals Mining and Dressing				10		
非金属矿采选业	Nonmetal Minerals Mining and Dressing	715		2	20		1
其他采矿业	Other Minerals Mining and Dressing						
制造业	**Manufacturing**	**784 805**	**269 327**	**20**	**1 114**		**166**
农副食品加工业	Food Processing	142 888	4 819		18		166
食品制造业	Food Manufacturing	22 251			1		
饮料制造业	Beverage Production	6 429					
烟草制品业	Tobacco Processing						
纺织业	Textile Industry	17 812			1		
纺织服装、鞋、帽制造业	Textile Clothing Shoes and Hats Manufacturing						
皮革、毛皮、羽毛(绒)及其制品业	Leather Furs Downand Related Products						
木材加工及木、竹、藤、棕、草制品业	Timber Processing Bamboo Cane Palm Fiber and Straw Products	19					
家具制造业	Furniture Manufacturing						
造纸及纸制品业	Paper making and Paper Products	1 273		1	2		
印刷业和记录媒介的复制	Printing Industry and Recording Media	2					
文教体育用品制造业	Cultural Educational and Sports Goods						
石油加工、炼焦及核燃料加工业	Petroleum,Processing Coking and Nucler Fuel	70 468			9		
化学原料及化学制品制造业	Raw Chemical Materials and Chemical Products	164 599	259 895	3	915		
医药制造业	Medical and Pharmaceutical Products	13 525					
化学纤维制造业	Chemical Fiber	130					
橡胶制品业	Rubber Products						
塑料制品业	Plastic Products	693					
非金属矿物制品业	Nonmetal Mineral Products	322 299		16	167		
黑色金属冶炼及压延加工业	Ferrous Metals Smelting and Rolling	11 452	4 613				
有色金属冶炼及压延加工业	Non-Ferrous Metals Smelting and Rolling	10 664					
金属制品业	Metal Products	9					
通用设备制造业	Ordinary Machinery	95					
专用设备制造业	Special Purpose Equipment	77			1		
交通运输设备制造业	Transport Equipment						
电气机械及器材制造业	Electric Equipment and Machinery						
工艺品及其他制造业	Arts and Crafts Products and Other Manufacturing						
废弃资源和废旧材料回收加工业	Worn-out Resource and Material Reclaim and Processing	120					
电力、燃气及水的生产和供应业	**Electricity Gasand Water Production and Supply**	**629 845**		**16**	**178**	**119**	
电力、热力的生产和供应业	Electricity and Heat Production and Supply	629 678		16	178	119	
燃气生产和供应业	Gas Production and Supply						
水的生产和供应业	Water Production and Supply	167					
按轻重工业分	**Grouped by Light & Heavy Industry**						
轻工业	Light Industry	205 150	4 819	2	22		166
重工业	Heavy Industry	1 213 052	264 508	48	1 325	119	1

14—10 各师规模以上工业企业主要能源年末库存量

Year-end Main Energy Inventory of Industrial Enterprises above Designated Size by Division

计量单位:吨 (2010 年) (ton)

单 位	Unit	原 煤 Coal	焦 炭 Coke	汽 油 Gasoline	柴 油 Diesel Oil	燃料油 Fuel Oil	其他石油制品 Other Petroleum Products
总 计	**Total**	**1 418 202**	**269 327**	**50**	**1 347**	**119**	**167**
一 师	Division 1	172 050		27	268		
二 师	Division 2	46 021	1 097	4	24		1
三 师	Division 3	18 851			100		
四 师	Division 4	243 118	5 776		1		
五 师	Division 5	40 018			5		166
六 师	Division 6	66 880		3	11		
七 师	Division 7	104 486	189		12		
八 师	Division 8	571 729	257 563	16	916	119	
九 师	Division 9	72 171	89				
十 师	Division 10	3 091					
建 工 师	Construction Division	160					
十 二 师	Division 12	21 907					
十 三 师	Division 13	40 044	4 613		10		
十 四 师	Division 14	360					
国资公司	State-owned Property Company	8 373					
中基公司	Chalkis Company	8 207					
兵团直属	Directly under XPCG	736					

14—11 各师交通运输法人企业主要能源及水消费

Main Energy and Water Consumption of Transportation Corporative Enterprises by Division

(2010 年)

单 位	Unit	原 煤(吨) Coal (ton)	汽 油(升) Gasoline (liter)	柴 油(升) Diesel Oil (liter)	天然气(立方米) Natrual Gas (cu. m)
总 计	**Total**	**5 796**	**9 811**	**62 363**	**9 719 961**
一 师	Division 1	4 692	1 603	3 329	510 000
二 师	Division 2		139	1 127	
三 师	Division 3	130	1 270	2 638	
四 师	Division 4	20	50	1 490	
五 师	Division 5	115	340	1 228	
六 师	Division 6	105	21	28 787	3 465 697
七 师	Division 7	65		1 854	225 402
八 师	Division 8		223	14 459	5 509 489
九 师	Division 9	32	42	427	
十 师	Division 10	600		1 168	
建 工 师	Construction Division		4 630	1 398	
十 二 师	Division 12	37	3	1 709	9 373
十 三 师	Division 13		4	18	
十 四 师	Division 14		1	8	
国资公司	State-owned Property Company		439		
中基公司	Chalkis Company				
兵团直属	Directly under XPCG		1 046	2 723	

2011 BING TUAN

第十五篇

对外贸易、经济技术协作和旅游业

Chapter 15 Foreign Trade, Economic and Technological Cooperation and Tourism

简要说明

本篇资料综合反映兵团主要年份对外贸易、经济技术协作、利用外资及旅游业概况。

一、兵团对外贸易基本情况

主要内容包括主要年份按国别（地区）分列的兵团、各师进出口总额及主要进出口商品量、金额和出口商品供货情况。兵团利用外资、外商投资及对外经济技术合作总体状况。统计范围为兵团范围内所有利用外资单位和部门，以及经批准在兵团范围内设立的中外合资经营企业、合作经营企业、外资企业、外商投资股份制企业、合作开发项目等法人企业（包括 港澳台地区投资企业）外资利用情况；对外承包工程、对外劳务合作及对外经济合作情况。资料来源于兵团商务局。

二、兵团经济技术协作基本情况

内容包括主要年份兵团与区外、区内签定的经济技术协作项目、人才协作及效益完成情况。资料由兵团经济协作办公室整理提供。

三、兵团旅游业概况

主要内容包括兵团旅游业基本情况、兵团星级旅游饭店情况以及兵团旅游景区其它旅游单位基本情况。统计范围包括国际旅游和国内旅游。资料由兵团旅游局整理提供。

Brief Introduction

Data in this chapter show the general situations of foreign trade, economic and technological cooperation, utilization of foreign capital and tourism.

1. The basic conditions of foreign trade in XPCG include total value of exports and imports by country(region) by division, and imports and exports of major commodities, value, and supply of exporting commodities; the conditions of economic and technological cooperation, utilization of foreign capital; The statistical scope of the general situations of foreign capital utilization, foreign investment and economic cooperation refers to units and department of foreign capital utilization, Sino-foreign joint ventures, cooperative enterprises, ventures exclusively with foreign own investment, shareholding enterprises with foreign investment, projects of cooperative development, and utilization of foreign capital of enterprises with corporate (including enterprises invested from Hong Kong, Macao and Taiwan), conditions of contracted projects and labor cooperation in foreign countries or regions and foreign economic cooperation. The data come from the Bureau of Commercial Affairs of XPCG.

2. The basic conditions of economic and technological cooperation in XPCG include mainly projects of economic and technological cooperation of XPCG signed with outside Xinjiang and inside Xinjiang, cooperation of talented persons and efficiency completio n. The data are compiled and provided by the Office of Economic and Technological Cooperation.

3. The situations of tourism in XPCG include mainly the basic conditions of tourism in XPCG, tourism hotels with stars, scenic spots, and tourism units in XPCG. The statistical scope includes international tourism and domestic tourism. The data come from the Tourism Bureau of XPCG.

15—1　进出口贸易总额

Total Imports and Exports

计量单位:万美元　　　　　　　　　　　　　　　　　　　　　　　　(USD 10 000)

单位 Unit	年份 Year	进出口总额 Total Imports and Exports	出口总额 Total Exports	# 一般贸易 General Trade	# 边境贸易 Border Trade	进口总额 Total Imports	# 一般贸易 General Trade	# 边境贸易 Border Trade
	1985	240	27			213		
	1990	2 022	1 299			723		
	1991	3 853	3 025			828		
	1992	7 132	4 179			2 953		
	1993	13 572	7 553	2 788	4 765	6 019	15	6 004
	1994	14 141	8 138	4 218	3 920	6 003	1 294	4 709
	1995	18 225	8 040	4 934	3 106	10 185	2 028	8 157
	1996	20 079	5 359	3 682	1 677	14 720	1 656	13 064
	1997	24 561	7 046	5 227	1 819	17 515	2 848	14 667
	1998	28 546	10 246	7 372	2 874	18 300	5 602	12 698
	1999	40 909	24 251	12 471	11 780	16 658	3 581	13 077
	2000	75 280	44 990	18 908	26 082	30 290	7 417	22 873
	2001	65 380	30 014	8 865	21 149	35 366	6 233	29 133
	2002	124 900	55 300	36 100	19 200	69 600	10 600	59 000
	2003	161 838	86 557	31 531	55 026	75 281	32 861	42 420
	2004	197 235	83 523	22 456	61 067	113 712	54 660	59 052
	2005	310 586	189 249	35 046	154 203	121 337	74 874	46 463
	2006	350 529	295 697	51 654	237 221	54 832	24 714	28 139
	2007	556 042	519 256	130 484	388 700	36 786	16 775	14 747
	2008	881 951	842 376	121 608	720 493	39 575	14 735	18 316
	2009	466 030	426 005	50 365	343 783	40 025	25 385	7 233
	2010	558 874	498 008			60 866		
一　师	Division 1	1 465	1 261			204		
二　师	Division 2	2 854	2 853			1		
三　师	Division 3	6 471	6 426			45		
四　师	Division 4	131 658	131 064			594		
五　师	Division 5	13 228	4 547			8 681		
六　师	Division 6	31 460	31 360			100		
七　师	Division 7	5 956	3 425			2 531		
八　师	Division 8	63 030	53 949			9 081		
九　师	Division 9	7 727	7 680			47		
十　师	Division 10	19 054	18 578			476		
建工师	Construction Division	274	274			…		
十二师	Division 12	7 060	7 026			34		
十三师	Division 13	10	10					
十四师	Division 14	25 375	22 469			2 906		
兵团直属	Directly under XPCG	243 252	207 086			36 166		

注:2001年以前为业务统计数据,2002年以后为海关统计数据。
Note: The data prior to 2001 is offered by the bureau of foreign economic and trade, data after 2002 is offered by Customs House。

15—2 主要进出口商品数量和金额

Main Imports and Exports in Volume and Value

计量单位:万美元 (USD 10 000)

指 标		Item		2010		2010年比2009年增减% Increase Rate in 2010 over 2009(%)	
				数 量 Volume	金 额 Value	数 量 Volume	金 额 Value
主要出口商品		**Main Export Commodities**					
棉 花(原棉)	(吨)	Cotton(Raw Cotton)	(ton)				
纺织纱线、织物及制品	(吨)	Cotton Yarm			54 396		−2.3
服 装		Garments			205 706		23.6
番茄酱	(吨)	Tomato Jam	(ton)	250 548	16 232	71.2	25.5
机电产品		Machine and Electricity Product			72 784		31.6
纸及纸板(未切成型的)	(吨)	Paper and Paperboard in Rolls	(ton)	2 761	739	−43.0	−44.6
塑料制品	(吨)	Plastic Products	(ton)	20 846	6 505	−9.9	−14.8
鲜、干水果及坚果	(吨)	Fresh,Dry Fruit and Nut	(ton)	49 572	2 666	−0.5	7.7
蔬菜	(吨)	Vegetable	(ton)	8 344	765	−31.4	39.2
焦炭、半焦炭	(吨)	Coke, Half Coke	(ton)	64 379	2 007	1 872.6	1 400.0
皮 鞋	(千双)	Leather Shoes	(1 000 pairs)		62 951		9.4
主要进口商品		**Main Import Commodities**					
钢 材	(万吨)	Rolled Steel	(10 000 tons)	8.11	4 155	−54.1	−42.7
原 木	(立方米)	Logs	(cu. m)	11 300	147	−41.1	−41.1
锯 材	(立方米)	Logs	(cu. m)	64 900	1 105	42.6	47.2
机电产品		Machine Electricity Product			14 695		87.5
成品油	(吨)	Finished Product Oil	(ton)	136 959	5 441	78.2	137.0
肥 料	(吨)	Fertilizers	(ton)	30 182	855	1 429.7	716.6
有色金属	(吨)	Nonferrous Metals	(ton)	135 679	5 101	36.8	115.3
羊 毛	(吨)	Wool	(ton)	3 808	500	29.2	44.7
高新技术产品		High and New Technical Product			1 018		267.6

15—3 出口商品分类金额

Value of Exports by Category of Commodities

计量单位:万美元 (USD 10 000)

指　标	Item	2000	2005	2009	2010
总　额	**Total**	**44 990**	**189 249**	**426 005**	**498 008**
初级产品	Primary Goods	12 046	12 914	76 260	89 634
食品及活动物	Food and Live Animals Used Chiefly for Food	599	11 128	48 859	7 353
饮料及烟草	Beverges and Tobacco	115	19	135	16 922
非食用原料	Non-edible Raw Materials	11 233	744	722	12 942
矿物燃料润滑油及有关原料	Mineral Fuels Lubricants and Related Materials	99	1 023	26 544	52 417
动、植物油脂及蜡	Animal and Vegetable Oils Fats and Wax				
工业制成品	Manufactured Goods	32 944	176 335	349 745	408 374
化学品及有关产品	Chemicals and Related Products	68	6 456	6 166	3 592
轻纺产品、橡胶制品、矿冶产品及其制品	Light and Textile Industrial Products Rubber Products Minerals Metal-Iurgical Products	73	40 329	277 510	262 422
机械及运输设备	Machinery and Transport Equipment	133	6 596	57 868	97 794
杂项制品	Miscellaneous Products	32 670	122 954	8 201	44 566

15—4 进口商品分类金额

Value of Imports by Category of Commodities

计量单位:万美元 (USD 10 000)

指　标	Item	2000	2005	2009	2010
总　额	**Total**	**30 290**	**121 337**	**40 025**	**60 866**
初级产品	Primary Goods	1 670	28 306	14 700	25 825
食品及活动物	Food and Live Animals Used Chiefly for Food	24	505	6 764	2 735
饮料及烟草	Beverges and Tobacco	39			
非食用原料	Non-edible Raw Materials	1 444	27 701	7 253	22 175
矿物燃料润滑油及有关原料	Mineral Fuels Lubricants and Related Materials	74	100	683	915
动、植物油脂及蜡	Animal and Vegetable Oils Fats and Wax	89			
工业制成品	Manufactured Goods	28 620	93 031	25 325	35 041
化学品及有关产品	Chemicals and Related Products	2 900	3 237	2 414	6 483
轻纺产品、橡胶制品、矿冶产品及其制品	Light and Textile Industrial Products Rubber Products Minerals Metal-Iurgical Products	19 143	69 050	15 842	14 238
机械及运输设备	Machinery and Transport Equipment	6 080	5 139	3 785	7 050
杂项制品	Miscellaneous Products	497	15 605	3 284	7 270

15—5 兵团同各国(地区)进出口总额

XPCG's Total Imports and Exports with Related Countries and Territories

计量单位:万美元 (USD 10 000)

国别(地区)	Country(Territory)	2009			2010		
		进出口 Total Imports and Exports	出口 Total Exports	进口 Total Imports	进出口 Total Imports and Exports	出口 Total Exports	进口 Total Imports
总 额	**Total**	**466 030**	**426 005**	**40 025**	**558 874**	**498 008**	**60 866**
亚 洲	**Asia**	**10 875**	**9 731**	**1 144**	**24 239**	**16 114**	**8 125**
阿富汗	Afghanistan	102	100	2	108	107	1
巴 林	Bahrain	4	4		83	83	
孟加拉国	Banglagdesh	29	29		3	3	
缅 甸	Myanmar	37	37		10	10	
塞浦路斯	Cyprus	16	16		14	14	
中国香港	HongKong,China	349	349		832	98	734
印 度	India	399	340	59	2 445	764	1 681
印度尼西亚	Indonesia	149	149		77	77	
伊 朗	Iran	13	12	1	711	711	
以色列	Israel	117	79	38	174	174	
日 本	Japan	893	497	396	5 404	825	4 579
约 旦	Jordan	162	162		42	42	
科威特	Kuwait	5	5		6	6	
黎巴嫩	Lebanon	41	41		50	50	
马来西亚	Malaysia	825	804	21	295	295	
蒙 古	Mongolia	100	100		2 194	2 194	
阿 曼	Aman	150	150		115	115	
巴基斯坦	Pakistan	3 376	3 375	1	5 034	5 024	10
菲律宾	The Philppines	470	467	3	436	436	
卡塔尔	Qatar	21	9	12	19	19	
沙特阿拉伯	Saudi Arbia	137	124	13	1 011	975	36
新加坡	Singapore	327	293	34	125	84	41
韩 国	Republic of Korea	826	420	406	876	288	588
斯里兰卡	Sri Lanka	46	46		28	28	
叙利亚	Syria	8	8		10	10	
泰 国	Thailand	148	137	11	543	467	76
土耳其	Turkey	30	30		500	372	128
阿联酋	United Arab Emirates	805	805		2 028	2 028	
也门共和国	ArabRepublicofYemen	1 017	1 017		409	409	
越 南	VietNam	65	65		123	123	
中国台湾	China	210	63	147	535	284	251
非 洲	**Africa**	**1 967**	**1 967**		**2 593**	**2 593**	
阿尔及利亚	Algeria	348	348		853	853	
安哥拉	Angola	4	4		20	20	
贝 宁	Beining						
喀麦隆	Cameroon	143	143		138	138	
刚 果	Congo	26	26		11	11	
吉布提	Jiebuti	3	3		8	8	
埃 及	Egypt	2	2		57	57	
埃塞俄比亚	Ethiopian				2	2	

15—5 续表 1 Continued

计量单位:万美元 (USD 10 000)

国别(地区)	Country(Territory)	2009			2010		
		进出口 Total Imports and Exports	出口 Total Exports	进口 Total Imports	进出口 Total Imports and Exports	出口 Total Exports	进口 Total Imports
冈比亚	Gambia	40	40		9	9	
加　纳	Ghana	196	196		156	156	
科特迪瓦共和国	Guinea	65	65		26	26	
肯尼亚	Kenya	34	34		28	28	
毛里求斯	Mauritius	11	11		32	32	
摩洛哥	Morocco	82	82		110	110	
尼日利亚	Nigeria	472	472		511	511	
塞内加尔	Senegal	23	23		183	183	
南　非	South Arfica	337	337		260	260	
苏　丹	Sudan	99	99		149	149	
坦桑尼亚	Tanzania	64	64		33	33	
多　哥	Congo	18	18		7	7	
其它国家	Other						
欧　洲	**Europe**	**448 720**	**411 956**	**36 764**	**526 669**	**476 269**	**50 400**
比利时	Belgium	172	43	129	646	8	638
丹　麦	Denmark	91	71	20	92	80	12
英　国	United Kingdom	453	370	83	849	733	116
德　国	Federal Repulic of Germany	2 868	364	2 504	1 551	657	894
法　国	France	1 594	1 364	230	1 016	429	587
爱尔兰	Ireland	119	6	113	106	17	89
意大利	Italy	5 113	2 382	2 731	6 109	2 858	3 251
荷　兰	Netherlands	149	108	41	216	98	118
希　腊	Greece	25	25		23	23	
葡萄牙	Portugal	259	259		18	18	
西班牙	Spain	238	238	…	256	256	
奥地利	Austria	2		2	4		4
保加利亚	Bulgaria	52	52		85	85	
芬　兰	Finland	22	18	4	28	28	
匈牙利	Hungary	24	24		18	18	
马耳他	Malta				49	49	
挪　威	Norway	3	3		64	22	42
波　兰	Poland	215	215		466	466	
罗马尼亚	Romania	242	242		419	419	
瑞　典	Sweden	69	31	38	83	52	31
瑞　士	Switzerland	216		216	1 885	5	1 880
爱沙尼亚	Estonian	10	10		11	11	
拉脱维亚	Latvia	70	70		187	187	
立陶宛	Lithuania	78	78		60	60	
格鲁吉亚	Venezuela				3	3	
阿塞拜疆	North America	10 268	10 268		16 761	16 740	21
白俄罗斯	Canada	88	84	4	37	32	5
俄罗斯联邦	United States	10 266	6 938	3 328	12 824	10 148	2 676

15—5 续表 2 Continued

计量单位:万美元 (USD 10 000)

国别(地区)	Country(Territory)	2009 进出口 Total Imports and Exports	2009 出口 Total Exports	2009 进口 Total Imports	2010 进出口 Total Imports and Exports	2010 出口 Total Exports	2010 进口 Total Imports
哈萨克斯坦	Kazakhstan	245 313	231 095	14 218	319 166	305 198	13 968
吉尔吉斯斯坦	Kirgizistan	124 966	122 899	2 067	96 851	93 749	3 102
塔吉克斯坦	Tajikistan	27 389	27 183	206	35 118	34 739	379
土库曼斯坦	Turkmenistan	1 771	1 082	689	2 923	1 938	985
乌兹别克斯坦	Uzbekistan	13 171	3 470	9 701	26 376	4 795	21 581
乌克兰	Ukraine	758	758		116	116	
克罗地亚	Croatia	23	23		37	37	
斯洛文尼亚	Slovenia	12	12		48	48	
捷克共和国	Czecho	130	130		103	103	
其他国家	Other	2 481	2 042	439	2 065	2 044	21
拉丁美洲	Latin America	**1 571**	**1 513**	**58**	**1 934**	**1 933**	**1**
阿根廷	Argentina	30	25	5	217	216	1
巴　西	Brazil	572	519	53	886	886	
智　利	Chile	138	138		139	139	
哥伦比亚	Colombia	176	176		49	49	
多米尼加	Dominican Republic	5	5		12	12	
哥斯达黎加	Costarica	28	28		11	11	
古　巴	Cuba				14	14	
多米尼加共和国	Dominican Republic	26	26		14	14	
厄瓜多尔	Ecuador	16	16		84	84	
格林纳达	Grenada	4	4				
危地马拉	Guatemala	12	12		6	6	
海　地	Haiti	220	220		66	66	
洪都拉斯	Honduras	16	16		25	25	
牙买加	Jamaica	63	63		69	69	
墨西哥	Mexico	26	26		97	97	
尼加拉瓜	Nicaragua	10	10		1	1	
巴拿马	Panama	10	10		11	11	
巴拉圭	Paraguay	75	75		60	60	
秘　鲁	Peru	50	50		124	124	
波多黎各	Puerto Rico	20	20		1	1	
萨尔瓦多	ElSalvador	24	24		20	20	
特立尼达和多巴哥	Trinidad				4	4	
乌拉圭	Uruguay	16	16		17	17	
委内瑞拉	Venezuela	34	34		7	7	
北美洲	**North America**	**2 654**	**624**	**2 030**	**3 013**	**693**	**2 320**
加拿大	Canada	182	169	13	333	223	110
美　国	The United States	2 472	455	2 017	2 680	470	2 210
大洋洲	**Oceania**	**243**	**214**	**29**	**426**	**406**	**20**
澳大利亚	Australia	213	184	29	370	350	20
斐　济	Fiji	5	5		5	5	
新西兰	New Zealand	9	9		33	33	
巴布亚新几内亚	Papua New Guinea	16	16		18	18	

15－6 按贸易方式和经济类型分进出口额

Total Imports and Exports by Trade Mode and Type of Economic

单位：万美元 (USD 10 000)

指 标	Item	2009			2010		
		进出口总额 Total Imports and Exports	出口总额 Total Exports	进口总额 Total Imports	进出口总额 Total Imports	出口总额 Total Exports	进口总额 Total Imports
总 计	**Total**	**466 030**	**426 005**	**40 025**	**558 874**	**498 008**	**60 866**
按贸易方式分	**Grouped by Trade Mode**						
一般贸易	General Trade	75 750	50 365	25 385	102 505	58 311	44 194
# 加工贸易	Processing Trade	8 487	7 872	615	8 467	8 188	279
边境贸易	Border Trade	351 016	343 783	7 233	396 289	386 253	10 036
其 他	Others	39 264	31 857	7 407	60 080	53 444	6 636
按经济类型分	**Grouped by Economic**						
国有企业	State-owned Enterprises	116 372	97 937	18 435	128 302	91 262	37 040
民营企业	Private-owned Enterprises	343 967	326 412	17 555	422 286	401 664	20 622
三资企业	Three Kinds of Ventures	2 451	1 656	795	6 097	3 511	2 586
集体企业	Collective-owned Enterprises				2 189	1 571	618

15－7 出口商品供货情况

Supply of Export Commodities

计量单位：万元 (2010 年) (10 000 yuan)

指 标		Item		数 量 Volume	金 额 Value
出口商品供货总额		**Supply Value Of Export Commodities**			**3 327 814**
主要出口商品		**Major Export Commodities**			
农产品类总额		Total Value of Agriculture Products			295 407
水 果	（吨）	Fruits	(ton)	49 572	17 816
# 苹 果	（吨）	Apple		29 036	10 158
食用干果	（吨）	Edible Dried Fruit	(ton)		
甘 草	（吨）	Lipuorice	(ton)	58	748
蔬 菜	（吨）	Vegetable	(ton)		
淀 粉	（吨）	Starch	(ton)		
其 他		Others			276 843
畜产品类总额		Total Value of Livestock Products			
工业产品类总额		Total Value of Industry Products			3 032 407
大 米	（吨）	Rice	(ton)	6 729	2 600
甘 草 膏	（吨）	Licorice	(ton)		
罐 头	（吨）	Can	(ton)	251 828	254 541
# 番茄罐头		Tomato Can		250 548	242 131
棉布、呢绒、丝制品	（万米）	Cotton Cloth, Woolen Goods, Silk Products	(10 000 m)		4 010
棉 纱	（万件）	Cotton Yarm	(10 000 units)		29 370
各种服装	（万件）	Garments	(10 000 units)	708 588	1 374 692
鞋 类	（万双）	Leather Shoes	(10 000 pairs)1	68 239	420 688
焦 炭	（吨）	Coke	(ton)	64 379	13 412
工作车	（台）	Work Vehicle	(set)	1 000	25 111
其 他		Others			907 983

15—8 人民币汇率(中间价)

Reference Exchange Rate of Renminbi(Middle Rate)

计量单位:人民币元 (RMB yuan)

年 份 Year	100 美元 100 US Dollars	100 日元 100 Japanese Yen	100 港元 100 Hong Kong Dollars	100 欧元 100 Euros
1985	293.66	1.25	37.57	
1990	478.32	3.32	61.39	
1991	532.33	3.96	68.45	
1992	551.46	4.36	71.24	
1993	576.20	5.20	74.41	
1994	861.87	8.44	111.53	
1995	835.10	8.92	107.96	
1996	831.42	7.64	107.51	
1997	828.98	6.86	107.09	
1998	827.91	6.35	106.88	
1999	827.83	7.29	106.66	
2000	827.84	7.69	106.18	
2001	827.70	6.81	106.08	
2002	827.70	6.62	106.07	800.58
2003	827.70	7.15	106.24	936.13
2004	827.68	7.66	106.23	1 029.00
2005	819.17	7.45	105.30	1 019.53
2006	797.18	6.86	102.62	1 001.90
2007	760.40	6.46	97.46	1 041.75
2008	694.51	6.74	89.19	1 022.27
2009	683.10	7.30	88.12	952.70
2010	676.95	7.73	87.13	897.25

15—9 经济技术协作情况

Conditions of Economic and Technical Cooperation

计量单位:个、万元 (2010 年) (unit,10 000 yuan)

指 标 Item	当年签订合同 New Signed Contracts in this Year		执行合同 Execution of Contract					
			合计 Total		当年签订 New Signed Contracts in this Year		往年结转 Carried Down in the Past	
	数量 Volume	金额 Value	数量 Volume	金额 Value	数量 Volume	金额 Value	数量 Volume	金额 Value
总 计 Total	**483**	**8 023 009**	**483**	**8 023 009**	**370**	**3 108 318**	**113**	**4 914 691**
# 产权交易 Property Right Transaction	3	27 258	3	27 258	2	24 708	1	2 550
按疆内、疆外分 Inside and Outside XJ								
疆 内 Inside XJ	249	1 283 760	249	1 283 760	203	873 910	46	409 850
疆 外 Outside XJ	234	6 739 249	234	6 739 249	167	2 234 408	67	4 504 841
# 引进兵团外到位资金 Funds Arrived from Other Region Outside XPCG				1 992 578		773 458		1 219 120
按性质分 Brouped by Nature								
经济联合 Economic Cooperation	181	2 567 632	181	2 567 632	141	1 154 306	40	1 413 326
技术协作 Technological Coordination								
兵团外独资 Sole Funded Outside XPCG	300	5 454 820	300	5 454 820	228	1 953 912	72	3 500 908
承包经营 Contract to Run								
租赁经营 Leasing Management	2	557	2	557	1	100	1	457

15—10　招商引资情况

Conditions of Attraction Investment

计量单位:万元　　　　(2010 年)　　　　(10 000 yuan)

指　标	Item	项目个数(个) Number of Item(unit)	总投资 Total Investment	兵团投资 XPCG Investment	客方投资 Investment Outside XPCG	客方当年已到位资金 Funds Arrived Outside XPCG in this Year	客方后续资金 Follow-up Funds Outside XPCG
总　计	**Total**	**483**	**8 023 009**	**1 130 028**	**6 892 981**	**1 992 578**	**4 633 651**
按产业分	**Grouped by Industry**						
第一产业	Primary Industry	77	82 835	8 348	74 487	37 467	23 691
第二产业	Secondary Industry	312	7 180 336	1 080 505	6 099 831	1 673 822	4 250 418
第三产业	Tertiary Industry	94	759 838	41 175	718 663	281 289	359 542
按所有制分	**Grouped by Ownership**						
国　有	State-owned	58	1 527 811	563 271	964 540	343 641	485 910
非国有	Non-state-owned	425	6 495 198	566 757	5 928 441	1 648 937	4 147 741
按新增或续建分	**Grouped by Newly Increased or Continue to Construction**						
新　增	Newly Increased	370	3 108 318	577 262	2 531 056	773 458	1 747 797
续　建	Continue to Construction	113	4 914 691	552 766	4 361 925	1 219 120	2 885 854
按引资区域分	**Grouped by Attraction Investment District**						
新　疆	Xin jiang	249	1 283 760	120 479	1 163 281	418 917	667 487
外　省	Other Province	219	6 172 891	709 305	5 463 586	1 484 348	3 781 614
港澳台	Hongkong, Macao and Taiwan	9	144 448	9 670	134 778	48 866	81 662
外　资	Foreign Investment	2	37 000	12 700	24 300	7 000	29 300
兵团上市公司	Listed Companies of XPCG	4	384 910	277 874	107 036	33 447	73 588
按师分	**Grouped by Division**						
一　师	Division 1	70	470 791	71 245	399 546	170 092	203 475
二　师	Division 2	19	78 842	14 731	64 111	31 011	24 100
三　师	Division 3	22	97 355	6 347	91 008	32 072	57 666
四　师	Division 4	105	430 840	188 272	242 568	64 886	139 626
五　师	Division 5	7	126 920	22 326	104 594	42 736	61 858
六　师	Division 6	44	2 791 418		2 791 418	559 489	2 280 657
七　师	Division 7	15	676 495	241 850	434 645	170 504	406 841
八　师	Division 8	55	2 166 861	526 815	1 640 046	511 466	906 720
九　师	Division 9	16	14 505	570	13 935	9 050	4 355
十　师	Division 10	20	80 094	16 982	63 112	31 581	29 615
建工师	Construcion Division	1	457		457	410	47
十二师	Division 12	27	914 586	7 625	906 961	300 335	496 519
十三师	Division 13	70	139 569	29 860	109 709	40 395	19 852
十四师	Division 14	10	13 076	3 405	9 671	7 351	2 320
国资公司	State-owned Property Company	2	21 200		21 200	21 200	

15—11 利用外资概况

Utilization of Foreign Capital

计量单位：个，万美元 (unit，USD 10 000)

年份 Year	总计 Total		对外借款 Foreign Loans		外商直接投资 Foreign Investments	
	项目 Number of Projects	金额 Value	项目 Number of Projects	金额 Value	项目 Number of Projects	金额 Value
签订利用外资(合同)外资额 Total Amount of Foreign Capital to Be Utilized through the Signed Agreements and Contracts						
2000	17	352	1	270	16	82
2001	6	1 524	4	1 074	2	450
2002	11	4 751	3	1 769	8	2 982
2003	18	4 646	9	2 409	9	2 237
2004	9	5 136	4	1 160	5	3 976
2005	17	4 791	9	3 494	8	1 297
2006	16	14 428	7	9 145	9	5 283
2007	15	13 552	3	7 122	12	6 430
2008	14	28 979	1	11 000	13	17 979
2009	6	8 739			6	5 706
2010	10	63 48			10	3 610
实际利用外资额 Total Amount of Foreign Capital Actually Used						
2000		363		270		93
2001		1 074		1 074		
2002		4 083		1 769		2 314
2003		3 108		1 280		1 828
2004		4 066		844		3 222
2005		3 136		2 503		634
2006	16	6 100	7	2 721	9	3 379
2007	15	7 007	3	4 160	12	2 847
2008	14	6 139	1	3 657	13	2 482
2009	6	4 170		2 946	6	1 224
2010	10	3 845			10	3 845

15—12 按方式分利用外资情况

Amount of Utilization of Foreign Capital and Foreign Investment by Mode

计量单位：个，万美元 (unit，USD 10 000)

指标	Item	2009 项目 Number of Projects	2009 合同金额 Contract Value	2009 实际使用金额 Used Value	2010 项目 Number of Projects	2010 合同金额 Contract Value	2010 实际使用金额 Used Value
总计	**Total**	**6**	**5 706**	**4 170**	**10**	**3 610**	**3 845**
对外借款	**Foreign Loans**			**2 946**			
外国政府贷款	Government Loans			2 946			
国际金融组织贷款	Loans from						
外国商业银行贷款	Commercial						
出口信贷	Export Loans						
对外发行债券	External Bonds						
外商直接投资	**Foreign Direct Investments**	**6**	**5 706**	**1 224**	**10**	**3 610**	**686**
外资企业	Foreign Investment Enterprises	4	3 591	392	2	34	9
合资经营企业	Joint Ventures Enterprises	2	2 115	226	8	3 576	677
合作经营企业	Cooperative Operation Enterprises						
股份制企业	Foreign Investment Share Enterprises						
其他：(历年外资到位)	Other：(Foreign Capital Arrived in Former Year)			607			3 159

15－13 外国和港澳台地区在兵团直接投资情况
Conditions of Direct Investment in XPCG by Foreign Countries and Compatriots from Hongkong, Macao and Taiwan

计量单位：个、万美元　　(2010 年)　　(unit, USD 10 000)

指标	Item	签订协议情况 Signed Agreements		客商实际投资额	年末实有企业个数
		合同数 Number of Contracts	客商投资额 Used Amount of Foreign Investment	Actually Used Amount offoreign Investment	Number of Enterprises
总　　计	**Total**	**10**	**3 610**	**3 845**	**10**
按投资方式分	**Grouped by Investment Mode**				
外资企业	Foreign Investment Enterprises	2	34	9	2
合资经营企业	Joint Ventures Enterprises	8	3 576	677	8
合作经营企业	Cooperative Enterprises				
其他：历年外资到位	Other: (Foreign Capital Arrived in Former Year)			3 159	
按国民经济行业分	**Grouped by Economic Sector**				
制造业	Manufacturing	5	2 807	54	5
批发零售贸易、餐饮业	Wholesale and Retail Trade and Catering Services	3	159	5	3
农业	Agriculture	1	622	627	1
服务业	Services	1	22		1
其他：历年外资到位	Other: (Foreign Capital Arrived in Former Year)			3 159	
按国别、地区分	**Grouped by country or Territory**				
香港特别行政区	Hong Kong SAR	6	3 427	656	6
台湾省	Taiwan Province	1	22		1
乌兹别克斯坦	Uzbekistan	1	5	5	1
比利时	Belgium	1	24	24	1
澳门特别行政区	Macao SAR	1	132		1
其他：历年外资到位	Other: (Foreign Capital Arrived in Former Year)			3 159	

15－14 各师利用外商直接投资情况
Foreign Direct Investment Used by Division

计量单位：个、万美元　　(unit, USD 10 000)

单　位	Unit	2009			2010		
		签订合同数 Number of Contracts	合同金额 Contract Value	实际利用投资 Amount of Foreign Capital Acturally Used	签订合同数 Number of Contracts	合同金额 Contract Value	实际利用投资 Amount of Foreign Capital Acturally Used
总　计	**Total**	**6**	**5 706**	**1 224**	**10**	**3 610**	**3 845**
四　师	Division 4				1	22	
五　师	Division 5				2	1 445	5
六　师	Division 6				1	622	627
七　师	Division 7	2	2 115	226			
八　师	Division 8	3	3 584	384	6	1 521	54
兵直企业	Directly Enterprises Under XPCG	1	7	7			
其他：历年外资到位	Other: (Foreign Capital Arrived in Former Year)			607			3 159

15—15　外商投资企业年底注册登记情况

Registration Status of Foreign Enterprises at Year-end

(2010 年)

指　标	Item	2010
企业数(户)	**Number of Enterprises(unit)**	**162**
合资企业	Joint-Venture Enterprises	81
合作企业	Cooperative Enterprises	7
独资企业	Private-Funds Enterprises	74
投资总额(万美元)	**Total Investment (USD 10 000)**	**94 519**
合资企业	Joint-Venture Enterprises	65 225
合作企业	Cooperative Enterprises	14 555
独资企业	Private-Funds Enterprises	14 739
注册资本(万美元)	**Registered Capital (USD 10 000)**	**59 515**
合资企业	Joint-Venture Enterprises	36 243
合作企业	Cooperative Enterprises	14 172
独资企业	Private-Funds Enterprises	9 100
外方出资(万美元)	**Foreign Investment (USD 10 000)**	**47 669**
合资企业	Joint-Venture Enterprises	19 984
合作企业	Cooperative Enterprises	17 434
独资企业	Private-Funds Enterprises	10 251

15—16　对外经济合作主要指标

Major Indicators of Foreign Economic Cooperation

年　份 Year	境外投资 Foreign Investment				对外工程承包 Foreign Contracted Projects		劳务合作 Labor Cooperation		外派劳务人员(人) Labor Force (person)
	项目数(个) Number of Projects (unit)	合同金额(万美元) Contracted Value (USD 10 000)	#中方合同金额 Contract Value of China	#中方实际投资额 Actually Investment of China	项目数(个) Number of Projects (unit)	合同金额(万美元) Contracted Value (USD 10 000)	项目数(个) Number of Projects (unit)	合同金额(万美元) Contracted Value (USD 10 000)	
1991	5	95	58						
1992	15	677	309	167	3	1 553	9	316	774
1993	12	429	222	60	4	111	1	50	233
1994	4	37	25	25	1	91	1	44	147
1995	5	79	50	16	2	296	2	55	262
1996	4	134	121	13					
1997	3	40	40	20			2	20	100
1998	6	3 386	3 385	313			2	150	80
1999	2	2 401	1 201	1 201					
2000	4	1 456	533	533					
2001	3	20	13	13					
2002	5	179	157	157	1	3 100			
2003	6	150	150	281	1	434			221
2004	13	1 972	1 216	1 216	5	6 739			740
2005	12	1 530	1 530	1 083	4	858			603
2006	12	1 692	1 354	1 354	6	35 227	4	338	1 386
2007	12	57 000	57 000	57 000	1	2 260	4	331	2 697
2008	8	3 000	3 000	3 000	10	54 719	1	257	3 422
2009	17	3 900	3 900	3 900	2	27 226			3 126
2010	7	10 281	9 684	9 684	10	18 253			3 813

15－17 对外承包工程和劳务合作

Contracted Projects and Labor Cooperation in Foreign Countries or Territoreis

指　标	Item	2009	2010
承包工程	**Contracted Projects**		
新签合同数　（个）	Newly SignedNumber of Contract　(unit)	2	10
新签合同金额　（万美元）	Newly Signed Contrcted Value　(USD 10 000)	27 226	18 253
劳务合作	**Labor Cooperation**		
新签合同数　（个）	Newly Signed Number of Contract　(unit)		
新签合同金额　（万美元）	Newly Signed Contrcted Value　(USD 10 000)		

15－18 旅游业发展情况

Development of Tourism

指　标	Item	2000	2005	2009	2010
旅行社总数　（个）	**Total Numberof Travel Agencies　(unit)**	**24**	**79**	**124**	**98**
# 出境组团社	Outbound Travel Agencies	3	3	4	6
旅行社职工人数　（人）	**Number of staff and Workers of Travel Agencies　(person)**	**347**	**743**	**460**	**562**
# 出境组团社	Outbound Travel Agencies	142	295	165	134
星级饭店　（个）	**Star-rating Tourist Hotal　(unit)**	**20**	**30**	**48**	**50**
入境旅游人数　（人）	**Total Number of International Tourists Inbound　(person)**	**45 656**	**80 945**	**100 002**	**130 000**
国内旅游人数　（人）	**Total Number of Domestic Tourist　(person)**	**1 284 821**	**2 188 452**	**3 300 091**	**3 874 950**
出境旅游人数　（人）	**Total Number of Domestic Outbound　(person)**	**779**	**5 976**	**4 539**	**5 050**
旅游总收入　（万元）	**Income of Tourism　(10 000 yuan)**	**41 924**	**58 735**	**100 007**	**169 000**
旅游景区及其它旅游单位（个）	**Scenic Spots and other Tourism Units　(unit)**		**12**	**30**	**35**
年末就业人数　（人）	Year-end Employed Persons　(person)		596	600	1 062
景区年接待人数　（万人）	Tourists of Scinic Area　(10 000 persons)		92.50	350.80	428.94
营业收入　（万元）	Business Income　(10 000 yuan)		1 653	4 238	18 037
年门票收入　（万元）	Tickets Income　(10 000 yuan)		385	758	3 226
利润总额　（万元）	Total Profits　(10 000 yuan)		309	950	1 443

15—19 旅游业情况
Tourism

指标	Item	旅游总收入(万元) Tourism Receipts (10 000 yuan)		入境旅游者(人次) International Tourists (person-time)		国内旅游者(人次) Domestic Tourists (person-time)	
		2009	2010	2009	2010	2009	2010
总计	**Total**	**100 007**	**169 000**	**100 002**	**130 000**	**3 300 091**	**3 874 950**
饭店	Hotel	32 249	46 047	50 150	60 148	1 528 639	1 499 209
旅行社	Travel Agencies	63 520	104 916	49 852	69 852	785 234	1 291 155
旅游景区	Scenic Area	4 238	18 037			986 218	1 084 586
其他	Others						

15—20 星级旅游饭店情况
Conditions of Tourism Star-rated Hotels

(2010年)

单位		Unit		合计 Total
星级饭店	(个)	Star-rated Hotels	(unit)	50
接待住宿人数	(人)	Persons Received	(person)	1 556 592
海外旅游者	(人)	Internationa Tourists	(person)	57 383
客房间数	(间)	Rooms	(unit)	6 008
床位张数	(张)	Beds	(unit)	11 235
从业人数	(人)	Employed Persons	(person)	3 832
固定资产	(万元)	Fixed Assets	(10 000 yuan)	156 658
营业收入	(万元)	Business Income	(10 000 yuan)	46 047
经营利润	(万元)	Business Profits	(10 000 yuan)	
营业税金及附加	(万元)	Business Taxes and Extra Charges	(10 000 yuan)	1 901
利润总额	(万元)	Total Profits	(10 000 yuan)	−1 173
客房收入	(万元)	Rooms Income	(10 000 yuan)	23 571
餐饮收入	(万元)	Catering Services Income	(10 000 yuan)	19 816

2011 BING TUAN

第十六篇

金融业

Chapter 16 Financial Intermediation

简要说明

一、本篇资料主要内容

本篇主要反映中国农业银行兵团分行本外币资产负债情况及中华联合财产保险公司机构、国内保险情况和兵团上市公司基本情况。

二、本篇资料来源

金融资料由中国农业银行兵团分行提供，兵团统计局国民经济综合统计处整理。保险资料由中华联合财产保险公司整理提供。上市公司资料由兵团发展和改革委员会整理提供。

Brief Introduction

1. Main Contents

Data in this chapter show mainly the basic conditions of total assets and liabilities in XPCG Branch of the Agricultural Bank of China, units and domestic Insurance of China United Property Insurance Company, and listed corporations of XPCG.

2. Sources of Data

Data on Banking are provided by XPCG Branch of the Agricultural Bank of China, and are prepared by the Comprehensive Office of Statistics Bureau of XPCG. Data on insurance are prepared and provided by China United Property Insurance Company. Data of listed companies are prepared and provided by the Development and Reform Commission of XPCG.

16－1 兵团农业银行本外币资产负债情况

Total Assets and Liabilities of the Agricultural Bank of XPCG

计量单位:万元 (10 000 yuan)

指　　标	Item	2010
资产总计	**Total Assets**	**7 689 130**
现金及银行存款	Cash and Bank Deposit	57 995
存放中央银行款项	Deposit the National Central Bank Amount of Money	7 875
存放同业款项	Due from Bank Amount of Money	493
往来资金净资产	Dealings in the Same Trade	5 084 321
应收利息	Receivable Interest	6 030
各项贷款	Loans	2 322 914
贴现及转贴现净值	Discount and turn the discount net worth	
贸易融资	Trade Margin	
贷　款	Loan	2 322 914
其他贷款	Other Loan	
拆借同业款项	Borrows the Same Profession Amount of Money	
其他应收款	Other Receivable Loan	3 871
投　资	Investment	21 551
买入回售票据、信贷资产	Bying Back to Sell Ticket,Credit Assets	60 040
待摊费用	Expenses	1 113
固定资产净值	Net Worth of Fixed Assets	79 303
固定资产原价	Original Value of Fixed Assets	102 120
减:累计折旧	Reduce:Accumulated Ddepreciation	22 817
在建工程	Under Construction	17 037
无形资产	Immaterial Assets	11 116
待处理抵债资产	The Assets Wait for to Handle	
其他资产	Other Assets	74 428
资产减值准备	The Preparation of Assets Reduced	58 956
# 贷款损失准备	The Preparation of Loan Loses	58 083
负债及所有者权益总计	**Total Liabilities and CreditordEquity**	**7 689 130**
负债总计	**Total Liabilities**	**7 614 467**
各项存款	Deposits	7 465 627
储蓄存款	Individual Deposits	3 422 180
公司类存款	Unit Deposits	4 025 093
# 保险公司存款	The Insurance Company Deposits	43 436
应解汇款及暂存款	Should Solve the Remittance and Temporary Deposit	693
保证金存款	Security Deposit	17 661
同业存放款项	Same profession Deposit	26 161
汇出汇款	Remit Remittance	5
应付利息	Payable Interest	71 411
应交税金	Payable Taxes	2 889
应付工资	Payable Wages	3 177
其他应付款	Other Payable	27 110
递延收益	Deferred Lncome	940
预计负债	Antecipate Liabilities	1 363
其他负债	Other Liabilities	15 784
所有者权益总计	**Total Creditord Equity**	**74 663**
实收资本	Paid-up Capital	
资本公积	Capital Reserve Fund	
盈余公积	Surplus Reserve Fund	
未分配利润	Did not Assign Profits	74 663
# 当期利润	Profits	76 035

注:本资料未包括七师、十三师、十四师。

Note:Data in this table is not including Division 7,Division 13 and Division 14.

16—2 保险机构与业务

Insurance Institutions and Business

指　　标		Item		2009	2010
机构数	**(个)**	**Number of Institution**	**(unit)**	**2 079**	**2 051**
总公司		National Corporations		1	1
省级分公司		Provincial Branches		18	18
计划单列市分公司		Branches at Separate Planning Cities		4	4
省会城市营业部		Business Departments at Provincial Capitals		3	3
地市级分公司		Prefecture/City Branches		15	15
地市营业部		Prefecture/City Business Departments		12	12
地市中心支公司		Prefecture/City Center Branches		173	173
县级支公司		County Branches		894	896
县级营业部		County Business Departments			
营销服务部		Sales Departments		959	929
年底实有职工人数	**(人)**	**Staff and Workers at the Year-end**	**(person)**	**27 486**	**25 738**
国内保险业务		**Domestic Insurance Business**			
保险金额	(亿元)	Amount Insured	(100 million yuan)	50 747	45 773
财产险		Property Insurance		30 590	31 109
人身险		Life Insurance		19 601	14 302
农业险		Agreculture Lnsurance		557	362
保险业务收入	(亿元)	Insurance Business Income	(100 million yuan)	194. 61	193. 49
财产险		Property Insurance		159. 46	164. 31
人身险		Life Insurance		9. 88	9. 88
农业险		Agreculture Lnsurance		25. 27	19. 30
赔款(理赔)件数	(万件)	Amount Compensated	(10 000 unit)	583. 97	369. 99
已　决		Already Settled		510. 17	333. 82
未　决		Not Settled		73. 80	36. 17
已决理赔(给付)金额	(亿元)	Settled Claim and Payment	(100 million yuan)	134. 62	120. 47
财产险		Property Insurance		112. 81	101. 89
人身险		Life Insurance		6. 16	5. 27
农业险		Agreculture Lnsurance		15. 65	13. 31
当年结案率	(%)	Settled Case Ratio in the Year	(%)	87. 4	90. 2
当年赔付率	(%)	Claimed and Payment Ratio in the Year	(%)	69. 1	62. 3

16—3 国内保险业务基本情况

Basic Conditions of Domestic Insurance Business

指 标		Item		1995	2000	2005	2009	2010
承保数量		**Quantity Insured**						
农业险	(千公顷)	Agriculture Insurance	(1 000 hectares)	594	642	687	6 675	6 794
企业财产险	(笔)	Enterprise Property Insurance	(unit)	1 557	1 441	42 141	52 204	59 393
家庭财产险	(户)	Family Property Insurance	(household)	54 170	26 933	47 165	98 064	123 759
机动车辆险	(辆)	Motorvehicles Insurance	(unit)	31 869	41 704	4 022 016	8 423 678	7 673 007
货物运输险	(笔)	Freight Transport Insurance	(unit)	25 114	1 013	81 336	79 207	84 289
船舶险	(艘)	Ships Insurance	(unit)			7 530	5 341	6 023
航空航天险	(笔)	Aviation Insurance	(unit)			42	31	8
其他财产险	(笔)	Other Property Insurance	(unit)	631	237	222 357	185 402	150 439
人身险	(人)	Life Insurance	(person)	691 276	1 086 421	25 248 401	21 308 300	18 079 623
保险金额	**(亿元)**	**Amount Insured**	**(100 million yuan)**	**163**	**533**	**22 152**	**50 747**	**45 773**
农业险		Agriculture Insurance		13	44	72	557	362
企业财产险		Enterprise Property Insurance		42	75	3 578	6 179	6 558
家庭财产险		Family Property Insurance		5	4	172	487	609
机动车辆险		Motorvehicles Insurance		26	52	5 995	17 290	17 240
货物运输险		Freight Transport Insurance		12	5	982	1 553	1 214
船舶险		Ships Insurance				167	159	163
航空航天险		Aviation Insurance				14	4	1
其他财产险		Other Property Insurance		12	2	1 947	4 918	5 324
人身险		Life Insurance		53	351	9 225	19 601	14 302
保险业务收入	**(万元)**	**Insurance Business Income**	**(10 000 yuan)**	**19 492**	**38 310**	**1 053 959**	**1 946 133**	**1 934 940**
农业险		Agriculture Insurance		8 715	16 389	24 843	252 685	193 062
企业财产险		Enterprise Property Insurance		1 279	2 165	42 633	63 052	63 341
家庭财产险		Family Property Insurance		242	134	2 397	9 630	12 324
机动车辆险		Motor Vehicles Insurance		4 757	12 169	851 138	1 456 479	1 503 213
货物运输险		Freight Transport Insurance		815	240	12 243	10 728	10 199
船舶险		Ships Insurance				12 035	12 059	11 341
航空航天险		Aviation Insurance				893	277	413
其他财产险		Other Property Insurance		478	112	44 446	42 445	42 275
人身险		Life Insurance		3 206	7 101	63 331	98 778	98 772
赔款件数	**(件)**	**Amount Compensated**	**(unit)**	**26 422**	**68 113**	**1 201 723**	**5 839 728**	**3 699 873**
已 决		Already Settled		25 977	65 422	1 133 701	5 101 720	3 338 162
未 决		Not Settled		445	2 691	68 022	738 008	361 711
已决赔款给付金额	**(万元)**	**Settled Claim and Payment**	**(10 000 yuan)**	**8 084**	**18 767**	**449 738**	**1 346 171**	**1 204 667**
农业险		Agriculture Insurance		4 854	11 172	16 857	156 527	133 130
企业财产险		Enterprise Property Insurance		158	433	24 107	40 844	31 763
家庭财产险		Family Property Insurance		53	39	687	1 911	1 455
机动车辆险		Motorvehicles Insurance		2 510	4 933	366 432	1 047 530	934 004
货物运输险		Freight Transport Insurance		20	43	3 375	5 635	6 232
船舶险		Ships Insurance				2 693	9 991	19 524
航空航天险		Aviation Insurance				11	1 365	664
其他财产险		Other Property Insurance		13	1	10 778	20 805	25 217
人身险		Life Insurance		476	2 146	24 798	61 563	52 677
未决赔款估损金额	**(万元)**	**Not Settled Claim and Payment**	**(10 000 yuan)**	**468**	**1 138**	**47 571**	**620 497**	**1 268 877**
当年结案率	**(%)**	**Settled Case Ratio in the Year**	**(%)**	**98. 3**	**96. 0**	**94. 3**	**87. 4**	**90. 2**
当年赔付率	**(%)**	**Claimed and Payment Ratio in the Year**	**(%)**	**41. 5**	**49. 0**	**56. 8**	**69. 1**	**62. 3**

16—4 各分公司保险业务收入

Insurance Business Income by Branch

计量单位:万元 (2010年) (10 000 yuan)

单 位	Unit	保险业务收入 Insurance Business Income	#财产保险业务 PropertyInsurance	#人身保险业务 Life Insurance
总 计	**Total**	**1 934 940**	**1 643 106**	**98 772**
新疆分公司	Xinjiang Branch	146 243	77 279	29 266
浙江分公司	Zhejiang Branch	133 920	130 907	3 013
四川分公司	Chengdu Branch	140 764	122 782	12 478
上海分公司	Nanjing Branch	50 285	47 742	2 543
江苏分公司	Shanghai Branch	134 226	119 622	6 064
北京分公司	Beijing Branch	67 905	58 512	1 245
广州分公司	Guangzhou Branch	178 342	170 785	7 557
陕西分公司	Xian Branch	51 841	50 098	1 451
大连分公司	Dalian Branch	18 027	17 596	407
重庆分公司	Chongqing Branch	23 780	23 323	457
福建分公司	Fujiang Branch	53 777	50 864	2 812
河南分公司	Henan Branch	113 283	106 352	2 928
河北分公司	Shijiazhuang Branch	177 683	164 839	2 812
山东分公司	Shandong Branch	161 653	152 301	3 418
内蒙古分公司	Neimenggu Branch	134 681	85 782	3 303
天津分公司	Tianjin Branch	12 189	11 834	355
宁波分公司	Ningbo Branch	19 826	19 171	529
甘肃分公司	Gansu Branch	19 527	18 697	777
湖北分公司	Hubei Branch	66 262	55 826	1 295
青岛分公司	Qindao Branch	10 177	10 118	59
湖南分公司	Hunan Branch	119 052	66 057	9 441
深圳分公司	Shenzhen Branch	11 371	10 925	446
辽宁分公司	Liaoning Branch	90 128	71 695	6 116

16—5 各分公司保险业务保险金额和赔款给付金额

Amount Insured and Compensation of Insurance Business by Branch

计量单位:万元 （2010 年） (10 000 yuan)

单 位	Unit	保险金额 Amount Insured	# 财 产 保险业务 Property Insurance	# 人 身 保险业务 Life Insurance	赔款给付金额 Claim and Payment	# 财 产 保险业务 Property Insurance	# 人 身 保险业务 Life Insurance
总 计	**Total**	**457 730 499**	**311 090 362**	**143 017 453**	**1 204 667**	**1 018 860**	**52 677**
新疆分公司	Xinjiang Branch	39 758 736	14 243 148	24 678 202	78 559	35 975	17 539
浙江分公司	Zhejiang Branch	37 143 943	30 516 528	6 627 416	94 662	92 647	1 985
四川分公司	Chengdu Branch	37 279 459	25 070 087	12 131 210	89 681	78 318	5 459
上海分公司	Nanjing Branch	23 055 523	20 355 924	2 699 598	38 644	37 386	1 258
江苏分公司	Shanghai Branch	35 959 664	30 321 001	5 472 925	108 632	99 642	2 644
北京分公司	Beijing Branch	15 494 584	13 417 103	1 920 289	39 925	34 268	1 618
广州分公司	Guangzhou Branch	41 659 926	37 111 582	4 548 344	107 018	102 827	4 191
陕西分公司	Xian Branch	8 302 772	6 969 539	1 326 091	38 111	36 430	1 145
大连分公司	Dalian Branch	3 242 518	2 863 138	378 407	12 473	12 178	271
重庆分公司	Chongqing Branch	5 518 320	4 005 851	1 512 469	17 043	15 705	1 339
福建分公司	Fujiang Branch	25 922 671	9 304 957	16 602 188	38 599	36 416	2 117
河南分公司	Henan Branch	23 140 686	17 503 176	5 558 176	67 360	63 796	1 363
河北分公司	Shijiazhuang Branch	24 636 171	22 437 568	2 009 399	81 927	78 242	967
山东分公司	Shandong Branch	25 230 153	19 876 615	5 041 515	95 847	90 943	2 190
内蒙古分公司	Neimenggu Branch	15 760 122	12 210 276	2 982 737	68 328	38 208	1 222
天津分公司	Tianjin Branch	3 233 837	2 690 218	543 619	8 285	8 160	125
宁波分公司	Ningbo Branch	3 560 215	3 283 855	264 620	14 740	14 546	92
甘肃分公司	Gansu Branch	2 933 912	1 966 437	966 428	10 807	10 427	334
湖北分公司	Hubei Branch	7 440 435	5 337 013	1 971 213	41 335	34 369	541
青岛分公司	Qindao Branch	1 236 915	1 208 239	28 675	7 287	7 168	119
湖南分公司	Hunan Branch	20 151 873	14 348 114	4 884 876	74 479	33 361	2 557
深圳分公司	Shenzhen Branch	29 592 389	2 685 223	26 907 166	15 729	15 526	203
辽宁分公司	Liaoning Branch	27 475 675	13 364 771	13 961 887	55 194	42 323	3 399

16—6 上市公司基本情况

Basic Conditions of Listed Companies

计量单位:万元　　　　(2010 年)　　　　(10 000 yuan)

指　　标	Item	新疆百花村股份有限公司 XJ Bai huacun Ltd. ,Co.	新疆天业股份有限公司 XJ Tianye Ltd. ,Co.	新疆塔里木农业综合开发股份有限公司 XJ Tarimu Agi-cultural Compr-ehensive Develo-pment Ltd. ,Co.	新疆伊力特实业股份有限公司 XJ Yilite Industry Ltd. ,Co.
股票简称	Stock Brief Name	百花村 Bai Huacun	新疆天业 Xinjiang Tiangye	新农开发 Xinnong Development	伊力特 Yilite
股票代码	Stock Code	600721	600075	600359	600197
股票上市时间	Listed Time	1996年6月26日	1997年6月17日	1999年4月29日	1999年9月16日
股票上市交易所	Listing Stock Exchange	上交所 SHSE	上交所 SHSE	上交所 SHSE	上交所 SHSE
董事长	President	刘威东	侯国俊	李新海	徐勇辉
总经理	General Manager	侯铁军	余天池	楚建江	梁志坚
公司地址	Company Address	新疆乌鲁木齐市中山路141号 141 Zhongshan Road Urumqi, XJ	新疆石河子市经济开发区北三东路36号 36 East Road Beisan Economic Development Zone Shihezi XJ	新疆阿克苏市南大街2号新农大厦18层 2 South Road Xinnong Mension Aksu, XJ	新疆新源县肖尔布拉克 XJ Xinyuan County
邮政编码	Post Code	830002	832000	843000	835811
发行时总股本 (万股)	Total Capital Stock (10 000 share)	6 127.50	6 300.00	29 400.00	22 050.00
国家股	National Stock	2 672.50	3 600.00	20 400.00	13 450.00
法人股	Corporative Stock	455.00			1 100.00
流通股	Circulating Stock	3 000.00	2 430.00	9 000.00	7 500.00
其　他	Other		270.00		
发行募集资金 (万元)	Floated Raised Funds (10 000 yuan)	12 600.00	16 896.00	34 740.00	46 950.00
年末总股本 (万股)	Stock Capital at the Year-end (10 000 share)	26 885.20	43 859.20	32 100.00	44 100.00
国家股	National Stock	18 171.46	18 976.00	16 305.00	22 744.65
法人股	Corporative Stock				788.22
其　他	Other				
流通股	Circulating Stock	8 713.73	43 859.20	32 100.00	44 100.00
年末累计募集资金 (万元)	Capital Raised Year-end (10 000 yuan)	112 753.00	44 218.00	65 790.00	46 950.00
流动资产合计 # 存　货	Circulating Funds Stock	82 869.71	199 578.09	249 101.14	96 280.04
非流动资产合计 (万元)	Non-Circulating Funds (10 000yuan)	18 175.75	134 590.72	105 348.90	43 809.55
资产总计 (万元)	Total Assets (10 000 yuan)	324 786.12	259 328.71	156 809.81	85 188.58
流动负债合计 (万元)	Liquid Liabilities (10 000 yuan)	407 655.83	458 906.80	405 910.95	181 468.62
非流动负债合计 (万元)	Non-Liquid Liabilities (10 000 yuan)	143 450.65	227 605.67	227 748.74	61 582.26
股东权益合计 (万元)	Share-holders Equity (10 000 yuan)	159 300.24	12 420.15	59 092.60	11 383.42
营业总收入 (万元)	Total Revenue of Business (10 000 yuan)	85 783.68	218 880.98	119 069.60	108 502.95
营业总成本 (万元)	Total Cost of Business (10 000 yuan)	69 656.43	343 739.66	193 209.50	108 512.90
管理费用 (万元)	Administrative Expenses (10 000 yuan)	58 232.12	330 726.83	187 711.15	87 131.06
财务费用 (万元)	Financial Expenses (10 000 yuan)	8 959.65	11 302.33	10 991.76	8 816.23
营业利润 (万元)	Business Profits (10 000 yuan)	5 647.05	8 565.70	5 724.58	808.10
投资收益 (万元)	Investment Income (10 000 yuan)	11 878.82	13 872.78	3 192.20	22 279.95
营业外收入 (万元)	Extra-business Revenue (10 000 yuan)	−26.58	1 232.61	−2 306.14	898.11
营业外支出 (万元)	Extra-business Expenditures (10 000 yuan)	658.93 295.62	1 660.28 274.31	3 134.87 1 999.23	158.11 107.22
利润总额 (万元)	Total Profits (10 000 yuan)	12 242.14	15 258.75	4 327.84	22 330.84
净利润 (万元)	Net Profits (10 000 yuan)	4 103.88	11 143.65	442.92	13 413.11
每股收益 (元)	Net Income per Share (yuan)	0.25	0.25	0.01	0.30
每股净资产 (元)	Net Assets per Share (yuan)	3.19	3.90	3.09	2.34
净资产收益率 (%)	Net Assets of Yield (%)	4.84	6.73	0.44	13.59

16—6 续表 1 Continued

计量单位:万元 (2010 年) (10 000 yuan)

指 标	Item	新疆中基实业股份有限公司 XJ Chalkis Industry Ltd. ,Co.	新疆天宏纸业股份有限公司 XJ Tianhong Paper Industry Ltd. ,Co.	新疆天富热电股份有限公司 XJ Tianfu Thermoelectricity Ltd. ,Co.	新疆冠农果茸股份有限公司 XJ Guannong guorong Ltd. ,Co.	新疆青松建材化工(集团)股份有限公司 XJ Qinsong Building Material and Chemical Industry Ltd. ,Co.
股票简称	Stock Brief Name	新中基 Xinzhongji	ST 天宏 ST Tianhong	天富热电 Tianfu Thermoelectricity	冠农股份 Guannong Shares	青松建化 Qinsongjianhua
股票代码	Stock Code	000972	600419	600509	600251	600425
股票上市时间	Listed Time	2000 年 9 月 26 日	2001 年 6 月 28 日	2002 年 2 月 28 日	2003 年 6 月 9 日	2003 年 7 月 24 日
股票上市交易所	Listing Stock Exchange	深交所 SZSE	上交所 SHSE	上交所 SHSE	上交所 SHSE	上交所 SHSE
董事长	President	刘 一	李 侠	刘 伟	李 愈	甘 军
总经理	General Manager			何嘉勇	崔建文	杨万川
公司地址	Company Address	新疆乌鲁木齐市青年路北一巷 8 号 8 North First Lane Youth RD. Urumqi, XJ	新疆石河子市西三路 17 号 17 Xisan RD. Shihezi, XJ	新疆石河子市红星路 54 号 54 Hongxin RD. Shihezi, XJ	新疆库尔勒市团结南路 48 号 48 Tuanjie South RD. korla, XJ	新疆阿克苏市林园街 Linyuan RD. Aksu, XJ
邮政编码	Post Code	830002	832009	832000	841000	843005
发行时总股本 (万股)	Total Capital Stock (10 000 share)	12 458.92	8 016.00	16 908.50	12 000.00	18 492.75
国家股	National Stock	6 559.27	4 752.00	10 672.50	8 000.00	12 426.08
法人股	Corporative Stock	1 399.65	264.00	236.00		
流通股	Circulating Stock	4 500.00	3 000.00	6 000.00	4 000.00	6 000.00
其 他	Other					66.67
发行募集资金 (万元)	Floated Raised Funds (10 000 yuan)	22 500.00	16 633.00	39 990.00	21 609.00	24 265.00
年末总股本 (万股)	Stock Capital at the year-end (10 000 share)	48 205.33	8 016.00	65 569.66	36 210.00	47 869.50
国家股	National Stock	17 316.10	3 359.04	31 270.49	18 932.57	19 768.38
法人股	Corporative Stock	21 905.74	83.74	96.63		
其 他	Other	2 479.00				
流通股	Circulating Stock	47 906.71	8 016.00	65 569.66	36 210.00	47 869.50
年末累计募集资金 (万元)	Capital Raised Year-end (10 000 yuan)	120 585.00	16 633.00	151 321.00	64 529.00	165 408.00
流动资产合计	Circulating Funds	300 840.15	11 353.82	323 102.53	111 480.90	165 628.09
# 存 货	Stock	150 136.20	4 371.71	125 580.90	68 067.38	35 889.73
非流动资产合计 (万元)	Non-Circulating Funds (10 000yuan)	253 197.96	18 566.74	449 008.53	118 134.13	278 752.26
资产总计 (万元)	Total Assets (10 000 yuan)	554 038.11	29 920.56	772 111.06	229 615.03	444 380.35
流动负债合计 (万元)	Liquid Liabilities (10 000 yuan)	317 023.22	15 898.32	311 680.35	103 423.73	87 631.49
非流动负债合计 (万元)	Non-Liquid Liabilities (10 000 yuan)	100 079.32	223.00	252 970.16	41 347.76	93 229.75
股东权益合计 (万元)	Share-holders Equity (10 000 yuan)	136 935.57	13 799.24	207 460.56	84 843.54	263 519.10
营业总收入 (万元)	Total Revenue of Business (10 000 yuan)	151 196.36	34 461.38	187 995.98	82 093.54	175 395.69
营业总成本 (万元)	Total Cost of Business (10 000 yuan)	238 881.08	37 169.97	170 418.09	92 404.06	150 914.18
管理费用 (万元)	Administrative Expenses (10 000 yuan)	11 113.34	2 465.67	17 362.37	7 455.29	14 810.76
财务费用 (万元)	Financial Expenses (10 000 yuan)	21 771.73	272.43	11 919.11	4 515.24	4 903.46
营业利润 (万元)	Business Profits (10 000 yuan)	−43 318.16	−413.94	17 494.01	131.19	26 306.74
投资收益 (万元)	Investment Income (10 000 yuan)	44 185.41	2 292.64	−83.88	11 215.53	1 825.23
营业外收入 (万元)	Extra-business Revenue (10 000 yuan)	2 670.66	1 468.82	3 094.33	628.78	11 385.29
营业外支出 (万元)	Extra-business Expenditures (10 000 yuan)	3 117.79	57.03	706.56	221.50	1 164.19
利润总额 (万元)	Total Profits (10 000 yuan)	−43 765.29	997.85	19 881.78	538.48	36 527.85
净利润 (万元)	Net Profits (10 000 yuan)	−34 896.53	994.24	14 544.08	592.96	30 481.00
每股收益 (元)	Net Income per Share (yuan)	−0.76	0.12	0.22	0.02	0.75
每股净资产 (元)	Net Assets per Share (yuan)	2.78	1.72	2.98	2.25	5.05
净资产收益率 (%)	Net Assets of Yield (%)	−26.01	7.47	7.60	0.72	16.63

16—6 续表 2　Continued

计量单位:万元　　(2010 年)　　(10 000 yuan)

指　标	Item	新疆赛里木现代农业股份有限公司 XJ Sarimu Modern Agricultural Stock Ltd. ,Co	新疆天业节水灌溉股份有限公司 Xj Tianye Water-Saving Irrigated Stock Ltd. ,Co.	新疆天康畜牧生物技术股份有限公司 Xj Tiankang Animal Husbandry Technical Stock Ltd. ,Co.	新疆北新路桥建设股份有限公司 Xj Beixin Roadway and Bridge Stock Ltd. ,Co.	新疆西部牧业股份有限公司 Xi West Animal Husbandry Stock Ltd. ,Co.
股票简称	Stock Brief Name	新赛股份 Xinsai Shares	天业节水 Tianye Jieshui	天康生物 Tiankang Shengwu	北新路桥 beixin luqiao	西部牧业 Xibumuye
股票代码	Stock Code	600540	8280	002100	002307	300106
股票上市时间	Listed Time	2004 年 1 月 7 日	2006 年 2 月 28 日	2006 年 12 月 26 日	2009 年 11 月 11 日	2010 年 8 月 20 日
股票上市交易所	Listing Stock Exchange	上交所 SHSE	香港联交所	深交所 SZSE	深交所 SZSE	深交所 SZSE
董事长	President	武宪章	郭庆人	杨　焰	朱建国	徐义民
总经理	General Manager	何　伟		成　辉	陈　刚	杨文博
公司地址	Company Address	新疆博乐市红星路 158 号 158 HongXin RD. Bole,XJ	新疆石河子市经济开发区北三东路 36 号 36 East Road Beisan Economic Development Zone Shihezhi XJ	新疆乌鲁木齐市高新区长春南路 528 号 528 Changchun South RD. Hightnew Zone Urumqi,XJ	新疆乌鲁木齐市高新区高新街 217 号 217 Hight-tech Rd. High-tech Zone,Urumqi,XJ	新疆石河子市西四路 5—2 号 5—2 Xisi RD. Shihezi,XJ
邮政编码	Post Code	833400	832000	830011	830011	832000
发行时总股本 (万股)	Total Capital Stock (10 000 share)	15 000.00	51 952.16	6 400.00	18 495.00	11 700.00
国家股	National Stock	10 000.00	20 216.50	3 462.00	11 184.94	5 485.61
法人股	Corporative Stock		9 722.95	698.40	3 010.06	2 604.30
流通股	Circulating Stock	5 000.00	20 240.00	1 600.00	4 750.00	3 000.00
其　他	Other		1 772.71	639.60		610.09
发行募集资金 (万元)	Floated Raised Funds (10 000 yuan)	31 441.00	24 838.00	17 376.00	37 635.00	35 700.00
年末总股本 (万股)	Stock Capital at the year-end (10 000 share)	23 285.27	51 952.20	22 673.69	18 945.00	11 700.00
国家股	National Stock	11 631.66	20 216.50	9 319.70	11 612.42	5 485.61
法人股	Corporative Stock		9 722.95	5 102.01	3 782.58	2 604.30
流通股	Circulating Stock		1 772.71	1 771.69		610.09
其　他	Other	23 285.27	20 240.00	19 468.77	7 809.67	3 000.00
年末累计募集资金 (万元)	Capital Raised Year-end (10 000 yuan)	62 307.00	24 838.00	58 319.00	37 635.00	35 700.00
流动资产合计	Circulating Funds	185 946.89	75 269.93	110 443.54	193 910.37	47 507.65
# 存　货	Stock	130 113.86	46 706.52	72 576.62	58 296.62	12 896.38
非流动资产合计 (万元)	Non-Circulating Funds (10 000yuan)	67 682.90	23 118.07	80 136.16	91 415.74	26 120.72
资产总计 (万元)	Total Assets (10 000 yuan)	253 629.78	98 388.01	190 579.70	285 326.11	73 628.38
流动负债合计 (万元)	Liquid Liabilities (10 000 yuan)	149 803.02	26 066.31	65 451.36	120 330.98	11 023.56
非流动负债合计 (万元)	Non-Liquid Liabilities (10 000 yuan)	4 045.62	2 205.00	20 505.00	87 237.68	9 404.30
股东权益合计 (万元)	Share-holders Equity (10 000 yuan)	99 781.15	70 116.70	104 623.34	77 757.45	53 200.52
营业总收入 (万元)	Total Revenue of Business (10 000 yuan)	188 626.88	58 849.07	236 904.60	240 901.51	29 463.36
营业总成本 (万元)	Total Cost of Business (10 000 yuan)	187 172.91	56 386.53	224 777.44	237 315.85	26 688.03
管理费用 (万元)	Administrative Expenses (10 000 yuan)	5 820.82	1 662.17	12 050.90	13 251.50	765.25
财务费用 (万元)	Financial Expenses (10 000 yuan)	2 769.94	297.05	3 753.12	4 624.95	502.29
营业利润 (万元)	Business Profits (10 000 yuan)	2 433.90	2 208.75	11 440.34	6 985.99	2 775.33
投资收益 (万元)	Investment Income (10 000 yuan)	979.93	194.97	—686.82	3 400.33	
营业外收入 (万元)	Extra-business Revenue (10 000 yuan)	2 118.32	71.42	1 267.96	1 277.44	747.74
营业外支出 (万元)	Extra-business Expenditures (10 000 yuan)	93.17	180.51	135.80	434.95	102.14
利润总额 (万元)	Total Profits (10 000 yuan)	4 459.05	2 099.66	12 572.51	7 828.48	3 420.93
净利润 (万元)	Net Profits (10 000 yuan)	6 224.03	1 634.53	10 742.51	6 303.06	3 415.70
每股收益 (元)	Net Income per Share (yuan)	0.27	0.03	0.48	0.33	0.35
每股净资产 (元)	Net Assets per Share (yuan)	3.98	1.35	4.60	3.98	4.43
净资产收益率 (%)	Net Assets of Yield (%)	6.92	2.33	11.62	8.69	11.95

2011 BING TUAN

第十七篇

科技、教育、文化、卫生和城市

Chapter 17 Science, Education, Culture, Health and City

简要说明

本篇资料主要反映兵团科学技术事业、教育文化事业、卫生事业以及兵团4个城市发展基本情况。

一、科技部分主要内容和资料来源

国有单位专业技术人员情况，由兵团组织部(人事局)整理提供。兵团、各师科技活动规模、科技人员构成以及科技经费收支情况由兵团科技局整理提供。兵团大中型工业企业科技开发基本情况由兵团统计局社会科技贸易统计处根据《兵团大中型工业企业科技活动统计报表制度》整理提供。

二、教育部分主要包括兵团高等教育、普通中等教育、初等教育以及各级各类成人教育基本情况，主要指标有学校数、在校学生数、招生数、毕业生数、教职工人数及构成情况、各类学校基本状况等。由兵团教育局整理提供。

三、文化部分主要包括兵团艺术团体、新闻出版以及广播电台、电视台基本情况。由兵团宣传部整理提供。

四、卫生部分主要反映兵团卫生事业发展情况。包括卫生机构、人员、床位数等。由兵团卫生局整理提供。

五、城市部分主要反映兵团石河子市、阿拉尔市、图木舒克市、五家渠市基本情况。由国家统计局兵团调查总队统计监测处整理提供。

Brief Introduction

The data in this chapter show the basic conditions of causes and development of XPCG′ s science and technology, health, education, culture and four cities of XPCG.

1. Main content and sources of data on science and technology.

The data n conditions of scientific and technical personnel in State-owned units are provided by the Organizational Department of XPCG. Number of institutions of XPCG and division, the situation on scales of scientific and technological activities, composition of scientific and technological personnel, and revenue and expenditure of scientific and technological funds are provided by the Science and Technology Bureau of XPCG. The data on technical development of large-scale and medium-scale industrial enterprise are collected from the Comprehensive Statistical Reporting on Technical Activities of Large-scale and Medium-scale Industrial Enterprise of XPCG, which are provided by the Society Science Trade Statistical Section of the Statistics Bureau of XPCG.

2.The data on education cover mainly the situation on higher Education, regular secondary education, primary education and adult education of various types and at various levels. The main indicators cover number of schools, number of student enrollment, number of new student enrollment, number of graduates, number of staff and workers, number and composition of teachers, basic conditions on schools by level and type, which are provided by the Education Bureau of XPCG.

3. The data on culture cover mainly the basic conditions on arts group, news and publication, and radio and TV broadcasting stations, which are provided by the Propaganda Department of XPCG.

4.The data on public health cover mainly the basic conditions on development of XPCG′ s public health, including number of health institutions, beds, persons and etc, which are provided by the Public Health Bureau of XPCG.

5.The data on city cover mainly the basic conditions on Shihezi City, Alaer City, Tumushuke City and Wujiaqu City, which are Compiled by the Statistical Monitoring Section of Survey Office of the National Bureau of Statistics of XPCG.

17—1 国有单位专业技术人员及构成

Number of Scientific and Technical Personnel and its Composition in State-owned Units

(2010 年)

指 标	Item	年末人数（万人） Personnel at the Year-end (10 000 persons)	构 成 (%) Composition (%)	每万职工拥有科技人员(人) Number of S&T Personnel per 10 000 Staff and Workers (person)
专业技术人员合计	**Total**	**11.85**	**100.0**	**1 756**
工程技术人员	Engineering	1.67	13.4	247
农业技术人员	Agriculture	1.42	11.4	210
卫生技术人员	Health Care	1.72	13.8	255
教学人员	Teaching	3.22	25.9	477
其他人员	Others	3.82	30.7	566

17—2 各师国有单位专业技术人员数

Number of Professional and Technical Personnel in State-owned Units by Division

计量单位：万人 (2010 年) (10 000 persons)

单 位	Unit	年末专业技术人员合计 Total Professional and Technical Personnel at the Year-end	# 工 程 Engineering	# 农 业 Agriculture	# 卫 生 Health Care	# 教 学 Teaching
总 计	**Total**	**11.85**	**1.67**	**1.42**	**1.72**	**3.22**
一 师	Division 1	1.20	0.16	0.17	0.20	0.31
二 师	Division 2	0.93	0.13	0.14	0.14	0.24
三 师	Division 3	0.73	0.06	0.13	0.11	0.24
四 师	Division 4	0.98	0.08	0.09	0.15	0.26
五 师	Division 5	0.62	0.07	0.09	0.09	0.17
六 师	Division 6	1.08	0.06	0.19	0.20	0.33
七 师	Division 7	0.85	0.11	0.12	0.14	0.21
八 师	Division 8	2.15	0.37	0.26	0.28	0.63
九 师	Division 9	0.36	0.03	0.05	0.06	0.08
十 师	Division 10	0.42	0.04	0.06	0.07	0.12
建工师	Construction Division	0.68	0.39	0.00	0.02	0.08
十二师	Division 12	0.27	0.03	0.03	0.02	0.08
十三师	Division 13	0.34	0.02	0.06	0.06	0.10
十四师	Division 14	0.13	0.01	0.02	0.02	0.04
兵团直属	Directly under XPCG	1.11	0.11	0.01	0.16	0.33

17－3 科技活动基本情况

Basic Statistics on Scientific and Technological Activities

指 标		Item		2010
从事科技活动人员情况		**Personnel Engaged in Scientific and Technological Activities**		
从业人员总数	（人）	Number of Employed Persons	(person)	1 152
科技活动人员	（人）	Persons Engaged in Scientific and Technological Activities	(person)	852
# 大学本科及以上学历		University Graguate or above		587
按工作性质分		By employment character		
科技管理人员		Scientific and manage		133
课题活动人员		Subject Activities		571
科技服务人员		Scientific and Technological Service		148
按学历分		By Records		
博 士		Doctor's Degree		8
硕 士		Master's Degree		179
本 科		Regular College Course		400
其 他		Other		265
按职称分		By Records and the Title of a Technical Post		
高 级		Senior		242
中 级		Intermediate		328
其 他		Other		282
科技活动课题情况		**Subjects of Scientific and Technological Activities**		
课题个数	（个）	Subject	(pcs)	379
# R&D课题		Subject of R&D		277
课题经费内部支出	（万元）	Inner Expenditure for Subject	(10 000 yuan)	5 601
# 政府资金		Government Funds		3 160
# R&D课题		Subject of R&D		3 893
课题投入人员(人年)		Personnel for Subjects	(Person-Year)	708
# R&D		R&D		510
# 外聘流动研究人员		Hired Transient Personnel		7
# 在读研究生		Graduate Student Enrollment		3
经费收入总额	（万元）	Total Fund revenue for S&T Subject	(10 000 yuan)	23 852
# 政府资金		Government Funds		11 953
经费支出总额	（万元）	Total Expenditure	(10 000 yuan)	20 980
# 科技经费支出		Total Expenditure for S&T		14 804
科技产出及成果情况		**Statistics on S&T Outputs and Results**		
发表科技论文	（篇）	Scientific Papers Issued	(piece)	323
出版科技著作	（种）	Publication on Science and Technology	(kind)	
科技成果登记数	（项）	Number of Major Achievements in Science and Technology	(item)	51
国家技术发明奖	（项）	Number of National Invention Prizes Awarded	(item)	
国家科学技术进步奖	（项）	Number of National Scientific and Technological Progress Prizes Awarded	(item)	1
专利申请受理数	（件）	Number of Patents Application Accepted	(piece)	41
# 发明专利		Inventions		13
专利申请授权数(件)		Number of Patents Application Granted	(piece)	38
# 发明专利		Inventions		12

注：科技活动情况仅包括兵、师两级科研单位情况，不包括团场科技活动情况。
Note: Scientific and technological activities only include science research institutions at the levels of XPCG and divisions and exclude datd at farm level.

17—4 国有科学研究与开发机构基本情况

Basic Statistics on State-owned Scientific Research and Development Institutions

指 标		Item		2010
机构基本情况		**Basic Statistics on Institutions**		
机构数	(个)	Number of R&D Institutions	(unit)	18
# 中央属		Subordinated to Central Level		
地方属		Subordinated to Local Level		18
研究与试验发展(R&D)投入情况		**Statistics on R&D Input**		
R&D 人员	(人)	R&D Personnel	(person)	713
R&D 人员全时当量	(人年)	Full-time Equivalent of R&D Personnel	(man-year)	617
# 基础研究		Basic Research		26
应用研究		Applied Research		93
试验发展		Experimental Development		498
R&D 经费内部支出	(万元)	Intramural Expenditure on R&D	(10000 yuan)	6429
# 基础研究		Basic Research		323
应用研究		Applied Research		913
试验发展		Experimental Development		5193
# 政府资金		Government Appropriation Funds		5459
企业资金		Self-raised Funds by Enterprises		443
R&D 项目(课题)情况		**Statistics on R&D Topics**		
R&D 项目(课题)数	(项)	Projects of R&D	(item)	277
R&D 项目(课题)人员全时当量	(人年)	Participants	(man-year)	617
R&D 项目(课题)经费内部支出	(万元)	Intramural Expenditure	(10000 yuan)	6429
科技产出及成果情况		**Statistics on S&T Outputs and Results**		
发表科技论文	(篇)	Scientific Papers Issued	(piece)	323
# 国外发表		Published in Foreign Periodicals		15
出版科技著作	(种)	Publication on Science and Technology	(kind)	2
专利申请受理数	(件)	Number of Patents Applications Accepted	(piece)	41
# 发明专利		Inventions		13
专利申请授权数	(件)	Number of Patents Applications Granted	(piece)	38
# 发明专利		Inventions		12

17—5 国有科学研究与开发机构经费情况

Fund Statistics on State-owned Scientific Research and Development Institutions

计量单位:万元 (2010 年) (10 000 yuan)

指标	Item	合计 Total	自然科学与技术领域机构 Institutions of Natural Sciences and Technology	社会科学与人文领域机构 Institutions of Social Sciences and Humanities	转制科学研究与技术开发机构 Institutions of Reformed Scientific research and Technical Development
科技活动收入	**S&T Activities Revenue**	**10 911**	**9 020**	**132**	**1 759**
政府资金	Government Funds	9 033	8 495	132	406
财政拨款	Finance Appropriate Fouds	3 792	3 641	98	53
承担政府科研项目收入	Income form Government A&T Item	2 327	1 974		353
其　他	Other	216	216		
非政府资金	Non-Government Funds	1 878	525		1 353
技术性收入	Technique Income	1 878	525		1 353
生产经营收入	**Production and Operation Revenue**	**3 684**	**3 147**		**537**
其他收入	**Other Revenue**	**9 257**	**9 210**	**43**	**4**
科技经费内部支出	**Total Inner Expenditure for S&T Activities**	**14 804**	**13 095**	**117**	**1 592**
科技经费日常支出	Total Daily Expenditure for S&T Activities	11 738	10 411	117	1 210
人员劳务费	Personnel Work fee	6 551	6 035	67	449
设备购置费	Equipment Purchase Fee	1 918	1 532	16	370
其他日常支出	Other Daily Expenditure for S&T Activities	3 269	2 844	34	391
科研基本建设	S&T Infrastructure	3 066	2 684		382
生产经营支出	**Production and Operation Expenditure**	**2 691**	**2 226**		**465**
其他支出	**Other**	**2 705**	**2 346**	**29**	**330**

17—6 国有科学研究与开发机构基本建设与固定资产情况

Infrastructure and Assets Statistics on State-owned Scientific Research and Development Institutions

计量单位:万元 (2010 年) (10 000 yuan)

指标	Item	合计 Total	自然科学与技术领域机构 Institutions of Natural Sciences and Technology	社会科学与人文领域机构 Institutions of Social Sciences and Humanities	转制科学研究与技术开发机构 Institutions of Reformed Scientific research and Technical Development
基本建设投资实际完成额	**Infrastructure Practically Accomplish Invest**	**3 847**	**2 772**		**1 075**
科研仪器设备	S&T Apparatus	533	385		148
科研土建工程	S&T Engineering	2 433	2 299		134
科研基本建设	**S&T Infrastructure**	**3 066**	**2 684**		**382**
政府资金	Government Funds	2 704	2 664		40
企业资金	Enterprises Funds	342			342
事业单位资金	Institutions Funds	20	20		
其他资金	Other Funds				
年末固定资产原价	**Fixed Assets**	**16 171**	**13 896**	**66**	**2 209**
科研房屋建筑物	Building of Scientific Research	6 385	5 177	20	1 188
科研仪器设备	Apparatus of Scientific Research	4 096	3 530	46	520
#进　口	Import	1 097	1 097		

17—7 大中型工业企业技术开发基本情况

Basic Statistics on Technical Development of Large-Scale and Medium-Scale Industrial Enterprise

计量单位:万元 (2010 年) (10 000 yuan)

指 标	Item	2010
科技活动人员总计(人)	**Total Personnel Scientific and TechnologicalActivities(Person)**	**2 671**
# 参加科技项目人员	Personnel Attend the Scientific and Technological Item	2 174
科技管理和服务人员	Personnel of Scientific and Technological Management and Service	497
# 女 性	Famel	526
# 高、中级技术职称人员	personnel with senior ,intermidiate technical titles	523
# 全时人员	Full-time personnel	929
科技活动经费支出总额	**Total Expenditures for Scientific and Technological Activities**	**64 742**
内部支出合计	Total Internal Expenditure	60 001
科技活动人员劳务费(含工资)	Labor Expenses for Scientific and Technological Activities Personnel(Including Wages)	11 612
原材料费	Raw Material Cost	26 506
折旧费用与长期费用摊销	Depreciation and Long-term Expenses Amortizes	2 247
无形资产摊销	Aeriform Asset Amortizes	1 371
其 他	Other	18 264
内部支出中:R&D 经费	Internal Expenditure: R&D Fund	17 928
外部支出合计	Total External Expenditures	4 888
当年形成用于科技活动的固定资产	Fixed Assets Form in the Year Used for Scientific and Tenchnological Activity	10 214
使用来自政府部门的科技活动资金	Fund of Scientific and Tenchnological Activity Form the Government Section	11 661
科技项目情况	Statistics on Scientific and Technological Item	
全部科技项目数(个)	Number of Scientific and Technological Item(unit)	150
全部科技项目经费内部支出	Internal Expenditure of Scientific and Technological Item	55 282
其他科技活动经费支出	**Expenditure for Other Scientific and Technological Activities**	
技术改造支出总额	Total Expenditures for Technical Renovation	32 367
技术引进支出总额	Total Expenditures for Technical Import	
购买国内技术经费支出	Fund for Purchasing Domestic Technology	
技术开发活动产出	**Output for Technical Development**	
新产品产值	Output for New Product	45 481
新产品销售收入合计	Total Income of New Product Sales	92 466
# 新产品出口	Export of New Products	1 950
新产品开发项目数	Item of New Products	
拥有发明专利数	Original Value of Production Equipment of Microelectronic Technical Control	12
企业技术开发机构数(个)	**Technical Development Institutions of Enterprises(pcs)**	**25**

17—8 教育事业基本情况

Basic Statistics on Education

指标	Item	1980	1985	1990	1995
学校数 (所)	**Number of Schools (unit)**				
普通高等学校	Regular Institutions of Higher Education	3	3	5	5
成人高等学校	Adult Education Schools		4	7	7
普通中等学校	Regular Secondary Schools	631	695	541	391
普通中等专业学校	Specialized Secondary Schools	5	8	6	7
技工学校	Technical Schools	7		6	12
普通中学	Regular Secondary Schools	616	654	477	330
高　中	Senior Secondary Schools		248	214	127
初　中	Junior Secondary Schools		406	263	203
职业中学	Vocational Secondary Schools	3	33	52	42
成人中等学校	Secondary Schools for Adults		22	33	38
小　学	Primary Schools	2 189	1 809	801	541
盲聋哑学校	Special Schools		1	1	1
幼儿园	Kindergartens		268	510	223
毕业生数 (人)	**Graduates (person)**				
普通高等学校	Regular Institutions of Higher Education	326	484	1 584	2 186
成人高等学校	Adult Education Schools		265	1 290	1 427
普通中等学校	Regular Secondary Schools		90 595	86 716	42 498
普通中等专业学校	Specialized Secondary Schools	219	388	629	931
技工学校	Technical Schools	148		1 380	2 614
普通中学	Regular Secondary Schools		84 748	77 066	34 889
高　中	Senior Secondary Schools		19 936	25 621	10 419
初　中	Junior Secondary Schools		64 812	51 445	24 470
职业中学	Vocational Secondary Schools		5 459	7 641	4 064
成人中等学校	Secondary Schools for Adults		125	5 774	3 513
小　学	Primary Schools	70 093	71 140	40 263	23 840
盲聋哑学校	Special Schools			10	15
幼儿园	Kindergartens			10 914	33 665
招生数 (人)	**New Student Enrollment (person)**				
普通高等学校	Regular Institutions of Higher Education	597	1 217	1 750	2 646
成人高等学校	Adult Education Schools		1 185	2 072	2 843
普通中等学校	Regular Secondary Schools	80 782	136 433	73 934	44 108
普通中等专业学校	Specialized Secondary Schools	366	607	917	1 751
技工学校	Technical Schools	420		1 228	2 585
普通中学	Regular Secondary Schools	79 996	97 542	61 354	35 709
高　中	Senior Secondary Schools		28 188	22 617	11 618
初　中	Junior Secondary Schools		69 354	38 737	24 091
职业中学	Vocational Secondary Schools		10 096	10 435	4 063
成人中等学校	Secondary Schools for Adults		11 181	5 995	8 872
小　学	Primary Schools	85 230	46 600	26 665	45 741
盲聋哑学校	Special Schools		40	16	10
幼儿园	Kindergartens			16 288	22 100
在校学生 (人)	**Student Enrollment (person)**				
普通高等学校	Regular Institutions of Higher Education	2 944	2 809	5 827	8 568
成人高等学校	Adult Education Schools		2 225	5 723	8 282
普通中等学校	Regular Secondary Schools	244 707	330 368	231 287	125 748
普通中等专业学校	Specialized Secondary Schools	1 024	1 571	2 621	4 327
技工学校	Technical Schools	870		3 507	4 365
普通中学	Regular Secondary Schools	242 592	307 214	200 822	107 491
高　中	Senior Secondary Schools		70 488	77 550	34 204
初　中	Junior Secondary Schools		236 726	123 272	73 287
职业中学	Vocational Secondary Schools	221	21 583	24 337	9 565
成人中等学校	Secondary Schools for Adults		18 499	12 725	16 940
小　学	Primary Schools	468 792	324 271	199 624	209 351
盲聋哑学校	Special Schools		183	107	80
幼儿园	Kindergartens		24 826	30 681	56 210
教职工数 (人)	**Number of Teachers and Staff (person)**				
普通高等学校	Regular Institutions of Higher Education	2 415	2 498	4 473	4 479
成人高等学校	Adult Education Schools		431	664	563
普通中等学校	Regular Secondary Schools	21 620	27 661	24 809	18 892
普通中等专业学校	Specialized Secondary Schools	226	508	436	522
技工学校	Technical Schools	81		497	1 093
普通中学	Regular Secondary Schools	21 313	25 747	22 126	15 953
高　中	Senior Secondary Schools		4 533	5 253	3 164
初　中	Junior Secondary Schools		13 275	9 040	6 650
职业中学	Vocational Secondary Schools		1 406	1 750	1 324
成人中等学校	Secondary Schools for Adults		702	1 380	1 242
小　学	Primary Schools	23 128	19 268	14 245	14 122
盲聋哑学校	Special Schools		26	43	21
幼儿园	Kindergartens		1 722	2 180	3 401

17—8 续表 Continued

指　　标	Item	2000	2005	2009	2010
学校数（所）	**Number of Schools (unit)**				
普通高等学校	Regular Institutions of Higher Education	2	4	4	4
成人高等学校	Adult Education Schools	3	2	2	2
普通中等学校	Regular Secondary Schools	337	314	288	283
普通中等专业学校	Specialized Secondary Schools	8	20	21	21
技工学校	Technical Schools	11	11	10	10
普通中学	Regular Secondary Schools	293	277	256	251
高　中	Senior Secondary Schools	95	77	61	51
初　中	Junior Secondary Schools	198	200	195	200
职业中学	Vocational Secondary Schools	25	6	1	1
成人中等学校	Secondary Schools for Adults	23	3	1	1
小　学	Primary Schools	463	317	105	85
盲聋哑学校	Special Schools				
幼儿园	Kindergartens	255	177	168	189
毕业生数（人）	**Graduates (person)**				
普通高等学校	Regular Institutions of Higher Education	2 101	6 136	9 674	10 243
成人高等学校	Adult Education Schools	934	6 681	3 602	3 463
普通中等学校	Regular Secondary Schools	37 880	66 021	76 747	78 052
普通中等专业学校	Specialized Secondary Schools	2 178	3 910	8 940	10 374
技工学校	Technical Schools	2 166	1 697	3 476	5 187
普通中学	Regular Secondary Schools	30 380	60 152	64 315	62 410
高　中	Senior Secondary Schools	9 322	16 420	21 428	20 368
初　中	Junior Secondary Schools	21 068	43 732	42 887	42 042
职业中学	Vocational Secondary Schools	3 156	262	16	81
成人中等学校	Secondary Schools for Adults	5 484	450	1 923	3 226
小　学	Primary Schools	41 124	49 187	42 582	40 186
盲聋哑学校	Special Schools				
幼儿园	Kindergartens	28 330	24 933	20 987	21 329
招生数（人）	**New Student Enrollment (person)**				
普通高等学校	Regular Institutions of Higher Education	3 700	9 428	12 666	13 370
成人高等学校	Adult Education Schools	3 190	5 351	3 344	3 909
普通中等学校	Regular Secondary Schools	59 778	82 359	83 248	81 307
普通中等专业学校	Specialized Secondary Schools	2 458	7 824	10 757	12 110
技工学校	Technical Schools	2 716	3 480	6 179	5 768
普通中学	Regular Secondary Schools	52 218	70 952	66 168	63 429
高　中	Senior Secondary Schools	10 814	21 748	20 908	20 921
初　中	Junior Secondary Schools	41 404	49 204	45 260	42 508
职业中学	Vocational Secondary Schools	2 386	103	144	
成人中等学校	Secondary Schools for Adults	1 114	300	2 500	3 000
小　学	Primary Schools	45 671	39 655	35 558	33 255
盲聋哑学校	Special Schools				
幼儿园	Kindergartens	35 070	28 221	27 648	28 130
在校学生（人）	**Student Enrollment (person)**				
普通高等学校	Regular Institutions of Higher Education	11 735	30 663	44 149	46 776
成人高等学校	Adult Education Schools	7 652	12 286	10 377	10 857
普通中等学校	Regular Secondary Schools	149 182	233 470	243 665	236 413
普通中等专业学校	Specialized Secondary Schools	7 820	19 563	31 572	30 120
技工学校	Technical Schools	4 653	7 086	13 979	15 753
普通中学	Regular Secondary Schools	129 812	206 440	197 801	190 362
高　中	Senior Secondary Schools	29 298	59 816	60 959	59 956
初　中	Junior Secondary Schools	100 514	146 624	136 842	130 406
职业中学	Vocational Secondary Schools	6 897	381	313	178
成人中等学校	Secondary Schools for Adults	5 708	468	5 726	5 500
小　学	Primary Schools	288 707	269 811	227 854	217 600
盲聋哑学校	Special Schools				
幼儿园	Kindergartens	57 603	49 676	47 685	51 313
教职工数（人）	**Number of Teachers and Staff (person)**				
普通高等学校	Regular Institutions of Higher Education	3 138	4 023	4 150	4 201
成人高等学校	Adult Education Schools	901	938	957	948
普通中等学校	Regular Secondary Schools	16 048	20 044	20 664	20 770
普通中等专业学校	Specialized Secondary Schools	550	1 662	1 993	1 968
技工学校	Technical Schools	851	755	1 155	1 190
普通中学	Regular Secondary Schools	13 952	17 548	17 490	17 589
高　中	Senior Secondary Schools	2 506			
初　中	Junior Secondary Schools	6 841			
职业中学	Vocational Secondary Schools	695	79	26	23
成人中等学校	Secondary Schools for Adults	1 624	201	84	84
小　学	Primary Schools	16 791	17 545	15 846	15 568
盲聋哑学校	Special Schools				
幼儿园	Kindergartens	3 762	2 882	2 885	3 253

17—9 各级各类学校基本情况

Basic Statistics on Schools by Level and Type of School

计量单位:人　　(2010 年)　　(person)

指　标	Item	校数(所) Number of Schools (unit)	毕业生数 Graduates	招生数 New Student Enrollment	在校学生数 Student Enrollment	教职工数 Staff and Teachers	#专任教师 Full-Time Teachers
普通高等学校	Regular Institutions of Higher Education	4	10 243	13 370	46 776	4 201	2 741
成人高等学校	Adult Institutions of Higher Education	2	3 463	3 909	10 857	948	612
# 普通高校成教院	Adult Colleges of Institutions of Higher Education	2	3 125	3 495	9 318		
普通中等专业学校	Regular Specialized Secondary Schools	21	10 374	12 110	30 120	1 968	1 220
成人中等专业学校	Specialized Secondary Schools for Adults	1	3 226	3 000	5 500	84	70
技工学校	Technical Schools	10	5 187	5 768	15 753	1 190	640
普通中学	Regular Secondary Schools	251	62 410	63 429	190 362	17 589	14 541
高　中	Senior Secondary Schools	51	20 368	20 921	59 956		4 267
初中(含九年一贯制)	Junior Secondary Schools	200	42 042	42 508	130 406		10 274
职业中学	Vocational Secondary Schools	1	81		178	23	15
小　学	Primary Schools	85	40 186	33 255	217 600	15 568	13 581
幼儿园	Kindergartens	189	21 329	28 130	51 313	3 253	2 006

注:本表普通高等学校毕业生数、招生数、在校学生数包括研究生数,其他表均不包括。
Note:Data in this table on regular institutions of higher education include postgraduates and other tables don't include it.

17—10 普通高等学校研究生情况

Postgraduates of Regular Institutions of Higher Education

计量单位:人　　(2010 年)　　(person)

指　标	Item	毕业生数 Graduates	授硕士学位的 With Master's Degree	招生数 New Student Enrollment	博士 doctor	硕士 master	在校生数 Student Enrollment
总　计	**Total**	**664**	**635**	**951**	**36**	**915**	**2 476**
# 女　生	Femal	323	310	474	19	455	1 228
哲　学	Philosophy						
经济学	Economics	47	47	30		30	112
法　学	LawScience	39	39	51		51	143
教育学	Pedagogy	13	13	9		9	39
文　学	Literature						
历史学	History						
理　学	Science	90	90	108		108	308
工　学	Engineering	101	101	124		124	347
农　学	Agriculture	156	134	153	21	132	434
医　学	Medicine	164	164	173		173	581
军事学	Military						
管理学	Mangement	54	47	74	15	59	227

17—11 普通高等学校本、专科学生数

Number of Students in Undergraduate or Specialized Courses in Institutions of Higher Education

计量单位：人　　　　(2010 年)　　　　(person)

指　标	Item	毕业生数 Graduates	本　科 Regular Colledge Course	专　科 Specialized Subject (Three Years)	招生数 New Student Enrollment	本　科 Regular Colledge Course	专　科 Specialized Subject (Three Years)	在校学生数 Student Enrollment	本　科 Regular Colledge Course	专　科 Specialized Subject (Three Years)
总　计	**Total**	**9 579**	**6 993**	**2 586**	**12 419**	**8 956**	**3 463**	**44 300**	**34 541**	**9 759**
经济学	Economics	278	182	96	328	273	55	1 209	966	243
法　学	Law Science	848	320	528	677	412	265	2 674	1 419	1 255
教育学	Pedagogy	217	156	61	288	238	50	964	844	120
文　学	Literature	877	762	115	980	944	36	4 153	3 919	234
#外　语	Foreign Language	175	175		300	300		1 241	1 151	90
艺　术	Arts	271	156	115	203	167	36	915	771	144
历史学	History	36	36		45	45		153	153	
理　学	Science	667	667		851	851		3 478	3 478	
工　学	Engineering	2 732	1 881	851	4 380	2 438	1 942	13 383	8 303	5 080
农　学	Agriculture	1 445	1 195	250	1 558	1 449	109	6 943	6 437	506
医　学	Medicine	986	606	380	1 267	915	352	4 634	3 682	952
管理学	Mangement	1 493	1 188	305	2 045	1 391	654	6 709	5 340	1 369

17—12 普通高等学校现有校舍面积

Floor Space of Present Buildings of Regular Institution of Higher Education

计量单位：平方米　　　　(2010 年)　　　　(sq. m)

单　位	unit	校舍建筑面积 Floor Space of Buildings	教学用房 Teaching Buildings	#教　室 Classrooms	#实验室及实习场所 Laboratories and Fieldwork Buildings	#图书馆 Library	其他用房 Life and Welfare Building	#教工宿舍 Teachers' Quarters	#学生宿舍 Dormitories	#教工住宅 Teachers' House
总　计	**Total**	**1 789 809**	**691 886**	**269 683**	**304 065**	**53 703**	**1 097 923**	**11 909**	**447 124**	**400 393**
塔里木大学	Tarim University	494 275	181 645	54 833	109 469	11 153	312 630	3 600	115 343	129 276
石河子大学	Shihezi University	1 093 060	401 856	159 276	159 593	28 262	691 204	6 700	266 336	271 117
兵团警官高等专科学校	XPCG Police Officer Junior College	32 968	14 307	10 557		3 750	18 661	1 529	10 896	
石河子大学科技学院	The Technological College of Shihezi University	45 084	19 488	10 077	2 693	6 718	25 596	80	20 083	
石河子职业技术学院	Shihezi Worker's University	124 422	74 590	34 940	32 310	3 820	49 832		34 466	

17—13 普通、成人高等学校教师专业职务情况

Teacher Professional Titles of Regular and Adult Institution of Higher Education

计量单位：人　　　　（2010 年）　　　　(person)

单　位	Unit	合　计 Total	#女　性 Female	教　授 Professors	副教授 Associate Professors	讲　师 Lecturers	助　教 Assistants	教　员 Instructors
普通高等学校	**Regular Institutions of Higher Education**	**2 741**	**1 355**	**210**	**742**	**1 315**	**380**	**94**
塔里木大学	Tarim University	806	375	42	146	383	167	68
石河子大学	Shihezi University	1 597	791	168	530	774	125	0
兵团警官高等专科学校	XPCG Police Junior College	81	44		14	48	17	2
石河子职业技术学院	Shihezi Vocational and Technical University	257	145		52	110	71	24
成人高等学校	**Adult Institutions of Higher Education**	**612**	**329**	**15**	**219**	**237**	**105**	**36**
新疆兵团教育学院	Xinjiang XPCG Educational College	366	213	2	120	163	45	36
新疆兵团电视大学	Xinjiang XPCG TV University	246	116	13	99	74	60	

17—14 普通中等专业学校教师专业职务情况

Teacher Professional Titles of Regular Specialized Secondary Schools

计量单位：人　　　　（2010 年）　　　　(person)

单　位	Unit	合　计 Total	#女　性 Female	高级教师 Senior Lecturers	讲　师 Lecturers	助理讲师 Assistants Lecturers	教员（含无职称） Instructors Without Professional Titles
总　计	**total**	**1 220**	**630**	**233**	**533**	**318**	**136**
一师阿拉尔职业技术学校	Alaer Vocational and Technical School of Division1	92	55	13	45	27	7
二师华山职业技术学校	Huashan vocational and Technical School of Division 2	218	104	12	119	75	12
三师图木舒克职业技术学校	The Vocational and Technical School of Tumushuke of Division 3	24	15	4	20		
四师伊犁职业技术学校	Yili Vocational and Technical School of Division4	47	21	11	25	11	
五师博乐职业技术学校	Bole Vocational and Technical School of Division5	31	16	8	12	3	8
六师五家渠职业技术学校	Wujiaqu Vocational Middle School of Division 6	54	40	4	24	19	7
七师奎屯职业技术学校	Kuytun Vocational and Technical School of Division 7	43	25	24	9	10	
八师中等职业教育中心	The Specialized Secondary Vocational Education Center of Division 8	120	68	20	60	29	11
九师中等职业技术学校	The Vocational and Technical School of Division 9	33	23	12	16	2	3
十师北屯职业技术学校	Beitun Vocational and Technical School ofDivision 10	26	14	11	6	7	2
建工师职业技术学校	The Vocational and Technical School of Construction Division	56	33	5	21	13	17
十二师职业技术学校	The Vocational and Technical School of Division 12	23	14	7	12	4	
十三师职业技术学校	The Vocational and Technical School of Division 13	33	10	3	29	1	
兵团工贸学校	The Industry and Trade School	180	77	35	52	62	31
兵团财经学校	The Financial and Economic School	16	9	5	5	3	3
石河子工程技术学校	Shihezi Engineering Technique School	70	29	18	33	10	9
石河子大学护士学校	The Nurse School of Shihezi University	14	12	8	2	4	
石河子卫生学校	Shihezi Health School	34	25	13	6	15	
兵团竞技体育运动学校	XPCG Athletics school	8	1		3	5	
兵团重竞技体育运动学校	XPCG Sport of Heavy Tournament Athletics School	26	7				26
兵团民族师范学校	The Nationality Teachers' School	72	32	20	34	18	

17—15 各级普通学校学生及教职工民族构成

Composition of Nationalities of Students and Staff and Workers in Regular Schools by Level of School

计量单位:人 （2010 年） （person）

指　　标	Item	合　计 Total	汉　族 Han	维吾尔族 Uygur	哈萨克族 Kazak	回　族 The Hui	其他民族 Others
普通中等专业学校	**Regular Specialized Secondary Schools**						
毕业生数	Graduates	10 374	9 186	431	175	247	335
招生数	New Student Enrollment	12 110	9 570	1 232	490	455	363
在校学生数	Student Enrollment	30 120	25 322	2 377	807	817	797
教职工数	Teachers and Staff	1 968	1 816	69	35	21	27
# 专任教师	Full-time Teachers	1 220	1 118	55	22	11	14
普通中学	**Reguar Secondary Schools**						
毕业生数	Graduates	62 410	55 405	4 239	944	1 260	562
初　中	Junior Secondary Schools	42 042	36 494	3 551	749	901	347
高　中	Senior Secondary Schools	20 368	18 911	688	195	359	215
招生数	New Student Enrollment	63 429	56 010	4 258	1 034	1 505	622
初　中	Junior Secondary Schools	42 508	36 841	3 309	839	1 154	365
高　中	Senior Secondary Schools	20 921	19 169	949	195	351	257
在校学生数	Student Enrollment	190 362	168 568	12 818	2 796	4 249	1 931
初　中	Junior Secondary Schools	130 406	113 195	10 533	2 273	3 230	1 175
高　中	Senior Secondary Schools	59 956	55 373	2 285	523	1 019	756
教职工数	Teachers and Staff	17 589	15 749	1 084	308	270	178
# 专任教师	Full-time Teachers	14 541	12 930	942	278	227	164
初　中	Junior Secondary Schools	10 274	8 991	751	236	171	125
高　中	Senior Secondary Schools	4 267	3 939	191	42	56	39
职业中学	**Vocational Senior Secondary Schools**						
毕业生数	Graduates	81	81				
招生数	New Student Enrollment						
在校学生数	Student Enrollment	178	172	2		4	
教职工数	Teachers and Staff	23	21				2
# 专任教师	Full-time Teachers	15	14				1
小　学	**Primary Schools**						
毕业生数	Graduates	40 186	34 663	3 225	840	1 201	257
招生数	New Student Enrollment	33 255	25 785	4 693	1 141	1 290	346
在校学生数	Student Enrollment	217 600	177 905	24 190	5 868	7 757	1 880
教职工数	Teachers and Staff	15 568	13 255	1 452	428	293	140
# 专任教师	Full-time Teachers	13 581	11 475	1 348	369	262	127

17—16 按专业职务、年龄分中小学教师数

Teachers of Primary and Secondary Schools by Professional Title and Age

计量单位：人　　　　(2010年)　　　　(person)

指　标	Item	合　计 Total	25岁以下 Under 25	26—30岁 Between 26—30	31—35岁 Between 31—35	36—40岁 Between 36—40	41—45岁 Between 41—45	46—50岁 Between 46—50	51—55岁 Between 51—55	56—60岁 Between 56—60	61岁以上 above 61
高中教师	**Teachers of Secondary Schools**	**4 267**	**606**	**1 037**	**634**	**571**	**627**	**573**	**182**	**37**	
# 女	Female	2 325	350	608	328	303	381	292	63		
# 民　族	Nationality	328	34	84	73	57	44	29	7		
高　级	Senior	1 042			13	109	338	401	147	34	
一　级	Level 1	1 265		103	356	355	251	166	31	3	
二　级	Level 2	1 424	229	801	242	105	37	6	4		
三　级	Level 3	50	16	10	22	1	1				
未评级	Not Evaluated	486	361	123	1	1					
初中教师	**Teachers of Junior Secondary Schools**	**10 274**	**964**	**1 926**	**1 857**	**1 787**	**1 659**	**1 326**	**620**	**135**	
# 女	Female	6 099	631	1 173	1 132	1 131	1 056	720	256		
# 民　族	Nationality	1 283	81	241	298	274	212	129	39	9	
高　级	Senior	1 308		1	12	136	363	448	284	64	
一　级	Level 1	4 257	23	147	809	1 119	1 030	765	302	62	
二　级	Level 2	3 278	166	1 208	980	516	257	111	31	9	
三　级	Level 3	312	76	153	53	16	9	2	3		
未评级	Not Evaluated	1 119	699	417	3						
小学教师	**Teachers of Primary Schools**	**13 581**	**1 211**	**2 078**	**2 617**	**2 530**	**2 015**	**1 744**	**1 205**	**181**	
# 女	Female	10 584	968	1 590	2 074	2 096	1 646	1 337	873		
# 民　族	Nationality	2 106	131	354	492	436	299	255	112	27	
中教高级	Senior for Secondary Education	35			1	3	6	8	11	6	
小学高级	Senior	6 245		156	848	1 374	1 379	1 362	1 000	126	
一　级	Level 1	5 498	255	1 324	1 642	1 101	602	358	174	42	
二　级	Level 2	500	119	225	83	31	15	11	11	5	
三　级	Level 3	144	58	23	24	15	11	4	7	2	
未评级	Not Evaluated	1 159	779	350	19	6	2	1	2		

17—17 普通中小学及幼儿园专任教师学历情况

Teacher Records of Formal Schooling of Regular and Secondary Schools and Vocational Middel Schools and Kindergartens

（2010 年）

指　　标	Item	专任教师人数（人）Full-time Teachers (person)	#民族 Nationality	专任教师学历构成（%）Composition of Schooling Records of Full-time Teacher (%)	#民族 Nationality
高　中	**Senior Secondary Schools**	**4 267**	**328**	**94.2**	**91.5**
大学本科毕业及以上	Graduation from Universities and above	4 019	300		
大学专科毕业	Graduation from Junior College	248	28		
高中阶段毕业	Graducation from Senior Secondary Schools				
高中毕业阶段以下	Graduation from Senior Secondary Schools and below				
初　中	**Junior Secondary Schools**	**10 274**	**1 283**	**99.8**	**99.7**
大学本科毕业及以上	Graduation from Universities and above	7 060	502		
大学专科毕业	Graduation from Junior College	3 190	777		
高中阶段毕业	Graducation from Senior Secondary Schools	23	4		
高中毕业阶段以下	Graduation from Senior Secondary Schools and below	1			
小　学	**PrimarySchools**	**13 581**	**2 106**	**99.8**	**99.4**
大学本科毕业及以上	Graduation from Universities and above	5 367	343		
大学专科毕业	Graduation from Junior College	7 585	1 523		
高中阶段毕业	Graduation from Senior Secondary Schools	599	228		
高中毕业阶段以下	Graduation from Senior Secondary Schools and below	30	12		
幼儿园	**Kindergartens**	**2 006**	**139**	**98.0**	**98.6**
大学本科毕业及以上	Graduation from Senior Secondary Schools and above	288	11		
大学专科毕业	Graduation from Secondary Teachers′ Schools	1 319	103		
高中阶段毕业	Graduation from Senior Secondary Schools	358	23		
高中毕业阶段以下	Graduation from Senior Secondary Schools and below	41	2		

17—18 中等教育结构状况

Secondary Education Structures

（2010 年）

指　标	Item	毕业生 Graduates 人数(人) Persons	构成(%) Composition	招　生 New Student Enrollment 人数(人) Persons	构成(%) Composition	在校学生 Student Enrollment 人数(人) Persons	构成(%) Composition
总　计	**Total**	**72 865**	**100.0**	**75 539**	**100.0**	**220 660**	**100.0**
普通中学	Regular Senior Secondary Schools	62 410	85.7	63 429	84.0	190 362	86.3
职业中学	Occupation Senior Secondary Schools	81	0.1			178	0.1
普通中专	Regular Specialized Secondary Schools	10 374	14.2	12 110	16.0	30 120	13.6

17—19 各师普通中学校数、学生数

Regular Secondary Schools and Student Enrollment by Division

计量单位：人　　（2010 年）　　(person)

单　位	Unit	校　数(所) School (Unit)	初　中 Junior Secondary Schools	高　中 Senior Secondary Schools	毕业生数 Graduates 初　中 Junior Secondary Schools	高　中 Senior Secondary Schools	招生数 New Student Enrollment 初　中 Junior Secondary Schools	高　中 Senior Secondary Schools	在校学生数 StudentEnrollment 初　中 Junior Secondary Schools	高　中 Senior Secondary Schools
总　计	**Total**	**251**	**200**	**51**	**42 042**	**20 368**	**42 508**	**20 921**	**130 406**	**59 956**
一　师	Division 1	26	22	4	5 337	2 958	4 924	3 132	15 846	8 619
二　师	Division 2	25	23	2	4 308	2 079	4 273	1 930	13 909	5 600
三　师	Division 3	26	21	5	5 007	1 826	4 721	2 093	14 607	5 781
四　师	Division 4	25	17	8	3 607	1 794	3 738	2 036	11 155	5 827
五　师	Division 5	14	11	3	2 341	1 395	2 612	1 375	8 019	4 052
六　师	Division 6	28	21	7	3 776	2 383	4 147	2 433	12 436	6 698
七　师	Division 7	14	10	4	2 624	1 367	2 669	1 292	7 799	3 711
八　师	Division 8	34	28	6	6 078	1 940	6 177	2 297	18 906	6 250
九　师	Division 9	13	12	1	1 266	549	1 404	620	3 838	1 890
十　师	Division 10	12	11	1	1 826	1 431	1 696	1 075	5 419	3 436
建工师	Construction Division	5	3	2	1 029	767	1 063	801	3 231	2 357
十二师	Division 12	8	6	2	1 153	445	1 172	505	3 636	1 600
十三师	Division 13	13	8	5	1 347	673	1 434	562	4 135	1 770
十四师	Division 14	3	3		625		649		2 092	
兵团直属	Directly under XPCG	5	4	1	1 718	761	1 829	770	5 378	2 365

17—20 各师普通中学教职工人数

Staff and Teachers in Regular Secondary Schools by Division

计量单位:人 （2010 年） (person)

单位	Unit	教职工合计 Total Staff and Teachers	专任教师 Full-Time Teachers	行政人员 Adminis-trative Staff	教辅人员 Teaching Auxiliaries	工勤人员 Logistic Staff	校办厂人员 Personnel of Factories Run by Schools	代课教师 Supply Teachers	兼任教师 Part-Time Teachers
总计	**Total**	**17 589**	**14 541**	**858**	**855**	**1 322**	**13**	**699**	**2**
一师	Division 1	1 876	1 547	100	66	163		10	
二师	Division 2	1 802	1 606	81	48	67			2
三师	Division 3	1 669	1 435	90	39	105		304	
四师	Division 4	1 602	1 346	81	67	106	2	29	
五师	Division 5	1 093	864	72	44	113		5	
六师	Division 6	1 897	1 527	62	135	172	1	1	
七师	Division 7	1 426	1 123	54	100	145	4	80	
八师	Division 8	2 426	1 925	129	157	214	1	27	
九师	Division 9	661	527	30	43	61		92	
十师	Division 10	764	655	29	36	39	5		
建工师	Construction Division	476	426	15	13	22		75	
十二师	Division 12	459	374	38	20	27		13	
十三师	Division 13	606	538	32	10	26		6	
十四师	Division 14	231	165	8	22	36			
兵团直属	Directly under XPCG	601	483	37	55	26		57	

17—21 各师普通中学现有校舍面积

Floor Space of Present Buildings of Regular Secondary Schools by Division

计量单位:平方米 （2010 年） (sq. m)

单位	Unit	学校占地面积 Areas of Schools	校舍建筑面积 Floor Space of Buildings	教学用房合计 Total Teaching Buildings	#教室 Classrooms	#实验室 Laborat-ories	#图书馆 Libraries	行政用房 Administr-ative Buildings	生活用房 Life Buildings	其他用房 Others
总计	**Total**	**10 209 028**	**2 044 226**	**1 004 269**	**610 161**	**183 138**	**55 284**	**202 307**	**748 500**	**89 150**
一师	Division 1	980 718	252 212	115 329	69 676	24 265	6 334	23 704	103 206	9 973
二师	Division 2	909 959	215 011	104 266	58 419	19 945	7 216	26 777	78 028	5 940
三师	Division 3	908 796	186 385	89 330	58 757	14 595	3 910	18 065	77 810	1 180
四师	Division 4	947 904	144 784	77 747	42 689	14 907	4 639	13 310	53 727	
五师	Division 5	577 044	115 570	56 520	39 391	9 790	2 499	8 755	44 788	5 507
六师	Division 6	1 327 562	232 149	111 602	68 664	19 927	8 401	24 932	94 915	700
七师	Division 7	925 431	123 895	59 836	41 105	9 732	2 425	11 210	43 359	9 490
八师	Division 8	1 413 710	285 681	148 044	85 723	28 367	7 137	25 686	91 758	20 193
九师	Division 9	354 086	87 589	40 922	24 838	7 015	2 271	8 225	27 230	11 212
十师	Division 10	699 844	99 997	53 486	32 897	10 838	4 535	7 642	36 745	2 124
建工师	Construction Division	102 986	29 959	16 250	11 114	1 902	782	1 981	11 291	437
十二师	Division 12	216 143	68 335	39 805	24 673	5 411	1 249	5 080	23 200	250
十三师	Division 13	638 552	98 984	54 580	31 710	9 487	2 108	8 021	34 182	2 201
十四师	Division 14	65 126	24 618	9 451	6 306	1 599	384	1 339	9 082	4 746
兵团直属	Directly under XPCG	141 167	79 057	27 101	14 199	5 358	1 394	17 580	19 179	15 197

17—22 各师中等专业学校基本情况

Basic Statistics on Specialized Regular Secondary Schools by Division

计量单位:人 （2010 年） (person)

单 位	Unit	校 数（所） Schools (unit)	毕业生数 Graduates	招生数 New Student Enrollment	在校学生数 Student Enrollment	教职工数 Staff and Teachers	专任教师 Full-Time Teachers
总 计	**Total**	**23**	**13 681**	**15 110**	**35 798**	**2 075**	**1 305**
一 师	Division 1	1	330	342	645	110	92
二 师	Division 2	1	471	779	2 047	290	218
三 师	Division 3	1		383	550	33	24
四 师	Division 4	1	117	1 407	1 675	93	47
五 师	Division 5	1		70	70	75	31
六 师	Division 6	1	462	498	1 524	78	54
七 师	Division 7	1	325	355	613	87	43
八 师	Division 8	2	768	882	2 353	179	135
九 师	Division 9	1	167	236	236	51	33
十 师	Division 10	1	19	154	209	44	26
建 工 师	Construction Division	2	1 001	796	2 560	130	72
十 二 师	Division 12	1	115	193	544	39	23
十 三 师	Division 13	1		85	214	38	33
十 四 师	Division 14						
兵团直属	Directly under XPCG	8	9 906	8 930	22 558	828	474

17—23 各师中等专业学校现有校舍面积

Floor Space of Present Buildings of Specialized Regular Secondary Schools by Division

计量单位:平方米 （2010 年） (sq. m)

单 位	Unit	学校占地面积 Areas of Schools	校舍建筑面积 Floor Space of Buildings	教学用房合计 Total Teaching Buildings	#教 室 Classrooms	#实验室 Laboratories	#图书馆 Libraries	行政用房 Administrative Buildings	生活用房 Life Buildings	教职工住房 Teachers and Staff Graduates Buidings
总 计	**Total**	**1 942 785**	**549 537**	**273 089**	**145 807**	**99 666**	**17 829**	**34 574**	**200 198**	**41 676**
一 师	Division 1	50 685	23 801	9 913	3 720	4 945	196	682	10 734	2 472
二 师	Division 2	62 000	35 000	15 200	9 200	6 000		2 400	8 400	9 000
三 师	Division 3	103 407	17 424	9 402	6 265	400	2 277	1 799	6 223	
四 师	Division 4	53 946	6 638	3 077	2 693			160	3 401	
五 师	Division 5	50 000	11 186	5 501	3 217	1 712	332	801	1 574	3 310
六 师	Division 6	400 500	33 172	15 107	5 700	7 681	1 125	868	11 944	5 253
七 师	Division 7	78 400	19 345	12 685	4 900	7 635	150	2 450	4 210	
八 师	Division 8	250 337	68 627	31 358	9 386	19 147	1 310	12 560	24 709	
九 师	Division 9	21 099	6 925	3 234	2 248	566	120	374	3 317	
十 师	Division 10	19 733	11 209	4 262	3 152	500	190	1 297	5 650	
建 工 师	Construction Division	54 310	26 159	16 008	11 035	4 973			10 151	
十 二 师	Division 12	16 983	13 780	4 596	800	3 296	100	1 131	8 053	
十 三 师	Division 13	22 013	4 465	3 245	1 130	1 795	320	550	670	
十 四 师	Division 14									
兵团直属	Directly under XPCG	759 372	271 806	139 501	82 361	41 016	11 709	9 502	101 162	21 641

17－24 各师小学校数、学生数

Primary Schools and Pupil Enrollment by Division

（2010 年）

单　位	Unit	学　校（所）Schools (unit)	毕业生数（人）Graduates (person)	招生数（人）New Student Enrollment (person)	在校学生数（人）Student Enrollment (person)
总　计	**Total**	**85**	**40 186**	**33 255**	**217 600**
一　师	Division 1	10	4 618	3 157	24 017
二　师	Division 2	4	4 004	3 003	21 754
三　师	Division 3	8	4 198	4 859	26 911
四　师	Division 4	3	3 798	3 046	20 171
五　师	Division 5	3	2 153	1 957	12 692
六　师	Division 6	18	4 103	3 954	21 874
七　师	Division 7	10	2 808	1 791	13 405
八　师	Division 8	22	6 223	4 320	30 707
九　师	Division 9		1 384	1 362	7 694
十　师	Division 10		1 738	1 274	9 391
建 工 师	Construction Division	1	1 226	1 189	7 062
十 二 师	Division 12		1 202	879	6 188
十 三 师	Division 13	2	1 504	1 222	8 164
十 四 师	Division 14	4	649	822	4 545
兵团直属	Directly under XPCG		578	420	3 025

17－25 各师小学教职工人数

Staff and Teachers in Primary Schools by Division

计量单位：人　　（2010 年）　　(person)

单　位	Unit	教职工合计 Total Staff and Teachers	专任教师 Full-Time Teachers	行政人员 Adminis-trative Staff	教辅人员 Teaching Auxiliaries	工勤人员 Logistic Staff	校办厂人员 Personnel of Factories Run by Schools	代课教师 Supply Teachers	兼任教师 Part-Time Teachers
总　计	**Total**	**15 568**	**13 581**	**505**	**491**	**987**	**4**	**539**	**1**
一　师	Division 1	1 463	1 298	34	25	106		20	
二　师	Division 2	1 509	1 393	61	28	27		6	1
三　师	Division 3	1 820	1 682	46	23	69		207	
四　师	Division 4	1 330	1 154	56	33	87		64	
五　师	Division 5	748	678	19	19	32		11	
六　师	Division 6	1 732	1 499	49	69	115		5	
七　师	Division 7	1 279	998	36	66	179		44	
八　师	Division 8	2 335	1 928	101	122	184		35	
九　师	Division 9	567	495	19	22	31		70	
十　师	Division 10	737	615	30	37	55			
建 工 师	Construction Division	511	458	14	17	18	4	48	
十 二 师	Division 12	439	383	16	15	25		7	
十 三 师	Division 13	578	549	10	5	14		21	
十 四 师	Division 14	342	287	10	2	43			
兵团直属	Directly under XPCG	178	164	4	8	2		1	

17－26 各师学龄儿童入学率及小学毕业升学率

Percentage of School-age Enrolled and Percentage of Primary School Pupils Graduated by Division

(2010 年)

单 位	Unit	学龄儿童入学率 Percentage of School-Age Children Enrolled			小学毕业升学率 Percentage of Graduates of Primary Schools Entering Junior Secondary Schools		
		学龄儿童数（人） School-Age Children (person)	已入学数（人） School-Age Children Enrolled in Schools(person)	入学率（%） Erollment Rate (%)	小学毕业生数（人） Graduates from Primary Schools (person)	初中招生数（人） Students Entering Junior Secondary Schools(person)	升学率（%） Enrollment Rate (%)
总 计	**Total**	**205 587**	**205 326**	**99.9**	**40 186**	**42 508**	**105.8**
一 师	Division 1	21 901	21 901	100.0	4 618	4 924	106.6
二 师	Division 2	20 121	20 121	100.0	4 004	4 273	106.7
三 师	Division 3	26 346	26 162	99.3	4 198	4 721	112.5
四 师	Division 4	18 447	18 445	100.0	3 798	3 738	98.4
五 师	Division 5	11 625	11 625	100.0	2 153	2 612	121.3
六 师	Division 6	20 596	20 596	100.0	4 103	4 147	101.1
七 师	Division 7	12 095	12 095	100.0	2 808	2 669	95.0
八 师	Division 8	29 785	29 779	100.0	6 223	6 177	99.3
九 师	Division 9	7 552	7 552	100.0	1 384	1 404	101.4
十 师	Division 10	9 161	9 146	99.8	1 738	1 696	97.6
建工师	Construction Division	7 022	7 022	100.0	1 226	1 063	86.7
十二师	Division 12	5 524	5 524	100.0	1 202	1 172	97.5
十三师	Division 13	8 185	8 138	99.4	1 504	1 434	95.3
十四师	Division 14	4 424	4 424	100.0	649	649	100.0
兵团直属	Directly under XPCG	2 803	2 796	99.8	578	1 829	316.4

17－27 各师小学现有校舍面积

Floor Space of Present Buildings of Primary Schools by Division

计量单位：平方米 (2010 年) (sq. m)

单 位	Unit	学校占地面积 Areas of Schools	校舍建筑面积 Floor Space of Buildings	教学用房合计 Total Teaching Buildings	#教 室 Classrooms	#实验室 Laboratories	#图书馆 Libraries	行政用房 Administrative Buildings	生活用房 Life Buildings	其他用房 Others
总 计	**Total**	**8 524 009**	**1 394 910**	**787 609**	**595 367**	**57 680**	**32 030**	**145 106**	**387 952**	**74 243**
一 师	Division 1	752 943	150 559	86 730	65 998	4 213	4 138	18 746	39 507	5 576
二 师	Division 2	805 701	129 307	73 150	51 774	10 501	2 999	15 540	36 254	4 363
三 师	Division 3	1 104 634	159 488	94 025	74 551	7 723	3 624	14 871	47 989	2 603
四 师	Division 4	711 927	135 811	79 561	55 200	5 946	3 585	12 675	43 575	
五 师	Division 5	367 864	62 435	38 208	33 242	1 499	786	6 651	14 725	2 851
六 师	Division 6	1 065 179	162 196	95 927	69 651	6 504	4 391	17 802	47 523	944
七 师	Division 7	385 431	98 397	50 176	39 721	3 294	1 543	9 547	31 730	6 944
八 师	Division 8	1 412 158	221 788	112 875	86 102	5 145	4 692	21 472	63 373	24 068
九 师	Division 9	289 571	45 563	23 138	16 524	2 681	898	5 057	12 721	4 647
十 师	Division 10	498 127	65 359	38 643	26 659	3 860	2 407	4 524	20 056	2 136
建工师	Construction Division	117 957	28 526	21 552	18 534	1 152	842	3 651	1 732	1 591
十二师	Division 12	173 262	35 848	16 986	13 123	1 561	415	3 600	7 000	8 262
十三师	Division 13	500 099	42 529	31 037	23 476	2 169	495	6 038	2 934	2 520
十四师	Division 14	232 278	33 647	16 480	13 264	904	759	1 770	13 157	2 240
兵团直属	Directly under XPCG	106 878	23 457	9 121	7 548	528	456	3 162	5 676	5 498

17—28 各师中小学平均每班学生数、教师数及每一教师负担学生数

Students and Teachers of Primary and Secondary Schools Per Class and Student-Teacher Ratio by Division

计量单位：人 (2010 年) (person)

单 位	Unit	平均每班学生数 Per Class Students			平均每班教师数 Per Class Teachers			平均每一教师负担学生数 Students-Teacher Ratio		
		高 中 Senior Secondary Schools	初 中 Junior Secondary Schools	小 学 Primary Schools	高 中 Senior Secondary Schools	初 中 Junior Secondary Schools	小 学 Primary Schools	高 中 Senior Secondary Schools	初 中 Junior Secondary Schools	小 学 Primary Schools
总 计	**Total**	**51.9**	**44.4**	**40.7**	**3.7**	**3.5**	**2.5**	**14.1**	**12.7**	**16.0**
一 师	Division 1	55.3	47.9	44.3	3.4	3.1	2.4	16.2	15.6	18.5
二 师	Division 2	49.6	42.5	40.4	3.9	3.6	2.6	12.7	11.9	15.6
三 师	Division 3	55.6	46.4	35.9	3.8	3.3	2.2	14.5	14.1	16.0
四 师	Division 4	48.2	40.1	37.9	3.5	3.3	2.2	13.8	12.1	17.5
五 师	Division 5	51.9	45.8	43.6	3.5	3.4	2.3	15.0	13.5	18.7
六 师	Division 6	47.8	39.7	34.9	3.6	3.3	2.4	13.4	12.1	14.6
七 师	Division 7	48.2	40.8	41.1	4.2	4.2	3.1	11.5	9.7	13.4
八 师	Division 8	53.0	44.7	44.2	3.4	3.6	2.8	15.5	12.4	15.9
九 师	Division 9	57.3	39.2	40.5	3.9	4.1	2.6	14.7	9.6	15.5
十 师	Division 10	57.3	51.1	48.4	4.0	3.9	3.2	14.5	13.0	15.3
建 工 师	Construction Division	53.6	55.7	53.5	4.5	3.9	3.5	11.9	14.2	15.4
十 二 师	Division 12	50.0	46.6	42.4	3.1	3.5	2.6	16.2	13.2	16.2
十 三 师	Division 13	40.2	39.0	36.3	3.4	3.7	2.4	12.0	10.6	14.9
十 四 师	Division 14		44.5	45.0		3.5	2.8		12.7	15.8
兵团直属	Directly under XPCG	65.7	59.8	46.5	4.8	3.5	2.5	13.8	17.2	18.4

17—29 各师幼儿园基本情况

Basic Statistics on Kindergartens by Division

(2010 年)

单 位	Unit	园 数（所） Kindergartens (unit)	班 数（个） Classes (unit)	幼儿数（人） Children (person)	教职工数（人） Staff and Teachers (person)	#教 师 Teachers
总 计	**Total**	**189**	**1 363**	**51 313**	**3 253**	**2 006**
一 师	Division 1	17	138	5 605	433	250
二 师	Division 2	19	112	4 113	292	169
三 师	Division 3	18	132	5 289	198	142
四 师	Division 4	20	189	7 074	441	245
五 师	Division 5	12	83	2 951	331	200
六 师	Division 6	21	119	4 886	293	199
七 师	Division 7	14	116	4 279	297	197
八 师	Division 8	13	109	3 997	257	178
九 师	Division 9	12	70	2 548	121	86
十 师	Division 10	12	73	2 824	186	105
建 工 师	Construction Division	4	27	830	68	47
十 二 师	Division 12	15	78	2 310	172	101
十 三 师	Division 13	9	60	2 002	67	40
十 四 师	Division 14		30	1 363		
兵团直属	Directly under XPCG	3	27	1 242	97	47

17－30 技工学校基本情况

Basic Statistics on Technical Schools

计量单位：人　　(2010 年)　　(person)

单　位	Unit	学生数 Students 毕业生数 Graduates	招生数 New Student Enrollment	在校学生数 Student Enrollment	教职工数 Staff and Teachers	专任教师 Full-Time Teachers	教辅人员 Auxiliary Teaching Staff	行政人员 Administrative Personnel	工勤人员 Logistic Personnel	兼任教师数 Part-time Teachers
总　计	**Total**	**5 187**	**5 768**	**15 753**	**1 190**	**640**	**79**	**70**	**44**	**357**
兵团高级技校	XPCG Senior Technical School	2 503	1 677	5 650	340	111	4	24	6	195
建工师技工学校	The Technical School of Construction Division	838	883	1 815	130	69	14	12	7	28
一师技工学校	The Technical School of Division 1	112	710	1 879	108	86	2	5	2	13
二师技工学校	The Technical School of Division 2	591	835	2 130	98	63	5	4	5	21
四师技工学校	The Technical School of Division 4		675	1 675	93	55	5	5	6	22
五师技工学校	The Technical School of Division 5				68	48	2	4	2	12
六师技工学校	The Technical School of Division 6	816	549	1 446	96	75	2	4	5	10
七师技工学校	The Technical School of Division 7	218	157	673	20	12	1	2	1	4
八师技工学校	The Technical School of Division 8	109	282	485	228	116	40	10	10	52
十师技工学校	The Technical School of Division 10				9	5	4			

17－31 文化艺术事业基本情况

Basic Statistics on Culture and Art

(2010 年)

单　位	Unit	主管机关 Departmentin Charge	剧　种 Type of Drama	职工人数(人) Staff and Workers (person)	#演　员 Actors	演出场次数(场次) Number of Performances (time)	观众人次数(人次) Number of Spectators (person-time)
三师文工团	The Art Troupe of Division 3	三　师 Division 3	歌　舞 Song and Dance	43	43	320	1 000 000
石河子歌舞话剧团	Sihezi Song, Dance and Drama Troupe	八　师 Dvision 8	歌舞、话剧 Song, Dance and Drama	88	82	120	130 000
石河子豫剧团	Shihezi Yu Opera Troupe	八　师 Dvision 8	豫　剧 Yu Opera	39	38	110	110 000
九师豫剧团	The Yuju Opera Troupe of Division 9	九　师 Division 9	豫　剧 Yu Opera	43	43	111	98 000
十师秦剧团	The Yu Opera Troupe of Division 10	十　师 Division 10	秦　腔 Qin Opera	27	27	46	36 800
兵团秦剧团	Qin Opera Troupe of XPCG	兵团宣传部 Propaganda Department of XPCG	秦　腔 Qin Opera	57	46	48	24 000
兵团豫剧团	Yu Opera Troupe of XPCG	兵团宣传部 Propaganda Department of XPCG	豫　剧 Yu Opera	84	76	96	115 200
兵团杂技团	The Acrobatic Troupe of XPCG	兵团宣传部 Propaganda Department of XPCG	杂　技 Acrobatics	87	67	232	116 000
兵团歌舞团	The Song, Dance and Drama Troupe of XPCG	兵团宣传部 Propaganda Department of XPCG	歌舞、话剧 Song, Dance and Drama	155	142	120	20 000

17－32 报刊、杂志出版发行情况

Publication and Distribution of Newspaper and Magazines

（2010 年）

报刊、杂志名称 Name of Newspaper and Magazines	出版单位 Publishers	创办时间 The Initial Issue Time	出版期数（期） Publishing Issues (issue)	平均每期发行份数（份） Average Distribution Copiesper Issue(copy)	全年发行总份数（万份） Total Distribution Copies (10 000 copy)
兵团日报(汉) XPCG Daily(Han)	兵团党委 The Party Committee of XPCG	1953 年	358	70 000	2 486. 0
兵团日报(维) XPCG Daily(Uygur)	兵团党委 The Party Committee of XPCG	1953 年	104	3 400	35. 4
生活晚报 Life Evening Paper	兵团日报社 XPCG Daily Office	2001 年	104	80 000	932. 0
塔里木报 Tarim Paper	一师党委 The Party Committee of Division 1	1938 年	210	10 000	252. 0
绿原报 Luyuan Paper	二师党委 The Party Committee of Division 2	1948 年	108	12 000	129. 6
叶尔羌报 Yerqiang Paper	三师党委 The Party Committee of Division 3	1984 年	156	10 000	156. 0
叶尔羌报(维) Yerqiang Paper(Uygur)	三师党委 The Party Committee of Division 3	2003 年	104	5 000	52. 0
伊犁垦区报 Yili Reclamation Region Paper	四师党委 The Party Committee of Division 4	1988 年	100	10 000	100. 0
北疆开发报 Northern Part of XJ Development Paper	五师党委 The Party Committee of Division 5	1944 年	156	7 000	109. 2
准噶尔时报 Zhunger Times	六师党委 The Party Committee of Division 6	1983 年	150	13 000	195. 0
奎屯晨报 Kutun Mornig	七师党委 The Party Committee of Division 7	1950 年	210	10 000	210. 0
石河子日报 Shihezi Daily	八师党委 The Party Committee of Division 8	1950 年	210	15 000	315. 0
西陲时报 Western Frontier Times	九师党委 The Party Committee of Division 9	1984 年	100	6 000	60. 0
新疆北屯报 Xinjiang Beitun Paper	十师党委 The Party Committee of Division 10	1989 年	100	5 500	55. 0
天山建设报 Tianshan Construction Paper	建工师党委 The Party Committee of Construction Division	1993 年	100	10 000	100. 0
哈密开发报 Hami Development Paper	十三师党委 The Party Committee of Division	1993 年	100	10 000	100. 0
石河子广播电视报 Shihezi Broadcasting and TV Paper	石河子广播电视局 Shihezi Broadcasting and TV Bureau	1986 年	100	5 000	50. 0
石河子大学 Shihezi University	石河子大学 Shihezi University	1996 年	18	8 500	15. 3
塔里木大学 Tarim University	塔里木大学 Tarim University	1958 年	10	5 000	5. 0
兵团建设 XPCG Construction	兵团党委 The Party Committee of XPCG	1999 年	24	23 000	55. 2
新疆农垦经济 Xinjiang Nongken Economics	石河子大学 Shihezi University	1981 年	12	3 000	3. 6
新疆农垦科技 Xinjiang Nongken Science and Technology	兵团科技局 The Science and Technology Bureau of XPCG	1978 年	6	3 000	1. 8
兵团医学 XPCG Medicine	兵团卫生局 XPCG Health Bureau	1984 年	4	3 000	1. 2
兵团工运 XPCG Worker's Movement	兵团工会 XPCG Trade Union	1984 年	12	3 000	3. 6
绿　洲 Oasis	兵团文联 XPCG Literary and Art Federation	1957 年	12	2 500	3. 0
兵团党校学报 The Academic Journal of XPCG Party School	兵团党校 XPCG Party School	1989 年	12	3 000	3. 6
石河子大学学报(自然科学版) The Academic Journal of Shihezi University(Natural Science Edition)	石河子大学 Shihezi University	1997 年	6	1 200	0. 7

17—32 续表 Continued

(2010 年)

报刊、杂志名称 Name of Newspaper and Magazines	出版单位 Publishers	创办时间 The Initial Issue Time	出版期数(期) Publishing Issues (issue)	平均每期发行份数(份) Average Distribution Copiesper Issue(copy)	全年发行总份数(万份) Total Distribution Copies (10 000 copy)
石河子大学学报(哲学社会科学版) The Academic Journal of Shihezi University(Philosophy and Social Science Edition)	石河子大学 Shihezi University	1983 年	6	1 200	0.7
兵团教育学院学报 The Academic Journal of XPCG Educational College	兵团教育学院 XPCG Educational College	1991 年	6	600	0.4
农垦医学 Nongken Medicine	石河子大学医学院 The Medical College of Shihezi University	1979 年	6	600	0.2
塔里木大学学报 The Academic Journal of Tarim University	塔里木大学 Tarim University	1978 年	12	2 000	2.4
石河子科技 Shihezi Science and Technology	石河子市科技局 The Science and Technology Bureau of Shiheze City	1976 年	6	1 300	0.8
绿 风 Green Wind	石河子市文联 The Literary and Art Federation of Shiheze City	1978 年	6	3 000	1.8
兵团年鉴 XPCG Yearbook	兵团史志编纂委员会 XPCG Chorography Editorial Board	1986 年	1	2 500	0.3

17—33 广播电视基本情况

Basic Statistics on Radio and Television Industry

(2010 年)

单 位	Unit	广播节目综合人口覆盖率(%) Radio Coverage Rate of the Population (%)	电视节目综合人口覆盖率(%) TV Coverage Rate of Population (%)	有线广播电视用户数(万户) Number of Users of Cable Radio and TV (10 000 households)	广播电视总收入(万元) Revenue of Radio and TV (10000 yuan)	广播电视从业人员数(人) Staff and Workers of Radio and TV (person)	调频转播发射台(座) Relaying Stations of Frequency Modulation road-casting (unit)	电视转播发射台(座) TV Transmission and Relaying Stations (unit)
总 计	**Total**	**96.0**	**98.2**	**52.54**	**9 192**	**1 909**	**180**	**93**
兵团电视台				1.90	2 760	223		
一 师	Division 1	96.0	98.2	6.85	450	128	18	9
二 师	Division 2	96.0	98.5	3.39	550	131	17	12
三 师	Division 3	95.0	98.0	2.29	268	90	19	10
四 师	Division 4	95.5	98.0	3.87	925	177	21	8
五 师	Division 5	98.0	98.0	4.34	440	92	11	5
六 师	Division 6	96.5	99.0	7.66	701	223	21	8
七 师	Division 7	96.0	99.0	6.45	355	165	10	9
八 师	Division 8	97.0	99.0	7.99	1 905	292	18	10
九 师	Division 9	94.5	98.0	1.85	186	77	11	6
十 师	Division 10	94.5	98.0	2.60	302	93	12	7
十 二 师	Division 12	97.5	98.5	0.95	60	35	7	1
十 三 师	Division 13	95.5	98.0	1.95	205	161	11	4
十 四 师	Division 14	96.5	97.0	0.45	85	22	4	4

17—34 主要年份卫生机构、人员数

Number of Health Institutions and Persons Engaged in Health Institutons in Major Years

年份 Year	机构数(个) Institutions	#医院 Hospitals	人员总数(人) Total Personnel (person)	#卫生技术人员 Medical Technical Personnel	#医生(士) Doctors	#护士 Nurses	床位数(张) Beds(pcs)
1954	68	15	3 937	3 150	675	866	3 981
1957	247	11	3 629	2 885	933	835	4 606
1962	511	25	8 741	7 396	1 754	2 394	9 672
1965	537	29	14 047	11 334	3 223	2 427	14 752
1970	506	34	13 893	11 184	2 954	5 222	18 101
1975	189	7	12 977	9 733	2 765	2 466	12 801
1980	475	26	27 016	20 280	4 639	5 562	20 258
1985	595	213	28 015	22 361	7 869	5 238	19 873
1990	680	217	28 666	22 763	9 824	6 302	20 058
1995	622	222	29 952	23 781	10 090	6 720	19 872
1996	638	222	29 748	23 611	10 058	6 856	19 248
1997	632	221	29 895	24 098	10 376	7 037	18 702
1998	628	222	28 891	23 305	10 099	7 063	18 049
1999	626	221	28 349	23 022	10 292	7 192	17 483
2000	665	221	27 636	22 664	10 331	9 641	17 253
2001	664	220	26 682	21 907	10 226	2 171	16 915
2002	643	222	23 470	19 390	8 334	6 891	16 284
2003	677	235	24 139	20 329	9 050	6 970	16 235
2004	623	228	23 759	20 121	8 849	6 958	16 473
2005	673	225	24 332	20 617	9 023	7 186	16 537
2006	648	222	24 576	20 780	8 886	7 083	16 518
2007	1 506	225	24 553	20 470	8 751	7 195	17 045
2008	1 555	216	23 779	20 052	8 112	7 249	17 084
2009	1 327	212	23 997	20 278	8 063	7 647	17 561
2010	1 339	209	24 186	20 559	8 058	7 967	18 193

注:自 2002 年度开始,本表中医生和护士人数反映的是执业医师、执业助理医师和注册护士的人数。2007 年起机构数包含营利性机构。

Note: Number of doctors and nurses in this table have reflected the number of doctors with license and nurses registered since 2002. Number of health institutions included mercantil institutions since 2007.

17—35 卫生机构、床位、人员数

Number of Health Institutions, Beds and Persons

(2010 年)

类别	Category	机构数(个) Instituti-ons(unit)	床位数(张) Beds(pcs) 编制床位 Planned beds	实有床位 Real Beds	人员总数(人) Total Personnel (person)	卫生技术人员 Medical technical Personnel	其他技术人员 Other technical Personnel	管理人员 Manag-erial Personnel	工勤人员 Logisgic Personnel
总计	**Total**	**1 339**	**16 690**	**18 193**	**24 186**	**20 559**	**787**	**1 480**	**1 360**
医院合计	Total Hospitals	209	16 230	17 758	20 031	16 773	698	1 288	1 272
综合医院	Comprehensive Hospitals	202	15 612	16 653	19 514	16 395	644	1 270	1 205
中医医院	Traditional Chinese Medicine Hospitals	3	258	235	250	191	28	11	20
专科医院	Specialty Hospitals	4	360	870	267	187	26	7	47
妇幼保健所、站	Maternity and Child Care Centers	1	30	30	72	66	4	2	
门诊部	Clinics	8	62	47	225	183	15	17	10
卫生院	Health Centers	1	20		20	17		3	
社区卫生服务中心(站)	Community Health Service Centers	112	348	358	911	828	30	38	15
卫生所、医务室、社区医疗服务站	Health Offices, Health Centers, Community Health Service Stations	866			1 532	1 511			21
紧急救援中心	Urgent Rescue Center	1			22	14	2	1	5
疾病预防控制中心(防疫站)	Disease Prevention and Control Hospitals or Stations	105			1 085	933	27	94	23
卫生监督所	Health Direct Offices	29			200	168	3	30	7
采供血机构	Blood Collection and Supply Units	7			88	66	8	7	7

17—36 各师卫生机构、床位、人员数

Number of Health Institutions, Beds and Persons by Division

（2010年）

指标	Item	合计 Total	一师 Division 1	二师 Division 2	三师 Division 3	四师 Division 4	五师 Division 5	六师 Division 6	七师 Division 7
卫生机构（个）	**Health Institutions (unit)**	**1 339**	**116**	**117**	**67**	**56**	**76**	**152**	**160**
#医院	Hospitals	209	20	20	18	21	13	21	14
编制床位（张）	**Planned Beds (unit)**	16 690	1 860	1 519	1 043	1 333	656	1 752	1 885
实有床位数（张）	Real Beds (unit)	18 193	2 220	1 390	1 028	1 385	725	1 724	2 410
人员总数（人）	**Total Personnel (person)**	24 186	2 376	2 076	1 400	1 748	1 186	2 560	2 343
卫生技术人员	Medical Technical Personel	20 559	2 039	1 858	1 181	1 455	1 001	2 195	2 006
执业医师	Doctors with Licence	6 448	507	623	258	456	305	645	633
执业助理医师	Asistan Doctors with Licence	1 610	183	172	73	130	96	171	222
注册护士	Nurses Registered	7 967	917	708	474	532	367	885	701
药剂人员	Pharmaceutical Personnel	1 004	85	97	47	80	64	119	89
检验人员	Laborotory Technical Personnel	843	86	78	39	55	40	87	86
影像人员	Shadow Personnel	354	41	22	31	27	13	40	39
其他卫生技术人员	Other Health Technical Personnel	2 165	201	135	258	172	106	224	223
卫生监督员	Sanitation Supervisors	168	19	23	1	3	10	24	13
其他技术人员	Other Technical Personnel	787	34	43	34	73	24	99	51
管理人员	Managerial Personnel	1 480	174	72	132	137	89	134	158
工勤人员	Logistic Personnel	1 360	129	103	53	83	72	132	128
平均每千人口拥有卫生技术人员（人）	**Number of Health Technical Personnel per 1 000 Population (person)**	**8**	**7**	**10**	**6**	**7**	**9**	**7**	**9**

指标	Item	八师 Division 8	九师 Division 9	十师 Division 10	建工师 Construction Division	十二师 Division 12	十三师 Division 13	十四师 Division 14	兵团直属 Directly under XPCG
卫生机构（个）	**Health Institutions (unit)**	**382**	**49**	**33**	**18**	**42**	**41**	**8**	**22**
#医院	Hospitals	30	12	12	2	7	13	4	2
编制床位（张）	**Planned Beds (unit)**	2 543	612	670	110	260	930	176	1 341
实有床位数（张）	Real Beds (unit)	4 116	612	650	80	230	970	175	478
人员总数（人）	**Total Personnel (person)**	4 694	727	923	200	384	1 090	175	2 304
卫生技术人员	Medical Technical Personel	3 958	605	783	176	334	940	150	1 878
执业医师	Doctors with Licence	1 340	170	240	75	114	305	26	751
执业助理医师	Asistan Doctors with Licence	315	69	51	21	26	55	9	17
注册护士	Nurses Registered	1 493	229	291	56	122	381	59	752
药剂人员	Pharmaceutical Personnel	185	32	35	6	15	58	3	89
检验人员	Laborotory Technical Personnel	173	27	29	7	16	29	6	85
影像人员	Shadow Personnel	64	11	17	2	6	7	3	31
其他卫生技术人员	Other Health Technical Personnel	344	59	117	6	31	98	44	147
卫生监督员	Sanitation Supervisors	44	8	3	3	4	7		6
其他技术人员	Other Technical Personnel	172	37	29	12	3	17	6	153
管理人员	Managerial Personnel	236	51	60	8	26	93	7	103
工勤人员	Logistic Personnel	328	34	51	4	21	40	12	170
平均每千人口拥有卫生技术人员（人）	**Number of Health Technical Personnel per 1 000 Population (person)**	**7**	**8**	**10**	**4**	**5**	**12**	**4**	**34**

17—37 城市主要经济与社会指标

Major Economic and Social Indicators by City

计量单位:万元 (2010 年) (10 000 yuan)

指标	Item	石河子市 Shihezi City	阿拉尔市 Alaer City	图木舒克市 Tumushuke City	五家渠市 Wujiaqu City
年末总人口 (万人)	Total Population(year-end) (10 000 persons)	34. 70	17. 00	15. 55	9. 66
年平均人口 (万人)	Annual Average Population (10 000 persons)	34. 57	17. 20	15. 40	9. 62
常住人口	People Residing (10 000 persons)	31. 53	16. 80	14. 84	8. 77
年末总户数 (万户)	Total Households(year-end) (10 000 households)	12. 18	5. 26	4. 43	4. 10
年末单位就业人员数 (万人)	Employed Persons in Units (10 000 persons)	9. 64	4. 20	5. 48	1. 99
第一产业	Primary Industry	1. 24	3. 00	4. 02	0. 67
第二产业	Secondary Industry	5. 16	0. 46	0. 53	0. 38
第三产业	Tertiary Industry	3. 24	0. 74	0. 93	0. 94
城镇私营和个体就业人员 (人)	Employed Persons with Private Enterprises and Individual (person)	49 088	9 066	4 488	16 132
年末城镇登记失业人数 (人)	Registered Persons of Unemployment in Towns and Cities (person)	4 525		1 782	2 995
行政区域土地面积 (平方公里)	Administrative Areas (sq. km)	460	4 196	1 927	711
# 建成区面积	Developed Areas	27. 05	24. 00	14. 40	14. 16
地区生产总值(当年价格)	Gross Domestic Product(the Current Prices)	1 349 995	578 330	206 825	510 500
第一产业	Primary Industry	91 825	363 190	118 973	62 870
第二产业	Secondary Industry	686 175	122 595	44 041	259 209
# 工 业	Industry	550 975	93 615	25 681	190 184
第三产业	Tertiary Industry	571 995	92 545	43 811	188 421
# 交通运输、仓储及邮政业	Transport, Storage and Postal Service	58 895	4 093	1 330	22 859
金融业	Finance	80 281	550		28 474
房地产业	Real Estate	46 198	7 368	1 892	24 307
地区生产总值(2005 年价格) (万元)	Gross Domestic Product(the Comparable Prices in 2005)	1 150 284	429 652	158 290	405 932
人均地区生产总值 (元)	Per Capita GDP (yuan)	39 051	33 624	13 430	53 067
地区生产总值增长率 (%)	Growth Rate of GDP (%)	18. 1	16. 2	24. 5	22. 8
地方财政一般预算内收入 (万元)	Local Governments Revenue	137 555	13 103	5 500	22 882
# 各项税收	Taxes	122 618	12 307	4 925	21 586
地方财政一般预算支出 (万元)	Local Governments Expenditures	172 440	20 915	15 111	29 424
年末金融机构存款余额 (万元)	Deposits of Finance Institution at the year-end	2 222 025	388 100	138 257	556 931
# 城乡居民储蓄年末余额	Balance of Saving Deposits in Urban and Rural Areas	1 376 356	248 394	127 028	260 651
年末金融机构各项贷款余额 (万元)	Loans of Finance Institution at the year-end	1 277 303	51 700	81 556	534 013
保费收入 (万元)	Premium Income	92 973		1 941	27 153
赔款、给付 (万元)	Claim and Payment	18 387		744	15 449
工业企业数 (个)	Number of Industrial Enterprises (unit)	113	49	12	32
# 内资企业	Domestic-funded Enterprises	102	48	12	32
工业总产值(当年价) (万元)	Total Output Value of Industry(at Current Prices)	2 029 595	359 195	60 558	368 420
# 内资企业	Domestic-funded Enterprises	1 864 287	343 806	60 558	368 420
流动资产合计 (万元)	Total Circulating Assets	1 496 929	231 968	50 203	391 321
利润总额 (万元)	Total Profits	237 788	30 316	4 685	11 462
年末邮政局数 (所)(处)数	Number of Post Offices (unit)	24	12	8	4
邮政业务收入 (万元)	Business Income of Post	3 392	1 231	309	1 015
电信业务收入 (万元)	Business Income of Telecommunications	35 213	2 860	2 714	3 607
固定电话年末用户数 (万户)	Number of Fixed Telephone Subscribers (10 000 subscriber)	16. 44	6. 11	1. 83	3. 20
移动电话年末用户数 (万户)	Number of Mobile Telephone Subscribers (10 000 subscriber)	50. 43	7. 35	3. 16	6. 30

17－37 续表　Continued

计量单位:万元　　　　(2010 年)　　　　(10 000 yuan)

指　　标	Item	石河子市 Shihezi City	阿拉尔市 Alaer City	图木舒克市 Tumushuke City	五家渠市 Wujiaqu City
综合能源消费量（万吨/标准煤）	General Energy Consumption (10 000 tons of SCE)	443.4	90.8	7.7	20.4
全年用电量（万千瓦时）	Electric Consumption (10 000 kwh)	910 500	57 040	29 000	52 633
# 城乡居民生活用电（万千瓦时）	Electric Consumption for Urban and Rural Residential Use	14 356	5 489	3 510	17 317
限额以上批发和零售业商品销售总额	Commodity Sales Value of Enterprises Above Designated Size in Wholesale and Retail Sale Trade	1 016 797	23 126	3 400	182 516
社会消费品零售总额	Total Retail Sales of Consumer Goods	434 506	90 844	39 770	143 000
限额以上批发和零售企业数（个）	Number of Enterprises Above Designated Size in Wholesale and Retail Sale Trade (Unit)	46	4	1	4
当年新签项目(合同)个数（个）	Number of Contract Signed Newly (Unit)	1			
当年实际使用外资金额（万美元）	Contractual Value of Actually Utilizing Foreign Capital (USD 10 000)	300			
全社会固定资产投资总额	Investment of Fixed Assets	1 091 168	300 553	125 303	665 320
商品房屋销售面积（万平方米）	Floor Space of Merchandise House Saled (10 000 sq. m)	52.55	16.30	1.63	21.10
学校数（所）	Number of Schools (unit)				
# 高等学校	Institutions of Higher Education	1	1		2
中等职业教育学校	Specialized Secondary Schools	9		1	1
普通中学	Regular Secondary Schools	25	13	14	6
小　学	Primary Schools	11	21	12	6
在校学生数	Student Enrollment				
# 高等学校（人）	Institutions of Higher Education (person)	31 716	13 659		3 397
中等职业教育学校（人）	Specialized Secondary Schools (person)	12 888		519	1 889
普通中学（万人）	Regular Secondary Schools (10 000 persons)	2.98	1.01	1.08	0.85
小　学（万人）	Primary Schools (10 000 persons)	2.46	1.39	1.68	0.76
体育场馆数（个）	Number of Gymnasium (unit)	4	1		
剧场、影剧院数（个）	Theaters and Music Halls (unit)	1			1
公共图书馆图书总藏量（千册、件）	Books Published of Public Libraries (1 000 copies)	171	460		302
医院、卫生院床位数（张）	Number of Beds in Health Institutions (unit)	3 066	885	426	795
在岗职工平均人数（万人）	Average Staff and Workers on the Job (10 000 persons)	10.82	4.27	1.69	1.93
在岗职工工资总额	Total Wages of Staff and Workers on the Job	320 530	128 442	45 610	50 249
城镇居民人均可支配收入（元）	Per Capita Annual Disposable Income of Urban Households (yuan)	15 043	14 722	13 419	13 974
城镇居民人均消费支出（元）	Per Capita Annual Living Expenditures for Consumption of Urban Households (yuan)	10 885	11 520	12 770	11 409
人均住房建筑面积（平方米）	Per Capita Floor Space of Residential Buiding (sq. m)	27.00	32.47	32.01	27.86
基本养老保险参保人数（人）	Basci Old-Pension Persons (person)	165 925	43 354	15 072	33 100
基本医疗保险参保人数（人）	Medical Insurance Persons (person)	311 958	45 397	21 880	38 600
失业保险参保人数（人）	Retired and Resigned Persons (person)	83 769	43 354	13 883	21 874
城市维护建设资金支出	Funds Expenditures of City Maintenance and Developments	32 043	950	2 930	2 844
年末实有城市道路面积（万平方米）	Area of Paved Roads (10 000 sq. m)	627	67	77	280
全年供水总量（万吨）	Supply of Tap Water (10 000 tons)	6 166	1 250	485	454
液化石油气供气量（吨）	Liquefied Petroleum Gas (ton)	1 000	880	1 248	1 740
年末实有公共汽车营运车辆（辆）	Number of Vehicles for Business Transportation (unit)	485	56	72	38
全年公共汽车客运总量（万人次）	Passenger Traffic of Buses (10 000 person-times)	7 800	180	123	641
年末实有出租汽车数（辆）	Number of Taxis (unit)	1 196	105	50	450
绿地面积（公顷）	Areas of Green Areas (hectare)	996	280	5 904	654
建成区绿化覆盖面积（公顷）	Greening Coverage Area of Urban Districts (hectare)	1 161	280	2 891	490

2011

BING TUAN

第十八篇

检查院、法院和司法局资料

Chapter 18 Data on Procurator's Offices, Courts and Judicial Affairs

简要说明

一、本篇资料主要内容

本篇资料主要反映兵团检察机关办理各类案件、律师工作及法院收案、结案的基本情况。

二、本篇资料来源

本篇资料分别由兵团检察院、法院、司法局提供，兵团统计局国民经济综合统计处整理。

Brief Introduction

1. Main Contents

The data in this chapter cover the basic conditions on cases dealt by procurator's offices, lawyer's work, case acceptance and settlement of courts in XPCG.

2. Sources of Data

The data in this chapter are provided by XPCG's Procuratorate, Court and the Bureau of Judicial Affairs and compiled by the Statistics Bureau of XPCG.

18—1 检察机关直接立案侦查案件情况

Cases under Direct Investigation by Procurator's Offices

(2010 年)

案件分类	Case Item	受案(件) Cases Accepted (case)	立案件数(件) Number of Cases Registered (case)	立案人数(人) Person of case Registered (person)	#要案 Key Case	结案件数(件) Number of Cases Settled (cases)	结案人数(人) Person of cases Settled(person)
总计	**Total**	**156**	**76**	**80**	**6**	**74**	**77**
贪污贿赂案件小计	**Sub-total of Cases on Corruption and Bribery**	**155**	**75**	**79**	**6**	**73**	**76**
贪污	Corruption	103	46	50	3	46	49
贿赂	Bribery	41	23	23	3	22	22
挪用公款	Misappropriation of Public Funds	11	6	6		5	5
集体私分	Collective Illegal Possession of Public Funds						
巨额财产来源不明	Unstated Source of Large Properties						
其他	Others						
渎职侵权案件小计	**Sub-total of Cases on Abuse and Dereliction of Duty**	**1**	**1**	**1**		**1**	**1**
滥用职权	Abuse of Power	1	1	1		1	1
玩忽职守	Dereliction o fDuty						
徇私舞弊	Fraudulent Practice						
其他	Others						

18—2 检察机关处理申诉案件情况

Appeals Handled by Procurator's Offices

计量单位:件 (2010 年) (case)

案件分类	Case Item	受理 Cases Accepted	立案复查 Cases Registered for Reinvestigation	结案 Cases Settled	改变原决定 Original Decision Changed
合计	**Total**	**4**	**3**	**2**	
不服检察机关处理决定小计	**Appealsagainst Decision of Procurator's Offices**	**1**	**1**	**1**	
不服不批捕	Appeals against Rejection of Arrest				
不服不起诉	Appeals against Rejection of Prosecuting	1	1	1	
不服撤案	Appeals against With drawal of the Case				
不服原免予起诉	Appeals against Original Exemption of Lawsuit				
其他	Others				
不服法院刑事判决裁定小计	**Appealsagainst Judgment of Criminal Case**	**3**	**2**	**1**	
刑罚执行中被害人申诉	Appeals of the Victimat the Punishment				
刑罚执行中被告人申诉	Appeals of the Defendant at the Punishment	2	1	1	
刑罚执行完毕后被害人申诉	Appeals of the Victim after the Punishment				
刑罚执行完毕后被告人申诉	Appeals of the Defendant after the Punishment	1	1		

18—3 检察机关审查批准、决定逮捕犯罪嫌疑人和提起公诉情况

Arrests of Criminal Suspects and Defendants under Public Prosecution Approved by Procurator's Offices

(2010 年)

指 标	Item	批捕、决定逮捕合计 Total of Arrests		决定起诉合计 Total of Public Prosecution	
		件 (Case)	人 (Person)	件 (Case)	人 (Person)
总 计	**Total**	**652**	**912**	**917**	**1 341**
公安、安全、监狱机关侦查案件小计	Sub-total of Requests by Departments of State and Public	612	868	851	1 271
危害国家安全案	Offences Against State Security	8	30	9	34
危害公共安全	Offences Against Public Security	29	31	90	93
破坏社会主义市场经济秩序案	Offences Against Socialist Economic Order	7	14	13	28
侵犯公民人身、民主权利案	Offences Against Citizens' personal and Democratic Rights	203	239	298	367
侵犯财产案	Offences Against Properties	326	482	385	641
妨害社会管理秩序案	Offences Against Social Management of Order	39	72	56	108
其他案件	Other Offences				
检察机关直接立案侦查案件小计	Sub-total of Cases Handled by Procuratorates	40	44	66	70
贪污贿赂案	Offences on Corruption and Bribery	39	43	65	69
渎职侵权案	Offences on Abuse and Dereliction of Duty	1	1	1	1

18—4 律师、公证、基层法律服务、人民调解工作基本情况

Basic Statistics on Lawyers, Notarization, Basic Law Servings and Demos Mediation

指 标		Item		2005	2009	2010
律师工作		**Lawyers**				
律师事务所	(所)	Law Offices	(unit)	37	39	39
执业律师	(人)	Lawyers	(person)	258	276	278
担任法律顾问	(家)	Units with Permanent Legal Advisers	(unit)	654	526	551
刑事诉讼辩护及代理	(件)	Agent of Criminal Defense	(case)	713	398	624
民事案件诉讼代理	(件)	Agent of Civil Case	(case)	4 028	2 865	3 168
经济案件诉讼代理	(件)	Agent of Economic Case	(case)	2 150	1 081	1 222
行政案件诉讼代理	(件)	Agent of Administration Action	(case)	52	240	215
非诉讼法律事务	(件)	Off-court Case	(case)	506	958	745
解答法律咨询	(人次)	Agent of Legal Advisory Services	(person)	8 275	12 475	13 500
索回赔欠款	(万元)	Claim for Compensation	(10 000 yuan)	9 764	12 500	12 900
公证工作		**Notarization**				
公证处	(个)	Notary Offices	(unit)	23	25	25
执业公证员	(人)	Notarial Personnel	(person)	56	56	58
办理公证文书	(件)	Notarized Document	(case)	50 985	31 338	48 096
基层法律服务工作		**Basic Law Servings**				
基层法律服务所	(所)	Basic Law Offices	(unit)	205	207	201
基层法律工作者	(人)	Basic Law Operator	(person)	494	569	484
担任法律顾问	(家)	Unitswith Permanent Legal Advisers	(unit)	2 841	2 648	2 687
代理民事经济诉讼事务	(件)	Agent of Civil Case	(case)	3 154	2 031	2 664
代理非诉讼事务	(件)	Agent of Off-court Case	(case)	1 869	988	1 025
审查办理合同和涉农事务	(件)	Censor and Transact Contract and Come Down to Agricultural Business	(case)		38 633	120 000
调解纠纷	(件)	Disputes Mediated	(case)		3 127	4 722
挽回经济损失	(万元)	Redeem Economic losing	(10 000 yuan)	11 900	13 750	12 300
人民调解工作		**People's Mediation**				
人民调解委员会	(个)	People's Mediation Committees	(unit)	4 723	3 962	3 734
调解人员	(人)	Mediators	(person)	23 731	21 428	21 402
调解民间纠纷	(件)	Civil Disputes Mediated	(case)	11 221	16 467	26 580
法律援助		**LawHelp**				
法律援助工作站	(个)	Law Help Station	(unit)		276	276
受理申请	(件)	Accepted	(unit)		1 989	2 450
获得批准	(件)	Approvaled	(unit)		1 840	2 399
办结	(件)	Settled	(unit)		1 840	2 399

18—5 法院民商事案件收案和结案情况

Civil and Commercial Cases Accepted and Settled by People's Court

计量单位:件 (2010 年) (case)

指 标	Item	收 案 Cases Accepted	结 案 Cases Settled	判 决 Judgement	裁 定 Adjudication	调 解 Mediation	移 送 Handover
民商事案件	**Civil and Commercial Case**	**11 452**	**11 589**	**3 077**	**3 524**	**4 930**	**58**
合同代位权纠纷	Contract Procuration Dispute	1	1			1	
合同撤消权纠纷	Contract Cancellation Dispute	9	8	4	3	1	
买卖合同纠纷	Business Contract Dispute	1 971	2 031	637	538	841	15
# 分期付款买卖合同	Installment Business Contracts	146	148	30	52	62	4
互 易	Reciprocity	4	34	9	9	16	
其 他	Other	1 512	1 497	474	369	643	11
房地产开发经营合同纠纷	Real Estate Development Contracts	53	52	21	21	8	2
# 土地使用权转让合同	Land Use Transfer Contracts	1	1		1		
商品房预售合同	Pre-sale Contracts of Commercial Houses	13	14	5	4	4	1
房屋拆迁合同	Building Dismanting Contracts	15	15	6	8	1	
其 他	Other	7	7	3	3	1	
供用电、水、气、热力合同纠纷	Electricity, Steam, Water and Heat Contract Disputes	263	263	22	194	47	
借款合同纠纷	Loan Contracts Disputes	1 091	1 096	296	302	494	4
# 金融机构同业拆借	Call Money of Financial Institutions	5	5	1	1	3	
企业之间借款	Loan Between Enterprises	3	4	1	1	2	
民间借贷纠纷	Non-governmental Loan Disputes	882	887	227	232	426	2
其 他	Other	90	88	16	32	38	2
借用合同纠纷	Borrow Contract Disputes	4	4	2		2	
租赁合同纠纷	Lease Contract Disputes	276	293	108	91	93	1
建设工程合同纠纷	Construction Engineering Contracts	248	258	105	74	73	6
# 设计合同纠纷	Design Contract Disputes	1					
施工合同纠纷	Construction Contract Disputes	118	124	57	33	30	4
其 它	Other	45	48	17	12	17	2
承揽合同纠纷	Undertake Contract Disputes	261	268	80	82	105	1
运输合同纠纷	Transportation Contract Disputes	105	104	38	31	30	5
仓储、保管合同纠纷	Warehouse and Storage Contract Disputes	6	7	5	1	1	
委托合同纠纷	Trust Contract Disputes	36	40	10	12	18	
居间合同纠纷	Intermediary Contracts	1	1			1	
担保合同纠纷	Guarantee Contract Disputes	105	104	29	13	62	
保险合同纠纷	Insurance Contract Disputes	29	30	13	10	7	
储蓄存款合同纠纷	Savings Deposit Contract Disputes	1	1			1	
信用卡纠纷	Credit Card	2	3	1		2	
证券合同纠纷	Security Contracts	6	6	4		2	
经营合同纠纷	Management Contract Disputes	150	150	60	41	49	
农村承包合同纠纷	Rural Contract Disputes	388	393	100	141	149	3
电信合同纠纷	Telecommunication Contracts	160	169	7	140	22	
服务合同纠纷	Service Contract Disputes	237	240	30	142	68	
劳动争议案件	Work Disputes	242	240	111	62	64	3
# 劳动合同	Labor Contracts	58	69	31	13	25	
集体劳动合同	Collective Labor Contracts		1	1			
事实劳动关系争议	Defact Labor Relation Disputes	3	3	2		1	
劳动保险	Labor Insurance	4	4	2	2		
其 他	Other	77	64	31	13	17	3
劳务合同纠纷	Labor Service Contract Disputes	649	648	142	198	306	2
其 他	Other	109	103	32	38	32	1
所有权及与所有权相关权利纠纷	Ownership and Relevant Ownership Ritht Disputes	673	675	248	211	216	
票据、证券权益纠纷	Bill and Securities Rithts and Interests Disputes	2	2	1	1		
股东权纠纷	Shareholder's Rights Disputes	19	15	8	6	1	
特殊侵权纠纷	Special Tort Disputes	363	370	58	166	144	2
人身权纠纷	Personal Rights Disputes	1 374	1 381	453	263	659	6
# 人身损害赔偿纠纷	Personal Harm Compensation Disputes	1 080	1 094	331	200	557	6
知识产权纠纷	Intellectual Property Disputes	8	8	3	5		
其 他	Other	39	38	6	28	4	
不当得利	Not Appropriate Make Profit	105	102	39	32	30	1
无因管理	No Reason Management	2	2		2		
适用特别程序案件	Apply the Special Procedure	86	97	8	89		
婚姻家庭纠纷	Marriages and Family Affairs	2 312	2 318	380	567	1 366	5
# 离 婚	Divorce	2 000	2 010	330	493	1 182	5
抚育费	Foster	71	73	11	20	42	
赡 养	Support	11	11	2	4	5	
继承纠纷	Inheritance Dispute	66	68	16	20	31	1
# 法定继承	Legal Inheritance	41	39	5	12	21	1
继承权确认纠纷	Inheritance Right Dispute	1	1	1			

18—6 法院各类申诉、申请再审案件收案和结案情况

Various Litigation, Application and Re-appeal Cases Accepted and Settled by People's Court

计量单位:件　　　　(2010 年)　　　　(case)

指　标	Item	收　案 Cases Accepted	结　案 Cases Settled	驳　回 Reject	撤　拆 Withdrawal	裁定或决定 Adjudication	终　结 Termination	其　他 Other
各类申诉、申请再审案件	**Various Litigation Application and Re-appeal Cases**	**438**	**435**	**181**	**132**	**110**	**2**	**10**
刑事案件	Criminal Cases	39	32	28	2	2		
民事案件	Civil Cases	380	384	141	130	106	2	5
# 婚姻家庭、继承案件	Marriages Family and Inheritance Cases	15	13	7	4	1		1
合同案件	Contract Cases	282	287	98	98	88	2	1
权属、侵权案件	Right Infringement Cases	83	84	36	28	17		3
行政案件	Administrative Cases	14	14	11		2		1
其　他	Others	5	5	1				4

18—7 法院执行案件收案和结案情况

Executive Cases Accepted and Settled by People's Court

计量单位:件　　　　(2010 年)　　　　(case)

指　标	Item	收　案 Cases Accepted	结　案 Cases Settled	不予执行 Rejection of Prosecuting	自动履行 Automatically Implement	和　解 Reconciliation	强制执行 Compulsory Execution	终　结 Termination	其他 Other
执行案件	**Executive Cases**	**3 227**	**3 627**	**4**	**721**	**404**	**1 802**	**483**	**213**
民事案件	Civil Cases	3 026	3 394	4	665	386	1 712	435	192
婚姻家庭、继承	Marriages Family and Inheritance	269	293		80	55	111	37	10
合　同	Contract	1 731	2 013	3	441	254	850	327	138
权属、侵权	Authorityed and Infringement	970	1 040		132	65	737	67	39
其　他	Others	56	48	1	12	12	14	4	5
行政案件	Administrative Cases	2	4				2	2	
行政非诉审查与执行	Administrative Examination and Exection	25	23		2	2	19		
仲　裁	Arbitration	21	22		7		11	1	3
公证债权文书	Notary Creditor Document	25	33		12	5	8	6	2
其　他	Others	128	151		35	11	50	39	16

18—8 法院行政案件收案和结案情况

Administrative Cases Accepted and Settled by People's Court

计量单位:件　　　　(2010 年)　　　　(case)

指　标	Item	收　案 Cases Accepted	结　案 Cases Settled	判　决 Judgement	裁　定 Adjudication	行政赔偿 Mediation
行政案件	**Adminstrative Case**	**71**	**78**	**45**	**33**	
公　安	Pubilc Security	15	15	9	6	
土　地	Land	4	5	1	4	
城　建	City Construction	4	4		4	
劳动和社会保障	Labor and Social Security	21	20	13	7	
卫　生	Health					
司法行政	Administrative					
药　品	Drugs					
其　他	Others	27	34	22	12	

第十九篇

企业景气调查

Chapter 19 Enterprise Climate Survey

简要说明

一、本篇资料主要内容

本篇资料主要反映兵团企业景气调查的基本情况。包括企业宏观经济运行和微观经营现状的企业家信心指数、企业景气指数、企业生产总量景气指数、企业利润景气指数、流动资金景气指数等。

二、本篇资料来源

本篇资料由国家统计局兵团调查总队统计监测处提供。

三、本篇资料调查方法

企业景气调查是采取抽样调查方法，通过对八大行业，136家企业家定期进行问卷调查，并根据企业 家对企业经营状况及宏观经济形势判断和预期编制景气指数，从而对现实经济运行状况及其发展趋势进 行分析和预测。

景气指数又称为景气度，它是对企业景气调查中的定性指标通过定量方法加工汇总，综合反映某一特定调查群体或某一社会经济现象所处的状态或发展趋势的一种指标。通过其上升和下降的动态变化，反映经济发展状态及其变化过程。景气指数取值于0-200之间，100为景气指数的临界值；当景气指数大 于100时，表明经济状况趋于上升或改善，处于景气状态；当景气指数小于100时，表明经济状况趋于下降或恶化，处于不景气状态。

企业家信心指数也称宏观经济景气指数，是根据企业家对企业外部市场经济环境与宏观政策的认识、 看法、判断与预期而编制的指数，用以综合反映企业家对宏观经济环境的感受与信心。

企业景气指数也称企业综合生产经营景气指数，是根据企业家对本企业综合生产经营情况判断与预期编制的指数，用以反映企业综合生产经营状况。

Brief Introduction

1. Main Contents

The data in this chapter mainly show the basic conditions on enterprise climate survey in XPCG, including entrepreneurs' confidence index in macroeconomic operation and microeconomic operating status of enterprises, enterprises climate index, enterprise gross product climate index, profit climate index and circulating Fund climate index.

2. Sources of Data

The data are provided by Statistical Monitoring Section of Survey Office of the National Bureau of Statistics of XPCG.

3. Methodology of Survey

Enterprise climate survey is sampled one, which by way of regular questionnaire survey of eight sectors and 136 entrepreneurs, and in accordance with entrepreneurs' judgment and anticipation of operation conditions of enterprises and macroeconomic situations, the climate index is compiled in order to analyze and predict actual economic operation conditions and development trend.

The climate index is also called climate degree. It is an indicator, which by way of quantitative method, quantitative indicators in enterprise climate index survey are disposed and compiled to show comprehensively a status or development trend of a surveyed group of a social phenomenon. The dynamic changes of rise and decline show economic development status and its change process. The climate index ranges from 0 to 200. 100 are the critical value. When the climate index is larger than 100, it shows that the economic performance tends to pick up or improve and it is in a climate status. When it is lower than 100, it shows that the economic performance tends to decline or worsen and it is not in a climate status.

Entrepreneur's confidence index is also called the macroeconomic climate index. It is an index based on entrepreneur's recognition, views, judgment and anticipation of market economic circumstance outside enterprises and macro-policies. It is used to show comprehensively entrepreneur's impression and confidence of the macroeconomic circumstances. Business climate index is also called the comprehensive production and operation climate index of enterprises. It is an index based on entrepreneur's judgment and anticipation of comprehensive production and situation conditions of his own enterprise. It is used to show the comprehensive production and operation conditions of the enterprise.

19—1 企业家信心指数

Enterprisers Confidence Index

计量单位:% (2010 年) (%)

指 标	Item	一季度 1st Quarter	二季度 2st Quarter	三季度 3st Quarter	四季度 4st Quarter
企业家信心指数	**Enterprisers Confidence Index**	**144.2**	**139.0**	**137.0**	**144.6**
按企业登记注册类型分	**Grouped by Types of Registration**				
国有企业	State-owned Enterprises	133.4	131.0	129.5	136.4
有限责任公司	Limited Liability Corporations	146.8	145.2	145.2	146.8
股份有限公司	Share-holding Corporations Ltd.	156.3	144.7	141.7	160.0
私营企业	Private Enterprises	50.0	100.0	100.0	100.0
外商及港、澳、台商投资企业	Enterprises with Invstment from Foreign, HongKong, Macao and Taiwan	50.0	100.0	100.0	100.0
按行业门类分	**Grouped by Sector**				
工 业	Industry	121.8	128.1	123.5	127.1
采掘业	Mining and Quarrying	100.0	100.0	80.0	140.0
制造业	Manufacturing	118.2	123.8	124.0	125.0
电力、煤气及水的生产和供应业	Electricity, Gas and Water Production and Supply	157.1	171.4	142.9	128.6
建筑业	Construction	165.1	152.8	165.1	171.2
交通运输、仓储及邮电通信业	Transport, Storage, Post and Telecommunications	140.0	130.0	140.0	130.0
批发和零售业	Wholesale and Retail Sale Trade	151.3	145.5	139.8	159.3
房地产业	Real Estate Industry	150.0	141.7	150.0	133.3
社会服务业	Social Services	125.0	125.0	100.0	125.0
信息传输、计算机服务和软件业	Information Transmission, Computer Servcie and Software Industries	166.7	166.7	133.3	166.7
住宿和餐饮业	Accommodation and Catering Trade	133.3	122.2	144.4	144.4
按企业规模分	**Grouped by Size of Enterprises**				
大型企业	Large Scale Enterprises	162.0	165.8	164.5	174.2
中型企业	Medium Scale Enterprises	138.7	146.8	140.3	146.8
小型企业	Small Scale Enterprises	138.3	123.3	130.0	135.0
按特殊群体分	**Grouped by Special Group**				
上市公司	Listed Companies	181.0	168.5	166.1	175.0
国有控股企业	State-owned Share Holding	146.8	144.7	142.9	149.1

19－2 企业景气指数

Enterprises Climate Index

计量单位：%　　　　(2010 年)　　　　(%)

指　　标	Item	一季度 1st Quarter	二季度 2st Quarter	三季度 3st Quarter	四季度 4st Quarter
企业景气指数	**Enterprises Climate Index**	**124.9**	**125.5**	**138.5**	**135.6**
按企业登记注册类型分	**Grouped by Types of Registration**				
国有企业	State-owned Enterprises	124.1	120.2	130.9	128.7
有限责任公司	Limited Liability Corporations	138.7	132.3	141.9	151.6
股份有限公司	Share-holding Corporations Ltd.	143.8	145.7	140.0	148.7
私营企业	Private Enterprises	100.0	50.0	100.0	50.0
外商及港、澳、台商投资企业	Enterprises with Invstment from Foreign, HongKong, Macao and Taiwan	50.0	100.0	150.0	200.0
按行业门类分	**Grouped by Sector**				
工　业	Industry	132.0	126.8	135.4	138.2
采掘业	Mining and Quarrying	160.0	160.0	120.0	180.0
制造业	Manufacturing	123.4	116.3	127.8	129.0
电力、煤气及水的生产和供应业	Electricity, Gas and Water Production and Supply	157.1	157.1	185.7	157.1
建筑业	Construction	125.5	136.5	155.6	165.1
交通运输、仓储及邮电通信业	Transport, Storage, Post and Telecommunications	140.0	120.0	130.0	110.0
批发和零售业	Wholesale and Retail Sale Trade	140.7	129.3	131.6	157.9
房地产业	Real Estate Industry	116.7	125.0	141.7	125.0
社会服务业	Social Services	100.0	100.0	125.0	100.0
信息传输、计算机服务和软件业	Information Transmission, Computer Servcie and Software Industries	100.0	133.3	166.7	166.7
住宿和餐饮业	Accommodation and Catering Trade	144.4	133.3	122.2	122.2
按企业规模分	**Grouped by Size of Enterprises**				
大型企业	Large Scale Enterprises	152.6	170.3	176.2	173.6
中型企业	Medium Scale Enterprises	137.1	133.9	140.3	150.0
小型企业	Small Scale Enterprises	123.3	113.3	126.7	126.7
按特殊群体分	**Grouped by Special Group**				
上市公司	Listed Companies	154.2	160.8	162.5	154.2
国有控股企业	State-owned Share Holding	137.3	133.5	139.2	147.3

19—3 企业生产总量景气指数

Enterprises Gross Product Climate Index

计量单位：% (2010 年) (%)

指 标	Item	一季度 1st Quarter	二季度 2st Quarter	三季度 3st Quarter	四季度 4st Quarter
企业生产总量景气指数	**Enterprises Gross Product Climate Index**	**94.5**	**128.6**	**138.3**	**108.0**
按企业登记注册类型分	**Grouped by Types of Registration**				
国有企业	State-owned Enterprises	107.1	120.8	135.6	103.8
有限责任公司	Limited Liability Corporations	101.6	127.4	122.6	127.4
股份有限公司	Share-holding Corporations Ltd.	107.8	123.2	111.7	138.1
私营企业	Private Enterprises	50.0	100.0	150.0	50.0
外商及港、澳、台商投资企业	Enterprises with Invstment from Foreign, HongKong, Macao and Taiwan		200.0	200.0	200.0
按行业门类分	**Grouped by Sector**				
工 业	Industry	106.1	118.1	114.5	106.3
采掘业	Mining and Quarrying	100.0	140.0	80.0	140.0
制造业	Manufacturing	104.6	120.4	115.5	101.2
电力、煤气及水的生产和供应业	Electricity, Gas and Water Production and Supply	128.6	100.0	142.9	100.0
建筑业	Construction	81.2	185.7	187.0	146.5
交通运输、仓储及邮电通信业	Transport, Storage, Post and Telecommunications	120.0	100.0	90.0	120.0
批发和零售业	Wholesale and Retail Sale Trade	115.6	99.6	109.6	155.1
房地产业	Real Estate Industry	83.3	133.3	133.3	100.0
社会服务业	Social Services	50.0	125.0	150.0	25.0
信息传输、计算机服务和软件业	Information Transmission, Computer Servcie and Software Industries	100.0	133.3	166.7	133.3
住宿和餐饮业	Accommodation and Catering Trade	100.0	133.3	155.6	77.8
按企业规模分	**Grouped by Size of Enterprises**				
大型企业	Large Scale Enterprises	96.5	119.5	126.2	105.4
中型企业	Medium Scale Enterprises	111.3	140.3	143.6	125.8
小型企业	Small Scale Enterprises	93.3	110.0	113.3	113.3
按特殊群体分	**Grouped by Special Group**				
上市公司	Listed Companies	99.0	121.2	124.6	112.9
国有控股企业	State-owned Share Holding	108.8	129.2	130.8	119.1

19—4 企业利润景气指数

Enterprises Profits Climate Index

计量单位:% (2010 年) (%)

指 标	Item	一季度 1st Quarter	二季度 2st Quarter	三季度 3st Quarter	四季度 4st Quarter
企业利润景气指数	**Enterprises Profits Climate Index**	**101.6**	**127.0**	**127.4**	**130.6**
按企业登记注册类型分	**Grouped by Types of Registration**				
国有企业	State-owned Enterprises	109.4	127.8	129.8	127.6
有限责任公司	Limited Liability Corporations	112.9	129.0	148.4	158.1
股份有限公司	Share-holding Corporations Ltd.	122.8	132.7	112.5	152.7
私营企业	Private Enterprises	50.0	50.0	100.0	50.0
外商及港、澳、台商投资企业	Enterprises with Invstment from Foreign, HongKong, Macao and Taiwan		100.0	100.0	200.0
按行业门类分	**Grouped by Sector**				
工 业	Industry	118.7	120.7	128.5	137.4
采掘业	Mining and Quarrying	80.0	100.0	140.0	140.0
制造业	Manufacturing	125.3	122.5	127.4	139.2
电力、煤气及水的生产和供应业	Electricity, Gas and Water Production and Supply	114.3	128.6	128.6	128.6
建筑业	Construction	66.5	155.5	166.5	190.5
交通运输、仓储及邮电通信业	Transport, Storage, Post and Telecommunications	90.0	90.0	90.0	110.0
批发和零售业	Wholesale and Retail Sale Trade	126.1	141.2	140.1	159.5
房地产业	Real Estate Industry	116.7	125.0	150.0	158.3
社会服务业	Social Services	50.0	150.0	100.0	100.0
信息传输、计算机服务和软件业	Information Transmission, Computer Servcie and Software Industries	100.0	133.3	100.0	100.0
住宿和餐饮业	Accommodation and Catering Trade	144.4	100.0	144.4	88.9
按企业规模分	**Grouped by Size of Enterprises**				
大型企业	Large Scale Enterprises	122.3	153.2	146.3	163.3
中型企业	Medium Scale Enterprises	111.3	135.5	140.3	154.8
小型企业	Small Scale Enterprises	110.0	115.0	130.0	130.0
按特殊群体分	**Grouped by Special Group**				
上市公司	Listed Companies	149.4	136.9	133.5	136.9
国有控股企业	State-owned Share Holding	120.3	133.2	139.9	148.6

19—5 企业流动资金景气指数

Enterprises Mobile Capital Climate Index

计量单位：%　　　　（2010 年）　　　　（%）

指　　标	Item	一季度 1st Quarter	二季度 2st Quarter	三季度 3st Quarter	四季度 4st Quarter
企业流动资金景气指数	**Enterprises Mobile Capital Climate Index**	**67.7**	**67.1**	**76.0**	**78.0**
按企业登记注册类型分	**Grouped by Types of Registration**				
国有企业	State-owned Enterprises	69.4	62.5	54.0	71.3
有限责任公司	Limited Liability Corporations	87.1	82.3	90.3	91.9
股份有限公司	Share-holding Corporations Ltd.	79.2	74.3	75.3	88.6
私营企业	Private Enterprises	50.0	50.0	100.0	50.0
外商及港、澳、台商投资企业	Enterprises with Invstment from Foreign, HongKong, Macao and Taiwan	200.0	200.0	200.0	200.0
按行业门类分	**Grouped by Sector**				
工　业	Industry	81.0	73.8	70.0	76.2
采掘业	Mining and Quarrying	80.0	100.0	100.0	100.0
制造业	Manufacturing	83.1	71.6	66.4	74.7
电力、煤气及水的生产和供应业	Electricity, Gas and Water Production and Supply	71.4	57.1	57.1	57.1
建筑业	Construction	76.3	67.8	82.1	82.1
交通运输、仓储及邮电通信业	Transport, Storage, Post and Telecommunications	60.0	70.0	30.0	60.0
批发和零售业	Wholesale and Retail Sale Trade	88.3	94.7	92.9	116.9
房地产业	Real Estate Industry	91.7	75.0	83.3	83.3
社会服务业	Social Services			50.0	50.0
信息传输、计算机服务和软件业	Information Transmission, Computer Servcie and Software Industries	33.3	66.7	100.0	66.7
住宿和餐饮业	Accommodation and Catering Trade	111.1	88.9	100.0	88.9
按企业规模分	**Grouped by Size of Enterprises**				
大型企业	Large Scale Enterprises	99.7	101.2	99.2	112.6
中型企业	Medium Scale Enterprises	83.9	69.4	79.0	85.5
小型企业	Small Scale Enterprises	71.7	75.0	68.3	76.7
按特殊群体分	**Grouped by Special Group**				
上市公司	Listed Companies	86.1	68.0	69.7	69.7
国有控股企业	State-owned Share Holding	79.8	74.1	74.7	83.8

19－6 企业货款拖欠景气指数

Climate Index of Enterprises Loan in Arrears

计量单位：%　　　　(2010 年)　　　　(%)

指　　标	Item	一季度 1st Quarter	二季度 2st Quarter	三季度 3st Quarter	四季度 4st Quarter
企业货款拖欠景气指数	**Climate Index of Enterprises Loan in Arrears**	**120.7**	**112.2**	**111.0**	**116.8**
按企业登记注册类型分	**Grouped by Types of Registration**				
国有企业	State-owned Enterprises	119.0	100.0	101.9	114.9
有限责任公司	Limited Liability Corporations	125.8	129.0	132.3	133.9
股份有限公司	Share-holding Corporations Ltd.	136.8	117.9	84.2	128.8
私营企业	Private Enterprises	150.0	100.0	100.0	100.0
外商及港、澳、台商投资企业	Enterprises with Invstment from Foreign, HongKong, Macao and Taiwan	100.0	100.0	100.0	100.0
按行业门类分	**Grouped by Sector**				
工　业	Industry	134.0	112.1	105.9	129.4
采掘业	Mining and Quarrying	160.0	140.0	80.0	160.0
制造业	Manufacturing	142.0	115.7	106.8	124.4
电力、煤气及水的生产和供应业	Electricity, Gas and Water Production and Supply	57.1	57.1	128.6	114.3
建筑业	Construction	100.1	109.3	109.5	111.2
交通运输、仓储及邮电通信业	Transport, Storage, Post and Telecommunications	120.0	140.0	120.0	140.0
批发和零售业	Wholesale and Retail Sale Trade	125.7	119.3	125.0	125.7
房地产业	Real Estate Industry	141.7	133.3	141.7	133.3
社会服务业	Social Services	100.0	50.0	75.0	50.0
信息传输、计算机服务和软件业	Information Transmission, Computer Servcie and Software Industries	133.3	100.0	100.0	100.0
住宿和餐饮业	Accommodation and Catering Trade	111.1	133.3	111.1	144.4
按企业规模分	**Grouped by Size of Enterprises**				
大型企业	Large Scale Enterprises	135.3	139.9	51.0	134.0
中型企业	Medium Scale Enterprises	129.0	117.7	122.6	121.0
小型企业	Small Scale Enterprises	120.0	110.0	116.7	130.0
按特殊群体分	**Grouped by Special Group**				
上市公司	Listed Companies	154.2	122.4	48.1	126.4
国有控股企业	State-owned Share Holding	129.4	117.3	113.6	126.7

19－7 企业固定资产投资景气指数

Enterprises Fixed Assets Investment Climate Index

计量单位：%　　　　(2010 年)　　　　(%)

指　　标	Item	一季度 1st Quarter	二季度 2st Quarter	三季度 3st Quarter	四季度 4st Quarter
企业固定资产投资景气指数	**Enterprises Fixed-Assets Investment Climate Index**	**101.7**	**134.1**	**117.1**	**95.0**
按企业登记注册类型分	**Grouped by Types of Registration**				
国有企业	State-owned Enterprises	111.9	132.6	114.9	90.0
有限责任公司	Limited Liability Corporations	80.7	117.7	125.8	96.8
股份有限公司	Share-holding Corporations Ltd.	128.8	163.0	109.8	136.0
私营企业	Private Enterprises	100.0	150.0	100.0	50.0
外商及港、澳、台商投资企业	Enterprises with Invstment from Foreign, HongKong, Macao and Taiwan	100.0	100.0	100.0	100.0
按行业门类分	**Grouped by Sector**				
工　业	Industry	100.9	128.1	123.8	106.1
采掘业	Mining and Quarrying	120.0	140.0	120.0	80.0
制造业	Manufacturing	87.9	126.5	122.5	108.6
电力、煤气及水的生产和供应业	Electricity, Gas and Water Production and Supply	157.1	128.6	142.9	114.3
建筑业	Construction	101.6	168.5	149.3	87.3
交通运输、仓储及邮电通信业	Transport, Storage, Post and Telecommunications	110.0	120.0	120.0	110.0
批发和零售业	Wholesale and Retail Sale Trade	98.4	111.6	107.6	95.3
房地产业	Real Estate Industry	83.3	116.7	100.0	91.7
社会服务业	Social Services	75.0	150.0	125.0	25.0
信息传输、计算机服务和软件业	Information Transmission, Computer Servcie and Software Industries	133.3	166.7	133.3	166.7
住宿和餐饮业	Accommodation and Catering Trade	111.1	111.1	77.8	77.8
按企业规模分	**Grouped by Size of Enterprises**				
大型企业	Large Scale Enterprises	144.1	167.5	100.3	123.8
中型企业	Medium Scale Enterprises	100.0	145.2	143.6	101.6
小型企业	Small Scale Enterprises	91.7	105.0	98.3	91.7
按特殊群体分	**Grouped by Special Group**				
上市公司	Listed Companies	142.6	181.0	130.5	186.7
国有控股企业	State-owned Share Holding	104.4	135.7	123.6	102.0

19—8 企业劳动力需求景气指数

Climate Index of Enterprises Labor Demand

计量单位：%　　(2010 年)　　(%)

指　标	Item	一季度 1st Quarter	二季度 2st Quarter	三季度 3st Quarter	四季度 4st Quarter
企业劳动力需求景气指数	**Climate Index of Enterprises Labour Demand**	**96.3**	**134.4**	**130.0**	**92.4**
按企业登记注册类型分	**Grouped by Types of Registration**				
国有企业	State-owned Enterprises	90.0	124.6	119.5	99.5
有限责任公司	Limited Liability Corporations	100.0	124.2	124.2	108.1
股份有限公司	Share-holding Corporations Ltd.	109.0	114.7	109.6	104.9
私营企业	Private Enterprises	100.0	150.0	100.0	50.0
外商及港、澳、台商投资企业	Enterprises with Invstment from Foreign, HongKong, Macao and Taiwan	50.0	150.0	150.0	150.0
按行业门类分	**Grouped by Sector**				
工　业	Industry	107.5	109.3	107.6	116.1
采掘业	Mining and Quarrying	120.0	140.0	80.0	100.0
制造业	Manufacturing	100.6	103.1	112.7	116.1
电力、煤气及水的生产和供应业	Electricity, Gas and Water Production and Supply	142.9	128.6	100.0	128.6
建筑业	Construction	103.2	195.2	188.4	76.3
交通运输、仓储及邮电通信业	Transport, Storage, Post and Telecommunications	100.0	120.0	130.0	140.0
批发和零售业	Wholesale and Retail Sale Trade	79.0	86.9	91.5	115.3
房地产业	Real Estate Industry	83.3	133.3	108.3	58.3
社会服务业	Social Services	75.0	175.0	125.0	
信息传输、计算机服务和软件业	Information Transmission, Computer Servcie and Software Industries	100.0	100.0	133.3	100.0
住宿和餐饮业	Accommodation and Catering Trade	122.2	155.6	155.6	133.3
按企业规模分	**Grouped by Size of Enterprises**				
大型企业	Large Scale Enterprises	100.3	112.1	105.2	104.1
中型企业	Medium Scale Enterprises	103.2	133.9	133.9	101.6
小型企业	Small Scale Enterprises	90.0	116.7	113.3	106.7
按特殊群体分	**Grouped by Special Group**				
上市公司	Listed Companies	119.7	105.6	108.3	96.8
国有控股企业	State-owned Share Holding	100.9	127.5	119.9	103.0

19—9 企业产品订货景气指数

Enterprisee Production Ordered Climate Index

计量单位：% (2010 年) (%)

指标	Item	一季度 1st Quarter	二季度 2st Quarter	三季度 3st Quarter	四季度 4st Quarter
企业产品订货景气指数	**Enterprisee Production ordered Climate Index**	**102.4**	**120.6**	**121.6**	**92.5**
按企业登记注册类型分	**Grouped by Types of Registration**				
国有企业	State-owned Enterprises	101.6	124.1	121.2	96.1
有限责任公司	Limited Liability Corporations	106.5	116.1	124.2	112.9
股份有限公司	Share-holding Corporations Ltd.	129.7	120.1	114.0	141.1
私营企业	Private Enterprises	50.0	50.0	50.0	
外商及港、澳、台商投资企业	Enterprises with Invstment from Foreign, HongKong, Macao and Taiwan	50.0	100.0	100.0	150.0
按行业门类分	**Grouped by Sector**				
工 业	Industry	94.7	114.7	115.5	110.9
采掘业	Mining and Quarrying	80.0	120.0	100.0	140.0
制造业	Manufacturing	96.0	117.2	118.2	106.5
电力、煤气及水的生产和供应业	Electricity, Gas and Water Production and Supply	100.0	100.0	100.0	114.3
建筑业	Construction	133.1	181.0	169.3	103.7
交通运输、仓储及邮电通信业	Transport, Storage, Post and Telecommunications	90.0	100.0	90.0	100.0
批发和零售业	Wholesale and Retail Sale Trade	112.2	83.0	100.3	139.1
房地产业	Real Estate Industry	116.7	116.7	116.7	75.0
社会服务业	Social Services	50.0	125.0	125.0	
信息传输、计算机服务和软件业	Information Transmission, Computer Servcie and Software Industries	100.0	100.0	100.0	100.0
住宿和餐饮业	Accommodation and Catering Trade	122.2	144.4	155.6	111.1
按企业规模分	**Grouped by Size of Enterprises**				
大型企业	Large Scale Enterprises	157.3	170.1	166.4	169.5
中型企业	Medium Scale Enterprises	101.6	125.8	127.9	108.1
小型企业	Small Scale Enterprises	101.7	100.0	105.1	95.0
按特殊群体分	**Grouped by Special Group**				
上市公司	Listed Companies	143.5	138.4	139.3	152.6
国有控股企业	State-owned Share Holding	112.6	125.9	126.7	110.7

19—10 企业融资景气指数

Enterprises Financing Climate Index

计量单位：% (2010 年) (%)

指标	Item	一季度 1st Quarter	二季度 2st Quarter	三季度 3st Quarter	四季度 4st Quarter
企业融资景气指数	**Enterprises Financing Climate Index**	**71.6**	**83.0**	**66.7**	**78.0**
按企业登记注册类型分	**Grouped by Types of Registration**				
国有企业	State-owned Enterprises	61.1	75.6	65.0	65.5
有限责任公司	Limited Liability Corporations	80.7	85.5	77.4	93.6
股份有限公司	Share-holding Corporations Ltd.	115.3	101.9	53.7	115.3
私营企业	Private Enterprises	50.0	50.0	50.0	50.0
外商及港、澳、台商投资企业	Enterprises with Invstment from Foreign, HongKong, Macao and Taiwan	150.0	150.0	150.0	150.0
按行业门类分	**Grouped by Sector**				
工　业	Industry	84.1	82.0	63.6	86.2
采掘业	Mining and Quarrying	100.0	60.0	60.0	120.0
制造业	Manufacturing	83.0	85.8	65.2	83.0
电力、煤气及水的生产和供应业	Electricity, Gas and Water Production and Supply	71.4	71.4	57.1	71.4
建筑业	Construction	83.8	69.5	69.5	79.0
交通运输、仓储及邮电通信业	Transport, Storage, Post and Telecommunications	60.0	100.0	70.0	80.0
批发和零售业	Wholesale and Retail Sale Trade	80.9	101.6	90.9	106.9
房地产业	Real Estate Industry	83.3	83.3	83.3	91.7
社会服务业	Social Services	25.0	50.0	25.0	25.0
信息传输、计算机服务和软件业	Information Transmission, Computer Servcie and Software Industries	100.0	100.0	66.7	100.0
住宿和餐饮业	Accommodation and Catering Trade	55.6	77.8	66.7	55.6
按企业规模分	**Grouped by Size of Enterprises**				
大型企业	Large Scale Enterprises	143.9	143.9	67.2	140.8
中型企业	Medium Scale Enterprises	82.3	77.4	77.4	83.9
小型企业	Small Scale Enterprises	60.0	80.0	61.7	76.7
按特殊群体分	**Grouped by Special Group**				
上市公司	Listed Companies	154.7	129.7	44.3	129.7
国有控股企业	State-owned Share Holding	80.0	85.8	70.9	88.0

2011 BING TUAN

第二十篇

其他资料

Chapter 20 Other Data

简要说明

本篇资料综合反映兵团劳动和社会保障、水利、开发区发展、扶贫团场及社会团体基本情况。

一、兵团社会保障统计资料主要包括兵团企事业单位及个人参加基本养老保险、基本医疗保险、工伤保险、生育保险、失业保险等各类社会保险人数、缴费和发放、支出情况。由兵团劳动和社会保障局整理提供。

二、水利基本情况统计资料主要包括水利资金投入、灌溉面积、饮水安全，堤防、渠道及机电井数量。由兵团水利局整理提供。

三、开发区情况主要包括兵团石河子市国家级经济技术开发区基本情况和主要经济社会情况。由兵团农八师统计局整理提供。

四、兵团扶贫农场基本情况主要包括列入国家和兵团扶贫范围的农牧团场基本情况和主要经济社会情况。由兵团发展和改革委员会整理提供。

五、兵团社会团体情况主要包括兵团各级社会团体、民办非企业基本情况，兵团级社会团体单位名录。由兵团民政局整理提供。

Brief Introduction

The data in this chapter show basic conditions of labor and social security, water conservancy, development zone, farms of poverty reduction and public organizations.

1. The data on social security of XPCG cover mainly the persons, funds collection and expenditure of enterprises, institutions and individuals, participating in basic old-pension, medical insurance, industrial injury insurance, birth insurance, unemployment insurance and etc, which are provided by the Bureau of labor and Social Security of XPCG.

2. The data cover mainly the basic conditions on water conservancy, including total water conservancy fund input, irrigated area, drinking water safety, canal length, electromechanical well, which are provided by the Bureau of Water Conservancy.

3. The data cover mainly the basic conditions on development zone, including conditions on economy and society of National Shihezi Economic and Technological Development Zone of XPCG, which are provided by the Statistics Bureau of Shihezi.

4. The data cover mainly the basic conditions on farms of poverty reduction, including conditions on economy and social of farms of poverty reduction at the level of XPCG and State, which are provided by the Development and Reform Commission of XPXG.

5. The data cover mainly the basic conditions on f public organizations, including basic statisies on public organization, civil-run non-enterprises units and names of public organizations at the level of XPCG, which are provided by the Bureau of Civil Affairs.

20—1 基本养老保险情况

Conditions of Basic Old-Pension

（2010 年）

指　标	Item	参保职工期末人数（人） Active Contributors at the Initial Stage (person)	实际缴费人员期末数（人） Active Contributors at the Final Stage (person)	离退休（职）人员期末数（人） Retirees and Retirees with Honours at the Final Stage(person)	#退休人员 Retirees	本期办理退休人员（人） Retirement in the Year (person)	应发养老金额（万元） Payable Persion (10 000 yuan)	#退休金 Retiement Pension	实发养老金额（万元） Actually Payed Persion (10 000 yuan)	#退休金 Retirement Pension
总　计	**Total**	**814 696**	**767 810**	**526 401**	**514 524**	**74 487**	**917 950**	**876 926**	**917 950**	**876 926**
企　业	**Enterprises**	**621 856**	**586 175**	**449 395**	**438 007**	**13 436**	**852 010**	**812 589**	**852 010**	**812 589**
国有企业	State-owned Enterprises	607 676	572 013	447 196	435 808	13 318	848 239	808 818	848 239	808 818
集体企业	Collective-owned Enterprises	140	140	590	590	2	824	824	824	824
其他企业	Others	13 930	13 920	1 608	1 608	115	2 945	2 945	2 945	2 945
港澳台及外资企业	Enterprises with Funds from Hong Kong, Macao, Taiwan and Foreign	110	102	1	1	1	2	2	2	2
机关、事业	**Institutions**	**1 132**	**1 132**	**1 211**	**722**	**16**	**3 138**	**1 535**	**3 138**	**1 535**
其　他	**Others**	**191 708**	**180 503**	**75 795**	**75 795**	**61 035**	**62 802**	**62 802**	**62 802**	**62 802**

指　标	Item	社会化发放人数（人） Retirees Payed by Social Institutions (person)	社会化发放养老金金额（万元） Pension Payed by Social Institutions (10 000 yuan)	缴费基数总额（万元） Payment Base Amount(10 000yuan)		全额缴拨（万元） Full Payment (10 000 yuan)			
				单　位 Unit	个　人 Individual	单位应缴金额 Payable Amount by Units	单位实缴金额 Actual Payment Amount by Units	个人应缴金额 Payable Amount by Individuals	个人实缴金额 Actual Payment Amount by Individuals
总　计	**Total**	**526 401**	**917 950**	**964 366**	**1 272 778**	**193 615**	**192 380**	**132 764**	**132 396**
企　业	**Enterprises**	**449 395**	**852 010**	**961 970**	**1 012 535**	**192 393**	**191 158**	**81 004**	**80 636**
国有企业	State-owned Enterprises	447 196	848 239	939 657	990 222	187 931	186 696	79 219	78 851
集体企业	Collective-owned Enterprises	590	824	186	186	37	37	15	15
其他企业	Others	1 608	2 945	21 954	21 954	4 390	4 390	1 756	1 756
港澳台及外资企业	Enterprises with Funds from Hong Kong, Macao, Taiwan and Foreign	1	2	173	173	35	35	14	14
事　业	**Institutions**	**1 211**	**3 138**	**2 396**	**2 396**	**1 222**	**1 222**	**191**	**191**
其　他	**Others**	**75 795**	**62 802**		**257 847**			**51 569**	**51 569**

20—2 各师基本养老保险情况

Conditions of Basic Old-Pension by Division

（2010 年）

单 位	Unit	参保职工期末人数（人） Active Contributors at the Initial Stage (person)	实际缴费人员期末人数（人） Active Contributors at the Final Stage (person)	离退休（职）人员期末人数（人） Retirees and Retirees with Honours at the Final Stage(person)	#退休人员 Retirees	本期办理退休人员（人） Retirement in the Year (person)	应发养老金额（万元） Payable Persion (10 000 yuan)	#退休金 Retiement Pension	实发养老金额（万元） Actually Payed Persion (10 000 yuan)	#退休金 Retirement Pension
总 计	**Total**	**814 696**	**767 810**	**526 401**	**514 524**	**74 487**	**917 950**	**876 926**	**917 950**	**876 926**
一 师	Division 1	86 417	83 411	50 952	49 670	3 716	94 429	89 320	94 429	89 320
二 师	Division 2	68 738	63 099	57 312	55 800	7 566	100 450	93 511	100 450	93 511
三 师	Division 3	33 668	33 426	22 058	21 226	2 347	40 127	37 037	40 127	37 037
四 师	Division 4	79 295	77 355	51 701	50 642	7 098	92 773	89 330	92 773	89 330
五 师	Division 5	39 613	38 110	17 518	17 140	2 739	32 399	30 564	32 399	30 564
六 师	Division 6	89 270	88 746	61 078	60 285	11 140	102 495	100 393	102 495	100 393
七 师	Division 7	75 685	57 859	50 343	49 459	7 080	84 603	82 347	84 603	82 347
八 师	Division 8	198 274	195 132	127 886	125 230	23 440	214 606	207 997	214 606	207 997
九 师	Division 9	24 705	23 608	18 938	17 846	2 148	34 408	30 464	34 408	30 464
十 师	Division 10	24 005	22 894	19 296	18 812	2 692	34 515	32 339	34 515	32 339
建 工 师	Construction Division	10 410	9 658	8 980	8 832	182	15 285	14 596	15 285	14 596
十 二 师	Division 12	19 374	19 284	12 052	11 895	1 163	20 308	19 537	20 308	19 537
十 三 师	Division 13	27 012	25 712	13 036	12 799	1 617	23 050	22 391	23 050	22 391
十 四 师	Division 14	9 585	9 578	4 259	4 159	170	8 335	7 880	8 335	7 880
兵团直属	Directly under XPCG	28 645	19 938	10 992	10 729	1 389	20 167	19 220	20 167	19 220

单 位	Unit	社会化发放人数（人） Retirees Payed by Social Institutions (person)	社会化发放养老金金额（万元） Pension Payed by Social Institutions (10 000 yuan)	缴费基数总额（万元） Payment Base Amount(10 000yuan)		全额缴拨（万元） Full Payment (10 000 yuan)			
				单 位 Unit	个 人 Individual	单位应缴金额 Payable Amount by Units	单位实缴金额 Actual Payment Amount by Units	个人应缴金额 Payable Amount by Individuals	个人实缴金额 Actual Payment Amount by Individuals
总 计	**Total**	**526 401**	**917 950**	**964 366**	**1 272 778**	**193 615**	**192 380**	**132 764**	**132 396**
一 师	Division 1	50 952	94 429	134 600	155 048	26 920	26 920	15 648	15 648
二 师	Division 2	57 312	100 450	89 090	117 720	17 818	17 818	12 891	12 891
三 师	Division 3	22 058	40 127	43 640	53 655	8 728	8 728	5 007	5 007
四 师	Division 4	51 701	92 773	69 928	136 913	14 728	14 728	14 224	14 224
五 师	Division 5	17 518	32 399	54 318	59 143	10 863	10 863	5 311	5 311
六 师	Division 6	61 078	102 495	82 133	133 316	16 427	16 427	15 165	15 165
七 师	Division 7	50 343	84 603	75 635	91 500	15 127	14 325	9 224	9 029
八 师	Division 8	127 886	214 606	246 634	315 221	49 327	49 327	33 448	33 448
九 师	Division 9	18 938	34 408	22 853	26 558	4 571	4 571	2 569	2 569
十 师	Division 10	19 296	34 515	24 484	32 024	4 897	4 897	3 466	3 466
建 工 师	Construction Division	8 980	15 285	17 838	20 588	3 566	3 566	1 977	1 977
十 二 师	Division 12	12 052	20 308	26 762	34 924	5 352	5 352	3 774	3 774
十 三 师	Division 13	13 036	23 050	30 406	40 926	6 082	6 082	4 537	4 537
十 四 师	Division 14	4 259	8 335	14 220	14 402	2 844	2 844	1 174	1 174
兵团直属	Directly under XPCG	10 992	20 167	31 825	40 840	6 365	5 932	4 349	4 176

20—3 参加职工基本医疗保险人员及缴费基数情况

Staff and Workers Participating in Medical Insurance and Fund Collection

(2010 年)

单 位	Unit	基本医疗参保人数(人) Active Contributors of Basic Medical Insurance (person)	年末在岗职工 Staff and Workers on the Job at the Final Stage	年末退休人员 Retirees at the Final Stage	统帐结合缴费基数总额(万元) Payment Base Amount (10 000 yuan)		单建统筹缴费基数总额(万元) Signal Payment Base Amount (10000 yuan)	特殊人员人数(人) Number of Special People(person)		
					单 位 Unit	个 人 Individual		医疗照顾人员 Persons Cared by Medical Treament	离休及老红军 Retirees with Honours and Veteran Red Army	1—6 级革命伤残军人 Disabled Army with Level 1 — Level 6
总 计	**Total**	**1 210 091**	**739 683**	**470 408**	**1 290 127**	**1 177 939**	**87 539**	**788**	**12 111**	**105**
企 业	Enterprises	1 015 416	578 284	437 132	1 095 257	989 892		20	11 198	100
事 业	Institutions	59 802	40 498	19 304	98 031	94 752		85	632	4
机 关	Governmental Organs	29 261	22 619	6 642	75 821	72 385		683	281	1
其 他	Other	105 612	98 282	7 330	21 018	20 910	87 539			

20—4 各师参加职工基本医疗保险人员及缴费基数情况

Staff and Workers Participating in Medical Insurance and Funds Collection by Division

(2010 年)

单 位	Unit	基本医疗参保人数(人) Active Contributors of Basic Medical Insurance (person)	年末在岗职工 Staff and Workers on the Job at the Final Stage	年末退休人员 Retirees at the Final Stage	统帐结合缴费基数总额(万元) Payment Base Amount (10 000 yuan)		单建统筹缴费基数总额(万元) Signal Payment Base Amount (10000 yuan)	特殊人员人数(人) Number of Special People(person)		
					单 位 Unit	个 人 Individual		医疗照顾人员 Persons Cared by Medical Treament	离休及老红军 Retirees with Honours and Veteran Red Army	1—6 级革命伤残军人 Disabled Army with Level 1 — Level 6
总 计	**Total**	**1 210 091**	**739 683**	**470 408**	**1 290 127**	**1 177 939**	**173 256**	**788**	**12 111**	**105**
一 师	Division 1	130 620	80 313	50 307	146 300	146 300	18 267	7	1 266	
二 师	Division 2	115 267	64 717	50 550	102 455	100 600	22 414	14	1 512	
三 师	Division 3	54 875	34 315	20 560	93 480	60 518	1 114	53	832	
四 师	Division 4	108 773	63 661	45 112	75 188	113 842	3 645		1 059	23
五 师	Division 5	57 044	41 091	15 953	66 653	66 653			378	
六 师	Division 6	136 349	84 390	51 959	103 699	103 699	26 868	48	807	22
七 师	Division 7	100 358	56 270	44 088	156 300	92 525		22	884	
八 师	Division 8	293 304	180 721	112 583	294 074	294 074	63 202	105	2 656	57
九 师	Division 9	40 574	23 847	16 727	47 089	12 895		10	1 092	
十 师	Division 10	42 598	25 481	17 117	32 125	32 125	7 540		484	
建工师	Construction Division	18 029	10 511	7 518	24 133	24 133	4 893	11	188	
十二师	Division 12	27 808	16 818	10 990	49 311	31 255		2	157	
十三师	Division 13	33 319	22 137	11 182	33 517	33 517	3 492	21	237	
十四师	Division 14	13 936	9 807	4 129	6 976	6 976			100	
兵团直属	Directly under XPCG	37 237	25 604	11 633	58 827	58 827	21 821	495	459	3

20—5 职工基本医疗保险费征缴情况

Couditions of Funds Collection in Staff and Workers Basic Medical Insurance Premium

计量单位:万元 （2010年） (10 000 yuan)

指标	Item	统帐结合缴费基数总额(万元) Payment Base Amount(10000 yuan)							单建统筹(万元) Signal Payment Base Amount (10000 yuan)	
		期初欠费 Arreas at the Initial Stage	应缴基本医疗保险费 Payable Basic Medical Insurance Premium			实缴基本医疗保险费 Actual Payment of Basic Medical Insurance Premium			应缴基本医疗保险费 Payable Basic Medical Insurance Premium	实缴基本医疗保险费 Actual Payment of Basic Medical Insurance Premium
			合计 Total	单位 Unit	个人 Individual	合计 Total	单位 Unit	个人 Individual		
总计	**Total**	**500**	**126 229**	**102 677**	**23 552**	**125 690**	**102 187**	**23 503**	**10 948**	**10 948**
企业	Enterprises	497	106 488	86 699	19 789	105 965	86 223	19 742		
事业	Institutions	3	10 095	8 199	1 896	10 079	8 185	1 894		
机关	Governmental Organs		7 651	6 203	1 448	7 651	6 203	1 448		
其他	Other		1 995	1 576	419	1 995	1 576	419	10 948	10 948

20—6 各师职工基本医疗保险费征缴情况

Conditions of Funds Collection in Staff and Workers Basic Medical Insurance Premium by Division

计量单位:万元 （2010年） (10 000 yuan)

指标	Item	统帐结合缴费基数总额(万元) Payment Base Amount(10000 yuan)							单建统筹(万元) Signal Payment Base Amount (10000 yuan)	
		期初欠费 Arreas at the Initial Stage	应缴基本医疗保险费 Payable Basic Medical Insurance Premium			实缴基本医疗保险费 Actual Payment of Basic Medical Insurance Premium			应缴基本医疗保险费 Payable Basic Medical Insurance Premium	实缴基本医疗保险费 Actual Payment of Basic Medical Insurance Premium
			合计 Total	单位 Unit	个人 Individual	合计 Total	单位 Unit	个人 Individual		
总计	**Total**	**500**	**126 229**	**102 677**	**23 552**	**125 690**	**102 187**	**23 503**	**10 948**	**10 948**
一师	Division 1		14 630	11 704	2 926	14 630	11 704	2 926	1 096	1 096
二师	Division 2		11 233	9 221	2 012	11 233	9 221	2 012	1 569	1 569
三师	Division 3		7 753	6 543	1 210	7 753	6 543	1 210	78	78
四师	Division 4		8 292	6 015	2 277	8 292	6 015	2 277	219	219
五师	Division 5		5 946	4 620	1 326	5 946	4 620	1 326		
六师	Division 6		10 370	8 296	2 074	10 370	8 296	2 074	1 746	1 746
七师	Division 7	495	11 481	9 631	1 850	10 942	9 141	1 801		
八师	Division 8		32 347	26 466	5 881	32 347	26 466	5 881	3 982	3 982
九师	Division 9		3 554	3 296	258	3 554	3 296	258		
十师	Division 10		3 533	2 891	642	3 533	2 891	642	678	678
建工师	Construction Division		2 655	2 172	483	2 655	2 172	483	245	245
十二师	Division 12		4 078	3 452	626	4 078	3 452	626		
十三师	Division 13		3 352	2 682	670	3 352	2 682	670	244	244
十四师	Division 14		533	393	140	533	393	140		
兵团直属	Directly under XPCG	5	6 472	5 295	1 177	6 472	5 295	1 177	1 091	1 091

20—7 职工基本医疗保险基金支出情况

Fund Paying in Staff and Workers Medical Insurance

（2010 年）

指 标	Item	在岗职工 Staff and Workers on the Job			退休人员 Retirees		
		费用支出（万元）Expenditure (10 000 yuan)	住院人次（人次）Inpatients (person)	累计院床日（床日）Accumulated Hospitalization Bed Days(day)	费用支出（万元）Expenditure (10 000 yuan)	住院人次（人次）Inpatients (person)	累计院床日（床日）Accumulated Hospitalization Bed Days(day)
总 计	**Total**	**36 802**	**80 320**	**1 022 385**	**96 953**	**168 137**	**2 391 631**
三级医疗机构	Medical Organswith Level3	16 468	17 727	252 180	39 787	34 746	532 447
二级医疗机构	Medical Organswith Level2	15 024	30 392	397 743	44 353	70 594	1 040 732
一级医疗机构	Medical Organswith Level1	5 310	32 201	372 462	12 813	62 797	818 452
未定级医疗机构	Not Evaluated Medical Organs						

20—8 各师职工基本医疗保险住院费用支出情况

Fund Paying for Hospitalization in Staff and Workers Medical Insurance by Division

（2010 年）

单 位	Unit	在岗职工 Staff and Workers on the Job			退休人员 Retirees		
		费用支出（万元）Expenditure (10 000 yuan)	住院人次（人次）Inpatients (person)	累计院床日（床日）Accumulated Hospitalization Bed Days(day)	费用支出（万元）Expenditure (10 000 yuan)	住院人次（人次）Inpatients (person)	累计院床日（床日）Accumulated Hospitalization Bed Days(day)
总 计	**Total**	**36 802**	**80 320**	**1 022 385**	**96 953**	**168 137**	**2 391 631**
一 师	Division 1	3 770	5 535	105 172	8 878	17 529	333 044
二 师	Division 2	3 592	7 386	83 858	11 319	19 179	248 863
三 师	Division 3	2 184	5 311	61 136	4 722	9 345	127 278
四 师	Division 4	1 317	5 386	66 469	4 403	8 275	199 406
五 师	Division 5	1 234	3 301	55 067	2 253	3 919	67 103
六 师	Division 6	4 166	8 756	108 197	12 407	23 409	291 052
七 师	Division 7	3 247	8 020	90 933	9 776	21 284	268 831
八 师	Division 8	9 081	22 396	254 479	23 599	34 273	415 840
九 师	Division 9	1 596	3 012	42 174	4 031	6 951	97 308
十 师	Division 10	1 144	2 457	30 268	3 083	6 104	80 794
建 工 师	Construction Division	814	987	12 583	2 928	3 444	45 098
十 二 师	Division 12	1 282	2 651	39 779	1 866	4 926	68 964
十 三 师	Division 13	1 051	2 420	35 869	2 562	4 047	72 143
十 四 师	Division 14	177	157	1 919	113	91	1 183
兵团直属	Directly under XPCG	2 147	2 545	34 482	5 013	5 361	74 724

20—9 参加工伤保险人员及基金征缴情况

Persons Participating in Industrial Injury Insurance and Fund Collection

（2010 年）

指 标 Item	参保职工人数（人） Active Contributors (person)	缴费基数总额（万元） Total Payment Base A mount (10 000 yuan)	应缴工伤保险费（万元） Payable Industrial Injury Insurance Premium(10 000 yuan)	实缴工伤保险费（万元） Actual Payment of Industrial Injury Insurance Premium(10 000 yuan)	本期补缴（万元） Overdue Payment at the Current Stage (10000 yuan)	期末累计欠费（万元） Accumulated Arrears at the Final Stage (10000 yuan)	享受待遇的受伤或致残人数（人） Number of Enjoying Industrial Injury and Disabled Treatment(person) 合 计 Total	# 职业病 Occupational Disease	一至四级 Level 1—Level 4	# 职业病 Occupational Disease
总 计 Total	**651 666**	**1 117 130**	**8 732**	**8 701**	**20**	**31**	**5 456**	**211**	**993**	**174**
企 业 Enterprises	610 406	1 025 145	8 209	8 178	20	31	5 380	211	991	174
事 业 Institutions	41 260	91 985	523	523			76		2	
其 他 Other										

单 位 Unit	享受待遇的受伤或致残人数（人） Number of Enjoying Industrial Injury and Disabled Treatment(person) 五至六级 Level 5—Level 6	# 职业病 Occupational Disease	七至十级 Level 7—Level 10	# 职业病 Occupational Disease	其 他 Other	# 职业病 Occupational Disease	因工死亡人数（人） Number of Death from Industrial Injury (person)	供养直系亲属（人） Number of Supporting Lineal Relative (person)
总 计 Total	**254**	**15**	**1 139**	**12**	**1 933**	**10**	**103**	**1 034**
企 业 Enterprises	250	15	1 114	12	1 899	10	102	1 024
事 业 Institutions	4		25		34		1	10
其 他 Other								

20—10 各师参加工伤保险人员及基金征缴情况

Persons Participating in Industrial Injury Insurance and Fund Collection by Division

(2010 年)

指 标	Item	参保职工人数（人） Active Contributors (person)	缴费基数总额（万元） Total Payment Base Amount (10 000 yuan)	应缴工伤保险费（万元） Payable Industrial Injury Insurance Premium (10 000 yuan)	实缴工伤保险费（万元） Actual Payment of Industrial Injury Insurance Premium (10 000 yuan)	本期补缴（万元） Overdue Payment at the Current Stage (10000 yuan)	期末累计欠费（万元） Accumulated Arrears at the Final Stage (10000 yuan)	享受待遇的受伤或致残人数（人） Number of Enjoying Industrial Injury and Disabled Treatment (person)			
								合 计 Total	# 职业病 Occupational Disease	一至四级 Level 1—Level 4	# 职业病 Occupational Disease
总 计	**Total**	**651 666**	**1 117 130**	**8 732**	**8 701**	**20**	**31**	**5 456**	**211**	**993**	**174**
一 师	Division 1	69 769	150 000	750	750			563	70	184	52
二 师	Division 2	50 762	93 781	958	958			695	83	182	78
三 师	Division 3	31 358	53 350	270	270			274	1	42	1
四 师	Division 4	62 727	75 609	104	104			141		25	
五 师	Division 5	38 929	62 528	565	565			512		29	
六 师	Division 6	64 154	98 872	606	606			605	29	218	15
七 师	Division 7	54 328	77 477	781	781	20		224		8	
八 师	Division 8	150 690	277 830	2 507	2 507			1 226		142	
九 师	Division 9	21 672	26 051	182	182			33		2	
十 师	Division 10	21 156	36 200	346	346			533		27	
建 工 师	Construction Division	23 511	47 941	516	516			46		3	
十 二 师	Division 12	14 176	26 296	280	280			170	6	29	6
十 三 师	Division 13	22 792	33 403	503	503			254	1	57	1
十 四 师	Division 14	9 498	14 391	25	25			43		1	
兵团直属	Directly under XPCG	16 144	43 401	339	308		31	137	21	44	21

单 位	Unit	享受待遇的受伤或致残人数（人） Number of Enjoying Industrial Injury and Disabled Treatment (person)						因工死亡人数（人） Number of Death from Industrial Injury (person)	供养直系亲属（人） Number of Supporting Lineal Relative (person)
		五至六级 Level 5—Level 6	# 职业病 Occupational Disease	七至十级 Level 7—Level 10	# 职业病 Occupational Disease	其 他 Other	# 职业病 Occupational Disease		
总 计	**Total**	**254**	**15**	**1 139**	**12**	**1 933**	**10**	**103**	**1 034**
一 师	Division 1	59	8	27	4	114	6	11	168
二 师	Division 2	27		91	5	111		17	267
三 师	Division 3	3		11		109		5	104
四 师	Division 4	1		20		68		3	24
五 师	Division 5	12		63		366		3	39
六 师	Division 6	24	7	121	3	182	4	13	47
七 师	Division 7	3		138		25		10	40
八 师	Division 8	47		513		353		20	151
九 师	Division 9			22		9			
十 师	Division 10	3		8		381		5	109
建 工 师	Construction Division	23		4				6	10
十 二 师	Division 12	11		35		67		1	27
十 三 师	Division 13	32		46		90		4	25
十 四 师	Division 14	1				34		2	5
兵团直属	Directly under XPCG	8		40		24		3	18

20—11 参加生育保险人员及基金征缴情况

Persons Participating in Birth Insurance and Fund Collection

(2010 年)

指 标 Item	参保职工人数（人） Active Contributors (person)	#女性 Female	缴费基数总额（万元） Payment Base Total Amount (10 000 yuan)	应缴生育保险费（万元） Payable Birth Insurance Premium (10 000 yuan)	实缴生育保险费（万元） Actual Payment of Birth Insurance Premium (10 000 yuan)	本期享受生育保险待遇人数（人） Persons Enjoying Birth Insurance Treatment (person)	#本期生育人数 Birth Number	#顺产人数 Birth Number	#计划生育手术人次 Family Planning Operations	#流产人数 Abortion Number
总 计 Total	**611 884**	**280 272**	**1 030 118**	**3 051**	**3 029**	**12 873**	**3 854**	**1 321**	**9 019**	**1 103**
企 业 Enterprises	576 015	264 249	951 381	2 828	2 806	12 186	3 287	1 207	8 899	1 049
事 业 Institutions	27 557	13 742	58 563	178	178	624	512	106	112	54
机 关 Governmental Organs	8 312	2 281	20 174	45	45	63	55	8	8	
其 他 Other										

20—12 各师参加生育保险人员及基金征缴情况

Persons Participating in Birth Insurance and Fund Collection by Division

(2010 年)

单 位 Unit	参保职工人数（人） Active Contributors (person)	#女性 Female	缴费基数总额（万元） Payment Base Total Amount (10 000 yuan)	应缴生育保险费（万元） Payable Birth Insurance Premium (10 000 yuan)	实缴生育保险费（万元） Actual Payment of Birth Insurance Premium (10 000 yuan)	本期享受生育保险待遇人数（人） Persons Enjoying Birth Insurance Treatment (person)	#本期生育人数 Birth Number	#顺产人数 Birth Number	#计划生育手术人次 Family Planning Operations	#流产人数 Abortion Number
总 计 Total	**611 884**	**280 272**	**1 030 118**	**3 051**	**3 029**	**12 873**	**3 854**	**1 321**	**9 019**	**1 103**
一 师 Division 1	69 769	32 095	134 000	134	134	1 220	711	142	509	87
二 师 Division 2	47 249	33 117	95 200	476	476	696	245	154	451	20
三 师 Division 3	29 926	13 466	47 700	205	205	778	403	322	375	150
四 师 Division 4	57 778	27 760	67 498	68	68	3 314	226	126	3 088	41
五 师 Division 5	37 914	16 631	61 628	196	196					
六 师 Division 6	64 539	26 259	101 878	232	232	934	394	51	540	284
七 师 Division 7	52 015	21 155	74 925	226	226	639	265	48	374	35
八 师 Division 8	150 696	62 714	278 180	563	563	2 125	745	121	1 380	67
九 师 Division 9	20 285	8 723	17 304	86	86	53	53	19		
十 师 Division 10	17 856	7 485	24 484	66	66	329	119	48	210	210
建工师 Construction Division	8 186	2 989	22 600	113	113	119	96	24	23	14
十二师 Division 12	13 904	9 382	25 677	128	128	772	101	25	671	101
十三师 Division 13	19 149	7 806	33 199	100	100	657	270	125	387	58
十四师 Division 14	9 382	4 780	14 145	141	141	1 029	70	65	959	5
兵团直属 Directly under XPCG	13 236	5 910	31 700	317	295	208	156	51	52	31

20—13 参加失业保险人员及基金征缴情况

Persons Participating in Unemployment Insurance and Fund Collection

(2010 年)

指 标	Item	参保职工人数(人) Active Contributors (person)	单位缴费基数总额(万元) Total Payment Fund (10 000yuan)	个人缴费基数总额(万元) Total Payment Fund (10 000yuan)	应缴失业保险费(万元) Payable Unemployment Insurance Premium (10 000yuan)	#个人 Individual	实缴失业保险费(万元) Actual Payment of Umenployment Insurance Premium (10 000yuan)	#个人 Individual
总 计	**Total**	**626 629**	**1 065 921**	**1 104 124**	**19 993**	**9 804**	**19 885**	**9 757**
企 业	Enterprises	585 414	966 338	1 004 663	18 088	8 882	17 980	8 835
事 业	Institutions	41 215	99 583	99 461	1 905	922	1 905	922
其 他	Other							

20—14 各师参加失业保险人员及基金征缴情况

Persons Participating in Unemployment Insurance and Fund Collection by Division

(2010 年)

指 标	Item	参保职工人数(人) Active Contributors (person)	单位缴费基数总额(万元) Total Payment Fund (10 000yuan)	个人缴费基数总额(万元) Total Payment Fund (10 000yuan)	应缴失业保险费(万元) Payable Unemployment Insurance Premium (10 000yuan)	#个人 Individual	实缴失业保险费(万元) Actual Payment of Umenployment Insurance Premium (10 000yuan)	#个人 Individual
总 计	**Total**	**626 629**	**1 065 921**	**1 104 124**	**19 993**	**9 804**	**19 885**	**9 757**
一 师	Division 1	69 818	137 400	137 200	1 373	686	1 373	686
二 师	Division 2	47 249	94 800	94 700	1 895	947	1 895	947
三 师	Division 3	31 358	53 350	53 350	1 067	534	1 067	534
四 师	Division 4	60 444	72 551	111 076	1 255	1 110	1 255	1 110
五 师	Division 5	37 396	59 491	59 491	318	106	318	106
六 师	Division 6	63 155	98 063	98 063	2 942	981	2 942	981
七 师	Division 7	59 710	78 187	78 165	1 563	782	1 499	757
八 师	Division 8	149 110	277 366	277 366	5 547	2 774	5 547	2 774
九 师	Division 9	21 433	27 846	27 846	835	279	835	279
十 师	Division 10	20 454	28 484	28 484	708	284	708	284
建 工 师	Construction Division	8 353	22 800	22 800	456	228	456	228
十 二 师	Division 12	13 955	26 200	26 200	524	262	524	262
十 三 师	Division 13	18 544	31 761	31 761	476	318	476	318
十 四 师	Division 14	9 501	14 422	14 422	170	78	170	78
兵团直属	Directly under XPCG	16 149	43 200	43 200	864	435	820	413

20—15 水利基本情况

Basic Statistics on Water Conservancy

指 标		Item		2009	2010
总灌溉面积	**(千公顷)**	**Total Irrigated Area**	**(1 000 hectares)**	**1 350. 57**	**1 362. 88**
有效灌溉面积		Effective Irrigated Area		1 009. 22	982. 35
# 机电提灌面积		Irrigated Area by Machines		757. 74	772. 61
# 机电井灌溉面积		Irrigated Area by Electric Wells		112. 74	110. 99
林地灌溉面积		Irrigated Woodland Area		173. 61	177. 75
园地灌溉面积		Irrigated Orchard Area		103. 93	137. 01
牧草地灌溉面积		Irrigated Pasture Area		23. 92	23. 88
其他灌溉面积		other Irrigated Area		39. 89	41. 88
节水灌溉面积	**(千公顷)**	**Water-Saving Irrigated Area**	**(1 000 hectares)**	**821. 36**	**841. 96**
# 喷灌面积		Sprinkling irrigated Area		37. 26	34. 99
微灌面积		Micro-Irrigation Area		657. 41	713. 83
渠道防渗面积		Canal Anti-Seepage Area		111. 58	83. 26
有效实灌面积	**(千公顷)**	**Effective Real Irrigated Area**	**(1 000 hectares)**	**999. 04**	**973. 64**
机电排灌面积	**(千公顷)**	**Machine-Irrigated Area**	**(1 000 hectares)**	**774. 63**	**774. 49**
# 纯排面积		Pure Discharging Area		16. 89	1. 88
饮水安全		**Drinking Water Safety**			
饮水安全达标人数	(万人)	People Drinking Water Attain Safety Standard	(10 000 persons)	131. 61	131. 14
其中:农村饮水基本安全人数	(万人)	Rural pelple Drinking Water Attain Safety Standard	(10 000 persons)	41. 44	55. 33
农村集中式供水人口	(万人)	Rural Concentrate of Water Supply Peoole	(10 000 persons)	182. 50	188. 72
农村自来水供水人口	(万人)	Rural Running Water Supply People	(10 000 persons)	181. 54	181. 61
堤 防		**Dike**			
堤防总长度	(公里)	Total Length of Dikes	(kilometer)	2 446. 46	2 477. 96
保护人口	(万人)	Protected Population	(10 000 persons)	152. 13	152. 77
保护耕地	(千公顷)	Cultivated Area Protected by Dikes	(1 000 hectares)	425. 46	422. 20
机电井		**Electromechanical Well**			
机电井眼数	(眼)	Number of Electromechanical Wells		14 833	15 651
# 深井眼数		Deep Wells			
已配套机电井眼数	(眼)	Number of Complete Electromechanical Wells		14 512	15 415
机电井装机容量	(千千瓦)	Installed Capacity of Electromechanical Wells	(Kilowatt)	629. 93	556. 84
水利总投入	**(万元)**	**Total Investment in Water Conservancy**	**(10 000 yuan)**		
本年水利资金总投入		Total Water Conservancy Fund Input in the Year		326 899	320 001
渠 道	**(公里)**	**Canal Length**	**(kilometer)**		
万亩以上灌区输水干渠总长度		Total Irrigation Canal Length above 10 000 acre		8 904	8 593
# 已防渗		Antiseepage		6 010	6 069
万亩以上灌区配水渠道(支、斗渠道)总长度		Total Trunk Canal above 10 000 acre		39 050	36 527
# 已防渗		Antiseepage		21 594	20 304

20—16 石河子市开发(合作)区主要情况

Basic Statistics on Development (Cooperation) Zones of Shihezi City

指标		Item		2009	2010
规划土地面积	**(公顷)**	**Planned Land Area**	**(Hectare)**	**1 121**	**1 121**
# 本年开发面积		Developed Area in the Year		77	139
土地出让面积	**(公顷)**	**Land Transfer Area**	**(Hectare)**	**86**	**124**
吸取土地出让金		Attracted Land Transfer Fund		16 190	28 255
就业人员平均人数	**(人)**	**Average Number of Employment Personnel**	**(Person)**	**45 076**	**56 100**
生产总值(当年价)	**(万元)**	**Gross Domestic Product(at Current Prices)**	**(10 000 yuan)**	**600 689**	**755 733**
第一产业		Primary Industry		710	1 000
第二产业		Secondary Industry		488 212	623 783
第三产业		Tertiary Industry		108 767	131 000
生产总值(2000 年价)	**(万元)**	**Gross Domestic Productat (at 2000 Prices)**	**(10 000 yuan)**	**529 967**	**644 188**
第一产业		Primary Industry		644	870
第二产业		Secondary Industry		434 101	533 235
第三产业		Tertiary Industry		95 222	110 084
固定资产投资完成额	**(万元)**	**Completion Value of Fixed Assets Investment**	**(10 000 yuan)**	**524 822**	**757 326**
# 基础设施投资		Infrastructure Investment		37 261	10 907
水		Water		44	517
电		Electricity		883	
路		Road		11 181	8 342
其他		Other		26 036	778
# 房屋建设投资额		Investment Value of Building Construction		36 022	61 459
房屋竣工面积	**(平方米)**	**Floor Space of Completed Buildings**	**(Sq. m)**	**858 824**	**2 044 000**
农业总产值	**(当年价,万元)**	**Total Out put Value of Agriculture**	**(at Current Prices,10 000 yuan)**	**1 918**	**2 703**
工业总产值	**(当年价,万元)**	**Total Out put Value of Industry**	**(at Current Prices,10 000 yuan)**	**1 621 578**	**2 010 649**
三资企业		Foreign-funded Enterprises		108 962	133 665
内资企业		Domestic-funded Enterprises		1 512 616	1 876 984
建筑业总产值	**(万元)**	**Total Out put Value of Construction**	**(10 000 yuan)**	**258 130**	**286 984**
实现税收	**(万元)**	**Realized Taxes Revenue**	**(10 000 yuan)**	**88 800**	**119 000**
进出口总额	**(万美元)**	**Total Value of Imports and Exports**	**(USD 10 000)**	**11 000**	**34 538**
进口		Imports		1 590	4 535
出口		Exports		9 410	30 003
当年注册登记企业数	**(个)**	**Number of Registered Enterprised in the Year**	**(unit)**	**100**	**113**
# 三资企业		Foreign-funded Enterprises		3	
内资企业		Domestic-funded Enterprises		97	113
当年注册登记企业资本	**(万元)**	**Capital of Registered Enterprises in the year**	**(10 000 yuan)**		**129 175**
# 三资企业	(万美元)	Foreign-funded Enterprises	(USD 10 000)	1 550	
内资企业	(万元)	Domestic-funded Enterprises	(10 000 yuan)	147 028	129 175
利用外资合同总额	**(万美元)**	**Total Contractual Value of Utilizing Foreign Capital**	**(USD 10 000)**	**2 560**	**378 000**
内联合同金额	**(万元)**	**Contractual Value of Domestic Co-operation**	**(10 000 yuan)**		**4 000 000**
外引内联实际利用外资总额	**(万美元)**	**Actually Utilized Foreign Capital Value of Foreign Attraction and Domestic Cooperation**	**(USD 10 000)**	**367**	**524 000**
期末全部投产(开业)企业数	**(个)**	**Number of Complete Operation(Starting Business) at Final Period**	**(unit)**	**812**	**692**
# 三资企业		Foreign-funded Enterprises		24	23
内资企业		Domestic-funded Enterprises		788	669
工业企业实现利税总额	**(万元)**	**Realized Profit and Tax Value of Industrial Enterprises**	**(10 000 yuan)**	**189 837**	**275 531**

20—17　扶贫团场基本情况

Basic Statistics on Helping Poverty-stricken Farms

指　　标		Item		2010
总人口	（人）	Total Population	(person)	785 650
# 职工总数		Total Staff and Workers		189 919
退休人数		Retired Persons		124 909
离休人数		Retired Veterans		3 618
土地面积	（千公顷）	Land Area	(1 000 hectares)	4 357.86
# 耕地面积		Cultivated Area		481.85
草原面积		Steppearea		1 874.95
林地面积		Woodland Area		239.44
果园面积		Orchard area		77.70
水产养殖面积		Culture Area		20.72
当年开工项目个数	（个）	Number of New-opened Works in the Year	(unit)	20
解决引用不安全水人口数	（万人）	Persons of Drinking Insecurity Water	(10 000 persons)	
解决饮水困难牲畜	（万头只）	Livestock of Drinks Difficultly Settled	(10 000 heads)	
住房年末实有面积	（万平方米）	Housing Area	(10 000 sq. m)	1 733.69
人均面积	（平方米）	Per Capita Area	(sq. m)	22
教学用房年末实有面积	（万平方米）	Housing Area for Teaching Use	(10 000 sq. m)	88.60
学生人均面积	（平方米）	Per Capita Floor Space of Students	(sq. m)	8
医疗用房年末实有面积	（万平方米）	Housing Area for Medical Treatment	(10 000 sq. m)	33.44
人均面积	（平方米）	Per Capita Area	(sq. m)	0.43
扶贫专项资金投入情况	（万元）	Poverty Reduction Fund Input	(10 000 yuan)	3 650
扶贫以工代赈资金		Work Relief Fund of Poverty Reduction		
财政专项扶贫资金		Governments Poverty Reduction Fund		2 000
扭亏措施费		Turnaround Fund		1 650
当年实现利润	（万元）	Profits	(10 000 yuan)	6 981

注：2010年兵团有97个贫困团场，其中：国家扶贫团场77个，兵团扶贫团场20个。
Note: There are 97 farms of poverty reduction in XPCG in 2010, of which there are 77 farms of poverty reduction at National level and 20 farms of poverty reduction at the XPCG level.

20—18 社会团体机构情况

Basic Statistics on Public Organization

计量单位:个 (2010年) (unit)

单位	Unit	年末实有社团 Actual Number of Public Organizations at the Year-end	按活动区域分 Grouped by Active District 省级社团 Public Organizations at the Provincial Level	地级社团 Public Organizations at the Prefectural Level	县级社团 Public Organizations at the County Level	职工人数(人) Staff and Workers (person)	#女性 Female
总计	**Total**	**684**	**100**	**236**	**348**	**7 077**	**2 969**
兵团本级	XPCG	100	100			721	201
一师	Division 1	116			116	482	217
二师	Division 2	111			111	2 533	1 178
三师	Division 3	17		12	5	17	9
四师	Division 4	39		16	23	126	36
五师	Division 5	19		14	5	110	29
六师	Division 6	55		20	35	386	109
七师	Division 7	35		34	1	187	122
八师	Division 8	101		101		1 310	654
九师	Division 9	18		17	1	332	71
十师	Division 10	41			41	467	184
建工师	Construction Division	4		3	1	8	6
十二师	Division 12	6		2	4	319	126
十三师	Division 13	8		8		23	8
十四师	Division 14	9		9		31	9
兵团直属	Directly under XPCG	5			5	25	10

20—19 民办非企业单位

Non-enterprises Units of Civil-Run

计量单位:个 (2010年) (unit)

单位	Unit	年末实有民办非企业单位 Actual Number of Non-enterprises Units of Civil-Run at the Year-end	按性质分 Grouped by Kindby Sector 法人 Corporation	合伙	个体 Individual	职工人数(人) Staff and Workers (person)	#女性 Female
总计	**Total**	**222**	**213**	**3**	**6**	**1 785**	**747**
兵团本级	XPCG	11	11			398	79
一师	Division 1	2			2	29	29
二师	Division 2	14	14			46	12
三师	Division 3	4	2	1	1	20	4
四师	Division 4	5	2		3	26	11
五师	Division 5						
六师	Division 6	6	5	1		41	
七师	Division 7						
八师	Division 8	170	170			1 120	521
九师	Division 9						
十师	Division 1	1		1		17	15
建工师	Construction Division	1	1			1	1
十二师	Division 12	8	8			87	75
十三师	Division 13						
十四师	Division 14						
兵团直属	Directly under XPCG						

20—20 兵团级社会团体名录

Names of Public Organizations at the Level of XPCG

(2010年)

社会团体名称	Name of Public Organizations	主管单位	Department in Charge
兵团工会	The Trade Union of XPCG	中华全国总工会	Annula Check and Only on Record National Labor Union of China
兵团妇女联合会	The Woman Union of XPCG	中华全国妇女联合会	National Women Federation of China
石河子大学纪检监察学会	The Disciplinary Supervision Society of Shihezi University	石河子大学	The Discipline Inspection Commission of XPCG Shihezi University
兵团农八师温州商会	Division 8 Wenzhou Commerce of XPCG	农八师经济技术协作办公室	The Division 8 Ecoomic Cooperation office of XPCG
兵团继续教育协会	The Continue Education Association of XPCG	兵团人事局	The Personnel Bureau of XPCG
兵团卫生思想政治工作促进研究会	The Thought Political Work Research Society of XPCG Health System	兵团卫生局	The Health Bureau of XPCG
兵团医学会	The Medicine Society of XPCG	兵团卫生局	The Health Bureau of XPCG
兵团医院协会	The Hospital Association of XPCG	兵团卫生局	The Health Bureau of XPCG
兵团护理学会	The Nursing Society of XPCG	兵团卫生局	The Health Bureau of XPCG
兵团预防医学会	The Preventive Medicine Society of XPCG	兵团卫生局	The Health Bureau of XPCG
兵团工人运动研究会	Labour Movement Reaearch Society of XPCG	兵团工会	The Trade Union of XPCG
兵团劳动模范协会	The Labor Model Association of XPCG	兵团工会	The Trade Union of XPCG
兵团职工技术协会	The Workers' Technology Association of XPCG	兵团工会	The Trade Union of XPCG
兵团生物有机肥行业商会	The Biology Organism Fertilizer Association of XPCG	兵团工商联	The Industry and Commerce Association of XPCG
兵团进出口商会	The Imports and Exports Chamber of XPCG	兵团工商联	The Industry and Commerce Association of XPCG
兵团公安文学艺术联合会	The Public Security Literature and Art Association of XPCG	兵团公安局	The Public Security Bureau of XPCG
兵团公安前卫体育协会	The Public Security Sports Association of XPCG	兵团公安局	The Public Security Bureau of XPCG
兵团警察协会	The Police Society of XPCG	兵团公安局	The Public Security Bureau of XPCG
兵团京剧戏迷票友协会	The Opera Fans Association of XPCG	兵团文联	The literature and Art Federation of XPCG
兵团诗词楹联家协会	The Verse Association of XPCG	兵团文联	The literature and Art Federation of XPCG
兵团摄影家协会	The Camerist Association of XPCG	兵团文联	The literature and Art Federation of XPCG
兵团人口理论研究会	The Population Theory Research Society of XPCG	兵团计生委	The Family Planning Commission
兵团计划生育协会	The Family Planning Association of XPCG	兵团计生委	The Family Planning Commission
兵团工程咨询协会	The Engineering Consultancy Association of XPCG	兵团发展与改革委员会	The Development and Reform Commission of XPCG
兵团企业联合会	The Enterprise Association of XPCG	兵团发展与改革委员会	The Development and Reform Commission of XPCG
兵团宏观经济学会	The Planning Society of XPCG	兵团发展与改革委员会	The Development and Reform Commission of XPCG
兵团律师协会	The Lawyer Association of XPCG	兵团司法局	The Judicial Bureau of XPCG
兵团老年人协会	The Old Man Association of XPCG	兵团民政局	The Civil Affairs Bureau of XPCG
兵团社区工作者协会	The Community Worker Association of XPCG	兵团民政局	The Civil Affairs Bureau of XPCG
兵团慈善总会	The Charity Federation of XPCG	兵团民政局	The Civil Affairs Bureau of XPCG
兵团公路学会	Accounting Society of XPCG	兵团交通局	The Ransportation Bureau of XPCG
兵团交通运输协会	The Transportation Conveyance of XPCG	兵团交通局	The Ransportation Bureau of XPCG
兵团道路运输协会	The Road Conveyance of XPCG	兵团交通局	The Ransportation Bureau of XPCG
兵团农产品加工业协会	The Farm Produce Process Association of XPCG	兵团农业局	The Agricultural Bureau of XPCG

20—20 续表 1 Continued

(2010 年)

社会团体名称	Name of Public Organizations	主管单位	Department in Charge
兵团花卉协会	The Floriculture Association of XPCG	兵团农业局	The Agricultural Bureau of XPCG
兵团学生联合会	The Student Union of XPCG	兵团团委	The Communist Youth League Commission of XPCG
兵团青少年工作研究会	The Juvenile Work Research Society of XPCG	兵团团委	The Communist Youth League Commission of XPCG
兵团青年企业家协会	The Youth Entrepreneur Association of XPCG	兵团团委	The Communist Youth League Commission of XPCG
兵团青年志愿者协会	The Youth Volunteer Association of XPCG	兵团团委	The Communist Youth League Commission of XPCG
兵团妇女理论婚姻家庭研究会	The Women Theories Marriage Family Research Society of XPCG	兵团妇女联合会	National Women Federation of XPCG
兵团纪检监察学会	The Disciplinary Supervision Society of XPCG	兵团纪检监察局	The Discipline Inspection Commission of XPCG
兵团机关妇女干部联谊会	The Woman Cadre Fraterity of XPCG Organ	兵团老干局	The Senile Cadres Bureau of XPCG
兵团老年书画协会	The Senile Painting and Caligraphy Association of XPCG	兵团老干局	The Senile Cadres Bureau of XPCG
兵团老年体育协会	The Senile Sports Association of XPCG	兵团老干局	The Senile Cadres Bureau of XPCG
兵团农垦经济研究会	Nongken Economics Research Society of XPCG	兵团党委政策研究室	The Policy Research office of the CPC of XPCG
兵团乒乓球协会	The Ping—pong Association of XPCG	兵团体育局	The Sports Bureau of XPCG
兵团人力资源管理协会	The Association Resource Control Association of XPCG	兵团劳动社会保障局	The Labour and Public Security Bureau of XPCG
兵团医疗保险研究会	The Medical Insurance Research Society of XPCG	兵团劳动和社会保障局	The Labour and Public Security Bureau of XPCG
兵团社会治安见义勇为协会	The XPCG Association of XPCG	兵团社会治安综合治理委员会	The Public Security Comprehensive Management Commission of XPCG
兵团会计学会	Accounting Society of XPCG	兵团财务局	The Financial Bureau of XPCG
兵团珠算心算学会	Abacus Society of XPCG	兵团财务局	The Financial Bureau of XPCG
兵团烟花爆竹行业协会	The Smoke Flower Firecracker Association of XPCG	兵团供销合作社	The Supply and Marketing Cooperation of XPCG
兵团棉花协会	The Cotton Association of XPCG	兵团供销合作社	The Supply and Marketing Cooperation of XPCG
兵团土地学会	The Land Society of XPCG	兵团国土资源局	The Land Resource Bureau of XPCG
兵团审计学会	The Auditing Society of XPCG	兵团审计局	The Auditing Bureau of XPCG
兵团城镇规划研究会	The Town Programming Research Society of XPCG	兵团建设局	The Building Bureau of XPCG
兵团女法官协会	The Woman Judge Association of XPCG	兵团法院	The People's Count of XPCG
兵团法官协会	The Judge Association of XPCG	兵团法院	The People's Count of XPCG
兵团国际人才交流协会	Xinjiang Association for International Expertise Exchange	兵团人事局	The Personnel Bureau t of XPCG
兵团党建研究会	The Party Building Theory Reaearch Society of XPCG	兵团党委组织部	The Organizational Department of XPCG
兵团张家港商会	Zhangjiagang Commerce of XPCG	兵团经济技术协作办公室	The Economic and Technological Co-operation Office of XPCG
兵团质量协会	The Quality Control Association of XPCG	兵团质量技术监督局	The Quality Control Bureau of XPCG
兵团软件行业协会	The Software Conveyance of XPCG	兵团信息化办公室	The Information Office of XPCG
兵团毛泽东屯垦思想研究会	The Garrison and Reclamation Research Society of Mao Zhedong Thought of XPCG	兵团党委宣传部	The Propaganda Department of XPCG
兵团职工思想政治研究会	The Workers' Thought Politics Research Society of XPCG	兵团党委宣传部	The Propaganda Department of XPCG
兵团新闻工作者协会	The Jounalist Association of XPCG	兵团党委宣传部	The Propaganda Department of XPCG
兵团作物学会	Farm Crop Association of XPCG	兵团科协	The Technology Association of XPCG

20—20 续表 2 Continued

(2010 年)

社会团体名称	Name of Public Organizations	主管单位	Department in Charge
兵团技术市场协会	The Market Technology Association of XPCG	兵团科技局	The Technology Bureau of XPCG
兵团棉花学会	The Cotton Society of XPCG	兵团科协	The Technology Association of XPCG
兵团统计学会	The Statistic Society of XPCG	兵团统计局	The Statistics Bureau of XPCG
兵团药学会	The Pharmaceutics Society of XPCG	兵团药监局	The Drugs Management Bureau of XPCG
兵团国际商会	International Commerce of XPCG	兵团贸促会	The Trade Promotes Commission of XPCG
兵团屯垦戍边理论研究会	United Guard Frontier Theories Research Society of XPCG	兵团党委宣传部	The Propaganda Department of XPCG
兵团工商业联合会	The Industry and Commerce Association of XPCG	兵团党委统战部	The United Front Deparment of the CPC of XPCG
兵团光彩事业促进会	The Gloss Career Promote Association of XPCG	兵团党委统战部	The United Front Deparment of the CPC of XPCG
兵团总商会	The Commerce Chamber of XPCG	兵团党委统战部	The United Front Deparment of the CPC of XPCG
兵团统一战线理论研究会	United Front Theories Research Society of XPCG	兵团党委统战部	The United Front Deparment of the CPC of XPCG
兵团海外联谊会	The Foreign Society of XPCG	兵团党委统战部	The United Front Deparment of the CPC of XPCG
兵团旅游协会	The Tour Association of XPCG	兵团旅游局	The Tour Bureau of XPCG
兵团监狱纪检监察学会	The Disciplinary Supervision Society of XPCG Prison	兵团监狱管理局	The Prison Management Bureau of XPCG
兵团监狱管理学会	The Prison Management Society of XPCG	兵团监狱管理局	The Prison Management Bureau of XPCG
兵团国际货运代理物流协会	The Goods Circulation and International Freight Transportation Agency of XPCG	兵团商务局	The Commerce Bureau of XPCG
兵团外语教育学会	The Foreign Language Education Society of XPCG	兵团教育局	The Education Bureau of XPCG
兵团石河子大学校友会	The Schoolfellow Society of Shihezi University	兵团教育局	The Education Bureau of XPCG
兵团青少年科技辅导员协会	The Juvenile Scientific and Technological Instructors Association of XPCG	兵团教育局	The Education Bureau of XPCG
兵团教育学会	The Education Society of XPCG	兵团教育局	The Education Bureau of XPCG
塔里木大学校友会	The Schoolfellow Society of Talimu University	兵团教育局	The Education Bureau of XPCG
兵团女检察官协会	The Female Procurator Association of XPCG	兵团检察院	XPCG Procuratorate
兵团检察官协会	The Procurator Association of XPCG	兵团检察院	XPCG Procuratorate
兵团老教授协会	The Old Professor of XPCG	兵团科协	The Technology Association of XPCG
兵团植物营养与肥料学会	The Plant Nourishment and Fertilizer Society of XPCG	兵团科协	The Technology Association of XPCG
兵团建设协会	The Building Association of XPCG	兵团建设局	The Building Bureau of XPCG
兵团红十字会	The Red Cross Association of XPCG	中国红十字会总会	The Red Cross Federation of China
兵团农资协会	The Agriculture Supplies Association of XPCG	兵团供销合作社	The Supply and Marketing Cooperation of XPCG
兵团老军垦文艺协会	The Old Garrison and Reclamation Literature Association of XPCG	兵团老干部局	The Senile Cadres Bureau of XPCG
兵团社会组织促进会	The Society Organizes Promote Association of XPCG	兵团民政局	The Civil Affairs Bureau of XPCG
兵团社区卫生协会	The Community Health Association of XPCG	兵团卫生局	The Health Bureau of XPCG
兵团机关事务工作协会	The Authority Affairs Association of XPCG	兵团机关事务管理局	The Authority Affairs Management Bureau of XPCG
兵团西域文化研究会	The Western Regions Culture Research Society of XPCG	兵团宣传部	The Propaganda Department of XPCG
兵团农二师华山中学教育基金会	The Education Foundation of Huashan Middle School Division 2 of XPCG	兵团教育局	The Education Bureau of XPCG
兵团青少年发展基金会	The Juvenile Development Foundation of XPCG	兵团团委	The Communist Youth League Commission of XPCG

2011

BING TUAN

第二十一篇

团场基本情况

Chapter 21 Basic Conditions of Farms

简要说明

一、本篇资料主要内容

本篇资料主要反映兵团各农牧团场基本概况和主要经济及社会指标完成情况。

二、本篇资料来源

本篇资料由兵团统计局、国家统计局兵团调查总队有关处室根据专业统计数据整理提供。

Brief Introduction

1. Main Contents

The data in this chapter mainly show the basic conditions of Farms and main indicators completed of economic and social.

2. Sources of Data

The data in this chapter are prepared and provided by relevant Section of the Statistics Bureau of XPCG and Survey Office of the National Bureau of Statistics of XPCG in accordance with professional statistical data.

21—1 团场基本情况

Basic Conditions of Farms

（2010 年）

指 标	Item	一师一团 Farm 1 Division 1	一师二团 Farm 2 Division 1	一师三团 Farm 3 Division1	一师四团 Farm 4 Division 1
法人代码	Enterprise Corporative Code	010628870	010628889	010628897	010633135
法人代表	Enterprise Corporative Representative	魏新元	乔国庆	吴宪文	李春生
所在县市	Under County or City	阿克苏市	阿克苏市	阿瓦提县	乌什县
邮政编码	Post Code	843008	843009	843011	843407
建场年份	The Year of Farm Establishment	1953	1956	1956	1956
行业分类	Sector Classification	种植业	种植业	种植业	种植业
团场占地面积 （千公顷）	Cover an Area of Farm Headquarters (1 000 hectares)	37.56	24.10	49.22	41.00
产业活动单位数合计 （个）	Number of Basic Units Engaged (unit)	38	27	28	23
# 农业连队	Agriculture Brigade	26	19	22	12
工 业	Industry	2	2		2
建筑业	Construction	1	1	1	
批发零售业	Wholesale and Retail Trade				
年末从业人员 （人）	Employed Persons (person)	6 940	4 133	5 898	3 031
第一产业	Primary Industry	5 107	2 945	4 552	2 231
第二产业	Secondary Industry	391	298	467	163
第三产业	Tertiary Industry	1 442	890	879	637
从业人员年平均人数 （人）	Annual Average Employed Persons (person)	6 954	4 225	4 487	3 155
境内公路里程 （公里）	Length of Highways (km)	147	80	118	122
团场电话年末用户 （户）	Telephone Customer of Farm at the Year-end (household)	1 865	3 100	1 689	2 319
移动电话年末用户 （户）	Mobile Phone Customer of Farm at the Year-end (household)	5 500	2 920	3 988	1 942
普通中学在校学生数 （人）	Student Enrollment in Regular Secondary Schools (person)	1 759	570	1 282	283
小学在校学生数 （人）	Student Enrollment in Primary Schools (person)	1 418	820	1 369	399
学龄儿童入学率 （%）	Percentage of School-age Enrolled (%)	100	100	100	100
初中升学率 （%）	Percentage of Junior Secondary Schools (%)	100	100	98	100
高中升学率 （%）	Percentage of Senior Secondary Schools (%)	74		89	96
医院、卫生院床位数 （床）	Beds of Hospitals and Health Centers (pcs)	95	50	50	38
医院、卫生院技术人员数 （人）	Medical Technical Personnel of Hospitals and Health Centers (person)	96	70	62	25
# 医 生	Doctors	20	20	41	8
卫生防疫人员数 （人）	Personnel of Epidemic Prevention (person)	11	6	11	4
参加基本养老保险人数 （人）	Persons Participation in Basic Old-Pension Insurance (person)	4 482	6 900	4 620	1 972
参加基本医疗保险人数 （人）	Persons Participation in Medical Insurance (person)	4 477	6 800	7 417	4 033
参加失业保险人数 （人）	Persons Participation in Unemployment Insurance (person)	4 482	3 441	4 620	1 972
团场居民最低生活保障人数 （人）	Bottommost Living Security of Farm Households (person)	876	153	131	464

21—1 续表 1

（2010 年）

指　　标	Item	一师五团 Farm 5 Division 1	一师六团 Farm 6 Division 1	一师七团 Farm 7 Division 1	一师八团 Farm 8 Division 1
法人代码	Enterprise Corporative Code	010633012	010633020	010633039	010633047
法人代表	Enterprise Corporative Representative	马金武	王永东	李世胜	张　塔
所在县市	Under County or City	温宿县	温宿县	阿拉尔市	阿拉尔市
邮政编码	Post Code	843015	843013	843016	843304
建场年份	The Year of Farm Establishment	1956	1958	1956	1958
行业分类	Sector Classification	种植业	种植业	种植业	种植业
团场占地面积　（千公顷）	Cover an Area of Farm Headquarters　(1 000 hectares)	79.10	12.64	17.13	22.09
产业活动单位数合计　（个）	Number of Basic Units Engaged　(unit)	31	23	26	17
# 农业连队	Agriculture Brigade	21	10	17	9
工　业	Industry	2	2	5	1
建筑业	Construction		1		1
批发零售业	Wholesale and Retail Trade				
年末从业人员　（人）	Employed Persons　(person)	8 246	4 059	3 779	5 035
第一产业	Primary Industry	6 193	2 938	2 648	4 110
第二产业	Secondary Industry	719	367	190	200
第三产业	Tertiary Industry	1 334	754	941	725
从业人员年平均人数　（人）	Annual Average Employed Persons　(person)	8 260	4 046	4 178	5 076
境内公路里程　（公里）	Length of Highways　(km)	104	125	52	97
团场电话年末用户　（户）	Telephone Customer of Farm at the Year-end　(household)	2 324	1 510	3 090	2 497
移动电话年末用户　（户）	Mobile Phone Customer of Farm at the Year-end　(household)	8 565	2 915	3 100	4 516
普通中学在校学生数　（人）	Student Enrollment in Regular Secondary Schools　(person)	972	552	835	808
小学在校学生数　（人）	Student Enrollment in Primary Schools　(person)	1 622	1 079	969	1 081
学龄儿童入学率　（%）	Percentage of School-age Enrolled　(%)	100	100	100	100
初中升学率　（%）	Percentage of Junior Secondary Schools　(%)	100	91	100	100
高中升学率　（%）	Percentage of Senior Secondary Schools　(%)	70	80	98	
医院、卫生院床位数　（床）	Beds of Hospitals and Health Centers　(pcs)	120	45	75	40
医院、卫生院技术人员数　（人）	Medical Technical Personnel of Hospitals and Health Centers　(person)	106	60	52	47
# 医　生	Doctors	54	15	25	21
卫生防疫人员数　（人）	Personnel of Epidemic Prevention　(person)	8	5	5	8
参加基本养老保险人数　（人）	Persons Participation in Basic Old-Pension Insurance　(person)	4 875	2 835	3 686	2 669
参加基本医疗保险人数　（人）	Persons Participation in Medical Insurance　(person)	6 680	4 588	5 098	2 677
参加失业保险人数　（人）	Persons Participation in Unemployment Insurance　(person)	3 539	2 835	2 965	2 669
团场居民最低生活保障人数　（人）	Bottommost Living Security of Farm Households　(person)	641	287	289	124

Continued

一师十团 Farm10 Division1	一师十一团 Farm 11 Division 1	一师十二团 Farm 12 Division 1	一师十三团 Farm 13 Division 1	一师十四团 Farm 14 Division 1	一师十六团 Farm 16 Division 1	二师三十一团 Farm 21 Division 2	二师三十二团 Farm 22 Division 2	二师三十四团 Farm 24 Division 2
010633063	010633071	01063308X	010633098	010628678	010628694	010633274	010633282	010633303
赵卫东	王立军	吴国丰	李平平	戚　麟	孙玉良	丁新民	程　伟	魏鸿彬
阿拉尔市	阿拉尔市	阿拉尔市	阿拉尔市	阿拉尔市	阿拉尔市	和静县	和静县	和硕县
843306	843303	843301	843302	843305	843018	841111	841303	841204
1958	1964	1958	1958	1958	1969	1950	1954	1959
种植业	种植业	种植业	种植业	种植业	种植业	种植业	种植业	种植业
52.48	40.67	24.19	23.33	61.20	15.30	28.33	62.32	21.32
29	24	24	25	19	23	31	35	27
17	15	7	15	10	14	13	16	16
1	3	1	2	3	2	2	3	3
	1		1	1	1	1	1	
		2				1		
6 280	4 696	3 916	6 096	3 660	5 433	3 901	6 959	4 130
3 774	3 650	2 546	4 756	2 934	3 888	2 792	4 725	2 858
527	351	243	276	104	505	164	608	267
1 979	695	1 127	1 064	622	1 040	945	1 626	1 005
6 790	4 702	3 952	6 205	3 706	5 433	3 952	6 737	4 098
90	113	97	25	172	44	102	45	105
4 200	2 132	3 856	3 302	1 833	3 213	3 319	5 289	3 378
4 000	1 702	3 995	2 912	2 346	3 201	1 985	3 598	3 420
898	551	1 348	1 224	464	1 002	417	827	747
3 143	735	1 842	1 684	711	1 752	625	1 254	1 362
100	100	100	100	100	100	100	100	100
100	100	100	100	100	100	86	100	100
90	74	100	100		98	58	94	63
121	54	100	110	50	63	55	100	65
149	55	83	62	44	78	56	107	67
44	20	17	10	21	41	36	55	45
8	6	8	11	4	9	7	6	7
3 980	2 190	1 839	3 850	3 082	3 655	3 075	5 030	3 169
4 100	3 600	2 290	6 315	3 082	3 655	3 083	5 030	3 177
4 100	2 200	1 839	3 850	3 082	3 655	3 079	5 030	3 172
257	1 236	576	292	240	582	819	856	934

21—1 续表 2

（2010 年）

指　　标	Item	二师 二十五团 Farm 25 Division 2	二师 二十七团 Farm 27 Division 2	二师 二十九团 Farm 29 Division 2	二师 三十团 Farm 30 Division 2
法人代码	Enterprise Corporative Code	010633311	010633338	010633354	010633362
法人代表	Enterprise Corporative Representative	陈　芳	隋健鹏	梁　永	王春瑞
所在县市	Under County or City	博湖县	焉耆回族自治县	库尔勒市	库尔勒市
邮政编码	Post Code	841403	841102	841005	841006
建场年份	The Year of Farm Establishment	1954	1959	1950	1954
行业分类	Sector Classification	种植业	种植业	种植业	种植业
团场占地面积　（千公顷）	Cover an Area of Farm Headquarters　(1 000 hectares)	5.39	27.84	70.61	27.71
产业活动单位数合计　（个）	Number of Basic Units Engaged　(unit)	14	25	54	31
# 农业连队	Agriculture Brigade	7	11	32	17
工　业	Industry	1	5	4	3
建筑业	Construction		1	1	1
批发零售业	Wholesale and Retail Trade				
年末从业人员　（人）	Employed Persons　(person)	1 790	3 805	9 391	3 858
第一产业	Primary Industry	1 092	2 742	6 910	2 661
第二产业	Secondary Industry	184	349	345	323
第三产业	Tertiary Industry	514	714	2 136	874
从业人员年平均人数　（人）	Annual Average Employed Persons　(person)	1 794	3 805	9 349	3 852
境内公路里程　（公里）	Length of Highways　(km)	42	55	85	33
团场电话年末用户　（户）	Telephone Customer of Farm at the Year-end　(household)	1 700	3 105	7 355	3 022
移动电话年末用户　（户）	Mobile Phone Customer of Farm at the Year-end　(household)	1 600	3 456	5 015	3 263
普通中学在校学生数　（人）	Student Enrollment in Regular Secondary Schools　(person)	285	1 005	1 482	561
小学在校学生数　（人）	Student Enrollment in Primary Schools　(person)	268	594	2 676	884
学龄儿童入学率　（%）	Percentage of School-age Enrolled　(%)	100	100	100	100
初中升学率　（%）	Percentage of Junior Secondary Schools　(%)	75	98	100	99
高中升学率　（%）	Percentage of Senior Secondary Schools　(%)		78	81	86
医院、卫生院床位数　（床）	Beds of Hospitals and Health Centers　(pcs)	30	50	94	50
医院、卫生院技术人员数　（人）	Medical Technical Personnel of Hospitals and Health Centers　(person)	31	58	129	60
# 医　生	Doctors	6	19	80	16
卫生防疫人员数　（人）	Personnel of Epidemic Prevention　(person)	6	5	12	4
参加基本养老保险人数　（人）	Persons Participation in Basic Old-Pension Insurance　(person)	1 937	3 142	5 923	3 130
参加基本医疗保险人数　（人）	Persons Participation in Medical Insurance　(person)	1 937	3 142	5 923	3 130
参加失业保险人数　（人）	Persons Participation in Unemployment Insurance　(person)	1 937	3 142	5 923	3 130
团场居民最低生活保障人数　（人）	Bottommost Living Security of Farm Households　(person)	625	805	636	619

Continued

二师三十一团 Farm 31 Division 2	二师三十三团 Farm 33 Division 2	二师三十四团 Farm 34 Division 2	二师三十六团 Farm 36 Division 2	二师二二三团 Farm 223 Division 2	二师三十八团 Farm 38 Division 2	三师四十一团 Farm 41 Division 3	三师四十二团 Farm 42 Division 3	三师四十四团 Farm 44 Division 3
01063236X	010633397	010632335	010645865	010633434	670220168	010645304	010645312	010645320
阮伯平	刘期国	薛　利	杨志成	游　明	丁利文	杨明超	曹开军	郑胜学
尉犁县	尉犁县	尉犁县	若羌县	和静县	且末县	疏勒县	岳普湖县	图木舒克市
841503	841505	841506	841802	841308	841900	844004	844405	843807
1958	1958	1960	1965	1960	2010	1950	1953	1969
种植业	种植业	种植业	种植业	种植业	种植业	种植业	种植业	种植业
30.43	54.34	88.81	66.86	64.22	19.48	9.33	14.66	61.33
30	40	23	26	30	18	23	14	46
12	20	13	5	15	4	12	6	24
2	2		5	4	1	2	1	5
1	1	1	1	1		1	1	1
1	1							
3 018	4 781	3 235	3 798	1 019	3 088	2 013	1 512	10 870
2 094	3 495	2 359	2 097	841	1 925	1 337	1 201	8 613
146	113	171	995	58	488	87	76	605
778	1 173	705	706	120	675	589	235	1 652
3 042	4 224	3 304	3 806	975	2 547	2 001	1 588	10 866
65	56	45	119	138		35	65	130
3 200	3 646	6 011	2 418	2 235	60	1 820	550	4 115
5 000	4 112	4 739	1 783	2 835	850	1 286	2 150	5 998
439	762	1 136	300	542		436	254	1 636
703	876	1 557	543	956	437	602	806	3 621
100	100	100	100	100	100	100	100	99
100	100	100	100	100		99	100	93
98	82	98		99			98	90
30	85	100	47	35	20	30	25	41
43	77	77	45	42	6	24	28	69
18	47	72	30	27	2	7	6	20
3	8	7	3	9	2	18	2	9
2 050	3 179	5 961	2 474	1 929	1 019	1 644	1 210	2 836
2 050	3 173	5 961	2 335	1 929	1 019	1 644	1 210	2 836
2 050	3 166	5 961	2 022	1 929	1 019	1 644	1 210	2 836
736	423	637	254	852		165	387	2 269

21—1 续表 3

（2010 年）

指　　标	Item	三　　师 四十五团 Farm 45 Division 3	三　　师 四十六团 Farm 46 Division 2	三　　师 四十八团 Farm 48 Division 2	三　　师 四十九团 Farm 49 Division 2
法人代码	Enterprise Corporative Code	010645339	010645347	010645275	010645355
法人代表	Enterprise Corporative Representative	冉春旺	刘　航	刘　军	王健虎
所在县市	Under County or City	麦盖提县	麦盖提县	巴楚县	图木舒克市
邮政编码	Post Code	844604	844612	843815	843809
建场年份	The Year of Farm Establishment	1960	1998	1966	1969
行业分类	Sector Classification	种植业	种植业	种植业	种植业
团场占地面积　（千公顷）	Cover an Area of Farm Headquarters　（1 000 hectares）	89.40	29.13	17.10	30.80
产业活动单位数合计　（个）	Number of Basic Units Engaged　（unit）	39	22	26	33
# 农业连队	Agriculture Brigade	23	9	12	20
工　业	Industry	6	3	5	3
建筑业	Construction		1	1	1
批发零售业	Wholesale and Retail Trade				
年末从业人员　（人）	Employed Persons　（person）	8 443	1 128	2 061	5 731
第一产业	Primary Industry	6 066	767	1 333	4 500
第二产业	Secondary Industry	952	93	183	313
第三产业	Tertiary Industry	1 425	268	545	918
从业人员年平均人数　（人）	Annual Average Employed Persons　（person）	8 286	1 107	2 060	5 738
境内公路里程　（公里）	Length of Highways　（km）	152	33	75	108
团场电话年末用户　（户）	Telephone Customer of Farm at the Year-end　（household）	5 276	1 015	1 580	2 300
移动电话年末用户　（户）	Mobile Phone Customer of Farm at the Year-end　（household）	4 900	1 652	1 960	4 094
普通中学在校学生数　（人）	Student Enrollment in Regular Secondary Schools　（person）	1 960	230	339	1 000
小学在校学生数　（人）	Student Enrollment in Primary Schools　（person）	2 960	472	694	1 914
学龄儿童入学率　（%）	Percentage of School-age Enrolled　（%）	100	99	100	98
初中升学率　（%）	Percentage of Junior Secondary Schools　（%）	98	99	100	99
高中升学率　（%）	Percentage of Senior Secondary Schools　（%）	96			
医院、卫生院床位数　（床）	Beds of Hospitals and Health Centers　（pcs）	128	20	38	40
医院、卫生院技术人员数　（人）	Medical Technical Personnel of Hospitals and Health Centers　（person）	152	43	39	64
# 医　生	Doctors	67	8	17	12
卫生防疫人员数　（人）	Personnel of Epidemic Prevention　（person）	15	4	15	6
参加基本养老保险人数　（人）	Persons Participation in Basic Old-Pension Insurance　（person）	6 902	861	1 689	3 546
参加基本医疗保险人数　（人）	Persons Participation in Medical Insurance　（person）	9 499	861	1 689	3 546
参加失业保险人数　（人）	Persons Participation in Unemployment Insurance　（person）	6 902	861	1 689	3 546
团场居民最低生活保障人数　（人）	Bottommost Living Security of Farm Households　（person）	618	152	315	207

Continued

三 师 五 十 团 Farm 50 Division 2	三 师 五十一团 Farm 51 Division 3	三 师 五十三团 Farm 53 Division 3	三 师 伽师总场 Jiashi Farm Division 3	三 师 东风农场 Dongfen Farm Division 3	三 师 红旗农场 Redflag Farm Division 3	三 师 叶城二牧场 Yechen Farm Division 3	三 师 托云牧场 Tuoyun Farm Division 3	四 师 六十一团 Farm 61 Division 4
010645363	010645371	010645398	010645400	010632482	010645267	010645283	010645240	010645523
宋向东	赵玉昌	葛统一	鲁维龙	李 明	聂伟如	王学义	王 剑	傅启军
图木舒克市	图木舒克市	图木舒克市	伽师县	英吉沙县	阿图什市	叶城县	乌恰县	霍城县
843804	843803	843805	844309	844500	845350	844911	845452	835216
1969	1969	1969	1958	1958	1958	1953	1953	1962
种植业	种植业	种植业	种植业	种植业	种植业	牲畜饲养放牧业	牲畜饲养放牧业	种植业
55.30	141.12	124.60	50.76	7.47	9.25	64.00	53.80	105.33
26	31	31	26	6	12	2	5	30
14	13	17	12	2	6	5	3	15
2	2	2	5		1			2
1	1	1	1					
								2
5 321	16 841	8 966	3 863	440	1 028	359	337	5 712
4 245	14 728	7 984	2 827	345	830	176	242	4 506
295	765	280	228	2	29	32	3	364
781	1 348	702	808	93	169	151	92	842
5 190	16 906	8 111	3 794	440	1 026	337	348	5 623
91	128	151	132	11	141	14	110	218
2 500	800	724	1 581	210	375	75	28	2 935
7 300	3 500	3 120	3 105	160	375	186	220	3 969
500	942	479	683	64	270		67	537
3 485	6 218	2 490	1 328	202	460	246	128	1 064
100	85	100	100	100	100	100	100	100
100	95	89	100	100	100		100	100
	80	45			70			82
80	150	55		6	6	10	4	60
96	52	45		9	6	8	7	66
30	18	12		5	3	2	3	24
6	12	4		1	1	1	1	5
1 784	1 665	1 306	2 820	269	319	252	240	7 729
1 784	1 665	1 306	2 820	269	319	252	240	7 310
1 784	1 665	1 306	2 820	269	319	252	240	4 637
2 001	5 100	1 450	639	287	988	140	190	475

21—1 续表 4

（2010 年）

指　　标	Item	四　师 六十二团 Farm 62 Division 4	四　师 六十三团 Farm 63 Division4	四　师 六十四团 Farm 64 Division4	四　师 六十六团 Farm 66 Division4
法人代码	Enterprise Corporative Code	010645531	01064554X	010645558	010645574
法人代表	Enterprise Corporative Representative	魏新平	黄新江	刘　杰	邓义华
所在县市	Under County or City	霍城县	霍城县	霍城县	霍城县
邮政编码	Post Code	835215	835206	835214	835219
建场年份	The Year of Farm Establishment	1962	1960	1953	1953
行业分类	Sector Classification	种植业	种植业	种植业	种植业
团场占地面积　（千公顷）	Cover an Area of Farm Headquarters　(1 000 hectares)	14. 50	30. 77	36. 31	32. 72
产业活动单位数合计　（个）	Number of Basic Units Engaged　(unit)	35	32	34	54
# 农业连队	Agriculture Brigade	14	13	22	22
工　业	Industry	6	1		2
建筑业	Construction	1	1	1	2
批发零售业	Wholesale and Retail Trade	3	1	2	6
年末从业人员　（人）	Employed Persons　(person)	6 592	4 050	9 005	9 956
第一产业	Primary Industry	4 121	3 111	6 991	6 327
第二产业	Secondary Industry	647	193	357	947
第三产业	Tertiary Industry	1 824	746	1 657	2 682
从业人员年平均人数　（人）	Annual Average Employed Persons　(person)	6 753	4 082	9 352	9 957
境内公路里程　（公里）	Length of Highways　(km)	115	201	175	176
团场电话年末用户　（户）	Telephone Customer of Farm at the Year-end　(household)	4 200	2 300	2 800	7 310
移动电话年末用户　（户）	Mobile Phone Customer of Farm at the Year-end　(household)	5 400	4 020	5 120	9 700
普通中学在校学生数　（人）	Student Enrollment in Regular Secondary Schools　(person)	1 323	467	2 168	1 765
小学在校学生数　（人）	Student Enrollment in Primary Schools　(person)	1 735	662	2 537	2 252
学龄儿童入学率　（%）	Percentage of School-age Enrolled　(%)	100	100	100	100
初中升学率　（%）	Percentage of Junior Secondary Schools　(%)	93	93	100	100
高中升学率　（%）	Percentage of Senior Secondary Schools　(%)	61. 2		86	85
医院、卫生院床位数　（床）	Beds of Hospitals and Health Centers　(pcs)	65	40	60	224
医院、卫生院技术人员数　（人）	Medical Technical Personnel of Hospitals and Health Centers　(person)	61	48	102	204
# 医　生	Doctors	25	40	26	104
卫生防疫人员数　（人）	Personnel of Epidemic Prevention　(person)	7	4	9	10
参加基本养老保险人数　（人）	Persons Participation in Basic Old-Pension Insurance　(person)	7 873	5 795	10 103	13 760
参加基本医疗保险人数　（人）	Persons Participation in Medical Insurance　(person)	6 750	5 411	13 494	11 297
参加失业保险人数　（人）	Persons Participation in Unemployment Insurance　(person)	4 081	3 636	5 873	5 867
团场居民最低生活保障人数　（人）	Bottommost Living Security of Farm Households　(person)	729	352	1 165	1 154

Continued

四 师 六十七团 Farm 67 Division4	四 师 六十八团 Farm 68 Division 4	四 师 六十九团 Farm 69 Division 4	四 师 七 十 团 Farm 70 Division 4	四 师 七十一团 Farm 71 Division 4	四 师 七十二团 Farm 72 Division 4	四 师 七十三团 Farm 73 Division 4	四 师 七十四团 Farm 74 Division 4	四 师 七十五团 Farm 75 Division 4
010645582	010645590	010633696	010645603	010645611	01064562X	010645638	010645646	010645654
努尔赛提	戴永林	陈 强	林文华	丁高峰	高文生	冷畅勤	唐献杰	刘建强
察布查尔锡伯自治县	察布查尔锡伯自治县	察布查尔锡伯自治县	伊宁县	新源县	新源县	巩留县	昭苏县	昭苏县
835304	835301	835312	835116	835801	835811	835407	835608	835605
1963	1959	1958	1958	1952	1950	1960	1963	1959
种植业	种植业	种植业	种植业	种植业	种植业	种植业	种植业	种植业
60.75	13.03	9.82	10.35	16.02	23.36	28.69	77.86	7.91
19	21	22	28	24	33	21	20	17
10	12	9	12	9	16	8	8	6
3	1	3		3	4	1		1
		1	1	1	1		1	1
1	1	2	2	2	1	1	2	2
2 714	3 007	2 933	5 641	5 498	4 613	2 499	1 707	1 644
1 723	2 272	1 386	3 691	3 472	2 609	1 473	1 235	1 080
160	139	1 051	715	1 026	625	345	101	218
831	596	496	1 235	1 000	1 379	681	371	346
2 160	3 044	3 245	5 609	5 502	4 601	2 584	1 691	1 564
300	66	66	83	109	101	112	284	90
1 450	1 835	1 986	3 210	3 865	3 045	1 420	489	872
3 985	3 244	988	5 700	4 020	4 065	1 928	1 558	1 223
621	477	453	664	634	1 284	490	81	142
821	753	768	1 253	596	972	799	264	321
100	100	100	100	100	100	100	100	100
98	100	97	100	56	100	100	100	100
83				89	99	78		
30	39	35	64	72	70	21	20	30
38	11	42	63	78	67	37	24	27
10	16	23	14	38	18	12	10	11
4	4	4	6	6	7	4	4	3
3 253	4 571	3 890	6 189	8 886	6 355	2 872	1 836	2 289
3 201	3 685	3 385	6 024	8 090	5 277	2 402	1 740	1 970
1 924	1 667	1 680	3 215	4 533	2 975	1 178	1 181	1 280
460	444	252	635	336	620	654	448	219

21—1 续表 5

（2010 年）

指　　标	Item	四师 七十六团 Farm 76 Division 4	四师 七十七团 Farm 77 Division 4	四师 七十八团 Farm 78 Division 4	四师 七十九团 Farm 79 Division 4
法人代码	Enterprise Corporative Code	010645662	010645670	010645689	010645718
法人代表	Enterprise Corporative Representative	钱存斌	陈历湘	罗忠海	齐福聚
所在县市	Under County or City	昭苏县	昭苏县	特克斯县	尼勒克县
邮政编码	Post Code	835609	835601	835502	835705
建场年份	The Year of Farm Establishment	1962	1956	1959	1956
行业分类	Sector Classification	种植业	种植业	种植业	种植业
团场占地面积　（千公顷）	Cover an Area of Farm Headquarters　(1 000 hectares)	59.85	39.07	69.45	26.48
产业活动单位数合计　（个）	Number of Basic Units Engaged　(unit)	25	25	17	15
# 农业连队	Agriculture Brigade	11	9	6	6
工　业	Industry	3		2	1
建筑业	Construction	1	1	1	1
批发零售业	Wholesale and Retail Trade	1	2	1	2
年末从业人员　（人）	Employed Persons　(person)	6 644	3 780	1 774	2 713
第一产业	Primary Industry	5 284	2 931	1 363	1 946
第二产业	Secondary Industry	262	238	77	308
第三产业	Tertiary Industry	1 098	611	334	459
从业人员年平均人数　（人）	Annual Average Employed Persons　(person)	6 040	3 731	1 757	2 404
境内公路里程　（公里）	Length of Highways　(km)	160	147	127	87
团场电话年末用户　（户）	Telephone Customer of Farm at the Year-end　(household)	1 810	802	903	566
移动电话年末用户　（户）	Mobile Phone Customer of Farm at the Year-end　(household)	5 806	3 350	1 202	3 286
普通中学在校学生数　（人）	Student Enrollment in Regular Secondary Schools　(person)	608	349	221	356
小学在校学生数　（人）	Student Enrollment in Primary Schools　(person)	792	631	490	712
学龄儿童入学率　（%）	Percentage of School-age Enrolled　(%)	100	100	100	100
初中升学率　（%）	Percentage of Junior Secondary Schools　(%)	100	97	100	100
高中升学率　（%）	Percentage of Senior Secondary Schools　(%)	94		80	
医院、卫生院床位数　（床）	Beds of Hospitals and Health Centers　(pcs)	55	37	22	23
医院、卫生院技术人员数　（人）	Medical Technical Personnel of Hospitals and Health Centers　(person)	72	43	29	40
# 医　生	Doctors	35	15	8	7
卫生防疫人员数　（人）	Personnel of Epidemic Prevention　(person)	8	4	2	4
参加基本养老保险人数　（人）	Persons Participation in Basic Old-Pension Insurance　(person)	6 321	4 686	1 946	1 412
参加基本医疗保险人数　（人）	Persons Participation in Medical Insurance　(person)	6 300	4 195	1 750	1 115
参加失业保险人数　（人）	Persons Participation in Unemployment Insurance　(person)	3 321	2 635	1 005	1 083
团场居民最低生活保障人数　（人）	Bottommost Living Security of Farm Households　(person)	842	632	1 014	757

Continued

五　师 八十一团 Farm 81 Division 5	五　师 八十三团 Farm 83 Division 5	五　师 八十四团 Farm 84 Division 5	五　师 八十六团 Farm 86 Division 5	五　师 八十七团 Farm 87 Division 5	五　师 八十八团 Farm 88 Division 5	五　师 八十九团 Farm 89 Division 5	五　师 九 十 团 Farm 90 Division 5	五　师 九十一团 Farm 91 Division 5
010646112	010646139	010646147	010646163	010646171	731816986	010646198	010646200	726976184
张华东	刘自发	宋守林	王如钦	孙美珍	麻　林	王　盛	曹立军	邓小军
博乐市	精河县	博乐市	博乐市	温泉县	温泉县	博乐市	博乐市	精河县
833411	833303	833405	833403	833417	833500	833408	833409	833307
1968	1958	1960	1960	1960	1960	1962	1960	1970
种植业	种植业	种植业	种植业	种植业	种植业	种植业	种植业	种植业
12.64	46.06	75.20	34.00	28.75	32.70	17.47	18.67	15.68
25	50	24	35	19	16	30	20	13
15	25	12	20	7	6	17	11	7
3	8	4	2	2	3	2	2	1
1	1	1	1	1	1	1		
1	2	1	1	1	1		1	1
4 409	8 087	2 914	5 152	1 859	1 504	5 772	3 890	1 618
3 391	5 545	1 963	3 838	1 292	926	4 132	2 986	1 247
202	619	284	372	153	156	406	318	65
816	1 923	667	942	414	422	1 234	586	306
4 297	7 770	2 873	5 140	1 878	1 527	6 328	3 900	1 738
132	159	63	199	65	43	62	235	35
6 051	14 710	6 365	13 793	5 375	1 498	7 600	6 200	2 866
2 658	6 980	4 135	9 118	2 112	912	4 500	4 200	2 221
848	1 914	493	759	260	258	1 403	491	326
1 351	1 857	760	1 486	471	508	1 082	583	398
100	100	100	99	100	100	100	100	100
80	100	98	95	100	100	90	100	98
	69					78		
52	80	40	65	30	23	64	40	20
82	95	53	76	44	25	81	68	18
49	28	35	28	27	10	46	28	7
6	7	3	7	5	4	11	7	4
5 129	9 308	4 352	6 628	3 057	2 294	6 790	4 475	1 509
6 930	17 422	6 614	8 389	4 451	3 693	13 350	4 475	2 959
3 855	6 263	2 527	4 313	1 610	1 255	5 220	3 613	1 509
590	956	542	1 128	375	390	560	340	232

21—1 续表 6

（2010 年）

指　　标	Item	六　师 一〇一团 Farm 101 Division 6	六　师 一〇二团 Farm 102 Division 6	六　师 一〇三团 Farm 103 Division 6	六　师 一〇五团 Farm 105 Division 6
法人代码	Enterprise Corporative Code	010644774	010630292	010630233	010630268
法人代表	Enterprise Corporative Representative	屈建法	刘金栋	董现荣	甘应枝
所在县市	Under County or City	五家渠市	五家渠市	五家渠市	呼图壁县
邮政编码	Post Code	831300	831302	831304	831308
建场年份	The Year of Farm Establishment	1949	1952	1953	1959
行业分类	Sector Classification	种植业	种植业	种植业	种植业
团场占地面积　（千公顷）	Cover an Area of Farm Headquarters　(1 000 hectares)	11. 20	33. 80	54. 60	22. 50
产业活动单位数合计　（个）	Number of Basic Units Engaged　(unit)	44	38	36	19
# 农业连队	Agriculture Brigade	9	13	13	12
工　业	Industry	14	7	6	
建筑业	Construction	1	3	1	1
批发零售业	Wholesale and Retail Trade	7	3	1	1
年末从业人员　（人）	Employed Persons　(person)	7 532	7 307	5 812	3 745
第一产业	Primary Industry	1 876	3 242	3 459	2 361
第二产业	Secondary Industry	1 692	1 473	694	216
第三产业	Tertiary Industry	3 964	2 592	1 659	1 168
从业人员年平均人数　（人）	Annual Average Employed Persons　(person)	7 195	7 002	5 800	3 727
境内公路里程　（公里）	Length of Highways　(km)	116	160	146	121
团场电话年末用户　（户）	Telephone Customer of Farm at the Year-end　(household)	3 910	4 980	4 800	3 665
移动电话年末用户　（户）	Mobile Phone Customer of Farm at the Year-end　(household)	1 600	3 200	5 600	9 989
普通中学在校学生数　（人）	Student Enrollment in Regular Secondary Schools　(person)	1 828	942	610	826
小学在校学生数　（人）	Student Enrollment in Primary Schools　(person)	1 651	1 718	1 146	1 351
学龄儿童入学率　（%）	Percentage of School-age Enrolled　(%)	100	100	100	100
初中升学率　（%）	Percentage of Junior Secondary Schools　(%)	100	100	100	100
高中升学率　（%）	Percentage of Senior Secondary Schools　(%)	73			
医院、卫生院床位数　（床）	Beds of Hospitals and Health Centers　(pcs)	100	60	65	30
医院、卫生院技术人员数　（人）	Medical Technical Personnel of Hospitals and Health Centers　(person)	111	57	52	46
# 医　生	Doctors	59	24	24	15
卫生防疫人员数　（人）	Personnel of Epidemic Prevention　(person)	15	7	9	4
参加基本养老保险人数　（人）	Persons Participation in Basic Old-Pension Insurance　(person)	3 493	3 694	5 742	4 059
参加基本医疗保险人数　（人）	Persons Participation in Medical Insurance　(person)	3 043	3 108	4 475	3 170
参加失业保险人数　（人）	Persons Participation in Unemployment Insurance　(person)	3 043	3 108	4 475	3 170
团场居民最低生活保障人数　（人）	Bottommost Living Security of Farm Households　(person)	470	307	184	238

Continued

六师 一〇六团 Farm 106 Division 6	六师 芳草湖农场 Fang Caohu Farm Division 6	六师 新湖农场 Xinhu Farm Division 6	六师 军户农场 Junhu Farm Division 6	六师 共青团农场 Communist League Tuan Farm Division 6	六师 六运湖农场 liu Yuhu Farm Division 6	六师 土墩子农场 TudunZi Farm Division 6	六师 红旗农场 Red Flag Farm Division 6	六师 奇台农场 Qitai Farm Division 6	六师 北塔山牧场 Bei Tashan Farm Division 6
010644803	010644723	010644715	010630241	010644731	010644766	01064482X	01064474X	010630284	010644790
李继军	李金平	王永信	李鹏	胡晓江	杨阜正	王晓明	王永福	郭怀安	巴合提拜
呼图壁县	呼图壁县	玛纳斯县	昌吉市	昌吉市	阜康市	阜康市	吉木萨尔县	奇台县	奇台县
831213	831208	832208	831111	831301	831504	831502	831702	831809	831304
1958	1959	1963	1958	1958	1965	1955	1965	1958	1952
种植业	种植业	种植业	种植业	种植业	种植业	种植业	种植业	种植业	牲畜饲养放牧业
18.80	95.40	98.10	9.10	19.40	6.50	11.50	146.80	76.40	225.30
13	90	84	17	16	12	15	27	62	7
8	48	45	10	9	6	6	15	29	6
1	4	7		1			4	3	1
			1				1	1	
1			2	1	1	2		2	
1 900	15 693	13 873	3 770	4 129	3 533	2 199	5 733	12 167	1 249
1 328	10 083	9 921	2 861	2 236	2 889	1 786	4 219	8 460	816
187	1 389	1 248	125	798	112	40	426	1 703	136
385	4 221	2 704	784	1 095	532	373	1 088	2 004	297
2 016	16 334	13 786	3 685	3 991	3 608	2 014	5 698	12 020	1 169
63	742	617	55	111	34	66	401	351	538
1 765	8 617	9 358	3 400	1 310	1 147	690	3 180	8 660	230
2 652	23 770	13 348	3 850	4 015	2 246	2 000	4 682	14 475	280
359	4 014	2 261	656	477	200	116	306	1 096	176
488	3 507	2 557	1 443	679	525	381	720	1 646	317
100	100	100	100	100	100	100	100	100	100
100	100	100	100	100	100	100	100	100	100
	99	94	71				95	79	
20	150	100	25	20	20	20	50	30	25
40	302	143	20	30	25	28	56	89	26
25	123	12	18	18	9	12	21	49	14
5	14	12	7	5	3	2	6	9	3
2 602	13 590	11 862	3 012	2 295	1 080	1 380	1 437	6 080	951
2 031	12 342	9 378	2 864	1 778	965	1 170	1 044	5 383	724
2 031	12 342	9 378	2 864	1 778	965	1 170	1 044	5 383	724
121	1 055	729	553	138	402	227	2 176	2 037	619

21—1 续表 7

（2010 年）

指　　标	Item	七　师 一二三团 Farm 123 Division 7	七　师 一二四团 Farm 124 Division 7	七　师 一二五团 Farm 125 Division 7	七　师 一二六团 Farm 126 Division 7
法人代码	Enterprise Corporative Code	010630591	010634146	01064722X	010647238
法人代表	Enterprise Corporative Representative	王宗洪	刘　孟	田永浩	王永安
所在县市	Under County or City	乌苏市	乌苏市	乌苏市	乌苏市
邮政编码	Post Code	833208	833011	833203	833211
建场年份	The Year of Farm Establishment	1950	1960	1954	1962
行业分类	Sector Classification	种植业	种植业	种植业	种植业
团场占地面积　（千公顷）	Cover an Area of Farm Headquarters　(1 000 hectares)	23.15	92.90	43.05	20.00
产业活动单位数合计　（个）	Number of Basic Units Engaged　(unit)	33	32	44	30
# 农业连队	Agriculture Brigade	20	20	23	14
工　业	Industry	5	3	7	4
建筑业	Construction	1	1	1	1
批发零售业	Wholesale and Retail Trade	1	1	1	1
年末从业人员　（人）	Employed Persons　(person)	8 711	6 863	8 527	3 803
第一产业	Primary Industry	4 196	4 080	5 288	1 889
第二产业	Secondary Industry	1 067	743	1 307	264
第三产业	Tertiary Industry	3 448	2 040	1 932	1 650
从业人员年平均人数　（人）	Annual Average Employed Persons　(person)	8 554	6 728	8 548	3 803
境内公路里程　（公里）	Length of Highways　(km)	119	120	206	110
团场电话年末用户　（户）	Telephone Customer of Farm at the Year-end　(household)	5 321	4 053	5 571	2 940
移动电话年末用户　（户）	Mobile Phone Customer of Farm at the Year-end　(household)	8 464	8 420	4 956	12 340
普通中学在校学生数　（人）	Student Enrollment in Regular Secondary Schools　(person)	1 473	728	877	605
小学在校学生数　（人）	Student Enrollment in Primary Schools　(person)	1 622	1 239	1 006	1 029
学龄儿童入学率　（%）	Percentage of School-age Enrolled　(%)	100	100	100	100
初中升学率　（%）	Percentage of Junior Secondary Schools　(%)	100	100	100	100
高中升学率　（%）	Percentage of Senior Secondary Schools　(%)	93		78	
医院、卫生院床位数　（床）	Beds of Hospitals and Health Centers　(pcs)	100	50	100	30
医院、卫生院技术人员数　（人）	Medical Technical Personnel of Hospitals and Health Centers　(person)	70	76	112	48
# 医　生	Doctors	25	41	70	16
卫生防疫人员数　（人）	Personnel of Epidemic Prevention　(person)	51	38	13	8
参加基本养老保险人数　（人）	Persons Participation in Basic Old-Pension Insurance　(person)	9 849	4 766	6 580	2 497
参加基本医疗保险人数　（人）	Persons Participation in Medical Insurance　(person)	9 849	4 766	5 625	2 497
参加失业保险人数　（人）	Persons Participation in Unemployment Insurance　(person)	4 473	4 766	5 490	2 497
团场居民最低生活保障人数　（人）	Bottommost Living Security of Farm Households　(person)	947	707	1 060	591

Continued

七师 一二七团 Farm 127 Division 7	七师 一二八团 Farm 128 Division 7	七师 一二九团 Farm 129 Division 7	七师 一三〇团 Farm 130 Division 7	七师 一三一团 Farm 131 Division 7	七师 一三七团 Farm 137 Division 7	八师 一二一团 Farm 121 Division 8	八师 一三三团 Farm 133 Division 8	八师 一三四团 Farm 134 Division 8	八师 一三六团 Farm 136 Division 8
010634170	010647262	010634197	010647270	010634218	010647289	010634234	010634912	010634269	010634285
武挺军	李新平	王天云	杨宝玉	李庆龙	孙洪波	李琦	杨德禄	夏东利	郑万里
乌苏市	乌苏市	克拉玛依区	乌苏市	奎屯市	乌尔禾区	沙湾县	沙湾县	沙湾县	克拉玛依区
833209	833207	834032	834034	833200	834014	832066	832064	832061	834018
1956	1958	1960	1958	1956	1958	1950	1958	1957	1952
种植业	种植业	种植业	种植业	种植业	种植业	种植业	种植业	种植业	种植业
18.55	28.60	30.46	63.68	37.41	64.11	58.50	74.34	58.00	19.30
30	37	31	36	27	22	58	46	36	28
16	19	15	20	22	9	38	30	25	13
4	6	6	3	2	5	6	4	3	4
1	2		1	1	1	1	1	1	2
1	2	1	2	1	2	1	1		5
3 775	4 998	7 267	6 904	7 882	4 119	13 990	7 431	7 799	3 910
2 031	3 125	3 031	4 351	4 430	2 071	8 475	5 576	6 154	2 190
380	418	914	321	1 236	378	1 842	305	263	471
1 364	1 455	3 322	2 232	2 216	1 670	3 673	1 550	1 382	1 249
3 898	4 977	7 260	6 130	7 882	4 308	12 806	7 774	7 863	3 867
120	179	146	138	161	143	313	231	180	52
3 600	3 795	5 936	5 417	8 120	3 260	8 733	6 650	6 255	2 480
8 000	5 002	4 613	9 911	13 500	5 600	30 600	12 500	7 233	8 900
830	645	713	1 261	1 126	397	2 743	934	1 185	459
1 300	921	1 068	1 252	1 832	538	2 502	1 273	1 519	1 619
100	100	100	100	100	100	100	100	100	100
100	100	100	100	100	100	100	76	100	85
		63		49	90	93	90	95	
40	80	150	80	210	30	120	80	140	40
68	59	120	121	205	48	224	127	120	58
25	16	45	86	151	28	105	38	47	23
42	32	11	9	55	18	15	16	17	7
2 715	3 960	4 290	2 957	5 150	1 975	9 201	6 573	6 550	3 526
2 715	3 960	4 290	2 957	5 150	1 975	9 201	19 351	6 230	3 400
2 715	3 960	4 290	2 957	5 150	1 975	9 201	6 573	5 900	3 526
560	556	1 032	807	956	505	1 283	1 204	801	319

21—1 续表 8

（2010 年）

指　　标	Item	八　师 一四一团 Farm 141 Division 8	八　师 一四二团 Farm 142 Division 8	八　师 一四三团 Farm 143 Division 8	八　师 一四四团 Farm 144 Division 8
法人代码	Enterprise Corporative Code	010634293	010634306	010634314	010632693
法人代表	Enterprise Corporative Representative	赵　军	杨靖宇	严桂花	任　晖
所在县市	Under County or City	沙湾县	沙湾县	沙湾县	沙湾县
邮政编码	Post Code	832028	832029	832021	832036
建场年份	The Year of Farm Establishment	1958	1950	1950	1969
行业分类	Sector Classification	种植业	种植业	种植业	种植业
团场占地面积　（千公顷）	Cover an Area of Farm Headquarters　(1 000 hectares)	20. 80	70. 00	172. 18	30. 30
产业活动单位数合计　（个）	Number of Basic Units Engaged　(unit)	27	49	59	25
# 农业连队	Agriculture Brigade	15	30	31	15
工　业	Industry	3	4	9	5
建筑业	Construction	1	1		
批发零售业	Wholesale and Retail Trade	3	1	6	1
年末从业人员　（人）	Employed Persons　(person)	3 940	12 315	13 986	4 407
第一产业	Primary Industry	2 446	7 139	10 592	2 908
第二产业	Secondary Industry	279	794	1 491	493
第三产业	Tertiary Industry	1 215	4 382	1 903	1 006
从业人员年平均人数　（人）	Annual Average Employed Persons　(person)	4 576	12 762	14 479	4 432
境内公路里程　（公里）	Length of Highways　(km)	96	674	339	88
团场电话年末用户　（户）	Telephone Customer of Farm at the Year-end　(household)	3 528	8 700	8 071	5 933
移动电话年末用户　（户）	Mobile Phone Customer of Farm at the Year-end　(household)	4 678	6 960	3 940	1 936
普通中学在校学生数　（人）	Student Enrollment in Regular Secondary Schools　(person)	530	1 742	2 389	563
小学在校学生数　（人）	Student Enrollment in Primary Schools　(person)	699	1 311	3 328	1 258
学龄儿童入学率　（%）	Percentage of School-age Enrolled　(%)	100	100	100	100
初中升学率　（%）	Percentage of Junior Secondary Schools　(%)	100	100	85	100
高中升学率　（%）	Percentage of Senior Secondary Schools　(%)	76	98	92	94
医院、卫生院床位数　（床）	Beds of Hospitals and Health Centers　(pcs)	50	90	110	108
医院、卫生院技术人员数　（人）	Medical Technical Personnel of Hospitals and Health Centers　(person)	66	148	203	90
# 医　生	Doctors	22	95	124	37
卫生防疫人员数　（人）	Personnel of Epidemic Prevention　(person)	7	13	22	9
参加基本养老保险人数　（人）	Persons Participation in Basic Old-Pension Insurance　(person)	2 963	4 463	7 884	3 588
参加基本医疗保险人数　（人）	Persons Participation in Medical Insurance　(person)	2 963	4 463	7 883	3 588
参加失业保险人数　（人）	Persons Participation in Unemployment Insurance　(person)	2 963	4 463	7 884	3 588
团场居民最低生活保障人数　（人）	Bottommost Living Security of Farm Households　(person)	556	1 323	1 473	645

Continued

八师 石河子总场 Shihezi Farm Division 8	八师 一四七团 Farm 147 Division 8	八师 一四八团 Farm 148 Division 8	八师 一四九团 Farm 149 Division 8	八师 一五〇团 Farm 150 Division 8	八师 一五二团 Farm 152 Division 8	九师 一六一团 Farm 161 Division 8	九师 一六三团 Farm 163 Division 8	九师 一六四团 Farm 164 Division 8	九师 一六五团 Farm 165 Division 8
010634330	010634349	010645064	010634365	010634373	01064423X	010634402	010631113	010630021	010634445
孟宪峰	王红军	王东升	张启全	蒋世义	王东旭	鲁刚	朱海安	孙尔祥	马道忠
石河子市	玛纳斯县	玛纳斯县	玛纳斯县	玛纳斯县	石河子市	裕民县	塔城市	塔城市	额敏县
832011	832045	832048	832052	832056	832000	834800	834704	834703	834609
1950	1953	1958	1958	1958	1965	1962	1962	1962	1962
种植业	种植业	种植业	种植业	种植业	种植业	种植业	种植业	种植业	种植业
47.50	22.40	30.80	34.19	45.00	3.70	124.10	19.06	18.50	114.19
63	31	40	30	32	16	22	33	19	24
42	18	20	17	21	7	11	15	10	8
7	4	6	5	2	4	2	2	1	2
	1	1	1	1		1	1	1	1
2	1	3		1	1	1		1	1
16 534	3 647	9 287	6 871	6 078	3 380	2 695	4 199	2 772	2 274
7 296	2 026	6 576	4 643	4 014	1 633	1 883	3 427	2 227	1 743
2 395	353	841	621	558	1 043	178	138	90	118
6 843	1 268	1 870	1 607	1 506	704	634	634	455	413
16 913	4 803	11 802	6 917	6 060	3 611	2 665	4 174	2 775	2 285
182	106	135	45	410	15	123	92	87	101
25 825	6 357	7 800	4 350	4 860	2 842	1 623	2 400	1 358	1 241
15 688	4 762	10 256	6 120	5 680	2 710	1 409	6 908	1 572	839
4 042	793	2 256	582	673	751	200	475	405	296
4 698	1 105	1 310	1 240	987	1 389	310	999	582	587
100	100	100	100	100	100	100	100	100	99.7
100	100	100	100	100	100	100	100	100	99.4
94	100	100	92	87					
180	60	80	60	87	30	35	55	30	30
269	112	159	150	85	43	38	47	34	39
60	61	103	60	47	24	8	25	25	15
28	12	11	10	8	7	3	6	5	5
13 795	3 524	8 473	5 539	4 530	2 043	3 098	3 154	2 200	1 313
9 687	3 524	8 473	5 539	4 534	2 043	3 029	3 154	3 770	1 313
8 226	3 524	8 473	5 539	4 530	2 043	1 688	3 154	2 200	1 313
1 869	531	1 103	630	714	341	936	352	690	332

21—1 续表 9

（2010 年）

指　　标	Item	九　师 一六六团 Farm 166 Division 9	九　师 一六七团 Farm 167 Division 9	九　师 一六八团 Farm 168 Division 9	九　师 一七〇团 Farm 170 Division 9
法人代码	Enterprise Corporative Code	010634453	010634461	01063447X	010634496
法人代表	Enterprise Corporative Representative	魏建山	翟钢成	种广虎	李保山
所在县市	Under County or City	额敏县	额敏县	额敏县	托里县
邮政编码	Post Code	834612	834611	834607	834615
建场年份	The Year of Farm Establishment	1962	1962	1962	1952
行业分类	Sector Classification	种植业	种植业	种植业	牲畜饲养放牧业
团场占地面积　（千公顷）	Cover an Area of Farm Headquarters　(1 000 hectares)	24. 72	24. 86	20. 35	106. 05
产业活动单位数合计　（个）	Number of Basic Units Engaged　(unit)	27	19	29	15
# 农业连队	Agriculture Brigade	14	9	16	7
工　业	Industry	4	2	3	1
建筑业	Construction		1	1	1
批发零售业	Wholesale and Retail Trade	1	1		
年末从业人员　（人）	Employed Persons　(person)	3 425	2 798	4 240	1 521
第一产业	Primary Industry	2 748	2 412	3 205	921
第二产业	Secondary Industry	61	43	204	114
第三产业	Tertiary Industry	616	343	831	486
从业人员年平均人数　（人）	Annual Average Employed Persons　(person)	3 445	2 851	4 363	1 544
境内公路里程　（公里）	Length of Highways　(km)	135	160	216	46
团场电话年末用户　（户）	Telephone Customer of Farm at the Year-end　(household)	1 520	1 530	3 018	987
移动电话年末用户　（户）	Mobile Phone Customer of Farm at the Year-end　(household)	1 950	3 110	3 905	1 139
普通中学在校学生数　（人）	Student Enrollment in Regular Secondary Schools　(person)	621	597	599	186
小学在校学生数　（人）	Student Enrollment in Primary Schools　(person)	545	339	1 312	387
学龄儿童入学率　（%）	Percentage of School-age Enrolled　(%)	100	100	100	100
初中升学率　（%）	Percentage of Junior Secondary Schools　(%)	100	100	100	100
高中升学率　（%）	Percentage of Senior Secondary Schools　(%)				
医院、卫生院床位数　（床）	Beds of Hospitals and Health Centers　(pcs)	35	35	63	20
医院、卫生院技术人员数　（人）	Medical Technical Personnel of Hospitals and Health Centers　(person)	35	27	66	18
# 医　生	Doctors	17	13	26	5
卫生防疫人员数　（人）	Personnel of Epidemic Prevention　(person)	5	3	6	4
参加基本养老保险人数　（人）	Persons Participation in Basic Old-Pension Insurance　(person)	2 964	2 565	3 515	740
参加基本医疗保险人数　（人）	Persons Participation in Medical Insurance　(person)	2 964	2 565	3 515	740
参加失业保险人数　（人）	Persons Participation in Unemployment Insurance　(person)	2 964	2 565	3 515	740
团场居民最低生活保障人数　（人）	Bottommost Living Security of Farm Households　(person)	534	460	633	267

Continued

九 师 团结农场 Tuanjie Farm Division 9	十 师 一八一团 Farm 181 Division 10	十 师 一八二团 Farm 182 Division 10	十 师 一八三团 Farm 183 Division 10	十 师 一八四团 Farm 184 Division 10	十 师 一八五团 Farm 185 Division 10	十 师 一八六团 Farm 186 Division 10	十 师 一八七团 Farm 187 Division 10	十 师 一八八团 Farm 188 Division 10	十二师 一〇四团 Farm 104 Division 12
010634509	010634517	010634525	010634533	010634541	01063455X	010634568	010634576	010634584	734462474
李 升	姜文斌	田秋礼	晏忠诚	王建江	赵传光	吴晓斌	李建军	李新建	徐志刚
额敏县	阿勒泰市	福海县	福海县	和布克赛尔县	哈巴河县	吉木乃县	福海县	福海县	沙依巴克区
834602	836001	836403	836004	834409	836705	836801	836002	836000	830009
1963	1953	1959	1959	1959	1963	1962	1965	1969	1956
种植业	种植业	种植业	种植业	种植业	种植业	种植业	种植业	种植业	种植业
4.35	76.00	37.70	35.30	72.40	90.80	6.20	29.00	39.00	227.00
16	49	34	54	33	33	24	45	45	33
6	16	13	17	6	11	6	15	16	11
2	7	3	1	2	1	2	7	2	2
1	2	1	2	1	1	1	1	2	1
	1		1	2	1	2	1		
1 157	3 933	2 104	2 776	2 199	1 363	1 034	2 363	3 595	5 343
794	2 603	1 343	1 774	1 153	909	497	1 367	1 877	1 663
70	353	198	329	276	61	145	483	602	1 282
293	977	563	673	770	393	392	513	1 116	2 398
1 103	4 311	2 097	2 776	2 165	1 392	1 087	2 218	3 294	7 089
32	93	143	73	40	140	38	55	117	159
876	2 001	1 219	1 388	1 392	840	802	1 300	3 663	4 520
963	2 994	2 536	3 090	3 500	1 900	727	2 700	3 012	5 805
210	609	402	457	513	226	197	360	1 492	1 466
366	728	695	696	1 015	369	312	496	738	2 016
100	100	100	100	100	100	100	100	100	100
100	67	70	80	96	90	100	85	52	64
									95
20	50	27	30	25	30	20	35	115	100
22	64	38	56	44	38	23	56	70	104
18	49	9	26	17	6	8	10	23	53
4	8	6	8	6	5	4	8	8	6
921	3 146	1 679	2 305	1 676	1 175	795	1 682	2 290	3 138
921	3 253	1 739	2 411	1 676	1 213	823	1 768	2 570	3 142
921	3 253	1 739	2 411	1 676	1 213	823	1 768	2 570	2 617
337	880	213	686	115	160	128	348	537	1 557

21—1 续表 10

（2010 年）

指标	Item	十二师 三坪农场 Sanping Farm Division 12	十二师 五一农场 May1st Farm Division 12	十二师 头屯河农场 ToutunHe Farm Division 12	十二师 西山农场 Xishan Farm Division 12
法人代码	Enterprise Corporative Code	457634003	731837656	457633385	457634177
法人代表	Enterprise Corporative Representative	秦筱枫	刘绍君	于永飞	张礼余
所在县市	Under County or City	头屯河区	头屯河区	头屯河区	沙依巴克区
邮政编码	Post Code	830032	830088	830022	830089
建场年份	The Year of Farm Establishment	1964	1957	1951	1959
行业分类	Sector Classification	种植业	种植业	种植业	种植业
团场占地面积（千公顷）	Cover an Area of Farm Headquarters (1 000 hectares)	7.50	2.90	4.13	9.30
产业活动单位数合计（个）	Number of Basic Units Engaged (unit)	22	43	21	21
# 农业连队	Agriculture Brigade	13	14	6	12
工　业	Industry	1	8	1	1
建筑业	Construction				
批发零售业	Wholesale and Retail Trade		3	1	
年末从业人员（人）	Employed Persons (person)	4 421	4 355	5 638	1 841
第一产业	Primary Industry	2 771	2 035	2 216	1 267
第二产业	Secondary Industry	694	600	621	113
第三产业	Tertiary Industry	956	1 720	2 801	461
从业人员年平均人数（人）	Annual Average Employed Persons (person)	4 252	4 730	5 638	1 871
境内公路里程（公里）	Length of Highways (km)	36	60	24	5
团场电话年末用户（户）	Telephone Customer of Farm at the Year-end (household)	2 725	1 623	2 075	1 105
移动电话年末用户（户）	Mobile Phone Customer of Farm at the Year-end (household)	1 530	1 378	2 695	1 503
普通中学在校学生数（人）	Student Enrollment in Regular Secondary Schools (person)	542	607	616	289
小学在校学生数（人）	Student Enrollment in Primary Schools (person)	857	839	971	520
学龄儿童入学率（%）	Percentage of School-age Enrolled (%)	100	100	100	100
初中升学率（%）	Percentage of Junior Secondary Schools (%)	100	100	89	100
高中升学率（%）	Percentage of Senior Secondary Schools (%)	42			
医院、卫生院床位数（床）	Beds of Hospitals and Health Centers (pcs)	40	30	20	30
医院、卫生院技术人员数（人）	Medical Technical Personnel of Hospitals and Health Centers (person)	31	39	19	23
# 医　生	Doctors	12	18	3	9
卫生防疫人员数（人）	Personnel of Epidemic Prevention (person)	3	4	3	5
参加基本养老保险人数（人）	Persons Participation in Basic Old-Pension Insurance (person)	2 516	2 050	1 427	743
参加基本医疗保险人数（人）	Persons Participation in Medical Insurance (person)	2 516	2 050	2 548	743
参加失业保险人数（人）	Persons Participation in Unemployment Insurance (person)	2 516	2 050	1 427	743
团场居民最低生活保障人数（人）	Bottommost Living Security of Farm Households (person)	253	319	562	372

Continued

十二师二二一团 Farm 221 Division 12	十三师红星一场 Red Star No. 1 Farm Division 13	十三师红星二场 Red Star No. 2 Farm Division 13	十三师红星四场 Red Star No. 4 Farm Division 13	十三师黄田农场 Huangtian Farm Division 13	十三师火箭农场 Huojian Farm Division 13	十三师柳树泉农场 Liushuqian Farm Division 13	十三师红山农场 Hongshan Farm Division 13	十三师淖毛湖农场 Lao Maohu Farm Division 13	十四师四十七团 Farm 47 Division 14
010598886	010632781	010632810	01063279X	010632773	010632722	010632853	710772144	010632837	742225313
景占斌	卢根昌	贾瑞强	吴江京	张世全	赵来疆	曹　萍	王忠明	龚安家	金文杰
吐鲁番市	哈密市	哈密市	哈密市	哈密市	哈密市	哈密市	巴里坤哈萨克自治县	伊吾县	墨玉县
838003	839108	839113	839105	839103	839000	839117	839202	839303	848112
1956	1953	1953	1959	1958	1958	1960	1958	1964	1953
种植业	种植业	种植业	种植业	种植业	种植业	种植业	种植业	种植业	种植业
78.30	15.00	20.30	125.50	65.00	18.15	120.00	305.90	2.90	13.51
18	32	31	37	40	35	24	52	16	13
9	7	12	9	13	21	8	15	2	11
3	9	6	3	10	8	2	7	2	1
1	1	1	2	1	2	1	1		
2	1	1	1	1	1	1	4	1	
1 994	2 953	2 853	2 874	5 587	5 510	5 424	4 184	1 290	1 370
1 558	1 712	1 841	1 812	2 103	2 853	4 265	2 348	693	1 079
95	226	270	173	1 995	1 028	306	772	262	29
341	1 015	742	889	1 489	1 629	853	1 064	335	262
2 028	2 875	2 816	2 639	5 102	5 502	5 359	4 101	1 278	1 371
89	73	74	107	156	130	70	97	65	65
825	2 270	2 091	1 993	2 498	4 902	2 508	2 513	680	315
1 133	1 869	2 312	1 845	2 368	4 512	1 500	2 760	990	688
207	748	387	760	460	863	382	222	198	275
300	1 071	577	1 386	1 009	1 315	760	930	310	425
100	100	100	100	100	100	98	100	100	100
100	100	100	100	99	100	100	100	100	100
89	86	90	90	86	76	51	82	86	
30	45	40	50	40	130	50	70	21	20
28	53	38	59	50	69	47	79	23	23
8	25	18	33	23	36	18	47	6	3
5	4	3	5	3	6	6	10	2	2
1 816	1 795	1 961	1 982	2 186	3 554	7 606	3 443	645	1 063
1 816	1 795	1 966	1 982	2 186	3 554	1 309	3 443	645	1 063
1 816	1 793	1 966	1 982	2 186	3 554	462	3 443	645	1 063
806	493	329	877	966	700	1 423	1 980	49	783

21—1 续表 11 continued

（2010 年）

指 标	Item	十四师皮山农场 Pishan Farm Division 14	十四师一牧场 Ranch 1 Division 14	十四师二二四团 Farm 224 Division 14	兵团直属二二二团 Directly under XPCG Farm 222
法人代码	Enterprise Corporative Code	751675113	742245904	731812280	010634824
法人代表	Enterprise Corporative Representative	刘惠明	肖安家	黄 然	王 军
所在县市	Under County or City	皮山县	策勒县	皮山县	阜康市
邮政编码	Post Code	845156	848306	848116	831505
建场年份	The Year of Farm Establishment	1955	1950	2004	1959
行业分类	Sector Classification	种植业	牲畜饲养放牧业	种植业	种植业
团场占地面积 （千公顷）	Cover an Area of Farm Headquarters (1 000 hectares)	34.49	80.71	20.85	22.50
产业活动单位数合计 （个）	Number of Basic Units Engaged (unit)	26	13	14	26
# 农业连队	Agriculture Brigade	11	5	8	8
工 业	Industry	1		1	2
建筑业	Construction			1	1
批发零售业	Wholesale and Retail Trade	1	1		3
年末从业人员 （人）	Employed Persons (person)	5 429	816	4 411	3 150
第一产业	Primary Industry	3 923	599	3 856	2 107
第二产业	Secondary Industry	137	44		418
第三产业	Tertiary Industry	1 369	173	555	625
从业人员年平均人数 （人）	Annual Average Employed Persons (person)	5 477	841	4 457	3 154
境内公路里程 （公里）	Length of Highways (km)	177	353	540	44
团场电话年末用户 （户）	Telephone Customer of Farm at the Year-end (household)	1 590	295	896	3 100
移动电话年末用户 （户）	Mobile Phone Customer of Farm at the Year-end (household)	1 830	456	2 341	2 310
普通中学在校学生数 （人）	Student Enrollment in Regular Secondary Schools (person)	1 268		513	618
小学在校学生数 （人）	Student Enrollment in Primary Schools (person)	2 823	230	957	727
学龄儿童入学率 （%）	Percentage of School-age Enrolled (%)	100	100	100	100
初中升学率 （%）	Percentage of Junior Secondary Schools (%)	69	98	100	100
高中升学率 （%）	Percentage of Senior Secondary Schools (%)	67			65
医院、卫生院床位数 （床）	Beds of Hospitals and Health Centers (pcs)	105	25	35	40
医院、卫生院技术人员数 （人）	Medical Technical Personnel of Hospitals and Health Centers (person)	76	17	21	43
# 医 生	Doctors	31	3	8	26
卫生防疫人员数 （人）	Personnel of Epidemic Prevention (person)	9	3	2	3
参加基本养老保险人数 （人）	Persons Participation in Basic Old-Pension Insurance (person)	4 237	369	3 114	2 819
参加基本医疗保险人数 （人）	Persons Participation in Medical Insurance (person)	4 237	369	3 114	2 819
参加失业保险人数 （人）	Persons Participation in Unemployment Insurance (person)	4 237	369	3 114	2 819
团场居民最低生活保障人数 （人）	Bottommost Living Security of Farm Households (person)	3 181	412	170	865

21—2 团场主要经济指标

Main Economic Indicators of Farms

（2010 年）

指标		Item		一师一团 Farm 1 Division 1	一师二团 Farm 2 Division 1	一师三团 Farm 3 Division1	一师四团 Farm 4 Division 1
生产总值	（万元）	Gross Domestic Products	（10 000 yuan）	56 613	45 558	56 259	15 109
第一产业		Primary Industry		44 715	35 118	45 742	10 716
第二产业		Secondary Industry		5 426	5 513	4 339	1 940
# 工　业		Industry		3 805	2 626	3 510	1 871
第三产业		Tertiary Industry		6 472	4 927	6 178	2 453
固定资产投资总额	（万元）	Investment in Fixed Assets	（10 000 yuan）	17 116	14 651	7 410	4 016
总播种面积	（千公顷）	Total Sown Areas	（1000 hectares）	14.20	9.90	11.53	5.86
粮食：播种面积	（千公顷）	Grain:Sown Areas	（1000 hectares）	1.86	2.66	0.70	4.51
总产量	（吨）	Total Output	（ton）	20 090	19 465	7 151	44 186
# 小麦：播种面积		Wheat:Sown Areas		0.31		0.05	2.00
总产量		Total Output		2 006		341	16 276
棉花：播种面积	（千公顷）	Cotton:Sown Areas	（1 000 hectares）	11.58	6.29	8.30	
总产量	（吨）	Total Output	（ton）	28 080	13 773	23 279	
油料：播种面积	（千公顷）	Oil-bearing Crops:Sown Areas	（1 000 hectares）				0.03
总产量	（吨）	Total Output	（ton）				91
甜菜：播种面积	（千公顷）	Beetroots:Sown Areas	（1 000 hectares）				
总产量	（吨）	Total Output	（ton）				
当年造林面积	（公顷）	Afforestation Area In the Current Year	（hectare）	40	41	142	173
年末果园面积	（公顷）	Planted Area of Fruits	（hectare）	2 957	2 006	3 573	1 154
水果产量	（吨）	Output of Fruits	（ton）	21 542	18 011	25 089	182
肉类总产量	（吨）	Total Output of Meat	（ton）	1 416	1 307	1 051	954
牲畜年底存栏头数	（万头）	Number of Livestock	（10000 heads）	3.62	2.35	3.29	4.39
# 大牲畜		Large Animals		0.38	0.29	0.10	0.55
猪		Pigs		1.27	1.20	0.49	0.18
羊		Sheep and Goats		1.97	0.86	2.70	3.66
工业总产值	（万元）	Gross Industrial Output Value	（10 000 yuan）	11 269	7 545	16 821	3 293
建筑业总产值	（万元）	Composition Output Value	（10 000 yuan）	10 406	15 038	5 318	443
全年用电量	（万千瓦时）	Electricity Consumed	（10 000 kwh）	2 691	1 870	2 648	417
# 工业用电量		Industry Electricity Consumed	（10 000 kwh）	651	578	680	154
农业用电量		Agriculture Electricity Consumed	（10 000 kwh）	1 501	971	1 886	141
民用汽车拥有量	（辆）	Civil Motor Vehicles	（unit）	1 250	651	358	160
# 私人汽车		Private Motor Vehicles		1 226	630	349	124
社会消费品零售总额	（万元）	Total Retail Sales of Consumer Goods	（10 000 yuan）	7 667	4 082	2 848	4 186
主营业务收入	（万元）	Main Business Income	（10000 yuan）	58 741	44 207	60 354	8 712
营业利润	（万元）	Business Profits	（10000 yuan）	4 439	4 643	5 966	564
利润总额	（万元）	Total Profits	（10000 yuan）	2 633	3 019	2 850	397

21—2 续表 1

(2010 年)

指　　标		Item		一师五团 Farm 5 Division 1	一师六团 Farm 6 Division 1	一师七团 Farm 7 Division 1	一师八团 Farm 8 Division 1
生产总值	(万元)	Gross Domestic Products	(10 000 yuan)	34 140	24 315	42 194	36 231
第一产业		Primary Industry		23 056	15 202	34 777	28 392
第二产业		Secondary Industry		7 802	4 944	3 146	4 266
# 工　业		Industry		1 529	2 207	2 151	3 109
第三产业		Tertiary Industry		3 282	4 169	4 271	3 573
固定资产投资总额	(万元)	Investment in Fixed Assets	(10 000 yuan)	9 205	23 263	9 114	8 673
总播种面积	(千公顷)	Total Sown Areas	(1000 hectares)	7.79	3.29	9.29	9.89
粮食：播种面积	(千公顷)	Grain:Sown Areas	(1000 hectares)	1.03	0.10	1.13	1.00
总产量	(吨)	Total Output	(ton)	7 783	1 441	9 510	10 257
# 小麦:播种面积		Wheat:Sown Areas		0.41		0.10	0.07
总产量		Total Output		2 103		475	300
棉花：播种面积	(千公顷)	Cotton:Sown Areas	(1 000 hectares)	4.37	2.43	7.59	7.91
总产量	(吨)	Total Output	(ton)	10 368	5 864	21 180	18 160
油料：播种面积	(千公顷)	Oil-bearing Crops:Sown Areas	(1 000 hectares)	0.07			
总产量	(吨)	Total Output	(ton)	138			
甜菜:播种面积	(千公顷)	Beetroots:Sown Areas	(1 000 hectares)				
总产量	(吨)	Total Output	(ton)				
当年造林面积	(公顷)	Afforestation Area In the Current Year	(hectare)	227	40	60	42
年末果园面积	(公顷)	Planted Area of Fruits	(hectare)	3 976	3 013	1 708	3 125
水果产量	(吨)	Output of Fruits	(ton)	51 513	19 040	16 149	20 053
肉类总产量	(吨)	Total Output of Meat	(ton)	1 203	804	1 080	1 186
牲畜年底存栏头数	(万头)	Number of Livestock	(10000 heads)	3.81	2.64	4.12	3.07
# 大牲畜		Large Animals		0.97	0.28	0.14	0.06
猪		Pigs		0.25	0.86	0.55	0.77
羊		Sheep and Goats		2.59	1.50	3.43	2.24
工业总产值	(万元)	Gross Industrial Output Value	(10 000 yuan)	7 939	7 939	8 309	12 526
建筑业总产值	(万元)	Composition Output Value	(10 000 yuan)	52 066	17 576	6 373	7 419
全年用电量	(万千瓦时)	Electricity Consumed	(10 000 kwh)	3 540	1 412	2 048	1 551
# 工业用电量		Industry Electricity Consumed	(10 000 kwh)	18	205	540	300
农业用电量		Agriculture Electricity Consumed	(10 000 kwh)	3 505	501	935	780
民用汽车拥有量	(辆)	Civil Motor Vehicles	(unit)	482	555	189	627
# 私人汽车		Private Motor Vehicles		462	538	178	617
社会消费品零售总额	(万元)	Total Retail Sales of Consumer Goods	(10 000 yuan)	4 463	2 887	6 066	4 491
主营业务收入	(万元)	Main Business Income	(10000 yuan)	31 059	23 057	45 131	36 941
营业利润	(万元)	Business Profits	(10000 yuan)	1 862	1 701	3 939	2 442
利润总额	(万元)	Total Profits	(10000 yuan)	1 300	583	1 339	1 653

Continued

一师十团 Farm10 Division 1	一师十一团 Farm 11 Division 1	一师十二团 Farm 12 Division 1	一师十三团 Farm 13 Division 1	一师十四团 Farm 14 Division 1	一师十六团 Farm 16 Division 1	二师三十一团 Farm 21 Division 2	二师三十二团 Farm 22 Division 2	二师三十四团 Farm 24 Division 2
68 737	31 374	36 266	37 176	32 259	57 750	22 248	41 705	20 355
49 681	24 343	20 600	28 809	22 961	37 241	15 905	18 722	14 456
10 499	2 651	11 889	2 337	4 321	11 384	3 021	15 494	2 074
8 579	2 007	3 827	2 148	4 202	8 369	2 609	14 552	1 841
8 557	4 380	3 777	6 030	4 977	9 125	3 322	7 489	3 825
12 200	4 703	11 570	8 928	7 919	7 768	3 775	5 230	7 243
8.64	8.58	5.47	8.02	5.04	9.81	6.17	10.06	6.78
1.72	0.20	0.91	0.11	0.98	0.63	1.42	2.07	1.83
16 000	900	5 205	850	8 280	5 930	12 384	13 782	11 645
0.17		0.53		0.07		0.94	1.53	1.67
820		2 381		210		6 624	11 277	10 675
6.37	4.31	3.54	6.50	3.22	7.59			0.24
18 800	11 168	9 520	16 861	9 167	21 407			322
							0.14	0.10
							299	171
						0.80	1.87	0.87
						72 000	145 756	60 143
73	40	135	100	16	47	12		3
4 211	3 589	2 030	2 680	4 380	1 771	995	698	674
28 160	20 000	17 002	28 025	19 016	10 079	510	1 457	6 281
1 800	1 205	501	858	805	1 239	3 354	3 242	3 552
4.50	1.56	1.56	1.95	2.15	1.98	6.61	14.01	7.02
0.38	0.12	0.07	0.16	0.18	0.14	0.17	0.16	0.04
1.25	0.39	0.45	0.21	0.41	1.05	2.45	0.35	4.55
2.87	1.05	1.04	1.58	1.56	0.79	3.99	13.50	2.43
20 160	9 104	12 219	7 404	14 506	33 184	17 459	48 479	7 721
8 665	4 129	34 507	1 210	761	13 970	1 276	1 684	685
1 728	1 926	3 041	1 959	1 512	1 454	655	1 251	859
398	626	1 198	705	358	942	247	754	72
1 330	1 300	388	1 254	442	512	256	213	698
642	547	845	1 453	732	230	103	171	110
619	537	828	1 434	721	208	92	164	95
14 287	4 395	5 496	6 948	5 624	7 559	2 466	2 588	5 768
39 395	26 623	21 689	42 007	23 242	37 101	12 705	23 883	21 231
4 002	2 163	1 521	3 279	3 329	2 165	−1 128	302	271
2 061	787	1 343	1 849	1 534	1 683	−1 534	204	277

21—2 续表 2

（2010 年）

指　　标		Item		二师三十五团 Farm 25 Division 2	二师三十七团 Farm 27 Division 2	二师二十九团 Farm 29 Division 2	二师三十团 Farm 30 Division 2
生产总值	（万元）	Gross Domestic Products	（10 000 yuan）	11 712	15 324	65 582	28 870
第一产业		Primary Industry		6 565	9 211	44 087	24 022
第二产业		Secondary Industry		3 316	3 451	10 296	1 704
# 工　业		Industry		3 244	3 052	9 852	1 607
第三产业		Tertiary Industry		1 831	2 662	11 199	3 144
固定资产投资总额	（万元）	Investment in Fixed Assets	（10 000 yuan）	14 883	5 093	7 672	3 576
总播种面积	（千公顷）	Total Sown Areas	（1000 hectares）	2. 18	4. 19	8. 99	5. 36
粮食：播种面积	（千公顷）	Grain：Sown Areas	（1000 hectares）	0. 53	1. 15	0. 13	0. 01
总产量	（吨）	Total Output	（ton）	4 720	7 054	600	68
# 小麦：播种面积		Wheat：Sown Areas		0. 27	0. 67		
总产量		Total Output		2 180	4 243		
棉花：播种面积	（千公顷）	Cotton：Sown Areas	（1 000 hectares）			8. 67	5. 33
总产量	（吨）	Total Output	（ton）			23 260	12 801
油料：播种面积	（千公顷）	Oil-bearing Crops：Sown Areas	（1 000 hectares）	0. 01			
总产量	（吨）	Total Output	（ton）	46			
甜菜：播种面积	（千公顷）	Beetroots：Sown Areas	（1 000 hectares）	0. 21	0. 73		
总产量	（吨）	Total Output	（ton）	19 200	64 408		
当年造林面积	（公顷）	Afforestation Area In the Current Year	（hectare）	3	13		18
年末果园面积	（公顷）	Planted Area of Fruits	（hectare）	88	61	4 907	1 575
水果产量	（吨）	Output of Fruits	（ton）	495	1 168	56 362	22 295
肉类总产量	（吨）	Total Output of Meat	（ton）	642	1 494	11 024	2 292
牲畜年底存栏头数	（万头）	Number of Livestock	（10000 heads）	0. 85	5. 20	11. 85	3. 70
# 大牲畜		Large Animals		0. 02	0. 34	0. 09	0. 25
猪		Pigs		0. 35	0. 40	11. 09	1. 62
羊		Sheep and Goats		0. 48	4. 46	0. 67	1. 83
工业总产值	（万元）	Gross Industrial Output Value	（10 000 yuan）	15 660	12 696	36 288	6 264
建筑业总产值	（万元）	Composition Output Value	（10 000 yuan）	233	2 230	1 200	256
全年用电量	（万千瓦时）	Electricity Consumed	（10 000 kwh）	614	678	3 850	1 843
# 工业用电量		Industry Electricity Consumed	（10 000 kwh）	478	266	980	332
农业用电量		Agriculture Electricity Consumed	（10 000 kwh）	97	296	2 018	1 287
民用汽车拥有量	（辆）	Civil Motor Vehicles	（unit）	62	304	914	242
# 私人汽车		Private Motor Vehicles		49	279	900	225
社会消费品零售总额	（万元）	Total Retail Sales of Consumer Goods	（10 000 yuan）	1 538	1 559	9 243	4 529
主营业务收入	（万元）	Main Business Income	（10000 yuan）	10 439	13 833	56 828	33 589
营业利润	（万元）	Business Profits	（10000 yuan）	−1 185	−1 476	2 559	1 761
利润总额	（万元）	Total Profits	（10000 yuan）	636	302	2 459	1 604

Continued

二师 三十一团 Farm 31 Division 2	二师 三十三团 Farm 33 Division 2	二师 三十四团 Farm 34 Division 2	二师 三十六团 Farm 36 Division 2	二师 二二三团 Farm 223 Division 2	二师 三十八团 Farm 38 Division 2	三师 四十一团 Farm 41 Division 3	三师 四十二团 Farm 42 Division 3	三师 四十四团 Farm 44 Division 3
19 326	28 904	19 862	17 091	13 090	2 259	11 388	11 941	35 862
15 032	22 808	17 383	13 456	6 878	1 218	8 146	9 276	26 678
1 135	1 479	420	1 190	4 082	19	843	786	2 915
984	1 195	215	1 114	3 706	19	503	350	2 573
3 159	4 617	2 059	2 445	2 130	1 022	2 399	1 879	6 269
4 020	4 318	4 903	7 293	4 002	1 007	10 798	7 995	11 784
3.27	4.78	3.51	1.81	2.40	3.47	3.75	3.82	12.21
0.20	0.27	0.27	0.20	1.22		0.47	0.80	2.67
920	1 225	1 200	905	5 690		3 200	3 850	15 115
				1.18			0.33	1.00
				5 210			1 530	6 015
2.63	4.01	3.07	1.49			2.60	2.52	4.63
6 980	11 118	8 114	3 269			3 850	6 800	11 524
				0.09				
				137				
				0.40				
				32 112				
21	7		70	1 349	500	4		333
3 276	5 403	5 360	3 132	1 968	3 467	1 699	253	4 577
22 184	39 500	30 738	12 539	19 550		8 048	2 450	21 640
743	1 520	981	1 147	1 248		945	452	2 140
1.90	1.30	2.28	4.45	5.56		0.94	0.97	8.60
0.08	0.13	0.16	0.04	0.32		0.01	0.04	0.27
0.22	0.26	0.15	0.05	0.13		0.79	0.14	0.60
1.60	0.91	1.97	4.36	5.11		0.14	0.79	7.73
2 289	2 811	515	15 273	13 100	36	1 492	987	7 004
190	942	638	255	1 189		1 429	1 720	1 435
1 415	1 374	1 318	1 987	1 125	63	440	410	3 910
56	153	164	1 046	366	3	151	190	175
1 033	1 012	1 154	678	97	60	268	180	2 350
270	360	336	147	192	18	158	98	874
257	338	312	143	123	10	150	84	858
2 308	2 819	2 948	2 469	865		5 276	1 405	6 404
21 272	28 741	23 354	14 814	4 974	1 046	3 020	14 527	24 006
1 333	1 907	1 307	1 513	−278	−2 632	−271	626	1 991
806	1 365	1 219	1 504	206	−2 549	229	1 233	1 459

21—2 续表 3

（2010 年）

指　　标	Item	三　师 四十五团 Farm 45 Division 3	三　师 四十六团 Farm 46 Division 3	三　师 四十八团 Farm 48 Division 3	三　师 四十九团 Farm 49 Division 3
生产总值　（万元）	Gross Domestic Products　(10 000 yuan)	55 715	9 777	21 449	33 235
第一产业	Primary Industry	38 090	7 667	17 189	25 487
第二产业	Secondary Industry	10 462	564	1 187	2 068
# 工　业	Industry	5 501	564	1 048	1 806
第三产业	Tertiary Industry	7 163	1 546	3 073	5 680
固定资产投资总额（万元）	Investment in Fixed Assets　(10 000 yuan)	16 082	6 792	7 557	7 512
总播种面积　（千公顷）	Total Sown Areas　(1000 hectares)	19.40	1.88	3.64	8.38
粮食：播种面积（千公顷）	Grain: Sown Areas　(1000 hectares)	2.06	0.56	0.31	1.65
总产量　（吨）	Total Output　(ton)	11 400	3 250	2 080	13 450
# 小麦：播种面积	Wheat: Sown Areas		0.47	0.17	
总产量	Total Output		2 450	900	
棉花：播种面积（千公顷）	Cotton: Sown Areas　(1 000 hectares)	11.05	0.73	2.04	4.89
总产量　（吨）	Total Output　(ton)	24 800	2 106	5 420	14 000
油料：播种面积（千公顷）	Oil-bearing Crops: Sown Areas　(1 000 hectares)			0.33	
总产量　（吨）	Total Output　(ton)			950	
甜菜：播种面积（千公顷）	Beetroots: Sown Areas　(1 000 hectares)				
总产量　（吨）	Total Output　(ton)				
当年造林面积　（公顷）	Afforestation Area In the Current Year　(hectare)		245		333
年末果园面积　（公顷）	Planted Area of Fruits　(hectare)	3 225	3 082	4 147	2 106
水果产量　（吨）	Output of Fruits　(ton)	24 335	11 882	26 700	13 382
肉类总产量　（吨）	Total Output of Meat　(ton)	2 131	533	1 135	1 162
牲畜年底存栏头数（万头）	Number of Livestock　(10000 heads)	7.43	1.84	1.89	2.15
# 大牲畜	Large Animals	0.56	0.03	0.04	0.03
猪	Pigs	1.07	0.85	1.44	0.41
羊	Sheep and Goats	5.80	0.96	0.41	1.71
工业总产值　（万元）	Gross Industrial Output Value　(10 000 yuan)	14 550	564	6 544	5 549
建筑业总产值　（万元）	Composition Output Value　(10 000 yuan)	21 105		552	1 093
全年用电量　（万千瓦时）	Electricity Consumed　(10 000 kwh)	2 920	592	2 279	1 660
# 工业用电量	Industry Electricity Consumed　(10 000 kwh)	406	41	350	450
农业用电量	Agriculture Electricity Consumed　(10 000 kwh)	2 510	424	1 760	1 210
民用汽车拥有量　（辆）	Civil Motor Vehicles　(unit)	815	124	369	464
# 私人汽车	Private Motor Vehicles	782	110	361	452
社会消费品零售总额（万元）	Total Retail Sales of Consumer Goods　(10 000 yuan)	5 986	95	2 160	6 799
主营业务收入　（万元）	Main Business Income　(10000 yuan)	18 963	5 657	11 609	29 215
营业利润　（万元）	Business Profits　(10000 yuan)	1 878	758	1 784	1 751
利润总额　（万元）	Total Profits　(10000 yuan)	2 349	227	747	1 632

Continued

三 师 五 十 团 Farm 50 Division 3	三 师 五十一团 Farm 51 Division 3	三 师 五十三团 Farm 53 Division 3	三 师 伽师总场 Jiashi Farm Division 3	三 师 东风农场 Dongfen Farm Division 3	三 师 红旗农场 Redflag Farm Division 3	三 师 叶城牧场 Yechen Farm Division 3	三 师 托云牧场 Tuoyun Farm Division 3	四 师 六十一团 Farm 61 Division 4
25 408	27 480	27 930	21 725	1 758	3 254	2 123	963	19 265
19 204	17 430	22 383	14 530	1 232	2 605	1 476	548	11 974
1 828	2 725	964	1 868	10	73	154	3	2 436
1 548	2 458	744	1 578	10	11	154	3	1 596
4 376	7 325	4 583	5 327	516	576	493	412	4 855
11 196	9 781	9 204	7 343	1 421	2 650	2 093	3 664	8 027
7.50	10.86	8.58	6.75	0.36	1.07	2.43	0.03	5.55
1.57	4.25	2.67	0.93	0.18	0.82	1.73	0.01	3.13
7 900	20 193	14 991	5 050	1 074	4 350	11 183	50	22 411
0.80	2.00	1.34	0.13	0.13	0.53	1.07	0.01	1.02
4 500	9 715	7 491	850	680	3 300	6 713	50	8 348
4.21	4.53	4.04	5.00		0.08	0.67		
10 590	8 778	11 339	9 200		140	878		
				0.02				0.62
				77				1 712
								0.21
								17 050
8	67	467		6	15	2		33
3 696	3 412	2 793	778	341	43	165		2 472
10 849	5 964	12 607	1 916	1 409	387	2 040		24 097
1 471	1 655	1 230	823	850	193	152	451	2 786
4.60	6.60	5.21	4.08	4.51	0.93	0.90	4.01	5.38
0.09	0.63	0.27	0.21	0.17	0.06	0.20	0.06	0.38
0.28	0.49	0.24	0.11	0.02	0.07		0.01	0.30
4.23	5.48	4.70	3.76	4.32	0.80	0.70	3.94	4.70
5 240	8 123	2 566	1 616	31	28	513	7	3 600
963	956	850	1 112		600			
2 000	1 326	1 510	1 359	30	44	21	19	450
120	496	60	247	5	1	13	2	200
1 600	681	1 300	875	25	42	3	3	250
112	129	91	85	21	35	17	28	180
96	106	83	65	17	32	13	25	160
3 769	9 600	6 190	4 200	44	208	65	101	3 098
23 725	23 883	22 473	15 472					6 534
691	592	1 717	306			−426		−200
1 196	1 100	1 106	1 320			−9		−38

21—2 续表 4

（2010 年）

指　　标	Item	四　师 六十二团 Farm 62 Division 4	四　师 六十三团 Farm 63 Division 4	四　师 六十四团 Farm 64 Division 4	四　师 六十六团 Farm 66 Division 4
生产总值　（万元）	Gross Domestic Products　（10 000 yuan）	30 501	19 742	22 451	36 068
第一产业	Primary Industry	13 687	12 991	15 410	17 427
第二产业	Secondary Industry	7 365	3 987	2 624	8 964
# 工　业	Industry	4 017	3 506	1 750	7 273
第三产业	Tertiary Industry	9 449	2 764	4 417	9 677
固定资产投资总额　（万元）	Investment in Fixed Assets　（10 000 yuan）	11 200	4 405	12 852	9 997
总播种面积　（千公顷）	Total Sown Areas　（1000 hectares）	4. 49	6. 50	8. 99	9. 24
粮食：播种面积　（千公顷）	Grain：Sown Areas　（1000 hectares）	2. 70	0. 56	2. 55	7. 02
总产量　（吨）	Total Output　（ton）	21 174	4 566	20 882	52 941
# 小麦：播种面积	Wheat：Sown Areas	0. 67	0. 24	0. 60	1. 78
总产量	Total Output	4 988	1 675	4 455	14 465
棉花：播种面积　（千公顷）	Cotton：Sown Areas　（1 000 hectares）	1. 20	2. 60	3. 21	0. 03
总产量　（吨）	Total Output　（ton）	2 023	4 123	5 002	35
油料：播种面积　（千公顷）	Oil-bearing Crops：Sown Areas　（1 000 hectares）		0. 50	0. 73	0. 42
总产量　（吨）	Total Output　（ton）		1 087	1 967	1 095
甜菜：播种面积　（千公顷）	Beetroots：Sown Areas　（1 000 hectares）	0. 33	0. 48	0. 86	0. 47
总产量　（吨）	Total Output　（ton）	30 120	42 397	64 440	39 694
当年造林面积　（公顷）	Afforestation Area In the Current Year　（hectare）	17	115	70	45
年末果园面积　（公顷）	Planted Area of Fruits　（hectare）	2 572	928	527	982
水果产量　（吨）	Output of Fruits　（ton）	20 887	1 722	1 508	9 042
肉类总产量　（吨）	Total Output of Meat　（ton）	2 077	1 460	2 799	4 852
牲畜年底存栏头数　（万头）	Number of Livestock　（10000 heads）	6. 11	1. 94	7. 04	8. 59
# 大牲畜	Large Animals	0. 53	0. 08	0. 52	0. 42
猪	Pigs	1. 35	0. 34	0. 50	2. 35
羊	Sheep and Goats	4. 23	1. 52	6. 02	5. 82
工业总产值　（万元）	Gross Industrial Output Value　（10 000 yuan）	13 807	8 249	3 116	20 902
建筑业总产值　（万元）	Composition Output Value　（10 000 yuan）	11 239	1 050	906	5 242
全年用电量　（万千瓦时）	Electricity Consumed　（10 000 kwh）	1 341	1 675	1 200	2 304
# 工业用电量	Industry Electricity Consumed　（10 000 kwh）	559	162	65	1 515
农业用电量	Agriculture Electricity Consumed（10 000 kwh）	182	1 200	795	258
民用汽车拥有量　（辆）	Civil Motor Vehicles　（unit）	290	217	320	606
# 私人汽车	Private Motor Vehicles	290	196	297	568
社会消费品零售总额　（万元）	Total Retail Sales of Consumer Goods　（10 000 yuan）	10 673	1 896	3 043	5 943
主营业务收入　（万元）	Main Business Income　（10000 yuan）	12 439	16 163	20 082	27 587
营业利润　（万元）	Business Profits　（10000 yuan）	266	192	－141	－19
利润总额　（万元）	Total Profits　（10000 yuan）	116	186	123	412

Continued

四　师 六十七团 Farm 67 Division 4	四　师 六十八团 Farm 68 Division 4	四　师 六十九团 Farm 69 Division 4	四　师 七 十 团 Farm 70 Division 4	四　师 七十一团 Farm 71 Division 4	四　师 七十二团 Farm 72 Division 4	四　师 七十三团 Farm 73 Division 4	四　师 七十四团 Farm 74 Division 4	四　师 七十五团 Farm 75 Division 4
20 985	14 816	14 317	22 069	26 133	19 016	12 208	8 478	13 906
14 735	8 590	6 597	10 598	12 540	7 507	6 268	5 462	7 292
2 108	4 030	5 319	8 199	8 881	5 229	2 128	744	4 869
496	3 220	4 562	7 113	7 921	3 059	1 165	370	4 713
4 142	2 196	2 401	3 272	4 712	6 280	3 812	2 272	1 745
21 715	3 654	3 459	5 895	17 151	5 255	12 075	2 682	1 681
6.70	5.92	4.46	5.05	7.88	6.46	4.73	4.14	6.94
2.45	5.45	2.78	2.19	6.08	4.49	2.66	2.18	4.06
20 265	51 991	19 140	19 242	59 411	34 055	19 025	15 635	31 037
1.78	0.72	0.86	0.67	0.83	1.39	1.45	2.12	3.32
14 260	4 759	6 345	5 550	6 376	8 970	9 821	15 239	24 911
2.38	0.22	0.05	0.10					
3 750	388	74	155					
0.22	0.02	0.16	0.67	0.08	1.20	0.71	1.60	2.65
655	39	374	1 800		2 242	1 568	5 277	8 156
0.82	0.14	0.47	0.52	1.00	0.20			
85 000	12 860	35 030	45 182	79 510	11 976	95		
33	13	40	38	33	36	40	6	3
625	167	203	441		41	289		
2 322	414	693	5 031	598	500	1 761		
3 650	2 701	1 410	3 043	5 137	2 438	1 888	1 106	761
6.71	3.13	2.06	5.29	8.43	4.52	3.96	2.96	1.46
0.30	0.18	0.23	0.32	0.92	0.45	0.33	0.53	0.12
0.30	1.53	1.09	1.36	3.23	0.98	0.38	0.09	0.14
6.11	1.42	0.74	3.61	4.28	3.09	3.25	2.34	1.20
2 090	9 274	12 289	23 547	20 896	6 013	2 546	795	13 592
		10 650	4 955	4 823	5 500		2 197	515
1 999	630	572	428	878	356	620	112	310
18	326	184	200	789	118	266	12	201
1 420	27	388	228	89	238	187	36	70
220	224	225	181	172	325	202	130	196
208	200	215	159	127	300	184	119	185
4 083	1 441	1 180	3 341	3 858	5 769	3 518	650	1 000
16 820	20 667	5 313	17 415	24 339	10 272	3 966	10 123	10 975
−141	942	−39	−458	1 205	426	750	−271	778
105	327	101	−28	263	−35	190	−32	150

21—2 续表 5

(2010 年)

指 标	Item	四 师 七十六团 Farm 76 Division 4	四 师 七十七团 Farm 77 Division 4	四 师 七十八团 Farm 78 Division 4	四 师 七十九团 Farm 79 Division 4
生产总值 (万元)	Gross Domestic Products (10 000 yuan)	26 137	22 043	8 598	8 864
第一产业	Primary Industry	16 278	11 990	6 066	5 608
第二产业	Secondary Industry	6 253	4 937	1 430	1 698
# 工 业	Industry	5 845	3 567	941	1 320
第三产业	Tertiary Industry	3 606	5 116	1 102	1 558
固定资产投资总额 (万元)	Investment in Fixed Assets (10 000 yuan)	3 392	3 344	3 004	2 948
总播种面积 (千公顷)	Total Sown Areas (1000 hectares)	14.28	13.09	1.59	2.14
粮食:播种面积 (千公顷)	Grain:Sown Areas (1000 hectares)	7.24	6.47	0.66	1.24
总产量 (吨)	Total Output (ton)	47 394	37 226	3 497	8 606
# 小麦:播种面积	Wheat:Sown Areas	4.65	6.27	0.52	0.97
总产量	Total Output	29 309	35 720	3 028	6 146
棉花:播种面积 (千公顷)	Cotton:Sown Areas (1 000 hectares)			0.37	
总产量 (吨)	Total Output (ton)			576	
油料:播种面积 (千公顷)	Oil-bearing Crops:Sown Areas (1 000 hectares)	6.48	6.55	0.07	0.32
总产量 (吨)	Total Output (ton)	16 582	18 765	188	786
甜菜:播种面积 (千公顷)	Beetroots:Sown Areas (1 000 hectares)	0.02	0.03	0.01	0.46
总产量 (吨)	Total Output (ton)			520	33 497
当年造林面积 (公顷)	Afforestation Area In the Current Year (hectare)	3	13	73	21
年末果园面积 (公顷)	Planted Area of Fruits (hectare)			1 413	95
水果产量 (吨)	Output of Fruits (ton)			25 065	41
肉类总产量 (吨)	Total Output of Meat (ton)	3 640	3 538	1 602	1 972
牲畜年底存栏头数 (万头)	Number of Livestock (10000 heads)	7.04	5.89	5.01	6.52
# 大牲畜	Large Animals	1.40	0.86	0.54	1.13
猪	Pigs	0.43	0.09	0.07	0.25
羊	Sheep and Goats	5.21	4.94	4.40	5.14
工业总产值 (万元)	Gross Industrial Output Value (10 000 yuan)	15 941	13 948	2 793	3 422
建筑业总产值 (万元)	Composition Output Value (10 000 yuan)	1 089	2 734	1 464	919
全年用电量 (万千瓦时)	Electricity Consumed (10 000 kwh)	500	392	28	109
# 工业用电量	Industry Electricity Consumed (10 000 kwh)	113	47	11	36
农业用电量	Agriculture Electricity Consumed (10 000 kwh)	176	129	17	38
民用汽车拥有量 (辆)	Civil Motor Vehicles (unit)	354	222	59	70
# 私人汽车	Private Motor Vehicles	339	202	48	62
社会消费品零售总额 (万元)	Total Retail Sales of Consumer Goods (10 000 yuan)	1 704	4 629	530	967
主营业务收入 (万元)	Main Business Income (10000 yuan)	18 931	15 381	1 736	2 313
营业利润 (万元)	Business Profits (10000 yuan)	—32	—263	—117	—354
利润总额 (万元)	Total Profits (10000 yuan)	142	151	—13	—12

Continued

五师八十一团 Farm 81 Division 5	五师八十三团 Farm 83 Division 5	五师八十四团 Farm 84 Division 5	五师八十六团 Farm 86 Division 5	五师八十七团 Farm 87 Division 5	五师八十八团 Farm 88 Division 5	五师八十九团 Farm 89 Division 5	五师九十团 Farm 90 Division 5	五师九十一团 Farm 91 Division 5
27 837	42 886	13 939	29 898	7 396	6 467	35 060	28 574	6 703
22 879	28 297	7 341	22 551	4 238	3 353	26 294	22 728	5 221
1 539	6 365	3 590	3 185	929	1 296	4 401	2 232	702
1 183	4 010	3 260	2 480	738	1 222	1 401	1 535	200
3 419	8 224	3 008	4 162	2 229	1 818	4 365	3 614	780
12 135	14 073	5 298	6 021	3 810	2 092	11 256	4 371	5 381
6.02	10.60	8.47	7.87	3.10	4.11	8.43	6.73	3.98
0.33	2.77	5.26	1.35	2.05	3.03	0.47	0.39	1.20
3 121	15 708	41 632	6 013	14 215	19 590	3 306	1 731	5 113
0.07	1.77	4.33	1.35	0.19	2.69	0.07	0.32	0.93
381	4 308	30 236	6 013	1 335	17 580	306	981	1 993
5.40	7.67	0.20	5.81			7.20	5.93	1.73
15 655	20 000	432	15 200			19 200	16 400	4 668
0.05	0.07	1.00		0.23	0.84	0.03	0.32	0.47
88	50	2 420		755	2 500	51	240	560
			0.13	0.03		0.13		0.20
			8 600	1 750		8 600		1 050
28	74	40	46	90	28	62	34	36
633	1 302	30	1 190	28	7	695	153	149
5 876	11 752	33	10 056	165		6 670	3 000	1 331
754	1 924	803	1 419	587	912	756	724	567
1.02	3.01	4.54	6.12	4.01	3.58	1.63	1.03	0.73
0.04	0.20	0.21	0.08	0.14	0.22	0.06	0.12	0.02
0.60	1.11	0.23	1.00	0.28	0.19	0.30	0.28	0.24
0.38	1.70	4.10	5.04	3.59	3.17	1.27	0.63	0.47
3 495	11 589	8 071	7 922	1 552	4 118	3 991	6 139	733
1 244	9 890	1 080	3 965	386	275	9 000	1 678	2 641
2 645	3 943	1 856	3 116	288	1 210	3 703	2 820	1 175
94	843	472	245	39	996	420	370	148
1 858	2 636	1 301	2 016	152	93	2 497	2 450	975
806	601	514	312	68	215	689	476	57
279	567	497	265	56	208	652	459	49
2 392	8 737	2 746	4 878	1 616	2 895	3 567	2 728	256
5 592	60 158	21 355	50 391	6 684	6 755	12 985	40 252	13 400
1 381	3 145	−90	3 062	198	110	856	2 296	280
752	1 859	36	1 952	42	29	222	1 899	280

21—2 续表 6

(2010 年)

指 标	Item	六 师 一〇一团 Farm 101 Division 6	六 师 一〇二团 Farm 102 Division 6	六 师 一〇三团 Farm 103 Division 6	六 师 一〇五团 Farm 105 Division 6
生产总值 (万元)	Gross Domestic Products (10 000 yuan)	50 712	45 098	33 867	28 593
第一产业	Primary Industry	20 817	15 174	18 810	18 040
第二产业	Secondary Industry	12 726	13 389	6 701	3 870
# 工 业	Industry	7 934	7 565	5 840	2 307
第三产业	Tertiary Industry	17 169	16 535	8 356	6 683
固定资产投资总额 (万元)	Investment in Fixed Assets (10 000 yuan)	12 717	18 017	2 991	10 172
总播种面积 (千公顷)	Total Sown Areas (1000 hectares)	3. 25	5. 35	7. 78	7. 85
粮食：播种面积 (千公顷)	Grain：Sown Areas (1000 hectares)	0. 84	2. 64	3. 10	1. 84
总产量 (吨)	Total Output (ton)	6 057	17 566	16 078	11 263
# 小麦：播种面积	Wheat：Sown Areas	0. 57	2. 52	2. 57	1. 60
总产量	Total Output	3 632	16 355	10 775	8 435
棉花：播种面积 (千公顷)	Cotton：Sown Areas (1 000 hectares)	0. 67	0. 95	2. 67	4. 75
总产量 (吨)	Total Output (ton)	1 250	1 680	4 695	8 781
油料：播种面积 (千公顷)	Oil-bearing Crops：Sown Areas (1 000 hectares)	0. 21	0. 37	0. 13	0. 05
总产量 (吨)	Total Output (ton)	704	1 288	507	67
甜菜：播种面积 (千公顷)	Beetroots：Sown Areas (1 000 hectares)				0. 03
总产量 (吨)	Total Output (ton)				1 959
当年造林面积 (公顷)	Afforestation Area In the Current Year (hectare)	14	13	1 542	9
年末果园面积 (公顷)	Planted Area of Fruits (hectare)	1 397	339	5	221
水果产量 (吨)	Output of Fruits (ton)	7 100	10	15	102
肉类总产量 (吨)	Total Output of Meat (ton)	6 858	6 994	5 047	3 797
牲畜年底存栏头数 (万头)	Number of Livestock (10000 heads)	3. 69	4. 74	5. 96	3. 68
# 大牲畜	Large Animals	0. 13	0. 05	0. 22	0. 06
猪	Pigs	3. 06	2. 03	4. 30	2. 99
羊	Sheep and Goats	0. 50	2. 66	1. 44	0. 63
工业总产值 (万元)	Gross Industrial Output Value (10 000 yuan)	26 296	29 622	28 113	7 740
建筑业总产值 (万元)	Composition Output Value (10 000 yuan)	7 145	17 207	2 397	7 249
全年用电量 (万千瓦时)	Electricity Consumed (10 000 kwh)	3 456	3 515	3 298	3 409
# 工业用电量	Industry Electricity Consumed (10 000 kwh)	686	1 196	507	300
农业用电量	Agriculture Electricity Consumed (10 000 kwh)	2 700	2 165	2 517	3 044
民用汽车拥有量 (辆)	Civil Motor Vehicles (unit)	1 036	1 023	565	600
# 私人汽车	Private Motor Vehicles	1 036	1 005	550	587
社会消费品零售总额 (万元)	Total Retail Sales of Consumer Goods (10 000 yuan)	32 000	22 870	6 721	5 363
主营业务收入 (万元)	Main Business Income (10000 yuan)	15 414	18 894	17 676	27 997
营业利润 (万元)	Business Profits (10000 yuan)	−1 249	−765	−3 981	2 183
利润总额 (万元)	Total Profits (10000 yuan)	−938	−1 426	−2 985	1 895

Continued

六师一〇六团 Farm 106 Division 6	六师芳草湖农场 Fang Caohu Farm Division 6	六师新湖农场 Xinhu Farm Division 6	六师军户农场 Junhu Farm Division 6	六师共青团农场 Communist League Tuan Farm Division 6	六师六运湖农场 liu Yuhu Farm Division 6	六师土墩子农场 TudunZi Farm Division 6	六师红旗农场 Red Flag Farm Division 6	六师奇台农场 Qitai Farm Division 6	六师北塔山牧场 Bei Tashan Farm Division 6
22 347	135 983	106 373	23 314	26 572	11 326	14 800	33 646	83 845	6 282
13 275	70 338	66 977	15 457	19 603	6 781	7 990	14 006	35 782	1 322
4 465	32 768	17 986	3 158	1 721	1 593	4 833	9 737	32 338	3 273
1 443	26 395	11 092	620	366	238	2 778	5 587	28 445	3 166
4 607	32 877	21 410	4 699	5 248	2 952	1 977	9 903	15 725	1 687
2 130	67 221	32 158	11 620	17 275	5 412	14 563	13 426	19 331	6 503
5.32	27.52	27.04	4.89	10.59	2.61	4.18	8.81	20.98	0.29
0.29	3.88	5.64	3.57	6.13	1.15	1.00	5.76	17.93	0.14
3 279	40 893	64 923	30 579	35 818	9 933	10 090	55 558	167 882	744
0.05	1.11	0.98	0.57	5.91	0.76	0.47	4.26	13.23	0.11
304	5 650	5 411	3 858	32 993	5 346	3 290	34 870	106 143	526
3.43	16.24	18.00		3.33	0.72	0.13	0.27		
7 535	33 000	37 383		7 590	1 398	240	525		
0.33	1.09	0.80	0.07	0.10	0.36	1.73	1.40	0.65	0.01
1 470	4 344	2 708	150	420	1 652	6 630	2 538	1 697	16
							0.29	0.46	
							19 531	41 820	
7	164	124	7	85	7	32	767	44	7
333	1 608	221	1 467	333	31			14	
	4 039	1 933	22 436	85	850	51	20	150	
776	8 739	6 080	3 874	1 620	1 255	1 425	2 619	9 644	809
1.63	12.86	10.62	4.11	4.06	2.86	3.13	11.62	19.21	5.10
0.02	0.35	0.46	1.04	0.13	0.16	0.29	0.68	0.75	0.42
0.08	4.40	1.38	0.86	0.96	0.30	0.07	0.50	6.12	
1.53	8.11	8.78	2.21	2.97	2.40	2.77	10.44	12.34	4.68
4 601	87 416	34 161	2 089	1 233	803	898	19 061	111 196	4 471
1 145	24 013	25 799	10 551	5 133	5 132	7 783	15 083	13 272	407
1 013	14 311	7 540	815	1 956	638	575	2 330	7 784	98
15	5 741	3 514	500	132	27	277	396	1 950	25
945	8 068	3 802	300	1 805	504	228	1 888	5 709	72
258	1 137	1 472	358	943	59	122	736	848	44
258	1 100	1 198	358	898	48	122	735	802	44
1 402	30 404	13 185	1 093	6 872	3 373	1 471	4 944	10 860	165
8 663	76 492	55 694	15 665	12 147	617	2 072	3 854	7 635	245
−628	−3 598	−3 069	1 547	581	93	218	508	−1 480	−340
−379	−3 824	−3 158	1 065	689	23	187	863	−104	−83

21—2 续表 7

（2010 年）

指　　标		Item		七　师 一二三团 Farm 123 Division 7	七　师 一二四团 Farm 124 Division 7	七　师 一二五团 Farm 125 Division 7	七　师 一二六团 Farm 126 Division 7
生产总值	（万元）	Gross Domestic Products	（10 000 yuan）	48 739	36 669	68 650	27 250
第一产业		Primary Industry		26 689	26 383	48 243	18 069
第二产业		Secondary Industry		8 567	2 651	14 505	1 195
# 工　业		Industry		7 088	1 956	12 799	565
第三产业		Tertiary Industry		13 483	7 635	5 902	7 986
固定资产投资总额	（万元）	Investment in Fixed Assets	（10 000 yuan）	22 042	9 033	15 473	3 425
总播种面积	（千公顷）	Total Sown Areas	（1000 hectares）	10. 74	10. 27	17. 01	7. 67
粮食：播种面积	（千公顷）	Grain：Sown Areas	（1000 hectares）	1. 74	4. 59	1. 68	1. 20
总产量	（吨）	Total Output	（ton）	11 950	44 982	16 144	10 500
# 小麦：播种面积		Wheat：Sown Areas		1. 53	2. 33	0. 67	0. 67
总产量		Total Output		9 470	17 150	4 120	4 100
棉花：播种面积	（千公顷）	Cotton：Sown Areas	（1 000 hectares）	3. 47	2. 20	10. 35	3. 67
总产量	（吨）	Total Output	（ton）	7 909	5 010	22 390	8 151
油料：播种面积	（千公顷）	Oil-bearing Crops：Sown Areas	（1 000 hectares）	0. 55	0. 20	0. 33	0. 97
总产量	（吨）	Total Output	（ton）	1 635	860	1 050	2 900
甜菜：播种面积	（千公顷）	Beetroots：Sown Areas	（1 000 hectares）	0. 20	0. 67		
总产量	（吨）	Total Output	（ton）	16 500	55 220		
当年造林面积	（公顷）	Afforestation Area In the Current Year	（hectare）	80	147	81	51
年末果园面积	（公顷）	Planted Area of Fruits	（hectare）	390	315	58	63
水果产量	（吨）	Output of Fruits	（ton）	5 745	5 547	825	1 100
肉类总产量	（吨）	Total Output of Meat	（ton）	4 660	4 613	2 122	1 828
牲畜年底存栏头数	（万头）	Number of Livestock	（10000 heads）	4. 64	5. 21	2. 47	1. 55
# 大牲畜		Large Animals		0. 25	0. 54	0. 26	0. 27
猪		Pigs		0. 78	0. 69	0. 51	0. 40
羊		Sheep and Goats		3. 61	3. 98	1. 70	0. 88
工业总产值	（万元）	Gross Industrial Output Value	（10 000 yuan）	23 501	7 846	48 945	2 292
建筑业总产值	（万元）	Composition Output Value	（10 000 yuan）	7 689	3 614	8 873	3 282
全年用电量	（万千瓦时）	Electricity Consumed	（10 000 kwh）	1 501	3 095	3 936	930
# 工业用电量		Industry Electricity Consumed	（10 000 kwh）	955	520	1 645	404
农业用电量		Agriculture Electricity Consumed	（10 000 kwh）	490	2 039	1 929	270
民用汽车拥有量	（辆）	Civil Motor Vehicles	（unit）	569	247	402	287
# 私人汽车		Private Motor Vehicles		558	241	390	281
社会消费品零售总额	（万元）	Total Retail Sales of Consumer Goods	（10 000 yuan）	30 291	10 389	8 294	11 853
主营业务收入	（万元）	Main Business Income	（10000 yuan）	16 819	15 624	71 032	24 742
营业利润	（万元）	Business Profits	（10000 yuan）	−2 644	−797	2 164	−1 723
利润总额	（万元）	Total Profits	（10000 yuan）	−1 835	589	1 175	−561

Continued

七师 一二七团 Farm 127 Division 7	七师 一二八团 Farm 128 Division 7	七师 一二九团 Farm 129 Division 7	七师 一三〇团 Farm 130 Division 7	七师 一三一团 Farm 131 Division 7	七师 一三七团 Farm 137 Division 7	八师 一二一团 Farm 121 Division 8	八师 一三三团 Farm 133 Division 8	八师 一三四团 Farm 134 Division 8	八师 一三六团 Farm 136 Division 8
24 387	37 038	51 923	62 089	56 601	14 159	99 410	51 701	49 980	26 354
17 204	29 045	30 261	39 476	31 872	5 365	61 923	38 958	36 488	19 865
2 029	1 526	7 098	9 349	12 069	4 120	20 283	3 855	4 168	1 524
1 495	1 058	5 766	7 832	10 231	2 879	18 514	3 202	3 537	866
5 154	6 467	14 564	13 264	12 660	4 674	17 204	8 888	9 324	4 965
1 767	4 347	8 098	12 857	4 635	6 453	13 174	16 772	14 703	6 870
7.93	14.33	11.87	14.64	9.23	2.39	22.84	14.74	12.87	7.34
2.00	2.73	3.70	4.32	3.11	0.63	0.83	0.20	0.60	0.20
20 200	29 450	36 524	31 743	26 310	4 065	5 937	1 200	6 257	2 400
0.67	0.80	1.77	3.29	2.04	0.60	0.53		0.17	
4 120	4 800	10 656	20 203	13 510	3 690	3 012		1 057	
4.00	6.00	4.33	5.04	2.33	0.53	19.53	12.41	11.22	6.47
9 009	13 340	9 523	11 500	5 132	1 040	38 815	27 900	26 778	16 450
0.87	2.79	1.10	1.39	0.06	0.07			0.03	
2 600	8 992	4 043	3 755	225	180			44	
0.13	0.27	0.20	0.07	1.47	0.07				
11 000	22 000	20 160	5 500	121 000	4 000				
72	83	51	51	267	40	847	413	348	793
20	120	284	78	110	17	576	544	489	21
534	638	3 580	1 519	2 790	120	5 258	4 915	2 873	44
1 287	2 016	2 673	2 237	5 708	1 898	1 650	2 477	925	656
0.76	2.17	3.65	2.87	6.61	9.60	3.30	2.85	1.76	0.66
0.20	0.30	0.21	0.37	0.52	0.68	0.92	0.33	0.31	0.04
0.21	0.72	1.33	0.67	1.56	0.48	1.75	1.87	0.85	0.41
0.35	1.15	2.11	1.83	4.53	8.44	0.63	0.65	0.60	0.21
6 042	9 752	21 214	29 886	37 078	6 872	62 004	11 489	19 548	2 270
2 777	2 435	6 928	7 896	9 560	6 452	5 893	2 808	2 527	2 632
890	1 883	3 096	7 993	4 350	789	14 588	6 055	6 013	1 808
201	503	857	3 191	1 015	491	2 641	1 340	1 844	297
689	1 113	1 608	1 425	2 985	87	9 184	4 071	2 501	1 365
237	279	618	662	817	243	3 280	620	1 992	427
232	269	605	651	809	239	3 265	516	1 922	389
6 316	9 723	26 762	10 472	12 837	9 220	16 773	5 794	2 222	9 851
4 528	5 759	14 202	8 168	25 483	4 594	66 594	78 507	57 165	25 082
−1 169	827	234	−3 284	−959	−2 008	3 525	1 104	−980	640
−469	565	699	−1 735	557	−746	2 088	442	−2 742	72

21—2 续表 8

(2010 年)

指　　标	Item	八　师 一四一团 Farm 141 Division 8	八　师 一四二团 Farm 142 Division 8	八　师 一四三团 Farm 143 Division 8	八　师 一四四团 Farm 144 Division 8
生产总值　(万元)	Gross Domestic Products　(10 000 yuan)	37 498	63 067	71 532	46 446
第一产业	Primary Industry	26 200	49 209	37 056	36 248
第二产业	Secondary Industry	5 297	5 938	20 399	2 903
#工　业	Industry	3 233	5 091	7 430	2 903
第三产业	Tertiary Industry	6 001	7 920	14 077	7 295
固定资产投资总额　(万元)	Investment in Fixed Assets　(10 000 yuan)	11 000	6 063	19 248	22 732
总播种面积　(千公顷)	Total Sown Areas　(1000 hectares)	8. 02	21. 70	13. 78	10. 20
粮食：播种面积　(千公顷)	Grain: Sown Areas　(1000 hectares)	0. 20	5. 37	3. 73	0. 30
总产量　(吨)	Total Output　(ton)	1 350	23 697	27 939	2 700
#小麦：播种面积	Wheat: Sown Areas	0. 20	4. 27	1. 20	0. 20
总产量	Total Output	1 350	14 480	10 810	1 500
棉花：播种面积　(千公顷)	Cotton: Sown Areas　(1 000 hectares)	6. 80	12. 14	7. 47	9. 36
总产量　(吨)	Total Output　(ton)	14 800	26 425	15 680	22 218
油料：播种面积　(千公顷)	Oil-bearing Crops: Sown Areas　(1 000 hectares)		0. 14	0. 13	
总产量　(吨)	Total Output　(ton)		388	523	
甜菜：播种面积　(千公顷)	Beetroots: Sown Areas　(1 000 hectares)		0. 27		
总产量　(吨)	Total Output　(ton)		9 782		
当年造林面积　(公顷)	Afforestation Area In the Current Year　(hectare)	133	133	84	84
年末果园面积　(公顷)	Planted Area of Fruits　(hectare)	966	831	878	627
水果产量　(吨)	Output of Fruits　(ton)	3 574	8 000	10 444	1 410
肉类总产量　(吨)	Total Output of Meat　(ton)	1 276	7 940	3 960	7 544
牲畜年底存栏头数　(万头)	Number of Livestock　(10000 heads)	1. 24	8. 69	4. 65	2. 85
#大牲畜	Large Animals	0. 29	0. 39	0. 56	0. 11
猪	Pigs	0. 85	7. 40	1. 80	2. 48
羊	Sheep and Goats	0. 10	0. 90	2. 29	0. 26
工业总产值　(万元)	Gross Industrial Output Value　(10 000 yuan)	11 358	19 076	62 333	10 477
建筑业总产值　(万元)	Composition Output Value　(10 000 yuan)	7 613		48 035	
全年用电量　(万千瓦时)	Electricity Consumed　(10 000 kwh)	1 713	8 340	6 119	2 893
#工业用电量	Industry Electricity Consumed　(10 000 kwh)	531	1 873	2 746	1 487
农业用电量	Agriculture Electricity Consumed　(10 000 kwh)	988	5 970	2 154	1 406
民用汽车拥有量　(辆)	Civil Motor Vehicles　(unit)	212	3 676	635	278
#私人汽车	Private Motor Vehicles	202	3 632	602	136
社会消费品零售总额　(万元)	Total Retail Sales of Consumer Goods　(10 000 yuan)	5 364	14 144	10 256	4 153
主营业务收入　(万元)	Main Business Income　(10000 yuan)	45 082	70 068	41 662	63 105
营业利润　(万元)	Business Profits　(10000 yuan)	1 734	2 610	3 185	3 340
利润总额　(万元)	Total Profits　(10000 yuan)	1 280	1 688	942	1 267

Continued

八 师 石河子总场 Shihezi Farm Division 8	八 师 一四七团 Farm 147 Division 8	八 师 一四八团 Farm 148 Division 8	八 师 一四九团 Farm 149 Division 8	八 师 一五〇团 Farm 150 Division 8	八 师 一五二团 Farm 152 Division 8	九 师 一六一团 Farm 161 Division 9	九 师 一六三团 Farm 163 Division 9	九 师 一六四团 Farm 164 Division 9	九 师 一六五团 Farm 165 Division 9
143 985	37 523	60 128	43 621	65 994	24 337	10 431	15 115	9 837	7 632
65 484	28 596	39 142	35 397	47 697	5 295	6 971	9 867	7 712	5 513
43 225	3 488	10 345	1 623	11 190	13 556	291	2 056	434	580
31 390	2 425	6 816	1 212	8 846	10 141	226	551	352	150
35 276	5 439	10 641	6 601	7 107	5 486	3 169	3 192	1 691	1 539
82 893	33 084	9 295	8 618	35 400	3 043	1 760	5 515	4 871	3 216
14.32	9.31	14.77	10.38	14.42	0.88	11.52	7.77	9.60	8.66
2.92	0.53	0.03	0.22		0.26	3.98	4.13	4.18	2.64
22 273	2 000	175	1 605		1 795	11 512	47 945	28 591	10 439
2.22	0.53					3.83	0.95	3.30	0.67
14 308	2 000					11 065	6 971	19 164	3 731
8.67	7.33	12.93	8.80	11.59					
20 880	19 995	31 076	22 240	31 368					
0.18			0.10			1.56	0.44	0.28	1.48
550			170		26	1 748	1 207	334	1 785
							0.80	1.74	
							44 235	89 125	
115	419	399	373	508		13	10	36	13
1 014	232	4	59	433	1 442	33	20	16	31
18 950	2 250	43	436	176	11 181	100	207	50	55
15 429	1 065	2 971	1 220	1 040	1 670	2 572	1 762	1 549	2 814
15.61	1.31	4.20	2.20	1.48	1.82	11.00	5.20	5.01	11.00
0.68	0.37	0.31	0.32	0.32	0.04	0.51	0.09	0.17	0.66
14.35	0.71	2.86	1.13	0.63	1.65	0.11	0.23	0.04	0.08
0.58	0.23	1.03	0.75	0.53	0.13	10.38	4.88	4.80	10.26
158 600	9 865	6 816	7 813	36 187	32 126	711	1 835	1 130	459
40 204	4 207	3 529	2 934	10 700	5 202	220	5 375	452	1 539
14 532	5 062	7 800	4 074	6 903	576	274	1 594	580	179
6 755	1 524	1 540	852	960	160	77	50	9	18
3 785	2 584	6 260	2 404	4 832	395	197	1 204	431	137
1 262	282	389	385	429	120	124	281	174	178
921	145	352	358	429	55	113	261	166	171
29 660	1 453	7 980	11 531	13 792	4 830	5 131	1 253	1 584	956
115 154	53 448	90 235	58 787	65 452	32 545	9 912	10 040	10 682	4 867
7 730	3 361	1 465	1 539	4 001	1 433	−821	−1 997	−1 074	−1 143
2 454	2 639	971	385	1 686	3 036	−79	−817	−784	−434

21—2 续表 9

（2010 年）

指　　标		Item		九　　师 一六六团 Farm 166 Division 9	九　　师 一六七团 Farm 167 Division 9	九　　师 一六八团 Farm 168 Division 9	九　　师 一七〇团 Farm 170 Division 9
生产总值	（万元）	Gross Domestic Products	（10 000 yuan）	12 588	10 605	17 806	4 036
第一产业		Primary Industry		10 605	8 457	9 820	2 456
第二产业		Secondary Industry		214	386	3 516	288
# 工　业		Industry		214	204	950	123
第三产业		Tertiary Industry		1 769	1 762	4 470	1 292
固定资产投资总额	（万元）	Investment in Fixed Assets	（10 000 yuan）	5 459	5 246	4 547	3 570
总播种面积	（千公顷）	Total Sown Areas	（1000 hectares）	14.79	11.46	10.72	0.32
粮食：播种面积	（千公顷）	Grain:Sown Areas	（1000 hectares）	5.53	2.81	3.20	0.02
总产量	（吨）	Total Output	（ton）	35 959	19 781	25 168	60
# 小麦:播种面积		Wheat:Sown Areas		4.30	2.34	2.34	0.01
总产量		Total Output		28 351	15 511	16 788	22
棉花：播种面积	（千公顷）	Cotton:Sown Areas	（1 000 hectares）				
总产量	（吨）	Total Output	（ton）				
油料：播种面积	（千公顷）	Oil-bearing Crops:Sown Areas	（1 000 hectares）	0.57	1.70	1.39	0.12
总产量	（吨）	Total Output	（ton）	1 037	3 728	3 289	211
甜菜:播种面积	（千公顷）	Beetroots:Sown Areas	（1 000 hectares）	1.75	1.76	1.74	
总产量	（吨）	Total Output	（ton）	95 537	92 952	104 465	
当年造林面积	（公顷）	Afforestation Area In the Current Year	（hectare）	35	52	49	1 308
年末果园面积	（公顷）	Planted Area of Fruits	（hectare）	5	82	62	3
水果产量	（吨）	Output of Fruits	（ton）	41	70	351	12
肉类总产量	（吨）	Total Output of Meat	（ton）	1 841	1 567	2 305	1 654
牲畜年底存栏头数	（万头）	Number of Livestock	（10000 heads）	6.51	6.53	8.52	4.53
# 大牲畜		Large Animals		0.03	0.05	0.06	0.22
猪		Pigs		0.03	0.07	0.06	0.05
羊		Sheep and Goats		6.45	6.41	8.40	4.26
工业总产值	（万元）	Gross Industrial Output Value	（10 000 yuan）	716	682	3 116	427
建筑业总产值	（万元）	Composition Output Value	（10 000 yuan）		649	9 116	594
全年用电量	（万千瓦时）	Electricity Consumed	（10 000 kwh）	1 524	498	796	181
# 工业用电量		Industry Electricity Consumed	（10 000 kwh）	98	5	82	21
农业用电量		Agriculture Electricity Consumed	（10 000 kwh）	1 208	315	598	144
民用汽车拥有量	（辆）	Civil Motor Vehicles	（unit）	341	145	357	107
# 私人汽车		Private Motor Vehicles		326	133	330	97
社会消费品零售总额	（万元）	Total Retail Sales of Consumer Goods	（10 000 yuan）	1 202	1 038	3 169	2 150
主营业务收入	（万元）	Main Business Income	（10000 yuan）	12 834	10 977	12 641	4 904
营业利润	（万元）	Business Profits	（10000 yuan）	－1 249	－1 454	－1 296	－742
利润总额	（万元）	Total Profits	（10000 yuan）	－376	－793	18	－588

Continued

九 师 团结农场 Tuanjie Farm Division 9	十 师 一八一团 Farm 181 Division 10	十 师 一八二团 Farm 182 Division 10	十 师 一八三团 Farm 183 Division 10	十 师 一八四团 Farm 184 Division 10	十 师 一八五团 Farm 185 Division 10	十 师 一八六团 Farm 186 Division 10	十 师 一八七团 Farm 187 Division 10	十 师 一八八团 Farm 188 Division 10	十二师 一〇四团 Farm 104 Division 12
5 227	17 588	10 308	20 663	32 948	5 607	3 505	14 219	19 410	52 147
4 004	8 302	5 531	10 755	19 885	3 246	1 416	7 453	6 611	6 895
265	4 966	2 038	6 797	9 709	664	1 159	4 327	8 002	12 237
201	3 880	1 636	3 864	7 155	313	868	3 364	6 026	8 426
958	4 320	2 739	3 111	3 354	1 697	930	2 439	4 797	33 015
3 825	9 322	6 117	10 236	9 872	2 200	1 460	4 085	11 041	28 128
2.46	6.98	5.51	8.86	11.60	3.67	2.34	6.91	5.25	1.17
0.35	0.99	0.47	1.08	1.00	0.34	0.94	0.70	0.54	0.37
3 860	5 577	3 860	8 114	9 600	2 861	5 807	4 016	3 341	2 627
0.10	0.41	0.27	0.55		0.15	0.91	0.41	0.10	
630	2 471	1 760	3 912		853	5 520	2 448	645	
				6.33					
				8 011					
0.05	2.78	1.69	1.96	1.45	1.34	0.44	2.23	1.35	0.12
157	7 940	4 656	6 452	3 427	5 086	1 365	6 165	3 557	306
0.67	0.16	0.80					0.22	0.05	
50 130	10 080	54 000					15 327	3 353	
17	53	47	40	33	27	13	40	113	10
3	10	7		112	2			54	82
61	150	30		1 540	2			1 394	268
1 142	2 931	910	1 857	1 354	644	186	2 280	2 857	2 573
1.81	5.45	1.85	2.56	1.74	1.12	0.20	2.65	4.17	5.21
0.11	0.37	0.14	0.18	0.10	0.12	0.01	0.22	0.31	0.42
1.21	0.52	0.23	0.18	0.33	0.10	0.08	0.47	1.67	0.67
0.49	4.56	1.48	2.20	1.31	0.90	0.11	1.96	2.19	4.12
825	9 242	3 494	12 682	20 555	898	2 806	7 981	13 490	27 555
210	5 200	1 652	14 860	10 755	1 532	1 133	4 280	10 230	17 400
589	710	357	736	3 127	296	184	318	656	1 530
26	417	125	144	736	80	90	263	209	785
499	293	174	505	1 431	168	36	28	250	485
175	302	254	210	588	168	41	305	270	418
166	289	247	198	573	153	29	289	266	337
752	6 098	3 353	3 814	6 454	2 850	708	4 995	3 164	20 920
5 953	4 851	2 704	9 353	14 914		3 866	7 996	14 028	38 285
−1 369	−543	−1 172	−1 271	−453	−544	−553	−747	802	−1 028
−799	−723	−764	−171	1 350	−748	−387	−405	1 009	1 211

21—2 续表 10

(2010 年)

指　　标		Item		十二师 三坪农场 Sanping Farm Division 12	十二师 五一农场 Wuyi Farm Division 12	十二师 头屯河农场 ToutunHe Farm Division 12	十二师 西山农场 Xishan Farm Division 12
生产总值	(万元)	Gross Domestic Products	(10 000 yuan)	18 689	25 038	15 694	10 853
第一产业		Primary Industry		9 737	8 101	6 242	3 305
第二产业		Secondary Industry		4 547	12 125	4 392	5 607
# 工　业		Industry		4 360	8 333	2 993	3 817
第三产业		Tertiary Industry		4 405	4 812	5 060	1 941
固定资产投资总额	(万元)	Investment in Fixed Assets	(10 000 yuan)	8 718	12 871	14 983	11 150
总播种面积	(千公顷)	Total Sown Areas	(1000 hectares)	3.27	2.77	1.31	1.84
粮食：播种面积	(千公顷)	Grain: Sown Areas	(1000 hectares)	1.19	0.81	0.67	1.06
总产量	(吨)	Total Output	(ton)	10 007	5 129	4 448	6 523
# 小麦：播种面积		Wheat: Sown Areas		0.77	0.70	0.55	
总产量		Total Output		4 990	3 861	3 145	
棉花：播种面积	(千公顷)	Cotton: Sown Areas	(1 000 hectares)		0.03		
总产量	(吨)	Total Output	(ton)		43		
油料：播种面积	(千公顷)	Oil-bearing Crops: Sown Areas	(1 000 hectares)	0.04	0.07	0.34	0.40
总产量	(吨)	Total Output	(ton)	135	116	1 002	1 083
甜菜：播种面积	(千公顷)	Beetroots: Sown Areas	(1 000 hectares)	0.03	0.11		
总产量	(吨)	Total Output	(ton)	2 454	6 441		
当年造林面积	(公顷)	Afforestation Area In the Current Year	(hectare)	10	24	47	7
年末果园面积	(公顷)	Planted Area of Fruits	(hectare)	1 213	637	1 381	
水果产量	(吨)	Output of Fruits	(ton)	16 962	7 360	22 337	
肉类总产量	(吨)	Total Output of Meat	(ton)	1 757	921	1 347	998
牲畜年底存栏头数	(万头)	Number of Livestock	(10000 heads)	0.83	1.46	1.36	1.16
# 大牲畜		Large Animals		0.26	0.52	0.09	0.15
猪		Pigs		0.30	0.64	0.97	0.82
羊		Sheep and Goats		0.27	0.30	0.30	0.19
工业总产值	(万元)	Gross Industrial Output Value	(10 000 yuan)	17 286	16 742	10 338	10 600
建筑业总产值	(万元)	Composition Output Value	(10 000 yuan)	650	10 251	4 101	6 030
全年用电量	(万千瓦时)	Electricity Consumed	(10 000 kwh)	702	2 119	745	1 098
# 工业用电量		Industry Electricity Consumed	(10 000 kwh)	312	1 209	496	781
农业用电量		Agriculture Electricity Consumed	(10 000 kwh)	383	910	12	65
民用汽车拥有量	(辆)	Civil Motor Vehicles	(unit)	1 273	707	499	191
# 私人汽车		Private Motor Vehicles		1 102	674	470	161
社会消费品零售总额	(万元)	Total Retail Sales of Consumer Goods	(10 000 yuan)	7 123	9 462	30 145	4 810
主营业务收入	(万元)	Main Business Income	(10000 yuan)	2 733	21 275	3 412	5 945
营业利润	(万元)	Business Profits	(10000 yuan)	552	1 168	516	—94
利润总额	(万元)	Total Profits	(10000 yuan)	655	807	395	190

Continued

十二师二二一团 Farm 221 Division 12	十三师红星一场 Red Star No. 1 Farm Division 13	十三师红星二场 Red Star No. 2 Farm Division 13	十三师红星四场 Red Star No. 4 Farm Division 13	十三师黄田农场 Huangtian Farm Division 13	十三师火箭农场 Huojian Farm Division 13	十三师柳树泉农场 Liushuqian Farm Division 13	十三师红山农场 Hongshan Farm Division 13	十三师淖毛湖农场 Lao Maohu Farm Division 13	十四师四十七团 Farm 47 Division 14
10 551	27 225	22 361	19 253	27 050	35 144	12 748	17 045	4 620	3 922
3 665	13 653	11 338	11 130	11 090	14 868	9 463	7 509	2 205	2 574
4 776	7 831	4 711	3 289	9 189	13 031	1 217	5 349	1 241	16
2 616	5 211	3 968	1 868	7 518	10 135	609	4 842	960	3
2 110	5 741	6 312	4 834	6 771	7 245	2 068	4 187	1 174	1 332
10 015	13 925	4 449	6 567	12 259	7 790	4 902	7 030	936	2 766
0.67	2.02	2.47	2.20	2.69	1.90	1.37	4.18	1.67	0.82
0.01		0.13		0.09	0.20	0.46	4.07	0.20	0.43
24		1 016		520	1 260	2 770	28 486	1 270	2 880
0.01					0.13	0.22	3.07	0.13	0.20
24					780	1 350	22 391	520	1 360
0.35	1.87	1.73	2.13	2.53	0.87	0.20			0.13
538	4 676	4 290	5 210	6 004	2 090	409			278
		0.03				0.10	0.01		0.01
		98				195	50		40
46	3	9	16	44	9	3	32	6	9
783	1 545	974	2 013	1 064	2 106	2 038	814		1 309
19 665	13 505	4 648	18 000	5 544	23 560	20 589	9 384		4 447
410	2 167	606	2 604	923	2 401	725	1 537	133	801
1.13	2.13	1.25	3.84	3.22	8.50	2.75	8.77	1.20	1.13
	0.11	0.03	0.17	0.19	0.50	0.17	0.29	0.09	0.15
0.14	1.16	0.12	1.80	0.03	0.49	0.33	0.11	0.11	0.22
0.99	0.86	1.10	1.87	3.00	7.51	2.25	8.37	1.00	0.76
9 022	16 730	12 191	5 235	21 984	11 805	1 845	19 533	2 900	1 006
659	10 476	2 969	5 683	6 684	11 584	2 643	2 029	1 124	48
621	1 685	2 880	1 943	2 066	3 814	941	2 649	631	374
50	487	560	339	313	862	112	758	215	67
301	754	1 867	1 223	1 373	2 458	631	1 398	160	215
146	342	539	374	723	365	239	654	473	157
130	322	522	362	703	343	238	649	466	145
7 283	5 834	3 723	4 917	258	5 508	440	2 933	259	319
10 149	20 139	14 497	9 349	11 990	26 961	4 061	22 319	3 955	6 094
36	1 527	1 122	1 147	606	1 735	701	1 234	−2 248	−937
−58	1 378	582	410	659	854	347	1 879	−2 290	−712

21—2 续表 11 continued

（2010 年）

指 标	Item	十四师皮山农场 Pishan Farm Division 14	十四师一牧场 Ranch 1 Division 14	十四师二二四团 Farm 224 Division 14	兵团直属二二二团 Directly under XPCG Farm 222
生产总值 （万元）	Gross Domestic Products （10 000 yuan）	11 007	1 886	13 318	23 039
第一产业	Primary Industry	7 340	1 344	11 925	11 921
第二产业	Secondary Industry	401	25		3 861
# 工 业	Industry	222	18		1 926
第三产业	Tertiary Industry	3 266	517	1 393	7 257
固定资产投资总额 （万元）	Investment in Fixed Assets （10 000 yuan）	8 402	1 497	5 680	4 543
总播种面积 （千公顷）	Total Sown Areas （1000 hectares）	1.59	0.27	4.45	7.48
粮食：播种面积 （千公顷）	Grain：Sown Areas （1000 hectares）	0.67	0.22	1.87	3.89
总产量 （吨）	Total Output （ton）	4 498	1 082	716	19 357
# 小麦：播种面积	Wheat：Sown Areas	0.33	0.18	1.87	3.37
总产量	Total Output	2 010	913	716	15 699
棉花：播种面积 （千公顷）	Cotton：Sown Areas （1 000 hectares）	0.67		0.09	0.20
总产量 （吨）	Total Output （ton）	1 520		187	353
油料：播种面积 （千公顷）	Oil-bearing Crops：Sown Areas （1 000 hectares）			0.03	1.70
总产量 （吨）	Total Output （ton）			88	4 929
甜菜：播种面积 （千公顷）	Beetroots：Sown Areas （1 000 hectares）				0.03
总产量 （吨）	Total Output （ton）				2 260
当年造林面积 （公顷）	Afforestation Area In the Current Year （hectare）	38		466	
年末果园面积 （公顷）	Planted Area of Fruits （hectare）	2 814	168	8 600	1 304
水果产量 （吨）	Output of Fruits （ton）	19 468	461	28 900	16 800
肉类总产量 （吨）	Total Output of Meat （ton）	1 366	789	295	363
牲畜年底存栏头数 （万头）	Number of Livestock （10000 heads）	3.47	5.76	0.48	0.75
# 大牲畜	Large Animals	0.27	0.06	0.06	0.12
猪	Pigs			0.28	0.13
羊	Sheep and Goats	3.20	5.70	0.14	0.50
工业总产值 （万元）	Gross Industrial Output Value （10 000 yuan）	703	63	131	5 124
建筑业总产值 （万元）	Composition Output Value （10 000 yuan）	1 053	26		4 137
全年用电量 （万千瓦时）	Electricity Consumed （10 000 kwh）	820	43	480	1 145
# 工业用电量	Industry Electricity Consumed （10 000 kwh）	97	1	329	135
农业用电量	Agriculture Electricity Consumed （10 000 kwh）	315	18	151	999
民用汽车拥有量 （辆）	Civil Motor Vehicles （unit）	202	52	619	304
# 私人汽车	Private Motor Vehicles	189	40	609	286
社会消费品零售总额 （万元）	Total Retail Sales of Consumer Goods （10 000 yuan）	1 027	160	1 173	3 989
主营业务收入 （万元）	Main Business Income （10000 yuan）	10 463	2 863	20 920	17 987
营业利润 （万元）	Business Profits （10000 yuan）	−2 072	−238	−582	977
利润总额 （万元）	Total Profits （10000 yuan）	−1 827	−48	−569	1 049

2011

BING TUAN

第二十二篇

各师、团主要经济指标排序

Chapter 22 Ranking of Main Economic Indicators by Division and Farm

简要说明

一、本篇资料主要内容

本篇资料为兵团各师、团各行业主要指标排序资料，主要包括分师生产总值、工农业总产值、工农业增加值及人均指标排序、农业主要统计指标、规模以上工业、道路交通运输企业、建筑施工企业及批发零售贸易业主要指标排序；农牧团场主要指标排序。

二、本篇资料来源

本篇资料由兵团统计局、国家统计局兵团调查总队有关处室根据统计年报资料加工整理。

Brief Introduction

1. Main Contents

The data in this chapter cover ranking data of main indicators by division and farm and by sector, including ranking data of Gross Domestic Product by division, Gross Output value of agriculture and industry, value-added of agriculture and industry, and per capita indicators, main indicators of agriculture, ranking data of main indicators of industrial communications and transportation, construction enterprises, wholesale and retail sale trades above designated size; and ranking data of main indicators by farm.

2. Sources of Data

The data in this chapter are compiled by relevant Section of the Statistics Bureau of XPCG and Survey Office of the National Bureau of Statistics of XPCG in accordance with annual reports.

22－1 各师生产总值、人均生产总值排序

Ranking of Gross Domestic Product,Per Capita Gross Domestic Product by Division

（2010 年）

单 位	Unit	生产总值（万元）Gross Domestic Product (10 000 yuan)	排 序 Ranking	单 位	Unit	人均生产总值（元）Per Gross Domestic Product(yuan)	排 序 Ranking
一 师	Division 1	1 043 212	2	一 师	Division 1	35 701	4
二 师	Division 2	500 142	6	二 师	Division 2	25 938	11
三 师	Division 3	386 345	7	三 师	Division 3	18 820	16
四 师	Division 4	546 010	5	四 师	Division 4	24 756	12
五 师	Division 5	276 030	9	五 师	Division 5	24 752	13
六 师	Division 6	974 993	3	六 师	Division 6	31 462	6
七 师	Division 7	645 039	4	七 师	Division 7	29 779	9
八 师	Division 8	1 885 049	1	八 师	Division 8	32 262	5
九 师	Division 9	139 690	14	九 师	Division 9	19 559	15
十 师	Division 10	170 177	13	十 师	Division 10	22 697	14
建 工 师	Construction Division	235 088	10	建 工 师	Construction Division	49 206	3
十 二 师	Division 12	232 005	11	十 二 师	Division 12	31 362	7
十 三 师	Division 13	218 126	12	十 三 师	Division 13	27 312	10
十 四 师	Division 14	47 938	16	十 四 师	Division 14	12 795	17
国资公司	State-owned Property Company	91 264	15	国资公司	State-owned Property Company	67 937	2
供销公司	Supply and Marketing Corporation General	5 714	17	供销公司	Supply and Marketing Corporation General	31 343	8
中基公司	Chalkis Company	－32 112	18	中基公司	Chalkis Company	－448 805	18
兵团直属	Directly under XPCG	341 442	8	兵团直属	Directly under XPCG	88 521	1

注：本表数按当年价格计算。

Note:Data in value terms in this table are calculated at current prices.

22－2 各师工业增加值率、农业增加值率排序

Ranking of the Ratio of Value-added of Industry and Agriculture by Division

计量单位：% （2010 年） (%)

单 位	Unit	工业增加值率 Ratio of Value-added to Gross Industrial Output Value	排 序 Ranking	单 位	Unit	农业增加值率 Ratio of Value-added to Farming Output Value	排 序 Ranking
一 师	Division 1	28. 2	7	一 师	Division 1	49. 3	8
二 师	Division 2	26. 9	11	二 师	Division 2	49. 3	7
三 师	Division 3	30. 7	5	三 师	Division 3	46. 6	12
四 师	Division 4	39. 9	1	四 师	Division 4	49. 2	9
五 师	Division 5	23. 9	13	五 师	Division 5	51. 3	1
六 师	Division 6	27. 1	8	六 师	Division 6	49. 7	6
七 师	Division 7	28. 6	6	七 师	Division 7	50. 8	2
八 师	Division 8	25. 1		八 师	Division 8	50. 2	4
九 师	Division 9	27. 0	9	九 师	Division 9	48. 2	10
十 师	Division 10	37. 2	2	十 师	Division 10	36. 1	15
建 工 师	Construction Division	20. 0	14	建 工 师	Construction Division	45. 2	13
十 二 师	Division 12	30. 8	4	十 二 师	Division 12	43. 9	14
十 三 师	Division 13	35. 9	3	十 三 师	Division 13	50. 2	3
十 四 师	Division 14	27. 0	10	十 四 师	Division 14	47. 1	11
国资公司	State-owned PropertyCompany	14. 7	15	国资公司	State-owned Property Company	18. 5	16
中基公司	Chalkis Company						
兵团直属	Directly under XPCG	9. 6	16	兵团直属	Directly under XPCG	50. 0	5

注：增加值率＝增加值/总产出×100%。

Note:Ratio of Value-added＝Value-added÷Total Output×100%.

22－3 各师人均农业增加值、人均工业增加值排序

Ranking of Per Capita Value-added of Agriculture and Industry by Division

计量单位：元　　(2010年)　　(yuan)

单　位	Unit	人均农业增加值 Per Capita Value-added of Agriculture	排　序 Ranking	单　位	Unit	人均工业增加值 Per Capita Value-added of Industry	排　序 Ranking
一　师	Division 1	19 074	1	一　师	Division 1	7 558	7
二　师	Division 2	11 207	4	二　师	Division 2	5 574	10
三　师	Division 3	10 743	5	三　师	Division 3	1 807	14
四　师	Division 4	8 692	10	四　师	Division 4	8 936	4
五　师	Division 5	13 044	2	五　师	Division 5	3 566	11
六　师	Division 6	10 728	6	六　师	Division 6	7 915	6
七　师	Division 7	12 924	3	七　师	Division 7	6 292	9
八　师	Division 8	9 460	8	八　师	Division 8	10 294	3
九　师	Division 9	9 172	9	九　师	Division 9	2 642	12
十　师	Division 10	8 430	11	十　师	Division 10	6 415	8
建工师	Construction Division	40	16	建工师	Construction Division	2 241	13
十二师	Division 12	6 066	13	十二师	Division 12	15 153	2
十三师	Division 13	10 174	7	十三师	Division 13	8 589	5
十四师	Division 14	6 198	12	十四师	Division 14	1 018	16
国资公司	State-owned Property Company	1 229	15	国资公司	State-owned Property Company	29 991	1
				中基公司	Chalkis Company	－403 955	17
兵团直属	Directly under XPCG	3 090	14	兵团直属	Directly under XPCG	1 027	15

注：本表按当年价格计算。

Note: Data in value terms in this table are calculated at current prices.

22－4 各师人均利润、在岗职工平均工资排序

Ranking of Per Capita Total Profit Value, Annual Averge Wage of Staff and Workers by Division

计量单位：元　　(2010年)　　(yuan)

单　位	Unit	人均利润 Per Capita Total Profit Value	排　序 Ranking	单　位	Unit	在岗职工平均工资 Annual Anerage Wage	排　序 Ranking
一　师	Division 1	3 130	3	一　师	Division 1	30 581	4
二　师	Division 2	584	11	二　师	Division 2	23 880	11
三　师	Division 3	716	9	三　师	Division 3	25 490	9
四　师	Division 4	2 145	5	四　师	Division 4	20 844	15
五　师	Division 5	858	8	五　师	Division 5	23 164	12
六　师	Division 6	127	13	六　师	Division 6	24 868	10
七　师	Division 7	211	12	七　师	Division 7	22 930	13
八　师	Division 8	2 660	4	八　师	Division 8	32 560	3
九　师	Division 9	－184	15	九　师	Division 9	15 627	18
十　师	Division 10	－98	14	十　师	Division 10	20 540	16
建工师	Construction Division	660	10	建工师	Construction Division	26 709	8
十二师	Division 12	1 297	7	十二师	Division 12	22 625	14
十三师	Division 13	1 313	6	十三师	Division 13	27 064	7
十四师	Division 14	－295	16	十四师	Division 14	17 764	17
国资公司	State-owned Property Company	15 351	1	国资公司	State-owned Property Company	30 301	5
				供销公司	Supply and Marketing Corporation General	51 275	1
				中基公司	Chalkis Company	27 981	6
兵团直属	Directly under XPCG	6 146	2	兵团直属	Directly under XPCG	44 194	2

22—5 各师人均农业总产值、人均工业总产值排序

Ranking of Per,Capita Gross Output Value of Agriculture and Industry by Division

计量单位:元 (2010 年) (yuan)

单 位	Unit	人均农业总产值 Per Capita Gross Output Value of Agriculture	排 序 Ranking	单 位	Unit	人均工业总产值 Per Capita Gross Output Value of Industry	排 序 Ranking
一 师	Division 1	38 701	1	一 师	Division 1	25 765	5
二 师	Division 2	22 716	6	二 师	Division 2	19 119	9
三 师	Division 3	23 040	5	三 师	Division 3	5 663	16
四 师	Division 4	17 655	11	四 师	Division 4	21 387	7
五 师	Division 5	25 429	3	五 师	Division 5	13 084	12
六 师	Division 6	21 583	7	六 师	Division 6	28 521	4
七 师	Division 7	25 430	2	七 师	Division 7	21 363	8
八 师	Division 8	18 843	10	八 师	Division 8	39 607	3
九 师	Division 9	19 048	9	九 师	Division 9	9 296	15
十 师	Division 10	23 337	4	十 师	Division 10	16 495	11
建工师	Con struction Division	89	16	建工师	Construction Division	10 911	13
十二师	Division 12	13 813	12	十二师	Division 12	18 683	10
十三师	Division 13	20 253	8	十三师	Division 13	22 751	6
十四师	Division 14	13 148	13	十四师	Division 14	3 693	17
国资公司	State-owned Property Company	6 659	14	国资公司	State-owned Property Company	206 643	2
				中基公司	Chalkis Company	878 230	1
兵团直属	Directly under XPCG	6 181	15	兵团直属	Direcly under XPCG	9 379	14

22—6 各师粮食、棉花总产量排序

Ranking of Yield Output of Grain and Cotton by Division

计量单位:吨 (2010 年) (ton)

单 位	Unit	粮食产量 Total Yield of Grain	排 序 Ranking	单 位	Unit	棉花产量 Total Yield of Cotton	排 序 Ranking
一 师	Division 1	193 524	4	一 师	Division 1	293 651	2
二 师	Division 2	61 645	9	二 师	Division 2	69 024	7
三 师	Division 3	117 489	7	三 师	Division 3	115 706	3
四 师	Division 4	488 762	1	四 师	Division 4	16 126	9
五 师	Division 5	110 786	8	五 师	Division 5	92 550	6
六 师	Division 6	473 732	2	六 师	Division 6	105 834	4
七 师	Division 7	237 273	3	七 师	Division 7	96 534	5
八 师	Division 8	133 764	6	八 师	Division 8	327 050	1
九 师	Division 9	183 315	5	九 师	Division 9		
十 师	Division 10	43 179	10	十 师	Division 10	8 011	10
建工师	Construction Division	273	15	建工师	Construction Division	53	14
十二师	Division 12	28 758	12	十二师	Division 12	581	12
十三师	Division 13	35 322	11	十三师	Division 13	22 679	8
十四师	Division 14	9 176	14	十四师	Division 14	1 985	11
兵团直属	Directly under XPCG	19 357	13	兵团直属	Directly under XPCG	353	13

22—7 各师人均粮食、人均棉花产量排序

Ranking of Per Capita Grain and Cotton Yields by Division

计量单位:公斤　　(2010 年)　　(kg)

单　位	Unit	人均粮食产量 Per Capita Grain	排　序 Ranking	单　位	Unit	人均棉花产量 Per Capita Cotton	排　序 Ranking
一　师	Division 1	662	6	一　师	Division 1	1 005	1
二　师	Division 2	320	12	二　师	Division 2	358	6
三　师	Division 3	572	8	三　师	Division 3	564	3
四　师	Division 4	2 216	2	四　师	Division 4	73	10
五　师	Division 5	993	5	五　师	Division 5	830	2
六　师	Division 6	1 529	3	六　师	Division 6	342	7
七　师	Division 7	1 095	4	七　师	Division 7	446	5
八　师	Division 8	229	14	八　师	Division 8	560	4
九　师	Division 9	2 567	1	九　师	Division 9		
十　师	Division 10	576	7	十　师	Division 10	107	9
建工师	Con struction Division	6	15	建工师	Construction Division	1	14
十二师	Division 12	389	11	十二师	Division 12	8	13
十三师	Division 13	442	10	十三师	Division 13	284	8
十四师	Division 14	245	13	十四师	Division 14	53	11
兵团直属	Directly under XPCG	502	9	兵团直属	Directly under XPCG	9	12

22—8 各师粮食、棉花单产排序

Ranking of Average Unit Yield of Grain and Cotton by Division

计量单位:公斤/公顷　　(2010 年)　　(kg/hectare)

单　位	Unit	粮食单产 Average Unit Yield of Grain	排　序 Ranking	单　位	Unit	棉花单产 Average Unit Yield of Cotton	排　序 Ranking
一　师	Division 1	8 757	2	一　师	Division 1	2 478	3
二　师	Division 2	6 395	11	二　师	Division 2	2 550	2
三　师	Division 3	5 662	12	三　师	Division 3	2 266	6
四　师	Division 4	7 642	4	四　师	Division 4	1 589	11
五　师	Division 5	6 563	9	五　师	Division 5	2 690	1
六　师	Division 6	8 673	3	六　师	Division 6	2 029	9
七　师	Division 7	8 917	1	七　师	Division 7	2 208	8
八　师	Division 8	6 416	10	八　师	Division 8	2 275	5
九　师	Division 9	6 835	8	九　师	Division 9		
十　师	Division10	7 125	5	十　师	Division 10	1 266	14
建工师	Construction Division	3 900	14	建工师	Construction Division	1 325	13
十二师	Division 12	6 997	6	十二师	Division 12	1 529	12
十三师	Division 13	6 872	7	十三师	Division 13	2 431	4
十四师	Division 14	2 876	15	十四师	Division 14	2 230	7
兵团直属	Directly under XPCG	4 976	13	兵团直属	Directly under XPCG	1 765	10

22—9 各师油料、甜菜总产量排序

Ranking of Yield of Oil-bearing and Beetroots by Division

计量单位:吨 (2010 年) (ton)

单 位	Unit	油料产量 Total Yield of Oil-bearing	排 序 Ranking	单 位	Unit	甜菜产量 Total Yield of Beetroots	排 序 Ranking
一 师	Division 1	229	13	一 师	Division 1		
二 师	Division 2	800	11	二 师	Division 2	396 149	3
三 师	Division 3	1 027	10	三 师	Division 3		
四 师	Division 4	62 293	1	四 师	Division 4	497 402	1
五 师	Division 5	6 664	6	五 师	Division 5	20 000	7
六 师	Division 6	25 101	4	六 师	Division 6	66 610	6
七 师	Division 7	27 772	3	七 师	Division 7	255 380	4
八 师	Division 8	2 008	9	八 师	Division 8	10 703	8
九 师	Division 9	13 496	5	九 师	Division 9	476 444	2
十师	Division 10	38 650	2	十 师	Division 10	82 760	5
建 工 师	Con struction Division	151	14	建 工 师	Construction Division		
十 二 师	Division 12	2 642	8	十 二 师	Division 12	8 895	9
十 三 师	Division 13	343	12	十 三 师	Division 13		
十 四 师	Division 14	128	15	十 四 师	Division 14		
兵团直属	Directly under XPCG	4 929	7	兵团直属	Directly under XPCG	2 260	10

22—10 各师人均油料、人均甜菜产量排序

Ranking of Per Capita Oil-bearing and Beetroots Yields by Division

计量单位:公斤 (2010 年) (kg)

单 位	Unit	人均油料产量 Per Capita Oil-bearing	排 序 Ranking	单 位	Unit	人均甜菜产量 Per Capita Beetroots Yields	排 序 Ranking
一 师	Division 1	1	15	一 师	Division 1		
二 师	Division 2	4	11	二 师	Division 2	2 054	3
三 师	Division 3	5	9	三 师	Division 3		
四 师	Division 4	282	2	四 师	Division 4	2 255	2
五 师	Division 5	60	7	五 师	Division 5	179	7
六 师	Division 6	81	6	六 师	Division 6	215	6
七 师	Division 7	128	4	七 师	Division 7	1 179	4
八 师	Division 8	3	12	八 师	Division 8	18	10
九 师	Division 9	189	3	九 师	Division 9	6 671	1
十 师	Division 10	516	1	十 师	Division 10	1 104	5
建 工 师	Construction Division	3	14	建 工 师	Construction Division		
十 二 师	Division 12	36	8	十 二 师	Division 12	120	8
十 三 师	Division 13	4	10	十 三 师	Division 13		
十 四 师	Division 14	3	13	十 四 师	Division 14		
兵团直属	Directly under XPCG	128	5	兵团直属	Directly under XPCG	59	9

22—11 各师油料、甜菜单产排序

Ranking of Average Unit Yield of Oil-bearing and Beetroots by Division

计量单位:公斤/公顷 （2010 年） (kg/hectare)

单 位	Unit	油料单产 Total Output of Oil-Bearing	排 序 Ranking	单 位	Unit	甜菜单产 Average Unit Yield of Beetroots	排 序 Ranking
一 师	Division 1	2 290	10	一 师	Division 1		
二 师	Division 2	2 162	13	二 师	Division 2	80 518	3
三 师	Division 3	2 934	3	三 师	Division 3		
四 师	Division 4	2 710	8	四 师	Division 4	82 762	2
五 师	Division 5	2 214	12	五 师	Division 5	40 000	9
六 师	Division 6	3 311	1	六 师	Division 6	76 563	4
七 师	Division 7	3 124	2	七 师	Division 7	83 186	1
八 师	Division 8	2 789	6	八 师	Division 8	36 907	10
九 师	Division 9	1 780	14	九 师	Division 9	56 251	8
十 师	Division 10	2 921	4	十 师	Division 10	67 836	6
建工师	Construction Division	1 510	15	建工师	Construction Division		
十二师	Division 12	2 752	7	十二师	Division 12	63 536	7
十三师	Division 13	2 287	11	十三师	Division 13		
十四师	Division 14	2 560	9	十四师	Division 14		
兵团直属	Directly under XPCG	2 899	5	兵团直属	Directly under XPCG	75 333	5

22—12 各师牲畜年底头数、肉类产量排序

Ranking of Number of Livestock at the Year-end and Output of Meat by Division

（2010 年）

单 位	Unit	牲畜年底头数（万头） Number of Livestock (10 000heads)	排 序 Ranking	单 位	Unit	肉类产量（吨） Output of Meat (ton)	排 序 Ranking
一 师	Division 1	54.55	7	一 师	Division 1	20 899	6
二 师	Division 2	65.27	3	二 师	Division 2	31 547	4
三 师	Division 3	55.58	6	三 师	Division 3	15 760	8
四 师	Division 4	93.10	2	四 师	Division 4	47 581	3
五 师	Division 5	26.43	10	五 师	Division 5	9 113	11
六 师	Division 6	93.70	1	六 师	Division 6	59 965	1
七 师	Division 7	40.13	8	七 师	Division 7	29 477	5
八 师	Division 8	57.14	5	八 师	Division 8	51 943	2
九 师	Division 9	60.11	4	九 师	Division 9	17 206	7
十 师	Division 10	19.74	11	十 师	Division 10	13 019	9
十二师	Division 12	11.15	12	十二师	Division 12	8 006	12
十三师	Division 13	31.66	9	十三师	Division 13	11 096	10
十四师	Division 14	10.84	13	十四师	Division 14	3 251	13
国资公司	State-owned Property Company	3.91	14	国资公司	State-owned Property Company	697	14
兵团直属	Directly under XPCG	0.75	15	兵团直属	Directly under XPCG	363	15

22－13 各师规模以上工业企业主营业务收入、利润总额排序
Ranking of Main Business Income and Total Profit Value of Industrial Enterprises above Designated Size by Division

计量单位:万元　　(2010 年)　　(10 000 yuan)

单　位	Unit	主营业务收入 Main Business Income	排　序 Ranking	单　位	Unit	利润总额 Total Profit	排　序 Ranking
一　师	Division 1	652 181	2	一　师	Division 1	96 042	2
二　师	Division 2	253 782	7	二　师	Division 2	27 344	5
三　师	Division 3	53 718	14	三　师	Division 3	5 473	13
四　师	Division 4	404 869	4	四　师	Division 4	84 012	3
五　师	Division 5	136 561	9	五　师	Division 5	6 700	11
六　师	Division 6	565 349	3	六　师	Division 6	47 652	4
七　师	Division 7	308 864	5	七　师	Division 7	15 125	7
八　师	Division 8	2 213 675	1	八　师	Division 8	253 045	1
九　师	Division 9	61 925	13	九　师	Division 9	6 018	12
十　师	Division 10	82 947	12	十　师	Division 10	13 704	8
建工师	Construction Division	30 934	16	建工师	Construction Division	1 825	14
十二师	Division 12	102 004	11	十二师	Division 12	9 144	10
十三师	Division 13	132 355	10	十三师	Division 13	19 217	6
十四师	Division 14	10 900	17	十四师	Division 14	1 301	16
国资公司	State-owned Property Company	275 122	6	国资公司	State-owned Property Company	12 952	9
中基公司	Chalkis Company	211 456	8	中基公司	Chalkis Company		
兵团直属	Direcly under XPCG	35 436	15	兵团直属	Direcly under XPCG	1 316	15

22－14 各师规模以上工业企业经济效益综合指数、全员劳动生产率排序
Ranking of Comprehensive Index of Industry Economic Results and Overall Labor Productivity of Industrial Enterprises above Designated Size by Division

(2010 年)

单　位	Unit	经济效益综合指数 Comprehensive Index of Industry Economic Results	排　序 Ranking	单　位	Unit	全员劳动生产率(元/人·年) Overall Labor Productivity (yuan/person. year)	排　序 Ranking
一　师	Division 1	245.12	2	一　师	Division 1	169 742	3
二　师	Division 2	213.33	5	二　师	Division 2	145 546	6
三　师	Division 3	195.86	10	三　师	Division 3	123 492	10
四　师	Division 4	310.01	1	四　师	Division 4	186 887	1
五　师	Division 5	137.74	16	五　师	Division 5	88 112	14
六　师	Division 6	205.00	6	六　师	Division 6	173 205	2
七　师	Division 7	178.44	12	七　师	Division 7	151 743	5
八　师	Division 8	203.21	7	八　师	Division 8	132 295	8
九　师	Division 9	197.22	9	九　师	Division 9	138 577	7
十　师	Division 10	232.72	3	十　师	Division 10	127 298	9
建工师	Construction Division	146.94	14	建工师	Construction Division	80 302	15
十二师	Division 12	145.83	15	十二师	Division12	70 400	16
十三师	Division 13	216.28	4	十三师	Division13	108 779	12
十四师	Division 14	202.77	8	十四师	Division14	116 972	11
国资公司	State-owned Property Company	193.02	11	国资公司	State-owned Property Company	164 519	4
中基公司	Chalkis Company	－137.85	17	中基公司	Chalkis Company	－123 460	17
兵团直属	Direcly under XPCG	171.26	13	兵团直属	Direcly under XPCG	93 883	13

22—15 各师道路运输法人企业固定资产原值、主营业务收入排序

Ranking of Original Value of Fixed Assets and Main Business Income of Road Transportation Corporative Enterprises by Division

(2010年)

计量单位:万元 (10 000 yuan)

单位	Unit	固定资产原值 Original Value of Fixed Assets	排序 Ranking	单位	Unit	主营业务收入 Main Business Income	排序 Ranking
一师	Division 1	5 422	2	一师	Division 1	1 396	9
二师	Division 2	1 122	8	二师	Division 2	847	12
三师	Division 3	4 420	3	三师	Division 3	2 721	4
四师	Division 4	1 073	9	四师	Division 4	1 780	7
五师	Division 5	2 046	6	五师	Division 5	1 051	10
六师	Division 6	3 704	4	六师	Division 6	1 031	11
七师	Division 7	3 167	5	七师	Division 7	5 284	3
八师	Division 8	17 849	1	八师	Division 8	23 062	1
九师	Division 9	1 698	7	九师	Division 9	2 459	5
十师	Division 10	721	11	十师	Division 10	346	13
十二师	Division 12	589	12	十二师	Division 12	1 920	6
十三师	Division 13	114	13	十三师	Division 13	1 629	8
十四师	Division 14	86	14	十四师	Division 14	39	14
兵团直属	Directl yunder XPCG	1 063	10	兵团直属	Directly under XPCG	6 386	2

22—16 各师建筑施工单位按年末自有机械设备净值、技术装备率排序

Ranking of Net Value of Self-owned Machinery and Equipment of Construction Units by Division

(2010年)

单位	Unit	年末自有机械设备净值(万元) Net Value of Self-owned Machinery and Equipment (10 000 yuan)	排序 Ranking	单位	Unit	技术装备率(元/人) Technical Equipment Rate (yuan/person)	排序 Ranking
一师	Division 1	14 868	2	一师	Division 1	8 747	4
二师	Division 2	2 814	7	二师	Division 2	3 398	8
三师	Division 3	5 080	5	三师	Division 3	8 231	5
四师	Division 4	2 620	8	四师	Division 4	3 384	9
五师	Division 5	3 590	6	五师	Division 5	11 009	2
六师	Division 6	2 126	9	六师	Division 6	1 098	13
七师	Division 7	5 445	4	七师	Division 7	3 370	10
八师	Division 8	10 617	3	八师	Division 8	2 131	11
九师	Division 9	1 991	10	九师	Division 9	6 560	6
十师	Division 10	1 808	11	十师	Division 10	4 243	7
建工师	Con struction Division	47 321	1	建工师	Construction Division	8 988	3
十二师	Division 12	289	13	十二师	Division 12	706	14
十三师	Division 13	1 205	12	十三师	Division 13	1 882	12
十四师	Division 14	41	15	十四师	Division 14	484	15
兵团直属	Directly under XPCG	279	14	兵团直属	Directly under XPCG	16 677	1

22—17 各师批发和零售业主营业务收入、商品销售总额排序

Ranking of Main Business Income and Total Sales Value of Commodities of Wholesale and Retail Enterprises by Division

计量单位:万元 (2010 年) (10 000 yuan)

单 位	Unit	主营业务收入 Main Business Income	排 序 Ranking	单 位	Unit	商品销售总额 Total Sales Value	排 序 Ranking
一 师	Division 1	518 476	3	一 师	Division 1	707 555	3
二 师	Division 2	165 284	10	二 师	Division 2	334 534	9
三 师	Division 3	229 928	7	三 师	Division 3	310 813	10
四 师	Division 4	173 837	8	四 师	Division 4	355 154	7
五 师	Division 5	265 854	6	五 师	Division 5	367 259	6
六 师	Division 6	166 782	9	六 师	Division 6	559 594	4
七 师	Division 7	93 858	11	七 师	Division 7	338 914	8
八 师	Division 8	724 338	2	八 师	Division 8	1 220 126	1
九 师	Division 9	19 615	15	九 师	Division 9	76 876	15
十 师	Division 10	6 857	17	十 师	Division 10	97 784	13
建 工 师	Con struction Division	29 772	14	建 工 师	Construction Division	34 254	17
十 二 师	Division 12	9 509	16	十 二 师	Division 12	88 970	14
十 三 师	Division 13	52 499	12	十 三 师	Division 13	100 006	12
十 四 师	Division 14	44 839	13	十 四 师	Division 14	54 039	16
国资公司	State-owned Property Company	895 945	1	国资公司	State-owned Property Company	1 034 421	2
供销公司	Supply and Marketing Corporation General	511 566	4	供销公司	Supply and Marketing Corporation General	513 263	5
中基公司	Chalkis Company			中基公司	Chalkis Company	1 653	18
兵团直属	Directly under XPCG	287 678	5	兵团直属	Directly under XPCG	298 436	11

22—18 农牧团场生产总值、利润总额前 20 名

Ranking of the First 20 Farms by Gross Domestic Product and Total Profit Value

(2010 年)

单 位	Unit	生产总值(万元) Gross Domestic Product (10 000 yuan)	排 序 Ranking	单 位	Unit	利润总额(万元) Total Profit Value (10 000 yuan)	排 序 Ranking
石河子总场	Shihezi Farm	143 985	1	一五二团	Farm 152	3 036	1
芳草湖农场	Fangcaohu Farm	135 983	2	二 团	Farm 2	3 019	2
新湖农场	Xinhu Farm	106 373	3	三 团	Farm 3	2 850	3
一二一团	Farm 121	99 410	4	一四七团	Farm 147	2 639	4
奇台农场	Qitai Farm	83 845	5	一 团	Farm 1	2 633	5
一四三团	Farm 143	71 532	6	二十九团	Farm 29	2 459	6
十 团	Farm 10	68 737	7	石河子总场	Shihezi Farm	2 454	7
一二五团	Farm 125	68 650	8	四十五团	Farm 45	2 349	8
一五〇团	Farm 150	65 994	9	一二一团	Farm 121	2 088	9
二十九团	Farm 29	65 582	10	十 团	Farm 10	2 061	10
一四二团	Farm 142	63 067	11	八十六团	Farm 86	1 952	11
一三〇团	Farm 130	62 089	12	九 十 团	Farm 90	1 899	12
一四八团	Farm 148	60 128	13	一〇五团	Farm 105	1 895	13
十 六 团	Farm 16	57 750	14	红山农场	Hongshan Farm	1 879	14
一 团	Farm 1	56 613	15	八十三团	Farm 83	1 859	15
一三一团	Farm 131	56 601	16	十 三 团	Farm 13	1 849	16
三 团	Farm 3	56 259	17	一四二团	Farm 142	1 688	17
四十五团	Farm 45	55 715	18	一五〇团	Farm 150	1 686	18
一〇四团	Farm 104	52 147	19	十 六 团	Farm 16	1 683	19
一二九团	Farm 129	51 923	20	八 团	Farm 8	1 653	20

22—19 农牧团场粮食、棉花产量前20名

Ranking of the First 20 Farms by Yield of Grain and Cotton

计量单位:吨 (2010年) (ton)

单 位	Unit	粮食产量 Yield of Grain	排 序 Ranking	单 位	Unit	棉花产量 Yield of Cotton	排 序 Ranking
奇台农场	Qitai Farm	167 882	1	一二一团	Farm 121	38 815	1
新湖农场	Xinhu Farm	64 923	2	新湖农场	Xinhu Farm	37 383	2
七十一团	Farm 71	59 411	3	芳草湖农场	Fangcaohu Farm	33 000	3
六师红旗农场	Hongqi Farm Divisoin 6	55 558	4	一五〇团	Farm 150	31 368	4
六十六团	Farm 66	52 941	5	一四八团	Farm 148	31 076	5
六十八团	Farm 68	51 991	6	一团	Farm 1	28 080	6
一六三团	Farm 163	47 945	7	一三三团	Farm 133	27 900	7
七十六团	Farm 76	47 394	8	一三四团	Farm 134	26 778	8
一二四团	Farm 124	44 982	9	一四二团	Farm 142	26 425	9
四团	Farm 4	44 186	10	四十五团	Farm 45	24 800	10
八十四团	Farm 84	41 632	11	三团	Farm 3	23 279	11
芳草湖农场	Fangcaohu Farm	40 893	12	二十九团	Farm 29	23 260	12
七十七团	Farm 77	37 226	13	一二五团	Farm 125	22 390	13
一二九团	Farm 129	36 524	14	一四九团	Farm 149	22 240	14
一六六团	Farm 166	35 959	15	一四四团	Farm 144	22 218	15
共青团农场	Gongqintuan Farm	35 818	16	十六团	Farm 16	21 407	16
七十二团	Farm 72	34 055	17	七团	Farm 7	21 180	17
一三〇团	Farm 130	31 743	18	石河子总场	Shihezi Farm	20 880	18
七十五团	Farm 75	31 037	19	八十三团	Farm 83	20 000	19
军户农场	Junhu Farm	30 579	20	一四七团	Farm 147	19 995	20

22—20 农牧团场粮食、棉花单产前20名

Ranking of the First 20 Farms by Grain and Cotton Average Unit Yield

计量单位:公斤/公顷 (2010年) (kg/hectare)

单 位	Unit	粮食单产 Grain Average Unit Yield	排 序 Ranking	单 位	Unit	棉花单产 Cotton Average Unit Yield	排 序 Ranking
六团	Farm 6	14 381	1	十团	Farm 10	2 952	1
一三六团	Farm 136	12 000	2	八十一团	Farm 81	2 899	2
一六三团	Farm 163	11 623	3	二二四团	Farm 224	2 899	3
新湖农场	Xinhu Farm	11 506	4	四十六团	Farm 46	2 872	4
一〇六团	Farm 106	11 438	5	四十九团	Farm 49	2 861	5
团结农场	Tuanjie Farm	10 925	6	十四团	Farm 14	2 850	6
一团	Farm 1	10 801	7	十六团	Farm 16	2 820	7
一二八团	Farm 128	10 774	8	五十三团	Farm 53	2 807	8
芳草湖农场	Fangcaohu Farm	10 550	9	三团	Farm 3	2 805	9
一三四团	Farm 134	10 428	10	七团	Farm 7	2 790	10
三团	Farm 3	10 248	11	三十三团	Farm 33	2 775	11
八团	Farm 8	10 222	12	九〇团	Farm 90	2 764	12
一二七团	Farm 127	10 100	13	一四七团	Farm 147	2 727	13
土墩子农场	Tudunzi Farm	10 090	14	一五〇团	Farm 150	2 707	14
一二九团	Farm 129	9 871	15	四十二团	Farm 42	2 695	15
四团	Farm 4	9 794	16	九十一团	Farm 91	2 693	16
一二四团	Farm 124	9 794	17	十二团	Farm 12	2 691	17
七十一团	Farm 71	9 778	18	二十九团	Farm 29	2 684	18
六师红旗农场	Hongqi Farm Divisoin 6	9 640	19	八十九团	Farm 89	2 667	19
一二五团	Farm 125	9 610	20	四十八团	Farm 48	2 657	20

22—21 农牧团场油料、甜菜产量前20名

Ranking of the First 20 Farms by Yield of Oil-bearing and Beetroots

计量单位:吨　　(2010年)　　(ton)

单　位	Unit	油料产量 Yield of Oil-bearing	排　序 Ranking	单　位	Unit	甜菜产量 Yield of Beetroots	排　序 Ranking
七十七团	Farm 77	18 765	1	二十二团	Farm 22	145 756	1
七十六团	Farm 76	16 582	2	一三一团	Farm 131	121 000	2
一二八团	Farm 128	8 992	3	一六八团	Farm 168	104 465	3
七十五团	Farm 75	8 156	4	一六六团	Farm 166	95 537	4
一八一团	Farm 181	7 940	5	一六七团	Farm 167	92 952	5
土墩子农场	Tudunzi Farm	6 630	6	一六四团	Farm 164	89 125	6
一八三团	Farm 183	6 452	7	六十七团	Farm 67	85 000	7
一八七团	Farm 187	6 165	8	七十一团	Farm 71	79 510	8
七十四团	Farm 74	5 277	9	二十一团	Farm 21	72 000	9
一八五团	Farm 185	5 086	10	六十四团	Farm 64	64 440	10
二二二团	Farm 222	4 949	11	二十七团	Farm 27	64 408	11
一八二团	Farm 182	4 656	12	二十四团	Farm 24	60 143	12
芳草湖农场	Fangcaohu Farm	4 344	13	一二四团	Farm 124	55 220	13
一二九团	Farm 129	4 043	14	一八二团	Farm 182	54 000	14
一三〇团	Farm 130	3 755	15	团结农场	Tuanjie Farm	50 130	15
一六七团	Farm 167	3 728	16	七〇团	Farm 70	45 182	16
一八八团	Farm 188	3 557	17	一六三团	Farm 163	44 235	17
一八四团	Farm 184	3 427	18	六十三团	Farm 63	42 397	18
一六八团	Farm 168	3 289	19	奇台农场	Farm 95	41 820	19
一二六团	Farm 126	2 900	20	六十六团	Farm 96	39 694	20

22—22 农牧团场油料、甜菜单产前20名

Ranking of the First 20 Farms of Oil-bearing and Beetroots Average Unit Yield

计量单位:公斤/公顷　　(2010年)　　(kg/hectare)

单　位	Unit	油料单产 Oil-bearing Average Unit Yield	排　序 Ranking	单　位	Unit	甜菜单产 Beetroots Average Unit Yield	排　序 Ranking
一五二团	Farm 152	6 500	1	六十七团	Farm 67	104 252	1
六运湖农场	Liuyunhu Farm	4 573	2	一二九团	Farm 129	100 800	2
一〇六团	Farm 106	4 500	3	六十八团	Farm 68	93 143	3
一二四团	Farm 124	4 234	4	二十五团	Farm 25	90 000	4
共青团农场	Gongqingtuan Farm	4 200	5	奇台农场	Qitai Farm	90 000	5
芳草湖农场	Fangcaohu Farm	3 997	6	六十二团	Farm 62	90 000	6
一四三团	Farm 143	3 903	7	二十一团	Farm 21	90 000	7
土墩子农场	Tudunzi Farm	3 825	8	六十三团	Farm 63	88 131	8
一八五团	Farm 185	3 787	9	二十七团	Farm 27	87 749	9
一〇三团	Farm 103	3 765	10	七〇团	Farm 70	87 000	10
一三一团	Farm 131	3 750	11	六十六团	Farm 66	84 204	11
红山农场	Hongshan Farm	3 750	12	一二四团	Farm 124	82 500	12
一二九团	Farm 129	3 675	13	一三一团	Farm 131	82 500	13
一〇二团	Farm 102	3 450	14	一二八团	Farm 128	82 500	14
二十五团	Farm 25	3 450	15	一二三团	Farm 123	82 500	15
新湖农场	Xinghu Farm	3 399	16	一二七团	Farm 127	82 500	16
三坪农场	Sanping F rm	3 375	17	六十一团	Farm 61	82 500	17
八十七团	Farm 87	3 311	18	一三〇团	Farm 130	82 500	18
一〇一团	Farm 101	3 300	19	二二三团	Farm 223	80 280	19
叶城牧场	Yecheng Farm	3 300	20	七十一团	Farm 71	79 499	20

22—23 农牧团场牲畜存栏头数、肉类产量前 20 名

Ranking of the First 20 Farms by Number of Livestock and Meat Production

（2010 年）

单 位	Unit	牲畜存栏头数（万头只） Number of Livestock (10 000 heads)	排 序 Ranking	单 位	Unit	肉类产量（吨） Out put of Meat (ton)	排 序 Ranking
奇台农场	Qitai Farm	19.21	1	石河子总场	Shihezi Farm	15 429	1
石河子总场	Shihezi Farm	15.61	2	二十九团	Farm 29	11 024	2
二十二团	Farm 22	14.01	3	奇台农场	Qitai Farm	9 644	3
芳草湖农场	Fangcaohu Farm	12.86	4	芳草湖农场	Fangcaohu Farm	8 739	4
二十九团	Farm 29	11.85	5	一四二团	Farm 142	7 940	5
六师红旗农场	Hongqi Farm Divisoin 6	11.62	6	一四四团	Farm 144	7 544	6
一六一团	Farm 161	11.00	7	一〇二团	Farm 102	6 994	7
一六五团	Farm 165	11.00	8	一〇一团	Farm 101	6 858	8
新湖农场	Xinhu Farm	10.62	9	新湖农场	Xinhu Farm	6 080	9
一三七团	Farm 137	9.60	10	一三一团	Farm 131	5 708	10
红山农场	Hongshan Farm	8.77	11	七十一团	Farm 71	5 137	11
一四二团	Farm 142	8.69	12	一〇三团	Farm 103	5 047	12
四十四团	Farm 44	8.60	13	六十六团	Farm 66	4 852	13
六十六团	Farm 66	8.59	14	一二三团	Farm 123	4 660	14
一六八团	Farm 168	8.52	15	一二四团	Farm 124	4 613	15
黄田农场	Hangtian Farm	8.50	16	一四三团	Farm 143	3 960	16
七十一团	Farm 71	8.43	17	军户农场	Junhu Farm	3 874	17
四十五团	Farm 45	7.43	18	一〇五团	Farm 105	3 797	18
六十四团	Farm 64	7.04	19	六十七团	Farm 67	3 650	19
七十六团	Farm 76	7.04	20	七十六团	Farm 76	3 640	20

22—24 各师规模以上工业企业综合能源消费量、产值能耗排序

Ranking of Comprehensive Energy Consumption and Output Value Energy Consumption of Industrial Enterprises above Designated Size by Division

（2010 年）

单 位	Unit	产值能耗（吨标准煤/万元） Output Value Energy Consumption (ton Standard Coal/ 10 000 yuan)	排 序 Ranking	单 位	Unit	综合能源消费量（吨标准煤） Comprehensive Energy Consumption (ton Standard Coal)	排 序 Ranking
一师	Division 1	1.3379	5	一师	Division 1	918 354	2
二师	Division 2	0.5542	12	二师	Division 2	166 016	7
三师	Division 3	0.8842	9	三师	Division 3	57 157	12
四师	Division 4	1.5898	4	四师	Division 4	673 540	3
五师	Division 5	0.9706	7	五师	Division 5	98 717	8
六师	Division 6	0.8625	10	六师	Division 6	555 519	5
七师	Division 7	2.2124	1	七师	Division 7	663 511	4
八师	Division 8	1.9893	3	八师	Division 8	4 272 061	1
九师	Division 9	1.0337	6	九师	Division 9	57 593	11
十师	Division 10	0.9346	8	十师	Division 10	81 617	9
建工师	Construction Division	0.7149	11	建工师	Construction Division	22 125	14
十二师	Division 12	0.4410	13	十二师	Division 12	43 938	13
十三师	Division 13	2.1082	2	十三师	Division 13	283 920	6
十四师	Division 14	0.0722	15	十四师	Division 14	860	17
国资公司	State-owned Property Company	0.0645	16	国资公司	State-owned Property Company	17 817	15
中基公司	Chalkis Company	0.4001	14	中基公司	Chalkis Company	64 061	10
兵团直属	Directly under XPCG	0.0565	17	兵团直属	Directly under XPCG	2 043	16

22—25　规模以上工业企业主营业务收入、利润总额前20名
Ranking of the First 20 Industrial Enterprises above Designated Size by Main Business Income and Total Profit Value

计量单位：万元　　(2010年)　　(10 000 yuan)

单　位	Unit	主营业务收入 Main Business Income	排　序 Ranking
八师天业天辰化工有限公司	Division 8 Tianchen Chemical Industry Co.,Ltd. of XPCG	400 774	1
八师天业股份有限公司(母公司)	Division 8 Tianye Co.,Ltd. Of XPCG	296 508	2
天津中辰番茄制品有限责任公司	Tianjin Zhongchen Tomato Products Co.,Ltd.	147 602	3
六师铝业有限责任公司	Division 6 Alumium Industry Co.,Ltd.	137 489	4
八师石河子开发区天业化工有限责任公司	Division 8 Shihezi Development Zones Tianye Chemical Industry Co.,Ltd.	123 103	5
八师天盛实业有限公司	Division 8 Tianshen Yilite Industry Co.,Ltd.	117 359	6
八师天富热电股份有限公司(母公司)	Division 8 Tianfu Thermoelectricity Co.,Ltd.	115 011	7
新疆海龙化纤有限公司	XJ Hailong Chemical Fiber Co.,Ltd.	107 782	8
四师伊力特实业股份有限公司	Division 4 Yilite Industry Co.,Ltd.	105 000	9
新疆天康畜牧生物技术股份有限公司	XJ Tian kang Biology Technique Co.,Ltd.	100 415	10
河南宏展实业有限责任公司	Henan Hongzhan Industry Co.,Ltd.	91 924	11
八师华芳石河子纺织有限公司	Division 8 Huafang Shihezi Spinning Co.,Ltd.	80 248	12
八师石河子开发区天业热电有限责任公司	Division 8 Shihezi Development Zones Tianye Thermoelectricity Co.,Ltd.	68 105	13
阿拉尔新农棉浆有限责任公司	Alaer Xinnong Cotton Slurry Co.,Ltd.	67 588	14
新疆青松建材化工(集团)股份有限公司	XJ Qingsong Building Material and Chemical Industry Co.,Ltd.	59 647	15
八师石河子中发化工有限责任公司	Division 8 Shihezi Zhongfa Chemical Industry Co.,Ltd. of XPCG	59 025	16
四师伊犁南岗建材有限责任公司	Division 4 Nangang Building Material Co.,Ltd.	57 709	17
八师天业节水灌溉股份有限公司	Division 8 Tianye Water-Saving Irrigates Area Co.,Ltd.	53 330	18
新疆万翔化纤有限公司	XJ Fanxiang Chemical Fiber Co.,Ltd.	47 961	19
新疆中基番茄制品有限责任公司	XJ Chalkis Tomato Products Co.,Ltd.	47 129	20

单　位	Unit	利润总额 Total Profit	排　序 Ranking
八师天业天辰化工有限公司	Division8 Tianchen Chemical Industry Co.,Ltd. of XPCG	114 972	1
四师伊力特实业股份有限公司	Division 4 Yilite Industry Co.,Ltd	30 896	2
新疆青松建材化工(集团)股份有限公司	XJ Qingsong Building Material and Chemical Industry Co.,Ltd.	26 022	3
八师华芳石河子纺织有限公司	Division 8 Huafang Shihezi Spinning Co.,Ltd.	22 493	4
八师石河子开发区天业热电有限责任公司	Division 8 Shihezi Development Zones Tianye Thermoelectricity Co.,Ltd.	18 369	5
八师天盛实业有限公司	Division 8 Tianshen Yilite Industry Co.,Ltd.	17 888	6
八师天富热电股份有限公司(母公司)	Division 8 Tianye Co.,Ltd. Of XPCG	16 015	7
八师石河子开发区天业化工有限责任公司	Division 8 Shihezi Development Zones Tianye Chemical Industry Co.,Ltd.	13 402	8
新疆青松水泥有限责任公司	XJ Qingsong Cement Co.,Ltd.	12 045	9
六师大黄山煤矿	Division 6 Dahuangshan CoalMinerals	10 527	10
新疆天康畜牧生物技术股份有限公司	XJ Tiankang Biology Technique Co.,Ltd.	9 839	11
八师石河子郑氏化纤有限公司	Division 8 Shihezi Zhengshi Chemical Fiber Co.,Ltd	9 100	12
四师伊犁南岗建材有限责任公司	Division 4 Nangang Building Material Co.,Ltd.	8 820	13
新疆万翔化纤有限公司	XJ Fanxiang Chemical FiberCo.,Ltd	8 257	14
六师铝业有限责任公司	Division 6 Alumium Industry Co.,Ltd.	7 894	15
库车县科兴煤炭实业有限责任公司	Kuchen Kexin Coal Industry Co.,Ltd.	7 580	16
八师石河子天富南热电有限公司	Division 8 TianfuSouth Thermoelectricity Co.,Ltd	6 185	17
哈密天隆镍业有限责任公司	Hami Tianlong Nickel Industry Co.,Ltd.	5 776	18
新疆库车青松水泥有限责任公司	XJ Kuche Qingsong Cement Co.,Ltd.	5 741	19
八师石河子顶津食品有限公司	Division 8 Shihezi Dingjin Food Co.,Ltd.	5 700	20

22—26 建筑业资质以上法人企业固定资产原值、工程结算利润前20名

Ranking of the First 20 Construction Corporative Enterprises of Qualification by Original Value of Fixd Assets and Net Profits of Construction Works

计量单位：万元　　（2010年）　　(10 000 yuan)

单　位	Unit	固定资产原值 Original Value of Fixed Assets	排　序 Ranking
兵团北新路桥建设股份有限公司	Beixin Road and Bridge Building Share-holding Co. ,Ltd. of XPCG Construction Group	78 702	1
七师北方建设集团公司	Division 7 The North Construction Group	30 765	2
兵团第八建筑安装工程有限责任公司	The 8th Construction and Installation Co. ,Ltd. of XPCG	16 951	3
新疆阿拉尔水利水电工程总公司	XJ Alaer Water Conservancy and water Electricity Engineering Company	16 321	4
兵团建设工程集团有限责任公司	XPCG Construction and Installation Co. ,Ltd.	16 089	5
兵团第一建筑安装工程有限责任公司	The 1th Construction and Installation Co. ,Ltd. of XPCG	12 222	6
二师天宇建设工程有限责任公司	Division 2 Tianyu Construction(Group) Co. ,Ltd	9 314	7
兵团道路桥梁工程总公司	Road and Bridge Engineering Company of XPCG	8 274	8
兵团第四建筑安装工程公司	The 4th Construction and Installation Co. ,Ltd. of XPCG	8 129	9
新疆塔里木建筑安装工程集团有限责任公司	XJ Talimu Construction and Installation Co. ,Ltd.	8 097	10
八师石河子天筑建设(集团)有限责任公司	Division 8 ShiHezi Taian Construction and Installation Company	7 128	11
四师伊犁宏远建设有限责任公司	Division 4 Yili Hongyuan Construction Co. ,Ltd.	5 933	12
二师天宇建设工程有限责任公司	Division 2 Tianyu Construction(Group) Co. ,Ltd.	5 725	13
八师石河子开发区汇能工业设备安装公司	Division 8 ShiHezi Huineng Industry Installation Company	5 602	14
兵团第六建筑安装工程公司	The 6th Construction and Installation Co. ,Ltd of XPCG	4 596	15
三师小海子水利建筑安装工程有限公司	Division 3 Xiaohaizi Water Conservancy and water Electricity Engineering Company	4 295	16
八师石河子泰安建筑工程有限公司	Division 8 ShiHezi Taian Construction and Installation Company	4 184	17
一师松鹤建筑安装公司	Division 1 Songhe Construction and Installation Company	4 029	18
新疆阿拉尔南口建筑有限责任公司	XJ Alaer Nankou Construction and Installation Co. ,Ltd.	3 728	19
九师绿翔建筑安装工程有限责任公司	Division 9 LuXiang Construction and Installation Co. ,Ltd.	3 456	20

单　位	Unit	工程结算利润 Net Profits of Construction Works	排　序 Ranking
兵团北新路桥建设股份有限公司	Beixin Road and Bridge Building Share-holding Co. ,Ltd. of XPCG Construction Group	21 983	1
兵团建设工程集团有限责任公司	XPCG Construction and Installation Co. ,Ltd.	10 853	2
兵团第一建筑安装工程有限责任公司	The 1th Construction and Installation Co. ,Ltd. of XPCG	7 049	3
兵团第八建筑安装工程有限责任公司	The 8th Construction and Installation Co. ,Ltd. of XPCG	5 838	4
八师石河子泰安建筑工程有限公司	Division 8 ShiHezi Taian Construction and Installation Company	3 789	5
七师北方建设集团公司	Division 7 The North Construction Group	3 091	6
一师松鹤建筑安装公司	Division 1 Songhe Construction and Installation Company	2 972	7
三师小海子水利建筑安装工程有限公司	Division 3 Xiaohaizi Water Conservancy and water Electricity Engineering Company	2 963	8
阿拉尔塔里木建筑工程有限公司	Alaer Talimu Construction and Installation Co. ,Ltd.	2 510	9
新疆塔里木建筑安装工程集团有限责任公司	XJ Talimu Construction and Installation Co. ,Ltd.	2 343	10
兵团第六建筑安装工程公司	The 6th Construction and Installation Co. ,Ltd. of XPCG	1 901	11
兵团第五建筑安装工程公司	The 5th Construction and Installation Co. ,Ltd. of XPCG	1 895	12
八师石河子泰安建筑工程有限公司	Division 8 ShiHezi Taian Construction and Installation Company	1 844	13
九师绿翔建筑安装工程有限责任公司	Division 9 LuXiang Construction and Installation Co. ,Ltd.	1 813	14
四师伊犁宏远建设有限责任公司	Division 4 YiliHongyuan Construction Co. ,Ltd.	1 693	15
五家渠天力建工有限责任公司	WuJiaQu TianLi Construction and Installation Co. ,Ltd.	1 682	16
二师天宇建设工程有限责任公司	Division 2 Tianyu Construction(Group) Co. ,Ltd.	1 579	17
十三师建筑安装总公司	Division 13 Construction and Installation Co. ,Ltd. of XPCG	1 539	18
七师三利建筑有限责任公司	Division 7 Sanli Construction Group	1 446	19
喀什前海建筑安装工程有限责任公司	Kashgar Qianhai Construction and Installation Co. ,Ltd.	1 430	20

22—27 道路运输法人企业主营业务收入、客货换算周转量前 20 名

Ranking of The First 20 Transportation Corporative Enterprises by Main Business Income and Turnover Volume of Passenger and Freight Traffic

(2010 年)

单 位	Unit	主营业务收入（万元） Main Business Income (10 000 yuan)	排 序 Ranking
石河子开发区鑫源公路运输有限责任公司	Shihezi Development Zones Xinyuan Road Treffic Company	8 532	1
兵团新大地实业有限责任公司	Xindadi Industry Co. ,Ltd of XPCG	6 386	2
七师奎屯旅客运输公司	Division 7 Kuytun Passenger Conveyance Company	5 284	3
八师石河子长运旅客运输有限责任公司	Division 8 Shihezi Changyun Passenger Conveyance Company	4 794	4
石河子丰尔达物流有限责任公司	Shihezi Fengerda Trade Co. ,Ltd	4 405	5
兵团第三运输公司	The 3th Motor Vehicles Conveyance Company of XPCG	2 721	6
新疆通联运输有限责任公司	XJ Tonglian Vehicles Conveyance Company of XPCG	2 599	7
九师第二汽车运输公司	Division 9 The 2th Motor Vehicles Conveyance Company	2 459	8
十二师新大陆运输公司	Division 12 Xindalu Conveyance Company	1 920	9
四师伊犁农垦交通运输有限责任公司	Division 4 Yili Nongken Transportation Conveyance Co. ,Ltd.	1 780	10
八师石河子市新建畅达客运有限责任公司	Division 8 Shihezi Xinjian Changda Passenger Conveyance Co. ,Ltd.	1 754	11
十三师五洲汽车运输有限责任公司	Division 13 Motor Vehicles Conveyance Company	1 629	12
一师运输公司	Division 1 Motor Vehicles Conveyance Company	1 330	13
五师赛里木运输有限责任公司	Division 5 Sailimu Conveyance Co. ,Ltd.	1 051	14
二师中联客运有限责任公司	Division 2 Zhonglian Passenger Conveyance Company	848	15
五家渠新建旅客运输有限责任公司	Wujiaqu Xinjian Changyun Passenger Conveyance Co. ,Ltd.	573	16
石河子新建鑫泰旅客运输有限责任公司	Shihezi Xinjian Xingtai Passenger Conveyance Co. ,Ltd.	539	17
石河子开发区天富燃料运输有限责任公司	Shihezi Tianfu Fuel Convevance Co. ,Ltd.	439	18
五家渠顺通城市公交公司	Wujiaqu Shuntong City Passenger Conveyance Company	358	19
十师旅客运输公司	Division 10 Passenger Conveyance Company	346	20

单 位	Unit	客货换算周转量（万吨公里） Turnover Volume of Passenger and Freight Traffic (10 000 ton-km)	排 序 Ranking
石河子开发区鑫源公路运输有限责任公司	Shihezi Development Zones Xinyuan Road Treffic Company	19 276	1
兵团第三运输公司	Division 3 Motor Vehicles Conveyance Company	14 833	2
石河子丰尔达物流有限责任公司	Shihezi Fengerda Trade Co. ,Ltd.	14 300	3
五家渠隆途运输有限责任公司	Wujiaqu Longtu Passenger Conveyance Co. ,Ltd.	12 818	4
十二师新大陆运输公司	Division 12 Xindalu Conveyance Company	12 600	5
新疆新大地实业有限责任公司	Xindadi Industry Co. ,Ltd. of XPCG	9 833	6
五师赛里木运输有限责任公司	Division 5 Sailimu Conveyance Co. ,Ltd.	9 331	7
四师伊犁农垦交通运输有限责任公司	Division 4 YiliNongken Transportation Conveyance Co. ,Ltd.	6 648	8
八师石河子长运旅客运输责任公司	Division 8 Shihezi Changyun Passenger Conveyance Company	5 210	9
二师中联客运有限责任公司	Division 2 Zhonglian Passenger Conveyance Company	4 663	10
七师奎屯旅客运输公司	Division 7 Kuytun Passenger Conveyance Company	4 236	11
新疆通联运输有限责任公司	XJ Tonglian Vehicles Conveyance Company of XPCG	4 182	12
十师旅客运输公司	Division 10 Passenger Conveyance Company	2 973	13
十三师五洲汽车运输有限责任公司	Division 13 MotorVehicles Conveyance Company	2 616	14
五家渠顺通城市公交公司	Wujiaqu Shuntong City Passenger Conveyance Company	2 403	15
一师运输公司	Division1 MotorVehicles Conveyance Company	1 783	16
五家渠新建旅客运输有限责任公司	Wujiaqu Xinjian Changyun Passenger Conveyance Co. ,Ltd.	1 630	17
九师第二汽车运输公司	Division 9The 2th MotorVehicles Conveyance Company	1 422	18
石河子开发区天富燃料运输有限责任公司	Shihezi Tianfu Fuel Convevance Co. ,Ltd.	1 197	19
石河子市新建畅达客运有限责任公司	Shihezi Xinjian Changda Passenger Conveyance Co. ,Ltd.	1 035	20

22－28 限额以上批发和零售企业主营业务收入、利润总额前20名

Ranking of the First 20 Wholesale and Retail Trade Enterprises above Designated Size by Main Business Income and Total Profit Value

（2010年）

计量单位：万元 (10 000 yuan)

单 位	Unit	主营业务收入 Main Business Income	排 序 Ranking
兵团石油有限责任公司	XPCG Petroleum Co. ,Ltd.	383 935	1
一师棉麻公司	Division 1 Cotton and Flax Company	356 787	2
新疆石河子西部银力棉业(集团)有限责任公司	XJWest Yinli Cotton Industry Group Co. ,Ltd.	301 408	3
兵团棉麻公司	XPCG Cotton and Flax Company	247 191	4
新疆银隆国际贸易股份有限责任公司	XJ Yinlong International Trade Co. ,Ltd.	203 386	5
五师棉麻公司	Division 5 Cotton and Flax Company	169 805	6
三师棉麻公司	Division 3 Cotton and Flax Company	138 768	7
兵团农业生产资料供应公司	XPCG Agricultural Production Materials Supplying Company	133 501	8
六师棉麻公司	Division 6 Cotton and Flax Company	128 755	9
四师供销合作联合社	Division 4 Supplying and Marketing Cooperation Company	112 847	10
新疆石河子银力实业投资有限责任公司	Shihezi Yinli Industry Investment Co. ,Ltd.	109 589	11
一师供销合作有限责任公司	Division 1 Supplying and Marketing Cooperation Company	108 855	12
二师永兴供销有限责任公司	Division 2 YongxinSupplying and Marketing Cooperation Company	89 571	13
七师供销合作总公司	Division 7 Supplying and Marketing Cooperation Company	80 955	14
三师农业生产资料公司	Division 3 Agricultural Production Materials Supplying Company	72 510	15
二师天润农资有限责任公司	Division 2 Tianrun Agrucultural Production Materials Co. ,Ltd.	65 371	16
兵团供销银花有限责任公司	XPCG Yinhua Supplying and Marketing Co. ,Ltd.	65 123	17
新疆农垦宏业棉花有限责任公司	XJ Nongken Hongye Cotton Co. ,Ltd.	58 644	18
新疆恒盛贸易有限责任公司	XJ Henshen Trade Co. ,Ltd.	45 376	19
新疆万达有限责任公司	XJ Wanda Co. ,Ltd.	44 964	20

单 位	Unit	利润总额 Total Profit	排 序 Ranking
新疆银隆国际贸易股份有限责任公司	XJY inlong International Trade Co. ,Ltd.	8 993	1
兵团石油有限责任公司	XPCG Petroleum Co. ,Ltd.	6 203	2
新疆农垦宏业棉花有限责任公司	XJ Nongken Hongye Cotton Co. ,Ltd.	4 727	3
一师棉麻公司	Division1 Cotton and Flax Company	4 142	4
中国彩棉(集团)股份有限责任公司	XJ China Colour Cotton Group StockCo. ,Ltd.	4 066	5
新疆石河子西部银力棉业(集团)有限责任公司	XJ West Yinli CottonIndustry Group Co. ,Ltd.	3 351	6
新疆康地种业科技股份有限责任公司	XJ Kangdi Seed Industry Technological Stock Co. ,Ltd.	3 248	7
兵团棉麻公司	XPCG Cotton and Flax Company	3 216	8
一师塔里木河种业股份有限责任公司	Division1 Talimuhe Seed Industry Stock Co. ,Ltd.	2 705	9
阿拉尔市天华棉业有限责任公司	Alaer Tianhua CottonIndustry Co. ,Ltd.	2 564	10
石河子开发区新捷燃气有限责任公司	Shihezi Development Zone Xinjie Gas Petroleum Co. ,Ltd.	2 551	11
一师供销合作有限责任公司	Division1 Supplying and Marketing Cooperation Company	2 108	12
四师供销合作联合社	Division4 Supplying and Marketing Cooperation Company	1 777	13
新疆烟草兵团石河子有限责任公司	XPCG Shihezi Tobacco Co. ,Ltd.	1 416	14
三师棉麻公司	Division3 Cotton and Flax Company	1 256	15
新疆石河子市银力实业股份有限责任公司	Shihezi Yinli Industry Investment Co. ,Ltd.	1 145	16
三师农业生产资料公司	Division3 Agricultural Production Materials Supplying Company	1 140	17
六师棉麻公司	Division6 Cotton and Flax Company	1 139	18
和田昆仑山枣业有限责任公司	Hetian Kunlunshan Jujubes Industry Co. ,Ltd.	1 067	19
石河子好家乡超市有限责任公司	Shihezi Goodhome Supermarket Co. ,Ltd.	876	20

2011

BING TUAN

附　录

各省（区）、直辖市主要经济指标排序

Appendix Ranking of Main Economic Indicators by Province

简要说明

一、本篇资料的主要内容

本篇资料主要反映全国各省（区）、直辖市主要经济指标的排序情况、新疆16地州市及天山北坡经济带情况、全国东、中、西部和东北三省主要指标对比情况。

二、本篇的资料来源

资料取自《2010年中国区域经济统计年鉴》和《2010年新疆统计年鉴》，反映2009年及以前年度资料，由兵团统计局国民经济综合统计处整理。

Brief Introduction

1. Main Contents

The data in this chapter mainly show the conditions on ranking of main economic indicators by province and comparison of main indicators on the economic belt of the northern slope of the Tianshan Mountains, 16 prefectures and cities of the Eastern, Middle, Western and 3 Northeastern provinces to national total.

2. Sources of Data

The data are collected from China Statistical Yearbook For Regional Economy-2010 and Xinjiang Statistical Yearbook-2010. Data in 2009 and before are prepared by the General office of the Statistics Bureau of XPCG.

附录 1－1　各省(区)、直辖市生产总值及指数、人均指标排序

Ranking of Gross Domestic Product and its Indices, Per Capita GDP by Region

(2009 年)

地　区	Region	生产总值(亿元) Gross Domestic Product (100 million yuan)	排　序 Ranking	生产总值指数(上年=100) Gross Domestic Product Indices (preceding year=100)	排　序 Ranking	人均生产总值(元) Per Capita GDP (yuan)	排　序 Ranking
全　国	**China**	**340 506.90**		**109.1**		**25 575**	
北　京	Beijing	12 153.03	13	110.2	25	70 452	2
天　津	Tianjin	7 521.85	20	116.5	2	62 574	3
河　北	Hebei	17 235.48	6	110.0	27	24 581	12
山　西	Shanxi	7 358.31	21	105.4	32	21 522	19
内蒙古	Inner Mongolia	9 740.25	15	116.9	1	40 282	7
辽　宁	Liaoning	15 212.49	7	113.1	11	35 239	9
吉　林	Jilin	7 278.75	22	113.6	7	26 595	11
黑龙江	Heilongjiang	8 587.00	16	111.4	21	22 447	16
上　海	Shanghai	15 046.45	8	108.2	30	78 989	1
江　苏	Jiangsu	34 457.30	2	112.4	14	44 744	4
浙　江	Zhejiang	22 990.35	4	108.9	29	44 641	5
安　徽	Anhui	10 062.82	14	112.9	13	16 408	27
福　建	Fujian	12 236.53	12	112.3	16	33 840	10
江　西	Jiangxi	7 655.18	19	113.1	11	17 335	26
山　东	Shandong	33 896.65	3	112.2	17	35 894	8
河　南	Henan	19 480.46	5	110.9	23	20 597	20
湖　北	Hubei	12 961.10	11	113.5	10	22 677	15
湖　南	Hunan	13 059.69	10	113.7	6	20 428	21
广　东	Guangdong	39 482.56	1	109.7	28	41 166	6
广　西	Guangxi	7 759.16	18	113.9	5	16 045	28
海　南	Hainan	1 654.21	28	111.7	20	19 254	24
重　庆	Chongqing	6 530.01	23	114.9	3	22 920	14
四　川	Sichuan	14 151.28	9	114.5	4	17 339	25
贵　州	Guizhou	3 912.68	26	111.4	21	10 309	32
云　南	Yunnan	6 169.75	24	112.1	18	13 539	30
西　藏	Tibet	441.36	32	112.4	14	15 295	29
陕　西	Shaanxi	8 169.80	17	113.6	7	21 688	18
甘　肃	Gansu	3 387.56	27	110.3	24	12 872	31
青　海	Qinghai	1 081.27	30	110.1	26	19 454	23
宁　夏	Ningxia	1 353.31	29	111.9	19	21 777	17
新　疆	Xinjiang	4 277.05	25	108.1	31	19 942	22
新疆建设兵团	XPCG	610.69	31	113.6	7	23 734	13

注:本表按当年价计算。

Note: Data in value in this table are calculated at current prices.

附录1－2　各省(区)、直辖市三次产业增加值排序

Ranking of Value-added of Three Industries by Region

计量单位:亿元　　　　(2009年)　　　　(100 million yuan)

地　区	Region	第一产业 Primary Industry	排　序 Ranking	第二产业 Secondary Industry	排　序 Ranking	第三产业 Tertiary Industry	排　序 Ranking
全　国	**China**	**35 226.00**		**157 638.80**		**147 642.10**	
北　京	Beijing	118.29	29	2 855.55	23	9 179.19	5
天　津	Tianjin	128.85	27	3 987.84	18	3 405.16	16
河　北	Hebei	2 207.34	5	8 959.83	6	6 068.31	7
山　西	Shanxi	477.59	24	3 993.80	17	2 886.92	20
内蒙古	Inner Mongolia	929.60	18	5 114.00	13	3 696.65	14
辽　宁	Liaoning	1 414.90	11	7 906.34	7	5 891.25	8
吉　林	Jilin	980.57	17	3 541.92	20	2 756.26	21
黑龙江	Heilongjiang	1 154.33	14	4 060.72	16	3 371.95	17
上　海	Shanghai	113.82	30	6 001.78	11	8 930.85	6
江　苏	Jiangsu	2 261.86	3	18 566.37	3	13 629.07	2
浙　江	Zhejiang	1 163.08	13	11 908.49	4	9 918.78	4
安　徽	Anhui	1 495.45	9	4 905.22	14	3 662.15	15
福　建	Fujian	1 182.74	12	6 005.30	10	5 048.49	13
江　西	Jiangxi	1 098.66	15	3 919.45	19	2 637.07	22
山　东	Shandong	3 226.64	1	18 901.83	2	11 768.18	3
河　南	Henan	2 769.05	2	11 010.50	5	5 700.91	9
湖　北	Hubei	1 795.90	8	6 038.08	9	5 127.12	12
湖　南	Hunan	1 969.69	7	5 687.19	12	5 402.81	10
广　东	Guangdong	2 010.27	6	19 419.70	1	18 052.59	1
广　西	Guangxi	1 458.49	10	3 381.54	22	2 919.13	19
海　南	Hainan	462.19	25	443.43	30	748.59	28
重　庆	Chongqing	606.80	21	3 448.77	21	2 474.44	24
四　川	Sichuan	2 240.61	4	6 711.87	8	5 198.80	11
贵　州	Guizhou	550.27	22	1 476.62	27	1 885.79	25
云　南	Yunnan	1 067.60	16	2 582.53	24	2 519.62	23
西　藏	Tibet	63.88	32	136.63	32	240.85	31
陕　西	Shaanxi	789.64	19	4 236.42	15	3 143.74	18
甘　肃	Gansu	497.05	23	1 527.24	26	1 363.27	27
青　海	Qinghai	107.40	31	575.33	29	398.54	30
宁　夏	Ningxia	127.25	28	662.32	28	563.74	29
新　疆	Xinjiang	759.74	20	1 929.59	25	1 587.72	26
新疆建设兵团	XPCG	204.73	26	206.57	31	199.39	32

注:本表按当年价计算。
Note: Data in value in this table are calculated at current prices.

附录1—3 各省(区)、直辖市生产总值指数排序

Ranking of Indices of Gross Domestic Product by Region

计量单位：% (2009年) (%)

地区	Region	第一产业 Primary Industry	排序 Ranking	第二产业 Secondary Industry	排序 Ranking	第三产业 Tertiary Industry	排序 Ranking
全国	**China**	**104.2**		**109.9**		**109.3**	
北京	Beijing	104.6	16	110.4	27	110.2	29
天津	Tianjin	103.4	25	118.0	6	115.2	2
河北	Hebei	103.3	26	110.5	26	111.4	17
山西	Shanxi	104.2	21	101.9	32	110.5	26
内蒙古	Inner Mongolia	102.3	31	121.1	3	115.0	3
辽宁	Liaoning	103.1	27	115.6	13	112.1	16
吉林	Jilin	102.8	29	117.1	9	113.0	10
黑龙江	Heilongjiang	105.2	5	113.1	19	110.7	24
上海	Shanghai	98.9	32	103.5	31	112.2	15
江苏	Jiangsu	104.5	17	112.5	21	113.6	6
浙江	Zhejiang	102.4	30	106.8	30	112.5	11
安徽	Anhui	105.0	10	116.8	11	111.0	22
福建	Fujian	104.7	15	113.7	17	112.3	13
江西	Jiangxi	104.5	17	117.1	9	110.7	24
山东	Shandong	104.2	23	113.9	15	111.2	19
河南	Henan	104.2	21	112.4	22	111.1	21
湖北	Hubei	105.2	5	116.8	11	112.3	13
湖南	Hunan	105.0	10	118.9	5	111.3	18
广东	Guangdong	104.9	13	109.2	28	110.8	23
广西	Guangxi	105.2	5	117.7	8	113.8	5
海南	Hainan	107.2	2	112.6	20	114.1	4
重庆	Chongqing	105.5	4	117.9	7	113.5	7
四川	Sichuan	104.0	24	119.5	4	112.4	12
贵州	Guizhou	104.3	20	112.1	23	113.1	8
云南	Yunnan	105.2	5	113.6	18	113.1	8
西藏	Tibet	103.0	28	121.7	2	110.4	27
陕西	Shaanxi	104.9	13	113.8	16	115.3	1
甘肃	Gansu	105.1	9	111.0	25	111.2	19
青海	Qinghai	105.0	10	111.3	24	109.8	31
宁夏	Ningxia	107.3	1	114.4	14	110.0	30
新疆	Xinjiang	104.5	17	108.5	29	109.2	32
新疆建设兵团	XPCG	107.0	3	125.3	1	110.4	27

注：本表按可比价格计算。

Note: Data in value in this table are calculated at comparable prices.

附录1—4　各省(区)、直辖市总人口排序(2007—2009年)

Ranking of Total Population by Region(2007—2009)

计量单位:万人　　　　(10 000 persons)

地　区	Region	2007	排　序 Ranking	2008	排　序 Ranking	2009	排　序 Ranking
全　国	**China**	**132 129**		**132 802**		**133 474**	
北　京	Beijing	1 633	26	1 695	26	1 755	26
天　津	Tianjin	1 115	27	1 176	27	1 228	27
河　北	Hebei	6 943	6	6 989	6	7 034	6
山　西	Shanxi	3 393	19	3 411	19	3 427	19
内蒙古	Inner Mongolia	2 405	23	2 414	23	2 422	23
辽　宁	Liaoning	4 298	14	4 315	14	4 319	14
吉　林	Jilin	2 730	21	2 734	21	2 740	21
黑龙江	Heilongjiang	3 824	15	3 825	15	3 826	15
上　海	Shanghai	1 858	25	1 888	25	1 921	25
江　苏	Jiangsu	7 625	5	7 677	5	7 725	5
浙　江	Zhejiang	5 060	10	5 120	10	5 180	10
安　徽	Anhui	6 118	8	6 135	8	6 131	8
福　建	Fujian	3 581	18	3 604	18	3 627	18
江　西	Jiangxi	4 368	13	4 400	13	4 432	13
山　东	Shandong	9 367	2	9 417	3	9 470	3
河　南	Henan	9 360	3	9 429	2	9 487	2
湖　北	Hubei	5 699	9	5 711	9	5 720	9
湖　南	Hunan	6 355	7	6 380	7	6 406	7
广　东	Guangdong	9 449	1	9 544	1	9 638	1
广　西	Guangxi	4 768	11	4 816	11	4 856	11
海　南	Hainan	845	28	854	28	864	28
重　庆	Chongqing	2 816	20	2 839	20	2 859	20
四　川	Sichuan	8 127	4	8 138	4	8 185	4
贵　州	Guizhou	3 762	16	3 793	16	3 798	16
云　南	Yunnan	4 514	12	4 543	12	4 571	12
西　藏	Tibet	284	31	287	31	290	31
陕　西	Shaanxi	3 748	17	3 762	17	3 772	17
甘　肃	Gansu	2 617	22	2 628	22	2 635	22
青　海	Qinghai	552	30	554	30	557	30
宁　夏	Ningxia	610	29	618	29	625	29
新　疆	Xinjiang	2 095	24	2 131	24	2 159	24
新疆建设兵团	XPCG	258	32	257	32	257	32

附录 1—5 各省(区)、直辖市城镇居民人均可支配收入排序(2007—2009 年)

Ranking of Per Capita Disposable Income of Urban by Region(2007—2009)

计量单位:元 (yuan)

地区	Region	2007	排序 Ranking	2008	排序 Ranking	2009	排序 Ranking
全国	**China**	**13 786**		**15 781**		**17 175**	
北京	Beijing	21 989	2	24 725	2	26 738	2
天津	Tianjin	16 357	6	19 423	5	21 402	5
河北	Hebei	11 690	14	13 441	14	14 718	14
山西	Shanxi	11 565	15	13 119	18	13 997	23
内蒙古	Inner Mongolia	12 378	10	14 433	9	15 849	9
辽宁	Liaoning	12 300	11	14 393	10	15 761	10
吉林	Jilin	11 286	21	12 829	23	14 006	22
黑龙江	Heilongjiang	10 245	31	11 581	30	12 566	30
上海	Shanghai	23 623	1	26 675	1	28 838	1
江苏	Jiangsu	16 378	5	18 680	6	20 552	6
浙江	Zhejiang	20 574	3	22 727	3	24 611	3
安徽	Anhui	11 474	19	12 990	19	14 086	19
福建	Fujian	15 506	7	17 961	7	19 577	7
江西	Jiangxi	11 452	20	12 866	21	14 022	21
山东	Shandong	14 265	8	16 305	8	17 811	8
河南	Henan	11 477	18	13 231	16	14 372	16
湖北	Hubei	11 486	17	13 153	17	14 367	17
湖南	Hunan	12 294	12	13 821	13	15 084	13
广东	Guangdong	17 699	4	19 733	4	21 575	4
广西	Guangxi	12 200	13	14 146	12	15 451	12
海南	Hainan	10 997	24	12 608	25	13 751	25
重庆	Chongqing	12 591	9	14 368	11	15 749	11
四川	Sichuan	11 098	23	12 633	24	13 839	24
贵州	Guizhou	10 678	27	11 759	28	12 863	28
云南	Yunnan	11 496	16	13 250	15	14 424	15
西藏	Tibet	11 131	22	12 482	26	13 544	26
陕西	Shaanxi	10 763	26	12 858	22	14 129	18
甘肃	Gansu	10 012	32	10 969	32	11 930	32
青海	Qinghai	10 276	30	11 640	29	12 692	29
宁夏	Ningxia	10 859	25	12 932	20	14 025	20
新疆	Xinjiang	10 313	29	11 432	31	12 258	31
新疆建设兵团	XPCG	10 521	28	11 836	27	12 929	27

附录1—6　各省(区)、直辖市农村居民家庭人均纯收入排序(2007—2009年)

Ranking of Per Capita Net Income of Rural Households by Region(2007—2009)

计量单位:元　　(yuan)

地　区	Region	2007	排序 Ranking	2008	排序 Ranking	2009	排序 Ranking
全　国	**China**	**4 140**		**4 761**		**5 153**	
北　京	Beijing	9 440	2	10 662	2	11 669	2
天　津	Tianjin	7 010	4	7 911	4	8 688	4
河　北	Hebei	4 293	11	4 795	13	5 150	13
山　西	Shanxi	3 666	20	4 097	23	4 244	23
内蒙古	Inner Mongolia	3 953	16	4 656	16	4 938	16
辽　宁	Liaoning	4 773	10	5 576	10	5 958	10
吉　林	Jilin	4 191	12	4 933	11	5 266	11
黑龙江	Heilongjiang	4 132	13	4 856	12	5 207	12
上　海	Shanghai	10 145	1	11 440	1	12 483	1
江　苏	Jiangsu	6 561	5	7 356	5	8 004	5
浙　江	Zhejiang	8 265	3	9 258	3	10 007	3
安　徽	Anhui	3 556	21	4 202	20	4 504	20
福　建	Fujian	5 467	8	6 196	8	6 680	8
江　西	Jiangxi	4 045	14	4 697	14	5 075	14
山　东	Shandong	4 985	9	5 641	9	6 119	9
河　南	Henan	3 852	18	4 454	18	4 807	18
湖　北	Hubei	3 997	15	4 656	15	5 035	15
湖　南	Hunan	3 904	17	4 512	17	4 909	17
广　东	Guangdong	5 624	7	6 400	7	6 907	7
广　西	Guangxi	3 224	24	3 690	24	3 980	25
海　南	Hainan	3 791	19	4 390	19	4 744	19
重　庆	Chongqing	3 509	23	4 126	21	4 478	21
四　川	Sichuan	3 547	22	4 121	22	4 462	22
贵　州	Guizhou	2 374	31	2 797	31	3 005	31
云　南	Yunnan	2 634	30	3 103	29	3 369	29
西　藏	Tibet	2 788	27	3 176	27	3 532	27
陕　西	Shaanxi	2 645	29	3 136	28	3 438	28
甘　肃	Gansu	2 329	32	2 724	32	2 980	32
青　海	Qinghai	2 684	28	3 061	30	3 346	30
宁　夏	Ningxia	3 181	26	3 681	25	4 048	24
新　疆	Xinjiang	3 183	25	3 503	26	3 883	26
新疆建设兵团	XPCG	6 193	6	6 771	6	7 668	6

附录 1—7　各省(区)、直辖市粮食总产量排序(2007—2009 年)

Ranking of Total Grain Yield by Region(2007—2009)

计量单位:万吨　　(10 000 tons)

地　区	Region	2007	排　序 Ranking	2008	排　序 Ranking	2009	排　序 Ranking
全　国	**China**	**50 160. 3**		**52 870. 9**		**53 082. 1**	
北　京	Beijing	102. 1	31	125. 5	29	124. 8	29
天　津	Tianjin	147. 2	27	148. 9	27	156. 3	28
河　北	Hebei	2 841. 6	7	2 905. 8	7	2 910. 2	7
山　西	Shanxi	1 007. 1	20	1 028. 0	20	942. 0	21
内 蒙 古	Inner Mongolia	1 810. 7	13	2 131. 3	11	1 981. 7	12
辽　宁	Liaoning	1 835. 0	12	1 860. 3	13	1 591. 0	13
吉　林	Jilin	2 453. 8	9	2 840. 0	8	2 460. 0	9
黑 龙 江	Heilongjiang	3 462. 9	3	4 225. 0	3	4 353. 0	2
上　海	Shanghai	109. 2	29	115. 7	30	121. 7	30
江　苏	Jiangsu	3 132. 2	4	3 175. 5	4	3 230. 1	4
浙　江	Zhejiang	728. 6	23	775. 6	23	789. 2	23
安　徽	Anhui	2 901. 4	6	3 023. 3	6	3 069. 9	6
福　建	Fujian	635. 1	24	652. 3	24	666. 9	24
江　西	Jiangxi	1 904. 0	11	1 958. 1	12	2 002. 6	11
山　东	Shandong	4 148. 8	2	4 260. 5	2	4 316. 3	3
河　南	Henan	5 245. 2	1	5 365. 5	1	5 389. 0	1
湖　北	Hubei	2 185. 4	10	2 227. 2	10	2 309. 1	10
湖　南	Hunan	2 692. 2	8	2 805. 0	9	2 902. 7	8
广　东	Guangdong	1 284. 7	16	1 243. 4	16	1 314. 5	16
广　西	Guangxi	1 396. 6	15	1 394. 7	15	1 463. 2	15
海　南	Hainan	177. 5	26	183. 5	26	187. 6	27
重　庆	Chongqing	1 088. 0	18	1 153. 2	18	1 137. 2	19
四　川	Sichuan	3 027. 0	5	3 140. 0	5	3 194. 6	5
贵　州	Guizhou	1 100. 9	17	1 158. 0	17	1 168. 3	17
云　南	Yunnan	1 460. 7	14	1 518. 6	14	1 576. 9	14
西　藏	Tibet	93. 9	32	95. 0	32	90. 5	32
陕　西	Shaanxi	1 067. 9	19	1 111. 0	19	1 131. 4	20
甘　肃	Gansu	824. 0	22	888. 5	22	906. 2	22
青　海	Qinghai	106. 2	30	101. 8	31	102. 7	31
宁　夏	Ningxia	323. 5	25	329. 2	25	340. 7	25
新　疆	Xinjiang	867. 0	21	930. 5	21	1 152. 0	18
新疆建设兵团	XPCG	120. 5	28	142. 3	28	217. 4	26

注:本表全国及新疆建设兵团农业数据按兵团第二次全国农业普查结果进行校验修订,下同。
Note:agriculture date of china and XPCG in this table are calculated at result of second china agriculture census,(the same as follow).

附录1—8　各省(区)、直辖市棉花总产量排序(2007—2009年)

Ranking of Cotton Yield by Region(2007—2009)

计量单位:万吨　　(10 000 tons)

地　区	Region	2007	排序 Ranking	2008	排序 Ranking	2009	排序 Ranking
全　国	**China**	**762.4**		**749.2**		**637.7**	
北　京	Beijing	0.2	21	0.1	22	0.1	23
天　津	Tianjin	9.3	13	8.3	14	7.1	14
河　北	Hebei	72.5	5	73.7	4	60.5	4
山　西	Shanxi	11.5	12	10.7	12	8.4	13
内蒙古	Inner Mongolia	0.4	17	0.3	19	0.1	20
辽　宁	Liaoning	0.2	19	0.2	20	0.1	21
吉　林	Jilin	0.1	24	0.5	17	0.2	19
黑龙江	Heilongjiang						
上　海	Shanghai	0.3	18	0.3	18	0.3	17
江　苏	Jiangsu	34.8	8	32.6	8	25.5	8
浙　江	Zhejiang	2.6	15	2.8	15	2.8	15
安　徽	Anhui	37.4	7	36.3	7	34.6	7
福　建	Fujian	0.1	22				
江　西	Jiangxi	12.8	11	11.2	11	12.5	10
山　东	Shandong	100.1	3	104.1	3	92.1	3
河　南	Henan	75.0	4	65.1	5	51.7	5
湖　北	Hubei	55.7	6	51.3	6	48.1	6
湖　南	Hunan	24.4	9	24.7	9	21.2	9
广　东	Guangdong						
广　西	Guangxi	0.2	20	0.2	21	0.2	18
海　南	Hainan						
重　庆	Chongqing						
四　川	Sichuan	1.7	16	1.6	16	1.5	16
贵　州	Guizhou	0.1	23	0.1	23	0.1	22
云　南	Yunnan						
西　藏	Tibet						
陕　西	Shaanxi	9.0	14	10.1	13	8.6	12
甘　肃	Gansu	12.9	10	12.3	10	9.5	11
青　海	Qinghai						
宁　夏	Ningxia						
新　疆	Xinjiang	301.3	1	302.6	1	252.4	1
新疆建设兵团	XPCG	124.7	2	131.3	2	113.4	2

附录1—9 各省(区)、直辖市油料总产量排序(2007—2009年)

Ranking of Oil-bearing Yield by Region(2007—2009)

计量单位:万吨 (10 000 tons)

地区	Region	2007	排序 Ranking	2008	排序 Ranking	2009	排序 Ranking
全国	**China**	**2 568.7**		**2 952.8**		**3 154.3**	
北京	Beijing	2.2	31	2.2	31	1.8	31
天津	Tianjin	0.5	32	0.5	32	0.5	32
河北	Hebei	138.1	7	152.6	6	143.3	8
山西	Shanxi	13.5	25	19.1	25	17.0	26
内蒙古	Inner Mongolia	79.4	10	117.5	9	119.6	9
辽宁	Liaoning	26.4	21	48.5	17	55.3	15
吉林	Jilin	28.7	18	51.8	15	50.4	17
黑龙江	Heilongjiang	21.3	24	28.5	23	28.2	23
上海	Shanghai	3.6	30	3.6	30	3.4	30
江苏	Jiangsu	145.1	6	150.3	7	162.2	7
浙江	Zhejiang	33.0	16	41.3	18	43.2	19
安徽	Anhui	199.2	5	228.0	5	240.3	5
福建	Fujian	23.3	22	25.4	24	26.3	24
江西	Jiangxi	82.7	9	91.2	10	102.0	10
山东	Shandong	328.6	2	340.6	2	334.5	2
河南	Henan	484.0	1	505.3	1	533.0	1
湖北	Hubei	254.8	3	285.7	3	314.1	3
湖南	Hunan	110.1	8	133.8	8	179.2	6
广东	Guangdong	77.7	11	81.5	11	84.6	11
广西	Guangxi	33.8	15	37.5	19	42.1	20
海南	Hainan	6.8	28	8.7	28	9.1	28
重庆	Chongqing	30.7	17	35.7	20	40.5	21
四川	Sichuan	204.3	4	249.9	4	261.8	4
贵州	Guizhou	69.7	12	68.4	12	78.7	12
云南	Yunnan	22.1	23	30.4	22	50.2	18
西藏	Tibet	5.2	29	6.0	29	5.8	29
陕西	Shaanxi	39.1	14	49.5	16	54.4	16
甘肃	Gansu	42.4	13	53.5	14	58.5	14
青海	Qinghai	28.0	19	35.2	21	36.6	22
宁夏	Ningxia	7.7	27	13.6	27	13.6	27
新疆	Xinjiang	26.9	20	56.8	13	63.9	13
新疆建设兵团	XPCG	10.3	26	16.9	26	18.6	25

附录 1－10　各省(区)、直辖市糖料总产量排序(2007—2009 年)

Ranking of Sugar Crops Yield by Region(2007—2009)

计量单位:万吨　　　　(10 000 tons)

地　　区	Region	2007	排　序 Ranking	2008	排　序 Ranking	2009	排　序 Ranking
全　　国	**China**	**12 188.2**		**13 419.6**		**12 276.6**	
北　　京	Beijing						
天　　津	Tianjin						
河　　北	Hebei	53.1	14	59.4	15	30.7	16
山　　西	Shanxi	21.1	18	23.4	19	15.4	20
内 蒙 古	Inner Mongolia	118.2	8	170.0	7	109.6	8
辽　　宁	Liaoning	5.0	24	7.5	24	6.2	24
吉　　林	Jilin	5.0	25	24.3	18	6.6	23
黑 龙 江	Heilongjiang	207.2	6	260.0	6	110.0	7
上　　海	Shanghai	1.0	26	1.0	25	1.6	25
江　　苏	Jiangsu	6.6	22	8.8	23	11.6	21
浙　　江	Zhejiang	57.4	12	85.5	10	81.4	10
安　　徽	Anhui	23.9	17	29.5	16	21.8	18
福　　建	Fujian	56.4	13	70.9	13	65.9	12
江　　西	Jiangxi	48.1	15	64.2	14	62.2	14
山　　东	Shandong			0.1	27	0.1	28
河　　南	Henan	16.6	19	20.7	20	28.3	17
湖　　北	Hubei	14.9	20	26.5	17	34.4	15
湖　　南	Hunan	70.0	10	77.0	11	78.2	11
广　　东	Guangdong	1 180.7	3	1 198.8	3	1 253.5	3
广　　西	Guangxi	7 737.5	1	8 215.6	1	7 509.4	1
海　　南	Hainan	405.8	5	518.8	4	479.2	4
重　　庆	Chongqing	11.3	21	11.2	22	11.6	22
四　　川	Sichuan	102.2	9	116.5	9	94.1	9
贵　　州	Guizhou	67.0	11	71.8	12	64.3	13
云　　南	Yunnan	1 491.2	2	1 898.9	2	1 761.4	2
西　　藏	Tibet						
陕　　西	Shaanxi	5.4	23	0.3	26	0.2	26
甘　　肃	Gansu	27.8	16	20.1	21	20.4	19
青　　海	Qinghai	0.7	27			0.1	27
宁　　夏	Ningxia	0.3	28	0.1	28		
新　　疆	Xinjiang	453.9	4	438.9	5	418.4	5
新疆建设兵团	XPCG	188.1	7	158.2	8	145.3	6

附录 1—11 各省(区)、直辖市人均粮食产量排序(2007—2009 年)

Ranking of Per Capita Grain Yield by Region(2007—2009)

计量单位:公斤/人 (kg/person)

地区	Region	2007	排序 Ranking	2008	排序 Ranking	2009	排序 Ranking
全国	**China**	**381**		**399**		**399**	
北京	Beijing	64	31	75	31	72	31
天津	Tianjin	134	30	130	30	130	30
河北	Hebei	411	14	417	13	415	13
山西	Shanxi	298	21	302	22	276	24
内蒙古	Inner Mongolia	754	3	885	3	820	4
辽宁	Liaoning	428	10	432	12	369	17
吉林	Jilin	900	2	1 040	2	899	2
黑龙江	Heilongjiang	906	1	1 105	1	1 138	1
上海	Shanghai	59	32	62	32	64	32
江苏	Jiangsu	413	13	415	14	419	12
浙江	Zhejiang	145	28	152	28	153	28
安徽	Anhui	475	6	493	7	501	8
福建	Fujian	178	27	182	27	184	27
江西	Jiangxi	437	9	447	9	453	11
山东	Shandong	444	8	454	8	457	9
河南	Henan	559	4	571	4	570	5
湖北	Hubei	384	16	390	16	404	14
湖南	Hunan	424	11	441	10	454	10
广东	Guangdong	137	29	131	29	137	29
广西	Guangxi	294	22	291	24	303	22
海南	Hainan	211	25	216	25	218	25
重庆	Chongqing	387	15	408	15	399	15
四川	Sichuan	372	17	386	17	391	16
贵州	Guizhou	293	23	307	21	308	21
云南	Yunnan	325	19	335	19	346	18
西藏	Tibet	332	18	333	20	314	20
陕西	Shaanxi	285	24	296	23	300	23
甘肃	Gansu	316	20	339	18	344	19
青海	Qinghai	193	26	184	26	185	26
宁夏	Ningxia	533	5	536	6	548	6
新疆	Xinjiang	418	12	440	11	537	7
新疆建设兵团	XPCG	467	7	552	5	823	3

附录 1－12　各省(区)、直辖市人均棉花产量排序(2007—2009 年)

Ranking of Per Capita Cotton Yield by Region(2007－2009)

计量单位:公斤/人　　　　(kg/person)

地　　区	Region	2007	排　序 Ranking	2008	排　序 Ranking	2009	排　序 Ranking
全　　国	**China**	**5.78**		**5.66**		**4.79**	
北　　京	Beijing	0.12	19				
天　　津	Tianjin	8.50	6	7.24	6	5.90	6
河　　北	Hebei	10.47	4	10.58	4	8.62	4
山　　西	Shanxi	3.40	12	3.14	12	2.46	13
内 蒙 古	Inner Mongolia	0.15	17	0.12	19		
辽　　宁	Liaoning	0.05	20				
吉　　林	Jilin	0.02	23	0.19	16		
黑 龙 江	Heilongjiang						
上　　海	Shanghai	0.14	18	0.17	18	0.14	17
江　　苏	Jiangsu	4.58	10	4.26	10	3.32	11
浙　　江	Zhejiang	0.51	15	0.55	15	0.55	15
安　　徽	Anhui	6.12	8	5.93	8	5.64	7
福　　建	Fujian	0.02	22				
江　　西	Jiangxi	2.93	13	2.55	14	2.83	12
山　　东	Shandong	10.72	3	11.08	3	9.75	3
河　　南	Henan	8.00	7	6.93	7	5.47	8
湖　　北	Hubei	9.78	5	9.00	5	8.41	5
湖　　南	Hunan	3.85	11	3.87	11	3.32	10
广　　东	Guangdong						
广　　西	Guangxi	0.04	21				
海　　南	Hainan						
重　　庆	Chongqing						
四　　川	Sichuan	0.21	16	0.19	17	0.18	16
贵　　州	Guizhou	0.01	24				
云　　南	Yunnan						
西　　藏	Tibet						
陕　　西	Shaanxi	2.40	14	2.68	13	2.28	14
甘　　肃	Gansu	4.96	9	4.70	9	3.63	9
青　　海	Qinghai						
宁　　夏	Ningxia						
新　　疆	Xinjiang	145.37	2	143.20	2	117.69	2
新疆建设兵团	XPCG	483.41	1	509.29	1	440.83	1

附录 1－13　各省(区)、直辖市人均油料产量排序(2007－2009 年)

Ranking of Per Capita Oil-bearing Yield by Region(2007－2009)

计量单位:公斤/人　　(kg/person)

地　区	Region	2007	排　序 Ranking	2008	排　序 Ranking	2009	排　序 Ranking
全　国	**China**	**19.49**		**22.29**		**23.69**	
北　京	Beijing	1.36	31	1.30	31	1.05	31
天　津	Tianjin	0.42	32	0.42	32	0.45	32
河　北	Hebei	19.95	9	21.91	11	20.43	16
山　西	Shanxi	3.98	29	5.62	29	4.98	29
内蒙古	Inner Mongolia	33.09	6	48.78	5	49.47	5
辽　宁	Liaoning	6.16	26	11.26	21	12.82	21
吉　林	Jilin	10.53	19	18.98	17	18.41	18
黑龙江	Heilongjiang	5.57	27	7.45	26	7.36	27
上　海	Shanghai	1.97	30	1.92	30	1.78	30
江　苏	Jiangsu	19.12	10	19.64	16	21.07	14
浙　江	Zhejiang	6.57	24	8.11	24	8.40	26
安　徽	Anhui	32.58	7	37.22	6	39.19	6
福　建	Fujian	6.53	25	7.07	27	7.26	28
江　西	Jiangxi	18.99	11	20.80	14	23.10	11
山　东	Shandong	35.19	5	36.27	7	35.42	7
河　南	Henan	51.62	1	53.79	3	56.35	3
湖　北	Hubei	44.72	3	50.09	4	54.95	4
湖　南	Hunan	17.34	14	21.01	13	28.04	10
广　东	Guangdong	8.29	21	8.59	23	8.83	24
广　西	Guangxi	7.13	23	7.84	25	8.70	25
海　南	Hainan	8.14	22	10.23	22	10.60	23
重　庆	Chongqing	10.91	18	12.62	20	14.23	20
四　川	Sichuan	25.07	8	30.73	8	32.07	8
贵　州	Guizhou	18.53	12	18.11	18	20.73	15
云　南	Yunnan	4.90	28	6.71	28	11.01	22
西　藏	Tibet	18.50	13	21.12	12	20.05	17
陕　西	Shaanxi	10.46	20	13.17	19	14.44	19
甘　肃	Gansu	16.22	15	20.41	15	22.25	12
青　海	Qinghai	50.94	2	63.68	2	65.85	2
宁　夏	Ningxia	12.76	17	22.09	10	21.96	13
新　疆	Xinjiang	12.98	16	26.90	9	29.80	9
新疆建设兵团	XPCG	40.04	4	65.57	1	72.04	1

附录1－14　各省(区)、直辖市人均糖料产量排序(2007－2009年)

Ranking of Per Capita Sugar Crops Yield by Region(2007－2009)

计量单位:公斤/人　　(kg/person)

地区	Region	2007	排序 Ranking	2008	排序 Ranking	2009	排序 Ranking
全国	**China**	**92.48**		**101.31**		**92.21**	
北京	Beijing						
天津	Tianjin						
河北	Hebei	7.67	16	8.52	16	4.38	18
山西	Shanxi	6.23	17	6.89	18	4.51	17
内蒙古	Inner Mongolia	49.21	8	70.57	7	45.32	7
辽宁	Liaoning	1.17	25	1.74	23	1.43	24
吉林	Jilin	1.83	21	8.88	15	2.42	22
黑龙江	Heilongjiang	54.20	7	67.98	8	28.75	8
上海	Shanghai	0.57	27	0.53	25	0.85	25
江苏	Jiangsu	0.87	26	1.14	24	1.51	23
浙江	Zhejiang	11.42	12	16.79	11	15.80	11
安徽	Anhui	3.91	19	4.82	19	3.55	20
福建	Fujian	15.79	10	19.74	9	18.21	9
江西	Jiangxi	11.05	13	14.65	12	14.09	12
山东	Shandong			0.01	28	0.01	28
河南	Henan	1.77	22	2.21	22	2.99	21
湖北	Hubei	2.62	20	4.64	20	6.02	16
湖南	Hunan	11.03	14	12.10	14	12.23	13
广东	Guangdong	125.92	6	126.24	6	130.70	6
广西	Guangxi	1 631.17	1	1 714.44	1	1 552.82	1
海南	Hainan	482.85	3	610.73	3	557.81	3
重庆	Chongqing	4.01	18	3.96	21	4.06	19
四川	Sichuan	12.54	11	14.32	13	11.53	14
贵州	Guizhou	17.81	9	19.00	10	16.93	10
云南	Yunnan	331.49	4	419.32	4	386.53	4
西藏	Tibet						
陕西	Shaanxi	1.44	23	0.07	27	0.04	27
甘肃	Gansu	10.65	15	7.66	17	7.76	15
青海	Qinghai	1.25	24			0.11	26
宁夏	Ningxia	0.51	28	0.09	26		
新疆	Xinjiang	219.00	5	207.72	5	195.09	5
新疆建设兵团	XPCG	728.88	2	613.44	2	565.15	2

附录1－15 各省(区)、直辖市粮食平均亩产排序(2007－2009年)

Ranking of Grain Average Unit Yield by Region(2007－2009)

计量单位:公斤/亩 (kg/acre)

地区	Region	2007	排序 Ranking	2008	排序 Ranking	2009	排序 Ranking
全国	**China**	**317**		**330**		**325**	
北京	Beijing	345	16	370	13	368	12
天津	Tianjin	336	17	338	17	340	17
河北	Hebei	307	21	315	20	312	21
山西	Shanxi	222	30	220	32	200	32
内蒙古	Inner Mongolia	236	27	270	24	244	29
辽宁	Liaoning	391	8	409	4	340	18
吉林	Jilin	377	9	431	2	370	10
黑龙江	Heilongjiang	213	31	256	27	255	26
上海	Shanghai	429	2	442	1	420	2
江苏	Jiangsu	400	4	402	8	408	4
浙江	Zhejiang	398	6	407	7	408	5
安徽	Anhui	299	22	307	22	310	22
福建	Fujian	353	14	359	15	361	13
江西	Jiangxi	360	13	365	14	370	11
山东	Shandong	399	5	408	5	409	3
河南	Henan	369	10	373	11	371	9
湖北	Hubei	366	11	380	10	384	8
湖南	Hunan	396	7	408	6	403	6
广东	Guangdong	345	15	332	18	345	15
广西	Guangxi	312	20	313	21	318	20
海南	Hainan	294	23	290	23	291	23
重庆	Chongqing	330	18	347	16	340	16
四川	Sichuan	313	19	326	19	332	19
贵州	Guizhou	260	24	264	26	261	25
云南	Yunnan	244	26	247	29	250	27
西藏	Tibet	364	12	371	12	356	14
陕西	Shaanxi	230	29	237	30	241	30
甘肃	Gansu	204	32	221	31	220	31
青海	Qinghai	235	28	250	28	248	28
宁夏	Ningxia	252	25	266	25	275	24
新疆	Xinjiang	419	3	391	9	387	7
新疆建设兵团	XPCG	481	1	420	3	461	1

附录1—16 各省(区)、直辖市棉花平均亩产排序(2007—2009年)

Ranking of Cotton Average Unit Yield by Region(2007—2009)

计量单位:公斤/亩 (kg/acre)

地区	Region	2007	排序 Ranking	2008	排序 Ranking	2009	排序 Ranking
全国	**China**	**85.76**		**86.80**		**85.85**	
北京	Beijing	78.97	12	121.74	13	85.22	10
天津	Tianjin	91.98	10	143.02	5	85.00	11
河北	Hebei	71.05	17	99.90	16	65.01	19
山西	Shanxi	73.77	14	74.27	21	76.42	14
内蒙古	Inner Mongolia	92.85	9	123.65	12	96.47	6
辽宁	Liaoning	129.63	2	115.74	14	73.26	15
吉林	Jilin	62.89	22	129.47	10	81.94	12
黑龙江	Heilongjiang						
上海	Shanghai	119.52	3			132.17	2
江苏	Jiangsu	70.87	18	130.00	8	67.45	17
浙江	Zhejiang	90.21	11			93.13	7
安徽	Anhui	66.37	21	130.00	8	65.58	18
福建	Fujian	56.25	23	85.99	20	51.04	23
江西	Jiangxi	104.19	6	113.84	15	110.45	5
山东	Shandong	74.15	13	128.33	11	76.73	13
河南	Henan	71.43	16	135.98	6	64.20	20
湖北	Hubei	72.25	15	72.44	22	69.63	16
湖南	Hunan	94.64	8	55.93	24	92.62	8
广东	Guangdong						
广西	Guangxi	56.03	24			61.52	21
海南	Hainan						
重庆	Chongqing	42.22	26	69.84	23		
四川	Sichuan	51.60	25	88.32	19	61.16	22
贵州	Guizhou	26.76	27	89.55	18	41.93	24
云南	Yunnan	102.63	7	133.99	7		
西藏	Tibet						
陕西	Shaanxi	67.15	19	94.99	17	92.55	9
甘肃	Gansu	108.86	5	165.76	2	114.28	4
青海	Qinghai						
宁夏	Ningxia	66.67	20	187.23	1		
新疆	Xinjiang	112.67	4	159.18	3	119.41	3
新疆建设兵团	XPCG	135.63	1	155.47	4	155.01	1

附录1－17 各省(区)、直辖市油料平均亩产排序(2007－2009年)

Ranking of Oil-bearing Average Unit Yield by Region(2007－2009)

计量单位:公斤/亩 (kg/acre)

地区	Region	2007	排序 Ranking	2008	排序 Ranking	2009	排序 Ranking
全国	**China**	**151.34**		**153.49**		**154.03**	
北京	Beijing	207.05	3	201.79	3	197.88	3
天津	Tianjin	175.38	6	176.80	6	181.31	6
河北	Hebei	184.76	4	196.82	4	192.33	4
山西	Shanxi	53.78	32	71.14	32	67.48	32
内蒙古	Inner Mongolia	99.45	28	111.13	24	113.57	24
辽宁	Liaoning	164.68	9	193.10	5	133.05	21
吉林	Jilin	78.67	31	162.77	9	138.30	19
黑龙江	Heilongjiang	80.37	30	86.82	31	92.47	31
上海	Shanghai	147.70	13	155.36	14	146.19	15
江苏	Jiangsu	178.85	5	176.58	7	182.29	5
浙江	Zhejiang	145.11	15	144.21	17	137.19	20
安徽	Anhui	153.64	10	162.30	11	165.39	9
福建	Fujian	152.99	11	157.71	12	158.58	10
江西	Jiangxi	91.33	29	92.28	30	94.94	30
山东	Shandong	273.16	1	279.48	1	283.13	1
河南	Henan	215.48	2	221.88	2	230.55	2
湖北	Hubei	144.95	16	139.49	19	143.89	17
湖南	Hunan	105.81	24	95.98	29	105.82	27
广东	Guangdong	166.80	8	167.83	8	170.26	8
广西	Guangxi	147.56	14	153.33	15	154.84	13
海南	Hainan	138.67	17	144.16	18	149.24	14
重庆	Chongqing	106.01	23	110.35	25	114.02	23
四川	Sichuan	136.71	19	144.25	16	144.78	16
贵州	Guizhou	107.22	22	100.17	28	102.22	29
云南	Yunnan	108.18	21	107.70	26	105.39	28
西藏	Tibet	150.63	12	162.57	10	157.49	12
陕西	Shaanxi	103.51	25	118.98	22	122.69	22
甘肃	Gansu	101.35	26	107.61	27	110.92	25
青海	Qinghai	124.03	20	135.94	20	141.53	18
宁夏	Ningxia	100.98	27	112.27	23	106.04	26
新疆	Xinjiang	137.97	18	132.19	21	157.78	11
新疆建设兵团	XPCG	172.47	7	156.60	13	180.73	7

附录1—18　各省(区)、直辖市糖料平均亩产排序(2007—2009年)

Ranking of Sugar Crops Average Unit Yield by Region(2007—2009)

计量单位:公斤/亩　　(kg/acre)

地　区	Region	2007	排序 Ranking	2008	排序 Ranking	2009	排序 Ranking
全　国	**China**	**4 510**		**4 496**		**4 344**	
北　京	Beijing						
天　津	Tianjin						
河　北	Hebei	2 257	24	2 523	19	1 636	25
山　西	Shanxi	2 441	22	2 442	22	2 476	19
内蒙古	Inner Mongolia	2 599	20	2 328	23	2 210	22
辽　宁	Liaoning	4 532	4	2 511	20	2 269	20
吉　林	Jilin	1 190	28	2 280	24	1 875	23
黑龙江	Heilongjiang	1 757	27	1 917	25	1 148	26
上　海	Shanghai	4 073	8	4 433	3	4 517	4
江　苏	Jiangsu	3 726	11	3 670	11	3 833	11
浙　江	Zhejiang	4 080	7	4 087	8	4 134	8
安　徽	Anhui	2 953	17	2 898	16	2 523	17
福　建	Fujian	4 122	6	4 416	4	4 282	6
江　西	Jiangxi	2 963	16	3 057	14	3 049	14
山　东	Shandong			549	27	768	27
河　南	Henan	3 656	13	3 962	10	4 125	9
湖　北	Hubei	2 759	18	2 666	18	2 218	21
湖　南	Hunan	3 670	12	3 579	12	3 397	12
广　东	Guangdong	5 336	1	5 340	1	5 502	1
广　西	Guangxi	5 095	2	5 024	2	4 722	3
海　南	Hainan	4 278	5	4 401	5	4 280	7
重　庆	Chongqing	2 598	21	2 502	21	2 513	18
四　川	Sichuan	3 299	14	3 347	13	3 136	13
贵　州	Guizhou	2 603	19	2 707	17	2 601	16
云　南	Yunnan	3 744	10	4 086	9	3 964	10
西　藏	Tibet						
陕　西	Shaanxi	1 897	26	990	26	1 774	24
甘　肃	Gansu	3 147	15	2 918	15	3 046	15
青　海	Qinghai	2 177	25				
宁　夏	Ningxia	2 297	23				
新　疆	Xinjiang	4 037	9	4 113	7	4 376	5
新疆建设兵团	XPCG	4 551	3	4 315	6	4 775	2

附录1－19　新疆各地、州、市主要国民经济指标

Main National Economic Indicators of XinJiang's Prefecture, Autonomous Prefecture and City

（2009年）

指　　标	Item	乌鲁木齐市 Urumqi-city	克拉玛依市 Karama-ycity	石河子市 Shi Hezicity	吐鲁番地区 Turpan Adminis-trative Offices
人口与劳动力　（万人）	**Population and Labor force　(10 000 persons)**				
年末总人口	Year-end Population	241.19	27.61	63.52	61.46
就业人员数	Employment	113.28	22.64	15.52	36.88
# 职工人数	Staff and Workers	46.85	14.01	8.93	6.83
全社会固定资产投资　（亿元）	**Total Investment in Fixed Assets　(100 million yuan)**	**598.03**	**186.61**	**69.79**	**80.48**
工　资	**Wages**				
职工工资总额　（亿元）	Total Wages of Staff and Workers　(100 million yuan)	181.95	50.80	27.19	22.74
职工平均货币工资　（元）	Average Wage of Staff and Workers　(yuan)	37 161	36 248	26 512	32 911
农　业	**Agriculture**				
总播种面积　（千公顷）	Total Sown Area　(1 000 hectares)	52.91	9.39		50.81
农林牧渔业总产值　（现价，亿元）	Gross Output Value of Farming, Forestry, Animal Husbandry and Fishery (the Current prices)　(100 million yuan)	23.02	7.22		33.55
农　业	Farming	9.98	2.32		25.73
林　业	Forestry	0.32	1.44		0.44
牧　业	Animal Husbandry	11.81	2.27		6.67
渔　业	Fishery	0.53	0.08		0.04
服务业	Services	0.38	1.13		0.67
主要农产品产量　（万吨）	Output of Major Farm Products　(10 000 tons)				
粮　食	Grain	15.87	0.62		1.54
棉　花	Cotton	0.16	1.03		2.67
油　料	Oil-bearing Crops	1.06	0.04		0.18
甜　菜	Beetroots	0.14	0.00		0.00
水　果	Fruits	1.40	0.00		81.50
牲畜存栏头数　（万头只）	Number of Livestock　(10 000 heads)	69.97	14.38		104.58
肉　类　（万吨）	Meat　(10 000 tons)	5.15	0.85		3.86
工　业	**Industry**				
工业总产值（规模以上）（亿元）	Gross Industrial Output Value (the Current prices)　(100 million yuan)	1 373.97	881.10	160.47	141.68
主要工业产品产量	Output of Major Industrial Products				
纱　（吨）	Yarn　(ton)	65 659		107 852	6 366
布　（万米）	Cloth　(10 000 meters)	4 437		3 981	
机制糖　（万吨）	Machine-made Sugar　(10 000 tons)				
原　煤　（万吨）	Crude Coal　(10 000 tons)	2 326.41			1 465.08
发电量　（亿千瓦小时）	Electricity　(100 Million kwh)	134.30	30.83	83.14	18.78
水泥　（万吨）	Cement　(10 000 tons)	401.38		123.78	64.61
机制纸及纸板　（吨）	Machine-made Paper and Paperboard　(ton)	177 138		27 842	
饮料酒　（千升）	Alcohol Beverage　(1 000 Liter)	156 376		34 589	6 783
建筑业施工产值　（亿元）	**Output Value of Contruction　(100 million yuan)**	**349.00**	**56.95**	**41.15**	**13.92**
贸易业	**Domestic Trade**				
社会消费品零售总额　（亿元）	Total Retail Sales of Consumer Goods (100 million yuan)	449.98	29.57		23.79
进出口总额　（万美元）	Total Exports and Imports　(USD 10 000)	368 300	18 121	22 943	1 072

附录1—19　续表

(2009年)

指　　标	Item	哈密地区 Hami [Kumul] Adminis-trative Offices	昌吉回族自治州 Changji Hui Auto-nomous Prefecture	伊犁哈萨克自治州 Ili Kazak Autonomous Prefecture	伊犁州直属县(市) Counties (Cities) Direct Under Ili Prefecture
人口与劳动力　(万人)	**Population and Labor force　(10 000 persons)**				
年末总人口	Year-end Population	56.78	140.65	444.32	276.30
就业人员数	Employment	22.04	71.46	195.14	109.63
# 职工人数	Staff and Workers	7.39	18.55	57.83	26.00
全社会固定资产投资(亿元)	**Total Investment in Fixed Assets　(100 million yuan)**	**95.65**	**205.08**	**395.60**	**193.29**
工　资	**Wages**				
职工工资总额　(亿元)	Total Wages of Staff and Workers　(100 million yuan)	22.46	55.06	126.61	60.26
职工平均货币工资　(元)	Average Wage of Staff and Workers　(yuan)	30 427	26 924	21 179	22 727
农　业	**Agriculture**				
总播种面积　(千公顷)	Total Sown Area　(1 000 hectares)	60.97	480.98	979.20	434.23
农林牧渔业总产值　(现价,亿元)	Gross Output Value of Farming, Forestry, Animal Husbandry and Fishery(the Current prices)　(100 million yuan)	24.75	170.78	266.08	111.29
农　业	Farming	13.17	79.77	154.40	58.12
林　业	Forestry	0.68	2.28	4.27	2.07
牧　业	Animal Husbandry	10.44	85.30	101.38	48.11
渔　业	Fishery	0.13	1.38	1.54	0.86
服务业	Services	0.34	2.06	4.49	2.13
主要农产品产量　(万吨)	Output of Major Farm Products　(10 000 tons)				
粮　食	Grain	13.76	177.42	349.23	194.01
棉　花	Cotton	2.06	13.11	15.55	1.37
油　料	Oil-bearing Crops	0.32	6.33	28.86	13.30
甜　菜	Beetroots	0.00	37.49	156.22	126.17
水　果	Fruits	9.17	16.45	17.24	14.94
牲畜存栏头数　(万头只)	Number of Livestock　(10 000 heads)	114.43	385.83	1 300.30	602.57
肉　类　(万吨)	Meat　(10 000 tons)	4.20	41.26	43.76	21.37
工　业	**Industry**				
工业总产值(规模以上)(亿元)	Gross Industrial Output Value (the Current prices)　(100 million yuan)	72.91	290.57	334.34	165.56
主要工业产品产量	Output of Major Industrial Products				
纱　(吨)	Yarn　(ton)	14 307	20 260	37 123	18 506
布　(万米)	Cloth　(10 000 meters)		2 122	792	519
机制糖　(万吨)	Machine-made Sugar　(10 000 tons)		6.17	22.55	16.12
原　煤　(万吨)	Crude Coal　(10 000 tons)	1 080.94	1 689.53	1 148.27	584.08
发电量　(亿千瓦小时)	Electricity　(100 Million kwh)	19.52	103.39	70.28	51.31
水泥　(万吨)	Cement　(10 000 tons)	53.81	154.75	434.73	193.75
机制纸及纸板　(吨)	Machine-made Paper and Paperboard　(ton)	2 565	42 388	6 046	308
饮料酒　(千升)	Alcohol Beverage　(1 000 Liter)	33 625	30 321	146 392	66 242
建筑业施工产值　(亿元)	**Output Value of Contruction　(100 million yuan)**	**16.15**	**41.40**	**75.41**	**44.69**
贸易业	**Domestic Trade**				
社会消费品零售总额(亿元)	Total Retail Sales of Consumer Goods (100 million yuan)	34.79	100.54	154.30	88.62
进出口总额　(万美元)	Total Exports and Imports　(USD 10 000)	6 190	226 651	501 149	370 729

Continued

塔城地区 Tacheng [Tarbagatai] Adminis -trative Offices	阿勒泰地区 Altay Admini -strative Offices	博尔塔拉蒙古自治州 Bortala Mongol Autonomous Prefecture	巴音郭楞蒙古自治州 Bayangol Mongol Autonomous Prefecture	阿克苏地区 Aksu Adminis -trative Prefecture	克孜勒苏克尔柯孜自治州 Kizilsu Kirgiz Autonomous Prefecture	喀什地区 Kashgar [Kaxgar] Adminis -trative Offices	和田地区 Hotan Adminis -trative Offices
102. 26	65. 77	47. 84	129. 32	230. 50	53. 02	387. 28	195. 58
57. 03	28. 48	21. 76	53. 11	96. 51	20. 59	124. 11	73. 11
21. 08	10. 75	8. 36	17. 13	16. 81	3. 43	17. 15	8. 64
124. 37	**77. 93**	**47. 27**	**252. 85**	**234. 03**	**27. 40**	**219. 37**	**76. 11**
43. 10	23. 24	17. 90	50. 75	40. 66	9. 25	44. 10	22. 85
19 615	20 587	20 421	27 715	24 327	26 946	25 713	26 445
413. 85	131. 12	109. 93	276. 55	577. 59	52. 58	852. 14	228. 64
113. 76	41. 03	34. 58	118. 05	141. 48	14. 92	239. 87	66. 14
77. 40	18. 87	25. 51	89. 99	107. 65	8. 57	147. 61	41. 51
1. 13	1. 07	0. 38	1. 61	6. 21	0. 29	20. 17	8. 03
33. 44	19. 83	7. 19	21. 40	20. 45	5. 03	64. 15	15. 27
0. 27	0. 42	0. 25	0. 89	0. 70	0. 02	0. 99	0. 21
1. 51	0. 85	1. 24	4. 16	6. 06	1. 02	6. 95	1. 11
130. 35	24. 87	46. 94	39. 57	161. 14	23. 33	258. 86	105. 07
14. 19	0. 00	7. 60	27. 24	46. 45	0. 81	30. 68	4. 56
9. 56	6. 00	3. 31	1. 25	2. 05	0. 09	0. 95	0. 85
25. 45	4. 60	19. 14	33. 68	26. 41	0. 00	0. 00	0. 00
2. 24	0. 06	0. 37	50. 14	90. 70	19. 07	139. 18	36. 84
423. 37	274. 36	108. 92	300. 44	425. 83	159. 87	799. 65	471. 43
14. 88	7. 51	1. 97	7. 94	14. 45	3. 35	32. 73	6. 89
116. 81	51. 98	23. 20	437. 24	176. 10	6. 13	48. 37	10. 71
18 617		11 924	28 637	31 686		45 656	2 953
273		199	1 007	936		1 054	48
5. 70	0. 73	2. 25	7. 76	2. 03		0. 02	
560. 74	3. 45		296. 32	718. 00	2. 96	22. 00	63. 04
11. 24	7. 72	1. 88	43. 17	33. 44	0. 26	21. 73	6. 21
184. 88	56. 10	51. 19	149. 00	361. 81	14. 09	125. 55	106. 11
5 150	588		89 373	1 165		8 045	
79 798	351	1 465	3 807	33 626	2	37 626	149
17. 38	**13. 34**	**10. 26**	**69. 19**	**38. 42**	**6. 23**	**38. 70**	**10. 53**
36. 97	28. 71	17. 37	47. 30	61. 52	6. 94	70. 11	18. 49
83 722	46 698	109 687	12 017	13 980	14 986	87 605	70

附录1—20　天山北坡经济带主要经济指标

(2009年)

指　　标	Item	全区合计 Total of the whole region	天山北坡经济带合计 Total	天山北坡经济带占全区比重(%) Ratio of the Economic Belt	乌鲁木齐市 Urumqi city
人　口　　(万人)	**Population　(10 000 persons)**				
年末总人口	Year-end Population	2 158.63	501.04	23.2	241.19
全社会固定资产投资　(亿元)	**Total Investment in Fixed Assets　(100 million yuan)**				
# 城镇固定资产投资总额	Fixed Assest Value of the Whole Society	2 299.98	774.59	33.7	352.29
工　资	**Wages**				
职工平均货币工资　(元)	Average Wage of Staff and Workers　(yuan)	27 753			37 161
农　业	**Agriculture**				
农林牧渔业总产值(亿元)	Gross Output Value of Farming, Forestry, Animal Husbandry and Fishery　(100 million yuan)	1 297.61	402.17	31.0	23.02
农　业	Farming	898.61	262.96	29.3	9.98
林　业	Forestry	26.65	5.16	19.4	0.32
牧　业	Animal Husbandry	318.37	114.32	35.9	11.81
渔　业	Fishery	11.14	3.28	29.4	0.53
农林牧渔服务业	Services for Farming, Forestry, Animal Husbandry and Fishery	42.84	16.46	38.4	0.38
主要农产品产量　(万吨)	Output of Major Farm Products　(10 000 tons)				
粮　食	Grain	1 152.00	229.15	19.9	15.87
棉　花	Cotton	252.40	80.08	31.7	0.16
油　料	Oil-bearing Crops	63.91	14.84	23.2	1.06
甜　菜	Beetroots	418.41	62.73	15.0	0.14
水　果	Fruits	565.15	40.51	7.2	1.40
肉　类	Meat	115.31	51.93	45.0	5.15
工　业	**Industry**				
工业总产值(规模以上)(亿元)	Gross Industrial Output Value　(100 million yuan)	4 001.12	2 807.37	70.2	1 373.97
轻工业	Light Industry	541.80	298.56	55.1	87.53
重工业	Heavy Industry	3 459.32	2 508.84	72.5	1 286.44
国有工业	State-owned Induretry	2 887.46	2 134.07	73.9	1 071.05
集体工业	Collective-owned Induretry	69.37	44.86	64.7	11.89
其他工业	Other Induretry	1 044.29	628.44	60.2	291.03
主要工业产品产量	Output of Major Industrial Products				
纱　(万吨)	Yarn　(10 000 tons)	38.61	23.09	59.8	6.57
布　(万米)	Cloth　(10 000 meter)	15 148.42	11 331.42	74.8	4 436.53
机制糖　(吨)	Machine-made Sugar　(ton)	40.77	5.47	13.4	
原煤　(万吨)	Crude Coal　(10 000 tons)	9 202.21	3 702.39	40.2	2 385.13
发电量　(万千瓦小时)	Electricity　(10 000 kwh)	571.31	369.72	64.7	134.30
水泥　(万吨)	Cement　(10 000 tons)	2 049.60	798.18	38.9	401.38
公路运输业	**Highways Transportation**				
客运量　(万人)	Passenger Traffic Volume　(10 000 persons)	41 604	7 358	18.0	2 521
货运量　(万吨)	Freihg Traffic　(10 000 tons)	46 787	20 979	45.0	11 988
货物周转量(万吨公里)	Freight Ton-Kilometers　(10 000 ton-km)	705.90	206.53	29.3	164.93
国内贸易	**Domestic Trade**				
社会消费品零售总额(亿元)	Total Retail Sales of Consumer Goods (100 million yuan)	1 177.53	711.54	60.4	449.98

Main Economic Indicators for Economic Belt on the Tianshan Northern Slope

克拉玛依市 Karamay city	石河子市 ShiHezi City	奎屯市 Kuitun City	乌苏市 Usu City	沙湾县 Shawan County	昌吉市 Changji City	阜康市 Fukang City	呼图壁县 HuTubi County	玛纳斯县 Manas County
27. 60	63. 52	30. 96	22. 35	21. 08	38. 32	16. 80	21. 76	17. 46
172. 33	60. 91	29. 90	23. 15	25. 96	39. 46	27. 12	10. 07	33. 40
36 248	26 512	36 485	16 611	21 153	28 551	25 777	22 121	27 063
7. 22	13. 91	0. 80	28. 49	37. 47	28. 69	15. 23	31. 90	33. 87
2. 31	9. 54	0. 41	22. 41	27. 14	14. 49	7. 05	13. 57	18. 36
1. 44	0. 09	0. 01	0. 52	0. 20	0. 28	0. 24	0. 37	0. 16
2. 27	3. 41	0. 29	5. 14	9. 55	12. 76	7. 83	16. 91	14. 48
0. 07	0. 31		0. 10	0. 11	0. 86	0. 02	0. 25	0. 17
1. 13	0. 56	0. 09	0. 32	0. 47	0. 30	0. 09	0. 80	0. 70
0. 62	7. 35	0. 09	20. 99	26. 61	26. 05	16. 31	19. 10	15. 38
1. 03	4. 62	0. 15	6. 59	6. 63	3. 56	0. 02	3. 69	5. 84
0. 04	0. 19	0. 02	0. 90	2. 31	1. 61	0. 96	0. 59	1. 47
	0. 03		2. 10	3. 48	7. 30	0. 20	6. 68	1. 57
	3. 76		0. 30	1. 09	5. 29	1. 31	0. 94	7. 76
0. 85	1. 61	0. 28	2. 71	4. 58	6. 82	5. 70	6. 15	5. 62
881. 10	160. 47	49. 75	25. 15	53. 09	126. 71	56. 59	33. 92	46. 62
1. 87	48. 04	31. 20	6. 42	30. 85	45. 16	2. 07	15. 91	29. 51
879. 23	112. 43	18. 55	18. 73	22. 24	81. 55	54. 52	18. 01	17. 11
836. 82	125. 52	40. 32	16. 87	12. 35	3. 47	15. 04	2. 55	10. 09
9. 13	1. 57	0. 23		16. 56		5. 44	0. 05	
35. 15	33. 38	9. 20	8. 28	24. 18	123. 24	36. 11	31. 32	36. 53
	10. 79	1. 85		1. 86	0. 52		0. 75	0. 75
	3 980. 89	519. 00	113. 00	160. 00			1 857. 00	265. 00
		3. 20			2. 27			
		9. 93	251. 97	35. 76	454. 28	229. 29	312. 56	23. 47
30. 83	83. 14	16. 42	0. 95	1. 38	15. 68	21. 02	0. 01	65. 99
	123. 78	0. 02	4. 23	114. 01	108. 37	46. 39		
536	785	629	990	910	279	150	558	
2 180	1 663	394	281	720	16	3 646	91	
	23. 04	7. 61	4. 95	6. 00				
29. 57	39. 54	11. 90	7. 90	8. 50	42. 18	13. 89	11. 83	12. 89

附录 1—20 续表　Continued

（2009 年）

指　　标	Item	六　师 XPCG Division 6	七　师 XPCG Division 7	八　师 XPCG Division 8	建工师 XPCG Construction Division	十二师 XPCG Division 12
人口与劳动力　（万人）	**Population and Labor force　(10 000 persons)**					
年末总人口	Year-end Population					
全社会固定资产投资　(亿元)	**Total Investment in Fixed Assets　(100 million yuan)**					
#城镇固定资产投资总额	Fixed Assest Value of the Whole Society					
工　资	**Wages**					
职工平均货币工资　（元）	Average Wage of Staff and Workers　(yuan)					
农　业	**Agriculture**					
农林牧渔业总产值（亿元）	Gross Output Value of Farming, Forestry, Animal Husbandry and Fishery　(100 million yuan)	51.76	43.02	78.01	8.75	0.03
农　业	Farming	36.94	32.61	61.99	6.13	0.03
林　业	Forestry	0.27	0.51	0.68	0.07	
牧　业	Animal Husbandry	10.14	6.79	10.75	2.19	
渔　业	Fishery	0.21	0.18	0.33	0.14	
农林牧渔服务业	Services for Farming, Forestry, Animal Husbandry and Fishery	4.20	2.94	4.26	0.22	
主要农产品产量　（万吨）	Output of Major Farm Products　(10 000 tons)					
粮　食	Grain	38.07	21.26	19.81	1.62	0.02
棉　花	Cotton	8.56	9.55	29.60	0.07	0.01
油　料	Oil-bearing Crops	2.35	2.71	0.34	0.28	0.01
甜　菜	Beetroots	6.42	34.18	0.03	0.60	
水　果	Fruits	3.32	2.11	6.42	6.81	
肉　类	Meat	4.97	2.31	4.38	0.80	
工　业	**Industry**					
工业总产值　（亿元）	Gross Industrial Output Value　(100 million yuan)					
轻工业	Light Industry					
重工业	Heavy Industry					
国有工业	State-owned Induretry					
集体工业	Collective-owned Induretry					
其他工业	Other Induretry					
主要工业产品产量	Output of Major Industrial Products					
纱　（万吨）	Yarn　(10 000 tons)					
布　（万米）	Cloth　(10 000 meter)					
机制糖　（吨）	Machine-made Sugar　(ton)					
原煤　（万吨）	Crude Coal　(10 000 tons)					
发电量　（万千瓦小时）	Electricity　(10 000 kwh)					
水泥　（万吨）	Cement　(10 000 tons)					
公路运输业	**Highways Transportation**					
客运量　（万人）	Passenger Traffic Volume　(10 000 persons)					
货运量　（万吨）	Freihg Traffic　(10 000 tons)					
货物周转量（万吨公里）	Freight Ton-Kilometers　(10 000 ton-km)					
国内贸易	**Domestic Trade**					
社会消费品零售总额（亿元）	Total Retail Sales of Consumer Goods (100 million yuan)	26.14	13.64	35.50	7.61	0.47

附录1－21 东、中、西部和东北三省国民经济和社会发展主要指标

Main Indicators of National Economic and Social Development of Eastern, Middle, Western and 3 Northeastern Provinces to National Total

（2009年）

指标		Item		东部10省(市)合计 Total of 10 Eastern Provinces	中部6省合计 Total of 6 Middle Provinces	西部12省(区、市)合计 Total of 12 Western Provinces	东北3省合计 Total of 3 North eastern Provinces
自然资源		Natural Resources					
土地面积	（万平方公里）	Area of Land	(10 000 sq. km)	91.6	102.8	686.7	78.8
人口		Population					
年底总人口	（万人）	Population at Year-end	(10 000 persons)	48 442.9	35 603.5	36 729.7	10 884.6
劳动就业		Employment					
城镇就业人员	（万人）	Number of Employed Persons in Urban Area	(10 000 persons)	10 962.8	4 458.9	4 760.0	2 180.3
城镇登记失业率	（%）	Registered Unemployment Rate in Urban Area	(%)	3.2	3.9	4.0	4.0
国民经济核算		National Accounting					
国内(地区)生产总值	（亿元）	Gross Domestic Product	(100 million yuan)	196 674.4	70 577.6	66 973.5	31 078.2
第一产业		Primary Industry		12 875.1	9 606.3	9 198.3	3 549.8
第二产业		Secondary Industry		97 050.1	35 554.2	31 782.9	15 509.0
# 工业		Industry		86 695.7	30 683.5	26 588.3	13 530.0
第三产业		Tertiary Industry		86 749.2	25 417.0	25 992.3	12 019.5
人均国内(地区)生产总值	（元）	Per Capita Gross Domestic Product	(yuan)	40 800	19 862	18 286	28 566
固定资产投资		Investment in Fixed Assets					
全社会固定资产投资总额	（亿元）	Total Investment in Fixed Assets	(100 million yuan)	95 548.0	49 851.8	49 686.3	23 732.9
# 房地产开发		Real Estate Development		18 462.1	6 620.4	7 198.1	3 961.2
国内商业		Domestic Trade					
社会消费品零售总额	（亿元）	Total Retail Sales of Consumer Goods	(100 million yuan)	71 058.5	26 409.7	23 038.7	12 171.7
对外贸易		Foreign Trade					
货物进出口总额	（亿美元）	Total Value of Exports and Imports	(USD 100 million)	19 470.5	779.0	916.7	909.1
出口额		Exports		10 610.4	419.1	520.4	466.2
进口额		Imports		8 860.1	359.9	396.3	442.8
财政		Government Finance					
地方财政收入	（亿元）	Local Government Revenue	(100 million yuan)	18 786.6	5 039.6	6 056.4	2 720.0
地方财政支出	（亿元）	Local Government Expenditures	(100 million yuan)	24 951.5	12 473.1	17 580.1	6 039.3
物价		Price Indices					
居民消费价格总指数(上年=100)		Consumer Price Index	(preceding year=100)	99.0	99.4	100.3	100.1
农业		Agriculture					
主要农产品产量	（万吨）	Output of Major Farm Products	(10 000 tons)				
粮食		Grain		13 817.4	16 615.2	14 245.4	8 404.0
棉花		Cotton		188.4	176.5	272.5	0.3
油料		Oil-bearing Crops		809.0	1 385.7	825.7	133.9

附录 1—21 续表　Continued

(2009 年)

指　　标		Item		东部 10 省(市)合　计 Total of 10 Eastern Provinces	中部 6 省 合　计 Total of 6 Middle Provinces	西部 12 省(区、市)合　计 Total of 12 Western Provinces	东北 3 省 合　计 Total of 3 North eastern Provinces
工　业		**Industry**					
主要工业产品产量		Output of Major Industrial Products					
原　煤	(亿吨)	Coal	(100 million tons)	2. 8	10. 6	14. 1	2. 0
原　油	(万吨)	Crude Oil	(10 000 tons)	7 280. 9	555. 4	5 472. 1	5 640. 6
发电量	(亿千瓦小时)	Electricity	(100 million kwh)	15 269. 6	8 628. 4	10 821. 3	2 427. 3
粗　钢	(万吨)	Crude Steel	(10 000 tons)	31 771. 9	11 855. 3	7 418. 2	6 172. 9
水　泥	(万吨)	Cement	(10 000 tons)	69 033. 8	42 764. 8	41 611. 0	10 988. 2
交通运输业		**Transportation**					
铁路营业里程	(公里)	Length of Railways in Operation	(km)	19 144	19 721	32 754	13 899
公路里程	(公里)	Length of Highways in Operation	(km)	970 830	1 044 440	1 504 532	341 017
# 高速公路		Expressway		23 834	17 546	18 589	5 087
旅客周转量	(亿人公里)	Total Passenger-kilometer	(100 million person-km)	8 378. 7	6 232. 4	5 115. 2	1 733. 5
货物周转量	(亿吨公里)	Total Freight Ton-kilometer	(100 million ton-km)	60 506. 9	22 279. 9	17 732. 6	10 565. 9
邮电通信业		**Postal and Telecommunication Services**					
邮电业务总量	(亿元)	Business Volume of Postal and Telecommunication Services	(100 million yuan)	14 161. 6	4 951. 9	5 891. 8	2 188. 2
教　育		**Education**					
普通高等学校		Institutions of Higher Education					
学校数	(个)	Number of Instiutions	(unit)	915	596	554	240
招生数	(万人)	New Students Enrollment	(10 000 persons)	257. 2	179. 0	143. 5	59. 7
在校学生数	(万人)	Students Enrollment	(10 000 persons)	876. 1	585. 3	474. 0	209. 2
毕业生数	(万人)	Number of Graduates	(10 000 persons)	221. 1	148. 9	110. 2	50. 8
卫　生		**Health Care**					
卫生机构数	(个)	Number of Hospitals	(unit)	298 988	262 433	280 053	75 097
# 医院、卫生院		Hospital and Health Centers		16 728	15 488	22 562	5 140
卫生技术人员	(万人)	Medical Technical Personel	(10 000 persons)	221. 0	140. 6	138. 5	53. 4
# 执业(助理)医师		Licensed (Assistant) Doctors		91. 3	58. 3	60. 2	23. 0
医疗机构床位数	(万张)	Number of Hospital Beds	(10 000 units)	163. 7	113. 6	119. 8	44. 6
# 医院、卫生院		Hospital and Health Centers		150. 2	104. 9	112. 1	40. 9
人民生活	**(元)**	**People's Living Conditions**	**(yuan)**				
城镇居民可支配收入		Per Capita Annual Displsable Income of Urban Households		20 953	14 367	14 213	14 324
农村居民人均纯收入		Per Capita Net Income of Rural Residents		7 156	4 793	3 816	5 457

附录 1—22 东、中、西部和东北三省国民经济和社会发展主要指标占全国比重

Percentage of Main Indicators of National Economic and Social Development of Eastern, Middle, Western and 3 Northeastern Provinces to National Total

计量单位:% (2009 年) (%)

指 标	Item	东部 10 省(市) 合 计 Total of 10 Eastern Provinces	中部 6 省 合 计 Total of 6 Middle Provinces	西部 12 省(区、市) 合 计 Total of 12 Western Provinces	东北 3 省 合 计 Total of 3 North eastern Provinces
自然资源	**Natural Resources**				
土地面积	Area of Land	9.5	10.7	71.5	8.2
人 口	**Population**				
年底总人口	Population at Year-end	36.8	27.0	27.9	8.3
劳动就业	**Employment**				
城镇就业人员	Number of Employed Persons in Urban Area	49.0	19.9	21.3	9.7
国民经济核算	**National Accounting**				
国内(地区)生产总值	Gross Domestic Product	53.8	19.3	18.3	8.5
第一产业	Primary Industry	36.5	27.3	26.1	10.1
第二产业	Secondary Industry	53.9	19.8	17.7	8.6
# 工 业	Industry	55.0	19.5	16.9	8.6
第三产业	Tertiary Industry	57.8	16.9	17.3	8.0
人均国内(地区)生产总值	Per Capita Gross Domestic Product				
固定资产投资	**Investment in Fixed Assets**				
全社会固定资产投资总额	Total Investment in Fixed Assets	43.7	22.8	22.7	10.8
# 房地产开发	Real Estate Development	50.9	18.3	19.9	10.9
国内商业	**Domestic Trade**				
社会消费品零售总额	Total Retail Sales of Consumer Goods	53.6	19.9	17.4	9.2
对外贸易	**Foreign Trade**				
货物进出口总额	Total Value of Exports and Imports	88.2	3.5	4.2	4.1
出口额	Exports	88.3	3.5	4.3	3.9
进口额	Imports	88.1	3.6	3.9	4.4
财 政	Government Finance				
地方财政收入	Local Government Revenue	57.6	15.5	18.6	8.3
地方财政支出	Local Government Expenditures	40.9	20.4	28.8	9.9
农 业	**Agriculture**				
主要农产品产量	Output of Major Farm Products				
粮 食	Grain	26.0	31.3	26.8	15.8
棉 花	Cotton	29.5	27.7	42.7	0.05
油 料	Oil-bearing Crops	25.6	43.9	26.2	4.2

附录 1—22 续表　Continued

计量单位:%　　(2009 年)　　(%)

指　标	Item	东部 10 省(市)合计 Total of 10 Eastern Provinces	中部 6 省合计 Total of 6 Middle Provinces	西部 12 省(区、市)合计 Total of 12 Western Provinces	东北 3 省合计 Total of 3 North eastern Provinces
工　业	**Industry**				
主要工业产品产量	Output of Major Industrial Products				
原　煤	Coal	9.6	35.9	47.8	6.7
原　油	Crude Oil	38.4	2.9	28.9	29.8
发电量	Electricity	41.1	23.2	29.1	6.5
粗　钢	Crude Steel	55.5	20.7	13.0	10.8
水　泥	Cement	42.0	26.0	25.3	6.7
交通运输业	**Transportation**				
铁路营业里程	Length of Railways in Operation	22.4	23.1	38.3	16.3
公路里程	Length of Highways in Operation	25.1	27.1	39.0	8.8
# 高速公路	Expressway	36.6	27.0	28.6	7.8
旅客周转量	Total Passenger-kilometer	39.0	29.0	23.8	8.1
货物周转量	Total Freight Ton-kilometer	54.5	20.1	16.0	9.5
邮电通信业	**Postal and Telecommunication Services**				
邮电业务总量	Business Volume of Postal and Telecommunication Services	52.1	18.2	21.7	8.0
教　育	**Education**				
普通高等学校	Institutions of Higher Education				
学校数	Number of Instiutions	39.7	25.9	24.0	10.4
招生数	New Students Enrollment	40.2	28.0	22.4	9.3
在校学生数	Students Enrollment	40.9	27.3	22.1	9.8
毕业生数	Number of Graduates	41.6	28.0	20.8	9.6
卫　生	**Health Care**				
卫生机构数	Number of Hospitals	32.6	28.6	30.6	8.2
# 医院、卫生院	Hospital and Health Centers	27.9	25.8	37.7	8.6
卫生技术人员	Medical Technical Personel	39.9	25.4	25.0	9.7
# 执业(助理)医师	Licensed (Assistant) Doctors	39.2	25.0	25.9	9.9
医疗机构床位数	Number of Hospital Beds	37.1	25.7	27.1	10.1
# 医院、卫生院	Hospital and Health Centers	36.8	25.7	27.5	10.0

中国统计出版社最新资料书简目

（仅供参考，以最后出书为准）

统计资料

中国统计年鉴-2011
中国统计摘要-2011
国际统计年鉴-2011
2011 中国发展报告
中国第三产业统计年鉴-2011
中国区域经济统计年鉴-2011
中国劳动统计年鉴-2011
中国社会统计年鉴-2011
中国城市统计年鉴-2009
中国建筑业统计年鉴-2011
中国人口和就业统计年鉴-2011
中国工业经济统计年鉴-2011
中国商品交易市场统计年鉴-2011
中国房地产统计年鉴-2011
中国能源统计年鉴-2011
中国民政统计年鉴-2011
中国贸易外经统计年鉴-2011
中国科技统计年鉴-2011
2011 中国地区经济监测报告
中国农村统计年鉴-2011
中国农产品价格调查年鉴-2011
中国高技术产业统计年鉴-2011
中国教育经费统计年鉴-2010
中国农村贫困监测报告-2011
全国农产品成本收益资料汇编-2011
中国科学技术协会统计年鉴-2011
工业企业科技活动资料-2011
大中型批发零售和住宿餐饮企业统计年鉴-2011
中国城市(镇)生活与价格年鉴-2011
中国县(市)社会经济调查年鉴-2011
中国农村住户调查年鉴-2011（中、英文）
中国农村全面建设小康监测报告-2011
第二次全国 R&D 资源清查资料汇编-综合卷
第二次全国 R&D 资源清查资料汇编-工业企业卷
中国零售和餐饮业连锁企业统计年鉴-2011
2010 年中国第六次人口普查公报

2011 年省级综合统计年鉴系列

北京 天津 河北 山西 内蒙古
辽宁 吉林 黑龙江 上海 江苏
浙江 安徽 福建 江西 山东
河南 湖北 湖南 广东 广西
海南 重庆 四川 贵州 云南
西藏 陕西 甘肃 青海 宁夏
新疆 新疆生产建设兵团

2011 年市(县)级综合统计年鉴系列

天津滨海新区 石家庄 唐山
邯郸 太原 大同 长治 阳泉
晋城 朔州 晋中 运城 忻州
临汾 呼和浩特 包头 沈阳
大连 长春 吉林市 四平
哈尔滨 黑龙江垦区
上海浦东新区 苏州 无锡
常州 徐州 南通 盐城 镇江
江阴 丹阳 杭州 宁波 绍兴
台州 温州 金华 嘉兴 衢州
福州 福州经济技术开发区
厦门经济特区 南昌 上饶
济南 青岛 潍坊 郑州
洛阳 三门峡 南阳 武汉 宜昌
十堰 荆州 咸宁 长沙 广州
东莞 惠州 深圳 桂林 南宁
柳州 来宾 河池 海口 成都
贵阳 昆明 庆阳 西安 兰州
银川 乌鲁木齐

“十一五”规划教材

非参数统计 医学统计学
概率论与数理统计 统计学
现代金融投资统计分析
多元统计分析 经济计量学教程
应用时间序列分析
统计指数理论及应用
统计数据处理概论
质量管理统计方法 社会统计学
多元统计分析实验
企业经营管理统计
市场调查与预测
统计学原理(非统计专业使用)
统计学:从数据到结论
国民经济核算教程(国民经济统计学)
概率论与数理统计（经济、管理类专业使用）

重点图书

挑大学选专业 2011—高考志愿填报指南
挑大学选专业 2011—考研择校指南

欲购以上图书请与中国统计出版社发行部联系
电　话:(010)63376907,63376908　同榍行书店电话:68783171,68783172
通讯地址:北京市西城区三里河月坛南街 57 号　邮政编码:100826

New Published Statistical Yearbook by China Statistics Press

Statisticses Data

China Statisticses Yearbook -2011
China Statisticses Abstract-2011
International Statisticses Yearbook -2011
China Development Reportin -2011
China Third Property Statisticses Yearbook -2011
China District Economy Statisticses Yearbook -2011
China labor Statisticses Yearbook -2011
China Society Statisticses Yearbook -2011
China City Statisticses Yearbook -2009
China Construction Statisticses Yearbook -2011
China Population and Labor Statisticses Yearbook -2011
China Industry Economy Statisticses Yearbook -2011
China Commodity Trade Market Statisticses Yearbook -2011
China Real Estate Statisticses Yearbook -2011
China Energy Statisticses Yearbook -2011
China Domestic Affairs Statisticses Yearbook -2011
China Foreign Economic Statisticses Yearbook -2011
China District Eoomony Monitor Report-2011
China Science Technique Statisticses Yearbook-2011
China Rural Statisticses Yearbook -2011
China Yearbook of Price of Farm Corps -2011
China High-technique Industry Statisticses Yearbook -2011
China Education Fund Yearbook -2010
China Rural Poor Monitor Report-2011
China Yearbook of Cost Income of Farm Corps -2011
China Science Technique Statisticses Yearbook -2011
Industry Enterprise Technology Movable data-2011
Large Scale and Medium Scale Cater Retail Trade and Catering Enterprises Statisticses Yearbook -2011
China City(Town) Life and Price Yearbook -2011
China County(City) Social Economy Survey Yearbook -2011
China Rural Household Survey Yearbook -2011 (Chinaese, English)
China Rural Completely Development Middle-class Monitor Report-2011
The Second National R&D Resource Check-General Survey
The Second National R&D Resource Check-Industry Enterprises
China Cater Retail Trade and Catering Enterprise Statisticses Yearbook -2011
The Sixth National Population Census Communipue

Provinces Statisticses Yearbook Series

Beijing Tianjin Hebei Shanxi Neimenggu
Liaoning Jilin Heilongjiang Shanghai Jiangsu
Zhejiang Anhui Fujian Jiangxi Shandong
Henna Hubei Hunan Guangdong Guangxi
Hainan Chongqing Sichuan Guizhou Yunnan
Xizang Shanxi Gansu Qinghai Ningxia
Xinjiang Xinjiang Production and Construction Group

City(County) Statisticses Yearbook Series

Tianjin Coastal New District Shijiazhuang Tangshan
Handan Taiyuan Changzhi Yangquan Jincheng
Shuozhou Jinzhong Yuncheng Xinzhou Linfen
Huhehaote Datong Baotou Shenyang Dalian
Changchun Jilin Siping Haerbin Heilongjiang
Shanghai Pudong New Area Suzhou Wuxi
Changzhou Xuzhou Nantong Yancheng
Jiangyin Danyang Hangzhou Ningbo
Shaoxing Taizhou Wenzhou Jinhua Jiaxing
Quzhou Fuzhou Fuzhou Economic Technique Development Area Xiamen Nanchang Shangrao
Jinan Qingdao Weifang Zhengzhou
Luoyang Sanmenxia Nanyang Wuhan Yichang
Shiyan Jingzhou XianNing Changsha Guangzhou
Dongguan Huizhou Shenzhen Guilin Nanning
Liuzhou Laibin Hechi Haikou Chengdu MianYan
Guiyang Kunming Qingyang Xi'an LanZhou Yinchuan
Urumqi

Distribution Department: Tel(010)63376907 63376908 68783171 68783172 Press Zip Code: 100826
Address: No. 57 Yuetan Nanjie, Sanlihe, Beijing P. R. China Statistics

2011

新疆生产建设兵团

统计年鉴

XINJIANG PRODUCTION & CONSTRUCTION GROUP

STATISTICAL YEARBOOK